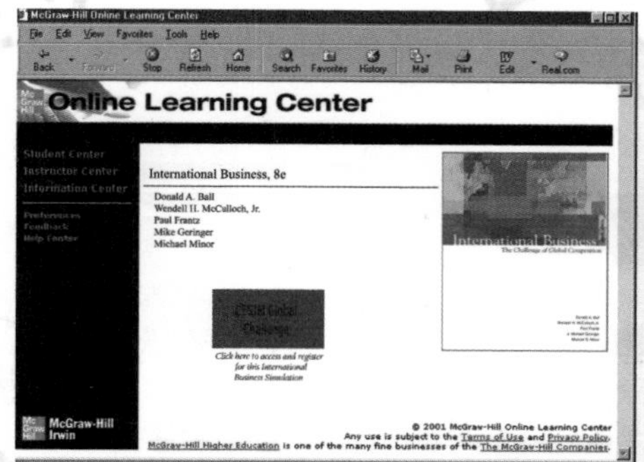

Online Learning Center

www.mhhe.com/ball8e

The *new* Online Learning Center includes a wealth of resources for professors and students such as:

- **Chapter self-quizzes** that help you review the material you have learned in each chapter and prepare for your exams.
- **e-Learning Session:** McGraw-Hill's unique, integrated, multimedia online study guide helps you prepare for tests with PowerPoint slides, concept checks and self-quizzes, key terms, and much more.
- **Internet assignments** for each chapter include concepts presented in the text and direct students to the Internet to complete the exercise. Answers are provided in the Instructor's Center.
- **e-Business cases** are included where relevant and provide cases/assignments based on recent e-commerce developments.
- **A career corner** that includes information and links to job hunting and interviewing resources, resume tips, and more.
- **Links to professional resources** are available so you can easily access the organizations you are reading about. The links can also give you more information that will be helpful in your course.

CESIM Global Challenge Simulation-NEW!

Included with each new text is a password that allows you to access the CESIM Global Challenge. The web-based simulation involves the hand-held digital device market (current generation of cell phones, plus potential future generations). There are three market areas (North America, Europe, and Asia, and players can choose which ones to market), four technologies (current, new emerging, and potential future technologies to invest in), a range of features that could be offered (impacting product differentiation), choice of production sites (within Asia or North America), pricing options, and exposure to exchange rate fluctuations. The simulation can be used with three to 12 teams (so six to 50 students per simulation) — and can involve teams from more than one class or university if the instructor wishes. You can access the simulation through the Online Learning Center as described above.

International Business PowerWeb

Current articles, interactive exercises, daily news, study tips, and web research are included in this interactive tool. Here you will find international business resources recommended by international business professors. You no longer have to wade through those long lists provided by traditional search engines. This PowerWeb can be accessed through the Online Learning Center, as described above. A registration code is provided with each new copy of this text.

See for yourself how both the book and these resources add to the teaching and learning possibilities with the eighth edition.

International Business

The Challenge of Global Competition

McGraw-Hill Higher Education

A Division of The McGraw-Hill Companies

INTERNATIONAL BUSINESS: THE CHALLENGE OF GLOBAL COMPETITION

Published by McGraw-Hill/Irwin, an imprint of The McGraw-Hill Companies, Inc., 1221 Avenue of the Americas, New York, NY, 10020.

This book is printed on acid-free paper.

domestic 1 2 3 4 5 6 7 8 9 0 VNH/VNH 0 9 8 7 6 5 4 3 2 1

international 1 2 3 4 5 6 7 8 9 0 VNH/VNH 0 9 8 7 6 5 4 3 2 1

ISBN 0-07-235676-6

Publisher: *John E. Biernat*

Developmental editor: *Sarah Reed*

Marketing manager: *Lisa Nicks*

Project manager: *Laura Griffin*

Production supervisor: *Debra R. Sylvester*

Coordinator freelance design: *Mary Kazak*

Photo research coordinator: *David A. Tietz*

Photo researcher: *Connie Gardner*

Supplement coordinator: *Matthew Perry*

Media technology producer: *Jenny R. Williams*

Cover design: © *PhotoDisc*

Compositor: *Carlisle Communications, Ltd.*

Typeface: *10.5/12 Times Roman*

Printer: *Von Hoffmann Press, Inc.*

Library of Congress Cataloging-in-Publication Data

Ball, Donald A.

International business: the challenge of global competition/Ball, McCulloch.—8th ed.

p. cm.

Includes bibliographical references and index.

ISBN 0-07-235676-6 (alk. paper)

1. International business enterprises—Management. 2. International business enterprises. 3. International economic relations. I. McCulloch, Wendell H. II. Title.

HD62.4.B34 2002

658'.049—dc21 2001030137

INTERNATIONAL EDITION ISBN 0-07-112296-6

www.mhhe.com

International Business

The Challenge of Global Competition

Eighth Edition

Donald A. Ball

Wendell H. McCulloch, Jr.

Paul L. Frantz

J. Michael Geringer

Michael S. Minor

McGraw-Hill Irwin

Boston Burr Ridge, IL Dubuque, IA Madison, WI New York San Francisco St. Louis
Bangkok Bogotá Caracas Kuala Lumpur Lisbon London Madrid Mexico City
Milan Montreal New Delhi Santiago Seoul Singapore Sydney Taipei Toronto

[About the Authors]

Don A. Ball

Don A. Ball, a consultant to multinational corporations, was a professor of marketing and international business for several years after leaving industry. He has a degree in mechanical engineering from Ohio State and a doctorate in business administration from the University of Florida. Ball has published articles in the *Journal of International Business Studies* and other publications. Before obtaining the doctorate, he spent 15 years in various marketing and production management positions in Mexico, South America, and Europe.

Wendell H. McCulloch, Jr.

Wendell H. McCulloch, Jr. is a professor of international business, finance, and law and the former director of international business programs at California State University, Long Beach. He earned a bachelor's degree in economics at George Washington University and a JD from Yale University. He has published articles in *The Wall Street Journal,* the *Journal of International Business Studies,* and the *Collegiate Forum.* The results of McCulloch's research have appeared in publications by the Joint Economic Committee of the U.S. Congress and the Heritage Foundation. Before beginning his academic career, McCulloch spent 19 years as an executive for American and European multinationals that offered banking, insurance, and investment products in many countries. While teaching and writing, he continues to act as an international business consultant.

Paul L. Frantz

Paul L. Frantz is on the faculty of the College of Business Administration at California State University, Long Beach, where he teaches international business and business law and is director of the international business program. He earned a bachelor's degree in finance at Montana State University, a JD from the University of Montana, a Master of International Management degree from Thunderbird, the American Graduate School of International Management, and a master of laws degree in transnational business practice from the McGeorge School of Law. He has published articles on international law, including laws of the European Union. In addition, he has spoken at conferences throughout the world on matters dealing with international law, international employment, and immigration.

J. Michael Geringer

J. Michael Geringer is a professor of strategy and international management and chair of the global strategy and law area at California Polytechnic University in San Luis Obispo. He earned a BS in business at Indiana University and MBA and PhD degrees at University of Washington. He has authored or edited eight books and monographs, over 95 published papers, and over 35 case studies; serves on the editorial boards of several leading academic journals; and is a past chair of the Academy of Management's International Management Division. His research has appeared in the *Journal of International Business Studies, Strategic Management Journal,* the *Academy of Management Journal,* and the *Journal of Applied Psychology,* among others. He has received 11 "best paper" awards for his research, including the Decade Award for most influential article from the *Journal of International Business Studies.* His teaching performance has earned numerous awards and recognition, including the University Distinguished Teacher Award. In addition to his work on the business faculty of universities in Europe, Africa, Australia, Asia, Canada, and the United States, Geringer is active in consulting and executive development for multinational corporations and executives from six continents.

Michael S. Minor

Michael S. Minor is professor of marketing and international business and director of the PhD program in international business at the University of Texas–Pan American. He was educated at the University of North Carolina–Chapel Hill, American University, and Cornell and holds a PhD from Vanderbilt University. His research focuses on comparative consumer behavior, international marketing strategy, and political risk issues. He has published in the *Journal of International Business Studies,* the *Journal of Consumer Marketing, International Studies of Management and Organization,* the *Journal of Services Marketing, International Business Review,* and elsewhere. He is active in the American Marketing Association and has served in leadership positions for the Global Marketing, Consumer Behavior, and Technology and Marketing Special Interest Groups of the AMA. He serves on multiple editorial advisory boards and is the coauthor with John C. Mowen of two consumer behavior books. His consulting experience includes work for the United Nations, and he lived in Asia for a number of years. He is the bass guitar player for the country/classic rock group RiverRock.

[Preface]

We are pleased to present the eighth edition of *International Business: The Challenge of Global Competition.* We thank everyone who has called or written us or made in-class suggestions for improvement.

Purpose and Scope of This Text

Students ask a number of questions in an international business course: about different cultures, why products are the same (or different) in different countries, why different peoples have different rituals, the effect of the Internet on international business, and many more. We wrote this book to provide answers to those questions and more, whether the students are advanced undergraduates or are in an MBA program. Earlier in our careers we, the authors, had similar questions. We still don't know all the answers, but in this text we hope to both provide answers and convey our continuing fascination with the subject matter. There are always new questions, and sometimes there are new answers to old questions.

International Business 8/e is organized into four sections in order to maximize its utility to instructors and students alike. The opening section defines the nature of international business and the three environments in which it is conducted. Section Two is devoted to the continuing importance of international organizations and the international monetary system and how they affect business. Section Three focuses on the uncontrollable forces at work in all business environments and discusses their inevitable impact on business practice. We devote the final section to a discussion of how managers deal with all the forces affecting international business.

Authorship

You may have noticed that the number of authors has swelled considerably in the 8th edition. Those who have used prior editions may have seen the names of these new authors in the acknowledgments section, as the authors of cases, or in other capacities. Paul Franz, Mike Geringer, and Michael Minor all bring new perspectives and new energy to the considerable task of revising such a large text. Each also brings his individual strengths and areas of expertise to this new edition. Paul specializes in international law, international employment, and immigration. Mike focuses on strategy and international management. Michael's research is mainly in comparative consumer behavior, international marketing strategy, and political risk issues. This new author team brings a dynamic new focus to this edition.

Changes to the Eighth Edition

With each new edition we have been blessed by an expanding network of those making helpful suggestions. Professors, reviewers, businesspeople who bought the book or received it at a conference, and our own graduate and undergraduate students have made useful and constructive comments. We believe that *International Business* 8/e continues to offer you a superior text in terms of quality, currency, and the infusion of current topics relevant to current challenges.

1. A resounding comment in the reviews of the seventh edition was that the strategy chapter needed to come earlier. We have moved the material on strategic planning from Chapter 20 to Chapter 14, which introduces the fourth and final section of the text.
2. Another consistent comment we received concerned Chapter 13. We have moved the discussion of distributive forces—long a part of Chapter 13—to Chapter 2.
3. Also, our presentation of the Internet has changed. In the 7th edition we viewed the Internet primarily as a source of materials for research. In this edition we reflect the current reality. The Internet is a concrete part of a firm's international strategy, across the marketing mix and across production issues—in fact, its influence is pervasive across the functions of the firm.
4. As we already have mentioned, the addition of three new authors to this edition brings a great deal of change, particularly to the strategy, marketing, and legal chapters of this text. This new author team has worked together to make sure this edition retains the style and strengths of the previous editions but also has made sure that this edition is a current, comprehensive, and relevant textbook for international business students.

Key Features and Resources

1. **The Internet Appendix:** As in the 7th edition, a comprehensive list of Internet addresses and resources is included at the end of Chapter 1. This helps make researching international business topics much easier for students. This comprehensive list is also included on the 8th edition Web site and will be updated/expanded periodically.
2. **Relevance for Businesspeople:** This feature links the concepts introduced in the text to real-world experiences of international businesspeople. Through these examples, students learn "why" these concepts are relevant and important.
3. **Student CD-Rom:** With every copy of the text, students will receive a free CD-ROM that contains what used to be the exam prep disk (20 to 100 questions per chapter for review), video clips, and word games to review key terms.
4. **Online Learning Center: http://www.mhhe.com/ball8e:** The *International Business* Web site is a great resource for students and professors alike. It has been greatly enhanced since the 7th edition. The 8th edition site provides company and E-commerce updates, book features, a career center, professional resources, internet assignments, downloadable supplements, a discussion board for instructors and students, chapter quizzes, and much more!
5. **Online simulation:** With each new copy of the text, you will receive a passcode to the online simulation specifically designed to accompany this text. The simulation, developed by CESIM, includes:
   - 3 market areas (North America, Europe, Asia) and players can choose which ones to market to
   - 4 technologies (current, new emerging, and potential future technologies to invest in)
   - a range of features that could be offered (affecting product differentiation)
   - choice of production sites (within Asia or in North America)

- pricing options
- exposure to exchange rate fluctuations

This is quite a robust simulation, lots of fun, and, more important, a great learning tool. It can be used with 3 to 12 teams (so 6 to 50 students per simulation)—and can involve teams from more than one class or university if the instructor wishes. It is resident on the web, and there is essentially no instructor management required (other than selecting a few variables regarding number of teams, length of time to run the simulation in terms of quarters, etc.). Instructor materials for the simulation can be found in the Online Learning Center under downloadable supplements.

6. PowerWeb: With each new copy of the text, you will also receive access to the International Business PowerWeb. This online supplement includes daily and weekly updates to international business news around the world. Access to PowerWeb is available through the Ball Online Learning Center (*http://www.mhhe.com/ball8e*)

We have updated the material in each chapter to reflect recent world events and new international business issues.

Chapter 1

There is a new discussion of the continual broadening of the term *globalization* by social scientists and businesspeople. A new word—*globality*—is introduced. New evidence of the rapid growth of global and multinational firms is offered by an UNCTAD report. Also, the Internet Appendix has been completely updated. It will also appear on the book's Web site, and so it can be updated if any links change or are deleted.

Chapter 2

New information on the role of small and medium-sized enterprises in international exporting and investment has been incorporated into the discussion. We have updated the discussion on recent changes and trends in the levels and direction of trade and investment among the major regions and nations of the world, including changes associated with China and other Asian nations. The discussion of distributive forces, which previously had been a part of Chapter 13, has been moved into this chapter to extend the discussion on ways in which companies enter into foreign markets for international trade and investment.

Chapter 3

Information on the EU ban of U.S. beef has been updated to include the WTO authorization for retaliation given to the United States. Also, new information has been added on the EU–U.S. pact to limit government subsidies to commercial aircraft makers.

Chapter 4

We have expanded the discussion of the European Union as well as coverage of the OECD and other international organizations. There is also a new section explaining the relationship between international organizations and international business.

Chapter 5

Obviously, the discussion of the euro and its strengths and weaknesses has been updated to reflect current developments. Also, developments in the euro zone where the European Central Bank sets monetary policy are included in this chapter.

Chapter 6

A new discussion of the euro and its impact on international business is included. There is also an expanded discussion of the role of the U.S. dollar in international transactions and of financial forces and how they affect business in countries throughout the world.

Chapter 7

The extensive tables in this chapter have been revised. New indicators of development such as cell phones, home computers, and Internet hosts are introduced. The importance of sociocultural forces is reemphasized. To illustrate the wide variability of inflation rates, we have added a historical perspective.

Chapter 8

There are a number of updates and additions to this chapter. Information on the biggest ecological disaster since Chernobyl is presented, the impact of the new bridge connecting Sweden to Denmark is described, a report on the blockage of the Rhine waterway caused by the NATO bombing of Yugoslavia is included, and new information on the progress made in the production of unconventional sources of petroleum has been added.

Chapter 9

The table comparing religious populations has been updated and changed to a graphical representation, which should make this information easier to understand. We changed the vignette on Disneyland Paris to reflect the successful changes made there. We indicate that the influx of scientists and engineers into the United States from other countries has subsided. A new bribe payer's index from Transparency International is introduced, as well as a new table describing the extent of the entrepreneurial spirit in various countries around the world.

Chapter 10

We have added an explanation of the importance to business of politics, including such concepts and labels as conservative and liberal, right and left.

Chapter 11

There is now a discussion of international litigation and alternative dispute resolution mechanisms. The discussion of extraterritorial application of U.S. laws and application of antitrust laws throughout the world has been expanded. Additionally, there is a discussion of the role of the U.S. Department of Justice.

Chapter 12

A new section on immigration, focusing on the entry of businesspeople into the United States, has been added. Also, we have expanded the discussion of how technology is influencing workers and the workplace and of trends in labor movements worldwide.

Chapter 13

The discussion in Chapter 13 of competitiveness at the macro level ("national competitiveness") has been completely revised and updated. The extensive tables in this chapter have been revised. Numerous new tables and figures have been added, including new measures of national competitiveness. Major changes in relative competitiveness of the U.S., the European Community, and Japan have been updated, including discussion of the changing role of keiretsu in Japan and the role of information and communication technologies in affecting relative rates and directions of development in the developed countries. We have included discussion of international e-commerce, as well as an expanded discussion of the newly industrialized economies and the leading developing nations of Asia, including China. The discussion of counterfeiting and piracy as important international business issues has been expanded and updated. Reflecting comments of our reviewers and prior users of this text, the discussion of distributive forces previously included in this chapter has been moved into Chapter 2.

Chapter 14

To more appropriately reflect the role of strategy and strategic planning as a key introductory and organizing focus for the discussion of how managers deal with the forces affecting international business, this chapter has been moved from the end of the text to the beginning of section 4. In this new Chapter 14, we have included a discussion of the concepts of strategy and competitive advantage, and their importance to international business. We have provided updated examples for many of the key concepts introduced in this chapter. The chapter includes a new strategic planning example (on 3M) and there is also a small and medium-sized enterprises box on ACT Manufacturing.

Chapter 15

We shift our focus from the notion of market screening on a per-country basis only and introduce the core idea that cross-country segments may be just as important. We reemphasize the fact that policy stability rather than political stability per se is more important as an international business risk factor. We also introduce several political risk forecasting services for the first time. The material on sociocultural forces has been changed extensively. An in-depth vignette on market research practices has been added, as well as a new table on the marketing potential of emerging economies.

Chapter 16

The eternal issue of standardization versus adaptation has been tackled again, with more attention given to the likelihood of the need for adaptation. Another general change is an increased focus on consumer products and services as compared to business-to-business marketing examples. We introduce a table illustrating Internet advertising agencies for the first time. We also discuss challenges to advertising, personal selling, channels of distribution, and prices on the Internet. A bit less emphasis is given to transfer prices as a pricing issue.

Chapter 17

We have added a new graphic that illustrates the risk/cost trade-off of export payment terms. There is also a new discussion on the successor to the Foreign Sales Corporation. The U.S. government agreed to eliminate the FSC after it lost an appeal to the WTO. Also, we have included information showing that large firms do export; information from a Census Bureau study confirms that a large proportion of the export value associated with large multinational manufacturers was between related parties. Also, the top 50 manufacturers accounted for 45 percent of the known export value.

Chapter 18

Chapter 18 includes new approaches to child labor, discussion of the difficulties companies have to find and recruit suitable executives for foreign assignments, changes in Japanese employment practices, new executive interview techniques, and new cost of living, business environment, office rents, and compensation comparison tables for various countries.

Chapter 19

Chapter 19 includes a further discussion of hedging against foreign currency exchange risks, new developments in the derivatives markets, and the growth of countertrade.

Chapter 20

In Chapter 20, we have expanded substantially our discussion of international outsourcing, and we have expanded our discussion of the linkage among outsourcing, value chains, and cycle time. We have provided an extensive new discussion of electronic purchasing and the impact of e-commerce on international operations management, including the challenges as well as opportunities associated with emerging business-to-business electronic purchasing practices. We have introduced an expanded discussion of international standards, with an emphasis on ISO standards, and have also expanded our discussion of the management of maintenance activities in international operations. We have provided updated examples for many of the key concepts introduced in this chapter, including examples from service-based companies to complement our existing coverage of more manufacturing-oriented firms. We have included a discussion of global concurrent engineering (or "chasing the sun") and have also added an extended example of international operations management within small and medium-sized enterprises (Cognizant Technology Solutions).

The 8th Edition International Business Package

For Instructors:

Instructors' Manual: This manual, written by the authors, will help save you invaluable time preparing for the course by providing suggestions for heightening your students' interest in the material. Each chapter-by-chapter discussion presents concept previews, an overview of the chapter, suggestions and comments, student involvement exercises, suggestions for guest lecturers, video case suggestions, and a detailed chapter outline.

Test Bank:

Written by the authors, the test bank contains approximately 100 questions per chapter in multiple choice, true/false, and short answer format. Each question is ranked for difficulty level, and the page references in the textbook are given for the answers.

PowerPoint CD-ROM:

Authored by Andrew Yap of Florida International University, this PowerPoint presentation includes key points from each chapter, sample figures from the text, and supplemental exhibits that help illustrate the main points in a chapter. Over 600 images are included. Students also have access to this presentation on the Student CD that accompanies each new book.

Instructor's Presentation CD-ROM:

This instructor's CD collects many features of the Instructor's Manual, videos, the PowerPoint presentation, and lecture material in an electronic format and offers a convenient tool that allows you to customize your own lecture and presentation.

Videos:

We realize that time is a scarce resource for instructors, and so this video program provides a carefully selected set of videos to accompany the text. The series includes videos, mostly from NBC archives, that focus on international business challenges, processes, and experiences. A video case highlighting each video and asking discussion questions is included with the Instructor's Manual.

For Students:

Student CD-ROM:

With each new book, students receive a free CD-ROM containing what used to be the Exam Prep Disk, which has been updated to reflect the changes in the 8th edition. Students can use these test questions to prepare for exams or to review the content they have learned in each chapter. The CD also includes video clips that reference specific sections of the text.

E-Learning Session:

This "online study guide" is a great resource for students as they review the key concepts from each chapter. Each chapter includes an outline of the chapter, and the most important supplements are brought into this outline to emphasize important concepts in the chapter. Each chapter contains a quiz for review, PowerPoint slides, figures from the text, concept checks, key term definitions, and much more!

For Both Students and Instructors:

Business Week Edition:

Keep your classroom up to date with the latest international business news. Now you can take advantage of a 15-week subscription to the world's leading business magazine. Instructors receive a free semester subscription and a weekly newsletter summarizing the articles. The newsletter will also include application questions for incorporating current events into your curriculum.

PowerWeb:

With the 8th edition, professors and students get free access to the International Business PowerWeb. This is an online supplement unlike any you have experienced before. It includes

- Easy-to-use instructor assessment for effective supplemental content.
- Self-assessment areas for students to use to check their comprehension.
- Current and relevant articles from leading periodicals and journals for students to use in researching assigned projects.
- Periodic posting of the most recent and dynamic articles along with relevant quizzing and assessment tools; new material that can be brought into class for discussion.
- The highest-quality peer-reviewed and refereed content. The content is vetted to uncover relevant course issues versus random Web-search results.
- Optional research and study skill tools.

Online Learning Center:

http://www.mhhe.com/ball8e: Students and professors have access to many great resources. Authored by Chula King of the University of West Florida, this Web site contains book features, Web exercises, E-commerce updates, links to national and international news, a career center for students, audio clips that take students and instructors through the text, and many other course-enhancing materials, including links to PowerWeb and the E-Learning Session described above.

International Business Simulation

With each new copy of the book, students and professors will receive access to the simulation developed to accompany this text. The simulation can be accessed through the book's Online Learning Center. As mentioned earlier, the instructor materials for this simulation are also available on the text Web site.

[Acknowledgments]

To the long list of people to whom we are indebted, we want to add professors Robert T. Aubey, University of Wisconsin–Madison; Mark C. Baetz, Wilfred Laurier University; Rufus Barton, Murray State University; Joseph R. Biggs, California Polytechnic State University; S. A. Billon, University of Delaware; James R. Bradshaw, Brigham Young University; Sharon Browning, Northwest Missouri State University; Dennis Carter, University of North Carolina–Wilmington; Mark Chadwin, Old Dominion University; Refik Culpan, Pennsylvania State University; Peter DeWill, University of Central Florida; Galpira Eshigi, Illinois State University; Christof Falli, Portland State University; Prem Gandhi, State University of New York at Plattsburgh; Stanley D. Guzell, Youngstown State University; Gary Hankem, Mankato State University; Baban Hasnat, State University of New York at Brockport; Paul Jenner, Southwest Missouri State University; Bruce H. Johnson, Gustavus Adolphus College; Michael Kublin, University of New Haven; Eddie Lewis, University of Southern Mississippi; Lois Ann McElroy Lindell, Wartburg College; Carol Lopilato, California State University–Dominguez Hills; Gary Oddon, San Jose State University; John Setnicky, Mobile College; Jesse S. Tarleton, William and Mary College; John Thanopoulos, University of Akron; Kenneth Tillery, Middle Tennessee State University; Hsin-Min Tong, Redford University; Dennis Vanden Bloomen, University of Wisconsin–Stout; and George Westacott, State University of New York at Binghamton. Attorney Mary C. Tolton, Esq., of the law firm Parker, Poe, Adams & Bernstein of Raleigh, North Carolina, provided valuable supplementary readings for the legal forces chapter; and we acknowledge the help of Danielle Acosta, Denalee Eaton, Nicolaus J. Roessler, and Rosemary Taylor, students at California State University, Long Beach.

We are also indebted to the following reviewers for helping us fine-tune the eighth edition to better meet market needs:

Aruna Chandras, Ashland University
John Cleek, University of Missouri, Kansas City
Kenneth Gray, Florida Agricultural and Mechanical University
Veronica Horton, University of Akron
Fraser McLeay, University of Montana
Jeanne McNett, Assumption College
Les Mueller, Central Washington University
Mike Peng, Ohio State University
V. N. Subramanyam, Lancaster University
Angelo Tarallo, Ramapo College
Terry Witkowski, California State University

Hundreds of professors have reviewed this text over the past eight editions and have shaped it into the solid textbook it is. Their suggestions and feedback have been invaluable to us, and we very much appreciate their efforts and time.

Finally, we would like to thank Andrew Yap for his work on the PowerPoint presentation and questions for the Student CD-ROM, Chula King for her work on the text Web site, and David Sturges for his work on the E-Learning Session that accompanies the text.

[Brief Table of Contents]

[Table of Contents]

[3] Economic Theories of International Business 106

[4] The Dynamics of International Organizations 146

[5] Understanding the International Monetary System 181

[6] Financial Forces: Influencing International Business 208

[7] Economic and Socioeconomic Forces 236

[8] Physical and Environmental Forces 266

[9] Sociocultural Forces 300

[10] Political Forces 346

[11] Legal Forces 376

[12] Labor Forces 404

[13] Competitive Forces 434

[14] International Strategy, Organizational Design, and Control 480

[17] Export and Import Practices 578

[18] Human Resource Management 616

Dedication

Don dedicates this edition to his wife, Vicki; children, Don, Jr., Lianne, and Dulce; their spouses, Susan and Jim; and his grandchildren, Alison, Sean, and Alexandra. Wendell would like to dedicate this edition to his wife, Sally, and his children, Malinda and Kevin. Paul would like to dedicate this book to Charlotte and Kirke Frantz, his parents. Mike dedicates this edition to his parents, Ray and JoAnn, and to his wife, Colette Frayne. Michael's thanks go to Karen and Amy, who suffered the most through the long hours at the office, and to his mother, Mary Ruth. He thanks Melinda Zuniga and Elia Ovalle, both of whom put up with his "working on the book" rather than attending to other responsibilities.

[Chapter]

The Rapid Change of Global Business

"There is no longer any such thing as a purely national economy. The rest of the world is just too big to ignore, either as a market or as a competitor. If business schools do nothing other than to train their students to think internationally, they would have accomplished an important task."

—*John Young, CEO, Hewlett-Packard*

Concept Previews

After reading this chapter, you should be able to:

- **appreciate** the dramatic internationalization of markets
- **understand** the various names given to firms that have substantial operations in more than one country
- **appreciate** the profound effect of the Internet on many international business firms
- **understand** the five kinds of drivers, all based on change, that are leading international firms to the globalization of their operations
- **comprehend** why international business differs from domestic business
- **describe** the three environments—domestic, foreign, and international—in which an international company operates

Howard Grey/Tony Stone Images

Why You Need International Business Experience and How to Get It

Gary Ellis, a young assistant controller for Medtronic, a Fortune 500 manufacturer of pacemakers and other medical equipment, was thought to be on the fast track for a top management position. However, company executives felt he first needed broader experience, so they sent him to head their European headquarters in Belgium. In his new job Gary was responsible for many top-level duties and worked with an array of officials (labor, government, production, and marketing, as well as financial).

Two years later, when the corporate controller's job in the company's home office in Minneapolis became vacant, Ellis was given the job. Bill George, Medtronic's CEO, summed up the company philosophy regarding necessary experience: "Successful executives of the future will have all lived in another country for several years."[a]

Medtronic is not the only firm with this policy. At FMC Corp., a heavy machinery and chemicals producer, the vice president for human resources says that his company believes that "no one will be in a general management job by the end of the decade who didn't have international exposure and experience."[b] Evidently, the boards of directors of the Big Three automakers have the same policy. All three CEOs were at one time heads of their firms' international operations.

The realization that overseas experience is important for career advancement has heightened the competition for foreign assignments. For example, nearly 500 midlevel engineering and technical managers in GE's aircraft engine unit applied for the 14 positions in the company's global marketing training program.[c] The global human resources manager at another GE unit, GE Medical Systems, claims, "We have far more candidates than we have jobs offshore."[d] In the face of such competition, what can you do to improve your chances to obtain an overseas post?

First, make your boss and the Human Resource Management department personnel aware of your interest and the fact that you have studied international business. Look for opportunities to remind them that you continue to be interested (performance review is a good time). Try to meet people in the home office who work with the foreign subsidiaries as well as visitors from overseas. As evidence of your strong interest in foreign employment, take additional international business courses and study foreign languages. Make sure that people in your company know what you are doing.

You have seen that many American managements want their top executives at company headquarters to have years of foreign experience, but do CEOs of the major firms recognize the value of internationalized business education for all employees in management? Do they, in fact, believe it is important that all business graduates they hire have some education in the international aspects of business? How important is the knowledge of foreign languages?

To find out, we surveyed the CEOs of *Forbes*'s "100 Largest Multinational Firms" and *Fortune*'s "America's 50 Biggest Exporters." We found that: (1) Seventy-nine percent believed that all business majors should take an introduction to international business course. (2) About 70 percent felt that business graduates' expertise in foreign languages, international aspects of functional areas (e.g., marketing, finance), and business, human, or political relations outside the United States is an important consideration in making hiring decisions. (3) A majority of the respondents believed that a number of courses in the international business curriculum (e.g., international marketing, international finance, export–import, international management) are relevant to their companies.

It appears from our study, then, that the CEOs of the major American firms doing business overseas are convinced that the business graduates they hire should have some education in the international aspects of business. Most seem to agree with the executive vice president of Texas Instruments, who said, "Managers must become familiar with other markets, cultures, and customs. That is because we operate under the notion that it is 'one world, one market,' and we must be able to compete with—and sell to—the best companies around the world."[e]

Table 1.1 Import Penetration, 1970 versus 1999 ($ billions)

	Import Penetration (%)		Goods and Services: Exports		Goods and Services: Imports		GDP*	
	1999	1970	1999	1970	1999	1970	1999	1970
United Kingdom	24.8%	23.4%	$268	$25	$321	$25	$1,241	$107
Germany	18.7	19.3	541	39	473	35	2,604	185
France†	17.3	15.5	299	16	286	22	1,665	143
United States	11.8	6.7	695	68	1,060	68	8,637	1,012
Japan	5.9	9.8	419	22	311	20	5,393	204

Notes: *At 1999 prices and exchange rates.
†Figures include overseas territories.

Sources: "Gross Domestic Product," *Main Economic Indicators,* March 2000, OECD Web site, www.oecd.org/std/gdp.htm (July 24, 2000); "Appendix Table 1," *Annual Report 2000,* www.wto.org/wto/english/res_e/anre00_e.pdf (July 24, 2000).

Clearly, the top executives from some of the largest corporations in the world are saying that they prefer business graduates who know something about markets, customs, and cultures in other countries. Companies that do business overseas have always needed some people who could work and live successfully outside their own countries, but now it seems that managers wanting to advance in their firms must have some foreign experience.

Did you note the reason for this emphasis on foreign experience for managers—increased involvement of the firm in international business? The top executives of many corporations want their employees to have a global business perspective. What about companies that have no foreign operations of any kind? Do their managers need this global perspective? They do indeed, because it will help them not only to be alert for both sales and sourcing opportunities in foreign markets but also to be watchful for new foreign competitors preparing to invade their domestic market.

Indicators of this expanding competition are the increases in import penetration defined as

$$\frac{\text{imports}}{\text{GDP} - \text{exports} + \text{imports}}$$

and the buildup of foreign investment. Note that import penetration has increased markedly for the five major importing nations over the past 29 years (Table 1.1).

In summary, we can say that every company's management, whether or not it has any direct foreign involvement, needs to be aware of what is occurring globally in its markets and its industry. ■

Sources: [a]"The Real Fast Track Is Overseas," *Fortune,* August 21, 1995, p. 129. [b]"Path to Top Job Now Twists and Turns," *The Wall Street Journal,* March 15, 1993, p. B1. [c]"Younger Managers Learn Global Skills," *The Wall Street Journal,* March 3, 1994, p. B1. [d]"The Fast Track Leads Overseas," *Business Week,* November 1993, pp. 64–68. [e]Donald A. Ball and Wendell H. McCulloch, Jr., "The Views of American Multinational CEOs on Internationalized Business Education for Perspective Employees," *Journal of International Business Studies,* 2nd Quarter, 1993, pp. 383–91.

What about you? Are you involved in the global economy yet? Think back to how you began your day. After you awoke, you may have looked at your Timex watch for the time and turned on your RCA TV for the news and weather while you showered. After drying your hair with a Conair dryer, you quickly swallowed some Carnation Instant Breakfast and Sanka coffee, brushed your teeth with Close-Up toothpaste, and drove off to class in your Honda with its Firestone tires and a tank full of Shell gasoline.

Meanwhile, on the other side of the world, a group of Japanese students dressed in Lacoste shirts, Levi's jeans, and New Balance shoes may be turning off their IBMs in the computer lab and debating whether they should stop for hamburgers and Cokes at McDonald's or coffee and doughnuts at Mister Donut. They get into their Ford Mustangs with Goodyear tires and drive off.

What do you and the Japanese students have in common? You are all consuming products made by *foreign-owned companies.* This is international business.

To further see the point we're making, answer this question: Which of the following companies or brands are foreign owned? Who are the owners?

1. Norelco (electric razors)
2. Chesebrough-Pond (Vaseline)
3. Ben & Jerry's Ice Cream
4. Lever Brothers (Lux, Dove)
5. Lenscrafters (eyeglasses)
6. Maybelline (cosmetics)
7. Comp USA (computer stores)
8. Greyhound Lines
9. Holiday Inn
10. Godiva Chocolate
11. Scott Paper (Kleenex)
12. Elizabeth Arden
13. General Tire (tires)
14. A&W Brands (root beer)
15. Motel 6
16. Pillsbury[1]

All that you have read so far points to one salient fact: *All businesspeople need to have a basic knowledge of international business to be able to meet the challenge of global competition.*

International Business Terminology

Part of this knowledge consists of learning its special terminology, an important function, as you already know, of every introductory course. To assist you in learning the international business "language," we've included a glossary at the end of the book and listed the most important terms at the end of each chapter. They also appear in bold print where they are first used in the text, with their definitions in the margin.

Multinational, Global, International, and Transnational Companies

Because international business is a relatively new discipline and is extremely dynamic, you will find that the definitions of a number of terms vary among users. For example, some people use the words *world* and *global* interchangeably with *multinational* to describe a business with widespread international operations, but others define a global firm as one that attempts to standardize operations in all functional areas but that responds to national market differences when necessary.[2]

According to this definition, a global firm's management

1. Searches the world for (*a*) market opportunities, (*b*) threats from competitors, (*c*) sources of products, raw materials, and financing, and (*d*) personnel. In other words, it has global vision.
2. Seeks to maintain a presence in key markets.
3. Looks for similarities, not differences, among markets.

Those who use *global* in this manner are defining a multinational company as a kind of holding company with a number of overseas operations, each of which is left to adapt its products and marketing strategy to what local managers perceive to be unique aspects of their individual markets. Some academic writers suggest using terms such as *multidomestic* and *multilocal* as synonyms for this definition of *multinational.*[3] You will also find those who consider *multinational corporation* to be synonymous with *multinational enterprise* and *transnational corporation.*

However, the United Nations and the governments of most developing nations have been using *transnational* instead of *multinational* for decades to describe a firm doing business in more than one country. The United Nations specialized agency, the United Nations Conference on Trade and Development (UNCTAD), for example, employs the following definition: "Transnational corporations comprise parent enterprises and their foreign affiliates: a parent enterprise is defined as one that controls assets of another entity or entities in a country or countries other than its home country, usually by owning a capital stake. An equity capital stake of at least 10 percent is normally considered as a threshold for the control of assets in this context."[4] More recently, some academic writers have employed the term for a company that combines the characteristics of global and multinational firms: (1) trying to achieve economies of scale through global integration of its functional areas while at the same time (2) being highly responsive to different local environments (a newer name is *multicultural multinational*).[5] You recognize, of course, that this is similar to the definition of a global company mentioned earlier. To be able to use this definition for *transnational,* these writers have simply redefined a global firm as one that responds weakly to local environments.

Businesspeople, though, usually define a transnational as a company formed by a merger of two firms of approximately the same size that are from two different countries. Four of the largest are Unilever (Dutch–English, food), Shell (Dutch–English, oil), Pharmacia & Upjohn (Swedish–American, pharmaceuticals), and ABB (electrotechnical, power generating), a 1988 merger between ASEA (Swedish) and Brown-Bovari (Swiss). Other European transnationals, now dissolved, were Dunlop-Pirelli (English–Italian, tires), Semperit-Kleber Colombes (Austrian–French, tires), and VFW-Fokker (Germany–Netherlands, aircraft). *Binational* is another name given to this kind of company.

Organization of a Transnational

Generally, there is a 50–50 ownership of a new company formed by the merger, as in the case of ABB, although there are notable exceptions. The Unilever Group was established in 1930 when Margarine Unie (Dutch) and Lever Brothers (British) decided to merge their interests while remaining separate legal entities. Now known as Unilever N.V. (Dutch) and Unilever PLC (British), they are the parent companies of one of the world's largest consumer goods businesses (31 in the Fortune Global 500 with 1999 sales of $44 billion), with corporate centers in Rotterdam and London. These companies, which serve as holding and service companies for their group companies around the world, have the same directors, and each company chairman is vice chairman in the other company. In most cases, shares in the group companies are held by either N.V. or PLC. Interestingly, Unilever describes itself as "international, not global, because it does not attempt to enter all markets with the same product."[6]

[Worldview]

Global Company—By Whose Definition?

After talking about having to be a multinational firm (a collection of national businesses) to gain a competitive advantage during the 1960s, management consultants and managements in the 1980s turned to the buzzword *globalization* as a strategy to beat their competitors. Unfortunately, *globalization* and its root, *global,* are overused and misused in international business because of the prestige that managements believe these words bring to their companies. Here are three of the various definitions of a global company—an organization that attempts to

1. Have a worldwide presence in its market.
2. Standardize operations worldwide in one or more of the firm's functional areas.
3. Integrate its operations worldwide.

There are those who believe a global firm must possess all three characteristics and have a worldwide locus of control and ownership. Critics of this definition claim there is no global firm by that definition. To see how firms define global firms to suit their purpose, compare these two situations.

Allen-Edmonds is a small shoe manufacturer in Port Washington, Wisconsin, whose sales in 17 years rose from $9.5 million in 1978 to $55 million in 1995. The president explains that the firm accomplished this by "choosing a market niche—manufacturing high-quality dress shoes for men, and by viewing the whole globe as our marketplace. Today, although we produce all our shoes in Port Washington, Allen-Edmonds is a *global manufacturing company.*" Contrast this with the way Procter & Gamble's (P&G) management describes its company: "Since 1980, the company has quadrupled the number of consumers it can serve with its brands—about five billion people around the world. P&G now has operations in more than 70 countries and its products are sold in over 140 countries, making P&G one of the biggest and most successful consumer goods companies in the world. P&G is also a major force for economic growth and well-being around the world, employing more than 103,000 people worldwide. Today, Procter & Gamble is a *truly global corporation.*"

Although the same term is used in both situations, the definitions are different. For example, some people, such as the Allen-Edmonds president, claim the

The other large Dutch–British transnational, Shell, has a similar organizational arrangement in that in 1903 a British petroleum company and a Dutch one formed a partnership, the Asian Petroleum Company, that worked so well that it was extended to worldwide operations with the formation of the Royal Dutch/Shell Group of Companies in 1907. The partnership continues. The two parent companies retain their separate businesses and own the Group, with over 1,700 companies in the proportion of 60 percent to Royal Dutch Petroleum and 40 percent to the Shell Transport and Trading Company. The Shell Group ranked eleventh in the 1999 Fortune Global 500 with sales of $105 billion. Note that neither Unilever nor Shell is a merger in the strictly legal sense.[7]

> In 1990, Brazil and Argentina signed a treaty establishing Argentina/Brazil Binational Companies, presumably because of their membership in the regional trade association Mercosur. The Colombian and Ecuadorian governments have also established regulations for the formation of binational companies.[8]

Other Possible Solutions to Multiple Definitions

Perhaps the Japanese have the solution to the use of terms with multiple definitions; they call the technique of adapting to local conditions *dochakuka,* meaning "global localization." The word comes from Japanese agriculture, where it means adjusting the planting, fertilizing, and harvesting methods to meet local soil conditions.

To complete this discussion, we need to mention that the term *supranational corporation* was described in a publication of the United Nations as one in which both the operation and the ownership are multinational, yet many reserve this term for a corporate form that does not exist now—one that would be chartered by an international agency such as the United Nations.

title *global* simply because their companies export to other countries. Presumably, he calls his firm a global manufacturing company because Allen-Edmonds does its own manufacturing instead of subcontracting from China, Indonesia, and other Asian nations as Nike and Adidas do. For other firms, such as P&G, attaining global company status requires meeting additional criteria, thereby reducing the number of companies able to reach that goal. Their definition, essentially based on marketing, production, and technological globalization, is one that focuses on customer similarities worldwide and producing in similar manufacturing facilities around the world essentially the same products, which are then sold under the same brand names in all markets.

Recently, however, the term *global company* has taken on still more new criteria. Compared to other definitions, a global company is now said to be more culturally diverse and incorporates much more worldwide standardization in its marketing, technical, and production functions than previously. To utilize its worldwide assets more efficiently against competitors, the new global company places production plants all over the world to gain the benefits of lower-cost labor and better-educated workers. Improvements in communications technology such as Electronic Data Interchange (EDI) data exchange (invoices, purchase orders) between computers of manufacturers and suppliers, international networking, and teleconferencing have made it possible for project teams around the world to meld ideas from different cultures for greater innovation.

Managements are also removing the barriers within their companies to allow the free flow of people as well as ideas. Many are offering top management positions to citizens from countries other than the home country. Some are even calling this newly defined global company by a new name: *multicultural multinational.*

The aims of the multicultural multinational are (1) to be responsive to local markets, (2) to produce and market its products worldwide, and (3) to exploit its technology on a global basis—elusive goals reached by few companies so far. Although it has become fashionable to speak of global corporations as being "stateless" or "borderless," measurement by any criterion shows that they don't exist. Each has a home government and tax authority and is owned by shareholders from primarily one nation. According to Professor Yao-Su Hu, a former World Bank economist, writing in *California Management Review,* these firms are national firms with international operations. ■

Sources: "Getting Your Foot in the Global Door," *Financial Executive,* May/June 1995, p. 23; "A Global Company, 1980–1996," www.pg.com/info/library/history/1980d.html, August 11, 1997; "The Discreet Charm of the Multicultural Multinational," *The Economist,* July 30, 1994, pp. 57–58; Yao-Su Hu, "Global or Stateless Corporations Are National Firms with International Operations," *California Management Review,* Winter 1992, pp. 107–26.

Definitions Used in This Text

In this text we will employ the definitions listed below, which are generally accepted by businesspeople. Although we primarily use the terms *global, multidomestic,* and *international* firms or companies, at times we may use *multinational enterprise (MNE)* or *multinational company (MNC)* interchangeably with *international company (IC)* inasmuch as both terms are employed in the literature and in practice.

1. *International business* is business whose activities are carried out across national borders. This definition includes not only international trade and foreign manufacturing but also the growing service industry in areas such as transportation, tourism, advertising, construction, retailing, wholesaling, and mass communications. Figure 1.1 demonstrates how widespread one service corporation has become.
2. *Foreign business* denotes the domestic operations within a foreign country. This term sometimes is used interchangeably with *international business* by some writers.
3. **Multidomestic company** (MDC) is an organization with multicountry affiliates, each of which formulates its own business strategy based on perceived market differences.
4. **Global company** (GC) is an organization that attempts to standardize and integrate operations worldwide in all functional areas.*
5. **International company** (IC) refers to both global and multidomestic companies.

*Note that in this definition global ownership is not a requirement. However, you should be aware that some people do include this along with other criteria, such as the ratio of foreign to total employment or foreign to total assets.

multidomestic company
An organization with multi-country affiliates, each of which formulates its own business strategy based on perceived market differences.

global company
An organization that attempts to standardize and integrate operations worldwide in all functional areas.

international company
Either a global or a multidomestic company.

[Figure 1.1] **Overseas Locations of McDonald's, an International Service Company**

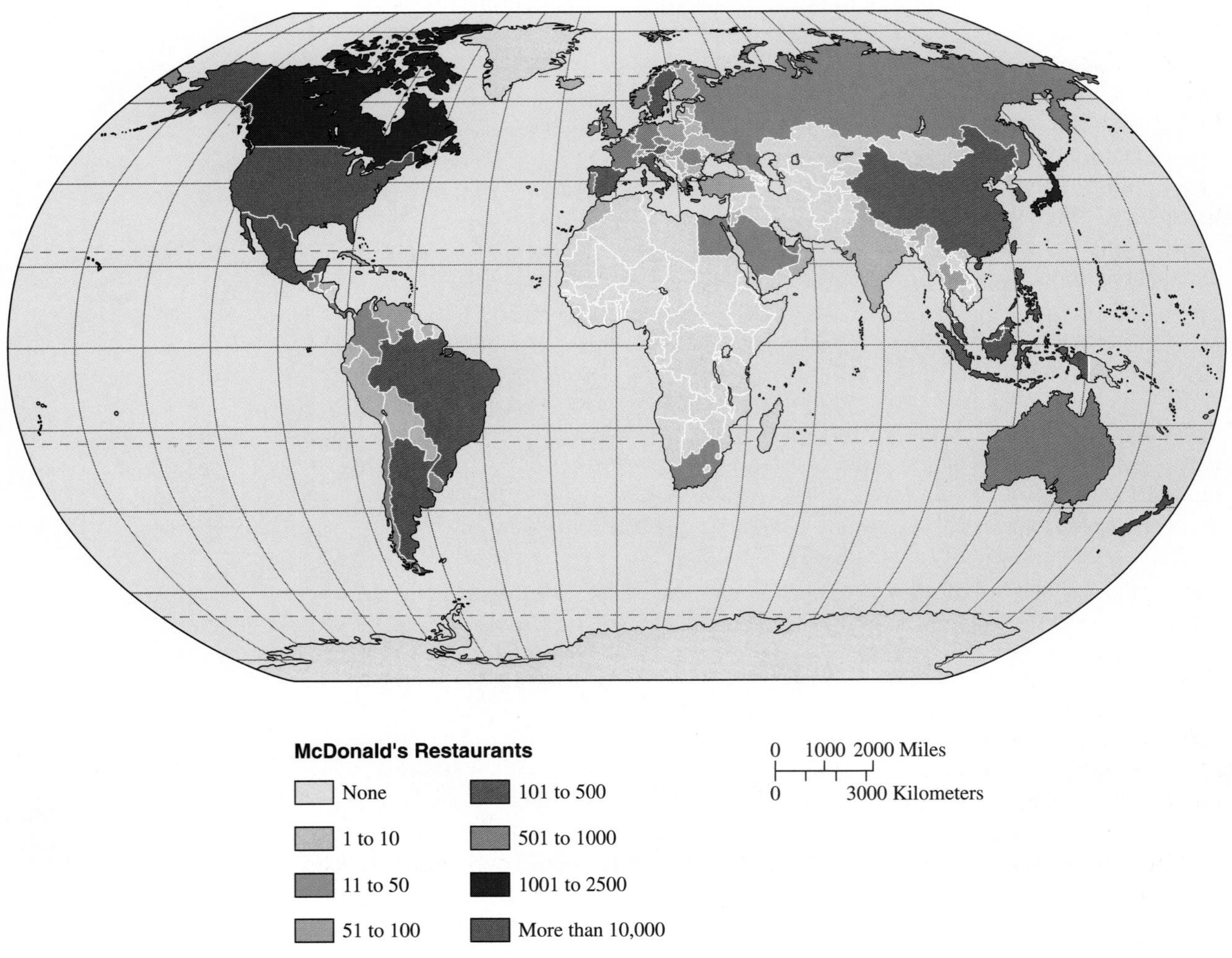

History of International Business

While international business as a discipline is relatively new, international business as a business practice is not, as we shall see in the next section, "History of International Business." Well before the time of Christ, Phoenician and Greek merchants were sending representatives abroad to sell their goods. In 1600, the British East India Company, a newly formed trading firm, established foreign branches throughout Asia. At about the same time, a number of Dutch companies, which had organized in 1590 to open shipping routes to the East, joined together to form the Dutch East India Company and also opened branch offices in Asia.[9] American colonial traders began operating in a similar fashion in the 1700s.

Early examples of American foreign direct investment are the English plants set up by Colt Fire Arms and Ford* (vulcanized rubber), which were established before the Civil War. Both operations failed, however, after only a few years.

A number of multinational companies existed in the late 1800s. One of the first to own foreign production facilities, have worldwide distribution networks, and market its products under global brands was Singer Sewing Machine. In 1868, it built a factory in Scotland, the first successful American venture into foreign production. By 1880, the company had become a global organization with an out-

*This Ford was no relation to Henry Ford.

standing international sales organization and several overseas manufacturing plants. Other firms, such as J&P Coats (United Kingdom) and Ford, soon followed, and by 1914, at least 37 American companies had production facilities in two or more overseas locations.[10]

Among those firms already established overseas were National Cash Register and Burroughs, with manufacturing plants in Europe; Parke-Davis, with a plant near London (1902); and Ford Motor Company, which had assembly plants or distribution outlets in 14 countries. General Motors and Chrysler followed soon afterward, so that by the 1920s all three companies had sizable foreign operations. Interestingly, and quite the reverse of today's situation, in the 1920s *all* cars sold in Japan were made in the United States by Ford and General Motors and sent to Japan in knocked-down kits to be assembled locally. Another early overseas investor was General Electric, which, by 1919, had plants in Europe, Latin America, and Asia.[11] Other well-known American firms in Europe at that time were Alcoa, American Tobacco, Armour, Coca-Cola, Eastman Kodak, Gillette, Quaker Oats, Western Electric, and Westinghouse.

Interestingly, American business moving overseas caused consternation among Europeans similar to that caused by Japanese investments in the United States today. One author wrote, "The invasion goes on unceasingly and without noise or show in 500 industries at once. From shaving soap to electric motors, and from shirtwaists to telephones, the American is clearing the field."[12]

Although American firms were by far the largest foreign investors, European companies were also moving overseas. Friedrich Bayer purchased an interest in a New York plant in 1865, two years after setting up his plant in Germany. Then, because of high import duties in his overseas markets, he proceeded to establish plants in Russia (1876), France (1882), and Belgium (1908).[13] Bayer, now one of the four largest chemical companies in the world ($29 billion in 1999 sales), has 350 companies with operations in 140 countries. After losing the right to use the name Bayer in North America as part of Germany's World War I reparations, the company regained that right in 1995 by buying the over-the-counter drug division from Kodak, which had been the manufacturer and owner of Bayer aspirin.[14]

Although multinational firms existed well before World War I, only in recent years have they become the object of much discussion and investigation, especially concerning the increasing globalization of their operations. What is globalization? What are the reasons for globalization?

Globalization

What Is It?

Although globalization is discussed everywhere—television shows, Internet chat rooms, political demonstrations, parliaments, management boardrooms, and labor union meetings—so far there is no widely accepted definition. In fact, its definition continues to broaden. Now, for example, social scientists discuss the political, social, environmental, historical, geographical, and even cultural implications of globalization.[15] Some also speak of technological globalization, political globalization, and the like.[16]

However, the most common definition and the one used in international business is that of economic globalization—the international integration of goods, technology, labor, and capital; that is, firms implement global strategies which link and coordinate their international activities on a worldwide basis.[17] Interestingly, at the 1999 World Economic Forum (WEF) annual meeting in Davos, Switzerland, a new word, *globality,* was introduced as the meeting's theme. Daniel Yergin, coauthor of *The Commanding Heights,* decided that since globalization is a process, a different word was needed for "the results of this process—a place, a condition, the situation that comes afterward." Professor Klaus Schwab, founder of the WEF, explained, "We wanted to look beyond the economic dimensions of what is happening. It is a globality." Bill Gates announced at the meeting that Microsoft would add *globality* to Microsoft's dictionary.[18]

Globalization Forces

There are five major kinds of drivers, all based on change, that are leading international firms to the globalization of their operations: (1) political, (2) technology, (3) market, (4) cost, and (5) competitive:[19]

1. **Political.** There is a trend toward the unification and socialization of the global community. Preferential trading arrangements, such as the North American Free Trade Agreement and the European Union, that group several nations into a single market have presented firms with significant marketing opportunities. Many have moved swiftly to enter either through exporting or by producing in the area.

   Two other aspects of this trend are contributing to the globalization of business operations: (*a*) the progressive reduction of barriers to trade and foreign investment by most governments, which is hastening the opening of new markets by international firms that are both exporting to them and building production facilities in them, and (*b*) the privatization of much of the industry in formerly communist nations and the opening of their economies to global competition.

2. **Technology.** Advances in computers and communications technology are permitting an increased flow of ideas and information across borders, enabling customers to learn about foreign goods. Cable TV systems in Europe and Asia, for example, allow an advertiser to reach numerous countries simultaneously, thus creating regional and sometimes global demand. Global communications networks enable manufacturing personnel to coordinate production and design functions worldwide so that plants in many parts of the world may be working on the same product.

   The Internet and network computing enable small companies to compete globally because they make possible the rapid flow of information regardless of the physical location of the buyer and seller. Internet videoconferencing allows sellers to demonstrate their products to prospective buyers all over the world without the need to travel. It also permits international companies to hold corporate meetings between managers from headquarters and overseas subsidiaries without expensive, time-consuming travel. In addition, communicating by E-mail on the Internet is faster and more reliable than using postal mail and much less expensive than using a fax machine. Both Internet uses have given home office managers greater confidence in their ability to direct overseas operations.

   The ease of obtaining information and making transactions on the Internet has started to have a profound effect on many firms and especially on business-to-business commerce.* Whereas companies formerly used faxes, telephones, or mail to complete their transactions, they now use the cheaper and faster Internet. For example, Cisco Systems, a network-equipment maker, makes 80 percent of its $12 billion annual sales from its Web site.[20] The concept of using the Web to find suppliers is already established in certain industries, and more are coming online. In February 1999, Ford, General Motors (GM), and DaimlerChrysler announced a joint venture to fund and develop a Web-based trading exchange connecting all the buyers and sellers in the entire automobile supply chain. Renault and Nissan also declared their intention to join. As an example of the savings to be obtained, Ford expects to save 10 percent on the $80 billion it buys from its suppliers annually plus another $1 billion in transaction costs. A typical purchase order costs Ford $150, but an order on the exchange will cost about $15.[21] The five automakers spend roughly $700 billion annually. Similar Internet exchanges have been announced by tire manufacturers, airlines, computer companies, aerospace companies, retailers, and chemical companies.[22]

3. **Market.** As companies globalize, they also become global customers. For years, advertising agencies established offices in foreign markets when their major clients entered those markets to avoid having a competitor steal the accounts. Likewise,

*See the Chapter 1 "Internet Appendix" for information on using the Internet for international business research.

A Little Guy Makes Global Business Easier for the Little Guys

Small and Medium-Sized Enterprises

DE Technologies, a tiny private company with only six employees, has patented a technology for processing sales globally using the Internet. With this system, which is called the Electronic Commerce Backbone System (ECBS), small and medium-sized firms can export and import goods and services without previous international trade experience. The ECBS allows buyers/sellers to buy American products in the currency of the destination country, view product descriptions in the language of the destination country, view digital still or motion video displays of the products for sale, and view the calculations and displays of prices for air, land, and sea transportation; it also ensures direct payment of goods via credit cards or documentary credit.

Procedures such as the preparation and filing of export–import documents, freight, insurance, titles, letters of credit, pro forma invoices, and bills of lading are done by the program. This eliminates the necessity of engaging foreign freight forwarders, export and import agents, and other international channel of distribution members. Thus, ECBS reduces the costs of ocean and air freight, banking, and human resources.

Small and medium-sized businesses can become members by paying a small membership fee, which gives them access to the ECBS. A small transactional fee of 0.3 percent also is levied. According to the founder of DE Technologies, "the capability of the system will allow thousands of SMEs to compete effectively in the Import/Export business with 'The Big Guys' as the barriers to entry will be lowered tremendously." ■

Sources: "Cutting through a World of Red Tape," *Business Week Online,* www.businesswe...m/small biz/0006/te000628.htm?scriptFramed (June 30, 2000); "Electronic Commerce Backbone System (ECBS)," *DE Technologies Web site,* www.detechnologies.com/ecbs.htm (August 1, 2000); and "Borderless Order Entry Systems," *DE Technologies Web site,* www.detechnologies.com/boes.htm (August 1, 2000).

when an automaker, about to set up a foreign plant where there was no tire factory, asked a tire company if it was interested in setting up a plant in this new market, the response was, "When do you want us there?" It is also quite common for a global supplier to make global supply contracts with a global customer.

Finding the home market saturated also sends companies into foreign markets, especially when the marketer realizes there is a convergence of customer tastes and lifestyles brought about by increasing tourist travel, satellite TV, and global branding.

4. **Cost.** Economies of scale to reduce unit costs are always a management goal. One means of achieving them is to globalize product lines to reduce development, production, and inventory costs. The company can also locate production in countries where the costs of the factors of production are lower.

5. **Competitive.** Competition continues to increase in intensity. New firms, many from newly industrialized and developing countries, have entered world markets in automobiles and electronics, for example. As you saw in the opening incident, import penetration has increased markedly for five of the six major trading nations over the past 29 years. Another competitive driving force for globalization is the fact that companies are defending their home markets from competitors by entering the competitors' home markets to distract them (example: Kodak–Fuji).

   Many firms that would not have entered a single country because it lacked sufficient market size have established plants in the comparatively larger trading groups (European Union, ASEAN, Mercosur). It's one thing to be shut out of Belgium, but it's another to be excluded from all Europe.

The result of this rush to globalization has been an explosive growth in international business.

Explosive Growth

There has been explosive growth in both the size and the number of U.S. and foreign international concerns.

Table 1.2 **FDI Indicators and Multinational Company Statistics (billions of dollars and percentages)**

	Value at Current Prices (billions of dollars)			Annual Growth Rate (percent)			
	1996	1997	1998	1991–1995	1996	1997	1998
FDI data							
Inflows	359	464	644	19.6	9.1	29.4	38.7
Outflows	380	475	649	15.9	5.9	25.1	36.6
Inward stock	3,086	3,437	4,088	9.6	10.6	11.4	19.0
Outward stock	3,145	3,423	4,117	10.5	10.7	8.9	20.3
Cross-border M&As*	163	236	411	30.2	15.5	45.2	73.9
Foreign affiliate data							
Sales	9,372	9,728	11,427	10.7	11.7	3.8	17.5
Total assets	11,246	12,211	14,620	13.8	8.8	8.6	19.7
Exports	1,841	2,035	2,338	13.1	−5.8	10.5	14.9
Employment (thousands)	30,941	31,630	35,074	5.6	4.9	2.2	10.9

Note: *Majority-held investment only.

Source: "Mega Mergers Reshaping Global Production System," *UNCTAD Press Release,* TAD/INF/2821, September 23, 1999, www.unctad.org/en/press/pr2821.htm (August 3, 2000).

Foreign Direct Investment

One variable commonly used to measure where and how fast internationalization is taking place is the increase in total foreign direct investment (FDI).* For example, the world stock of FDI is estimated to have risen from $519 billion in 1980 to $4.117 *trillion* in 1998, an eightfold increase in just 18 years (see Table 1.2).

Note also that total FDI rose by nearly 40 percent to $644 billion for a record increase, while total assets of multinational foreign affiliates grew by 19.7 percent in 1998 to reach $14.62 trillion. Majority-owned cross-border mergers and acquisitions (M&As) registered a 1998 growth of $411 billion, up almost 75 percent, after rising 45 percent in 1997. Preliminary 1999 results reveal that cross-border M&As ($720 billion) continue to be the driving force behind the growth of FDI flows ($827 billion in 1999). The United States, the nation with the highest sales of companies in 1999, was replaced by the United Kingdom as the largest acquirer of foreign companies. These two countries also represent for each other the principal home country as well as host country.[23]

Number of International Companies

We also have estimates of the number of global and multidomestic firms in the world. In 1999, UNCTAD, the United Nations agency in charge of all matters relating to FDI and international corporations, estimated that there were over 60,000 companies with half a million foreign affiliates that accounted for 25 percent of global output. They accounted for two-thirds of world trade. Foreign affiliates' sales ($11 trillion) are far in excess of global trade ($7 trillion).[24] Only four years ago, UNCTAD estimated that there were only 45,000 parent companies with 280,000 foreign affiliates with sales of US$7 trillion.[25]

UNCTAD reports, "The world's largest 100 transnational corporations, measured in terms of foreign assets, hold a dominant position in the new international production system. They now account for US$4 trillion in total sales and hold a stock of total assets in excess of US$4.2 trillion." General Electric is the world's largest TNC, closely followed by the Ford Motor Company and the Royal Dutch Shell Group. What is striking is that

**Foreign direct investment* is sufficient investment to obtain significant management control. In the United States, 10 percent is sufficient; in other countries, it is not considered a direct investment until a share of 20 or 25 percent is reached.

85 of the top 100 have been on the UNCTAD list for several years. Only two, Petroleos of Venezuela and Daewoo Corporation of Korea, are from developing countries.[26]

As a result of this expansion, the foreign company's subsidiaries have become increasingly important in the industrial and economic life of many nations, developed and developing. This situation is in sharp contrast to the one that existed when the dominant economic interests were in the hands of local citizens. The expanding importance of foreign-owned firms in local economies came to be viewed by a number of governments as a threat to their autonomy. However, beginning in the 1980s, there has been a marked liberalization of government policies and attitudes toward foreign investment in both developed and developing nations. Leaders of these governments know that local firms must obtain modern commercial technology in the form of direct investment, purchase of capital goods, and the right to use the international company's expertise if they are to be competitive in world markets.*

Despite this change in attitude, there are still critics of large global firms who cite such statistics as the following to "prove" that host governments are powerless before them:

1. In 1998, only 23 nations had gross national products (GNPs) greater than the total annual sales of General Motors, the world's largest international company.
2. Also in 1998, the total amount of money spent in Wal-Mart worldwide was greater than the sum of the GNPs of over 100 nations.

As Table 1.3 indicates, these statements must be true. In fact, when nations and industrial firms are ranked by GNP and total sales, respectively, 48 of the first 100 on the list are industrial firms. While a nation's GNP and a company's sales are not comparable, they are indicators of potential power, as you will see in Chapter 10, "Political Forces." Also, regardless of the parent firm's size, each subsidiary is a local company that must comply with the laws in the country where it is located. If it does not, it can be subject to legal action or even government seizure. From 1970 to 1975 there were 336 acts of seizure, but a decade later that number dropped to just 15. Now most differences are settled by arbitration.**[27]

Recent Developments

Lessening of American Dominance?

You may have noticed in Table 1.3 that there are more Asian and European international firms than there are American. It was not always this way. Until the 1960s American multinationals clearly dominated world business, but then the situation began to change. European firms began challenging American multinationals, first in their home countries and then in third-country markets dominated by U.S. companies. By the 1970s large European and Japanese businesses were expanding their overseas production facilities faster than were American firms. To realize the change in the relative importance of American, European, and Japanese multinationals, it is helpful to compare *Fortune*'s list of the top 100 industrial firms in the world ranked according to *sales* in 1980, 1996, and 1999.[28]

1980		1996		1999	
45	United States	32	United States	35	United States
42	Western Europe	38	Western Europe	45	Western Europe
8	Japan	23	Japan	20	Japan
1	South Korea	4	South Korea		
1	Brazil	1	Brazil		
1	Mexico	1	Mexico		
1	Venezuela	1	Venezuela		
1	Canada				
100		100		100	

*Granting the right to use a firm's expertise for a fee is called *licensing*. See Chapter 2 for more details.

**These and related subjects are discussed in Chapters 10 and 11.

Table 1.3 Ranking of International Firms and Nations According to GNP or Total Sales in 1998

Ranking	Nation or Firm	GNP or Total Sales for 1998 ($ billion)
1.	United States	7,903.0
2.	Japan	4,089.1
3.	Germany	2,179.8
4.	France	1,465.4
5.	United Kingdom	1,264.3
6.	Italy	1,157.0
7.	China	923.6
8.	Brazil	767.6
9.	Canada	580.9
10.	Spain	555.2
11.	India	427.4
12.	Korea, Republic of	398.8
13.	Netherlands	389.1
14.	Australia	387.0
15.	Mexico	368.1
16.	Russian Federation	331.8
17.	Argentina	290.3
18.	Switzerland	284.1
19.	Belgium	259.0
20.	Sweden	226.5
21.	Austria	216.7
22.	Turkey	200.5
23.	Denmark	175.2
24.	*General Motors (US)*	161.3
25.	Hong Kong, China*	158.2
26.	*DaimlerChrysler (G)*	154.6
27.	Norway	152.0
28.	Poland	151.3
29.	*Ford Motor (US)*	144.4
30.	Saudi Arabia	143.4
31.	*Wal-Mart Stores (US)*	139.2
32.	South Africa	136.9
33.	Thailand	131.9
34.	Indonesia	130.6
35.	Finland	125.1
36.	Greece	123.4
37.	*Mitsui (J)*	109.4
38.	*Itochu (J)*	108.7
39.	*Mitsubishi (J)*	107.2
40.	Portugal	106.4
41.	Iran	102.2
42.	Colombia	100.7
43.	*Exxon (US)*	100.7
44.	*General Electric (US)*	100.5
45.	*Toyota (J)*	99.7
46.	Israel	96.5
47.	Singapore	95.5
48.	*Royal Dutch Shell (UK–Neth)*	93.7
49.	*Marubeni (J)*	93.6
50.	*Sumitomo (J)*	89.0

Table 1.3 *(continued)*

Ranking	Nation or Firm	GNP or Total Sales for 1998 ($ billion)
51.	Venezuela	82.1
52.	*IBM (US)*	81.7
53.	Malaysia	81.3
54.	Egypt	79.2
55.	Philippines	78.9
56.	*AXA (F)*	78.7
57.	*Citigroup (US)*	76.4
58.	*Volkswagen (G)*	76.3
59.	*Nippon T & T (J)*	76.1
60.	Chile	73.9
61.	Ireland	69.3
62.	*BP Amoco (UK)*	68.3
63.	*Nissho Iwai (J)*	67.7
64.	*Nippon Life Ins. (J)*	66.3
65.	*Siemens (G)*	66.0
66.	*Allianz (G)*	64.9
67.	*Hitachi (J)*	62.4
68.	Pakistan	61.5
69.	Peru	60.5
70.	*U.S. Postal Service (US)*	60.1
71.	*Matushita Elec. (J)*	59.8
72.	*Philip Morris (US)*	57.8
73.	*Ing Group (Neth)*	56.5
74.	*Boeing (US)*	56.2
75.	New Zealand	55.4
76.	*AT&T (US)*	53.6
77.	*Sony (J)*	53.2
78.	Czech Republic	53.0
79.	*Metro (G)*	52.1
80.	*Nissan Motors (J)*	51.5
81.	*Fiat (It)*	51.0
82.	*Bank of America (US)*	50.8
83.	*Nestlé (S)*	49.5
84.	Ukraine	49.2
85.	*Credit Suisse (S)*	49.1
86.	*Honda Motor (J)*	48.7
87.	United Arab Emirates	48.7
88.	*Assicurazioni Gen. (It)*	48.5
89.	*Mobil (US)*	47.7
90.	*Hewlett-Packard (US)*	47.1
91.	Algeria	46.4
92.	Hungary	45.7
93.	*Deutsche Bank (G)*	45.2
94.	*Unilever (UK–Neth)*	44.9
95.	*State Farm Ins. (US)*	44.6
96.	*Dai-Ichi Ins. (J)*	44.5
97.	Bangladesh	44.2
98.	*Veba Group (G)*	43.4
99.	*HSBC Holdings (UK)*	43.3
100.	*Toshiba (J)*	41.5

*Value is gross domestic product (GDP), not GNP.

Letters in parentheses indicate a firm's nationality: F = France, G = Germany, It = Italy, J = Japan, K = South Korea, Neth = Netherlands, S = Switzerland, UK = United Kingdom, US = United States.

Sources: "Total GNP 1998, Atlas Method," Washington, DC: World Bank, www.worldbank.org/databytopic/GNP.pdf (July 16, 2000); and "Fortune Global 5 Hundred," *Fortune,* August 2, 1999, pp. 144–F11.

Another basis for comparison is market value. The number of firms ranked according to market capitalization in the top 100 Companies in *Business Week*'s "The Global 1000" are as follows:

1996		1999	
52	United States	62	United States
23	Western Europe	32	Western Europe
21	Japan	4	Japan
2	Hong Kong	1	Canada
1	Singapore	1	Australia
1	Australia		
100		100	

Note the difference when firms are ranked according to market capitalization instead of total sales.

We can also compare lists over time of the largest firms in a number of industries to see if there has been a change of leadership in sales volume. Following is an analysis of the automobile industry.

1981	1996	1999
1. General Motors (U.S.)	1. General Motors (U.S.)	1. General Motors (U.S.)
2. Ford (U.S.)	2. Ford (U.S.)	2. Ford (U.S.)
3. Fiat (Italy)	3. Toyota (Japan)	3. DaimlerChrysler (Germany)
4. Renault (France)	4. Daimler-Benz (Germany)	4. Toyota (Japan)
5. Volkswagen (Germany)	5. Volkswagen (Germany)	5. Volkswagen (Germany)
6. Daimler-Benz (Germany)	6. Daewoo (South Korea)	6. Honda (Japan)
7. Peugeot (France)	7. Chrysler (U.S.)	7. Nissan (Japan)
8. Toyota (Japan)	8. Nissan (Japan)	8. Fiat (Italy)
9. Nissan (Japan)	9. Fiat (Italy)	9. Peugeot (France)
10. Mitsubishi (Japan)	10. Honda (Japan)	10. Renault (France)

A similar analysis of the top ten firms in five other industries that American firms dominated in 1959 showed that by 1999 they continued to lead in only two of them.[29]

Industry	1959		1999	
Aerospace	8	United States	6	United States
	2	European	2	European*
Chemicals	7	United States	6	European
	3	European	2	United States
			2	Japanese
Metal manufacturing	9	United States	5	Japanese
	1	European	3	European
			1	United States
			1	South Korean
Electronics	7	United States	6	Japanese
	3	European	2	European
			2	United States
Pharmaceuticals	7	United States	5	United States
	3	European	5	European

*Only eight firms in this industry are in the Fortune Global 500.

It would appear from this analysis that American firms have lost ground to European and Japanese multinationals, as a few writers claim. However, when you compare the number of companies on the first Fortune Global 500 list (1989 sales) with the 1999 results, you come to a different conclusion.

Countries with the Most Companies on Fortune Global 500 List			
	1999	1995	1989
United States	179	153	167
Japan	105	141	111
France	36	42	29
Germany	38	40	32
United Kingdom	39	32	43

Sources: "World's Largest Corporations," *Fortune,* August 4, 1997, p. F-1; "Fortune's New Global 500," *Fortune,* July 30, 1989, p. 265; and "The Global 500 List," *Fortune,* www.fortune.com/fortune/global500/ (July 22, 2000).

Why Is International Business Different?

International business differs from domestic business in that a firm operating across borders must deal with the forces of three kinds of environments—domestic, foreign, and international. In contrast, a firm whose business activities are carried out within the borders of one country needs to be concerned essentially with only the domestic environment. However, no domestic firm is entirely free from foreign or international environmental forces because the possibility of having to face competition from foreign imports or from foreign competitors that set up operations in its own market is always present. Let us first examine these forces and then see how they operate in the three environments.

Forces in the Environments

Environment as used here is the sum of all the forces surrounding and influencing the life and development of the firm. The forces themselves can be classified as *external* or *internal.* Furthermore, management has no direct control over them, though it can exert influences such as lobbying for a change in a law and heavily promoting a new product that requires a change in a cultural attitude. The external forces are commonly called **uncontrollable forces** and consist of the following:

environment
All the forces surrounding and influencing the life and development of the firm

uncontrollable forces
External forces over which management has no direct control, although it can exert an influence

1. *Competitive*—kinds and numbers of competitors, their locations, and their activities.
2. *Distributive*—national and international agencies available for distributing goods and services.
3. *Economic*—variables (such as GNP, unit labor cost, and personal consumption expenditure) that influence a firm's ability to do business.
4. *Socioeconomic*—characteristics and distribution of the human population.
5. *Financial*—variables such as interest rates, inflation rates, and taxation.
6. *Legal*—the many kinds of foreign and domestic laws by which international firms must operate.
7. *Physical*—elements of nature such as topography, climate, and natural resources.
8. *Political*—elements of nations' political climates such as nationalism, forms of government, and international organizations.
9. *Sociocultural*—elements of culture (such as attitudes, beliefs, and opinions) important to international businesspeople.
10. *Labor*—composition, skills, and attitudes of labor.
11. *Technological*—the technical skills and equipment that affect how resources are converted to products.

The elements over which management does have some control are the internal forces, such as the factors of production (capital, raw materials, and people) and the activities of the organization (personnel, finance, production, and marketing). These are the **controllable forces** management must administer in order to adapt to changes in the uncontrollable environmental variables. Look at how one change in the political force—the passage of the North American Free Trade Agreement—is affecting all the controllable forces of firms worldwide that do business in or with the three member-nations: the United States, Mexico, and Canada. Suddenly these companies must examine their business practices and change those affected by this new law. For example, some American concerns and foreign subsidiaries in the United States have relocated part of their operations to Mexico to exploit the lower wages there. There are European and Asian companies that have set up production in one of the member-countries to supply this giant free trade region. By doing this, they avoid paying import duties on products coming from their home countries.

controllable forces
Internal forces that management administers to adapt to changes in the uncontrollable forces

The Domestic Environment

domestic environment
All the uncontrollable forces originating in the home country that surround and influence the firm's life and development

The **domestic environment** is composed of all the uncontrollable forces originating in the home country that surround and influence the life and development of the firm. Obviously, these are the forces with which managers are most familiar. Being domestic forces does not preclude their affecting foreign operations, however. For example, if the home country is suffering from a shortage of foreign currency, the government may place restrictions on overseas investment to reduce its outflow. As a result, managements of multinationals find that they cannot expand overseas facilities as they would like to do. In another instance from real life, a labor union striking the home-based plants learned that management was supplying parts from its foreign subsidiaries. The strikers contacted the foreign unions, which pledged not to work overtime to supply what the struck plants could not. The impact of this domestic environmental force was felt overseas as well as at home.

The Foreign Environment

foreign environment
All the uncontrollable forces originating outside the home country that surround and influence the firm

The forces in the **foreign environment** are the same as those in the domestic environment except that they occur in foreign nations.* However, they operate differently for several reasons, including the following:

Different Force Values

Even though the kinds of forces in the two environments are identical, their values often differ widely, and at times they are completely opposed to each other. A classic example of diametrically opposed political force values and the bewilderment they create for multinational managers was the case of Dresser Industries and the gas pipeline in the Soviet Union. When President Reagan extended the American embargo against shipments of equipment for the pipeline to include foreign companies manufacturing equipment under license from U.S. firms, the Dresser home office instructed its French subsidiary to stop work on an order for compressors. Meanwhile, the French government ordered Dresser-France to defy the embargo and begin scheduled deliveries under penalty of both civil and criminal sanctions. As a Dresser's vice president put it, "The order put Dresser between a rock and a hard place."

A similar case occurred when, because of the American export embargo on shipments to Cuba, that country could not buy buses from the U.S. manufacturer with which it had done business for years. To circumvent the embargo, the government

**Foreign* has multiple definitions according to the *American Heritage Dictionary,* including (1) originating from the outside—external, (2) originating from a country other than one's own, and (3) conducted or involved with other nations or governments. *Extrinsic* is a synonym. Note that we are not using another definition—unfamiliar or strange. Some writers have this last definition in mind when they state that overseas markets in which the firm does business are not foreign because their managers know them well. However, according to any of the first three definitions, the degree of familiarity has no bearing.

ordered the buses from the firm's Argentine subsidiary. When word came from the firm's American headquarters that the order should not be filled because of the American embargo, the Argentine government ordered the Argentine subsidiary to fill the order, saying that Argentine companies, of which the Argentine subsidiary was one, did not answer to the demands of a foreign government. The Argentine management of the subsidiary was in a quandary. Finally, headquarters relented and permitted its Argentine subsidiary to fill the order.

Changes Difficult to Assess

Another problem with foreign forces is that they are frequently difficult to assess, especially their legal and political elements. A highly nationalistic law may be passed to appease a section of the population. To all outward appearances, a government may appear to be against foreign investment, yet pragmatic leaders may actually encourage it. A good example is Mexico, which until 1988 had a law prohibiting foreigners from owning a majority interest in a Mexican company. However, a clause permitted exceptions "if the investment contributes to the welfare of the nation." IBM, Eaton, and others were successful in obtaining permission to establish a wholly owned subsidiary under this clause.

Forces Interrelated

In the chapters that follow, it will be evident that the forces are often interrelated. This in itself is not a novelty, because the same situation confronts a domestic manager. Often different, however, are the types and degrees of interaction that occur. For instance, the combination of high-cost capital and an abundance of unskilled labor in many developing countries may lead to the use of a lower level of technology than would be employed in the more industrialized nations. In other words, given a choice between installing costly, specialized machinery needing few workers and installing less expensive, general-purpose machinery requiring a larger labor force, management will frequently choose the latter when faced with high interest rates and a large pool of available workers. Another example is the interaction between physical and sociocultural forces. Barriers to the free movement of a nation's people, such as mountain ranges and deserts, help maintain pockets of distinct cultures within a country.

The International Environment

The **international environment** is the interactions (1) between the domestic environmental forces and the foreign environmental forces and (2) between the foreign environmental forces of two countries when an affiliate in one country does business with customers in another. This agrees with the definition of international business: business that involves the crossing of national borders.

international environment
Interaction between domestic and foreign environmental forces or between sets of foreign environmental forces

For example, personnel at the headquarters of a multidomestic or global company work in the international environment if they are involved in any way with another nation, whereas those in a foreign subsidiary do not unless they too are engaged in international business through exporting or the management of other affiliates. In other words, the sales manager of Goodyear-Chile does not work in the international environment if he or she sells tires only in Chile. If Goodyear-Chile exports tires to Bolivia, then the sales manager is affected by forces of both the domestic environment of Chile and the foreign environment of Bolivia and therefore is working in the international environment. International organizations whose actions affect the international environment are also properly part of it. These organizations include (1) worldwide bodies (e.g., World Bank), (2) regional economic groupings of nations (e.g., North American Free Trade Agreement), and (3) organizations bound by industry agreements (e.g., Organization of Petroleum Exporting Countries).

Decision Making More Complex

Those who work in the international environment find that decision making is more complex than it is in a purely domestic environment. Consider managers in a home office who must make decisions affecting subsidiaries in just 10 different countries (many internationals are in 20 or more countries). They not only must take into account the domestic forces, they must also evaluate the influence of 10 foreign national environments. Instead of having to consider the effects of a single set of 10 forces, as do their domestic counterparts, they have to contend with 10 sets of 10 forces, *both individually and collectively,* because there may be some interaction.

For example, if management agrees to labor's demands at one foreign subsidiary, chances are, it will have to offer a similar settlement at another subsidiary because of the tendency of unions to exchange information across borders. Furthermore, as we shall observe throughout the text, not only are there many sets of forces, there also are extreme differences among them.

self-reference criterion
Unconscious reference to one's own cultural values when judging behavioral actions of others in a new and different environment

Another common cause of the added complexity of foreign environments is managers' unfamiliarity with other cultures. To make matters worse, they will ascribe to others their own preferences and reactions. Thus, the foreign production manager, facing a backlog of orders, offers the workers extra pay for overtime. When they fail to show up, the manager is perplexed: "Back home they always want to earn more money." This manager has failed to understand that the workers prefer time off to more money. This unconscious reference to the manager's own cultural values, called **self-reference criterion,** is probably the biggest cause of international business blunders. Successful administrators are careful to examine a problem in terms of the local cultural traits as well as their own.

International Business Model

The relationships of the forces in the three environments we have been discussing form the basis for our international business environments model shown in Figure 1.2. The external or uncontrollable forces in both the domestic and the foreign environments surround the internal forces controlled by management. The domestic environment of the international firm's home country is surrounded by as many sets of foreign environments as there are countries in which the company does business. Solid lines connecting the internal forces at the home office to the internal forces in the foreign affiliates indicate the lines of control. The beige areas indicate the international environment in which personnel in the headquarters of the international firm work. If, for example, the affiliate in foreign environment A exports to or manages the affiliate in foreign environment B, then its personnel are also working in the international environment, as shown by the beige section.

We shall be using this model throughout the book. After describing the nature of international business in Section I, we examine the international organizations and the international monetary system in Section II. In Section III, we analyze the uncontrollable forces that make up the foreign and domestic environments and illustrate their effect on management functions. Finally, we reverse the procedure in Section IV and deal with the management functions, demonstrating how they are influenced by the uncontrollable forces.

A solid understanding of the business concepts and techniques employed in the United States and other advanced industrial nations is a requisite for success in international business. However, because transactions take place across national borders, three environments—domestic, foreign, and international—may be involved instead of just

[Figure 1.2] **International Business Environments**

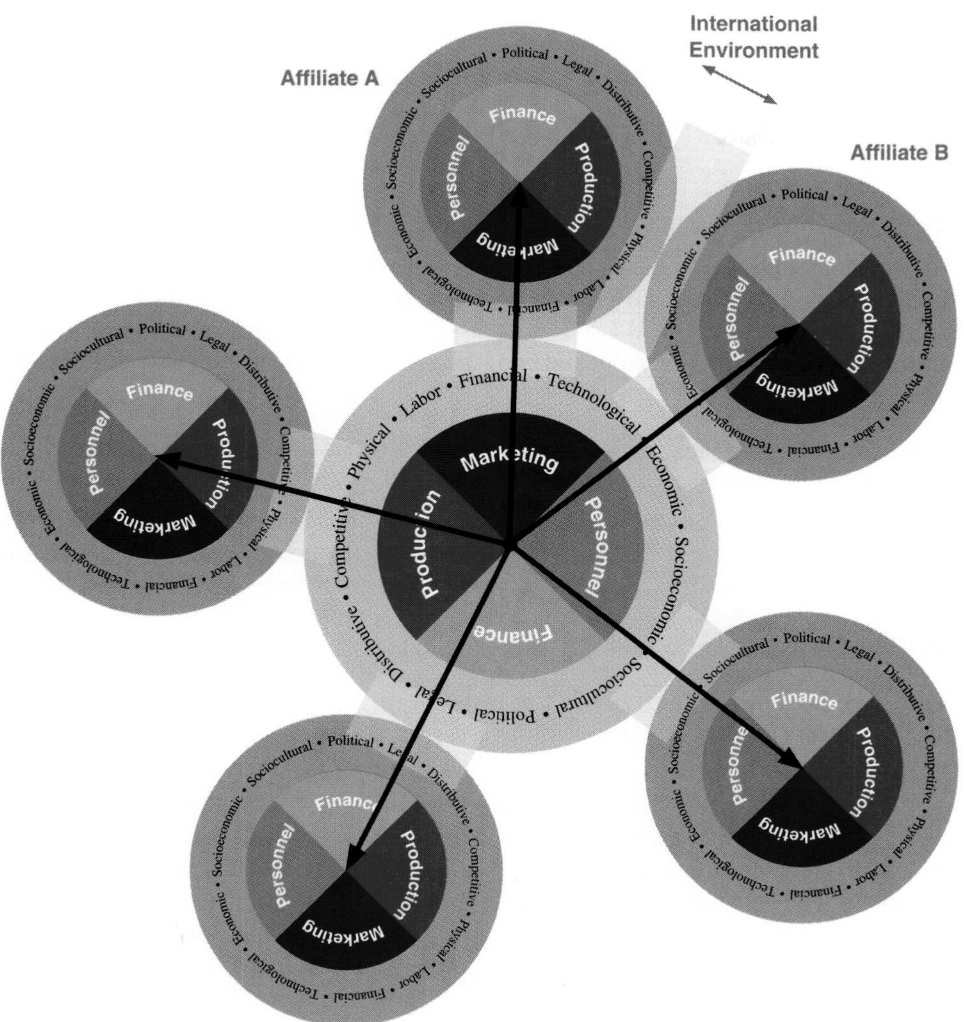

Domestic environment
(Includes socioeconomic, sociocultural, political, legal, distributive, competitive, physical, labor, financial, technological, and economic environments)

Foreign environment
(Includes socioeconomic, sociocultural, political, legal, distributive, competitive, physical, labor, financial, technological, and economic environments)

one; thus, in international business, the international manager has three choices in what to do with a concept or a technique employed in domestic operations: (1) transfer it intact, (2) adapt it to local conditions, or (3) not use it overseas. International managers who have discovered that there are differences in the environmental forces are better prepared to decide which option to follow. To be sure, no one can be an expert on all these forces for all nations, but just knowing that differences may exist will cause people to "work with their antennas extended." In other words, when they enter international business, they will know they must look out for important variations in many of the forces that they take as given in the domestic environment. It is to the study of the three environments that this text is directed.

[Summary]

Appreciate the dramatic internationalization of markets.

Global competition is mounting. The huge increase in import penetration, plus the massive amounts of overseas investment, means that firms of all sizes face competitors from everywhere in the world. This increasing internationalization of business is requiring managers to have a global business perspective gained through experience, education, or both.

Understand the various names given to firms that have substantial operations in more than one country.

The following definitions are used in this text. A *global company* is an organization that attempts to standardize operations worldwide in all functional areas. A *multidomestic* firm, by contrast, is an organization with multicountry affiliates, each of which formulates its own business strategy based on perceived market differences. The term *international company* is often used to refer to both global and multidomestic firms.

Appreciate the profound effect of the Internet on many international business firms.

The Internet enables small firms to compete globally because they can contact foreign customers without expensive and time-consuming travel. Sellers can demonstrate their products to prospects inexpensively and rapidly with video teleconferencing. Home office managers have closer, more rapid, and less expensive contact with their overseas operations by using E-mail on the Internet. By means of Web sites on the Internet, firms advertise, recruit personnel, and provide customer support with a minimum of expense and effort.

Understand the five kinds of drivers, all based on change, that are leading international firms to the globalization of their operations.

There are five kinds of drivers, all based on change, that are leading international firms to the globalization of their operations. Following are the five drivers with an example for each kind: (1) *political*—preferential trading agreements, (2) *technology*—advances in communications technology, (3) *market*—global firms become global customers, (4) *cost*—globalization of product lines and production helps reduce costs by achieving economies of scale, and (5) *competitive*—firms are defending their home markets from foreign competitors by entering the foreign competitors' markets.

Comprehend why international business differs from domestic business.

International business differs from its domestic counterpart in that it involves three environments—domestic, foreign, and international—instead of one. Although the kinds of forces are the same in the domestic and foreign environments, their values often differ, and changes in the values of foreign forces are at times more difficult to assess. The international environment is defined as the interactions (1) between the domestic environmental forces and the foreign environmental forces and (2) between the foreign environmental forces of two countries when an affiliate in one country does business with customers in another. An international business model helps explain this relationship.

Describe the three environments—domestic, foreign, and international—in which an international company operates.

The *domestic environment* is composed of all the uncontrollable forces originating in the home country that surround and influence the firm's life and development. The *for-*

eign environment is composed of all the forces originating outside the home country that surround and influence the firm. The *international environment* is the interaction between the domestic and foreign environment forces or between sets of foreign environmental forces.

[Key Words]

multidomestic company (p. 9)
global company (p. 9)
international company (p. 9)
environment (p. 19)
uncontrollable forces (p. 19)
controllable forces (p. 20)
domestic environment (p. 20)
foreign environment (p. 20)
international environment (p. 21)
self-reference criterion (p. 22)

[Questions]

1. What are the differences between international, global, and multidomestic companies?
2. Give examples to show how an international business manager might manipulate one of the controllable forces in answer to a change in the uncontrollable forces.
3. A nation whose GNP is smaller than the sales volume of a global firm is in no position to enforce its wishes on the local subsidiary of that firm. True or false? Explain.
4. Discuss the forces that are leading international firms to the globalization of their production and marketing.
5. Business is business, and every firm has to produce and market its goods. Why, then, cannot the managers apply the techniques and concepts they have learned in their own country to other areas of the world?
6. What do you believe makes foreign business activities more complex than purely domestic ones?
7. Discuss some possible conflicts between host governments and foreign-owned companies.
8. Why, in your opinion, do the authors regard the use of the self-reference criterion as "probably the biggest cause of international business blunders"? Can you think of an example?
9. You have decided to take a job after graduation in your hometown. Why should you study international business?
10. Although forces in the foreign environment are the same as those in the domestic environment, they operate differently. Why is this so?

[Internet Exercises]

Using the Internet

1. The myths and realities of globalization. Following are a number of myths and realities about globalization:
   a. Globalization lowers wages and exports jobs in developed countries and increases the income gap between high-income and low-income countries.
   b. Multinational firms can take their capital and leave to invest in lower-wage countries.
   c. Globalization has weakened the administrative power of states to mandate social protection, such as rules on working hours, minimum-wage laws, and health and safety laws.
   d. Globalization is the automatic and unstoppable consequence of the emergence of new technologies.
   e. Globalization is a relatively new phenomenon. How new is it?
   f. It is possible that globalization will make multinational firms less necessary. Why or why not?

Various articles in the Internet Appendix address one or more of these points. Choose three of the points above and determine whether each is a myth or a reality according to the Internet sources.

2. In "Organization of a Transnational" in the text, there is a brief discussion of Argentina/Brazil Binational Companies. (*Hint:* See endnote #8 for Chapter 1.)
   a. Must such a company be owned 100 percent by Argentine and Brazilian nationals?
   b. Must the participation in the ownership of the firm be evenly divided between Brazilians and Argentineans?
   c. Must the investors from each country be citizens of that country?
   d. What kind of restrictions are there for the importation of capital goods of Argentine or Brazilian origin when these goods are brought in from that country to the other country for use in the Binational Company?

[Minicase 1.1]

Key Differences between the Global and the Multidomestic Corporation

They seem to be similar, but in fact the concepts of the global corporation and the multidomestic are dissimilar. The multidomestic firm sells to several countries but adjusts its products, manufacturing processes, and business strategies to local conditions. The global firm also sells to several countries but does so with the same products, the same manufacturing processes, and a single business strategy. Management regards the entire world as a single market.

Which of the following characteristics commonly define the global corporation and which are attributes of the multidomestic corporation as defined in Chapter 1?

1. Localized decision making.
2. Home country is the major market.
3. Research and design implemented wherever necessary, often in foreign laboratories.
4. Shareholders spread around the world.
5. Trade barriers not a threat to the company's business.
6. Company stock listed on home country's stock exchange only.
7. Has no legal nationality and home tax authority.
8. Considerable number of foreign directors on company board of directors.
9. Research conducted principally in home (headquarters) country.
10. Headquarters makes the major decisions, not the overseas subsidiaries.
11. Global image bolstered, not confined, by a strong home-country identity (if it has one).
12. Products designed at headquarters.
13. Decision making greatly affected by national borders and barriers to trade.
14. Multiple identities and loyalties successfully managed through a fluid chain of command.
15. Less than 50 percent of the company's sales come from overseas.
16. Overseas management staffed and directed chiefly from headquarters with few nonnationals on fast track to upper management.
17. A significant number of non–home-country nationals on the board of directors.
18. Company stock generally listed on stock exchanges in several countries.
19. Clear, unambiguous chain of command.
20. Global ownership and control at the level of the parent company.

Sources: Rolf Leppanen, "Globalization and Its Organizational Implications: The ABB Experience," http://www.mbs.umd.edu/Ciber/wp31.html (August 11, 1997); "Globalization Starts with Company's Own View of Itself," *Business International,* June 10, 1991, pp. 197–98; and Yao-Su Hu, "Global or Stateless Corporations Are National Firms with International Operations," *California Management Review,* Winter 1992, pp. 107–26.

[Internet Appendix]

Using the Internet for International Business Research

By the time students take an introductory course in international business, they usually have taken at least one CIS or MIS course in which they had an opportunity to connect to the Internet. However, if you have no Internet experience, we recommend that you either take a course or get a book from the library to learn the basics of the Internet, an extremely valuable business tool.

In Chapter 1, we discussed briefly the numerous uses of the Internet, such as the following:

1. E-mail for fast, inexpensive global communication.
2. Videoconferencing for worldwide sales demonstrations and to hold meetings among people stationed in various countries.
3. Posting Web sites to market products, recruit employees globally, and provide customer support.

In this Appendix, we (1) examine the Internet as a global information source and (2) provide a directory of Web sites you can use to gather information on a wide range of topics.

The Internet: A Dynamic Global Information Source

The Internet is a network of thousands of computer networks that allows you to access information stored on computers around the world. No government or organization controls the Internet, nor does any one person or organization pay for it.

Ways to Access Information on the Internet

There are a number of ways you can access information on the Internet, including (1) the World Wide Web, (2) Gopher, (3) FTP, and (4) Telnet.

World Wide Web (WWW)

The World Wide Web is the most popular and fastest-growing part of the Internet because it is easy to use and has excellent graphics, image, and sound capabilities; this is why corporations use it to promote and sell their products. Want to see the latest Ford models? Go to the firm's home page at http://www.ford.com to see them in full color with complete specifications. Every home page has a specific address called a Uniform Resource Locator (URL). Incidentally, if you do not know the URL of a firm, try entering www.companyname.com.

The WWW uses a computer language—hypertext markup language (HTML)—that allows one document to be linked to another. If you click on words that are underlined in color or are of a different color, you will be transferred either to another Web site or to another document in the same site.

Gopher

This is a navigational tool, developed at the University of Minnesota, that uses a simple menu system to move among numerous sites on the Internet. Before the Web, this was the most common method of navigating the Internet. Gophers are easy to use and are accessible through the Web, as are FTP and Telnet.

FTP

File Transfer Protocol (FTP) allows you to send and receive data and program files stored on other computers. You can use FTP to obtain copies of software, games, and documents that are available to the public. Generally, you need access privileges, although some sites permit you to use "anonymous" as your user name and "guest" or your E-mail name as the password.

Telnet

This allows your computer to connect to host computers on the Internet and act as though you were directly connected. If, for example, you want to browse the University of Texas's computerized library catalog from home, you can connect to it through Telnet. Although you usually need permission to access the remote computer, as in the case of FTP, some sites are available to the public.

Browsers

Browsers are software programs that enable you to move from site to site or move within a site. Two of the most popular browsers are Netscape and Explorer, which function similarly. With a browser, you can move forward to new documents or retrace your steps by pressing the Forward and Backward buttons. Netscape and other browsers allow you to store the addresses of favorite sites to which you expect to return. Called Bookmarks by Netscape and Favorites by others, these lists of URLs enable you to revisit a site simply by clicking on it in your Bookmark list. All browsers have a dialog box in which you can type the URL to reach a Web site. You can also reach other areas of the Internet by using the dialog box: enter ftp://,gopher://, or telnet://, followed by the name of the site.

Search Engines

Unless you know the URL of the site you want to view or have a directory of URLs such as the one that follows this section, you have little chance of finding what you want on the Web without search engines, which are (1) indexes made by human classifiers, (2) software programs that travel around the Web collecting information on new Web sites, which they assemble into searchable databases, or (3) hybrids.[1] Because some search engines actively look for new sites while others depend on site developers to include them in their databases, the results of a search differ among search engines.[2] As a result, no single Internet search engine is best for every job, and you may have to use several to get the information you want.

Useful Search Engines

We recommend using meta search engines because each one searches a number of individual search engines. SavvySearch (http://savvy.search.com), for example, searches 11 search engines simultaneously. You can choose to add other groups of search engines by clicking on a list of categories. Click on "International," for example, and you will be able to add search engines from over 30 countries. This is a good way to see a variety of results quickly in just one search. Google (www.google.com) and DogPile (www.dogpile.com) are two other useful meta search engines. Click on the search engine name you wish to use and you will go to a page where you will get a short explanation of how it functions and will be able to use it for your search.

Improving Your Search Returns

You can improve your returns substantially by using Boolean operators such as AND, OR, and NOT to specify the relation between keywords. You can also enclose a phrase with quotation marks to request an exact matching of it.

Read the instructions for the search engine you are using to learn about its language so that you can improve your efficiency in working with it. Take the time to study the requirements for advanced searches. It's worth the effort.

Some Helpful Suggestions

Here are a few things we have learned while using the Internet:

1. Be prepared for constant change on the Web. Daily, there are additions and deletions of sites. Addresses also change. A considerable number of Gopher sites seem to be moving to the WWW. When you log on the old address, you will find a link to the new one.
2. If you get an error message saying, "There was no response. Server could be down. Try later," it may be because there are too many people trying to reach the site at the same time. Try a second time. If there is still no connection, try 30 minutes later. Of course, the server may really be down so that you cannot reach it.
3. Sometimes you can enter a long URL and get the response that it doesn't exist. This is irritating, especially when you know that it does. Try entering the URL and omitting some of the last part. For example, instead of entering www.oas.org/EN/PINFO/HR/jobstudy.htm to get information on the Organization of American States student intern program, try entering the address up to the last slash. If that doesn't help, enter only up to the slash before that. You can continue this until you arrive at the first slash, where you have only www.oas.org, which is the URL of the OAS. Once you are at the OAS site, it shouldn't be difficult to find the student intern information.
4. To save time entering site addresses on the Web, omit the http://. It's not necessary. Begin instead with www. If the URL begins with www. and ends with com, type only the part in the middle between www. and .com. When you enter Gophers, FTP, and Telnet, you need to begin with gopher, ftp, or telnet, respectively, however.
5. If you get a message saying that "there are no pages to print" when you try to print a page from the screen, don't give up. Hit the Print button again. Usually, it works the second time.
6. Keep a list of the search words you use that produce good results.

The Internet Directory for International Business

Africa

Region

African Development Bank www.afdb.org/
African Resources (country data) www.ibrc.bschool.ukans.edu/country/africa/africa.htm
Africa Studies Server (links to African countries)
www.sas.upenn.edu/African_Studies/Home_Page/Country.html
Common Market for Eastern and Southern Africa (COMESA) www.comesa.int/home1024.asp
Investment Guide for African Nations (extensive country profiles, including investment rules)
www.unido.org/start/business/InvGuideAfrica/navigator.htmls
Regional or Country-Specific Information (Africa) ciber.bus.msu.edu/busres/africa.htm

Country

Angola Business and Investment Center (investment and economic news)
www.angola.org/business/index.htm
Cote d'Ivoire (business guide) www.cotedivoire.com/sommaus.htm
Doing Business in and Profiles of Countries in Middle East and Africa
www.dfait-maeci.gc.ca/middle_east/menu-e.asp?name=Africa
Kenya (economy, Preferential Trade Area) www.kenyaweb.com/

Asia and Australia

Region

Arabia Net (Arabian news, links to Arabian nations) www.arabia.com
Arabia-on-line (Arab country information) www.awo.net
Arabia Web (Arabian national information on business, culture, religion) http://arabiaweb.com
Arab Net (country information, culture, business) www.arab.net/
ASEAN Web (Association of Southeast Nations) www.aseansec.org/
ASEAN statistics (extensive data on member nations). Click on "Country Focus" and "Asia Recovery Information Center."
Asia (country data) www.ibrc.bschool.ukans.edu/. Click on "Country Resources."
Asian Business and Financial News www.asia-inc.com
Asian Development Bank (economic data of member countries, industrial outlook) www.adb.org
Asian Studies (broad information on Asian nations, including parts of the former USSR and its satellites) coombs.anu.edu.au/WWWVL-AsianStudies.html
Asia-Pacific Economic Cooperation (APEC) www.apecsec.org.sg
APEC-U.S. Trade Agreement (description of U.S. trade agreements) www.ustr.gov/reports/tpa/. Click on "Parent Directory"
Tariff Schedules for APEC Countries www.apectariff.org
Asia/Pacific Information (U.S. Department of Commerce Trade Information Center: APEC, ASEAN, and country information) http://ita.doc/gov/. Click on "Countries and Regions."
Asia Pacific Information (information on India and Japan) http://SunSITE.sut.ac.jp/asia/
Asia Worldwide Web (directories of Asian firms, Asia-related business links)
www.asiawww.com/index.htm
Australia and Oceania (country information)
www.ibrc.bschool.ukans.edu/country/austral/austral.htm
Business Links to Business World (business directories to European, Asian, and American companies and a detailed directory for South Korea) www.kotra.co.kr/e_main/links/bizlink/. Click on "biz_corpo1.htm."
Middle East (country information) www.ibrc.bschool.ukans.edu/country/middleE/middlee.htm
Middle East and North Africa (country profiles) www.dfait-maeci.gc.ca/middle_east/menu-e.asp/
Regional or Country-Specific Information (Asia and Oceania) ciber.bus.msu.edu/busres/asia.htm
Webasia (links to Asian, Japanese, Korean, and Indian sources)
www.gyoza.com/lapres/html/webasia.html#gen
West Asia: Major Environmental Concerns (UN) www.grida.no/prog/global/geo1/ch/ch2_13.htm

Country

Australia
Bureau of Statistics www.abs.gov.au. Click on "Statistics."

Doing Business in Australia www.business.gov.au/
Federal Government Entry Point (links to government agencies) www.fed.gov.au/
Links to country information www.anu.edu.au/
National Library of Australia (many on-line databases and publications) www.nla.gov/au/
Virtual Library (news sources, information technology, business news) www.austudies.org/vl/index.html

Brunei, Business Guide (investing and doing business in) www.brunet.bn/homepage/bus_com/brubusin.htm

China
China News Digest International (nonprofit organization for balanced news coverage) www.cnd.org
Chinese government links www.china-embassy.org/Links/Links.htm
Country Data http://SunSITE.sut.ac.jp. Click on "Index" and then on China.
Country information, laws and regulations, and investment climate www.ccpit.org/engVersion/ccpit.html
Economic and Commercial Office, PRC Embassy www.china-embassy.org
Emerging Market (exporting, statistics, links) www.ita.doc.gov/bems/China.html
Negotiating Business Relationships gopher://hoshi.cic.sfu.ca:70/00/dlam/business/forum/china/rittenbe

Egypt (journals, maps, country studies, politics, business and economy) www.winsor.ig.net/~ddupuis/egypt.htm
Egypt Economic Bulletin www.economic.idsc.gov.eg/
Investing in Egypt (starting business in Egypt, information service) http://its-idsc.gov.eg/invest/

Hong Kong (economic outlook, government information) www.hongkong.org
Hong Kong Trade Development Council (database containing thousands of Hong Kong company profiles and business and trade contacts) www.tdctrade.com/

Indonesian Business Center Online (business news) www.indobiz.com/

India
Culture, government agencies, maps, media, general, and business and economic news SunSITE.sut.ac.jp/asia/india
Emerging market (exporting, statistics, links) www.ita.doc.gov/bems/India.html
Indian business, economic, and political news www.indiaserver.com
Indian Economic Times (political and business news) www.economictimes.com
Invest in India (business opportunities, how to) www.india-invest.com/index.htm
Links to Indian business sites www.india-invest.com/links.htm

Israel
Economy in Israel (Israel–U.S. Free Trade Agreement and business news) gopher://israel-info.gov.il:70/11/econ
Facts About (history, culture, science) gopher://israel-info.gov.il:70/11/facts
Foreign Ministry (peace process, facts about Israel) www.israel-mfa.gov.il/
Legal Issues, Maps and Pictures, Culture, Economic News gopher://israel-info.gov.il

Japan www.embjapan.org.uk
Business and Economic Information, General Information and Maps sunSITE.sut.ac.jp/asia/japan/corp/index.html
Doing Business in (practical information) www.jetro.org/biz5.html
Negotiating with the Japanese www.jetro.go.jp/it/e/pub/negotiating1994.index.html
Economic Stimulus Package of Japan www.miti.go.jp/press-e/f410001e.html
Electronic Industries Association in Japan (data on electronics industry) www.eiaj.or.jp/english/index.htm
Japan (U.S. Department of Commerce) (market access and compliance) www.mac.doc.gov/japan/index.html
Japan-Asia (how to do business in Japan, database of market reports, JETRO offices in United States) www.jetro.org/jetro.html
Japanese reports, news, statistics (Ministry of International Trade and Industry) www.miti.go.jp/index-e.html
Japanese Trade Organization (JETRO) site map (good starting point for doing business in Japan) www.jetro.org/sm.html OR http://jin.jcic.or.jp
Japan Incorporated (the complex interweaving of all aspects of Japanese society, including family, business, government) http://vikingphoenix.com/public/JapanIncorporated/japaninc.htm
Japan in Figures, Japan Statistical Yearbook (population, labor, foreign trade, finance, manufacturing) www.stat.go.jp/english/143.htm
Japan Information Network (Ministry of Foreign Affairs—Japanese statistics) www.jinjapan.org/stat/index.html

JETRO in Japan (trade and investment information for Japan–U.S. and Japan–EU) www.jetro.go.jp

Keidanren (Japanese nonprofit organization representing 970 Japanese firms, including 53 foreign ones in Japan) www.keidanren.or.jp

Keiretsu (extensive coverage of the history and structure and way of doing business) http://vikingphoenix.com/public/JapanIncorporated/postwar/keiretsu.htm

Overseas Business Activities of Japanese Companies www.miti.go.jp/intro-e/a225101e.html

Retail Revolution (supermarkets, department stores, discounting, case studies) www.jetro.go.jp/it/e/pub/Changing1995/index.html

Statistical Bureau of Japan (demographics, consumer price indices, family income and expenses) www.stat.go.jp.english/1.htm

Tokyo Stock Exchange (company data and market information) www.tse.or.jp/

Korea

Access Korea (doing business in Korea, Korea's market) www.accesskorea.com/index.html

Chaebol Update www.gyoza.com/lapres/html/webasia.html#gen. Click on "Korea" and then on "Chaebol Update."

Culture and Communication Patterns in Korean Firms gopher://hoshi.cic.sfu.ca:70/00/dlam/business/forum/korea/steers

Korean business practices, maps, culture, general information http://SunSITE.sut.ac.jp/asia/korea

Korean Chamber of Commerce (guide to doing business, economic news) www1.kcci.or.kr/

Korean government home page (organization of Korean government) www.kipa.re.kr/painfo/govern/e_gorg.htm

Korean Overseas Information Service www.kois.go.kr

Korean National Statistical Office (economic and socioeconomic data) www.nso.go.kr/eindex.html

Korea Trade-Investment Promotion Agency (KOTRA) (investment and tax news, economic trends) www.kotra.co.kr

New Zealand Trade (trade and investment information) www.tradenz.govt.nz/

Pakistan (economy, culture) www.alephinc.com/pakistan/html/profile.htm

Pakistan, Government of (government, economy, investment) www.pak.gov.pk/

Russia: General information, maps http://SunSITE.sut.ac.jp/asia/russia/

General information www.emulateme.com/russia.htm

Russia and Eastern Europe (news and data on Eastern European nations with search capacity) www.ucis.pitt.edu/research/

Singapore

Financial and Economic Data www.gov.sg/mti/mti6.html

Links to www.webcraftsg.com/cybersling/_singlink/main_spore.html

Singapore-Inc (doing business in, economy) www.singapore-inc.com/home.html

Statistics www.singstat.gov.sg/

Taiwan

General information (culture, news, business, search engines) www.roc-taiwan.org AND www.emulate.com/taiwan.htm

Trade: China External Trade Development Council (CETRA) Trade Kit (statistics, doing business with, links to Taiwan) www.cetra.org.tw/mycetra/tradekit/frameset.htm

Thailand

Board of Investment (investment information) www.boi.go.th/

General Information www.nectec.or.th/thailand/index.html

Virtual Library (current events, business news) www.nectec.or.th/WWW-VL-Thailand.html

Vietnam: Business protocol, investment information, business news www.batin.com.vn/vninfo/vninfo.htm

Center for Global Trade Development www.cgtd.com/global/directory/vietnews.htm

Vietnamese Business Journal (Vietnamese news) www.viam.com

Companies

Databases and Listings

Annual reports

U.S. firms www.reportgallery.com/

International firms www.reportgallery.com/international.htm

Annual Reports Library www.zpub.com/sf/arl/

Annual reports and other company news www.prnewswire.com/cnoc/cnoc.html
Asian Public Companies (press releases) www.irasia.com/index.htm
Company Directories, Yellow Pages, and country-specific Web sites http://ciber.bus.msu.edu/busres/company.htm
Corporate Information (corporate information by country, country commercial guides, links to countries' laws) www.corporateinformation.com/
Corporate World (links to Asian, European, Latin American, and American companies) www.kotra.co.kr/e_main/links/bizlink/. Click on "biz_corpo1.html."
Forbes International 800 (ranking of international firms) www.forbes.com/tool/toolbox/int500/
Fortune Global 500 (ranking of international firms) www.fortune.com/fortune/global500/
Hoover's Online (company directory listings searchable by company name, location, industry, and sales figures and company news) www.hoovers.com
International Firms (large manufacturers, service firms, small firms, and trade service firms) http://web.idirect.com/~tiger/worldbea.html
Russian companies and banks www.emergingeconomies.net/russiancompanies.html
Top 100 Saudi Firms www.arab.net/saudi100/
U.S. corporate information (SEC filings) www.edgar-online.com
US Securities and Exchange Commission (offers 10-Ks) (Edgar database) www.sec.gov
Wright Investors' Service (profiles on over 14,000 firms worldwide, including stock charts, financial data, company descriptions) http://profiles.wisi.com/

Individual Firms

Advanced Microsoft Devices www.amd.com
Airbus Industrie www.airbus.com/
AMP www.amp.com
Andersen Consulting www.ac.com
Arthur Andersen (global and country-specific links) www.ArthurAndersen.com
Asea Brown Bovari (ABB) (Swedish-Swiss transnational) www.abb.com
Bell-Howell www.bellhowell.com
Boeing www.boeing.com/
Daewoo Trading (Daewoo's trading company) www.dwc.co.kr
Disney www.disney.com
Federal Express www.fedex.com
Ford www.ford.com
IBM www.ibm.com
Kodak www.kodak.com
Pepsi in Russia www.pepsi.ru.
P&G www.pg.com
Rockwell International www.rockwell.com/
SKF www.skf.com
Toyota www.global.toyota.com/
Wal-Mart www.wal-mart.com

Competition

Anti-Piracy Web Index (Software and Information Industries Association) www.spa.org/piracy/
Barriers to Foreign Trade www.ustr.gov/index.html
Benchmarking, The "Best Practice" and Other Benchmarking Myths www.benchnet.com/bestpracticeco.htm
Benchmarking: Past, Present, and Future www.benchnet.com/bppf.htm
Benchmarking in Australia (articles, news, links) www.benchmarkingplus.com.au
Benchmarking in Outsourcing www.outsourcing-benchmarking.com/
Business Software Alliance (organization of software producers that fights software piracy) www.bsa.org
Competitiveness, British (analysis by the Department of Trade and Industry) www.dti.gov.uk/comp/
Competitiveness in the European Union www.coopers.co.uk/coopers/management consulting/economics/competitiveness/index.html
Competitive Intelligence (thorough coverage of the topic) http://strategis.ic.gc.ca/se_indps/service/engdoc/steps.html
Competitive Intelligence Guide www.fuld.com/

Economic Intelligence (chapter from UNESCO's *World Information Report* about business and economic intelligence) www.unesco.org/webworld/wirerpt/wirenglish/chap22.pdf
European Community R&D Information Service www.cordis.lu/
Generalized System of Preferences (GSP) www.tradelaw.com/gspren.htm AND www.ustr.gov/reports/gsp/
Global Competitiveness Report (country rankings) www.weforum.org/publications/GCR/
Japan: Japan, Incorporated (interweaving of all aspects of Japanese society: family, business, religion, government, education, extragovernmental organizations) www.ccnet.com/~suntzu75/japaninc.htm
Distribution in Japan www.jetro.go.jp/it/e/pub/distribution1993/index.html
The Japanese Consumer (income and expenditures) www.jetro.go.jp/it/e/pub/consumer1993/index.html
Japanese market for semiconductors www.csjapan.doc.gov/isa99/semicon.html
Keiretsu www.swadishi.com/keiretsu/keirhist/keiintro.htm
Sogo Shosha www.jetro.go.jp/it/e/pub/distribution1993/4-2gen.html
The Retail Revolution (35-page article) www.jetro.go.jp/it/e/pub/changing1995/ret.html
Trading Companies in International Commerce www.jetro.go.jp/it/e/pub/role1993/index.html
OECD Competition and Antitrust Policy www.oecd.org/daf/clp/
Research and Development Country Indicators www.unesco.org/
Section 301 of the 1974 Trade Act www.ita.doc.gov/legal/301.html
Special 301 on Intellectual Property Rights and Specific Country Decisions www.ustr.gov/reports/special/factsheets.html
Super 301 (WTO enforcement actions) www.ustr.gov/reports/
Society of Competitive Intelligence Professionals www.scip.org/news/cimagazine.html. Click on magazine articles.
World Competitiveness Yearbook (country ranking) www.imd.ch/index_4.cfm. Click on "Faculty & Research" and then on "World Competitiveness Yearbook."

Country Data

Army Area Handbooks http://lcweb2.loc.gov/frd/cs/cshome.html
Big Emerging Markets (commercial opportunities in the future) www.ita.doc.gov/bems
Business Practices in 88 Countries (how foreign business is allowed to operate in each country) www.smartbiz.com/sbs/browse.htm. Highlight "International Business," click on "International Business," and go to "International Business Guides."
Central European Countries (statistical database and Web sites for 13 Central European nations, worldwide company research) www.bcemag.com/
Central European Countries and China (links to these countries for country information and business news) www.einnetworks.com
Chinese government links www.china-embassy.org/Links/Links.htm
Classification of Economies (World Bank classification system) www.worldbank.org/data/databytopic/keyrefs.html. Click on "country classification."
Country Commercial Guides (Department of Commerce reports on individual nations) www.state.gov/www/about_state/business/com_guides/index.html OR www1.usatrade.gov/website.ccg.nsf
Country Commercial Guides (from Canada's Industry Department) http://strategis.ic.gc.ca/sc_mrkti/ibin/engdoc/dyna_ccg.html
Country Commercial Guides (U.S. Department of Commerce) www1.usatrade.gov/website/ccg.nsf
Country Data (geography, economy, population, social indicators)
U.S. Dept. of Commerce www.ita.doc.gov/uscs/ccglist.html
Country Data Comparison (compare UN statistical data on up to seven countries) www.un.org/Pubs/CyberSchoolBus/infonation/e_infonation.htm
Country Health Profiles (data on sanitary conditions) www.paho.org/english/country.htm
Country Information (commercial, trade, and financial data) www.dis.strath.ac.uk/business/countries.html
Country Library (information on over 200 countries) http://tradeport.org/ts/countries/index.html
Country Profiles (geography and population) www.xist.org
Country Profiles www.tradenz.govt.nz/. Click on "Country Profile" and then on "All."
Country Profiles (prepared by Library of Congress) http://lcweb2.loc.gov/frd/cs/cshome.html
Countries and Regions (International Trade Administration Web sites covering big emerging markets and other leading world markets) www.ita.doc.gov/ita_home/itacnreg.htm

Country Reports on Economic Policy and Trade Practices (U.S. Department of State)
www.state.gov/www/issues/economic/trade_reports/index.html
Country Reports (of over 100 nations on numerous international business practices)
http://strategis.ic.gc.ca/sc_mrkti/ibin/engdoc/dyna_ibp.html
Country Reports (links to army, country studies, and international economic statistics handbooks)
www.umsl.edu/services/govdocs/#alphalist
Country Reports and Statistics www.lib.lsu.edu/bus/marketin.html
Country Resources and Information (links to 150 countries)
www.yahoo.com/government/countries
Country Statistics (U.S. Department of State background notes on history, geography, economy, government) www.state.gov/www/background_notes/index.html
Developing Country Data www.unido.org/doc/f330692.htmls
Doing Business Guides (32 countries) www.hg.org/guides.html
Foreign Government and Country Background
www.lib.umich.edu/libhome/Documents.center/foreign.html. On page "Foreign Govt. Resources on the Web," click on "Country Information" at bottom of page.
Foreign government statistical agencies www.census/gov/main/www/stat_int.html
Foreign Government: Statistical Resources on the Web
www.lib.umich.edu/libhome/Documents.center/stats.html. Click on "Foreign Governments" at bottom right of page.
International Trade Links (country Web sites, export assistance, industry)
www.tradeport.org/ts/countries.index.html
Japan in Figures 2000 (very extensive collection of economic and socioeconomic indicators)
www.stat.go.jp/english/16.htm
Links to U.S. and Foreign Statistical Agencies www.cbs.nl/eng/link/index.htm
Middle East/North Africa Business Country Commercial Information www.ita.doc.gov/ita_home/siteindexer.htm. Click on "Africa and the Near East" under "Countries and Region."
OECD member statistics www.oecdwash.org/PRESS/CONTENT/frstat.htm
Regional and Country Information www.usitc.gov/tr/REGION3.HTM
Regional or Country-Specific Information (General) ciber.bus.msu.edu/busres/general.htm
World Bank Statistics (national statistics, debt and finance data)
www.worldbank.org/html/extdr/data.htm
World Factbook (all countries) www.odci.gov/cia/publications/factbook/
World Information (all countries) www.ibrc.bschool.ukans.edu/. Click on "Country Resources."
Worldwide Governments on the WWW (links to individual countries)
www.gksoft.com/govt/en/world.html

Culture

AntiCorruption
- *World Bank Anti-Corruption Program* (how to report fraud and corruption, helping countries reduce corruption) www.worldbank.org/public sector/anticorrupt/
- *OECD Anti-Corruption Unit* www.oecd.org/nocurruption/index.htm

Body Language Around the World www.webofculture.com/refs/gestures.html
Bribery
- *Bribe Payers Index and Corruption Perception Index* www.GWDG.DE/~uwvw/. Click on "Press Release."
- *Bribery-Country Updates* (Transparency International newsletter) www.transparency.de/documents/index.html#newsletter

Corruption Perception Index (compiled by Transparency International, which ranks public perception of corruption in over 100 countries)
www.transparency.de/documents/cpi/index.html
Culture (including doing business with various Asian-Pacific nations)
gopher://hoshi.cic.sfu.ca:70/11/dlam/business
Education
- *Global Education Database 1999* (statistical data from over 200 countries) www.info.usaid.gov/educ_training/ged.htm

Educational Attainment (by age groups and countries) http://unescostat.unesco.org/
Feng Shui (articles on) www.bartlettdesigns.com
Foreign Corrupt Practices Act: Antibribery Provisions
http://tradeport.org.ts/ntdb/express/fcpa.html AND www.ita.doc.gov/legal/fcparev.html

Foreign Corrupt Practices Act (FCPA) and International Corporate Due Diligence (rules applicable to selection of independent distributors and elements of gift and entertainment policy) http://tht.com/ClientBulletinForeignCorruptPracticesAct.htm

FCPA: Elements, Due Diligence, and Affirmative Defenses—A Practical Guide www.abanet.org/cle/articles/turza.html

Illiteracy rates www.un.org/Depts/unsd/social/literacy.htm

Japan: Business Relationships in www.jetro.go.jp/it/e/negotiating1994/2.html

Changing Face of Japanese Retail www.jetro.go.jp/it/e/changing1995/index.html

Consumer Attitudes Changing www.jetro.go.jp/it/e/changing1995/6.html

Doing Business in Japan www.jetro.go.jp/it/e/pub/doing1999/index.html

25 Japanese Business Secrets www.smartbiz.com/sbs/arts/bly9.htm

Korean Business Culture gopher://cic.sfu.ca:70/00/dlam/business/forum/korea/steers

Religion

All Religions (links to most religions, large and small) www.worldculture.com/religion.htm

All Religions www.studyweb.com/Religion

Chinese Religions (Taoism, Confucianism) www.gio.gov.tw/info/yb97/html/content.htm. Click on "Religion."

Geography of Religions (overview of major world's religions) www.morehead-st.edu/people/t.pitts/mainmenu.htm

Islam, Articles and Pillars of www.usc.edu/dept/MSA/fundamentals/pillars/intropillars.html

Sikhism Compared with Other Religions www.sikhs.org/religion.htm

Transparency International (TI) (organization to counter corruption in governments) www.transparency.org

TI Documents and Publications www.transparency.de/documents/index.html

Demographics

Country and Urban Data (World Resources International) www.wri.org/facts/country-data.html

Divorce statistics (world) www.divorcereform.org/nonus.html

Health Statistics (diseases, environmental health, World Health Organization) www-nt.who.int/whosis/statistics/menu.cfm

Human Development Indicators (education, poverty, demographics) www.undp.org/htro/report.html#stats

International Data Base (demographic and socioeconomic data, including population pyramids, for all nations in world) www.census.gov/ipc/. Click on "www" and then on "International Data Base."

Population (demography, migration, urbanization patterns) www.undp.org/popin/wdtrends/wdtrends.htm

Regional Resources: Country-Level Data www.wri.org/sdia/index.html

Social Indicators (Latin American countries) www.lanic.utexas.edu/la/region/aid/aid96/Social/index.html

Social Indicators (water supply, health, education, literacy, economic activity, etc.) www.un.org/Depts/unsd/social/main2.htm

Urban Data Tables (safe drinking water, air pollution, other urban indicators) www.igc.org/wri/facts/data-tables-urban.html

Women and children (indicators on health, education) www.unicef.org/sowc98/

Women, Statistical Indicators on www.un.org/Depts/unsd/gender/intro.htm

World Culture Report (statistics on media, communications, economics) www.unesco.org/general/eng/publish.cult.html

World Population Information (data and projections) www.census.gov/. Click on "International" and then on "World Population Information."

World Population Profile: 1998 (links to Census Bureau on population issues) www.census.gov/ipc/www.wp98.html

World Population Trends www.undp.org/popin/popin.htm

U.S. Statistical Abstract tables www.census.gov/statab/www/

Directories for International Business

Business Information Sources on the Internet (guides to business sites) www.dis.strath.ac.uk/business/index.html

Comprehensive Guide to International Trade Terms (200 pages) www.ntia.doc.gov/lexcon.txt

Directories of International Organizations www.imf.org/external/np/sec/decdo/about.htm

Directory of Economic, Commodity, and Development Organizations (by IMF) www.imf.org/external/np/sec/decdo/contents.htm

Ethics in International Business (list of international ethics sites) www.ethics.ubc.ca/resources/business/

Everything International (country data, international organizations, and export assistance) http://faculty.philau.edu/russow.html

Facts about Nations and Other International Resources www.intergov.gc.ca/world/orge.html

General International Business References (SUNY Empire State College) www.esc.edu/library/ibol/default.html

Global Business Centre (links to international trade, culture, Asian and European business) www.glreach.com/gbc/en.php3

Guide to Internet Export Trade Leads (100 government and nongovernment sites from around the world furnished by Commerce Trade Information Center) http://infoserve2.ita.doc.gov/tic.nsf. Click on "Trade Lead Information" and then "Internet Guide to Export Trade Leads."

Institute for International Economics Links to Useful Sites www.iie.com/LINKS/linkjour.htm

International Business Resources: Michigan State University (global statistics, links to private and government-sponsored business sites) www.ciber.bus.msu.edu/busres.htm

International Business Resources: University of North Carolina (statistics, export and import information, indexes to periodicals) http://metalab.unc.edu/reference/moss/business/

International Business and Technology: World and Local www.brint.com/International.htm

International Import-Export Institute (international trade links—major organizations, trade law, country links) www.intlimport-export.com

International Organizations www.library.nwu.edu/govpub/resource/internat/igo.html

International Trade (federal site with links to government agencies) www.business.gov/. Click on "International Trade."

I.O.M.A. Business Directory (guide to business resources on the Internet) www.ioma.com/dir

Language Resources (bilingual dictionaries, quotations, acronyms, thesauruses, translations) www.pscw.uva.nl/sociosite/Language.html

Latin America—LATCO Tools of the Trade (over 200 links to useful sites for international trade with Latin America) www.latco.org/tools.htm

Links to sources of international business information (no fee-based services or business directories) (University of North Carolina–Charlotte) http://libweb.uncc.edu/ref-bus/vibehome.htm

Official Sources of Trade and Investment Information (Organization of American States) www.sice.oas.org/stidre.stm

Related International Web Sites (National Telecommunications and Information Administration list of hundreds of international telecommunications and international Internet information) www.ntia.doc.gov/oiahome/dianelist.html

Resources for International Research (Rutgers) (guidebooks, data sources, electronic texts) www.libraries.rutgers.edu/rul/rr_gateway/besearch_guides/busi/business.shtml

Small Business Administration Hotlist of International Links www.sbaonline.sba.gov/hotlist/internat.html

Statistical Resources on the Web (University of Michigan) www.lib.umich.edu/libhome/Documents.center/stats.html

Statistics from Developed Nations (OECD statistics) www.oecdwash.org/PRESS/CONTENT/frstat.htm

Statistical Sites on the WWW (international and U.S. federal) www.bls.gov/oreother.htm

SUNY Oneonta International Business (international business links) www.oneonta.edu/~libweb/subject/intbus.html

Trade Information Sources on the Internet www.intracen.org/itc/infobase/infsourc/index.htm

University of Kansas Business Resources Web Site (statistics, country information, international news, trade leads) www.ibrc.bschool.ukans.edu/KU/ku.htm

KU GovDocs Library: International Links (search by agencies, subject, countries, or regions) www.ukans.edu/cwis/units/kulib/docs/govdocs.html

Virtual International Business and Economic Sources (VIBES) (comprehensive sources) http://libweb.uncc.edu/ref-bus/vibetabl.htm

The WWW Virtual Library: International Business and Economics www.etown.edu/vl/intlbus.html

Economic Data

Big Emerging Markets (BEMs) (key economic indicators for ASEAN, South Africa, Poland, Argentina, Mexico, Brazil, Turkey) www.stat-usa.gov/itabems.html

Bureau of Economic Analysis (Department of Commerce—national and international economic data) www.bea.doc.gov/
Canada: Imports and Exports www.statcan.ca/english/Pgdb/Economy/International/gblec02a.htm
Comparative International Statistics (U.S. Census) www.census.gov/prod/99pubs/99statab
Data series (36 data series for UN member-countries) www.un.org/Pubs/CyberSchoolBus/infonation/e_infonation.htm
Economic Data Sources (for OECD countries) www.oecd.org/statlist.htm
Economic Freedom Index for 150 Countries www.heritage.org/heritage/index/execsum.html
European Economic Outlook www.pwcglobal.com/gx/eng/ins-sol/spec-int/eeo/pwc_eeo_jar
Facts and Figures (U.S.–Japan and ASEAN–Japan economic relations) www.jetro.go.jp/FACTS/index.html
Federal and foreign statistical agencies on WWW http://stats.bls.gov:80/oreother.htm
Government (U.S.) Information Locator Service (browse federal government agency databases) www.access.gpo.gov/su_docs/gils/gils.html
Human Development Report (includes Human Development Index) www.undp.org/hdro/indicators.html
Income Distribution (Latin American countries) www.iadb.org/int/sta/ENGLISH/staweb
International Comparisons of Manufacturing Productivity and Unit Labor Costs (unit labor costs in U.S. dollars and national currency, output per hour) http://stats.bls.gov.news.release/prod4.toc.htm
Industry data www.industrylink.com/
International Data Base (U.S. Census) www.census.gov/ipc/www/idbinst.html
International Economic Statistics Handbook www.umsl.edu/services/govdocs/#alphalist
International and national economic statistics (Federal Reserve Bank of Cleveland) www.clev.frb.org/research/index.htm
International and National Statistical Sites (compiled by the U.S. Bureau of Labor) http://stats.bls.gov/oreother.htm
National Accounts, technical notes www.oecd.org.std/natechn.htm
Searchable U. California Database of Government Publications http://infomine.ucr.edu/Main.html
Sources of Trade and Investment Information (multinational, regional and Latin America, United States and Canada) www.sice.oas.org/
Statistical Abstract of the U.S. (1999) (U.S. trade and investment data) www.census.gov/prod/99pubs/99statab/sec28.pdf
Statistical Agencies, National (list of 70 national agencies) www.census.gov/main/www/stat_int.html
Statistics, global and regional www.xist.org/
Steel production in major producing nations www.jetro.go.jp/FACTS/t_10.html
Trade and Economic Analysis (data from U.S. Department of Commerce) www.ita.doc.gov/

Employment

International Career Opportunities (many searchable links) www.montana.edu/wwwcp/national.html
Organization of American States (OAS) Student Intern Program www.oas.org/EN/PINFO/HR/internshipstudy.htm
United Nations Jobs Available www.un.org/Depts/OHRM/intern.htm

Europe

Region

Austria, OECD, and Eastern Europe databases www.wsc.ac.at/datenangebot.htm#wifo
Center for Russian, East European, and Euroasian Studies http://reenic.utexas.edu/reenic.html
Central and Eastern Europe (country information) www.ibrc.bschool.ukans.edu/country/eeurope/eeurope.htm
Central and Eastern Europe country information www.bcemag.com. Click on "Statistics."
Central European Free Trade Agreement www.gzs.si/eng/slovenia/cefta.htm
Eastern Europe and Former USSR (industrial output, unemployment statistics, inflation rates) www.planecon.com/
EU Business (industry news, economic data, country data) www.eubusiness.com/

Eurobarometer (attitude surveys of Europeans on various subjects) http://europa.eu.int/comm/dg10/epo/eb.html

European country listings (euro information from various governmental departments of European nations) www.euro-emu.co.uk/navigation/europelinks.shtml

European Economic Outlook, January 2000 www.pwcglobal.com/gx/eng/ins-sol/spec-int/eeo/pwc_eeo_jar

European Free Trade Association www.efta.int/structure/main/index.html

European Union (subject index of all official sites) www.eurunion.org/infores/euindex.htm

Community R&D Information Service www.cordis.lu/

EU (Washington, DC) www.eurunion.org

European Bank for Reconstruction and Development www.ebrd.com

European Parliament www.europarl.eu.int

European trade agreements, trade barriers http://europa.eu.int/comm/trade/index_en.htm. Click on "Download Documents."

European Union Institutions http://europa.eu.int/en/inst.html

Online Publications and Statistical Indicators www.europa.eu.int/en/comm/eurostat/serven/part3/indic.htm

Publications (free) http://europa.eu.int/comm/dg10/publications/index_en.html

Statistical Comparison of the EU and the United States www.eurunion.org/profile/facts.htm

Statistical Office of the European Union http://europa.eu.int/en/comm/eurostat/serven/home.htm

Regional or Country-Specific Information (Europe) ciber.bus.msu.edu/busres/europe.htm

Western Europe (country information) www.ibrc.bschool.ukans.edu/countryeurope/europe.htm

Country

Austria

Austrian Business Agency (doing business in) www.aba.gv.at/english/main_s.htm

Austrian business database www.austria.org

Austrian government www.austria.gv.at

Austrian tourism www.austria-info.at

Belarus, Virtual Guide to www.belarusguide.com/main/index.html

Belgian Foreign Trade Board (market organization, foreign trade statistics) www.obcebdbh.be/en/obce/index.html

Bulgaria Country Report (many business facts, geography, tax guide) www.business-europa.co.uk/bsmenu.html

Czech Republic www.czech.cz/washington/

Estonia Ministry of Foreign Affairs (economic and business news) www.vm.ee/eng/index.html

Finland www.siba.fi/finland.html

An Internet Guide to Finnish Customs and Manners (religion, languages, greeting) www.virtual.finland.fi/finfo/english/guide.html

France

General information www.franceway.com/welcome.html

The Paris Pages (information on Paris) http:paris.org

Germany

Embassy (Washington, DC) (business news, culture, doing business in, statistics) www.germany-info.org/f_index.html

Embassy (Canada) www.docuweb.ca/germany/

Federal Ministry of Economics (business reports) www.bmwi.de/

Hungary, Business in: The Essential Guide www.isys.hu/business

Irish Trade Web (doing business in, trade facts) www.itw.ie/

Malta, Business in (geography, history, international trade) www.u-net.com/metcowww/bim_02_a.htm

Netherlands (statistics) www.cbs.nl/index.htm

Poland: Business Polska (commercial guide, economy, opportunities in Poland) www.polska.net/

Portugal (guide for investors—geography, population, EU membership) www.portugal.org/

Romania (business, government, geography) www.odci.gov/cia/publications/factbook/ro.html

Russia: Economics, Politics, Culture http://SunSITE.sut.ac.jp/asia/russia/

Sweden: statistics www.scb.se/indexeng.htm

United Kingdom

Bank of England www.bankofengland.co.uk/

British Information Service (comprehensive information source on UK) www.britain-info.org

Office of National Statistics (international trade, socioeconomic data) www.ons.gov.uk/ons_f.htm

Yugoslavia (official government site) www.gov.yu/index.html

Export and Import Information

AES Direct (internet system for filing SED information to AES) www.aesdirect.gov/

Antiboycott Compliance Program www.bxa.doc.gov/AntiboycottCompliance/Default.htm

Automated Export System (AES) (U.S. Customs electronic collection system)
(1) www.customs.gov/impoexpo/abaesint.htm
(2) www.census.gov/foreign-trade/aes/aesfact.html

Big Emerging Markets (fast-growing export markets) www.stat-usa.gov/itabems.html

Bureau of Export Administration (U.S. export controls and Department of Commerce export licensing agency) www.bea.doc.gov/

Business Plan (20 pages, based on a fictitious company) www.sb.gov.bc.ca/smallbus/workshop/ Click on "Sample."

Business Plan, How to Prepare http://strategis.ic.gc.ca/SSG/mi02687e.html

Cargo Theft Prevention www.iccwbo.org/index_ccs.asp

Commerce Department Help to Exporters www.ita.doc.gov/

Common Questions and Answers on International Trade (exporting, importing, financing, insurance, laws and regulations, taxes for overseas employers) www.tradenet.gov/

Customs (U.S.) information for exporters www.customs.ustreas.gov/impoexpo/impoexpo.htm

Dictionary of International Trade Terms www.ibnogny.org/export/glossary.html

EU–U.S. Trade Relations http://europa.eu.int/comm/trade/bilateral/usa/usa.htm OR http://europa.eu.int/comm/dg01/euus.htm

Export Assistance Centers (U.S. Department of Commerce) www.ita.doc.gov/

Export Compliance (U.S. laws) www.bxa.doc.gov/AntiboycotCompliance/Default.htm

Export Documents (forms and instructions for preparing certificate of origin, invoice, shipper's export declaration, bill of lading) http://tradeport.org/ts/transport/expdocs.html

Export Glossary http://royalbank.ca/sme/guides/export/glossary.html

Export-Import Bank (US) (loan guarantees, credit insurance, and a reference library of links to other sites on trade, finance, and international organization) www.exim.gov/

Ex-Im Bank Programs (summary of programs and links to explanation of each) www.exim.gov/mprograms.html

Export Credit Insurance Program (Exim Bank) www.exim.gov/minsprog.html

Exporting for Small Business http://royalbank.ca/sme/guides/export/index.html

Export Zone U.S.A. (assistance for exporters) www.exportzone.com/

Fairs and Trade Shows (links to trade shows and fairs in many countries) www.euromktg.com/gbc/en/events.html

Financing Exports (obtaining financing for exports) http://tradeport.org/ts/financing/

Foreign Sales Corporation (provisions of the law) www.ita.doc.gov/legal/fsc.html

Present Status www.ustr.gov/releases/2000/09/00-65.pdf

Foreign Tariff, Tax, and Customs Information (determine tariffs on U.S. products shipped to another country) http://tradeinfo.doc.gov/. Click on "Tariff and Tax Information."

Foreign Trade Barriers, National Trade Estimated Reports on www.ustr.gov/. Click on "Reports."

Foreign Trade Information System [Free Trade Area of the Americas Process, Trade Agreements (full text), Harmonized Tariff Schedule] www.sice.oas.org/

Foreign Trade Zones Board (FTZ applications, annual reports, FTZ list) www.ita.doc.gov/import_admin/records/ftzpage/

Foreign Trade Zone statistics and locations in states www.naftz.org/ AND http://imex.com/naftz.html

Free Trade Zones (list of free trade zones organized by country) www.ceemail.com/free_zones.html

General Export Assistance Web Sites http://tradeport.org/links/general.htm

Getting Started in Exporting (data and advice on export issues) www.inc.com/advice/going_global/

Glossary of international trade terms and international organizations http://tradeport.org/ts/refs/gloss/

Harmonized Tariff Schedule www.usitc.gov/taffairs.htm

Help with International Trade www.ibrc.bschool.ukans.edu/resources/articles/articles.htm

INCOTERMS 2000 (exact text of latest INCOTERMS) www.worldcargoalliance.co/library/incoterms/incoterms.htm

The International Import-Export Institute (NAFTA and trade law links, foreign exchange rates)
www.intlimport-export.com/IIEI%20Links.html

International Terms and Codes
International Trade Dictionary www2.tradecompass.com/TermCode/msearch.asp
International Trade Acronyms www2.tradecompass.com/TermCode/acrosearch.asp
Harmonized System (HS) Classifier www2.tradecompass.com/TermCode/codesearch.asp
NAICS Classifier www2.tradecompass.com/TermCode/naicssearch.asp

International Trade (federal site with links to government agencies)
www.business.gov/busadv/index.cfm. Click on "International Trade."

International Trade Administration www.ita.doc.gov

1. Commercial Service
2. Export Programs Guide
3. Export Assistance Centers
4. Import Administration (administers antidumping and countervailing duty laws)
5. U.S. Industry and Trade Outlook
6. U.S. Global Trade Outlook
7. U.S. Foreign Trade Highlights
   a. Trade in goods and services
   b. Top 50 foreign trading partners
8. State Export Data

International Trade Administration (Department of Commerce source for export information)
www.ita.doc.gov/

International Trade Administration Information on ITA Web sites
www.ita.doc.gov/ita_home/itafind.html

International Trade Desk (trade information sources) http://users.aol.com/tradedesk/trade.html

International Trade, Foreign Direct Investment, Glossaries, Maps, and Flags)
www.internationaltrade.org/webindex.html

International Trade Infobases www.intracen.org/. Click on "infobase/infobase.htm/ITC infobases."

International Trade leads www.cob.ohio-state.edu/ciberweb/International/
internatframe.htm. Click on "International Trade."

1. Export Process Assistant (interactive tutorial and guide to exporting)
2. Legal and regulatory information
3. Finance links

International trade links (country, industry, and export assistance) www.tradeport.org/ts/

International trade links (guides to exporting) ciber.bus.msu.edu/busres/inttrade.htm

International Trade Shows and Conferences ciber.bus.msu.edu/busres/tradshow.htm

Japan External Trade Organization (JETRO) (Japanese trade performance with APEC, United States, EU, and Latin America; Japanese firms' overseas operating strategies)
www.jetro.go.jp/

Marine Insurance Links www.sowest.net/users/jthomp1/

Market Access and Compliance (information on accessing foreign markets) www.mac.doc.gov/

Market Access Information and Trade (U.S. Department of Commerce links)
www.ita.doc.gov/ita_home/itacnreg.html

Product Classification Systems (SITC, NAIC–NAFTA)
http://faculty.philau.edu/russow/product.html

Research for Export Markets http://tradeport.org/ts/planning/index.htmlresources.html

Schedule B Commodity Numbers (required for all U.S. export shipments)
www.census.gov/foreign-trade/misc/guidance.html

Small Business Administration Assistance to Exporters www.business.gov/busadv/index.cfm.
Click on "International Trade."

Tariff Schedules for APEC Countries www.apectariff.org

Tips to Help You to Export More Successfully (from Dun & Bradstreet)
www.dnb.com/global/hglobal.htm

Trade Agreements (WTO, NAFTA, CARICOM, LAIA, bilateral agreements)
http://sice.oas.org/tradee.asp

Trade Assistance for Small Business www.sba.gov/OIT/

Trade Compliance Center (reports on foreign trade agreements and trade barriers) www.mac.doc.gov/

Trade Development (in-depth information on market trends around the world) www.ita.doc.gov/ita_home/itatdhom.html

Trade Expert (international trade tutorial) http://tradeport.org/ts/trade_expert/index.html

Trade fair directories www.expoworld.net/class.asp?class=10000

Trade finance (online guide to export finance for small businesses) www.sba.gov/OIT

Trade Information Center (U.S. Department of Commerce first stop for information on export assistance, country and foreign tariff information) http://tradeinfo.doc.gov.

Trade information (Automated Export System, Foreign Trade Regulations, Shipper's Export Declaration form, Guide to Foreign Trade Statistics) www.ibrc.bschool.ukans.edu/stats/stats.htm

Trade leads (Web search engine visits 30 leading sites for trade leads) www.tradecompass.com/tradebroker/content.html

Trade Link Library (help for international traders) www.online-trade-show.com/it.htm

Trade Port [(1) How to Export, (2) Export Bibliography, (3) International trade links] http://tradeport.org/ts/

TradeExpert (international trade tutorial for all levels of exporters) http://tradeport.org/ts/trade_expert/index.html

Trade Shows, Import and Export Training, Payment Systems www.fita.org/webindex.html

Trade shows (search by product, theme, or country) http://exporthotline.com/tshows/asp/tshow_search.asp

Tutorials on Exporting www.gb.net/content/Global/Tutorials/tutorials.htm

U.S. Census Bureau Foreign Trade Index (links to all documents in Census Bureau's foreign trade site for latest trade information from federal government) www.census.gov/foreign-trade/siteindex/site_index.html

U.S. Census Bureau statistics and information (AES, Foreign Trade Regulations, Schedule B numbers, Guide to Foreign Trade Statistics) www.census.gov/ftp/pub/foreign-trade/www/

U.S. Commercial Service (counseling, market research, trade events, exporting resources) www1.usatrade.gov/website/

U.S. Customs Guide to Importing (complete 34-chapter manual) www.insidex.com/

U.S. Customs information for exporters www.customs.ustreas.gov/impoexpo/impoexpo.htm

U.S. Foreign Trade Data Sources www.lib.umich.edu/libhome/Documents.center/stectrad.html

U.S. Foreign Trade Data Sources (frequently asked questions—good sources) www.ita.doc.gov/industry/otea/usfth/fth_faq.html

U.S. Generalized System of Preferences (GSP) (United States, EU, Japan, Canada) www.unctad.org.gsp

Countries Designated Beneficiary GSP Countries (177 countries and territories) www.ustr.gov/reports/gsp/

U.S. International Trade Commission www.usitc.gov

U.S. Trade Representative National Trade Estimate Report on Foreign Trade Barriers www.ustr.gov/reports/nte/usguide_importing.htm

World Trade Sites (export leads, links to importing firms) www.worldtrade-sites.com/

Foreign Investment

Bureau of Economic Analysis (BEA) (U.S. foreign direct investment, foreign direct investment in the United States, operations of U.S. multinationals, U.S. intrafirm trade) www.bea.doc.gov/

BEA International Accounts Data (U.S. investment position, foreign direct investment in United States) www.bea.doc.gov/bea/di1.htm

BEA International Investment Guide (list of BEA materials on international investment) www.bea.doc.gov/. Click on "Data" under "Investment" and then on "International Investment Division's Product Guide."

BEA Survey of Current Business (monthly publication) www.bea.doc.gov/bea/pubs.htm

Canada: Department of Foreign Affairs and International Trade (NAFTA, doing business with Canada) www.dfait-maeci.gc.ca/menu-e.asp

Caribbean Basin Initiative Act www.ustr.gov/reports/cbera/

Official Sources of Trade and Investment Information www.sice.oas.org/stidre.stm

U.S. Direct Investment Abroad www.bea.doc.gov/bea/di1.htm

Geography, Natural Resources, and Pollution

Country Library (geographical, political, and economic profiles of hundreds of countries)
www.tradeport.org/ts/countries/index.html
Distance between two cities anywhere in the world www.indo.com/distance/
Energy
Energy Information Administration www.eia.doe.gov/index.html
Annual Energy Review (U.S. data) www.eia.doe.gov/aer/contents.html
Energy and Statistical Information on the Web (5 pages of links to energy sites—international statistics, foreign and U.S. energy companies, trade associations)
www.eia.doe.gov/links.html
Fossil Energy on a Country Basis (links to business information sources)
www.fe.doe.gov/international
Gas and Coal Conversion to Liquid Fuel (South Africa) www.sasol.com
Global Energy Marketplace (renewable energy, energy systems, world regions)
http://gem.crest.org/
Hybrid Vehicle Propulsion Program (information on progress of automakers' programs to produce hybrid vehicles) www.ott.doe.gov/hev/
Hybrid Electrical Vehicle Program www.ott.doe.gov/hev/related.html
Hydrogen and Fuel Cells (newsletter) www.hfcletter.com/
International Energy Information (petroleum, gas, coal, electricity, consumption, production, CO_2 emissions) www.eia.doe.gov/emeu/international/contents.html
International Renewable Energy www.eia.doe.gov/fuelrenewable.html
Internet Addresses of Renewable Energy Information
www.eia.doe.gov/cneaf/solar.renewables/renewable.energy.annual/appi.html
Fuel Cells www.fuelcells.org/
Geothermal Energy in Use www.demon.co.uk/geosci/igahome.html
Wind Energy News www.awea.org/
OPEC Fact Sheet (production, quotas) www.eia.doe.gov/emeu/cabs/opec.html
Petroleum Industry in Canada http://strategis.ic.gc.ca/sc_indps/sectors/engdoc/petr_hpg.html
National Renewable Energy Laboratory (renewable energy resources, industrial technologies, international initiatives) www.nrel.gov/textonly.html
Renewable Energy and Energy Efficiency (alternative energy, wind, ocean, solar, geothermal)
www.eren.doe.gov/
Renewable Energy Information (biomass, geothermal, hydro, solar, wind)
http://solstice.crest.org/renewables/index.shtml
Renewable Energy Annual www.eia.doe.gov/cneaf/solar.renewables/rea_data/rea.pdf
Renewable Energy Center (solar, wind, biomass) www.nrel.gov/energy_resources/
Synthetic Crude Production (Canada)
Suncor Energy www.suncor.com
Syncrude Canada, Ltd. www.syncrude.com/00.html
Unconventional Sources of Petroleum in Canada www.aec.ca/
World Energy 1998, Statistical Review www.bpamoco.com/worldenergy/index.htm
Environment: World Resources International www.wri.org/wr-98-99/
Flags www.wave.net/upg/immigration/flags.html
Flags of All Countries (flags and geography) www.theodora.com/flags/flags.html
ISO 14000 (standards on environmental management tools—how to get registered)
www.isogrooup.simplenet.com/
Law of the Sea Convention and U.S. Policy (extensive discussion of Convention provisions)
www.cnie.org/nle/mar-16.html
Mapquest (creates maps from all over the world) www.mapquest.com
Map-related Web sites (links to many kinds of maps)
www.lib.utexas.edu/Libs/PCL/Map_collection/map_sites/map_sites.html
Maps (hundreds of links to topography, subway, and satellite maps)
www.cgrer.uiowa.edu/servers/servers_references.html
Maps on other Web sites (University of Texas map collection)
www.lib.utexas.edu/Libs/PCL/Map_collection/map_sites/map_sites.html
Tunnel, English Channel http://212.111.25.40/english/netscape_e.htm
University of Texas (world map collection)
www.lib.utexas.edu/Libs/PCL/Map_collection/Map_collection_guide.html
World Energy Consumption Tables (energy consumption by regions, major users, and energy types)
www.eia.doe.gov/oiaf/ieo99/appa1.html

World Factbook (world and country maps) www.odci.gov/cia/publications/factbook/index.html
World Resources (urban and global environment—pollution, population, energy, economic variables, including purchasing power parity) www.wri.org/wri/geograph.html. Click on geographical area

Globalization

Articles on Globalization (a series of eight articles on globalization that appeared in *The Economist*) www.economist.com/3oix11n0/editorial/freeforall/18-1-98/contents_page.html
Assessing Globalization (World Bank Group Fact Sheets—four briefing papers) www.worldbank.org/html/extdr/pb/globalization/
Globalization Is a Fuzzy Term (various definitions) www2.hawaii.edu/~fredr/ipsaglo.htm
Globalization and Labor www2.dol.gov/dol/asp/public/futurework/conference/trends/trendsVI.htm
Globalization Ledger (globalization index and other research by AT Kearney on globalization truths and falsehoods), April 2000 www.atkearney.com/pdfs/GLBL_LDGR_FINAL.pdf
Globalization: Myths, Reality and Ideology http://aidc.org.za/archives/gl_myth_realty.html
Globalization: Threat or Opportunity? (IMF staff paper covering definition, history, and aspects of globalization) www.imf.org/external/np/exr/ib/2000/041200.htm
Important Aspects of Globalization ("The Globalization of Economy and Society" by Professor R. F. M. Lubbers) www.globalize.org/globview.htm
Issues and Debates: Towards Defining Globalization (links to articles on globalization) www.globalpolicy.org/globaliz/define/index.htm
World Link Online Magazine (global management articles in the online magazine of the World Economic Forum, publisher of the *Global Competitiveness Report*) www.worldlink.co.uk/

Global Marketing

Advertising, links to the world of http://advertising.utexas.edu/world/International.html#Top
Advertising Age (international advertising publication) http://adage.com
- *International Agency Report* (top ad agencies ranked by revenue in regions and countries, world's top advertising organizations) http://adage.com/dataplace/
- *Top 50 Global Marketers by Ad Spending* http://adage.com/dataplace/archives/dp152.html
- *Top 50 Ad Organizations* (groups with more than one agency) http://adage.com/dataplace/archives/dp097.html

Asia Pacific marketing resources (culture, communication patterns with businesspeople from various Asian-Pacific nations) gopher://hoshi.cic.sfu.ca/11/dlam/business/forum
Global Branding www.pangaea.net/ign/chev0496.htm
Global Online Retailing Survey www.ey.com/GLOBAL/ger.nsf/International/International_Home. Click on "Global Online Retailing Survey."
Global Retail & Consumer Products (Ernst & Young articles) www.ey.com/GLOBAL/ger.nsf/International/International_Home. Click on Global Online Retailing Survey" and then on "Download the Global Online Retailing Report." Go to "By Category" menu and click on "Retail & Consumer Products."
International Advertising Sources http://advertising.utexas.edu/world/International.html#Top
International Consumer Studies www.euromonitor.com. Click on title list in lower half of page.
Japan
- *Automobile manufacturers* www.japanauto.com/news/
- *Distribution in Japan* www.jetro.go.jp/it/e/pub/distribution1993.html
- *Fundamental Change in Consumer Patterns* www.jetro.go.jp/it/e/pub/meeting1993/fundamental.html
- *General Traders or "Sogo Shosha"* www.jftc.or.jp/e_sogo.htm
- *Large-Scale Retail Store Law* www.jetro.go.jp/it/e/pub/changing1995/2.html
- *The Japanese Retail Industry* (retail revolution, discounters) www.jetro.go.jp/it/e/pub/changing1995/index.html OR 23MIS41.html
- *The Rise of Discounting* www.jetro.go.jp/it/e/pub/changing1995/3.html

Newspapers, Radio, and Television (number, circulation, or ownership in most nations) http://unescostat.unesco.org/yearbook/ybframe.htm. Click on "Culture and Communications" and then on "Daily Newspapers," "Radio," or "Television."
Trade Fairs (a guide to world's major trade shows) http://203.116.80.102/

Transfer Pricing (Ernst & Young articles) www.ey.com/global/ger.nsf/US/Library_-_Transfer_Pricing
TV stations by country (links to Web sites)
http://archive.comlab.ox.ac.uk/publishers/broadcast.html

Governments (Foreign)

Government Resources ciber.bus.msu.edu/busres/govrnmnt.htm
Links to Statistical Agencies of Foreign Governments www.cbs.nl/en/services/links/default.asp
Rulers and Heads of State (lists of heads of state worldwide)
www.geocities.com/Athens/1058/rulers.html

Government (U.S.)

Agriculture Department (Foreign Agricultural Service—world agricultural production, U.S.–EU hormone dispute, U.S.–China WTO Accession Agreement) www.fas.usds.gov/
Bureau of Labor Statistics http://stats.bls.gov/blshome.htm
Commerce Department (trade and economic data, copy of federal budget) www.doc.gov
Bureau of Economic Analysis (GDP, industry and wealth data, international data) www.bea.doc.gov/
Bureau of Export Administration (responsible for export controls) www.bxa.doc.gov/
Census Bureau (international trade and world population statistics) www.census.gov/foreign-trade/www
International Programs Center (part of the Population Division of the Census Bureau—conducts demographic and socioeconomic studies) www.census.gov/ipc/www/index.html

1. *International Data Base* (computerized source of demographic and socioeconomic statistics for all countries) www.census.gov/ipc/www/idbnew.html
2. *World Population Information* (data and projections) www.census.gov/ipc/www/world.html

International Trade Administration www.ita.doc.gov

1. Commercial Service www.usatrade.gov/website/
2. Export Programs Guide
3. Export Assistance Centers
4. Import Administration (administers antidumping and countervailing duty laws)
5. U.S. Industry and Trade Outlook
6. U.S. Global Trade Outlook
7. U.S. Foreign Trade Highlights
   a. Trade in goods and services
   b. Top 50 foreign trading partners
8. State Export Data

Customs (U.S.) information for exporters and importers www.customs.gov/impoexpo/impoexpo.htm
Defense Department http://defenselink.mil/
Air Force (links to Air Force sites) www.af.mil/
Army Corps of Engineers (recreation and flood control) www.usace.army.mil/
Navy Department (connect to news service, library, postgrad school) www.ncts.navy.mil
Department of the Treasury www.treas.gov/
Energy, Department of (International Energy—country briefs, database, forecasts, petroleum, gas, electricity) www.eia.doe.gov/emeu/international/contents.html
Export-Import Bank of the United States (bank programs, project fees, support for U.S. aircraft exports) www.exim.gov
Ex-Im Bank Programs (summary of programs and links to explanation of each) www.exim.gov/mprograms.html
Export Credit Insurance Program www.exim.gov/minsprog.html
Federal Communication Commission (FCC) (daily news, public notices) www.fcc.gov/
Federal Trade Commission (FTC) http://ftc.gov/
Fedstats (site to find statistics of over 70 federal agencies) www.fedstats.gov/
Government Information Locator Service (GILS) www.access.gpo.gov/su_docs/gils/gils.html

Government Printing Office www.access.gpo.gov/

Labor Department (employment statistics, consumer price index) gopher://marvel.loc.gov. [Page through menus to Government Information/Federal Information Resources/Information by Branch of Federal Government/Executive Branch/Labor Department.] http://stats.bls.gov/blshome.html

International Comparisons of Manufacturing Hourly Compensation Costs http://stats.bls.gov/news.release/prod4.toc.htm

Market Access and Compliance (Big Emerging Markets, NAFTA, Central and Eastern Europe market data) www.mac.doc.gov

National Institute for Standards and Technology (U.S. representative for ISO) www.nist.gov/

Security Exchange Commission filings www.sec.gov/edgarhp.htm

State Department (human rights, travel advisories) www.state.gov

Country Commercial Guides www.state.gov/www/ind.html. Click on "Country Commercial Guides."

United States International Trade Commission (provides trade expertise to government agencies, publishes updates to Harmonized Tariff Schedule) www.usitc.gov

U.S. Trade Representative (reports on U.S. trade issues such as National Trade Estimate Report on Foreign Trade Barriers and on Section 301) www.ustr.gov/reports/index.html

International Business

Advertising (international advertising news from major magazine *Advertising Age International*) www.adageinternational.com/

Business Monitor (international business magazine) www.businessmonitor.co.uk/

Business Software Alliance www.bsa.org

Company extensions (definitions and acronyms for company forms used in various countries) www.corporateinformation.com/definitions.html

G-7 Information Center (University of Toronto) (G-7 info) www.g7.utoronto.ca

Global Business Centre (hundreds of links to international business topics) http://glreach.com/gbc/en.php3

Holidays, National www.rubicon.com/passport/holidays/holidays.htm

Industrial Espionage (National Counterintelligence Center) www.nacic.gov/

International Affairs Resources (WWW virtual library of over 1,100 links to maps, intergovernmental organizations, national governments, and news sources) www.etown.edu/vl

International Business Resources (useful interbusiness sites) www.ibrc.bschool.ukans.edu/resources/gen/gen.htm

International Business Terms, Guide to (194-page list) www.ntia.doc.gov/lexcon.txt

International Organization for Standardization (ISO) (product standards) www.iso.ch/

Language Resources (bilingual dictionaries, translations, acronyms, style and grammar guides) www.pscw.uva.nl/sociosite/Language.html

Links to International and National Statistical Sources www.cbs.nl/eng/link/index.htm

Management and marketing surveys (Ernst & Young International) www.eyi.com

PriceWaterhouseCoopers (articles on international business by this global management consulting firm) www.pwcglobal.com/. Click on "Insights and Solutions" and then on "Publications."

Product Classification Systems

1. *U.N. Standard International Trade Classification (SITC)* www.tradeport.org/ts/trade_expert/.arket/classify/sitc1.html
2. *U.S. Standard Industrial Classification (SIC)* www.immigration-usa.com/sic_index.html
3. *North American Industry Classification System (NAICS)* (standard for United States, Canada, and Mexico) www.census.gov/epcd/www.naics.html

Regional Search Directory (numerous topics, such as culture and news for the world's geographical regions) www.orientation.com

Unit Conversions (convert nearly every unit in the world to another) www.legacy.com/convert2/convert_old.html

World Time (correct local time for every country in the world) www.worldtimesaver.com

World Travel (general information about world travel) www.webcom.com/one/world/

International Finance

Asian Crisis www.imf.org/External/np/exr/facts/asia.HTM
Bank for International Settlements (BIS) www.bis.org
Briefings on Business Issues (latest developments in international business, economic, and political developments) www.pwcglobal.com/extweb/newcolth.nsf/ExecutivePerspectives. Click on "International Briefings."
Central Banks and Bank for International Settlements www.bis.org/cbanks.htm
CNN Financial News www.cnnfn.com/news/
Countertrade www.cob.ohio-state.edu/citm/expa/countert.html
Forms of Countertrade www.cob.ohio-state.edu/citm/expa/countertrade_list.html
Country Research, Asian Crisis (ING Bank) www.ingbarings.com/pweb/research/research_frame.htm. Click on "Global Market Links."
Currency Converter (exchange rates) www.xe.net/currency/
Currency Site (currency converter, currency forecasts, historical table) www.oanda.com/
Doing Business in Guides (PriceWaterhouseCooper guides for many countries) www.pwcglobal.com/. Click on "Insights and Solutions" and then on "Publications."
Euromoney (European financial news online) www.euromoney.com
Exchange Rates
Current Week www.bog.frb.fed.us/Releases/H10/Update/
Euro foreign exchange reference rates (daily) www.ecb.int/home/home01.htm
Hamburger Standard—Big Mac Price www.oands.com/products/bigmac/bigmac.shtml
Historical Data www.bog.frb.fed.us/Releases/H10/hist/
Universal Currency Converter www.xe.net/ict/
Financial Accounting Standards Board (FASB) (international activities) www.rutgers.edu/Accounting/raw/fasb/IASC/iascfeb.htm
Foreign Direct Investment in the United States www.bea.doc.gov/bea/ail.htm
ING Bank International www.ingbank.com
ING Barings Global Strategy www.liquidity.com. Click on icon in upper left hand corner.
International Global Markets www.ino.com/
Madrid Stock Exchange www.bolsamadrid.es/
Multilateral Development Banks (African, Asian, European, Inter-American, World Bank Group) www.worldbank.com/html/extdr/institutions/mdb.htm
Tax information
Latest tax law changes of numerous countries www.pwcglobal.com. Go to "Online Solutions" and click on "Tax News Network."
Country Tax Facts (country-specific tax information on 50 countries by KPMG) www.tax.kpmg.net/country_tax_facts/
Users' Guide to the SDR (Special Drawing Rights) www.imf.org/external/pubs/FT/usrgsdr/usercon.htm
U.S. Exports, Imports, and Foreign Direct Investment www.bea.doc.gov/bea/sitemap.htm. Click on "International Accounts Articles."

International Trade

Agricultural Trade and Production (FAO) www.fao.org
Anti Dumping and Countervailing Duty Statistics (products, countries involved) www.ita.doc.gov/import_admin/records/stats/iastats1.html
Big Emerging Markets (10 growing markets with huge business potential) www.stat-usa.gov/itabems.html
Country Barriers to U.S. Exports (reports on trade barriers and their negotiations) www.ustr.gov/reports/nte/2000/contents.html
Country by Commodity Trade Data (monthly 1-digit SITC commodity code trade data between the United States and 226 nations) www.census.gov/foreign-trade/www.index.html
Country Reports on Economic Policy and Trade Practices (U.S. State Department) www.state.gov/www/issues/economic/trade_reports/
Country Trade Data (U.S.) www.census.gov/foreign-trade/www/statistics.html
Export Controls (information on U.S. Bureau of Export Administration, agency in charge of export controls) www.bxa.doc.gov/
Export Sales of U.S. Metropolitan Areas www.ita.doc.gov/industry/otea/metro/

Export Trade Data by 3 digit SITC code (country and total dollar value by UN International Trade Center) www.intracen.org/itc/infobase/itcinfb.htm/. Click on "International Trade Statistics by Product Group and Country" under "Trade Statistics."

Foreign Trade Data (37 different tables on various aspects of U.S. foreign trade) www.ita.doc.gov/industry/otea/usfth/tabcon.html

FT900 (U.S. International Trade in Goods and Services Report (menu includes reports for current month and year as well as previous years) www.census.gov/ftp/pub/foreign-trade/www/press.html

Generalized System of Preferences (list of member countries) ustr.gov/reports/gsp/

Guide to U.S. Foreign Trade Statistics (covers various aspects of international trade) www.census.gov/foreign-trade/www/sec2.html

Industries Information (links to ITA Web sites that cover key industries) www.ita.doc.gov/ita_home/itakeyin.html

International and National Statistical Sites (compiled by the U.S. Bureau of Labor) http://stats.bls.gov/oreother.htm

International Trade for the Newcomer ciber.bus.msu.edu/busres/inttrade.htm

International Trade Sites (links to over 150 sites) www.geocities.com/WallStreet/Floor/1325/trade_info.html

Legal Aspects of Trade and Investment (U.S. Department of Commerce) www.ita.doc.gov/legal/

Major Trading Countries of the World (importing and exporting) www.tdc.org.hk/. Click on "Statistics."

North American Industry Classification System [replaces Standard Industrial Classification (SIC)] www.census.gov/epcd/www/naics.html

Office of Trade and Economic Analysis (foreign trade highlights, U.S. industry sector data) www.ita.doc.gov/td/industry/otea

Office of Trade and Economic Analysis (U.S. Industry and Trade Outlook, U.S. Foreign Trade Highlights, State Export Data) www.ita.doc.gov/td/industry/otea/

Official Sources of Trade and Investment Information (global, multinational, and national) www.sice.oas.org/stidre.asp

Section 301 of the 1974 Trade Act www.ita.doc.gov/legal/301.html

Semiconductor Industry in Japan www.eiaj.or.jp/

Statistical Data and Information Sources www.ciber.bus.msu.edu/busres/statinfo.htm

Trade balances for U.S. trade partners (ranked according to U.S. exports) www.ustr.gov/reports/nte/2000/appendix.pdf

Trade Data Sources (sites for trade data) intracen.org/itc/infobase/infsourc/index.htm

Trade Leads www.ciber.bus.msu.edu/busres/tradlead.htm

Trade statistics and information (U.S. Census Bureau) www.census-gov/ftp/pub/foreign-trade/www/

UN International Trade Center www.intracen.org/

Country-Specific Export Profiles (Trade Performance Index—ranks a nation's competitiveness in export performance, National Export Trade Maps—assessment of a country's export portfolio) www.intracen.org/services/mas/smr_inde.htm

International Trade Statistics (by SITC code and product group or exports and imports by country) www.intracen.org/infobase/itcinfb.htm#Statistics

U.S. foreign trade data sources www.lib.umich.edu/libhome/Documents.center/stectrad.html AND www.bea.doc.gov

U.S. International Trade in Goods and Services Highlights (bimonthly) www.census.gov/indicator/www/ustrade.html

U.S. International Trade Summary (merchandise and service totals, end use commodities, trade by principal countries) www.ita.doc.gov/td/industry/otea/usftu/current.pdf

U.S. Merchandise Trade (FT925 Exports and Imports Report—terminated by Department of Commerce in 1996) www.census.gov/prod/1/ftd/ft925/ft925.html

U.S. Top Trading Partners (trade balances, percent changes) www.ustr.gov/reports/. Click on "National Trade Estimate Reports" and then on "Foreign Trade Barriers."

U.S. Trade Balance by Partners http://dataweb.usitc.gov/scripts/cy_m3.asp

U.S. Trade Commission's Investigations and Fact-Finding Reports (complaints about foreign governments' trade barriers) www.usitc.gov

U.S. Trade Representative Press Releases (international trade relations) www.ustr.gov/releases/

U.S. Trade Representative's 2000 National Trade Estimate Report on Foreign Trade Barriers by Country www.ustr.gov/reports/nte/2000/contents.html. Click on "Country."

U.S. trade statistics, export and import counseling www.ita.doc.gov

Internet

A Short Internet Guide (a 20-page introduction to the Internet and the World Wide Web prepared by UNESCO) www.unesco.org/webworld/infotech/guide.pdf

The Internet (16-page discussion of the Internet and the WWW from UNESCO's World Information Report) www.unesco.org/webworld/wirerpt/wirenglish/chap18.pdf

Lessons on Internet (27-lesson training workshop: see syllabus and register for lessons delivered by E-mail) http://netsquirrel.com/roadmap96/syllabus.html

Internships

International Internships (many links to internships) www.whittier.edu/career/intlintern1.html#intldirectories

International Trade Administration (Trade Information Center Intern Program) http://infoserv2.ita.doc.gov/tic.nsf. Click on "College Intern Opportunities."

Organization of American States www.oas.org. Click on "Fellowships" in menu at upper right corner.

Project Chile (study Spanish and work in Chile for four to six months to gain management experience. Financial assistance provided. Information and application forms at Web site) www.docp.wright.edu/projectchile

United Nations Headquarters Internship Programme (unpaid internships for students in graduate school; program consists of three two-month periods from mid-January to mid-November) www.un.org/Depts/OHRM/brochure.htm

U.S. Department of State (overseas and in United States; paid and unpaid internships for 10 weeks, employment after graduation) www.state.gov/www/careers/rinterncontents.html

World Bank (summer internships in Washington, DC for students enrolled in graduate programs; monthly salaries paid) www.worldbank.org/. Click on "site map" and then on "Summer Internship Program" under "CAREERS."

Labor

Foreign Labor Statistics (FLS) (statistics for 18 developed nations) http://146.142.4.24/cgi-bin/surveymost?in

International Comparisons of FLS http://stats.bls.gov/flsdata.htm

International Comparison of Hourly Compensation Costs for Production Workers in Manufacturing http://stats.bls.gov/news.release/ichcc.toc.htm

Languages

Dictionaries and Translations www.june29.com/HLP/

Language Resources (bilingual dictionaries, thesauruses, encyclopedia) www.pscw.uva.nl/sociosite/Language.html

Language Tools (translators, dictionaries, thesaurus, famous quotes) www.iTools.com/research-it/ AND www.facstaff.bucknell.edu/rbeard/diction.html

Languages of the World (geographical distribution of languages, top 100 languages by population) www.sil.org/ethnologue/

Silent Language (gestures, speaking distance) www.webofculture.com/edu/gestures.html

Translation (translate phrases from the language you speak to the language you want to learn)

1. www.travlang.com/languages/
2. http://babelfish.altavista.digital.com/
3. www.systransoft.com

Latin America and the Caribbean

Region

Business and Finance in Latin America (sources organized by Latin American country) www.lanic.utexas.edu/

Business Practices, Economic, and Socioeconomic Data www.latinworld.com

Caribbean (country information) www.ibrc.bschool.ukans.edu/country/carib/carib.htm
Central America (country information) www.ibrc.bschool.ukans.edu/country/centA/centa.htm
Country-Specific and Regional Information (Central and South America) ciber.bus.msu.edu/busres/samerica.htm
Economic Commission for Latin America and the Caribbean www.eclac.org
Economic, Trade, and Social Databases www.iadb.org/int/sta/ENGLISH/staweb/statshp.htm
Free Trade Area of the Americas (FTAA) http://alca-ftaa.org/
Handbook for Latin American Studies (Library of Congress searchable bibliography on Latin America) lcweb.loc.gov/rr/tools.html#hlas
Information for Trade with Latin America www.latco.org/tools.htm
Inter-American Development Bank (country reports, international trade data, databases for income distribution and socioeconomic data) www.iadb.org
Latin American Country and Caribbean Selected Economic and Social Data http://lanic.utexas.edu/la/region/aid/aid96/
Latin American economic and social statistics (searchable) www.iadb.org. Follow "Research and statistics" path.
Latin America On-Line (country briefs, business intelligence) www.dfat.gov.au/geo/americas/la/index.html
Links of the AMERICAS (excellent maps, links to newspapers, periodicals, and country information, Internet search engines) www.iadb.org. Click on "Links of the Americas."
Mercosur (organization and operation of Mercosur) www.mercosur.org AND http://uscommerce.org.mx AND www.americasnet.com/mauritz/mercosur/english/
NAFTA
- *NAFTA Countries and the Americas* www.nafta.net/naftacos.htm
- *NAFTA Information Center* (search databases) www.tamiu.edu/coba/usmtr/
- *NAFTANET* (NAFTA links) www.plattsburgh.edu/centers/tac/qmib/misc/nafta.html

NAFTA Information Center (U.S. Customs) www.customs.gov/nafta/center.htm
Organization of American States www.oas.org/
- *Trade Agreements* (Mercosur, G3, LAIA, CARICOM, and more) www.sice.oas.org/tradee.asp
- *Trade and Investment Information Sources* (global and regional) www.sice.oas.org/stidre.asp

Statistics (regional and national) http://lanic.utexas.edu/la/region/statistics/

Country

Argentina
- *Argentina Business* (business culture, marketing in, macroeconomic data, news) www.invertir.com
- *The Southernmost South* (history, culture, and economic activities) www.surdelsur.com/economia/indexingles.html

Brazil
- *Geographical and Statistical Institute* (maps, economic data) www.ibge.gov.br
- *Infonet* (culture, geography, maps) www.brazilinfo.net

Chile (economy, demographics, government) www.emulateme.com/chile.htm
Colombia, a Country Study http://lcweb2.loc.gov/frd/cs/cotoc.html
Guatemala Online (country profile, business and economic overviews) www.quetzalnet/.com/default.html
Guyana Economy and Investment www.guyana.org/Economy/economy.html
Mexico
- *Institute of Statistics, Geography, and Informatics* www.inegi.gob.mx
- *Exporting to Mexico* (U.S. Commercial Service in Mexico) http://uscommerce.org.mx

Legal Information

Antiboycott Compliance Requirements www.bxa.doc.gov/Antiboycott Compliance/default.htm
- *Arab boycott of Israel* www.ustr.gov/reports/nte/2000/arab.html

Arbitration (International Chamber of Commerce) www.iccwbo.org/home/menu_international_arbitration.asp
Association of International Law (general information, publications) www.asil.org/
Canadian Legal Resources on the WWW (sources of Canadian law and government) www.mbnet.mb.ca/~psim/can_law.html
Competition and Antitrust (OECD) www.oecd.org/daf/clp/
Corporate Forms, Description (forms used in various countries) www.corporateinformation.com/definitions.html

Country Tax Facts (KPMG's site for country-specific tax information)
www.tax.kpmg.net/country_tax_facts/default.htm
Doing Business in Germany www.germany-info.org/f_index.html. Click on "Business and Economy."
Doing Business Guides (for 32 countries) www.hg.org/guides.html
FCPA: Antibribery Provisions www.ita.doc.gov/legal/fcpa1.html
Foreign Corrupt Practices Act (FCPA) www.dhlaw.com/DOCS/FCPAHTM
Foreign and International Law (Washburn University Law Library) www.washlaw.edu/. Click on "Foreign Law."
Foreign and International Law Resources (Cornell Law Library)
www.lawschool.cornell.edu/library/International_Resources/foreign.htm
Global Legal Information Network (database of searchable legal abstracts and some full texts of national laws from 35 contributing countries) http://rs6.loc.gov/glin/mdbquery.html
Guide to Law Online (worldwide sources) http://lcweb2.loc.gov/glin/worldlaw.html
INCOTERMS 2000 (terms of sale) www.worldcargoalliance.com/Library/Incoterms
Intellectual Property
Worldwide www.ipww.com/
Intellectual Property Alliance www.iipa.com/
Intellectual Property Rights (post-Uruguay Round) www.ita.doc.gov/legal/ipr.html
International Arbitration Rules (rules, procedures, links to other arbitration resources)
www.adr.org/
International Chamber of Commerce www.ibnet.com/icchp.html
International Court of Justice (judicial organ of the UN) www.icj-cij.org/
International Economic Law Web Sources www.tufts.edu/fletcher/inter_econ_law/iellinks.htm

a. *International Trade Law*

b. *International Finance Law*

c. *Law and Development*

d. *World Intellectual Property Law*
World Intellectual Property Organization (WIPO) www.wipo.org

e. *International Business Regulation*
Transparency International (coalition against corruption in international business transactions) www.transparency.de

International Trade Law (Legal Information Institute, Cornell Law School—treaties, trade laws)
www.law.cornell.edu/topics/trade.html
International Trade Law (APEC, NAFTA, European Union, and individual countries)
www.findlaw.com/01topics/25interntrade/index.html
Laws of Other Nations (House of Representatives Library)
www.priweb.com/internetlawlib/52.htm
Legal Aspects of International Trade and Investment www.ita.doc.gov/legal/
Measuring Units Conversion Tables (convert from/to metric, imperial, U.S. measuring systems)
www.french-property.com/ref/convert.htm
Mercosur Treaty (Treaty of Asuncion) www.sice.oas.org/trade/mrcsr/MRCSRTOC.asp
News on International Trade Law (export, import, Customs) www.exportimportlaw.com
Product Standards, International
International Electrotechnical Commission (world standards for electrotechnical products)
www.iec.ch/
International Organization for Standardization (ISO) (product standards) www.iso.ch/
Trade Agreements and Treaties (between United States and its trading partners)
www.mac.doc.gov/tcc/
Trade and Commercial Treaties and Agreements
www.tufts.edu/departments/fletcher/multi/trade.html
U.N. Commission on International Trade Law (contains abstracts of cases beginning with 1993)
www.unicitral.org/
U.N. Convention on Contracts for the International Sale of Goods
www.cisg.law.pace.edu/
U.N. International Law Resources (International Court of Justice, Law of the Sea, International Trade Law) www.un.org/law/
U.S. Bilateral Investment Treaties www.state.gov/www.issues.economic/7treaty.html
U.S. Trade Laws (FCPA and Foreign Sales Corporations) http://ita.doc/gov/legal/

Newspapers, Periodicals, and Radio and Television Stations

World Links

AJR News Link (worldwide links to newspapers, magazines, radio and TV)
http://ajr.newslink.org/mag.html
Index to Business Journals and Newspapers
http://metalab.unc.edu/reference/moss/business/journals.html
Kidon Media-Link (links to radio, TV, newspapers, and magazines by country worldwide)
www.kidon.com/media-link/index.shtml
Newslink (links to media worldwide) www.ajr.newslink.org
News Media www.lib.umich.edu/libhome/Documents.center/psnews.html
Newspapers around the World www.freenet.mb.ca/community/media/newspapers/
Online Newspaper Indexes www.uwstout.edu/lib/serials/news.htm
Periodicals from around the world www.euromktg.com/gbc/en/journals.html
TV Net (lists of TV station stations by country)
http://archive.comlab.ox.ac.uk/publishers/broadcast.html
Wire Services (global, national—many countries) www.trib.com/NEWS/
World Business Magazines (31 world, industry-specific, and regional)
web.idirect.com/~tiger/magazine.htm

World Coverage

Bloomberg Business News (international business news) www.bloomberg.com/
Business Week (international business news) www.businessweek.com/
Euromoney (money and banking magazine) www.euromoney.com
Finance and Development (publication of the World Bank and IMF) www.imf.org/fandd
Financial Times (British business newspaper) www.ft.com/
Forbes www.forbes.com
Fortune www.fortune.com
International Herald Tribune (international business newspaper) www.iht.com
Journal of Commerce (world business news) www.joc.com/
Links to foreign newspapers worldwide www.kidon.com/media-link/
Links to U.S. and foreign newspapers www.trib.com/NEWS/news/
Worldwide links to newspapers, magazines, broadcasters, and news services http://ajr.newslink.org/

African Coverage

Africa News (business, financial, and technological news) www.africanews.org
South Africa
Cape Business News www.cbn.co.za/
Financial Mail (weekly financial news) www.fm.co.za/

Asian Coverage

Arab net (business information from several Arab countries) www.arab.net
Arab World Online www.awo.net/
Asia Business News www.nb-pacifica.com
Asia One Business Center (Asian on-line newspapers) www.asia1.com.sg/bizcentre
China
China News Digest www.cnd.org/
China News Service www.chinanews.com.hk/
Inside China Today www.insidechina.com/
South China Morning Post (Hong Kong and China) www.scmp.com/
Far Eastern Economic Review (Dow-Jones Asian news) www.feer.com
Hong Kong Mail (Chinese and Hong Kong news) www.hk-standard.com/
netscape-welcome.html
India
Business Line India (business information on India) www.indiaserver.com/news/bline/
Economic Times (business news; check "Brand Equity" for case studies on international brands in India) www.economictimes.com/
Iran Weekly Press Digest www.neda.net/iran-wpd/
Israel: Jerusalem Post (economic and company news) www.jpost.com

Japan

Asahi News (top stories from Tokyo) www.asahi.com/english/asahi/index.html

The Japanese Times Online www.japantimes.co.jp

Nikkei Net (Japanese stock market news) www.nni/nikkei.co.jp

Jordan: The Star (political, economic, and cultural weekly) http://star.arabia.com/

Korea Herald (in-depth information in English on North and South Korea) www.koreaherald.co.kr/

Korea Web Weekly www.kimsoft.com/korea.htm

Malaysia Star www.jaring.my/

Nepal: Nepal News (economic and businessnews) www.nepalnews.com/

Pakistan Dawn (business news from Pakistan and West Asia) www.dawn.com

Russia: Russia Today (political and business news) www.russiatoday.com/

The St. Petersburg Times (English) www.sptimes.ru/index.htm

Singapore Business Times http://biztimes.asia1.com/

Vietnam Business Journal www.viam.com/

Vietnam Business Magazines www.cgtd.com/global/

Latin American Coverage

Brazil Financial Wire www.estadao.com.br/agestado

Buenos Aires Herald Weekly (news in English on Mercosur and Argentine economy) www.buenosairesherald.com

Costa Rica Tico Times Online-Business News www.ticotimes.co.cr/business.html

Inter-American Development Bank www.iadb.org/

LATCO's list of Useful Sites for International Trade with Latin America (includes a Latin American company database, Latin American trade links, and links to numerous Latin American newspapers; also has a NAFTA database) www.latco.org/tools.htm

LatinoWeb (links to Latin American, including Mexican newspapers and magazines) www.latinoweb.com/header_index.html

Mexico

Excelsior (major Mexico City newspaper) www.excelsior.com.mx/

The News (political and financial news) www.novedades.com. Click on "The News."

Mundo Latino (links to newspapers in Latin American countries, Portugal, and Spain—some are in English) www.mundolatino.org/prensa

European Coverage

Athens News Agency Bulletin (business and political news) www.ana.gr

Baltic Information Links (includes business periodicals) http://eurasianews.com/erc/0faltic.htm

Central Europe Online (news from Czech Republic, Hungary, Poland, Slovakia) www.centraleurope.com

Ireland

Belfast Telegraph (Northern Ireland daily and political news) www.belfasttelegraph.co.uk/

Finfacts Ireland (business and financial news) www.finfacts.ie

The Irish Times www.irish-times.ie/

Norway Post www.norwaypost.no/. Click on "Guestbook" for business and cultural news.

The Papers of Europe for 27 Countries www.reach.net/notw/eu.html

Portugal (news, business) http://members.aol.com/Alduarte/portugalnewspapers.html

Russia—The St. Petersburg Times www.sptimes.ru/index.htm

Spain

La Gaceta de los Negocios http://negocios.com/

Tenerife News (business news from Spanish tourist region) www.tennews.com/

United Kingdom

The Economist (British business magazine) www.economist.com

Electronic Telegraph www.telegraph.co.uk

Financial Times (London) www.ft.com OR www.usa.ft.com

Internet News www.ananova.com

Marketing Week (leading business magazine from UK) www.mad.co.uk/mw/

The Times (London) www.the-times.co.uk/

Virtual Manchester (news of Manchester, UK) www.manchester.com

U.S. Coverage

Business Week www.businessweek.com/index.html

CNN www.CNN.com

Editor & Publisher magazine www.mediainfo.com/

Frontline (PBS documentaries) www2.pbs.org/wgbh/pages/frontline
Hot-Wired (Internet news) www.hotwired.com
Journal of International Marketing ciber.bus.msu.edu/jim/
Knight-Ridder Financial News www.cnnfn.com/news/
Los Angeles Times www.latimes.com/
MSNBC 24-Hour News (Microsoft and NBC) www.msnbc.com
Newslink (over 3,000 links to news-oriented sites) www.ajr.newslink.org
PBS www.pbs.org
Positive Press www.positivepress.com
San José Mercury www.mercurycenter.com/
Thomas (information on U.S. legislation) http://thomas.loc.gov
USA Today www.usatoday.com
US News & World Report www.usnews.com
Wall St. Journal www.wsj.com
Washington Post Online www.washingtonpost.com
WGN TV www.WGNTV.COM

Canadian Coverage

Canadian Business www.canbus.com/
Montreal Gazette www.montrealgazette.com
Toronto Globe & Mail www.globeandmail.ca/
Vancouver Sun www.vancouversun.com

North America

Regional

North America (country information) www.ibrc.bschool.ukans.edu/country/northA/northa.htm
North American Free Trade Agreement (NAFTA) (complete agreement) www.sice.oas.org/trade/nafta/naftatce.asp
- *NAFTA Facts* (NAFTA's automated information for background information, reports, and agreement provisions) www.mac.doc.gov/nafta/
- *NAFTA by U.S. Congress, Canada and Mexico* www.worldwideschool.org/library/books/hst/northamerican/Nafta/toc.html
- *NAFTA* (Annual Report of the President of the U.S.) www.ustr.gov/reports/
  - *Commission for Environmental Cooperation* (NAFTA agency) www.cec.org/
  - *Impact of NAFTA on doing business in Mexico* www.ustr.gov/reports/nte/1996/mexico.html
  - *Impact of NAFTA on U.S. auto exports to Mexico* www.ustr.gov/reports/nafta/auto_96/index.html
  - *North American Development Bank* (NAFTA bank) www.quicklink.com/mexico/nadbank/ning2.htm

Regional or Country-Specific Information (North America) ciber.bus/msu.edu/busres.htm

Country

Canada
- *Canada* (trade statistics, geography, culture) http://canada.gc.ca/main_e.html AND (federal statistics) www.statcan.ca/start.html
- *Government of Canada: Department of Foreign Affairs and International Trade* www.dfait-maeci.gc.ca/dfait/sitemap-e.asp
- *Mineral Production in Canada* www.nrcan.gc.ca/mms/efab/mmsd/production/default.html
- *Petroleum Industry in Canada* http://strategis.ic.gc.ca/sc_indps/sectors/engdoc/petr_hpg.html
- *Statistics Canada* www.statcan.ca/start.html
- *Strategis Canada* (Canadian equivalent of U.S. Department of Commerce—good source of international business information) http://strategis.ic.gc.ca/engdoc/main.html see also http://strategis.ic.gc.ca/SSG/mi02712e.html
- *Virtual Library* (information on business and government) www.kpmg.ca/main/vl.htm

Caribbean Area (country information) www.ibrc.bschool.ukans.edu/country/carib/carib.htm
Caribbean Nations
- *Caribbean Basin Initiative Report to Congress* www.ustr.gov/reports/cbera/index.html
- *Cuba: CubaWeb* (U.S.-based) www.cubaweb.com
- *Cubaweb* (Cuba-based) www.cubaweb.cu

Latin American Network Information Center (trade and statistics of Cuba and other Latin American nations) www.lanic.utexas.edu

Mexico

Ministry of Finance www.shcp.gob.mx/english/

National Statistics Institute (data on resources, population, and manufacturing) www.inegi.gob.mx/economia/ingles/fieconomia.html

Global Operations Management

Agile Manufacturing Links http://catt.okstate.edu/catt2/resources/agile.htm

Association for Quality and Participation (AQP) (professionals in quality and management participation processes) www.aqp.org

Concurrent Engineering http://dfca.larc.nasa.gov/dfc/ce.html

Deming Web Site (Dr. Deming's writings) http://deming.eng.clemson.edu/pub/den/deming_info.htm

Engineering Technologies for Competitive Advantage (various kinds of engineering with links to technologies such as cost, human, quality) http://dfca.larc.nasa.gov/dfc/etec.html

How Companies Improve Performance through Quality Effort, Survey of www.dbainc.com/dba2/library/survey/index.html

Information-Driven Manufacturing www.mel.nist.gov/informat.html

Integrated Product and Process Development http://dfca.larc.nasa.gov/dfc/ipd.html

ISO (global federation of national standards organizations) www.iso.ch/

What Is ISO 9000 and ISO 9001? www.isoeasy.org

ISO/TC176 (umbrella committee for ISO 9000 series) www.tc176.org/abouttc176/index.htmlb

ISO Translated into Plain English www.connect.ab.ca/~praxiom/webindex.htm

ISO 9000: 4 Steps in Making It Work www.dbainc.com/dba2/implementation/iso9000/isowork.html

ISO 14000 Information Center www.iso14000.com/

Malcolm Baldrige National Quality Awards (annual winners, criteria, fees) www.quality.nist.gov/

Outsourcing (numerous articles from the Outsourcing Institute) www.outsourcing.com

Poka-Yoke Techniques for Early Defect Detection www.geocities.com/SiliconValley/Lab/5320/pokasoft.htm

Poka-Yoke: Role of Mistake-Proofing Systems in Zero-Defect-Oriented Environments http://ayame.seg.kobe-u.ac.jp/ghinzto/paper3.html

Price of Non-Quality Elements www.dbainc.com/dba2/library/price.html

Quality Digest (articles from *Quality Digest* magazine) www.qualitydigest.com

Quality Technologies for Competitive Advantage (Design for Quality, Kaizen, Statistical Quality Control, Poka-Yoke, Taguchi methods) http://dfca.larc.nasa.gov/dfc/qtec.html

Technologies Enabling Agile Manufacturing (TEAM) cewww.eng.oml.gov/team/home.html

Total Quality Management (TQM) http://larc.nasa.gov/dfc/tqm.html

Value Engineering (function or value analysis) http://akao.larc.nasa.gov/dfc/ve.html

Organizational Design

Horizontal Corporation: David Theel, The Horizontal Corporation and Its Use of Self Managed Teams www.emporia.edu/bed/jpur/www.emporia.edu/bed/jpur/jour23ot/davidt.htm

Virtual Corporation, A Framework for Analyzing www.fintec.com/97vc/VCintro.html

Virtual Corporation Page www.cba.uga.edu/~ntaylor/virtual/#VirtualCorporation

Virtual Corporation and Cottage Industries wsrv.clas.virginia.edu/~jeb2n/virtual.html

Virtual Corporation

Everything's Coming Up Virtual www.acm.org/crossroads/xrds4-1/organ.html

The Virtual Corporation www.opengroup.org/opencomments/winter96/1_text/htm#Top AND http://bcn.boulder.co.us/business/BCBR/december/virtual.dec.html

Virtual Corporations and Outsourcing www.brint.com/EmergOrg.htm

Virtual Teaming and Virtual Organizations: 25 Principles of Proven Practice www.skyrme.com/updates/u11.htm#Feature

Political Systems

Corruption Perceptions Index www.GWDG.DE/~uwvw/1999.html

Country Risk Analysis (political, economic, financial risk) www.duke.edu/~charvey/index.html

Country Risk Providers, Comparison of www.duke.edu/~charvey/Country_risk/pol/poltab6.htm

Country Risk Providers, Products of www.duke.edu/~charvey/Country_risk/pol/polappa.htm

Index of Economic Freedom for 100 Nations www.heritage.org/heritage/library/categories/forpol/econ_index/ch5toc.html.cgi

Political Resources on the Internet (sorted by country) www.politicalresources.net/

Small Business

Breaking into the Trade Game (information for beginning exporters) www.sbaonline.gov/OIT/
Central and Eastern Europe Business Information Center's Small Business Facility
www.mac.doc.gov/eebic/. Click on "sbsfhome."
European small business links www.europages.com
How to Start a Small Business Internet Resources www.inreach.com/sbdc/book/netresources.html
Small Business Administration Guide to Exporting www.sba.gov/OIT/txt/Guide-to-Exporting/
Small Business Information
www.yahoo.com/Business_and_Economy/Small_Business_Information
Small Business Links www.bizoffice.com/index.html
Trade Finance Programs www.sbaonline.sba.gov/OIT/. Click on "Export Finance."

Sources of Information (Libraries, Lists, and Centers)

Britannica Online (Encyclopedia Britannica) www.eb.com
Internet Public Library (guide to 1,900 home pages of prominent organizations) www.ipl.org
Library of Congress (searchable databases for books and periodicals) www.loc.gov/
National Security Archive (collection of declassified documents) www.gwu.edu/~nsarchive
Research-It (word translator, geography, CIA Factbook, currency converter)
www.iTools.com/research-it/research-it.html
Resources for Economics on Internet
www.library.ualberta.ca/library_html/subjects/economics/sites.html
Statistical Abstract of U.S. www.census.gov/prod/www./statistical-abstract-us.htm
Yellow Pages (find people, businesses, E-mail) www.bigyellow.com

South America

South America (country information)
www.ibrc.bschool.ukans.edu/country/samerica/samerica.htm
South America Search Engines www.internets.com/ssouthamerica.htm

Strategic Planning

Planning and Organization (short articles on planning)
www.hci.com.au/hcisite/articles/index.htm
Scenario Planning (Global Business Network—organization for scenario training)
www.gbn.org/home.html
Strategic Planning www.entarga.com/stratplan/index.htm AND
www.strategyplanning.com/article.htm AND www.planware.org/strategy.htm
Strategic Planning (with checklists) http://strategis.ic.gc.ca/SSG/sv00050e.html
Tips to Help You Export More Successfully www.dnb.com/global/hglobal2.htm

Telecommunication Technology

Telecommunication Technologies (Chapter 17 from UNESCO's *World Information Report,* covering infrastructure and applications)
www.unesco.org/webworld/wirerpt/wirenglish/chap17.pdf
Telecommunication Technology Briefs http://gold.sao.nrc.ca/ims/ittb/ittb.html

Think Tanks

Heritage Foundation (regulatory studies, statistics) www.heritage.org
Institute for International Economics (analyses of key international economic problems with proposed solutions) www.iie.com
Links to Public Policy Organizations and Think Tanks www.heritage.org/links/policy.html

Videos

European Union Videos (free) www.eurunion.org/infores/index.htm. Under "Research and Academic Resources," click on "Video—Free, Educational."
OAS TV Videos (free) (documentaries on American countries, arts, culture, and OAS operations)
www.oas.org/en/pinfo/week/aveng.htm. Click on "Videos."
Videos on Japan (on loan from JETRO) www.jetro.org/sm.html. Click on "Videos."

World Organizations (Governments)

Bank for International Settlements www.bis.org
Directories of International Organizations

1. www.imf.org/external/np/sec/decdo/about.htm
2. www.intergov.gc.ca/world.orge.html

International Electrotechnical Commission (electrical product standards) www.iec.ch/
International Governmental Organizations (links to many organizations) www.library.nwu.edu/govpub/resource/internat/igo.html
International Monetary Fund (IMF) (IMF Staff Country Reports, World Economic Outlook, various publications) www.imf.org
International Organization for Standardization (ISO) (product standards) www.iso.ch/welcome.html
Links to Government Sources and Information (international, regional, national) www.eff.org/govt.html
Links to International Development Sources w3.acdi-cida.gc.ca/Virtual.nsf/pages/index_e.htm
Links to World Bank data sources (international organizations) www.worldbank.org/data/links.html
Organization for Economic Cooperation and Development (OECD) www.oecd.org
Free Online OECD Documents www.oecd.org/products
Main Economic Indicators; Country Graphs www.oecd.org/std/MEI.HTM
OECD in Figures (demography, trade, tourism, education, taxation, etc.) www.oecd.org/publications/figures
OECD monthly information bulletin www.oecd.org/media/index.htm
OECD Washington DC office (*OECD in Figures,* GDP, income tax rates, and more) www.oecdwash.org/PRESS/CONTENT/frstat.htm
United Nations www.un.org
Group of 77 (home page of organization of 133 developing nations) www.g77.org/index.htm
Index of UN System of Organizations (in alphabetical order) www.unsystem.org/index8.html
Web Site Locator for UN System of Organization www.unsystem.org/index7.html
UN Official Classification System www.unsystem.org/index2.html
International Trade Centre: UNCTAD/WTO (trade statistics) www.intracen.org/itcinfo/itcinfo.htm. Click on "ITC infobases."
UN specialized agencies
Food and Agricultural Organization (FAO) (trade and production data) www.fao.org
International Civil Aviation (ICAO) www.icao.int/
International Court of Justice www.icj-cij.org/
International Labor Organization (ILO) www.ilo.org
International Telecommunication Union (ITU) www.itu.int/
UN Conference on Trade and Development (UNCTAD) www.unctad.org/en/enhome.htm
UN Development Programme www.undp.org
UN Human Development Index www.undp.org/hdro/HDI.html
UN Educational, Scientific, and Cultural Organization www.unesco.org
UN Industrial Development Organization (UNIDO) www.unido.org
Universal Postal Union (UPU) www.upu.int/
U.S. Central Intelligence Agency Statistics (geography, maps, political) www.odci.gov/cia/publications/factbook/index.html
World Bank www.worldbank.org (for publications, click on "Publications")
International Development Association (IDA) www.worldbank.org/ida/
International Finance Corporation (IFC) www.ifc.org/
Multilateral Investment Guarantee Agency (MIGA) www.miga.org
National Statistics www.worldbank.org/data/
World Health Organization (WHO) www.who.ch
World Intellectual Property Organization www.wipo.org/
World Trade Organization (WTO) site map (international trade, services and textile agreements, intellectual property rights, trade dispute settlement) www.wto.org/english/info_e/site2_e.htm
WTO and GATT—are they the same? (no, they're different) www.law.nyu.edu/library/wto_gatt.html
WTO Information www.ustr.gov/

World Organizations (Nongovernment)

International Chamber of Commerce www.iccwbo.org/
ICC International Court of Arbitration www.ibnet.com/iccarb.html

[Chapter]

2

Trading and Investing in International Business

"Creating overseas production sites merely in order to meet local consumption looks an increasingly fragile basis for foreign investment. A much better one is the ability to make the best use of a company's competitive advantages by locating production wherever it is most efficient. Today's multinationals create widespread networks of research, component production, assembly, and distribution."

—Martin Wolfe, global business analyst, Financial Times, *October 1, 1997, p. 12.*

Concept Previews

After reading this chapter, you should be able to:

- **appreciate** the magnitude of international trade and how it has grown
- **identify** the direction of trade, or who trades with whom
- **explain** the size, growth, and direction of U.S. foreign direct investment
- **identify** who invests and how much is invested in the United States
- **understand** the reasons for entering foreign markets
- **understand** the international market entry methods
- **comprehend** that globalization of an international firm occurs over at least seven dimensions and that a company can be partially global in some dimensions and completely global in others
- **discuss** the channel members available to companies that export indirectly or directly or manufacture overseas
- **explain** the structural trends in wholesaling and retailing

Dave Bartruff/Stock Boston

Large International Firms Invest Overseas, and They Also Export

Large American international firms, responding to such factors as (1) global competition, (2) liberalization by host governments in regard to foreign investment, and (3) advances in technology, caused foreign direct investment (FDI) to soar in 1999 to an unprecedented level (from $84 billion in 1996 to $151 billion in 1999, an 80 percent increase). The increase from an average of $41 billion annually from the period 1985–1995 to the 1999 figure amounted to 268 percent.[a] Inasmuch as foreign direct investment generally is used to set up foreign production, have U.S. exports dropped as a result of the more than $480 billion in U.S. FDI in the period 1996–1999?

Apparently not, because American exports of goods and services also experienced a sizable increase (78 percent) in the 1990–1999 period, rising from $537 billion in 1990 to $795 billion in 1995 and $956 billion in 1999. Even with a dollar that was strong relative to many other currencies, such as the euro, American exports rose by more than 20 percent from 1995 to 1999.[b] Are small firms, large firms, or both kinds responsible for this growth? It is a common belief that small and medium-sized companies, because they lack the financial and human resources, supply their foreign markets by exporting to rather than producing in them and that large international companies do just the opposite. In fact, the U.S. Department of Commerce states that approximately two-thirds of U.S. exports of goods are by U.S.-owned multinational corporations, with over one-third of those exports being shipped by the U.S. parent to foreign affiliates.[c]

The latest study by *Forbes* (2000) of the largest U.S. multinationals lists 28 companies with foreign sales of at least $9 billion. Among those companies, the ratio of foreign sales to total sales ranged from 77.1 percent for Texaco to 13.8 percent for Wal-Mart Stores (see Table 2.1).[d] Many of these companies sell to 100 countries or more. Even though large international companies such as these typically have numerous production facilities overseas, it is usually not feasible for them to have a factory in every market. The foreign investment would be too great for them to attempt to set up production facilities in each market. Also, many markets are too small to support local manufacturing; they must be served by exports.

To appreciate the importance of international trade and foreign investment for these companies, examine the last column in Table 2.1, which shows the ratio of net profit from foreign sales to total net profit. For 17 of the 28 companies (61 percent), more than 40 percent of net profits were attributed to foreign sales. Without sales and profits generated from foreign operations, the competitiveness of many of these companies would be seriously damaged and some of them might be unable to remain in business. ■

Note: Forbes defines foreign sales as sales from *foreign production* and excludes exports and intercompany sales, and so total levels of foreign sales may be understated.

Sources: [a]"Country Fact Sheet: United States," *World Investment Report 2000,* www.unctad.org/en/pub/ps4wir00fs.en.htm (October 2000). [b]"U.S. International Trade in Goods and Services, Balance of Payments Basis, 1960–1999," International Trade Administration, U.S. Department of Commerce, www.ita.doc.gov/td/industry/otea/usfth/aggregate/H99t01.txt (September 9, 2000). [c]"U.S. Trade Facts," *Business America,* May 1996, p. 22. [d]Brian Zajac, "Global Giants: The Largest 100 U.S. Multinationals," *Forbes,* July 24, 2000, pp. 335–38.

The opening section of this chapter illustrates the fact that both means of supplying overseas markets—*exporting* to and *production* in those markets—are essential to most major U.S. corporations. Moreover, these two international business activities are not confined to manufacturing concerns. Among the companies *Forbes* lists as the 100 largest U.S. multinationals, 21 are service companies with primary activities in banking, finance, insurance, business services, entertainment, computer software and services, transportation and travel, and retailing. However, smaller firms also have operations overseas. According to *World Investment Report,* small and medium-sized international firms account for 20.8 percent of the total 3,470 U.S. international corporations and also play an important role in generating exports (see Small and Medium-Sized Enterprises on page 64).*[1]

foreign sourcing
The overseas procurement of raw materials, components, and products

In this chapter, we examine two topics directly related to exporting and production in foreign countries: (1) *international trade,* which includes exports and imports, and (2) *foreign direct investment,* which internationals must make to establish and expand their overseas operations.[2] Later, in the chapters on production and importing, we shall

*The United Nations defines small and medium-sized international firms for this study as bank and nonbank parent companies whose affiliates had assets, sales, and net income under $3 million.

Table 2.1 Foreign Sales and Profits of Largest U.S. Multinationals ($ billions)

Company	Foreign Sales	Rank in Forbes Largest 100 U.S. Multinationals	Total Sales	Rank in Fortune 1000	Foreign Sales as Percentage of Total Sales	Net Profit from Foreign Operations	Total Net Profit	Net Profit from Foreign Operations as Percentage of Total Net Profit
ExxonMobil	$115.46	1	$160.88	3	71.8%	$5.31	$8.47	62.7%
IBM	50.38	2	87.55	6	57.5	3.83	7.71	49.6
Ford Motor	50.14	3	162.56	4	30.8	n.a.	7.24	n.a.
General Motors	46.49	4	176.56	1	26.3	3.28	5.93	55.3
General Electric	35.35	5	111.63	5	31.7	3.93	17.23	22.8
Texaco	32.70	6	42.43	28	77.1	0.64	1.18	54.1
Citigroup	28.75	7	82.01	7	35.1	n.a.	9.99	n.a.
Hewlett-Packard	23.40	8	42.37	13	55.2	1.80	3.10	58.0
Wal-Mart Stores	22.73	9	165.01	2	13.8	.81	10.00	8.2
Compaq Computer	21.17	10	38.53	20	55.0	.58	0.57	101.4
American International Group	20.31	11	40.66	17	50.0	n.a.	5.06	n.a.
Chevron	20.02	12	45.20	35	44.3	1.09	2.07	52.9
Philip Morris	19.67	13	61.75	9	31.9	2.76	7.68	35.9
Procter & Gamble	18.35	14	38.13	23	48.1	1.42	3.76	37.6
Motorola	17.76e	15	30.93	37	57.4	1.46	0.82	179.1
Intel	16.65	16	29.39	39	56.7	3.66	7.31	50.1
E.I. du Pont de Nemours	13.26	17	26.92	42	49.3	0.69	0.28	244.6
Xerox	12.69	18	23.10	87	54.9	0.60	1.41	42.8
Lucent Technologies	12.19	19	38.30	22	31.8	0.47	3.46	13.7
Coca-Cola	12.12	20	19.81	83	61.2	1.58	2.43	65.1
Johnson & Johnson	12.09	21	27.47	43	44.0	2.01	4.17	48.3
Dow Chemical	11.45	22	18.93	89	60.5	0.84	1.40	59.7
Ingram Micro	11.26	23	28.07	41	40.1	0.00	0.18	1.7
Pfizer	10.74e	24	27.60	107	38.9	n.a.	4.96	n.a.
Halliburton	10.12	25	14.90	115	67.9	0.30	0.56	53.7
Enron	9.94	26	40.11	18	24.8	0.57	1.02	55.3
Caterpillar	9.53	27	19.70	85	48.4	0.21	0.97	21.3
United Technologies	9.52	28	24.13	57	39.5	0.58	0.93	62.7

Note: Because of rounding, values in the percentage columns do not always equal the proportion of figures shown in corresponding columns. Figures are from continuing operations.

n.a. = not available. e = estimate.

Forbes defines foreign sales as revenues from foreign production and excludes exports and intercompany sales.

Sources: "The Largest 100 U.S. Multinationals," *Forbes,* July 24, 2000, pp. 335–36; and "The Fortune 1000 List," www.fortune.com/fortune/global500 (October 8, 2000).

discuss the third activity of international business—**foreign sourcing,** the overseas procurement of raw materials, components, and products.

International Trade

Volume of Trade

In 1990, a milestone was reached when the volume of international trade in goods and services measured in current dollars surpassed $4 trillion. Nine years later, despite a global economic slowdown associated with the Asian financial crisis that began in 1997, international trade in goods and services reached $6.8 trillion.[3] The dollar value of total world exports in 1999 was greater than the gross national product of every nation in the world except the United States. One-fourth of everything grown or made

Table 2.2 World Trade in Merchandise Exports (FOB Values; in Billions of Current U.S. Dollars)

	1970	1980	1990	1995	1999
Total world exports	$314	$2,001	$3,436	$5,004	$5,478
Developed countries	225	1,269	2,449	3,435	3,690
Germany[a]	35	193	423	508	541
United States	43	217	394	585	702
Japan	19	130	288	443	418
France	18	111	210	287	300
United Kingdom	19	110	185	242	268
Italy	13	78	170	234	230
Developing countries[b]	56	587	806	1,384	1,586
EU	88[c]	690[d]	1,477[e]	2,038	2,166
EFTA	51[f]	112	99[g]	122	123
LAIA	13	80	113	173	209

Notes: EU = European Union.
EFTA = European Free Trade Association.
LAIA = Latin American Integration Association (formerly Latin America Free Trade Association).
[a]Includes exports to East Germany before reunification.
[b]Defined by the World Bank as low- and middle-level-income nations as indicated by GNP/capita.
[c]Original six members only (Belgium, Luxembourg, France, West Germany, Italy, and the Netherlands).
[d]Includes original six members plus Denmark, Ireland, and the United Kingdom.
[e]Includes Greece, Spain, and Portugal and excludes Austria, Finland, and Sweden before 1995.
[f]Includes Finland as associate member with the original seven states: Austria, Denmark, Norway, Portugal, Sweden, United Kingdom, and Switzerland.
[g]Includes Iceland, Austria, Finland, and Sweden before 1995 and excludes the United Kingdom and Denmark.
Sources: *Monthly Bulletin of Statistics* (New York: United Nations, June 1997), pp. 92–102, 266–71; and *Monthly Bulletin of Statistics* (New York: United Nations, August 2000), pp. 92–111, 122.

in the world is now exported, another measure of the significance of international trade.[†]

Of the $6.8 billion in international trade in goods and services in 1999, exports of merchandise were $5.5 trillion, more than 17 times what they had been 29 years earlier (see Table 2.2). While smaller in absolute terms at more than $1.3 trillion, worldwide trade in services grew faster during the 1990s than did trade in merchandise (see Table 2.3). As we will discuss in Chapter 13, trade in goods and services related to information technology (including personal computers, semiconductors, and cellular phones) was a major driving force for continued growth in world trade in the latter part of the 1990s.

True, inflation was responsible for a large part of this trade increase, but using a quantum index that eliminates the effects of inflation from the data, we see that the volume of world trade in 1999 was nearly four times what it had been in 1970 (a 5.2 percent annual increase). Figure 2.1 compares the increase in exports measured in current dollars, including the effects of inflation, with volume increases measured by quantum indexes that eliminate the effects of inflation.

How even has this growth been? Have some nations fared better than others? Although there are some differences, the exports of most of the major exporting nations have increased at about the same rate as the world average. However, the European Union (EU) and the developing nations as a whole did surpass the world rate. Note that much of the EU's increase has come from the admission of six new members, and the relatively slow growth rate of the European Free Trade Agreement (EFTA) is the result of losing six members to the EU.

[†]Divide total world exports of goods and services ($6.4 trillion for 1995), as shown on page 212 of the *1997 World Development Indicators,* by the world's GDP ($27.8 trillion), as shown on page 136.

Table 2.3 World Trade in Services Exports (FOB Values; in Billions of Current U.S. Dollars and in Percentage Share)

	1990	1995	1999	Percentage Share of Worldwide Exports
World	$782.0	$1,187.0	$1,339.2	100.0%
United States	132.2	197.2	251.7	18.8
Japan	41.4	64.0	59.8	4.5
European Union	369.9	506.1	565.8	42.2
France	66.3	83.1	79.3	5.9
Germany	51.6	75.2	76.8	5.7
Italy	48.6	61.2	64.5	4.8
Netherlands	29.6	46.8	53.1	4.0
United Kingdom	53.2	74.6	101.4	7.6
East Asia	68.1	160.3	161.2	12.0
Korea	46.9	101.1	98.1	7.3
Taiwan	6.9	14.9	14.8	1.1
Hong Kong	18.1	34.3	35.4	2.6
Singapore	12.7	29.7	22.9	1.7
Thailand	6.3	14.7	14.1	1.1
Malaysia	3.8	11.4	10.8	0.8
China	5.7	18.4	26.6	2.0
Latin America	29.7	44.5	53.5	4.0
Middle East	n.a.	n.a.	n.a.	n.a.
Africa	18.6	25.2	28.4	2.1
Russia and Central and Eastern Europe	n.a.	n.a.	n.a.	n.a.

Note: n.a. = not available.

Source: Excerpted from *JETRO White Paper on Foreign Direct Investment 2000* (Tokyo: Japan External Trade Organization, 2000), p. 5, based on World Trade Organization data.

[Figure 2.1] 1996/1970 Export Ratios Based on Current Dollars and Quantum Indexes

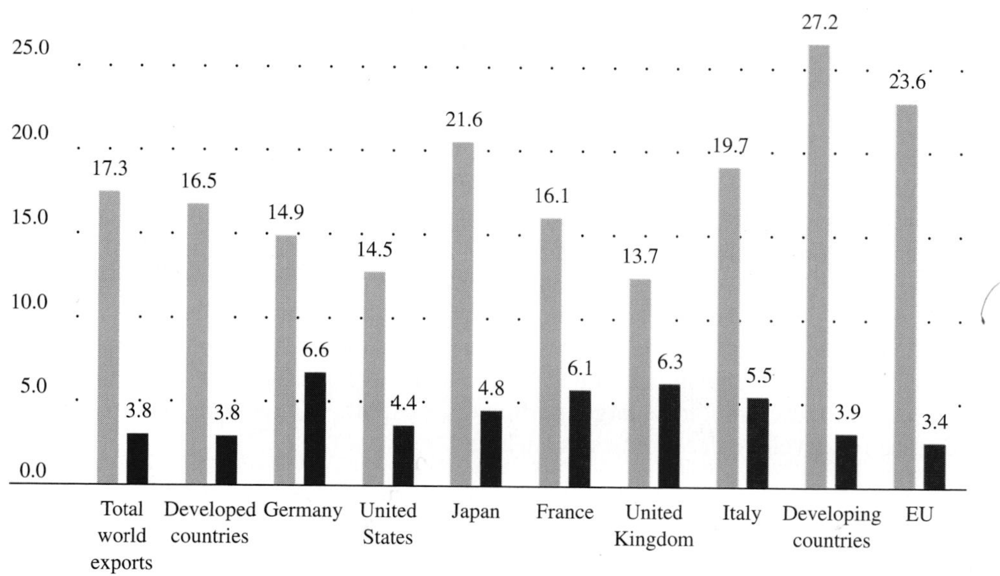

How Important Are Small and Medium-Sized Enterprises in Generating Export Sales?

Small and Medium-Sized Enterprises

The Exporter Data Base (a joint project of the International Trade Administration and the Census Bureau) provides some insight into the relative importance of small and medium-sized enterprises (SMEs) in generating U.S. exports. If SMEs are categorized as companies with fewer than 500 employees, an analysis of the 1997 Exporter Data Base reveals the following:

SMEs accounted for 96.5 percent of all U.S. exporters in 1997 (an increase from 95.7 percent in 1992). In 47 states, over half the manufacturing firms that exported goods in 1997 were SMEs.

Very small companies, with fewer than 20 employees, accounted for 65 percent of all U.S. exporting firms in 1997 (an increase from 59 percent in 1992) and for 14 percent of U.S. merchandise exports (an increase from 11.1 percent in 1992). Firms with fewer than 100 employees generated 21.5 percent of U.S. merchandise exports in 1997.

The proportion of U.S. merchandise exports generated by SMEs has been increasing, rising from 26.4 percent in 1987 to 30.6 percent in 1997.

Almost 40 percent of exports by SMEs in 1997 went to Canada, Japan, and Mexico (representing \$31.2, \$18.5, and \$16.7 billion in sales, respectively).

Emerging markets were increasingly important to SME exporters, with the following percentage changes in exports from 1992 to 1997: Brazil (291 percent), Malaysia (224 percent), China (107 percent), Philippines (102 percent), and Thailand (97 percent). Over 80 percent of all firms that exported to China in 1997 were SMEs. With exports valued at \$8.9 billion, SMEs accounted for 38 percent of goods exports to China and Hong Kong in 1997 (an increase from 33 percent in 1992).

In 1997, 63 percent of SME exporters sold goods to only one foreign market, and less than 6 percent sold to 10 or more countries.

Most of the SMEs that exported were wholesalers or other nonmanufacturing companies (69 percent of all SME exporters in 1997). Those nonmanufacturing companies generated 69 percent of all SME exports. ■

Note: The Exporter Data Base may slightly understate the total number of exporters. The database excludes exporters of services and includes only direct exporters. Only exporters with shipments exceeding \$2,500 were included in the database.
Source: *Small and Medium-Sized Exporting Companies: A Statistical Profile* (Washington, DC: International Trade Administration, Office of Trade and Economic Analysis, U.S. Department of Commerce), December 1999.

The quadrupling of world exports in less than 30 years demonstrates that the opportunity to increase sales by exporting is a viable growth strategy. As you saw in Table 2.1, there are numerous large international firms that need these sales to survive. At the same time, however, the export growth of individual nations should be a warning to businesspeople that they must be prepared to meet increased competition from exports to their own domestic markets.

Direction of Trade

What are the destinations of this \$5.5 trillion in merchandise exports? If you never have examined trade flows, you may think that international trade consists mainly of manufactured goods exported by the industrialized nations to the developing nations in return for raw materials. However, Table 2.4 shows that this is only partially correct. While more than half the exports from developing nations do go to developed countries, this proportion has been declining. Also, nearly three-fourths of exports from developed economies go to other industrialized nations, not to developing countries. As shown in the table, Japan, the United States, and Australia and New Zealand are exceptions, with each sending a larger portion of its exports to developing nations than is the case for developed economies as a whole.

The Three Exceptions—Japan, the United States, and Australia/New Zealand

One reason Japan sells more to developing nations than most developed nations do is that it has had an extensive distribution system in those markets since the early 1900s. Because the country has no local sources for many raw materials, it has used

Table 2.4 Direction of Trade for Selected Regions and Countries (percentage of region's or country's total merchandise exports to regions or country in columns)

Exports from	Year	DE	U.S.	Can.	Jap.	EU	EFTA	Dev.	DA	D. Am.	East Eur.	LAIA	Aus.
		Exports to											
Developed economies (DE)	1970	76.9	12.8	5.1	6.9	39.5	9.4	18.4	4.1	6.2	n.a.	4.4	2.0
	1980	70.8	19.1	4.0	9.9	43.1	8.4	25.1	5.2	6.1	3.4	4.8	1.4
	1990	71.1	19.5	4.5	8.2	46.2	7.9	19.5	2.4	3.9	2.0	2.9	1.8
	1999	72.8	14.6	4.7	3.3	44.9	2.8	22.4	1.8	6.2	3.4	5.0	1.3
United States (U.S.)	1970	69.5	—	20.7	10.8	26.6	4.0	28.8	2.3	15.2	n.a.	11.4	2.6
	1980	59.5	—	15.7	9.5	26.7	3.3	36.2	2.1	17.6	1.8	14.6	2.1
	1990	64.7	—	20.9	12.3	24.8	2.8	34.0	1.6	14.0	1.1	11.2	2.5
	1999	57.3	—	21.7	8.6	22.1	1.2	41.6	1.2	21.4	1.1	18.2	2.1
Canada (Can.)	1970	90.9	65.4	—	4.7	16.4	1.8	7.4	0.7	4.3	n.a.	2.3	1.5
	1980	85.1	63.4	—	5.7	13.2	1.4	11.7	1.4	5.1	2.7	3.7	1.0
	1990	91.1	75.0	—	5.5	8.1	1.5	8.0	0.7	1.8	0.9	1.3	0.7
	1999	94.7	85.9	—	2.4	5.6	0.4	5.2	0.4	1.6	0.2	1.2	0.3
Japan (Jap.)	1970	54.6	31.1	2.9	—	11.2	3.0	39.2	5.6	5.8	n.a.	3.5	3.6
	1980	47.5	24.5	1.9	—	14.0	2.5	49.8	4.6	6.6	2.8	4.6	3.1
	1990	59.3	31.7	2.3	—	18.8	2.9	39.5	1.3	3.4	1.2	1.9	2.8
	1999	54.6	31.1	1.7	—	17.9	0.9	45.0	0.9	4.3	0.4	2.2	2.4
European Union (EU)†	1970	81.0	8.2	1.3	1.2	51.0	12.5	14.0	4.9	3.9	n.a.	2.6	1.6
	1980	76.5	5.6	0.7	1.0	55.8	11.1	19.2	6.6	3.2	3.5	2.4	0.8
	1990	83.1	7.1	0.9	2.1	60.7	10.3	13.3	3.2	1.9	2.6	1.3	0.8
	1999	78.9	8.4	0.8	1.7	61.8	4.2	13.7	2.3	2.6	5.2	2.1	0.8
European Free Trade Association (EFTA)‡	1970	82.2	6.6	1.3	1.3	49.4	18.6	10.7	3.5	3.6	n.a.	2.9	1.0
	1980	78.4	4.8	0.7	1.4	54.7	14.7	14.9	3.5	2.9	6.8	2.2	0.7
	1990	85.1	6.8	1.2	2.6	57.9	13.4	11.2	1.4	1.4	2.2	1.3	0.9
	1999	85.0	10.3	1.8	3.4	66.8	0.8	12.4	1.0	2.4	2.7	1.9	0.7
Developing countries (Dev.)	1970	72.3	18.4	1.8	10.8	33.9	3.0	19.8	2.8	6.7	n.a.	3.1	1.4
	1980	68.4	19.8	1.2	14.0	29.4	2.3	26.5	2.6	7.6	3.9	3.8	1.2
	1990	60.5	21.3	1.3	12.4	22.0	2.0	33.1	2.5	3.7	2.9	2.2	1.3
	1999	55.6	23.0	1.1	9.2	19.2	0.9	39.2	1.8	5.2	1.7	3.8	1.5
Developing Africa (DA)	1970	81.2	6.7	0.7	4.0	61.2	4.3	10.7	5.6	2.0	n.a.	0.6	6.5
	1980	82.9	26.1	0.2	2.1	46.2	2.5	13.7	3.1	6.4	2.6	1.6	2.6
	1990	82.8	18.4	1.1	2.2	58.9	1.4	13.2	5.9	1.6	2.7	0.7	4.3
	1999	74.0	18.1	1.1	2.1	50.2	0.9	22.5	7.6	3.4	2.4	2.8	0.2
Developing America (D. Am.)	1970	74.2	32.4	3.4	5.4	26.3	3.4	19.1	0.7	17.3	n.a.	7.7	0.2
	1980	64.3	32.2	2.6	4.2	22.2	1.9	27.5	2.2	21.3	6.5	10.2	0.2
	1990	62.8	32.6	1.2	5.3	21.0	1.6	21.4	1.0	13.6	3.0	8.9	0.5
	1999	68.2	47.1	1.4	2.8	15.5	0.8	28.2	1.1	21.0	1.1	16.0	0.2
Eastern Europe and former USSR–Europe (East Eur.)	1980	27.9	0.9	0.2	1.1	19.3	6.4	20.9	2.8	3.3	50.7	0.5	0.1
	1990	38.3	1.4	0.2	1.7	27.9	6.2	23.0	2.1	4.8	40.1	0.4	0.1
	1999	57.7	4.4	0.2	1.3	48.4	2.5	13.4	1.1	1.5	23.3	0.6	0.1
Latin American Integration Association (LAIA)	1970	76.5	30.0	3.4	5.7	30.2	3.3	20.8	0.6	19.0	n.a.	10.1	0.1
	1980	65.2	29.4	3.1	5.2	24.1	2.0	29.6	2.2	23.1	4.5	13.8	0.2
	1990	63.3	32.2	1.0	6.0	21.7	1.3	22.2	1.4	13.8	1.7	16.3	0.5
	1999	70.1	49.4	1.3	3.0	15.1	0.7	28.0	1.1	20.7	0.9	17.6	0.3
Australia and New Zealand (Aus.)	1970	76.9	13.8	3.0	23.9	27.1	0.7	17.8	1.5	1.4	n.a.	0.8	—
	1980	58.2	10.5	2.0	22.7	15.6	0.6	31.1	2.3	1.3	5.7	1.0	—
	1990	61.8	11.5	1.6	24.9	14.3	2.2	35.0	1.3	1.5	1.5	1.3	—
	1999	55.8	9.8	1.5	19.1	14.7	1.2	42.4	1.3	1.9	0.6	1.6	—

Note: The European Union, the European Free Trade Association, and the Latin American Integration Association are three different forms of regional trading groups. The member-nations in each one have reduced or eliminated their import duties on goods and services from the other members. n.a. = not available.

†1980 data include Denmark, Great Britain, and Ireland. Greece, Spain, and Portugal are included in 1990 data. Before 1999, data exclude Austria, Finland, and Sweden.

‡Excludes Denmark and Great Britain and includes Iceland in 1980. Before 1995, data include Austria, Finland, and Sweden.

Sources: *Monthly Bulletin of Statistics* (New York: United Nations, July 2000, pp. 258–61; June 1997, pp. 255–62; June 1993, pp. 266–71; and *Statistical Yearbook*, 1969 (New York: United Nations), pp. 376–83.

general trading companies (*sogo shosha* in Japanese) to import many of the raw materials and components necessary for Japanese industry. The trading companies' offices in developing nations—where these raw materials and components are obtained—also market Japanese manufactured products to those nations (including components for industrial and consumer markets, such as electronic equipment and parts, as well as capital goods such as machine tools). Many Japanese companies in consumer electronics, computers, and other areas have moved manufacturing operations to lower-cost nations such as China and various Southeast Asian countries, producing substantial "reverse imports" to Japan as these goods replace products traditionally manufactured in Japan. The value of reverse exports to Japan from just the nations of Thailand, Malaysia, Indonesia, and the Philippines increased from 751 billion yen in 1995 to 2,169 billion yen in 1997 (an increase of 189 percent in 2 years).[4] Moreover, when other industrialized nations have imposed import restrictions on Japanese exports to protect their home industries, the Japanese trading companies have expanded their efforts to sell to developing nations.[5] Their efforts have achieved some success. Although the Asian economic crisis of 1997 affected trade throughout the region, Japanese exports to Thailand, Malaysia, Indonesia, and the Philippines rose from $30.3 billion in 1998 to $36.3 billion in 1999 (an increase of 12 percent).[6]

The United States also exported a smaller proportion to other developed countries (DCs) and more to the developing nations than did developed countries generally, but for reasons somewhat different from those of Japan. American firms have significantly more subsidiaries in developing nations than Japanese companies do; these subsidiaries are captive customers for their American owners. In addition, some buyers in Southeast Asian countries, remembering that Japan was an aggressor nation in World War II and before, prefer to buy from American firms. Notice also the high percentage of American exports that go to Latin America; this indicates the relative importance of this market to American firms. They account for 21.4 percent of the U.S. total in 1999, which is 3.5 times the 6.2 percent of the total exports of all developed nations that go to Latin America. U.S. exports to that region have three times the dollar value of the goods and services that all the Latin American nations export to each other ($148.4 billion versus $49.9 billion in 1999).[7]

There has been a notable change in the direction of Australia and New Zealand's trade, which has moved from Europe and North America to Southeast Asia. For example, the proportion of exports sent to Europe declined from 27.1 percent in 1970 to 14.7 percent in 1999. In contrast, 37 percent of Australia and New Zealand's exports in 1999 went to Asia (an 80 percent increase since 1990).[8]

The Changing Direction of Trade

The data in Table 2.4 illustrate how the direction of trade frequently changes over time among nations or regions of the world. The development of expanded (or contracted, as with the European Free Trade Association) regional trade agreements (discussed in Chapter 4), such as the Association of Southeast Asian Nations (ASEAN) and the EU, can substantially alter the level and proportion of trade flows within and across regions. For example, in Table 2.4, you see that most of Canada's exports go to the United States, mainly as a result after 1989 of the U.S.–Canada Free Trade Agreement and now the North American Free Trade Agreement. Although the percentage of total American exports to Canada changed little from 1990 to 1999 (approximately the period during which the trade agreement has been in effect), their dollar value in 1999 was 193 percent of that in 1990.[9] The share of world trade accounted for by members of regional trade agreements increased from 37.3 percent in 1980 to 59.9 percent in 1990 and to 70.7 percent in 1999.[10]

It appears that the American exporters have made major inroads in developing country markets, which in turn are selling more to the United States. This is due in part to their increasing ability to export manufactured goods and the growing intercompany trade among international firms' affiliates. The fact that members of trade groups are increasingly selling more to each other is a development that will influence international companies' choices of locations for their plants and other operations. Note too that the United States, Japan, and Australia, but not Europe, are fast approaching a 50–50 split in their exports to developing and developed nations.

Major Trading Partners: Their Relevance for Businesspeople

An analysis of the major trading partners of a firm's home country and those of the nations where it has affiliates that export can provide valuable insights to management.

Why Focus on Major Trading Partners?

There are a number of advantages to focusing attention on a nation that is already a sizable purchaser of goods coming from the would-be exporter's country:

1. The business climate in the importing nation is relatively favorable.
2. Export and import regulations are not insurmountable.
3. There should be no strong cultural objections to buying that nation's goods.
4. Satisfactory transportation facilities have already been established.
5. Import channel members (merchants, banks, and customs brokers) are experienced in handling import shipments from the exporter's area.
6. Foreign exchange to pay for the exports is available.
7. The government of a trading partner may be applying pressure on importers to buy from countries that are good customers for that nation's exports. We have seen the efforts of the Japanese, Korean, and Taiwanese governments to persuade their citizens to buy more American goods. They have also sent buying missions to the United States.

Major Trading Partners of the United States

Table 2.5 shows the major trading partners of the United States. The data indicate that the United States, an industrialized nation, generally follows the tendency we found in Table 2.4; that is, developed nations trade with one another. Mexico and Canada are major trading partners in great part because they share a common border with the United States. Freight charges are lower, delivery times are shorter, and contact between buyers and sellers is easier and less expensive. Now that both nations are joined with the United States in the North American Free Trade Agreement, we can be confident that their importance as trading partners will grow.

Note the marked change in the rankings of America's trading partners in just three decades. Not only have the rankings changed, some nations have been added while others have become relatively less important. Nations from East and Southeast Asia have become increasingly important trade partners in recent years. South Korea, Taiwan, Malaysia, Singapore, Thailand, and the Philippines are supplying the United States with huge quantities of electronic products and components and other labor-intensive goods, many of which are produced by affiliates of American internationals. Between 1991 and 1999, China rose from 6th to 4th place in exports to the United States (from \$18.97 to \$81.79 billion, a 331 percent increase in eight years), although it was only in 13th place as an importer in 1999 (\$13.11 billion).

Many of the same Asian countries appear as importers of American goods as well because (1) their rising standards of living enable their people to afford more imported products, and the countries' export earnings provide the foreign exchange to pay for them, (2) they are purchasing large amounts of capital goods to further their industrial expansion, and (3) their governments, pressured by the American government to lower their trade surpluses with the United States, have sent buying missions to this country to look for products to import.

Table 2.5 Major Trading Partners of the United States, 1965, 1991, and 1999 ($ billions)

1965		1991		1999	
Imports from	**Amount**	**Imports from**	**Amount**	**Imports from**	**Amount**
1. Canada	$4.83	1. Japan	$91.51	1. Canada	$198.71
2. Japan	2.41	2. Canada	91.06	2. Japan	130.86
3. United Kingdom	1.41	3. Mexico	31.13	3. Mexico	109.72
4. West Germany	1.34	4. Germany	26.14	4. China	81.79
5. Venezuela	1.02	5. Taiwan	23.02	5. Germany	55.23
6. Mexico	0.64	6. China	18.97	6. United Kingdom	39.24
7. Italy	0.62	7. United Kingdom	18.41	7. Taiwan	35.20
8. France	0.62	8. South Korea	17.02	8. South Korea	31.18
9. Brazil	0.51	9. France	13.33	9. France	25.71
10. Belgium and Luxembourg	0.49	10. Italy	11.76	10. Italy	22.36
11. Philippines	0.37	11. Saudi Arabia	10.90	11. Malaysia	21.42
12. India	0.35	12. Singapore	9.96	12. Singapore	18.19
13. Hong Kong	0.34	13. Hong Kong	9.28	13. Thailand	14.33
14. Netherlands Antilles	0.32	14. Venezuela	8.18	14. Philippines	12.35
15. Australia	0.31	15. Brazil	6.72	15. Venezuela	11.34

1965		1991		1999	
Exports to	**Amount**	**Exports to**	**Amount**	**Exports to**	**Amount**
1. Canada	5.64	1. Canada	$85.15	1. Canada	$166.60
2. Japan	2.08	2. Japan	48.13	2. Mexico	86.91
3. West Germany	1.65	3. Mexico	33.28	3. Japan	57.47
4. United Kingdom	1.62	4. United Kingdom	22.05	4. United Kingdom	38.41
5. Mexico	1.11	5. Germany	21.30	5. Germany	26.80
6. Netherlands	1.09	6. South Korea	15.51	6. South Korea	22.96
7. France	0.97	7. France	15.35	7. Netherlands	19.44
8. India	0.93	8. Netherlands	13.51	8. Taiwan	19.13
9. Italy	0.89	9. Taiwan	13.18	9. France	18.88
10. Australia	0.80	10. Belgium and Luxembourg	10.79	10. Singapore	16.25
11. Belgium and Luxembourg	0.65	11. Singapore	8.80	11. Belgium and Luxembourg	13.37
12. Venezuela	0.63	12. Italy	8.57	12. Brazil	13.20
13. Spain	0.47	13. Australia	8.40	13. China	13.11
14. South Africa	0.44	14. Hong Kong	8.14	14. Hong Kong	12.65
15. Switzerland	0.37	15. Saudi Arabia	6.56	15. Australia	11.82

Source: "U.S. Aggregate Foreign Trade Data, 1999 and Prior Years," *U.S. Foreign Trade Highlights,* Tables 10 and 11, U.S. Department of Commerce International Trade Administration, www.ita.doc.gov/td/industry/otea/usfth/aggregate/H99t10.txt, www.ita.doc.gov/td/industry/otea/usfth/aggregate/H99t.11.txt.

Notes: Exports are stated on an f.a.s. (free alongside ship) value basis. Services not included.

Imports are stated on a CIF (Cost, Insurance, Freight) value basis. Services not included.

The analysis of foreign trade that we have described would be helpful to anyone just starting to search outside the home market for new business opportunities. The preliminary steps of (1) studying the general growth and direction of trade (Table 2.4) and (2) analyzing major trading partners (Table 2.5) would provide an idea of where the trading activity is. What kinds of products do these countries import from the United States? The Department of Commerce's Office of Trade and Economic Analysis maintains a site on the Internet with downloadable files of trade statistics. One entry, "U.S. Foreign Trade Highlights," contains over 100 tables of goods and services, including one that reports on the top U.S. exports to and imports from its 80 largest trading partners. There are also tables from the new Commerce Department publication *U.S. Industry and Trade Outlook 2000,* which replaces the *U.S. Industrial Outlook.* These tables compare the imports and exports of more than 100 industries for the last four years, providing an idea of their competitiveness in world markets.[11] Foreign trade reports are no longer available in hard copy. Trade data with much more information are available on CD-ROMs that are sent monthly to government depositories, such as many college and university libraries. The new reports have been expanded to contain additional data on units which permit analysts to make price comparisons by calculating average prices on exports and imports on a country basis.[12]

The topic we have been examining—international trade—exists because firms export. As you know, however, exporting is only one aspect of international business. Another—overseas production—requires foreign investment, the topic of the next section.

Foreign Investment

Foreign investment can be divided into two components: **portfolio investment,** which is the purchase of stocks and bonds solely for the purpose of obtaining a return on the funds invested, and **direct investment,** by which the investors participate in the management of the firm in addition to receiving a return on their money. The distinction between these two components has begun to blur, particularly with the growing size and number of international mergers, acquisitions, and alliances in recent years. For example, investments by a foreign investor in the stock of a domestic company generally are treated as direct investment when the investor's equity participation ratio is 10 percent or more. In contrast, deals that do not result in the foreign investor obtaining at least 10 percent of the shareholdings are classified as portfolio investments. With the increasing pace of business globalization, it is not uncommon for companies to form strategic relationships with firms from other nations in order to pool resources (such as manufacturing, marketing, and technology and other know-how) while still keeping their equity participation below 10 percent. Financing from foreign venture capitalists also tends to be treated as a portfolio investment, although these investors frequently become actively involved in the target company's business operations, with the goal of ultimately realizing substantial capital gains when the target company goes public.

portfolio investment
The purchase of stocks and bonds to obtain a return on the funds invested

direct investment
The purchase of sufficient stock in a firm to obtain significant management control

Portfolio Investment

Although portfolio investors are not directly concerned with the control of a firm, they invest immense amounts in stocks and bonds from other countries. For example, data from the Department of Commerce show that persons residing outside the United States owned American stock and bonds other than U.S. Treasury securities with a value of $2,509 billion in 1999 (including $1,446 billion in corporate stocks). This represents a 59 percent increase over 1997. Of the total of stock and bond holdings, 64 percent is owned by Europeans, 9 percent by Japanese, and 6 percent by Canadians. Americans, by contrast, own $2,583 billion in foreign securities, of which $2,027 billion is in corporate stocks. The valuation of foreign corporate stockholdings represents an increase of 68 percent over the corresponding level for 1997.[13] This dramatic increase reflects net U.S. purchases of foreign stocks, including exchanges associated with the large number and scale of acquisitions of U.S. companies by foreign companies, and price appreciation in many foreign stocks. The increase in the valuation of foreign stock held by Americans is notable because it occurred despite a substantial depreciation of the euro and many other currencies against the dollar. As you can see, foreign portfolio investment is sizable and will continue to grow as more international firms list their bonds and equities on foreign exchanges.

Foreign Direct Investment

Volume

The book value of all foreign investments is over $4.7 trillion. Table 2.6 shows how this total is divided among the largest investor nations. In 1999, the United States had 1.7 times the foreign direct investment of the next largest investor, the United Kingdom, and 2.7 times that of the third largest investor, Germany. The proportion

Table 2.6	Stocks of Outward Foreign Direct Investment, Selected Countries, 1985, 1990, 1995, and 1999 ($ billions)

Country	1985 Amount	1985 Share	1990 Amount	1990 Share	1995 Amount	1995 Share	1999 Amount	1999 Share
United States	$251.0	35.5%	$430.5	25.1%	$699.0	24.4%	$1,131.5	23.8%
United Kingdom	100.3	14.2	229.3	13.4	304.9	10.6	664.1	14.0
Japan	44.0	6.2	201.4	11.7	238.5	8.3	292.8	6.2
Germany	59.9	8.5	151.6	8.8	268.4	9.3	420.9	8.8
France	37.1	5.2	110.1	6.4	184.4	6.4	298.0	6.3
Netherlands	47.8	6.8	109.0	6.4	179.6	6.3	306.4	6.4
Belgium and Luxembourg	9.6	1.4	40.6	2.4	88.5	3.1	159.5	3.4
Switzerland	25.1	3.5	66.1	3.9	142.5	5.0	199.5	4.2
Italy	16.6	2.3	57.3	3.3	109.2	3.8	168.4	3.5
Canada	43.1	6.1	84.8	4.9	118.1	4.1	178.3	3.7
Developing countries	32.4	4.6	81.9	4.8	258.3	9.0	468.7	9.8
Other	40.2	5.7	153.8	8.9	279.2	9.7	471.2	9.9
World total	707.1	100.0%	1,716.4	100.0%	2,870.6	100.0%	4,759.3	100.0%

Source: Various "Country Fact Sheets," *World Investment Report 2000,* United Nations Conference on Trade and Development, Geneva, October 2000.

of foreign direct investment accounted for by the United States declined by nearly one-third between 1985 and 1999, however, from 35.5 percent to 23.8 percent.

Investment outflows hit a new high in 1999—$799.9 billion, an increase of nearly 105 percent over 1996 (see Table 2.7). The United States was the leader in foreign direct investment inflows at $275.5 billion (the United Kingdom was second with $82.2 billion) and was second in outflows at $150.9 billion (the United Kingdom was the leader with $199.3 billion).

Direction

Even though it is impossible to make an accurate determination of the present value of foreign investments, we can get an idea of the rate and amounts of such investments and of the places in which they are being made. This is the kind of information that interests managers and government leaders. It is analogous to what is sought in the analysis of international trade. If a nation is continuing to receive appreciable amounts of foreign investment, its investment climate must be favorable. This means that the political forces of the foreign environment are relatively attractive and that the opportunity to earn a profit is greater there than elsewhere. Other reasons for investing exist, to be sure; however, if the above factors are absent, foreign investment is not likely to occur.

In which countries are investments being made, and where do the investments come from? Table 2.7 indicates that the industrialized nations invest primarily in one another just as they trade more with one another.

Trade Leads to FDI

Historically, foreign direct investment has followed foreign trade. One reason is that foreign trade is less costly and less risky. Also, management can expand the business in small increments rather than through the considerably greater amounts of investment and market size that a foreign production facility requires. Typically, a firm would use domestic or foreign agents to export. As the export business increased, the firm would set up an export department and perhaps hire sales representatives to live in overseas markets. The firm might even establish its own sales company to import in its own name.

Meanwhile, managers would watch the total market size closely because they would know that their competitors were making similar studies. Generally, because the local

Table 2.7 Direction of Foreign Direct Investment (Annual Flows) for Selected Regions and Countries, 1985–1995, 1996, and 1999 ($ billions)

Where Funds Originate (Net Investment)	1985–1995 (annual average)	1996	1999
World	$203.1	$390.8	$799.9
Developed countries	182.5	332.0	731.8
Developing countries	20.5	57.8	65.6
North America	47.3	97.5	169.5
United States	41.0	84.4	150.9
Canada	6.1	13.1	17.8
Mexico	0.2	0.0	0.8
European Union	97.1	182.3	509.8
United Kingdom	26.0	34.0	199.3
Germany	17.6	50.8	50.6
France	18.4	30.4	108.0
Netherlands	11.9	31.2	45.9
Belgium and Luxembourg	5.2	8.0	24.9
Switzerland	6.8	16.2	17.9
Italy	4.7	8.7	3.0
Africa	0.9	0.0	0.9
South, East, and Southeast Asia	16.3	49.5	35.7
Japan	25.2	23.4	22.7
Hong Kong, China	8.0	26.5	19.9
Korea, Republic of	1.2	4.2	2.5
Malaysia	0.7	3.8	1.6
Singapore	1.7	6.9	3.9
Taiwan	2.7	3.8	4.4
China	1.6	2.1	2.5
Latin America and Caribbean	3.0	5.8	27.3
Brazil	0.5	0.5	1.4
Chile	0.2	1.2	4.9
Venezuela	0.3	0.5	0.6
Argentina	0.4	1.6	1.2
Peru	0.0	0.0	0.2
Where Funds Go (Net Investment)			
World	182.6	277.5	865.5
Developed countries	129.3	219.8	636.4
Developing countries	50.1	145.0	207.6
North America	54.5	103.3	311.8
United States	44.4	84.5	275.5
Canada	5.6	9.6	25.1
Mexico	4.5	9.2	11.2
European Union	67.3	108.6	305.1
United Kingdom	17.0	24.4	82.2
Germany	3.7	6.6	26.8
France	12.2	22.0	39.1
Netherlands	6.9	15.1	33.8
Belgium and Luxembourg	6.8	14.1	15.9
Switzerland	2.1	3.1	3.4
Italy	3.3	3.5	4.9
Africa	3.5	5.5	8.9
South, East, and Southeast Asia	29.7	88.0	96.1
Japan	0.7	0.2	12.7
Hong Kong, China	4.0	10.5	23.1
Korea, Republic of	0.9	2.3	10.3
Malaysia	2.9	7.3	3.5
Singapore	4.1	9.0	7.0
Taiwan	1.0	1.9	2.9
China	11.7	40.2	40.4
Latin America and Caribbean	14.8	45.9	90.5
Brazil	1.8	10.5	31.4
Chile	1.2	4.6	9.2
Venezuela	0.5	2.2	2.6
Argentina	2.2	6.5	23.2
Peru	0.6	3.2	2.1

Source: Various "Country Fact Sheets," *World Investment Report 2000,* United Nations Conference on Trade and Development, Geneva, October 2000.

Table 2.8 **United States Direct Investment Position Overseas on a Historical-Cost Basis, 1985 and 1999 ($ billions)**

Country or Region	1985 Total	1985 Percent of Total	1999 Total	1999 Percent of Total	Manufacturing
Total	$184.6	100.0%	$988.7	100.0%	$291.0
Canada	17.1	9.3	79.7	8.1	26.3
Europe	121.4	65.8	685.8	69.4	305.5
France	6.7	3.6	77.6	7.8	39.1
Germany	14.8	12.2	111.1	11.2	59.3
Netherlands	37.1	20.1	130.7	13.2	42.9
Switzerland	10.6	5.7	55.3	5.6	27.8
United Kingdom	43.6	23.6	183.1	18.5	68.2
Latin America and other Western Hemisphere	16.8	9.1	44.6	4.5	6.0
South and Central America	3.5	1.9	10.6	1.1	2.0
Mexico	n.a.	—	3.6	0.4	2.2
Other Western Hemisphere	13.3	7.2	34.0	3.4	4.0
Africa	n.a.	—	1.5	0.2	−0.2
Middle East	5.0	2.7	7.1	0.7	1.2
Asia and Pacific	n.a.	—	167.9	17.0	52.2
Japan	19.3	10.5	148.9	15.1	47.3

Notes: S = suppressed to avoid disclosure of individual firms; n.a. = not available; — = cannot be calculated.
[a]Includes finance, banking, real estate, and insurance.
[b]Includes transportation, communications, public utilities, petroleum, mining, and wholesale trade.
Source: "Foreign Direct Investment Position in the United States on a Historical-Cost Basis, 1999," www.bea.doc.gov/bea/ai/0700dip/table4-2.htm (October 19, 2000); and *Survey of Current Business*, June 1986, p. 34.

market would not be large enough to support local production by all the firms exporting to it, the situation would become one of seeing who could begin manufacturing there first. Experienced managers know that governments often limit the number of local firms making a given product so that those which do set up local operations will be assured of having a profitable and continuing business. This is especially important to developing countries that are dependent on foreign investment to provide jobs and tax revenue.

Does Trade Lead FDI or Does FDI Lead Trade?

The previous section described the linear path to market expansion that many international firms have taken and still take today. However, the new business environment of fewer government barriers to trade, increased competition from globalizing firms, and new production and communications technology is causing many international firms to disperse the activities of their production systems to locations close to available resources. They then integrate the entire production process either regionally or globally. As a result, the decision about where to locate may be either an FDI or a trade decision, illustrating just how closely FDI and trade are interlinked.[14]

U.S. Foreign Direct Investment

You saw in Table 2.6 that the United States is by far the largest foreign investor (nearly one-quarter of the total investment flow in 1999), and as Table 2.8 indicates, American firms have invested much more in the developed nations than they have in the developing nations. During the 14-year period 1985–1999, the proportion of total U.S. investment that went to Europe increased by 12.0 percent (45.9 percent to 51.4 percent), while Canada declined by more than 50 percent (from 20.5 percent to 9.9 percent).

Percent of Manufacturing	Finance[a]	Percent of Finance	Services	Percent of Services	Other[b]	Percent of Other
100.0%	$52.1	100.0%	$57.6	100.0%	$488.0	100.0%
6.7	10.7	20.5	1.4	2.4	41.3	8.5
78.1	18.6	35.7	45.6	78.9	316.1	64.8
10.0	5.1	9.8	3.7	6.4	29.7	6.1
15.2	−0.1	0.2	4.5	7.8	47.4	9.7
11.0	3.6	6.9	6.0	10.4	78.2	16.0
7.1	1.0	2.0	3.1	5.4	23.4	4.8
17.4	6.1	11.7	16.9	29.3	91.9	18.9
1.5	2.3	4.4	1.6	2.8	34.7	7.1
0.5	0.7	1.3	0.3	0.5	7.6	1.6
0.6	S	—	0.2	0.3	1.2	0.2
1.0	1.6	3.1	1.3	2.3	27.1	5.6
0.1	0.5	1.0	0.2	0.3	1.0	0.2
0.3	0.3	0.6	0.1	0.2	5.5	1.1
13.4	19.6	37.6	8.6	14.9	87.5	17.9
12.1	17.6	33.8	8.0	13.9	76.0	15.6

Note also that the United Kingdom (31 percent increase) and the Netherlands (194 percent increase) received the largest percentage increases. In Asia, the tigers (South Korea, Taiwan, Singapore, and Hong Kong) and Japan all received a larger proportion of American FDI in 1999 than they did in 1985. Although American firms invested more in Africa and the Middle East in 1999, the percentages of their total investment were lower than they were in 1985.

During the early and middle 1990s, the focus of Japan's FDI outflows shifted from developed nations (83 percent in the period 1989–1991, down to 58 percent in 1994–1995) to Southeast Asia (17 percent, up to 42 percent). However, the level of Japanese FDI going to Asian locations declined substantially at the end of the decade, falling from 22.6 percent in 1997 to 16.0 percent in 1998 and 10.7 percent in 1999.[15] Table 2.7 shows that the developing countries as a whole obtained a sizable increase in investment between 1996 and 1999. African nations participated relatively little in that flow, however. The small nation of Singapore (population 3 million) received almost as much foreign investment as the entire African continent did, and Hong Kong received more than twice as much. For Asia as a whole, total inflows to the region soared to a record $96 billion in 1999, with China receiving $40 billion and Hong Kong receiving $23 billion as the second largest recipient. In Latin America, which experienced a doubling of investment inflow from 1996 to 1999, Brazil and Argentina were the leaders.

Foreign Direct Investment in the United States

Rapid Increase

Foreign direct investment in the United States rose rapidly from $185 billion in 1985 to $989 billion in 1999 (see Table 2.9). This is an average annual increase of nearly

Table 2.9 Foreign Direct Investment Position in United States on a Historical-Cost Basis, 1985 and 1999 ($ billions)

Country or Region	1985 Total	1985 Percent of Total	1999 Total	1999 Percent of Total	1999 Manufacturing
Total	$184.6	100.0%	$988.7	100.0%	$291.0
Canada	17.1	9.3	79.7	8.1	26.3
Europe	121.4	65.8	685.8	69.4	305.5
France	6.7	3.6	77.6	7.8	39.1
Germany	14.8	12.2	111.1	11.2	59.3
Netherlands	37.1	20.1	130.7	13.2	42.9
Switzerland	10.6	5.7	55.3	5.6	27.8
United Kingdom	43.6	23.6	183.1	18.5	68.2
Latin America and other Western Hemisphere	16.8	9.1	44.6	4.5	6.0
South and Central America	3.5	1.9	10.6	1.1	2.0
Mexico	n.a.	—	3.6	0.4	2.2
Other Western Hemisphere	13.3	7.2	34.0	3.4	4.0
Africa	n.a.	—	1.5	0.2	−0.2
Middle East	5.0	2.7	7.1	0.7	1.2
Asia and Pacific	n.a.	—	167.9	17.0	52.2
Japan	19.3	10.5	148.9	15.1	47.3

Notes: n.a. = not available; — = cannot be calculated.
[a]Includes finance, banking, real estate, and insurance.
[b]Includes transportation, communications, public utilities, petroleum, mining, and wholesale trade.
Source: "Foreign Direct Investment Position in the United States on a Historical-Cost Basis, 1999," www.bea.doc.gov/bea/ai/0700dip/table 4-2.htm (October 19, 2000); and *Survey of Current Business,* June 1986, p. 34.

13 percent. Observe how concentrated FDI is in the United States. Nearly three-quarters of the total stock was owned by firms or individuals from just six nations: (1) United Kingdom (19 percent), (2) Japan (15 percent), (3) Netherlands (13 percent), (4) Germany (11 percent), (5) Canada (8 percent), and (6) France (8 percent).

Acquire Going Companies or Build New Ones?

Of the record investment outlays in the United States by foreign firms, much more has been spent to acquire going companies than to establish new ones. A number of reasons are responsible: (1) Corporate restructuring in this country caused management to put on the market businesses or other assets that either did not meet management's profit standards or were considered to be unrelated to the company's main business, (2) foreign companies wanted to gain rapid access in this country to advanced technology, especially in computers and communications, and (3) management of foreign firms felt that entrance into the large and prosperous American market could be more successful if they acquired known brand names rather than spending the time and money to promote new, unknown ones.

According to data from the U.S. Department of Commerce, 90 percent of the total amount of foreign investment (over $72 billion) was spent in 1996 to acquire American businesses and only 10 percent was spent in starting from the ground up.

In the previous section, we mentioned briefly some of the reasons why foreign investors acquire companies more than they establish them in this country. Now let us examine the reasons why international firms enter foreign markets, which are all linked to the desire to increase profits and sales or protect them from being eroded by competitors.

Percent of Manufacturing	Finance[a]	Percent of Finance	Services	Percent of Services	Other[b]
100.0%	$52.1	100.0%	$57.6	100.0%	$488.0
6.7	10.7	20.5	1.4	2.4	41.3
78.1	18.6	35.7	45.6	78.9	316.1
10.0	5.1	9.8	3.7	6.4	29.7
15.2	−0.1	0.2	4.5	7.8	47.4
11.0	3.6	6.9	6.0	10.4	78.2
7.1	1.0	2.0	3.1	5.4	23.4
17.4	6.1	11.7	16.9	29.3	91.9
1.5	2.3	4.4	1.6	2.8	34.7
0.5	0.7	1.3	0.3	0.5	7.6
0.6	S	—	0.2	0.3	1.2
1.0	1.6	3.1	1.3	2.3	27.1
0.1	0.5	1.0	0.2	0.3	1.0
0.3	0.3	0.6	0.1	0.2	5.5
13.4	19.6	37.6	8.6	14.9	87.5
12.1	17.6	33.8	8.0	13.9	76.0

Why Enter Foreign Markets?

Increase Profits and Sales

Enter New Markets

Managers are always under pressure to increase the sales and profits of their firms, and when they face a mature, saturated market at home, they begin to search for new markets outside the home country. They find that (1) markets with a rising GNP per capita and population growth appear to be viable candidates for their operations and (2) the economies of some nations where they are not doing business are growing at a considerably faster rate than is the economy of their own market.

New Market Creation. Table 2.10 shows the great variety in growth rates among the top and bottom countries ranked by GNP per capita. Note the disparity among and between the two groups.

Although nearly everyone looks to GNP per capita as a basis for making comparisons of nations' economies, extreme care must be exercised to avoid drawing unwarranted conclusions. In the first place, because the statistical systems in many developing nations are deficient, the reliability of the data provided by such nations is questionable.

Second, to arrive at a common base of U.S. dollars, the World Bank and other international agencies convert local currencies to dollars. The Bank uses an average of the exchange rate for that year and the previous two years after adjusting for differences in relative inflation between the particular country and the United States.[16] World Bank economists admit that official exchange rates do not reflect the relative domestic purchasing powers of currencies. "However," they say, "exchange rates

Table 2.10 **Top and Bottom Countries for GNP/Capita (1999) and Average Growth Rates of GNP/Capita (1998–1999) and Population (1990–1999)**

		1999		Annual Growth Rates (percentage)	
Ranking	Country*	GNP/Capita (current US$)	Population (millions)	GNP/Capita†	Population
1	Switzerland	$38,350	7	$1.2	0.7%
2	Norway	32,880	4	0.1	0.5
3	Japan	32,230	127	0.8	0.3
4	Denmark	32,030	5	1.0	0.4
5	United States	30,600	273	3.1	1.0
6	Singapore	29,610	3	3.6	1.9
7	Austria	25,970	8	2.2	0.5
8	Germany	25,350	82	1.2	0.4
9	Sweden	25,040	9	3.8	0.4
10	Belgium	24,510	10	1.7	0.3
11	Netherlands	24,320	16	2.3	0.6
12	Finland	23,780	5	3.5	0.4
13	Hong Kong	23,520	7	0.1	2.1
14	France	23,480	59	2.0	0.5
15	United Kingdom	22,640	59	1.6	0.3
16	Australia	20,050	19	2.5	1.2
17	Italy	19,710	58	0.9	0.2
18	Canada	19,320	31	2.8	1.1
19	Ireland	19,160	4	8.0	0.7
20	Spain	14,000	39	3.6	0.2
109	Kyrgyz Republic	300	5	1.7	0.8
110	Central African Republic	290	4	1.9	2.1
111	Tajikistan	290	6	2.0	1.8
112	Lao PDR	280	5	1.5	2.6
113	Cambodia	260	12	2.2	2.8
114	Madagascar	250	15	2.3	2.9
115	Rwanda	250	8	4.8	2.0
116	Burkina Faso	240	11	2.7	2.4
117	Mali	240	11	2.7	2.8
118	Tanzania	240	33	3.1	2.9
119	Mozambique	230	17	6.6	2.2
120	Angola	220	12	−37.4	3.2
121	Nepal	220	23	2.2	2.4
122	Chad	200	7	−4.1	2.9
123	Eritrea	200	4	0.8	2.7
124	Malawi	190	11	4.4	2.6
125	Niger	190	10	−1.1	3.4
126	Sierra Leone	130	5	−9.8	2.4
127	Burundi	120	7	−2.5	2.2
128	Ethiopia	100	63	4.8	2.8

*Countries were selected from the 128 countries for which complete data were reported to the World Bank and listed in the *World Development Report.*

†GNP/capita growth rates are real.

Source: *World Development Report,* 2000 (Washington, DC: World Bank, 1997), pp. 274–75, 278–79.

remain the only generally available means of converting GNP from national currencies to U.S. dollars."[17]

Finally, you must remember that GNP per capita is merely an arithmetic mean obtained by dividing GNP by the total population. However, a nation with a lower GNP but more evenly distributed income may be a more desirable market than one whose GNP is higher. On the other hand, as you will note in the chapter on economic forces

(Chapter 7), a skewed distribution of income in a nation with a low GNP per capita may indicate that there is a viable market, especially for luxury goods.

The data from Table 2.10 indicate that from a macro perspective, markets around the world are growing, but this does not mean that equally good opportunities exist for all kinds of business. Perhaps surprisingly, economic growth in a nation causes markets for some products to be lost forever while simultaneously markets for other products are being created. Take the case of a country in the initial stage of development. With little local manufacturing, it is a good market for exporters of consumer goods. As economic development continues, however, businesspeople see profit-making opportunities in (1) producing locally the kinds of consumer goods that require simple technology or (2) assembling from imported parts the products that demand a more advanced technology. Given the tendency of governments to protect local industry, the importation of goods being produced in that country will normally be prohibited or discouraged through taxes, tariffs, or other means once local production of those goods has been established. Thus, exporters of easy-to-manufacture consumer goods, such as paint, adhesives, toilet articles, clothing, and almost anything made of plastic, will begin to lose this market, which now becomes a new market for producers of the inputs to these "infant industries."

Preferential Trading Arrangements. The fact that most nations have experienced growth in population and GNP per capita does not necessarily mean they have attained sufficient size to warrant investment by an international firm in either (1) an organization for marketing exports from the home country or (2) a local manufacturing plant. For many products, a number of these nations still lack sufficient market potential. When such nations have made some kind of a **preferential trading arrangement** (for example, the EU or the North American Free Trade Agreement), the resultant market has been much larger. As a result, firms frequently have bypassed what is often the initial step of exporting to make their initial market entry with local manufacturing facilities.

preferential trading arrangement
An agreement by a small group of nations to establish free trade among themselves while maintaining trade restrictions with all other nations

Faster-Growing Markets. Not only are new foreign markets appearing, many of them are growing at a faster rate than is the home market. One outstanding example has been the growth of Singapore, which has had 4.5 times the average annual growth of Japan, with a similar GNP/capita. However, because it is a small market, the country would not be a candidate for every firm searching for overseas growth opportunities. It is attractive for exporters of luxury products and food chains such as McDonald's, which, incidentally, already has over 50 restaurants there.

A firm looking for a market large enough to support the local production of appliances or machinery, for example, would be attracted by the wealth, growth, and population size of Japan and Spain. When you examine the low GNP/capita and negative growth rates of so many of the African nations, you realize why foreign direct investment in that entire continent is so low. Clearly, market analysts will investigate other factors, such as the legal and competitive situations (discussed in Chapter 15), but an examination of the variables in Table 2.10 is a good place to start. Interestingly, of the 128 countries in the World Bank table on which Table 2.10 is based, 52 (41 percent) had average annual GDP growth rates higher than the U.S. growth rate for the period 1990–1999.

Faster growth in the markets of developing nations frequently occurs for another reason. When a firm that has supplied the market by exporting builds a factory for local production, the host government generally prohibits imports. The firm, which may have had to share the market with 10 or 20 competitors during its exporting days, now has the local market all to itself or shares it with only a small number of other local producers. Before General Tire began manufacturing tires in Chile, probably a dozen exporters, including General Tire, were competing in the market. However, once local production got under way, there was only one supplier for the entire market—General Tire. That is growth.

Improved Communications. This might be considered a supportive reason for opening up new markets overseas, because certainly the ability to communicate rapidly and less expensively with customers and subordinates by electronic mail and videoconferencing, as we discussed in Chapter 1, has given managers confidence in their ability to control foreign operations. Advances in computer-based communications are allowing virtual integration, which permits firms to become more physically fragmented as their managements search the world for lower-cost inputs. For example, anyone in the home office or in a subsidiary anywhere in the world can instantly access databases and computer-generated drawings.

Good, relatively inexpensive international communication enables large insurance, banking, and software firms to "body shop," that is, transmit computer-oriented tasks worldwide to a cheap but skilled labor force. New York Life, for example, employs 50 people in Ireland to process insurance claims on a computer linked to the firm's computer in New Jersey. American employees coming to work in the morning find that the claims processed during the night in Ireland have been transmitted to their computers in the United States. In India, the clients of numerous software companies are in the United States. A few years ago, software teams were required to fly back and forth between the two countries. Now, at the end of the day, customers in the United States E-mail their problems to India, and while they are sleeping, the Indians work on the solutions and have them back in the United States before the Americans have had breakfast. For their work, Indian software engineers receive only 20 percent as much as do their American counterparts.[18]

Obtain Greater Profits

As you know, greater profits may be obtained by either increasing total revenue or decreasing the cost of goods sold, and often conditions are such that a firm can do both.

Greater Revenue. Rarely will all of a firm's domestic competitors be in every foreign market in which it is located. Where there is less competition, the firm may be able to obtain a better price for its goods or services. For example, Goodrich had only one competitor in the Mexican market when it began producing V belts locally, whereas it had dozens of competitors in the United States.

Increasingly, firms are obtaining greater revenue by simultaneously introducing products in foreign markets and in their domestic markets as they move toward greater globalization of their operations. This results in greater sales volume while lowering the cost of the goods sold.

Lower Cost of Goods Sold. Going abroad, whether by exporting or by producing overseas, can frequently lower the cost of goods sold. Increasing total sales by exporting not only will reduce research and development (R&D) costs per unit but also will make other economies of scale possible. The management of Warner-Lambert, a global health care and consumer products manufacturer, evidently agrees as it states, "Warner-Lambert is addressing each new product as a global opportunity, particularly pharmaceuticals. Only in the context of a worldwide marketplace can Warner-Lambert hope to recapture the escalating costs of bringing new drugs to market."[19] The head of research for Bristol-Myers Squibb, a U.S. pharmaceuticals manufacturer that ranks as the fourth largest in the world, claims that of every 5,000 substances examined, only 1 is likely to prove safe and effective. It takes on average $350 million to bring a new drug on the market, and only 3 out of 10 prescription medicines recover that average cost.[20]

Another factor that can positively affect the cost of goods sold is the inducements that some governments offer to attract new investment. For example, Greece offers the following to new investors: (1) investment grants of up to 50 percent of the investment, (2) interest subsidies to cover up to 50 percent of the interest cost of bank loans, and (3) reduction of up to 90 percent of a firm's taxes on profits. Incentives such as these are designed to attract prospective investors and generally are not a sufficient motive for foreign investment. Nevertheless, they do have a positive influence on the cost of goods sold.

Higher Overseas Profits as an Investment Motive. There is no question that greater profits on overseas investments were a strong motive for going abroad in the early 1970s and 1980s. *Business International* reported that 90 percent of 140 Fortune 500 companies surveyed had achieved higher profitabilily on foreign assets in 1974, for example.[21] This trend continued into the 1990s. As an example, in 1993, only 18 of the 100 largest multinationals earned more than 50 percent of their revenue overseas but 33 earned more than 50 percent of their profits from foreign operations.[22] However, the ratio of firms earning more than 50 percent of their profits overseas to those whose foreign revenues exceed 50 percent of total revenues declined during the mid-1990s.[23] In 1999, for the largest 100 U.S. multinationals, the ratio was 33 to 28. Apparently, the cost and competition drivers to globalization we examined in Chapter 1 are acting to reduce the differences between overseas and home country profits.

Test Market

Occasionally, an international firm will test-market a product in a foreign location that is less important to the company than its home market and major overseas markets. This provides an opportunity to make changes, if necessary, to any part of the marketing mix (product, promotion, price, channels of distribution) or drop the entire venture if the test indicates that this should be done. Management's thinking is that any mistakes made in the test market should not adversely affect the firm in any of its major markets. Since companies usually monitor their competitors' actions in all markets, there is always the danger that a market test will give those competitors an early warning. We shall examine this point again in Chapter 15, "Assessing and Analyzing Markets."

Let's now look at some reasons for going abroad that are more related to the protection of present markets, profits, and sales.

Protect Markets, Profits, and Sales

Protect Domestic Market

Frequently, a firm will go abroad to protect its home market.

Follow Customers Overseas. Service companies (for example, accounting, advertising, marketing research, banking, law) will establish foreign operations in markets where their principal accounts are to prevent competitors from gaining access to those accounts. They know that once a competitor has been able to demonstrate to top management what it can do by servicing a foreign subsidiary, it may be able to take over the entire account. Similarly, suppliers to original equipment manufacturers (for example, battery manufacturers supplying automobile producers) often follow their large customers. These suppliers have an added advantage in that they are moving into new markets with a guaranteed customer base.

This is true for the over 250 Japanese auto parts makers that have come to the United States, the world's largest auto parts producer, to supply the Japanese auto plants in this country. For example, Tokyo Seat established a subsidiary to make seats, exhaust systems, and other parts for Honda, which also asked Nippodenso, a Japanese producer of radiators and heaters, to put up a plant.[24]

Researchers at the University of Michigan found that American companies supplied only 16 percent of the auto parts for Honda's Marysville, Ohio, plant. The remaining 84 percent was provided by Japanese imports (38 percent) and by Japanese suppliers that had set up plants in the United States (46 percent). And it is not only parts suppliers: Mitsubishi Bank for Toyota in Japan opened an office in Columbus, Ohio, to serve Honda's Ohio plant.[25] Toyota also heavily favors Japanese-owned parts suppliers to its American plant. Of 63 U.S. parts suppliers, only 32 are American-owned.[26]

Attack in Competitor's Home Market

Occasionally, a firm will set up an operation in the home country of a major competitor with the idea of keeping it so occupied defending that market that it will have less energy to compete in the home country of the first company. Although Kodak claimed its decision to open a manufacturing plant in Japan had nothing to do with its Japanese competitor (Fuji), its announcement came just 10 days after Fuji began construction of its first manufacturing facility in the United States.[27]

Using Foreign Production to Lower Costs. A company may also go abroad to protect its domestic market when it faces competition from lower-priced foreign imports. By moving part or all of its production facilities to the countries from which its competition is coming, it can enjoy such advantages as less costly labor, raw materials, and energy. Management may decide to produce certain components abroad and assemble them in the home country, or, if the final product requires considerable labor in the final assembly, it may send the components overseas for this final operation.

Zenith Electronics announced in 1992 that it would move its television assembly operations from Missouri to Mexico. Zenith, which had not earned a profit since 1984, expected to save many millions of dollars in annual labor costs from the move.[28] Zenith was able to take advantage of the lower-cost Mexican labor because of the in-bond (*maquiladora* in Mexico) program, a version of the export processing zones that began in the 1960s in Hong Kong, Taiwan, and Singapore. These all pertain to using foreign production to lower costs.

in-bond plants (maquiladoras)
Production facilities in Mexico that temporarily import raw materials, components, or parts duty-free to be manufactured, processed, or assembled with less expensive local labor; the finished or semifinished product is then exported

In-bond (maquiladora) industry. **In-bond plants (maquiladoras)** came into existence because of an arrangement between Mexico and the United States. The Mexican government permitted plants in the in-bond area to import parts and processed materials to be assembled, packaged, and processed without paying import duties provided that the finished products were reexported; the American government permitted the finished product containing the American-made parts and materials to be imported with import duty being paid only on the value added in Mexico. Originally, the in-bond plant program was called the *twin-plant program* because it was thought that a plant on the Mexican side would do the labor-intensive processes for a twin located on the American side. However, fewer than 10 percent of the Mexican plants have a twin on the U.S. side.

Although Mexican law required the in-bond plants to locate on the border in the beginning, later they were permitted into the interior of the country. Despite this relaxation, approximately 70 percent of the plants and nearly 85 percent of in-bond plant employment are still in Mexico's northern states bordering the United States. There were over 3,600 in-bond plants in 2000 (see Figure 2.2), an increase of 75 percent since 1994. More than 1.3 million workers (over 15 percent of the total employment in Mexico's manufacturing sector) were employed in maquiladoras in July 2000. Their production, led by electronics, electronic machinery, transportation equipment, and textiles, amounted to more than $82 billion in 2000. According to the Mexican Commerce Industry, 81 percent of Mexican trade with the United States is from the maquiladora industry.[29]

North American Free Trade Agreement (NAFTA)
A treaty establishing a free trade area consisting of the United States, Mexico, and Canada; quotas on each other's goods were eliminated in January 1994, and import duties will be phased out over 10 years

Because of the **North American Free Trade Agreement (NAFTA),** in the year 2001 in-bond plants will have to pay Mexican import duties on components coming from outside the NAFTA member-nations. As a result, the advantage of using an in-bond plant will be lost to the hundreds of Japanese, Korean, and other Asian firms that currently import most of their raw materials, especially for electronic products, from Asia. Because Mexican suppliers currently provide only 2 percent of the total inputs used by the in-bond plants, Japanese companies are concerned that they will then have to purchase components from American manufacturers. To avoid this, Japan has sent experts to advise Mexico on how to foster greater development of suppliers to the Japanese industry.[30]

Another factor will change the way the in-bond plants operate. Since the beginning of 1994, they could sell 50 percent of their production in Mexico, and as of January 1, 2001, all their production may be sold in the domestic market.[31] However, because most plants produce subassemblies that are sent out of Mexico to the parent company for further processing, they have practically nothing to sell locally. Most home offices are only beginning to realize the importance of this change in the Mexican law. Eventually, they will have to change the scope of the in-bond plants to include the production of finished products.[32]

Caribbean Basin Initiative. This was started by President Reagan to stimulate investment in the Caribbean nations. The advantages are similar to those enjoyed by Mexican in-bond industries. There is a wide range of products either grown or manufactured in 24 Caribbean countries that have duty-free entry into the United States. Although most

[Figure 2.2] Number of Maquila Plants and Maquiladora Employment

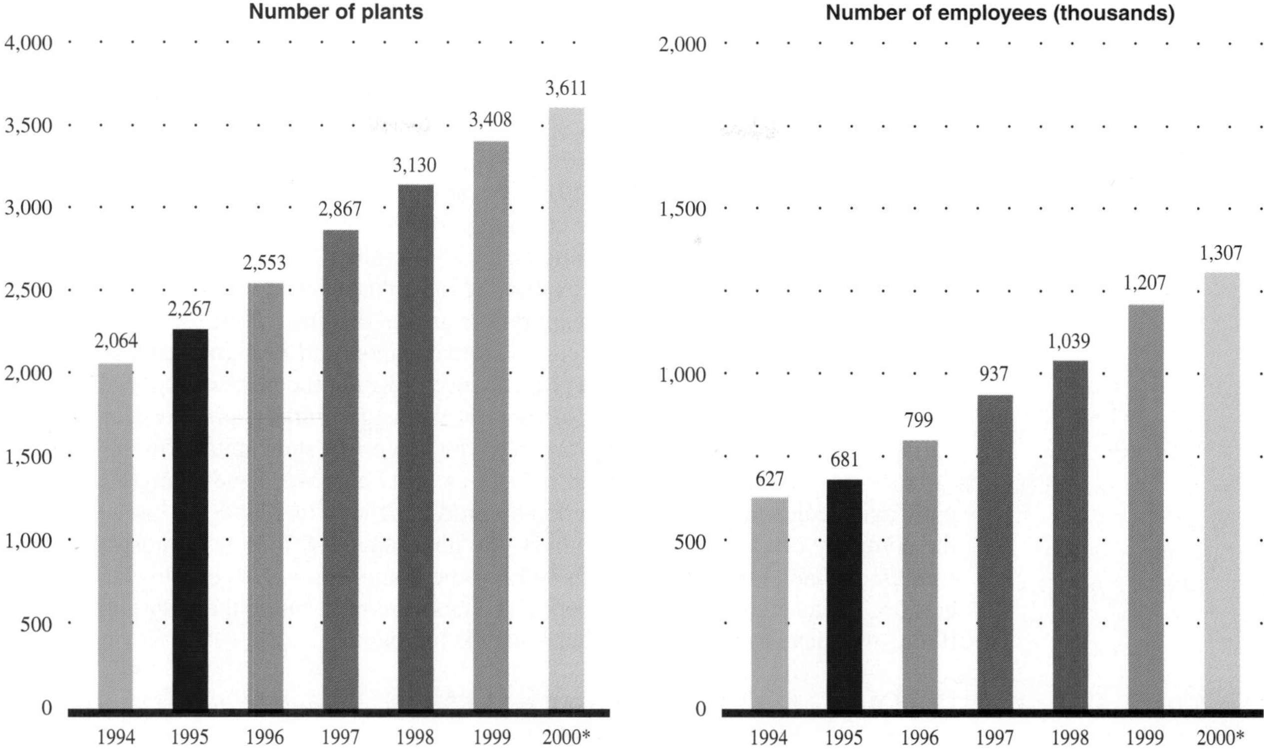

*Data are for July, 2000.

Source: "Maquila Overview," www.maquilaportal.com/Visitors_Site/maquilaoverview/MOVERVIEW1.htm (November 18, 2000).

textiles and apparel are excluded from duty-free status, apparel assembled from U.S.-formed and U.S.-cut material can enter the United States free of duty. The American apparel industry sends precut pieces to these countries, where they are assembled and returned for sale in the United States. This work has created over 100,000 jobs in Haiti, the Dominican Republic, Jamaica, and other nearby countries.[33]

Andean Trade Preference Act (ATPA). This is a unilateral trade benefit program similar to the Caribbean Basin Initiative, but it was designed to promote economic development in Bolivia, Colombia, Ecuador, and Peru. It was a major component of President Bush's Andean Trade Initiative that was designed to combat the production of coca by offering broader access to the U.S. market. ATPA's provisions are similar to those of the Caribbean Basin Initiative with some limitations.[34]

Growth Triangles. To remain competitive in attracting new industry in the face of rising wages, Singapore introduced the concept of localized economic cooperation zones, or **growth triangles.** They consist of a group of countries that complement each other economically and are close to each other geographically. The original one is the Southern Growth Triangle covering a 30-mile radius encompassing Singapore, the Malaysian state of Johore, and Indonesia's Riau Islands. Singapore furnishes management, financing, transportation, and telecommunications capabilities, while Riau and Johore provide land, labor, and natural resources. At least five other growth triangles in Asia are being organized.[35]

growth triangles
Transnational economic zones spread over large, geographically proximate areas covering three or more countries where differences in factor endowments are exploited to promote external trade and investment

Export Processing Zones. Many developing nations have a form of the export processing zone in which firms, mostly foreign manufacturers, enjoy almost a complete absence of taxation and regulation of materials brought into the zones for processing and subsequent reexport.

Protect Foreign Markets

Changing the method of going abroad from exporting to overseas production is often necessary to protect foreign markets. The management of a firm supplying a profitable overseas market by exporting may begin to note some ominous signs that this market is being threatened.

Lack of Foreign Exchange. One of the first signs is a delay in payment by the importers. The importers may have sufficient local currency but may be facing delays in buying foreign exchange (currency) from the government's central bank. The credit manager in the exporting firm, by checking with his or her bank and other exporters, learns that this condition is becoming endemic—a reliable sign that the country is facing a lack of foreign exchange. In examining the country's balance of payments, the financial manager may find that its export revenue has declined while the import volume remains high. Experienced exporters know that import and foreign exchange controls are in the offing and that there is a good chance of losing the market, especially if they sell consumer products. In times of foreign exchange scarcity, governments will invariably give priority to the importation of raw materials and capital goods.

If the advantages of making the investment outweigh the disadvantages, the company may decide to protect this market by producing locally. Managers know that once the company has a plant in the country, the government will do its utmost to provide foreign exchange for raw materials to keep the plant, a source of employment, in operation. Because imports of competing products are prohibited, the only competition, if any, will have to come from other local manufacturers.

Local Production by Competitors. Lack of foreign exchange is not the only reason a company might change from exporting to manufacturing in a market. For instance, while a firm may enjoy a growing export business and prompt payments, it still may be forced to set up a plant in the market. It may be that its competitors have also noticed their export volumes will support local production.

Should a competing firm move to put up a factory in the market, management must decide rapidly whether to follow suit or risk losing the market forever. Managers know that many governments, especially those in developing nations, not only will prohibit further imports once the product is produced in the country but also will permit only two or three other companies to enter so as to maintain a sufficient market for these local firms. General Motors tried for years to enter Spain, but the Spanish government, believing there were already enough automobile manufacturers in the country, refused the company entry. Only when Spain joined what was then the European Community was General Motors permitted to enter.

Downstream Markets. A number of Organization of Petroleum Exporting Countries (OPEC) nations have invested in refining and marketing outlets, such as filling stations and heating oil distributors, to guarantee a market for their crude oil at more favorable prices. Petróleos de Venezuela, owner of Citgo, is one of the largest foreign investors in the United States. Kuwait bought Gulf Oil's refining and marketing network in three European countries and also owns 20 percent of British Petroleum, which has the second-largest foreign investment in the United States. Lukoil, Russia's largest oil company, bought the Getty Oil chain of gasoline retailers in the eastern United States. These are just three examples.

Protectionism. When a government sees that local industry is threatened by imports, it may erect import barriers to stop or reduce them.* Even threats to do this can be sufficient to induce the exporter to invest in production facilities in the importing country. This and a high-priced yen, which makes it difficult for Japanese exports to compete with American products, are important reasons for Japanese investment in the United States.

*See Chapter 3 for a discussion of import barriers.

[Worldview]

Reverse Maquila, a New Concept

A new concept called *reverse maquila* is gaining attention in the Rio Grande Valley on the Texas–Mexico border, where over 200 in-bond plants (maquiladoras) are located. The term is so new that its definition is still fluid. Users are applying it to two different manufacturing situations: (1) a Mexican firm sets up production on the American side of the border and produces for sale in Mexico, and (2) a Mexican firm establishes production facilities on the American side of the border and sells the output in the United States.

Anyone familiar with the maquiladora concept recognizes that the first situation is the reverse of the usual maquiladora operation, in which an American or other non-Mexican company builds a plant on the Mexican side of the border to produce products by using foreign-made components and the cheaper Mexican labor and then exports them to the United States. Here is an example of the reverse of that operation. A Mexican snack company owned by Pepsico International is building a plant in the Texas border city of Weslaco to make snacks that will be sold in Mexico. Why build the plant on the American side of the border, where labor is more expensive?

There are a number of reasons being offered for locating on the U.S. side:

1. Many of the American materials used in the manufacturing process are of consistently superior quality to what the firm can obtain in Mexico. According to Pepsico, the quality of the American potatoes is better for their needs.
2. There are far fewer problems with organized labor on the American side.
3. Operational services such as electricity and waste disposal are less expensive.
4. NAFTA-level import duties for both nations are becoming progressively lower.
5. Less bureaucracy and less corruption exist on the American side.
6. The finished product does not have to undergo what can be a time-consuming process: passing through U.S. customs.
7. Roads, telecommunications, and waste disposal on the American side are far superior.
8. There has been a lessening of the difference in effective hourly wages: $6 average in Mexico compared with less than $16 in the American border area. For products produced by automated manufacturing processes, labor costs commonly range from 15 to 20 percent of production costs compared with 45 to 55 percent of production costs for raw materials.
9. Workers on the American side of the border are better educated and more accustomed to factory work. They are bilingual.
10. Far less housing is available on the Mexican side for the workers, many of whom literally live in cardboard boxes. Because of the poor living conditions, a large number leave after a short time, causing the turnover of the workers to be much higher on the Mexican side of the border.

An example of the second situation is the case of a Mexican manufacturer of elastic for the underwear industry. The company, Select Elastics of America, is now constructing a plant in McAllen, Texas, also in the Rio Grande Valley and near the Pepsico plant mentioned above. This firm has been supplying elastic to American producers of underwear, such as Playtex and VF, from Mexican production, using Mexican raw materials. To maintain these customers, the company recognizes that it must deliver, on time, a consistently top-quality product. To do so, it must have raw materials of superior quality, and they must be constantly available. The labor cost is 16 to 18 percent of the production cost compared to 48 to 52 percent for the raw materials cost. Thus, the savings in labor costs are insignificant compared to the expense caused by the factors listed above. A company representative believed that the management chose a location close to the border and still far from its clients in the north because the Mexican owners felt more comfortable with an operation in an area with a strong Mexican culture and where most people speak both Spanish and English. It is also much closer to their headquarters in Mexico City.

Representatives of the McAllen Economic Development Corporation are talking with numerous companies from both sides of the border about moving to the area and are finding a high level of interest because of the reasons stated above. ■

Source: Personal interviews.

Guarantee Supply of Raw Materials

Few developed nations possess sufficient domestic supplies of raw materials. Japan and Europe are almost totally dependent on foreign sources for many important materials, and even the United States depends on imports for more than half of its aluminum, chromium, manganese, nickel, tin, and zinc. Furthermore, the Department of the Interior estimates that iron, lead, tungsten, copper, potassium, and sulfur will be added soon to the critical list.*

To ensure a continuous supply, manufacturers in the industrialized countries are being forced to invest primarily in the developing nations, where most new deposits are being discovered. Interestingly, although Japan does this as well, for years it has also looked to the United States as a source of raw materials. A Japanese deputy general consul once stated,

> The United States offers an abundance of raw materials. Because Japan has long depended on the United States for various materials, such as grain, coking coal, and lumber, it is entirely logical for Japanese firms to establish facilities close to the sources of these essential raw materials.

Some analysts claim that the Japanese-American trade flows approximate those between an industrialized country and a developing country: the industrialized nation sends manufactured goods to the developing nation in return for raw materials. This is somewhat exaggerated, but in 1999 practically all of Japan's exports to the United States consisted of manufactured goods and services, while approximately one-third of American exports to Japan consisted of foodstuffs, raw materials, and mineral fuels.

Acquire Technology and Management Know-How

A reason often cited by foreign firms for investing in the United States is the acquisition of technology and management know-how. Nippon Mining, for example, a Japanese copper mining company, came to Illinois and paid $1 billion for Gould Inc. to acquire technology leadership and market share in producing the copper foil used in printed circuit boards. In a similar situation, Taiwan's Acer Inc. wanted to learn about small business computers, and so it bought Counterpoint Computers in California for $20 million, saving millions in research.

Geographic Diversification

Many companies have chosen geographic diversification as a means of maintaining stable sales and earnings when the domestic economy or their industry goes into a slump. Often, in other parts of the world, the industry or the other economies are at their peak. Remember that 12 of the 28 firms in Table 2.1 obtained at least 50 percent of their revenues overseas and that 14 of the 28 obtained over 50 percent of their profits abroad.

Satisfy Management's Desire for Expansion

The faster growth mentioned previously helps fulfill management's desire for expansion. Stockholders and financial analysts also expect firms to continue to grow, and those companies operating only in the domestic market have found it increasingly difficult to sustain that expectation. As a result, many firms have expanded into foreign markets. This, of course, is what companies based in small countries, such as Nestlé (Switzerland), SKF Bearing (Sweden), and Nokia (Finland), discovered decades ago.

Another aspect of this reason sometimes motivates a company's top managers to begin searching for overseas markets. Being able to claim that the firm is a "multinational" creates the impression of importance, which can influence the firm's customers. Sun Microsystems, a manufacturer of computer workstations, opened a technical center in Germany and built a factory in Scotland. "To be a major player in the marketplace, you have to be internationally recognized," said the head of Sun's European operations.[36]

*See Chapter 8 for a discussion of scarce industrial minerals.

We also know of instances in which a company has examined and then entered a market because its president brought it to the attention of the market planners after enjoying a pleasant vacation there.

> How else can you explain the fact that in pre-Castro Cuba there were three American tire factories in Havana, the "fun capital" of the world, with Miami just 90 miles away? Delivery of tires to Cuba could have been made in hours and at better prices. One of the authors found out why when he spent a winter in Akron working for a tire company. That was the time of the year when the Cuban subsidiary customarily had financial, marketing, and production problems that required the presence of Akron executives.

How to Enter Foreign Markets

As you learned in Chapter 1, all of the means for supplying foreign markets may be subsumed in just two activities: (1) exporting to a foreign market and (2) manufacturing in it.

Exporting

Most firms began their involvement in overseas business by exporting—that is, selling some of their regular production overseas. This method requires little investment and is relatively free of risks. It is an excellent means of getting a feel for international business without committing any great amount of human or financial resources. If management does decide to export, it must choose between *direct* and *indirect* exporting.

Indirect Exporting

indirect exporting
The exporting of goods and services through various types of home-based exporters

Indirect exporting is simpler than direct exporting because it requires neither special expertise nor large cash outlays. Exporters based in the home country will do the work. Management merely follows instructions. Among the exporters available are (1) *manufacturers' export agents,* who sell for the manufacturer, (2) *export commission agents,* who buy for their overseas customers, (3) *export merchants,* who purchase and sell for their own accounts, and (4) *international firms,* which use the goods overseas (mining, construction, and petroleum companies are examples).

Indirect exporters, however, pay a price for such service: (1) They will pay a commission to the first three kinds of exporters, (2) foreign business can be lost if exporters decide to change their sources of supply, and (3) firms gain little experience from these transactions. This is why many companies that begin in this manner generally change to direct exporting.

Direct Exporting

direct exporting
The exporting of goods and services by the firm that produces them

To engage in **direct exporting,** management must assign the job of handling the export business to someone within the firm. The simplest arrangement is to give someone, usually the sales manager, the responsibility for developing the export business. Domestic employees may handle the billing, credit, and shipping initially, and if the business expands, a separate export department may be set up. A firm that has been exporting to wholesale importers in an area and servicing them with visits from either home office personnel or foreign-based sales representatives frequently finds that sales have grown to a point that will support a complete marketing organization.

sales company
A business established for the purpose of marketing goods and services, not producing them

Management may then decide to set up a **sales company** in the area. The sales company will import in its own name from the parent and will invoice in local currency. It may employ the same channels of distribution, though the new organization may permit the use of a more profitable arrangement. This type of organization can grow quite large, often invoicing several millions of dollars annually. Before building a plant in Mexico, for many years Eastman Kodak imported and resold cameras and photographic supplies while doing a large business in local film developing. Many firms that began with local repair facilities later expanded to produce simple components.

Gradually, they produced more of the product locally until, after a period of time, they were manufacturing all the components in the country.

A firm's foreign business may evolve sequentially over the path just traced, or a company may move directly to foreign production (nonsequentially) for any of the reasons discussed previously in the section "Why Enter Foreign Markets?"

Before examining foreign manufacturing, we want to describe briefly the *turnkey project,* which is an export of technology, management expertise, and in some cases capital equipment. The contractor agrees to design and erect a plant, supply the process technology, provide the necessary suppliers of raw materials and other production inputs, and then train the operating personnel. After a trial run, the facility is turned over to the purchaser.

The exporter may be a contractor that specializes in designing and erecting plants in a particular industry, such as petroleum refining or steel production. It may also be a company in the industry that wishes to earn money from its expertise by delivering a plant ready to run rather than merely selling its technology. Chemical companies sold numerous turnkey projects to the communist countries, for example. Another kind of supplier of turnkey projects is the producer of a key input that sells a complete plant in order to obtain a contract to provide its product to the finished factory.

> One of the writers used to sell Goodyear latex to a U.S. manufacturer of paint driers. The client found it could lock in contracts to supply its products overseas by selling investors in developing countries a complete paint factory. It designed the plant, hired a contractor to erect it, trained the people to operate it, and provided ongoing technical assistance after the factory was delivered to the owners. The company also acted as a distributor for American producers of other inputs and manufacturers of paint-making machinery.

Foreign Manufacturing

When management does decide to become involved in foreign manufacturing, it generally has five distinct alternatives available, though not all of them may be feasible in a particular country. They are

1. Wholly owned subsidiary
2. Joint venture
3. Licensing agreement
4. Franchising
5. Contract manufacturing

A sixth arrangement—the *management contract*—is utilized by both manufacturing and service companies to earn income by providing management expertise for a fee.

Wholly Owned Subsidiary

A company that wishes to own a foreign subsidiary outright may (1) start from the ground up by building a new plant, (2) acquire a going concern, or (3) purchase its distributor, thus obtaining a distribution network familiar with its products. In this last case, of course, production facilities will typically have to be built.

Historically, American companies generally have preferred wholly owned subsidiaries, but they have not had a marked preference for any of the three means of obtaining them. However, this has not been the case for foreign investors in the United States, who have demonstrated a general preference for acquiring going concerns for the instant access to the market they provide. Moreover, they also have one less competitor after the purchase.

In 1998, 90 percent of the $201 billion spent by foreign investors was used for acquiring American firms. Only $20.3 billion was spent to create new businesses. Figure 2.3 points out an interesting fact: The average size of an acquisition in 1998 was *5.5 times* that of an investment to create a new firm ($268.5 million versus $49.1 million).

Sometimes it is not possible to have a wholly owned foreign subsidiary. The host government may not permit it, the firm may lack either capital or expertise to under-

[Figure 2.3] **Investment Outlays and Number of Investments, 1985–1998**

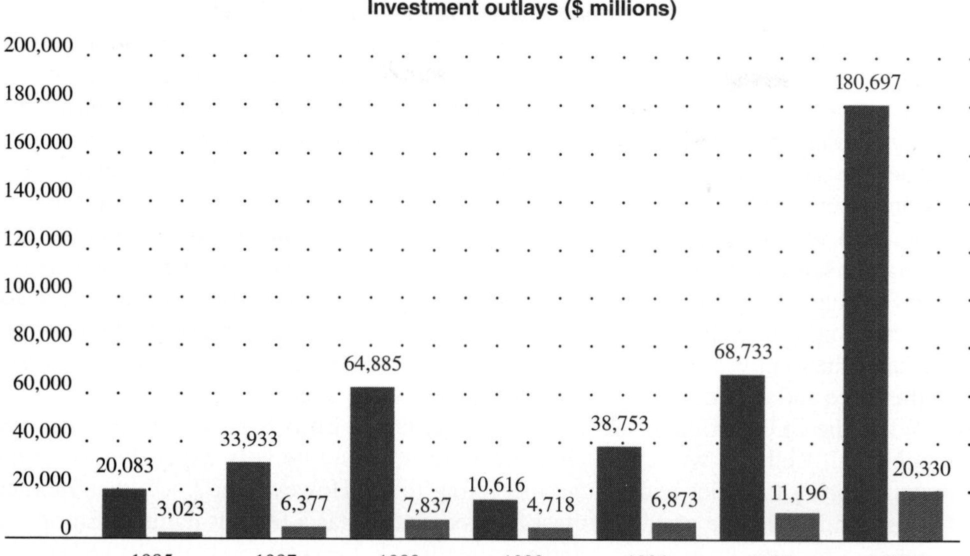

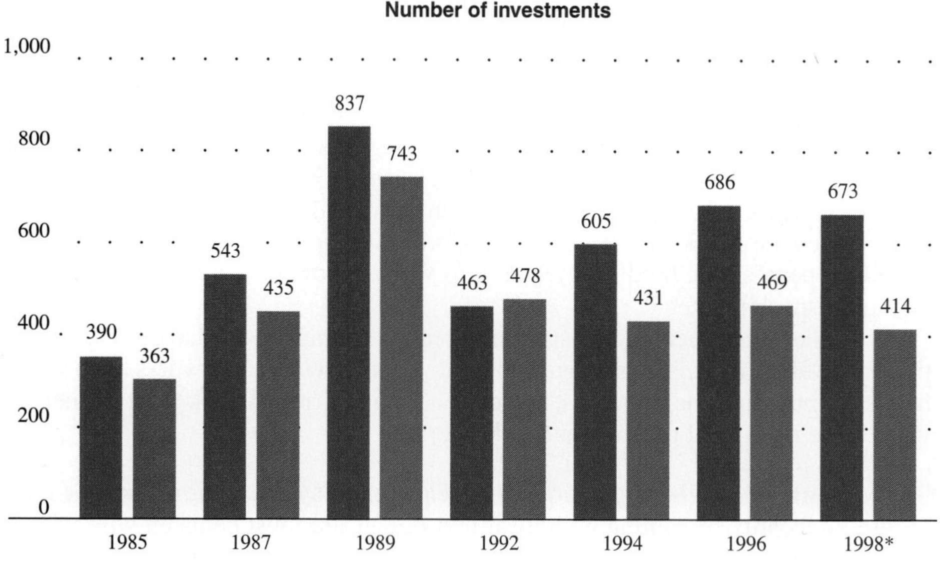

*1998 figures are preliminary.

Sources: *Survey of Current Business,* June 1997, p. 45; and *Survey of Current Business,* June 1999, www.bea.doc.gov/bea/ai/0699fdi/table2.htm (October 19, 2000).

take the investment alone, or there may be tax and other advantages that favor another form of investment, such as a joint venture.

Joint Venture

A **joint venture** may be (1) a corporate entity formed by an international company and local owners, (2) a corporate entity formed by two international companies for the purpose of doing business in a third market, (3) a corporate entity formed by a government agency (usually in the country of investment) and an international firm, or (4) a cooperative undertaking between two or more firms of a limited-duration

joint venture
A cooperative effort among two or more organizations that share a common interest in a business enterprise or undertaking

project. Large construction jobs such as a dam or an airport are frequently handled by this last form.

In 1987, Ford and Volkswagen formed a novel joint venture in which their operations in Argentina and Brazil were merged into a holding company, Autolatina, in an effort to eliminate the losses suffered by both. The joint venture, owned 51 percent by Volkswagen and 49 percent by Ford, assembled products based on VW and Ford designs, but both companies marketed the vehicles through their own distribution channels. Although 1993 sales reached $7.58 billion, the companies decided to terminate the operation. One industry expert says that Ford wanted to leave because Autolatina did not fit its new global strategy of having global vehicles. The two companies clashed about sharing models when they were facing increasing pressure from General Motors, which had sold so many of its Corsa subcompacts that it undertook an ad campaign telling consumers not to be in a hurry to buy the car. In 1994, Volkswagen dealers refused to share the company's new subcompact with Ford, prompting Ford to rush its program to produce the small Fiesta. In a news release, the companies said the termination of the joint venture reflected "the necessity of the companies to make better use of the force and resources of their worldwide organizations."[37]

When the CEO of General Mills decided to enter the European market, where a very tough rival, Kellogg, was entrenched, he knew it would be very expensive to set up manufacturing facilities and a huge marketing force. However, he knew that another food giant, Nestlé, the world's largest food company, has a famous name in Europe, a number of manufacturing plants, and a strong distribution system. It also lacked strong cereal brand names, something that General Mills, the number two American cereal company, has. Just two weeks after the initial discussions, General Mills and Nestlé formed a joint venture, Cereal Partners Worldwide. General Mills provided the cereal technology, brand names, and cereal marketing expertise. Nestlé supplied its name, distribution channels, and production capacity. Cereal Partners Worldwide distributes cereals everywhere in the world except the United States. Within two years, the new company had already passed Quaker Oats, the longtime number two in Europe after Kellogg. According to General Mills's vice chairman, building factories and distribution channels from scratch would have taken years and years: "We felt a sense of urgency." General Mills and Pepsico won approval from the European Union to merge their European snack food businesses into what is now the largest company in the European snack market.[38]

When the government of a host country requires companies to have some local participation, foreign firms must engage in joint ventures with local owners to do business in that country. In some situations, however, a foreign firm will seek local partners even when there is no local requirement to do so.

Strong Nationalism. Strong nationalistic sentiment may cause the foreign firm to try to lose its identity by joining with local investors. Care must be taken with this strategy, however. Although a large number of people in many developing countries dislike multinationals for "exploiting" them, they still believe, often with good reason, that the products of the foreign companies are superior to those of purely national firms. One solution to this ambivalence has been to form a joint venture in which the local partners are highly visible, give it an indigenous name, and then advertise that a foreign firm (actually the partner) is supplying the technology. Even wholly owned subsidiaries have followed this strategy.

> Eastman Kodak has eliminated the word *Kodak* from the names of its 100-percent-owned subsidiaries in Venezuela, Mexico, Chile, Peru, and Colombia. Kodak-Venezuela has become Foto Interamericana, and Kodak's large manufacturing company in Mexico is now called Industria Fotografica Interamericana.

Acquire Expertise, Tax, and Other Benefits. Other factors that influence companies to enter joint ventures are the ability to acquire expertise that is lacking, the special tax benefits some governments extend to companies with local partners, and the need for additional capital and experienced personnel.

Merck, the largest U.S. maker of ethical drugs, spent $313 million to acquire 50.5 percent of Banyu Pharmaceutical in Japan. Management had been dissatisfied with the performance of Merck's Japanese subsidiary in the world's second-largest ethical drug market. With this acquisition, the 600-person sales force of Merck-Japan was augmented by Banyu's 350 sales representatives. Merck's chairman said, "To bring new products effectively to market in Japan required a larger and more effective marketing organization. With a controlling interest in Banyu, I would hope for a better penetration of the Japanese market."[39]

To take advantage of Israel's lower labor costs and the 1985 U.S.–Israel Trade Agreement, which (1) reduced import duties on Israeli-made shirts and (2) gave them quota-free access to the United States, Van Heusen decided to buy the production facilities of an insolvent Israeli clothing manufacturer. When the government refused to sell on Van Heusen's terms, the company formed a joint venture with another Israeli textile-and-apparel conglomerate. Van Heusen will purchase the plant's output for five years, with the option to extend the agreement if satisfied with the local partner's performance and will have exclusive control over marketing. Although it has trained Israeli engineers and will maintain its own engineers at the operation, the Israeli partner has had to invest all of the capital to expand an existing plant.[40]

Some firms, as a matter of policy, enter joint ventures to reduce investment risk. Their strategy is to enter into a joint venture with either native partners or another worldwide company. Still others, such as Ford and Volkswagen, have joined together to achieve economies of scale. Incidentally, any division of ownership in a joint venture is possible unless there are specific legal requirements.

Disadvantages. Although a joint venture arrangement offers the advantage of a smaller commitment of financial and managerial resources and thus less risk, there are some disadvantages for the foreign firm. One, obviously, is that profits must be shared. Furthermore, if the law allows the foreign investors to have no more than a 49 percent participation (common in developing countries), they may not have control. This is because the stock markets in these countries are either small or nonexistent, and so it is generally impossible to distribute the shares widely enough to permit the foreign firm with its 49 percent to be the largest stockholder.

Lack of control over the joint venture is the reason why many companies resist making such arrangements. They feel that they must have tight control of their foreign subsidiaries to obtain an efficient allocation of investments and production and to maintain a coordinated marketing plan worldwide. For example, local partners might wish to export to markets that the global company serves from its own plants, or they might want to make the complete product locally when the global company's strategy is to produce only certain components there and import the rest from other subsidiaries.[41]

In recent years, numerous governments of developing nations have passed laws requiring local majority ownership for the purpose of giving control of firms within their borders to their own citizens. Despite these laws, control with a minority ownership may still be feasible.

Control with Minority Ownership

There have been occasions when the foreign partner has been able to circumvent the spirit of the law and ensure its control by taking 49 percent of the shares and giving 2 percent or more to its local law firm or another trusted national.

Another method is to take in a local majority partner, such as a government agency, an insurance company, or a financial institution, that is content to invest merely for a return while leaving the venture's management to the foreign partner. If neither arrangement can be made, the foreign company may still control the joint venture, at least in the areas of major concern, by means of non-ownership-based control mechanisms such as a *management contract.*

management contract
An arrangement by which one firm provides management in all or specific areas to another firm

Management Contract

The **management contract** is an arrangement under which a company provides managerial know-how in some or all functional areas to another party for a fee that typically ranges from 2 to 5 percent of sales. International companies make such contracts with (1) firms in which they have no ownership (examples: Hilton Hotel provides management for nonowned overseas hotels that use the Hilton name, and Delta provides management assistance to foreign airlines), (2) joint venture partners, and (3) wholly owned subsidiaries. The last arrangement is made solely for the purpose of allowing the parent to siphon off some of the subsidiary's profits. This becomes extremely important when, as in many foreign exchange–poor nations, the parent firm is limited in the amount of profits it can repatriate. Moreover, because the fee is an expense, the subsidiary receives a tax benefit.

Used in Joint Ventures. Management contracts can enable the global partner to control many aspects of a joint venture even when holding only a minority position. If it supplies key personnel, such as the production and technical managers, the global company can be assured of the product quality with which its name may be associated as well as be able to earn additional income by selling the joint venture inputs manufactured in the home plant. This is possible because the larger global company is more vertically integrated. A local paint factory, for example, might have to import certain semiprocessed pigments and driers that the foreign partner produces in its home country for domestic operations. If these can be purchased elsewhere at a lower price, the local majority could insist on other sources of supply. This rarely happens, because the production and technical managers can argue that only inputs from their employer will produce a satisfactory product. They are the experts, and they generally have the final word.

Purchasing Commission. There is another source of income that a global or multinational company derives not only from firms with which it has a management contract but also from joint ventures and wholly owned subsidiaries. That source is a commission for acting as a purchasing agent of imported raw materials and equipment. This relieves the affiliates of having to establish credit lines with foreign suppliers and assures them that they will receive the same materials used by the home company. The commission received for this service averages about 5 percent of invoice value and is in addition to the management contract fee.

licensing
A contractual arrangement in which one firm grants access to its patents, trade secrets, or technology to another for a fee

Licensing. Frequently, worldwide companies are called on to furnish technical assistance to firms that have sufficient capital and management strength. By means of a **licensing** agreement, one firm (the licensor) will grant to another firm (the licensee) the right to use any kind of expertise, such as manufacturing processes (patented or unpatented), marketing procedures, and trademarks for one or more of the licensor's products.

The licensee generally pays a fixed sum when signing the licensing agreement and then pays a royalty of 2 to 5 percent of sales over the life of the contract (five to seven years with an option for renewal). The exact amount of the royalty will depend on the amount of assistance given and the relative bargaining power of the two parties.

In the past, licensing was not a primary source of income for international firms. This changed in the 1980s, however, especially in the United States, because (1) the courts began upholding patent infringement claims more than they used to, (2) patent holders became more vigilant in suing violators, and (3) the federal government pressed foreign governments to enforce their patent laws.[42]

This forced foreign companies to obtain licenses instead of making illegal copies. Texas Instruments (TI), for example, sued nine Japanese electronics manufacturers for using its patented processes without paying licensing fees. The defendants have paid the company over $1 billion since 1986. Although the company does not publish its royalty receipts in its income statements, to give you an idea of the magnitude of the earnings from royalties associated with its 6,000 patents, TI announced 10-year agreements with both Hyundai Electronics and Samsung Electronics. Each of these agreements is projected to yield royalty payments of more than $1 billion to Texas Instruments.[43]

We do know that the total paid to American firms in royalties and license fees amounted to $36.5 billion in 1999 versus only $13.3 billion that those firms paid out to foreign licensors.[44]

Technology is not the only thing that is licensed. In the fashion industry, a number of designers license the use of their names. Pierre Cardin, one of the largest such licensors, reported 900 licenses in 140 countries for everything from skis to frying pans. These licenses earned the company $75 million annually, including $12 million from 32 American licensees. Even Russia paid the firm three-quarters of a million dollars every year.[45]

Are you giving Coca-Cola free advertising on your T-shirt? The company's manager for merchandise licensing expects the company to make millions from an agreement with the founder of Gloria Vanderbilt. He says the firm agreed to the arrangement because "clothes enhance our image. The money is not important."

Another industry, magazine publishing, is licensing overseas editions. You can buy *Cosmopolitan* in the native language in over 12 countries, *Playboy* in 10, and *Penthouse* in 5.

Despite the opportunity to obtain a sizable income from licensing, many firms, especially those that produce high-tech products, will not grant licenses. They fear that a licensee will become a competitor upon expiration of the agreement or that it will aggressively seek to market the products outside of its territory. At one time, licensors routinely inserted a clause in the licensing agreement that prohibited exports, but most governments will not accept such a prohibition.

Franchising

In recent years, American firms have gone overseas with a new kind of licensing—**franchising.** Franchising permits the franchisee to sell products or services under a highly publicized brand name and a well-proven set of procedures with a carefully developed and controlled marketing strategy. Of some 500 U.S. franchisers with approximately 50,000 outlets worldwide, fast-food operations (such as McDonald's, Kentucky Fried Chicken, and Tastee-Freeze) are the most numerous—McDonald's alone has approximately 15,000 restaurants in 119 countries outside of the United States.[46] Other types of franchisers are hotels (Hilton), business services (Muzak, Manpower), soft drinks (Coca-Cola, Canada Dry), home maintenance (Servicemaster, Nationwide Exterminating), and automotive products (Midas).

franchising
A form of licensing in which one firm contracts with another to operate a certain type of business under an established name according to specific rules

Contract Manufacturing

International firms employ **contract manufacturing** in two ways. One way is as a means of entering a foreign market without investing in plant facilities. The firm contracts with a local manufacturer to produce products for it according to its specifications. The firm's sales organization markets the products under its own brand, just as Montgomery Ward sells washing machines made by Norge.

contract manufacturing
An arrangement in which one firm contracts with another to produce products to its specifications but assumes responsibility for marketing

> When Gates Rubber licensed its V belt technology to General Tire's Chilean plant, it drew up a novel licensing agreement that included contract manufacturing. General Tire was obliged to produce part of its output with the Gates label. Gates executives knew that in Chile, once General Tire began production, the government would stop the importation of all V belts, including theirs. Gates would gain in a number of ways: (1) it would earn a royalty on all belts made in Chile, (2) it would have belts made in Chile to Gates specifications without making any investment in production facilities, and (3) competition from a dozen importers would be eliminated. There would be only one local competitor, General Tire. General Tire gained because it increased its product mix and offered another product to its present channels of distribution.

The second way is to subcontract assembly work or the production of parts to independent companies overseas. Although the international firm has no equity in the subcontractor, this practice does resemble foreign direct investment. When the international firm is the largest or only customer of the subcontractors, it has in effect created in another country a new company that generates employment and foreign exchange for the host nation. Frequently, the international firm will lend capital to the foreign contractor in the same way that a global or multinational firm will lend funds to its subsidiary. Because of these similarities, this practice is called *foreign direct investment without investment.*

Strategic Alliances

strategic alliances
Partnerships between competitors, customers, or suppliers that may take one or more of various forms

Faced with (1) expanding global competition, (2) the growing cost of research, product development, and marketing, and (3) the need to move faster in carrying out their global strategies, many firms are forming **strategic alliances** with customers, suppliers, and competitors (these are referred to as *competitive alliances, competitive collaborations, or coopetition* to reflect the simultaneous existence of collaborative and competitive forces in the relationship among the partners). Their aim is to achieve faster market entry and start-up; gain access to new products, technologies, and markets; and share costs, resources, and risks.

Alliances include various types of partnerships. Companies wanting to share technology may cross-license their technology (each will license its technology to the other). If their aim is to pool research and design resources, they may form an R&D partnership. For example, in late 1997, Intel, Motorola, and Advanced Micro Devices, three of the most prominent names in the computer chip industry, announced the formation of a not-for-profit company named EUV (Extreme Ultraviolet). Valued at $250 million, the project is the largest American commercial research partnership ever formed between industry and government. The three government laboratories will get the rights to use the resulting technologies as they wish, and the computer chip companies will have the right to use them to create faster chips. European and Asian chip makers may have the opportunity to join if they desire.[47] In 1998, Nokia, Ericsson, and Motorola (which jointly accounted over 75 percent of the world's mobile phone sales) formed a joint venture with Psion (a major manufacturer of handheld computers). An objective of the venture was to license Psion's software and develop it into an operating system for the next generation of "smart" mobile phones that could link to the Internet and perform many of the functions of a palmtop computer. Matsushita Electric of Japan, which also manufactures cellular phones, later joined the venture. The alliance is intended to enhance the competitiveness of the partners' future lines of wireless phones and other handheld devices as well as reduce their potential dependence on Microsoft and its Windows CE operating software.[48]

Alliances May Be Joint Ventures. Other companies carry the cooperation further by forming joint ventures in manufacturing and marketing. Westinghouse and Toshiba formed an equity joint venture to produce color display tubes for computer terminals and picture tubes for TV sets. Westinghouse, which was making monochrome tubes, formed the alliance to get the technology to produce color tubes. The joint venture gave Toshiba an opportunity to be involved in a manufacturing facility that could supply tubes to its TV plant in Tennessee. The Japanese also expected that another U.S.-based venture would help deflect protectionist pressure from Toshiba. Toshiba provided the technology, and Westinghouse provided a factory building and helped arrange financing, including $46 million in low-cost public loans. However, within just two years, Westinghouse had sold its interest to Toshiba, which then became the sole owner of the facility.[49]

Alliances Can Be Mergers and Acquisitions. Swedish ASEA and Swiss Brown Bovari, both energy generation and transmission specialists, merged to form an $18 billion company. The reason, according to the CEO of the new firm, was that the two firms individually were too small to compete with U.S. and Japanese rivals such as Westinghouse, General Electric, Hitachi, and Toshiba. Sandoz, a Swiss pharmaceutical manufacturer, acquired Gerber for $3.7 billion in order to double the size of its food products division. Two years later, because of the increased global competition and the mounting cost of technology, Sandoz and Ciba Geigy, another Swiss drug company, merged to form Novartis, which would then become the second-largest pharmaceutical firm in the world (and now ranks third).

Future of Alliances. Many alliances fail or are taken over by one of the partners. The existence of two or more partners, which are often competitors as well as partners and typically have differences in strategies, operating practices, and organizational cultures, often causes alliances to be difficult to manage, particularly in rapidly changing international competitive environments.[50]

The management consulting firm McKinsey & Co. surveyed 150 companies involved in alliances that had been terminated. It found that three-quarters of the alliances had been taken over by Japanese partners.[51] Professor Chalmers Johnson, an expert on Japan, warns, "I find the idea of joint ventures no longer makes any sense at all. They are a way for the Japanese to acquire technology."[52]

Despite the challenges involved with forming and managing alliances successfully, there is no question that some alliances have accomplished what they set out to accomplish. CFM International, the alliance between General Electric and France's Snecma, has been producing jet engines for more than two decades. Airbus Industrie, an alliance among British, French, German, and Spanish aircraft manufacturers, is now the world's second-largest commercial aircraft producer. It seems that alliances in their various forms will continue to be used as important strategic and tactical weapons, particularly given the financial, technological, political, and other challenges facing companies involved in increasingly competitive international marketplaces.

Multidomestic or Global Strategy?

Many large global and multidomestic firms with numerous manufacturing subsidiaries all over the world began their foreign operations by exporting. Once they succeeded at this stage, they often established sales companies overseas to market their exports. Where sales companies were able to develop sufficiently large markets, their firms set up plants to assemble imported parts. Finally, complete products were produced locally. However, this sequence of foreign trade to foreign direct investment does not represent the only way firms have entered foreign markets. In some countries, if a company was entering a new market because its competitor was already in production there, it too would have to establish a production facility.

The World Environment Is Changing

While this linear relationship still holds, changes in the world environment that affect trade and foreign investment are occurring: (1) Governments generally have liberalized the flows of capital, technology, people, and goods, and (2) improvements in information technology enable managers to direct company activities in diverse areas over long distances. As a result, global competition has increased, forcing companies to strive for better quality and lower-cost products. To reduce costs, they have moved some production activities to lower-cost countries and, through acquisitions and mergers, have increased company size to achieve economies of scale. Increasing sales by opening up new markets also will provide more economies of scale for the manufacturing system, especially if the firm sells the same products in all markets.

The aforementioned increased global competition will drive companies to open up new markets either to take market share from their competitors or to go to markets where there is less competition. It is evident that numerous conditions are forcing companies to enter foreign markets. Which strategy will management follow—multidomestic or global? In other words, what can the company standardize worldwide?

Seven Global Dimensions

There are at least seven dimensions along which management can globalize (standardize): (1) product, (2) markets, (3) promotion, (4) where value is added to the product, (5) competitive strategy, (6) use of non–home-country personnel, and (7) extent of global ownership in the firm. The possibilities range from zero standardization (multidomestic) to standardization along all seven dimensions (completely global). The challenge for company managers is to determine how far the firm should go with each one. Usually the amount of globalization will vary among the dimensions. For example, the promotion for washing machines might be standardized to a great extent: People use them to get their clothes clean, but for economic reasons, in poorer countries the machines must be simpler and less costly. Therefore, the product is not standardized worldwide. We shall return to this topic in various parts of the text, particularly in Chapter 14.

Whether a firm attempts to enter a foreign market through exporting or direct investment, a critical issue facing managers is how to distribute the firm's products or services in that market. Achieving the potential benefits of foreign market entry as described earlier in this chapter often depends on the firm's ability to understand and effectively operate within the channels of distribution in the nation or nations being entered. Channels of distribution is the topic of the final section of this chapter.

Channels of Distribution

Channels of distribution—systems of agencies through which a product and its title pass from the producer to the user—involve both controllable and uncontrollable variables. We shall discuss the uncontrollable aspects in this section, where we examine all the uncontrollable forces, and then return to them in Chapter 16, when we will consider them as controllable variables in the marketing mix.

How can a channel of distribution be both controllable and uncontrollable? It is controllable to the extent that the channel captain* is free to choose from the available channel members those that will enable the firm to reach its target market, perform the functions it requires at a reasonable cost, and permit it the amount of control it desires. If the company considers that the established channels are inadequate, it may assemble a different network.

Coca-Cola, dissatisfied with the complex Japanese system of distributing through layers of wholesalers, created its own system in which 17 bottlers sell directly to over 1 million retailers. The dramatic reduction in distributive costs, coupled with the fact that each bottler was well versed in its own market, enabled Coca-Cola to obtain 60 percent of the Japanese market. Note, however, that although a new system was created, new agencies were not.

The distributive *structure*—the agencies themselves—is generally beyond the marketer's control, and so it must use the agencies that are available. Yet new agencies are occasionally created when the established institutions do not fulfill the channel captain's requirements.

Compaq's Japanese subsidiary expected to sell its computers in Japan at prices well below those charged by Japanese PC makers. Part of its strategy in lowering prices was to sell directly to dealers, thus eliminating wholesalers. After the firm authorized dealers to buy directly from the factory, it learned that a number of them wanted to get part of their stock from wholesalers even though the price was higher. In that way, they could preserve old business and sometimes old school relationships. By agreeing to what was an odd arrangement for it, Compaq created a different type of retailer—one that bought the same product from both the factory and the wholesaler.[53]

International Channel of Distribution Members

The selection of channel of distribution members to link the producer with the foreign user will depend first of all on the method of entry into the market. As was discussed earlier in this chapter, to supply a foreign market, a firm must either export to a foreign country or manufacture in it. If the decision is to export, the firm may do so *directly* or *indirectly.* Figure 2.4 shows that management has considerable latitude in forming the channels.

Indirect Exporting

For indirect exporting, a number of U.S.-based exporters (A) sell for the manufacturer, (B) buy for their overseas customers, (C) buy and sell for their own account, or (D) pur-

*The *channel captain* is the dominant and controlling member of a channel of distribution.

[Figure 2.4] International Channels of Distribution

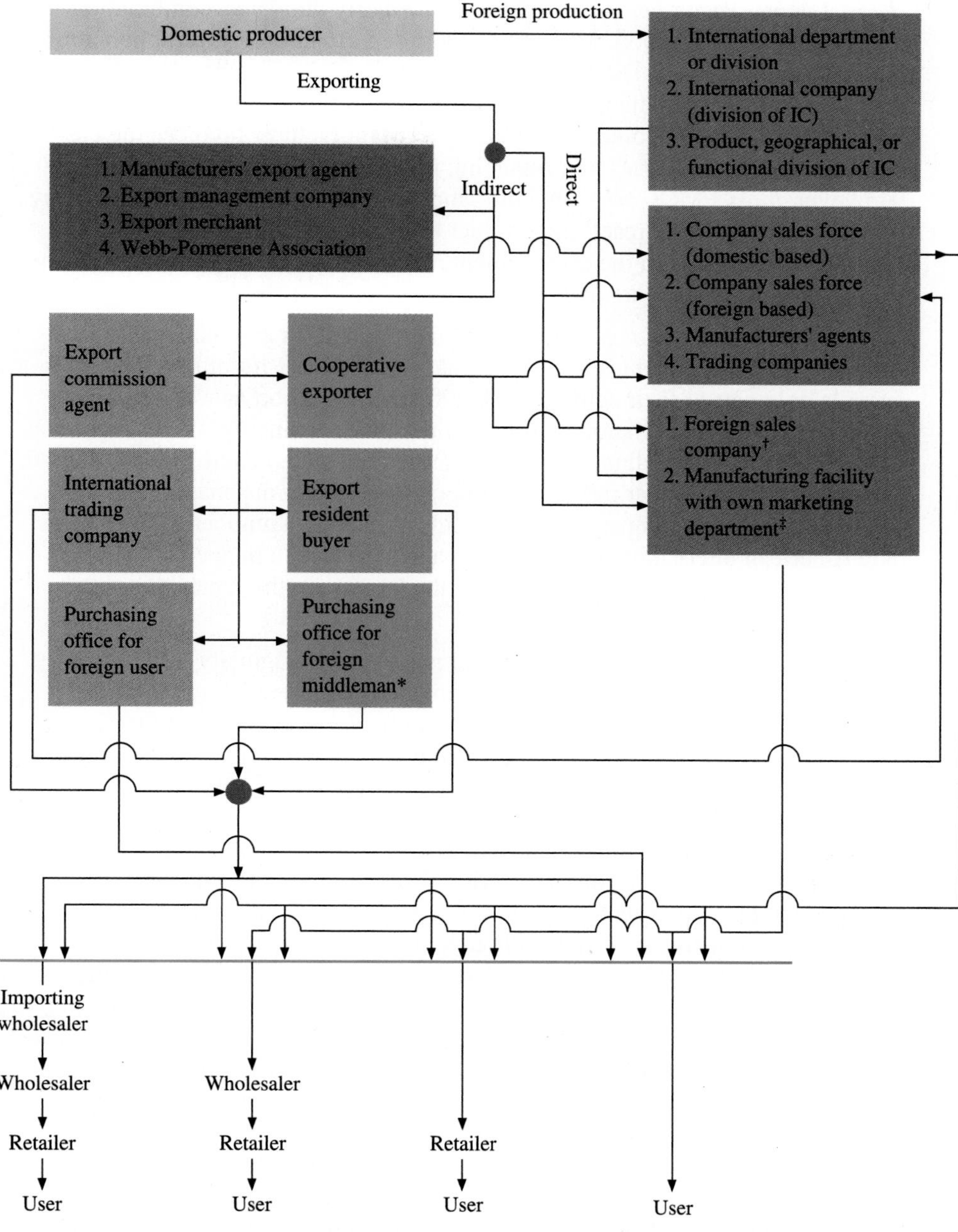

*There should be no direct connection between this category and the user. For simplification, a separate line to eliminate the user is not shown.

†Can be wholly owned or a joint venture. The foreign sales company may sell imports as well as local production from the licensee, contract manufacturer, or joint venture.

‡Can be wholly owned, a joint venture, or a licensee.

Source: Republished with permission of World Bank, from *World Development Report* 1999/2000, p. 274–275, 278–279. Permission conveyed through Copyright Clearance Center, Inc.

chase on behalf of foreign middlemen or users. Although each type of exporter usually operates in the following manner, any given company may actually perform one or more of these functions.

A. Exporters that sell for the manufacturer.

1. *Manufacturers' export agents* act as the international representatives for various noncompeting domestic manufacturers. They usually direct promotion, consummate sales, invoice, ship, and handle the financing. They commonly

are paid a commission for carrying out these functions in the name of the manufacturer.

2. *Export management companies* (EMCs), formerly known as combination export managers (CEMs), act as the export department for several noncompeting manufacturers. They also will transact business in the name of the manufacturer and handle the routine details of shipping and promotion. When the EMC works on a commission basis, the manufacturer invoices the customer directly and carries any financing required by the foreign buyer. However, most EMCs work on a buy-and-sell arrangement under which they pay the manufacturer, resell the product abroad, and invoice the customer directly. Depending on the arrangement, the EMC may act in the name of the firm it represents or in its own name.

3. *International trading companies* are similar to EMCs in that they also act as agents for some companies and as merchant wholesalers for others. This, however, is only part of their activities. They frequently export as well as import, own their own transportation facilities, and provide financing. W. R. Grace was at one time a major trading company that operated on the Pacific coast of South America. It owned sugar mills, large import houses, various manufacturing plants, a steamship company, and an airline. Although a number of European and American international trading companies have been in operation for centuries, certainly the most diversified and the largest are the Japanese **sogo shosha** (general trading companies).

sogo shosha
The largest of the Japanese general trading companies

a. *Sogo shosha.* The general trading companies were originally established by the *zaibatsu*—centralized, family-dominated economic groups, such as Mitsui, Mitsubishi, and Sumitomo—to be the heart of their commercial operations. The general trading companies obtained export markets, raw materials, and technical assistance for other companies of the zaibatsu and also imported goods for resale. Included in the zaibatsu in addition to banks and general trading companies were transportation, insurance, and real estate companies and various manufacturing firms. Although the zaibatsu were forced to dissolve after World War II, the companies that had been their major components survived. Although unified ownership and management ceased after World War II, cross-shareholdings and collaborative relationships resulted in the close coordination of many business activities among the affiliated companies. In recent years, the level of cross-shareholdings and coordination has evidenced some decline, a development promoted by liberalization of financial markets, pressures for improved performance and corporate governance, and other factors.

There are 20 general trading companies with more than 2,000 Japanese and overseas business locations. Their combined sales amount to over $1 trillion annually.[54] Mitsui, for example, had sales of $128 billion in 2000, employed 10,702 employees in 123 offices worldwide, and had 882 domestic and foreign consolidated or affiliated companies in its group. Mitsubishi Corporation had $127 billion in sales in 2000, employed 12,000 people in 160 offices worldwide, and had 653 consolidated or affiliated companies in its group.[55]

Although Mitsui & Co. is huge, it is only one company in the Mitsui Group (formerly the Mitsui zaibatsu), which consists of several hundred companies encompassing a wide range of businesses, including steelmaking, shipbuilding, banking, insurance, paper, electronics, petroleum, warehousing, tourism, and nuclear energy. The Mitsui Group is not a legal entity but exists as an informal organization of major enterprises that have related interests and related financial structures. They cooperate in promoting the economic interests of group members. To ensure cooperation, the top executives of the 68 major components of the former Mitsui zaibatsu meet for a weekly luncheon.

b. *Korean general trading companies.* Similar in scope to the Japanese sogo shosha, these are owned by the huge Korean diversified conglomerates called *chaebol.* They are responsible for a major part of Korea's exports and are also that country's principal importers of key raw materials.

c. *Export trading companies.* You will read in Chapter 11 that the Reagan administration, impressed by the success of the Japanese, Taiwanese, and Korean general trading companies, obtained passage of the Export Trading Company Act. The measure provides the mechanism for creating a new indirect export channel, the **export trading company (ETC).** For the first time in U.S. history, businesses were permitted to join together to export goods and services or offer export-facilitating services without fear of violating antitrust legislation. Bank holding companies also may participate in ETCs. This not only increases the ability of trading companies to finance export transactions but also gives them access to the banks' extensive international information systems. Furthermore, because ETCs can import as well as export, they can engage in countertrade by selling their customers' products in other markets.

export trading company (ETC)
A firm established principally to export domestic goods and services and to help unrelated companies export their products

Any potential exporter may apply to the Department of Commerce for a *certificate of review,* a legal document that provides immunity from state and federal antitrust prosecution and significant protection from certain private antitrust lawsuits. The certificate allows firms and associations to engage in joint price setting and joint bidding and gives them the freedom to divide up export markets among companies and jointly own warranty, service, and training centers in various overseas markets. Note that the benefits of the ETC Act are available to *all exporters,* not just export trading companies.

The Commerce Department has issued over 100 certificates covering 4,400 companies. Most companies that have received certificates are export intermediaries for two or more firms from the same industry, although now the majority of the certificates are being issued to groups of companies. For example, the National Tooling and Machining Association is a national trade association with 3,150 members. The American Film Marketing Association (67 members) is another example.

B. Exporters that buy for their overseas customers.

1. *Export commission agents* represent overseas purchasers, such as import firms and large industrial users. They are paid a commission by the purchaser for acting as resident buyers in industrialized nations.

C. Exporters that buy and sell for their own account.

1. *Export merchants* purchase products directly from the manufacturer and then sell, invoice, and ship them in their own names so that foreign customers have no direct dealings with the manufacturer, as they do in the case of an export agent. If export merchants have an exclusive right to sell the manufacturer's products in an overseas territory, they are generally called *export distributors.* Some EMCs may actually be export distributors for a number of their clients.

2. Sometimes called piggyback or mother hen exporters, **cooperative exporters** are established international manufacturers that sell the products of other companies in foreign markets along with their own. Carriers (exporters) may purchase and resell in their own name, or they may work on a commission basis. Carriers, like EMCs, serve as the export departments for the firms they represent. Large companies, such as General Electric and Borg-Warner, have been acting as piggyback exporters for years. A single carrier usually represents between 10 and 20 suppliers, although there is one large manufacturer of industrial machinery that has more than 1,000.

cooperative exporters
Established international manufacturers that export other manufacturers' goods as well as their own

3. *Webb-Pomerene Associations* are organizations of competing firms that have joined together for the sole purpose of export trade. The Export Trade Act of

1918 provides for the formulation of such groups and generally exempts them from antitrust laws. They are permitted to buy from their members and sell abroad, set export prices, or simply direct the promotional activities that are destined for overseas markets. At this time, there are only 30 associations, of which those in phosphate rock, wood pulp, movies, and sulfur are the most active. Webb-Pomerene Associations failed to become an important export channel because (1) the antitrust exemption was very vague and (2) the exporting of services was not included. The intent of the Export Trading Act is to remedy these deficiencies.

D. Exporters that purchase for foreign users and middlemen.

1. Large foreign users, such as mining, petroleum, and international construction companies, buy for their own use overseas. The purchasing departments of all the worldwide companies are continually buying for their foreign affiliates, and both foreign governments and foreign firms maintain purchasing offices in industrialized countries.

2. *Export resident buyers* perform essentially the same functions as export commission agents. However, they are generally more closely associated with a foreign firm. They may be appointed as the official buying representatives and paid a retainer, or they may even be employees. This is in contrast to the export commission agent, who usually represents a number of overseas buyers and works on a transaction-by-transaction basis.

Direct Exporting

If the firm chooses to do its own exporting, it has four basic types of overseas middlemen from which to choose: (A) manufacturers' agents, (B) distributors, (C) retailers, and (D) trading companies. These may be serviced by sales personnel who either travel to the market or are based in it. If the sales volume is sufficient, a foreign sales company may be established to take the place of the wholesale importer. The manufacturing affiliates of most worldwide companies also import from home country plants or from other subsidiaries products that they themselves do not produce.

manufacturers' agents
Independent sales representatives of various noncompeting suppliers

distributors
Independent importers that buy for their own account for resale

A. *Manufacturers' agents* are residents of the country or region in which they are conducting business for the firm. They represent various noncompeting foreign suppliers, and they take orders in those firms' names. **Manufacturers' agents** usually work on a commission basis, pay their own expenses, and do not assume any financial responsibility. They often stock the products of some of their suppliers, thus combining the functions of agent and wholesale distributor.

B. *Distributors* or wholesale importers are independent merchants that buy for their own account. They import and stock for resale. **Distributors** are usually specialists in a particular field, such as farm equipment or pharmaceuticals. They may be given exclusive representation and, in return, agree not to handle competing brands. Distributors may buy through manufacturers' agents when the exporter employs them, or they may send their orders directly to the exporting firm. Instead of manufacturers' agents, exporters may employ their own salespeople to cover the territory and assist the distributors. For years, worldwide companies such as Caterpillar and Goodyear have utilized field representatives in export territories.

C. *Retailers,* especially of consumer products that require little after-sales servicing, are frequently direct importers. Contact on behalf of the exporter is maintained either by a manufacturers' agent or by the exporter's sales representative based in the territory or traveling from the home office.

D. *Trading companies* are relatively unknown in the United States but are extremely important importers in other parts of the world. In a number of African nations,

trading companies not only are the principal importers of goods ranging from consumer products to capital equipment but also export such raw materials as ore, palm oil, and coffee. In addition, they operate department stores, grocery stores, and agencies for automobiles and farm machinery. Although many trading companies are large, they are in no way comparable in either size or diversification (products and functions performed) to the sogo shosha.

trading companies
Firms that develop international trade and serve as intermediaries between foreign buyers and domestic sellers and vice versa

Trading companies in Brazil, Korea, Taiwan, and Malaysia are a recent development. They are of little use to exporters to those countries inasmuch as their primary function is to promote their own country's exports. On the other hand, the English *importer/factor,* which performs some of the functions of a trading company, is of value to exporters. It will, on behalf of foreign manufacturers, warehouse goods, price them for the local market, deliver anywhere in the country, and factor (buy the seller's accounts receivable). The exporter must still develop the sales, however.

Another form of trading company is owned by the state. State trading companies handle all exports and imports in Vietnam, North Korea, and Cuba, and in noncommunist nations where an industry is a government monopoly, such as petroleum in Mexico, exporters or their agents must deal with these government-owned entities.

Foreign Production

When a firm is selling products produced in the local market, whether they are manufactured by a wholly owned subsidiary, a joint venture, or a contract manufacturer, management is concerned only with the local channels of distribution. Generally, the same types of middlemen are available as in the home country, although the established channels and their manner of operating may differ appreciably from those to which management is accustomed. Differences between the foreign and domestic environmental forces are responsible for this situation.

Wholesale Institutions

In other developed nations, as in the United States, the marketer will be able to select wholesalers that take title to the goods (merchant wholesalers, rack jobbers, drop shippers, cash-and-carry wholesalers, truck jobbers) and those that do not (agents, brokers). However, just as in the United States, as retailers have become larger, they have sought to bypass wholesalers and purchase directly from local manufacturers and foreign suppliers.

Diversity of Wholesaling Structures. Generally, wholesaling and retailing structures vary with the stage of economic development. In less developed countries (LDC) that depend on imports to supply the market, the importing wholesalers are large and few in number and the channels are long. Historically, many of the importers were trading companies formed by international companies to import the machinery and supplies required by their local operation and to export raw materials for use in the home country plants. To obtain distributor prices, they were required by their suppliers to sell to other customers as well. Some of these operations became extremely diversified, owning automobile and industrial machinery agencies, grocery stores, and department stores. They literally could and did supply a complete city and an industry with all of its requirements.

As colonies became nations, the new governments began applying pressure to convert these trading companies to local ownership. Furthermore, these countries were industrializing, which meant more goods were being produced locally and fewer goods were being imported. Many of the local manufacturers were able to take control of the channels from the import jobber. To obtain more extensive market coverage, they canceled the importing wholesaler's exclusivity and gave their product lines to new wholesalers, many of which were formed by ex-employees of the importer. As economic development continued, markets broadened, permitting greater specialization by more and smaller wholesalers.

parallel importers
Wholesalers that import products independently of manufacturer-authorized importers or buy goods for export and divert them to the domestic market

Parallel Importers and Gray Market Goods. **Parallel importers** are wholesalers that import products independently of the manufacturer-authorized importer or that buy products for export and then sell them in the domestic market. Four transactions are possible:

1. An importer buys from an overseas dealer in the home country. This occurs when authorized dealers in the importer's country charge more for the import than do the home country dealers.
2. An unauthorized dealer imports from the foreign subsidiary and competes in the home country against locally made products. Honda and other Japanese manufacturers are legitimately *reverse exporting:* exporting American-made products to Japan.
3. An unauthorized importer buys products overseas from the home office and competes with the local subsidiary. Most international companies can price lower for the export market than for the domestic market because they have less promotional expense. The subsidiary's price may be higher than the home office's price because of lower production volume, higher raw material costs, and so forth.
4. Goods are bought for export but are sold on the domestic market instead, creating parallel trading, or a "gray market." Gray market goods are not counterfeits, although differences may exist between these export-oriented goods and goods intended for domestic markets (for example, differences may involve warranty coverage or compliance with regulations such as environmental standards for automobile emissions). Gray markets may occur when a manufacturer's export prices are lower than its domestic prices. For example, Quality King Distributors in New York annually sells millions of dollars' worth of items such as Pampers, Tylenol, and Johnson & Johnson toothbrushes to dealers at prices 30 percent lower than domestic wholesalers can. The firm buys such products from exporters that sell to it rather than sell them in export markets. In some cases the merchandise never physically leaves the domestic market, while at other times the items are actually sent to a foreign port, where they may be repackaged and shipped back to the United States as "American goods returned." The false exporter then sells it to an American retailer at a price lower than the usual wholesaler price in the United States but higher than the export price.[56]

gray market
The sale of goods that are either legal-but-unauthorized imports bearing domestic manufacturers' trade names or exports that have been diverted to the domestic market

Although American manufacturers have gone to court to try to stop these **gray market** operations, they have had only limited success. There are gray markets in numerous products, including perfume, photographic equipment, cigarettes, electronic goods, and high-fashion apparel. U.S. gray market sales are estimated to total more than $10 billion annually.[57]

Retail Institutions

The variation in size and number of retailers among countries is even greater than that for wholesalers. Generally, *the less developed the country, the more numerous, more specialized, and smaller the retailers.* Exceptions to this generalization are France, Japan, and Italy, where the extensive presence of small retailers has been maintained by stringent laws that have kept the expansion of supermarkets and mass merchandisers at a rate much lower than that of similarly developed countries. When retailing methods in the developing and developed nations are compared, the following generalizations are notable: *in going up the scale from developing to developed nations, one encounters more mass merchandising; more self-service, large-sized units; and a trend toward retailer concentration.*

hypermarkets
Huge combination supermarkets/discount stores where soft and hard goods are sold

Typical of this trend is the emergence of the European **hypermarket**—a huge combination supermarket/discount house with five or six acres of floor space where both soft goods and hard goods are sold. A similar type of outlet in Japan, the **superstore,** is a recent phenomenon that now accounts for over 10 percent of all retail sales there. In Scandinavia and Switzerland, there is also a marked trend toward retailer concentration, but it is occurring for the most part through retailer-controlled voluntary chains and consumer cooperatives rather than through company-owned chains.

superstores
Name given to hypermarkets in Japan, some parts of Europe, and the United States

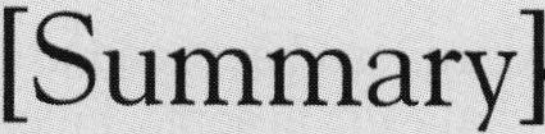

[Summary]

Appreciate the magnitude of international trade and how it has grown.

The volume of international trade in goods and services measured in current dollars approached $7 trillion in 1999. Merchandise exports, at $5.5 trillion, were more than 17 times what they were in 1970.

Identify the direction of trade, or who trades with whom.

The percentage of total exports of all the categories of developed nations to other developed nations is declining with the exception of Canada's. Most of Canada's exports to developed countries go to the United States, and they have been increasing since the U.S.–Canada Free Trade Agreement went into effect. Developing nations are selling more to each other, and U.S.–developing country trade is on the rise.

Explain the size, growth, and direction of U.S. foreign direct investment.

The book value of foreign direct investment has grown and now totals over $4.7 trillion. The American FDI is 1.7 times that of the United Kingdom, the next largest investor, and 2.7 times that of Germany, the third-largest investor. The proportion of global foreign direct investment accounted for by the United States has been declining, falling from 36 percent in 1985 to 24 percent in 1999. The direction of FDI follows the direction of foreign trade; that is, developed nations invest in each other just as they trade with each other. Note that because of the new business environment, many international firms are dispersing the activities of their manufacturing systems to locations closer to available resources. The decision where to locate may be either an FDI or a trade decision.

Identify who invests and how much is invested in the United States.

Foreign direct investment in the United States rose from $185 billion in 1985 to nearly $1 trillion in 1999. Firms from just six nations—United Kingdom, Japan, Netherlands, Germany, Canada, and France—own about three-quarters of the total stock of foreign direct investment in the United States.

Understand the reasons for entering foreign markets.

Companies enter foreign markets (exporting to and manufacturing in) to increase sales and profits and to protect markets, sales, and profits. Foreign firms often buy American firms to acquire technology and marketing know-how. Foreign investment also enables a company to diversify geographically.

Understand the international market entry methods.

The two basic methods of entering foreign markets are exporting to and manufacturing in them. Exporting may be done directly or indirectly. A firm may become involved in foreign production through various methods: (1) wholly owned subsidiaries, (2) joint ventures, (3) licensing, (4) franchising, and (5) contract manufacturing.

Comprehend that globalization of an international firm occurs over at least seven dimensions and that a company can be partially global in some dimensions and completely global in others.

A firm can have, and usually does have, an international strategy that is partially multidomestic in some dimensions and partially global in others. Management must decide the extent to which the firm should globalize along each dimension.

Discuss the channel members available to companies that export indirectly or directly or manufacture overseas.

Channel members are available to those who (1) indirectly export or are exporters that sell for manufacturers, (2) buy for their overseas customers, or (3) purchase for foreign users or middlemen. Direct exporters use manufacturers' agents, distributors, retailers, and trading companies. Firms that manufacture overseas generally have the same kinds of channel members they have in their domestic market, although their manner of operation may be different from what they are accustomed to.

Explain the structural trends in wholesaling and retailing.

The retailing trend in Europe and Japan, as well as in many developing nations, is toward more discounters. Rigid, inefficient distribution systems that depend on high prices are breaking up. Small retailers as well as large department stores are losing out to discounters. Wholesalers are being bypassed by retailers.

[Key Words]

foreign sourcing (p. 60)
portfolio investment (p. 69)
direct investment (p. 69)
preferential trading arrangement (p. 77)
in-bond plants (maquiladoras) (p. 80)
North American Free Trade Agreement (NAFTA) (p. 80)
growth triangles (p. 81)
indirect exporting (p. 85)
direct exporting (p. 85)
sales company (p. 85)
joint venture (p. 87)
management contract (p. 89)
licensing (p. 90)
franchising (p. 91)
contract manufacturing (p. 91)
strategic alliances (p. 92)
sogo shosha (p. 96)
export trading company (ETC) (p. 97)
cooperative exporters (p. 97)
manufacturers' agents (p. 98)
distributors (p. 98)
trading companies (p. 99)
parallel importers (p. 100)
gray market (p. 100)
hypermarkets (p. 100)
superstores (p. 101)

[Questions]

1. The greater part of international trade consists of an exchange of raw materials from developing nations for manufactured goods from developed nations. True or false? Explain.
2. The volume of exports has increased, but the ranking of U.S. trading partners in order of importance remains the same year after year. True or false? Of what use is this information to a businessperson?
3. What is the value of analyzing foreign trade data? For example, what should the quadrupling in real terms of exports in just 29 years indicate to businesspeople?
4. Knowing that a nation is a major trading partner of another signifies what to a marketing analyst?
5. Why has FDI historically followed foreign trade? What about the new international business environment is causing this path to market expansion to change?

6. How can a firm protect its domestic market by investing overseas?
7. How is it possible for a firm to be multidomestic on one dimension of globalization and global on another?
8. Under what conditions might a company prefer a joint venture to a wholly owned subsidiary when making a foreign investment?
9. a. Why would the foreign partner in a joint venture wish to have a management contract with the local partner?
   b. Why would a global or multinational require a wholly owned foreign subsidiary to sign a management contract when it already owns the subsidiary?
10. What are in-bond plants? Why might they be an attractive alternative for a manufacturing company?
11. How do sogo shosha differ from their American counterparts?

[Internet Exercises]

Using the Internet

1. a. What are the five largest importing nations of U.S. exports? What are the top five imports of each country?
   b. What are the five largest foreign suppliers to the United States? What are the top five products that each sells to the United States?
2. a. According to the U.S. Census Bureau's *FT900—U.S. International Trade in Goods and Services* final report for 1999, Exhibit 6 (www.census.gov/foreign-trade/Press-Release/99_press_releases/Final_Revisions_1999/exh6.txt) and Exhibit 7 (www.census.gov/foreign-trade/Press-Release/99_press_releases/Final_Revisions_1999/exh7.txt), in 1999 was there a trade surplus (exports greater than imports) or a deficit in the following industries: (1) telecommunications equipment, (2) semiconductors, (3) computers, (4) wine and related products, (5) lumber, (6) records, tapes, and disks, and (7) auto vehicles, parts, and engines?
   b. How much was the surplus or deficit for each of these categories?

[Minicase 2.1]

Method of Entry for Local Manufacturing— The McGrew Company

The McGrew Company, a manufacturer of peanut combines, has for years sold a substantial number of machines in Brazil. However, a Brazilian firm has begun to manufacture them, and McGrew's local distributor has told Jim Allen, the president, that if McGrew expects to maintain its share of the market, it will also have to manufacture locally. Allen is in a quandary. The market is too good to lose, but McGrew has had no experience with foreign manufacturing operations. Because Brazilian sales and repairs have been handled by the distributor, no one in McGrew has had any firsthand experience in that country.

Allen has made some rough calculations that indicate the firm can make money by manufacturing in Brazil, but the firm's lack of marketing expertise in the country troubles him. He calls in Joan Beal, the export manager, and asks her to prepare a list of all the options open to McGrew, with their advantages and disadvantages. Allen also asks Beal to indicate her preference.

1. Assume you are Joan Beal. Prepare a list of all the options and give the advantages and disadvantages of each.
2. Which of the options would you recommend?
3. Assuming the president's calculations are correct and a factory to produce locally the number of machines that McGrew now exports to Brazil will offer a satisfactory return on investment, what special information about Brazil will you want to gather?

[Chapter] 3

Economic Theories of International Business

"If a foreign country can supply us with a commodity cheaper than we ourselves can make it, better buy it of them with some part of our own industry, employed in a way in which we have some advantage."
—Adam Smith, *The Wealth of Nations*

Concept Previews

After reading this chapter, you should be able to:

- **understand** the theories that attempt to explain why certain goods are traded internationally
- **comprehend** the arguments for imposing trade restrictions
- **explain** the two basic kinds of import restrictions: tariff and nontariff trade barriers
- **state** the agreements reached during the Uruguay Round
- **appreciate** the relevance of the changing status of tariff and nontariff barriers to businesspeople
- **recognize** the weaknesses of GNP/capita as an economic indicator
- **identify** the common characteristics of developing nations
- **understand** the new definition of economic development, which includes more than economic growth
- **understand** why some governments are changing from an import substitution strategy to one of export promotion and the implications of this change for businesspeople
- **explain** some of the theories of foreign direct investment

Christian Lagereck/Tony Stone Images

Knowing Economic Theory Is Essential

Business managers must have a good knowledge of economic theory to be able to understand a nation's development strategy, which depends greatly on the beliefs and education of the government's economic planners. By closely following the actions and speeches of government leaders, managers often can discover the economic theories on which those actions and speeches are based. If they know the underlying theories, they can anticipate changes in government strategy and use that knowledge to their advantage. As an example, look at what happened when Chile's new government took over from the Marxist regime of Salvador Allende.

The economy was in a shambles. Inflation was running over 1,000 percent annually, and the nation's debt load was totally unmanageable. The previous government had been following the policy of many developing nations at that time—heavy involvement in the economy. This included placing high import duties on imports to protect local industry, levying high income taxes on the private sector to obtain funds for government-directed investment, and granting huge subsidies to selected industries.

Realizing that drastic changes had to be made, the new government appointed a group of conservative Chilean economists to design a new program. Known as the Chicago Boys for having graduated from the University of Chicago, they were followers of the free-market teachings of its economics professor and Nobel Prize winner Milton Friedman.

The contents of the Chicago Boys' program and its impact on Chilean business did not surprise anyone with a knowledge of economic theory. In fact, much of what they proposed was based on the theory of comparative advantage. Managers who understood the significance of the proposals knew that Chile soon would have a free-market economy which would require a massive restructuring of Chilean manufacturing plants.

One of the most important reforms recommended by the economists and put into effect by the government was to reduce import duties from a high of 1,000 percent to a basic level of 10 percent. Moreover, all other import barriers were removed so that virtually anyone was free to import anything. As a result, manufacturers and growers were forced to compete in world markets to stay in business. In addition, the lower import duties reduced the cost of imported capital equipment, which encouraged business investment. What was the reaction of the managers who were prepared to change to the new system?

The president of Chile's largest appliance maker, whose industry had been protected from foreign competition by a 1,000 percent import duty, gave his opinion of the new program: "We used to have 5,000 workers and an annual productivity of only $9,000 per worker. Now we have 1,860 workers and a productivity of $43,000 per worker, and we are finally showing a profit."

It was no surprise to those with a knowledge of economics that there would be a contraction of local industry when companies lost their protection from imports. Although the leading appliance maker mentioned above was able to compete after losing its import protection, a number of other local appliance makers were forced to go out of business or contract their operations. "We're going to lose a large part of our appliance industry," conceded Alvaro Bardon, a 37-year-old Chicago Boy who was then the head of the central bank of Chile, "and also our electronics industry and our automobile assembly plants." Bardon was hardly disappointed, however. "Those are products we should be importing," he said. "We have other things based on our farm products, our timberlands, our fisheries, and our mineral resources that we should be making because they give us a natural advantage over other countries."

How successful were these free-market measures taken by the government? Exports certainly increased just as economic theory says they would—from less than $2 billion in 1976 to $19 billion in 1998. Gross national product (GNP) per capita rose over the same period from $1,050 to $5,000. Its purchasing power was equivalent to a GNP/capita of $8,500. Chile's latest Country Commercial Guide (CCG) prepared by the combined efforts of various U.S. government agencies, reported, "Chile is among the region's most dynamic and promising markets. Market-led reforms have yielded 16 straight years of economic growth which averaged 8.1 percent annually from 1988–1997. Prudent economic policy-making has secured long-term stability unknown elsewhere in Latin America." ■

Sources: Various tables in *World Development Indicators 2000* (Washington, DC: World Bank, 2000); Dennis R. Appleyard and Alfred J. Field, Jr., *International Economics,* 2nd ed. (Chicago: Irwin, 1995); *Country Commercial Guide–Chile* (Washington, DC: U.S. Commercial Service, 2000), www1.usatrade.gov/website/ccg.nsf (August 23, 2000); and "Why Chile's Economy Roared While the World's Slumbered," *The Wall Street Journal,* January 22, 1993, p. A11.

The economic program that the Chilean economists put into effect is a practical application of the keystone of international trade theory—the law of comparative advantage. Note the education of the head of Chile's central bank. Economists are commonly found in governments as policymakers and advisers to government leaders worldwide. When they have a particularly strong influence in government affairs, they are frequently dubbed with such pejorative names as the "Chicago Boys" in Chile, "tecnicos" in Mexico, and the "Berkeley Mafia" (economists educated at the University of California–Berkeley) in Indonesia.

What is the significance for international businesspeople? For one thing, since they frequently will be dealing with government officials trained in economics, businesspeople must be prepared to speak their language. When presenting plans requiring governmental approval, businesspeople must take care that the plans are economically sound, for they are almost certain to be studied by economists and will often need to be approved by them. Marketers proposing large projects to government planners must be aware that the key determinant now is economic efficiency rather than mere financial soundness.[1] Moreover, as you have seen in the case of Chile, knowledge of economic concepts, especially in the areas of (1) international trade, (2) economic development, and (3) foreign direct investment, frequently provide insights into future government action.

International Trade Theory

Why do nations trade? This question and the equally important proposition of predicting the direction, composition, and volume of goods traded are what international trade theory attempts to address. Interestingly, as is the case with numerous economic writings, the first formulation of international trade theory was politically motivated. Adam Smith, incensed by government intervention and control over both domestic and foreign trade, published *An Inquiry into the Nature and Causes of the Wealth of Nations* (1776), in which he tried to destroy the mercantilist philosophy.

Mercantilism

Mercantilism, the economic philosophy Smith attacked, held that it was essential to a nation's welfare to accumulate a stock of precious metals. These metals were, in the mercantilists' view, the only source of wealth. Because England had no mines, the mercantilists looked to international trade to supply gold and silver. The government established economic policies that promoted exports and stifled imports, resulting in a trade surplus to be paid for in gold and silver. Import restrictions such as import duties reduced imports, while government subsidies to exporters increased exports. Those acts created a trade surplus.

mercantilism
An economic philosophy based on the belief that (1) a nation's wealth depends on accumulated treasure, usually gold, and (2) to increase wealth, government policies should promote exports and discourage imports

Although the mercantilist era ended in the late 1700s, its arguments live on. A "favorable" trade balance still means that a nation exports more goods and services than it imports. In balance-of-payment accounting, an export that brings dollars to this country is called *positive,* but imports that cause dollar outflow are labeled *negative.*

An example of modern-day mercantilism, called *economic nationalism* by some, was the industrial policy based on heavy state intervention that the socialists were creating for France. They nationalized key industries and banks so as to use the power of the state as both (1) stockholder and financier and (2) customer and marketer to revitalize the nation's industrial base. With nearly one-third of France's productive capacity and 70 percent of its high-tech electronic capabilities in the hands of the government, its power was approaching the level of state intervention in the 17th century. Some writers were calling this *high-tech mercantilism.* In 1986, after five years of little growth and high unemployment, the government reversed its policy when a conservative was elected premier.

In the United States, many businesspeople believe that Japan, because of its protectionism, remains largely a nearly impenetrable market—a present-day "fortress of mercantilism." American businesspeople are concerned that Japan's barriers to their imports are the result of Japanese insularity, traditional preoccupation with self-sufficiency, and "us against them" mentality. A U.S. secretary of commerce once said, "They tell us they have to protect their markets because of their culture. They haven't joined the world yet." Comments from the Japanese seem to confirm what some Americans are saying. "The public is not in favor of perfect markets," says a Japanese bank manager. "We would like to preserve the substance of our culture. If we move to free trade, we may lose Japanese virtue in the process."[2]

Theory of Absolute Advantage

Adam Smith claimed that market forces, not government controls, should determine the direction, volume, and composition of international trade. He argued that under free, unregulated trade, each nation should specialize in producing those goods it could produce most efficiently (had an absolute advantage, either natural or acquired). Some of these goods would be exported to pay for imports of goods that could be produced more efficiently elsewhere. Smith showed by his example of **absolute advantage** that both nations would gain from trade.

absolute advantage
The capability of one nation to produce more of a good with the same amount of input than another country

An Example

Assume there is perfect competition and no transportation costs in a world of two countries and two products. Suppose that (1) one unit of input (combination of land, labor, and capital) can produce the following quantities of rice and automobiles in the United States and Japan, (2) each nation has two input units it can use to produce either rice or automobiles, and (3) each country uses one unit of input to produce each product. If neither country imports or exports, the quantities shown in the table are also what is available for local consumption. The total output of both nations is 4 tons of rice and six automobiles.

Commodity	United States	Japan	Total
Tons of rice	3	1	4
Automobiles	2	4	6

In the United States, 3 tons of rice or two automobiles can be produced with one unit of output. Therefore, 3 tons of rice should have the same price as two automobiles. In Japan, however, since only 1 ton of rice can be produced with the input unit that can produce four automobiles, 1 ton of rice should cost as much as four automobiles.

The United States has an absolute advantage in rice production (3 to 1), while Japan's absolute advantage is in automobile manufacturing (4 to 2). Will anyone anywhere give the Japanese automaker more than 1 ton of rice for four automobiles? According to the example, all American rice producers should because they can get only two automobiles for 3 tons of rice at home. Similarly, Japanese automakers, once they learn that they can obtain more than 1 ton of rice for every four automobiles in the United States, will be eager to trade Japanese autos for American rice.

Each Country Specializes

Suppose each nation decides to use its resources to produce only the product at which it is more efficient. The following table shows each nation's output. Note that with the same quantity of input units, the total output is now greater.

Commodity	United States	Japan	Total
Tons of rice	6	0	6
Automobiles	0	8	8

Terms of Trade (Ratio of International Prices)

With specialization, now the total production of both goods is greater, but to consume both products, the two countries must trade some of their surplus. What are the limits within which both countries are willing to trade? Clearly, the Japanese automakers will trade some of their cars for rice if they can get more than the 1 ton of rice that they get for four cars in Japan. Likewise, the American rice growers will trade their rice for Japanese automobiles if they get a car for less than the 1.5 tons of rice it costs them in the United States.

If the two nations take the mean of the two trading limits so that each shares equally in the benefits of trade, they will agree to swap 1.25 tons of rice for one car. Both will gain from specialization because each now has the following quantities:

Commodity	United States	Japan	Total
Tons of rice	3	3	6
Automobiles	4	4	8

Gains from Specialization and Trade

Because each nation specialized in producing the product at which it was more efficient and then traded its surplus for goods that it could not produce as efficiently, both gained the following:

Commodity	United States	Japan
Tons of rice		2
Automobiles	2	

Certainly, both nations have gained by trading. But what if one country has an absolute advantage in the production of *both* rice and automobiles? Will there still be a basis for trade?

Theory of Comparative Advantage

Ricardo demonstrated in 1817 that even though a nation held an absolute advantage in the production of two goods, the two countries could still trade with advantages for each as long as the less efficient nation was not *equally* less efficient in the production of both goods.[3] Let us slightly change our first example so that now the United States has an absolute advantage in producing *both* rice and automobiles. Note that compared to the United States, Japan is less inefficient in automaking than in producing rice. Therefore, it has a relative advantage, or **comparative advantage**, according to Ricardo, in producing automobiles.

comparative advantage
A nation having absolute disadvantages in the production of two goods with respect to another nation has a comparative or relative advantage in the production of the good in which its absolute disadvantage is less

Commodity	United States	Japan	Total
Tons of rice	6	3	9
Automobiles	5	4	9

Each Country Specializes

If each country specializes in what it does best, its output will be as follows:

Commodity	United States	Japan	Total
Tons of rice	12	0	12
Automobiles	0	8	8

Terms of Trade

In this case, the terms of trade will be somewhere between the 1 ton of rice for five-sixths of an auto that American rice growers must pay in the United States and the one and one-third automobiles Japanese automakers must pay for 1 ton of Japanese rice.

Let us assume that the traders agree on an exchange rate of one car for 1 ton of rice. Both will gain from this exchange and specialization, as the following table shows:

Commodity	United States	Japan
Tons of rice	8	4
Automobiles	4	4

Note that this trade left the United States with some surplus rice and one fewer automobile than it had before. Japan has more rice and the same quantity of automobiles. However, the American rice growers should be able to trade the 2 tons of surplus rice for two automobiles elsewhere. Then the final result will be as follows:

Commodity	United States	Japan
Tons of rice	6	4
Automobiles	6	4

Gains from Specialization and Trade

Gains from specialization and trade in this case are the following:

Commodity	United States	Japan
Tons of rice		1
Automobiles	1	

Production Possibility Frontiers

We can also illustrate the gains from trade graphically, using production possibility frontiers. Figure 3.1 graphs the Japanese and U.S. production possibility frontiers using constant costs for simplicity. These curves, in the absence of trade, also illustrate the possible combinations of goods for consumption. Before trade, the United States might be producing and consuming 6 tons of rice and five automobiles (point A), while Japan is producing and consuming 3 tons of rice and four automobiles (point A).

With each nation specializing in the production of the goods in which it has a comparative advantage and trading its surplus with the other, both nations are able to consume at point B. The shaded areas under each curve indicate the gains from trade.

The simple concept of comparative advantage is the basis for international trade.

Note that in our examples we mentioned a unit of input. This is a more modern version of the examples of Ricardo and Smith, who used only labor input. They did so because at that time only labor was considered important in calculating production costs.[4] Also, no consideration was given to the possibility of producing the same goods with different combinations of factors and no explanation was given as to why production costs differed. Not until 1933 did Ohlin, a Swedish economist building on work begun by the economist Heckscher, develop the theory of **factor endowment**.[5]

factor endowment
Heckscher-Ohlin theory that countries export products requiring large amounts of their abundant production factors and import products requiring large amounts of their scarce production factors

[Figure 3.1] **Production and Consumption Possibility Frontiers Before and After Trade**

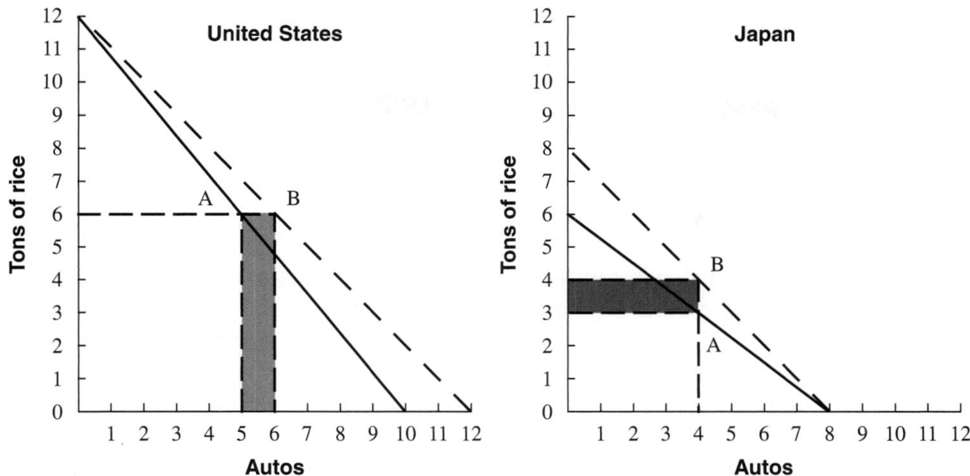

Heckscher-Ohlin Theory of Factor Endowment

The Heckscher-Ohlin theory states that international and interregional differences in production costs occur because of differences in the supply of production factors. Those goods that require a large amount of the abundant—thus less costly—factor will have lower production costs, enabling those goods to be sold for less in international markets. For example, China, relatively well endowed with labor compared to the Netherlands, ought to concentrate on producing labor-intensive goods; the Netherlands, with relatively more capital than labor, should specialize in capital-intensive products. When these countries trade, each will obtain the goods that require large amounts of the relatively scarce production factor at a lower price, and both will benefit from the transaction.

How useful is this theory for explaining present-day trading patterns? Countries with relatively large amounts of land (such as Australia) do export land-intensive products (such as grain and cattle), whereas Hong Kong exports labor-intensive goods.[6] There are exceptions, however, due in part to Ohlin's assumptions. One assumption was that the prices of the factors depend only on the factor endowment. We know this is untrue. Factor prices are not set in a perfect market. Legislated minimum wages and benefits force the cost of labor to rise to a point greater than the value of the product that many workers can produce. Investment tax credits reduce the cost of capital below market cost, and so forth. As a result, factor prices do not fully reflect factor supply.

Ohlin also assumed that a given technology is universally available, but this is not so. There is always a lag between the introduction of a new production method and its worldwide application. As a result, superior technology often permits a nation to produce goods at a cost lower than that of a country better endowed with the required factor. A closely related assumption was that a given product is either labor- or capital-intensive. Yet anyone who has watched construction methods in less developed nations knows that wet concrete can be poured either by a gang of laborers with buckets or by a crane and its operator.

Leontief Paradox

A study made in 1953 by the economist Wassily Leontief disputed the usefulness of the Heckscher-Ohlin theory as a predictor of the direction of trade. The study, known as the *Leontief paradox,* found that the United States, one of the most capital-intensive countries in the world, was exporting labor-intensive products. Economists have speculated that this occurred because the United States exports technology-intensive products produced by highly skilled labor requiring a large capital investment to educate and train and imports goods made with mature technology requiring capital-intensive mass production processes operated by unskilled labor. A study by the Harvard economists Sachs and Shatz in 1994 did in fact show that the United States has increased its exports of skill-intensive goods to developing nations while reducing its production of unskilled goods.[7] Another possible explanation is that many products may be produced by either capital- or labor-intensive processes, as was noted in the previous paragraph.

Heckscher-Ohlin also ignored transportation costs, but there are goods for which freight charges are so high that the landed cost (export sales price plus transportation charges) is greater than the cost of a locally made product. In that case, there will be little trade. Why not say there will be no trade?

Differences in Taste

It is because of a demand-side construct that is always difficult to deal with in economic theory and that we have so far neglected—*differences in taste.* Businesspeople, however, cannot neglect this difference, which enables trade to flow in a direction completely contrary to that predicted by the theory of comparative advantage—from high- to low-cost nations. France sells us wine, cosmetics, clothing, and even drinking water, all of which are produced here and generally sold at lower prices. Germany and Italy send Porsches and Maseratis to one of the largest automobile producers in the world. We buy these goods not only on the basis of price, the implied independent variable in the theory we have been examining, but also because of taste preferences.

We have presented the theory of comparative advantage without mentioning money; however, a nation's comparative advantage can be affected by differences between the costs of production factors in that country's currency and their costs in other currencies. As we shall see in the next section, money can change the direction of trade.

Introducing Money

Suppose the total cost of land, labor, and capital to produce the daily output of rice or automobiles in the example on absolute advantage is $10,000 in the United States and 2.5 million yen in Japan. The cost per unit is as follows:

	Price per Unit	
Commodity	**United States**	**Japan**
Ton of rice	$\frac{\$10{,}000}{3} = \$3{,}330/\text{ton}$	$\frac{2.5 \text{ million yen}}{1} = 2.5 \text{ million yen/ton}$
Automobiles	$\frac{\$10{,}000}{2} = \$5{,}000/\text{auto}$	$\frac{2.5 \text{ million yen}}{4} = 0.625 \text{ million yen/auto}$

To determine whether it is more advantageous to buy locally or to import, the traders need to know the prices in their own currencies. To convert from foreign to domestic currency, they use the *exchange rate.*

Exchange Rate

exchange rate
The price of one currency stated in terms of another currency

The **exchange rate** is the price of one currency stated in terms of the other. If the prevailing rate is $1 = 250 yen, then 1 yen must be worth 0.004 dollar.* Using the exchange rate of $1 = 250 yen, the prices in the preceding example appear to the U.S. trader as follows:

	Price per Unit (dollars)	
Commodity	**United States**	**Japan**
Ton of rice	$3,330	$10,000
Automobile	5,000	2,500

*If $1 = 250 yen, to find the value of 1 yen in dollars, divide both sides of the equation by 250. Then 1 yen = 1/250 = $0.004.

The American rice producers can earn $6,670 more by exporting rice to Japan than they can by selling locally, but can the Japanese automakers gain by exporting to the United States? To find out, they must convert the American prices to Japanese yen.

	Price per Unit (yen)	
Commodity	United States	Japan
Ton of rice	0.83 million yen	2.5 million yen
Automobile	1.25 million yen	0.625 million yen

It is apparent that the Japanese automakers will export cars to the United States because they can sell at the higher price of 1.25 million yen. The American automobile manufacturers, however, will need some very strong sales arguments to sell in the United States if they are to overcome the $2,500 price differential. Ricardo did not consider this possibility; in his time, products were considered homogeneous and therefore were sold primarily on the basis of price.

Influence of Exchange Rate

Rice to Japan and cars to the United States will be the direction of trade as long as the exchange rate remains in a range around $1 = 250 yen. But if the dollar strengthens to $1 = 750 yen, the American rice will cost as much in yen as does the Japanese rice, and importation will cease. On the other hand, should the dollar weaken to $1 = 125 yen, then a Japanese car will cost $5,000 to American traders, and they will have little reason to import.

Actually, when the dollar reached 100 yen in 1993, sales of Japanese cars dropped as the manufacturers were forced to increase sharply the dollar prices of their exports to the United States in order to maintain their yen profits. Because their cars produced in the United States contain so many Japanese parts, they had to increase these prices as well. Analysts figure that by 1993 Japanese cars cost $2,500 more than their American counterparts.[8] The following example demonstrates the impact of the yen's appreciation against the dollar on the dollar prices of Japanese imports.

> Suppose Toyota wanted 3,000,000 yen for its Camry in 1985. At an exchange rate of 250 yen = $1, the company would have had to charge $12,000 for the car. To get 3,000,000 yen for the car in 1994 with the exchange rate at 100 yen = $1, it would have to charge $30,000 (3,000,000 yen ÷ 100 yen/$).

Another way a nation can avoid losing markets and regain competitiveness in world markets is through **currency devaluation** (lowering its price in terms of other currencies). Note that this leaves the domestic prices unchanged.

currency devaluation
Lowering its price in terms of other currencies

> In the 1980s, Mexico, which depends on American tourists for a large part of its foreign exchange earnings, was faced with losing this business because inflation had driven peso prices so high that at the rate of 12.5 pesos = $1, dollar prices to the Americans were excessive. Mexican officials had three alternatives: (1) deflate to drive peso prices down (time-consuming and painful to the Mexicans), (2) lower prices by government edict (bureaucratic difficulties as with any system of price controls), or (3) devalue the peso. Overnight the rate was decreased to 25 pesos = $1, and without disturbing the peso prices, the prices in dollars were halved. Suddenly, trips to Mexico were a bargain for Americans.

The international trade theory we have been discussing was the only explanation of trade available to us until the 1960s, when a new concept—the international product life cycle—was formulated.[9] Note that this concept, unlike the Heckscher-Ohlin theory, applies only to manufactured goods.

International Product Life Cycle (IPLC)

This concept, which is related to the product life cycle, concerns the role of innovation in trade patterns. It can be applied to new product introduction by firms in any of the industrialized nations, but because more new products have been successfully introduced

[Figure 3.2] International Product Life Cycle

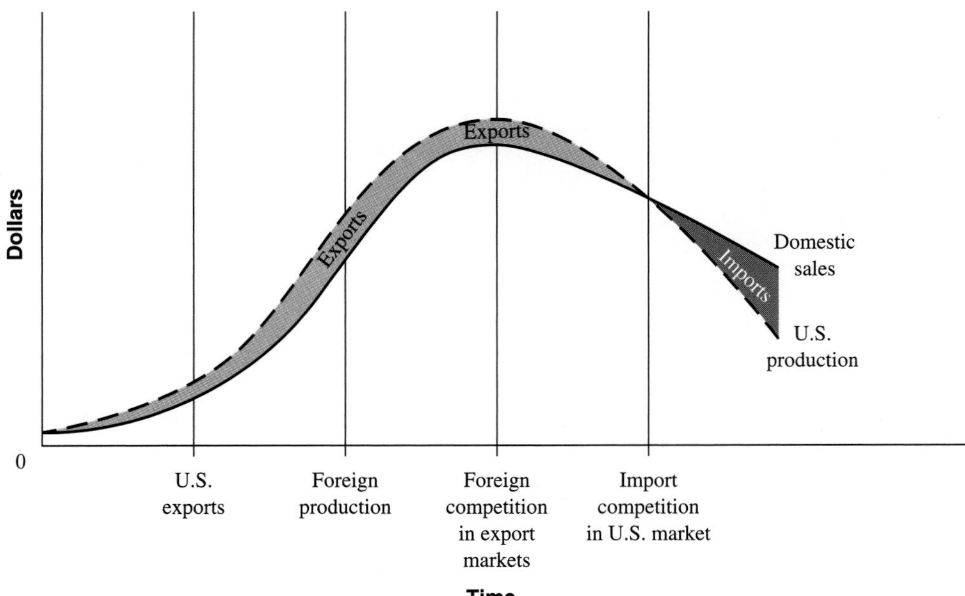

international product life cycle (IPLC)
A theory explaining why a product that begins as a nation's export eventually becomes its import

on a commercial scale in the United States, let us examine the **international product life cycle (IPLC)** as it applies to this country. The four stages through which a new product is said to pass are illustrated in Figure 3.2 and described as follows.

1. *U.S. exports.* Because the United States possesses the largest population of high-income consumers in the world, competition for their patronage is intense. Manufacturers are therefore forced to search constantly for better ways to satisfy their customers' needs. To provide new products, companies maintain large research and development laboratories, which must be in constant contact with suppliers of the materials they need for product development. The fact that their suppliers are also in this country facilitates the contact.[10] In the early stages of the product life cycle, the design and the production methods are changing. By being close to the market, management can react quickly to customer feedback. These factors combine to make the United States a leader in new product introduction. For a while, American firms will be the only manufacturers of the product; overseas customers, as they learn of the product, will therefore have to buy from American firms. The export market develops.

2. *Foreign production begins.* Overseas consumers, especially those in developed nations, have similar needs and the ability to purchase the product. Export volume grows and becomes large enough to support local production. If the innovator is a multinational firm, it will be sending its subsidiaries new product information with complete details on how to produce it. Where there are no affiliates, foreign businesspeople, as they learn of the product, will obtain licenses for its production. Foreign production will begin. The American firm will still be exporting to those markets where there is no production, but its export growth will diminish.

3. *Foreign competition in export markets.* Later, as early foreign manufacturers gain experience in marketing and production, their costs will fall. Saturation of their local markets will cause them to look for buyers elsewhere. They may even be able to undersell the American producers if they enjoy an advantage in labor or raw material costs. In this stage, foreign firms are competing in export markets, and as a result, American export sales will continue to decline.

4. *Import competition in the United States.* If domestic and export sales enable foreign producers to attain the economies of scale enjoyed by the American firm, they may reach a point where they can compete in quality and undersell American firms in the American market. From that point on, the U.S. market will be served by imports only. Black-and-white television sets are an example of such a product.

The authors of the IPLC concept also claim that this cycle may be repeated as the less developed countries (LDC) with still lower labor costs obtain the technology and thus acquire a cost advantage over the more industrialized nations. Although little research has been done to substantiate the IPLC concept, the World Bank study mentioned previously seems to provide a plausible reason for these changes in production locations.

> With countries progressing on the comparative advantage scale, their exports can supplement the exports of countries that graduate to a higher level. . . A case in point is Japan, whose comparative advantage has shifted towards highly capital-intensive exports. In turn, developing countries with a relatively high human capital endowment, such as Korea and Taiwan, can take Japan's place in exporting relatively human capital-intensive products, and countries with a relatively high physical capital endowment, such as Brazil and Mexico, can take Japan's place in exporting relatively physical capital-intensive products. Finally, countries at lower levels of development can supplant the middle-level countries in exporting unskilled labor-intensive commodities.[11]

Some Newer Explanations for the Direction of Trade

Economies of Scale and the Experience Curve

In the 1920s, economists began to consider the fact that most industries benefit from economies of scale; that is, as a plant gets larger and output increases, the unit cost of production decreases. This occurs because larger and more efficient equipment can be employed, companies can obtain volume discounts on their larger-volume purchases, and fixed costs such as those of research and design and administrative overheads can be allocated over a larger quantity of output. Production costs also drop because of the *learning curve.* As firms produce more products, they learn ways to improve production efficiency, causing production costs to decline by a predictable amount.[12]

Economies of scale and the experience curve affect international trade because they permit a nation's industries to become low-cost producers without having an abundance of a certain class of production factors. Then, just as in the case of comparative advantage, nations specialize in the production of a few products and trade with others to supply the rest of their needs.

First Mover Theory

Some management theorists argue that firms that enter the market first (first movers) will soon dominate it. The resultant large market share will enable them to obtain the benefits of economies of scale mentioned in the preceding section. One study across a broad range of industries revealed that first movers held a 30 percent market share compared to just 13 percent for late entries. Another found that 70 percent of the leaders in present-day markets were first movers.

New research, however, indicates that previous studies were flawed because they were based on surveys of surviving firms and did not include a large number of the true pioneers. As an example, it was an American firm, Ampex, that made the first VCRs, but because it charged so much ($50,000), it sold only a few. Sony and Matsushita saw the market potential and worked for 20 years to make one to sell for $500. They reached that goal and cornered the market. The authors argue that the early success has gone to the companies that entered the market on average 13 years after the "first movers."[13]

The Linder Theory of Overlapping Demand

Another Swedish economist, Stefan Linder, recognized that although the supply-oriented Heckscher-Ohlin theory, which depended on factor endowments, was adequate to explain international trade in primary products, another explanation was needed for trade in manufactured goods. His demand-oriented theory stated that customers' tastes are strongly affected by income levels, and therefore a nation's income per capita level determines the kinds of goods they will demand. Because industry will produce goods to meet this demand, the kinds of products manufactured reflect the country's level of income per capita. Goods produced for domestic consumption will eventually be exported.

The Linder theory deduces that international trade in manufactured goods will be greater between nations with similar levels of per capita income than between those with dissimilar levels of per capita income. The goods that will be traded are those for which there is an *overlapping demand* (consumers in both countries are demanding the same good).[14] Note that the Linder model differs from the model of comparative advantage in that it does not specify in which direction a given good will go. In fact, Linder specified that a good may go in either direction. You recognize, of course, that this intraindustry trade occurs because of *product differentiation;* for example, Ford exports its Mustangs to Japan and Nissan sends its 300ZXs to the United States because consumers in both countries perceive a difference in the brands.

Porter's Competitive Advantage of Nations. Michael Porter, an economics professor at Harvard, studied 100 firms in 10 developed nations to learn if a nation's prominence in an industry can be explained more adequately by variables other than the factors of production on which the theories of comparative advantage and Heckscher-Ohlin are based. The Porter theory claims that four kinds of variables will have an impact on the ability of the local firms in a country to utilize the country's resources to gain a competitive advantage:

1. Demand conditions—nature of the domestic demand. If a firm's customers are demanding, it will strive to produce high-quality and innovative products and in doing so will obtain a global competitive advantage over companies located where domestic pressure is less. This might have been the case in the past, when international firms introduced their new products in home markets first (a condition of the product life cycle theory), but as more firms introduce new products globally, this variable will lose importance.

2. Factor conditions—level and composition of factors of production. Porter distinguishes between the basic factors (Heckscher-Ohlin theory) and the advanced factors (a nation's infrastructure). Lack of natural endowments has caused nations to invest in the creation of the advanced factors, such as education of its work force, free ports, and advanced communications systems, to enable their industries to be competitive globally. Various Caribbean nations have upgraded their communications systems to attract banking and other service companies that have little dependence on the basic factors of production.

3. Related and supporting industries—suppliers and industry support services. For decades, firms in an industry with their suppliers, the suppliers' suppliers, and so forth, have tended to form a group in a given location, often without any apparent reason. For example, all the major American rubber companies, with the exception of U.S. Rubber, have been located in Akron, Ohio, since the beginning of the 20th century, when they dominated the world's tire industry. Logically, many of their major suppliers, such as rubber chemical producers, synthetic rubber companies, and manufacturers of rubber processing machinery, have had production facilities, extensive laboratories, and/or service organizations there as well.

4. Firm strategy, structure, and rivalry—the extent of domestic competition, the existence of barriers to entry, and the firms' management style and organization. Porter points out that companies subject to heavy competition in their domestic markets are constantly working to improve their efficiency, which makes them more competitive internationally. For decades, firms in oligopolistic industries have carefully watched their competitors' every move and have even entered foreign markets because their competitors had gone there.

> One of the writers recently employed by Goodyear International came to work to find the executives discussing a new market in which the company was going to set up a subsidiary. When he asked them where they had heard this news, they replied that they were discussing an announcement in the morning newspaper about Firestone's going into this market. They also patiently explained, "Where Firestone goes, Goodyear will follow and vice versa."

Porter's work complements the theories of Ricardo and Heckscher-Ohlin. However, as Dunning stated, there is nothing new in Porter's analysis, but Porter does set out a model in which the determinants of national competitiveness may be identified.[15] One other problem is that Porter's evidence is anecdotal. There is no empirical evidence yet.[16]

Summary of International Trade Theory

In summary, we can say that international trade occurs primarily because of relative price differences among nations. These differences stem from differences in production costs, which result from

1. Differences in the endowments of the factors of production.
2. Differences in the levels of technology that determine the factor intensities used.
3. Differences in the efficiencies with which these factor intensities are utilized.
4. Foreign exchange rates.

However, taste differences, a demand variable, can reverse the direction of trade predicted by the theory.

International trade theory clearly shows that nations will attain a higher level of living by specializing in goods for which they possess a comparative advantage and importing those for which they have a comparative disadvantage. Generally, trade restrictions that stop this free flow of goods will harm a nation's welfare. If this is true, why is every nation in the world surrounded by trade restrictions?

Trade Restrictions

This apparent contradiction occurs because the government officials who make decisions about import restrictions are particularly sensitive to the interest groups that will be hurt by the international competition. These groups consist of a small, easily identified body of people—as contrasted to the huge, widespread number of consumers who gain from free trade. In any political debate over a proposed import restriction, the protectionist group will be united in exerting pressure on government officials, whereas pro-trade consumers rarely mount an organized effort. For example, steel companies and steelworker unions have protested vehemently to Congress and government officials about lower-priced imported steel, yet consumer organizations have said nothing. In other words, if you are employed by a chemical manufacturer, you probably are not going to fight for unrestricted steel imports even though you may believe they contribute to a lower price for your automobile.

In the next section, note the importance of special interest groups.

Arguments for Trade Restrictions and Their Rebuttal

One argument for trade restrictions involves national defense.

National Defense

Certain industries need protection from imports because they are vital to the national defense and must be kept operating even though they are at a comparative disadvantage with respect to foreign competitors. If competition from foreign firms drives these companies out of business and leaves this country dependent on imports, those imports may not be available in wartime.

One problem with this argument is that the armed forces require hundreds of products, ranging from panty hose to bombs.

> In 1984, the U.S. shoe industry, after failing to obtain relief from imports with arguments about loss of jobs, requested Congress to impose restrictions based on the fact that growing reliance on imported footwear was "jeopardizing the national security of the United States." In the event of war, shoemakers claimed that there would be insufficient manufacturing capacity in this country.
>
> A Defense Department spokesman said he knew of no plan to investigate the prospects of a wartime shoe crisis. Furthermore, federal law already requires the armed forces to buy U.S.-made footwear exclusively.[17]

Critics of the defense argument claim it would be far more efficient for the government to subsidize a number of firms to maintain sufficient capacity for wartime use only. The output of these companies could be varied according to the calculated defense needs. Moreover, a subsidy would clearly indicate to taxpayers the cost of maintaining these companies in the name of national security—something, however, that some interests do not want known. Currently, most American steamship companies receive government subsidies without which they could not remain in business because of the competition from foreign firms with lower operating costs. In this way, we have a merchant marine ready in case of hostility, and we know what this state of readiness costs us.

Protect Infant Industry

Advocates for the protection of an infant industry may claim that in the long run the industry will have a comparative advantage but that its firms need protection from imports until the labor force is trained, production techniques are mastered, and they achieve economies of scale. When these objectives are met, import protection will no longer be necessary. Without the protection, they argue, a firm will not be able to survive because lower-cost imports from more mature foreign competitors will underprice it in its local market.

The protection is meant to be temporary, but realistically, a firm will rarely admit it has matured and no longer needs this assistance. Protected from foreign competition by high import duties, the company's managers have little reason to improve efficiency or product quality.

International businesspeople will find that the infant-industry argument is readily accepted by the governments of most developing nations. The first firm in an industry new to the country generally gets protection with no date stipulated for its removal. However, some of the larger developing nations, such as Brazil and Mexico, have been reducing their protection to force these companies to lower their prices and become more competitive in world markets.

Protect Domestic Jobs from Cheap Foreign Labor

The protectionists who use this argument will compare lower foreign hourly wage rates to those paid here and conclude that exporters from these countries can flood the United States with low-priced goods and put Americans out of work. The first fallacy of this argument is that wage costs are neither all of the production costs nor all of the labor costs. In many LDCs, the legislated fringe benefits are a much higher percentage of the direct wages than they are in this country.

> In Mexico, the base pay in 1994 of the typical worker was the peso equivalent of US$1.80, less than half the American minimum wage. This is deceiving, however, as the base pay was less than 30 percent of the total hourly pay, whereas in the United States, it amounted to over 70 percent. The difference was due to the pay supplements that the Mexicans received—a month's pay for Christmas, up to 80 percent extra pay at vacation time, and punctuality bonuses. With these supplements, the hourly rate rose to around US$6.00 per hour. In addition, Mexican employers were required to pay workers for 365 days annually, even though they did not work weekends; that is, their weekly income was the US$6.00 hourly rate times eight hours daily times seven days, not five. This raised the hourly rate on a weekly basis to about US$8.40.[18]

Furthermore, the productivity per worker is frequently so much greater in developed countries because of more capital per worker, superior management, and advanced technology that the labor cost is lower even though wages are higher.

The second fallacy results from failure to consider the costs of the other factors of production. Where wage rates are low, the capital costs are usually high, and thus production costs may actually be higher in a low-wage nation. Ironically, one of the arguments for protection used by manufacturers in developing nations is that they cannot compete against the low-cost, highly productive firms in the industrialized countries. Those who might be persuaded by this argument to stop imports to save domestic jobs should remember that American exports create jobs—every $1 billion in exports creates 25,000 new jobs. If we stop a country's imports, its government may retaliate with greater import duties on our exports. The result could be a net loss of jobs rather than the gain that was anticipated.

Scientific Tariff or Fair Competition

Supporters of this argument say they believe in fair competition. They simply want an import duty that will bring the cost of the imported goods up to the cost of the domestically produced article. This will eliminate any "unfair" advantage that a foreign competitor might have because of superior technology, lower raw material costs, lower taxes, or lower labor costs. It is not their intent to ban exports; they wish only to equalize the process for "fair" competition. If this were law, no doubt the rate of duty would be set to protect the least efficient American producer, thereby enabling the more efficient domestic manufacturers to earn large profits. The efficient foreign producers would be penalized, and, of course, their comparative advantage would be nullified.

Retaliation

Representatives of an industry whose exports have had import restrictions placed on them by another country may ask their government to retaliate with similar restrictions. An example of how retaliation begins is the ban by the European Union (EU) on imports of hormone-treated beef from the United States on January 1, 1989. Because the use of hormones is considered a health hazard in the EU, it closed the market to $100 million worth of beef (12 percent of total U.S. meat exports). American beef producers complained that no scientific evidence supports the claim, and the United States promptly retaliated by putting import duties on about $100 million worth of EU products, including boneless beef and pork, fruit juices, wine coolers, tomatoes, French cheese, and instant coffee. The EU then threatened to ban U.S. shipments of honey, canned corn, walnuts, and dried fruit worth $140 million. In reply, the United States announced that it would follow the EU ban with a ban on all European meat. If that had happened, about $500 million in U.S.–EU trade would have been affected.[19]

Generally, disputes like these go to the World Trade Organization (WTO). After having U.S. beef banned by the EU for over 10 years, the United States launched a formal dispute settlement procedure with the WTO in May 1996, challenging the ban. When the WTO Appellate Body announced that the EU ban had been imposed without reason, the EU declared in March 1998 that it would implement the Appellate Body ruling, but it did not comply by May 1999, the date set by the WTO. When the United States asked the WTO for permission to retaliate, the EU requested arbitration to settle the amount. On July 26, 1999, the WTO authorized the United States to retaliate, resulting in the imposition of a 100 percent import duty on a list of EU products with an annual trade value of $116.8 million. Both the United States and the EU continue to discuss this matter.[20] The EU's ban on hormone-treated beef keeps out most American and Canadian production.[21]

dumping
Selling a product abroad for less than the cost of production, the price in the home market, or the price to third countries

Dumping. Retaliation will also be made for **dumping**. This is the selling of a product abroad for less than (1) the cost of production, (2) the price in the home market, or (3) the price to third countries.

A foreign manufacturer may take this action because it wishes to sell excess production without disrupting prices in its domestic market, or it may have lowered the export price to force all domestic producers in the importing nation out of business. The exporter expects to raise prices in the market once that objective is accomplished. This is called *predatory dumping.*

In the United States, when a manufacturer believes a foreign producer is dumping a product, it can ask the Office of Investigation in the Department of Commerce to make a preliminary investigation. If Commerce finds that products have been dumped, the case goes to the International Trade Commission* to determine if the imports are injuring U.S. producers. If the commission finds that they are, U.S. Customs is authorized to levy antidumping duties. Unlike most trade restrictions, which are applied to all exporters of a product, antidumping measures are applied to specific producers in selected nations.

Most governments retaliate when dumping injures local industry. The EU, for example, levied antidumping duties of 39.2 percent on handbags from China in spite of a warning from European retailers and importers that such a move would cost more jobs than it would create. The EU's *Official Journal* found that Chinese manufacturers of handbags had "significantly undercut EU producers' prices, eroding profitability and causing a gradual reduction in employment as well as a number of company closures." In fact, antidumping suits have become the favorite means of manufacturers in the EU, the United States, and, increasingly, other nations to protect themselves from less expensive imports. In 1999, 328 antidumping investigations were begun, compared with 232 cases in 1998. The EU, the United States, Australia, and Canada combined initiated 42 percent of all the cases in 1999, up from 34 percent in 1998. Interestingly, 17 of the 22 initiating nations were developing countries. India led with 60 cases. The biggest targets were Japan, China, Korea, and Taiwan.[22]

New Types of Dumping. There are at least four new kinds of dumping for which fair-trade lobbies consider sanctions to be justified in order to level the playing field for international trade. In reality, these special interest groups calling for level playing fields are seeking to raise the production costs of their overseas competitors to protect their local high-cost manufacturers. The classes of dumping are

1. *Social dumping*—unfair competition by firms in developing nations that have lower labor costs and poorer working conditions.
2. *Environmental dumping*—unfair competition caused by a country's lax environmental standards.
3. *Financial services dumping*—unfair competition caused by a nation's low requirements for bank capital/asset ratios.
4. *Cultural dumping*—unfair competition caused by cultural barriers aiding local firms.[23]

subsidies
Financial contribution, provided directly or indirectly by a government, which confers a benefit. Include grants, preferential tax treatment, and government assumption of normal business expenses

Subsidies. Another cause of retaliation may be **subsidies** that a government makes to a domestic firm either to encourage exports or to help protect it from imports. Some examples are cash payments, government participation in ownership, low-cost loans to foreign buyers and exporters, and preferential tax treatment. For example, Airbus, the European consortium that produces passenger jet aircraft, has, according to a U.S. Department of Commerce study, received over $13.5 billion in government subsidies, without which the company could not have been established or survived. Airbus did not make a profit during its first 20 years of operation.[24]

In 1992, the United States and the EU made a pact to limit government subsidies to their commercial aircraft makers, but according to the U.S. Trade Representative, the Airbus governments continue to subsidize their member companies. In the year 2000, the Spanish, German, and French members of the consortium formed the European Aeronautic Defense and Space Company (EADS), which now owns 80 percent of Airbus Industries. British Aerospace Systems, the fourth partner in Airbus Industries,

*The International Trade Commission is a government agency that provides technical assistance and advice to the president and Congress on matters of international trade and tariffs.

holds the remaining 20 percent in a new firm, Airbus Integrated Company. One of the new co-CEOs said in a news conference that EADS would play strictly by the rules of the 1992 agreement between the EU and the United States that limits the amount of aid that governments can give to an aerospace project to one-third of the development costs. He emphasized that the United States would have no cause to complain about unfair subsidizing under the terms of the 1992 agreement.[25]

Competitors in importing nations frequently ask their governments to impose **countervailing duties** to offset the effects of a subsidy. In the United States, when the Department of Commerce receives a petition from an American firm claiming that imports from a particular country are subsidized, it first determines if a subsidy actually was given. If the findings are positive, Commerce proceeds to impose countervailing duties equal to the subsidy's amount. In most cases involving members of the WTO, another independent government agency, the U.S. International Trade Commission, must determine if the firm has been injured by the subsidy before Commerce assesses the duty (see Table 3.1 for the countries and the quantity of countervailing duty and antidumping measures they had in force in 1999).

countervailing duties
Additional import taxes levied on imports that have benefited from export subsidies

Other Arguments

The arguments we have examined are probably the ones most frequently given. Others include the use of protection from imports to (1) permit diversification of the domestic economy or (2) improve the balance of trade. You should have gathered from this discussion that protection from imports generally serves the narrow interests of a special interest group at the expense of many. Although their application can sometimes buy time for the protected industry to modernize and become more competitive in the world market, a real danger exists that a nation's trading partners will retaliate with

Table 3.1 **Number of Countervailing Duty (CD) and Antidumping (AD) Measures in Force by WTO Members on December 31, 1999**

Measures and Country	Number
CD measures*	
United States	61
Mexico	11
Canada	10
European Union	6
Brazil	6
Australia	5
Argentina	3
New Zealand	3
Venezuela	3
Total	108
AD measures*	
United States	336
European Union	183
Mexico	88
South Africa	86
Canada	77
Australia	48
Argentina	42
Brazil	35
Others	202
Total	1,097

*The table is based on member's semiannual reports and is incomplete because of a significant number of missing notifications.
Source: "Countervailing Actions" and "Antidumping Actions," *Annual Report* (Geneva: World Trade Organization, 2000), pp. 45–49, www.wto.org/english/res_e/anrep_e/anre00_e.pdf.

Table 3.2 Kinds of Import Restrictions

Tariff Barriers	Nontariff Barriers
Import duties	Quantitative
Ad valorem	Quotas
Specific	• Tariff-rate quotas
Compound	• Global
Variable levies	• Discriminatory
Official prices	Voluntary export restraints
	Orderly marketing arrangements
	Nonquantitative
	Direct government participation in trade
	• Subsidy
	• Buy domestically
	• Import licenses
	• Manipulation of exchange rates
	• Local content
	Customs and other administrative procedures
	• Tariff classifications
	• Documentation requirements
	• Product valuation
	Standards
	• Health, safety, and product quality
	• Packaging and labeling
	• Product testing methods

restrictions, causing injury to industries that have received no protection. Let's examine these restrictions.

Kinds of Restrictions

Import restrictions are commonly classified as *tariff* (import duties) and *nontariff* barriers (see Table 3.2).

tariffs
Taxes on imported goods for the purpose of raising their price to reduce competition for local producers or stimulate their local production

Tariff Barriers

Tariffs, or import duties, are taxes levied on imported goods primarily for the purpose of raising their selling price in the importing nation's market to reduce competition for domestic producers. A few smaller nations also use them to raise revenue on both imports and exports. Exports of commodities such as coffee and copper are commonly taxed in developing nations.

ad valorem duty
An import duty levied as a percentage of the invoice value of imported goods

specific duty
A fixed sum levied on a physical unit of an imported good

compound duty
A combination of specific and ad valorem duties

Ad Valorem, Specific, and Compound Duties. Import duties are (1) *ad valorem,* (2) *specific,* or (3) a combination of the two called *compound*. An **ad valorem duty** is stated as a percentage of the invoice value. For example, the U.S. tariff schedule states that flavoring extracts and fruit flavors not containing alcohol are subject to a 6 percent ad valorem duty. Therefore, when a shipment of flavoring extract invoiced at \$10,000 arrives in the United States, the importer is required to pay \$600 to U.S. Customs before taking possession of the goods. A **specific duty** is a fixed sum of money charged for a physical unit. A company importing dynamite in cartridges or sticks suitable for blasting would have to pay \$.37 per pound irrespective of the invoice value. When the flavoring extracts and fruit flavors mentioned above contain over 50 percent alcohol by weight, they are charged \$.12 per pound plus 3 percent ad valorem. On a \$10,000 shipment weighing 5,000 pounds, the importer would have to pay a **compound duty** of \$900 (\$.12 × 5,000 pounds + 0.03 × \$10,000 = \$600 + \$300). Note that a specific duty, unless changed frequently in an inflationary period, soon loses its importance, whereas the amount collected from an ad valorem duty increases as the invoice price rises. Sometimes, however, an exporter may charge prices so much lower than domestic prices that the ad valorem duty fails to close the gap. Some governments set *official prices* or use *variable levies* to correct this deficiency.

Official Prices. These prices are included in the customs tariff of some nations and are the basis for ad valorem duty calculations whenever the actual invoice price is lower. The official price guarantees that a certain minimum import duty will be paid irrespective of the actual invoice price. It thwarts a fairly common arrangement that numerous importers living in high-duty nations have with their foreign suppliers whereby a false low invoice is issued to reduce the amount of duty to be paid. The importer sends the difference between the false invoice price and the true price separately.

Variable Levy. One form of **variable levy**, which guarantees that the market price of the import will be the same as that of domestically produced goods, is used by the EU for imported grains. Calculated daily, the duty level is set at the difference between world market prices and the support price for domestic producers.

variable levy
An import duty set at the difference between world market prices and local government-supported prices

Lower Duty for more Local Input. Import duties are set by many nations in such a way that they encourage local input. For example, the finished product ready for sale to the consumer may have a 70 percent ad valorem duty. However, if the product is imported in bulk so that it must be packaged in the importing nation, the duty level may be 30 percent. To encourage some local production, the government may charge only 10 percent duty on the semifinished inputs. These situations can provide opportunities for foreign manufacturers of low-technology products, such as paint articles and toiletries, to get behind a high tariff wall with very modest investments.

Nontariff Barriers

Nontariff barriers (NTBs) are all forms of discrimination against imports other than the import duties we have been examining. As nations progressively reduced import duties, nontariff barriers assumed greater importance. This trend continued until the 117 member nations of GATT, the world's international trade organization, concluded negotiations in 1994 that created the WTO and provided for the elimination of nontariff barriers, both quantitative and nonquantitative, over a 10-year period.[26]

nontariff barriers (NTBs)
All forms of discrimination against imports other than import duties

Quantitative. **Quotas**, one type of quantitative barrier, are numerical limits for a specific kind of good that a country will permit to be imported without restriction during a specified period. If the quota is *absolute,* once the specified amount has been imported, further importation for the rest of the period (usually a year) is prohibited.

quotas
Numerical limits placed on specific classes of imports

> China is the biggest clothing supplier of the American market, a market ruled by quotas. And when it comes to evading quotas, China has no equal. For example, China is notorious for overshipping, that is, sending goods after the quota is filled. Because of overshipping, China's quotas are often filled after only six months into the new year.
>
> Another kind of quota evasion—transshipping—is plain fraud. Chinese producers ship finished goods to other countries with unfilled quotas, where they are labeled as a product of that country. This deceptive labeling scheme brings $2 billion in illegal clothing imports from China into the United States annually. Gitano, for example, pled guilty to charges of fraud for importing Chinese blouses labeled "Made in the Maldive Islands."[27]
>
> The American Textile Manufacturers Institute accused The Limited and several of its subsidiaries, including Victoria's Secret, Lane Bryant, and Abercrombie & Fitch, of importing clothing made in China but labeling it as made elsewhere to avoid U.S. quotas and import duties. This case, which was intended to recover millions of dollars in import duties, was the first to be filed to bring civil actions on behalf of the government to recover losses incurred by fraud. However, twice in 1998, federal courts in Ohio refused to accept the American Textile Manufacturers Institute's evidence suggesting that The Limited was illegally importing textiles from China.[28]

Some goods, such as sugar, are subject to *tariff-rate quotas,* which permit a stipulated amount to enter the United States duty-free or at a low rate, but when that amount

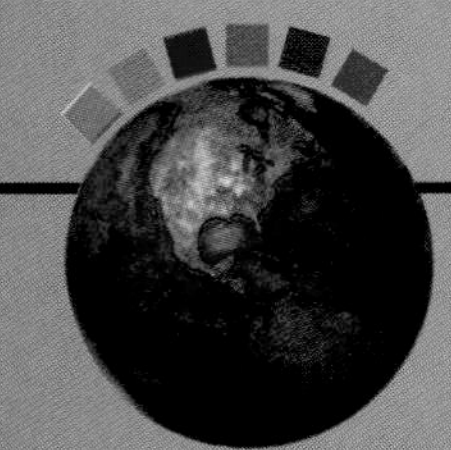

[Worldview]

Our Taxing Tariff Code

In 1790, the U.S. tariff code was written on just one page; it now requires two volumes with 8,753 different rates. Although it's true that the average American import duty is only 5 percent of the product's value—one of the lowest average duty levels in the world—the United States still levies over 100 percent duty on some products. Why must importers pay a 35 percent duty rate for apricot jam when they pay only 3 percent on jam made with currants? Has an apricot jam cartel gotten to Congress? How do you explain this difference? Although vitamin B_{12} is no longer produced in this country, it carries a 16.2 percent duty rate while vitamin E is levied less than half that amount, 7.9 percent, and vitamin C at only 3.1 percent. The reason, of course, is that the government adds new tariffs to satisfy interest groups and no one is vitally interested in removing a tariff just because nobody is benefiting from it now.

Frank Grant/International Stock

Barry Johnson/Gamma Liaison

Besides Congress, the U.S. Customs Service also has the ability to raise import duties or even keep some products from entering the country. It does this by putting goods in more restrictive tariff classifications. For example, an American importer had been bringing in girls' ski jackets at a 10.6 percent import duty. Suddenly, Customs declared that a shipment of 33,000 jackets should now pay 27.5 percent of the invoice value plus 17 cents per pound because they had small strips of corduroy trim on the sleeves. The strips, which accounted for only 2 percent of the jacket's materials, were ruled to have changed the jackets from being "garments designed for rainwear, hunting, fishing, or similar uses" (skiing might be one) to the more expensive category "other girls' wearing apparel, not ornamented." The importer brought this case to the Court of International Trade (the U.S. court that handles such disputes), and the judge not only ruled against Customs but also ordered the government to refund all the extra duty that the importer had paid.

Tariff classification disputes and the thousands of import categories are the bases for these absurd situations. They also make it difficult for the United States to call for other nations to reduce their tariff and nontariff barriers. In fact, every year since 1984, the European Union has published its *Report on United States Barriers to Trade and Investment.* This 115-page publication lists, as the EU puts it, "a significant number of barriers and impediments to international trade that the European Union wants the United States to remove. These barriers, some of which have been in existence for decades, reduce the benefits which can be gained from free trade, they cause distortions to the efficient flow of capital and investment, and in many cases cause significant market distortions and losses of business to European firms in the U.S." To give you an idea of the contents, the topics cover such areas as public procurement, tariffs as trade impediments, standards, testing, labeling, and the application of countervailing duty legislation.

It is apparent that while the United States pursues the reduction of tariff and nontariff barriers that other nations have erected, there are also many in this country that must be eliminated. ■

Sources: James Bovard, *The Wall Street Journal,* March 28, 1990, p. A14; "The Customs Service's Fickle Philosophers," *The Wall Street Journal,* July 3, 1991, p. A10; "Trade Barriers' Cost Put at $19 Billion," *The Press Democrat* (*Santa Rosa*), November 27, 1993, p. E3; and *Report on United States Barriers to Trade and Investment 2000* (Brussels: Services of the European Commission, 2000), http://europa.eu.int/en/comm/trade/pdf/usrbt 2000.pdf (August 28, 2000).

is reached, a much higher duty is charged for subsequent importations. Sugar imported above the low duty quantities (quotas) is subject to a second-tier duty of 16 cents a pound, which results in a domestic price that is double the world price. In effect, American consumers are subsidizing American sugar producers.[29]

Quotas are generally *global;* that is, a total amount is fixed without regard to source. They may also be *allocated,* in which case the government of the importing nation assigns quantities to specific countries. The United States allocates quotas for specific tonnages of sugar to 40 nations. Because of their nature, allocated quotas are sometimes called *discriminatory quotas.*

For many years there has been an agreement among nations against imposing quotas unilaterally on goods (agricultural products excepted). Therefore, governments have negotiated **voluntary export restraints (VERs)** with other countries. Although a VER is a generic term for all bilaterally agreed measures to restrict exports, it has a stricter legal definition in the United States: "an action unilaterally taken to restrict the volume or number of items to be exported during a given period and administered by the exporting country. It is 'voluntary' in the sense that the country has a formal right to eliminate or modify it." It is also voluntary in that the exporting nation may prefer its consequences to any trade barriers the importing nation might impose.

voluntary export restraints (VERs)
Export quotas imposed by the exporting nation

To avoid having the United States place import quotas on Japanese automobiles, the Japanese government established a VER to restrict the number of automobiles that its manufacturers could export to the United States annually. However, as we mentioned previously, nontariff barriers such as quotas, VERs, and orderly marketing arrangements are being eliminated as a result of the 1994 negotiations (Uruguay Round). Also, agricultural products and textiles, which have always had special treatment, are being brought under the general trading rules of all products during a 10-year period. At the end of the transition period on January 1, 2005, all remaining products will lose their special status.[30]

Orderly Marketing Arrangements. **Orderly marketing arrangements** are VERs consisting of formal agreements between the governments of exporting and importing countries to restrict international competition and preserve some of the national market for local producers. Usually, they stipulate the size of the export or import quotas that each nation will have for a particular good.

orderly marketing arrangements
Formal agreements between exporting and importing countries that stipulate the import or export quotas each nation will have for a good

The largest and oldest such arrangement is the Multifiber Arrangement (MFA), which began in 1973 and regulated about 80 percent of the world's textile and clothing exports to the industrialized nations. As we mentioned previously, by the year 2005, special treatment for textiles and clothing will be terminated by WTO member-nations.

Nonquantitative Nontariff Barriers. Many international trade specialists claim that the most significant nontariff barriers are the nonquantitative type. Governments have tended to establish nontariff barriers to obtain the protection formerly afforded by import duties. A study of nonquantitative barriers revealed over 800 distinct forms, which may be classified under three major headings: (1) direct government participation in trade, (2) customs and other administrative procedures, and (3) standards.

1. *Direct government participation in trade.* The most common form of direct government participation is the *subsidy.* Besides protecting industries through subsidies, as was mentioned earlier, nearly all governments subsidize agriculture. The EU, for example, paid European farmers an export refund of $150 per ton to get them to sell their wheat in the export markets for the world price of $80 per ton when the government-guaranteed price within the EU was $230. In 1999, the EU paid out the most in farm subsidies: $114.5 billion, or 49 percent of its total farm output. However, as a percentage of the value of production, Korea led with 74 percent, Switzerland paid 73 percent, Norway and Iceland paid 69 percent each, and Japan paid 65 percent. Interestingly, the subsidies paid by the governments of Australia and New Zealand, two major exporters of agricultural products, were extremely small percentages of the total value of production, unlike those of the United States and other developed nations (see Figure 3.3).

[Figure 3.3] Value of OECD Member Farm Subsidies ($ billions)

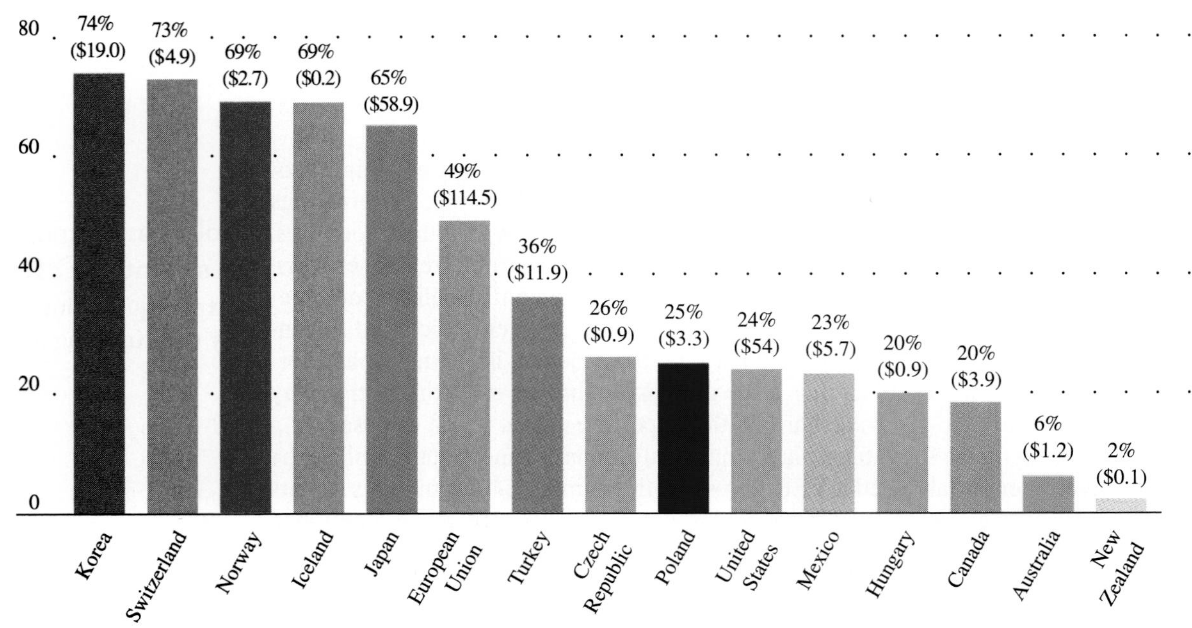

Source: "Agriculture: Support Estimates, 1999," *OECD in Figures,* 2000 ed., www.oecdwash.org/PRESS/CONTENT/oecdinfig2000.pdf (August 28, 2000). Reprinted with permission of OCED Washington.

Government procurement policies also are trade barriers because they usually favor domestic producers and severely restrict purchases of imported goods by government agencies. Policies may also require that products purchased by government agencies have a stipulated minimum *local content.* Under an EU Utilities Directive for purchases by the public utilities sector, bids with less than 50 percent EU value (local content) could be excluded without additional justification. In 1994, an agreement was reached with the United States to eliminate this provision.[31] Since the WTO Government Procurement Agreement went into effect, most nations have opened their government business to foreign bidders to comply with its requirements.

2. *Customs and other administrative procedures.* These barriers cover a large variety of government policies and procedures that either discriminate against imports or favor exports. For example, in China, a product being imported may be subject to different rates of duty, depending on the port of duty and an arbitrary determination of the customs value. Because of this flexibility, customs charges often depend on negotiations between Chinese customs officials and businesspeople. It is alleged that corruption is often involved.[32]

   Governments have also found ways to discriminate against the exportation of services. Overseas, U.S. airlines face a number of situations in which the national airline receives preferential treatment, such as in the provision of airport services, airport counter locations, and number of landing slots. Other examples of discrimination are the Canadian government's giving tax deductions to local businesses that advertise on Canadian TV, but not when they use American stations across the border, and Australia's requiring television commercials to be shot in Australia.

3. *Standards.* Both governmental and private standards to protect the health and safety of a nation's citizens certainly are desirable, but for years exporting firms have been plagued by many that are complex and discriminatory. The European

A Small Business Fights the Standards Barrier

Small and Medium-Sized Enterprises

If you sell in one EU member country, you can sell in them all, right? Wrong. EU rules allow member-countries to prohibit imports that threaten public safety, and there is no agreement on that. Dermont Manufacturing Co., a small firm ($25 million in sales), makes hoses that connect gas appliances to gas outlets. It had been selling them throughout Europe when, suddenly, one day a U.S. manufacturer of deep-fat fryers who was supplying McDonald's told Dermont's president, Evan Seagal, that McDonald's could no longer use his hoses in its British restaurants. Similar situations began occurring elsewhere: French health inspectors ordered Euro Disney to replace Dermont hoses before it opened to the public. The reason for the different national standards was that the gas hoses were considered essential to the safe operation of the gas appliances and therefore fell under product safety rules, thus permitting each nation to establish its own standards.

Seagal studied the various rules and realized that his product could not meet them. As is often the case, the rules were written by committees composed of a nation's experts. Who were they? The producers of the hoses who were Dermont's competitors. Designs varied from country to country, and all were different from Dermont's hose. Seagal argues that there were no reasons for the differences in design except to keep his product out of the local market. They had no bearing on either the safety or the performance. The president of the American National Standards Institute, the U.S. standards organization, claimed that the Dermont case is "clearly a case of European standards being used as a barrier to trade."

Meanwhile, Dermont has begun obtaining product approval from individual EU countries. The U.S. government has been urging the European Committee for Standardization to begin developing a harmonized standard for Europe for the past three years but has made little progress. ■

Source: "Europe's 'Unity' Undoes a U.S. Exporter," *The Wall Street Journal,* April 1, 1996, p. B1; and Office of the Foreign Trade Representative, "The 2000 Estimate Report on Foreign Trade Barriers," www.ustr.gov/reports/nte/2000//contents.html (August 28, 2000).

Union complains that the United States is causing a problem for foreign imports because it pays little attention to standards set by international standardizing bodies. The American complaint is that the EU has not completed EU-wide standards. These barriers concern exporters who either (1) make a product that will meet the standards of some countries and not attempt to cover all of the market or (2) make a variety of types in an attempt to meet the requirements of the entire market (see "A Small Business Fights the Standards Barrier" on hose standards).

These few examples will give you an idea of the complexity involved in trying to eliminate nontariff barriers. You have seen that as a consequence of the Uruguay Round,* considerable progress has been made.

Creating New Markets

Exporting companies need to be informed about the changing status of tariff and nontariff barriers in the countries where they are doing business or would like to do business. Those that have stayed away from markets with extremely high import duties or nontariff barriers, such as product standards or customs procedures designed to keep out foreign products, may find these barriers no longer exist.

From Multinational to Globally Integrated Manufacturing Systems

The lowering of import duties and the elimination or weakening of nontariff barriers are making it easier and less costly for companies to locate their production activities in lower-cost countries. Paying lower import duties on components manufactured elsewhere reduces their landed cost, and not having to overcome nontariff barriers makes the international dispersion of production activities possible and more economical. It is also possible that a multidomestic company with numerous manufacturing plants,

*The Uruguay Round is discussed completely in Chapter 4.

Table 3.3 Annual Costs to American Consumers for Import Protection

Product Group	Cost per American Job Saved	Number of Jobs Involved	Total Cost ($ millions)
Benezoid chemicals	$1,000,000	216	$216
Luggage	933,628	226	211
Softwood lumber	758,678	605	459
Sugar	600,177	2,261	1,357
Polyethylene resins	590,604	298	176
Dairy products	497,897	2,378	1,184
Frozen concentrated orange juice	461,412	609	281
Ball bearings	438,356	146	64
Maritime	415,325	4,411	1,832
Ceramic tiles	400,576	347	139
Machine tools	348,349	169	59
Apparel and textiles	340,727	12,624	4,301

Source: Gary C. Hufbauer and Kimberly Ann Elliott, *Measuring the Cost of Protection in the United States* (Washington, DC: Institute for International Economics, 1994), pp. 11–13. Reprinted with permission.

each of which has a complete manufacturing system to supply the country where it is located, may find that with lower barriers to importation, it has two possibilities for improving operational efficiency:

1. Close the least efficient plants and supply their markets with imports from other subsidiaries.
2. Change the multidomestic manufacturing system to a globally integrated system in which each plant performs the activities at which it is most efficient.

Costs of Barriers to Trade

You may have been surprised to read that because of the U.S. quota system for sugar, American consumers have to pay double the world price. But this is just a small part of what trade restraints cost consumers. In a study that was done in 1994, economists of the Institute for International Economics studied 21 product groups, each of which had a domestic market of at least $1 billion and, after removal of import restraints, potential imports of $100 million. They estimated that the average consumer cost per job saved is $170,000 per year. This means that consumers pay over six times the average annual compensation of manufacturing workers to preserve jobs through import restraints. With the exception of lumber and machine tools, the sectors studied have been shielded from imports for 35 years or more. Table 3.3 summarizes the findings for the 12 product groups most affected.

This is why your jeans cost you what they do. Protection makes sugar, a commodity for which the United States has no comparative advantage, cost you 50 percent more than the world price. The United States has lost valuable wetlands in the Florida Everglades to sugar growers. A single family controls most of the Florida sugar industry, and annually American consumers make involuntary contributions to that family.[33] Note, too, how much it costs to save one American job. Studies done in other countries show similar results.[34]

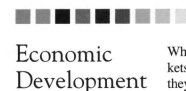

section [1]

Economic Development

When businesspeople move from domestic to international business, they encounter markets with far greater differences in levels of economic development than those in which they have been working. It is important to understand this because a nation's level of economic development affects all aspects of business—marketing, production, and finance. Although nations vary greatly with respect to economic development levels, we commonly group them into categories based on their level of economic development.

Categories Based on Levels of Economic Development

Developed is the name given to the industrialized nations of Western Europe, Japan, Australia, New Zealand, Canada, Israel, and the United States. The term **developing** is a classification for the world's lower-income nations, which are less technically developed. At one time, **newly industrializing countries (NICs)** was a category which included the four Asian tigers (Taiwan, Hong Kong, Singapore, and South Korea), Brazil, Mexico, and three emerging NICs—Malaysia, Thailand, and Chile. These countries (1) had what the World Bank considers to be fast-growing, middle-income or higher economies, (2) possessed a heavy concentration of foreign investment, and (3) exported large quantities of manufactured goods, including high-tech products.

developed
A classification for all industrialized nations, which are most technically developed

developing
A classification for the world's lower-income nations, which are less technically developed

newly industrializing countries (NICs)
The four Asian tigers and the middle-income economies of Brazil, Mexico, Malaysia, Chile, and Thailand

newly industrialized economies (NIEs)
Fast-growing upper-middle-income and high-income economies of South Korea, Taiwan, Hong Kong, and Singapore

Because the economies of the four tigers have grown faster than those of other NICs and are approximating the size of developed nations' economies, the term *NIC* has generally given way to **newly industrialized economies (NIEs)**, which is used primarily to refer to the tigers.

You will also find that various different classification systems are employed by international agencies such as the United Nations (UN), the International Monetary Fund (IMF), and the World Bank for reporting statistics.* For example, the IMF in 1997 combined the NIEs with the industrialized nations to form the *advanced economies.*

The rest of the noncommunist nations are in the category *developing countries,* which has a subcategory, *emerging market economies,* that includes Chile, Malaysia, China, Thailand, and Indonesia. The third category, called *transition countries,* includes the former communist countries. The UN uses simply *developed* and *developing economies* and refers to the former communist nations as *Eastern Europe* and the *former USSR.* When speaking of developed and developing nations as a block, UN economists frequently use the terms *North* and *South,* respectively. The World Bank, by contrast, uses a classification system based on GNP/capita:[35]

1. *Low income* ($755 or less)
2. *Lower middle income* ($756–$2,995)
3. *Upper middle income* ($2,996–$9,265)
4. *High income* ($9,266 or more)

Since *developed* and *developing* are used in industry as a kind of shorthand to describe the characteristics of two distinct groups of nations, we shall use them in this text. Note that GNP/capita is the basis for this classification scheme.

GNP/Capita as an Indicator

We mentioned in Chapter 2 that although GNP/capita is widely used to compare countries with respect to the well-being of their citizens and for market or investment potential, businesspeople must use it with caution. What does this value signify? Is a country with an $800 GNP/capita a better market for a firm's products than one whose GNP/capita is only $750? To assume this gives excessive credence to its accuracy. For example, to arrive at the GNP, government economists must impute monetary values to various goods and services not sold in the marketplace, such as food grown for personal consumption. Moreover, many goods and services are bartered in both low-income nations (because people have little cash) and high-income countries (because

*These agencies are discussed in Chapter 4.

[Figure 3.4] Underground Economies (percentage of GDP, 1998)

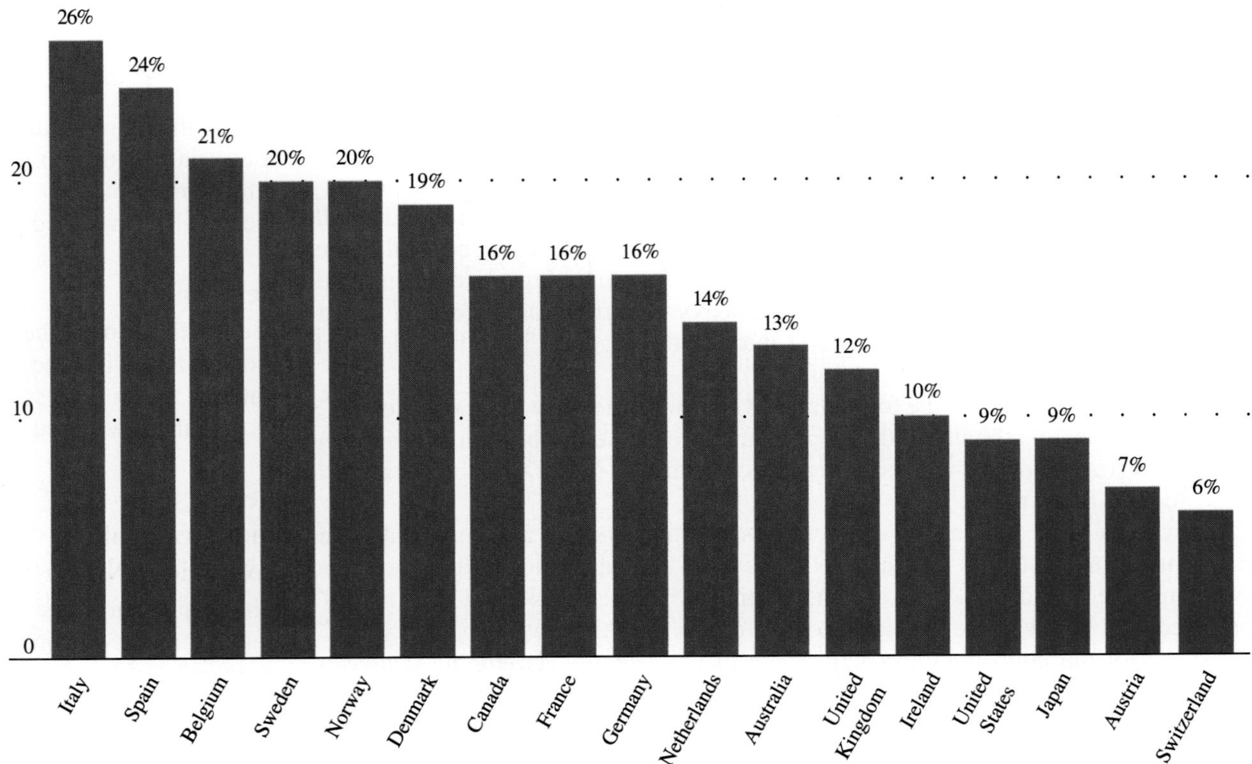

Source: "Black Hole," *The Economist,* August 28, 1999, p. 59.

people wish to reduce reported income and thus pay less income tax). Transactions of this type are said to be part of the *underground economy.*

Underground Economy

underground economy
The part of a nation's income that, because of unreporting or underreporting, is not measured by official statistics

Much has been written about the part of the national income that is not measured by official statistics because it is either underreported or unreported. Included in this **underground** (black, parallel, informal, submerged, shadow) **economy** are undeclared legal production, production of illegal goods and services, and concealed income in kind (barter). As a rule, the higher the level of taxation and the more onerous the government red tape are, the bigger the underground economy will be.[36] Figure 3.4 shows estimates of some underground economies. They vary widely because of the different methodologies used to compile them; also, people who have undeclared income are not likely to admit it and be liable to prosecution for tax evasion. But there are many humorous incidents that people tell about others.

> In Bonn, a gardener completed a large landscaping job and when asked for a bill replied, "If you want one, it will be DM1,500 plus 14 percent tax. If you don't need one, just pay me DM1,400 cash." In Greece, when a patient tried to pay with a check, the physician was reluctant to accept one or to give a receipt, and when he opened his desk drawer, it was crammed with cash. A visitor to an Italian company was talking to the chief executive when his secretary announced the unexpected arrival of a tax inspector. He told her to stall the inspector and then called the company's financial director. A few minutes later, the visitor looked out the window and saw the financial director running across the field with an armload of ledgers.[37]

In addition to reducing the total taxes paid to government, the underground economy is responsible for all kinds of distortions of economic data. In Italy, for example, there was no record that a single pair of gloves was produced in Naples, yet it is now known that Naples is one of Italy's biggest glove-making centers—the unreported output is produced by small groups of workers in kitchens and garages. Italy's shadow economy is so well known that in 1987 the government began to increase the official figures to take the missing output into account. With the first adjustment of 18 percent, the country overtook the United Kingdom in the World Bank GDP rankings, much to the pride of officials in the Italian government.[38] A Mexican economist calculated that his country's GNP was actually 38 percent higher than the official total of the finance ministry.[39]

Although government officials have yet to learn it, it is a general rule that the higher the taxation and the more oppressive the regulations in the formal economy are, the larger the informal economy is likely to be.

Currency Conversion

Another problem with GNP estimates is that to compare them, the GNPs in local currency must be converted to a common currency—conventionally the dollar—by using an exchange rate. If the relative values of the two currencies accurately reflected consumer purchasing power, this conversion would be acceptable. However, the World Bank recognizes that "the use of official exchange rates to convert national currency figures to U.S. dollars does not reflect domestic purchasing powers of currencies."[40]

To overcome this deficiency, the UN International Comparison Program (ICP) has developed a method of comparing the GNP that is based on **purchasing power parity (PPP)** rather than on the international demand for currency (exchange rates). Here is how purchasing power parity rates are calculated.

purchasing power parity (PPP)
The number of units of a currency required to buy the same amounts of goods and services in the domestic market that one dollar would buy in the United States

Suppose Thailand reports to the World Bank that its GNP/capita for last year is 46,370 baht/capita. The Bank must translate this value to U.S. dollars. It uses the current exchange rate of 25.2 baht = $1 to convert 46,370 baht to $1,840 (46,370/25.2). How well does this measure Thailand's welfare? What can a Thai citizen consume with the 46,370 baht compared with what an American can consume with the $23,240 per capita income of the United States?

Compare local prices in both countries of the same basket of goods.

Goods	Thailand (baht)	U.S. ($)
Soap (bar)	15	0.45
Rice (lb.)	10	0.30
Shoes (pair)	450	60.00
Dress	350	45.00
Socks (pair)	25	2.00
	850	$107.75

In Thailand 850 baht buys what $107.75 buys in the United States. Therefore, comparing the purchasing power of the currencies, 850 baht/$107.75 = 7.9 baht per $1. Using the exchange rate of 7.9 baht per dollar, Thailand's GNP/capita is now 46,370/7.9 = $5,870. At the official exchange rate of 25.2 baht/$1, Thailand's GNP is $1,840. At the purchasing power parity rate of 7.9 baht/$1, Thailand's GNP is $5,870.

Table 3.4 illustrates that comparisons based on purchasing power parity result in GNP/capita values that are considerably higher than those regularly given for developing nations and lower for most developed nations; that is, in considering purchasing power, the differences between the GNPs of developing and developed nations are smaller than those generally published. Note how the smaller buying power of the yen compared to that of the U.S. dollar affects the GNP/capita based on PPP.

More Than GNP/Capita Is Required

Even if the problems we have examined did not exist, businesspeople still would not obtain a true picture of the relative strengths of markets by comparing GNP/capita alone. Remember that GNP/capita is a mean, which infers that every inhabitant receives an

Table 3.4 **GNP/Capita Based on UN ICP for Selected Countries in 1994**

Country	GNP/Capita in US$s Converted at World Bank Adjusted Exchange Rates	GNP/Capita in US$s Based on Purchasing Power Parity
Switzerland	$40,080	$26,620
Norway	34,330	24,290
Denmark	33,260	23,830
Japan	32,380	23,180
United States	29,340	29,340
Mexico	3,970	8,190
China	750	2,790
Indonesia	680	2,790
India	430	1,700
Ethiopia	100	500

Source: *World Development Indicators 2000,* Table 1.1, pp. 10–12. Republished with permisson of World Bank; permission conveyed through Copyright Clearance Center, Inc.

equal share of the national income. This is patently untrue, especially in developing nations, where the national income is much less evenly divided than it is in developed countries. Thus, businesspeople who conclude from a low GNP/capita that a nation is too poor to buy their products will certainly miss some lucrative markets.

The dissatisfaction with GNP/capita as an indicator of a nation's level of living (it is an index of production, not consumption) has led to various attempts to create indexes by combining variables such as the consumption of steel, concrete, newsprint, and electricity with the ownership of automobiles, telephones, TVs, and radios. In Chapter 15 on market analysis, we shall examine an index to compare market size that *Business International* has constructed by combining population and GDP with the consumption and production of certain key commodities. Although GNP/capita is an imperfect yardstick for comparing the purchasing power and market size of nations, it does serve as a rough indicator of whether a country is in the developed or the developing category. This is valuable because it gives a set of common characteristics that provide some insight into the approximately 170 developing nations.

Characteristics of Developing Nations

Although there is great diversity among the many developing nations, most share the following common characteristics:

1. GNP/capita of less than $9,265 (World Bank criterion).*
2. Unequal distribution of income, with a very small middle class.
3. *Technological dualism*—a mix of firms employing the latest technology and companies using very primitive methods.
4. *Regional dualism*—high productivity and incomes in some regions and little economic development in others.
5. A preponderance (80 to 85 percent) of the population earning its living in a relatively unproductive agricultural sector.
6. Disguised unemployment or underemployment—two people doing a job that one person can do.
7. High population growth (2.5 to 4 percent annually).
8. High rate of illiteracy and insufficient educational facilities.

*The World Bank uses the term *developing economies* to include low- and middle-income economies.

9. Widespread malnutrition and a wide range of health problems.
10. Political instability.
11. High dependence on a few products for export, generally agricultural products or minerals.
12. Inhospitable topography, such as deserts, mountains, and tropical forests.
13. Low saving rates and inadequate banking facilities.

You can see from these characteristics that a tremendous gap exists between the levels of living of Third World inhabitants and those of industrialized nations. Although economists have studied and theorized about the various aspects of economic development for over two centuries, their preoccupation with the poor nations of the world really began only after World War II.

A Human-Needs Approach to Economic Development

Until the 1970s, economists generally considered economic growth synonymous with economic development. A nation was considered to be developing economically if its real output per capita as measured by GNP/capita was increasing over time. However, the realization that economic growth does not necessarily imply development—because the benefits of this growth so often have applied to only a few—has led to the widespread adoption of a new, more comprehensive definition of economic development.

The **human-needs approach** defines economic development as the reduction of poverty, unemployment, and inequality in the distribution of income. The definition of poverty also has been broadened. Instead of being defined in terms of income, as is common in developed countries, a reduction in poverty has come to mean less illiteracy, less malnutrition, less disease and early death, and a shift from agricultural to industrial production.[41]

human-needs approach
Defines economic development as the elimination of poverty and unemployment as well as an increase in income

Because of the increased emphasis on human welfare and the lack of a clear link between income growth and human progress, the United Nations Development Program has devised a Human Development Index (HDI) based on three essential elements of human life: (1) a long and healthy life, (2) the ability to acquire knowledge, and (3) access to resources needed for a decent standard of living. These elements are measured by (1) life expectancy, (2) adult literacy, and (3) GDP/capita, adjusted for differences in purchasing power (see Figure 3.5 for the distribution of one of the variables). In its latest report, the program ranked Canada as the most developed with respect to social progress; the United States ranked third, below Canada and Norway.[42]

No Accepted General Theory

The inclusion of noneconomic variables has made it impossible to formulate a widely accepted general theory of development. Instead of pursuing a general theory, development economists are concentrating on specific problem areas, such as population growth, income distribution, unemployment, transfer of technology, the role of government in the process, and investment in human versus physical capital.

What is the relevance of a lack of consensus among specialists about development theory? If a particular theory has fallen into disfavor among the experts, can businesspeople neglect it when dealing with government officials? That depends. Perhaps those officials still subscribe to it. In that case, businesspeople should emphasize the parts of their proposals that are germane to the theory, which is generally not too difficult because nearly every proposal will provide not only investment in physical capital but also training of employees, employment, and the transfer of technology. There will even be some redistribution of income through the creation of a middle class composed of managers and highly skilled technicians. As an example, let's look at how businesspeople might emphasize investment in human capital when making a proposal.

[Figure 3.5] **Life Expectancy at Birth, 1998**

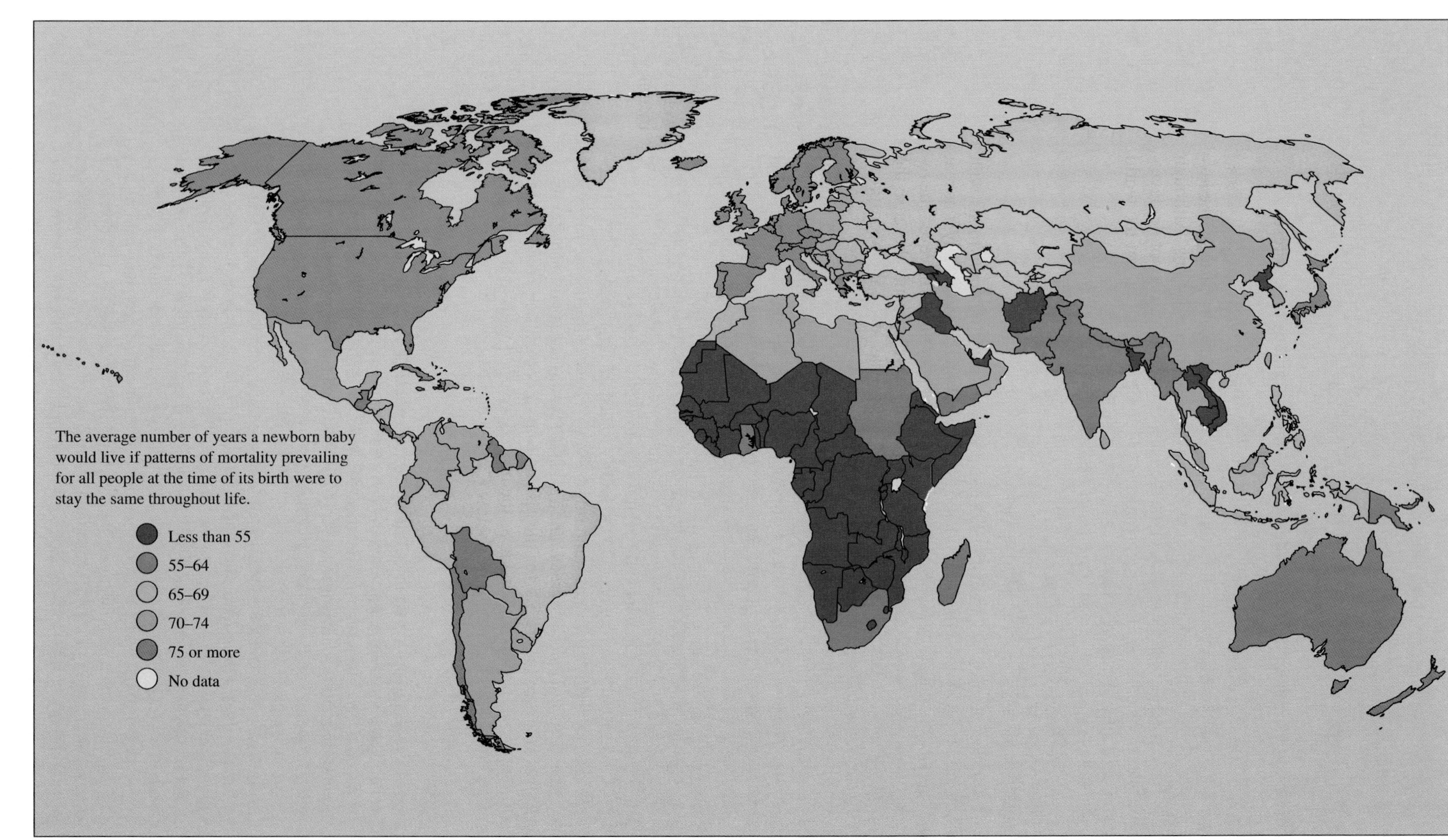
The average number of years a newborn baby would live if patterns of mortality prevailing for all people at the time of its birth were to stay the same throughout life.
Less than 55
55–64
65–69
70–74
75 or more
No data

Source: 2000 World Bank Atlas (Washington, D.C.: World Bank, 2000), p. 18. Republished with permission from World Bank Atlas; permission conveyed through Copyright Clearance Center, Inc.

Investment in Human Capital

This development theory recognizes that more than just capital accumulation is needed for growth. There must also be investment in the education of people so there will be managers to ensure that the capital is productive and skilled workers to operate and maintain the capital equipment.

If managers know that this theory has strong acceptance in the country where they have an operation or are seeking permission to establish one, they should emphasize this aspect of their investment. A multinational or global firm that does not have training programs for workers is rare, and nearly all send local managers to the home office to update their skills.

Import Substitution versus Export Promotion

Another strategy followed by some developing nations has been **import substitution.** Although developing nations have long considered the exporting of primary products (agricultural and raw materials) an important facet of their development strategy, they have not aggressively promoted the exporting of manufactured goods. Instead, they have concentrated on substituting these domestically manufactured products for imports as a way to lessen their dependence on developed countries.

import substitution
The local production of goods to replace imports

Unfortunately, import substitution has not reduced their dependence on developed nations as much as it has changed the composition of imports from finished products to capital and semiprocessed inputs. Often, however, developing nations are unable to obtain these inputs because of a lack of foreign exchange, which can stop entire industries and throw thousands of people out of work, further increasing dependence on developed nations. An example was the closing of automobile and agricultural machinery plants when the Turkish government could not obtain foreign exchange to import the necessary intermediate products.

Another serious problem with the import substitution strategy stems from the protection to local industry that governments grant by levying high import duties on goods that also are made domestically. Under this umbrella, local manufacturers feel no pressure to either lower their costs or improve their quality. Without such pressure, they rarely become competitive in world markets and thus cannot export. Furthermore, other domestic firms that must buy imports from these high-priced, protected industries cannot export either because their costs are excessive.

Problems such as these have caused numerous governments to change from a strategy of import substitution to one of promoting exports of manufactured goods. Spurring them on to this decision have been the rapid export growth of the newly industrializing nations and the general opening of world markets as a result of the Uruguay Round.

This change in strategy affects international firms in a variety of ways. First, local affiliate managers must be prepared for demands to export by government officials. They may even be given ultimatums, as were automobile manufacturers in Mexico: "If you need to import parts for your output, you must earn the foreign exchange to pay for them by exporting part of your production." A company asking for permission to set up a foreign manufacturing facility now will certainly be asked by government administrators about its plans for exporting. This is a new phenomenon to longtime managers accustomed to restricting an affiliate's sales to its internal market to save the export market for home-country production. Second, managers can no longer count on having permanent protection from competing imports, as they once could. In some countries, they are likely to be told that after a certain date they will lose their protection and will be expected to compete internationally. Last, in a situation where two firms are competing for permission to establish a plant, the deciding factor may be that one offers its multinational channels of distribution to the affiliate's exports.

The Importance of Keeping Current

These few examples illustrate (1) some of the concepts that underlie the strategies and policies of developing nations and (2) the relationship among the theories of international trade, economic development, and international investment. Moreover, they show why experienced international businesspeople keep abreast of developments in these areas.

International Investment Theories

Contemporary international investment theory has been expanded considerably from the classical theory, which postulated that differences in interest rates for investments of equal risk are the reason international capital moves from one nation to another. For this to happen, there had to be perfect competition, but as Kindleberger, a noted economist, stated, "Under perfect competition, foreign direct investment would not occur, nor would it be likely to occur in a world wherein the conditions were even approximately competitive."[43]

Contemporary Theories of Foreign Direct Investment

Monopolistic Advantage Theory

monopolistic advantage theory
Foreign direct investment is made by firms in oligopolistic industries possessing technical and other advantages over indigenous firms

The modern **monopolistic advantage theory** stems from Stephen Hymer's dissertation in the 1960s, in which he demonstrated that foreign direct investment occurred largely in oligopolistic industries rather than in industries operating under near-perfect competition. This means that the firms in these industries must possess advantages not available to local firms. Hymer reasoned that the advantages must be economies of scale, superior technology, or superior knowledge in marketing, management, or finance. Foreign direct investment takes place because of these product and factor market imperfections.[44]

Product and Factor Market Imperfections

Caves, a Harvard economist, expanded Hymer's work to show that superior knowledge permitted the investing firm to produce differentiated products that the consumers would prefer to similar locally made goods and thus would give the firm some control over the selling price and an advantage over indigenous firms. To support these contentions, he noted that companies investing overseas were in industries that typically engaged in heavy product research and marketing efforts.[45]

International Product Life Cycle

We have already examined this theory to help explain international trade flows, but as we said, there is a close relationship between international trade and international investment. As you saw, the IPLC concept also explains that foreign direct investment is a natural stage in the life of a product. To avoid losing a market that it services by exporting, a company is forced to invest in overseas production facilities when other companies begin to offer similar products. This move overseas will be heightened during the third and fourth stages as the company that introduced the product strives to remain competitive, first in its export markets (stage 3) and later in its home market (stage 4), by locating in countries where the factors of production are less expensive. In-bond factories on the Mexican–American border are an example.

Other Theories

Another theory was developed by Knickerbocker, who noted that when one firm, especially the leader in an oligopolistic industry, entered a market, other firms in the industry followed. The follow-the-leader theory is considered defensive because competitors invest to avoid losing the markets served by exports when the initial investor begins local production. They may also fear that the initiator will achieve some advantage of risk diversification that they will not have unless they also enter the market.[46] In addition, suspecting that the initiator knows something they do not, they may feel it is better to be safe than sorry.

cross investment
Foreign direct investment by oligopolistic firms in each other's home countries as a defense measure

Graham noted a tendency for **cross investment** by European and American firms in certain oligopolistic industries; that is, European firms tended to invest in the United States when American companies had gone to Europe. He postulated that such investments would permit the American subsidiaries of European firms to retaliate in the home market of U.S. companies if the European subsidiaries of these companies initiated some aggressive tactic, such as price cutting, in the European market.[47] Of course, as we noted in

Chapter 2, there are a number of other reasons investment in the United States by foreign multinationals takes place, such as *following the customer* (Japanese parts manufacturers following Japanese auto manufacturers), *seeking knowledge* (Japanese and European investment in Silicon Valley), and *benefiting from the stability of the American government.*

The **internalization theory** is an extension of the market imperfection theory. A firm has superior knowledge, but it may obtain a higher price for that knowledge by using it than by selling it in the open market. By investing in a foreign subsidiary rather than licensing, the company is able to send the knowledge across borders while maintaining it within the firm, presumably realizing a better return on the investment made to produce it.[48]

internalization theory
An extension of the market imperfection theory: to obtain a higher return on its investment, a firm will transfer its superior knowledge to a foreign subsidiary rather than sell it in the open market

Other theories relate to financial factors. Aliber believes that the imperfections in the foreign exchange markets may be responsible for foreign investment. Companies in nations with overvalued currencies are attracted to invest in countries whose currencies are undervalued.[49] Although empirical tests are inconclusive, it does seem that a sizable number of U.S. takeovers by European globals and multinationals occurred during the late 1970s, when the dollar was relatively weak. Another financially based theory (portfolio theory) suggests that international operations allow for a diversification of risk and therefore tend to maximize the expected return on investment.[50]

Dunning's Eclectic Theory of International Production. This theory combines elements of some of those we have discussed. Dunning maintains that if a firm is going to invest in production facilities overseas, it must have three kinds of advantages:

1. *Ownership-specific*—This is the extent to which a firm has or can get tangible and intangible assets not available to other firms.
2. *Internalization*—It is in the firm's best interests to use its ownership-specific advantages (internalize) rather than license them to foreign owners (externalize).
3. *Location-specific*—The firm will profit by locating part of its production facilities overseas.

The **eclectic theory of international production** provides an explanation for an international firm's choice of its overseas production facilities. The firm must have both location and ownership advantages to invest in a foreign plant. It will invest where it is most profitable to internalize its monopolistic advantage.[51]

eclectic theory of international production
For a firm to invest overseas, it must have three kinds of advantages: ownership-specific, internalization, and location-specific

There is one commonality to nearly all of these theories that is supported by empirical tests—the major part of direct foreign investment is made by large, research-intensive firms in oligopolistic industries. Also, all these theories offer reasons companies find it *profitable* to invest overseas. However, as we stated in Chapter 2, all motives can be linked in some way to the desire to increase or protect not only profits but also *sales* and *markets.*

[Summary]

Understand the theories that attempt to explain why certain goods are traded internationally.

Why do nations trade? Mercantilists did so to build up storehouses of gold. Later, Adam Smith showed that a nation would export goods that it could produce with less labor than other nations. Ricardo then proved that even though it was less efficient than other nations, a country could still profit by exporting goods if it held a comparative advantage in the production of those goods.

The idea that a nation would tend to export products requiring a large amount of a relatively abundant factor was offered by Heckscher and Ohlin in their theory of factor endowment. The international product life cycle theory states that many products first produced in the United States or other developed countries are eventually produced in less developed nations and become imports to the very countries in which their production began.

In the 1920s, economists realized that economies of scale affect international trade because they permit the industries of a nation to become low-cost producers without having an abundance of a class of production factors. As in the case of comparative advantage, nations specialize in the production of a few products and trade to supply the rest. The Linder theory of overlapping demand states that because customers' tastes are strongly affected by income levels, a nation's income level per capita determines the kind of goods they will demand. The kinds of goods produced to meet this demand reflect the country's income per capita level. International trade in manufactured goods will be greater between nations with similar levels of per capita income. Porter claims that four classes of variables affect a country's ability to gain a competitive advantage: demand conditions, factor conditions, related and supporting industries, and firm strategy, structure, and rivalry.

Comprehend the arguments for imposing trade restrictions.

Special interest groups demand protection for defense industries so that this country will have their output in wartime and will not depend on imports that might not be available. Critics say that it would be far more efficient to subsidize some firms, that is, pay them to be ready. Taxpayers would know exactly what the cost is, as we do in the case of American steamship companies. New industries in developing nations frequently request barriers to imports of competing products from developed countries. The argument is that the infant industry must have time to gain experience before having to confront world competition. Protectionists argue for protection from cheap imports by claiming that countries with lower hourly labor rates than their nation's rates can flood the United States with low-priced goods and put Americans out of work. However, hourly labor rates are just a small part of production costs. There are legislated fringe benefits that are a much higher percentage of the direct wages than is the case in developed nations. Productivity per worker may be considerably lower in developing nations so that less is produced for a given hourly rate. Commonly, also, the costs of the other factors of production that must be included in the cost of production often are higher in developing nations. Others want "fair" competition, that is, an import duty to raise the cost of the imported good to the price of the imported article to eliminate any "unfair" advantage that the foreign competitor may have. This, of course, nullifies the comparative advantage. Companies will also demand that their government retaliate against dumping and subsidies offered by their competitors in other countries.

Explain the two basic kinds of import restrictions: tariff and nontariff trade barriers.

In response to demands for protection, governments impose import duties (tariff barriers) and nontariff barriers, such as quotas, voluntary export restraints, and orderly marketing arrangements, and nonquantitative nontariff barriers, such as direct government participation in trade, customs and other administrative procedures and standards for health, safety, and product quality.

State the agreements reached during the Uruguay Round.

As a result of negotiations during the Uruguay Round, governments agreed to eliminate nontariff barriers such as quotas, VERs, and orderly marketing agreements and bring textiles and agricultural products under the general trading rules for all products during a 10-year period.

Appreciate the relevance of the changing status of tariff and nontariff barriers to businesspeople.

Exporting firms may find that because tariff and nontariff barriers have been eliminated or lowered, they can now enter markets that were closed to them. It also is easier for firms to locate production activities in lower-cost nations to improve the efficiency of their manufacturing systems. Multidomestic firms may be able to close less efficient plants and supply those markets by exporting from more efficient ones.

Recognize the weaknesses of GNP/capita as an economic indicator.

For a number of reasons, GNP/capita is a weak market indicator. Transactions worth billions of dollars go unrecorded because people do business in the underground economy, paying cash without demanding receipts and invoices. Exchange rates for converting economic data usually do not reflect consumer purchasing power. International institutions such as the World Bank and the United Nations have developed a method of comparing GNPs that is based on purchasing power parity.

Identify the common characteristics of developing nations.

Developing nations have certain common characteristics: unequal distribution of income, technological and regional dualism, large percentage of the population in agriculture, high population growth, high illiteracy rate, insufficient education, and low saving rates.

Understand the new definition of economic development, which includes more than economic growth.

The human-needs approach defines economic development as the reduction of poverty, unemployment, and inequality in the distribution of income.

Understand why some governments are changing from an import substitution strategy to one of export promotion and the implications of this change for businesspeople.

Governments are changing from using an import substitution strategy to one of export promotion to become less dependent on developed nations. Also, governments are opening their borders to imports to force local producers to raise quality and improve prices so that they can enter world markets. Managers of foreign-owned affiliates can be expected to export even though the company may prefer to keep exporting and keep the profits for the home office.

Explain some of the theories of foreign direct investment.

International investment theory attempts to explain why foreign direct investment (FDI) takes place. Product and factor market imperfections provide firms, primarily in oligopolistic industries, with advantages not open to indigenous companies. The international product life cycle theory explains international investment as well as international trade. Some firms follow the industry leader, and the tendency of European firms to invest in the United States and vice versa seems to indicate that cross investment is done for defensive reasons. The internalization theory states that firms will seek to invest in foreign subsidiaries rather than license their superior knowledge to receive a better return on the investment used to develop that knowledge.

There are two financially based explanations of foreign direct investment. One holds that foreign exchange market imperfections attract firms from nations with overvalued currencies to invest in nations with undervalued currencies. The second theory postulates that FDI is made to diversify risk. Empirical tests reveal that most FDI is made by large, research-intensive firms in oligopolistic industries.

The eclectic theory of international production explains an international firm's choice of its overseas production facilities. The firm must have location and ownership advantages to invest in a foreign plant. It will invest where it is most profitable to internalize its monopolistic advantage.

[Key Words]

mercantilism (p. 109)
absolute advantage (p. 110)
comparative advantage (p. 111)
factor endowment (p. 112)
exchange rate (p. 114)
currency devaluation (p. 115)
international product life cycle (IPLC) (p. 116)
dumping (p. 121)
subsidies (p. 122)
countervailing duties (p. 123)
tariffs (p. 124)
ad valorem duty (p. 124)
specific duty (p. 124)
compound duty (p. 124)
variable levy (p. 125)
nontariff barriers (NTBs) (p. 125)
quotas (p. 125)
voluntary export restraints (VERs) (p. 127)
orderly marketing arrangements (p. 127)
developed (p. 131)
developing (p. 131)
newly industrializing countries (NICs) (p. 131)
newly industrialized economies (NIEs) (p. 131)
underground economy (p. 132)
purchasing power parity (PPP) (p. 133)
human-needs approach (p. 135)
import substitution (p. 137)
monopolistic advantage theory (p. 138)
cross investment (p. 138)
internalization theory (p. 139)
eclectic theory of international production (p. 139)

[Questions]

1. a. Explain Adam Smith's theory of absolute advantage.
   b. How does Ricardo's theory of comparative advantage differ from the theory of absolute advantage?
2. What is the relationship between the Heckscher-Ohlin factor endowment theory and the theories in question 1?
3. Name some products that you believe have passed through the four stages of the international product life cycle.
4. It seems that free, unrestricted international trade, in which each nation produces and exports products for which it has a comparative advantage, will enable everyone to have a higher level of living. Why, then, does every country have import duty restrictions?
5. We certainly need defense industries, and we must protect them from import competition by placing restrictions on competitive imports. True or false? Is there an alternative to trade restrictions that might make more economic sense?
6. "Workers are paid $20 an hour in the United States but only $4 in Taiwan. Of course we can't compete. We need to protect our jobs from cheap foreign labor." What are some possible problems with this statement?

7. There are two general classifications of import duties: tariff and nontariff barriers.
   a. Describe the various types of tariff barriers.
   b. What are some of the nontariff barriers?
8. Of what importance to marketers is a nation's level of economic development?
9. What problems with the import substitution strategy have caused some governments to increase their emphasis on export promotion?
10. A firm entering the market first will soon dominate it, and the large market share it acquires will enable it to obtain the benefits of economies of scale. True or false? Remember that there are at least two studies showing that first movers held large market shares.

[Internet Exercises]

Using the Internet

1. According to the World Trade Organization's Agreement on Textiles and Clothing (ATC), textiles and clothing products are being integrated progressively into GATT 1994 rules.
   a. Describe the stages of the integration process.
   b. What is the body that is monitoring the application of the agreement? Who are the members?
   c. As you read in Chapter 3, U.S. clothing importers circumvent the Chinese quotas by transshipping clothing made in China to other countries, where it is relabeled as coming from those countries. What are the agreement's provisions for dealing with the circumvention of quotas by transshipment and false declarations of origin?
   d. What were the four WTO members which maintained import restrictions under the former Multifiber Agreement (United States, Canada, European Union, and Norway) required to do under the ATC?
2. Assume you own an exporting company that specializes in American-made construction machinery. You have been selling to the larger Latin American markets, such as Mexico, Brazil, and Argentina, but now you have a request for a quotation from a construction firm in Honduras, a market where you have not previously sold your products. As usual, you go to the Department of Commerce's *Country Commercial Guides* (CCGs) on the Internet for background information. What does the U.S. embassy in Honduras think of American business opportunities? For example:
   a. You heard somewhere that Honduran imports have quadrupled over the last decade primarily because of the Honduran government's program of trade liberalization. According to the CCG Executive Summary, what actions did the government take? What has been the response to its program?
   b. Does Honduras buy much from the United States, or is it supplied primarily from the European Union? (Check the Executive Summary.)
   c. In Chapter VI, "Trade Regulations and Standards," you will find the tariff rate for capital goods. Do capital goods such as your construction equipment pay high import duties?
   d. What does the U.S. embassy say has been the size of the market for the last three years? (See Chapter V.)

e. According to Chapter VI of the *Country Commercial Guide,* what does the U.S. embassy think the future is for the importation of construction equipment? Why?
f. Will Honduran construction firms accept American construction machinery as readily as European or Japanese machinery?
g. On what economic development strategy was the Honduran development strategy based until the mid-1980s? (See Chapter IV.)
h. Is there a possibility that the Honduran government will place trade barriers to the importation of construction machinery to protect local production?
i. Can you export directly to construction firms, or must you sell through local agents or distributors? (Check Chapter IV, "Marketing U.S. Products and Services.")
j. What does the U.S. embassy say about exporters trying to sell directly to Honduran customers?
k. If the U.S. exporter wants to find a local agent or distributor, how should it go about it?

[Minicase 3.1]

Tarus Manufacturing

John Baker, vice president of Tarus Manufacturing, called in Ed Anderson, the export manager, to discuss the sales results for the new adhesive that Tarus was exporting to its sales subsidiary in Colombia.

Baker: *Ed, how is Tarus Colombiana doing with the new adhesive we're sending them?*

Anderson: *They're doing well. In the first six months they've sold 6,000 quarts at 1,800 pesos, or $3 a quart.*

Baker: *Not bad for a small operation. If they keep it up, that cement is going to be a best-seller.*

Anderson: *That's true, and our profit is good. Moreover, I've been studying Colombia's import tariff, and I think I've found a way to improve our profit.*

Baker: *Great. How are you going to do it? It has to be honest, Ed.*

Anderson: *Well, you know that they have to pay a 40 percent ad valorem import duty on our $1.60 invoice price plus 60 pesos per quart specific duty. If, however, we send them the adhesive in 55-gallon drums, the import duty drops to 30 percent ad valorem plus a specific duty of 6,600 pesos per drum.*

Baker: *Yes, but then they'll have to buy 1-quart cans and labels and fill them in Colombia. This adds to their expense.*

Anderson: *True, but because we won't have to fill the cans or charge them for cans and labels, we will save 20 cents per quart, which we'll pass on to them.*

Baker: *How much will it cost to fill the cans locally?*

Anderson: *They tell me the cans, labels, and labor to fill the cans will come to 180 pesos per can, and the only investment required is a shut-off valve, which they screw in the drumhead when the cans are filled.*

Baker: *I'm not sure I see the advantage, Ed. The cans, labels, and labor are more expensive in Colombia than they are here. Where is the advantage?*

Anderson: *Let me show you, John.*

Show Ed Anderson's calculations. Disregard any possible freight savings for shipping in bulk.

[Minicase 3.2]

The Impact of Galawi's Development Policy

Armando Suarez, CEO, and Pedro Garcia, Director of International Operations for Industrias Globales, are discussing a statement made today by the secretary of treasury in Galawi.

Suarez: *Pedro, did you listen to the secretary's comments today about the proposed change in development strategy?*

Garcia: *Yes, I did, and I'm concerned. We have spent considerable time and money planning our entry into the Galawi market, and if the government proceeds with the new economic strategy, we've got to change our plant design, plan to produce different product lines, and completely change our marketing plans.*

Suarez: *This apparently is more serious than I thought. How can a change in their development strategy from import substitution to export promotion affect us?*

Garcia: *Hang on to your chair, Chief, and I'll explain each strategy and how the change will affect our entire startup program in Galawi. Oh, and by the way, our Galawi competitors are going to have to make changes, too.*

Imagine you are Pedro Garcia.

1. Describe the two strategies for the CEO.
2. Explain how the change in development strategy will affect the firm in many ways.
3. What changes in the entry plans will the firm have to make?

[Chapter] 4

The Dynamics of International Organizations

"If one word encapsulates the changes we are living through, it is 'globalization.' We live in a world that is interconnected as never before—one in which groups and individuals interact more and more directly across State frontiers, often without involving the State at all. This has its dangers, of course. Crime, narcotics, terrorism, disease, weapons—all these move back and forth faster, and in greater numbers, than in the past. People feel threatened by events far away. But the benefits of globalization are obvious too: faster growth, higher living standards, and new opportunities—not only for individuals but also for better understanding between nations, and for common action."

—*Kofi A. Annan, Secretary-General, United Nations, Millennium Report, April 3, 2000*

Concept Previews

After reading this chapter, you should be able to:

- **understand** the influence international organizations have on international businesses
- **explain** the activities of the United Nations in the economic and social fields as well as those as a peacekeeper/peacemaker in the World's trouble spots
- **explain** the three major parts of the World Bank: its regular loan window, its International Finance Corporation, and its International Development Association
- **explain** the original and changed activities of the International Monetary Fund
- **understand** the importance of the World Trade Organization to world business and trade
- **understand** the European Union and how it affects business
- **understand** the North American Free Trade Agreement and its impact on business
- **know** about the Organization for Economic Cooperation and Development

Fabian Falcon/Stock Boston

The United States and the United Nations: A Close but Sometimes Strained Relationship

As indicated in the following piece from the U.S. Department of State, the United States was closely involved in the creation of the United Nations. The UN headquarters is located in the United States, and the United States is one of five permanent members of the Security Council. Nonetheless, the UN has many critics in the United States and the United States has made many recommendations for improvement of the UN. The following is part of the background notes on the UN prepared by the U.S. Department of State:

> The idea for the United Nations was elaborated in declarations signed at the wartime Allied conferences in Moscow and Tehran in 1943. The name "United Nations" was suggested by President Franklin Roosevelt. From August to October 1944, representatives of the U.S., U.K., France, U.S.S.R., and China met to elaborate the plans at the Dumbarton Oaks Estate in Washington, DC. Those and later talks produced proposals outlining the

purposes of the organization, its membership and organs, as well as arrangements to maintain international peace and security and international economic and social cooperation. These proposals were discussed and debated by governments and private citizens worldwide.

On April 25, 1945, the United Nations Conference on International Organizations began in San Francisco. The 50 nations represented at the conference signed the Charter of the United Nations two months later on June 26. Poland, which was not represented at the conference, but for which a place among the original signatories had been reserved, added its name later, bringing the total of original signatories to 51. The UN came into existence on October 24, 1945, after the Charter had been ratified by the five permanent members of the Security Council—China, France, U.S.S.R., U.K., and U.S.—and by a majority of the other 46 signatories.

The U.S. Senate, by a vote of 89 to 2, gave its consent to the ratification of the UN Charter on July 28, 1945. In December 1945, the Senate and the House of Representatives, by unanimous votes, requested that the UN make its headquarters in the U.S. The offer was accepted and the UN headquarters building was constructed in New York City in 1949 and 1950 beside the East River on donated land, which is considered international territory. Under special agreement with the U.S., certain diplomatic privileges and immunities have been granted, but generally the laws of New York City, New York State, and the U.S. apply.

It is important that the UN operate efficiently and effectively. The U.S. seeks a UN that both gets back to basics and is ready to meet the challenges of the 21st century. U.S. efforts include:

Reducing bureaucracies. Important progress has been made in streamlining the UN personnel system and holding the line on budgets;

Improving management. The U.S. applauds the initiatives of Secretary General Annan in consolidating programs and implementing a more transparent and consultative approach to management;

Security Council reform. The U.S. supports permanent seats on the Security Council for Japan and Germany and a modest further enlargement of the Council to include permanent seats for developing nations from Asia, Africa, and Latin America;

Improving responsiveness. The U.S. seeks a UN able to respond to humanitarian crises more rapidly and effectively. ■

Source: U.S. Department of State, Bureau of International Organization Affairs, www.state.gov/www/background_notes/un_0007_bgn.html, (July 2000).

Given the immense and growing numbers and importance of private and governmental international transactions, it is not surprising that a variety of international organizations exist to facilitate, regulate, measure, or finance them. It is advantageous for the business student—who is likely to be exposed to international opportunities and problems soon after graduation—to be aware of the existence and functions of a number of these organizations.

Some are worldwide organizations, and some are regional organizations with members from only one geographic area. Some are large, and some are small. Most are groupings of governments, but a few are private.

The element common to all the organizations discussed in this chapter is that they all can be important to businesses. They may be sources of orders or sources of financing. They may be regulatory, or they may aim at standardization of weights and measurements. Last but not least, they may be sources of jobs. The United Nations, the World Bank, and the Organization for Economic Cooperation and Development are a few of the organizations that routinely have career positions to fill in such fields as economics, languages, law, and information technology. You can obtain information by contacting the specific organization through its Web page; many of those pages are listed in the Internet Appendix at the end of Chapter 1.

Relationship between International Organizations and International Businesses

It is important for people involved in international business to understand the impact international organizations have on businesses and businesspeople throughout the world. No longer is it sufficient for a businessperson simply to understand the political environment and the laws in her or his own country. It is now important to understand political environments and laws throughout the world. Since most organizations discussed in this chapter are organizations of governments, businesspeople should understand how and when they speak for their member governments and the impact their power has. Some international organizations have governmental powers and act as supranational entities. For example, a merger of two companies based in the United States may need approval from the European Union if the merger would significantly affect markets or business operations in Europe.

The United Nations

Possibly the best-known worldwide organization is the **United Nations (UN)**. Conceived and born amid the idealism and hope that came with peace following World War II, the UN has been both a source of pride and a disappointment to many of its supporters.

United Nations (UN)
International organization of 189 member-countries dedicated to the promotion of peace; also has many functions related to business

The UN's peacekeeping efforts have taken place in many areas throughout the world. Some have been successful while others have not been. In addition to its peacekeeping functions, the United Nations has been responsible for the creation of many international entities that facilitate business transactions around the world. One example is the International Telecommunication Union (ITU), which is a UN agency headquartered in Geneva, Switzerland, that assists governments and the private sector in coordination of global telecommunications networks and services. Another example is the International Trade Center of the UN, which provides trade information to assist developing countries in their efforts to realize their full business potential. A third example is the International Civil Aviation Organization (ICAO), which is headquartered in Montreal, Canada, and works with civil aviation throughout the world. A complete listing of the institutions in the UN system is given in Table 4.1.

The United Nations also has been responsible for many international agreements and much of the creation of international law since 1945. For example, the Universal Declaration of Human Rights, which the General Assembly adopted in 1948, seeks to ensure basic human rights for all people worldwide.

The UN is a collection of scattered offices, which can be a source of frustration for the student or businessperson. The UN's Web page, www.un.org, is a good source of information about the UN and its operations.

Table 4.1 Official Classification of the United Nations System

Programs of the United Nations

United Nations Headquarters (UN): New York, USA
United Nations Compensation Commission (UNCC): Geneva, Switzerland
United Nations Staff College (UNSC): Turin, Italy
United Nations Office at Geneva (UNOG): Geneva, Switzerland
United Nations High Commissioner for Human Rights, Office of the (UNHCHR): Geneva, Switzerland
United Nations Office at Vienna (UNOV): Vienna, Austria
Office for Outer Space Affairs (OOSA): Vienna, Austria
United Nations Commission on International Trade Law (UNCITRAL): Vienna, Austria
United Nations Office for Project Services (UNOPS): New York, USA
Economic Commission for Africa (ECA): Addis Ababa, Ethiopia
Economic Commission for Europe (ECE): Geneva, Switzerland
Economic Commission for Latin America and the Caribbean (ECLAC): Santiago, Chile
Economic and Social Commission for Asia and the Pacific (ESCAP): Bangkok, Thailand
Economic and Social Commission for Western Asia (ESCWA): Beirut, Lebanon
United Nations Children's Fund (UNICEF): New York, USA
United Nations Conference on Trade and Development (UNCTAD): Geneva, Switzerland
United Nations Development Program (UNDP): New York, USA
United Nations Development Fund for Women (UNIFEM): New York, USA
United Nations Volunteers (UNV): Bonn, Germany
United Nations Environment Program (UNEP): Nairobi, Kenya
United Nations Population Fund (UNFPA): New York, USA
United Nations International Drug Control Program (UNDCP): Vienna, Austria
World Food Program (WFP): Rome, Italy
United Nations Relief and Works Agency for Palestine Refugees in the Near East (UNRWA): Gaza, Gaza Strip, and Amman, Jordan
United Nations Center for Human Settlements [UNCHS (Habitat)]: Nairobi, Kenya
United Nations High Commissioner for Refugees, Office of the (UNHCR): Geneva, Switzerland
United Nations University (UNU): Tokyo, Japan
International Court of Justice (ICJ): The Hague, Netherlands
International Research and Training Institute for the Advancement of Women (INSTRAW): Santo Domingo, Dominican Republic
United Nations Institute for Disarmament Research (UNIDIR): Geneva, Switzerland
United Nations Institute for Training and Research (UNITAR): Geneva, Switzerland
International Institute on Ageing (INIA): Valetta, Malta
United Nations Research Institute for Social Development (UNRISD): Geneva, Switzerland
United Nations Interregional Crime and Justice Research Institute (UNICRI): Rome, Italy
International Trade Center UNCTAD/WTO: Geneva, Switzerland
Advisory Committee on Administrative and Budgetary Questions (ACABQ): New York, USA
International Civil Service Commission (ICSC): New York, USA
Joint Inspection Unit (JIU): Geneva, Switzerland
Panel of External Auditors of the United Nations, the Specialized Agencies and the International Atomic Energy Agency: New York, USA
United Nations Board of Auditors: New York, USA
United Nations Joint Staff Pension Fund (UNJSPF): New York, USA

Specialized Agencies of the United Nations System

International Labor Organization (ILO): Geneva, Switzerland
International Training Center (ILO/ITC): Turin, Italy
Food and Agriculture Organization of the United Nations (FAO): Rome, Italy
United Nations Educational, Scientific and Cultural Organization (UNESCO): Paris, France
International Bureau of Education (IBE): Geneva, Switzerland
International Civil Aviation Organization (ICAO): Montreal, Canada
World Health Organization (WHO): Geneva, Switzerland
World Bank (IBRD): Washington, DC, USA
Multilateral Investment Guarantee Agency (MIGA): Washington, DC, USA
International Monetary Fund (IMF): Washington, DC, USA
Universal Postal Union (UPU): Berne, Switzerland
International Telecommunication Union (ITU): Geneva, Switzerland
World Meteorological Organization (WMO): Geneva, Switzerland

(continued)

Table 4.1 *(continued)*

Specialized Agencies of the United Nations System (continued)
International Maritime Organization (IMO): London, United Kingdom
World Intellectual Property Organization (WIPO): Geneva, Switzerland
International Fund for Agricultural Development (IFAD): Rome, Italy
United Nations Industrial Development Organization (UNIDO): Vienna, Austria
International Center for Science and High Technology (ICS): Trieste, Italy
World Trade Organization: Geneva, Switzerland
Autonomous Organizations
International Atomic Energy Agency (IAEA): Vienna, Austria
World Tourism Organization: Madrid, Spain
Convention Secretariats
United Nations Framework Convention on Climate Change (UNFCCC): Bonn, Germany
United Nations Convention to Combat Desertification (UNCCD): Bonn, Germany

Source: United Nations Administrative Committee on Coordination, www.unsystem.org/index2.html (April 4, 2000). Reprinted with permission of the UN Publications Board.

The work of the United Nations is carried out through five main bodies or organs:* the General Assembly, the Security Council, the Economic and Social Council, the International Court of Justice, and the Secretariat. Even though the UN conducts its work throughout the world, all the main UN organs are headquartered in New York City except for the International Court of Justice, which is located in The Hague in the Netherlands. The United Nations has six official languages: Arabic, Chinese, English, French, Russian, and Spanish.

UN Growth and Change

All UN member-nations are members of the **General Assembly,** in which each nation has one vote regardless of its size, wealth, or power. The General Assembly is able to express its intentions through resolutions it adopts. Decisions on important questions, such as those involving peace and security, the admission of new member-nations, and budgetary matters, require a two-thirds majority, while decisions on other matters require a simple majority. Decisions of the General Assembly have no legally binding force for governments or citizens in the member-nations, but they carry the weight of world opinion. The number of members has grown rapidly since the UN's establishment in 1945, and new nations continue to join as they gain independence and become sovereign in their territory. The UN charter was signed in San Francisco, California, in 1945 by the 51 original member-nations. Today there are 189 members. Although there have been proposals to allow nongovernmental agencies to join the UN, at the current time, only recognized nations may join.

General Assembly Deliberative body of UN made up of all member-nations, each with one vote regardless of size, wealth, or power

The second major organ of the UN is the **Security Council.** It is composed of 15 members—5 permanent members and 10 chosen (5 each year) by the General Assembly for two-year terms. The five permanent members—the People's Republic of China, France, Russia, the United Kingdom, and the United States—each have the power to veto any measure. Five of the nonpermanent members are elected from among member-countries in Africa and Asia. One of the nonpermanent members comes from a member-country in Eastern Europe, two come from Latin American member-countries, and the remaining two come from member-countries in Western Europe and other areas.

Security Council Body of UN composed of 5 permanent members with veto power and 10 chosen (5 each year) for two-year terms

*The UN has a sixth organ, the Trusteeship Council, but it suspended operations in 1994.

Members of the UN Security Council in session.
AP Photo (Mikhail Metzel)

The Secretariat, which is headed by the Secretary-General, is the staff of the UN. It carries out day-to-day administrative functions and is headquartered in New York City even though it has offices in other cities around the world. The Secretariat services the other principal organs and administers the UN's programs and policies. The Secretary-General, who is appointed by the General Assembly on the recommendation of the Security Council for a five-year renewable term, supervises the Secretariat. The current Secretary-General, Kofi A. Annan of Ghana, is the seventh Secretary-General of the United Nations. He was the first Secretary-General to be elected from the ranks of United Nations staff and began his term on January 1, 1997. About 8,600 people from 170 countries make up its staff. As international civil servants, they and the Secretary-General answer to the United Nations alone for their activities and take an oath not to seek or receive instructions from any governmental or outside authority.[1]

The Economic and Social Council (ECOSOC) is concerned with economic problems, such as trade, transport, industrialization, and economic development, and social issues, including population, children, housing, women's rights, racial discrimination, illegal drugs, crime, social welfare, youth, the human environment, and food. It makes recommendations on how to improve education and health conditions and promote respect for and observation of the human rights and freedoms of people everywhere.

The International Court of Justice (ICJ) is also called the World Court. The ICJ renders legal decisions involving disputes between national governments because it was established to resolve disputes between sovereign states, not between individuals. As a result, only nations may be parties to litigation before the court. Governments can, and often do, intervene on behalf of private parties such as corporations and individuals in their countries. Even though the court has worldwide jurisdiction to hear disputes between governments, it hears relatively few cases, usually fewer than 10 a year. The ICJ has 15 judges who must come from 15 different countries. The judges serve nine-year terms. A majority of the General Assembly and a majority of the Security Council must agree on appointment of judges to the ICJ. The activities of the ICJ are explored more fully in Chapter 11.

Over 52,000 people work for the UN and its related organizations worldwide. As was mentioned above, during its existence, the United Nations has promoted many programs and agreements that assist with the smooth operations of businesses worldwide. Table 4.2 includes a statement from the UN outlining contributions made by the UN to world business.

Table 4.2 Contribution of the UN System to Commercial Order and Openness

International markets require global rules of the road. This is virtually a truism in the business world, which must deal with the complications of operating across borders and in distant regions on an everyday basis. Not as widely appreciated is the extent of the soft infrastructure—as UN Secretary-General Kofi Annan terms it—that is already in place to facilitate the international exchange of goods, money and information.

- When ships sail freely across the seas and through international straits, they are protected by rules legitimized in UN conferences.
- Commercial airlines have the right to fly across borders, and to land in case of emergency, due to agreements negotiated by the International Civil Aviation Organization, part of the UN system.
- The World Health Organization sets criteria for pharmaceutical quality and standardizes the names for drugs.
- Universal Postal Union protocols prevent losses and allow the mail to move across borders.
- International Telecommunication Union allotment of frequencies keeps the air waves from becoming hopelessly clogged, and thus avoids interference among radio transmissions.
- Data collected and re-distributed from member states by the World Meteorological Organization makes possible worldwide and country-specific weather forecasts.
- The UN Sales Convention and the UN Convention on the Carriage of Goods by Sea help to establish rights and obligations for buyers and sellers in international commercial transactions.

In short, without these and other public goods generated by the UN system, it would truly be a jungle out there for firms from developing, industrialized and transition countries alike that cared to venture beyond their own national borders. Within the UN system, there are 28 different organizations. Virtually all of these bodies contribute in one way or another to the maintenance of commercial order and openness.

The establishment of states' jurisdictional rights clarifies which nation is the legitimate political authority on land, on the sea, and in the air. This makes it possible to invest in oil exploration and drilling or to send ships and planes across oceans and continents.

Before the United Nations got in the business of setting international laws governing commercial transactions, such standardization was promoted by a number of international organizations. Now the UN Commission on International Trade Law is the most important body in the field.

In summary, it is not practical for rules for commercial conduct to be negotiated on an ad hoc basis. In our present world of close to 200 states, it is important to win universal, or virtually universal, support for standards of economic as well as political behavior. International regimes require legitimacy, and the consent and willing participation of the international community is obtained most reliably via the United Nations.

Source: United Nations, www.un.org/partners/business/fs2.htm. Reprinted with permission of the UN Publications Board.

The World Bank and Other Multilateral Development Banks

Multilateral development banks International lending institutions that work primarily with developing countries to promote economic and social progress

Multilateral development banks are international lending institutions owned by member-nations. They work primarily with developing countries. Their objective is to promote economic and social progress in developing member-nations by providing loans, technical assistance, capital investment, and help with economic development plans. The term *multilateral development banks* (MDBs) typically refers to the five main development banks worldwide: the Bank for Reconstruction and Development (commonly called the World Bank) and the four regional development banks: the African Development Bank, the Asian Development Bank, the European Bank for Reconstruction and Development, and the Inter-American Development Bank Group.

The member-nations of the banks include both borrowing developing countries and donor developed countries. Even though each bank has its own independent legal and operational status, the MDBs maintain a high level of cooperation. The MDBs provide financing for development activities through several types of financial facilities:

1. Long-term loans, which are based on market interest rates. The banks borrow on the international capital markets to fund these loans and relend to borrowing governments in developing countries.

2. Very long-term loans (often termed credits), which are loans with interest rates well below market rates. These facilities are funded through direct contributions from governments in donor countries.

3. Grant financing, mostly for technical assistance, advisory services, or project preparation.[2]

The World Bank

As its name indicates, this organization operates all over the world, in contrast to the regional development banks, whose geographic ranges are indicated by their names. We shall examine first the World Bank and then the regional ones.

The International Bank for Reconstruction and Development (IBRD) is usually referred to—in its own publications and elsewhere—as the World Bank. The World Bank Group consists of the Bank itself, the International Finance Corporation (IFC), the International Development Association (IDA), the Multilateral Investment Guarantee Agency (MIGA), and the International Center for Settlement of Investment Disputes (ICSID). The World Bank is the world's largest source of development assistance, providing nearly $16 billion in loans a year to its client countries.[3] The great majority of Group loans or credits are made to developing countries. You can obtain further information on the World Bank at www.worldbank.org.

Hard Loans

hard loans
Made and repayable in hard, convertible currencies at market interest rates with normal market maturities

The World Bank makes **hard loans.** This means its loans are at prevailing market interest rates with normal market maturities and are granted only to sound borrowers. The Bank must make relatively safe loans with high assurance of repayment because its own funds are acquired through sale of securities that must compete with government and private business offerings. Investors would not buy World Bank securities, even at advantageous interest rates, if they felt the Bank's loans were insecure.

Some countries have been unable to make payments when called for by the original loan terms. The Bank has rescheduled many of these loans, giving the debtor countries more time to repay them; however, it is quite possible that unless economic conditions improve for debtor developing countries, some World Bank loans will have to be recognized as being in default.

International Finance Corporation (IFC)

The International Finance Corporation (IFC) is the World Bank Group's investment banker. Its sphere is exclusively private risk ventures in the developing countries. The purpose of the IFC is to further economic development by encouraging growth of productive enterprise in member-countries, thus supplementing the activities of the World Bank.[4]

Joint Ventures Favored

The IFC's policy is to favor joint ventures that have some local capital committed at the outset or at least the probability of local capital involvement in the foreseeable future.[5] This is not to say that the IFC will not cooperate with capital sources outside the host country (the country in which the investment is being made), and there are many examples of such cooperation. Among the industries thus capitalized have been fertilizers, synthetic fibers, tourism, paper, and cotton fabric. The outside capital sources, if in related lines of business, are usually international companies (ICs). A few ICs that have cooperated with the IFC have been Phillips Petroleum, AKV Netherlands, ICI, Intercontinental Hotels, and Pechiney-Gobain.

Creation of Local Capital Markets

In return for its investment in a company, the IFC takes securities in the form of stock (equity ownership) or bonds (debt). One objective of the IFC is to sell its securities into

IFC's Small Enterprise Fund Reaches Out

Small and Medium-Sized Enterprises

Historically, the IFC has not normally financed projects of less than $5 million owing to the processing time and costs associated with the appraisal process. However, to reach out to small and medium-sized enterprises that are expected to become engines of economic growth, the IFC will now consider smaller ones, as low as $250,000.

The identification and appraisal procedure for these small projects will be simple and fast. They will be approved by the immediate management, not—as is the common practice—by the Board of Directors. To accelerate the program, the IFC will assign investment officers full-time to each country. Those officers will work to determine where the IFC can make a significant developmental impact through advisory work, technical assistance, investments, and financial intermediary lending in nine transition countries. They are Albania, Azerbaijan, Bosnia-Herzegovina, Cambodia and Laos, FYR Macedonia, Kazakhstan, Mongolia, Slovakia, and Uzbekistan.[6] ■

a local capital market. To do that, it will help create and nurture such a market. For example, the IFC extended a $5 million credit line to a syndicate of private Brazilian investment banks to provide support for those banks' securities underwriting activities. The banks work with Fondo do Desenvolvimento do Mercado de Capitais, a revolving capital market development fund maintained by the Brazilian central bank. The objectives are (1) to induce the investment banks to assume a greater role in underwriting Brazilian securities in Brazil, (2) to improve the access of Brazilian companies to long-term domestic source capital, and (3) to encourage Brazilians to invest in sound domestic securities.

Thanks to the IFC, investors from both poor and rich countries can now buy and sell securities (stocks and bonds) of companies operating in the developing countries through funds traded on the New York, London, and other stock exchanges.

International Development Association (IDA)

The IDA is the *soft* loan (or *credit,* as an IDA loan is called) section of the World Bank. Although it shares the Bank's administrative staff and grants credits for projects covering the same sorts of projects in developing countries as the Bank's loans, its **soft loans** differ from the hard loans of the Bank in several important ways. Soft loans have up to 40-year maturities, compared to the 15- to 25-year maturities of the Bank. The IDA may grant 10-year grace periods before repayment of principal or interest must begin, whereas the grace periods of the World Bank usually do not exceed 5 years. As is evident from these differences, borrowers from the IDA are the poorest of the poor developing countries, which need credit for development projects but cannot carry the burden on their economies or foreign exchange reserve positions that would result from normal commercial term loans. Determination of which countries qualify as poor enough for IDA credits is based on per capita incomes.

soft loans
May be repayable in soft, nonconvertible currencies; carry low or no interest obligations; are frequently long term, up to 40 years; and may grant grace periods of up to 10 years during which no payments are required

Unlike the World Bank, the IDA cannot raise capital in competitive capital markets and depends instead on subscriptions donated by the developed countries and some developing countries. Generally, developed countries members make contributions in convertible currencies; the developing countries donate their own currencies. IDA resources are renewed periodically by a process called *replenishment,* whereby supporting nations donate money.

The Multilateral Investment Guarantee Agency (MIGA)

MIGA was created in 1988 to encourage foreign investment. It provides guarantees to foreign investors against losses caused by noncommercial risks in developing countries, thus creating investment opportunities. MIGA also provides capacity-building and advisory services to help countries attract foreign direct investment and disseminate information on investment opportunities. MIGA issued its first contract in 1990, when it had 46 member-countries. Its membership now is 152 countries. Since its creation, MIGA has raised its per project and per country limits, expanded its constructive reinsurance and coinsurance relationships with other political risk insurers, streamlined its internal guarantee business processes, and extended its marketing efforts to better reach and serve investors from developing countries. As of January 1, 2000, MIGA had issued more than 420 contracts to private investors for projects in some 70 developing countries, facilitating more than $30 billion in private investment.[7]

International Center for Settlement of Investment Disputes (ICSID)

The ICSID provides facilities for settlement by conciliation or arbitration of investment disputes between foreign investors and their host countries. Founded in 1966, the ICSID now has 131 member-countries. The ICSID has certain types of proceedings, including proceedings for the settlement of investment disputes that arise between parties that are not member-countries or nationals of member-countries. Under the ICSID Convention, ICSID proceedings need not be held at the Center's headquarters in Washington, DC. The parties to an ICSID proceeding are free to agree to conduct their proceeding at any other place. ICSID has agreements with the Permanent Court of Arbitration at The Hague, the Regional Arbitration Centers of the Asian-African Legal Consultative Committee at Cairo and Kuala Lumpur, the Australian Center for International Commercial Arbitration at Melbourne, the Australian Commercial Disputes Center at Sydney, the Singapore International Arbitration Center, and the Commercial Arbitration Center at Bahrain. The number of cases submitted to the Center has increased significantly in recent years. In addition to its dispute settlement activities, ICSID carries out advisory and research activities. It also has a number of publications, which are available from the World Bank's Web page. The publications include multivolume collections of Investment Laws of the World and Investment Treaties, which are updated periodically by the ICSID staff. The ICSID also collaborates with other World Bank Group units in meeting requests by governments for advice on investment and arbitration law. Since 1983, the Center has also cosponsored, with the American Arbitration Association (AAA) and the International Chamber of Commerce (ICC) International Court of Arbitration, informational sessions on international arbitration.[8]

Privatize the World Bank?

The World Bank was designed to serve the nationalized industries and state sectors of developing nations. But as one author argues, "it is being made obsolete by privatization in the Third World. . . Opportunities for loans to finance state enterprise, the reason for being of the World Bank and of other multilateral development banks, will become scarcer if developing nation governments continue to sell state companies."[9]

The World Bank has become the target of increasingly adverse criticism. Another observer says it should be much stricter about not lending to countries without institutions such as basic property rights, well-run legal systems, and effective and uncorrupt bureaucracies. It should help countries build them.[10]

African Development Bank (AfDB)

The AfDB has tried to lower the percentage of loans it makes to governments because of public sector mismanagement and to increase the percentage that goes to private companies, some of which have been privatized recently from government ownership. The bank is also channeling more money to two of Africa's most vital human resources largely ignored in the past. They are the rural women who produce more than two-thirds of Africa's food and the small business entrepreneurs who keep many national economies afloat with their informal market trading.

However, by the mid-1990s, the AfDB was in deep trouble. A report by external consultants, headed by a former vice president of the World Bank, found a chaotic, top-heavy bureaucracy riddled with political intrigue and suspicion. The consultants could not assess the quality of AfDB loans because of unreliable and insufficient data. They could not find a central file on any project.

One thing the consultants did find was mounting arrears and defaults on loan repayments. Africa's growing impoverishment is placing greater demands on the African Development Fund, which is the soft loan arm of the AfDB as the IDA is of the World Bank. But its coffers are empty, and industrial countries that periodically donate funds for its use are refusing to replenish its coffers until it streamlines its bureaucracy, tightens its lending policies, and improves its record keeping.[11]

Asian Development Bank (AsDB)

The AsDB's equivalent of the World Bank's concessionary-finance arm, the IDA, is called the Asian Development Fund (AsDF). The AsDF should have lots of lending opportunities because Asia is still home to about three-quarters of the world's 1 billion poorest people. However, as is the case with the African Development Fund, the AsDF is running out of money, although for different reasons. The American, Japanese, and European developed countries, which put up the great majority of the AsDF funds, want the newly rich Asian countries to pick up more of the tab; East Asian countries, excluding Japan, despite their newfound prosperity, contribute less than 0.3 percent of the AsDF's resources. There are several reasons why.

For example, Singapore objects to aid in principle, saying it prefers to bless the poor through technical assistance and direct investment. South Korea says it wants a bigger say in running the AsDB before it gives more money. It also wants to save up for the day when it may have to absorb bankrupt North Korea.[12]

European Bank for Reconstruction and Development

This bank, known by its acronym EBRD, was created in 1990 to assist the countries of the former Soviet Union and its one-time Eastern European satellites. There are 60 shareholders: 58 governments plus the European Union and the European Investment Bank.

The bank borrows in the international capital markets to meet the bulk of its capital needs, and its AAA debt rating permits it to get the most favorable interest costs on its borrowings. Strong backing for that AAA rating was given in 1996, when the bank's shareholders voted to double its capital base to $25.2 billion.[13]

Inter-American Development Bank (IDB)

The IDB finances projects in Latin America and the Caribbean for social and economic development such as building roads, installing power lines, operating health clinics, providing safe drinking water, and encouraging small and medium-sized private businesses. The projects financed by the IDB generate substantial business opportunities. Over 3,500 contracts are awarded each year for a great variety of goods, civil works, and consultant services.

The IDB is the oldest and largest regional multilateral development institution. It was established in 1959 to help accelerate economic and social development in Latin America and the Caribbean. The bank was created in response to a long-standing desire on the part of the Latin American nations for a development institution that would focus on the pressing problems of that region. The bank's original membership included 19 Latin American and Caribbean countries and the United States. Its membership now totals 46 member-nations, including 18 member-countries from outside the region.

The bank has become a major catalyst in mobilizing resources for the region. In carrying out its mission, the bank has mobilized financing for projects that represent a total investment of $240 billion. Annual lending has grown dramatically from the $294 million in loans approved in 1961 to $10 billion in 1998.

The bank's operations cover the entire spectrum of economic and social development. In the past, its lending emphasized the productive sectors of agriculture and industry, the physical infrastructure sectors of energy and transportation, and the social sectors of environmental and public health, education, and urban development. Current lending priorities include poverty reduction and social equity, modernization and integration, and the environment.[14]

International Monetary Fund (IMF)

Although the IMF deals solely with governments, its policies and actions have a profound impact on business worldwide. Its influence may become even greater. Before explaining that statement, we should look briefly at the objectives and activities of the IMF and how they developed. Most of them continue to be important.

The IMF Articles of Agreement were adopted at the Bretton Woods Conference in 1944.[15] In general terms, the IMF's objectives were, and continue to be, to foster (1) orderly foreign exchange arrangements, (2) convertible currencies, and (3) a shorter duration and lesser degree of balance-of-payments disequilibria. The premise of the IMF is that the common interest of all nations in a workable international monetary system far transcends conflicting national interests.[16] One of the IMF's original objectives, since abandoned, was maintenance of fixed exchange rates among member-countries' currencies, with par value related to the U.S. dollar, which was valued at $35 per ounce of gold.

Each member-country has a quota equal to the amount it subscribes to the IMF. Votes at IMF meetings are weighted according to quota size, and the amount a member can draw is related to its quota.[17]

The IMF agreement was entered before the founding conference of the United Nations, and when the UN was formed, the IMF was brought into a relationship with the UN by an agreement. This agreement preserved the IMF's independence, which was justified by the need for independent control of monetary management. This need results from the temptations of every government to overspend and cause inflation.[18]

Changes in the IMF

The 1970s and 1980s saw some fundamental changes in the IMF's activities and roles. As was stated above, the IMF abandoned the objective of maintaining the fixed exchange rate system. More accurately stated, the obligation of maintaining such a system remained in the Articles of Agreement, but the IMF was powerless to uphold it in the face of a situation in which all major currencies were floating* rather than fixed in value. In recognition of reality, the articles were amended to legalize the actual current practice, that is, floating exchange rates.

Greater Power for the IMF?

firm surveillance
Permits the IMF to influence or even dictate fiscal and monetary policies of member-countries if the economically strong countries allow such intrusion

The amended articles also included a new Article IV, which, among other things, empowers the IMF to "exercise **firm surveillance** over the exchange rate policies" of members. Some observers feel that this new surveillance power may permit the IMF to move toward the position in the world occupied by central banks nationally.[19] That, of course, would require the member-countries to surrender a great deal of sovereignty, which many governments will stoutly resist.

The IMF fulfills its surveillance responsibilities in two principal ways. First, its board of governors regularly examines in depth each member's economic policies

*Discussion of floating exchange rates compared to fixed exchange rates appears in Chapter 5.

and performance and the interaction of those policies with economic developments in other countries. Second, the board holds regular discussions on the world economic outlook and periodic discussions on exchange rate developments in the major industrial countries.

The IMF contributes to policy coordination among the major industrial countries through its work on the economic indicators and the medium-term economic outlook. Those major industrial countries (Canada, France, Germany, Italy, Japan, the United Kingdom, and the United States) are sometimes referred to as the **Group of Seven,*** and the IMF managing director participates in the group's meetings. There are 176 other IMF member-countries, making a total of 183.

Group of Seven (G7)
The major industrial countries, namely, Canada, France, Germany, Italy, Japan, the United Kingdom, and the United States

Conditionality and Cooperation with the World Bank

Scarcity of trained personnel and lack of political will or strength are reasons countries are unable or unwilling to take the steps necessary to correct their economic problems. To ensure better use of their funds, the IMF and the World Bank cooperate with each other in working with borrowing member-countries in what are called *structural adjustment facilities* (SAFs) or, if the problems are greater, enhanced structural adjustment facilities (ESAFs).

Funding by the IMF or the Bank is conditional and linked to the member's progress in implementing policies geared to restoring balance-of-payment viability and sustainable economic growth. The borrowing member must file a policy framework paper that details annual programs it will undertake to reach the established goal. The Bank and the IMF monitor the progress of the programs. Often, the Bank and the IMF require members to implement austerity measures, which usually include cutting government spending and reducing government debt.

As is the case with the World Bank, the IMF has its skeptics. One says, "The time has come for a change in the way the IMF prescribes remedies for irresponsible economic problems in developing nations. The biggest impediment to development in these nations is deeply entrenched public and private-sector corruption. The IMF must insist in the future that its aid packages are contingent on tangible progress in attacking these problems. . . ."[20]

Bank for International Settlements (BIS)

The round tower of the BIS is the first landmark in Basel, Switzerland, for anyone leaving the main railway station and heading toward the city center. There is, however, no sign saying "BIS" because this is the most discreet financial institution in the world, the place where central bankers of major industrial countries meet ten times a year to discuss the global financial system. The BIS is an international organization that fosters cooperation among central banks and international financial institutions. The BIS deals with governments and governmental agencies; it does not accept deposits from or provide financial services to private individuals or corporations.

In addition to providing a congenial and confidential meeting place for central bankers, the BIS provides secure, anonymous cover for shareholder countries as they transfer large amounts of currency or gold among themselves. When they do this through the BIS, currency and gold traders may not be able to figure out the identity of the real buyers and sellers.

The BIS has four main functions. It serves as

1. A forum for international monetary cooperation. The forum function was touched on in the second paragraph of this section.
2. A center for research. Applied economic research finds an outlet in the series of economic papers published by the BIS. Probably the best known is the BIS *Annual Report,* published in June of each year. Typical of other research is

*The G7 is often referred to now as the G8, which includes the original seven industrialized nations and Russia.

"International Banking and Financial Market Developments," published in 1997. This report shows acceptance of more bond market risk by investors and the growth in popularity of asset-backed structures that repackage financial assets and cash flows ranging from bank loans to aircraft leases.[21]

3. A banker for central banks. Some 80 central banks from around the world have deposits with the BIS. In addition to placing surplus funds in the international markets, the BIS occasionally makes liquid resources available to central banks. The Bridge loans and more traditional types of lending are other banking services the BIS provides.

4. An agent or trustee with regard to various international financial arrangements. As an agent and trustee, the BIS books and settles the balances that arise from currency exchange market interventions by EU* central banks in observation of European Monetary System (EMS) rules. Officially, the BIS is the agent for the European Monetary Co-operation Fund, which holds 20 percent of EU countries' gold and dollar reserves.[22]

Since several Eastern European countries broke out of the Soviet empire in 1989, a fifth function has been developed. A number of their central bankers now meet their Western counterparts at BIS headquarters to study free-market banking. Training courses have been established.[23]

When the BIS was founded in 1930, the United States turned down an invitation to join, but it changed its mind in 1994. The decision was made by the U.S. Federal Reserve, whose current chairman, Alan Greenspan, now regularly attends the monthly meetings of central bank officials of member-countries. Jim Leach, former chair of the U.S. House of Representatives Financial Services Committee, said that "in a time of intertangled and intertwined international finances, it would be irresponsible for the U.S. not to ensure that its interests are represented."[24]

World Trade Organization (WTO)

World Trade Organization (WTO)
A multinational organization designed to deal with rules of trade between nations

The **World Trade Organization** (WTO) is a multinational organization designed to deal with rules of trade between nations. The WTO works with its core agreements, which were negotiated, signed, and ratified by most of the world's trading nations. The goal is to help producers of goods and services, exporters, and importers conduct their business by reducing or eliminating trade barriers and restrictions worldwide. The WTO's headquarters are in Geneva, Switzerland. It currently has 140 member-countries.

The Early Years of Global International Trade Cooperation

Arising from the optimism among the Western allies following World War II was the ideal of an international organization that would function in the trade areas much as it was hoped the UN would function in the political and peacekeeping areas. A charter was drawn for an International Trade Organization (ITO) at the Havana Conference in 1948. However, the ITO never came into existence because not enough governments ratified its charter.

At what were thought of as preliminaries to and preparations for an ITO, the American negotiators presented what they envisioned as a step toward an acceptable ITO treaty, which was to embody the numerous bilateral trade treaties in one multilateral treaty. They suggested, in the absence of any established international trade rules, that the commercial policy rules of the draft ITO charter be incorporated into a general agreement on tariffs and trade as an interim measure pending ITO ratification. The American suggestions were accepted, and so the General Agreement on Tariffs and

*The EU is introduced later in this chapter.

Trade (GATT) was born in 1947.[25] Differently stated, the ITO was not ratified as a de jure organization, and GATT became a de facto international trade organization.[26]

Some observers felt GATT to be a "slender reed" on which to base world progress toward free international trade. Nevertheless, it still exists and has been extremely successful in some areas of tariff reduction as well as in other fields.[27]

GATT 1947–1995

GATT set up business in the Palais des Nations of the old League of Nations, which was superseded by the UN. The Palais is in Geneva, where GATT has since erected its own headquarters building to house its secretariat.

GATT negotiations to reduce tariffs and other trade obstacles were conducted in sessions referred to as *rounds,* of which there were eight, from the first in 1947 through the Uruguay Round, which was launched in 1986 in Punta del Este, Uruguay. A main achievement of the first seven rounds was reduction of tariffs among industrial countries from an average of 40 percent to 5 percent. In addition, 9 out of 10 disputes among trading nations brought to GATT were settled satisfactorily, discreetly, and without publicity. The volume of trade in manufactured goods multiplied 20-fold.

The Uruguay Round

This was a hugely ambitious undertaking. As indicated, the seven preceding rounds had reduced industrial product tariffs from 40 to 5 percent, and the Uruguay negotiators succeeded in lowering them by more than their target of one-third more. But Uruguay broke new GATT ground by writing new international rules for trade in services and agriculture and for protection of intellectual properties. Agreement was reached to phase out the multifiber arrangement, which is Byzantine and the oldest managed-trade system. It covers textiles and clothing. Procedures to speed settlements of trade disputes were agreed on, as were means to reduce trade subsidies.

Many regarded a successful conclusion of the Uruguay Round as hopelessly overambitious, but the negotiators met a GATT-imposed December 15, 1993, deadline by initialing an agreement late on that day. There was disappointment that antidumping laws were not limited, and the American entertainment industry wanted greater access to the European markets than the agreement allowed. Presumably, these and many other carryover and new issues will be brought up in the WTO.[28]

Creation of the World Trade Organization

As provided by the successful conclusion of the Uruguay Round GATT negotiations, on January 1, 1995, the WTO replaced the GATT secretariat and began to administer the system of international trade law. A trade policy review mechanism will raise issues for discussion on a regular agenda, replacing the previous practice of periodic rounds of negotiation with a permanent process of revising the rules of international trade. By November 2000, there were 140 WTO member-countries.

Clouds on WTO's Horizon

Regional trade agreements (RTAs) may weaken the WTO. A committee of international trade experts has warned that the WTO needs to develop effective disciplines soon to stop RTAs from weakening its authority and obstructing global economic integration.

RTAs could distort trade at the expense of countries that are not party to the agreements. In the two years after the 1994 enlargement of the EU to include Austria, Finland, and Sweden, the relative importance of intra-EU trade to its members grew 10 percent but the importance of EU members in the rest of the world's trade fell 44 percent. Much of the same shift occurred in trade among the six members of the Gulf Co-operation Council after their free trade pact took effect in 1993. Trade among members of the North American Free Trade Agreement (NAFTA) exhibited a similar but less marked trend. Mercosur has seen trade among its members increase faster than has trade with nonmembers.

The committee was chaired by Professor Jamie Serra, a former Mexican finance minister. Its members included Carla Hills, a former U.S. trade representative, and Professor John Jackson of the University of Michigan, a leading trade lawyer. It made strong recommendations, among which are that RTAs move toward common trade rules, remain open to new members, avoid distorting foreign direct investment flows, and encourage members to use WTO procedures to settle disputes.[29]

The WTO also has been hindered by protests from many sides in regard to its purpose. In late 1999, in Seattle, Washington, the WTO attempted to start another round of trade negotiations. The talks, however, were overshadowed by demonstrators in the streets of Seattle protesting what they thought was insensitivity and outright disdain by the WTO toward matters of concern in such diverse areas as environmental issues, human rights, working conditions, and labor protection in the United States. The WTO is attempting to recover from the problems in Seattle, but it may take a long time before it gains the clout it needs to succeed at reducing trade barriers around the world. An article in *The Asian Wall Street Journal Weekly Edition* shortly after the failed Seattle meeting set forth many reasons why the talks failed. One concern expressed in the article is that the WTO has become too large for traditional negotiating tools to work. Many delegates to the meeting also were bothered by the failure of the United States to show adequate leadership at the meeting. For example, the U.S. position on the inclusion of labor rights issues in worldwide trade negotiations disturbed many delegates from developing countries. While many expressed discouragement, the leadership of the WTO sought to assure people with those concerns that the Seattle demonstrations were a mere setback and that the work of the WTO in setting rules for a new negotiating session would continue.[30]

Another problem for the WTO is the question of whether its member-countries will abide by its decisions. The WTO relies on the goodwill of its members to implement its decisions. During the late 1990s, the WTO was wrestling with several trade disputes between the United States and the European Union. Many disputes involved products such as bananas and beef. For example, the United States has complained that the EU ignores WTO rulings directing the EU to open its markets to bananas from American companies. As the United States and the EU continue to argue, disputes such as this call into question the effectiveness of the WTO in reducing trade barriers. The United States and the EU have been fighting over banana imports since 1993, when the EU introduced an EU-wide banana import scheme. The EU's 1993 scheme was based on quotas. Its aim was to create a single market for bananas in the EU without causing a fall in prices for the African, Caribbean, and Pacific (ACP) banana-growing countries, many of which are former colonies of EU member-states. The WTO has twice ruled the EU scheme illegal, but the EU has refused to modify the scheme.[31]

Organization of Petroleum Exporting Countries (OPEC)

Realizing that if the oil-exporting countries were united they could bargain more effectively with the large oil companies, Iran and Venezuela joined the Arab Petroleum Congress at a Cairo meeting in 1959. Discussions and secret agreements at that meeting became the seeds for the Organization of Petroleum Exporting Countries (OPEC).[32] Of the 11 OPEC member-countries, most are in the Middle East (Iran, Iraq, Kuwait, Qatar, Saudi Arabia, and United Arab Emirates), but there are three in Africa (Algeria, Libya, and Nigeria) and two elsewhere in the world (Indonesia and Venezuela). There are other large oil-exporting countries (such as Mexico, Norway, and the United Kingdom) that are not members of OPEC.

Early in 1960, the Venezuelan minister of mines and hydrocarbons and the Saudi oil minister wrote to the oil companies operating in Venezuela and the Middle East, requesting that they consult with the host governments before making any price changes. In August 1960, the oil companies reduced oil prices, and it is said that the host governments learned of it only when they read it in the newspapers. In any event,

Table 4.3 Demand for Petroleum by Groups of Countries

	1974	1978	1982	1986	1990	1994	1998	1999	2000	2001
	Million Barrels per Day									
World	**56.4**	**64.3**	**59.5**	**61.82**	**66.43**	**68.57**	**74.29**	**74.73**	**75.69**	**77.53**
OECD countries*	40.7	44.4	37.9	38.60	41.52	44.38	46.89	47.61	47.87	48.77
North America	19.8	22.3	19.2	19.61	20.71	21.67	23.15	23.86	24.03	24.52
Europe	14.6	15.3	13.0	13.18	13.63	14.28	15.30	15.12	15.11	15.31
Pacific	6.3	6.8	5.7	5.81	7.19	8.43	8.43	8.63	8.74	8.95
Non-OECD Countries	15.7	19.9	21.6	23.22	24.91	24.19	27.40	27.12	27.82	28.76
Former Soviet Union	6.7	8.3	9.1	8.91	8.40	4.86	4.27	3.50	3.50	3.42
Europe	1.0	1.3	0.9	0.97	1.03	0.68	0.81	0.74	0.75	0.76
China	1.2	1.8	1.6	1.98	2.32	3.06	4.15	4.48	4.68	4.97
Other Asia	1.8	2.5	2.8	3.25	4.42	5.50	6.75	7.04	7.32	7.69
Latin America	2.7	3.1	3.2	3.42	3.58	4.06	4.76	4.77	4.84	4.98
Middle East	1.4	1.7	2.3	2.96	3.24	3.92	4.28	4.26	4.35	4.52
Africa	1.0	1.3	1.6	1.73	1.92	2.11	2.37	2.33	2.38	2.43
	Percent of Total									
World	**100.0**	**100.0**	**100.0**	**100.0**	**100.0**	**100.0**	**100.0**	**100.0**	**100.0**	**100.0**
OECD Countries	72.2	69.1	63.7	62.4	62.5	64.7	63.1	63.7	63.2	62.9
North America	35.1	34.7	32.3	31.7	31.2	31.6	31.2	31.9	31.7	31.6
Europe	25.9	23.8	21.8	21.3	20.5	20.8	20.6	20.2	20.0	19.7
Pacific	11.2	10.6	9.6	9.4	10.8	12.3	11.3	11.5	11.5	11.5
Non-OECD Countries	27.8	30.9	36.3	37.6	37.5	35.3	36.9	36.3	36.8	37.1
Former Soviet Union	11.9	12.9	15.3	14.4	12.6	7.1	5.7	4.7	4.6	4.4
Europe	1.8	2.0	1.5	1.6	1.6	1.0	1.1	1.0	1.0	1.0
China	2.1	2.8	2.7	3.2	3.5	4.5	5.6	6.0	6.2	6.4
Other Asia	3.2	3.9	4.7	5.3	6.7	8.0	9.1	9.4	9.7	9.9
Latin America	4.8	4.8	5.4	5.5	5.4	5.9	6.4	6.4	6.4	6.4
Middle East	2.5	2.6	3.9	4.8	4.9	5.7	5.8	5.7	5.7	5.8
Africa	1.8	2.0	2.7	2.8	2.9	3.1	3.2	3.1	3.1	3.1

*Note: OECD = Organization for Economic Cooperation and Development.
Source: International Energy Agency, *Monthly Oil Market Report*, September 2000, and *Annual Statistical Supplement* for 1998.

they had not been consulted. This made them angry and also increased their anxiety about the control and conservation of their natural resources. In that atmosphere, they called a meeting on September 14, 1960, in Baghdad.

Attending the meeting were representatives of Iran, Iraq, Kuwait, Saudi Arabia, and Venezuela. OPEC was formed, and the OPEC members took charge of pricing.

Economic Muscle and Political Strength

OPEC soon began to test its strength, and the price of petroleum began to rise. At the end of 1973 and in early 1974, OPEC demonstrated its potentially devastating strength with the oil embargo by its Arab members against the Netherlands and the United States, accompanied by very large price increases to all customers. Its strength stemmed from the comparative cohesiveness of the members and from the fact that it controlled some 68 percent of the world's known petroleum reserves.[33] OPEC supplied some 84 percent of Europe's oil needs and over 90 percent of Japan's.[34]

Using its strength, OPEC drove up petroleum prices from about \$3 a barrel* in 1973 to close to \$35 in 1980. Such a drastic increase in energy prices caused recession and unemployment in oil-importing countries, but it also sparked conservation measures

*Forty-two gallons constitutes one barrel of oil.

and increased oil exploration in non-OPEC countries and research into alternative energy sources.

Thanks to those initiatives, OPEC's market weakened, but its members refused to cut their production, and thus an oversupply developed. OPEC had seized control of pricing in the mid-1970s, but by the early 1980s the free markets were setting prices with major markets in Rotterdam, New York, and Chicago.[35]

"Isn't it time to regain control of the price of oil?" asked Arrieta Valera, Venezuela's new oil minister, at an OPEC meeting in March 1994. But that may be difficult to achieve, considering the huge oil and gas projects being developed in such former Soviet republics as Kazakhstan and Azerbaijan and even bigger ones in Russia.

On the other hand, the OPEC share of the world supply of oil is up to 40 percent from just over 20 percent in 1984. In addition, sustained low oil prices have weakened conservation efforts and have made exploration, investment, and extraction unprofitable; moreover, demand is increasing in developing countries, with China and Indonesia becoming net importers by the year 2000, and so OPEC may have a shot at regaining oil price control.[36]

Table 4.3 on page 163 shows demand for petroleum by countries and country groups in millions of barrels per day (mbd) and percent of totals for the years from 1974 to 2001. Note the growth in demand in developing countries.

On the production side, OPEC's numbers grew from 23 mbd in 1990 to 27 mbd in 1996, with 28.5 projected for 2000. Non-OPEC production went from 41.9 mbd in 1990 to 43.8 in 1996, with 47.8 mbd projected for the year 2000.[37]

Economic Integration

The Four Major Forms of Economic—and Finally Political—Integration

Free Trade Area (FTA)

Tariffs are abolished among the members of the FTA, but each member-country maintains its own external tariffs on imports from nonmember countries.

Customs Union

In this form, member-countries add a common external tariff to the FTA form wherein the member-countries have abolished tariffs among themselves.

Common Market

This is a customs union plus the abolition of restrictions on the mobility of capital and labor among the member-countries.

Complete Economic Integration

This form involves a high degree of political integration as member-countries surrender important elements of their sovereignty. A supercentral bank is created together with a supranational authority that will determine monetary and fiscal policies as well as labor and social policies for all member-countries. There would probably be a single currency that would replace members' currencies. The EU is endeavoring to reach these goals.

[2] The European Union (EU)

Background

In the aftermath of World War II, the continent of Europe was in shambles as a result of the fighting and the need to devote almost all resources and investments to the war effort. The war devastated not only buildings and highways but also businesses and people's lives. Europeans found themselves with the enormous task of rebuilding European society—economically, politically, and culturally. In beginning the task of rebuilding Europe, there was concern throughout the continent that the previous economic and political systems had failed. Out of this concern came a willingness to relinquish certain aspects of national sovereignty for the greater economic and political good. Since the old political systems known before and during World War II had been destroyed or discredited, it became apparent that Europe needed a fresh start.

While most Europeans understood the need to establish national democracies and free market economies, many argued for greater continentwide cooperation. Much of the support for European unity came from resistance movements during the war. During the war, resistance fighters put aside their national ideological conflicts to fight for a common objective. One of the most ardent proponents of a united Europe was an Italian resistance fighter, Altiero Spinelli. In 1944, Spinelli argued "for a federal Europe with a written constitution, a supranational government directly responsible to the people of Europe and not national governments, along with an army under its control, with no other military forces being permitted."[38] The end of the war, though, brought many changes in Europe, and with those changes, support for a United States of Europe waned. Exiled or imprisoned political leaders reemerged in their respective countries. Ideological and traditional divisions between socialists, communists, and conservatives that had been put aside during the resistance movement resurfaced. The emergence of the Cold War and the resulting division of Europe helped shatter the dream of a united Europe. Many of the proponents of greater European unity, including Britain's Winston Churchill, lost political power in their own nations. In addition to these factors, as a practical matter, many Europeans were concerned not with philosophical debates about politics and economics but with seemingly basic problems such as food supplies, fuel, shelter, and physical reconstruction. It is hard to think in terms of grand European unification when it is hard to find food. To help Europeans get back on their feet and encourage strong, friendly governments, U.S. Secretary of State George C. Marshall recommended that the United States provide large amounts of financial assistance to European countries to help in their reconstruction. Thus was born the Marshall Plan, which was immensely successful.[39] It swung into action in 1948, and by the first quarter of 1950, European industrial production was already 138 percent ahead of the level reached in 1938, the last year of general European peace. The Organization for European Economic Cooperation (OEEC) was established in 1947 to ensure economic integration within Europe. The OEEC controlled the distribution of U.S. aid from the Marshall Plan. After the task of administering the Marshall Plan was complete, the OEEC continued in its role of encouraging economic and trade relationships among countries. In 1961, the OEEC became the Organization for Economic Cooperation and Development (OECD), which is discussed later in this chapter.

In 1948, three of Europe's smallest countries—the Netherlands, Belgium, and Luxembourg—formed the Benelux Union. Although the Benelux Union planned to merge into a full economic union in the future, it was merely a customs union in the beginning. A third organization, the Western European Union (WEU), was created in 1948. The WEU consisted of the United Kingdom, France, Belgium, the Netherlands, and Luxembourg. It provided "for collaboration in economic, social and cultural matters and for the collective self-defense." The subsequent creation of the North Atlantic Treaty Organization (NATO), which provided a mechanism for military security, made the WEU unnecessary. Twelve nations (the United States, Canada, and 10 Western European countries) created NATO in 1949, in large part to guard against the Soviet threat. The United States was a leader in the formation of NATO and continues to play a dominant role. NATO today has 19 members, including the Czech Republic,

Leaders of the NATO nations gathered in Washington, DC, in 1999 for NATO's 50th anniversary.
Gamma Liaison

Hungary, and Poland, which were admitted in 1999 as the newest members. These three new members are former Soviet bloc countries. Even though NATO replaced the need for the WEU, the WEU nevertheless showed that European cooperation was possible on matters beyond the economy.

European Union (EU)

A supranational entity of 15 European countries dedicated to European economic and political integration

Out of the cooperation generated by these and other organizations came the seeds for greater European integration, which led eventually to what is now the **European Union (EU).** In addition to European cooperation to rebuild the European economy, there was also a sense of urgency that the destruction of World War II must never be allowed to happen again. The Europeans thought that if closer relationships were formed between the economies of the European countries, the devastation of war could be prevented.

Early EU history shows that European integration was largely a continental European movement. Even though Britain's Winston Churchill in 1945 called for the building of a kind of United States of Europe, the United Kingdom stayed out of the process until the 1970s. The 1950s saw the formation of three separate yet related European communities. Those three communities combined to create what is now the European Union. In 1952, six countries began by creating the first of the three communities, the European Coal and Steel Community (EC&SC). The original six members were Belgium, France, the Federal Republic of Germany (West Germany), Italy, Luxembourg, and the Netherlands. In 1957, those six countries created the other two communities by signing two Treaties of Rome, which came into force in 1958. One of the Treaties of Rome created the European Economic Community (EEC), and the other created the European Atomic Energy Community (Euratom). The purpose of the EEC was to extend the common market for coal and steel to all sectors of the economy. Euratom's purpose was to create a common market for the atomic energy industry. Both the EC&SC and Euratom attempted to integrate the European economies one sector at a time. This would later prove ineffective with the emergence of the EEC as the dominant one of the three initial European communities.

By 1973, the United Kingdom, along with Ireland and Denmark, finally joined the EU. By waiting so long to join, the United Kingdom yielded to France and, to a lesser extent, Germany, Italy, and the three smaller original countries (Belgium, Luxembourg, and the Netherlands) any voice it most likely would have had in the formation of what would become the EU. Germany and Italy had just been defeated in World War II and the three smaller original countries were too small to play a meaningful leadership role, and so the responsibility for creating a united Europe became a French task. The decisions made in the early years of European integration therefore fell largely to the French. As a result, the EU of today shows clear signs of the early French influence. By the time the United Kingdom joined in 1973, the British were left to adapt to a largely French institution, which made their transition into the EU even harder than it otherwise would have been.

During the 1980s and 1990s, the EU continued to expand by adding Greece (1981), Spain (1986), Portugal (1986), Austria (1995), Finland (1995), and Sweden (1995). Those additions brought the number of member-nations to 15, which is the current number. Noticeably absent from the EU are two major Western European nations—Switzerland and Norway—both of which rejected EU membership in national elections.

Future Expansion

The EU is currently in membership talks with Cyprus, the Czech Republic, Estonia, Hungary, Poland, and Slovenia. Bulgaria, Latvia, Lithuania, Malta, Romania, Slovakia, and Turkey also have expressed an interest in joining. In addition to complying with economic criteria, which include market economies, all new members must meet other membership criteria, including showing evidence of respect for democracy, the rule of law, human rights, and the protection of minorities.

Purpose of the EU

The EU is a supranational entity, meaning that it is a regional government. In order to join the EU, member-nations give a certain amount of their sovereignty to the EU. This supranational status distinguishes the EU from other international organizations, such as the United Nations, and from treaties, such as the North American Free Trade Agreement (NAFTA). The United Nations relies on the goodwill of its member-nations for cooperation and even for its income. The UN is not a world government. Likewise, the countries in NAFTA (Canada, Mexico, and the United States) remain sovereign nations. The EU, by contrast to both the UN and NAFTA, has certain powers because of its supranational status. For example, it has the power to tax member-nations directly. The EU does not rely on voluntary contributions from its member-nations. It also has the power to implement legislation directly in each of the member-nations. The EU also has a court, the European Court of Justice, with the power to impose fines and other sanctions on individuals, companies, and even member-nations that violate the Treaty of Rome.

As originally established in the 1950s, European integration was limited to economic issues. As the years went on, it grew to include monetary and possible political integration as well. In the 1957 Treaty of Rome, which still serves as the fundamental law of the EU, the EU member-nations sought to achieve four fundamental freedoms: freedom of movement of goods, services, capital, and people. Goods, services, capital, and people are to move freely among all member-nations of the EU. For example, a citizen of the United Kingdom has the right to work in Greece without any additional approval from the Greek government. This is in sharp contrast to NAFTA, under which a citizen of Mexico must obtain the proper visa in order to work in the United States.

Institutions of the EU

There are four main institutions of the EU, which perform functions similar to those performed by a national government: the Commission, the Council of Ministers, the Parliament, and the Court. The **European Commission** is the executive institution and is in charge of administering the daily operations of the EU. It is called the "Guardian of the Treaty," because it is charged with ensuring proper implementation of the provisions of the Treaty of Rome. The Commission consists of 20 commissioners, who come from the member-nations. Each member-nation is entitled to one commissioner, with the larger member-nations having two. The current president of the European Commission is Romano Prodi, who is a former prime minister of Italy. The Commission's offices are located mostly in Brussels, Belgium, which has become the unofficial capital of the EU.

European Commission
Institution that runs the day-to-day operations of the EU

The **Council of Ministers** is the primary policy-setting institution of the EU. This is where important decisions are made. The ministers who make up the Council are members of their respective national governments. The presidency of the Council rotates among the member-nations, with each member-nation holding the presidency for six months. Here is the current order of the rotation of the Council presidency:

Council of Ministers
Institution that serves as the primary policy-setting institution of the EU

	First half	*Second half*
2001	Sweden	Belgium
2002	Spain	Denmark
2003	Greece	

The holder of the presidency sets the agenda and the location of any meetings. This makes holding the presidency quite important and gives the holder of the presidency great power to influence the future of the EU.

The Council sets forth regulations (self-executing) and directives (for each member-nation to implement). One goal of the EU is to harmonize legislation throughout the EU, and this is accomplished though the EU's legislative process, which includes the regulations and directives. Recent directives dealt with issues of health and safety including the use of workplace safety equipment,

European Union Parliament.
Courtesy European Commission Delegation, Washington, DC

rules for the use of computer terminals, and protection of workers from exposure to dangerous elements in the environment.

Parliament of the EU
EU institution containing representatives popularly elected from the member-nations

The **Parliament of the EU** was first elected in 1979 and is now elected by popular vote throughout Europe every five years. It holds its sessions in Strasbourg, France. Members of the Parliament are seated by political party affiliation rather than by national origin. The EU Parliament currently has 626 members from the 15 member-nations, representing over 100 European political parties. This party identification underscores the nature of the EU as a European rather than a national institution. Recent changes have given the Parliament more power, but the Council remains the primary policy-setting institution. The Parliament has been given certain specific powers, including the power to reject the EU budget.

European Court of Justice
Court designed to decide issues pertaining to the implementation of EU policies

The **European Court of Justice** decides all cases arising under the Treaty of Rome, and its authority supersedes that of the member-countries' courts. Because the treaty covers many subjects and more and more cases are being decided by the Court of Justice, its influence is growing steadily. It is assisted by the Court of First Instance, which has more limited jurisdiction.

The EU joins most of the economic and industrial might of Western Europe and most of its population. The EU is the largest import and export market in the world. It is second only to the United States in the size of its gross domestic product, and it accounts for 20 percent of world trade, compared with 14 percent for the United States and 9 percent for Japan.

A United States of Europe?

The countries involved have made great strides toward union, and the EU is now a major world force. There is a historic dream among Europeans of a United States of Europe in which the movement of people, money, and goods would be as free as it is in America, but a wall of obstacles stands in the way of realizing that dream.

There are 15 sovereign nations in the EU—and more want to join—with long, proud histories and loyalties and different cultures and languages, and of course there have been bitter, bloody wars among Europeans. Each country has its own laws, taxes, armed forces, and police. Also several of the countries have shown strong and growing reluctance to surrender their national currencies, central banks, and other powers to a distant authority, particularly an unelected authority.

In December 1991, representatives of the then 12 EU member-nations met in the Dutch city of Maastricht, where they signed a treaty that bears that city's name. This treaty has numerous provisions, but it is the broad sweep that fits this "United States of Europe" discussion. Its goals include economic and monetary union, with a European central bank to replace the national central banks and a European currency instead of the national ones.

For the first time, in the Maastricht Treaty, the parties spoke of political as well as economic unity. It is in the Maastricht Treaty that the parties first used the term *union,* which replaced *community* and *communities.* The Maastricht Treaty calls for the EU "to assert its identity on the international scene, in particular through the implementation of a common foreign and security policy including the eventual framing of a common defense policy, which might in time lead to a common defense."

Fortress Europe?

The term *Fortress Europe* was used by outsiders, Americans, Japanese, and others to express their fears that the EU would deny its privileges to them, their companies, and their products.[40] Although those fears persist, the term is now being used in another context: prevention of countries joining as new EU members. It is difficult for many countries, including many former Soviet bloc countries, to meet the admission requirements.

Some current EU members want a "wider" organization and would admit any European democracy that met certain criteria, such as stable prices, sound public finances and monetary conditions, and a sustainable balance of payments. Other current

[Figure 4.1] European Union

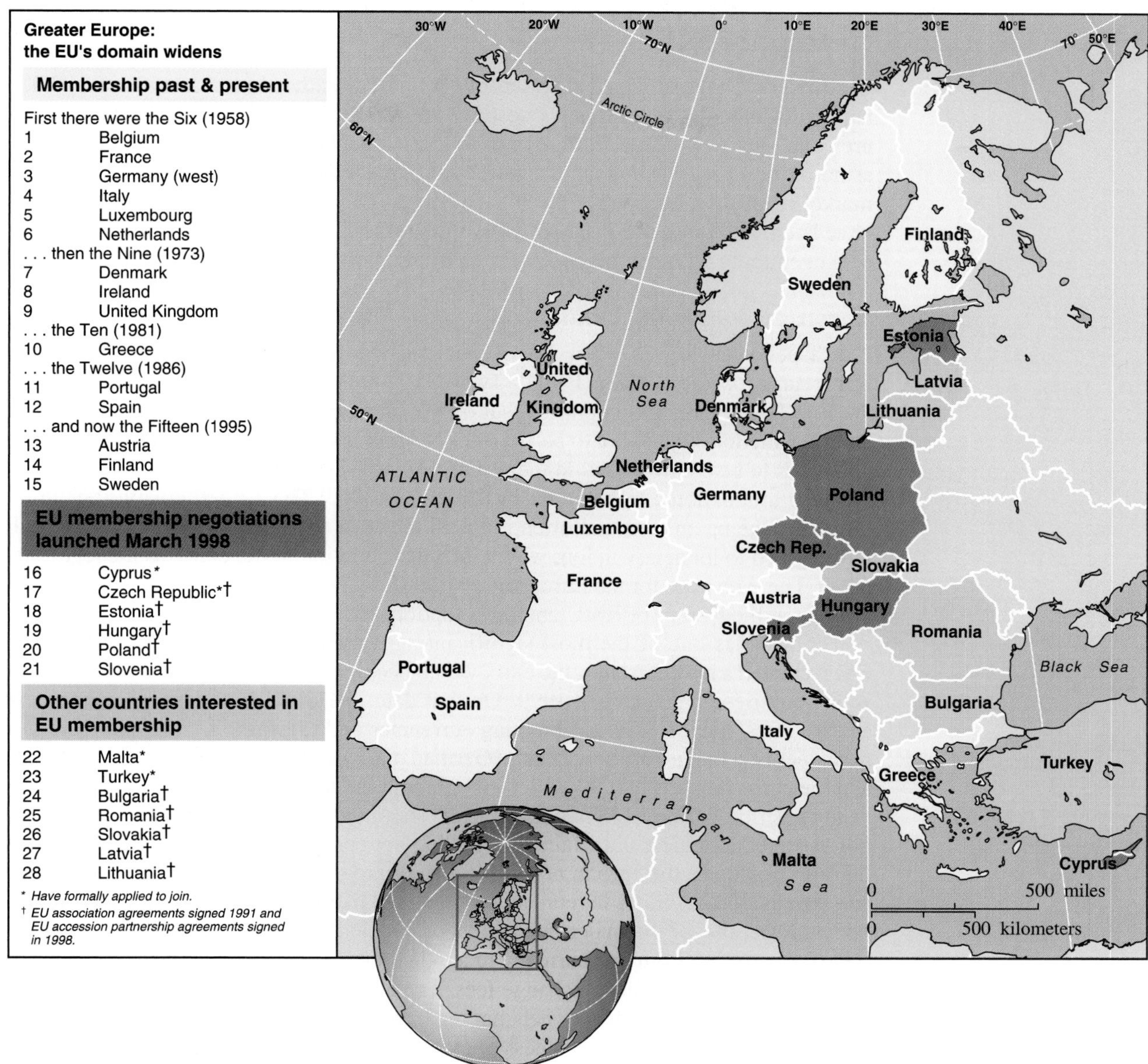

Source: Republished with permission from World Bank Atlas, 1997, p. 17. Permission conveyed through Copyright Clearance Center, Inc.

members want a "deeper" organization giving EU members and institutions time to digest Maastricht before bringing in new members (see Figure 4.1).

Problems

EU members cannot agree whether they want to implement Maastricht and have a centralized federal system with most of the power held by the EU institutions (i.e., the parliament, council, and commission) or leave the power with the member-countries in a Europe-of-countries form. They disagree on whether to admit new member-countries, which ones, and when.

But one subject about which there is unhappy agreement is that fraud is costing the EU about $7 billion a year from the agriculture budget, which at 48.6 percent is the largest item in the EU budget. Another leak from the EU budget is due to Mafia gangs defrauding the EU of at least $5 billion a year in unpaid customs duties, value-added taxes, and export subsidies. Some sources say the losses could be as high as "tens of billions of dollars." To combat this, the EU plus Norway, Switzerland, Malta, and Iceland set up a customs intelligence unit in 1997.[41]

EU Actions

EU directives have superseded 15 sets of national rules; they have harmonized 100,000 national standards, labeling laws, testing procedures, and consumer protection measures covering everything from toys to food, to stockbrokering, to teaching. As many as 60 million customs and tax formalities at borders were scrapped. Thanks to single-market measures, Europe's GDP is now most likely higher than it would otherwise have been. Although these successes are impressive, many Europeans and others expect even more with continued European integration.

European Monetary Union

One aspect that affects every businessperson who does business in the EU is the European Monetary Union (EMU). Twelve EU nations are currently participating in the EMU. The three EU countries that do not participate (Denmark, Sweden, and the United Kingdom) opted not to participate for various reasons. The adoption of the euro continues to be controversial in these three countries. Denmark, for example, rejected the euro in a national referendum in September 2000. The 12 participating member-nations make up an area that often is called the euro zone because these countries all have agreed to monetary union, which includes adoption of the euro* as the legal currency. The Web page for the European Central Bank, www.ecb.int, contains a good discussion of the history of EMU and the adoption of the euro.

The EMU is one of the most significant agreements to come out of the EU. The EMU created a new currency, the euro, which became the official currency of the euro-zone countries on January 1, 1999. On that date, the EMU set irrevocable fixed exchange rates between the participating currencies and the euro. As a result, there is a permanent exchange rate between the German mark and the other euro-zone currencies and the euro. January 1, 1999, saw the beginning in the euro-zone countries of a three-year transition period from national currencies to the euro. Euronotes and coins were not expected to appear until January 1, 2002, but consumers, retailers, and public authorities could use the euro in noncash form during the transition period. Many financial statements and prices in retail stores appeared in both euros and the local currency.

For years, one of the major complaints of people doing business in Europe was the cost of converting from one currency to another. One could lose significant amounts of money by paying currency exchange fees. The adoption of the euro eliminated the necessity of changing currencies when moving from one euro-zone country to another. The euro is expected to facilitate business transactions throughout the euro-zone countries.

Relations with the United States

When dealing with trade matters involving member-nations of the EU, on a national level the U.S. government negotiates with the EU as the representative of all EU member nations. On an individual level, many businesses in the United States are realizing the vast potential for trade opportunities in the EU. The United States and Europe have always enjoyed a well-established commercial relationship, and the increase in European prosperity has made this relationship even stronger. According to statistics compiled by the International Trade Administration of the United States Department of Commerce, in 1999, the United States exported $152 billion worth of goods to the EU nations and imported $195 billion worth of goods from those nations. In 1999, the United States exported $19.7 billion dollars worth of aircraft to the EU, making it the largest single export item to the EU nations in terms of value. Likewise, in terms of value, the largest single item imported from the EU nations in 1999 to the United States was motor vehicles. The United States imported $20.1 billion worth of motor vehicles in 1999, $13.5 billion of which came from Germany.

*The euro is discussed in Chapter 5.

Table 4.4 **Top 10 States Exporting to the European Union**

State	Total Value ($ billions)
California	23.2
New York	10.9
Washington	10.5
Texas	9.7
Massachusetts	6.5
Illinois	6.4
Ohio	5.2
New Jersey	5.1
Virginia	4.6
North Carolina	4.4

Source: www.eurunion.org/partner/usstates/sld052.htm.

[Figure 4.2] **Sources of Foreign Direct Investment in the United States by Region**

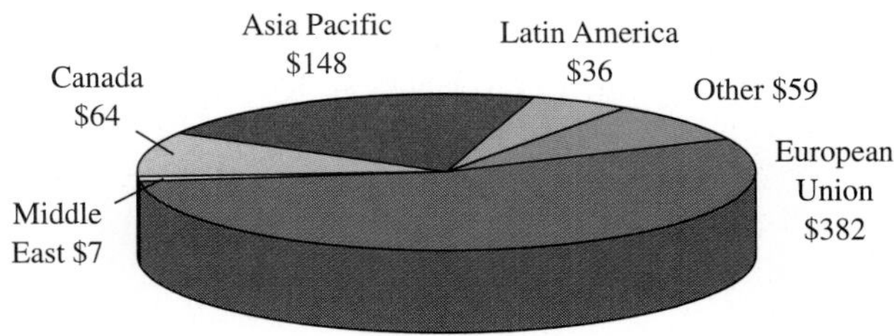

1998 ($US BILLIONS)
TOTAL FOREIGN INVESTMENT IN THE UNITED STATES: $812 BILLION
Source: U.S. Department of Commerce, Bureau of Economic Analysis, 1998.

EU member-nations account for significant export markets for the United States and foreign direct investment in the United States. Table 4.4 shows the top 10 states exporting to the EU. Figure 4.2 shows the EU is the largest source of foreign direct investment* in the United States. For those who want more information about EU, the EU Web page, www.europa.eu.int, has a wealth of information in all 11 EU official languages (Danish, Dutch, English, Finnish, French, German, Greek, Italian, Portuguese, Spanish, and Swedish). The EU has a special Web page that focuses on matters of interest concerning EU–U.S. relations, www.eurunion.org, which includes information about the EU's trade activities with individual states in the United States.

Other Regional Groupings of Nations

The success of the EU has led nations to form a number of other groupings with similar, but usually more limited, objectives. It is important to understand the authority and power regional organizations have over businesses that operate within their areas. The number of international organizations has grown significantly as more and more governments have reached out to seek formal relationships with other countries.

*Foreign direct investment is discussed in Chapter 1.

[Figure 4.3] Map of ASEAN Members

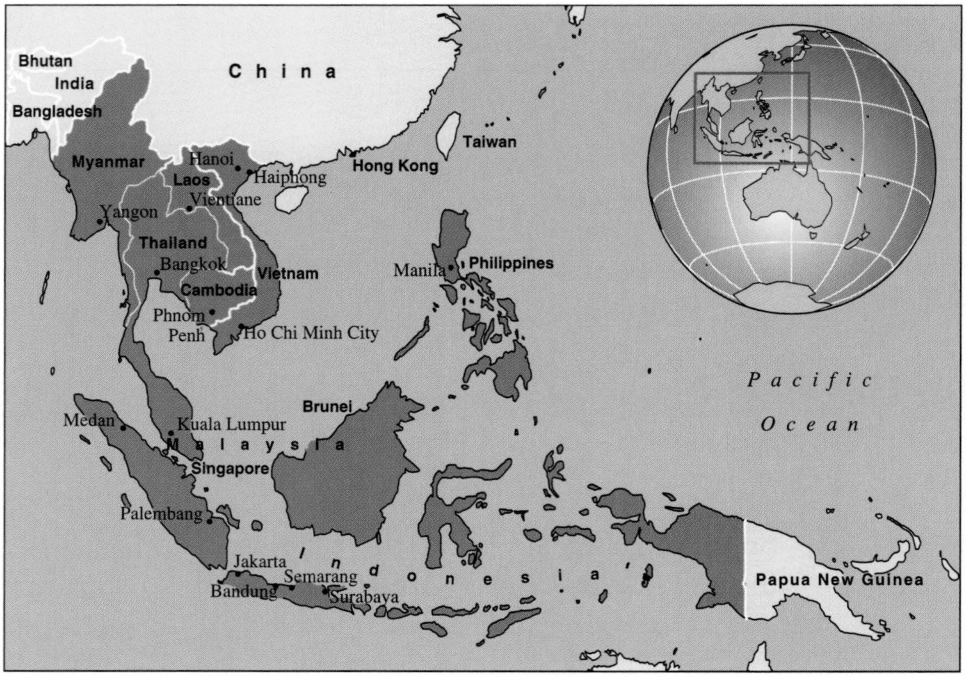

● Members of the Association of Southeast Asian Nations (ASEAN) as of October 2000

Association of Southeast Asian Nations (ASEAN)

Created in 1967, ASEAN is one of the most dynamic and fastest-developing economic regions in the world. Taken together, its members—Brunei, Cambodia, Indonesia, Malaysia, Myanmar (formerly Burma), the Philippines, Singapore, Thailand, and Vietnam—are major trading partners of the United States. Figure 4.3 presents a map of ASEAN members. ASEAN's purpose is to promote economic growth and peace in the region.

European Free Trade Association (EFTA)

The EFTA, created in 1960 in reaction to the EU, consisted of many European countries that were not EU members. EFTA countries wanted to stimulate trade among themselves and enable bargaining with the EU as an organization rather than as individual countries. As EFTA countries observed EU progress toward unification, they realized that a potentially powerful European force was in the making. They feared being excluded from it and reacted in different ways. Many former EFTA members are now members of the EU. Others have reached other agreements with the EU on various matters.

The original EFTA members were Austria, Denmark, Norway, Portugal, Sweden, Switzerland, and the United Kingdom. The current EFTA members are Iceland, Liechtenstein, Norway, and Switzerland.

African Trade Agreements

To promote economic growth throughout the continent, several African countries have formed trade and investment groups. Three of those groups are the Economic Community of West African States (ECOWAS), the Common Market for Eastern and Southern Africa (COMESA), and the Southern African Development Community (SADC). Figure 4.4 includes their locations and the member-countries.

[Figure 4.4] African Trade Agreements

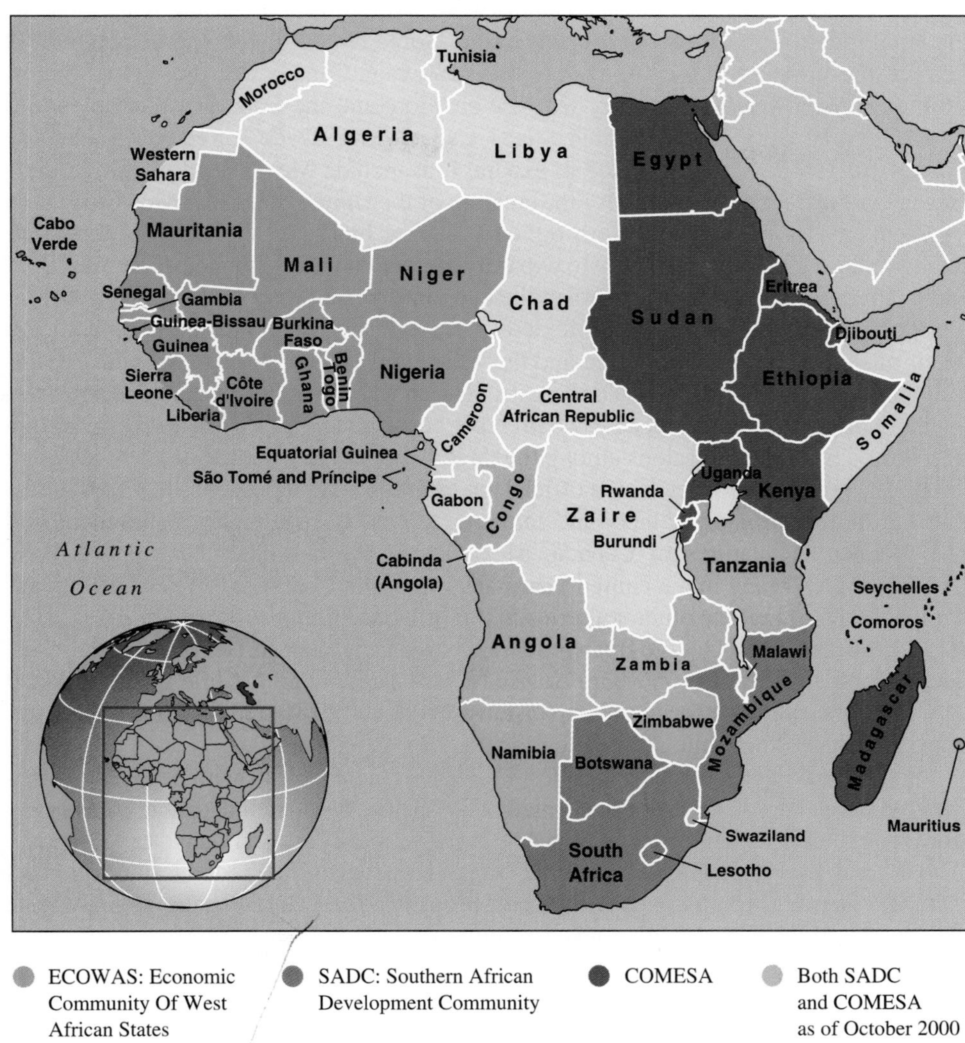

ECOWAS: Economic Community Of West African States; SADC: Southern African Development Community; COMESA; Both SADC and COMESA as of October 2000

North American Free Trade Agreement (NAFTA)

The **North American Free Trade Agreement** (NAFTA), which created a free trade area among Canada, Mexico, and the United States and two supplemental agreements on labor and environmental issues, came into existence on January 1, 1994. NAFTA does not operate as a separate entity but is part of the national law of each party to the agreement. While NAFTA did create several agencies for implementation of certain parts of the agreement, it created no EU-style entity and did not establish any sort of regional government. NAFTA is a trade agreement that is intended to facilitate trade within the areas of the countries that are parties to the agreement.

North American Free Trade Agreement (NAFTA)
Agreement creating a free trade area consisting of Canada, Mexico, and the United States

The impetus for the creation of NAFTA and its 1989 predecessor, the United States–Canada Free Trade Agreement, was the desire of the United States to remain as competitive as possible in the world marketplace. NAFTA's purpose is to eliminate trade barriers among the three countries, creating a free trade area. Import duties were eliminated or reduced among the three countries. In the 1980s, the United States was a leader in developing free trade agreements; it is now reluctant to enter into such agreements. By contrast, Canada was reluctant in the 1980s to enter into trade agreements and is now aggressively seeking out trade agreement partners. Mexico, along with the rest of Latin America, also is looking for trading partners.

The original 1988 debate in Canada over whether that country should be part of the United States–Canada Free Trade Agreement led to a national election. Proponents, including Prime Minister Brian Mulroney, argued that the agreement would be good for Canada and that free trade would open up large markets to the south to Canadian businesses. Opponents argued that Canadians would lose jobs and Canada would lose its national identity by approving the agreement. Some feared that the agreement would lead to the virtual elimination of the border between Canada and the United States. Prime Minister Mulroney's party won the election, and the Canadian Parliament approved the agreement. The United States–Canada Free Trade Agreement proved so successful that the parties wanted to expand it to include Mexico and possibly others at a later date. Since one reason for the creation of the United States–Canada Free Trade Agreement was competition from regional trading blocs, by including Mexico, the United States saw an opportunity to expand potential markets even more. The result of such expansion could only strengthen the economies of all three countries. Many also believed that opening markets in Mexico to U.S. interests would have the added benefit of raising the standard of living and the wage rate of the citizens of Mexico. An improvement in the economy would increase Mexico's ability to retain valuable members of the work force who otherwise would have been attracted by a higher wage rate in the United States. Discussions among the three nations were successful, and the agreement was presented to the elected officials in each country for approval. Despite fierce opposition from organized labor and some politicians, the negotiations succeeded and the national legislatures of Canada, Mexico, and the United States approved the NAFTA treaty. Many in the United States and throughout Latin America wanted to extend NAFTA to include other countries in the free trade area.

In 1990, President George Bush proclaimed as a goal "Enterprise for the Americas," envisioning a free trade zone from Alaska to Tierra del Fuego.[42] Chile was mentioned as a possible candidate for initial expansion and the parties started discussions, but enthusiasm for adding Chile seemed to fade.

Tired of waiting for the United States, Chile cut free trade deals with nearly all its major commercial partners except the United States. Those deals included a preliminary accord with the EU and agreements with America's NAFTA partners, Canada and Mexico. The Chilean president, Eduardo Frei, said that "the status of the U.S. as Latin America's number one trading partner—and with a positive trade balance for Washington—will be lost quickly if the U.S. doesn't retake the initiative."[43]

Canada also tired of waiting for the United States. Art Eggleton, Canada's trade minister, said, "We're going to certainly move ahead with our relationships in Latin America. If we wait, we will be left behind."[44]

Brazil has filled the vacuum created by America's absent leadership with a proposal to consolidate Mercosur into a regional "building block" before negotiating as a single entity to establish a free trade area of the Americas.[45]

Despite the U.S. failure to enlarge NAFTA, it remains important for American business. Many commentators point to increased trade among the three countries and argue that NAFTA has been a great success. Many argue that NAFTA has created more problems by moving lower-wage jobs to Mexico. The debate over the success of NAFTA continues to this day.

Organization of American States (OAS)

The Organization of American States (OAS) is an organization of 35 countries in the Western Hemisphere dedicated to promoting cooperation in the region. The OAS was formed in 1948 with the United States as one of the original 21 countries, even though its origins date back to 1890, when the First International Conference of American States, held in Washington, DC, established the International Union of American Republics. The OAS has expanded to other countries in the hemisphere and now includes the present 35 members. The OAS is headquartered in Washington, DC. Information about the OAS can be found at its website, **www.oas.org.**

The 21 original OAS Members in 1948 were Argentina, Bolivia, Brazil, Chile, Colombia, Costa Rica, Cuba, the Dominican Republic, Ecuador, El Salvador, Guatemala, Haiti, Honduras, Mexico, Nicaragua, Panama, Paraguay, Peru, the United States, Uruguay, and Venezuela. Even though Cuba is a member of the OAS, in 1962, the organization excluded the Cuban government from participation in its activities. The 14 additional members and their years of admission are Barbados (1967), Trinidad and Tobago (1967), Jamaica (1969), Grenada (1975), Suriname (1977), Dominica (1979), Saint Lucia (1979), Antigua and Barbuda (1981), Saint Vincent and the Grenadines (1981), the Bahamas (1982), St. Kitts and Nevis (1984), Canada (1990), Belize (1991), and Guyana (1991).[46]

Asia-Pacific Economic Cooperation (APEC)

In response to the growing importance of the economies of the Pacific Rim countries, the Asia-Pacific Economic Cooperation (APEC) was established in 1989. It now serves as a regional vehicle for promoting open trade and practical economic cooperation. Today, APEC includes all the major economies in the region. The United States is one of the 21 current members. Information about APEC can be found at its website, apec.org.

Mercosur—Mercosul in Portuguese

In either language it is an acronym for the Common Market of the South, and it was created in 1991 by the Treaty of Asunción, which united Argentina, Brazil, Paraguay, and Uruguay. Although its title uses the term *common market,* **Mercosur** has not yet achieved that state. But it has come a long way.

Mercosur
Economic free trade area consisting of Argentina, Brazil, Paraguay, and Uruguay

Most trade within Mercosur is already tariff-free, and free trade in all products is an objective. A common external tariff has been adopted on most products, but the group will not become a full customs union until 2006.

Mercosur is expanding (see Figure 4.5). Chile and Bolivia acceded in 1996 and 1997, respectively, as associate members, meaning they will become part of the group's free trade zone without adopting the common external tariff. Negotiations with Colombia, Ecuador, Mexico, Peru, and Venezuela for a free trade association began in 1997. The group is also in talks with the EU for freer trade.

Since its inception, trade within Mercosur has grown rapidly at an average of 27 percent a year while trade with the rest of the world expanded an annual 7.5 percent. One-fifth of the four countries' foreign trade is now conducted with each other, up from 9 percent in 1990. All this growth has highlighted the area's poor infrastructure. Roads and bridges are inadequate.

The growth has also shown the need for coordinated policies in a number of areas, including competition codes, antidumping policies, and tax harmonization. Services need to be incorporated in the Mercosur agreement. Such coordination will be particularly difficult for Mercosur because it lacks an institution such as the European Commission of the EU, and Brazil, which accounts for 70 percent of the grouping's production and population, has strongly resisted a supranational bureaucracy or court for Mercosur.[47]

Organization for Economic Cooperation and Development (OECD)

The members of the **Organization for Economic Cooperation and Development (OECD)** are the world's developed countries, and its headquarters is in Paris. As of 2000, there were 30 member-countries. The OECD publishes extensive research on a wide variety of international business and economic subjects. These publications and resource materials contain valuable information for students and businesspeople.

The OECD is often called the "rich man's club" because it is composed of 30 of the wealthiest nations in the world. Membership, though, is open to all nations committed to a market economy and a pluralistic democracy. The OECD provides information on economic and other activities within its member-countries and also gives member-governments a setting in which to discuss economic and social policy. The governments seek answers to common problems and work to coordinate domestic and international policies. The OECD has been instrumental in many areas, including encouraging member-countries to eliminate bribery and establish a code of conduct for multinational companies. The OECD has a formal mechanism to propose legislation for adoption in the member countries.

[Figure 4.5] Regional Trade Agreements in Central America and South America

Regional Trade Agreements in Central America and South America as of October 2000

● Andean Community ● Central American Free Trade Zone ● Mercosur ● None

Organization for Economic Cooperation and Development (OECD) International organization of primarily developed countries dedicated to promoting economic expansion in its member-countries

The 30 OECD member-countries with their years of admission are Australia (1971), Austria (1961), Belgium (1961), Canada (1961), the Czech Republic (1995), Denmark (1961), Finland (1969), France (1961), Germany (1961), Greece (1961), Hungary (1996), Iceland (1961), Ireland (1961), Italy (1961), Japan (1964), Korea (1996), Luxembourg (1961), Mexico (1994), the Netherlands (1961), New Zealand (1973), Norway (1961), Poland (1996), Portugal (1961), Slovak Republic (2000), Spain (1961), Sweden (1961), Switzerland (1961), Turkey (1961), the United Kingdom (1961), and the United States (1961). Information about the OECD can be found at its website, www.OECD.org.

The OECD has several committees, including the Business and Industry Advisory Committee (BIAC), which was created in 1962 to represent business and industry. The BIAC works in various areas, such as trade liberalization, sustainable development, E-commerce, taxation, and biotechnology. Information about the BIAC can be found at www.biac.org.

[Summary]

Understand the influence international organizations have on international businesses.

International organizations can have profound influence on businesses and businesspeople worldwide. Most of the organizations discussed in this chapter are organizations of governments. As a result, they often speak for their member governments and can have significant power over businesses.

Explain the activities of the United Nations in the economic and social fields as well as those as a peacekeeper/peacemaker in the world's trouble spots.

The UN organization consists of (1) a 15-member Security Council, of which 5 are permanent members, which is responsible for the UN's peacekeeping operations, (2) the General Assembly, of which every country is a member and in which every country has one vote, and (3) specialized agencies that conduct studies and assist member-countries in many fields.

Explain the three major parts of the World Bank: its regular loan window, its International Finance Corporation, and its International Development Association.

The World Bank lends money to developing countries for projects and has begun to insist that the borrowers put their economic houses in order as a condition for getting loans. The International Finance Corporation, a very successful arm of the Bank, encourages private business in developing countries.

Explain the original and changed activities of the International Monetary Fund.

The International Monetary Fund helps developing countries with balance-of-payments deficits and cooperates with the World Bank's efforts to correct borrowers' fiscal and monetary policies. It began loan renegotiation procedures that have helped deal with the sovereign debt crisis that came to light in the 1980s.

Understand the importance of the World Trade Organization to world business and trade.

The WTO attempts to remove trade barriers worldwide.

Understand the European Union and how it affects business.

The EU is a supranational entity with 15 European member-nations. Its purpose is to integrate the economies of its member-nations, creating a trading region where goods, services, people, and capital move freely. In recent years, the EU has made major steps toward political union as well.

Understand the North American Free Trade Agreement and its impact on business.

NAFTA was ratified by Canada, Mexico, and the United States. Negotiations are afoot to admit all Western Hemisphere countries, and some want to open it to the world. However, NAFTA's potential may not be realized because the U.S. government lost interest and its leadership position in enlarging membership. Into the resulting void has stepped Mercosur, led by Brazil. The EU has approached Mercosur to negotiate free trade between their areas.

Know about the Organization for Economic Cooperation and Development and its use as a source of valuable information.

The OECD is an excellent source of research on many subjects. New countries are joining as they become more market oriented democracies.

[Key Words]

United Nations (p. 149)
General Assembly (p. 151)
Security Council (p. 151)
multilateral development banks (p. 153)
hard loans (p. 154)
soft loans (p. 155)
firm surveillance (p. 158)
Group of Seven (G7) (p. 159)
World Trade Organization (WTO) (p. 160)
European Union (EU) (p. 166)
European Commission (p. 167)
Council of Ministers (p. 167)
Parliament of the EU (p. 168)
European Court of Justice (p. 168)
North American Free Trade Agreement (NAFTA) (p. 173)
Mercosur (p. 175)
Organization for Economic Cooperation and Development (OECD) (p. 176)

[Questions]

1. What are some reasons businesspeople and business students should be aware of important international organizations?
2. How does the UN operate?
3. When the World Bank makes a loan, what interest rates are used?
4. a. Which part of the World Bank Group is referred to as its investment banker? b. Why?
5. Multilateral development banks work primarily with which countries? Why?
6. How does the IMF function?
7. How did the WTO come into existence?
8. What are the four main institutions of the EU? What is the purpose of each institution?
9. The North American Free Trade Agreement passed the U.S. Congress despite strong opposition from organized labor. What motivated labor's stand? Have labor's forecasts turned out to be correct?
10. Explain why NAFTA has not expanded as originally envisioned and describe how Mercosur is stepping into the resulting void.
11. What is the importance of the OECD for business and students?

[Internet Exercises]

Using the Internet

1. As the text explains, the European Union (EU) is a union of 15 European nations. Using the Internet, such as the EU website, find information on the EU, including:
   a. The role of the European Union.
   b. Competition policy in the European Union.
   c. The role of EU institutions, including the Council and the Commission.
   d. How is the EU financed?

   After visiting the EU website, discuss the similarities and differences between the structure of the government of the United States and that of the European Union.

2. The text discusses the World Bank. Visit the World Bank's website and answer the following questions about the World Bank:
   a. What are the institutions in the World Bank Group? How are the institutions related? In what projects are the institutions involved?
   b. What are the current major World Bank programs?
   c. What information is contained in the annual report of the World Bank?
   d. Who is able to use the services of the World Bank?

[Minicase 4.1]

Use of International Organizations—Setting Up a 100-Percent-Owned Subsidiary

You are an international business consultant in the United States. Your specialty is exporting to and investing, licensing, or franchising in developing countries.

One of your clients is a hotel company that wants to build, operate, and 100 percent own a hotel in Guatemala. Your client is willing to put up about half of the original capital but wants to be assured that its share of the profits can be converted to U.S. dollars and repatriated as dividends.

To what organizations discussed in Chapter 4 might you look for assistance in raising the rest of the needed capital? To what organizations might you look for information concerning a Guatemalan company's ability to convert profits into U.S. dollars and remit them to the United States?

[Chapter]

5

Understanding the International Monetary System

European central banks announced they would limit future gold sales, and the IMF sales of its gold reserve have been blocked. America's Federal Reserve, which owns most of the remaining stocks of gold, said it would not be selling.

"Without these supply overhangs, the equilibrium price of gold would be around $600 an ounce."

—Frank Veneroso, author of the influential Gold Book Annual.

Concept Previews

After reading this chapter, you should be able to:

- **understand** the historical and present uses and attractiveness of gold
- **explain** the developments shaping the world monetary system from the end of World War II to the present
- **understand** balance of payments (BOP)
- **compare** the relative strengths and weaknesses of currencies and reasons for them
- **understand** how "Big MacCurrencies" and the purchasing power parity theory are related
- **identify** the major foreign exchange (Fx) markets of the world
- **understand** changes being caused in the FX markets by electronic currency broking machines
- **understand** the central reserve asset/national currency conflict of the U.S. dollar and the reasons and uses for special drawing rights (SDRs)
- **discuss** the euro and its present state of acceptance by EU countries

Scott Olson/Liaison

Europe Can't Handle the Euro: Blame USA?

The European Central Bank (ECB) must make monetary policy for all twelve countries that have joined the economic and monetary union (EMU), which is called the euro zone. That means doing what is appropriate for Germany, France, and Italy, the euro zone's three largest economies. In 1999, demand conditions in those countries were relatively weak while demand conditions in Ireland and Spain were very strong. That meant a monetary policy that was too expansionary, causing inflation and threatening Irish and Spanish competitiveness.

Such disparities in economic conditions undoubtedly will persist because European countries differ substantially in industrial and labor composition and in a variety of economic policies. Europe lacks the unity of the United States, where labor can move easily to regions where demand is stronger and where net fiscal transfers from Washington occur as higher unemployment in a region results in lower federal tax liability in that region. Almost none of this occurs among the twelve separate countries of the euro zone.

One way for European governments to create greater unity is to have a common adversary. With the Soviet Union gone, there is worry that Europe will come to see the United States in that role. ■

Source: Martin Feldstein, "Europe Can't Handle the Euro," *The Wall Street Journal,* February 8, 2000, p. A26.

Since the end of World War II in 1945, the U.S. dollar has been a central currency in the world's transactions. In the beginning it was dominant because the U.S. economy emerged from the war relatively undamaged and far and away the most powerful. Fairly rapidly in historical context, however, Japan and countries in Western Europe and elsewhere developed powerful economies, and their currencies were increasingly used together with or instead of the U.S. dollar.

Although the American consumer pays U.S. dollars (US$s) for a German car or Scottish woolens purchased in the United States, the car manufacturer in Germany and the wool processor in Scotland must have, respectively, deutsche marks (DM) and pounds sterling (£) to meet their local expenses. At some point, the US$s must be exchanged for the necessary DM and £. Underlying the mechanics and rates of exchange (both of which are discussed in some detail in Chapter 6) is the international monetary system. The currencies mentioned above are **convertible currencies** (that is, they are readily convertible in the market), but most currencies are not. For example, the currencies of most developing countries are not convertible or are legally convertible only at artificial, government-established rates.

convertible currencies
Also called hard currencies; exchangeable for any other currency at uniform rates at financial centers worldwide

The international businessperson or student should have some knowledge of the history and current state of the international monetary system. We discuss history in this chapter because of its lessons and also because a vocal minority wants to resurrect elements of it, namely, the *gold standard* and *fixed currency exchange rates.* We then look at post–gold standard, 20th-century developments before examining the current practices of businesspeople, economists, governments, and institutions. The forecasting and planning that each of those groups must do involve informed guesses about the future.

A Brief Gold Standard History and Comment

From about A.D. 1200 to the present, the direction of the price of gold has been generally up.[1] True, there have been wide fluctuations in that price, and an investor in gold should have steady nerves, though law-abiding American investors were for a time spared that source of nervousness because it was illegal for them to own gold bullion between 1933 and 1976. During that period, the price of gold rose from about $21 per ounce to just under $200 in December 1976, when Americans were again legally free to own gold in bullion form. As it developed, Americans did not rush into the market, and the price has fluctuated between a bit over $100 and over $800 per ounce since 1976.

The historical upward direction of the price of gold mentioned in the preceding paragraph has been at least interrupted; some believe it has been ended. Since about 1980, the metal's price has been in broad decline. Given that there are some 140,000 tons above ground compared with annual demand for around 4,000 tons, the situation is intrinsically unstable.

It is said that gold should be marketed as are diamonds and platinum, but those commodities have a very important advantage over gold. De Beers, the giant in diamonds, happily calls itself a monopoly. Platinum is an oligopoly of which Amplats is the dominant member as the world's largest platinum miner. By contrast, gold mining is highly fragmented, and many gold companies have declined to join the marketing arm, the World Gold Council.

De Beers and the diamond industry spend around one percent of the retail value of diamond jewelry on marketing, and De Beers is trying to raise that proportion to 6 to

10 percent. For platinum, Amplats is the main power behind the retail marketing arm, the Platinum Guild, and it also orchestrates research on its already large number of industrial uses, such as for car exhaust catalysts, electronics, and fuel cells. For gold, the World Gold Council plus a few other sources can come up with less than 0.2 percent of the product value for promotion. While these are inexact and not apples-to-apples comparisons, they illustrate that many more efforts are being devoted to promoting sales and uses of diamonds and platinum than are being made for gold.[2]

Nevertheless, it is too early to write off gold as an important element in the international economy and business. Its history as a store of value, an international currency, and a haven in periods of inflation is long. The London bullion market alone trades around 750 to 1,000 tons of gold a day, while platinum markets are relatively illiquid. See also the commentary about gold at the beginning of this chapter.

On December 22, 1717, Sir Isaac Newton, master of the English mint, established the price of gold at 3 pounds, 17 shillings, 10.5 pence per ounce. England was then on the gold standard and stood willing to convert gold to currency, or vice versa, until World War I, except during the Napoleonic Wars. During that period, London was the dominant center of international finance. It has been estimated that more than 90 percent of world trade was financed in London.[3]

Most trading or industrial countries adopted the **gold standard.** Each country set a certain number of units of its currency per ounce of gold, and the comparison of the numbers of units per ounce from country to country was the exchange rate between any two currencies on the gold standard.

gold standard
When countries agree to buy or sell gold for an established number of currency units

The financial burdens of World War I forced Britain to sell a substantial portion of its gold, and the gold standard ended. Between World War I and World War II there was a short-lived flirtation with the gold standard, but it was not successfully reestablished.

Return to the Gold Standard?

Although the gold standard has not been the international monetary system for many years, it has had some ardent and influential advocates recently. One of the staunchest was Jacques Rueff, who until his death in 1978 was a member of the French Academy and an adviser to the French government. The heart of Rueff's argument may be expressed by one word: *discipline.*

Under the gold standard, a government cannot create money that is not backed by gold. Therefore, no matter how great the temptation to create more money for political advantage, without regard for economic results, a government cannot do so without the established amount of gold. This is the discipline that Jacques Rueff argued is the only effective means of avoiding inflation.[4]

One argument for a return to the gold standard, thus making gold the reserve asset of nations, is based on the premise that the current situation, in which the U.S. dollar is the reserve asset, is unsustainable. As world trade, investment, and economies grow, countries need more reserves. With the US$ as the reserve asset, other countries can increase their reserves only if the United States increases its net reserve indebtedness with a balance-of-payments (BOP) deficit.* The United States can increase its liquidity only at the expense of other countries; a U.S. BOP surplus would drain US$ reserves from other countries. Thus, under the present system, the reserves of other countries can increase only if the United States continues to run a BOP deficit.

It has been suggested that the five nations with the largest economies should agree to settle their accounts with one another in gold, not US$s.[5] If a gold standard is established, what should be the price of gold? Lewis Lehrman advocates $500 an ounce, based on production costs. Arthur Laffer picks a price in the $200 range, based on the increase in the consumer price level since gold was $35 an ounce. A third school of thought, identified with Robert Mundell, suggests pegging the price where it happens to be on the day that the five nations agree to institute a gold standard.[6]

*BOP is discussed later in this chapter.

Present-Day Uses of Gold

In addition to its uses in jewelry and dentistry, gold has some industrial uses. It is an excellent conductor of heat and is used as protective insulation in space programs.

In India, gold is a very popular dowry at weddings; at a typical wedding, about $500 worth is given. It also serves as a currency in the pervasive black market in India.[7] The Indian government also has uses for gold. In 1991, it shipped 45 tons to Switzerland and London. The Swiss shipment was to secure a $200 million loan from a Swiss bank. The Indian gold in London would permit India to borrow from the Bank of England and serve to "shore up the confidence of the international community."[8]

Because of its high value, gold is very portable. Thousands of people, including refugees from Hitler's National Socialists, Mao's terror, and Pol Pot's killing fields, owe their lives to small bars of bullion they managed to smuggle out. American agents and paratroopers are equipped with "escape and evasion" kits containing gold coins.[9]

The world's interest in gold remains high. Figure 5.1 is an advertisement in one of the most important international financial papers for gold bullion, coins, and bars for sale.

Bretton Woods and the Gold Exchange Standard

Bretton Woods
A New Hampshire town where treasury and central bank representatives met near the end of World War II; they established the IMF, the World Bank, and the gold exchange standard

central reserve assets
Gold, SDRs, or hard currencies held in a nation's treasury

During World War II, the countries of the world were much too involved with the hostilities to consider the gold standard or any other monetary system. However, many officials realized some system had to be established to operate when peace returned. Actually, consideration of it did not await the firing of the last shot. Before that, in 1944, representatives of the major Allied powers, with the United States and Britain assuming the dominant roles, met at **Bretton Woods,** New Hampshire, to plan for the future.

There was a consensus that (1) stable exchange rates were desirable but experience might dictate adjustments, (2) floating* or fluctuating exchange rates had proved unsatisfactory, though the reasons for this opinion were little discussed, and (3) the government controls of trade, exchange, production, and so forth, that had developed from 1931 through World War II were wasteful, discriminatory, and detrimental to expansion of world trade and investment. Despite the third consensus, the conferees recognized that some conditions—for example, reconstruction from war damage or the development of less developed countries (LDCs)†—would require government controls.

To achieve its goals, the Bretton Woods Conference established the International Monetary Fund (IMF). Article I of the IMF Articles of Agreement set forth its purposes, which reflected the consensus referred to above.[10] The IMF Articles of Agreement entered into force in December 1945.

The IMF agreement was the basis for the international monetary system from 1945 until 1971. It is doubtful, however, that the future role assumed by, or thrust upon, the US$—which became the major **central reserve asset**—was fully foreseen.[11]

The US$ was agreed to be the only currency directly convertible into gold for official monetary purposes. An ounce of gold was agreed to be worth US$35, and other currencies were assigned so-called par values in relationship to the US$. For example, the British pound's par value was US$2.40, the French franc's was US$0.18, and the German mark's was US$0.2732.[12]

It was recognized that each member-country would be subject to different pressures at different times. The pressures could be caused by political or economic events or trends and could render the par values (currency exchange rates) established at Bretton Woods unrealistic. A major force that affects currency exchange rates is the BOP of the member-countries.

*A currency is said to float freely when the governments do nothing to affect its value in the world currency markets. Other varieties of floating are discussed later in this chapter.

†New terminology is developing, and less developed countries are sometimes called *developing countries* and, more recently, *emerging economies.*

[Figure 5.1] Advertisement of a Major Gold Market Maker

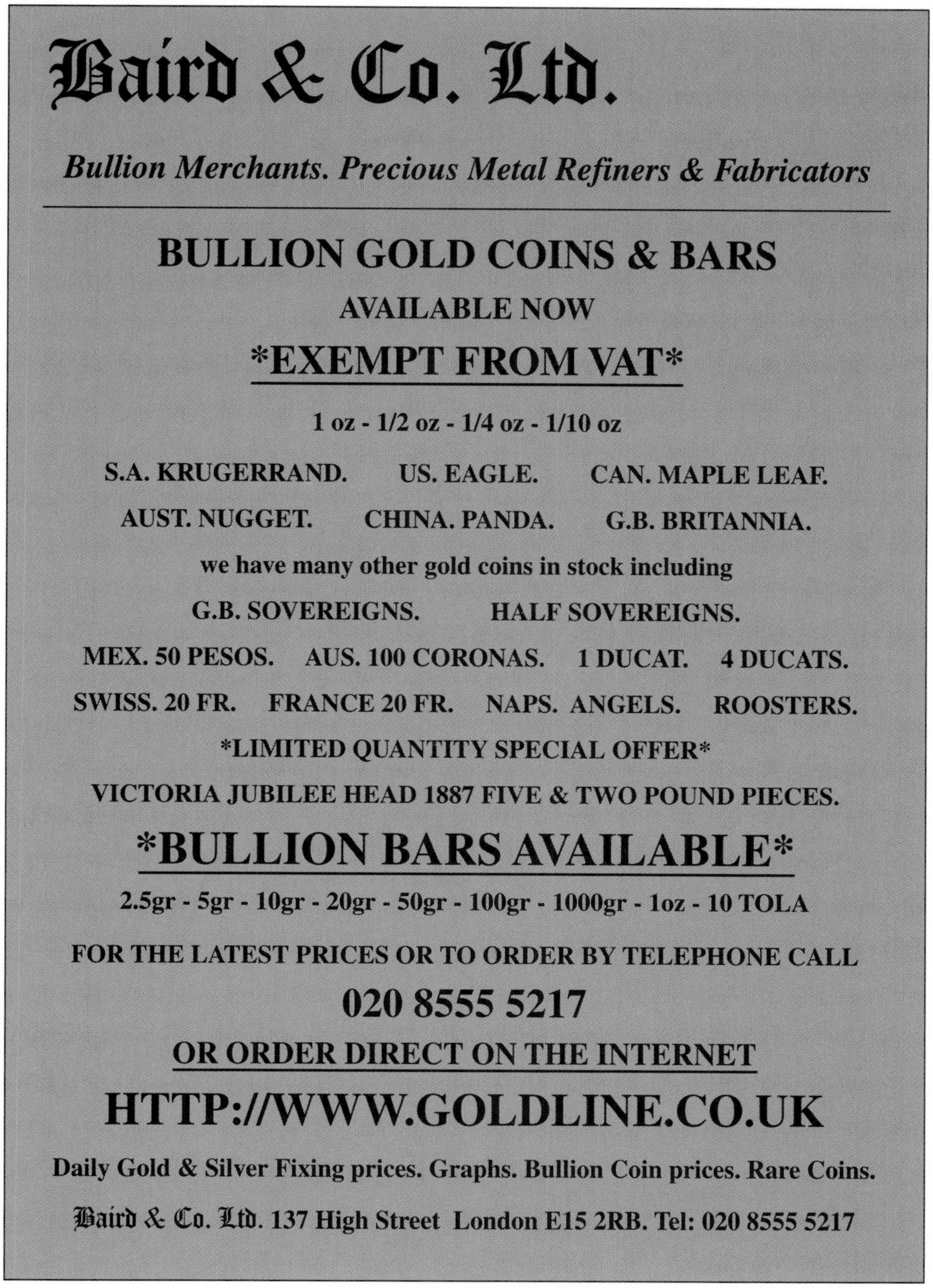

Baird & Co. Ltd.

Bullion Merchants. Precious Metal Refiners & Fabricators

BULLION GOLD COINS & BARS

AVAILABLE NOW

EXEMPT FROM VAT

1 oz - 1/2 oz - 1/4 oz - 1/10 oz

S.A. KRUGERRAND. US. EAGLE. CAN. MAPLE LEAF.

AUST. NUGGET. CHINA. PANDA. G.B. BRITANNIA.

we have many other gold coins in stock including

G.B. SOVEREIGNS. HALF SOVEREIGNS.

MEX. 50 PESOS. AUS. 100 CORONAS. 1 DUCAT. 4 DUCATS.

SWISS. 20 FR. FRANCE 20 FR. NAPS. ANGELS. ROOSTERS.

LIMITED QUANTITY SPECIAL OFFER

VICTORIA JUBILEE HEAD 1887 FIVE & TWO POUND PIECES.

BULLION BARS AVAILABLE

2.5gr - 5gr - 10gr - 20gr - 50gr - 100gr - 1000gr - 1oz - 10 TOLA

FOR THE LATEST PRICES OR TO ORDER BY TELEPHONE CALL

020 8555 5217

OR ORDER DIRECT ON THE INTERNET

HTTP://WWW.GOLDLINE.CO.UK

Daily Gold & Silver Fixing prices. Graphs. Bullion Coin prices. Rare Coins.

Baird & Co. Ltd. 137 High Street London E15 2RB. Tel: 020 8555 5217

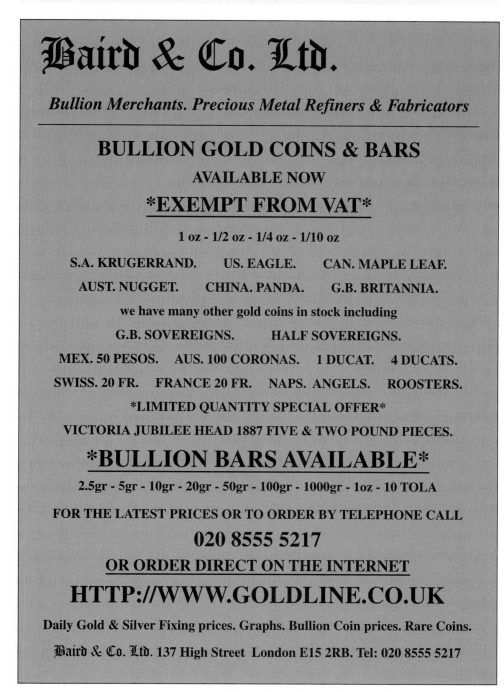

Source: *Financial Times,* June 28, 2000, p. Survey IV. Reproduced by permission of Baird & Co. All rights reserved.

Balance of Payments

One task assumed by the IMF was assistance to member-countries having difficulty keeping their balance of payments out of deficit.* A country's BOP is a very important indicator of what may happen to the country's economy, including what the government may cause to happen. If the BOP is in deficit, inflation is often the cause, and a company doing business there must adjust its pricing, inventory, accounting, and other

*A deficit occurs when the residents of a country are paying nonresidents more than they are earning or otherwise getting from nonresidents. The opposite is a surplus.

market measures
Steps taken to end a BOP deficit, including deflating the economy or devaluing the currency

nonmarket measures
Steps taken to end a BOP deficit, such as setting tariffs, quotas, and currency exchange controls

practices to inflationary conditions. The government may take measures to deal with inflation and the deficit. These may be so-called **market measures,** such as deflating the economy or devaluing the currency, or **nonmarket measures,** such as currency controls, tariffs, or quotas.

Even if a company does not consider itself international, it will be affected by inflation and by the government's methods of combating inflation and a BOP deficit. All those methods have the common goal of causing the country's residents to buy fewer foreign goods and services and to sell more to foreigners.

Debits and Credits in International Transactions

International debit transactions involve payments by domestic residents to foreign residents, and international credit transactions are the opposite. Taking America as the domestic economy, a list of debit transactions would include

1. Dividend, interest, and debt repayment services on foreign-owned capital in America.
2. Merchandise imports.
3. Purchases by Americans traveling abroad.
4. Transportation services bought by Americans on foreign carriers.
5. Foreign investment by Americans.
6. Gifts by Americans to foreign residents.
7. Imports of gold.

The opposite would be examples of credit transactions. For example, dividend, interest, and debt repayment services on American-owned capital abroad are credits on the American ledger.

Double-Entry Accounting

Although writers use debit and credit transaction language, each international transaction is an exchange of assets with debit and credit sides. Thus, the BOP is presented as a double-entry accounting statement in which total credits and debits are always equal. The statement of a country's BOP is divided into several accounts (see Table 5.1).

Current Account. Three subaccounts are included in the current account: (a) goods or merchandise, (b) services, and (c) unilateral transfers. The first two subaccounts are sometimes treated together, and they include the real (as opposed to the financial) international transactions, that is, exports and imports.

a. The goods or merchandise account deals with "visibles," such as autos, grain, machinery, and equipment, that can be seen and felt as they are exported or imported. The net balance on merchandise transactions is referred to as the country's trade balance.

b. The services account deals with "invisibles" that are exchanged or bought internationally. Examples include dividends or interest on foreign investments, royalties on patents or trademarks held abroad, travel, insurance, banking, and transportation.

c. Unilateral transfers are transactions with no quid pro quo; some of these transfers are made by private persons or institutions, and some by governments. Some private unilateral transfers are for charitable, educational, or missionary purposes; others are gifts from migrant workers to their families in their home countries and bequests or the transfer of capital by people migrating from one country to another. The largest government unilateral transfers are aid—which may be in money or in kind—from developed countries to developing countries. Pension payments to nonresidents and tax receipts from nonresidents are two other government-related unilateral transfers.

Table 5.1 Balance-or-Payments Accounts

	Debits	Credits
1. Current account		
a. Goods or merchandise—imports and exports		
b. Services		
Net goods and services balance		
c. Unilateral transfers		
To abroad		
From abroad		
Net current account balance		
2. Capital account		
a. Direct investment		
To abroad		
From abroad		
b. Portfolio investment		
To abroad		
From abroad		
c. Short-term capital		
To abroad		
From abroad		
Net capital account balance		
3. Official reserves account		
a. Gold export or import (net)		
b. Increase or decrease in foreign exchange (net)		
c. Increase or decrease in liabilities to foreign central banks (net)		
Net official reserves		
4. Net statistical discrepancy		

Capital Account. The capital account records the net changes in a nation's international financial assets and liabilities over the BOP period, which is usually one year. A capital inflow—a credit entry—occurs when a resident sells stock, bonds, or other financial assets to nonresidents. Money flows to the resident, while at the same time the resident's long-term international liabilities are increased, because dividends (profit) may be paid on the stock, rent will be paid on other assets, and interest must be paid on the bonds. And at maturity the bonds' face amounts must be repaid.

Subaccounts under the capital account are (*a*) direct investment, (*b*) portfolio investment, and (*c*) international movements of short-term capital.

a. Direct investments are investments in enterprises or properties located in one country that are effectively controlled by residents of another country. Effective control is assumed for BOP purposes (1) when residents of one country own 50 percent or more of the voting stock of a company in another country or (2) when one resident or an organized group of residents of one country own 25 percent or more of the voting stock of a company in another country.

b. Portfolio investments include all long-term—more than one year—investments that do not give the investors effective control over the object of the investment. Such transactions typically involve the purchase of stocks or bonds of foreign issuers for investment—not control—purposes, and they also include long-term commercial credits to finance trade.

c. Short-term capital flows involve changes in international assets and liabilities with an original maturity of one year or less. Some of the fastest-growing types of short-term flows are for currency exchange rate and interest rate hedging in the forward, futures, option, and swap markets. (These subjects are dealt with in Chapter 19, "Financial Management.") Among the more traditional types of short-term capital flow are payments and receipts for international finance and trade, short-term borrowings from foreign banks, exchanges of foreign notes or coins, and purchases of foreign commercial paper or foreign government bills or notes.

The volatility, private nature, and wide varieties of short-term capital flows make them the most difficult BOP items to measure—and therefore the least reliable. The wide fluctuations of currency exchange rates and interest rates during the 1980s and 1990s caused the surge in hedging activities mentioned above, with attendant surges in short-term capital movements.

Official Reserves Account. The official reserves account deals with *(a)* gold imports and exports, *(b)* increases or decreases in foreign exchange (foreign currencies) held by the government, and *(c)* decreases or increases in liabilities to foreign central banks.

Total credits and debits must be equal because of the double-entry accounting system used to report the BOP. Because some BOP figures are inaccurate and incomplete (notably true of the short-term capital flows item), the statistical discrepancy item is plugged in to bring total credits and debits into accounting balance.

Balance-of-Payment Equilibrium and Disequilibrium

Although the BOP is always in accounting balance, the odds are astronomical that it would be so without the statistical discrepancy item. There would be a surplus or a deficit in almost every case, but the BOP would nevertheless be considered in equilibrium if over a three- to five-year period the surpluses more or less canceled out the deficits.

Temporary and Fundamental BOP Deficits

monetary policies
These regulate the amount of growth or contraction of a nation's monetary stock

fiscal policies
These regulate a government's money receipts through taxes and its expenditure

In IMF terminology, a *temporary* BOP deficit is one that can be corrected by the country's **monetary policies** or **fiscal policies** and perhaps by short-term IMF loans and advice.

A *fundamental* BOP deficit is too severe to be repaired by any monetary or fiscal policies the country can apply; there are economic, social, and political limits to how much a country can deflate its economy, which causes unemployment, or devalue its currency, which causes higher prices for imports.

In these cases, the IMF rules permitted the countries' currencies to be devalued from the par values per US$ set at Bretton Woods; the amount of the devaluation was agreed on by the country and the IMF. Although many par value changes occurred between 1946 and 1971, none led to international financial crises of the kind that followed the devaluations of 1931. This was due at least in part to the performance of the IMF; it was able to maintain generally stable exchange rates, and when changes became necessary, it was able to prevent the competitive devaluations that proved so futile and destructive in the 1930s.

The devaluations of the 1946–71 period were in terms of the US$, and so its relative value went up in terms of the devalued currencies. This caused the prices of American goods and services to go up in terms of other currencies, because after devaluation, more units of those currencies were required to buy US$s. This, in turn, was one cause of an American BOP deficit that began in 1958.

American BOP Deficit

From the end of World War II until about 1958, there was a shortage of US$s for the development of world trade and investment. Even during that era many dollars flowed abroad due to government aid, private investment, and tourism. Around 1958 the United States began to run a series of BOP deficits, the flow of dollars became a flood, and the US$ shortage ended. The United States could have tried market methods (deflating its economy or devaluing the US$) to slow or reverse the deficit, but it did not, and its trading partner countries did not urge it to do so.

Why Market Methods Were Not Attempted

Vivid recollections of the hunger and hardships of the 1930s Depression caused U.S. leaders to see deflation as the greater danger, and until the late 1960s the U.S. government did not perceive inflation as a possible cause of another depression. The US$ had been enshrined at Bretton Woods as the key currency in the gold exchange standard and had become, along with gold, the central reserve asset of most countries. Those countries were understandably reluctant to see a reduction in the value of part of their reserves, and U.S. authorities seemed to feel that this nation's prestige would be tarnished by a devaluation of the US$.[13]

Moreover, foreign competitors of U.S. exports derived a price advantage from the overvaluation of the US$. As was pointed out above, almost all the 1946–71 currency value changes were devaluations in terms of the US$. Thus, foreign goods and services became relatively less expensive for holders of US$s, but at the same time, U.S. exports were becoming relatively more expensive for holders of other currencies, who bought fewer of those more expensive goods and services. The foreign competitors of U.S. firms did not want to lose that advantage, and their governments discouraged any U.S. inclination to devalue the US$.

Raising the US$ price of gold would amount to a dollar devaluation in terms of other currencies unless they also devalued. It was generally recognized that the US$ was overvalued and that, if permitted to float, its value would fall vis-à-vis the currencies of most developed countries.

The United States had thousands of troops stationed in Europe and Asia and could have saved billions of dollars in expenditures abroad by bringing them home. But the host countries—for example, Germany, Japan, South Korea, and South Vietnam—brought strong pressure on the U.S. government not to reduce its forces, and the United States felt obliged to maintain them.

Gold Exchange Standard

As the United States failed to even try market methods to end its BOP deficit and other, rather halfhearted attempts had little success, dollars piled up in foreign hands, including those of government **central banks.** At this point, beginning in 1958, the "exchange" part of the **gold exchange standard** began to function.

central bank
A government institution that manages the monetary policy of a country

gold exchange standard
Cast the U.S. dollar as the central currency at $35 per ounce of gold, at which price the U.S. agreed to buy gold from or sell it to other central banks

Gold for Dollars

The exchange feature agreed on at Bretton Woods required the United States to deliver an ounce of gold to any central bank of an IMF member-country that presented US$35 to the U.S. Treasury. As dollars accumulated in foreign hands in amounts greater than were needed for trade and investment, the central banks began turning them in to the U.S. Treasury for gold.

Gold and Dollars Go Abroad

From 1958 through 1971, the United States ran up a cumulative deficit of $56 billion. The deficit was financed partly by use of the U.S. gold reserves, which shrank from $24.8 billion to $12.2 billion,[14] and partly by incurring liabilities to foreign central banks. During this period, those liabilities increased from $13.6 billion to $62.2 billion.[15] This is illustrated in Figure 5.2.

The foreign central banks were willing to accept so many dollars primarily because those dollars were treated as a central reserve asset; they provided liquidity growth to support growing world trade and finance. But in the late 1960s and into 1971, the central banks became increasingly nervous about the volume of US$ accumulation. A number of them turned in excess dollars for gold, but by the mid-1960s, the banks held more dollars than there was gold left in the U.S. Treasury. By 1971, the Treasury held only 22 cents' worth of gold for each US$ held by those banks.[16]

As indicated, another reason foreigners accepted so many US$ was that those dollars provided liquidity to support world trade and investment, which grew rapidly in

[Figure 5.2] **Accumulation of US$s in Non–U.S. Resident Hands and Loss of U.S. Gold**

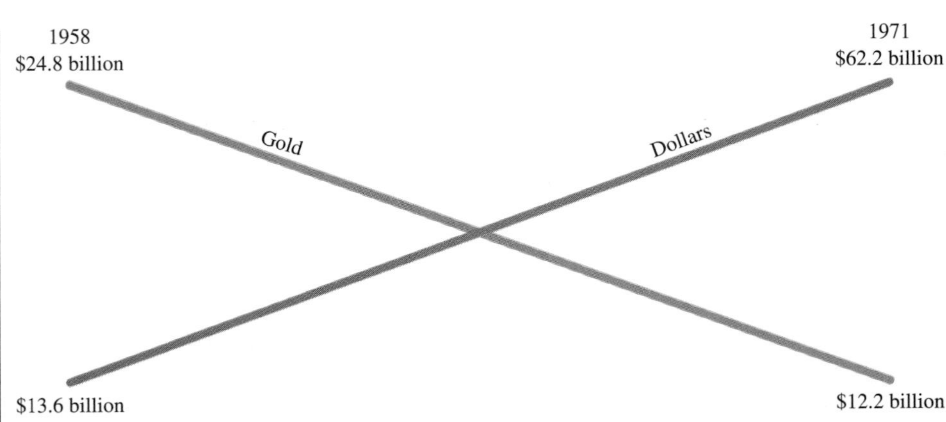

The gold value was set at $35/ounce

the post–World War II era. Of course, this meant liquidity growth depended on U.S. BOP deficits, but such deficits could not continue indefinitely without deterioration of confidence in the strength of the U.S. economy and the US$. Here is illustrated the inherent contradiction of the gold exchange standard. Foreigners needed and wanted growing numbers of dollars for many purposes but became nervous when the amounts of dollars they held exceeded the amount of gold held by the United States at the established price of $35 per ounce of gold.[17]

August 15, 1971, and the Next Two Years

As was noted above, by 1971 many more dollars were in the hands of foreign central banks than the gold held by the U.S. Treasury could cover. The event said to have triggered the drastic decisions made at Camp David* on the weekend beginning Friday, August 13, 1971, was a request by the British government that the United States cover US$3 billion of its reserve against loss.[18] President Nixon, with Treasury Secretary John Connally, Treasury Undersecretary Paul Volcker, and others, made the decisions that the president announced on Sunday night (the 15th). Those decisions shook the international monetary system to its roots.[19]

The president announced that the United States would no longer exchange gold for the paper dollars held by foreign central banks. He was said to have "closed the gold window."

The shock caused currency exchange markets to remain closed for several days, and when they reopened, they began playing a new game for which few rules existed. Currencies were floating, and the stated US$ value of 35 dollars per ounce of gold was now meaningless because the United States would no longer exchange any of its gold for dollars. The gold exchange standard was ended.

The president also imposed and announced a 10 percent surcharge on imports from all developed countries except Canada. He demanded that those countries lower their obstacles to imports from the United States in return for canceling the surcharges. Agreement on trade obstacles was reached in December 1971 along with new currency exchange rates that devalued the US$. The agreement was called the Smithsonian Accord because the final negotiations and signing ceremonies were held at the

*Camp David is a relatively isolated retreat in the Maryland mountains that U.S. presidents frequently use to escape from the pressures of Washington.

Smithsonian Institution in Washington, DC. The new rates could not be maintained, and by 1973 currencies were floating.

Politicians versus Speculators

Two attempts were made to agree on durable, new sets of **fixed currency exchange rates,** one in December 1971 and the other in February 1973. Both times, however, banks, businesses, and individuals (collectively referred to as speculators by unhappy politicians) felt that the central banks had pegged the rates incorrectly, and the speculators were correct each time. Of course, the speculators' prophecies could be said to have been self-fulfilling in that they put billions of units of the major currencies into the currencies they felt to be strong—for example, the deutsche mark, the Dutch guilder, and the Swiss franc—thereby making them even stronger. The speculators profited, and one writer commented, "It wasn't a holdup. It was more like an invited robbery."[20]

In March 1973 the major currencies began to float in the foreign exchange markets, and the system of **floating currency exchange rates** still prevails.[21] However, Western Europe moved back toward a fixed system, the European Monetary System, and in January 1999, eleven European countries began to phase out of their national currencies and move into the euro.

fixed currency exchange rates
When two or more countries agree on the exchange rate(s) of their currencies and undertake to maintain those rates

floating currency exchange rates
Values are set not by governments but by markets, although governments intervene frequently

1973 to the Present

The two kinds of currency floats are referred to by various commentators as free or managed or as clean or dirty. The free (clean) float is one of the world's closest approaches to perfect competition, because there is no government intervention and because billions of the product (units of money) are being traded by thousands of buyers and sellers. Buyers and sellers may change sides on short notice as information, rumors, or moods change or as their clients' needs differ. In the managed (dirty) float, governments intervene in the currency markets as they perceive their national interests to be served. Nations may explain their interventions in the currency market in terms of "smoothing market irregularities" or "assuring orderly markets."[22]

Beginning in September 1985, governments' reasons for intervening in currency markets have been expressed more forthrightly. The US$ soared in value from 1981 to its peak in February 1985, gaining some 80 percent against a trade-weighted basket of other major currencies. Although there were many other reasons for the huge growth of the American trade deficit, the powerful US$ was probably the biggest single reason.[23]

The unprecedented U.S. trade deficit, which was $134 billion in 1985 and reached $170 billion at its peak in 1987, greatly concerned the United States and its trading partners. To seek a solution, the finance ministers of the Group of Five (Britain, France, Germany, Japan, and the United States) met at the Plaza Hotel in New York in September 1985. Although the US$ exchange rate had begun to move down in March, they decided it was still too high and agreed in the so-called Plaza Accord to cooperate in bringing it lower. The Plaza meeting was the first of several—including one in Paris at the Louvre in February 1987—whose objective was to set the US$ at the "right" exchange rate, particularly in terms of the Japanese yen and the German deutsche mark (the currencies of the other two major world economies). And so, since 1985, the governments of the Group of Five have been intervening in currency markets to maintain their currencies' exchange rates at the "right" levels or within "target zones."

The Group of Five grew to be the Group of Seven (G7)* as Canada and Italy joined the meetings and deliberations. The G7 heads of state meet each year, and between those summits there are frequent private discussions among G7 finance ministers and central bankers on economic policy issues.[24] This is one of the important uses of the Bank for International Settlements: Its low-key facilities in Basel permit private, confidential meetings and discussions.

*The July 1994 G7 meeting in Naples, Italy, was attended by President Yeltsin of Russia, and some writers began to refer to the G8.

[Figure 5.3] **Pegged LDC Currencies**

23 LDC currencies	pegged to	U.S. dollar
12 LDC currencies	pegged to	French franc
7 LDC currencies	pegged to	SDR basket
32 LDC currencies	pegged to	non-SDR basket
1 LDC currency	pegged to	Indian rupee
2 LDC currencies	pegged to	South African rand
1 LDC currency	pegged to	Australian dollar
1 LDC currency	pegged to	German mark

Source: From *International Monetary Fund Survey,* July 17, 2000, p. 235. Reprinted with permission.

Economic policy coordination as practiced by the G7 has emerged as a key factor in the foreign exchange (Fx) markets. And although there is little doubt the G7 central banks have become more adept in influencing currency movements, another development can overwhelm their efforts. That is the explosive growth in the volume of currencies being traded in the world's foreign exchange markets. From an annual volume of roughly $18 billion in 1979, Fx transactions are now estimated at $2 trillion to $3 trillion daily.[25]

Even the richest countries have government reserves of "only" a few billion dollars available to influence exchange rates. Obviously, that is a lot of money, but it pales in the light of over a trillion being traded every day. For example, if the Fx market players believe the Japanese yen should be stronger in US$ terms, the yen will strengthen in spite of government market intervention.

Currency Areas

The U.S. dollar, Canadian dollar, Japanese yen (¥), Swiss franc, and several other currencies are floating in value against one another and against the euro. Most currencies of developing countries are pegged (fixed) in value to one of the major currencies or to a currency basket such as special drawing rights (SDRs) or some specially chosen currency mix or basket (see Figure 5.3).

Current developments may make the growth of currency areas, trading blocs, and currency blocs more likely. The most important of those developments are the continuing European Union (EU) progress toward unification and enlargement, the implementation and extension of the North American Free Trade Agreement (NAFTA) throughout the Western Hemisphere, and the growing economic importance of Pacific Rim countries.

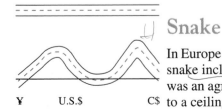

Snake

¥ U.S.$ C$

In Europe during the mid-1970s, a currency grouping called the *snake* was created. The snake included several European currencies, led by the German deutsche mark. There was an agreed central exchange rate, but currencies' values could fluctuate up or down to a ceiling or floor exchange rate shown by the solid lines.

Will Shortage of Euro Money Cause Them to Crash?

Small and Medium-Sized Enterprises

Retailers have warned European finance ministers that the cash economy will crash hours after the introduction of euro notes and coins on "E day," January 1, 2002. A study by Insead and WHU Koblenz indicates that there will be insufficient euro notes and coins in circulation to make change for customers paying in national currencies or large-denomination euro notes from bank machines. The solution to that problem creates another problem, which is the security risk of having very big amounts of euro cash in so many retail stores. ■

Source: Robert Shrimsley, "Euro Changeover Will Create Cash Crisis, Warn Retailers," *Financial Times,* August 28, 2000, p. 1.

The snake was so called because of how it appeared in a graph showing the member currencies floating against nonmember currencies, such as the yen or the Canadian or U.S. dollar.

The reptile's health was damaged by the departure of several currencies, including the pound sterling, the Italian lira, and the Swedish krona, and by the in-and-out relationship of the French franc.[26] The system's inflexibility, the major reason those currencies were removed, explains the snake's ultimate demise. Each member-country was responsible for keeping its currency's value within the agreed relationship to the other members' currencies, but each country had different inflation rates, fiscal and monetary policies, and BOP balances. Thus, market pressures pushed currency exchange rates out of the agreed ranges, and the countries lacked the political will or resources to restore the agreed exchange rate. Then the currency automatically fell out of the system.

The snake was the forerunner of the European Monetary System (EMS), which is discussed later in this chapter.

Experience with Floating

Such immense amounts of major currencies were being bought and sold each trading day that governments' efforts to keep their currencies at fixed exchange rates failed. The central banks stopped trying to peg the major currencies' exchange rates in 1973. The Organization of Petroleum Exporting Countries (OPEC) hiked the price of petroleum over 400 percent early in 1974, and there were fears that the banking and monetary systems would not be able to handle the resulting changes in the amounts and directions of currency flows.

Fears Not Realized

However, despite occasional flare-ups and sharp changes in the relative values of currencies, the system did not collapse. Indeed, the volatility of exchange rate movements diminished after a period of uncertainty with the new system from 1973 to 1974. Uncertainty was heightened by the sudden, drastic increase in oil prices by OPEC. In those days, it could be difficult and costly to engage in a foreign exchange transaction. By 1977 the cost of undertaking foreign exchange transactions was about the same as it had been under the Bretton Woods system.[27]

The system has still not collapsed, even though the value of the US$ fluctuated widely between 1977 and 1997, continuing market experiences since World War II. In March and April 1995 it reached post–World War II lows, but by March 1997 the dollar had climbed 26 percent against the mark and 52 percent against the yen. Even those levels are not the strongest it has been in terms of those currencies since World War II; in April 1957 the U.S. currency bought 4.20 marks, and in July 1963 it purchased 362.98 yen.[28] By the summer of 2000 it was well below those lofty levels; at the quoted exchange rates on August 28, 2000, one U.S. dollar bought 2.1713 marks and 106.47 yen.[29]

In January 1999, a new major currency joined the world markets. That was the euro, which began trading at 1 euro for US$1.14. During 1999 and into 2000 the euro fell in value to a low below US90¢; by August 28, 2000, it had recovered to .9008¢ for one euro.[30]

The most important purpose of this experience with floating section is to bring forcibly to your attention the fact that currencies change value in terms of each other in large amounts. For international business managers those changes create big uncertainties. They protect their organizations and themselves by what is called hedging, which is explained in Chapter 19.

Effect of the 1997 Asian Financial Crisis on Dollar Values

In 1997, several Asian nations suffered falling stock and property values as foreign and local investors alike sold and tried to convert local currencies to dollars. The region's troubles began to show in July 1997 in Thailand and spread. By January 1998, the value of the Indonesian rupiah had fallen 70 percent. The Indian rupee lost about 10 percent of its value, and the South Korean won and the Philippine peso were significantly weaker in dollar terms. By the year 2000, most of the Asian economies were back on their feet and their currencies had regained their values in US$s and other currencies.

Before the region's troubles, when those economies were soaring in unison, there were two schools of thought as to why that was happening. One camp attributed their success to strong and wise governments; the other emphasized the power of free markets. When those economies began crashing, the two camps changed sides, blaming respectively hysterical markets and stupid and corrupt governments.

A less clever but far more verifiable explanation is that the economies of East Asia are close to each other. Half of East Asian trade takes place within the region. As intraregional trade has become more dependable, East Asia has begun to outgrow its reliance on the U.S. economy. That reliance has been weakened further by growth in the European and Japanese markets.[31]

Forecasting Float Direction

Such large changes in short time periods prompt efforts by everyone affected to forecast currency value changes. Such changes have many causes, including political events and expectations and government economic policies. A major cause is present and forecast relative inflation from country to country. One means of measuring relative inflation is purchasing power parity (PPP), the theory of which is that an exchange rate between the currencies of two countries is in equilibrium when it equates the prices of a basket of goods and services in both countries.

One product sold worldwide that is, or is supposed to be, the same everywhere is McDonald's Big Mac hamburger. In 1989, *The Economist* published the first of what became an annual study of worldwide PPP using the price of a Big Mac as its "basket" of goods. The Worldview entitled "Big MacCurrencies" presents the 2000 update of this hamburger index on pages 198–99.

Money Markets, Foreign Exchange

money markets
Places where moneys can be bought, sold, or borrowed

Since currencies began floating freely in 1973, the daily volume of foreign exchange trading in the world's **money markets** grew at a rapid pace into 2001, when growth slowed in the European and North American markets. Even so, average daily market turnover in 2000 was $1.2 trillion. London is the world's largest market, with a 30 percent share of Fx turnover. New York is in second place, while in Asia, Tokyo, Hong Kong, and Singapore are fighting for supremacy.

The end of growth and even the contraction of European and North American Fx markets were due to several factors. The onset of the European Monetary Union stopped trading among member-country currencies, and even before it came into force, the German mark, the French franc, the Benelux currencies, and even the Italian lira barely moved against one another.

Another factor that slowed the Fx markets was that central banks ceased targeting unrealistic exchange rates. In the early 1990s, traders made billions betting against currencies such as sterling and the lira.

A further factor that will contract the old Fx markets even more is the electronic currency broking machine provided by the electronic brokers Reuter and EBS. They allow even small banks to learn the best price in the market for any major currency. Ultimately, they will be available in the offices of international business managers, who then will be able to trade currencies through the broking machine without contacting—or paying—any bank or live broker.

Asian Currencies to the Rescue

Once referred to as "exotic" currencies traded in "emerging" markets, Asian currencies are no longer thought of as exotic, and their markets have emerged.

The more liquid currencies are the Singapore dollar, the Thai baht, the Indonesian rupiah, the Malaysian ringgit, and the Hong Kong dollar. Other, less liquid currencies, such as the South Korean won, the Taiwan dollar, the Philippine peso, and the Vietnamese dong, are sometimes called "Asia minors."

Standard Chartered Bank set up its biggest currency dealing room in Singapore, which is the fourth-largest currency trading center in the world and the largest center of non-yen trade in Asia. Tokyo, of course, surpasses it if yen trade is included.

Turnover in Singapore was US$190 billion in 1996, up from US$111 billion in 1995 and US$100 billion in 1994. Some 220 international and merchant banks keep offices in Singapore.[32]

The US$ is the most traded currency. The US$–deutsche mark market is the busiest, closely followed by that of the US$–yen. Third, fourth, and fifth are US$–sterling, US$–Swiss franc, and mark–yen. The percentage of the dominance of the US$ as the most traded currency is increasing. That is due to the rapid growth of the Asian Fx markets mentioned above. Virtually all trading there is conducted through the dollar.

Although the US$ is the most traded currency, it need not be a part of every transaction. As indicated, the mark–yen market is big, and other major currencies are traded without going through the US$. Therefore, they are quoted in terms of each other, referred to as cross rates of exchange.

London has a pivotal role in world currency trading. Because the London market shares trading hours with markets in Asia and the Middle East during its morning session and with the New York market during its afternoon session, it has more transaction opportunities than do the New York and Tokyo markets. Figure 5.4 shows the trading hours of major financial centers.

The growth of foreign exchange trading in recent years has greatly outpaced world trade even though trade has also expanded. This has been due to the near explosions in international investment and in derivatives and hedge and swap transactions. Derivatives, hedges, and swaps are explained in Chapter 19.

London, New York, and Tokyo have the biggest currency markets but by no means the only ones. Other important markets are in Los Angeles and San Francisco, Hong Kong, Singapore, Bahrain, Frankfurt, Zurich, and Paris. Trades can be made 24 hours a day at one or more of these markets.

Billions of US$s are traded around the world in the various currency markets. Smaller—but still large—amounts of the other currencies of major market countries are also traded outside the borders of the issuing countries, and all these currencies are used as countries' national reserve assets as well as in trade, investments, hedges, swaps, and derivatives.

Beginning in the 1960s, there was a growing feeling that national currencies or gold should be replaced as central reserve assets. In 1970, the IMF established special drawing rights for that purpose.

[Figure 5.4] Trading Hours of the World's Major Financial Centers

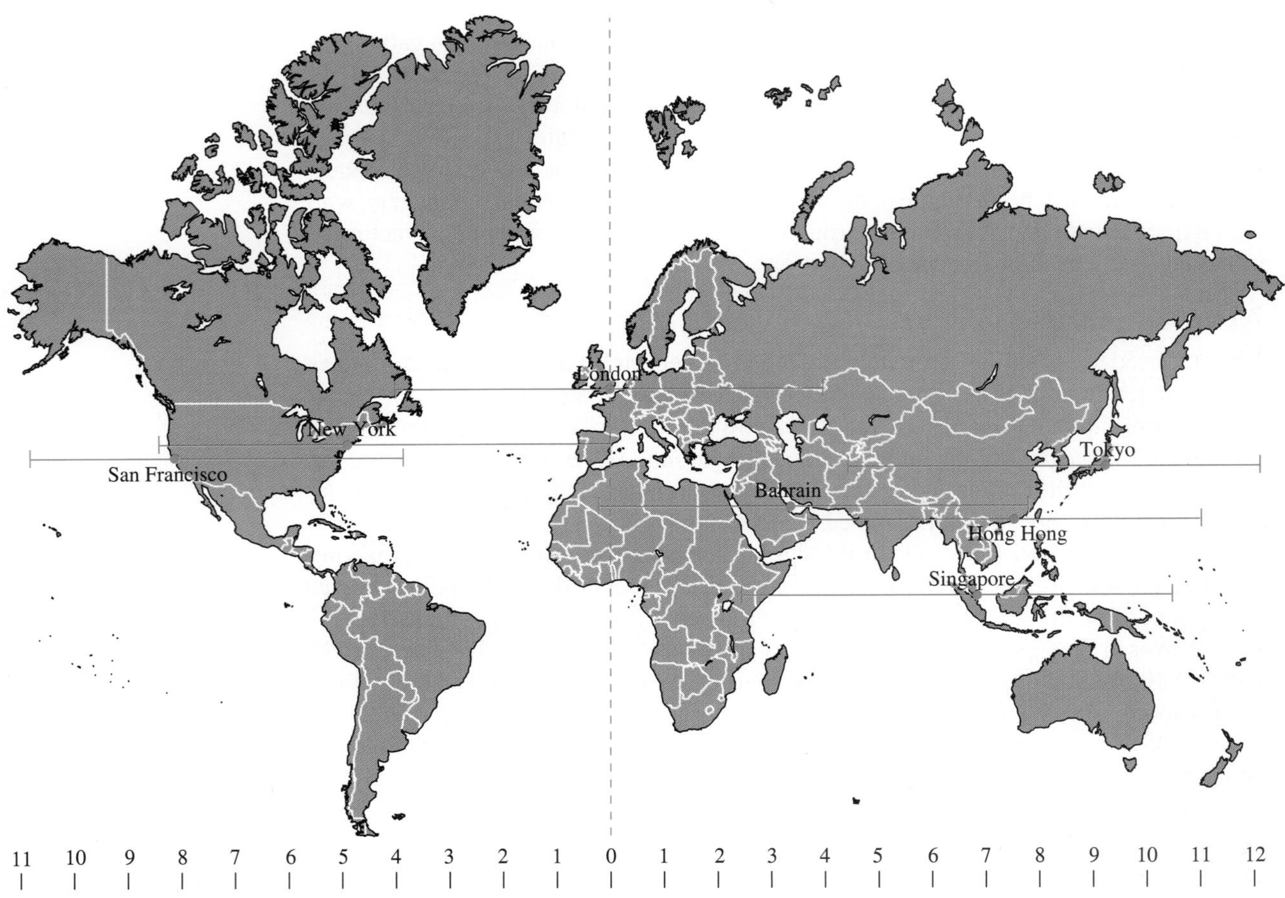

Source: Bank for International Settlements, *63rd Annual Report,* June 14, 1993, p. 194.

SDRs in the Future

special drawing rights (SDRs)
Established by the IMF as units of value to replace the dollar as a reserve asset

Special drawing rights (SDRs) may be a step toward a truly international currency. The US$ has been the closest thing to such a currency since gold in the pre–World War I gold standard system, but the US$ must also serve as a national currency, and the roles sometimes conflict (see the Worldview on page 200).

SDRs, bookkeeping entries at the IMF, were created in 1970 by agreement among the IMF members, whose accounts are credited with certain amounts of SDRs from time to time. The objective was to make the SDR the principal reserve asset in the international monetary system.[33]

Value of the SDR

The SDR's value is based on a basket of the following five currencies (the percentage of each currency is in parentheses): U.S. dollar (41.3), euro Germany (19), euro France (10.3), Japanese yen (17), and British pound (12.4). The weights broadly reflect the relative importance of the currencies in trade and payments, based on the value of the exports of goods and services by the member-countries issuing these currencies. The percentages are changed periodically. When the 7th edition of this book went to print, they were as follows: U.S. dollar (39), German mark (21), Japanese yen (18), British pound (11), and French franc (11).[34]

The value of the SDR in US$ terms is calculated daily by the IMF as the sum of the values in US$s based on market exchange rates of specified amounts of the currencies in the valuation basket.

As you saw in the preceding paragraph, the percentages of the currencies in the basket change periodically. We have observed before in this chapter that currency exchange rates fluctuate constantly in terms of each other. Because of these changes and fluctuations, the SDR values and their quotations move up or down in terms of currencies.

Uses of the SDR

The SDR's value remains more stable than that of any single currency, and that stability has made the SDR increasingly attractive as a unit for denominating international transactions. Future payment under a contract, for example, may be agreed to be made in a national currency at its rate in terms of the SDR on the payment date, and some Swiss and British banks now accept accounts denominated in SDRs.

Holders of SDRs

SDRs are held by the IMF, most of its 181 members, and 16 official institutions, which typically are regional development or banking institutions prescribed by the IMF. All holders can buy and sell SDRs both spot and forward* and receive or use SDRs in loans, pledges, swaps, grants, or settlement of financial obligations. Holders receive interest at a rate determined weekly by reference to the weighted-average interest rate on short-term obligations in the money markets of the five countries with currencies in the SDR valuation basket. Thirty-eight of the newer IMF member-countries have never received an SDR allocation, and they complain that this is unfair. This has come to be referred to as the "equity issue."

SDRs as Central Reserve Assets

A major purpose envisioned for SDRs was to replace currencies and gold as central reserve assets of nations. That has not happened. After the first allocation of 9 billion SDRs to members in 1972, they constituted 6.1 percent of the central reserves, while foreign exchange made up 65.3 percent and gold made up 24.5 percent at $35 per ounce. There was a second SDR allocation in 1979 of 13 billion, but total reserves went up faster so that by 1983 SDRs constituted only 3.4 percent of the central reserves. Currencies had increased to 78.7 percent, and gold had fallen to 8.2 percent, but that was on the basis of valuing gold at $35 per ounce. In the gold markets, the price of gold had soared to over $800 in 1980, and gold traded between $256 and $465 per ounce from then into 2000.

The most recent SDR allocation to the 141 IMF member-countries at that time was on January 1, 1981, in the amount of SDR 4.1 billion. As of the end of 1997, the IMF had allocated a total of SDR 21.4 billion in six allocations, but SDR holdings by member-countries amounted to only 2.3 percent of their total nongold reserves. At a 1996 "Seminar on the Future of the SDR," Stanley Fischer, first deputy managing director of the IMF, conceded that the SDR does not appear likely to become the principal reserve asset of the international monetary system. He also doubted that it would evolve into a full-fledged world currency. The seminar resolved nevertheless that the SDR should not be abolished because it possesses the ability to serve as a "safety net" should the international monetary system run into serious difficulty.[35]

Such lack of enthusiasm for SDRs as central reserve assets may have several explanations. Dollars and other hard currencies are more flexible and have more uses, usually yield higher interest returns, and can officially be credited and debited by anyone—in contrast to the limited numbers with official access to SDRs.

*Spot and forward rates are discussed in Chapter 6.

[Worldview]

Big MacCurrencies

Some People Read Tea Leaves to Predict the Future. We Prefer Hamburgers.

It is that time of the year when *The Economist* munches its way around the globe in order to update our Big Mac index. We first launched this 14 years ago as a lighthearted guide to whether currencies are at their "correct" exchange rate. It is not intended as a precise predictor of exchange rates, but a tool to make economic theory more digestible.

Burgernomics is based on the theory of purchasing-power parity, the notion that a dollar should buy the same amount in all countries. Thus in the long run, the exchange rate between two currencies should move towards the rate that equalizes the prices of an identical basket of goods and services in each country. Our "basket" is a McDonald's Big Mac, which is produced in about 120 countries. The Big Mac PPP is the exchange rate that would mean hamburgers cost the same in America as abroad. Comparing actual exchange rates with PPPS indicates whether a currency is under- or overvalued.

The first column of the table shows local-currency prices of a Big Mac; the second converts them into dollars. The average price of a Big Mac (including tax) in four American cities is $2.51. The cheapest burger among the countries in the table is once again in Malaysia ($1.19); at the other extreme the most expensive is $3.58 in Israel. This is another way of saying that the Malaysian ringgit is the most undervalued currency (by 53%), and the Israeli shekel the most overvalued (by 43%).

The third column calculates Big Mac PPPS. For instance, dividing the Japanese price by the American one gives a dollar PPP of ¥117. On April 25th the actual rate was ¥106, implying that the yen is 11% overvalued against the dollar.

Despite a single currency, the price of a Big Mac varies considerably within the euro area—from a bargain $2.09 in Spain to a beefy $3.12 in Finland. The average price (weighted by GDPS) in the 11 countries is €2.56, or $2.37 at current exchange rates. The euro's Big Mac PPP against the dollar is €1 = $0.98, which suggests that the euro is 5% undervalued—considerably less than many market commentators claim.

The most undervalued of all the rich-world currencies is the Australian dollar, currently 38% below McParity. In contrast, most of the West European currencies outside the euro—notably, sterling, the Danish krone and the Swiss franc—are hugely overvalued, by 20–40%.

Most emerging-market currencies are undervalued against the dollar on a Big Mac PPP basis. Besides the Israeli shekel, the other main exception is the South Korean won which, as a result of currency appreciation, is now 8% overvalued against the dollar. In early 1998, at the height of the Asian crisis, it was 31% undervalued.

Adjustment back to PPP does not always come about through a shift in exchange rates, but sometimes through price changes. In 1994, for instance, Argentina's peso was 60% overvalued against the dollar; today it is spot on McParity—not because the peso has fallen (it is fixed against the dollar), but because the price of a Big Mac has tumbled in Argentina.

Some readers beef that our Big Mac index does not cut the mustard. They are right that hamburgers are a flawed measure of PPP, because local prices may be distorted by trade barriers on beef, sales taxes or big differences in the cost of non-traded inputs such as rents. Thus, whereas Big Mac PPPS can be a handy guide to the cost of living in countries, they may not be a reliable guide to future exchange-rate movements. Yet, curiously, several academic studies have concluded that the Big Mac index is surprisingly accurate in tracking exchange rates over the longer term.

European Monetary System (EMS)
A grouping of most Western European nations cooperating to maintain their currencies at fixed exchange rates

European Monetary System (EMS)

As evidenced by the snake, the European countries prefer fixed currency exchange rates to floating ones. Due to inflexibility and weaknesses, the snake expired in the mid-1970s. Not daunted, a larger group of European countries banded together in 1979 and created the **European Monetary System (EMS),** which was a large step back toward fixed currency exchange rates. It was an enlarged and improved version of the snake.

Indeed, the Big Mac has had several forecasting successes. When the euro was launched at the start of 1999, most forecasters predicted that it would rise. But the euro has instead tumbled—exactly as the Big Mac index had signaled. At the start of 1999, euro burgers were much dearer than American ones. Burgernomics is far from perfect, but our mouths are where our money is. ■

Source: From *The Economist*, April 29, 2000, p. 75. Copyright © 2000. The Economist Newspaper Group, Inc. Reprinted with permission. Further reproduction prohibited. www.economist.com

The Golden-Arched Standard

	Big Mac Prices				Under (−)/ Over (+) Valuation
	In Local Currency	In Dollars	Implied PPP* of the Dollar	Actual $ Exchange Rate 25/04/00	Against the Dollar, %
United States[†]	**$2.51**	**2.51**			
Argentina	Peso2.50	2.50	1.00	1.00	0
Australia	A$2.59	1.54	1.03	1.68	−38
Brazil	Real2.95	1.65	1.18	1.79	−34
Britain	£1.90	3.00	1.32[‡]	1.58[‡]	+20
Canada	C$2.85	1.94	1.14	1.47	−23
Chile	Peso1,260	2.45	502	514	−2
China	Yuan9.90	1.20	3.94	8.28	−52
Czech Rep.	Koruna54.37	1.39	21.7	39.1	−45
Denmark	DKr24.75	3.08	9.86	8.04	+23
Euro area	€ 2.56	2.37	0.98§	0.93[§]	−5
France	FFr18.50	2.62	7.37	7.07	+4
Germany	DM4.99	2.37	1.99	2.11	−6
Italy	Lire4,500	2.16	1,793	2,088	−14
Spain	Pta375	2.09	149	179	−17
Hong Kong	HK$10.20	1.31	4.06	7.79	−48
Hungary	Forint339	1.21	135	279	−52
Indonesia	Rupiah14,500	1.83	5,777	7,945	−27
Israel	Shekel14.5	3.58	5.78	4.05	+43
Japan	¥294	2.78	117	106	+11
Malaysia	M$4.52	1.19	1.80	3.80	−53
Mexico	Peso20.90	2.22	8.33	9.41	−11
New Zealand	NZ$3.40	1.69	1.35	2.01	−33
Poland	Zloty5.50	1.28	2.19	4.30	−49
Russia	Rouble39.50	1.39	15.7	28.5	−45
Singapore	S$3.20	1.88	1.27	1.70	−25
South Africa	Rand9.00	1.34	3.59	6.72	−47
South Korea	Won3,000	2.71	1,195	1,108	+8
Sweden	SKr24.00	2.71	9.56	8.84	+8
Switzerland	SFr5.90	3.48	2.35	1.70	+39
Taiwan	NT$70.00	2.29	27.9	30.6	−9
Thailand	Baht55.00	1.45	21.9	38.0	−42

*Purchasing-power parity: local price divided by price in United States

[†]Average of New York, Chicago, San Francisco, and Atlanta.

[‡]Dollars per pound.

[§]Dollars per euro.

Source: From *The Economist*, April 29, 2000, p. 75. Copyright © 2000. The Economist Newspaper Group, Inc. Reprinted with permission. Further reproduction prohibited. www.economist.com

The EMS member-countries agreed to maintain their currency values within a specified range in relation to one another. An important feature, not available to the old snake, is the European Monetary Cooperation Fund (EMCF). Composed of dollars, gold, and member-country currencies, it was used to support the efforts of member-countries to keep their currency values within the agreed relationship to the other currencies. The EMCF has the equivalent of about $32 billion with which to work.

[Worldview]

Central Reserve/National Currency Conflict

The US$ has been the most used central reserve asset in the world since the end of World War II. Somewhat analogous to a savings account, the dollars were available when needed to finance trade or investments or to intervene in currency markets. Held in the form of U.S. Treasury bonds, the US$s earn interest, and the more held in the savings/central reserve account, the better. But the countries don't want their central reserve asset US$s to lose value, and there lies a contradiction: at some point, greater numbers of US$s (or any other product) in supply cause them to lose value—supply and demand.

At the same time, the US$ is the national currency of the United States of America, whose government must deal with inflation, recession, interest rates, unemployment, and other national, internal problems. The U.S. government uses fiscal and monetary policies to meet those problems—higher or lower taxes, decisions as to how to spend available revenue, growth or contraction of the money supply, and rate of its growth or contraction.

It would be only accidental if the national interests of the United States in dealing with its internal problems coincided with the interests of the multitude of countries holding US$s in their central reserve asset accounts. The United States may be slowing money supply growth and raising taxes to combat U.S. inflation while the world needs more liquidity, in the form of US$s, to finance growth, trade, or investment. Or the United States may be stimulating its economy through faster money supply growth and lower taxes at a time when so many US$s are already outstanding that their value is dropping—not a happy state of affairs for countries holding US$s.

It was a quirk of history that thrust the US$ into this conflicting role. It was the hope of the IMF that a nonnational asset, the SDR, would rescue the US$ and the world from the conflict. ■

Another difference between the EMS and its ancestor, the snake, is that the exchange rates of the EMS are flexible. If one currency proves weaker than another and the governments cannot or will not take steps to correct the situation, the EMS exchange rates can be changed. There have been several rate rearrangements since 1979. If a snake member-country could not keep its currency up to the agreed strength, it dropped out and ceased to be a member.

Two of the EMS fathers, former French president Valery Giscard d'Estaing and former West German chancellor Helmut Schmidt, think it's time their child was allowed to grow up. They are pushing hard for the never-implemented second stage of their plan, the economic and monetary union of Europe. This union would be accomplished through a European Central Bank and free use of the European Currency Unit (see the next section) by banks, companies, and consumers in all 15 EU countries.

Despite opposition from the German central bank (the Bundesbank) and the British government, the two men are optimistic the European Bank will be created. Schmidt says, "All the talk about European union will be rubbish if we don't do anything. We must create a European Central Bank because we must have a currency with which you could as easily buy a dress or a train ticket in Paris or Madrid."[36]

The EU took large steps toward those goals at a summit meeting in Maastricht, the Netherlands, during December 1991. There, the then members signed a commitment to proceed toward EMU involving a single currency governed by a European Central Bank by 1999.

But does Maastricht make sense? In Chapter 4, we discussed the growing opposition to Maastricht goals (e.g., a European central bank and a single European currency). And during 1993, the EMS suffered a blow as several countries were unable to keep their currencies close in value to the deutsche mark; those currencies were devalued, and the permissible range of values was enlarged to 15 percent below and 15 percent above the agreed central exchange rate, a range so wide, it almost constituted a free currency float system.

From the European Currency Unit (ECU) to the Euro

The European Currency Unit (ECU) was established as the EMS bookkeeping currency. It had much the same uses as does the SDR (see above), and the international market for ECU-denominated bonds increased greatly in liquidity and issuance during the 1990s. All sorts of borrowers entered the market: international agencies, numerous national governments, municipalities, and public and private companies. It came to be that more bonds were denominated in ECUs than in any other currency except the US$, and the ECU easily surpassed the SDR in that use.

One reason the ECU became more popular than the SDR was that neither the US$ nor the yen was included in the currency basket that determined its value. The exchange rates of the US$ and the yen have fluctuated much more widely than have those of the European currencies in the ECU basket. Both the US$ and the yen are in the SDR basket, and so the SDR's value has been less stable than that of the ECU.

Another reason the ECU's use surpassed that of the SDR was active sponsorship of the ECU by European governments, banks, and businesses; the SDR has received no such support. The ECU was being used for various purposes, and support and supplementary networks were put in place. Bank accounts could be denominated in ECUs, and ECU traveler's checks were available. Between units of some international companies, debits and credits were denominated in ECUs as they bought, sold, or borrowed from one another.

The ECU was a weighted basket of currencies, and its uses, in addition to denominating bonds, included calculating the EU budget, raising levies, and distributing funds that were translated into domestic, national currencies. Nowhere was the ECU a domestic currency.

The euro has replaced the ECU and is supposed to replace some national currencies. The **euro** will be a retail currency, whereas the ECU was only a wholesale and debt market currency. The euro's value and integrity will be supervised by the European Central Bank.[37]

euro
A currency established by the EU

The first euro coins were issued in 1996 by the Isle of Man. Although the Isle of Man is geographically part of the British Isles, it has an independent government and tax regime and has money-issuing powers.[38] Figure 5.5 shows how euro bills will probably appear. They were designed by Robert Kalina, an artist at the Austrian National Bank, for a competition sponsored by the European Monetary Institute.

Transition to the Euro: How, When, Whether

In terms of the Maastricht Treaty, the transition from national currencies and the ECU to the euro began on January 1, 1999. Under one scenario, the national currencies and the euro will coexist until the year 2002, and a French study predicts a "fiendishly complex transition period." The study sees problems for many companies if they are asked to pay suppliers in euros while their customers are paying them in francs. Some companies have already decided to use the euro as quickly as possible but will need to pay their employees in francs. Benoit Jolivet, president of the National Credit Council, says most small and medium-sized companies are still ignorant of the issues and could have big trouble if larger customers or suppliers move rapidly to the euro.[39]

As to the "when" question for the euro, one influential observer says, "The Maastricht Treaty plan for the euro should be delayed to avoid a financial fiasco." He is Wilhelm Nolling, who was president of the Hamburg Land Central Bank and a member of the Bundesbank (the German central bank) council between 1982 and 1992. He is currently a professor at Hamburg University. Mr. Nolling calls the euro a "test tube currency" and gives several reasons for delaying its introduction. One reason is the "grave mistake" he sees in making a fundamental change in monetary arrangements without any new political institutions. He says monetary union needs to come after political union, not the other way around. Another reason for delay, he says, is the colossal technical and organizational challenge and huge costs of preparing for European monetary union, including the euro.

[Figure 5.5] Euro Currency Bills Scheduled to Begin Circulating in 2002

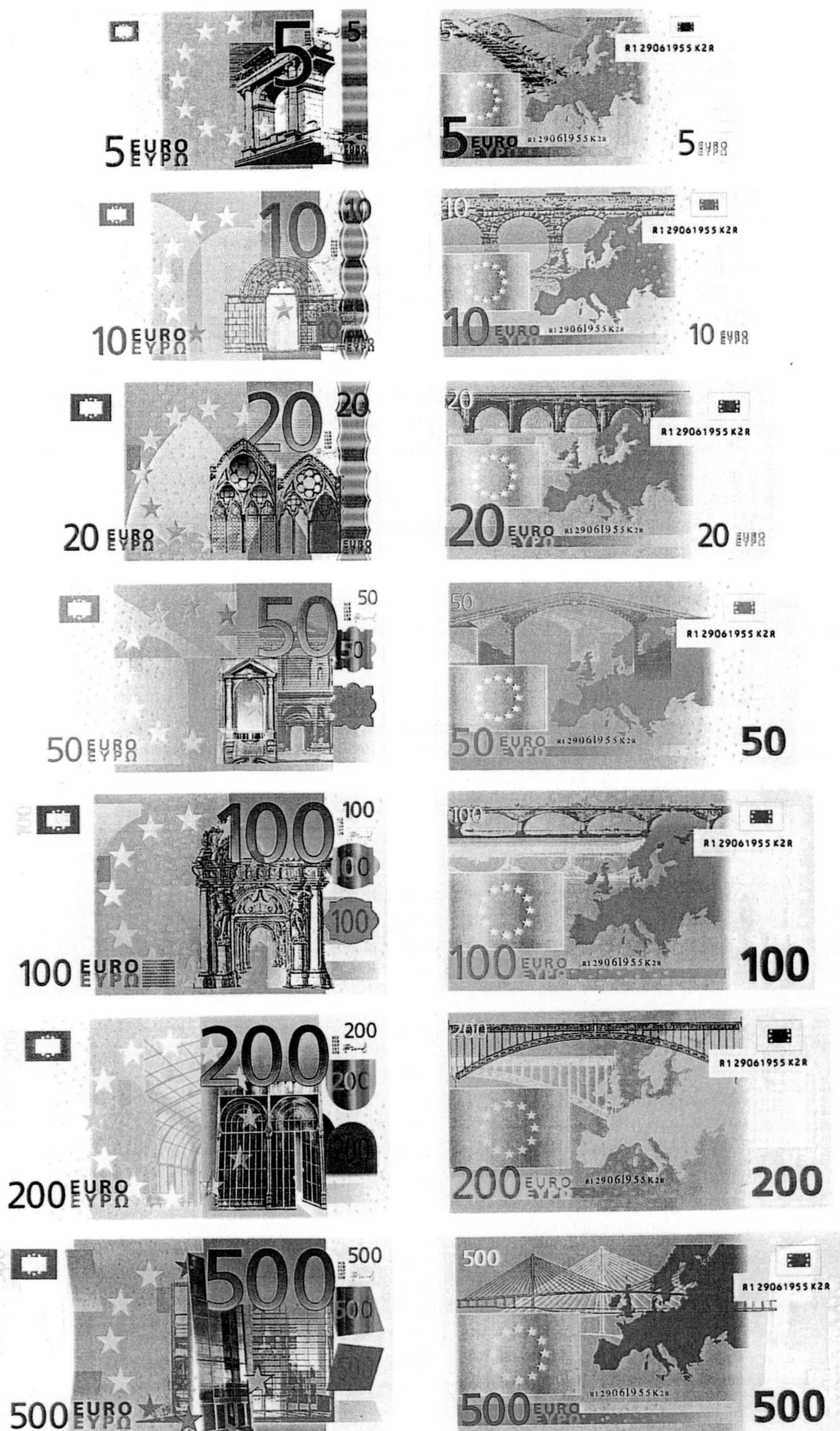

[Figure 5.6] **One of the Earliest Capital Market Offerings Denominated in Euros**

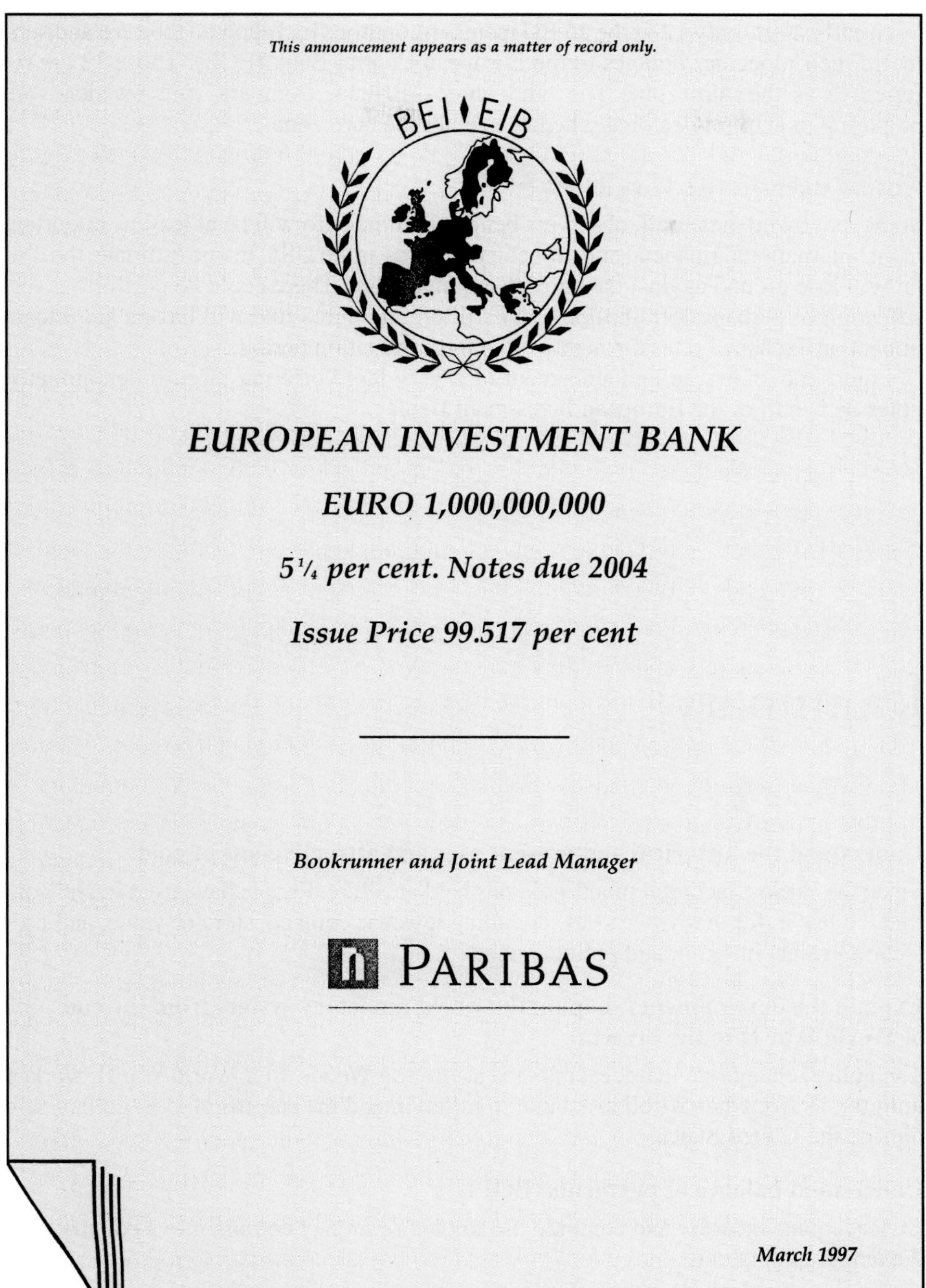
This announcement appears as a matter of record only.

BEI EIB

EUROPEAN INVESTMENT BANK

EURO 1,000,000,000

5¼ per cent. Notes due 2004

Issue Price 99.517 per cent

Bookrunner and Joint Lead Manager

PARIBAS

March 1997

Mr. Nolling worries also that in meeting the Maastricht convergence criteria, Europe's successes in bringing down inflation and stabilizing exchange rates have been accompanied by "a sensational degree of upward harmonization of unemployment and public sector debt."[40]

There remains a "whether question": whether to go the euro route at all. People of this mind say that currency union has not had the political analysis it deserves and was something of an improvisation to begin with, a superficially appealing idea. Others have said that Europeans misuse the American analogy when arguing for monetary union, since in the United States a powerful central bank, the Federal Reserve, faces an even more powerful central government. They point out that Europe is giving itself an effectively unaccountable bank with enormous power and say that "major European governments seem fecklessly ready today to commit their nations' future to a committee of bankers."[41]

In early 2001, only 12 of the 15 EU member-countries had adopted the euro and subjected their monetary policies to the European Central Bank (ECB). Those 12 are referred to as the euro zone. The other three—Britain, Denmark, and Sweden—are preparing to enter or deciding whether to enter the euro zone.

Euro Effect on the U.S. Dollar

Some, but by no means all, observers believe that the euro will be at least as important in the international financial and monetary systems as the US$. In one estimate, the dollar will lose ground against the euro on a global scale. There could be portfolio diversification of perhaps $500 billion to $1 trillion into euros that will have a significant impact on exchange rates throughout a longish transition period.[42]

Figure 5.6 shows an announcement of a very large offering of euro-denominated notes on behalf of the European Investment Bank.

[Summary]

Understand the historical and present uses and attractiveness of gold.

Since the earliest recorded times, gold has held an allure. People have used it, and continue to use it, for many purposes, including jewelry, coinage, store of value, and protection against inflation and political unrest.

Explain the developments shaping the world monetary system from the end of World War II to the present.

The gold exchange standard, established at Bretton Woods after World War II, worked until the 1970s, when it collapsed due to inflation and the surplus of U.S. dollars held outside the United States.

Understand balance of payments (BOP).

BOP accounts measure and compare the amount of money coming into a country with the amount going out.

Compare the relative strengths and weaknesses of currencies and reasons for them.

Causes for a currency's relative strengths and weaknesses include relative inflation, balance of payments, political developments, and confidence in the country's leaders.

Understand how "Big MacCurrencies" and the purchasing power parity theory are related.

A Big Mac hamburger is supposed to be the same at every McDonald's around the world. Therefore, according to the PPP theory, its cost in the currency of one country compared with its cost in the currency of a second country should equal the exchange rate between those currencies.

Identify the major foreign currency exchange (Fx) markets of the world.

London is the largest Fx market, New York the second largest, and Tokyo the third. In Asia, if trading in yen is disregarded, Singapore is the largest market and is growing rapidly.

Understand that as electronic brokering is becoming more available to smaller banks and international businesses, the spot currency trading activities of large banks are diminishing in Europe and North America.

Identify the growth areas for currency traders, which are derivatives, hedges, swaps, and Asian currencies.

Understand the central reserve asset/national currency conflict of the U.S. dollar and the reasons and uses for special drawing rights (SDRs).

The U.S. dollar is the currency of the United States, but it is also the major reserve asset of other countries. It is usually desirable for countries to increase their reserve assets, but that depends on growing amounts of US$s being in the hands of foreign holders, which may not be in the best interest of the United States. SDRs were established by the IMF to replace the U.S. dollar as the main central reserve asset.

Discuss the euro and its present state of acceptance by EU countries.

The euro became an official currency value in January 1999, but euro coins and bills were not scheduled to be in circulation until 2002. Eleven of the 15 EU countries accepted the euro, and they are referred to as the euro zone; as of the end of 2000, the other 4 EU countries are either striving to qualify for euro-zone membership, as in the case of Greece, or deciding whether to join, as in the case of Britain, Denmark, and Sweden.

[Key Words]

convertible currencies (p. 182)
gold standard (p. 183)
Bretton Woods (p. 184)
central reserve assets (p. 184)
market measures (p. 186)
nonmarket measures (p. 186)
monetary policies (p. 188)
fiscal policies (p. 188)
central bank (p. 189)
gold exchange standard (p. 189)
fixed currency exchange rates (p. 191)
floating currency exchange rates (p. 191)
money markets (p. 194)
special drawing rights (SDRs) (p. 196)
European Monetary System (EMS) (p. 198)
euro (p. 201)

[Questions]

1. Explain the appeal gold holds for people. Discuss the pros and cons of a gold standard.
2. Identify and discuss causes for currencies to strengthen or weaken in Fx markets.
3. Why were SDRs created? Discuss their success in their original mission and their current uses.
4. Why do people in Europe fear the new European Central Bank in the current European political situation?
5. Explain the national currency/central reserve conflict.
6. The Maastricht objectives to unify Europe are being opposed. By whom and why?
7. What difficulties is the EMS encountering? Why?
8. Why should managers be aware and wary of the BOP of the country in which their business operates?

[Internet Exercises]

Using the Internet

1. The text discusses balance-of-payment accounts. Using the Web site of the U.S. Bureau of Economic Administration, find the U.S. balance-of-payments account and answer the following questions:
   a. What does the U.S. balance-of-payments account show?
   b. Using the entries on the U.S. balance-of-payments account, explain why the United States is in a balance-of-payment deficit.
2. As discussed in the text, one function of the International Monetary Fund (IMF) is to provide assistance to member-countries having balance-of-payments problems. For example, the IMF may provide assistance in the form of a loan to a country. Go to the IMF's Web site and find information on the role of the IMF. Using the IMF's Web site, answer the following questions:
   a. What is the role of the IMF?
   b. What is the responsibility of the IMF in providing debt relief for low-income countries?
   c. What are the arrangements for IMF surveillance?
   d. How does the IMF differ from the World Bank?
   e. What are the current research projects in which the IMF is currently involved?

[Minicase 5.1]

SDR Exchange Risk

The Bowling Green National Bank has made loans denominated in SDRs to several of its MNE customers. It has built up a portfolio to the amount of SDR 8 million. Management decides to hedge by selling in the forward market the currencies that make up the SDR basket. How much of each currency must be hedged?

"May I have my allowance in Deutsche Marks, Dad?"

From *The Wall Street Journal.* Copyright Cartoon Features Syndicate.

[Chapter] 6

Financial Forces: Influencing International Business

"Do the wrong thing. That's the best advice anyone could possibly offer an ambitious young person eager to get ahead in banking."

—Alan Abelson, Barron's

Concept Previews

After reading this chapter, you should be able to:

- **realize** that much money is made, and lost, in the foreign exchange (Fx) markets
- **understand** the role of the U.S. dollar in the world
- **understand** Fx quotations, including cross rates
- **recognize** currency exchange risks
- **understand** currency exchange controls
- **anticipate** financial forces such as balance of payments, tariffs, taxes, inflation, fiscal and monetary policies, and differing accounting practices that affect business
- **understand** sovereign debt, its causes, and its solutions
- **know** that a new small business in a developing country might be a better credit risk than the government in a developing country.

Gamma Liaison

One Big Mac, Hold the Fluctuations

McDonald's (Japan) imports many items used in its restaurants, including French fries, paper napkins, and some ingredients for its famous Big Mac, such as beef patties and sesame seed buns. Therefore, in early 1997, when the yen's value sank to a 44-month low against the U.S. dollar, falling to 122 from its high of 80, one would expect its yen costs for the imports to have soared, forcing McDonald's to raise Big Mac prices to its customers. Instead, in January, it began a 22-day campaign of discounting hamburgers. So is McDonald's an international company that is immune from the effects of currency fluctuations?

It is not immune, and its ability to hold and even lower Big Mac prices was due to two reasons. First, McDonald's had signed forward currency contracts with its bank under which it could buy U.S. dollars through the end of 1997 for 103 yen. Second, McDonald's global purchasing system buys for more than 19,500 McDonald's shops in 101 countries, and this permits it to drive hard bargains as it buys materials in bulk. It has developed software that finds and identifies the least expensive suppliers. ■

Source: Keiko Kambara, "International Manager" *International Herald Tribune,* January 30, 1997, p. 11.

The "uncontrollable" financial forces that we will discuss include foreign currency exchange risks, national balances of payment, taxation, tariffs, national monetary and fiscal policies, inflation, and national business accounting rules. *Uncontrollable* means that these forces originate outside the business enterprise. It does not mean that the financial management of a company is helpless to minimize its disadvantages; those disadvantages may even be turned to the company's advantage (see the Big Mac story on the preceding page).

sovereign debt
Debt of the government of a sovereign nation

We will look at what causes exchange rates to change and at how governments sometimes intervene in foreign exchange markets. We will emphasize the importance for management of remaining aware of balance-of-payments developments, exchange rate forecasts, inflation forecasts, government fiscal and monetary policies, and other financial forces. And at the end of the chapter, we will look at the **sovereign debt** of a number of countries.

Fluctuating Currency Values

In Chapters 4 and 5, we spoke of efforts to unify European countries with a central bank and a single currency, and we learned there is powerful opposition in some countries to giving up their own historical—and in some cases strong—currencies as well as the powers of their national central bank. Efforts toward unification are continuing, but progress is slow and uncertain. Indeed, the euro's drop of over 25 percent against the U.S. dollar in the two years after its introduction on January 1, 1999, caused many to question whether European monetary integration is viable. Outside Europe, there are no comparable efforts by countries to tie major currency values to each other.

Most currencies in the world are free to fluctuate against each other. You will recall that the Bretton Woods conference (discussed in Chapter 5) established fixed exchange rates. That system was eliminated in 1971 and replaced with freely floating exchange rates. Although central banks occasionally intervene in the foreign exchange markets by buying and selling large amounts of a currency, for the most part, currencies fluctuate freely against each other. These fluctuations may be quite large. Financial managers must understand how to protect against losses or optimize gains from such fluctuations. Another level of currency exchange risk is encountered when a nation suspends or limits convertibility of its currency, and managers must try to foresee and minimize or avoid losses resulting from large holdings of inconvertible and otherwise limitedly useful currencies.

When you want to convert one currency into another currency, you might first look for the value of the currency you have in terms of the one you want. You can find international currency exchange quotations in business publications such as *The Wall Street Journal* and the *Financial Times* and in the business section of most major newspapers. Xenon Laboratories, Inc., has developed what it calls the Universal Currency Converter, which allows you to see exchange rates on the Internet, www.xe.net/currency.

Foreign Exchange Quotations

Foreign exchange quotations—the price of one currency expressed in terms of another—can be confusing until you have examined how they are reported. In the world's currency exchange markets, the U.S. dollar (US$) is the common unit being exchanged for other currencies. Even if a holder of Japanese yen (¥) wants British pounds (£), the trade, particularly if it involves a large amount, usually will be to buy US$s with the ¥ and then to buy £s with the US$s. The reasons for this procedure are historical and practical.

Historically, the international monetary system established at Bretton Woods just before the end of World War II set the value of the US$ in terms of gold at $35 per ounce. The values of all the other major currencies were then stated in terms of the US$. For example, the yen was worth 0.28 of a U.S. cent, the French franc (Ff) was worth 18 cents, the German mark (DM) was worth 27 cents, and the £ was worth $2.40. In other words, the US$ was established as the keystone currency at the center of the world's monetary system.

The practical reasons for the continuing central position of the US$ are the several functions it has come to perform in the world. It is the main **central reserve asset** of many countries. It is the most used **vehicle currency** and **intervention currency.**

central reserve asset
Asset, usually currency, held by a government's central bank

vehicle currency
A currency used as a vehicle for international trade or investment

intervention currency
A currency used by a country to intervene in the foreign currency exchange markets (e.g., using some of its U.S. dollar reserve to buy—and thus strengthen—its own currency)

Liberia, Panama, and El Salvador use the US$ as their official currency, and Israel uses it as a parallel currency to its shekel. It has been the preferred medium of exchange and store of value in Poland, the former Soviet Union, and many other countries. Ecuador, for example, in the year 2000, adopted the US$ as its currency. After a six-month transition period, the US$ replaced the local Ecuadorean currency, the sucre. The decision by the Ecuadorean government to dollarize the Ecuadorean economy came as a surprise to many people in and outside that country even though Ecuador had experienced recession and inflation. In 1999, the sucre lost two-thirds of its value and the economy shrank by 7.5 percent. These economic problems convinced the Ecuadorean government to replace the sucre with the US$.[1] Even though many in Ecuador lament the loss of the local currency, most recognize that acceptance of the dollar was necessary to ensure financial security. As is shown in Figure 6.1, another South American country, Argentina, tied its currency, the peso, to the US$. As the US$ fluctuates, so does the Argentine peso.

Among the reasons the US$ is in great demand worldwide are its so-called **safe haven** aspect and its universal acceptance. Even if U.S. interest rates and investment opportunities were less attractive, many would still feel that money is safe in American securities or property. Inflation has been brought to a low level, and the country is seen as less likely than others to be invaded or to have its government collapse. It is seen as a safe haven. As to universal acceptance, if you have traveled internationally with U.S. dollars, you have found the currency welcome almost everywhere. One problem with universal use of U.S. dollars is the possibility of counterfeiting. This is especially true in certain countries. The U.S. government estimates that one-third of counterfeit money circulating in the United States was made in Colombia. In November 2000, local Colombian police working with agents of the U.S. Secret Service (the U.S. agency charged with prevention of counterfeiting) raided a counterfeiting operation in Colombia that may have produced more than US$1 billion in counterfeit bills.[2]

safe haven
In reference to the U.S. dollar, a political concept based on the belief that the United States is less likely than most countries to have communist government or to be subjected to a military coup or revolution

In the United States, the symbol $ generally refers to U.S. dollars. One must be careful, as the $ symbol is also used elsewhere in the world to denote local currencies. For example, Australia and New Zealand both call the local currency the dollar and use the $ symbol to refer to the local currency. The same is true in Hong Kong. Even Mexico, which calls its currency the peso, uses the $ symbol to denote the Mexican peso.

Exchange Rates

Figure 6.1 is the listing from *The Wall Street Journal* for currency transactions of major currencies against the U.S. dollar for the two days preceding Thursday, November 9, 2000. For the European currencies that have adopted the euro (€), the rates have been calculated using the official euro rates that went into effect on January 1, 1999, and the most recent US$–€ exchange rates. On January 1, 1999, the European Monetary Union (EMU) set irrevocable fixed exchange rates between the participating currencies and the euro. There is a permanent exchange rate between the German mark and the other euro-zone currencies and the euro. As was explained in Chapter 4, January 1, 1999, saw the beginning in the euro-zone countries of the three-year transition period from national currencies to the euro.

Figure 6.1 shows the US$ equivalent rate and the currency per US$ rate. The US$ equivalent rate is the cost in U.S. dollars of one unit of another currency. For example, Figure 6.1 shows that the price (indicated as the US$ equivalent rate) of Switzerland's currency, the franc, on Wednesday, November 8, 2000, was .5635. This means that one Swiss franc costs US$.5635, or about 56 cents. For another example, look at the Japanese yen, which is quoted at .009320. Each yen costs that fraction of a dollar. One yen is less than one cent. This does not mean that prices are inexpensive in Japan. A Big Mac in Japan costs ¥294, or about US$2.66. A one-night stay at a four-star business

[Figure 6.1] Exchange Rates (from The Wall Street Journal, Thursday, November 9, 2000)

The New York foreign exchange mid-range rates below apply to trading among banks in amounts of $1 million and more, as quoted at 4 p.m. Eastern time by Reuters and other sources. Retail transactions provide fewer units of foreign currency per dollar. Rates for the 11 Euro currency countries are derived from the latest dollar-euro rate using the exchange ratios set 1/1/99.

	U.S. $ Equiv.		Currency per U.S. $	
Country	Wed	Tue	Wed	Tue
Argentina (Peso)	1.0003	1.0003	.9997	.9997
Australia (Dollar)	.5273	.5297	1.8966	1.8880
Austria (Schilling)	.06217	.06254	16.086	15.990
Bahrain (Dinar)	2.6525	2.6525	.3770	.3770
Belgium (Franc)	.0212	.0213	47.1564	46.8769
Brazil (Real)	.5080	.5120	1.9685	1.9530
Britain (Pound)	1.4250	1.4343	.7018	.6972
1-month forward	1.4258	1.4351	.7014	.6968
3-months forward	1.4277	1.4370	.7004	.6959
6-months forward	1.4299	1.4392	.6993	.6948
Canada (Dollar)	.6485	.6520	1.5421	1.5338
1-month forward	.6489	.6524	1.5410	1.5327
3-months forward	.6499	.6534	1.5388	1.5304
6-months forward	.6510	.6546	1.5362	1.5277
Chile (Peso)	.001738	.001736	575.25	576.05
China (Renminbi)	.1208	.1208	8.2772	8.2769
Colombia (Peso)	.0004715	.0004693	2121.00	2131.00
Czech. Rep. (Koruna)				
Commercial rate	.02469	.02478	40.506	40.356
Denmark (Krone)	.1148	.1155	8.7080	8.6615
Ecuador (US Dollar)-e	1.0000	1.0000	1.0000	1.0000
Finland (Markka)	.1439	.1447	6.9504	6.9092
France (Franc)	.1304	.1312	7.6680	7.6225
1-month forward	.1306	.1314	7.6572	7.6115
3-months forward	.1310	.1317	7.6365	7.5908
6-months forward	.1314	.1322	7.6104	7.5658
Germany (Mark)	.4374	.4400	2.2863	2.2728
1-month forward	.4380	.4406	2.2831	2.2695
3-months forward	.4392	.4418	2.2770	2.2633
6-months forward	.4407	.4433	2.2691	2.2559
Greece (Drachma)	.002516	.002532	397.49	394.98
Hong Kong (Dollar)	.1282	.1282	7.7985	7.7985
Hungary (Forint)	.003241	.003262	308.51	306.58
India (Rupee)	.02142	.20143	46.685	46.665
Indonesia (Rupiah)	.0001086	.0001077	9205.00	9285.00
Ireland (Punt)	1.0862	1.0927	.9206	.9152
Israel (Shekel)	.2429	.2433	4.1170	4.1095
Italy (Lira)	.0004418	.0004444	2263.45	2250.04
Japan (Yen)	.009320	.009347	107.30	106.99
1-month forward	.009370	.009399	106.73	106.40
3-months forward	.009471	.009494	105.58	105.33
6-months forward	.009609	.009637	104.07	103.77
Jordan (Dinar)	1.4065	1.4094	.7110	.7095
Kuwait (Dinar)	3.2520	3.2520	.3075	.3075
Lebanon (Pound)	.0006605	.0006607	1514.00	1513.50
Malaysia (Ringgit)-b	.2632	.2632	3.8000	3.8000
Malta (Lira)	2.1711	2.1805	.4606	.4586
Mexico (Peso)				
Floating rate	.1036	.1041	9.6550	9.6085
Netherlands (Guilder)	.3882	.3905	2.5761	2.5608
New Zealand (Dollar)	.3985	.3997	2.5094	2.5019
Norway (Krone)	.1076	.1082	9.2957	9.2441
Pakistan (Rupee)	.01783	.01778	56.100	56.250
Peru (new Sol)	.2833	.2839	3.5298	3.5228
Philippines (Peso)	.01994	.02030	50.150	49.250

[Figure 6.1] *(Continued)*

Country	U.S. $ Equiv. Wed	U.S. $ Equiv. Tue	Currency per U.S. $ Wed	Currency per U.S. $ Tue
Poland (Zloty)-d	.2184	.2190	4.5780	4.5655
Portugal (Escudo)	.004267	.004292	234.36	232.97
Russia (Ruble)-a	.03596	.03595	27.809	27.819
Saudi Arabia (Riyal)	.2666	.2666	3.7513	3.7513
Singapore (Dollar)	.5748	.5759	1.7398	1.7363
Slovak Rep. (Koruna)	.01991	.01992	50.214	50.209
South Africa (Rand)	.1299	.1313	7.7000	7.6150
South Korea (Won)	.0008811	.0008791	1135.00	1137.50
Spain (Peseta)	.005141	.005172	194.50	193.35
Sweden (Krona)	.0998	.1004	10.0190	9.9610
Switzerland (Franc)	.5635	.5656	1.7747	1.7681
1-month forward	.5651	.5673	1.7696	1.7628
3-months forward	.5682	.5702	1.7600	1.7537
6-months forward	.5723	.5744	1.7474	1.7409
Taiwan (Dollar)	.03120	.03115	32.050	32.100
Thailand (Baht)	.02287	.02290	43.730	43.670
Turkey (Lira)	.00000147	.00000147	682450.00	680460.00
United Arab (Dirham)	.2723	.2723	3.6729	3.6730
Uruguay (New Peso)				
Financial	.08042	.08055	12.435	12.415
Venezuela (Bolivar)	.001439	.001440	694.75	694.40
SDR	1.2852	1.2883	.7781	.7762
Euro	.8555	.8606	1.1689	1.1620

Note: Special Drawing Rights (SDR) are based on exchange rates for the U.S., German, British, French, and Japanese currencies. Source: International Monetary Fund.

a-Russian Central Bank rate. b-Government rate. d-Floating rate; trading band suspended on 4/11/00.

e-Adopted U.S. dollar as of 9/11/00. Foreign Exchange rates are available from Readers' Reference Service (413) 592-3600.

Source: *The Wall Street Journal,* November 9, 2000, p. C20. Republished with permission of *The Wall Street Journal.* Permission conveyed through Copyright Clearance Center.

hotel in Tokyo is ¥30,000 a night, or about US$272.00. An example of a currency that costs more than a U.S. dollar is the British pound at $1.4250. A Big Mac in Britain costs £1.81, or about $2.53. A one-night stay at a four-star business hotel in London is £139, or about US$195.00.

The currency per US$ rate, on the other hand, is the price of one U.S. dollar in another currency. The currency per U.S. dollar rate of the Australian dollar for Wednesday, November 8, 2000, was 1.8966. That means one US$ costs about 1.90 Australian dollars.

Depending on what transaction is occurring, it may be necessary to convert from the US$ equivalent rate to the currency per US$ rate. By using the reciprocal of the US$ equivalent rate, one can reach the currency per US$ rate, and vice versa:

$$\frac{1}{\text{US\$ equivalent rate}} = \text{currency per US\$ rate}$$

$$\frac{1}{\text{currency per US\$ rate}} = \text{US\$ equivalent rate}$$

£.7018 = US$1.00

There is more to be learned from reading the exchange rates quotes. Using Figure 6.1, you will see the figure 1.4343 to the right of the "Britain (pound)" 1.4250 quote. Now look at the tops of the columns in which those numbers appear, and you will find the abbreviations "Wed" and "Tue." As you probably have surmised, the 1.4250 quote is the price at the close of trading on Wednesday, November 8, 2000, while 1.4343 was the quote at the close of the previous trading day. Those two prices tell you the US$ strengthened vis-à-vis the British pound during Wednesday's trading; one pound cost US$1.4250, at Wednesday's close, while it had cost more, US$1.4343, at Tuesday's close.

There is another way of expressing the value relationships between currencies, and that is the currency per US$ rate discussed above. Look again at the "Britain (pound)" line in Figure 6.1 and move to the right of the number about which we spoke. There you find another "Wed" and another "Tue" column; the quote in the "Wed" column is .7018, while it is .6972 under "Tue." These quotes inform us how many British pounds it took to buy one US$ at the close of trading on each of those days, and they are the reciprocals of the two quotes to the left. Observe that slightly more was needed to buy one US$ after Wednesday's trading than was needed after Tuesday's trading; in other words, the £ had weakened a little vis-à-vis the US$.

Spot Rates

spot rate
The exchange rate between two currencies for delivery within two business days

The **spot rate** is the exchange rate between two currencies for their immediate trade for delivery within two days. The rate on the same line as the name of the country is the spot rate. You will note in Figure 6.1 that the spot rate for Swiss francs was .5635 for Wednesday.

Forward Rates

forward rate
The exchange rate between two currencies for delivery in the future, commonly 30, 60, 90, or 180 days

The **forward rate** is the cost today for a commitment by one party to deliver to or take from another party an agreed amount of a currency at a fixed, future date. The commitment is a forward contract, and for frequently traded currencies such contracts are usually available on a 30-, 60-, 90-, or 180-day basis. You may be able to negotiate with banks for different time periods or for contracts in other currencies.

In Figure 6.1, look under Switzerland and refer to the Swiss franc one-month forward rate quotation. For Wednesday, November 8, 2000, it was .5651. Compare that rate with the spot rate of .5635, and you will see that it would cost more in US$ to buy a Swiss franc for delivery in one month than for delivery today. The Swiss franc is said to be **trading at a premium** in the one-month forward market. Look then at the three-month and six-month rate quotations, and you see that on Wednesday, the Swiss franc costs .5682 and .5723, respectively, for three-month and six-month delivery. These prices are also *more* expensive, or stronger, than the .5635 Wednesday spot rate, and so the Swiss franc is trading at a *premium* in all the report forward periods. Conversely, if a currency's forward rate quotes are *less* expensive, or weaker, than the spot rate, the currency is said to be **trading at a discount** in the forward markets.

trading at a premium
When a currency's forward rate quotes are stronger than spot

trading at a discount
When a currency's forward rate quotes are weaker than spot

So Many Yen, So Few Pounds

Look again at Figure 6.1, and you will see that it took about 107 yen to buy 1 US$, whereas less than 1 pound was enough for a dollar. Glancing up and down the column, you find that an Indonesian rupiah holder would need over 9,200 rupiahs for US$1 and that a different number is required by holders of each of the other currencies quoted. It might seem that the fewer units of a currency required to buy a dollar, the "harder" or better that currency is compared to the others, but as we have seen before, that is not necessarily correct.

As we mentioned before, the currencies of the world's major countries were set in value relative to the US$ at the end of World War II. Those exchange rates were the rates in the markets at that time. Since then, and particularly since 1973, the relative values of currencies, their convertibility, and their hardness or softness have been set by the supply and demand volumes of the foreign exchange markets. Those volumes are influenced by the policies of the various governments—their monetary and fiscal policies, their trade policies, and so on. Thus, the number of units of a currency per US$ on any given day does not indicate the relative strength of that currency. Many other factors must be examined to determine that.

The cost of a forward contract is the premium or discount compared to the spot rate. Whether there is a premium or a discount and its size depend on the expectations of the world financial community, businesses, individuals, and governments about what the future will bring. These expectations factor in such considerations as supply and demand forecasts for the two currencies, relative inflation in the two countries, relative productivity and unit labor cost changes, expected election results or other political developments, and expected government fiscal, monetary, and currency exchange market actions.

Values of currencies in terms of each other do not remain fixed but change, sometimes rapidly, as the currencies are traded in the world's financial centers. Currencies are traded around the world. What happens in the Tokyo foreign exchange market affects the London and New York markets.

An international traveler will need currencies for use in the countries in which that traveler is visiting. Often credit cards and automatic teller machine (ATM) cards can be used instead of the local currency.

Automatic teller machines (ATMs) are often used as a source of currency worldwide.
Dave Bartroff/Stock Boston

Bid and Asked Prices

When travelers or businesses contact a bank or an exchange agency to buy or sell a currency, they find a bid price and an asked price. The bid is the lower. The quotation for the Swiss franc may be .53 bid and .58 asked. If the customer has francs to sell, the bank or agency is bidding—offering—53 cents (U.S. pennies) for each franc. If the customer wants to buy francs, the bank or agency is asking 58 cents, a higher price. The difference provides a margin—profit—for the bank or agency. The rates listed in financial publications, such as those shown in *The Wall Street Journal* (Figure 6.1), are for customers buying large quantities, usually US$1 million or more. The rates charged to small customers are much less favorable to the customer. As was explained above, banks intend to make a profit in currency transactions.

International financial transactions are increasingly common.
Andres Hernandez/Gamma Liaison

Cross Rates

Although the US$ remains the most used currency, the currencies of other industrialized countries are also important in world transactions and are becoming more important. This is particularly true of the Japanese yen (¥) and the European euro (€). Many expect the euro to become as frequently used as the dollar. Although most large currency exchanges go through the US$ (see the ¥–£ example above), it is possible to find exchange rates for trading directly between non-US$ currencies. These rates are called **cross rates.** See Figure 6.2 for an example of the quotes for cross rates from *The Wall Street Journal.*

cross rates
Currency exchange rates directly between non-US$ currencies; usually determined by comparing the US$ exchange rates of the other currencies

Fluctuating Exchange Rates Create Risk

When your activities involve more than one country, you must deal with more than one currency. For example, a U.S. company exporting to Switzerland will, in most cases, want to receive US$s. If credit is involved, payment is not made when the goods are delivered, and one of the parties will have a currency exchange risk. If the Swiss importer agrees to pay Swiss francs, then the U.S. exporter bears a risk that the value of the Swiss franc will fall and thus the Swiss francs will buy fewer US$s when received than they would have at the earlier goods delivery date. On the other hand, if the Swiss importer agrees to pay in US$ at a future time, then the importer bears that risk (see Figure 6.3.)

Company financial managers are not without weapons for dealing with this type of risk. These weapons are presented in Chapter 19. Another potential hazard for a company is that a country in which it has assets may institute currency exchange controls.

[Figure 6.2] Key Currency Cross Rates

Late New York Trading Wed, November 8, 2000

	Dollar	Euro	Pound	Sfranc	Guilder	Peso	Yen	Lira	D-mark	Ffranc	Cdndlr
Canada	1.5421	1.3193	2.1975	0.8689	.59862	.15972	.01437	.00068	.67450	.20111	....
France	7.6680	6.5600	10.9269	4.3207	2.9766	.79420	.07146	.00339	3.3539	....	4.9724
Germany	2.2863	1.9559	3.2580	1.2883	.88750	.23680	.02131	.00101	....	.29816	1.4826
Italy	2263.5	1936.4	3225.4	1275.4	878.64	234.43	21.095	....	990.01	295.18	1467.8
Japan	107.30	91.80	152.90	60.461	41.652	11.113	....	.04741	46.932	13.993	69.580
Mexico	9.6550	8.2599	13.758	5.4404	3.7479	....	.08998	.00427	4.2230	1.2591	6.2609
Netherlands	2.5761	2.2039	3.6709	1.4516	....	.26682	.02401	.00114	1.1268	.33595	1.6705
Switzerland	1.7747	1.5183	2.5289	....	.68891	.18381	.01654	.00078	.77623	.23144	1.1508
U.K.	.70180	.6004	....	.3954	.27241	.07268	.00654	.00031	.30694	.09152	.45506
Euro	1.16890	....	1.6657	.65865	.45375	.12107	.01089	.00052	.51127	.15244	.75800
U.S.	....	.8555	1.4250	.56348	.38818	.10357	.00932	.00044	.43739	.13041	.64847

Source: *The Wall Street Journal,* November 9, 2000, p. C20. Republished with permission of *The Wall Street Journal.* Permission conveyed through Copyright Clearance Center.

[Figure 6.3] Currency Exchange Risk

February 1	Goods delivery date exchange rate	August 1	Payment date exchange rate
Suppose:	US$1 = 1.78 Swiss francs Whichever party bore the currency exchange risk, neither gained or lost.		US$1 = 1.78 Swiss francs
Suppose:	US$1 = 1.78 Swiss francs Whichever party bore the currency exchange risk lost. It now requires 1.80 Swiss francs to buy the US$1, which could have been bought for 1.78 Swiss francs at the time the goods were delivered.		US$1 = 1.80 Swiss francs
Suppose:	US$1 = 1.78 Swiss francs Whichever party bore the currency exchange risk gained. It now requires only 1.76 Swiss francs to buy the US$1, which would have cost 1.78 Swiss francs at the time the goods were delivered.		US$1 = 1.76 Swiss francs

Note: Parties agree to payment in US$.

Currency Exchange Controls

currency exchange controls
Government controls that limit the legal uses of a currency in international transactions

Currency exchange controls limit or prohibit the legal use of a currency in international transactions. Typically, the value of the currency is arbitrarily fixed at a rate higher than its value in the free market, and it is decreed that all purchases or sales of other currencies be made through a government agency. A black market inevitably springs up, but it is of little use to a finance manager, who usually wants to avoid breaking the laws of a country in which the company is operating. In addition, the black market is rarely able to accommodate transactions of the size involved in a multinational business.

Thus, the company, along with all other holders of the controlled or blocked currency, must pay more than the free market rate if the government grants permission to buy foreign currency. If permission is not granted or if the cost of foreign currency is uneconomically high, the blocked currency can be used only within the country. This usually presents problems of finding suitable products and investments within the country.

Official rates for currencies are considered currency exchange controls. When you see the notation "official rate" next to a currency rate quotation, you know that the country has currency exchange controls.

The currency exchange controls discussed here are a result of some governmental action. A government must be involved. For example, if a private-sector bank charges a

Table 6.1 Comparative Table of Worldwide Exchange Controls

Country (currency)	Regulatory Environment	Borrowing from Abroad	Incoming Direct Investment	Incoming Portfolio Investment
Argentina (peso)	Two Fx* tiers since October; official rate for trade and foreign loans; free market rate for other transactions.	Terms must be fixed in advance, with minimum of 1 year.	Amounts under $5 million and equity injections under 30% of firm's capital freely permitted.	Freely permitted for listed shares of amounts under $2 million.
Chile (peso, $)	Ongoing liberalization; official Fx rate set by Banco Central used for most transactions.	Registration and approval of loan required.	Investments over $5 million or in certain sectors require approval.	Freely permitted.
China (renminbi, RmB)	Severe Fx shortage; new foreign exchange centers offer minimal volume and high premiums.	A few local entities may borrow abroad, subject to restrictions.	Time-consuming approval process; minimum foreign equity, 25%.	No markets exist.
Egypt (pound, £E)	All transactions are the free market rate, except basic commodity imports, traditional exports (e.g., cotton), and oil company transactions. These are at a rate of E0.7:US$1.	Permitted for new projects if within approved financing plan and for ongoing projects if they generate Fx to service the debt.	Approval required; freely given in sectors needing foreign expertise or capital.	Approval required; foreign ownership limited in banking, insurance; priority given to export-oriented and import-substitution projects.
France (franc, F)	In the process of eliminating remaining controls.	Freely permitted.	Freely permitted, but advance notification required so authorities can check source of funds.	Regulations gradually being relaxed.
Germany (deutsche mark, DM)	Extremely liberal.	Freely permitted.	No approval needed; stringent antitrust laws should be considered.	Freely permitted.
Hong Kong (dollar, $)	All controls abolished in December 1972.	Freely permitted.	Freely permitted; local business-registration procedures must be followed.	Freely permitted.
India (rupee, Rs)	Strict controls; managed Fx rate; parallel market exists at 15–20% premium.	Approval required; borrowing usually limited to capital investments.	Approval required; maximum foreign equity; 40% in most cases.	Limited to authorized mutual funds.
Japan (yen, ¥)	Liberalization continuing; controls persist in certain areas (e.g., netting).	Freely permitted; must be reported to Ministry of Finance	3 months' prior notice required.	Notification usually required.
Nigeria (naira, N)	Highly controlled; two different exchange rates—interbank rate and FEM‡ rate. FEM rate determined at fortnightly auctions.	Subject to Finance Ministry approval.	Approval needed from Finance Ministry and Ministry of Internal Affairs; limits on foreign equity vary, 100% ownership not allowed.	Finance Ministry approval required.
Saudi Arabia (riyal, Sr)	No restrictions are placed on the inward or outward movement of funds.	Freely permitted.	Freely permitted.	Freely permitted.
Switzerland (franc, SwF)	Controls usually avoided, but government has applied restrictions in the past.	Freely permitted.	Freely permitted, except for a few public services.	Freely permitted for registered shares.
United Kingdom (pound sterling, £)	All controls have been removed.	Freely permitted.	Freely permitted, although takeovers scrutinized by Department of Trade.	Freely permitted.
United States (dollar, $)	Virtually no controls.	Freely permitted.	Freely permitted in most sectors; some states have their own restrictions.	Freely permitted in most sectors.

(continued)

Table 6.1 Comparative Table of Worldwide Exchange Controls *(continued)*

Remittance of Dividends and Profits	Remittance of Interest and Principal	Remittance of Royalties and Fees	Repatriation of Capital	Documentation for Remittances
Freely permitted at free market rate; heavy taxes on excess over 12% of capital base.	Freely permitted at commercial rate for approved loans.	Freely permitted at free market rate; fees must reflect market value.	Fully remittable 3 years after initial investment at free rate.	Authorization forms must be filed with the CB.†
Freely permitted	Freely permitted for registered loans.	Freely permitted for approved contracts.	Freely permitted for full amount after 3 years.	Requests must be filed with the CB.
Fx income and expense must be balanced before remitting.	Fx income and expense must be balanced before remitting.	Limited to 4% and 10-year period; low Fx priority for fees.	Freely permitted, but Fx shortage makes conversion difficult.	Onerous and complex requirements.
Approval required; 20% reserve required; firms without Fx to cover remittance must apply to banks for Fx allocation.	Freely permitted if the project generates sufficient Fx to cover payment; if not, approval required.	Freely permitted if the project generates Fx for payment; if not, approval required.	Allowed after 5 years, to be remitted in 5 equal annual payments; exceptions sometimes made.	Accountant's certificate of source of funds and proof of tax payment required.
No restrictions if minimum capital and reserve requirements met.	No restrictions on bonds or loans; prepayment requires approval.	No restrictions, but the CB requires the account number.	Freely permitted if repatriated within 3 months of liquidation.	Notification needed; local bank must run transaction.
Freely permitted.	Freely permitted.	Freely permitted.	Freely permitted.	Notification required for statistical purposes.
Freely permitted.	Freely permitted.	Freely permitted.	Freely permitted.	No official requirements.
Approval required; no ceiling on amount.	Freely permitted for approved loans.	Approval required; generally restricted to 4% of sales.	Approval required; amounts may be limited.	Onerous; Fx must be obtained from authorized banks.
Freely permitted.	Freely permitted for approved loans.	Freely permitted for approved contracts; tax authorities monitor rate changes.	Freely permitted.	Handled by Fx banks; mainly for reporting purposes.
Finance Ministry approval required; frequent delays. No ceilings if paid out of current-year after-tax profits.	Finance Ministry approval required.	Finance Ministry approval required; royalties limited to 1% of sales, fees to 2% of pretax profits.	Finance Ministry approval required, followed by authorized Fx dealer's approval.	Onerous and complex requirements; transfers via authorized dealers only.
Freely permitted.	Freely permitted.	Freely permitted.	Freely permitted.	No official requirements.
No restrictions except for reserve requirements.	Freely permitted.	Freely permitted.	Freely permitted.	Only that needed for ordinary bank transactions.
Freely permitted.	Freely permitted.	Freely permitted.	Freely permitted.	No official requirements.
Freely permitted.	Freely permitted.	Freely permitted.	Freely permitted.	Foreign bank transaction records must be kept for 5 years.

*Fx = foreign exchange, †CB = national central bank, ‡FEM = foreign exchange market.

Source: *Business International Money Report,* July 27, 1997. This table includes only a partial listing. For a more comprehensive list of countries and restrictions, see the *Business International Money Report.*

commission for exchanging currency, that may restrict the use of that currency to some, but it is not a currency exchange control since it does not involve the government.

People will go to remarkable extremes to get blocked money out of exchange-controlled countries. In New Delhi, the local manager of a major international airline gave a case of Scotch to a government official. Shortly thereafter, the agency for which that official worked granted the airline permission to use blocked rupees to buy almost US$20 million and transfer them to the airline's home country. This was an extreme method of converting blocked currencies to convertible currencies. It was also illegal. Most financial managers do not resort to such methods, but they can take legal steps to protect their firms from the adverse effects of currency exchange controls. Those steps are considered in Chapter 19.

Table 6.1 shows the currency exchange control laws and regulations of several countries.* You can see that the controls differ greatly from country to country and even within a country, depending on the type of transaction. In general, only the relatively rich industrialized countries have few or no currency exchange controls. They are a minority of the world's countries, and thus the great majority of countries do impose exchange controls. The international businessperson must carefully study those laws and regulations both before and while doing business in any country. Even the industrialized countries may have some restrictions.

Balance of Payments

Balance of payments (BOP) was discussed in some detail in Chapter 5, but we would be remiss not to mention it as a major financial force. The state of a nation's BOP will tell observant management much about the state of that country's economy. If the BOP is slipping into deficit, the government is probably considering one or more market or nonmarket measures to correct or suppress that deficit. Management should be alert for either currency devaluation or restrictive monetary or fiscal policies to induce deflation. Another possibility is that currency or trade controls may be coming. With foresight, the firm's management can adjust to the changing government policies or at least soften their impact.

On the export side, the company may start shopping for **export incentives**—government incentives to make exporting easier or more profitable. Lower-cost capital may be available if the company can demonstrate that exports will be increased.

export incentives
Tax breaks, lower-cost financing, foreign aid, or other advantages that governments give to encourage businesses to export and foreign customers to buy goods and services

One of the most common export incentives is the financing of exports by a government agency that offers foreign buyers lower interest rates than they could get from other money sources. Sometimes the agency's loans are accompanied by an aid grant, which need not be repaid.

Countries that levy value-added taxes (see Chapter 11) are permitted by World Trade Organization (WTO) rules to rebate them to exporters. This makes the exports less expensive and thus more competitive.

When firms are engaged in tough competition for major export contracts, their home governments may intervene to assist them. Often, the potential customer is a government agency, and the intervention may be contact with the customer's decision makers by their counterparts in the home government.

Tariffs or Duties

The words *tariffs* and *duties* are used interchangeably and refer to taxes usually on imported goods. These can be high or low, and it is of great importance to business to minimize them. They are discussed in the "Trade Restrictions" section of Chapter 3 and as one of the legal forces in Chapter 11, but they can certainly be classified as financial forces and therefore should be mentioned in this chapter.

*The information in Table 6.1 comes from *Business International Money Report,* July 25, 1997, pp. 210–15. Many more countries are covered in that publication; we have presented only a few to give you an idea of the types of controls and how countries differ.

The European Union (EU) and the other groupings of nations that we discussed in Chapter 4 have lowered or abolished tariffs on trade among member-countries. Such developments add new dimensions to the decision-making processes of companies located outside the groupings. For example, would the expenses and legal and personnel problems involved in establishing operations within a grouping be justified by tariff savings?

Taxation

Since much international business is conducted by companies operating in a corporate form, we are concerned with tariffs paid by and taxes levied on corporations. The point may be made that corporations don't pay taxes; they only collect them. In the end, people pay taxes.[3] The taxes may be collected from customers in higher prices, from employees in lower wages, from stockholders in lower dividends or capital gains, or from suppliers in smaller orders. However, even though corporations act as tax collectors rather than bearing the ultimate burden, it is very much in their best interest to minimize taxes. If a corporation can achieve a lower tax burden than its competitors, it can lower prices to its customers or make higher profits with which to pay higher wages and dividends. The price of its stock tends to rise, and it can be a better customer for the suppliers of its components and raw materials.

All this is true for all corporations, but international companies have more taxes—more countries—to consider and therefore more risks. They also have more opportunities to save taxes.

Different Taxes in Different Countries

In almost every country, the income tax is the biggest revenue earner for governments. Then there are sales or value-added taxes on goods or services, capital gains taxes, property taxes, and social security. A company must study carefully the tax laws of each country in which it operates. This subject is dealt with further in Chapter 11, and in Chapter 19 we shall see how financial managers can sometimes use different tax regimes and other measures to lower their taxes legally.

The amount of taxes paid is affected by inflation. At one time, some thought that inflation was a problem limited to developing countries and that industrialized countries need not worry about it. Recent experience has shown that view to be false.

Inflation

The phenomenon of increasing prices for almost everything over a period of time is familiar. Contagious inflation was probably the major cause of the end of the unprecedented world economic boom that lasted from the end of World War II until 1973. As prices of internationally traded goods rose due to a combination of rising demand and increased money supplies in all the developing countries, inflation fever spread from one developing country to the others.[4]

Inflation's Effects on Interest Rates

Inflation is clearly a financial force external to companies that finance managers must deal with as best they can. Almost every company must borrow money occasionally, and the inflation rate determines the real cost of borrowing. Real interest rates are found by subtracting inflation from the nominal interest rates. Figure 6.4 shows the difference between the real and nominal rates in selected regions of the world. When borrowed money is repaid in the future after inflation, it is worth that much less to the lender and, of course, is that much cheaper to the borrower.

Figure 6.5 illustrates inflation rates for countries in the Organization for Economic Cooperation and Development (OECD). Turkey has the highest inflation rate, while Japan has the lowest.

[Figure 6.4] Nominal and Real Interest Rates (1992–2000)

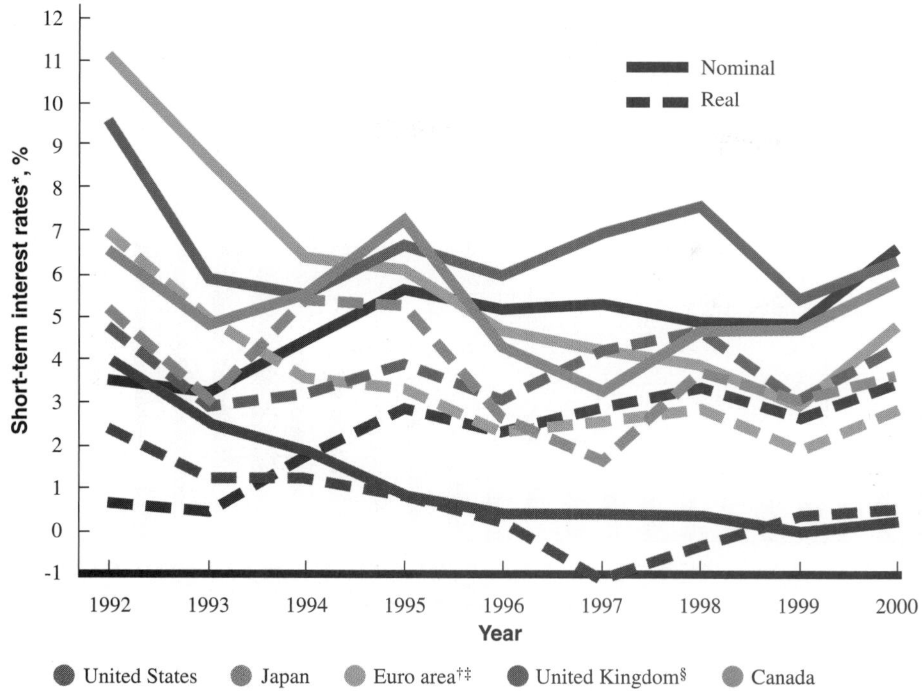

*For the United States, three-month certificates of deposit (CDs) in secondary markets; for Japan, three-month CDS; for Germany, France, and the United Kingdom, three-month interbank deposits; for Italy, three-month Treasury bill gross rate; and for Canada, three-month prime corporate paper.

†Germany, France, Italy.

‡Based on the revised consumer price index for united Germany introduced in September 1995.

§Retail price index excluding mortgage interest.

Source: *World Economic Outlook,* IMF, September 2000.

Monetary and Fiscal Policies Affect Inflation

Nations may conduct their monetary and fiscal policies in ways that cause an increase or decrease in inflation. *Monetary policies* control the amount of money in circulation, whether it is growing, and, if so, at what pace. *Fiscal policies* address the collecting and spending of money by governments. What kinds of taxes at what rates? On what and in what amounts does the government spend money?

Successful policies have two common denominators: (1) they remove artificial economic controls, such as wage and price controls, and (2) they apply fiscal and monetary restraint. The restraint includes lower taxes and slower growth in the nation's money supply.[5]

Japan, Germany, and the United States have had relatively good records in keeping inflation down in recent years. At the other extreme, many believe the infamous hyperinflation of the German mark in 1923 is the world's record. It is not. That dubious distinction belongs to the Hungarian pengö; inflation in Hungary in 1946 was a thousand times worse than the earlier German inflation. In 1939, 1 US$ bought 3.38 Hungarian pengös; in July 1946, the same dollar was worth 500 million trillion pengös. Never before or since has so much official money been worth so little.

Most Latin American countries have inflation troubles, although not as drastic as the Hungarian example. From 1970 into the 1990s, the worst inflation in Latin America occurred in Bolivia in 1985 at a rate of 11,750 percent. That far outstripped Brazil, in second place with 3,118 percent in 1990.

In a dramatic turnaround, Bolivia slashed its inflation to only 7.9 percent in 1996. Chile is a Latin American economic success story, decreasing inflation from 505 percent in 1974 to 7.4 percent in 1996 while increasing per capita income substantially.

[Figure 6.5] **Inflation Rates in OECD Countries**

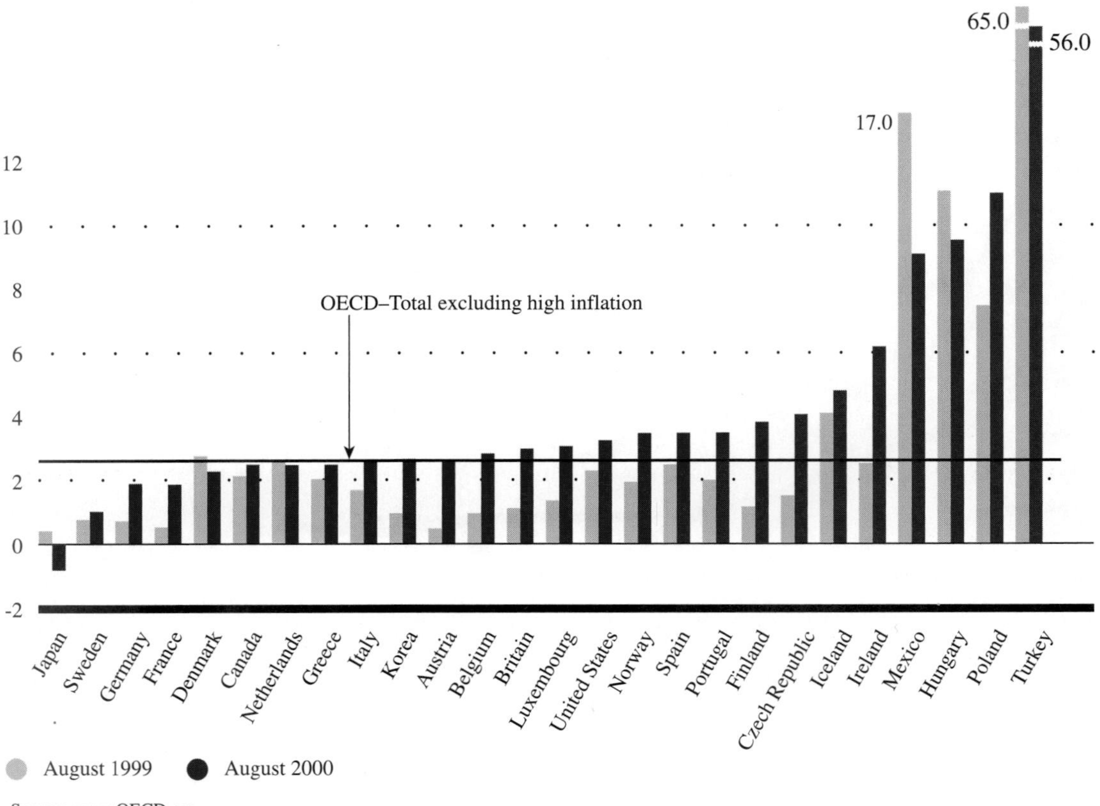

Source: www.OECD.org

Argentina reduced inflation from 3,080 percent in 1989 to 0.2 percent in 1996 while achieving a slight increase in per capita income; Mexico brought down inflation from 132 percent in 1988 to 34.4 percent in 1996, although Mexico's per capita income also came down.[6]

Importance of Inflation to Business

Even within a single country, inflation is of concern to management. Should it raise capital, and if so, should this be done through equity or debt? High inflation rates encourage borrowing because the loan will be repaid with cheaper money. But high inflation rates bring high interest rates or may discourage lending. Potential lenders may fear that even with high interest rates, the amount repaid plus interest will be worth less than the amount lent. Instead of lending, the money holder may buy something that is expected to increase in value, thereby further fueling inflation.

Lenders have begun to use variable interest rates, which rise or fall with inflation, to shift the risk to the borrower. Of course, that risk requires the borrower to be much more careful about borrowing. The original rate and any future changes are based on a reference interest rate, such as the U.S. prime rate or the London Interbank Offer Rate (LIBOR).

High inflation rates make capital expenditure planning more difficult. Management may allocate US$1 million for a plant and be forced to pay much more to complete construction.

Inflation and the International Company

All this also applies to international business, with the complication that inflation rates differ in different countries. For this reason, the management of an international company must try to forecast the rates for each of the countries in which it is active. The comparative inflation rates will affect the comparative currency values as the curren-

[Figure 6.6] **Misery Index**

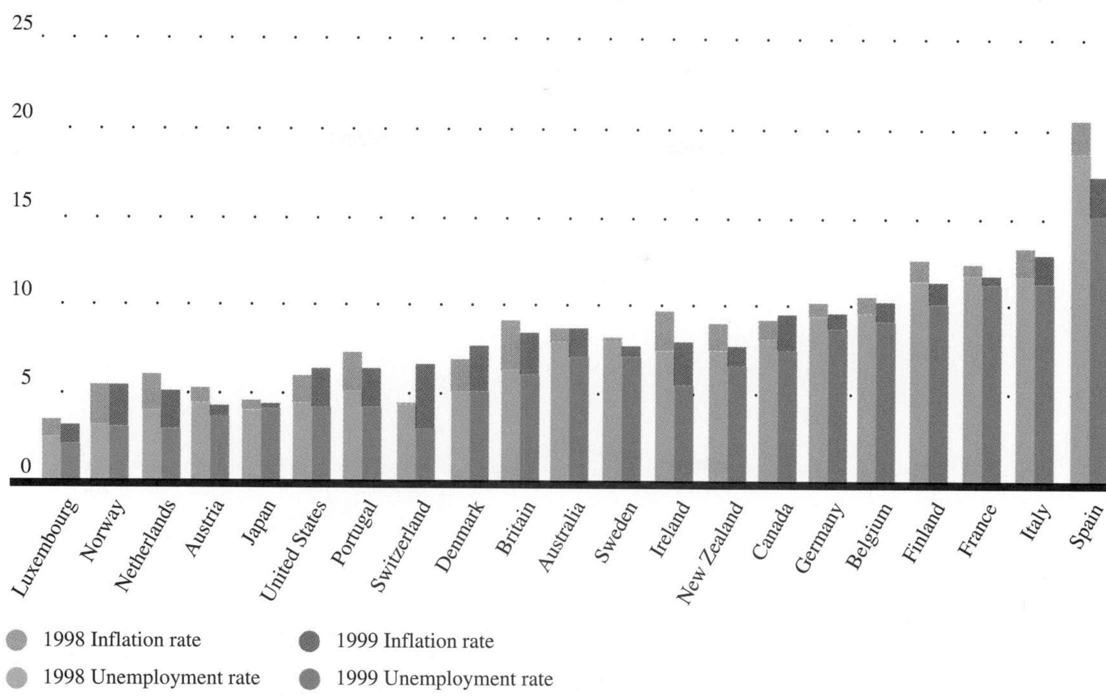

Sources: The Economist, October 25, 1997, p. 114. IMF, *World Economic Outlook Database,* March 2001.

cies of high-inflation countries weaken vis-à-vis the currencies of countries with lower inflation rates. Management will try to minimize holdings of the weaker currencies.

Higher inflation rates cause the prices of the goods and services produced or offered by a country to rise, and thus the goods and services become less competitive. The company's affiliate in that country finds it more difficult to sell its products in export, as do all other producers there. Such conditions tend to cause balance of payments (BOP) deficits, and management must be alert to changes in government policy to correct these deficits. Such changes could include more restrictive fiscal or monetary policies, currency controls, export incentives, and import obstacles.

Relative inflation rates affect where the international company raises and invests capital. Interest rates tend to be higher where inflation is higher, and high inflation discourages new investment for all the reasons we have seen.

The Misery Index

The term *misery index* had its origin in American politics during the 1980 presidential campaign, when both inflation and unemployment were high. A simple total of a country's unemployment and inflation rates, it is a sort of indicator of economic success; the higher the total score, the worse the misery. Figure 6.6 is a comparison of the misery levels of various countries. It also indicates for each country whether misery had increased or diminished from 1998 to 1999.

Accounting Practices

Accounting practices vary widely from country to country. When dealing with its foreign subsidiaries, an international company must be prepared to use the accounting practices of the host country. It must then translate these results into home country practices so that home country investors, creditors, and government regulators understand

[Figure 6.7] Rates of Savings (United States and Japan)

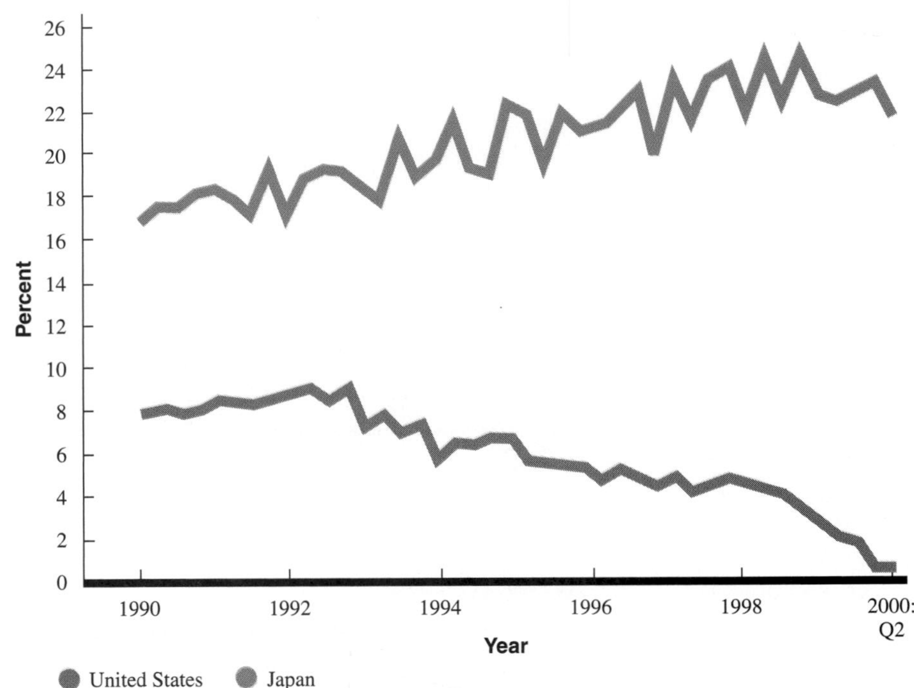

Sources: IMF, Bloomberg Financial Markets, LP; and WEFA, Inc., 2000.

them. Accounting practices are financial forces, which is why we include the topic here. In Chapter 19 we shall examine some of management's solutions.

Household Savings

Household savings as a percentage of disposable income is a good measure of the savings rate in a country. Saving is important because it allows the creation of capital for new investment. Traditionally, the United States, which is a consumer-driven economy, has a low savings rate, while Japan, which has a culture that encourages savings, has a high savings rate. Many argue that the high savings rate in Japan has helped boost that country's economy since the end of World War II by allowing capital investment that has helped build Japan's manufacturing base. Figure 6.7 shows dramatically the differences between the United States and Japan in terms of the rate of savings.

Countries Went Bust

During the lending binge by banks to developing countries in the 1970s, the head of a major bank said, "Countries don't go bust." That statement was proved wrong, and a new and ominous financial force hit international business: sovereign debt. Contrary to many expectations, a number of developing countries found themselves unable to pay even the interest, much less the principal, on their debts. The sovereign debt crisis for Poland occurred in 1981; for Mexico, Brazil, Argentina, and others it occurred in 1982 and later.

We examined this matter in Chapter 4 from the point of view of the International Monetary Fund (IMF) and the Bank for International Settlements (BIS). As was discussed, the IMF took the lead role in trying to resolve these crises as they arose, and the BIS made bridge loans while the IMF was preparing to act.

Because these crises were so important and still affect international business, we will discuss some of the background in this chapter. Also, we will suggest some possible solutions.

Causes of Increasing Indebtedness in Developing Countries

The immediate causes of the growing debts were the jumps in oil prices (crude oil represents an average of 16 percent of the merchandise imports of the nonoil developing countries). In 1973–74, oil prices quadrupled; they then doubled in 1979–80, and that increase from a higher base represented an even larger increase in absolute terms than the 1973–74 rise.

Those oil price increases made the already severe inflation that much worse, and the combination brought on a worldwide recession. The resulting drop in prices of primary nonoil commodities, which account for 45 percent of developing country (excluding Mexico and OPEC developing countries) exports, was a serious blow to the economies of developing countries and their ability to pay their heavy debts. Mexico and the OPEC developing countries were hurt by drops in oil prices beginning in 1981 as well as by uneconomic uses of oil revenue and borrowed moneys they received during the 1970s and 1980s.

Then, after the 1979–80 oil price jump, interest rates increased. That increase affected all new loans and the many existing loans that carried variable rather than fixed interest rates. Every 1 percent increase in US$ interest rates costs the developing countries some $2.5 billion per year more in interest payments.

On top of all that, the US$ began to strengthen in value in the foreign exchange markets during 1980. It continued up into 1985 and gained over 80 percent by March 1985. Developing countries borrow mainly in dollars but export in many currencies, and so the rise in the value of the US$ created new burdens; they had to earn that much more in hard currencies to pay the US$ debts.

Since that time and through the 1990s, the dollar has fluctuated in value but has remained strong vis-à-vis the currencies of most of the debtor developing countries. Of course, those countries can, and increasingly do, borrow in currencies other than the US$, but those borrowings are almost always in the currency of another developed country that also is strong in comparison with the borrower's money.

Debt Problem Solutions

The IMF, the BIS, national central banks, and commercial banks have been scrambling for solutions.

Short-Term Solutions

The short-term answers have included rescheduling of debts for countries that were unable to pay as they came due. But renegotiations are becoming more and more difficult. The BIS, the commercial banks, and the central banks are reluctant to come up with more money, and the IMF's resources are finite.

The debtor countries are balking at the stringent austerity programs being insisted on by the IMF. The economic growth of some developing countries has halted as they must use new money they receive from exports or loans to repay debt rather than for productive investments. Social unrest, including rioting, has broken out in several countries, notably Venezuela, Argentina, and Brazil.

The debtor countries are in desperate straits, but the industrialized countries are also being damaged. As the debtor countries use money to repay debts, they do not buy goods and services from the developed countries. As a result, the developed countries have lost billions of dollars of export business and thousands of jobs.

The debtor developing countries can reduce their debts only by exporting more than they import and thus running balance of payments (BOP) surpluses. Some of the debtor developing countries have been able to run BOP surpluses and make debt payments. However, these surpluses have been achieved as much by cutting imports as by expanding exports, and that has slowed or stopped economic development in the debtor countries and also hurt exports from countries that had been suppliers before the imports were curtailed.

Most of the debtor developing countries have needed more money from private banks and international agencies and have been lent more. This has caused the debt burdens of these countries to increase at the same time that their economic development has been retarded, a process that cannot be sustained.

Long-Term Solutions

The debt renegotiations accompanied by stringent austerity were part of the first phase of the world's efforts to solve the debt problems. This phase led to declines in living standards and curtailed economic growth and exports.

The second phase saw a growing awareness that short-term adjustment policies would not do the job alone. The problem for the developing countries was not the outstanding debt per se but the economic policies they followed and the cultural and attitudinal barriers they faced.

Recognizing this, the Baker Plan (named for then U.S. secretary of the treasury James Baker) called for market-oriented strategies to encourage growth and bring inflation under control. Measures were needed to rebuild confidence in and lure flight capital and new investment back to debtor countries.[7]

The Baker Plan was followed by the Brady Plan, which built on its predecessor and made debt relief conditional on a debtor country's pursuit of an IMF-approved economic adjustment program. The plan called on private banks for more money backed by funds from the IMF, the World Bank, and developed country governments.

Brady debt relief is provided through three mechanisms: (1) the exchange of old debt for new at a discount, (2) the exchange of old debt for new at a lower interest rate, and (3) the buying back of debt from creditor banks at a discount.[8]

Growing Developing Country Debt Market

The third mechanism has resulted in debtor countries buying their own debt and retiring it. The creditor banks have also sold debt of developing countries and countries in transition* to other banks and investors, resulting in a large secondary debt market. The debts are in several instrument forms, including loans, Brady bonds, corporate and non-Brady sovereign bonds, local market instruments, options, and warrants on debt.

Even as the Latin American debt market has flourished, developing country debt traders have begun to focus on Eastern Europe. The list of major players reflects how important the financial community feels the Eastern European market will be. They include Morgan Grenfell, Indosuez, Salomon Brothers, Merrill Lynch, Chase Manhattan, J. P. Morgan, Chemical, and Continental Bank of London.

So far, debts of Russia and Poland are the most traded of the Eastern European countries, with some Bulgarian issues thrown in. The other Eastern European countries are described by one banker as "flies on the back of the elephant." Strangely enough, Latin American money has been going into Russia as investors seek yield and capital appreciation, demonstrating how small a financial world it has become.[9]

200-Year History of Sovereign Debt Defaults

Investment banks are preparing a new generation of sovereign credits. Enthusiasm for emerging-market bonds is so great that one banker said, "I honestly think that any sovereign can access the market." Evidence of the correctness of that statement is provided by the many dubious credit-risk countries in or about to enter the market. Among them are Jordan, Lebanon, Morocco, Slovakia, Slovenia, and Tunisia.

*"Countries in transition" refers to countries in Central and Eastern Europe and elsewhere that are in transition from centrally controlled to market economies.

Investors and investment bankers seem to have forgotten or are ignoring history, which is littered with sovereign defaults. Since 1800, Ecuador has been through periods of default and rescheduling totaling 113 years. Greece is not far behind with 87 years in three separate periods of default. Such prestigious names as the Netherlands, Austria, Japan, and China have all failed to meet their external obligations at some point during the last two centuries.[10]

Of course, investors and investment bankers do not have to look 200 years into history to find problems with government repayment. We have been discussing efforts of lenders, investors, and sovereign borrowers to work themselves out of the debt crises of the 1980s.

Some Positive Developments

The Paris Club, which is a group of Western creditor governments, forgave half of Poland's debt. That is a reduction of some $17.5 billion. The United States forgave the Egyptian debt as an expression of thanks for Egypt's support in the war against Iraq. More recently, the World Bank, the IMF, and the Paris Club approved a plan to relieve the massive debt load of some of the world's most heavily indebted poor countries (HIPCs). As a whole, HIPCs have a debt-to-export ratio of over 500 percent, more than three times as high as the average for all developing countries. Assistance for such countries can certainly be defended on a humanitarian basis, and tying relief to economic reforms encourages them to take steps toward improving their economic performance. However, programs such as this are controversial from an economic standpoint because of what one author calls "moral hazard": special treatment of highly indebted countries might reduce the disincentives for nations to run up large debts in the future.[11]

Figure 6.8 is a world map showing the location of HIPCs. Most are in sub-Saharan Africa. Figure 6.9 is a chart showing HIPC debt from 1992 to 2001. At the current rate, HIPCs will never get out of debt because they constantly increase their long-term debt at high interest rates and, at the same time, are dependent on essential imports (such as fuel). Figure 6.9 shows continued bad news for HIPCs. Even though the ratio of external debt to gross domestic product (GDP) decreased from 92.2 to 42.5 percent during the time period shown in Figure 6.9, the percentage of exports of goods and services also decreased and the balance of current account remained consistently negative.

[Figure 6.8] **HIPC Debt**

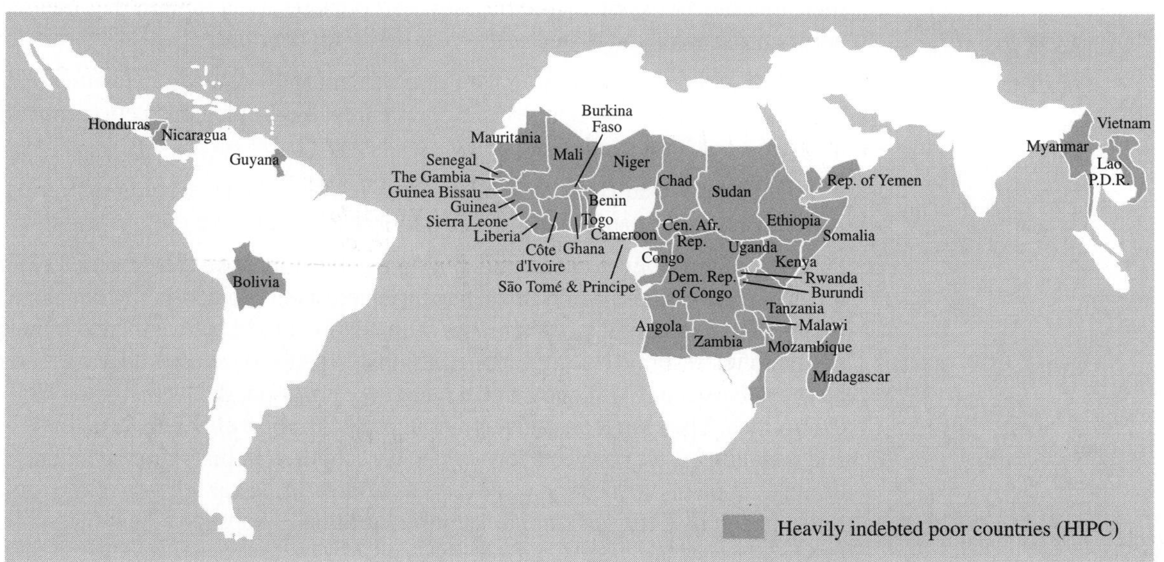

Source: World Bank Group, 2000.

[Figure 6.9] Debt of all HIPCs (1992–2001)

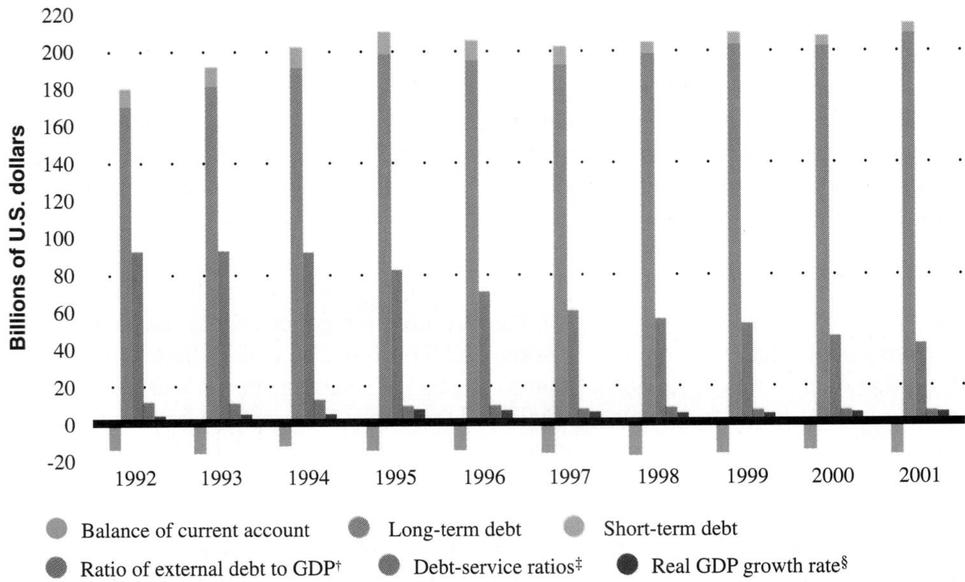

†Debt at year end in percent of GDP in year indicated.

‡Percent of exports of goods and services.

§Annual percent change.

Source: *World Economic Outlook,* IMF, September 2000.

Longer-Term Solutions

A number of cures have been suggested. We will list a few.

1. Borrowing countries will have to pursue policies ensuring that new money they obtain is used for economic growth rather than for consumption, capital flight, or overambitious government schemes or armaments.
2. Borrowers should build up reserves in good years to enable them to withstand the fluctuations in commodity export prices that are inevitable even if no more oil price shocks occur.
3. The developed countries must strive for their own economic growth and open their markets to exports from developing countries even though that means competition with some industries in developing countries.
4. The IMF and other creditors must not try to enforce austerity measures that are too stringent on debtor countries. Social unrest and trade contraction must be avoided or at least minimized.
5. The IMF, the World Bank, and other agencies that aid developing countries must be assured of sufficient funding so that they can take long-term views.
6. Parts of the huge developing country external debts must be changed in form to types of equity. These could be ownership interests in projects being developed or shares of export earnings. Other parts of the debts should be lengthened in maturity, with interest rate ceilings applied. A novel use for sovereign debt was arranged by the debtor country Senegal and a Dutch organization, the Netherlands UNICEF Committee. The Dutch organization bought $24 million of Senegalese foreign debt and converted it into projects for women and children in that African nation. Child immunization and education of the street children of Dakar are two of the projects. Since begun by Senegal, similar "debt for children" swaps have benefited children in Madagascar, Jamaica, and the Philippines.
7. The developing countries must relax their restrictions on foreign investments and on repatriation of profits from existing investments. They must encourage

new money from foreign private sources—nonbank sources—because the banks are now overcommitted with existing loans to developing countries and are not likely prospects for new, economic growth money.

8. Blame for the debt crises belongs to several parties. The developing countries borrowed more than they could productively invest, and much of the borrowed money was wasted at home or sent abroad for the personal accounts of corrupt political leaders. The lending banks were encouraged to lend by the governments of their countries because the governments were thus relieved to that extent of foreign aid demands by the developing countries. But the banks must also bear a share of the blame; they made limited inquiries regarding the uses of the borrowed money or the soundness of the projects in which the money would be invested. They failed to get collateral to secure the loans, and one reason they were so casual was that the loans were almost always to governments or guaranteed by governments. They seem to have forgotten how wrong the banker we mentioned above was when he said during the 1970s that "countries don't go bust."

Do the Wrong Thing, Young Bankers

That was the title of an article Alan Abelson wrote for Barron's several years ago, pointing out that bankers during the 1960s and 1970s made fortunes by shoveling out loans that exploded into the debt crises and problems of the 1980s and 1990s. And indeed, in the 1990s, U.S. bankers seemed to have followed that advice.[12]

The United States in Debt?

After 70 years as the world's leading creditor, the United States is said by some to have become the world's biggest debtor, a situation which causes them to forecast adverse effects for America. Before looking at some of those effects, we should define the debt, see how it differs from the debts of developing countries, and put its growth into perspective with the growth rates of the other G7 countries.*

U.S. Debt Defined

Conceptually, the U.S. foreign debt—what the Department of Commerce calls a **net negative international investment position**—is the difference between the value of overseas assets owned by Americans and the value of U.S. assets owned by foreigners. These assets consist of commercial bank deposits, foreign exchange holdings, corporate securities, real estate, physical plant, and other direct investments. The popular press calls the difference *debt,* but the Commerce phrase, *net negative investment position,* is more accurate. One reason is the differences between U.S. debt and debt in developing countries.

net negative international investment position
The U.S. Commerce Department's description of what is commonly called the U.S. international debt

Figure 6.10 on page 232 shows foreign holdings in the United States as a percentage of total privately held public debt. You will notice that foreign holdings increased significantly during the late 1990s. Figure 6.11 also on page 232 shows the countries that are major foreign holders of U.S. Treasury securities. Japan and the United Kingdom together account for over one-third of all foreign holders of Treasury securities.

Differences between U.S. and Developing Country Debt

First, over $300 billion of the U.S. foreign-owned assets are obligations of the U.S. Treasury or U.S. corporations that are traded daily in world financial markets. Their worth, unlike the face value of a developing country debt, is subject to constant change.

Second, U.S. foreign assets are often measured at book value, which results in an estimated undervaluation of up to $200 billion. Book value would be cost when bought, which may have been years ago, less depreciation. Inflation alone would result in prices much higher than book value if the assets were sold today.

*The G7 countries are discussed in Chapter 4.

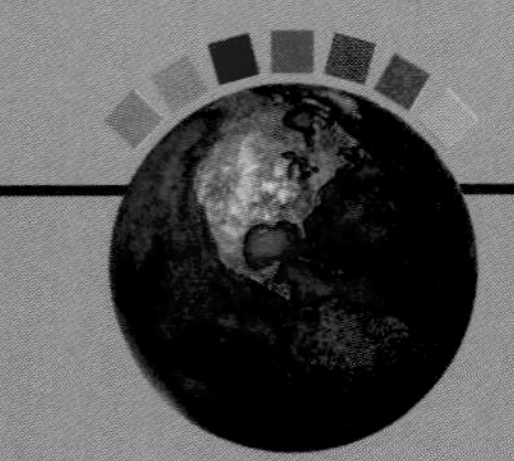

[Worldview]

Third World Debt That Is Almost Always Paid in Full

You think it would be utter folly to lend money to a developing country. So how about a new small business such as a vegetable stand in a developing country?

U.S. development organizations are finding that some of the world's poorest entrepreneurs repay their debts at rates approaching 100 percent. To encourage grass-roots private business in Latin America, Asia, and Africa, these organizations are expanding programs that already lend thousands of these struggling entrepreneurs amounts ranging from $50 to several hundred dollars.

Tiny businesses in developing countries commonly repay these "microloans" faithfully because they crave the security of a favorable credit rating. This rescues them from the clutches of loan sharks—microloans typically charge the prevailing commercial loan rate—and lets them borrow again in hard times. The money helps them start or expand their businesses—selling vegetables, sewing, repairing shoes, making furniture, and the like—and boosts their local economies.

Their repayment performance shines when compared with that of many sovereign nations. It also looks good compared with a default rate of 17 percent among U.S. recipients of federally guaranteed student loans.

Though microlending has been around for years, it is now booming. With the decline of communism, U.S. development groups believe they are exporting free market economics to tiny businesses that can fuel growth in the developing world.

"Micro-enterprise lending is the hottest thing in development since the Green Revolution. Everybody does it," says Accion International spokesperson Gabriela Romanow. The Green Revolution sent farm output surging in many poor nations.

Romanow cites the case of Aaron Aguilar, an unemployed factory worker in Monterrey, Mexico, who borrowed $100 to buy clay and glazes for making figurines with his wife in their backyard. In six years, the couple took out and repaid five loans and built their business to 18 full-time employees.

Sometimes borrowers have to struggle against setbacks that might seem comical in the prosperous West. One group of women in Cameroon received $100 from Trickle Up to start a rabbit-breeding business, but the rabbit ate her offspring, recalls Mildred Leet, cofounder of the U.S. agency. Undaunted, the women switched to chickens and made enough money selling eggs to branch out into tomatoes and tailoring, ultimately opening two shops, Leet says.

Microlending at One Development Agency, Accion International

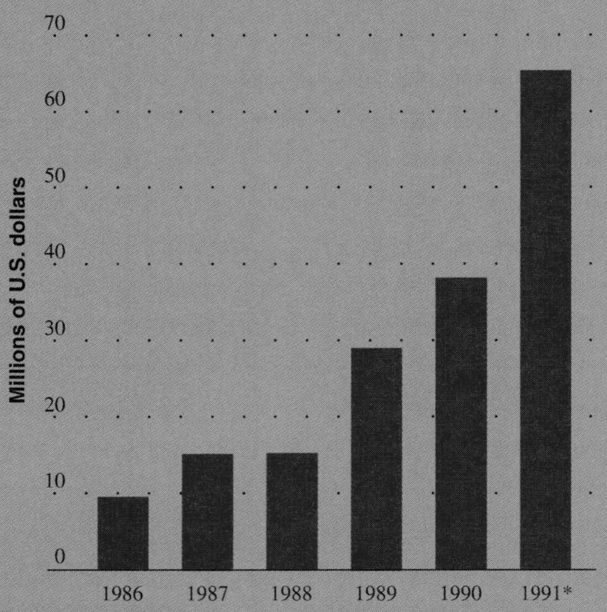

*Projection
Source: Accion International.

Third, U.S. assets abroad reportedly earn more in interest and dividend per dollar of investment than foreign holdings earn in America.

Fourth, although current U.S. net liabilities are immense in absolute terms, they are relatively small in terms of other economic indicators. Total U.S. debt amounts to 6 percent of U.S. GDP—compared to 35.6 percent for developing countries as a group. The annual service cost of the U.S. debt is less than 1 percent of U.S. exports of goods and services. The corresponding cost for the same group of developing countries ranged from a low of 6.6 percent to that of Hungary, the highest at 39.1 percent.[13]

[Internet Exercises]

Using the Internet

1. The text discusses financial markets around the world. These financial markets move very fast, and it is important to be able to keep up with financial information. One of the advantages of the Internet is its ability to provide accurate up-to-the-minute information. Using the Internet, such as CNNfn's Web site, find the current exchange rates of the following currencies:
   a. French franc.
   b. Japanese yen.
   c. Thai baht.
   d. Portuguese escudo.
   e. Cyprus pound.
   f. Jordanian dinar.
   g. Kenyan schilling.
2. Using the Internet, find stock quotes from major stock exchanges around the world. This information can be found on sites such as CNNfn's Web site. You should also visit Web sites from other countries to see the variety of country- or region-specific financial information that is available on the Internet.

[Minicase 6.1]

Management Faces a BOP Deficit

You are the chief executive officer of a multinational's subsidiary in a developing host country. The subsidiary has been in business for about eight years, making electric motors for the host country's domestic market, with mediocre financial results. Before you left the home country a month ago, you were told to make the sub profitable or consider closing it.

After a month in the host country, you have discovered that it is running a worsening balance of payments (BOP) deficit and that the government officials are very concerned about the situation. They are considering various measures to stanch or reverse the deficit flow.

What measures might be adopted? Can you think of some ways your company might profit from them or at least minimize the damage?

[Chapter]

7

Economic and Socioeconomic Forces

"There is so much information—some of it quite meaningless—put out every day about every conceivable aspect of the U.S. economy that companies, banks, and individual investors can find reasons to justify almost any move they make."

—*Paul Fabra, leading French economist,* Columbus Dispatch, *August 9, 1994, p. 1-D*

Concept Previews

After reading this chapter, you should be able to:

- **understand** the purpose of economic analyses
- **recognize** the economic and socioeconomic dimensions of the economy
- **understand** the importance of a nation's consumption patterns and the significance of purchasing power parity
- **understand** the degree to which labor costs can vary from country to country
- **understand** the significance for businesspeople of the large foreign debts of some nations
- **ascertain** the reasons for the worldwide downward trend in birthrates and its implications for businesspeople
- **understand** indicative plans and their importance for businesspeople

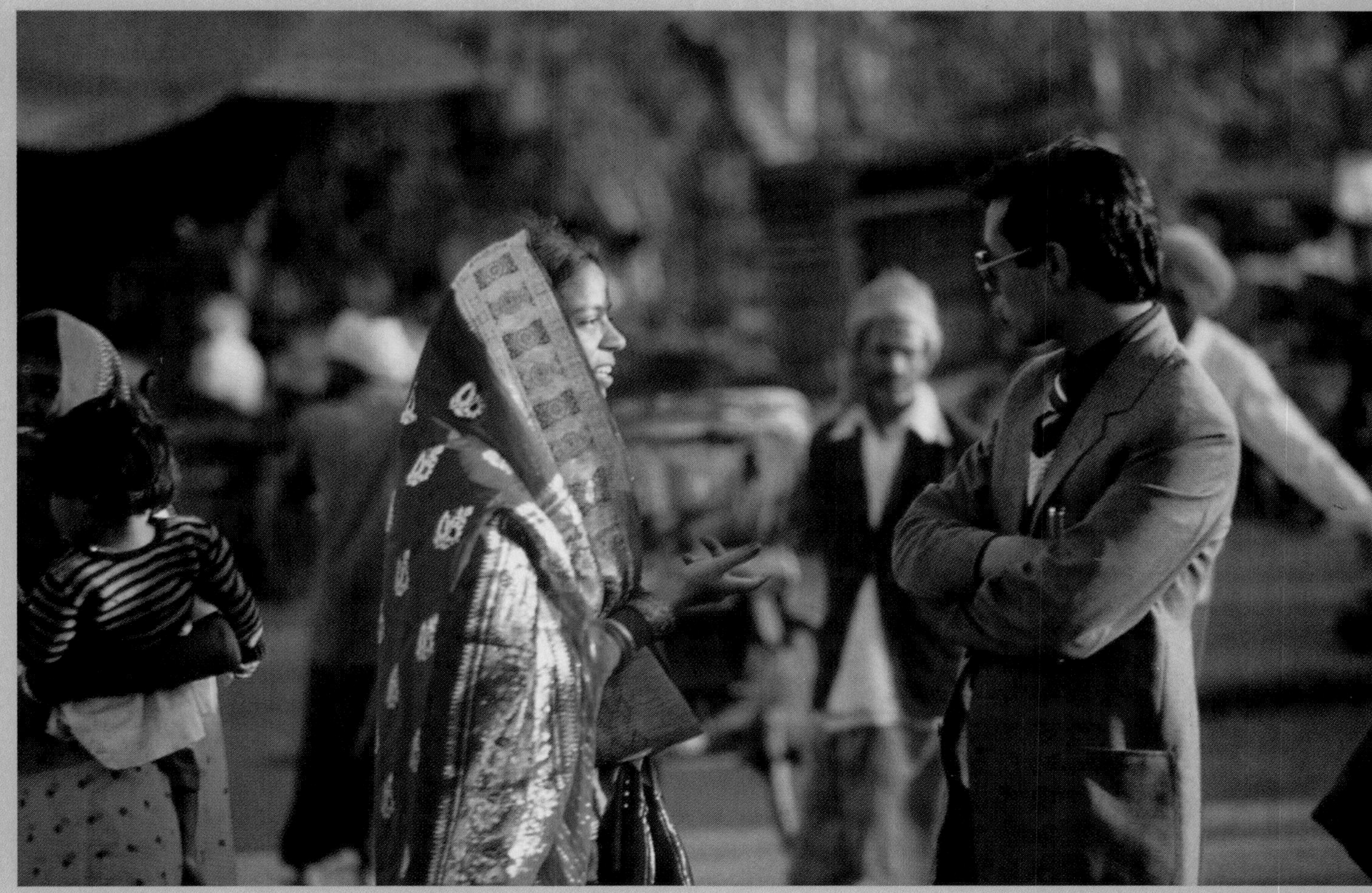

Alan Oddie/PhotoEdit

Can Indians Afford Cars and TV Sets? The Size and Average Income of India's Consuming Class

International companies searching for new markets to enter are seeing tremendous opportunities in India as a result of its economic liberalization. With a population of well over 1 billion and the fifth-largest economy in the world (based on purchasing power parity), India is said to have a rapidly growing consuming class (rich and middle class). The National Council of Applied Economic Research (NCAER), an independent research organization in India, estimated in 1998 that the country's middle-income population was 494 million people, or 86.6 million households of 5.7 persons each.[a]

But is this really a middle class as American and European multinationals define it? Managers unfamiliar with international economic data might conclude that India is not a market for their appliances or automobiles.

(1) But economists know that because India's living costs are considerably lower than American costs, its income translated to U.S. dollars represents more purchasing power than is evident from the \$430/capita figure the World Bank obtained by converting Indian rupees to American dollars using the foreign exchange rate. To find out how much, analysts can go to World Bank data and discover that based on a comparison of the purchasing power of the two currencies, \$430 in rupees is equivalent to \$1,700.[b] This is the purchasing power parity (PPP) that we examined in Chapter 3.

(2) Next, the analysts want to know the purchasing power of the middle and upper classes. They first obtain the GNP in dollars of equivalent purchasing power by multiplying the PPP dollar equivalent of India's GNP/capita by the population: \$1,700 × 980 million (in 1988) = \$1,666 billion.[c]

(3) How much of gross national product goes to the middle and upper classes? Table 7.2 provides the percentage share of per capita expenditure accruing to percentile groups ranked by per capita expenditure. The values for India are as follows:

First (lowest) quintile	8.1%
Second quintile	11.6%
Third quintile	15.0%
Fourth quintile	19.3%
Fifth (upper) quintile	46.1%
Top 10 percent	33.5%

Assume that the fourth quintile represents the upper middle class and the fifth quintile represents the upper class. The upper middle class has 19.3 percent of the consumer expenditures, and the upper class has 46.1 percent. Using the World Bank assumption that the distribution of consumer expenditures represents the distribution of income, the upper middle class has 0.193 × \$1,666 billion = \$21.5 billion, and the upper class has 0.461 × \$1,666 billion = \$768 billion.[c] The income of the highest 10 percent is 0.335 × \$1,666 billion = \$558.11 billion.

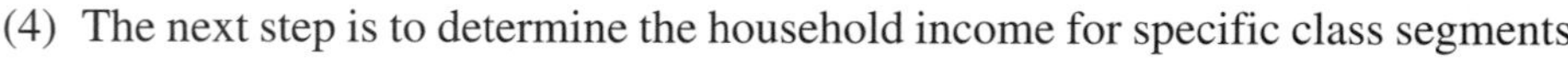

(4) The next step is to determine the household income for specific class segments:

$$\text{Population per quintile} = \frac{980\text{ million}}{5} = 196\text{ million people}$$

$$\text{Top 10 percent per capita} = \frac{\$558.11\text{ billion}}{98\text{ million people}} = \$5{,}695$$

$$\text{Upper-class per capita income} = \frac{\$768\text{ billion}}{196\text{ million people}} = \$3{,}918.4$$

$$\text{Upper-middle-class per capita income} = \frac{\$321.5\text{ billion}}{196\text{ million people}} = \$1{,}640.3$$

(5) The Research Council states that there is an average of 5.7 people per household in India. Using this number, analysts can estimate the per capita income per household in each of the three classes under investigation.

$$\text{Income per household in top 10 percent of population} \\ = 5.7 \times \$5,695 = \$32,461.5$$

$$\text{Income per household in upper class} = 5.7 \times \$3,918.4 = \$22,334.9$$

$$\text{Income per household in upper middle class} \\ = 5.7 \times \$1,640.3 = \$9,349.7$$

Add to this the rapidly rising incomes of computer software professionals in Bangalore and Hyderabad as well as a large underground economy which does not appear in the official statistics. It appears that India is quite likely to have 400 million or more people who have the purchasing power to buy refrigerators, TV sets, and automobiles. ■

Sources: [a]"Rising Incomes Foretell Durable Goods Consumerism, Shows NCAER Report," *Financial Express,* November 28, 1998; [b]1998 values from *World Development Report 1999–2000* (Washington, DC: World Bank, 2000), p. 230; [c]980 million is used as India's population total to assure comparability with other statistics.

You have just read an example of an economic analysis—one that attempts to measure the size of the population segment capable of buying the typical consumer products of industrialized nations. This information is necessary input for any firm considering investment in a local production facility.

As you can imagine, this and other economic forces are among the most significant uncontrollable forces for managers. To keep abreast of the latest developments and also to plan for the future, firms for many years have been assessing and forecasting economic conditions at the national and international levels.

Even though the data published by governments and international organizations such as the World Bank and the International Monetary Fund (IMF) are not as timely or as accurate as business economists would like, these are what they have, and they must work with them. However, analysts do not work solely with government-published data. Private economic consulting specialists—such as Data Resources, Inc., Chase Econometric Associates, Business International, the Economist Intelligence Unit, and Wharton Economic Forecasting Associates—provide economic forecasts (some do industry forecasts as well) to which many multinationals subscribe. Other sources are various industry associations, which generally provide industry-specific forecasts to their members.

In addition, economists and marketers use certain economic indicators that they have found predict trends in their industry. Pitney Bowes' Data Documents division, for example, uses changes in the growth of the U.S. GNP to predict the sales of its business forms because its sales have for years generally lagged changes in GNP growth by six months. We shall discuss the use of market indicators in Chapter 15, "Assessing and Analyzing Markets."

The purpose of economic analyses is first to appraise the overall outlook of the economy and then to assess the impact of economic changes on the firm. An examination of Figure 7.1 will illustrate how a change in just one factor in the economy can affect all the major functions of the company.

A forecast of an increase in employment would cause most marketing managers to revise their sales forecasts upward, which in turn would require production managers to augment production. This might be accomplished by adding another work shift, but if the plant is already operating 24 hours a day, new machinery will be needed. Either situation will require additional workers and raw materials, which will result in an extra workload for the personnel and purchasing managers. Should both the raw materials and labor markets be tight, the firm will probably have to pay prices and wage rates that are higher than normal. The financial manager may then have to negotiate with the banks for a loan to enable the firm to handle the greater cash outflow until additional revenue is received from increased sales.

[Figure 7.1] Impact of Economic Forecast on Firm's Functional Areas

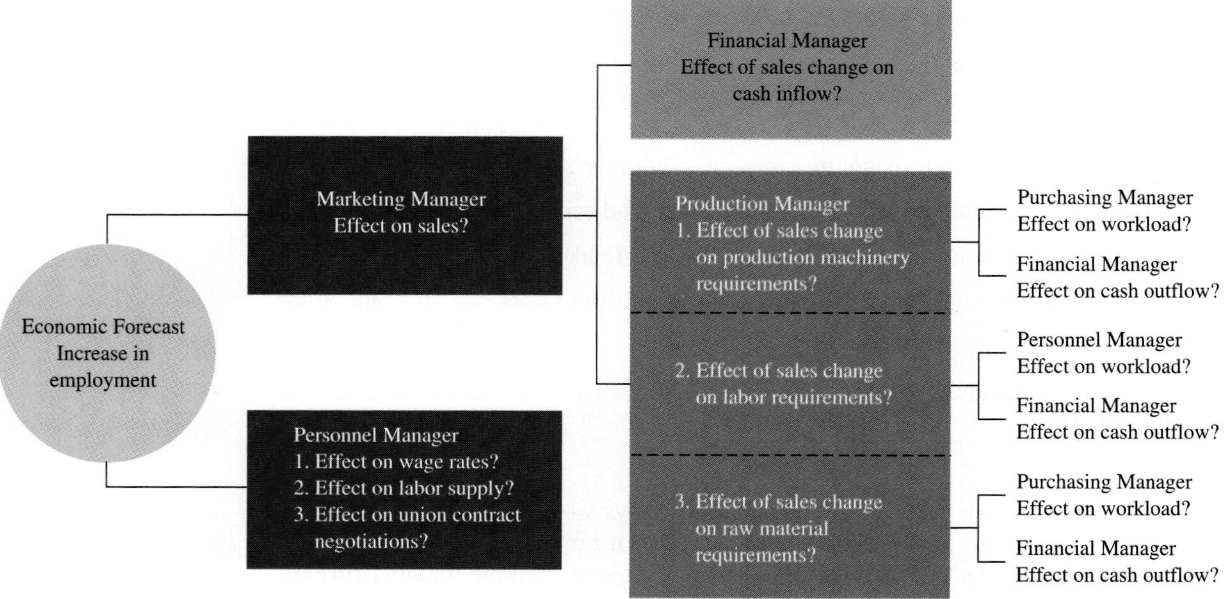

Note that all of this occurs because of a change in only one factor. Actually, of course, many economic factors are involved, and their relationships are complex. The object of an economic analysis is to isolate and assess the impact of those factors believed to affect the firm's operations.

International Economic Analyses

When a firm enters overseas markets, economic analyses become more complex because now managers must operate in two new environments: foreign and international. In the foreign environment, not only are there many economies instead of one, they are also highly divergent. Because of these differences, policies designed for economic conditions in one market may be totally unsuitable for economic conditions in another market. For example, headquarters may have a policy requiring its subsidiaries to maintain the lowest inventories possible, and the chief financial officer may decree that they make only foreign currency–denominated loans because of more favorable interest rates. For nations whose annual inflation rates are low (0 to 15 percent), these policies usually work well. But what about for countries such as Georgia, with a 1995 inflation rate of 2,280 percent, and Brazil, with 965 percent? The last thing headquarters wants is for the subsidiaries in these countries to have cash or foreign currency–denominated loans, and so the policy for markets with high inflation rates will be just the reverse of what it is for countries with low inflation rates (see Table 7.1).

Besides monitoring the foreign environments, analysts must keep abreast of the actions taken by components of the international environment, such as regional groupings [European Union (EU), North American Free Trade Agreement (NAFTA)] and international organizations [United Nations (UN), IMF, World Bank]. American firms are very attentive to the EU's progress in reaching its goals and to the impact this will have on EU–U.S. trade relations. They are also following closely the UN's progress in developing world pollution standards, health standards, and so forth. Any of these actions can seriously affect firms.[1]

International economic analyses should provide economic data on both actual and prospective markets. Also, as part of the competitive forces assessment, many companies monitor the economic conditions of nations where their major competitors are lo-

Table 7.1 **Annual Rates of Inflation for Selected Countries**

Country	1995	1999
Georgia	2,280%	19%
Turkmenistan	1,167	30
Ukraine	1,041	20
Brazil	965	5
Angola	775	270
Russian Federation	517	86
Zambia	108	27
Nicaragua	98	12
Peru	62	5
Uruguay	56	4

Source: *World Development Indicators 1997* (Washington, DC: World Bank, 1997), pp. 206–08; and www.cia.gov/publications/factbook/docs/guide.html, various country pages.

cated, because changing conditions may strengthen or weaken their competitors' ability to compete in world markets.

Because of the importance of economic information to the control and planning functions at headquarters, the collection of data and the preparation of reports must be the responsibility of the home office. However, foreign-based personnel (subsidiaries and field representatives) will be expected to contribute heavily to studies concerning their markets. Data from areas where the firm has no local representation can usually be somewhat less detailed and are generally available in publications from national and international agencies.[2] The reports from central or international banks are especially good sources for economic information on single countries. Other possible sources are the American chambers of commerce located in most of the world's capitals, the commercial officers in U.S. embassies, the United Nations, the World Bank, the International Monetary Fund, and the Organization for Economic Cooperation and Development.[3]

Dimensions of the Economy and Their Relevance for Businesspeople

To estimate market potentials as well as to provide input to the other functional areas of the firm, managers require data on the sizes and the rates of change of a number of economic and socioeconomic factors. For an area to be a potential market, it must have sufficient people with the means to buy a firm's products. Socioeconomic data provide information on the number of people, and the economic dimensions tell us if they have purchasing power.

Economic Dimensions

Among the more important economic indicators are gross national product (GNP), distribution of income, private consumption expenditures, personal ownership of goods, private investment, unit labor costs, exchange rates, inflation rates, and interest rates.

GNP. Gross national product, the total of all final goods and services produced, and gross domestic product (GNP less net foreign factor incomes) are the values used to measure an economy's size. GNPs range from $8.0 trillion for the United States to $44 million for São Tomé and Príncipe (in the Gulf of Guinea off the coast of Gabon).[4] What is the relevance of GNP for the international businessperson? Is India, with a GNP of $421 billion, a more attractive market than Denmark, with $176 billion?

Imagine the reaction of managers who receive a (fictional) report containing Figure 7.2, which shows a high *real* growth rate of **gross domestic product (GDP)** projected for Asia, at an annual rate of 6 percent. They will want to examine the data for

gross domestic product (GDP)
The total value of all goods and services produced domestically, not including (unlike GNP) net factor income from abroad

[Figure 7.2] Five-Year Projected Growth in GDP (Cumulative Percentage Change 2000–2005)*

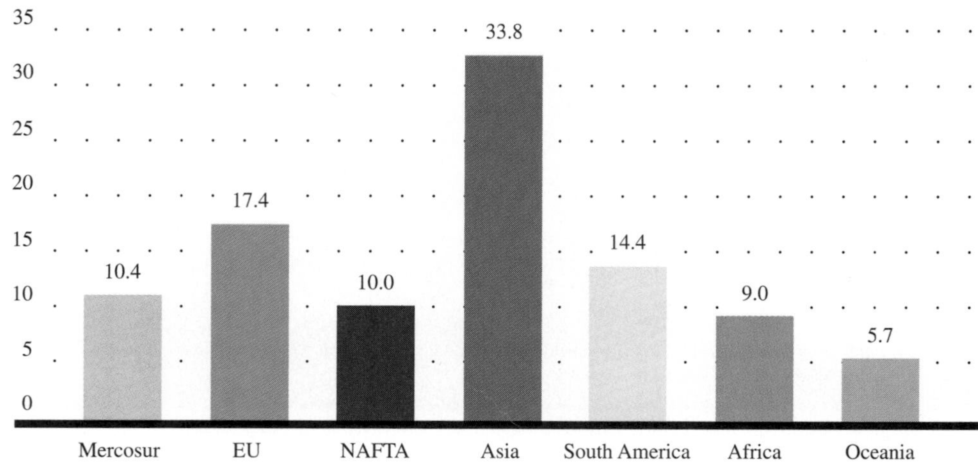

*EU—European Union; NAFTA—North American Free Trade Agreement. Figure 7.2 serves only as an example.

individual countries in the area and compare growth rates with their subsidiaries' growth rate. The data might indicate that some markets where they have no operations need to be investigated. Of course, this is only the initial step. To compare the purchasing power of nations, managers also need to know among how many people this increase in GNP or GDP is divided.

GNP/Capita and GDP/Capita. The not altogether satisfactory method of employing GNP/capita or GDP/capita to compare purchasing power reveals that Denmark is far richer than India, with a GDP/capita of $33,260 versus $430. In other words, although India's pie is over twice as big as Denmark's, there are 180 times as many people to eat it. However, as you saw in the opening section of this chapter, an economist will use purchasing power parity (PPP) to obtain the exchange rate that equates the purchasing power of the two currencies. In this case, Denmark's GDP/capita based on PPP is worth $23,800 and India's is worth $1,700.

What can we learn from GNP/capita? As we saw in Chapter 3, we can generally assume that the higher its value, the more advanced the economy. Generally, however, the rate of growth is more important to marketers because a high growth rate indicates a fast-growing market—for which they are always searching. Frequently, given the choice between investing in a nation with a higher GNP/capita but a low growth rate and a nation in which the conditions are reversed, management will choose the latter.

Although differences in GNP/capita do tell us something about the relative wealth of a nation's inhabitants, the information is somewhat misleading because few of them have the equal share indicated by an arithmetic mean. This first crude estimate of purchasing power must be refined by incorporating data on how national income is actually distributed.

income distribution
A measure of how a nation's income is apportioned among its people, commonly reported as the percentage of income received by population quintiles

Income Distribution. Data on **income distribution** are gathered by the World Bank from a number of sources and published yearly in the *World Development Indicators.* Note that the data in Table 7.2 refer to the distribution of either income or consumption expenditures. The footnotes to the table indicate whether the data are ranked by per capita expenditure, per capita income, or household income. World Bank economists prefer consumption expenditures as indicators of living standards, as they are more evenly distributed than are incomes.[5]

Table 7.2 Percentage Share of Income or Consumption

Country	Lowest 20 Percent	20–40 Percent	40–60 Percent	60–80 Percent	Highest 20 Percent	Highest 10 Percent
Australia (94)	5.9%	12%	17.2%	23.6%	41.3%	25.4%
Brazil (96)*	2.5	5.5	10.0	18.3	63.8	47.6
Bulgaria (95)*	8.5	13.8	17.9	22.7	37.0	22.5
Canada (94)	7.5	12.9	17.2	23.0	39.3	23.8
Chile (94)*	3.5	6.6	10.9	18.1	61.0	46.1
China (98)*	5.9	10.2	15.1	22.2	46.6	30.4
Colombia (96)	3.0	6.6	11.1	18.4	60.9	46.1
Costa Rica (96)*	4.0	8.8	13.7	21.7	51.8	34.7
Czech Rep. (96)*	10.3	14.5	17.7	21.7	35.9	22.4
Ecuador (95)†	5.4	9.4	14.2	21.3	49.7	33.8
France (95)	7.2	12.6	17.2	22.8	40.2	25.1
Germany (94)	8.2	13.2	17.5	22.7	38.5	23.7
Ghana (97)†	8.4	12.2	15.8	21.9	41.7	26.1
Hungary (96)†	8.8	12.5	16.6	22.3	39.9	24.8
India (97)†	8.1	11.6	15.0	19.3	46.1	33.5
Indonesia (96)	8.0	11.3	15.1	20.8	44.9	30.3
Israel (92)	6.9	11.4	16.3	22.9	42.5	26.9
Italy (95)	8.7	14.0	18.1	22.9	36.3	21.8
Jamaica (96)†	7.0	11.5	15.8	21.8	43.9	28.9
Japan (93)	10.6	14.2	17.6	22.0	35.7	21.7
Kazakhstan (96)†	6.7	11.5	16.4	23.1	42.3	26.3
Latvia (98)	7.6	12.9	17.1	22.1	40.3	25.9
Malaysia (95)*	4.5	8.3	13.0	20.4	53.8	37.9
Mexico (95)*	3.6	7.2	11.8	19.2	58.2	42.8
Morocco (98–99)†	6.5	10.6	14.8	21.3	46.6	30.9
Netherlands (94)	7.3	12.7	17.2	22.8	40.1	25.1
Norway (95)	9.7	14.3	17.9	22.2	35.8	21.8
Pakistan (96–97)†	9.5	12.9	16.0	20.5	41.1	27.6
Peru (96)†	4.4	9.1	14.1	21.3	51.2	35.4
Philippines (97)†	5.4	8.8	13.2	20.3	52.3	36.6
Poland (96)	7.7	12.6	16.7	22.1	40.9	26.3
Russian Fed. (98)†	4.4	8.6	13.3	20.1	53.7	38.7
Senegal (95)†	6.4	10.3	14.5	20.6	48.2	33.5
Slovenia (95)*	8.4	14.3	18.5	23.4	35.4	20.7
Sri Lanka (95)†	8.0	11.8	15.8	21.5	42.8	28.0
United Kingdom (91)	6.6	11.5	16.3	22.7	43.0	27.3
United States (97)	5.2	10.5	15.6	22.4	46.4	30.5
Venezuela (96)*	3.7	8.4	13.6	21.2	53.1	37.0
Vietnam (98)	8.0	11.4	15.2	20.9	44.5	29.9
Zimbabwe (91) †	4.0	6.3	10.0	17.4	62.3	46.9

Note: Numbers in parentheses indicate year of study.

No superscript: Data refer to household income and percentiles of households.

*Data refer to per capita income and percentiles of population.

†Data refer to per capita expenditure and percentiles of population.

Source: *World Development Indicators 2000* (Washington, DC: World Bank, 2000), Table 2.8, pp. 66–68. Republished with permission of World Bank. Permission conveyed through Copyright Clearance Center, Inc.

Despite the difficulties associated with income distribution studies, such as inconsistent measuring practices and wide variations in the representativeness of samples, the data provide some useful insights for businesspeople:

1. They confirm the belief that, generally, income is more evenly distributed in the advanced nations, although there are important variations among both developed and developing nations.
2. From comparisons over time (not shown), it appears that income redistribution proceeds very slowly, so that older data are still useful.

3. The same comparisons indicate that income inequality increases in the early stages of development, with a reversal of this tendency in the later stages. This is true for both developed and developing nations. For example, China's income inequality grew in urban areas by over 42 percent during the period 1988–1995, while the overall economy was booming.[6] The fact that the middle quintiles are growing at the expense of the top and bottom 20 percent signifies an increase in middle-income families, which are especially significant to marketers.

Contingent on the type of product and the total population, either situation (relatively even or uneven income distribution) may represent a viable market segment. For example, although Costa Rica's GNP is $9.8 billion, the fact that just 20 percent of the population receives over 50 percent of that income (10 percent gets 34.7 percent) indicates that there is a sizable group of people who are potential customers for low-volume, high-priced luxury products. On the other hand, the market is rather small (4 million population) for low-priced goods requiring a high sales volume.

This simple calculation based on GNP, total population, and income distribution may be all that is required to indicate that a particular country is not a good market; however, if the results look promising, the analyst will proceed to gather data on private consumption.

Private Consumption. One area of interest to marketers is the manner in which consumers allocate their disposable income (after-tax personal income) between purchases of essential and nonessential goods. Manufacturers of household durables, for instance, will want to know the amounts spent in that category, whereas producers of nonessentials will be interested in the magnitude of **discretionary income** (disposable income less essential purchases), for this is the money available to be spent on their products. Fortunately, disposable incomes and the amounts spent on essential purchases are available from the *UN Statistical Yearbook,* and discretionary income may be obtained by subtracting the total of these items from disposable income. More detailed expenditure patterns can be found in the *World Development Indicators* published by the World Bank. Data from that publication are reproduced in Table 7.3, which ranks the 10 largest and the 10 smallest economies according to private consumption expenditures using PPP equivalents.

discretionary income
The amount of income left after paying taxes and making essential purchases

This table also gives you the opportunity to compare GNP/capita in U.S. dollars converted from the local currency using market exchange rates with GNP/capita in what the World Bank calls "international dollars," which are based on estimates of the relative purchasing power of the different currencies. Note that the GNP values measured in international dollars tend to be higher for developing countries than are those converted from national currencies using market-based exchange rates (their currencies are undervalued), while seven of the currencies of the 10 developed nations appear to be overvalued compared to the international dollar.

Because PPP-based consumer expenditures eliminate differences in relative prices, marketers use these data to analyze how the composition of consumption changes with the level of development. For example, the percentages of household expenditures spent on food and clothing by residents of developing nations are double the percentages consumers in industrialized nations spend. On the other hand, the percentages spent on (1) transport and communication, (2) consumer durables, (3) health care, and (4) other consumption (beverages, tobacco, and services, including meals eaten in restaurants or taken out) by households of developed nations are twice the percentages of those in developing nations.

Note that the percentage differences within a consumption category do not vary with the consumption expenditures per capita. An example is clothing and footwear. Interestingly, in spite of the fame of French haute-couture, the percentage spent on clothing in France is less than half that spent by the residents of Hong Kong and only 78 percent of U.S. expenditures. International businesspeople know better than to underestimate the importance of small percentage differences among nations. They are

Table 7.3 Private Consumption Based on Purchasing Power Parity

Country	GNP/Capita Based on Exchange Rates 1998 (US$)	GNP/Capita Based on PPP 1998 (US$)	Private Consumption Expenditures/ Capita 1998 (US$)	Percentage of Household Consumption: Food	Clothing and Footwear	Education	Health Care	Transport and Communication	Other Consumption
1. United States	$29,340	$29,340	$21,515	13%	9%	6%	4%	8%	60%
2. Denmark	33,260	23,830	16,385	16	6	17	3	5	53
3. Canada	20,020	24,050	15,643	14	5	21	4	9	47
4. Belgium	25,380	23,480	15,591	17	6	1	3	7	66
5. Germany	25,850	20,810	15,577	14	6	10	2	7	61
6. Switzerland	40,080	26,620	15,536	19	6	18	3	8	46
7. France	24,940	22,320	14,115	22	7	8	3	12	48
8. Austria	26,850	22,740	13,886	20	10	9	4	9	48
9. Japan	32,380	23,180	13,568	12	7	22	2	13	44
10. Hong Kong	23,670	22,000	12,648	10	17	8	2	6	57
105. Yemen, Rep.	300	740	768	25	5	5	3	5	57
106. Kenya	330	1,130	677	31	9	8	2	3	47
107. Tajikistan	350	. . .	660	48	7	14	0	5	26
108. Madagascar	260	900	608	61	8	2	2	5	22
109. Zambia	330	860	481	52	10	11	2	3	22
110. Malawi	200	730	469	50	13	6	2	9	20
111. Mali	250	720	452	53	15	5	4	2	21
112. Nigeria	300	820	448	51	5	8	2	2	22
113. Sierra Leone	140	390	404	47	9	13	3	8	20
114. Tanzania	210	490	375	67	6	12	4	6	5

Source: "Structure of Consumption in PPP Terms," *World Development Indicators 2000*, pp. 222–23; and *World Development Report 1999–2000*, pp. 230, 231.

aware that each percentage point is worth a large sum of money. To appreciate its value, try multiplying the total per capita consumption expenditure by 1 percent of the population. If American consumers had spent 1 percent more on clothing in 1993, for example, this would have amounted to $21,515 × 0.01 × 275.6 million, or $59.3 billion greater sales for the clothing industry.

Other indicators that add to our knowledge of personal consumption are those concerned with (1) the ownership of goods and (2) the consumption of key materials. For example, commercial energy use per capita is related to the size of the modern sectors—*urban areas, industry,* and *motorized transport.* The World Bank has found that "people in high-income economies use nearly seven times as much commercial energy as do people in developing economies," and the quantity and mix of energy constitute a rough indicator of a country's level of development.[7] As Table 7.4 illustrates, the more industrialized nations have considerably higher values for these indicators than do the developing nations. See the Worldview for an Asian Development Bank expert's opinion about the most significant indicator.

Gross Domestic Investment. The amount of private investment (the part of national income allocated to increasing a nation's productive capacity) is another factor that contributes to the analysis of market size and growth. New investment brings about increases in GNP and the level of employment, which are signals of a growing market. A history of continual investment growth signifies, furthermore, that a propitious investment climate exists; that is, there are numerous profitable investment opportunities, and the government enjoys the confidence of the business community.

Table 7.5 shows how the slow recovery from the worldwide recession affected the growth of investment. In the original table from which Table 7.5 was derived,

Table 7.4 Per Capita Ownership or Consumption of Key Goods and Services for Selected Countries

Country	1998 Motor Vehicles/ 1,000 Population*	1998 Telephone Mainlines/ 1,000 Population	1998 Mobile Phones/ 1,000 Population	1998 TV Sets/ 1,000 Population	1998 Personal Computers/ 1,000 Population	1997 Commercial Energy Use (kg of oil equiv/capital)	2000 Internet Hosts/ 10,000 People
Europe							
Switzerland	516	675	235	535	421.8	3,629	429.0
Germany	522	567	170	580	304.7	4,128	207.6
France	530	570	188	601	207.8	4,042	131.5
Sweden	468	674	464	531	361.4	5,723	670.8
United Kingdom	439	557	252	645	263.0	3,772	321.4
Italy	591	451	355	486	173.4	2,707	114.4
Middle East							
Israel	264	471	359	318	217.2	2,717	225.1
Kuwait	462	236	138	491	104.9	8,622	20.5
Saudi Arabia	166	143	31	262	49.6	4,566	1.3
Egypt	30	60	1	122	9.1	600	0.73
Africa							
Mauritius	92	214	53	226	87.1	387	4.56*
South Africa	n.a.	115	56	125	47.4	2,146	39.2
Cameroon	12	5	0	32	n.a.	103	0
Ghana	7	8	1	99	1.6	93	0.06
Ethiopia	2	3	0	5	n.a.	22	0.01
Asia							
Japan	560	503	374	707	237.2	3,856	208.1
Korea, Republic	226	433	302	346	156.8	2,982	60.0
China	8	70	19	272	8.9	664	0.6
India	7	22	1	69	2.7	248	0.23
Bangladesh	1	3	1	6	n.a.	197	0
South America							
Uruguay	169	250	60	241	91.2	622	76.1
Chile	110	205	65	232	48.2	1,012	26.4
Brazil	77	121	47	316	30.1	1,051	26.2
Colombia	40	173	49	217	27.9	622	9.6
Bolivia	52	69	27	116	7.5	373	1.1
Eastern Europe							
Hungary	268	336	105	437	58.9	2,383	113.4
Czech Republic	402	364	94	447	97.3	3,868	109.8
Poland	273	228	50	413	43.9	2,401	47.3
Russian Federation	154	197	5	420	40.6	4,014	14.7
Kazakhstan	82	104	2	231	n.a.	3,371	2.5
North America and Caribbean							
United States	767	661	256	847	458.6	7,819	1,940
Canada	560	634	176	715	330.0	7,854	540.2
Trinidad and Tobago	108	206	20	334	46.8	5,436	28.2[†]
Mexico	144	104	35	261	47.0	1,561	40.9
Haiti	7	8	0	5	n.a.	29	0

n.a. = not available.

*Includes cars and trucks but excludes buses.

[†]1999 data

Source: *World Development Indicators 2000, 2001,* pp. 106–08, 138–40, 158–60, 178–80, 284–86, 296–98, 300–02, 310–11.

60 percent of the 100 nations for which there are data experienced positive investment growth in the period 1990–95 compared to 67 percent in the period 1980–90. Interestingly, the three income levels had different percentages of nations with positive growth rates: middle-income nations led with 74 percent, low-income nations followed with 54 percent, and then came high-income nations with only 42 percent.

Table 7.5 Average Annual Growth Rate of Consumption and Investment for Selected Countries (Percent)

	Government Consumption*		Private Consumption		Gross Domestic Investment†	
Country	1980–90	1990–98	1980–90	1990–98	1980–90	1990–98
Low-income countries						
Cote d'Ivoire	−0.1%	1.7%	1.5%	1.0%	−9.8%	17.7%
Burundi	3.2	−3.9	3.4	−1.8	6.9	−16.1
India	7.7	9.2	4.6	5.8	6.5	7.3
Chad	14.5	−3.2	5.3	1.4	n.a.	3.8
Lower-middle-income countries						
Philippines	0.6	3.4	2.6	3.7	−2.1	4.5
Gabon	0.6	7.3	1.5	−1.6	−5.7	4.3
Chile	0.4	3.5	2.0	8.7	6.4	13.5
Thailand	4.2	5.7	5.9	4.7	9.5	2.0
Upper-middle-income countries						
Uruguay	1.8	2.15	0.5	5.9	−7.8	9.9
Mexico	2.4	1.3	1.1	1.6	−3.3	−3.1
Brazil	7.3	−1.4	1.6	4.8	0.2	3.9
Malaysia	2.7	6.2	3.7	5.0	2.6	9.5
Industrial market economies						
United Kingdom	1.1	1.2	4.1	2.0	6.4	1.8
Japan	2.4	2.3	3.7	1.9	5.3	1.1
United States	2.8	0.0	3.4	3.0	2.9	7.0
Switzerland	3.1	0.8	1.6	0.5	4.0	−0.4

*Included all levels of government and defense spending.
†Includes changes in inventory levels.
n.a. = not available.
Source: Adapted from *World Development Indicators 2000* (Washington, DC: World Bank, 2000), pp. 218–20.

For 1980–90, the ranking was reversed (high income 100 percent, low income 67 percent, middle income 28 percent). Check Ivory Coast's 1990–98 increase.

Private and Government Consumption. Market analysts must have been pleased to learn that growth in private spending increased in 84 of the 106 nations in the original World Bank table (79 percent), with only 22 nations experiencing a reduction in average percentage growth. Pleasant for both taxpayers and industry was the continuing trend of governments to reduce spending: 63 percent of the governments reduced their growth rate of spending from the 1980–90 levels in 1990–95. The former communist nations were especially active in making large reductions.

Unit Labor Costs. One factor that contributes to a favorable investment opportunity is the ability to obtain **unit labor costs** (total direct labor costs/units produced) lower than those currently available to the firm. Foreign trends in these costs are closely monitored because each country experiences a different rate of increase.

unit labor costs
Total direct labor costs divided by units produced

Countries with slower-rising unit labor costs attract management's attention for two reasons. First, they are investment prospects for companies striving to lower production costs, as discussed in Chapter 2; second, they may become sources of new competition in world markets if other firms in the same industry are already located there.

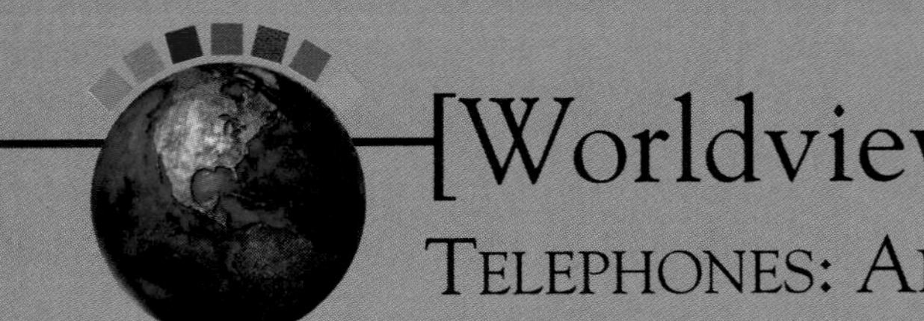

[Worldview]

TELEPHONES: AN ECONOMIC INDICATOR?

What is the best gauge for measuring a country's level of development? Is it (1) per capita income, (2) state of the construction industry, (3) density of pollution, or (4) number of telephones? If you selected number four, you are right, according to the International Telecommunications Union (ITU), a specialized agency of the United Nations. The ITU published an article in which the author claimed that the total number of telephone lines installed in a country is often a better indicator of a nation's level of development than is even per capita income.

Generally, the wealthier a country is, the more telephone lines it has. In 1998, the richest countries had more than one phone line for every two people. The increase in mobile phone use has also been extremely rapid in rich countries: Since 1995, the mobile phone ratio rose from 84 per 1,000 people to 265 per 1,000 people, an increase of some 315 percent in only three years.

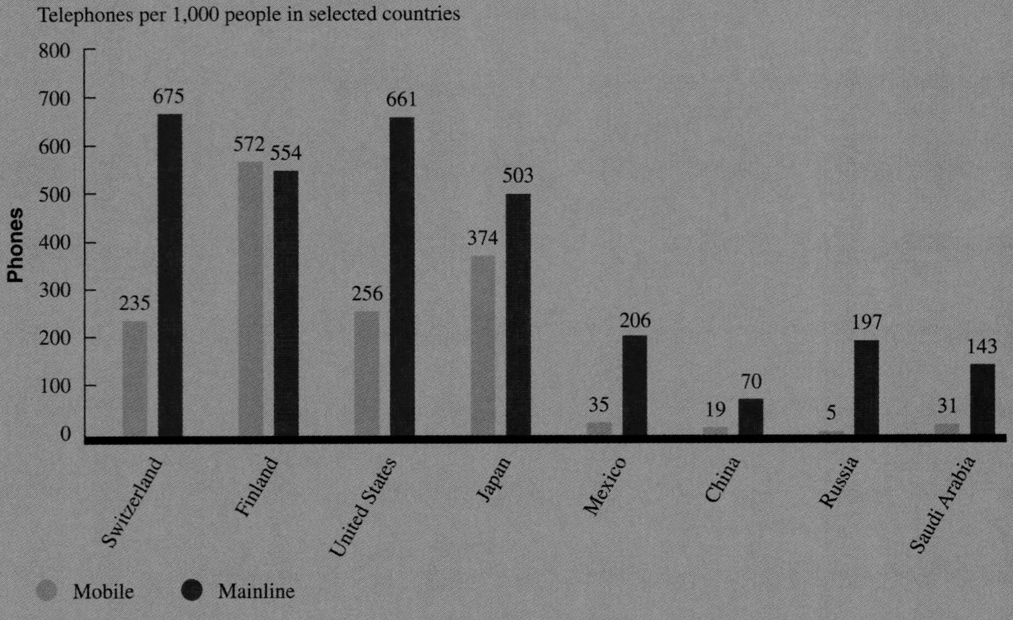

Changes in wage rates may also cause a multinational firm that obtains products or components from a number of subsidiaries to change its sources of supply.

> Nike, which produces none of the shoes it sells in the United States, began using Japanese plants in 1964. When labor costs rose there in the mid-1970s, the company changed to factories in South Korea and Taiwan. Later, Nike added Thailand, and by 1989 that country was the company's second-largest source of production. But as labor costs rose in those countries, Nike began buying in over 50 Indonesian factories and in China, which now account for two-thirds of its production requirements. Alarmed because its $75 to $100 (retail) shoes are costing as much as $10 to produce and ship to the United States, Nike contracted for production in Vietnam and now depends primarily on China and Vietnam for shoes.[8]

What are the reasons for the relative changes in labor costs? Three factors are responsible: (1) compensation, (2) productivity, and (3) exchange rates. Hourly compensation tends to vary more widely than wages because of the appreciable differences in the size of fringe benefits. Unit labor costs will not rise in unison with compensation rates if the gains in productivity outstrip the increases in hourly compensation. In fact, if productivity increases fast enough, the unit costs of labor will decrease even though the firm is required to pay more to the workers.

In fact, mobile phone use has increased across countries at all income levels. In Cambodia and Sri Lanka, for example, the number of cell phones per 1,000 people was already greater than that for mainlines by the late 1990s. As the figure shows, this was also the case for Finland. For poor countries, in some cases it is faster and less expensive to add cell phone networks than to put in a mainline infrastructure.

Telephone mainlines per 1,000 people	
World	146
Low income (GNP/capita $765 or less)	37
Middle income (GNP/capita $766–$9,385)	145
High income (GNP/capita $9,386 or more)	567

Mobile Telephones per 1,000 people	
World	55
Low income (GNP/capita $765 or less)	8
Middle income (GNP/capita $766–$9,385)	39
High income (GNP/capita $9,386 or more)	265

Arab man in Yemen using a radio phone.
Gary John Norman/Tony Stone Images

In contrast to the average 567 telephone lines per 1,000 people in the high-income developed nations, World Bank statistics show that in sub-Saharan Africa the telephone density is 14 lines per 1,000 compared to 19 in South Asia, 81 in the Middle East and North Africa, and 123 in Latin America. In countries such as Chad, there is just one telephone per 1,000 persons.

It is evident that most developing nations therefore have a serious communications problem. For example, the World Bank reports that in Pakistan the telephone density is 19 per 1,000 persons. But in rural areas the situation is much worse, with as little as one telephone per 1,000 persons. In fact, out of Pakistan's 45,000 villages, only about 1,900 have access to telephone service. One reason for this is that fewer than 15,000 villages have electricity.

In spite of difficulties such as these, the demand for phone service continues unabated. In India, for example, you need to get on a waiting list of 2,706, and in Russia, 7,120,000 people are ahead of you! ■

Source: *World Development Indicators 2000*, pp. 296–98, 300–02.

Table 7.6 reveals why international firms' managements keep a close watch on labor compensation rates around the world.[9] For example, in 1975 Sweden had the highest hourly rate, with the United States and Germany tied for fifth place. Note that Japan's average hourly rate was less than half the American rate. However, by 1985, the U.S. rate was the world's highest and American managers were searching for overseas production sites. Yet just ten years later, the United States had fallen to thirteenth place in the hourly compensation cost ranking. Every European nation but the United Kingdom and Spain had higher costs. In 1995, American costs were still in eleventh place but there was one important change in the rankings: Japan's labor compensation rate, which was less than half of the U.S. rate in 1985, had jumped to 138% of the U.S. compensation rate. By that point many Japanese firms had moved significant parts of their production to other Asian countries with lower labor costs, such as Thailand, China, and Indonesia. (This movement abroad was also influenced by the retirement of many skilled machinists and other artisans in Japan, which made foreign labor more attractive). See Figure 7.3 for a graphical presentation.

If you wish to prepare a table of average wage costs for countries not included in Table 7.6, you will find a method for doing so in endnote 9 of this chapter.

Table 7.6 Labor Compensation Costs, 1975–1999*

	Average Hourly Rate Including Fringe Benefits (US$ and local currencies)								Relative Index (US = 100)	
	1999		1995		1985		1975			
Country	US$	Local	US$	Local	US$	Local	US$	Local	1999	1975
Germany[†]	$26.93	49.44	$31.85	45.61	$9.60	28.23	$6.35	15.59	140	100
Norway	23.91	186.67	24.38	154.46	10.37	89.11	6.77	35.29	125	106
Switzerland	23.56	35.45	29.30	34.61	9.66	23.71	6.09	15.72	123	96
Denmark	22.96	160.49	24.26	135.86	8.13	86.18	6.28	36.00	120	99
Belgium	22.82	864.11	26.88	792.10	8.97	532.39	6.41	235.10	119	101
Austria	21.83	281.99	25.38	255.87	7.58	156.75	4.51	78.46	114	71
Sweden	21.58	178.52	21.64	154.51	9.66	83.12	7.18	29.73	112	113
Finland	21.10	117.75	24.83	108.64	8.16	50.56	4.61	16.88	110	72
Netherlands	20.94	43.32	24.18	38.79	8.75	29.04	6.58	16.59	109	103
Japan	20.89	2,375.00	23.66	2,223.00	6.34	1,512.00	3.00	889.00	109	47
United States	19.20	19.20	17.19	17.19	13.01	13.01	6.36	6.36	100	100
France	17.98	110.71	19.34	96.45	7.52	67.49	4.52	19.34	94	71
Italy	16.60	30,170	16.52	26,911.00	7.63	14,563.00	4.67	3,048.00	86	73
United Kingdom	16.56	10.24	13.73	8.70	6.27	4.84	3.37	1.52	86	53
Canada	15.60	23.17	16.04	22.02	10.94	14.94	5.96	6.07	81	94
Spain	12.11	1,891	12.70	1,582.00	4.66	792.00	2.53	145.00	63	40
Taiwan	5.62	181.69	5.82	154.26	1.50	59.60	0.40	15.17	29	6
Hong Kong	5.44	42.20	4.82	37.30	1.73	13.46	0.76	3.73	28	12
Mexico	2.12	20.24	1.51	9.66	1.59	409.00	1.47	18.00	11	23

*Dollar conversions are at average annual exchange rates.
[†]Former West Germany.
Source: Bureau of Labor Statistics, http://stats.bls.gov/news.release/ichcc, various tables.

[Figure 7.3] **Comparison of Labor Costs for Selected Countries**

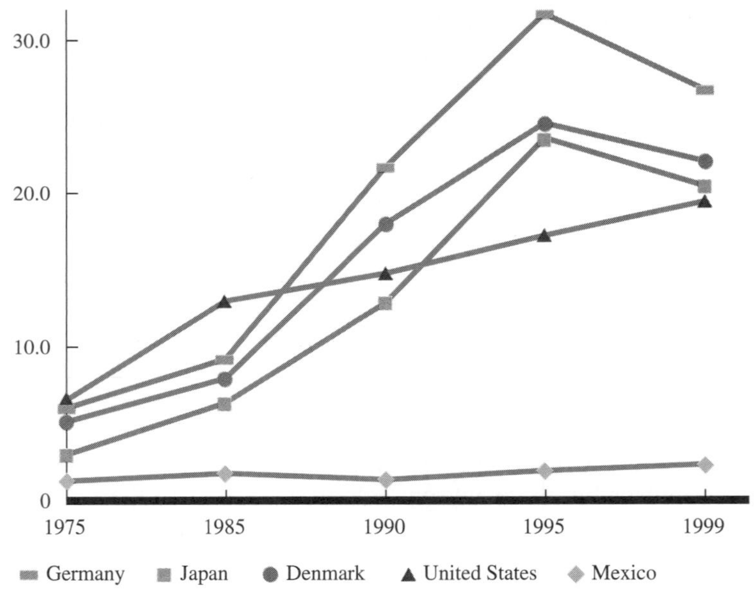

Other Economic Dimensions

[3] section

We have mentioned only a few of the many economic indicators that economists study, and you learned about the importance to businesspeople of interest rates, balances of payments, and inflation rates in Chapter 6, "Financial Forces." Which of the economic measures the analyst chooses to study will depend on the industry and the purpose of the study. Executives

Table 7.7 Major International Debtors

Country	Total External Debt ($ billion) 2000	1980	Change in Debt since 1980 (percent)
Brazil	$167.70	$71.50	234
Mexico	149.2	57.4	260
Argentina	136.8	27.2	503
Korea	131.2	47*	279
China	105.3	4.5	2,347
Russian Federation	84.1	5.9*	1,425
Indonesia	80.5	20.9	385
Turkey	69.6	19.1	364
India	56.9	20.6	276

*1990 data.
Sources: www.oecd.org/dac/debt/htm/data_index.htm, various country files; and *World Bank Indicators 1999.*

of an automobile manufacturer, for example, will want the economist's opinion as to where interest rates are headed and what is the rate of growth of a nation's GNP. GNP, as you saw earlier, is important to other producers of industrial products, such as Pitney Bowes.

The large international debts of a number of middle- and low-income nations are causing multiple problems not only for their governments but also for multinational firms. Just look at the situation of the countries with the highest debts that are listed in Table 7.7. Note that there are no high-income nations, including the United States, with international debt.

Is this a problem for international bankers only, or should it concern multinational managements as well? Is it significant to global and multidomestic firms with subsidiaries in these countries that high indebtedness indicators such as debt to GDP and debt service to exports are a cause for concern? The World Bank claims that an empirical analysis of developing countries' experience shows that "debt service difficulties become increasingly likely when the ratio of the present value of debt to exports reaches 200–250 percent and the debt service ratio exceeds 20–25 percent."[10] If management agrees, then it will expect periodic reports on this situation from its analysts. Let's examine the ramifications of these large foreign debts for an international firm.

If a large part of the foreign exchange a nation earns cannot be used to import components used in local products, then either local industries must manufacture them or the companies that import them must stop production. Either alternative can cause the multinational to lose sales if it has been selling the parts made in one of its home country plants to its subsidiary, a common occurrence because the home plant is usually more **vertically integrated** than its subsidiaries. A scarcity of foreign exchange can also make it difficult for the subsidiary to import raw materials and spare parts for its production equipment. If headquarters wants its affiliate to continue production, it may have to lend the foreign exchange and wait for repayment. Campbell Soup, Revlon, and Gerber closed their operations in Brazil because of this problem. Other multinationals have resorted to barter or have begun to export their subsidiaries' products even though these actions have reduced exports or even local sales of their domestic plants.

vertically integrated
Describes a firm that produces inputs for its subsequent manufacturing processes

Governments may impose price controls (which make it difficult for a subsidiary to earn a profit), cut government spending (which reduces company sales), and impose wage controls (which limit consumer purchasing power). The economic turmoil that follows can turn into a political crisis, as occurred in Venezuela and Peru when rioting resulted after their presidents tried to impose austerity measures. During the Asian financial crisis, South Korea experienced nationwide strikes in response to laws passed to ease that country's economic problems.[11]

An aspect of debt reduction that has interested some multinationals has been debt-for-equity swaps, which we discussed in Chapter 6. Argentina is one country that makes them. Foreigners have been able to buy Argentine dollar debt at a discount and convert it into Argentine currency at a rate closer to face value. They then invest the money in local firms. Campbell Soup took advantage of this situation to build a new meatpacking plant. The company purchased $60 million worth of Argentine foreign-debt paper in the world market at 17 percent of the par value. Argentina's central bank agreed to redeem the paper in Argentine currency at the equivalent of 30 cents on the dollar if the company used the money to build the plant. The debt-for-equity swap saved Campbell $8 million.[12] Grupo Visa, a Mexican conglomerate, reduced its foreign debt from $1.7 billion to $400 million with a private debt-for-equity swap. The company gave its foreign creditors a 40 percent share in the company in return for debt cancellation.[13]

Scarcity of foreign exchange can affect even firms that merely export to nations with high foreign debt because the governments will surely impose import restrictions. When Latin American debt increased rapidly from 1981 to 1983, that region's share of U.S. exports dropped by one-third. To protect these export markets, firms had to extend long-term credit. From this you can see that managements will expect to receive information on the status of the foreign debt in nations where it is high in addition to the other economic data we have been examining. This is especially important now that the same American banks that were involved in the Third World debt crisis in the 1980s are once again lending huge sums to developing nations.[14]

Socioeconomic Dimensions

A complete definition of market potential must also include detailed information about the population's physical attributes as measured by the socioeconomic dimensions. Just as we began with GNP in the study of purchasing power, we shall begin this section with an analysis of total population.

Total Population. Total population, the most general indicator of potential market size, is the first characteristic of the population that analysts examine. They readily discover that there are immense differences in population sizes, which range from more than a billion inhabitants in China and India to 7,000 each for Saint Pierre and Miquelon and Saint Helena. The fact that many developed nations have fewer than 10 million inhabitants makes it apparent that population size alone is a poor indicator of economic strength and market potential. Switzerland, for example, with only 7.0 million people, is far more important economically than Bangladesh, with 160 million. Clearly, more information is needed; only for a few low-priced, mass-consumed products, such as soft drinks, cigarettes, and soap, does population size alone provide a basis for estimating consumption.

For products not in this category, large populations and populations that are increasing rapidly may not signify an immediate enlargement of the market, but if incomes grow over time, eventually at least a part of the population will become customers. Insight into the rapidity with which this is occurring may be obtained by comparing population and GNP growth rates (see Table 2.10). Where GNP increases faster than the population, there is probably an expanding market, whereas the converse situation not only indicates possible market contraction but may even point out a country as a potential area of political unrest. This possibility is strengthened if an analysis of the educational system discloses an accruement of technical and university graduates. These groups expect to be employed as and receive the wages of professionals, and when enough new jobs are not being created to absorb them, the government can be in serious trouble. Various developing nations already face this difficulty: Egypt and India are two notable examples.[15]

Age Distribution. Because few products are purchased by everyone, marketers must identify the segments of the population that are more apt to buy their goods. For some firms, age is a salient determinant of market size, but unfortunately, the distribution of age groups within populations varies widely. Generally, because of higher birth and fertility rates, developing countries have more youthful populations than do industrial countries. Figure 7.4 illustrates the tremendous difference in age distribution between developed and developing

[Figure 7.4] Population by Age and Sex—1996 and 2020 (Millions)

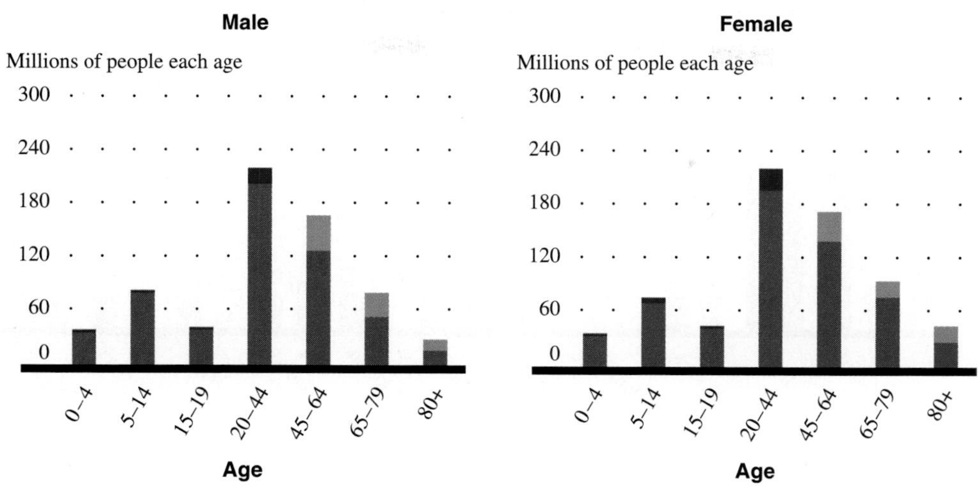

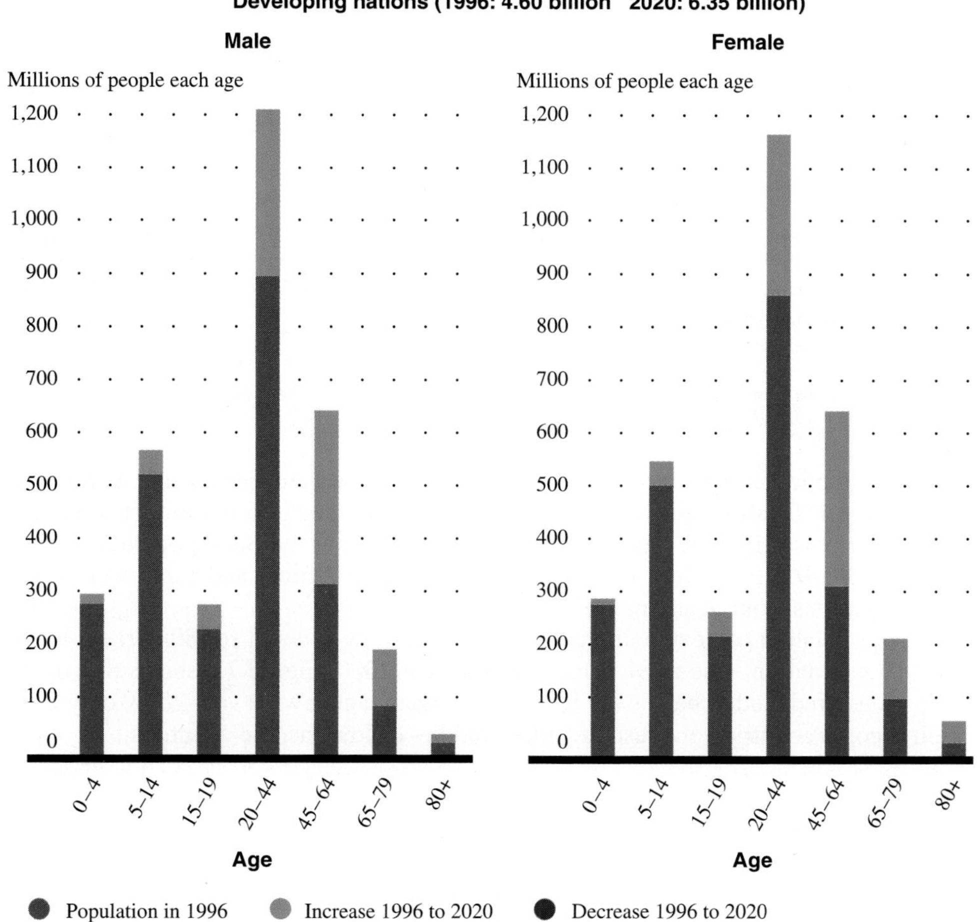

Population in 1996 · Increase 1996 to 2020 · Decrease 1996 to 2020

Source: Based on U.S. Bureau of Census projections, www.census.gov/ipc/pred/wp96/wp96a1.pdf (December 7, 1997).

[Figure 7.5] **Population Growth of Countries with Over 100 Million Inhabitants in the Year 2010 (Millions of Inhabitants)**

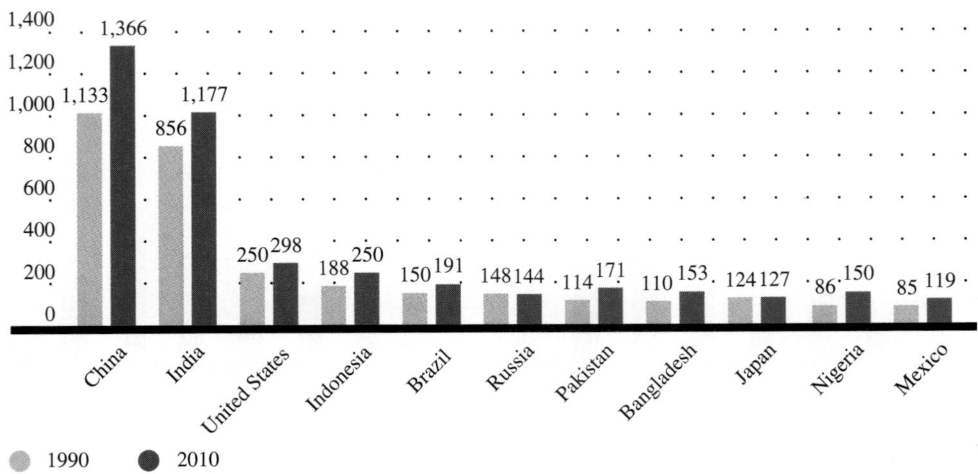

Source: "Table A-4: Population by Region and Country: 1950 to 2025," U.S. Census Bureau, *The Official Statistics,* March 1, 1999. pp. A6–A10.

countries, which is the result of much higher birthrates in the developing nations. According to the World Bank, past and estimated average annual population percentage increases for nations grouped according to income are as shown in the following table.

Average Annual Population Increases

	1970–80	1980–95	1998–2015
Low-income economies	2.2%	1.9%	1.3%
Middle-income economies	3.8	1.7	1.0
High-income economies	0.8	0.7	0.3

Source: *World Development Indicators 2000* (Washington, DC: World Bank, 2000), p. 40. Republished with permission of World Bank. Permission conveyed through Copyright Clearance Center, Inc.

This situation is far from static, however; birthrates are decreasing worldwide. Among the 146 nations for which the World Bank provided information, only 8 experienced increases in their crude (born alive) birthrates per thousand population in the period 1980–95. Five were low-income nations from Africa, and three were high-income nations from Scandinavia.[16]

The population of developing countries, which now account for 80 percent of the world's population, rose to 81 percent by the year 2000. Figure 7.5 shows that of the 10 nations predicted to have over 100 million inhabitants by the year 2010, only 2 are high-income countries; the rest are either middle- or low-income countries.[17]

What does this signify for businesspeople? In the developed nations, there will be a decrease in the demand for products used in schools and for products bought by and for children, a smaller market for furniture and clothing, but an increased demand for medical care and related products, tourism, and financial services. Firms confronted by a decreasing demand for their products will have to look for sales increases in the developing economies, where the age distribution is reversed. The high growth rates in the developing nations will provide markets for transportation systems, higher-yield food grains, fertilizers, agricultural tools, appliances, and so forth.

Whirlpool, concerned about the decline in the number of householders age 25 or less in the United States while noting the opportunities in overseas markets, acquired 53 percent of the Dutch electronics giant Philips' domestic appliance business in 1988. The acquisition enabled Whirlpool to become the world's largest major home appliance company, with manufacturing facilities in 11 countries and a distribution network covering 45 countries. In August 1991, Whirlpool bought the remaining 47 percent of the business from Philips.[18]

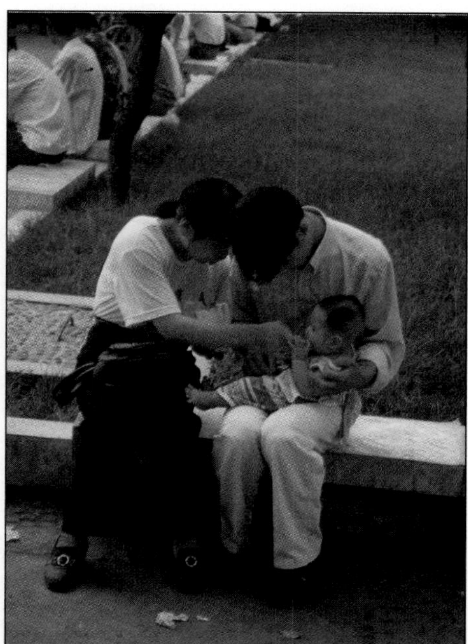
Couple feeds their baby in a park in Chengdu, China.
Paul Conklin/PhotoEdit

Many forces are responsible for reductions in birthrates. Governments are supporting family planning programs, to be sure, but there is ample evidence that improved levels of health and education along with an enhanced status for women, a more even distribution of income, and a greater degree of urbanization are all acting to reduce the traditional family size. Figure 7.6*a* and *b* illustrates the influence of female educational attainment and urbanization on the rate of contraceptive usage in some developing nations. In fact, experts have been claiming for some time that the combined effect of an effective family planning program and female education beyond the primary level is extremely powerful in reducing family size.[19]

Concern in Developed Nations. While this is welcomed in developing nations, such as those in Africa and the Middle East, where fertility rates are as high as eight children per woman, declining birthrates are causing concern in the governments of industrialized nations. The World Bank reports that the fertility rates in these countries are considerably below the *replacement number* of 2.1 children.* Only the United States and New Zealand have that rate.[20]

An increasing number of young Europeans are not marrying, and those who do are marrying later and having fewer children. By the year 2025 the present 11 percent unemployment rate in the European Union will be replaced by a shortage of workers. European governments will have to provide medical care and pensions for the 22 percent of their population that will be over 65 years old, and there will be fewer working taxpayers (see Figure 7.7).

Japan's situation seems to be even more serious. Its fertility rate is only 1.5 children per woman, well below the 2.1 population replacement value, and in the year 2025 Japan's population age 65 and older will make up 26.8 percent of its total population, whereas the same age group in the United States will amount to only 18.5 percent of the total population. As you can see in Table 7.6, the labor shortage has inflated wages to the point where the average manufacturing pay in Japan is $20.89 an hour compared to $19.20 in the United States.

By the year 2025 Japan, which is the fastest-graying nation in the industrial world, will have twice as many old people as it has children. The government's reserve of social security funds will have run dry because retirement and health costs for the elderly are forecast to consume 73 percent of national income. According to the Health and Welfare Ministry, the only solution is to levy significantly higher taxes and reduce benefits. An analysis by the advisory council to the prime minister concluded that if the current system is not changed, the "economy will collapse."[21]

Early retirements and the fact that retirees are living longer are also straining the social security systems of many other countries. In the industrialized nations, not only are the costs of social security systems rising because of the growing number of retirees, but there are fewer people working and paying into the system to support them. However, in developing nations, just the opposite is occurring. The higher birthrates result in a younger population, as shown in Figure 7.4, and this reduces the dependency ratios and the costs to the workers supporting the system. Figure 7.8 shows the dependency ratios for selected industrialized and developing nations.

population density
A measure of the number of inhabitants per area unit (inhabitants per square kilometer or square mile)

population distribution
A measure of how the inhabitants are distributed over a nation's area

Population Density and Distribution. Other aspects of population that concern management are **population density** and **population distribution.** Densely populated countries tend to make product distribution and communications simpler and less

*Number of children that will be born to a woman if she lives to the end of her childbearing years and bears children according to present age-specific fertility rates.

[Figure 7.6a] **Contraceptive Prevalence Rate for Selected Countries by Rural/Urban Residence: Mid-1990s**

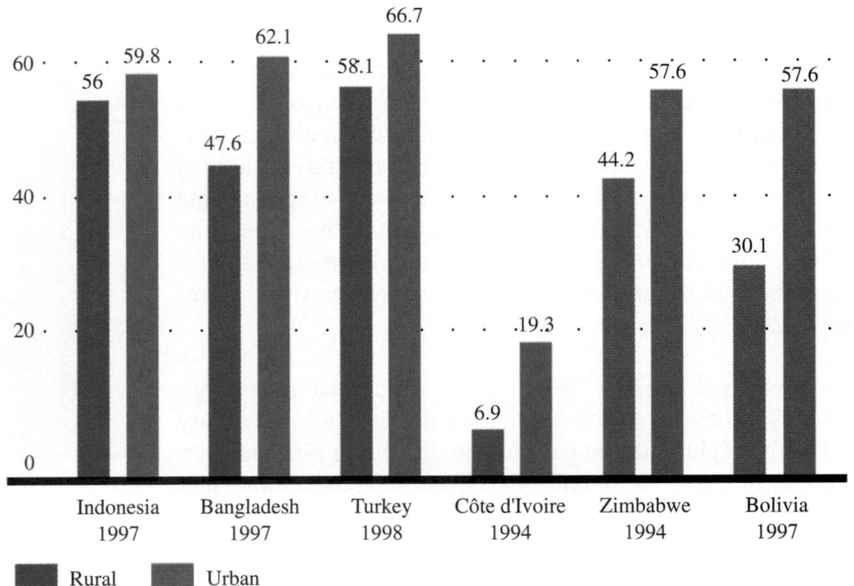

[Figure 7.6b] **Contraceptive Prevalence Rate for Selected Countries by Level of Education: Mid-1990s**

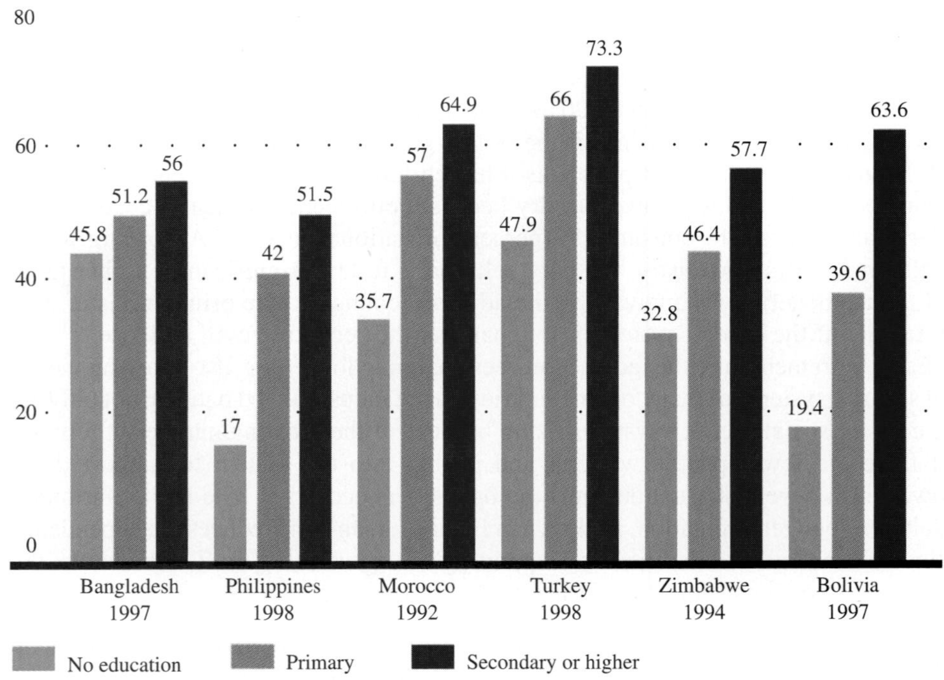

Source: "Current Use of Contraception by Background Characteristics: Custom Table," www.measuredhs.com/data/indicators (September 10, 2000).

[Figure 7.7] Percentages of Elderly (Over 65) in Population

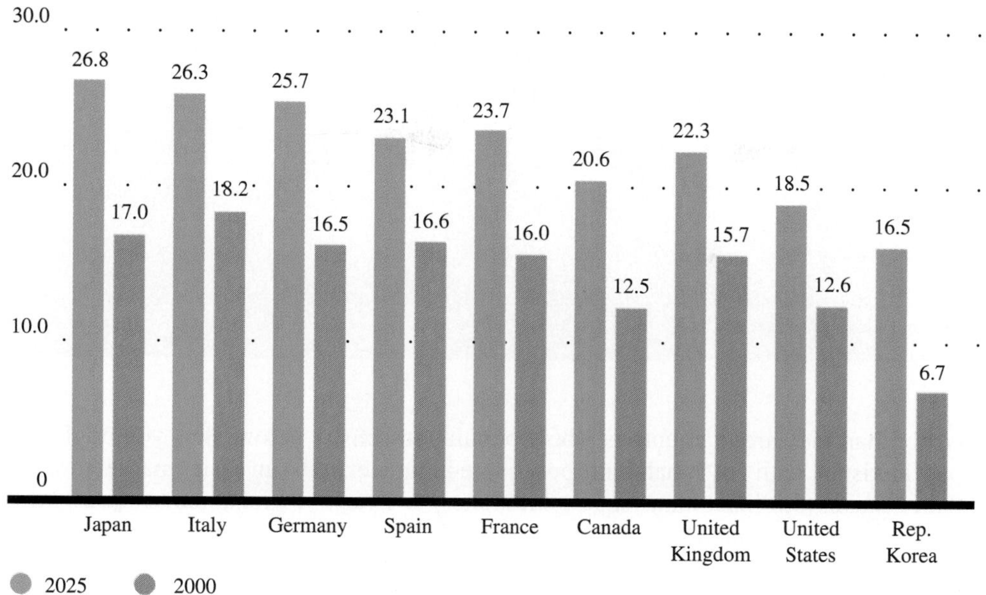

Sources: "No. 1350. Age Distribution by Country: 1999 and 2000," *Statistical Abstract of the U.S.,* U.S. Census Bureau, 1999; and U.S. Census Bureau, *The Official Statistics,* March 1, 1999.

[Figure 7.8] Dependency Ratio Per 100 People of Working Age

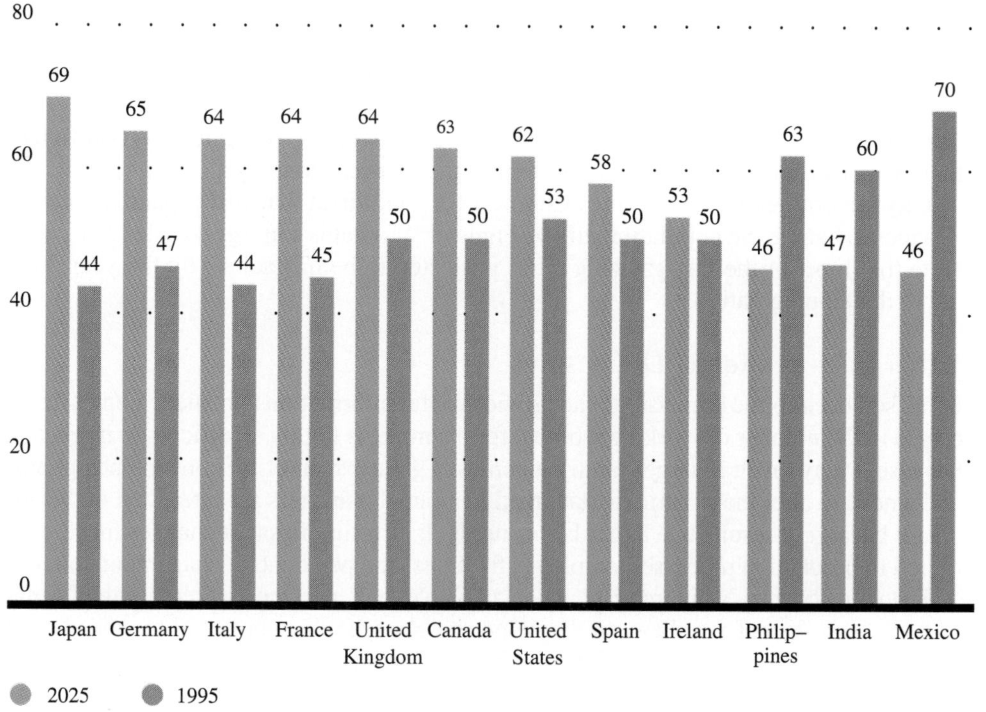

Sources: *World Development Indicators 1997* (Washington, DC: World Bank), p. 34; and *World Development Report 1996* (Washington, DC: World Bank), pp. 194–199.

Table 7.8 Rural-to-Urban Shift

	Percentage of Population in Urban Areas		
	1970	1999	Percentage Increase
Low-income countries	18%	31%	7.2%
Middle-income countries	46	50	8.7
High-income countries	74	77	4.1

Source: *World Development Report 2000/2001* (Washington, DC: World Bank, 2000), p. 277. Permission conveyed through Copyright Clearance Center, Inc.

costly than they are in countries where population density is low; thus you might expect Pakistan, with 169 inhabitants per square kilometer, to be an easier market to serve than Canada (3.0 inhabitants/square kilometer) or Brazil (19 inhabitants/square kilometer).[22] The expectation, though, is another of those based on an arithmetic mean. We must know how these populations are distributed.

One needs only to compare the urban percentages of total population to learn that Canada and Brazil possess population concentrations that facilitate the marketing process. While only 35 percent of Pakistan's population is urban, the percentages for Brazil and Canada are 80 and 77 percent, respectively.[23] The physical forces, as we shall see in Chapter 8, contribute heavily to the formation of these concentrations.

rural-to-urban shift
The movement of a nation's population from rural areas to cities

An important phenomenon that is changing the population distribution is the **rural-to-urban shift,** which is occurring everywhere, especially in developing countries, as people move to cities in search of higher wages and more conveniences.

An indicator of the extent of this movement is the change in the percentages of urban population. As Table 7.8 indicates, the greatest urban shifts are occurring in the low- and middle-income countries. In only four nations is there a net flow in the other direction.*

This shift is significant to marketers because city dwellers, being less self-sufficient than persons living in rural areas, must enter the market economy.

City governments also become customers for equipment that will expand municipal services to handle the population influx. Figure 7.9 contains some good sales prospects. Note that most of the fast-growing cities projected to be megacities by the year 2015 are in developing nations.

Other Socioeconomic Dimensions

Other socioeconomic dimensions can provide useful information to management. The increase in the number of working women, for example, is highly significant to marketers because it may result in larger family incomes, a greater market for convenience goods, and a need to alter the **promotional mix.** Personnel managers are interested in this increase because it results in a larger labor supply. It also signifies that changes may be required in production processes, employee facilities, and personnel management policies.

promotional mix
A blend of the promotional methods a firm uses to sell its products

Data on a country's divorce rate, when available, will alert the marketer to the formation of single-parent families and single-person households, whose product needs and buying habits differ in many respects from those of a two-parent family (see Figure 7.10). In many countries, important ethnic groups require special consideration by both marketing and personnel managers.

> Wal-Mart has had language problems on both sides of the border. In a country where labels and communications are made in English and French, the retailer mailed English-only circulars to residents of Quebec, where 83 percent of the population are French

*Australia, Mauritius, Tajikistan, and Turkmenistan.

[Figure 7.9] 25 Megacities 1970–2015 (Millions)

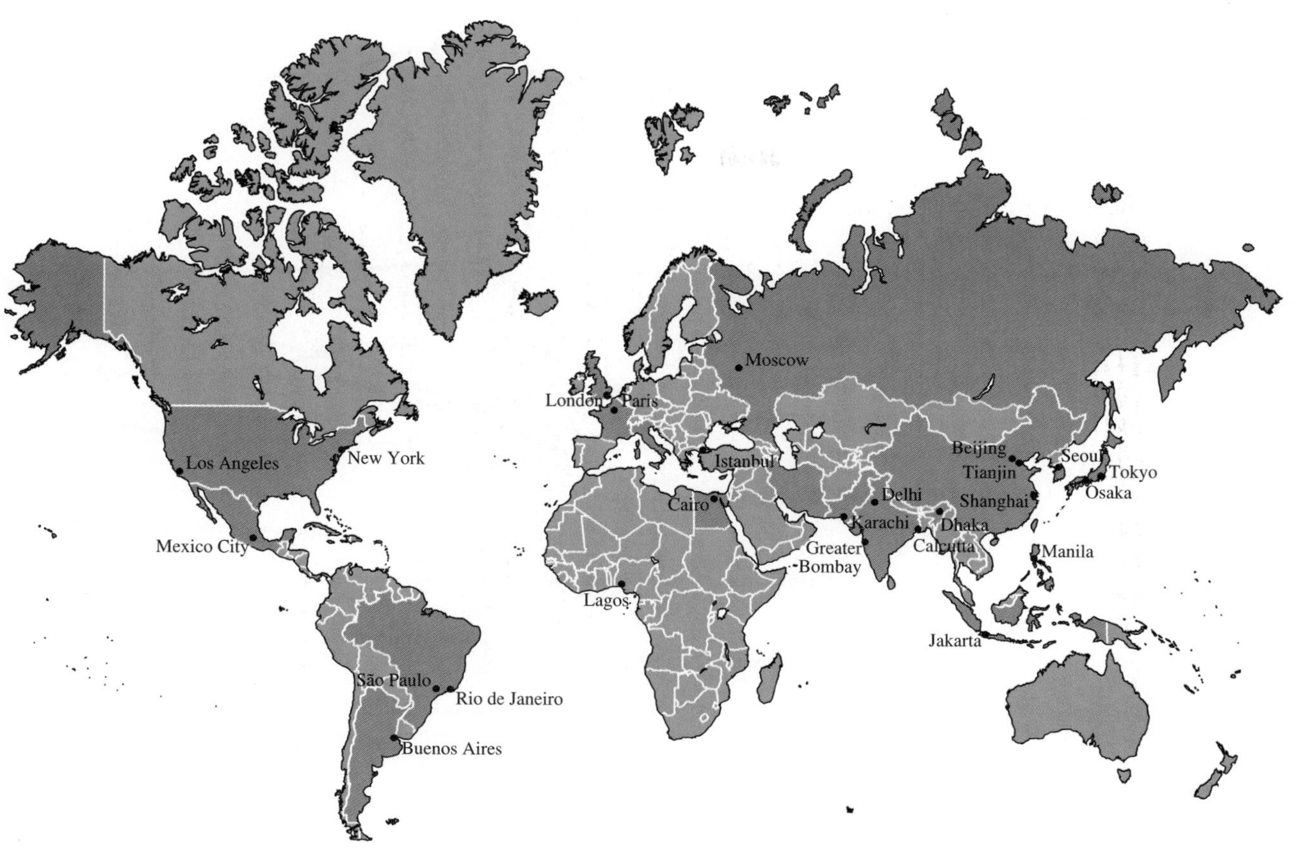

	1970	2015
Beijing	8.3	19.4
Calcutta	7.1	17.6
Greater Bombay	6.0	27.4
Karachi	3.1	20.6
Los Angeles	8.4	14.3
Moscow	7.1	9.3
Paris	8.3	9.6
Seoul	4.5	13.1
Tokyo	14.9	28.7
Buenos Aires	8.6	12.1
Dhaka	4.3	19.0
Istanbul	1.8	12.3
Lagos	1.51	24.4
Manila	3.6	14.7
New York	16.3	17.6
Rio de Janeiro	7.2	11.6
Shanghai	11.4	23.4
Cairo	5.7	14.5
Delhi	3.6	17.6
Jakarta	4.5	21.2
London	10.6	7.1
Mexico City	9.1	18.8
Osaka	7.6	10.7
São Paulo	8.2	20.8
Tianjin	6.9	17.0

Source: United Nations, 1995, www.megacities.nl/top 15/topworld/.html; *The Economist,* April 29, 1995, p. 122; and *World Development Report 1994,* pp. 222–23.

speakers. After apologizing for this mistake, Wal-Mart officials had to apologize a week later when the company was criticized severely for ordering Canadian employees to work 12 hours a week extra without pay by means of memos that also were in English only.

One month later, the company had language-law problems on the other border when Mexican trade inspectors temporarily closed its Mexico City superstore, claiming that the firm had violated a 40-year-old law that requires the seller to place Spanish-language labels on all products on display.[24]

national economic plans
Plans prepared by governments stating their economic goals and means for reaching them, usually for periods of up to five years

National Economic Plans

One other source of economic data that may prove useful to a firm, especially for its marketers, is the **national economic plans** that many countries publish. These range from the annual and five-year plans (in reality, budgets) used as production control instruments by such nations as Cuba, Vietnam, and China to the **indicative plans** of others. Instead of production targets, the five-year indicative plans contain the basic

indicative plans
Forecasts made by governments with industry collaboration of the direction they expect the economy to take

[Figure 7.10] **Changing Divorce Rates in Selected Countries**

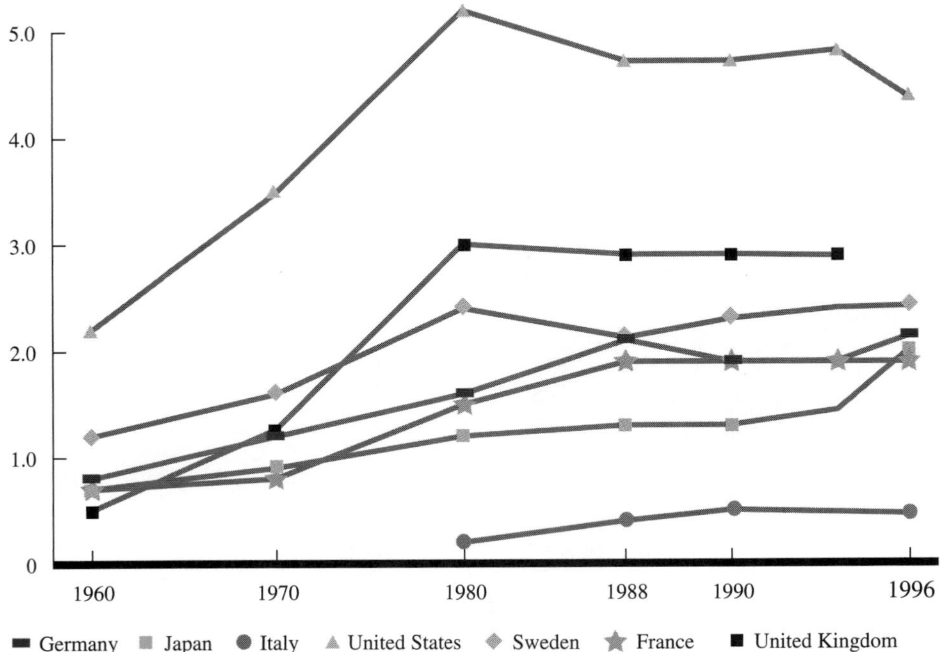

Sources: Statistical Office of the European Communities, *Demographic Statistics,* various years; United Nations *Demographic Yearbook,* 1997 edition; and "International Comparison of Divorce Rates," Japan Ministry of Health and Welfare, jin.jcic.or.jp/stat/stats/02VIT33.html. Data for Italy and the United Kingdom are for 1995; data for Japan are for 1999.

targets set by the government and some general policy statements on how the goals will be achieved. The government then attempts by means of the usual monetary and fiscal tools to create favorable conditions for business so that the targets may be attained. This favoritism may be manifested in many ways, among which are special tax concessions to investors and foreign exchange allocations (when foreign exchange is controlled) to purchase imported capital equipment and raw materials.

Information about national development plans and budgets is regularly reported in such publications as *Business International* and *Business America.* Commercial attachés in American embassies and the overseas American chambers of commerce are additional sources of information.

Industry Dimensions

Every firm is concerned about the general economic news because of its impact on consumer purchases, prices of raw materials, and investment decisions, but certain factors are more significant than others to a given industry or to a specific functional area of a firm. The size and growth trend of the automobile industry are of paramount importance to a tire manufacturer, for example, but are of no interest to an appliance manufacturer. Nor would the quantity of machine operators graduated by technical schools be useful to financial officers, although these data are of vital interest to human resources managers of manufacturing plants. Managers want data not only about the firm's industry but also about industries that supply and purchase from the company. The minicase at the end of this chapter illustrates the use of both macroeconomic and industry-specific data.

Industry studies are generally made by the firm's economists or its trade association, but they can also be purchased from independent research organizations, such as Fantus (New York) and The Economist Intelligence Unit (London). Government agencies, chambers of commerce, and trade publications such as *Advertising Age* publish them as well. Many international banks publish free newsletters containing useful economic data.

Use the Internet for Economic Research

Small and Medium-Sized Enterprises

You own a small business, and you don't have the money to hire an economic analyst. Yet you need economic and socioeconomic data to help you plan for market expansion just as the big multinationals do. What can you do? Do you have a personal computer with an Internet connection? Use it to get the information free of charge that the analyst you were going to hire would have gotten and then charged you for.

Suppose that up to now you have confined yourself to the U.S. market, but because you have been reading about NAFTA, you are curious about the possibilities of expanding into the Canadian and Mexican markets. They are both nearby and relatively easy to get to. Can you find information about doing business with these countries on the Internet?

For a free online report on key economic trends, trade regulations, and standards, go to the Canada Commercial Guide at www.state.gov/www/about_state/business/com_guides/2001/wha/canada_ccg2001.pdf. There is also a marketing section with help for American exporters in finding agents and distributors, mailing products, and establishing a Canadian office. For trade statistics, geography, and culture, go to http://canada.gc.ca/main_e.html.

To get data on Mexico, go to www.latinworld.com/norte/mexico/ for economic forecasts and an extensive Mexican financial commentary. The University of Texas has an excellent site, "Business and Finance in Latin America." The sources are organized by country. For Mexico, go to www.lanic.utexas.edu/la/region/business and then click on MexicoNAFTA. There are at least 25 different sites at this location with useful information for your business. You can also go to the Commercial Section of the U.S. embassy in Mexico City, which offers services to companies that want to do business in Mexico. Go directly from the University of Texas site or go directly to www.uscommerce.org.mx/. Another site, www.zonalatina.com will provide even more information.

With the information you obtain from these sites, you should be able to decide whether you want to move into these new international markets. ■

[Summary]

Understand the purpose of economic analyses.

To keep abreast of the latest economic developments and also to plan for the future, firms regularly assess and forecast economic conditions at the local, state, and national levels. When they enter international operations, the economic analysis increases in complexity because managers are operating in two new environments: foreign and international. There are more economies to study, and these economies are frequently highly divergent.

Recognize the economic and socioeconomic dimensions of the economy.

The various functional areas of a firm require data on the size and rates of change of a number of economic and socioeconomic factors. Among the more important economic dimensions are GNP, GNP/capita, distribution of income, personal consumption expenditures, private investment, unit labor costs, and financial data, such as exchange rates, inflation rates, interest rates, and the amount of a nation's foreign debt. The principal socioeconomic dimensions are total population, rates of growth, age distribution, population density, and population distribution.

Understand the importance of a nation's consumption patterns and the significance of purchasing power parity.

Marketers must know how consumers allocate their discretionary incomes, since this is money spent on their products. They must also use purchasing power parity (PPP) to understand what the true purchasing power of a nation is. Consumers in a nation whose GDP appears to be too low to be a viable market may have some discretionary buying power when the GDP based on market exchange rates is converted to a GDP based on PPP.

Understand the degree to which labor costs can vary from country to country.

Hourly labor rates, especially when stated in U.S. dollars, change rather rapidly. There are three factors that are responsible: (1) real changes in compensation, (2) changes in productivity, and (3) changes in exchange rates.

Understand the significance for businesspeople of the large foreign debts of some nations.

Large foreign debts may indicate that the government will impose exchange controls on its country's businesses. If a large part of the country's export earnings go to service its external debt, there will be little remaining for use by firms in the country to pay for imports of raw materials, components used in their products, and production machinery. The government could impose price and wage controls. There is also the possibility that firms can buy some of the discounted debt to obtain local currency at a favorable exchange rate.

Ascertain the reasons for the worldwide downward trend in birthrates and its implications for businesspeople.

Birthrates are declining in nearly all nations because (1) governments are providing family planning programs, (2) women are continuing their education and marrying later, and (3) a greater degree of urbanization is enabling women to become employed and self-supporting, which contributes to a delay of marriage.

Understand indicative plans and their importance for businesspeople.

National economic plans, for which no American counterpart exists, provide an insight into government expectations. In centrally planned economies, national plans are often the equivalent of market studies. Many developed and developing nations use indicative plans to set out their goals and provide some general policy statements as to how they will be achieved.

[Key Words]

gross domestic product (GDP) (p. 241)
income distribution (p. 242)
discretionary income (p. 244)
unit labor costs (p. 247)
vertically integrated (p. 251)
population density (p. 255)
population distribution (p. 255)
rural-to-urban shift (p. 258)
promotional mix (p. 258)
national economic plans (p. 259)
indicative plans (p. 259)

[Questions]

1. Management learns from the economic analysis of Country A that wage rates are expected to increase by 10 percent next year. Which functional areas of the firm will be concerned? Why is management concerned?
2. What are "international dollars"? What is their significance to international businesspeople?
3. What common problem does the use of GNP per capita and population density values present?
4. Compare the GNP/capita of the highest quintile in Canada and the Netherlands using the GNP/capita shown in Table 2.10 and the percentage shares given in Table 7.2. Which country has the higher average GNP/capita in the highest 20 percent of the population?
5. If the clothing industry association to which your firm's Swiss subsidiary belongs could mount a successful promotional program to cause the Swiss to increase their clothing expenditures by 1 percent annually, what would be the total increase in sales for the clothing industry?
6. In 1996, Italy's average hourly labor compensation costs stated in U.S. dollars were $18.08 compared to $16.52 in 1995 and 27,894 lira compared to 26,911 lira.
   a. What was the percentage increase in dollars?
   b. What was the percentage increase in labor costs stated in Italian lira?
   c. What percentage of the change when stated in dollars was due to changes in the lira–dollar exchange rate?
7. The staff economist of a large multinational with an Argentine subsidiary has given to the firm's chief financial officer a report on Argentina's foreign debt situation, as shown in Table 7.7. What concerns might the chief financial officer have?
8. What would be the concerns of the chief financial officer if he or she were to receive the information on annual inflation rates from Table 7.1?
9. What problems is the reduction in birthrates causing for European governments?
10. Choose a country and a product and estimate the market potential of the product based on the economic and socioeconomic dimensions. What other environmental forces should you investigate?

[Internet Exercises]

Using the Internet

1. Compare the relative social indicators of the developing countries in Latin America with those of the industrialized nations.
   a. Which developing country has the lowest life expectancy index?
   b. Which country has the lowest daily calorie supply index?

c. Compared to the average of the industrialized nations, which developing nation has the lowest relative adult literacy rate?
d. Which developing nation has the lowest indicator for safe drinking water?
e. Which developing nation has the lowest value for mean years of schooling?

2. According to *OECD in Figures,*
a. What are the two members with the largest land area?
b. Which were the two most populous members in 1995?
c. Which two countries are the most densely populated?
d. In which two countries is the population growing the fastest?
e. Which country has the largest percentage of the total population under 15 years of age? 65 and over?

[Minicase 7.1]

World Laboratories

World Laboratories (WL) is a large multinational pharmaceutical manufacturer specializing in the production of ethical pharmaceuticals (available to the public only by prescription). These products are characterized by a high degree of research, and because of the limited protection offered by patents, they have a relatively short product life. WL does make some over-the-counter products, but these products account for only about 20 percent of total company sales.

The South American division manager must make a sales forecast for ethical drugs, which he will use to set quotas for the six countries in his division that have manufacturing plants. These products produce about 75 percent of the total sales in each market. At present, WL's market share and sales by category of drug (pediatric, general, geriatric) in each country are as shown in the table below.

Total health care has grown faster than world population and world income since 1970. A conservative average of the total amount per capita spent on health care, both private and public, for pharmaceuticals in South America is 20 percent. This is lower than in the United States and Europe, but in government clinics, medicine is generally offered without charge or at a substantial discount from the price charged in pharmacies. According to WL's subsidiaries, the patients at clinics pay, on average, 40 percent of the drugs' listed price when those drugs given at no charge are included. Obviously, private drugstores that get only 40 percent off list (60 percent of list price is their cost) cannot compete. WL, however, still earns a 12 percent profit based on its selling prices when it sells to governments at list less 50 percent because of the low marketing costs on such large volumes, compared to an average 20 percent of selling price on sales to private pharmacies.

Here are the data that the staff economist has just given to the South American division manager. Help him do the forecast. If you have to make any assumptions, please make a note of them. If marketing costs for government sales average 6 percent of WL's selling price while they average 11.5 percent to private pharmacies, should the division manager try to change the present government–private pharmacy sales ratio that now prevails in any of the six markets? Should he have any other concerns based on these data?

	Market Share (percent)	Pediatric (0–14 years)	General (15–64 years)	Geriatric (65 and older)
Argentina	30%	32.0%	58.0%	10.0%
Brazil	24	29.3	65.7	5.0
Chile	55	32.1	62.8	5.1
Paraguay	65	41.2	55.4	3.4
Peru	45	42.0	56.5	1.5
Uruguay	38	27.0	63.9	9.1

	GNP (billions of dollars)			Foreign Debt (billions of dollars)			Percent Change from Previous Year		
	1986	1989	1992	1986	1989	1992	1986	1989	1992
Argentina	$ 73.1	$ 67.8	$200.3	$ 51.4	$ 64.7	$ 49.1	+4.5%	+9.8%	+4.0%
Brazil	249.8	375.1	425.4	111.0	111.3	99.2	+4.2	−2.4	+4.3
Chile	16.6	22.9	37.1	20.7	18.2	14.9	+4.7	−7.1	−1.3
Paraguay	3.6	4.3	6.0	1.9	2.5	1.5	+8.1	0	−16.6
Peru	21.4	23.0	21.3	14.5	19.9	15.6	+2.3	−7.0	+2.0
Uruguay	5.8	8.1	10.4	5.2	3.8	3.4	+4.6	0	−8.8

	Total Debt Service as Percentage of Export Receipts			Total Government Expenditures as Percentages of GNP			Percentage of Government Expenditures on Health Care		
	1986	1989	1992	1986	1989	1992	1986	1989	1992
Argentina	50.9%	36.1%	34.4%	12%	15.5%	13.1%*	1.3%	2.0%	3.0%*
Brazil	41.4	31.3	23.1	9†	30.6	25.6	6.4	6.1	6.9
Chile	37.9	27.5	20.9	13	32.5	22.1	6.0	5.9	11.1
Paraguay	18.5	11.9	40.3	7	8.9	9.4	3.1	3.0	4.3
Peru	26.2	6.8	23.0	11	11.6	12.5	5.8†	5.5	5.6*
Uruguay	24.7	29.4	23.2	14	25.8	28.7	4.8	4.5	5.0

*1991.
†1988.

	Population per Physician*			Annual Inflation Rate			Population (millions)			Population Distribution 1991		
	1980	1984	1990	1986	1989	1992	1986	1989	1992	0–14 Years	15–64 years	65+ years
Argentina	430	370	n.a.	82%	3,072%	25%	31.0	31.9	33.1	29.4%	62.2%	8.4%
Brazil	1,200	1,080	n.a.	58	1,234	1,056	138.4	147.3	153.9	34.2	62.8	3.0
Chile	1,930	1,230	2,150	17	14	15	12.2	13.0	13.6	30.6	63.3	6.1
Paraguay	1,310	1,460	1,250	24	31	15	3.8	4.2	4.5	40.3	56.7	3.0
Peru	1,390	1,040	960	63	3,121	74	19.8	21.2	22.4	37.1	60.8	2.1
Uruguay	510	510	n.a.	76	73	68	3.0	3.1	3.1	25.4	63.3	11.3

n.a. = Not available.
*Latest estimate available from World Health Organization.

	Percentage of GNP for Private Consumption Expenditure		Percentage of Private Consumption Expenditure for Health Care (1989–1992)
	1989	1992	
Argentina	54.8%	73.3%	3%
Brazil	55.3	60.0	5
Chile	72.7	65.8	4
Paraguay	75.9	69.3	2
Peru	84.6	72.6	3
Uruguay	64.0	65.8	5

Sources: Various *World Development Reports* and Banco Nacional de Comercio Exterior, *Comercio Exterior,* February and March 1989 issues.

[Chapter] 8

Physical and Environmental Forces

"If you do this. . .
Look at a map of the world as large a map as possible. At first sight, it seems to be a maze of lines, colors, and unfamiliar names. Go on looking and studying until the mere mention of a town, country, or river enables it to be picked out immediately on the map. Those who are concerned with overseas marketing must, as a basis, know their export geography as well as the streets around their home."

—*Henry Deschampneufs*, Selling Overseas

"You won't be told this. . .
Middle East consultant, piqued by his clients' ignorance of the region, begins his briefings by saying, 'Iraq isn't the past tense of Iran.' "

—The Wall Street Journal, *July 5, 1985, p. 32.*

Concept Previews

After reading this chapter, you should be able to:

- **appreciate** the relevance to businesspeople of four elements of geography: (1) location, (2) topography, (3) climate, and (4) natural resources
- **understand** the importance of a country's location in political and trade relationships
- **understand** how surface features contribute to economic, cultural, political, and social differences among nations and among regions of a single country
- **comprehend** the importance of inland waterways and outlets to the sea
- **recognize** that climate exerts a broad influence on business
- **understand** why managers must monitor changes in the discovery and the use of mineral resources and energy sources
- **understand** why managers must be alert to changes in a nation's infrastructure
- **appreciate** the impact of industrial disasters such as the Alaskan oil spill and the Bhopal accident on global and multinational firms

Cosmo Condina/Tony Stone Images

Why Switzerland Makes Watches

Watches, lace, carvings, chocolate, cheese, precision machinery, pharmaceuticals—what do they have in common? All are produced in Switzerland; all have a high value per kilo; the Swiss versions are known for their quality; and physical forces are primarily responsible for their being produced in Switzerland.

To appreciate why this is so, consider the following: (1) Switzerland is mostly mountainous, with little level land, (2) it is close to the heavily populated lowlands of Western Europe, (3) transportation across the mountains to these markets is relatively expensive, and (4) Switzerland has practically no mineral resources.

One way to overcome the lack of local sources of raw materials and high transportation costs is to import small amounts of raw materials, add high value to them, and export a lightweight finished product. The Swiss have done precisely this with the manufacture of watches. They import small volumes of high-quality Swedish steel costing 40 cents per ounce that they then convert to watch movements selling for $60 per ounce. Because of their light weight, the cost of transporting these movements to market is minimal. Precision machinery and pharmaceuticals are other products that minimize the need for importing bulky raw materials. For all of these products, emphasis is placed on the value added by manufacturing, which is based on skill, care, and tradition.

Although the Swiss slopes do not support much agriculture, they are adequate for raising cattle and goats. Production of milk is no problem, but getting it to its major markets outside Switzerland is. Fluid milk is bulky in relation to its value and expensive to transport. The dairymen do to the milk what the watchmakers do to the steel—convert it to a concentrated, high-value product: cheese. Because Swiss cheesemakers have no advantage over their counterparts in the lowland dairying areas nearer to the important markets, they have to compete on the basis of high quality and reputation, which they have carefully promoted.

The plentiful supply of milk is responsible for another product: milk chocolate. The Swiss import the raw chocolate and convert the milk into another high-value-per-kilo product. Certainly the Swiss manufacturer pays higher transportation costs to bring sugar and chocolate in and ship the finished product out than does Hershey in Pennsylvania. Again, the Swiss product must be perceived to be superior so that it will bring a higher price to offset the greater costs.

What about the lace and carvings? Physical forces are responsible for these also. The heavy snowfall and cold temperatures of the Swiss winter leave the dairymen and their wives with little to do. About the only work necessary is feeding the animals with stored hay. To help pass the time and earn some money, Swiss women make lace and embroidery while the men carve figures and cuckoo clocks. ■

Source: Adapted from Rhoads Murphey, *The Scope of Geography,* 2nd ed. (Skokie, IL: Rand McNally, 1973), pp. 65–67.

The opening article illustrates what one writer meant when he wrote that "the physical character of a nation is perhaps the principal and broadest determinant of both the society found there and the means by which that society undertakes to supply its needs."[1]

Strictly speaking, the physical elements are not forces because, except for natural disasters (such as earthquakes, floods, and hurricanes), they are passive. However, there are similarities between them and the uncontrollable forces we describe in this section: their effects are not constant, and although they have a profound impact on the way people organize their activities, the physical forces are only one set of the many factors that influence humanity. In fact, cultural, political, and economic factors may be more important than the physical factors in determining land use and the nature of the economy. How else can you explain the great differences between southeast China and the U.S. Southeast? Their physical environments are very similar, but they support different people with wide divergences in their cultures and land use.

Probably the most important reason for considering the physical elements as uncontrollable forces is that they have many aspects of the foreign environmental forces we discussed in Chapter 1. Also, as we shall illustrate, managers must adjust their strategies to compensate for differences among markets of the physical forces just as they do for the other uncontrollable forces.

Although the scope of geography is extremely broad, it is possible to select some elements that are particularly significant for the businessperson: (1) location, (2) topography, (3) climate, and (4) natural resources.

Location

Where a country is located, who its neighbors are, and what its capital and major cities are should be part of the general knowledge of all international businesspeople. Location is important because it is a factor in explaining a number of a nation's political and trade relationships, many of which directly affect a company's operations.

Political Relationships

At the height of the cold war, the location of Austria enabled that country to be a political bridge between the noncommunist nations of the West and the communist nations of the East. It was bounded on the west by Germany, Italy, and Switzerland and on the east by Czechoslovakia, Hungary, and Yugoslavia. In addition, Austria's political neutrality made it a popular location for the offices of international firms servicing Eastern European operations. Vienna, Austria's capital, is only 40 kilometers from the Czech Republic and 60 kilometers from Hungary.

Because of the recent political and economic changes in both Western and Eastern Europe, Austria is taking advantage of its location to (1) increase trade with the East, (2) become the principal financial intermediary between the two regions, and (3) strengthen its role as the regional headquarters for international businesses operating in Eastern Europe.

The collapse of COMECON (the economic grouping of former communist satellite nations) forced Eastern enterprises to reorient their trade toward the West. Because of their location on the borders of the former communist nations Czechoslovakia and Hungary, Austrian entrepreneurs have captured an important share of the Western nations' exports to the East. For example, after Germany, Austria is the second-largest exporter to Hungary. East–West traffic via Austria is projected to increase five- to sevenfold over the next 20 years. Because of low wage costs in the East and low transport costs due to Austria's proximity to its Eastern neighbors, Austrian producers send textiles, furniture, and machinery components to Eastern countries for further processing and assembly and then bring them back to Austria. Called **passive processing,** this is similar to what foreign firms do in the Mexican maquiladoras. This trade is seven times greater than what it was before the opening of the East.[2]

passive processing
The finishing or refining in Eastern European countries of semifinished goods from the West; after finishing, the goods are returned to the West; similar to Mexican maquiladora operations

Austria's location enabled the country to develop close trading links with the European Union members, especially the two on its borders: Germany and Italy. As Austria's main trading partner, the EU supplies nearly 70 percent of its imports and takes 65 percent of its exports. In recent years, Austria has been fifth as a supplier to the EU and third, ahead of Japan and behind only the United States and Switzerland, as an export market for the EU. After many years of close association with the EU, Austria became a full member in 1995.[3]

Finland is another country whose location has shaped its political relationships. For years, Finland, which shared a 780-mile border with the Soviet Union, thrived on a balancing act it did between that country and Western Europe while maintaining a policy of neutrality. It was the only nation in the world that was at the same time a member of the Soviet trading bloc, the Council for Mutual Economic Assistance (COMECON), and the European Free Trade Association (EFTA). However, Finland lost an important market with the Soviet collapse and turned toward the West. As a result of its active participation in the earlier EC/EFTA negotiations, Finland had already established a high level of integration with the European Union (EU). Finland became a full member of the EU on January 1, 1995.[4]

Trade Relationships

Geographical proximity is often the major reason for trade between nations. As you saw in Chapter 2, the largest and the third-largest trading partners of the United States—Canada and Mexico—lie on its borders. Deliveries are faster, freight costs are lower, and it is less expensive for sellers to service their clients. This is also one reason so many American firms have plants on the Mexican side of the common border. Geographic proximity has always been a major factor in the formation of trading groups, such as the EU, EFTA, and the North American Free Trade Agreement. The latter, which took effect on January 1, 1994, created a trading block of 362 million people and $6 trillion in GDP.

Nearness to the market is also why Japan's sales to the Association of Southeast Asian Nations (ASEAN)* are over twice those of either the United States or Europe.[5] Because it is closer to Japan, China has been able to take over part of the sales of soybeans and wheat formerly supplied by the United States.

Did you ever stop to think where the fresh grapes, peaches, and raspberries that you eat in the dead of winter come from? Probably not. But Chile's U.S. sales of such fruit, averaging nearly $1 billion annually, are possible because of its location in the southern hemisphere, where the growing seasons are the opposite from those of the northern hemisphere (Europe and the United States).

Topography

topography
The surface features of a region

Let us examine some of the principal surface features to give you an idea of what businesspeople should look for. Surface features such as mountains, plains, deserts, and bodies of water contribute to differences in economies, cultures, politics, and social structures both among nations and among regions of a single country. Physical distribution is aided by some features but hindered by others. Differences in **topography** may require products to be altered. For example, the effects of altitude on food products begin to be seen at heights above 3,000 feet, and so producers of cake mixes must change their baking instructions, and internal combustion engines begin to lose power noticeably at 5,000 feet, which may require the manufacturer of gasoline-powered machinery to use larger engines.

Mountains and Plains

Mountains are barriers that tend to separate and impede exchange and interaction, whereas level areas (plains and plateaus) facilitate them. The extent to which mountains serve as barriers depends on their height, breadth, and length; the ruggedness of the terrain; and whether there are any transecting valleys.

An example of such a barrier is the Himalaya Mountains. Travel across them is so difficult that transportation between India and China has been by air or sea rather than overland. The contrast between the cultures of the Indo-Malayan people living to the south of the mountains and those of the Chinese living to the north is evidence of the Himalayas' effectiveness as a barrier. In similar fashion, the Alps, Carpathians, Balkans, and Pyrenees have long separated the Mediterranean cultures from those of northern Europe.

Mountains Divide Markets

A greater problem for businesspeople is posed by those nations divided by mountain ranges into smaller regional markets, each with its own distinctive industries, climate, culture, dialect, and sometimes even language.

Spain. Such is the case of Spain, where there are five separate regions (see Figure 8.1). The cultural differences between two of them, Catalonia and the Basque country, are so great that they have separate languages, not dialects, and each has a sizable minority that wishes to secede from Spain to form a separate nation. Although the Basques and the Catalans can speak Spanish, when they are among themselves they use their

*ASEAN members are Indonesia, Malaysia, Philippines, Singapore, Thailand, Laos, Vietnam, Myanmar, and Brunei.

[Figure 8.1] **Map of Spain**

own languages, which are completely unintelligible to other Spaniards in both commerce and the home. This creates the same kind of problems found wherever there are language differences: Spanish-speaking managers do not attain the empathy with their local employees that they do in other parts of Spain, and sales representatives who speak the local language are more effective.[6] Moreover, the language differences increase promotional costs if, to be more effective, Spanish companies choose to prepare their material in Basque, Catalan, and Spanish.[7]

Political unrest is prevalent among the Basques on the northern Spanish–French border and, to a lesser extent, among the Catalans on the southern Spanish–French border. Since 1968 an armed terrorist group called ETA, the Basque-language acronym for Basque Homeland and Liberty, has killed about 800 people, mostly members of the security forces, in its campaign for independence of the Basque country. They have financed their attacks by bullying local businesses into paying their "revolutionary tax" or by holding wealthy businesspeople for ransom.

The ETA ended its truce with the Spanish government in December 1999 after a 14-month cease-fire. By September 2000, the Basque separatists had killed twelve people, two of them in Madrid and one in Malaga. Apparently, this is a signal to the Spanish government that the ETA is strong enough to kill anyone anywhere in Spain. Prime Minister José Maria Aznar told a news conference, "The terrorist band has mobilized all of its criminal capacity against those who refuse to accept their final aim, which is to convert the Basque Country into a camp of ethnic cleansing and ideological cleansing." He

[Figure 8.2] The Cantons and Major Language Areas of Switzerland

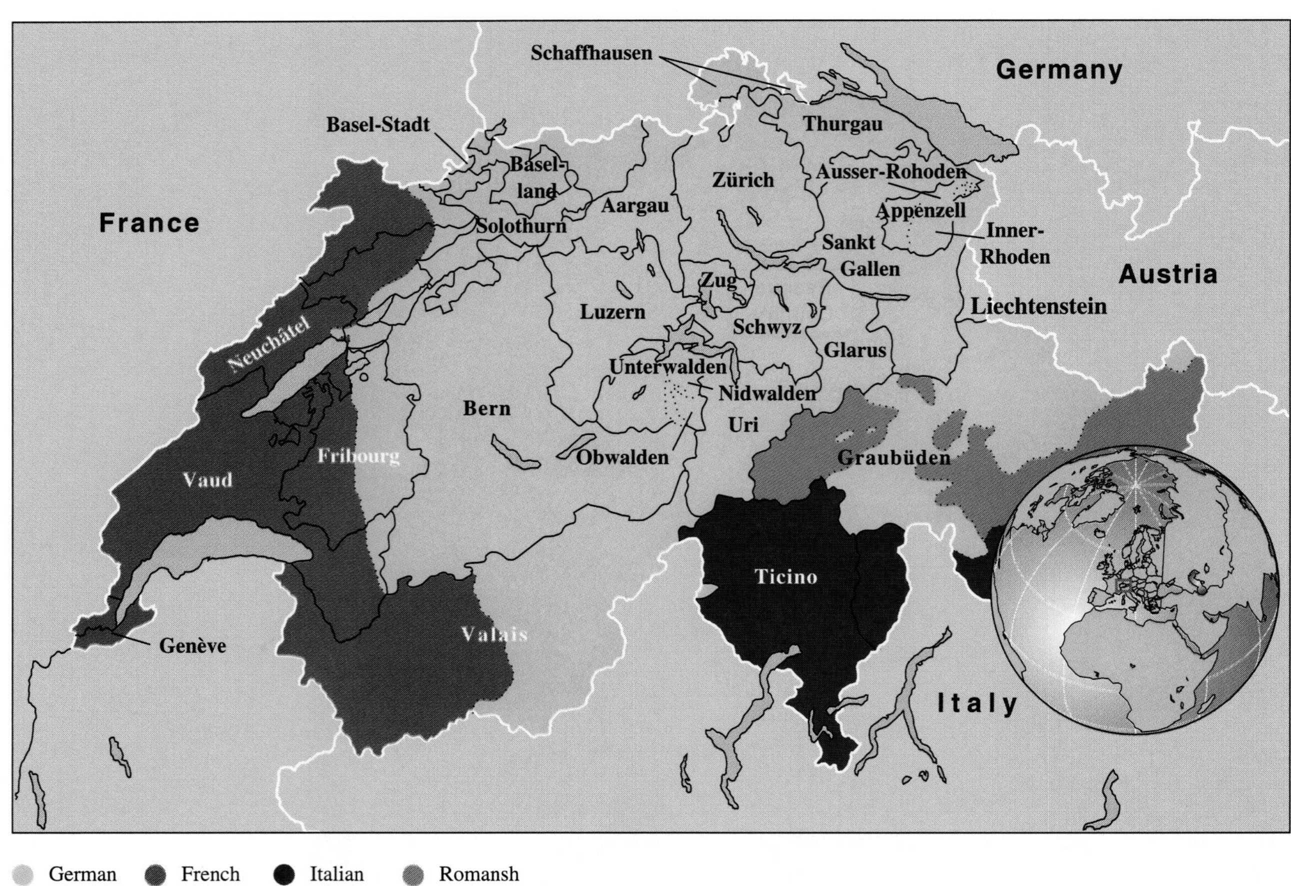

vowed not to waver in using force against a guerrilla offensive that had killed seven people in July and August 2000.[8]

Switzerland. Switzerland is another country separated into distinctive cultural regions by mountains. In a country one-half the size of Maine, four different languages and 35 different dialects are spoken—Italian, French, German, and Romansh (see Figure 8.2). To the consternation of advertising managers attempting to reach all the regions of the country, each of the three major language groups has its own radio and television network, and the fourth, Romansh (Latin), is also used by the German stations.

China. In China, dozens of dialects or languages were developed in villages segmented by mountains. This caused a communications problem that hindered economic development until the government decreed Mandarin to be the official language.

Colombia. Colombia is similar to Switzerland in that mountains divide its markets. Three ranges of the Andes divide Colombia from north to south into four separate markets, each with its own culture and dialects (see Figure 8.3). Depending on the product, this could require marketers to create four distinctive promotional mixes.

Colombia differs from Switzerland, however, in that besides containing distinct cultures within its borders, it experiences a range of distinct climates. Because of its location near the equator, Colombia has no seasons, but the great differences in altitude throughout the country result in a variety of climates. These range from hot and humid at sea level (mean average temperature of 82 degrees in Barranquilla) to cold and dry in the 10,000-foot-high snowcapped mountains (57 degrees in Bogotá). Imagine the production and inventory problems that such differences occasion for a manufacturer

[Figure 8.3] Map of Colombia

Colombia

—— Department, Intendencia and Comisaría Boundaries ● Elevations above 14,000 meters

that must produce a distinct product and package for each zone. A product with adequate cooling and lubrication for the temperate zone would function well in Bogotá but might be woefully deficient in Barranquilla. Similarly, a machine powered with an internal combustion engine might perform well in Barranquilla but be severely underpowered in the 10,000-foot altitude of Bogotá.

Because these climatic conditions are not peculiar to Colombia, market analysts should examine topographical maps to see which tropical countries possess this combination of lowlands and mountains. If the firm's products will not function properly in such climatic extremes, either they must be redesigned or the company must bypass this market.

Population Concentration

Mountains also create concentrations of population either because the climate is more pleasant at higher altitudes or because they are barriers to population movement. For example, nearly 80 percent of Colombia's population is located in the western highlands (only one-third of the nation's area) because the climate there is moderate. Eighty percent of Brazil's 166 million people inhabit a 300-mile-wide coastal strip separated from the remainder of the country by a mountain range. Except in the tropics, the population density generally decreases as the elevation increases. If you were to place a population map over a topographical map, the blank areas on the population map would generally coincide with the areas of higher elevation. For example, 90 percent of Switzerland's population is located in a narrow belt at the base of the Alps. The reason for this is that dense population requires commerce, manufacturing, and agriculture, which all depend on the good transportation and ease of communication afforded by the plains.

Deserts and Tropical Forests

Deserts and tropical forests, like mountains, separate markets, increase the cost of transportation, and create concentrations of population.

Deserts

Over one-third of the earth's surface consists of arid and semiarid regions located either on the coasts where the winds blow away from the land or in the interior where mountains or long distances cause the winds to lose their moisture before reaching these regions. Every continent has them, and every west coast between 20 and 30 degrees north or south of the equator is dry. Since people, plants, and animals must have water to exist, the climatic and vegetational deserts are also the human deserts. Only where there is a major source of water, as in Egypt, is there a concentration of population.

Australia. Nowhere is the relationship between water supply and population concentration better illustrated than in Australia, a continent the size of the continental United States but with only 19 million inhabitants. Its surrounding coastline is humid and fertile, whereas the huge center of the country is mainly a desert closely resembling the Sahara (see Figure 8.4).

Because of its geography, Australia's population has tended to concentrate (1) along the coastal areas in and around the state capitals, which are also major seaports, and (2) in the southeastern fifth of the nation, where more than one-half of the population lives. This gives Australia one of the highest percentages of urban population in the world. The 85 percent of the total population living in cities is surpassed by only nine other countries.[9]

The distances between these cities and the fact that they are seaports make coastal shipping preferred over road and rail transportation.[10] However, these long distances between major markets result in transportation accounting for as much as 30 percent of the final cost of the product, compared with the more usual 10 percent in the United States and Europe.

The population distribution also has a profound impact on Australia's media. First of all, there are only three upper-socioeconomic-group newspapers and a few magazines that can be considered national media. All other media are concentrated in capital city areas. This requires advertisers to buy space or time on a state-by-state or city-by-city basis. Although most capital city areas have three commercial TV channels, there is little networking.

Even though 70 percent of the country is arid or semiarid, some areas in the northern rim receive up to 100 inches of rainfall annually, much like the monsoon areas of

[Figure 8.4] Map of Australia

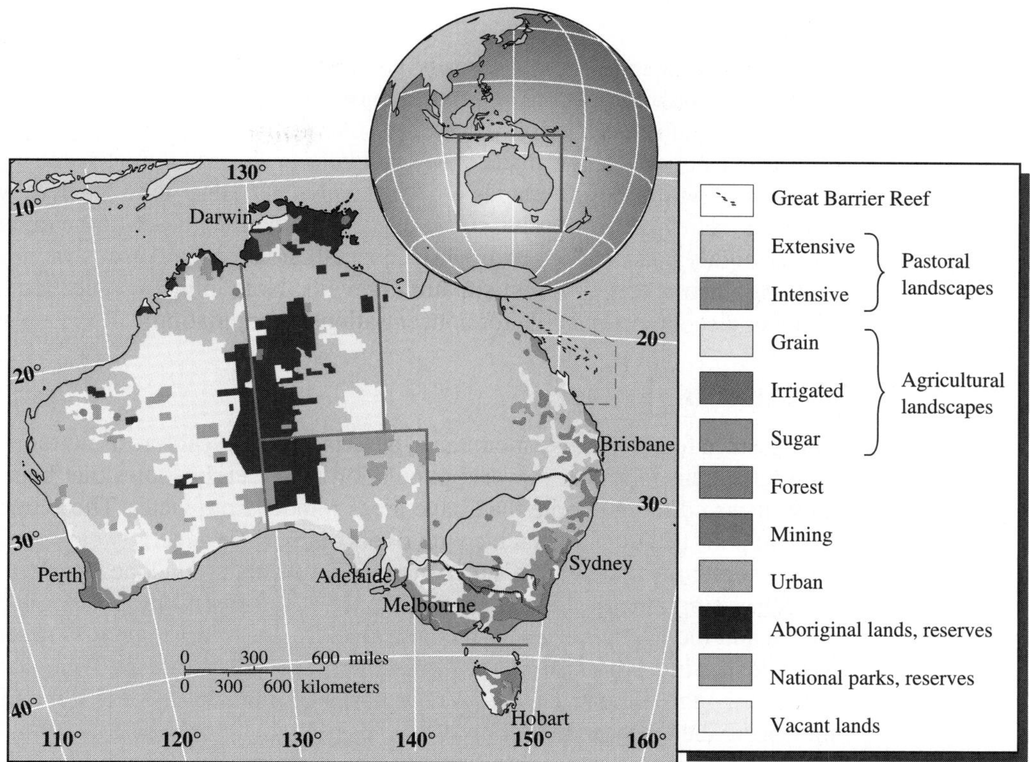

India. Thus, firms entering the Australian market face the same extreme differences of temperature and humidity encountered in Colombia.

Were it not for the uniform topography of Australia, the temperature differences would be even greater, as they are in countries with large, hot desert areas and irregular surfaces. Iran is such a nation. In the summer, temperatures may reach 130°F, whereas winter temperatures in high altitudes may drop to −18°F. From December to March, it is possible to ski just an hour and a half's drive from Teheran, the capital. Like Australia, Iran's population distribution is heavily influenced by climate and topography. More than 70 percent of the country—consisting mostly of mountains and deserts—is uninhabited, and one-half of the population lives in urban areas.

Tropical Rain Forests

Vegetation can be an effective barrier to economic development and human settlement, especially when it is combined with a harsh climate and poor soil. This occurs in the world's tropical rain forests located in the Amazon basin, Southeast Asia, and the Congo. Except in parts of West Africa and Java, they are thinly populated and little developed economically. For example, the greatest rain forest of them all—in the Brazilian Amazon—has been called one of the world's greatest deserts because of its low population density. Although it covers more than 1 million square miles (one-fourth of the U.S. land area) and occupies one-half of Brazil, it is inhabited by just 4 percent of the country's population. Only true deserts have a population density lower than the Amazon's one person per square mile.

Canadian Shield

Although the **Canadian Shield** is neither a desert nor a tropical forest, this massive area of bedrock covering one-half of Canada's land mass has most of their characteristics—forbidding topography, poor soil, and harsh climate. The Shield is swept by polar air, which permits a frost-free growing season of only four months. During that time,

Canadian Shield
A massive area of bedrock covering one-half of Canada's land mass

residents are molested by swarms of black flies and mosquitoes. Like deserts and tropical forests, its population density is very low: only 10 percent of Canada's population inhabits the region.

Managers know that in more densely populated nations, it costs less to market their products (population centers are closer, and communication systems are better), more people are available for employment, and so forth. Therefore, when they compare population densities such as Canada's 3 inhabitants per square kilometer, Australia's 2, and Brazil's 20 with the Netherlands' 463 or Japan's 336, they may draw the wrong conclusions.[11] However, if they are aware that the population in each of the first three countries is highly concentrated in a relatively small area for the reasons we have been examining, then a very different situation prevails. Note in the next section how bodies of water also are responsible for concentrations of population.

Bodies of Water

This surface feature, unlike mountains, deserts, and tropical forests, attracts people and facilitates transportation. A world population map clearly shows that bodies of water have attracted more people than have areas remote from water. Those densely populated regions that do not coincide with rivers or lakes are generally close to the sea. You would note from a population's map that people cluster around the Amazon, the Congo, the Mississippi, the St. Lawrence, and the Great Lakes. In Europe, the plain of the Po (Italy) and the Rhine are easily recognizable. So are rivers that cross deserts, such as the Nile, the Indus (Pakistan), the Tigris-Euphrates (Iraq), and the Amu Darya (central Asia), although these rivers are more important for the irrigation water and fertile soil they bring than for transportation.

Bodies of water that are significant because they provide inexpensive access to markets in the interior of various nations are the inland waterways.

Inland Waterways

Before the construction of railways, water transport was the only economically practical carrier for bulk goods moving over long distances. Water transport increased even after the building of railroads, although its importance relative to railroads has diminished everywhere with one exception—the Rhine waterway, the world's most important inland waterway system.

Cargo ships passing through Germany on Europe's main transportation artery, the Rhine waterway.
Hans Wolf/The Image Bank

[Figure 8.5] European Waterway System

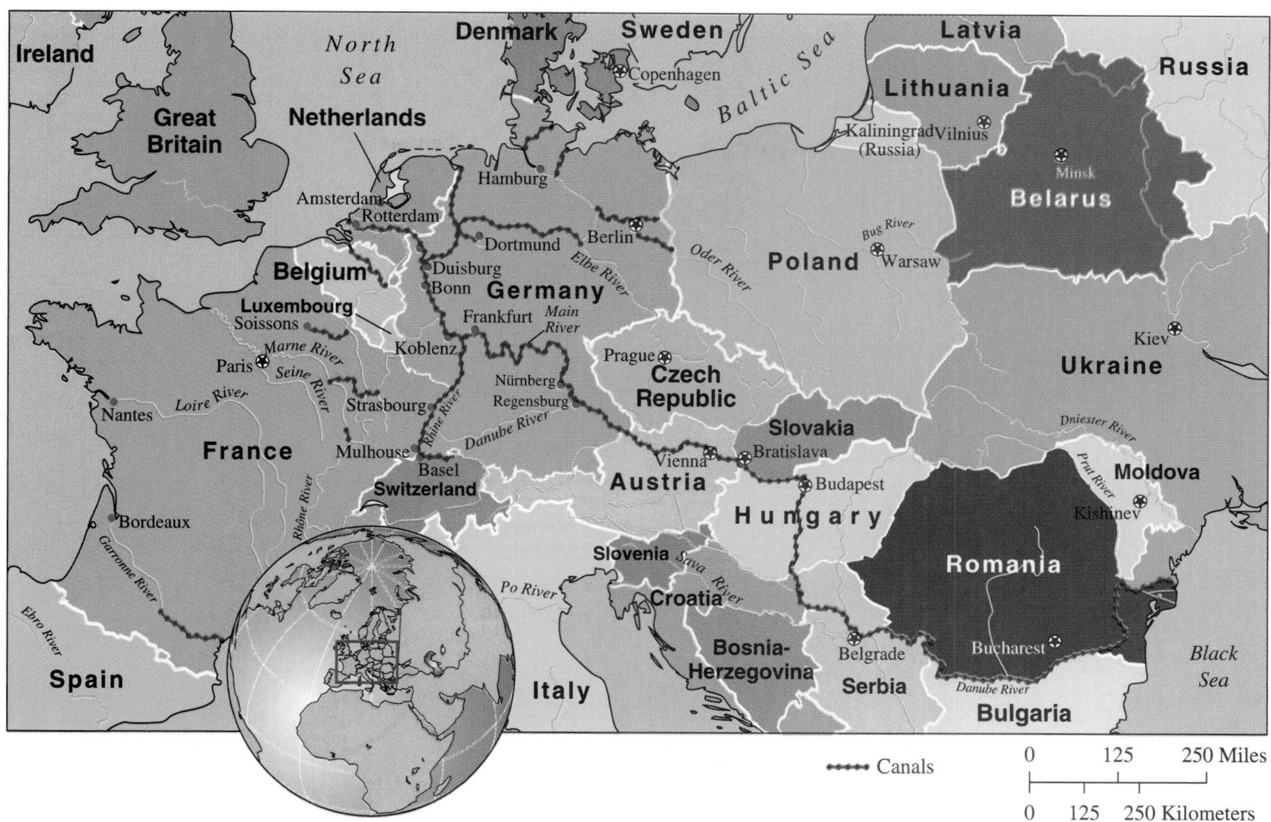

Source: Karte der Wasserstraβen in Deutschland und Benelux

Rhine Waterway. The **Rhine waterway,** the main transportation artery of Europe, carries a greater volume of goods than do the combined railways that run parallel to it. As an illustration of the Rhine's significance, one-half of Switzerland's exports and nearly three-fourths of its imports pass through Basel, the Swiss inland port. This cargo is carried on the country's own 31-vessel oceangoing fleet via the Rhine waterway to Rotterdam, 500 miles to the north (see Figure 8.5).

Rhine waterway
A system of rivers and canals; the main transportation artery of Europe

For years, shipments have moved between the Netherlands, Belgium, Germany, France, Austria, and Switzerland by means of the Rhine and its connecting waterways, but the Rhine-Main-Danube canal completed in 1992 gives access to the Atlantic Ocean, 13 countries, and the Black Sea. From there, shipments can continue to Moscow over the interconnected system of the Volga and Don rivers. Not many ships undertake the entire 30-day voyage from Rotterdam to the Black Sea (3,500 kilometers), but it has stimulated shipping over shorter east–west routes, such as Nuremburg to Budapest and Vienna to Rotterdam. Increasingly, firms have been turning to the Rhine waterway as an environmentally friendly alternative to road transportation (see the Worldview on page 279).

Since 1999, the Danube has been blocked by the wreckage of bridges bombed by NATO at Novi Sad, Yugoslavia, a river port hundreds of miles upstream from the Main-Danube Canal. It is this canal that connects the Danube through the Main River to the Rhine River and makes river shipping possible from Rotterdam all the way to the Black Sea. The general director of a Hungarian shipping company that is losing $4 million annually because of the blockage asked, "Can you imagine someone bombing the Mississippi in the middle?"[12]

Other Waterways. In every continent except Australia, which has no inland waterways, extensive use is made of water transportation. In South America, the Amazon and

[Figure 8.6] **Paraná-Paraguay Rivers Trade Corridor**

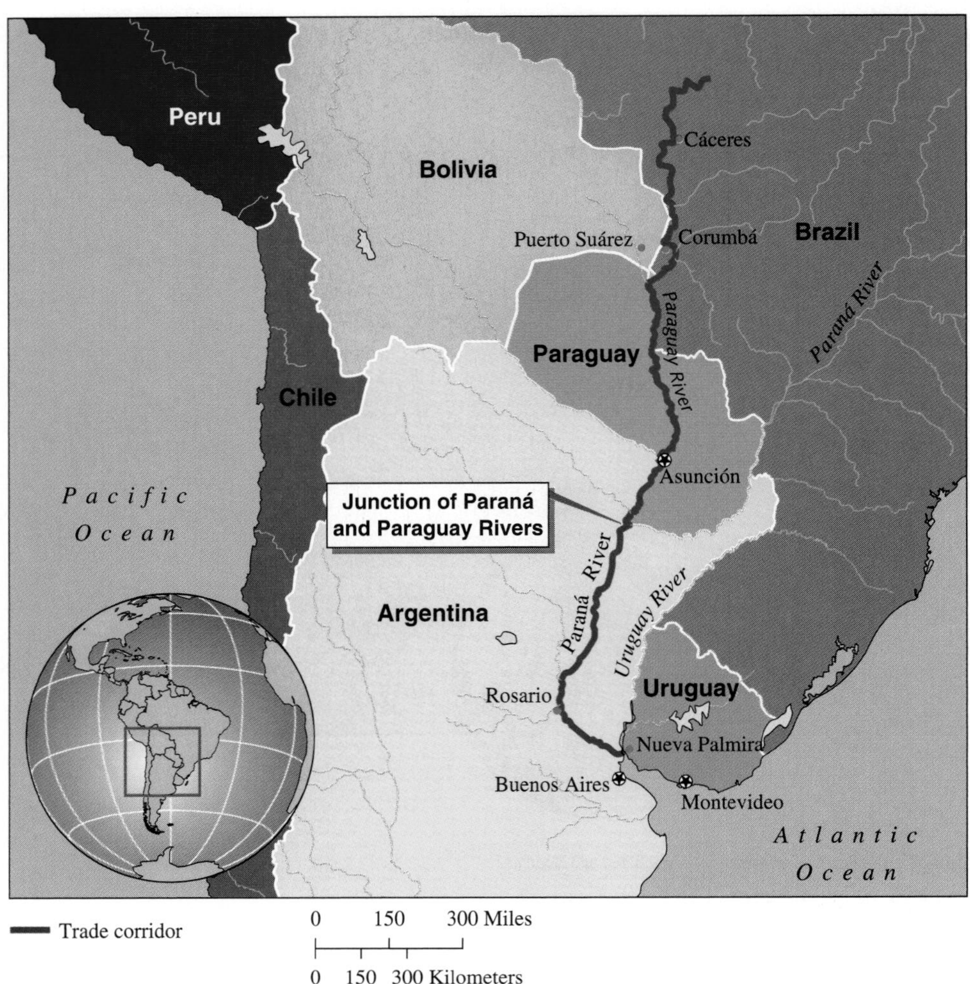

its tributaries offer some 57,000 kilometers of navigable waterways during the flood season. Oceangoing vessels can reach Manaus, Brazil (1,600 kilometers upstream), and smaller river steamers can go all the way to Iquitos, Peru (3,600 kilometers from the Atlantic).

Farther south, the Mercosur governments of Argentina, Brazil, Paraguay, and Uruguay are working to develop the Paraná and Paraguay rivers as a trade corridor connecting the vast landlocked interior of South America with seaports at the River Plate estuary near Montevideo (see Figure 8.6). Although at present the rivers are only partly navigable, Argentina uses river ports on the Paraná to handle 25 percent of its exports and Paraguay imports most of its fuel on the Paraguay River. The Mercosur governments have embarked on a $1 billion project called Hidrovia to dredge the 3,400-kilometer river system. This will permit reliable barge transport year-round from the heart of South America's farmland in northern Argentina, eastern Bolivia, and western Brazil to the port of Rosario, near Buenos Aires. Already Brazil is the world's second-largest soybean producer after the United States.[13]

In Asia, the major waterways are the Yangtze (China), the Ganges (India), and the Indus (Pakistan). Rivers are especially important in China because water is the least expensive, and often the only, means of moving industrial raw materials to the manufacturing centers. Oceangoing vessels can travel up the Yangtze as far as Wuhan, 1,000 kilometers from the sea.

However, when the Three Gorges dam is finished in the year 2010 and the reservoir is filled by the year 2019, oceangoing vessels will be able to continue past Wuhan to

[Worldview]

HELPING THE ENVIRONMENT WHILE SAVING MONEY

The management of Neckermann, a $2.4 billion German mail-order firm, wanted to help protect the environment, so it formulated a policy directing its employees to work to this end. The logistics department, responsible for handling imports from European countries and Asia, proposed sending more imports to Rotterdam, from where they would be forwarded in barges via the Rhine waterway to the firm's three warehouses in Frankfurt. Under the old arrangement, imports arriving in Hamburg were sent by rail or road to Frankfurt. The 120,000 tons of merchandise from European suppliers now comes by rail instead of truck as it formerly did. These changes have provided two benefits: less environmental damage and lower costs.

Based on estimates by the prestigious Planco Institute, the company calculates that the new environmentally friendly system of waterways and rail has reduced total costs to the environment (air, ground, water, and noise pollution) from $1.6 million under the old road-intensive arrangement to $722,000. In addition, the firm is saving $241,000 annually by shipping containers over the Rhine waterway from Rotterdam to Frankfurt instead of using rail from Hamburg to Frankfurt. It is now considering supplying its Mannheim warehouse by barge, and it may also use barges on the Rhine waterway to handle the 500 containers that come each year from Eastern Europe. This has been made possible by the new Main-Danube canal that extends the Rhine waterway all the way to the Black Sea.

Other firms, among them Ford and Unilever, had already changed to the more environmentally friendly river system. These companies predict that others will increase their use of waterways when, as expected, the European Union deregulates waterway rates. ■

Source: "Why Neckermann Chose the Rhine Option," *Business Europe*, January 24–30, 1994, p. 7.

Chongquing, which will become an island seaport 2,400 kilometers from the ocean. When the largest concrete dam ever constructed is completed, the reservoir it creates will be 760 kilometers long. An estimated 1.8 million persons will lose their homes. Because of the environmental issues as well as the human-rights issues involved, the World Bank refused to fund the dam. Governmental export credit agencies from Canada, Germany, Switzerland, and Japan are providing financing and insurance to companies bidding on the project although the U.S. Export-Import Bank has denied support to American exporters. The Chinese government estimates that the total cost of the dam will reach $24.5 billion by the time it is finished. The world's largest public works has been plagued with charges of corruption and malfeasance since January 1999, when the Chinese press reported that over 100 project officials had been arrested on suspicion of corruption.[14]

Although the United States possesses extensive rail and highway systems, it also depends heavily on two waterways. One, the Great Lakes–St. Lawrence, enables ocean freighters to travel 3,700 kilometers inland, thus transforming lake ports into ocean ports. The other waterway, the Mississippi, connects the Great Lakes to the Gulf of Mexico and is especially important for carrying bulky commodities, such as wheat, cotton, coal, timber, and iron ore.

Outlets to the Sea. Historically, navigable waterways with connections to the ocean have permitted the low-cost transportation of goods and people from a country's coast to its interior, and even now they are the only means of access from the coasts of numerous developing nations.

This has been a particularly troublesome problem for Africa, in which 14 of the world's 20 landlocked developing countries are located. Almost one-third of all sub-Saharan countries are landlocked, and some are more than 1,000 kilometers from the sea by the shortest land route. The implications for these poor nations are obvious: they must construct costly, long truck routes and extensive feeder networks for relatively

[Figure 8.7] Bolivia's Export Corridor

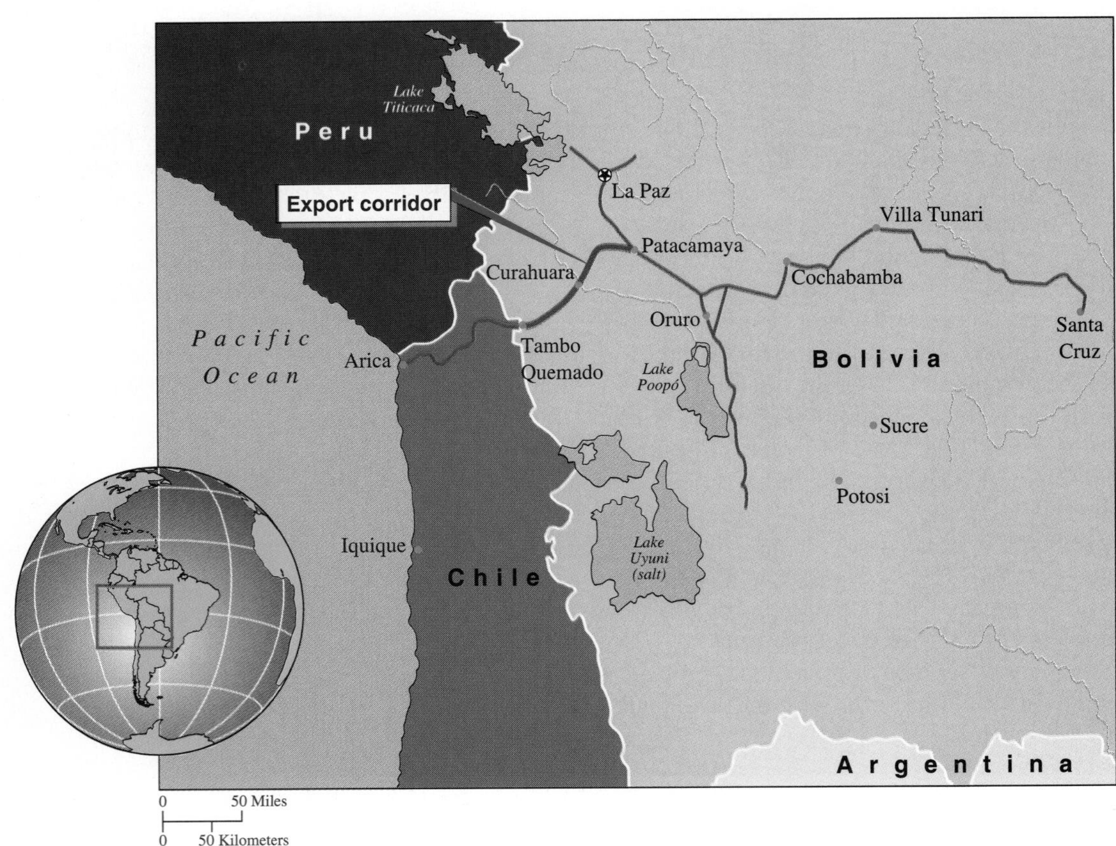

low volumes of traffic. Furthermore, governments in countries with coastlines through which the imports and exports of the landlocked nations must pass are in a position to exert considerable political influence. Small wonder that struggles for outlets to the sea still exist and are important political and economic factors.

Bolivia Demands an Outlet to the Sea. One outstanding example is the centurylong struggle by Bolivia to regain from Chile an outlet to the Pacific Ocean that it lost in an 1879 attack. The two countries have held discussions for decades without reaching a workable agreement. Until Bolivia has its own coastline, it must use Arica, the free port in northern Chile, and inland waterways.

Bolivia's Export Corridor. At the end of 1996, Bolivia inaugurated its first paved road link to the Pacific Ocean, a 192-kilometer highway to the Bolivian–Chilean border (see Figure 8.7). This highway is the last section of Bolivia's 1,000-kilometer "Export Corridor" which has opened Asian markets to Bolivian and Brazilian farmers, thus creating new competition for American growers. Although Bolivia uses a Chilean port as an outlet to the sea, the country still does not maintain diplomatic relations with Chile. Citing Chilean military exercises on the border, President Banzer of Bolivia stated that he doubted that relations with Chile, suspended in 1978, would be restored any time soon.[15]

This dispute affects business relations between the two countries. One of the writers, representing a Chilean subsidiary of an American multinational, called on a large government-owned mine in Bolivia to sell Chilean-made products. The purchasing agent asked how anyone could expect her, a Bolivian, to buy goods made in Chile. Although appreciating that the parent company was American, she said, "The products are still made in Chile."

Climate

climate Meteorological conditions, including temperature, precipitation, and wind, that prevail in a region

Climate (temperature and precipitation) is probably the most important element of the physical forces because it, more than any other factor, sets the limits on what people can do both physically and economically. Where the climate is harsh, there are few human settlements, but where it is permissive, generally there are great clusters of population. However, climate is not deterministic—it allows certain developments to occur, but it does not cause them. Nonclimatic factors, such as mineral deposits, accessibility to an area, economic and political organizations, cultural tradition, availability of capital, and the growth of technology, are more important than climate in the development of trade and manufacturing.

Similar climates occur in similar latitudes and continental positions, and the more water-dominated an area, the more moderate its climate. Thus, the northwest United States and northwest Europe, which are at similar latitudes and are both influenced by the sea, have mild, moist climates. Southeast Australia, New Zealand, and part of South Africa are at the same latitude and close to the sea. They too have mild, moist climates. At the other extreme, Kansas and Central Asia, which are far from the sea and at the same latitude, are dry and have cold winters and hot summers.

Climate and Development

For centuries, writers have used climatic differences to explain differences in human and economic development. They have suggested that the greatest economic and intellectual development has occurred in the temperate climates of northern Europe and the United States because the less temperate climates limit human energy and mental powers.[16] However, marketers must not be taken in by this ethnocentric reasoning, which fails to explain the difference in the level of technology employed in the 1600s by the inhabitants of northeastern North America and the inhabitants of northern Europe. Clearly there were other factors involved, such as the Industrial Revolution, population size, and location.

This is not to say that climate has not had some influence on economic development. Studies by the World Bank have shown that many of the factors responsible for the underdeveloped state of most tropical nations are present because of the tropical climate. Continuous heat and the lack of winter temperatures to constrain the reproduction and growth of weeds, insects, viruses, birds, and parasites result in destroyed crops, dead cattle, and people infected with debilitating diseases.[17]

As grim as this may sound, there is hope. The World Bank points out that techniques are becoming available to control pests and parasites. Once this is accomplished, the very characteristics that are now detrimental to tropical Africa will give it sizable advantages over the temperate zones in agriculture. The resulting income would create a market in tropical Africa that could easily surpass that of the Middle East at the time when oil prices were at their highest.

Climatic Implications

The differences in climatic conditions among a firm's markets can have a significant impact on its product mix. For example, internal combustion engines designed for temperate climates generally require extra cooling capacity and special lubrication to withstand the higher temperatures of the tropics. Goods that deteriorate in high humidity require special, more expensive packaging, machinery operating in dusty conditions needs special dust protection, and so forth.

When climatic extremes exist in a single market and the product is temperature- or humidity-sensitive, the company may have to produce and stock two distinct versions to satisfy the entire market. Severe winters, such as those in Canada, or the heavy monsoon rains that fall in northern Australia and India can impede distribution. This may require the firm to carry extraordinarily large inventories in its major markets to compensate for delays in delivery from the factory. All these conditions, of course, have an adverse effect on profitability. Let us turn now to **natural resources,** the fourth major element of geography that is extremely relevant to businesspeople.

Natural Resources

natural resources
Anything supplied by nature on which people depend

What are **natural resources?** There is no commonly accepted definition among the professionals who work with them. One well-known economic geographer, Joseph H. Butler, states, "To meet their economic needs—including the basic ecological requirements of water, food, clothing, and shelter—people undertake the production of goods and services by extracting *natural resources* from the environment." He adds that all three sectors of the natural environment provide raw materials: the solid portion of the earth, the water portion, and the atmosphere.[18] For our purposes, we can define natural resources as anything supplied by nature on which people depend. Some of the principal types of natural resources important to businesspeople are energy and nonfuel minerals.

Energy

Petroleum

During the Arab–Israeli war in 1973, Arab exporters of petroleum used an oil embargo on some nations and the threat of an embargo on others to obtain political support from Western Europe. Realizing that not only their industries but also their national defense depended on a substance other nations could use as a political force, the United States and other oil-importing nations initiated a worldwide campaign to conserve mineral fuels and search for new energy sources. The 1990 Iraqi invasion of Kuwait, followed by Operation Desert Storm, reminded industry and government officials of the necessity to continue searching for new sources of petroleum, both conventional and unconventional.

Conventional Sources. According to some analysts, the world is running out of oil, but according to other sources, there are reserves sufficient to last for 50 years at the present rate of consumption.[19] Estimates of reserves change because (1) new discoveries continue to be made in proven fields with the aid of improved prospecting equipment and (2) governments open up their countries to exploration and production, such as the countries of the former Soviet Union allowing commercial exploitation of the reserves under the Caspian Sea. Also, (3) new techniques, such as steam and hot water injection, enable producers to obtain greater output from wells already in operation, thus increasing the recoverable amount in an oil field, and (4) automated, less expensive equipment lowers drilling costs, such as wellheads located on the ocean floor that replace expensive offshore drilling platforms. This allows a company to work smaller-sized discoveries at a profit that otherwise it would not touch.[20]

Unconventional Sources. Among the many unconventional sources of synthetic petroleum are (1) oil sands, (2) oil-bearing shale, (3) coal, and (4) natural gas. You recognize, of course, that the last two are also employed without conversion to synthetic petroleum to generate energy.

1. **Oil sands.** One unconventional source of petroleum is the oil sands, located primarily in Athabasca, Alberta, Canada. The sands, which contain bitumen, a tarlike crude, account for about 20 percent (500,000 barrels per day) of Canada's crude oil production. However, the oil companies are increasing their production capacity, and the latest estimates are that oil sands production will reach 1 million barrels per day by the year 2010 and will amount to over 25 percent of the crude oil produced in Canada.

   At the current rate of US$12.64 per barrel, the cost of extracting bitumin is competitive with that of conventional crude. The oil that can be recovered economically from the Canadian oil sands is estimated to be 300 billion barrels, exceeding the proven oil reserves of Saudi Arabia, the world's largest producer of conventional crude.

A new technology, steam-assisted gravity drainage (SAGD), will enable producers to exploit additional resources that are too deep to mine from the surface. Industry specialists expect that the oil sands will be able to supply up to 50 percent of Canada's crude by 2005 at less than US$7 per barrel. Although the extraction cost is lower with the new technology, it is still considerably higher than that of conventional crude oil produced by Middle Eastern producers (US$2.50/barrel) and American producers (US$3.50–$4.50/barrel).[21]

2. **Oil-bearing shale.** Oil shale is the name given to fine-grained sedimentary rocks that yield 25 liters or more of liquid hydrocarbons per ton of rock when heated to 500°C. The largest source of this material is the three-state area of Utah, Colorado, and Wyoming, which has remained undeveloped because of the availability of less expensive conventional oil, the environmental problems of waste rock disposal, and the great quantities of water needed for processing.

   Because Australia is predicted to be only 50 percent self-sufficient in crude oil by the year 2001, two local oil companies joined with Suncor, a Canadian firm, to build a demonstration plant using Canadian technology to process the country's huge deposits. A decision about the technical and commercial viability of the process will be made by the year 2001. The new technology minimizes danger to the environment. No chemicals are required, only a small amount of energy is required, and there is no contaminated waste. The production cost should compete with the Australian cost of US$25/barrel for conventional crude.[22]

shale
A fissile rock (capable of being split) composed of laminated layers of claylike, fine-grained sediment

3. **Coal.** When many nations refused to sell crude oil to South Africa because of its apartheid policy, the government of that country erected a factory to obtain oil from coal, using a process developed in Germany. The company, Sasol, utilizes more than 40 million tons of low-grade coal for which there is no other use. This process begins in the gasification plant, where coal under pressure and high temperature, in the presence of steam and oxygen, is converted to crude gas. After cooling and purification, the gas passes through either a high- or a low-temperature conversion process where high-value chemical components and synthetic oil are produced. Most of the oil stream is routed to a refinery where it is converted to gasoline, liquefied petroleum gas (LPG), diesel fuel, and jet fuel.[23]

4. **Natural gas.** You saw in the coal-to-liquid process that the purified gas passes through conversion processes to become liquids. Oil companies have always had a problem disposing of large, isolated gas reserves that are too far from markets to be profitable. However, converting the gas to a liquid enables it to be produced profitably and moved less expensively to world markets. Using the Sasol process, the oil companies utilize gas that otherwise would be burned off and also produce cleaner fuels than are produced with other refining methods. In 1999, Chevron formed a joint venture with Sasol for worldwide use of its gas-to-liquid technology. The new company is building a conversion plant in Nigeria. Scheduled to be completed in 2002, the $1 billion project will be the world's largest natural gas-to-liquid facility. Shell, Exxon, and BP Amoco are working on similar technology.[24]

Coal and Nuclear Power

Because of public concern about the safety of nuclear power plants and waste disposal, this energy source is losing market share. Worldwide nuclear capacity is expected to increase from 349 gigawatts in 1998 to 368 gigawatts in 2010 and then begin to decline to 303 gigawatts by 2020, an 18 percent decrease. Only the developing nations are expected to have continuous nuclear power growth through 2020.

A wind turbine farm on the border of Denmark and Germany. Six of the world's top 10 turbine producers are Danish.
Peter Mueller

Although coal has lost market share to petroleum products, natural gas, and nuclear power, it continues to be a primary source for electric power generation. The consumption of coal has increased in the United States, Japan, and the developing Asian nations, especially China and India, but declined 33 percent in Europe between 1985 and 1997, where it has been replaced by the growing use of natural gas and nuclear power.[25]

Natural Gas

Natural gas is the fastest-growing energy source, and its use is expected to more than double between 1997 and 2020. The developing nations of Asia and Latin America will experience the greatest annual growth rates in demand (5.6 percent versus 3.1 percent for coal and oil), and there will be increases in all regions except the Middle East and Africa, where usage is relatively stable. Global gas reserves have more than doubled over the last 20 years, whereas oil reserves have grown 62 percent in the same period.[26]

Sources of Renewable Energy

Most people in the energy industry believe that one day renewable energy sources will replace fossil fuels. There are at least eight types: hydroelectric, solar, wind, geothermal, waves, tides, biomass, and ocean thermal energy conversion. None is universal, but all appear to have an application under appropriate conditions. Of the eight, hydroelectric has had an extensive application—7 percent of the total energy consumed in the world comes from hydroelectric installations.

Currently, the costs of generating electricity per kilowatt hour for various fuels in the United States are as follows:

Coal	4–5¢	Wind	4–7¢
Gas	3–5¢	Biomass	6–8¢
Hydro	4–7¢	Solar	10–12¢
Geothermal	5–8¢	Photovoltaic	30–40¢

Figure 8.8 compares the percentages of each type of energy for American and world energy sources.

[Figure 8.8] **U.S. and World Energy Supplies by Source**

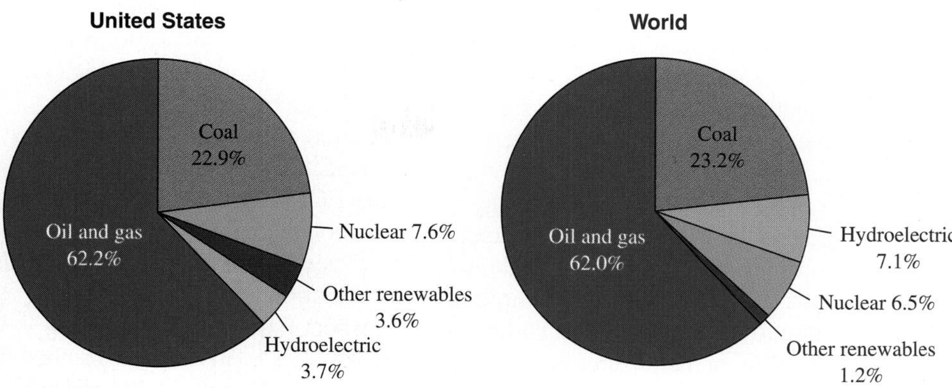

Source: "Overview," *International Energy Annual 1998* (Washington, DC: Energy Information Administration), www.eia.doe.gov/emeu/iea/overview.html (September 19, 2000).

Table 8.1 **Top Wind Energy Markets (Megawatts)**

	1998 Additions	1998 Total	1999 Additions	1999 Total
Germany	793	2,872	1,200	4,072
United States	193	1,770	732	2,502
Denmark	310	1,433	300	1,733
Spain	368	822	650	1,722
India	82	1,015	62	1,077
United Kingdom	10	334	18	534
Netherlands	50	375	53	428
China	55	224	76	300
Italy	94	199	50	249
Sweden	54	176	40	216

Note: Additions include only projects that have been installed and are operating in the calendar year. The year-end total for the United States is net of retired projects.

Source: "1999 Best Year Ever for Wind Energy," *Global Wind Energy Market Report,* American Wind Energy Association, www.awea.org/faq/global99.html (September 20, 2000).

Improved technology has resulted in new support for wind and solar energy in many parts of the world. Wind energy–generating capacity in 1999 increased by more than 36 percent over installed capacity in 1998. This seems to confirm the claim that wind energy is the fastest-growing energy technology in the world. The installed capacity increased 6½ times from 1990 to 1999 [2000 megawatts (MW) to 13,400 MW].

Only 3 of the 10 countries with the highest installed capacity at the end of 1999 lie outside of Europe: the United States, India, and China (see Table 8.1).

Global sales of photovoltaic (PV) cells and modules for converting solar energy to electricity increased fivefold during the period 1988–1998, while installed costs fell. Developing nations such as India, Kenya, and Indonesia are using them for rural electrification in isolated communities that are far from power lines and have small electricity requirements. In developed countries, on the other hand, their primary use is for water and space heating.

Small Business: Big Idea

Small and Medium-Sized Enterprises

Imagine a computer that uses neural computing techniques that imitate the way a brain works to find mineral deposits. A small nine-year-old company, Neural Technologies, working with a major Australian mining company, has written software that analyzes raw exploration data and then detects and prioritizes anything abnormal that could indicate the presence of new deposits.

The sophisticated remote sensing methods, such as satellite mapping, that geologists use in their surveys produce massive volumes of data that must be sifted in a tedious and costly procedure to identify mining prospects. Geologists must move quickly to collect and analyze data from a number of different surveys before they can establish areas for test drilling.

Usually, the mining company pays a fee to a government for permission to test for mineral deposits. The firm has only a limited time to decide whether it should develop the land or return it to the government. The process of analyzing data from a 300-square-mile plot can take a team of geologists six months and cost $100,000. Typically, they will study at least six sets of survey data covering airborne geophysics, topography, gravity, and geochemistry and then plot and examine them on a light table. Computers with conventional software cannot display simultaneously all the data for interpretation, and the usual expert systems rely heavily on subjective opinion.

Neural Technologies used a different approach. The software, Prospect Explorer, runs on an ordinary PC. The geologists use interrogation techniques and search facilities to look deeper for detailed information to analyze. Using Prospect Explorer for analyzing survey data is 50 times faster than using manual methods. According to the director of the American Institute of Mining, the software is bringing about "the biggest revolution in the mining industry in 25 years." ■

Source: "Rich Seam for Neural Systems," *Financial Times,* December 11, 1996, p. 10.

American shipments, aided by exports accounting for 72 percent of the total, reached a record level in 1999, up 52 percent from 1998. Germany (36.1 percent of U.S. exports) and Japan (26.9 percent) were the most important customers, followed by Brazil and Spain (3.4 percent each).[27]

Nonfuel Minerals

Although much of the world's attention has centered on the discovery of new energy sources, Figure 8.9 shows that there are also other mineral resources about which governments and industry are apprehensive. Nearly all of the world's chrome, manganese, platinum, and vanadium are produced by South Africa and the former Soviet Union. Chrome and manganese are indispensable for hardening steel; platinum is a vital catalytic agent in the oil-refining process and is used in automotive catalytic converters; and vanadium is used in forming aerospace titanium alloys and in producing sulphuric acid. The United States depends on South Africa to supply 79 percent of its platinum, 78 percent of its chromium, 41 percent of its manganese, and 20 percent of its vanadium. Although South Africa never threatened to stop exports of these strategic metals, government and industry leaders are well aware that if the South African source had been lost, the major industrial societies in the West would have been heavily dependent on their communist enemies for their supply in both wartime and peacetime.

Bleak Situation?

The situation appears bleak, but remember that we are discussing known reserves. Do other sources exist? Consider this. Only relatively small areas, mostly in the traditional mining countries, have been adequately explored. For example, it is estimated that only 5 percent of the potential mineral-containing areas in Mexico and only 10 percent of those in Bolivia have been studied extensively.

[Figure 8.9] **Who Has the Non-Fuel Mineral Wealth**

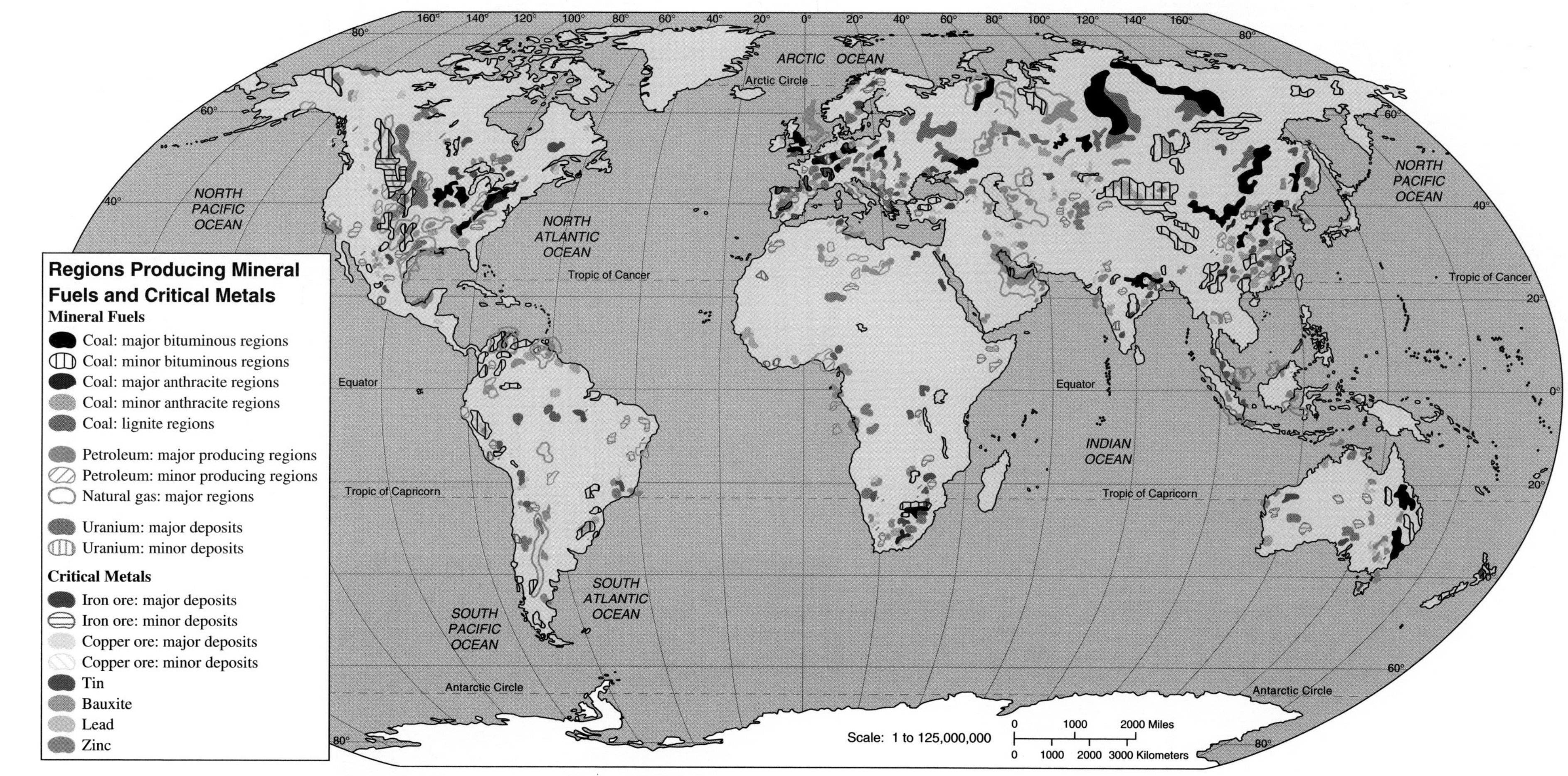

ARCTIC OCEAN
Arctic Circle
NORTH PACIFIC OCEAN
NORTH ATLANTIC OCEAN
Tropic of Cancer
Equator
Tropic of Capricorn
SOUTH PACIFIC OCEAN
SOUTH ATLANTIC OCEAN
INDIAN OCEAN
Antarctic Circle
Regions Producing Mineral Fuels and Critical Metals
Mineral Fuels
Coal: major bituminous regions
Coal: minor bituminous regions
Coal: major anthracite regions
Coal: minor anthracite regions
Coal: lignite regions
Petroleum: major producing regions
Petroleum: minor producing regions
Natural gas: major regions
Uranium: major deposits
Uranium: minor deposits
Critical Metals
Iron ore: major deposits
Iron ore: minor deposits
Copper ore: major deposits
Copper ore: minor deposits
Tin
Bauxite
Lead
Zinc
Scale: 1 to 125,000,000
0 1000 2000 Miles
0 1000 2000 3000 Kilometers

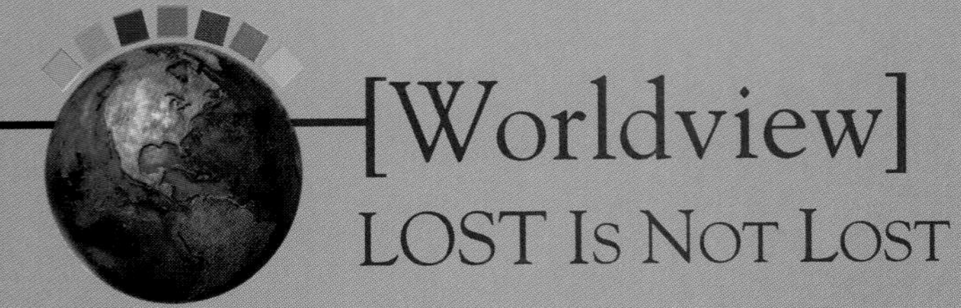

[Worldview]
LOST Is Not Lost

After four years of negotiations over the provisions of the United Nations Law of the Sea Treaty (LOST), representatives of 127 nations agreed on rules governing deep seabed mining to be administered by the UN organization the International Seabed Authority (ISA). This is the first time regulations have been made to govern deep seabed resources beyond national jurisdiction.

The ISA's code regulates the exploration and mining of potato-sized polymetallic nodules lying outside the 200-mile economic zone of any country as well as the metal deposits found in the crust of 100-foot-high chimneylike structures formed when hot water rushes up from volcanic vents in the sea floor. The recovery of hydrocarbons is also regulated. The new regulations also empower the ISA to sign exploration contracts with registered pioneer investors (the first firms to make large investments in the survey of nodules). They include five companies, one each from Japan, France, Russia, and China and one jointly owned by Poland, Cuba, Bulgaria, Slovakia, and the Czech Republic. Mining proposals by India and Korea have been approved. American firms, however, are not involved because the United States is an observer, not yet a member. ■

Sources: Marjorie Ann Browne, "The Law of the Sea Convention and U.S. Policy," CRS Issue Brief for Congress, June 16, 2000, www.cnei.org/nle/mar-16.html (September 22, 2000); and "Mines at Bottom of the Sea Move a Step Closer," *Financial Times,* August 15, 2000, p. 22.

The water emitted from this single black smoker in the East Pacific Rise has been measured at 660° F.
Woods Hole Oceanographic Institution, Woods Hole, MA 02543

Furthermore, a relatively new technology—satellite mapping—has enabled geologists to locate new sources. Before this discovery, geologists believed Brazil to have few minerals, but they now know that it possesses extensive deposits of chromium, nickel, copper, lead, zinc, and manganese.

Ocean Mining—the Last Frontier?

In 1997, a mining company for the first time filed a claim to mine the world's richest underseas deposit of gold, silver, copper, and zinc. The deposit, located in Papua New Guinea a mile below the surface, has about 10 times the gold and five times as much copper found in land-based mines. Temperatures as high as 800°F caused by underwater volcanic activity make gold, silver, and other metals separate from rocks deep in the earth and form chimneylike towers (see Worldview above). Robots crush a portion of the sea floor, and then the ore is scooped up and sent to the surface through piping.

The world's two largest diamond mining companies, De Beers and Namibian Mining Company, are mining diamonds off the coast of Namibia by using truck-sized remote-controlled crawlers to excavate seabed sediment with a powerful pump and transport the sediment to a surface ship where the diamonds are sorted and classified. De Beers and Namibian produce over 500,000 carats and 200,000 annually respectively. The average size is 35 points, but 2-carat and larger diamonds are frequently found. Sales revenue averages US$153 per carat with a production cost of US$63 per carat.[28]

Changes Make Monitoring Necessary

Mineral Resources

You saw how crude oil prices spurred the discovery of oil by non-OPEC members as they sought to lessen their dependence on imported oil. New land-based sources of strategic nonfuel minerals have also been discovered, and we have learned that the oceans contain vast amounts of these minerals in the form of nodules and seafloor crusts.

Concomitantly, important discoveries are being made that could lessen our need for these minerals. Reinforced plastics have lessened our dependence on steel alloys that require imported cobalt and manganese, for example.

One of the most fascinating discoveries is the fuel cell, first used by NASA in space capsules, that chemically converts fuel directly to electricity without having to burn it. In 1992, Ford, General Motors, and Chrysler formed the United States Council for Automotive Research (USCAR) to strengthen the base of the U.S. auto industry by collaborating in noncompetitive areas. One goal is to develop automobiles that use advanced fuel cell technology. Then, in 1993, USCAR formed the Partnership for a New Generation of Vehicles (PNGV) with the U.S. government. The PNGV aims to implement technologies to increase the efficiency of conventional vehicles, work on fuel-cell-powered cars, and develop a new class of vehicles that will get 80 miles per gallon.

Although interest in fuel cell technology has grown rapidly because of the increased fuel economy potential, a barrier to its use has been the fact that current fuel cells can be operated only on methanol or hydrogen—fuels that are not readily available. In 1999, however, PNGV researchers introduced a fuel processor that converts gasoline into a hydrogen-rich gas that can be used to power a fuel cell. Nevertheless, reducing the size and the cost of fuel cell systems remains a significant barrier to overcome before fuel cells can be competitive with internal combustion engines. One advantage: Unlike Japanese gasoline-electric hybrid cars, which get lower mileage and have higher emissions, fuel-cell-driven automobiles require no battery.[29]

Do these discoveries have any significance for businesspeople? Obviously, sellers of commodities and products that are being threatened by the discoveries must monitor them and prepare for new competition. More important, all firms supplying goods and services to nations that depend on the traditional minerals for foreign exchange to pay for those goods and services must be aware of developments that can destroy old markets and create new ones. Imagine the loss of purchasing power in the Middle Eastern countries if lower-cost hydrogen available from water takes the place of gasoline. We have already seen cutbacks in the purchases of these countries because of lower crude oil prices, but what if petroleum were needed only by the petrochemical industry and not for transportation?

Other Changing Physical Forces

Mineral resources are not the only physical forces that change. Modifications of infrastructure, most of which are of great significance to businesspeople, are being made constantly. For example, new settlements and new industries are attracted to areas in which dams have been built to control flooding and provide power and irrigation water. New highways and new railways reduce delivery times to present markets and thus enable firms to cut their distribution costs by reducing their inventories. For example, improved highways now permit regularly scheduled overland delivery service from London to cities as far east as Moscow. One Russian trucking firm now makes the London–Moscow run in just eight days, a trip that formerly took months by sea.

However, when the Brazilian government sought a World Bank loan to construct a paved highway to connect the mineral-rich but economically stagnant state of Acre to the rest of Brazil, American environmentalists complained, and the loan was postponed. The environmentalists' concern was that the road would destroy the Amazon tropical forest, which they say converts carbon dioxide to oxygen and absorbs heat, thus reducing the greenhouse effect. Nevertheless, Brazil's foreign minister said, "Brazil isn't going to become the ecological reserve for the rest of the world. Our biggest commitment is with

A Gnat and the Elephant

Small and Medium-Sized Enterprises

A tiny nine-person company, A-55 LP, has formed a joint venture with Caterpillar, a multinational with 50,000 employees. What's the attraction? A German inventor and owner of A-55 LP, Rudolf W. Gunnerman, claims he has invented a technology that enables internal combustion engines to burn a mixture of half fuel and half water. The mixture gets 40 percent more mileage with less pollution. He believes the water breaks down into oxygen and hydrogen, with the hydrogen supplying the energy.

Actually, the drivers do not simply mix water with gasoline; they have to buy a prepared mixture, 0.5 percent of which is an emulsifier that enables the water and fuel to mix. The inventor says the conversion of a gasoline motor to run on the mixture would cost less than $500. The city of Reno, Nevada, used the product to power a city bus for five months and experienced a 29 percent increase in miles per gallon of diesel fuel.

After 11,000 miles, the engine was removed and sent to Caterpillar for evaluation. Caterpillar was so interested that it has now formed a joint venture with the inventor's company to perfect and market the product. It is expected that the new product will find a global market.

Caterpillar's technical manager and acting general manager of the joint venture, called Advanced Fuels LLC, says, "It's certainly a very exciting technology. But a lot of work still needs to be done, and a lot of surprises can crop up as you go to product development." How big is this new fuel? An expert who tracks emerging transportation technology claims that if it works as expected, the United States will no longer have to import crude oil.

Unfortunately, the joint venture lasted only two years. Later, an arbitrator ruled that Caterpillar improperly patented and then sought to market clean-fuel technology for diesel engines that rightfully belonged to the former joint venture partner. ■

Sources: "Arbitrator Says Cat Committed Fraud," *World Mining Equipment,* January 20, 2000, www.wme.com/wme/headlines/head0120.htm (September 23, 2000); and "Engines That Run on Water," *Business Week,* August 8, 1994, p. 47.

economic development."[30] Despite its cost (the picture illustrates why), one of Latin America's major infrastructural achievements, the Trans-Andean Highway, has greatly increased trade and tourism between Argentina and Chile.

New infrastructure is responsible for economic development in developed nations also. The 31-mile Channel Tunnel, or Chunnel, connecting England and France, which began service in November 1994, has attracted heavy investment. The population of Calais, the city at the French end of the tunnel, is expected to double to 200,000, many of whom will be British citizens attracted by cheaper housing and the ability to live in France and commute daily to work in Great Britain. Distribution costs are expected to be significantly lower because the trip from London to Paris takes about three hours through the tunnel compared to seven hours using ferries and trains. The trip from London to Brussels, Belgium, takes just three hours and 15 minutes.[31]

Another time-saver is the Oresund bridge, the first land link between Denmark and Sweden. The 16-kilometer bridge and tunnel with a four-lane roadway and a double-track railway have joined southern Sweden and eastern Denmark for the first time since the Ice Age 7,000 years ago. Commuting time has been reduced from 45 minutes on a ferry to about 20 minutes on the new US$3.5 billion bridge. With 3.5 million inhabitants, the Oresund Region created by the bridge is the largest domestic market in Northern Europe.

The new connection has already begun to influence the location of company offices. To improve communication between its Danish and Swedish offices, DaimlerChrysler moved its Swedish offices from Stockholm to Malmo at the Swedish end of the bridge and its Danish offices from northern Denmark to Copenhagen on the Danish end. Malmo's population is expected to increase 20 percent over the next 10 years as a result of Danes seeking less expensive housing and an influx from other parts of Sweden. Copenhagen's mayor says, "The feeling that we are part of Europe is the main reason we built this bridge. Twenty years ago, even 10 years ago, we would not have spent bil-

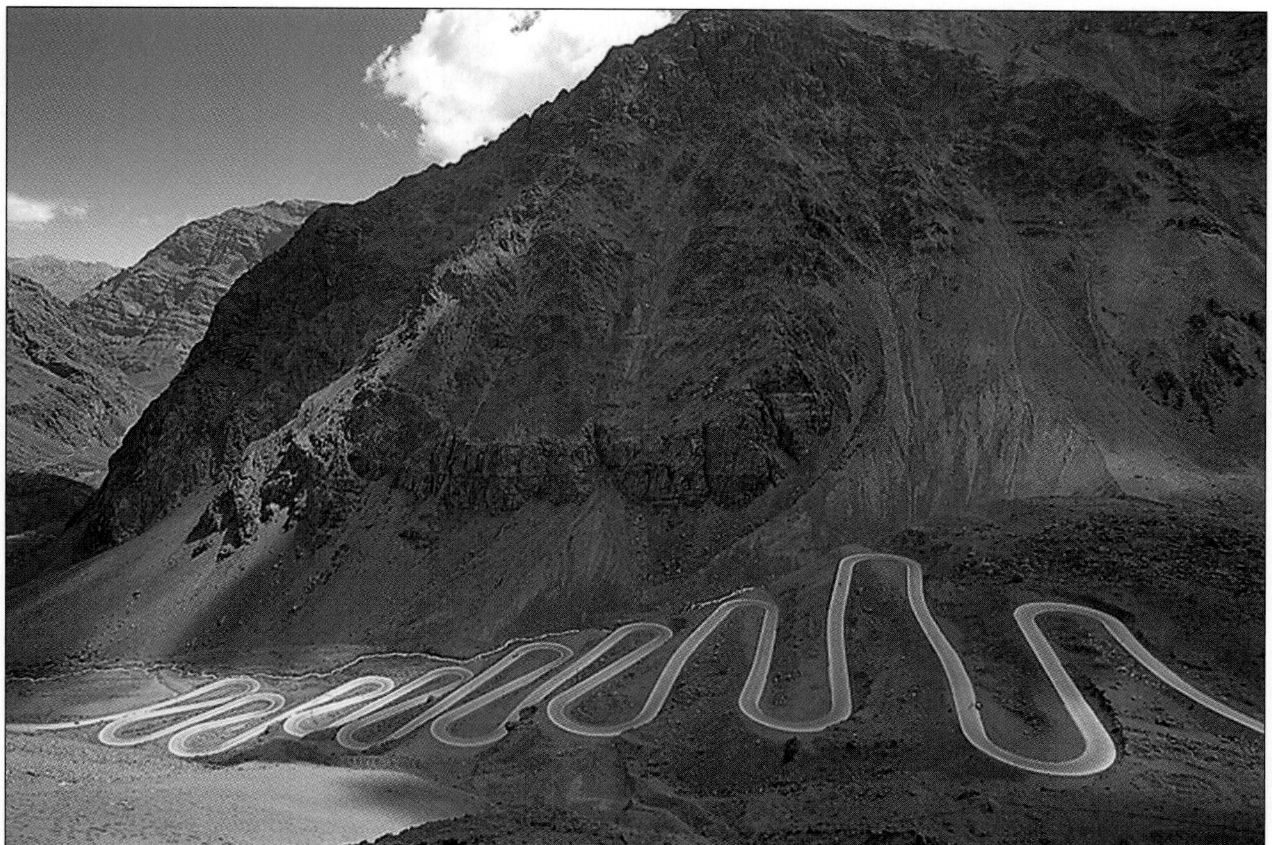

The Trans-Andean Highway
Loren McIntyre

lions on a link between Denmark and Sweden. But now, we are no longer just Danes and Swedes—we are Europeans. We needed to have that mental bridge before we could build the concrete one."[32]

Destruction of Natural Resources

Historically, nations have paid relatively little attention to the contamination and destruction of the world's natural resources. Entire forests have been destroyed by people wanting to get firewood or to clear land and by contaminated air and water. Pollution control of air and water was considered a luxury that governments, anxious to attract new industry and to keep the industry they had, could ill afford to impose. As the secretary of mines and energy for the state of Bahia, Brazil, stated, "Brazil can't afford pollution control like Japan or the United States. It's cultural imperialism."

However, such tragedies as the Bhopal disaster and the world's largest radiation catastrophe at the Chernobyl nuclear power plant in Ukraine have forced officials to realize that the price for such negligence is too high.

The Bhopal Disaster

What is described as the world's worst human-made industrial disaster killed at least 7,000 people. On December 4, 1984, the deadly gas methyl isocyanate, which is used in the production of insecticides, leaked from storage tanks at the Bhopal plant of Union Carbide (India), a joint venture of Union Carbide (50.9 percent) and Indian capital. Government financial institutions owned nearly 26 percent of the company.

Although suits totaling $250 billion were filed on behalf of Bhopal victims, in 1989 the Indian supreme court reached an out-of-court settlement with Union Carbide (U.S.) for $470 million.[33] Ten years after the accident, Indian courts had paid out only $20 million to settle 94,000 compensation claims, or $213 per claimant. A key issue of great interest to American multinationals was whether the lawsuits seeking damages should be tried in American or Indian courts. Attorneys for the victims fought to have the case tried in the United States, but an American judge ruled that it should be heard in India.

However, in 1999, 15 years after the disaster, a lawsuit was filed in New York City charging the Union Carbide Corporation and its former CEO, Warren Anderson, with "violating international law and fundamental human rights of the victims and survivors of the 1984 release of toxic gases." Union Carbide said that the company was reviewing the suit, but all personal injury claims were settled in 1989 when US$470 million was paid to the Indian government in a final settlement. That settlement was initially approved by the Supreme Court of India and then upheld by that body in 1991.

Over 95 percent of those who received payment were paid only US$600 in the case of injury or less than US$3,000 in the case of death. More than 120,000 survivors still need medical attention, and 10 to 15 people die monthly from exposure-related illnesses.[34]

Chernobyl: The World's Worst Nuclear Disaster

On April 26, 1986, a nuclear explosion at the Chernobyl power plant caused 190 tons of highly radioactive uranium and graphite to be released into the air. Called by the United Nations the world's worst human-made disaster, the explosion caused the population of the Republic of Belarus to be exposed to radioactivity 90 times greater than that released at Hiroshima.

A 1995 United Nations report claimed that at least 9 million people were affected in the three countries of Belarus, Ukraine, and Russia. According to the Ukrainian government, 125,000 have already died. Over half a million inhabitants of 2,000 towns were evacuated from their homes in a heavily contaminated area, and it is believed that the evacuations will continue into the 21st century.[35]

Although Chernobyl's reactor number 4, the one that exploded and caused the world's worst nuclear disaster, was encased in concrete after the explosion, the site's only functioning reactor (No. 3) was permitted to operate for nearly 15 years before being shut down in December, 2000. The government of Ukraine obtained an international loan to complete the construction of two nuclear power plants that will make up for the loss of reactor that was closed down.[36]

Alaskan Oil Spill

Called America's Chernobyl, the worst oil spill in this country's history occurred near Valdez, Alaska, in 1989, when an Exxon tanker hit a reef and spilled 10 million gallons of crude oil (see Figure 8.10). Exxon's cleanup group involved more than 11,000 people, 1,200 vessels, and 80 aircraft.[37] The company spent over $2.5 billion for the cleanup and $1 billion to settle federal and state criminal charges. In addition, in 1994 Exxon was ordered by a federal jury in Alaska to pay $5 billion to fishers and other Alaskans, the largest punitive award ever against a corporation. In an earlier phase of the trial, the jury awarded $287 million to 10,000 fishers. Another group of 4,000 native Alaskans settled their claims for $20 million.[38]

Eco-Terrorism in the Gulf War

An ecological disaster far worse than the Valdez oil spill was caused by the Iraqi army before its retreat from Kuwait. A total of 732 oil wells were sabotaged by the army or

[Figure 8.10] Oil Spill Disaster I: Prince William Sound

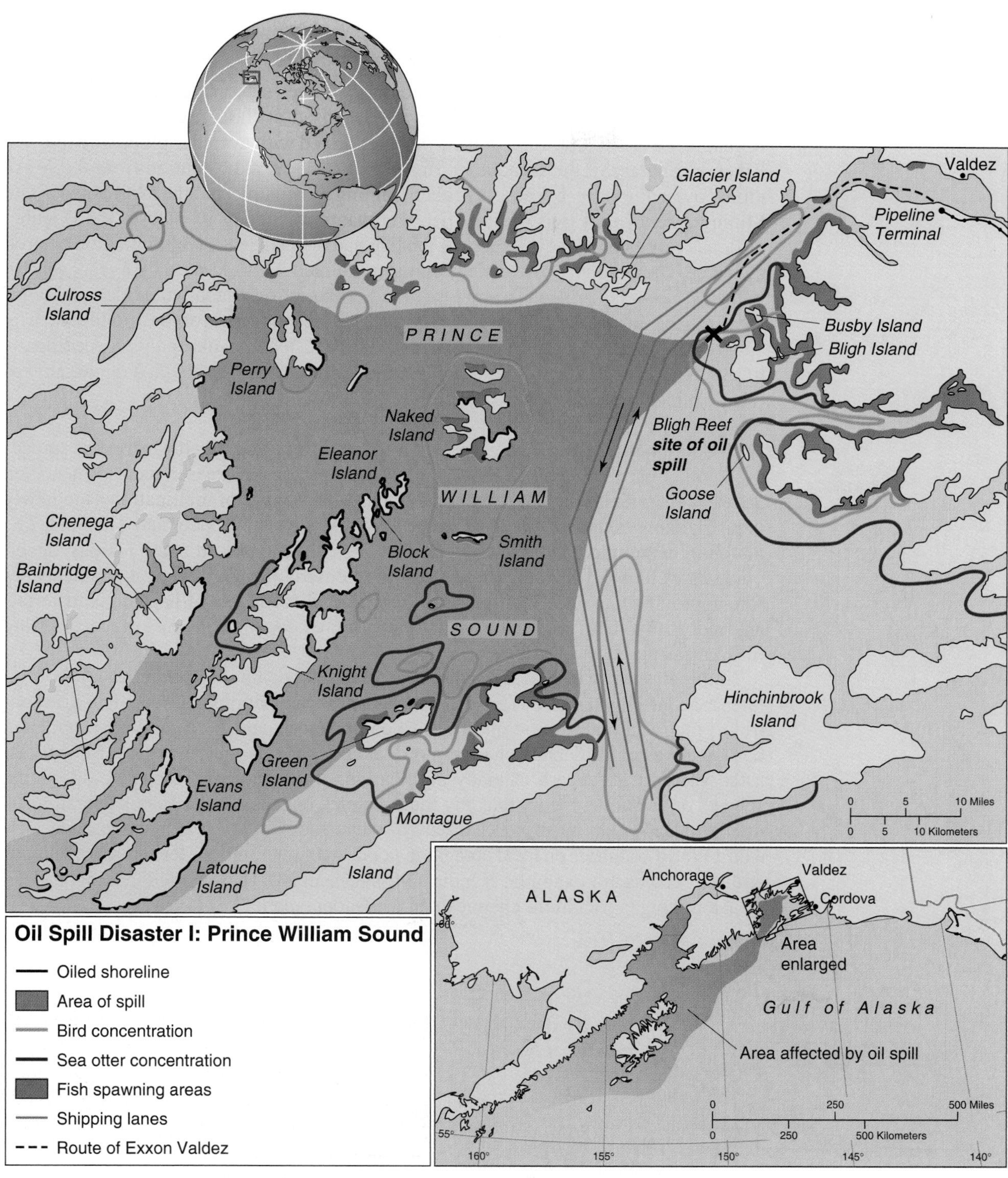

were set on fire during combat. Moreover, 75 million barrels of oil spilled out over the desert, forming lakes that birds mistakenly took for real ones, flying to their deaths.[39] Iraqi troops also let oil escape from Kuwait's Sea Island terminal, creating a spill 27 times larger than the Valdez disaster.

The estimated 42 billion gallons of oil that spread over the desert into the Persian Gulf, along with the oil well fires and the war damage, have resulted in an enormous ecological disaster. Years after the war, no one knows if the ecology suffered a crippling blow or if the damage can be absorbed. Although the oil made Kuwait's beaches look like an asphalt highway after the war, the Kuwaitis did little to clean it up.[40]

Biggest Ecological Disaster since Chernobyl

What has been called the biggest ecological disaster since Chernobyl occurred on January 30, 2000, when a reservoir wall collapsed at the Aurul mine in northern Romania. Over 100,000 cubic meters of water mixed with cyanide spilled into the Tisa River, a tributary of the Danube in Yugoslavia. The cyanide solution from the Aurul mine, owned jointly by an Australian mining company and the Romanian State Mining Agency, left tons of dead fish and waterbirds along its path to the Danube. Officials estimated that 80 percent of the fish had died since the contamination entered the river. The Serbian environment minister claimed it would take five years for life in the Tisa to recover. He also said that the Serbian government would demand compensation at an international court from those responsible for the pollution. The Australian partner went into receivership—the first step in bankruptcy proceedings—in anticipation of multi-million-dollar compensation claims, although it denies any direct responsibility.[41]

Antipollution activism, already a potent force in Europe and North America, is spreading to other parts of the world. Local citizen groups have increased their influence on government policies and have worked to delay the projects of multinationals in newly industrializing countries, such as Brazil, India, Malaysia, Mexico, and Thailand. The notion of economic growth at any cost is being challenged, and many nations, developing as well as developed, are now requiring environmental impact assessments before approving new industrial plants. Multinational producers of hazardous materials are finding that these changes are resulting in higher costs and are making the locating of overseas plants more difficult.

Multinationals in hazardous industries will resist the minority positions in joint ventures mandated by numerous governments when such positions cause them to lose control to the local majority on questions of equipment, plant safety, and environmental controls. Warren Anderson, chairman of Union Carbide at the time of the Bhopal disaster, voiced the concern of many multinational managements when he said, "India sued us on the novel theory that any multinational engaged in hazardous operations is totally liable for any mishap, regardless of what share it may own. Is the insistence by Third World countries on local content in goods manufactured for local markets always realistic? It was, for example, at India's insistence that Carbide started making, instead of just mixing, agricultural chemicals in the Bhopal plant."[42]

[Summary]

Appreciate the relevance to businesspeople of four elements of geography: (1) location, (2) topography, (3) climate, and (4) natural resources.

Throughout this chapter, we present practical examples to show you why these four geographical elements are relevant to businesspeople. Frequently, you will find a section headed "Relevance for Businesspeople."

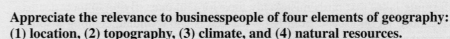

Understand the importance of a country's location in political and trade relationships.

A nation's location is a significant factor in its political and trading relationships. Austria, for example, located on the borders of both Eastern and Western Europe, has become the financial intermediary between the two regions as well as regional headquarters for numerous international firms that have Eastern European operations. Two major trading partners of the United States, Canada and Mexico, are located on its borders.

Understand how surface features contribute to economic, cultural, political, and social differences among nations and among regions of a single country.

Mountains divide nations into smaller regional markets that often have distinct cultures, industries, and climates. Sometimes even the languages are different. Deserts and tropical forests act as barriers to people, goods, and ideas.

Comprehend the importance of inland waterways and outlets to the sea.

Bodies of water attract people and facilitate transportation. Water transportation has increased even after the building of railroads and highways. Various European firms are shipping goods in barges on the Rhine waterway instead of using highways.

Recognize that climate exerts a broad influence on business.

The differences in climatic conditions among a firm's markets can significantly affect its marketing mix. A product sold for use in northern Canada may need protection against cold weather, while the same product used in the tropics may require extra cooling to resist the heat. Heavy seasonal rains can require the firm to carry large inventories because of the difficulty in replenishing stock in inclement weather.

Understand why managers must monitor changes in the discovery and the use of mineral resources and energy sources.

The discovery of a new energy source or the reduction in the cost of producing an alternative source may offer a company an opportunity to economize on its use of energy. A new oil or mineral find might provide a country with new income, which in turn could make it a valuable customer for international firms, as occurred in the Middle East when crude oil prices tripled. On the other hand, imagine what would happen to the income of oil-producing nations if hydrogen became an economical fuel.

Understand why managers must be alert to changes in a nation's infrastructure.

New roads, bridges, and canals often open new markets in developed and developing countries.

Appreciate the impact of industrial disasters such as the Alaskan oil spill and the Bhopal accident on global and multinational firms.

Industrial accidents such as the Bhopal disaster and the Alaskan oil spill have caused both developed and developing nations to be more concerned about the protection of natural resources. International chemical manufacturers are reassessing their positions concerning joint ventures when they cannot control the choice of equipment, plant safety, and maintenance.

[Key Words]

passive processing (p. 269)
topography (p. 270)
Canadian Shield (p. 275)
Rhine waterway (p. 277)
climate (p. 281)
natural resources (p. 282)
shale (p. 283)

[Questions]

1. Of the 25 nations listed by the UN as the least developed nations, 14 are landlocked. Is this a coincidence, or does the lack of a seacoast contribute to their slower development?
2. Analyze the potential of oil shale and oil sands as future energy sources.
3. Assume you are a member of your company's long-range planning committee. You have heard that experiments have been successful in separating hydrogen from water and that the hydrogen is then combined with carbon to form hydrocarbons. It is said that the product may cost 20 percent less than crude oil obtained from wells. Discuss with your colleagues how this development may affect your marketing plans in the Middle East and in the oil-poor developing countries.
4. a. Why do you suppose the blank areas on a population map generally coincide with the areas of higher elevation on a topographical map?
   b. Why are the tropics an exception to this rule?
5. International businesspeople, unless they are in the business of refining minerals or petroleum, have no need to concern themselves with world developments in natural resources. True or false? Explain.
6. Mountains, deserts, and tropical rain forests are generally culture barriers. Explain.
7. Explain how bodies of water are responsible for concentrations of population.
8. What will be the consequences for international firms of such disasters as the Bhopal accident and the Alaskan oil spill?
9. How can climatic differences affect a firm?
10. What is the relationship between Australia's water supply and its physical distribution costs?

[Using the Internet]

Internet Exercises

1. The Hudson Electric Company, a midsize ($178 million in annual sales) manufacturer of generating and switch gear equipment for electric power plants, wants to expand sales by persuading the governments of developing nations to build power plants. Electrical production is a capital-intensive industry, however, and many countries that need more generating capacity lack the capital. The company has noted that it has lost sales when some developing nations have purchased photovoltaic (PV) cells to furnish power for rural communities with small electricity requirements. The CEO and members of the executive committee are discussing the possibility of manufacturing PV cells to supply that market and build a customer base for future sales of their generating equipment.

   The marketing manager calls you, the market analyst, to explain that top management wants a report on future consumption of various kinds of energy. Fortunately, you know that the U.S. Department of Energy has its *International Energy Outlook 2001* on the Internet that should be a good source of information. Top management wants to know:

2. What are the projections for regions or energy types for the period 1999–2020 according to the world energy consumption tables?
   a. Which North American country is projected to have the highest average annual percentage change in its total energy consumption?
   b. Which type of energy will have the greatest average annual percentage increase in the world?
   c. Of all the countries listed, which one will have the greatest average annual percentage increase in oil consumption?
   d. Which country will have the greatest average annual percentage increase in coal consumption?
   e. Is the use of nuclear power on the rise in the industrialized nations? In the developing nations?
   f. Which nation has the greatest average annual percentage increase of nuclear power consumption?
   g. Which nation has the greatest average annual percentage increase in the consumption of hydroelectricity and other renewable energy?
   h. Which nation has the greatest average annual percentage increase in energy consumption measured in oil-equivalent units?
   i. Is this information of any use to international businesspeople?

[Minicase 8.1]

Bhopal Fallout

Harry Johnson, CEO of International Chemical, called a meeting of the newly formed crisis management committee, which consists of the vice president of manufacturing; the vice president–legal; the vice president of health, safety, and environment; the chief financial officer; and the public relations officer. Johnson had formed the committee after Union Carbide's Bhopal disaster to examine International Chemical's contingency plans. Because the two companies have similar international organizations and produce similarly toxic products, he asked the members to review the information they had on the Bhopal disaster and make recommendations as to what each person's area would do should their company have a similar accident. Johnson also asked the vice president of health, safety, and environment to begin the meeting by giving the committee a synopsis of the series of events that occurred during the first days after the disaster.

He begins, "As you know, on the night of December 2, a series of runaway chemical reactions heated the interior of a partially buried tank holding 10,000 gallons of methyl isocyanate (MIC) used in the manufacture of Sevin and other pesticides. An escape valve opened, which released a lethal cloud over Bhopal. No one knows how it happened, but Union Carbide investigators say that, by accident or through sabotage, a large quantity of water had been poured into the tank, which then reacted with the MIC to produce heat and open the valve. A refrigeration unit that could have kept the tank temperature at a manageable level had broken down five months previously and had not been repaired. A temperature alarm that would have alerted workers was not properly set. Last of all, a scrubber designed to neutralize toxic vapors was not turned on until the reaction was out of control.

"Union Carbide headquarters in Connecticut first heard of the accident at 3 A.M. on December 3, when employees from Union Carbide in Bhopal called Lutz (chairman of UC Eastern, the division responsible for Asian operations) at his home. By 6 A.M., Lutz, Oldfield (president of the agricultural products division, which markets the insecticides produced at Bhopal), Browning (director of health, safety, and environment), and Van Den Ameele (manager of press relations) met at headquarters. Although they were skeptical about the accuracy of the growing estimate of the numbers of dead and injured, they agreed that a swift response was needed and that top management would need to make some decisions. By midmorning, they called UC's president and went to a hastily called meeting of the senior management committee. When Carbide board chairman Warren Anderson, in bed with a bad cold, was informed by telephone of the problem, he organized a crisis committee of legal, finance, and public affairs people.

"Within 12 hours, the committee dispatched a medical and technical team to arrange relief for the victims, to investigate the incident, and to assist with the safe disposal of the remaining MIC supplies at the plant. They held a press conference even though they did not have all the answers for the press. The next day, as the death toll continued to mount, Anderson took the company jet to Bhopal. On arrival, he was arrested, held briefly, and then sent to New Delhi, the capital. There, Indian officials told him to leave for his own good. His offer of $1 million in aid and the use of the company guest house to shelter orphans of the victims was refused.

"Because Carbide managers did not know what had caused the leak, they stopped production of MIC in the United States and converted all of their stocks of MIC worldwide into pesticides. The crisis caused the price of Carbide stock to fall, so the team began to stress the company's financial soundness in press releases and briefings. To bolster employee morale, the UC president made a videotape for Carbide employees worldwide in which he assured them of the company's ability to handle any likely damage settlement. By the way, even though Carbide provided the specifications for the Indian plant, it was designed and built in India at the insistence of the Indian government, which has a 25 percent interest in the Indian company. Carbide has 50.9 percent, but it has been essentially an Indian operation. The other investors are Indian."

"Thanks for the rundown," says Johnson. "I don't need to tell you that managements of multinational producers all over the world are studying Union Carbide's situation very closely. I read that one executive said this accident could rewrite the whole book on how to operate in foreign countries and how one covers one's risks overseas. Who wants to start the discussion on (1) what we need to do now to avoid both an accident and risk to the company if there should be one and (2) what should our plan be in case—and I hope it never happens—we should have a similar accident?"

Sources: "Women Protest Decade after Anniversary of Deadly Disaster," *McAllen Monitor,* December 4, 1994, p. 2A; "Indian Gassing Victims Endure Another Disaster—No Aid," *San Antonio Express-News,* November 29, 1994, p. 4A; "Union Carbide: Coping with Catastrophe," *Fortune,* January 7, 1985, pp. 50–53; "Anderson Reflects on Managing Bhopal," *Industry Week,* October 13, 1986, p. 21; "For Multinationals It Will Never Be the Same," *Business Week,* December 24, 1984, p. 57; and "Bhopal Report," *C&EN,* February 11, 1985, pp. 14–52.

[Chapter]

9

Sociocultural Forces

"Speaking about cultural differences among Europeans . . . It is no good focusing on similarities and common interests and hoping things will work out. We have to recognize the differences and work with them."

—*Dr. Allan Hjorth, Copenhagen Business School, trainer in cross-cultural behavior*

Concept Previews

After reading this chapter, you should be able to:

- **understand** the significance of culture for international business
- **understand** the sociocultural components of culture
- **appreciate** the significance of religion to businesspeople
- **comprehend** the cultural aspects of technology
- **grasp** the pervasiveness of the Information Technology Era
- **understand** why businesspeople must follow the worldwide trends of formal education
- **discuss** the impact of the "brain drain" and the "reverse brain drain" on developed and developing nations
- **appreciate** the importance of the ability to speak the local language
- **recognize** the importance of unspoken language in international business
- **discuss** the two classes of relationships within a society
- **discuss** Hofstede's four cultural value dimensions

Gary A. Conner/PhotoEdit

Six Rules of Thumb for Doing Business across Cultures

Knowing your customer is just as important anywhere in the world as it is at home, whether one is aiming to sell computers in Abidjan or soft drinks in Kuala Lumpur. Each culture has its logic, and within that logic are real, sensible reasons for the way foreigners do things. If the salesperson can figure out the basic pattern of the culture, he or she will be more effective interacting with foreign clients and colleagues. The following six rules of thumb are helpful.

(1) *Be prepared.* Whether traveling abroad or selling from home, no one should approach a foreign market without doing his or her homework. A mentor is most desirable, complemented by endless reading on social and business etiquette, history and folklore, current affairs (including current relations between your two countries), the culture's values, geography, sources of pride (artists, musicians, sports), religion, political structure, and practical matters such as currency and hours of business. Mimi Murphy, an exporter who trades primarily in Indonesia, says, "Whenever I travel, the

first thing I do in any town is read the newspaper. Then when I meet my customer, I can talk about the sports or the news of the day. He knows that I am interested in the things he is interested in, and he will want to do business with me."

(2) *Slow down.* Americans are clock-watchers. Time is money. In many countries, Americans are seen to be in a rush, in other words, unfriendly, arrogant, and untrustworthy. Almost everywhere, we must learn to wait patiently.

(3) *Establish trust.* Often American-style crisp business relationships will get the sales representative nowhere. Product quality, pricing, and clear contracts are not as important as the personal *relationship and trust* that are developed carefully and sincerely over time. The marketer must be established as *simpatico,* worthy of the business, and dependable in the long run.

(4) *Understand the importance of language.* Obviously, copy must be translated by a professional who speaks both languages fluently, with a vocabulary sensitive to nuance and connotation, as well as talent with idiom and imagery in each culture. An interpreter is often critical and may be helpful even when one of the parties speaks the other's language.

(5) *Respect the culture.* Manners are important. The traveling sales representative is a guest in the country and must respect the hosts' rules. As a Saudi Arabian official states in one of the *Going International* films, "Americans in foreign countries have a tendency to treat the natives as foreigners, and they forget that actually it is *they* who are the foreigners themselves!"

(6) *Understand components of culture.* A region is a sort of cultural iceberg with two components: *surface culture* (fads, styles, food, etc.) and *deep culture* (attitudes, beliefs, values). Less than 15 percent of a region's culture is visible, and strangers to the culture must look below the surface. Consider the British habit of automatically lining up on the sidewalk when waiting for a bus. This surface cultural trait results from the deep cultural desire to lead neat and controlled lives.

Knowledge about other cultures and how they affect the way people do business may show businesspeople working in a culture different from their own that their solutions are not always the appropriate ones for a given task. Understanding this is the first step in learning to use cultural differences to gain a strategic advantage.

Mishandling or ignoring cultural differences can cause numerous problems, such as lost sales, the departure of competent employees, and low morale that contributes to low productivity. However, when these differences are blended successfully, they can result in innovative business practices superior to those that either culture could produce by itself. ■

Sources: Lisa Hoecklin, "Managing Cultural Differences," www.latinsynergy.org/strategicjointventure.htm#CHILE (December 27, 2000); "About Global Culture," www.globe.or.jp/gcc/src/gcc01.html; "How to Negotiate European Style," *Journal of European Business,* July–August 1993, p. 46; and U.S. Department of Commerce, *Business America,* June 25, 1984, p. 7.

The national characteristics you encounter in this chapter and elsewhere are generalizations. They are broadly true, but there are always exceptions. Furthermore, characteristics change over time. The Scandinavians were considered by a 10th-century writer to be "the filthiest race God ever created," and a noted 18th-century writer was amazed at the lack of German military spirit and how easygoing Germans were compared to the French.[1] Before we examine the significance of culture for international businesspeople, let us first define culture.

What Is Culture?

Although there are almost as many definitions of culture as there are anthropologists, most anthropologists view **culture** as the *sum total of the beliefs, rules, techniques, institutions, and artifacts that characterize human populations.*[2] In other words, culture consists of the learned patterns of behavior common to the members of a given society—the unique lifestyle of a particular group of people.[3] Most anthropologists also agree that

culture
Sum total of beliefs, rules, techniques, institutions, and artifacts that characterize human populations

1. Culture is *learned,* not innate.
2. The various aspects of culture are *interrelated.*
3. Culture is *shared.*
4. Culture *defines the boundaries* of different groups.[4]

Because society is composed of people and their culture, it is virtually impossible to speak of one without referring to the other. Anthropologists often use the terms interchangeably or combine them into one word—*sociocultural.*[5] This is the term we shall use, because the variables in which businesspeople are interested are both social and cultural.

When people work in societies and cultures that differ from their own, the problems they encounter in dealing with a single set of cultures are multiplied by the number of cultural sets they find in each of their foreign markets.

All too often, unfortunately, people who are familiar with only one cultural pattern may believe they have an awareness of cultural differences elsewhere, when in reality they do not. Unless they have had occasion to make comparisons with other cultures, they are probably not even aware of the important features of their own. They are probably also oblivious to the fact that many societies consider their culture superior to all others (**ethnocentricity**) and that their attempts to introduce the "German way" or the "American way" may be met with stubborn resistance.

ethnocentricity
Belief in the superiority of one's own ethnic group

How do international businesspeople learn to live with other cultures? The first step is to realize that there are cultures different from their own. Then they must go on to learn the characteristics of those cultures so that they may adapt to them. E. T. Hall, a famous anthropologist, claims this can be accomplished in only two ways: (1) spend a lifetime in a country or (2) undergo an extensive, highly sophisticated training program that covers the main characteristics of a culture, including the language. The program he mentions must be more than a briefing on a country's customs. It should be a study of what culture is and what it does, imparting some knowledge of the various ways in which human behavior has been institutionalized in a country.[6]

Culture Affects All Business Functions

Marketing

In marketing, for example, the wide variation in attitudes and values prevents many firms from using the same marketing mix in all markets.

> In Japan, Procter & Gamble (P&G) used an advertisement for Camay soap in which a man meeting a woman for the first time compared her skin to that of a fine porcelain doll. Although the ad had worked well in South America and Europe, it insulted the Japanese. "For a Japanese man to say something like that to a Japanese woman means he's either unsophisticated or rude," said an advertising man who worked on the account. Interestingly, P&G used the ad despite the warning from the advertising agency.
>
> Another Camay ad that failed in Japan shows a Japanese woman bathing when her husband walks into the bathroom. She begins to tell him about her new beauty soap, but

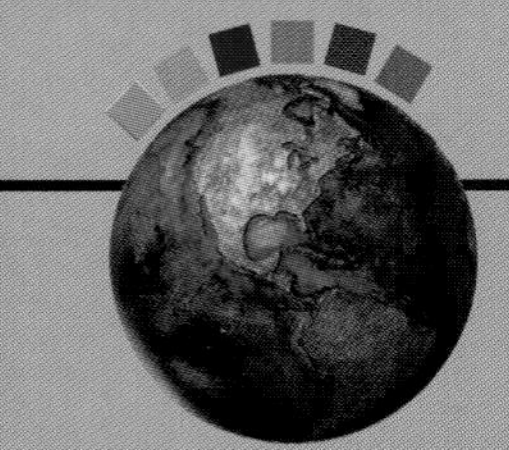

[Worldview]

Cultural Success and Failure in Disneyland

Why is it that Disneyland Paris had problems with falling attendance and losses while Tokyo Disneyland had steadily increasing attendance and is the most profitable Disney park? The many experts who predicted that Tokyo Disneyland attendance would peak in the first year and then taper off were wrong; instead, it has increased steadily. Over 16 million people visited the park in 1993 and spent an average of $85. Visitors to Disneyland in Los Angeles and Disney World in Florida spend between $60 and $70, while those going to Disneyland Paris spend only $45 on average.

Unfortunately for Disney, Tokyo Disneyland is wholly owned by a Japanese firm, the Oriental Land Co., which licenses Disney characters and other copyrighted material from the American firm. The park owes some of its success to its location in a metropolitan area of 30 million people, but a cultural change is believed to be a major reason for its success. Some say that Walt Disney Productions has written a new chapter in Japanese social history by popularizing the idea that family outings can be fun. Families now account for half of the park's visitors. An executive of the park owners states, "Leisure was not always a part of the Japanese lifestyle. Fathers used to see family outings as a duty."

The early staggering losses at Disneyland Paris stemmed from the high interest costs and high overheads, many of which were caused by cultural errors. To cover the project's $4 billion cost, Disney put up just $170 million for 49 percent of the operation and public shareholders paid $1 billion for the 51 percent they own. The $2.9 billion balance was borrowed at interest rates of up to 11 percent. Disney management expected to reduce the debt by selling the six big hotels it had built, but the $340-per-night price it charged had kept them about half full. Moreover, the guests weren't staying as long or spending as much as Disney had calculated.

the husband, stroking her shoulder, hints that suds are not what is on his mind. Although it was well received in Europe, it failed badly in Japan, where it is considered bad manners for a husband to intrude on his wife.

P&G also erred because it lacked knowledge about the business culture. The company introduced Cheer detergent by discounting its price, but this lowered the soap's reputation. Said a competitor, "Unlike in Europe and the United States, once you discount your product here, it's hard to raise the price again." Wholesalers were alienated because they made less money due to lower margins. Moreover, apparently P&G didn't realize that Japanese housewives do not have a family car to carry groceries, so they shop in the neighborhood mom-and-pop stores close to home. These small retailers, who sell 30 percent of all the detergent bought in Japan, have limited shelf space and thus do not like to carry discounted products because of the lower profit earned.[7]

Although acquiring knowledge about Japanese culture was both time-consuming and expensive, evidently P&G was a good learner. It wasn't until 1995, eight years after its difficulties with Cheer detergent, that the company reentered the soap market, which was completely controlled by two powerful Japanese consumer products concerns, Kao and Lion Corporation. Just two years later P&G held 20 percent of the market. What did it do differently this time?

In 1992, when the home office told the Japanese affiliate to find new markets for products in which the firm was strong elsewhere in the world, P&G–Japan sent researchers to study Japanese dish-washing habits. They found that Japanese homemakers used much more detergent than was needed. This indicated that consumers wanted a more powerful soap, which P&G's laboratory created. The marketing message was simple: a little bit of Joy cleans better yet is easier on the hands. This message hit home. Said a Japanese homemaker who, after seeing the pilot commercials, rushed to buy a bottle, "Grease on Tupperware, that's the toughest thing to wash off. I had to try it."

Disney executives believed, incorrectly, that they could change the French attitude of not wanting to take their children from school during the school year as Americans do or to take more short breaks during the year instead of one long vacation during the month of August. This would have given Euro Disney steady, high attendance all year rather than for just one month.

One reason the visitors didn't spend more was the extremely high prices. Almost two years passed before Disney lowered them. Another reason the guests didn't spend more, even though in this case they wanted to, was also due to a cultural problem: the breakfast debacle. Apparently, a decision involving millions of dollars in revenue was based not on research but only on what someone told Disney. One executive said, "We were told that Europeans don't take breakfast, so we downsized the restaurants." However, when the park opened, everyone wanted breakfast and wouldn't settle for just croissants and coffee; they wanted bacon and eggs. Disney tried to serve 2,500 breakfasts in hotel restaurants seating 350 people. The Disney solution for the French public, known worldwide as connoisseurs of good eating: prepackaged breakfasts delivered to hotel rooms.

As a French banker put it, "Euro Disney is a good theme park married to a bankrupt real estate company—and the two can't be divorced."

After 1995, Disneyland Paris worked to correct the cultural and financial errors that kept attendance down and losses up. Under new management, the park cut admission prices by 22 percent and hotel rates by one-third. In addition to the original expensive, sit-down restaurants that Disney mistakenly believed all Europeans would demand, cheaper fast food is available in self-service restaurants. Instead of marketing the park to Europe as if it were a single country, Disneyland Paris has offices in all the main European capitals, and each office tailors tour packages to fit its own market. By 1998 Disneyland Paris was France's biggest tourist attraction. And a new theme park, Disney Studios, is to open next to Disneyland Paris in April 2002. Not only has Disney recovered from its mistakes in Europe, it is continuing its success in Asia. A second park near Tokyo—DisneySea—opened in late 2001, and Hong Kong Disneyland will be launched in 2005. ■

Source: "Euro Disney's Fortunes Turn as Number of Visitors Rises," *Financial Times,* November 14, 1997, p. 13; "The Kingdom Inside a Republic," *The Economist,* April 13, 1996, pp. 66–67; "Tokyo Disney Shifts Japanese Ideas on Leisure," *The Columbian,* May 1, 1994, p. F7; "Mickey n'est pas fini," *Forbes,* February 14, 1994, p. 42; "Euro Disney's Wish Comes True," *The Economist,* March 19, 1994, p. 83; www.findarticle.com/cf_0/mOEIN/1998_Oct_22/53111449/pl/article.jhtml; and www.findarticle.com/cf_0/mOEIN/1999_Nov_2/57088089/pl/article.jhtml.

Retailers wanted it because P&G did the things it hadn't done with Cheer. For example, this time the profit margins for the retailers were high. P&G also exploited a weakness in the competing Japanese products: their long-necked bottles wasted space, but Joy bottles were compact cylinders that took up less space in stores, warehouses, and delivery trucks. A buyer for a large Japanese store chain estimated that the bottle improved the efficiency of the store's distribution by 40 percent.

The P&G ad campaign also delighted Japanese retailers. Its agency designed a TV commercial in which a famous comedian dropped in on homemakers unannounced with a camera crew to test Joy on dirty dishes in the home. The camera focused on a patch of oil in a pan full of water. After a drop of Joy, the oil dramatically disappeared. Japanese soapmakers did research on the effectiveness of the campaign and found that over 70 percent of Joy users had begun using it after seeing the commercial. "We mistakenly assumed Japanese didn't care much about grease-fighting power in dish soaps," the Kao dish-soap brand manager said. P&G, which had studied this part of Japanese culture, did know.[8]

Unlike P&G, Disney seemed to have an ideal global product and global promotion. According to the *Tokyo Disneyland Guidebook,* the Tokyo theme park is the same as those in California and Florida. Disneyland Paris is also similar, although, because of the French insistence on protecting their language and culture, Mickey and Donald developed French accents, and the Sleeping Beauty castle is called *Le Chateau de la Belle au Bois Dormant.*[9] The Worldview illustrates the problems a global firm can have when its management errs when making culturally sensitive decisions.

Human Resource Management

The national culture is also a key determinant for the evaluation of managers. In the United States, results are generally the criteria for the selection and promotion of executives, but in Great Britain, an American general manager complained that people were promoted because of the school they had attended and their family background but not for their accomplishments. School ties are important in France, too.[10] IBM would hire an Italian who fit within the IBM way of doing things, but Olivetti, whose corporate culture is informal and nonstructured with little discipline, looks for strong personalities and not "too good grades."[11]

Production and Finance

Personnel problems can result from differences in attitudes toward authority, another sociocultural variable. Latin Americans have traditionally regarded the manager as the *patron,* an authoritarian figure responsible for their welfare. When American managers accustomed to a participative leadership style are transferred to Latin America, they must become more authoritarian, or their employees will consider them weak and incompetent and they will encounter serious difficulties in having their orders carried out.

> A production manager who had been sent to Peru from the United States was convinced that he could motivate the workers to achieve higher productivity by instituting a more democratic decision-making style. He brought in trainers from the home office to teach the supervisors how to solicit suggestions and feedback from the workers.
>
> Shortly after the new management style was introduced, the workers began quitting their jobs. When asked why, they replied that the new production manager and his supervisors apparently didn't know what to do and were therefore asking the workers for advice. The workers thought the company wouldn't last long with that kind of management, and they wanted to quit before the collapse, because then everyone would be hunting for a job at the same time.

Production managers have found that attitudes toward change can seriously influence the acceptance of new production methods; even treasurers realize the strength of the sociocultural forces when, armed with excellent balance sheets, they approach local banks, only to find that the banks attach far more importance to who they are than to how strong their companies are.[12] One reason for Disney's financial problems in Paris was the insensitive attitude of Disney executives toward European business culture. A top French banker involved in the negotiations to restructure the park's debt claimed, "The Walt Disney group is making a major error in thinking it can impose its will once more."[13] These are just a few examples to show that sociocultural differences do affect all the business functions. As we examine the components of the sociocultural forces, we shall mention others.

Sociocultural Components

It should be apparent that to be successful in their relationships with people in other countries, international businesspeople must be students of culture. They must have factual knowledge, which is relatively easy to obtain, but they must also become sensitive to cultural differences, and this is more difficult. Hall, as we saw, recommended spending a lifetime in a country or, in lieu of this, undergoing an extensive program to study what the culture is and what it does. But most newcomers to international business do not even have the opportunity for area orientation. They can, however, take the important first step of realizing that there are other cultures. In this short chapter, we cannot do more than point out some of the important sociocultural differences as they concern businesspeople in the hope that you will become more aware of the need to be culturally sensitive—to know that there are cultural differences for which you must look. Remember that the more you know about another person's culture, the better will be your predictions of that person's behavior.

The concept of culture is so broad that even ethnologists (cultural anthropologists) have to break it down into topics to facilitate its study. A listing of such topics will give us a better understanding of what culture is and may also serve as a guide to international managers when they are analyzing a particular problem from the sociocultural viewpoint.

As you can imagine, experts vary considerably as to the components of culture, but the following list is representative of their thinking:

1. Aesthetics
2. Attitudes and beliefs
3. Religion
4. Material culture
5. Education
6. Language
7. Societal organization
8. Legal characteristics
9. Political structures[14]

We shall examine the first seven components in this chapter and leave the legal characteristics and political structures for later chapters.

Aesthetics

Aesthetics pertains to a culture's sense of beauty and good taste and is expressed in its art, drama, music, folklore, and dances.

aesthetics
A culture's sense of beauty and good taste

Art

Of particular interest to international businesspeople are the formal aspects of art, color, and form because of the symbolic meanings they convey. Colors, especially, can be deceptive because they mean different things to different cultures. The color of mourning is black in the United States and Mexico, black and white in the Far East, and purple in Brazil. Because green is a propitious color in the Islamic world, any ad or package featuring green is looked at favorably there. While in the United States mints are packaged in blue or green paper, in Africa the wrapper is red. These examples illustrate that marketers must be careful to check if colors have any special meanings before using them for products, packages, or advertisements.

Be careful of symbols, too. Seven signifies good luck in the United States but the opposite in Singapore, Ghana, and Kenya. In Japan, the number four is unlucky. If you are giving a Japanese client golf balls, make sure there are more or less than four in the package. Also, in general, avoid using a nation's flag or any symbols connected with religion.

> Nike, the athletic shoe marketer, recalled 38,000 pairs of shoes carrying the word *air* written in flaming letters because, according to Muslims, it resembles the word "Allah" in Arabic. Another 30,000 pairs have been diverted from Arabian countries to less-sensitive countries.[15]

It is also important to learn whether there are local aesthetic preferences for form that could affect the design of products, packaging, or even the building in which the firm is located. The American style of steel and glass in the midst of oriental architecture will be a constant reminder to the local population of the outsider's presence.

Music and Folklore

Musical commercials are generally popular worldwide, but the marketer must know what kind of music each market prefers, because tastes vary. Thus, a commercial that used a ballad in the United States might be better received to the tune of a bolero in Mexico or a samba in Brazil. However, if the advertiser is looking to the youth market with a product that is patently American, then American music will help reinforce its image.

Nike's logo: Air or Allah?
Associated Press

Those who wish to steep themselves in a culture find it useful to study its folklore, which can disclose much about a society's way of life. Although this is usually more than a foreign businessperson has time for, the incorrect use of folklore can sometimes cost the firm a share of the market. For example, associating a product with the cowboy would not obtain the same results in Chile or Argentina that it does in the United States, because in these countries the cowboy is a far less romantic figure—it's just a job. On the other hand, Smirnoff's use of an image of late revolutionary leader Ernesto "Che" Guevara in an advertisement for spicy vodka sparked controversy in Cuba, where Guevara is a national hero.[16] In another instance, a U.S. company may be paying handsome royalties to use American cartoon characters in its promotion, only to find they are considerably less important in foreign markets. In Mexico, songs of the "Singing Cricket" are known to all youngsters and their mothers, and a commercial tie-in with that character would be as advantageous to the firm as its use of Peanuts or Mickey Mouse. In many areas, especially where nationalistic feeling is strong, local firms have been able to compete successfully with foreign affiliates by making use of indigenous folklore in the form of slogans and proverbs. Tales of folklore are valuable in maintaining a sense of group unity.[17] Knowing them is an indication that one belongs to the group, which recognizes that the outsider is unfamiliar with its folklore.

Attitudes and Beliefs

Every culture has a set of attitudes and beliefs that influence nearly all aspects of human behavior and help bring order to a society and its individuals. The more managers can learn about certain key attitudes, the better prepared they will be to understand why people behave as they do, especially when their reactions differ from those that the managers have learned to expect in dealing with their own people.

Among the wide variety of subjects covered by attitudes and beliefs, some are of prime importance to the businessperson. These include attitudes toward time, toward achievement and work, and toward change.

Attitudes toward Time

This cultural characteristic probably presents more adaptation problems for Americans overseas than does any other. Time is important in the United States, and much emphasis is placed on it. If we must wait past the appointed hour to see an individual, we feel insulted. This person is not giving our meeting the importance it deserves. Yet the wait could mean just the opposite elsewhere. Latin American or Middle Eastern executives may be taking care of the minor details of their business so that they can attend to their important visitor without interruption.[18]

> An American who has worked in the Middle East for 20 years explains the Middle Eastern concept of time this way: "At worst, there is no concept at all of time in the Middle East. At best, there is a sort of open-ended concept." The head of Egypt's Industrial Design Center, an Egyptian, states, "The simple wristwatch is, in some respects, much too sophisticated an instrument for the Middle East. One of the first things a foreigner should learn in Egypt is to ignore the second hand. The minute hand can also be an obstacle if he expects Egyptians to be as conscious as he of time ticking away.[19]

Probably even more critical than short-term patience is long-term patience. American preoccupation with monthly profit and loss statements is a formidable barrier to the es-

Establishing Web Communities in Africa

Small and Medium-Sized Enterprises

Tanya Accone, 29, is executive producer for M-Web Africa (www.mwebafrica.com), an Internet services provider based in Johannesburg, South Africa. M-Web Africa is growing by acquiring ISPs in other African countries such as Zimbabwe and Namibia as well as South Africa. At present, Africa's potential for Internet growth is mostly that—potential. According to Accone, "Today, less than 1% of the world's 360 million Internet users live in Africa. Imagine a place with postal delivery, where the nearest telephone is more than 100 kilometers away."

Despite these relatively poor conditions in terms of commercial infrastructure, the potential seems to be real. Sub-Saharan Africa has 2.73 Internet hosts per 1,000 people, putting Africa ahead of the poorer regions of South Asia and the Middle East–North African region. Sub-Saharan Africa also exceeds the average in low-income countries for the number of personal computers on a per-capita basis. Finally, the region is ahead of the poor-country average for the number of mobile telephones.

Says Accone, "Now consider the Internet in that environment. It will fundamentally transform Africa. Africa, which is now divided by many regional languages, will be united through localized online channels such as touch-screen kiosks beefed up with auditory and visual features. The Net will drive commercial activity, allowing us to leapfrog stages of development." ■

Sources: Christine Canabou, "Report from the Futurist: Africa.Net," *Fast Company*, December 2000, p. 82; World Bank, *World Development Report 2000/2001*, p. 311.

tablishment of successful business relationships with Asian and Middle Eastern executives, especially during the development of joint ventures and other business relationships that have good potential in the long run—precisely the factors in which these people are most interested.[20]

Americans, Be Prompt. Few cultures give the same importance to time that Americans and Germans do. If an appointment is made with a group of Germans to see them at 12 noon, we can be sure they will be there, but to get the same response from a Brazilian, we must say noon English hour. If not, the Brazilian may show up anytime between noon and 2 o'clock. Compare this with Japan, where a description of an apartment in the rental contract includes the time in minutes required to walk to the nearest train station.

Should Americans follow the local custom or be prompt? It depends. In Spain, a general rule is to never be punctual. If you are, you will be considered early. However, in the Middle East, the American penchant for punctuality is well known and lateness by Americans is considered impolite. The Arabian executives, nonetheless, usually will not arrive at the appointed hour; why should they change their lifetime habits just for a stranger?

Mañana. Probably one of the most vexing problems for a newcomer to Latin America is the *mañana* attitude. Ask the maintenance man when the machine will be ready, and he responds "*mañana*." The American assumes this means "tomorrow," the literal translation, but the maintenance man means "some time in the near future," and if he is reprimanded for not having the machine ready the next day, he is angry and bewildered. He reasons that everyone knows *mañana* means "in the next few days."

This example illustrates that the ability to speak the local language is only half the task of communicating. A manager of an American subsidiary in Saudi Arabia says, "You can be talking the same language with someone, but are you talking on the same wavelength?" He states that he has met few Japanese or Koreans fluent in Arabic, yet they are able to understand and adapt to local conditions much better than Westerners can because they seem to be more sensitive to the Middle Easterner's mentality.[21]

Adios, Siesta. The revered three-hour siesta is disappearing from both Mexico and Spain. In April 1999 the federal government issued new regulations that brought a cultural revolution to Mexico. Most public employees from clerks to cabinet ministers are expected to begin work at 9 A.M. and leave work at 6 P.M., and instead of three hours for lunch, they now have only one hour. To be sure that people leave at 6 P.M. and not at 8 P.M. as they used to, the lights and air-conditioning are turned off at 6 P.M. sharp. Because so many private firms conduct business with government agencies, their employees have also had to change their schedules. One result of this change is that people are finding that much work is being done before noon, a rarity under the old schedule. Since people are no longer drowsy in the afternoon as a result of the banquet they used to eat at lunchtime, they now tend to make decisions in the afternoon instead of waiting until the evening.[22]

In Spain the three-hour siesta is disappearing for other reasons. The country is under pressure to take the shorter lunch breaks that the populations of most of the other European Union (EU) members take. Increasingly, large firms are reducing the lunch hour to two hours, and corporate culture is against the concept of napping during the day. As the human resources director of a major bank says, "Those who can take siestas do, but those who are really serious about working, do not."

Spain's growing economy, with the highest level of job creation of any EU nation, has increased traffic in the cities and allowed young people to move to the suburbs, but this has created longer commutes, making it more difficult to dash home for a siesta. Because both the husband and the wife are working, no one is at home to prepare the hot meal that precedes the siesta. A survey on siestas taken by a Spanish mattress company found that only 25 percent of all Spaniards surveyed still take a siesta and few people actually get into bed anymore. The company's marketing director explained, "The siesta is nothing more than a cliché for most working people in Spain. They don't have time for it."[23]

Directness and Drive. The American pride in directness and drive is interpreted by many foreigners as being brash and rude. Although we believe it expedient to get to the point in a discussion, this attitude often irritates others. Time-honored formalities are a vital part of doing business and help establish amicable relations, which are considered by people in many countries to be a necessary prerequisite to business discussions. Any attempt to move the negotiations along by ignoring some of the accepted courtesies invites disaster.

Deadlines. Our emphasis on speed and deadlines is often used against us in business dealings abroad. In Far Eastern countries such as Japan, an American may be asked how long he or she plans to stay at the first meeting. Then negotiations are purposely not finalized until a few hours before the American's departure, when the Japanese know they can wring extra concessions from the foreigner because of his or her haste to finish and return home on schedule.

> Three Americans, none of whom had ever been to Japan, went to sell tractors to Japanese buyers. They thought the discussions had gone well and prepared to wrap up the deal. However, there was no reaction from the Japanese. The silence became disquieting, and so the Americans lowered the price. Because there was still no reaction, they again lowered the price. This went on until their price was far lower than they had planned. What they didn't know was that the Japanese had become silent not to indicate rejection of the proposition but merely to think it over, a customary Japanese negotiating practice.[24]

Attitudes toward Achievement and Work

"Germans put leisure first and work second," says a German-born woman now living in the United States. "In America, it's the other way around."

> Angela Clark was born in Germany but now works for J.C. Penney as a merchandising manager in Washington, DC. Andreas Drauschke has a comparable job for comparable pay in Berlin. There is no comparison, however, in the hours each works. Drauschke works a 37-hour week, with a six-week annual vacation. The store closes at 2:00 P.M. on Saturday and opens again on Monday. It is open one night a week. Clark works a minimum of 44 hours a week, including evenings and often Saturdays and Sundays. She brings

work home and never takes more than one week's vacation at a time. "If I took any more, I'd feel like I was losing control," she says.

In the United States, Germans are known for their industriousness, but a comparison of workloads shows that there is little basis now for that stereotype. The average workweek in U.S. manufacturing plants is 37.7 hours and is increasing, whereas in Germany it is 30 hours and has been falling over recent years. All German workers are guaranteed by law a minimum of five weeks' annual vacation.[25]

Like the Germans, the Mexicans say that "Americans live to work, but we work to live." This is an example of the extreme contrasts among cultural attitudes toward work. Where work is considered necessary to obtain the essentials for survival, once these things have been obtained, people may stop working. They do not make the accomplishment of a task an end in itself. This attitude is in sharp contrast to the belief in many industrial societies that work is a moral, even a religious, virtue.

To the consternation of the production manager with a huge back order, the promise of overtime often fails to keep workers on the job. In fact, raising employees' salaries frequently results in their working less (economists call this effect the backward-bending labor supply curve).

It is important, however, to note that an additional change has occurred repeatedly in many developing countries as more consumer goods have become available. The **demonstration effect** (seeing others with these goods) and improvements in infrastructure (roads to bring the products to them and electric power to operate the products) cause workers to realize they can have greater prestige and pleasure by owning more goods. Thus, their attitude toward work changes not because of any alteration of their moral or religious values but because they now want what only money can buy.

demonstration effect
Result of having seen others with desirable goods

A Mexican distributor came to one of the writers to complain that a number of his salesmen were producing well for the first week or two of the month but were then slacking off. Investigation showed that the commissions plus salary earned during the periods of high production were about the same each time. It was apparent that the salesmen had earned what they required to live so that they could loaf the rest of the month. By instituting contests and informing the salesmen's wives about the prizes to be won, the company obtained considerable improvement.

In the industrialized nations, the opposite trend is observed. After peaking at 43.3 hours per week in 1994, the U.S. weekly average for production workers fell to 42.6 hours in 1996. The 1996 averages for Germany and France were 39.0 and 38.3 hours, respectively. Even in Japan the weekly average, which reached 43 hours in 1988, fell to 39.5 hours in 1996. In fact, by 1999 Japanese workers were putting in nearly 23 hours less per month than their counterparts in 1988.[26]

Job Prestige. Another aspect of the attitude toward work is the prestige associated with certain kinds of employment. In this country, some types of work are considered more prestigious than others, but there is nowhere near the disdain for physical labor here that there is in many developing countries. The result is an overabundance of attorneys and economists and a lack of toolmakers and welders even when the wages are higher for the latter. The distinction between blue-collar workers and office employees is especially great, as typified by the use of two words in Spanish for the worker—*obrero* (one who labors) signifies a blue-collar worker, whereas *empleado* (employee) signifies an office worker.[27]

The lesson to be learned from this discussion is that managers are likely to encounter sharp differences in attitudes toward work and achievement in other cultures compared to their own. However, they must recruit subordinates with a need to "get ahead," whatever the underlying motive. One good source for such people is among relatively well-educated members of the lower social class who view work as a route to the prestige and social acceptance that have been denied them because of their birth.

Attitudes toward Change

The American firm, accustomed to the rapid acceptance by Americans of something new, is frequently surprised to find that newness does not carry that kind of magic in markets where something tried and proven is preferred to the unknown. Europeans are fond of reminding Americans that they are a young nation lacking traditions. The near reverence for traditional methods makes it more difficult for a production manager to install a new process, a marketer to introduce a new product, or a treasurer to change an accounting system.

The New Idea. Yet undeniably, international firms are agents of change, and their personnel must be able to counter resistance to it. The new idea will be more readily acceptable the closer it can be related to the traditional one while at the same time being made to show its relative advantage. In other words, the more consistent a new idea is with a society's attitudes and experiences, the more quickly it will be adopted.

Tourists walk along the Great Wall of China.
Jeff Greenberg/PhotoEdit

Religion

Religion, an important component of culture, is responsible for many of the attitudes and beliefs affecting human behavior. A knowledge of the basic tenets of some of the more popular religions will contribute to a better understanding of why people's attitudes vary so greatly from country to country. Figure 9.1 presents a map of the major religions of the world.

Work Ethic

We have already mentioned the marked differences in attitudes toward work and achievement. Europeans and Americans generally view work as a moral virtue and look unfavorably on the idle. This view stems in part from the **Protestant work ethic** as expressed by Luther and Calvin, who believed it was the duty of Christians to glorify God by hard work and the practice of thrift.

In Asian countries where Confucianism is strong, the same attitude toward work is called the **Confucian work ethic,** and in Japan, it's called the Shinto work ethic after the principal religion of that nation. Interestingly, because of other factors—such as a growing feeling of prosperity and a shift to a five-day workweek (with two days off, workers develop new interests)—Japanese employers are finding that younger workers no longer have the same dedication to their jobs that their predecessors had. Workers rarely show up early to warm the oil in their machines before their shifts start, and some management trainees are actually taking all of their 15 days of vacation time. A representative of the Employers Association states, "Our universities are leisure centers." A recent college graduate claims, "Students ski in the winter and play tennis in the summer. What the companies sometimes find out is that some new employees like skiing better than working."[28]

Protestant work ethic
Christian duty to glorify God by hard work and the practice of thrift

Confucian work ethic
Same as Protestant work ethic

Asian religions
The primary ones are Hinduism, Buddhism, Jainism, and Sikhism (India); Confucianism and Taoism (China); and Shintoism (Japan)

Asian Religions

People from the Western world will encounter some very different notions about God, people, and reality in **Asian religions.** In the Judeo-Christian tradition, this world is real and significant because it was created by God. Human beings are likewise significant; so is time, because it began with God's creation and will end when His will has been fulfilled. Each human being has only one lifetime to heed God's word and achieve everlasting life.

In Asian religions, especially in the religions of India, the ideas of reality are different. There is a notion that this world is an illusion because nothing is permanent. Time is cyclical, and so all living things, including humans, are in a constant process of birth,

[Figure 9.1] **Major Religions of the World**

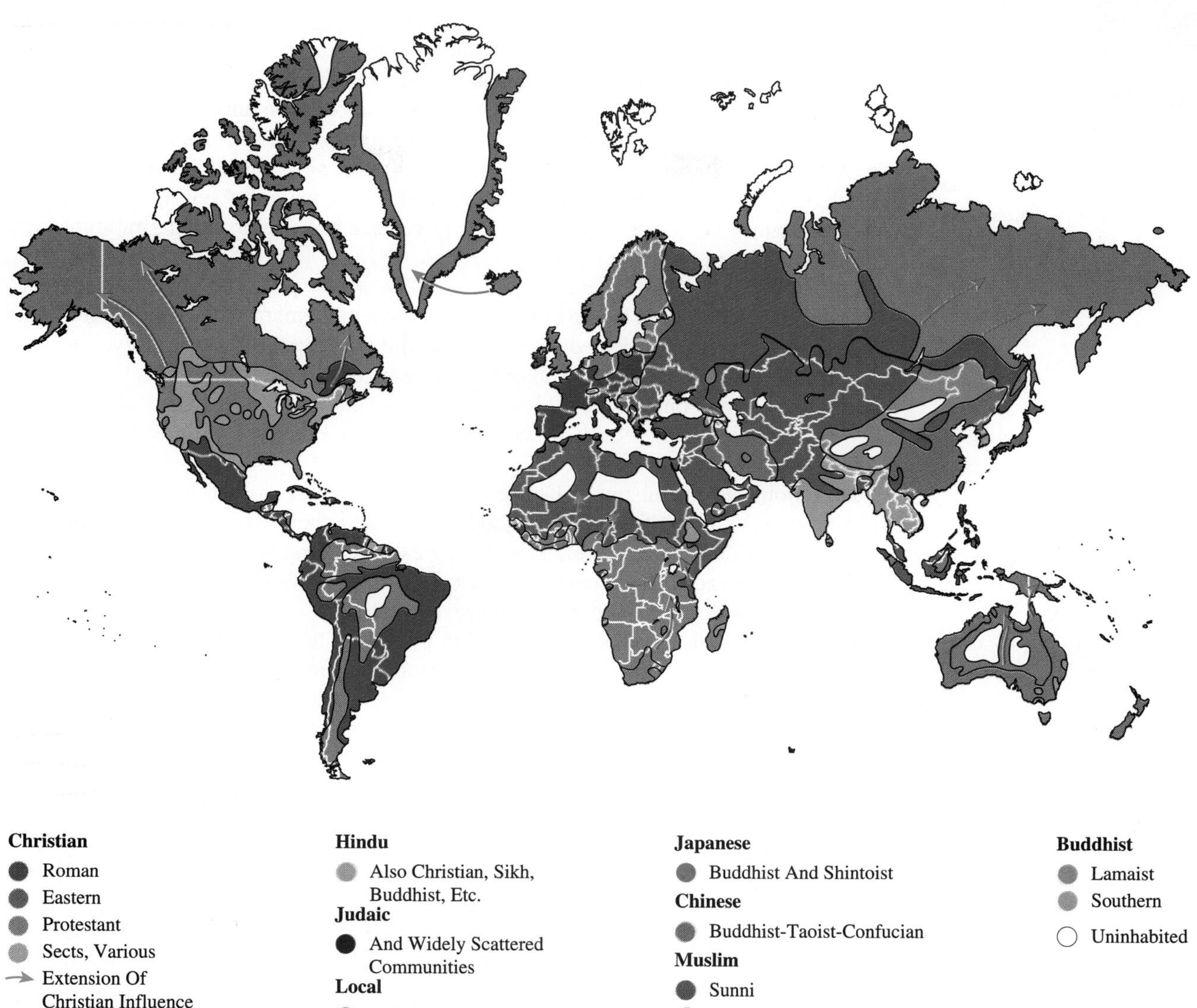

death, and reincarnation. The goal of salvation is to escape from the cycle and move into a state of eternal bliss (*nirvana*). The notion of *karma* (moral retribution) holds that evil committed in one lifetime will be punished in the next. Thus, *karma* is a powerful impetus to do good so as to achieve a higher spiritual status in the next life. Asians who hold these views cannot imagine that they have not had past lives when they may have been plants, animals, or human beings. Of the seven best-known religions that originated in Asia, four came from India (Hinduism, Buddhism, Jainism, and Sikhism), two from China (Confucianism and Taoism), and one from Japan (Shintoism).

Hinduism. This is a conglomeration of religions, without a single founder or a central authority, that is practiced by more than 80 percent of India's population. Although there is great diversity among regions and social classes, Hinduism has certain characteristic features. Most Hindus believe that everything in the world is subject to an eternal process of death and rebirth (*samsura*) and that individual souls (*atmans*) migrate from one body to another. They believe one can be liberated from the samsura cycle and achieve that state of eternal bliss (nirvana) through (1) yoga (purification of mind and body), (2) devout worship of the gods, or (3) good works and obedience to the laws and customs (*dharmas*) of one's caste.

A knowledge of the **caste system** is important to managers because the castes are the basis of the social division of labor. The highest caste, the Brahmins or priesthood, is followed by the warriors (politicians, landowners), the merchants, the peasants, and the *dalits,* a Hindi word meaning "downtrodden" or "oppressed" that has replaced *untouchable.*[29] An individual's position in a caste is inherited, as is that person's job within the caste, and movement to a higher caste can be made only in subsequent lives. Although the government of India has officially outlawed discrimination based on the caste system and in fact has worked to improve the situation of those in the lower castes, such discrimination still exists. Mercedes cars were not selling in India until management realized that it would have to replace the dealers with Brahmins who could deal with upper-caste clients.

caste system
An aspect of Hinduism by which the entire society is divided into four groups (plus the outcasts) and each is assigned a certain class of work

Buddhism. This religion began in India as a reform movement of Hinduism. At the age of 29, Prince Gautama rejected his wife, son, and wealth and set out to solve the mysteries of misery, old age, and death. After six years of experimenting with yoga, which brought no enlightenment, he suddenly understood how to break the laws of *karma* and the endless cycle of rebirth (*samsura*). Gautama emerged as the Buddha (the Enlightened One).

He renounced the austere self-discipline of the Hindus as well as the extremes of self-indulgence, both of which depended on a craving that locked people into the endless cycle of rebirth. Gautama taught that by extinguishing desire, his followers could attain enlightenment and escape the cycle of existence into nirvana. By opening his teaching to everyone, he opposed the caste system.

Because Buddhist monks are involved in politics in the areas where their religion is prevalent and because they are a mobilizing force for political and social action, managers working in these areas need to be aware of what these religious leaders are doing.

A Buddhist teaching is that if people have no desires, they will not suffer. This is important to marketers and production managers because if Buddhists and Hindus have no desires, they have little motive for achievement and for the acquisition of material goods.

Jainism. This religion was founded by Mahavira, a contemporary of Buddha. The Jain doctrine teaches that there is no creator, no god, and no absolute principle. Through right faith, correct conduct, and right knowledge of the soul, Jains can purify themselves, become free of samsura, and achieve nirvana. Although relatively few in number, Jains are influential leaders in commerce and scholarship. Their greatest impact on Indian culture is manifested in the widespread acceptance of their doctrine of nonviolence, which prohibits animal slaughter, war, and even violent thoughts.

Sikhism. This is the religion of an Indian ethnic group, a military brotherhood,* and a political movement that was founded by Nanek, who sought a bridge between Hinduism and Islam. Sikhs believe there is a single god, but they also accept the Hindu concepts of samsura, karma, and spiritual liberation. The Sikhs' holiest temple was partly destroyed by Indian troops that suppressed their movement for self-government. More than 80 percent of all Sikhs live in the Indian state of Punjab, which they hope to make an autonomous state.[30]

Confucianism. The name of Confucius is inseparable from Chinese culture and civilization, which were already well developed when he set out to transform ancient traditions into a rational system capable of guiding personal and social behavior. Confucianism may be considered a religion inasmuch as Confucius built a philosophy on the notion that all reality is subject to an eternal mandate from heaven; however, he refused to speculate on the existence of Chinese folk deities and was agnostic on the question of life after death.

Confucius taught that each person bears within himself or herself the principle of unselfish love for others, *jen,* the cultivation of which is its own reward. A second prin-

*Baptism into the Sikh brotherhood requires all members to take Singh as a second name.

ciple, *li,* prescribes a gentle decorum in all actions and accounts for the Chinese emphasis on politeness, deference to elders, and ritual courtesies such as bowing.

Taoism. This is a mystical philosophy founded by Lao-tzu, a contemporary of Confucius. It is just as likely that he never existed, and that the *Lao Tzu* is an anthology. Taoism, which means "philosophy of the way," holds that each of us mirrors the same forces, the male and the female energies (yin and yang) that govern the cosmos. The aim of Taoist meditation and rituals is to free the self from distractions and become empty to allow the cosmic forces to act.[31]

Feng Shui. This ancient custom, with roots in Taoism and nature worship, is based on a simple concept. If buildings, furniture, roads, and other human-made objects are placed in harmony with nature, they can bring good fortune. If they are not, they will cause a disaster. Before building a house, scheduling a funeral, or making an investment, a master of *feng shui* (pronounced "fung shway") is called in to give his seal of approval.

> Occupancy in a five-star hotel in Shanghai was down to just 5 percent. Desperate to find a remedy, the management called in a master of *feng shui* to examine the hotel. His analysis—very bad *feng shui* because the building was at the end of a very long street, "like a river rushing toward the hotel." To overcome this, he had them change the color of the roof, put reflective material over the main entrance, and dig up the flagpoles outside and put them at an angle to the street instead of being parallel to it. This, he claimed, was done "to diversify the energy flow." He also asked management to put a fountain in front of the hotel, nine dragons and nine turtles in the fountain, and a pair of lions in the front garden. The hotel's occupancy rate has shot up to 80 percent.[32]

Shintoism. This is the indigenous religion of Japan. It has no founder or sacred text. Shinto legends define the founding of the Japanese empire as a cosmic act, and the emperor was believed to have divine status. As a part of the World War II settlement, the emperor was forced to renounce such a claim. Shintoism has no elaborate theology or even an organized weekly worship. Its followers come to the thousands of Shinto shrines when they feel moved to do so.

Islam

About 1.1 billion followers make this youngest faith the second largest after Christianity, which has 2 billion adherents. Islam accepts as God's eternal word the Koran, a collection of Allah's (God's) revelations to Muhammad, the founder of Islam. Unlike the founders of other major religions, Muhammad was not only the prophet of God but also the head of state. In Muslim nations, *there is no separation of church and state.*

The basic spiritual duties of all Muslims consist of the five pillars of faith: (1) accepting the confession of faith ("There is no God but God, and Muhammad is the Messenger of God"), (2) making the five daily prayers while facing Mecca (Muhammad's birthplace, where he was inspired to preach God's word in the year A.D. 610), (3) giving charity, (4) fasting during the daylight hours of Ramadan, a 29- or 30-day month in Islam's lunar calendar, and (5) making a pilgrimage to Mecca at least once in a person's lifetime. Some Muslims claim there is a sixth duty, *jihad,* which refers to the various forms of striving for the faith, such as the inner struggle for purification. However, this term is often translated as "holy war."

A major division in Islam was created by a dispute over the succession to the caliphate (the political and religious leadership of the community). As a result, two major divisions, the Sunnis and the Shiites, were formed. Although the Shiites and the Sunnis agree on the fundamentals of Islam, they differ in other respects. The Sunnis are an austere sect that is less authoritarian and more pragmatic than the Shiites. In their view, as long as Muslims accept Allah, they are free to interpret their religion as they like. The Shiites, in contrast, insist that those claiming to be Muslim must put themselves under the authority of a holy man (*ayatollah*).[33]

"The Protestant work ethic isn't cutting it, so we're switching to Shinto."

Source: From *The Wall Street Journal*-copyright Cartoon Features Syndicate.

This has created a clergy that wields enormous temporal and spiritual power, with the result that religious leaders affect business as well as religion. Consider two harmless consumer products, Coca-Cola and Pepsi-Cola. Both were banned from Iran for 15 years after the Islamic revolution in 1979 but returned in 1993 and are now extremely popular with Iranians. However, Iran's spiritual leader, Ayatollah Ali Khamenei, has ruled that Coca-Cola and Pepsi-Cola contribute to the enhancement of Zionism and therefore are forbidden.[34] Khamenei has since made overtures toward the United States, and the ban may not be permanent.

Sunni–Shia Conflict. Businesspeople doing business with Muslim countries should understand the Sunni–Shia conflict, because much of what occurs in those countries is the result of it. Although most Muslim countries are Sunni-governed, many of them, such as Kuwait, the emirates, Bahrain, and other small states in the Gulf, have substantial Shia populations. Furthermore, small Shia minorities can cause trouble for the government. For example, Saudi Arabia's Shia population is very small—only 250,000—and is concentrated in the eastern oil fields. Iran's Shia government continually broadcasts appeals to the Saudi Shiites to overthrow the regime. In Iraq, the ruler Saddam Hussein and his army are Sunnis, but 52 percent of the population is Shiite. As you can imagine, this division has given rise to violent clashes between religious dissidents and government forces. On the other hand, Syria is predominantly Sunni, but its government is controlled by a Shia sect.[35]

Even where the Sunni–Shia conflict is not a problem, two of the five pillars of faith can be bothersome to Western managers. The dawn-to-dusk fasting during the month of Ramadan causes workers' output to drop sharply, and the requirement to pray five times daily also affects output, because when they hear the call to prayer, Muslim workers stop whatever they are doing and pray where they are.

> An American manager in Pakistan for the purpose of getting a new factory into production came to the plant the first day, saw that production had started as it should, and went into his office to do some work. Suddenly, all of the machinery stopped. He rushed out, expecting to find a power failure. Instead, he found workers on their prayer rugs. The manager returned to his office and lowered his production estimates.

Animism

In a number of African and Latin American countries, animism, a kind of spirit worship that includes magic and witchcraft, is a major religion. It is often combined with Catholicism to present a strange mixture of mysticism, taboos, and fatalism. Animists believe their dead relatives are ever present and will be pleased if the living act in the same way as their ancestors. The resultant strong tendency to perpetuate traditions makes it extremely difficult for marketers and production managers to initiate changes. To be accepted, these changes must relate to the animists' beliefs. A foreign manager

[Figure 9.2] Estimated Religious Population of the World

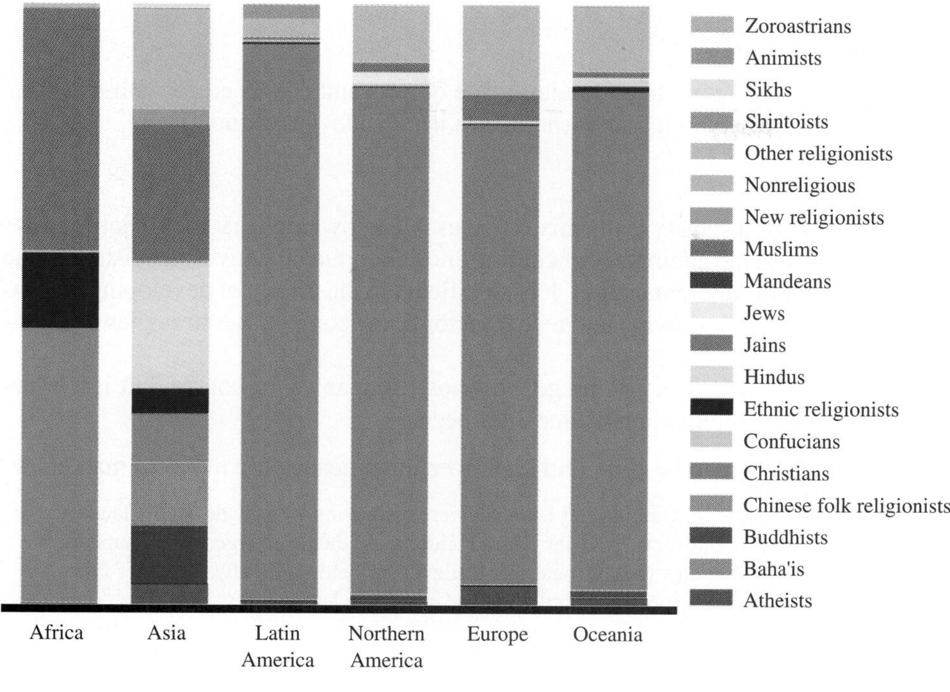

Source: No. 1348, Religious Population of the World: 1998. *Statistical Abstract of the United States 1999,* p. 831.

must also be cognizant of the proper religious protocols in situations such as factory and store dedications. If the evil spirits are not properly exorcised, they will remain to cause all sorts of problems, such as worker injuries, machinery breakdowns, and defective products.

> Evil spirits wreaked havoc in an American-owned semiconductor factory in Kuala Lumpur, Malaysia. The plant consists of an enormous room filled with hundreds of women looking into microscopes and television monitors.
>
> One afternoon, a girl claimed she saw an ugly woman in her microscope. The operator was pulled screaming to the first-aid room. The manager admitted that was a mistake: "Before I knew it, we had girls all over being held down by supervisors. It was like a battlefield."
>
> The factory was evacuated, but when the night crew arrived, the spirit returned. "Word had gone out that evil spirits were loose in the factory because of a dance we had the previous weekend. At night, it was worse. All we could do was hold them down, carry them out to the buses, and send them home."
>
> The next morning, a licensed healer was brought in. His recommendation—sacrifice a goat. That afternoon, a goat was killed and its blood was sprinkled on the factory floor. It was cooked in the cafeteria and eaten by the workers.
>
> "Next morning, we started up, and everything was fine."[36]

Figure 9.2 shows the religious populations of the world.

You have seen that religions have a pervasive influence on business. How effective can offers to pay time and a half for overtime and bonuses based on productivity be in a company whose workers are mainly Buddhists or Hindus? Strict adherents to these religions attempt to rid themselves of desires, and thus they have little need for an income beyond that which permits them to attain the basic necessities of life. When their incomes begin to rise, they have a tendency to reduce their efforts so that personal incomes remain unchanged.

Religious holidays and rituals can affect employee performance and work scheduling. When members of different religious groups work together, there may even be strife, division, and instability within the work force. Managers must respect the religious beliefs of others and adapt business practices to the religious constraints present in other cultures. Of course, to be able to do this, they must first know what those beliefs and constraints are.

Material Culture

material culture
All human-made objects; concerned with *how* people make things (technology) and *who* makes *what* and *why* (economics)

Material culture refers to all human-made objects and is concerned with *how* people make things (technology) and *who* makes *what* and *why* (economics).

Technology

The technology of a society is the mix of the usable knowledge that the society applies and directs toward the attainment of cultural and economic objectives; it exists in some form in every cultural organization. It is significant in the efforts of developing nations to improve their level of living and a vital factor in the competitive strategies of multinational firms.

Technological superiority is the goal of most companies, of course, but it is especially important to international companies because

1. It enables a firm to be competitive or even attain leadership in world markets.

   At one time, Procter & Gamble and Unilever were competing worldwide for the laundry detergent market, but then P&G introduced Tide, a synthetic detergent with superior cleaning power. Its sales took off and left Unilever far behind. Finally, Unilever introduced its own synthetic detergent, but P&G had stolen the lead.

2. It can be sold (via licensing or management contract), or it can be embodied in the company's products.
3. It can give a firm confidence to enter a foreign market even when other companies are already established there.
4. It can enable the firm to obtain better than usual conditions for a foreign market investment because the host government wants the technology that only the firm has (for example, permission for a wholly owned subsidiary in a country where the government normally insists on joint ventures with a local majority).

   IBM, confident of its superior technology, insisted on and obtained permission from the Mexican government to set up a wholly owned subsidiary when other computer manufacturers were forced to accept local partners.

5. It can enable a company with only a minority equity position to control a joint venture and preserve it as a captive market for semiprocessed inputs that it—but not the joint venture—produces.
6. It can change the international division of labor. Some firms that moved production overseas where labor was cheaper have returned to their home countries because production methods based on new technology have reduced the direct labor content of their products. With labor costs as low as 5 percent of total production costs, going overseas to save 30 to 40 percent in labor costs, for example, produces only about a 2 percent cost saving. This is more than offset by the transportation costs to bring the finished merchandise to the United States. Numerous electronics manufacturers, such as Radio Shack, Compaq, and Xerox, have brought production back to this country.
7. It is causing major firms to form competitive alliances in which each partner shares technology and the high costs of research and development. This is known as *strategic technology leveraging,* which is the concept of using external technology to complement rather than substitute for internal technology.

   To reduce the development costs for new low-pollution, fuel-efficient diesel engines to be used in European trucks and farm equipment, Cummins Engine of the United States and two Fiat subsidiaries formed a three-way joint venture to share costs and technology. It is believed that Fiat examined a number of options before choosing to collaborate with Cummins.[37]

Cultural Aspects of Technology. Technology includes not only the application of science to production but also skill in marketing, finance, and management. Its cultural aspects concern governments because their people may not be ready to accept the cultural changes a new technology may bring. Some say the shah of Iran's overthrow resulted in part from his trying to introduce new technology too rapidly.

Technology's cultural aspects are certainly important to international managers, because new production methods and new products often require people to change their beliefs and ways of living. A self-employed farmer frequently finds the discipline required to become a factory worker excessively demanding. If workers have been accustomed to the production conditions of cottage industries in which each individual performs all the production operations, they find it difficult to adjust to the monotony of tightening a single bolt. The "throw away instead of repair" philosophy behind the design of so many new products necessitates a change in the use habits of people who have been accustomed to repairing something to keep it operating until it is thoroughly worn out. Generally, the greater the difference is between the old and the new method or product, the more difficult it is for the firm to institute a change.

High GNP—High Level of Technology. The differences in levels of technology among nations are used as a basis for judging whether nations are developed or developing. Generally, a nation with a higher GNP per capita utilizes a higher level of technology than does one whose per capita income is smaller. Because of **technological dualism,** however, analysts must not assume that since the general technological level in a market is low, the particular industry they are examining is employing a simple technology.

technological dualism
The side-by-side presence of technologically advanced and technologically primitive production systems

Technological Dualism. Technological dualism is a prominent feature of many developing nations. In the same country, one industry sector may be technologically advanced, with high productivity, while the production techniques of another sector may be old and labor-intensive. This condition may be the result of the host government's insistence that foreign investors import only the most modern machinery rather than used but serviceable equipment that would be less costly and could create more employment.

Sometimes the preferences are reversed. A host government beset by high unemployment may argue for labor-intensive processes, while the foreign firm prefers automated production both because it is the kind the home office is most familiar with and because its use lessens the need for skilled labor, which is usually in short supply. To understand which policy the host government is following, management must study its laws and regulations and talk with host country officials.

Appropriate Technology. Rather than choosing between labor-intensive and capital-intensive processes, many experts in economic development are recommending **appropriate technology,** which can be labor-intensive, intermediate, or capital-intensive. The idea is to choose the technology that most closely fits the society using it. For example, in Africa, bricks are usually made in large-city factories using modern technology or locally in hand-poured, individual molds. In Botswana, an American group, AT International, designed an inexpensive small press with which four people can produce 1,500 bricks a day.[38] This is an intermediate technology that is also an appropriate technology.

appropriate technology
The technology (advanced, intermediate, or primitive) that most closely fits the society using it

In India a small manufacturer, Patel, took three-fourths of the detergent market from Lever, the giant multinational, by using a more appropriate technology, which was labor-intensive in this situation. Lever's Surf dominated the market until Patel, realizing that a high-quality, high-priced product was not appropriate for a poor country, set up a chain of shops in which people mixed the ingredients by hand. This primitive method tailored to Indian conditions enabled the company to outsell Lever on the basis of price. Patel's operation is one example of a large variety of production processes involving numerous distinct operations in which this technique can be employed. A large integrated production facility such as Lever had can be broken down into many small and more labor-intensive units, as Patel did with great success.[39]

[Worldview]

DON'T TRAVEL—USE CYBERSPACE

Silver Hammer, a California production firm that provides cable networks and television shows with graphics and promotional material, gets 30 percent of its business without leaving its office. The company, founded in 1996, won awards for five of its first six projects, among which were the *Oprah Winfrey Show* and the TV series *Dark Skies*. A new British TV network, attracted by the firm's success in the United States, asked Silver Hammer to create promotional spots for its debut. However, there were concerns about how the two companies could work together, being so far apart.

Silver Hammer's solution? It set up on its Web site something it called a "cyberbin" that was accessible by password only to a particular client. It posted storyboards, graphics, scripts, and correspondence that the client could see, comment on, and approve from a computer anywhere in the world. The cyberbin saved time by eliminating shipping delays of three days per package. The two companies took advantage of the eight-hour time difference between California and London in the same way Indian software engineers and American software firms do. Work Silver Hammer posted on the Internet at the end of the business day in Los Angeles was ready to be checked the first hour of the business day in London. The client could spend the entire day evaluating the material and send its commentary to California before the office opened in the morning.

Silver Hammer now uses the cyberbin to win other European jobs. Said CEO Holly Diefenderfer, "This has been so effective for us to open doors to other areas of the global marketplace." ■

Source: "The Cyber Screening Room," *World Trade*, January 1998, p. 12.

boomerang effect
When technology sold to companies in another nation is used to produce goods to compete with those of the seller of the technology

Boomerang Effect. One reason firms sometimes fear to sell their technology abroad is the **boomerang effect.** For example, Japanese firms have been less willing to sell their technology to newly industrialized economies (NIEs), such as Korea. Interestingly, fear of the boomerang effect has caused some American firms to restrict the sale of their technology to the Japanese. However, a recent study of the flat panel display industry suggests that there was no difference between U.S. and Japanese firms' tendency to share, or appropriate, knowledge from the rest of the world.[40]

Government Controls. The level of technology used by a foreign investor in a new manufacturing facility has a widespread impact. It affects the size of the investment, the quality and number of workers employed, the kinds of production inputs, what the facility can produce, and even what the host country can export. If the product cannot compete in the world market because production costs are excessive, quality is inferior, or the design is obsolete, the host government will not obtain the foreign exchange it otherwise would have. For these reasons, plus what many governments consider abuses in the sale of technology, some developing countries enacted strong laws that control the purchase of technical assistance by, for example, limiting the royalties paid to multinationals. This could include requiring licensees to transfer to licensors any improvements they make in the technology, prohibiting licensees from exporting, and obliging licensees to purchase raw materials from the licensor. However, host governments have recognized that technology is probably the most powerful stimulus to economic growth there is, so many are loosening controls as they pursue policies to attract foreign investment.[41]

The Information Technology Era

The information technology industry is changing at a pace that is bewildering to many business executives. Managing the flood of data available electronically is a challenge, but capturing information from transaction data, for example, offers profitable opportunities to mine the data for trend spotting. The Internet's worldwide reach has enabled firms to enter global markets with a minimal investment. It also, of course, has brought new competition to these companies in their own home markets. Apparently, the investment in new information technology is worth it. By the year 2000 the Internet economy had already reached $850 billion, exceeding the size of the automobile and truck and life insurance industries.[42]

Economics

The decision headquarters makes as to the kind of technology to be used by a subsidiary will, within any constraints imposed by the host government, depend on various measurements of the material culture. Economic yardsticks such as power generated per capita and number of high school graduates can uncover possible problems in the distribution and promotion of the product, help determine market size, and provide information on the availability of such resources as raw materials, skilled and unskilled labor, capital equipment, economic infrastructure (communications, financial system), and management talent. You studied these resources in Chapter 7.

Material Culture and Consumption

One of the unique expressions of Japanese material culture is the wide use of automation—not only in robots for manufacturing but in vending machines for a variety of items, including hot meals and (until recently) alcohol. Until a ban was enacted in 2000, Japan had nearly 170,000 alcohol vending machines. The major problem was that teenage males were buying beer that they were too young to buy in a store (Japan's official age for alcohol purchase is 20). Of course, it is feared that the vacuum will be filled by convenience stores which won't bother to check the age of patrons.[43]

Education

Although education in its widest sense can be thought of as any part of the learning process that equips an individual to take his or her place in the adult society, nearly everyone equates education with formal schooling.

Education Yardsticks

A firm contemplating foreign investment has no indicators of the educational level of a country's inhabitants except the usual yardsticks of formal education: literacy rate, kinds of schools, quantity of schools and their enrollments, and possibly the amount per capita spent on education. Such data underestimate the size of the vocationally trained group in the many countries where people learn a trade through apprenticeships. Like other international statistics, the published literacy rate must be suspect.

UNESCO recommends defining a literate person as "one who can both read and write a short, simple statement on his or her everyday life."[44] In some countries, the literacy census consists of asking respondents whether they can read and write, and the signing of their names is taken as proof of their literacy. Nevertheless, these data do provide some assistance. Marketers are interested in the literacy rate because it helps them decide what type of media to employ and at what level they should prepare advertisements, labels, point-of-purchase displays, and owner's manuals. The personnel manager will use the literacy rate as a guide in estimating what kinds of people will be available to staff the operation.

As with most kinds of data, the trends in education should be studied. It is important to realize that the general level of education is rising throughout the world. Figure 9.3 illustrates the extent of this increase in higher education.

Note that in a little over 25 years the percentage of adults age 20 to 24 in post–high school education increased threefold in the low-income nations and nearly tripled in the middle- and high-income countries. Businesspeople must be prepared to meet the needs of better-educated and more sophisticated consumers. They can also expect a better-educated work force.

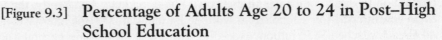

[Figure 9.3] **Percentage of Adults Age 20 to 24 in Post–High School Education**

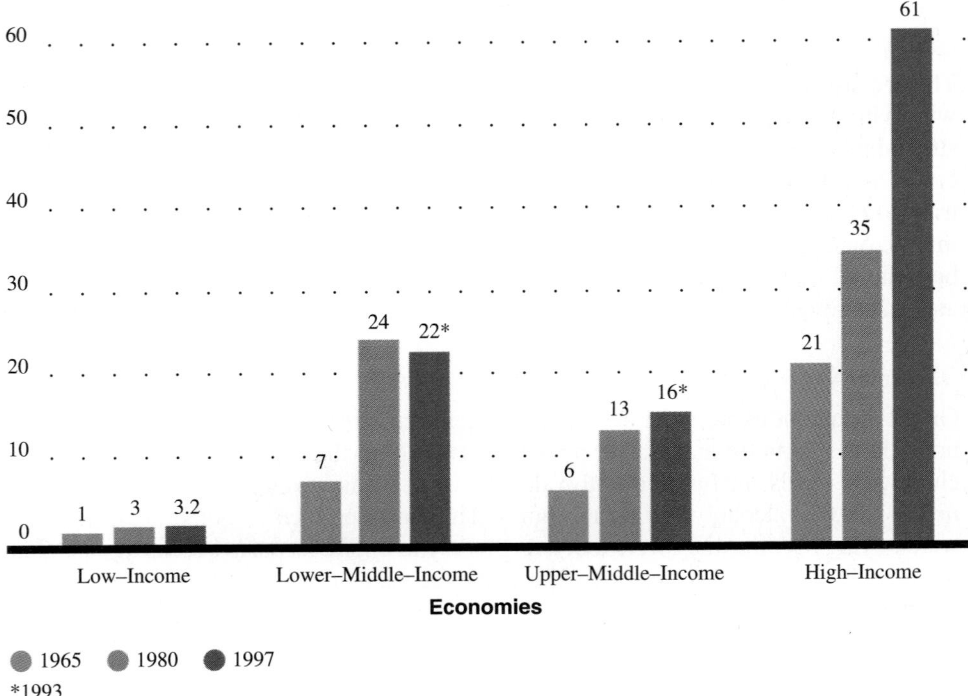

Source: *World Development Report,* 1991, 1993, 1997 (New York: World Development Bank, 1991, 1993, 1997), pp. 260–61, 216–17, 226–27; www.unesco.org/education/information/wer/WEBtables/regtabweb/xls (Dec. 27, 2000).

Although these data are indicative of the general level of education, unfortunately they tell us nothing about the quality of education or indicate how well the supply of graduates meets the demand.

Educational Mix

Until the 1970s, there was a feeling in Europe that managers were born, not made and that they could be trained only on the job. Thus, there was little demand for formal business education.

However, a combination of factors has caused a proliferation of European business schools patterned on the American model:

1. Increased competition in the European Union, resulting in a demand for better-trained managers.

2. The return to Europe of American business school graduates.

3. The establishment of American-type schools with American faculties and frequently with the assistance of American universities. Among elite European business schools we might find the London School of Economics and Political Science, the University of Mannheim in Germany, the University of St. Gallen and the IMD in Switzerland, INSEAD in France, and the London Business School.

This trend has been much slower in developing countries, where, historically, higher education has emphasized the study of the humanities, law, and medicine. Business education has been less popular than other fields because a business career lacked prestige.

In Chile, one of the writers was asked to train an engineer to be a V-belt technician. Noticing that the engineer could not comprehend engineering terms, the writer asked him what kind of engineer he was. To the writer's surprise, the answer was *commercial engi-*

neer. In a land of professional titles, apparently the government thought this was the best way to give professional recognition to business graduates. In many Latin American countries (such as Mexico, Argentina, Venezuela, and Colombia), a person is commonly addressed by his professional title—*Ingeniero* Garcia (engineer) or *Licenciado* Lopez (economist, attorney). However, in other countries, such as Chile, Peru, Bolivia, and Ecuador, this is not a common practice.

As developing nations industrialize, there is greater competition in the marketplace, and the job opportunities for engineers and business school graduates increase. Not only do the multinationals recruit such personnel, but the local firms do too when they find that the new competition forces them to improve the efficiency of their operations.

Brain Drain

Most developing nations are convinced that economic development is impossible without the development of human resources, and for the last two decades especially, governments have probably overinvested in higher education in relation to the demand for students. The result has been rising unemployment among the educated, which has led to a **brain drain,** the emigration of professionals to the industrialized nations. A study done by the United Nations Conference on Trade and Development (UNCTAD) estimated that about 500,000 professionals had left Third World countries since World War II. However, the incidence of brain drain varied enormously because most come from a limited number of countries in Asia, such as India, Pakistan, Egypt, and Korea.[45]

brain drain
The emigration of highly educated professionals to another country

The prime minister of Jamaica made an interesting observation. During the 1977–80 period, over 8,000 top professionals, 50 percent of the country's most highly trained citizens, emigrated, primarily to the United States. He estimated that the education of these people cost his nation $168.5 million, or $20,000 per person. During the same period, U.S. aid to Jamaica totaled only $116.3 million.[46]

Because of the salary and research opportunities available in the United States, the country continues to attract scientists and engineers from other countries (see Table 9.1). The number of women immigrants increased threefold from 1,167 in 1988 to 5,020 in 1993, whereas the number of male immigrants rose from 9,251 in 1988 to 18,511 in 1993. Note that the largest proportion of the scientists and engineers entering the United States as permanent residents came from the Far East (Figure 9.4). In 1997, among foreign-born science and engineering degree holders living in the United States, the top three places of birth were India, China, and the Philippines.[47]

Table 9.1 INS Permanent Visas Issued, by S&E Occupation (Thousands)

Year	Total, All Immigrant S&E	Engineers	Natural Scientists	Mathematical Scientists and Computer Specialists	Social Scientists
1988	11.0	8.1	1.2	1.2	0.5
1989	11.8	8.7	1.2	1.5	0.4
1990	12.6	9.3	1.2	1.6	0.5
1991	14.1	10.5	1.3	1.7	0.6
1992	22.9	15.6	2.8	3.4	1.1
1993	23.6	14.5	3.9	4.2	1.0
1994	17.2	10.7	3.1	2.8	0.7
1995	14.1	9.0	2.4	2.1	0.6
1996	19.4	11.6	3.7	3.3	0.8
1997	17.1	10.3	3.5	2.6	0.7
1998	13.5	7.9	2.5	2.5	0.6

Source: Appendix Table 3-24, *Science & Engineering Indicators—2000,* www.nsf.gov/sbe/srs/seind00/frames.htm.

[Figure 9.4] **Place of Birth of Foreign-Born Science and Engineering Degree Holders, 1997**

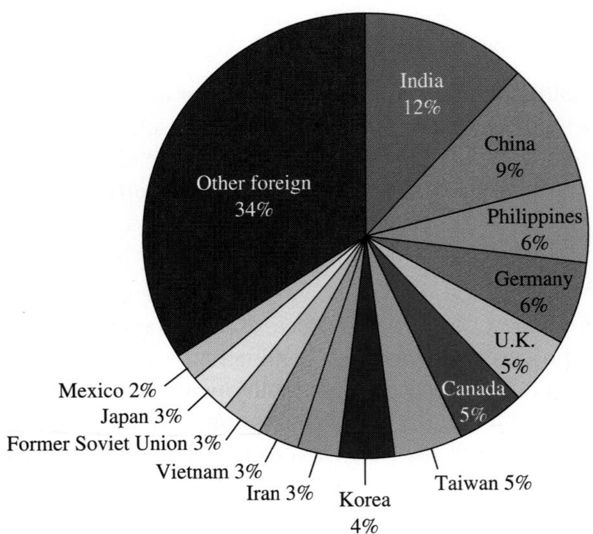

Source: National Science Foundation, *Science and Engineering Indicators—2000,* Figure 3-15, www.nsf.gov/sbe/srs/seind00/c3/fig03-15.htm

Brain drain facts:

1. Currently, the United States permits temporary admission of scientists and engineers (S&E) from Canada and Mexico under NAFTA's temporary entry provisions, which do not require a visa. Entry requirements are expected to be even easier in the year 2004.
2. Roughly 75 to 80 percent of foreign students remain in the United States after receiving doctorates in science.
3. Women represented 21.3 percent of the S&E who were admitted in 1993. Their ages ranged from 30 to 44 years, and the majority were born in the Far East.
4. As an indication of their professional positions, the median family income of Indians in the United States is $53,000. This is higher than the median income of native-born Americans.
5. Five times more Japanese research scientists work in the United States than Americans work in Japan.
6. A U.S. State Department report stated that the value of expert labor power migrating to the United States in one year was equal to $1.8 billion.
7. A United Nations report pointed out that the value of the human capital that emigrated to the West from developing nations during the years 1961–1972 exceeded $40 billion.[48]

Government authorities are deeply concerned about the loss of skills and have come to realize that there must be faster creation of new jobs not only to stop the costly loss but also to avoid serious political repercussions. To provide more jobs, they are adopting developmental plans that encourage labor-intensive exports and discourage the introduction of labor-saving processes. The pressure of the unemployed educated is also forcing officials in many areas to soften the terms for foreign investment.

[Figure 9.5] Gross Enrollment Ratios for Primary Education by Sex (Percent)

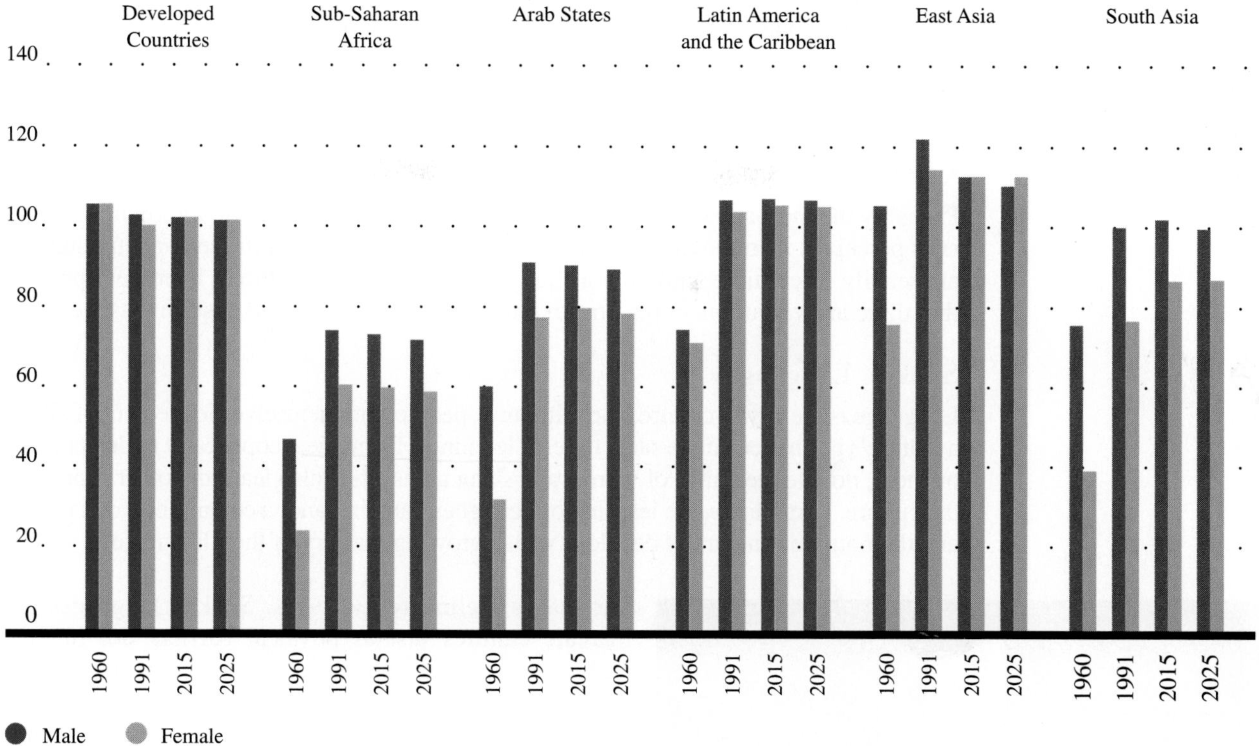

Source: UNESCO, *UNESCO Statistical Yearbook,* http://unesco.uneb.edu/unesco/educprog/stat/g155e_yc.html (January 12, 1998).

Reverse Brain Drain

reverse brain drain The return of highly educated professionals to their home countries

A **reverse brain drain** is preoccupying American educators and businesspeople. After suffering a severe brain drain for over 30 years, Korea and Taiwan are luring home Korean and Taiwanese engineers and scientists with American doctorates and 10 or more years of experience in American high-tech firms. More money and the opportunity to start businesses in these industrializing countries are the attractions.[49] The returnees are having a visible effect on their countries' competitiveness. The director of the science office at Sun Microsystems says, "Half the engineering vice presidents in Taiwan electronics companies went to school in the United States, worked at Sun, worked at Hewlett-Packard, and brought back cash to Taiwan to start companies."

In some developing countries from which scientists and engineers have gone to industrialized nations, organizations sponsored by local industry and occasionally by governments have "reverse brain drain" programs. For example, a business organization in Turkey whose aim is to "win Turkish college graduates back to Turkey" maintains a Web site to which Turkish people who are considering returning home can submit résumés. The organization then contacts leading Turkish firms in the fields specified by the applicant and puts the résumé in its database, which local companies search when they need scientists.[50]

Women's Education

An important trend is the fall in the illiteracy rate for women. The literacy differences between older and younger female age groups is striking. In Africa, which has the world's highest illiteracy rate, the percentage of women who could read and write grew from 18 percent in 1970 to 51 percent in 2000.

Nearly every government now has a goal, if not an actual policy, of providing free and compulsory education for both genders. Note in Figure 9.5 the improvement in female primary education from 1960 to 1991.

These statistics are extremely relevant for businesspeople because in almost every country, educated women have fewer, healthier, and better-educated children than do uneducated women. They achieve higher labor force participation rates and higher earnings. Undoubtedly, this is leading to an increased role for women in the family's decision making, which will require marketers to redo their promotional programs to take advantage of this important trend.

Language

Probably the most apparent cultural distinction that the newcomer to international business perceives is in the means of communication. Differences in the spoken language are readily discernible, and after a short period in the new culture it becomes apparent that there are variations in the unspoken language (manners and customs) as well.

Spoken Language

Language is the key to culture, and without it, people find themselves locked out of all but a culture's perimeter. At the same time, in learning a language, people can't understand the nuances, double meanings of words, and slang unless they also learn the other aspects of the culture. Fortunately, the learning of both goes hand in hand; a certain feel for a people and their attitudes naturally develops with a growing mastery of their language.

Stop signs appear in English and French in bilingual Montreal.
Walter Bibliow/The Image Bank

Languages Delineate Cultures. Spoken languages demarcate cultures just as physical barriers do. In fact, nothing equals the spoken language for distinguishing one culture from another. If two languages are spoken in a country, there will be two separate cultures (Belgium); if four languages are spoken, there will be four cultures (Switzerland); and so forth.

A poll taken of the German-speaking and French-speaking cultures in Switzerland illustrates how deeply opinions on crucial issues diverge even in a small country.[51] For example, 83.3 percent of the German Swiss regard environmental protection as one of that country's five major problems, compared to 45.1 percent of the French Swiss.

The results of a 1994 opinion poll "prove that there is no such thing as an average Swiss citizen. Each linguistic region attaches different importance to the particular problem. In German-speaking Switzerland, drugs head the list of worries. In French-speaking Switzerland and the Ticino (Italian-speaking), where jobless figures are higher, unemployment is seen as the number one problem by far, ahead even of drugs." The energy tax that receives only guarded support among the German-speaking Swiss is opposed by the majority in the French-speaking area and totally rejected in Ticino.[52]

Further, the Swiss are divided on what languages their children should be taught. A meeting of education officials broke up over disagreements about whether English should be taught as the first foreign language learned instead of any of the four official languages. The 64 percent of German-speaking Swiss learn French as their first foreign language, as do the small number of Romansh speakers. French- and Italian-speaking Swiss now learn German. However, many cantons intend to switch to English as the primary second language.[53]

What is occurring in Canada because of the sharp divisions between the English- and French-speaking regions is ample evidence of the force of languages in delineating cultures. The differences among the Basques, Catalans, and Spaniards and the differences between the French and Flemish in Belgium (see Figure 9.6) are other notable examples of the sharp cultural and often political differences between language groups. However, it does not follow from this generalization that cultures are the same wherever the same language is spoken. As a result of Spain's colonization, Spanish is the principal language

[Figure 9.6] How Language Divides Belgium

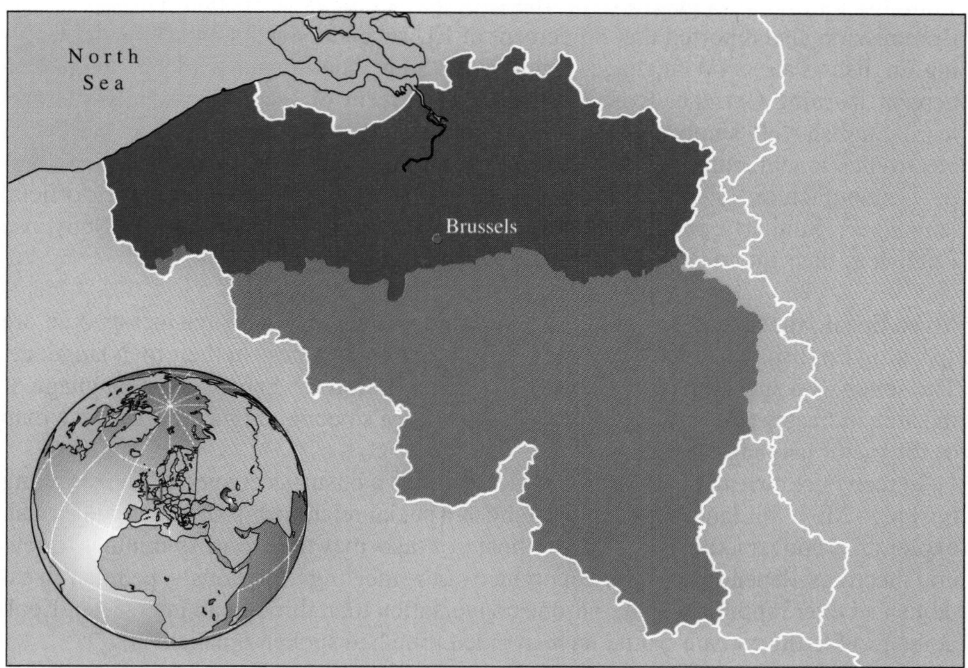

● Flemish-Speaking ● French-Speaking

of 21 Latin American nations, but no one should believe that they are culturally similar. Moreover, generally because of cultural differences, many words in both the written and the spoken languages of these countries are completely different. A Chilean told one of the authors of her surprise at seeing Puerto Rican coffee selling under the "El Pico" brand. In Chile, she said, *el pico* is a reference to the male sex organ.

Foreign Language. When many spoken languages exist in a single country (India and many African nations), one foreign language usually serves as the principal vehicle for communication across cultures. Nations that were formerly colonies generally use the language of their ex-rulers; thus, French is the **lingua franca,** or "link" language, of the former French and Belgian colonies in Africa, English in India, and Portuguese in Angola. Although they serve as a national language, these foreign substitutes are not the first language of anyone and consequently are less effective than the native tongues for reaching mass markets or for day-to-day conversations between managers and workers. Even in countries with only one principal language, such as Germany and France, there are problems of communication because of the large numbers of Greeks, Turks, Spaniards, and others who were recruited to ease labor shortages. A German supervisor may have workers from three or four countries and be unable to speak directly with any of them. To ameliorate this situation, managements try to separate the work force according to origin; for instance, all Turks are placed in the paint shop, all Greeks on the assembly line, and so on. But the preferred solution is to teach managers the language of their workers. Invariably, such training has resulted in an increase in production, fewer product defects, and higher worker morale.

lingua franca
A foreign language used to communicate among a nation's diverse cultures that have diverse languages

> General Tire–Chile sponsored a reverse language training program in which every employee could take free English courses given on the premises after work. Not only managers but also supervisors and even workers attended classes. The program was an excellent morale builder.

English, the Link Language of Business. When a Swedish businessperson talks with a Japanese businessperson, the conversation generally will be in English. The use of

English as a business *lingua franca* has spread so rapidly in Europe that in 1996, over half the European Union's adults could speak English, according to a European Commission report. One-third of the EU speaks it as a second language. The Commission also reported that 83 percent of EU secondary school students are learning English as a second language, compared to 32 percent learning French and just 16 percent learning German. Even in France, 84 percent of secondary school students learn English.[54] A number of European multinationals—such as Philips, the Dutch electronics manufacturer ($32 billion in annual sales), and Olivetti, the Italian computer manufacturer ($9 billion in annual sales)—have adopted English as their official language.[55] Similarly, some major Japanese firms, such as Matsushita and Sony, use English as their international business language.

Must Speak the Local Language. Even though more and more businesspeople are speaking English, when they buy, they insist on doing business in their own language. The seller who speaks it has a competitive edge. Moreover, knowing the language of the area indicates respect for its culture and the area's people. Figure 9.7 shows a map of the major languages of the world.

In many countries, it is a social blunder to begin a business conversation by talking business. Most foreigners expect to establish a social relationship first, and the casual, exploratory conversation that precedes business talks may take from 15 minutes to several meetings, depending on the importance of the meetings. Obviously, people can establish a better rapport in a one-on-one conversation than through an interpreter. Look at the trouble this person would have avoided if he had spoken Spanish.

> A German engineer, in Colombia to work on a pipeline, arrived at a hotel in the interior, where he tried to explain to the desk clerk that he had a suitcase full of cash that he wanted the hotel to keep. Because he knew no Spanish, he was having difficulty making himself understood. During the conversation, the desk clerk opened the suitcase in front of everyone in the lobby. A week later, the engineer was kidnapped by a guerrilla group and held for a month.[56]

Translation. The ability to speak the language well does not eliminate the need for translators. The smallest of markets requires technical manuals, catalogs, and good advertising ideas, and a lack of local talent to do the work does not mean that the organization must do without these valuable sales aids. The solution, even when the parent firm does not insist on international standardization, is to obtain this material from headquarters and have it translated if the costs are not prohibitive and suitable reproduction facilities are available locally. If the catalog or manual cannot be reproduced locally, the translation can be made and sent to the home office for reproduction. The home office already has the artwork, so the only additional cost is setting the type for the translations. Remember, though, a French or Spanish translation will be up to 25 percent longer.

Allowing headquarters to translate can be extremely risky because words from the same language frequently vary in meaning from one country to another or even from one region to another, as was mentioned earlier. A famous example that illustrated how only a single word incorrectly translated can ruin an otherwise good translation occurred in Mexico. The American headquarters of a deodorant manufacturer sent a Spanish translation of the manufacturer's international theme, "If you use our deodorant, you won't be embarrassed in public." Unfortunately, the translator used the word *embarazada* for "embarrassed," which in Mexican Spanish means "pregnant." Imagine the time that the Mexican subsidiary had with that one.[57]

Back Translations. To avoid translation errors, the experienced marketer will prefer what are really two translations. The first will be made by a bilingual native, whose work will then be translated back by a bilingual foreigner to see how it compares with the original. This work preferably should be done in the market where the material is to be used. No method is foolproof, but the back-translation approach is the safest way devised so far.

[Figure 9.7] Major Languages of the World

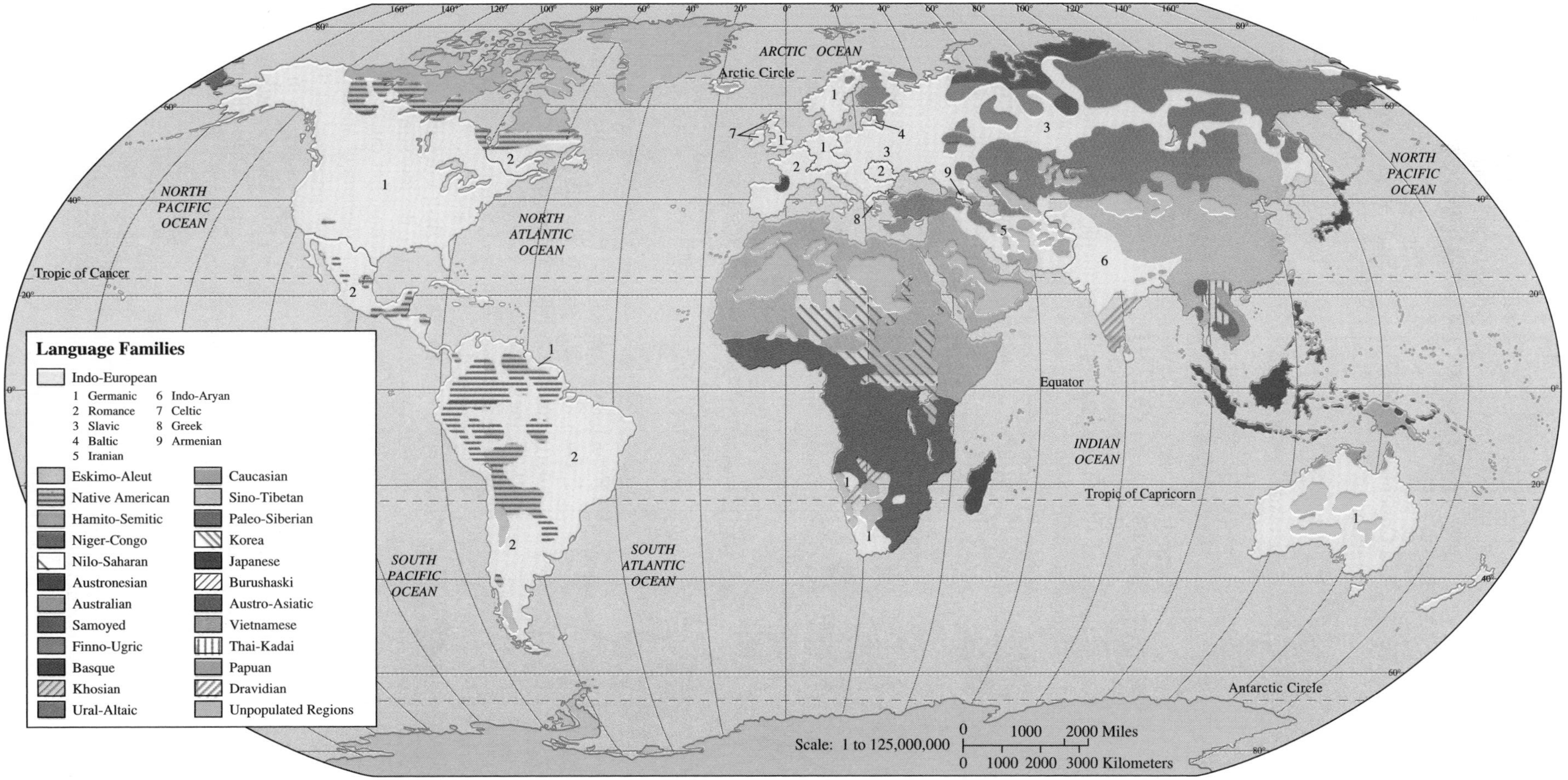

ARCTIC OCEAN
Arctic Circle
NORTH PACIFIC OCEAN
NORTH ATLANTIC OCEAN
Tropic of Cancer
Equator
INDIAN OCEAN
Tropic of Capricorn
SOUTH PACIFIC OCEAN
SOUTH ATLANTIC OCEAN
NORTH PACIFIC OCEAN
Antarctic Circle

Language Families

- Indo-European
  - 1 Germanic
  - 2 Romance
  - 3 Slavic
  - 4 Baltic
  - 5 Iranian
  - 6 Indo-Aryan
  - 7 Celtic
  - 8 Greek
  - 9 Armenian
- Eskimo-Aleut
- Native American
- Hamito-Semitic
- Niger-Congo
- Nilo-Saharan
- Austronesian
- Australian
- Samoyed
- Finno-Ugric
- Basque
- Khosian
- Ural-Altaic
- Caucasian
- Sino-Tibetan
- Paleo-Siberian
- Korea
- Japanese
- Burushaski
- Austro-Asiatic
- Vietnamese
- Thai-Kadai
- Papuan
- Dravidian
- Unpopulated Regions

Scale: 1 to 125,000,000
0 1000 2000 Miles
0 1000 2000 3000 Kilometers

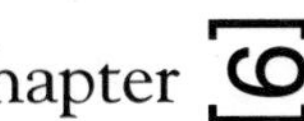

Some problems with translations:

1. A sign in a Paris hotel that sought to discourage Americans from wearing slacks in the plush dining room: "A sports jacket may be worn to dinner, but no trousers." The menu advised patrons that they could enjoy "tea in a bag just like mother."

2. In a Copenhagen airline ticket office: "We take your bags and send them in all directions."

3. In a Japanese hotel: "You are invited to take advantage of the chambermaid."

4. A Bangkok dry cleaner's boast: "Drop your trousers here for best results."

5. An Acapulco hotel that wanted to reassure guests about the drinking water: "The manager has personally passed all the water served here."

6. Sign in a Czech tourist office: "Take one of our horse-driven city tours—we guarantee no miscarriages."

Technical Words. Translators have difficulty with technical terms that do not exist in a language and with common words that have a special meaning for a certain industry. Portuguese, for example, is rich in fishing and marine terms, a reflection of Portugal's material culture, but it is exceedingly limited with respect to technical terms for the newer industries. The only solution is to employ the English word or fabricate a new word in Portuguese. Unless translators have a special knowledge of the industry, they will go to the dictionary for a literal translation that frequently makes no sense or is erroneous.

Resolving such problems by using English words may not be a satisfactory solution even if the public understands them, especially in France and Spain, which have national academies to keep the language "pure." The French, in their continuous effort to keep their language free of English words, passed a bill in 1994 prohibiting the use of foreign words and phrases in all business and government communications, radio and TV broadcasts, and advertising when there are suitable French equivalents.

ROTHCO
" First, le coca cola. Now peanut butter. Who will save La Belle Langue Française ?"

Source: *Pearson/Knickerbocker News,* NY/Rothco. Reprinted with permssion.

French Crackdown on English. In a continuing effort to protect the French language against the encroachment of other languages, various French watchdog groups, partially funded by the Culture Ministry, regularly sue those who in their opinion have violated the 1994 law. In 1997, they filed suits against the French campus of Georgia Tech for writing its Internet site in English, the Body Shop for selling products in France without French labels, and an electronics chain for selling computer games with English-only instructions. A French court dismissed the charges because the law stipulates that prosecutions must be brought by public prosecutors, not directly by associations.[58]

Although the French government and other defenders of the French language are struggling to maintain a French presence on the Internet, they are losing. An estimated 85 percent of the world's Internet sites are in English, and 80 percent of the information stored on computers is in English. According to the language experts, increasingly people will have two languages: one for talking to their friends and the other for communicating with the formal world.[59]

International businesspeople need to know that other governments have similar programs to keep the local culture pure. For example, Canada has a heritage minister whose job is to "safeguard Canadian culture," and Mexico, as Wal-Mart learned, has tough laws requiring labels in Spanish and metric measurements on imported goods.[60]

Wal-Mart has had language problems with the governments of both of America's NAFTA partners. Its New York stores broke the laws of Quebec by mailing circulars in English to residents of that French-speaking province; then the company was criticized for sending memos in English ordering Canadian employees to work extra hours without extra pay. Two months later, Mexican trade inspectors closed Wal-Mart's first supercenter store in Mexico City, charging the company with violating import regulations by not putting Spanish-language labels on its merchandise.

More than pride is involved here. The president of the Association of French-Speaking Computer Specialists, a former air force general, says the foreign jargon makes work more difficult for French computer specialists who are not fluent in English, and worse, it creates the impression among consumers that computing is a uniquely American science and that French computers are imitations that French buyers should avoid. The French culture minister says the time has come to head off an aggressive expansion of English in culture and trade: "A foreign language often becomes a tool of domination, uniformization, a factor of social exclusion, and, when used snobbishly, a language of contempt."[61]

Note the economic reason for keeping the language pure and separate from other languages. Those learning a foreign language not only are potential tourists but are likely to be empathetic toward anything that comes from that country. An Argentine engineer who reads French and not English will turn to French technical manuals and catalogs before specifying the machinery for the new power plant he is designing. However, if he constantly finds English technical terms in the French text, forcing him to consult his Spanish–English dictionary, he may decide to learn English and read American manuals and catalogs. Moreover, as the French general stated, if the French language doesn't have the technical terms and American English does have them, this indicates that the discovery and development of the industry have been occurring in the United States, not France, and that the Americans are the experts.

In Japan, the reverse situation exists, probably because for decades the country coveted foreign products while it struggled to overtake the West. Even now, most Japanese cars sold in the domestic market have almost nothing but English on them. A Nissan official explains that English is thought to be more attractive to the eye. Perhaps this is why people quench their thirst with a best-selling soft drink called "Pocari Sweat" and order from menus announcing "sand witches" and "miss Gorilla" (mixed grill). They also puff away on a cigarette called Hope.[62]

No Unpleasantness. One last aspect of the spoken language worthy of mention is the reluctance in many areas to say anything disagreeable to the listener. The politeness of the Japanese makes *no* a little-used word even when there are disagreements. An American executive, pleased that her Japanese counterpart is nodding and saying yes to all of her proposals, may be shaken later to learn that all the time the listener was saying yes (I hear you) and not yes (I agree). Western managers who ask their Brazilian assistants whether something can be done may receive the answer *meio deficil* (somewhat difficult). If managers take this answer literally, they will probably tell the assistants to do it anyway. The assistants will then elaborate on the difficulties until, they hope, it will dawn on the executives that what they ask is impossible but the Brazilians just don't want to give them the bad news.

Unspoken Language

Nonverbal communication, or the **unspoken language,** can often tell businesspeople something that the spoken language does not—if they understand it. Unfortunately, the differences in customs among cultures may cause misinterpretations of the communication.

unspoken language Nonverbal communication, such as gestures and body language

Gestures. Although gestures are a common form of cross-cultural communication, the language of gestures varies from one region to another. For instance, Americans and most Europeans understand the thumbs-up gesture to mean "all right," but in southern Italy and Greece, it transmits the message for which we reserve the middle finger. Making a circle with the thumb and the forefinger is friendly in the United States, but it means "you're worth zero" in France and Belgium and is a vulgar sexual invitation in Greece and Turkey.[63]

Department store greeter in Tokyo bows politely to a customer.
Charles Gupton/Stock Boston

In 2000, Japanese Prime Minister Yoshiro Mori climbed on a platform and paid his respects to his predecessor, Keizo Obuchi, by bowing two times before an urn containing Obuchi's ashes. Unfortunately, Japanese etiquette requires bowing *three* times to show respect for the deceased. Mori's gaffe was obvious to the 6,000 mourners in the hall and to millions watching on TV.[64]

Closed Doors. Americans know that one of the perquisites of an important executive is a large office with a door that can be closed. Normally, the door is open as a signal that the occupant is ready to receive others, but when it is closed, something of importance is going on. Contrary to the American open-door policy, Germans regularly keep their doors closed. Hall, the noted anthropologist mentioned at the beginning of this chapter, says that the closed door does not mean that the person behind it wants no visitors but only that he or she considers open doors sloppy and disorderly.[65]

Office Size. Although office size is an indicator of a person's importance, it means different things in different cultures. In the United States, the higher the status of the executive, the larger and more secluded the office, but in the Arab world, the president may be in what for us is a small, crowded office. In Japan, the top floor of a department store is reserved for the "bargain basement" (bargain penthouse?), not for top management. The French prefer to locate important department heads in the center of activities, with their assistants located outward on radii from this center. To be safe, never gauge people's importance by the size and location of their offices.

Conversational Distance. Anthropologists report that conversational distances are smaller in the Middle East and Latin America, though our personal experience in Latin America has not shown this to be the case.[66] Whether this generality is true or false, we must remember that generalities are like arithmetic means; perhaps more people do than do not act in a certain way in a culture, but the businessperson will be dealing with just a few nationals at a time. Luck may have it that he or she will meet exceptions to the stereotype.

The Language of Gift Giving

Gift giving is an important aspect of every businessperson's life both here and overseas. Entertainment outside office hours and the exchange of gifts are part of the process of getting better acquainted. However, the etiquette or language of gift giving varies among cultures, just as the spoken language does, and although foreigners will usually be forgiven for not knowing the language, certainly they and their gifts will be better received if they follow local customs.

Acceptable Gifts. In Japan, for example, one never gives an unwrapped gift or visits a Japanese home empty-handed. A gift is presented with the comment that it is only a trifle, which implies that the humble social position of the giver does not permit giving a gift in keeping with the high status of the recipient. He in turn will not open the gift in front of the giver because he knows better than to embarrass him by exposing the trifle in the giver's presence.

The Japanese use gift giving to convey one's thoughtfulness and consideration for the receiver, who over time builds up trust and confidence in the giver. White and yellow flowers are not good choices for gifts because in many areas they connote death. In Germany, red roses given to a woman indicate strong feelings for her, and if you give cutlery, always ask for a coin in payment so that the gift will not cut your friendship. Cutlery is a friendship cutter for the Russians and French also. Traditions vary greatly throughout the world, but generally safe gifts everywhere are chocolates, red roses, and a good Scotch whiskey (not in the Arab world, however—instead, bring a good book or something useful for the office).[67]

Gifts or Bribes? The questionable payments scandals (called bribery scandals by the press) exposed the practice of giving very expensive gifts and money to well-placed government officials in return for special favors, large orders, and protection. Some payments were **bribes;** that is, payments were made to induce the payee to do something for the payer that is illegal. But others were **extortion** made to keep the payee from harming the payer in some way. Still others were tips to induce government officials to do their jobs.[68]

bribes
Gifts or payments to induce the receiver to do something illegal for the giver

extortion
Payments to keep the receiver from causing harm to the payer

All three are payments for services, and usually they are combinations of two or possibly all three types. To distinguish among them, look at this example. If you tip the headwaiter to get a good table, that is a bribe, but if you tip him because you know that without it he'll put you near the kitchen, that's extortion. If you tip him for good service after eating, that is a tip. Part of the problem of adhering to American laws is the difficulty in making this distinction.

Although media exposure of questionable payments is fairly recent, for a long time it has been common knowledge in the international business community that gifts or money payments are necessary to obtain favorable action from government officials, whether to obtain a large order, avoid having a plant shut down, or receive faster service from customs agents. Their pervasiveness worldwide is illustrated by the variety of names for bribes—*mordida* ("bite"—Latin America), *dash* (West Africa), *pot de vin* ("jug of wine"—France), *la bustarella* (envelope left on Italian bureaucrat's desk), and *grease* (United States). Even the Soviets were not exempt according to a *Business International* study of multinational managers, who declared that representatives of the Russian state trading organization permitted gifts to be deposited in their Swiss bank accounts.

In 1999, Transparency International (an organization discussed below) began publishing a bribe payers index that ranks 19 major exporting nations according to the degree to which their companies are perceived to be paying bribes. The survey was conducted in 14 developing nations. Firms in Sweden, Australia, and Canada were thought to be least willing to bribe, while those in China, South Korea, and Taiwan were thought to be the most willing (see Table 9.2).

Questionable Payments. These come in all forms and sizes, from the petty "expediting" payments that have been necessary to get poorly paid government officials to do their normal duties to huge sums to win large orders.

> One of the writers was able to reduce by one-half the average age of receivables from a major Mexican governmental customer through the payment of $4 a month to a clerk whose sole job was to arrange suppliers' invoices according to their dates, so that the oldest were

Table 9.2 **1999 Bribe Payers Index**

Rank	Country	Score	Rank	Country	Score
1	Sweden	8.3	11	Singapore	5.7
2	Australia	8.1	12	Spain	5.3
2	Canada	8.1	13	France	5.2
4	Austria	7.8	14	Japan	5.1
5	Switzerland	7.7	15	Malaysia	3.9
6	Netherlands	7.4	16	Italy	3.7
7	United Kingdom	7.2	17	Taiwan	3.5
8	Belgium	6.8	18	South Korea	3.4
9	Germany	6.2	19	China	3.1
9	United States	6.2			

Source: From Transparency International (TI), *B & M 2000–2001 Update,* p. 27. Copyright Transparency International. Reprinted with permission.

on top and would be paid first. His company's invoices were placed on top regardless of their date and were paid promptly.

Included by the Securities and Exchange Commission (SEC) as questionable payments are contributions to foreign political parties and the payment of agents' commissions, even when these actions are not illegal in the country where they are done.[69] By means of the Foreign Corrupt Practices Act,* the United States is in effect requiring American firms to operate elsewhere according to this country's laws, which frequently places these firms at a competitive disadvantage. Many managements have responded by issuing strict orders not to make any questionable payments, legal or illegal, and some have been surprised to find that their business has not fallen off as they expected. Their action has been reinforced by a number of governments that have either passed stricter laws or begun to enforce those they already have. Given the combination of the low salaries of foreign officials and the intense competition for business, one should not be too sanguine about the prospects for completely eliminating this practice.

There is, nevertheless, a nongovernmental agency, Transparency International (TI), founded in Berlin in May 1993 and modeled after Amnesty International, the human rights agency. Its mission is to "curb corruption through international and national coalitions encouraging governments to establish and implement laws, policies and anti-corruption programmes."[70] The Corruption Perception Index (CPI) draws on seven surveys of businesspeople and political analysts, among which are those taken by Gallup and Political Risk Services. The CPI is designed so that countries perceived to be the *least corrupt* are given the highest score of 10. TI urges analysts to look at scores, not rankings, to understand how business perceives corruption in individual countries. Frequently, a country will have a higher score from one year to the next but will still fall in the ranking. The United States is an example of a country whose score has generally dropped over the years. It went from 8.41 for the period 1980–1985 to 7.76 for the survey covering the period 1988–1992, 7.66 in 1996, and 7.8 in 2000.

TI's chairman states that the "CPI has had a significant political impact in a number of countries as it has contributed to public awareness of the cancer of corruption"[71] (see Figure 9.8 for 2000 scores and rankings).

Societal Organization

Every society has a structure or an organization that is the patterned arrangement of relationships defining and regulating the manner by which its members interface with one another. Anthropologists generally study this important aspect of culture by breaking down its parts into two classes of institutions: those based on *kinship* and those based on the *free association* of individuals.

*The Foreign Corrupt Practices Act is discussed in Chapter 11.

[Figure 9.8] 2000 Corruption Perception Index Scores and Ranking

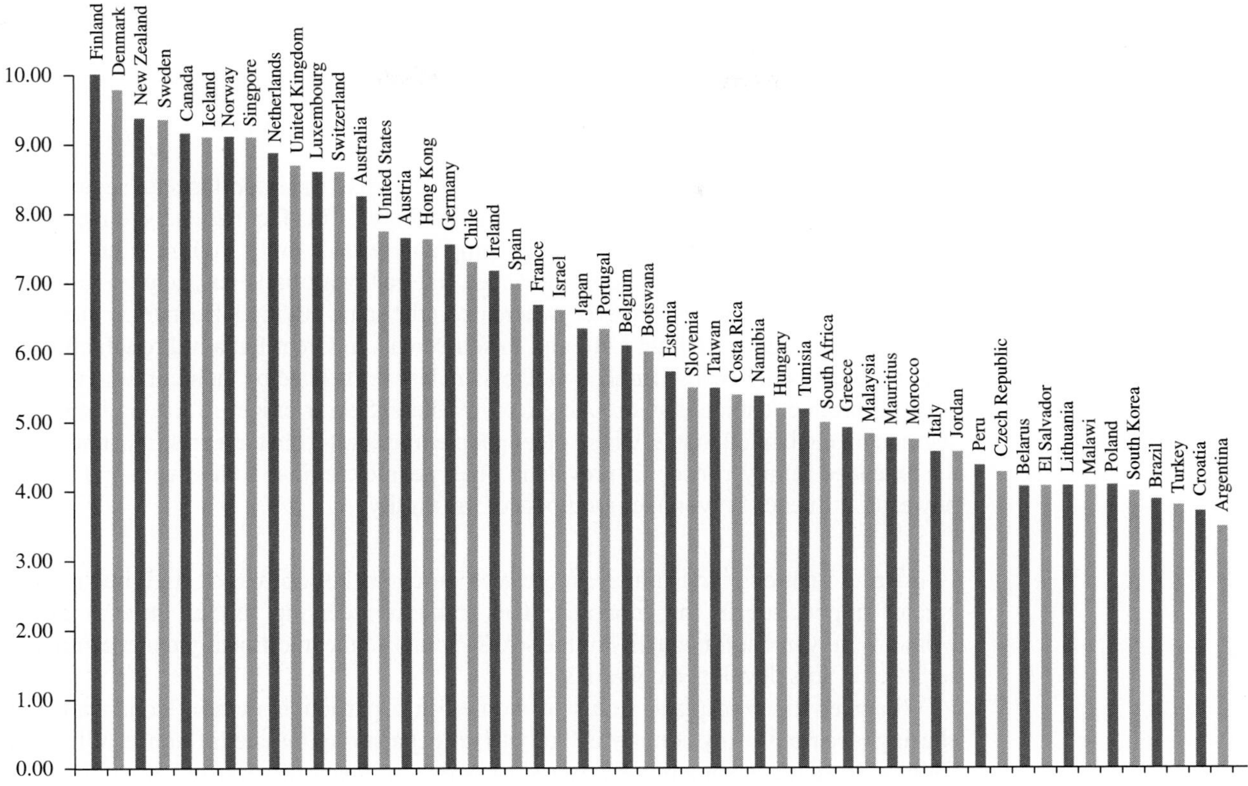

Source: "TI Press Release," http://www.gwdg/de/~uwvw/2000Data.html (November 14, 2000).

Kinship

The family is the basic unit of institutions based on kinship. Unlike the American family, which is generally composed of the parents and their children, families in many nations—especially the developing ones—are extended to include all relatives by blood and by marriage.

extended family
Includes blood relatives and relatives by marriage

Extended Family. For the foreign firm, the **extended family** is a source of employees and business connections. The trust that people place in their relatives, however distant, may motivate them to buy from a supplier owned by their cousin's cousin, even though the price is higher. Local personnel managers are prone to fill the best jobs with family members, regardless of their qualifications.

Member's Responsibility. Although the extended family is large, each member's feeling of responsibility to it is strong. An individual's initiative to work is discouraged if he or she is asked to share personal earnings with unemployed extended family members no matter what the kinship is. Responsibility to the family is frequently a cause of high absenteeism in developing countries where the worker is called home to help with the harvest. Managements have spent large sums to provide comfortable housing for workers and their immediate families, only to find them living in crowded conditions when members of their extended families have moved in.

Pedro Diaz Marin

In Latin America, where the extended family form is common, individuals use the maternal family surname (Marin) as well as the paternal (Diaz) to indicate both branches of the family. It is common to see two people, when meeting for the first time, exploring each other's family tree to see whether they have common relatives. If they find any kinship at all, the meeting goes much more smoothly, since they're relatives. By the way, in Korea, China, and Japan, the paternal family name appears first of all.

Associations

associations
Social units based on age, gender, or common interest, not on kinship

Social units not based on kinship, known as **associations** by anthropologists, may be formed by age, gender, or common interest.[72]

Age. Manufacturers of consumer goods are well aware of the importance of segmenting a market by age groups, which often cut across cultures. This fact has enabled marketers to succeed in selling such products as clothing and records to the youth market in both developed and developing nations. However, international marketers may go too far if they assume that young people everywhere exert the same buying influence on their parents as they do here. Kellogg's attempt to sell cereals in Great Britain through children was not successful because English mothers are less influenced by their children with respect to product choice than are American mothers. Senior citizens form an important segment in the United States, where older people live apart from their children, but where the extended family concept is prevalent, older people continue to live with and exert a powerful influence on younger members of the family.

Gender. As nations industrialize, more women enter the job market and thus assume greater importance in the economy. This trend is receiving further impetus as the women's movement for equality of the sexes spreads to the traditionally male-dominated societies of less developed countries.

Whatever the workplace status of women in a particular market, consumer purchasing in virtually any country is likely to reflect a strong female influence. While the Chinese husband is sometimes referred to as the "minister of defense," the wife is the "minister of the interior."

Free Association. Free association groups are composed of people joined together by a common bond, which can be political, occupational, recreational, or religious. Even before entering a country, management should identify such groups and assess their political and economic power. As we will see in later chapters, consumer organizations have forced firms to change their products, promotion, and prices, and investments have been supported or opposed by labor unions, which are often a powerful political force.

Entrepreneurial Spirit

One common interest which may be unexpected by many people is the desire to be an entrepreneur. We commonly assume that some countries may have a more intrinsically entrepreneurial culture than others, and this turns out to be true, but the countries with more would-be entrepreneurs are not quite what we might expect. In a straightforward study where researchers asked whether citizens would prefer to be an employee or to be self-employed, Blanchflower and Oswald found that the percentage of the would-be self-employed is high. And even in countries at the bottom of their sample, a quarter of the working-age population wanted to be self-employed. Figure 9.9 shows the results of their survey.

section [3]

Understanding National Cultures

To help managers of IBM understand the many national cultures in which the company operates, Geert Hofstede, a Danish psychologist, interviewed thousands of employees in 67 countries. He found that the differences in their answers to 32 statements could be based on four value dimensions: (1) individualism versus collectivism, (2) large versus small power distance, (3) strong versus weak uncertainty avoidance, and (4) mas-

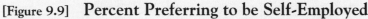

[Figure 9.9] **Percent Preferring to be Self-Employed**

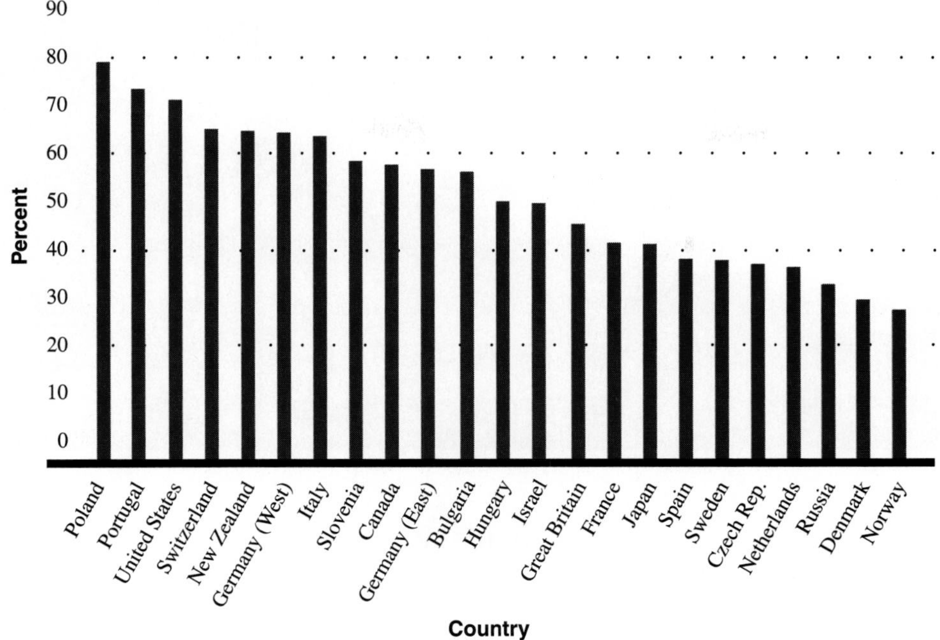

Source: David Blanchflower and Andrew Oswald, "Countries with the Spirit of Enterprise," *The Financial Times,* February 17, 2000, p. 27. Reprinted with permission of *The Financial Times.*

culinity versus femininity.[73] (Hofstede later added a fifth dimension, Long Term Orientation).

Individualism versus Collectivism

According to Hofstede, people in collectivistic cultures belong to groups that are supposed to look after them in exchange for loyalty, whereas people in individualistic cultures are only supposed to look after themselves and the immediate family.[74] Therefore, organizations operating in collectivistic cultures are more likely to rely on group decision making than are those in individualistic cultures where the emphasis is on individual decision making.

Large versus Small Power Distance

Power distance is the extent to which members of a society accept the unequal distribution of power among individuals. In large power distance societies, employees believe their supervisors are right even when they are wrong, and thus employees do not take any initiative in making nonroutine decisions. On the other hand, a participative management style of leadership is likely to be productive for an organization in a low power distance country.[75]

Strong versus Weak Uncertainty Avoidance

This is the degree to which the members of a society feel threatened by ambiguity and are reluctant to take risks. Employees in high risk-avoidance cultures such as Japan, Greece, and Portugal tend to stay with their organizations for a long time. Those from low risk-avoidance nations such as the United States, Singapore, and Denmark, however, are much more mobile. It should be apparent that organizational change in high uncertainty-avoidance nations is likely to receive strong resistance from employees, which makes the implementation of change difficult to administer.[76]

Table 9.3 Scores for Hofstede's Value Dimensions

Country	Power Distance	Uncertainty Avoidance	Individualism	Masculinity
Mexico	81	82	30	69
Venezuela	81	76	12	73
Colombia	64	80	13	64
Peru	90	87	16	42
Chile	63	86	23	28
Portugal	63	104	27	31
United States	50	46	91	62
Australia	49	51	90	61
South Africa (SAF)	49	49	65	63
New Zealand	45	49	79	58
Canada	39	48	80	52
Great Britain	35	35	89	66
Ireland	28	35	70	68

Masculinity versus Femininity

This is the degree to which the dominant values in a society emphasize assertiveness, acquisition of money and status, and achievement of visible and symbolic organizational rewards (masculinity) compared to the degree to which they emphasize relationships, concern for others, and the overall quality of life (femininity).[77]

Scores for the Four Dimensions

Table 9.3 presents the scores for Hofstede's four dimensions for about one-third of the countries in his sample.[78]

Plots of Dimensions and Management Implications

Figure 9.10 plots the scores for selected Anglo and Latin American (Hofstede's terms) nations on the power distance and uncertainty avoidance dimensions. The Latin American countries in the second quadrant scored relatively high on power distance and uncertainty avoidance. The lines of communication in organizations in these countries are vertical, and employees know who reports to whom. By clearly defining roles and procedures, the organizations are very predictable. The Anglo nations in the fourth quadrant scored low on both dimensions. Organizations in these countries are characterized by less formal controls and fewer layers of management. More informal communication is used.[79]

The scores for individualism and power distance are plotted in Figure 9.11. The Latin countries (first quadrant) scored relatively high on power distance and low on individualism. Employees tend to expect their organizations to look after them and defend their interests. They expect close supervision and managers who act paternally. On the other hand, people in the Anglo countries (third quadrant), which scored low on power distance and high on individualism, prefer to do things for themselves and do not expect organizations to look after them.[80]

Hofstede's four dimensions have given managers a basis for understanding how cultural differences affect organizations and management methods. They assist in showing that management skills are culturally specific; that is, "a management technique or philosophy that is appropriate in one national culture is not necessarily appropriate in another." Clearly, managing in different Western countries requires different activities, and thus generalizations are not justified. However, other researchers, using other data, have found the same or closely similar dimensions, leading Hofstede to conclude that "there is solid evidence that the four dimensions are, indeed, universal."[81]

[Figure 9.10] **Plot of Selected Nations on Power Distance and Uncertainty Avoidance**

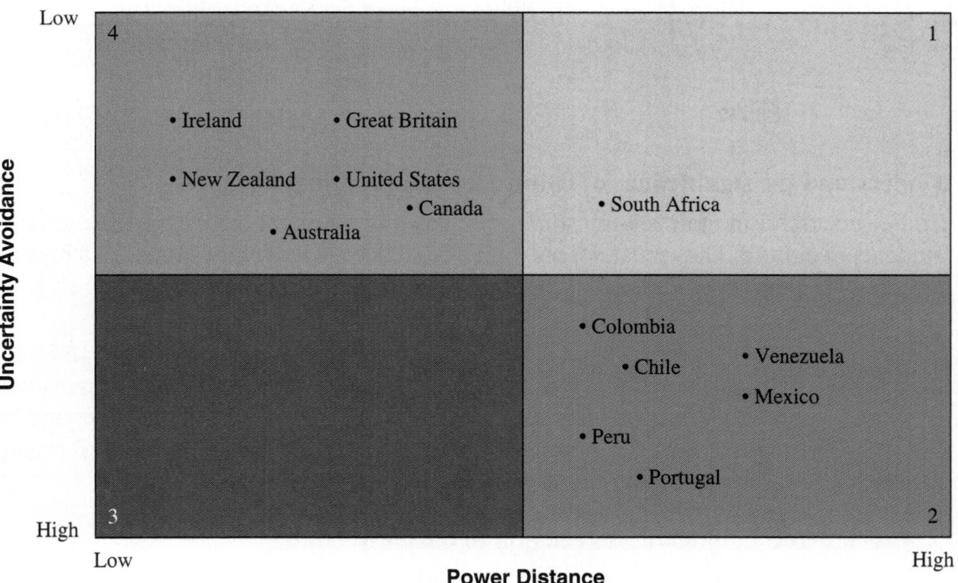

[Figure 9.11] **Plot of Selected Nations on Individualism and Power Distance**

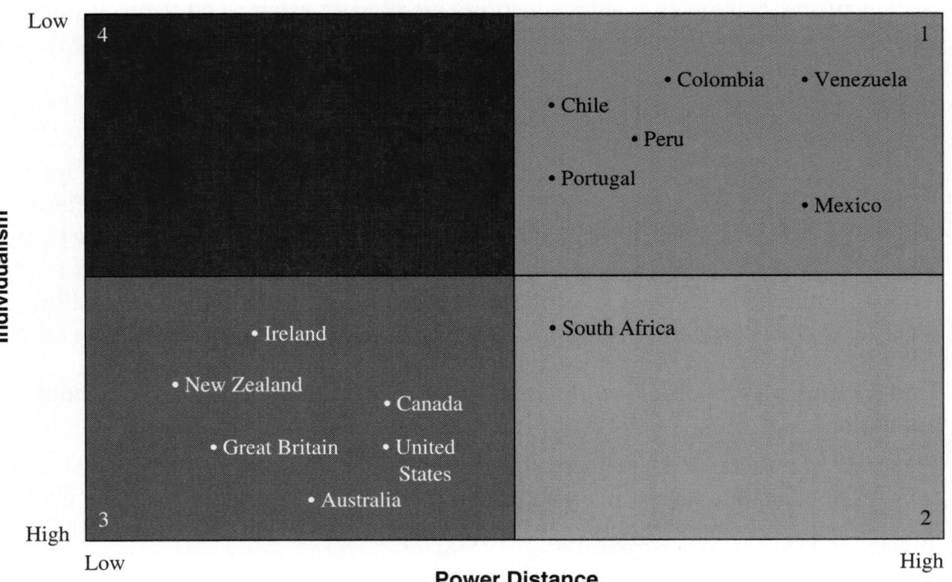

chapter [9]

[Summary]

Understand the significance of culture for international business.

To be successful in their relationships overseas, international businesspeople must be students of culture. They must not only have factual knowledge; they must also become culturally sensitive. Culture affects all functional areas of the firm.

Understand the sociocultural components of culture.

Although experts differ about the components of culture, the following is representative of what numerous anthropologists believe exist: (1) aesthetics, (2) attitudes and beliefs, (3) religion, (4) material culture, (5) education, (6) language, (7) societal organization, (8) legal characteristics, and (9) political structures.

Appreciate the significance of religion to businesspeople.

Knowing the basic tenets of other religions will contribute to a better understanding of their followers' attitudes. This may be a major factor in a given market.

Comprehend the cultural aspects of technology.

Material culture, especially technology, is important to managements contemplating overseas investment. Foreign governments have become increasingly involved in the sale and control of technical assistance. Technology may enable a firm to enter a new market successfully even if its competitors are already established there. It often enables the firm to obtain superior conditions for an overseas investment because the host government wants the technology.

Grasp the pervasiveness of the Information Technology Era.

Businesspeople must keep abreast of the changes in information technology to avoid falling behind their competitors. The Internet enables small firms to compete in the global market, a fact that provides new opportunities for some firms and new competition for others. Businesspeople who can capture information from transaction data have a significant advantage over those who cannot. The opinion in the retailing industry is that this capability is the primary reason for Wal-Mart's success, for example.

Understand why businesspeople must follow the worldwide trends of formal education.

Figure 9.5 shows the dramatic increase in the educational levels of adults living in countries of all economic levels. International firms must be prepared to meet the needs of better-educated and more sophisticated customers as well as a better-educated work force.

Discuss the impact of the "brain drain" and the "reverse brain drain" on developed and developing nations.

Developed nations have received thousands of scientists and highly trained professionals from developing nations without contributing any part of the cost of their education. They also have lost hundreds of scientists who obtained industry experience in developed countries to recruiters from their countries of origin.

Appreciate the importance of the ability to speak the local language.

Language is the key to culture. A feel for a people and their attitudes naturally develops with a growing mastery of their language.

Recognize the importance of the unspoken language in international business.

Because the unspoken language can often tell businesspeople something that the spoken language does not, they should know something about this form of cross-cultural communication.

Discuss the two classes of relationships within a society.

A knowledge of how a society is organized is useful because the arrangement of relationships within it defines and regulates the manner in which its members interface with one another. Anthropologists have broken down societal relationships into two classes: those based on kinship and those based on free association of individuals.

Discuss Hofstede's four cultural value dimensions.

Geert Hofstede, a Danish psychologist, interviewed IBM employees in 67 countries and found that the differences in their answers to 32 statements could be based on four value dimensions: (1) individualism versus collectivism, (2) large versus small power distance, (3) strong versus weak uncertainty, and (4) masculinity versus femininity. These dimensions help managers understand how cultural differences affect organizations and management methods.

[Key Words]

culture (p. 303)
ethnocentricity (p. 303)
aesthetics (p. 307)
demonstration effect (p. 311)
Protestant work ethic (p. 312)
Confucian work ethic (p. 312)
Asian religions (p. 312)
caste system (p. 314)
material culture (p. 318)
technological dualism (p. 319)
appropriate technology (p. 319)
boomerang effect (p. 320)
brain drain (p. 323)
reverse brain drain (p. 325)
lingua franca (p. 327)
unspoken language (p. 331)
bribes (p. 333)
extortion (p. 333)
extended family (p. 335)
associations (p. 336)

[Questions]

1. Why is it helpful for international businesspeople to know that a national culture has two components?
2. A knowledge of culture has been responsible for Disney's success in Tokyo, and ignorance of culture was responsible for the company's large losses in Paris. Discuss.
3. Why do international businesspersons need to consider aesthetics when making marketing decisions?

4. How can the demonstration effect be used to improve productivity? To improve sales?

5. Some societies view change differently than do Americans. What impact does this have on the way American marketers operate in those markets? The way American production people operate?

6. Why must international businesspeople be acquainted with the beliefs of the major religions in the areas in which they work?

7. What Buddhist belief would cause American marketing and production managers to think carefully before transferring their marketing plans or bonus plans to an area where Buddhists are present in large numbers?

8. Why is technological superiority especially significant for international firms?

9. What is the significance of the extended family for international managers?

10. Use Hofstede's four dimensions to analyze this situation: John Adams, with 20 years of experience as general foreman in the United States, is sent as production superintendent to his firm's new plant in Colombia. He was chosen because of his outstanding success in handling workers. Adams uses the participative management style. Can you foresee him having any problems on this new job?

[Internet Exercises]

Using the Internet

1. Research the following questions about body language.
   a. What is the gesture in Bulgaria that means the exact opposite of what it means in the United States?
   b. How do you beckon someone in Spain?
   c. How do you signal a waiter in a restaurant for a bill in the United Kingdom?
   d. If you are served tea during a business meeting in Hong Kong and your host does not touch his tea for a long time, what does this signify?
   e. In Brazil, if you see a Brazilian in a restaurant reach behind his head and grab the opposite earlobe, what is he indicating?

2. The 1998 amendment to the Foreign Corrupt Practices Act (FCPA) explicitly permits a certain kind of payment.
   a. What is it?
   b. What are the examples that the statute lists as permissible payments?

[Minicase 9.1]

Be Attuned to Business Etiquette

The proverb "When in Rome, do as the Romans do" applies to business representatives as well as tourists. Being attuned to a country's business etiquette can make or break a sale, particularly in countries where 1,000-year-old traditions can dictate the rules for proper behavior. Anyone interested in being a successful marketer should be aware of the following considerations:

- *Local customer, etiquette, and protocol.* An exporter's behavior in a foreign country can reflect favorably or unfavorably on the exporter, the company, and even the sales potential for the product.
- *Body language and facial expressions.* Often, actions do speak louder than words.
- *Expressions of appreciation.* Giving and receiving gifts can be a touchy subject in many countries. Doing it badly may be worse than not doing it at all.
- *Choices of words.* Knowing when and if to use slang, tell a joke, or just keep silent is important.

The following informal test will help exporters rate their business etiquette. See how many of the following you can answer correctly. (Answers follow the last question.)

1. You are in a business meeting in an Arabian Gulf country. You are offered a small cup of bitter cardamom coffee. After your cup has been refilled several times, you decide you would rather not have any more. How do you decline the next cup offered to you?
   a. Place your palm over the top of the cup when the coffeepot is passed.
   b. Turn your empty cup upside down on the table.
   c. Hold the cup and twist your wrist from side to side.
2. In which of the following countries are you expected to be punctual for business meetings?
   a. Peru.
   b. Hong Kong.
   c. Japan.
   d. China.
   e. Morocco.
3. Gift giving is prevalent in Japanese society. A business acquaintance presents you with a small wrapped package. Do you:
   a. Open the present immediately and thank the giver?
   b. Thank the giver and open the present later?
   c. Suggest that the giver open the present for you?
4. In which of the following countries is tipping considered an insult?
   a. Great Britain.
   b. Iceland.
   c. Canada.

5. What is the normal workweek in Saudi Arabia?
   a. Monday through Friday.
   b. Friday through Tuesday.
   c. Saturday through Wednesday.

6. You are in a business meeting in Seoul. Your Korean business associate hands you his calling card, which states his name in the traditional Korean order: Park Chul Su. How do you address him?
   a. Mr. Park.
   b. Mr. Chul.
   c. Mr. Su.

7. In general, which of the following would be good topics of conversation in Latin American countries?
   a. Sports.
   b. Religion.
   c. Local politics.
   d. The weather.
   e. Travel.

8. In many countries, visitors often are entertained in the homes of clients. Taking flowers as a gift to the hostess is usually a safe way to express thanks for the hospitality. However, both the type and the color of the flower can have amorous, negative, or even ominous implications. Match the country where presenting them would be a social faux pas.

a. Brazil.	1 Red roses.
b. France.	2 Purple flowers.
c. Switzerland.	3 Chrysanthemums.

9. In Middle Eastern countries, which hand does one use to accept or pass food?
   a. Right hand.
   b. Left hand.
   c. Either hand.

10. Body language is just as important as the spoken word in many countries. For example, in most countries, the thumbs-up sign means "OK." But in which of the following countries is the sign considered a rude gesture?
    a. Germany.
    b. Italy.
    c. Australia.

Answers:
1—*c.* It is also appropriate to leave the cup full. 2—*a, b, c, d,* and *e.* Even in countries where local custom does not stress promptness, overseas visitors should be prompt. 3—*b.* 4—*b.* 5—*c.* 6—*a.* The traditional Korean pattern is surname, followed by two given names. 7—*a, d,* and *e.* 8—*a* and 2. Purple flowers are a sign of death in Brazil, as are chrysanthemums in France (*b* and 3). In Switzerland (*c* and 1), as well as in many other north European countries, red roses suggest romantic intentions. 9—*a.* Using the left hand would be a social gaffe. 10—*b, c.*

How's Your Business Etiquette?

8–10 Congratulations, you have obviously done your homework when it comes to doing business overseas.
5–7 Although you have some sensitivity to the nuances of other cultures, you still might make some social errors that could cost you sales abroad.
1–4 Look out, you could be headed for trouble if you leave home without consulting the experts.

Where to Turn for Help

Whether you struck out completely in the business etiquette department or just want to polish your skills, there are several sources you can turn to for help.

- *Books.* Most good bookstores today carry a variety of resource materials to help the traveling business representative.
- *Workshops and seminars.* Many private business organizations and universities sponsor training sessions for the exporter interested in unraveling the mysteries of doing business abroad.
- *State marketing specialists.* In some states, your first contact should be your state commerce or agriculture department, where international specialists can pass on their expertise or put you in touch with someone who can.

Source: *Foreign Agriculture,* U.S. Department of Agriculture, February 1987, pp. 18–19.

[Chapter]

Political Forces

"Politics have no relation to morals."

—Niccoló Machiavelli

Concept Previews

After reading this chapter, you should be able to:

- **identify** the ideological forces that affect business and understand the terminology used in discussing them
- **understand** that although most governments own businesses, they are privatizing them in growing numbers
- **explain** the changing sources and reasons for terrorism and the methods and growing power of terrorists
- **explain** steps that traveling international business executives should take to protect themselves from terrorists
- **understand** the importance to business of government stability and policy continuity
- **discuss** the power sources of international organizations, labor unions, and international companies
- **understand** country risk assessment by international business

Steven Weinberg/Tony Stone Images

I'm from the Government, and I'm Here to Help You

In 1991, John Much, a North Sea fisherman, bought the *Pornstrom,* a rotting prawn-fishing boat, not to go fishing in but for the fishing license that came with it. His accountant advised him to create a tax deduction by donating the boat to the national coastal parks as a tourist attraction.

The German environment ministry vetoed the gift because Much didn't have an official "gift contract." Clearing that hurdle took 10 months. Then objections came from the office for land and water industry, which wanted to know where the boat would be wintered, and from the harbor master, who refused to allow a crane on his jetty to haul the boat from the water. Then the Tonning city planning office demanded planning permission, including regional permission from the interior ministry, which in turn required permission from the listed objects and monuments department.

The federal shipping and hydrographers' office demanded written confirmation that the boat was to be put on land. That confirmation was from the Tonning town council, but the construction office refused to build foundations for the boat, and a private firm had to be contracted to build it.

Finally, 18 months after Mr. Much offered the boat as a gift, it was lowered into place in the national park. Mr. Much was not present for the handing-over ceremony—he had gone fishing in frustration.

Today, few visitors will understand the purpose of the fishing boat in a field. The explanatory notices have been removed. There was no planning permission for them. ■

Source: Tony Paterson, "The Not So Everyday Tale of Fishing Folk," *The European,* February 4–7, 1993, p. 5.

Chapter 11 deals with the legal forces affecting international business. Of course, laws and their interpretation and enforcement reflect political ideologies and outlooks as well as government stability and continuity. Therefore, this chapter is intended as background for and a companion to Chapter 11.

In a number of ways, the political climate of the country in which a business operates is as important as the country's topography, its natural resources, and its meteorological climate. Indeed, we shall see examples in which a hospitable, stable government can encourage business investment and growth despite geographic or weather obstacles and a scarcity of natural resources. The opposite is equally true. Some areas of the world that are relatively blessed with natural resources and manageable topography and weather have been very little developed because of government instability. Occasionally, a country's government is hostile to investment in its territory by foreign companies even though they might provide capital, technology, and training for development of the country's resources and people.

Many of the political forces with which business must cope have ideological sources, but there are a large number of other sources. These sources include nationalism, terrorism, traditional hostilities, unstable governments, international organizations, and government-owned business. Figure 10.1 presents a world map of freedom.

It should be pointed out that the international company itself can be a political force. Some firms have budgets or sales larger than the gross national product (GNP) of some of the countries with which they negotiate. Although budgets and GNPs do not translate directly or necessarily into power, it should be clear that companies with bigger budgets and countries with bigger GNPs possess more assets and facilities with which to negotiate. Refer to Table 1.3 for some examples.

This chapter will provide an indication of the types of risks to private business posed by political forces. As we shall see, some of the risks can stem from more than one political force.

Ideological Forces

Such names as communism, socialism, capitalism, liberal, conservative, left wing, and right wing are used to describe governments, political parties, and people. These names indicate ideological beliefs.

Communism

communism
Marx's theory of a classless society, developed by his successors into control of society by the Communist party and the attempted worldwide spread of communism

It is communist doctrine that the government should own all the major factors of production. With exceptions, all production in these countries is done by state-owned factories and farms. Labor unions are government-controlled.

Communism as conceived by Karl Marx was a theory of social change directed toward the ideal of a classless society. As developed by Lenin and others, communism typically involves the seizure of power by a conspiratorial political party, the maintenance of power by stern suppression of internal opposition, and commitment to the ultimate goal of a worldwide communist state.

[Figure 10.1] 2000 Map of Freedom

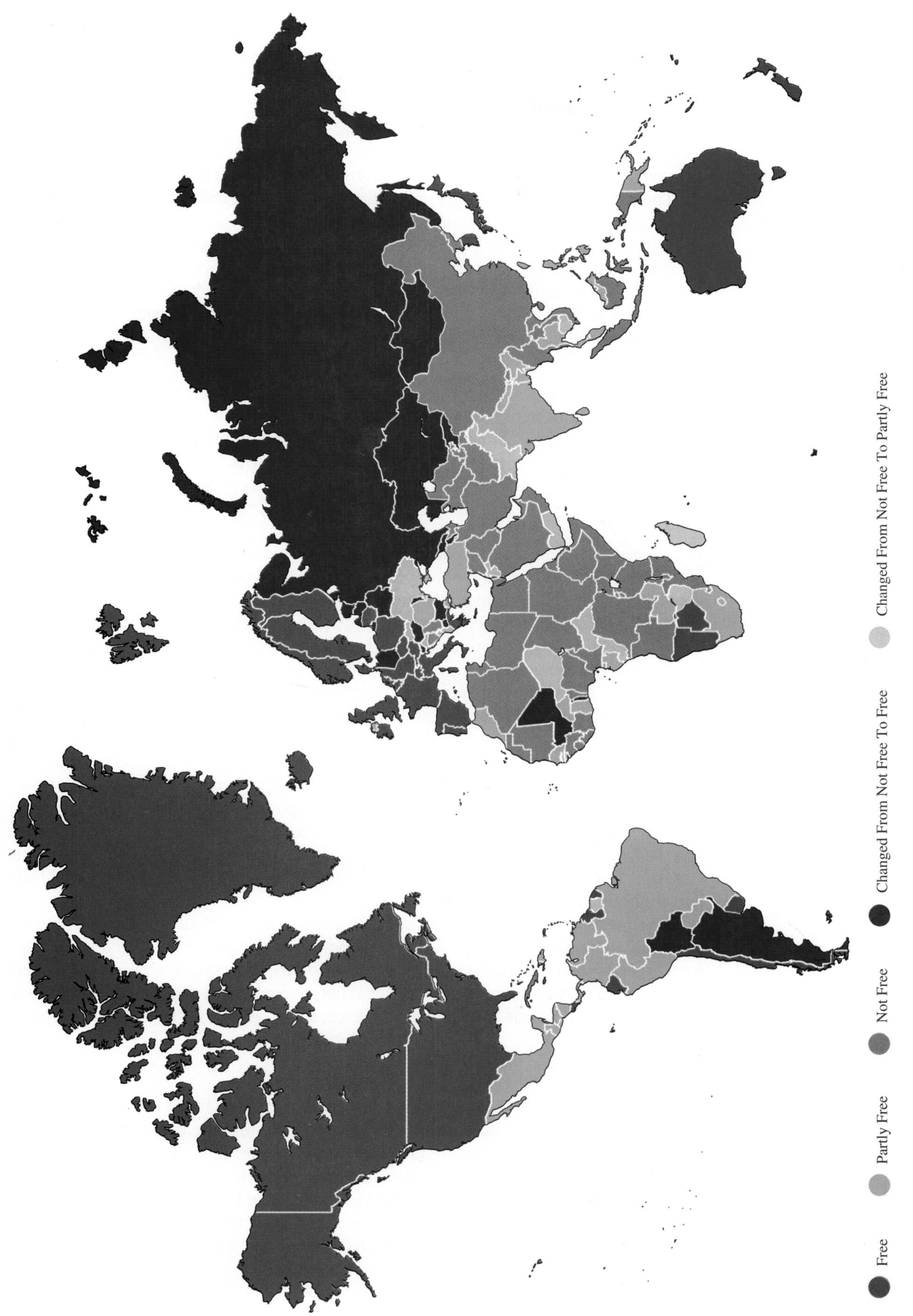

Communist Government Takeover of a Previously Noncommunist Country

Given one of communism's basic tenets—state ownership of all the productive factors—the government will take over private business. This occurred in Russia after the 1917 Bolshevik Revolution, and it has been repeated after each communist takeover of a country.

Compensation for Expropriated Property. To date, none of the new communist governments has compensated the foreign former owners directly. A few of the owners have gotten some reimbursement indirectly out of assets of the communist government seized abroad after the communist government confiscated foreign private property within its country. For example, the U.S. government seized assets of the Soviet Union in the United States after American property in the Union of Soviet Socialist Republics (U.S.S.R.) was confiscated. American firms or individuals whose property had been confiscated in the U.S.S.R. could file claims with a U.S. government agency, and if they could substantiate their loss, a percentage of it was paid.

Expropriation and Confiscation. The rules of traditional international law recognize a country's right to expropriate the property of foreigners within its jurisdiction. But those rules require the country to compensate the foreign owners, and *in the absence of compensation,* **expropriation** *becomes* **confiscation.**[1]

expropriation
Government seizure of the property within its borders owned by foreigners, followed by prompt, adequate, and effective compensation paid to the former owners

confiscation
Government seizure of the property within its borders owned by foreigners without payment to them

Communism Collapses

We have insufficient space to detail the reasons for communism's failure as an economic and social system. We shall present a couple of basic reasons and a few anecdotes that illustrate the results. See the endnotes for more.

The U.S.S.R. concentrated its best scientists, engineers, managers, and raw materials in production for the military; it neglected production of consumer goods. Gross production was the goal, and managers would go to ridiculous extremes to report the production figures set by government central planners.

Since Soviet central planning allowed only one condom factory and birth control pills were very expensive under the communist regime, the two products were rarely available except to the privileged. As a result, abortion was by far the country's most common form of birth control. All these abortions were then counted as part of doctors' gross production and therefore swelled the reported national income.

Factories under construction got a certificate putting them into commission on the scheduled completion date even though they were almost never actually completed on schedule. Because of the certificate, the factory had to report production coming from it even though it had not yet produced anything.

The first deputy chairman of the U.S.S.R. Committee for National Control, with the splendidly appropriate name of A. Shitof, reported that at least half the enterprises lied to exaggerate their output. Some enterprises used other deceptions. For instance, a factory reaching only 50 percent of its targeted output could have made a small change in its next shipped machine and doubled the price, say, from $10,000 to $20,000—presto, doubled output.[2]

Tale of Two Cities

A spectacular result of communism's collapse was the reunification of East Germany with West Germany, accompanied by the revival of Berlin as the capital of the new Germany. The capital of West Germany had been in Bonn, while East Germany's capital had been in its part of the divided Berlin. As reunited Berlin was renovated in the east and as hundreds of new buildings were constructed throughout the city, it resembled and was called a high-construction site. The picture at the beginning of this chapter illustrates a small part of that.

Capitalism

The capitalist, free enterprise ideal is that all the factors of production should be privately owned. Under ideal **capitalism,** government is restricted to those functions that the private sector cannot perform: national defense; police, fire, and other public services; and government-to-government international relations. No such government exists.

Reality in so-called capitalist countries is quite complex. The governments of such countries typically regulate privately owned businesses quite closely, and these governments own businesses.

capitalism
An economic system in which the means of production and distribution are for the most part privately owned and operated for private profit

Regulations and Red Tape

All businesses are subject to countless government laws, regulations, and red tape in their activities in the United States and all other capitalist countries. Special government approval is required to practice such professions as law and medicine. Tailored sets of laws and regulations govern banking, insurance, transportation, and utilities. States and local governments require business licenses and impose use restrictions on buildings and areas.

Complying with all the laws and regulations and coping with the red tape require expertise, time, and, of course, expense. A business found in noncompliance may incur fines or even the imprisonment of its management. The true story at the beginning of this chapter—entitled "I'm from the Government, and I'm Here to Help You"—is a ridiculous example of how bureaucracies can delay and sometimes prevent safe and sensible actions.

Socialism

Socialism advocates government ownership or control of the basic means of production, distribution, and exchange. Profit is not an aim.

In practice, so-called socialist governments have frequently performed in ways not consistent with the doctrine. One of the most startling examples of this is Singapore, which professes to be a socialist state but in reality is aggressively capitalistic.[3]

socialism
Public, collective ownership of the basic means of production and distribution, operating for use rather than profit

European Socialism

In Europe, socialist parties have been in power in several countries, including Great Britain, France, Spain, Greece, and Germany. In Britain, the Labour party—as the socialists there call their political party—in the past nationalized some basic industries, such as steel, shipbuilding, coal mining, and the railroads, but did not go much further in that direction. A vocal left wing of the Labour party advocates nationalizing all major British business, banks, and insurance companies.

Social Democrats is the name the Germans use for their socialist political party. During the several years that this party was in power before it lost to the Christian Democrats in 1982, it nationalized nothing and, in action and word, seemed more capitalist than socialist. By the time of the writing of the current edition of this book, the Social Democrats were back in power. In 1999, they took another page from the Christian Democratic book by passing into law a substantial tax decrease for German business. The socialist governments of France and Spain have embarked on programs to privatize government-owned businesses; such programs do not conform to pure socialist doctrine.

Socialism in Developing Countries

The developing countries often profess and practice some degree of socialism. The government typically owns and controls most of the factors of production. Shortages of capital, technology, and skilled management and labor are characteristic of developing countries, and developed countries (DCs) or international organizations often provide aid through a developing country's government. Also, many of the educated citizens of a developing country tend to be in or connected with the government. It follows that the government would own or control major factories and farms.

Unless the government of a developing country is communist, it will make occasional exceptions and permit capital investment. This happens when the developing country perceives advantages that would not be possible without the private capital, such as more jobs for its people, new technology, skilled managers or technicians, and export opportunities.

Conservative or Liberal

conservative
A person who wishes to minimize government activities and maximize private ownership and business

right wing
A more extreme conservative position

We should not leave the subject of ideology without mention of these words as they have come to be used in the middle and late 20th and now 21st centuries. Politically, in the United States, the word **conservative** connotes a person, group, or party that wishes to minimize government activity and maximize the activities of private businesses and individuals. *Conservative* is used to mean something similar to **right wing,** but in the United States and the United Kingdom, the latter term is more extreme. For instance, the Conservative party, one of the major political parties in the United Kingdom, is said to have a right-wing minority.

In the United States there is at least one exception to the generalization that conservatives wish to minimize government activities: the antiabortion movement calling for governmental control of abortion decisions. Although not all antiabortionists are conservative, the media present their position as such.

Also, connotations of *conservative* can differ depending on the application. For example, as the People's Republic of China and the countries of Eastern Europe and the former Soviet Union move from centrally planned economies to market economies and from dictatorships toward democracies, the people and groups trying to impede, stop, or reverse such movements are called *conservatives.* These people, typically members of communist (usually renamed) parties or the armed forces, long for "the good old days" when the governments owned and ran everything. That is precisely opposite to the wishes of conservatives in the United States and the United Kingdom, who want the least possible government involvement.

liberal
In the contemporary United States, a person who urges greater government involvement in most aspects of human activities

left wing
A more extreme liberal position

Politically, in the United States in the 20th century, the word **liberal** came to mean, and continues in the 21st century to mean, the opposite of what it meant in the 19th century. It now connotes a person, group, or party that urges greater government participation in the economy and regulation or ownership of business. Liberal and **left wing** are similar, but the latter generally indicates more extreme positions closer to socialism or communism.

Unique to the United States

This usage has not spread outside the United States.

> A conversation one of the authors had with an Italian lawyer at lunch in Rome turned to politics. The Italian identified himself as a liberal, and the author understood it in the American sense. As the conversation proceeded, the author learned that he had been wrong. The lawyer meant it in the Italian sense; he was a member of the Liberal party, a political party near the right end of the Italian political spectrum.

There are other Liberal parties in Europe that are not liberal in the American sense.

We do not want to overemphasize the importance of the labels *conservative, liberal, right wing,* and *left wing.* For one thing, individuals and organizations may change over time or may change as they perceive shifts in the moods of voters. Some feel that these labels are too simplistic or even naive and that reality is more complex. Nevertheless, we wanted to bring them to your attention because they are much used in discussions of international events and because different political forces flow from, for example, a right-wing government than from a left-wing one. Businesspeople must do their best to influence those political forces and then forecast and react to them.

Examples of "left" and "right" terminology in current international political reporting are widespread. Excerpts from one article include "the far right gains control of another town" and "the Socialist Party and the centre-right government had been shocked to the core by the election victories."[4] In another article it is said, "Europe wheels to the right"

Right and Left—What Do These Terms Mean?

After the French Revolution, an assembly was chosen, and it settled down to face the problems of reform. The radicals sat on the president's left, and the conservatives on his right. This disposition provided thereafter—in other countries as well as France—a useful addition to the terminology of politics.

A former member of the British Parliament made some interesting points on this subject. He found the Far Left similar to the Far Right. The terms "Right" and "Left" are losing their purchase. Under conventions established earlier in our century, people on the Far Right are seen as "Fascists" and people on the Far Left as "Communists," so that on the Left–Right axis, the two are supposed to be opposites, or at least at opposite extremes as far away from each other as it is possible to get. But a majority of observers seem to agree that the kinds of society they establish when they get into power have fundamental features of a striking nature in common—and are a good deal more like each other than either of them is like Liberal Democracy, which is supposed to separate them in the middle, halfway between them. ■

Source: *Forbes*, May 23, 1983, p. 20.

and "the mainstream parties of the left have realized."[5] One more article states that "the two traditional *frères ennemis* of the left have agreed to form a united front."[6]

Importance to Business of Left versus Right

Political advocacy organizations, both left and right, grow in size and power every year. In the United States alone, they have total annual revenues of some $5 billion, and they spend over $840 million a year on lobbying in Washington, DC, and the state capitals. They are equally influential and powerful in the corridors of power of the European Union and other countries.

Less well known but just as important, these organizations litigate precedent-setting lawsuits that affect judicial decisions for years to come. These court decisions, as well as the laws that result from their lobbying, powerfully affect business at every level.[7]

Government Ownership of Business

One might reasonably assume that government ownership of the factors of production is found only in communist or socialist countries, but that assumption is not correct. Large segments of business are owned by the governments of numerous countries that do not consider themselves either communist or socialist. From country to country, there are wide differences in the industries that are government-owned and in the extent of government ownership.

Why Firms Are Nationalized

There are a number of reasons, sometimes overlapping, why governments put their hands on firms. Some of them are (1) to extract more money from the firms—the government suspects that the firms are concealing profits; (2) an extension of the first reason—the government believes it could run the firms more efficiently and make more money; (3) ideological—when left-wing governments are elected, they sometimes nationalize industries, as has occurred in Britain, France, and Canada; (4) to catch votes as politicians save jobs by putting dying industries on life-support systems, which can be disconnected after the election; (5) because the government has pumped money into a firm or an industry, and control usually follows money; and (6) happenstance, as with the nationalization after World War II of German-owned firms in Europe. All governments are in business to some degree.

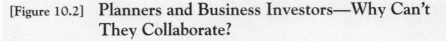

[Figure 10.2] **Planners and Business Investors—Why Can't They Collaborate?**

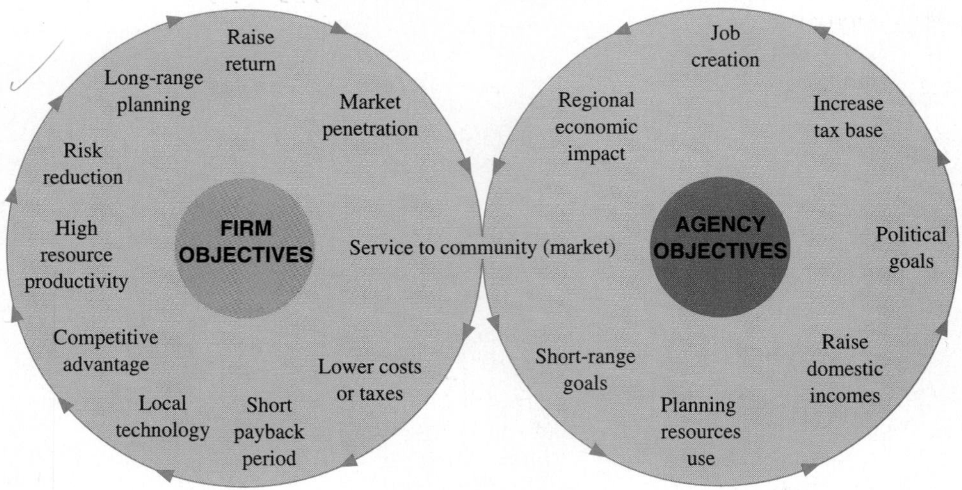

Source: Reprinted from *Long Range Planning,* Vol. 3, p. 83. Vichas et al., "Public Planners and Business Investors—Why Can't They Collaborate?" Copyright 1981 with permission of Elseviev Science.

Unfair Competition?

Where government-owned companies compete with privately owned companies, the private companies sometimes complain that the government companies have unfair advantages. Some of the complaints are that (1) government-owned companies can cut prices unfairly because they do not have to make profits, (2) they get cheaper financing, (3) they get government contracts, (4) they get export assistance, and (5) they can hold down wages with government assistance.

Another huge advantage state-owned companies have over privately owned business comes in the form of direct subsidies: payments by the government to those companies. The EU Commission is trying to discourage such subsidy payments. In 1991, it began requiring annual financial reports from state-controlled companies as part of a crackdown on the subsidies that can distort competition.[8]

Government–Private Collaboration Difficult

The objectives of private firms and those of government agencies and operations usually differ. Figure 10.2 illustrates some of the differences.

Privatization

Britain's former prime minister, Margaret Thatcher, was the acknowledged leader of the **privatization** movement. During her 11 years in office, Thatcher decreased state-owned companies from 10 percent of Britain's GNP to 3.9 percent. She sold over 30 companies, raising some $65 billion.[9] Thatcher pioneered in what has become a worldwide movement to privatize all sorts of government activities.

Airports, Garbage, Postal Services, and?

The American Lockheed Company, after quietly and profitably running Burbank Airport in California for decades, is expanding abroad. As owner or manager, Lockheed is operating or bidding to operate airports in Canada, Russia, Turkmenistan, Australia, Turkey, Hungary, Argentina, and Venezuela. Hughes Aircraft Company is in that business with Trinidad and Tobago and has completed studies for Ukraine on ways to upgrade that country's airports.[10]

The British airport operator BAA, which was privatized in 1987, manages terminals in numerous countries. It has run the Pittsburgh airport's retail facilities since 1992, increasing the average spending per passenger from $2.40 to more than $7.00. It is part of the management and/or ownership of similar facilities in Indianapolis; Melbourne, Australia; and Naples, Italy.

The management of Amsterdam's Schiphol airport has found that the management of foreign airports is an excellent export commodity. In partnership with the U.S. investment bank Lehman Brothers, Schiphol will build and operate a $1 billion terminal at New York's JFK airport. It is active also in Brisbane, Australia, and Vienna, Austria, and it and BAA are scouting the world for more business.[11]

One study found that it cost the New York Department of Sanitation $40, of which $32 was for labor, to deal with a ton of rubbish. It cost private collectors only $17 (of which $10 was for labor).[12]

Several countries are privatizing their postal services; the British are studying such a move, and the Germans are moving. In Germany, the three operating divisions of the Federal Bundespost—postal services, telecommunications, and the postal bank—are being converted into three public companies, the stock of which can be sold to nongovernment owners.[13]

In 1997, the government of Mozambique brought in the British company Crown Agents to run its customs service. Given the absurdly low levels of public-sector pay, it was scarcely surprising that bribery was endemic from top to bottom. Crown Agents set up antismuggling teams, and successes came quickly. They included cigarettes, alcohol, electrical goods, meat, condensed milk, and even yoghurt.[14]

Even the formerly rigid communist government of the People's Republic of China in Beijing has reached a consensus to allow state-run enterprises to diversify ownership. They don't call it privatization, but private and even foreign investors may acquire stakes.[15]

In the previously communist government–controlled economies of Central and Eastern Europe, the change to market economies is referred to as transition. The European Bank for Reconstruction and Development (EBRD) issued a Transition Report on privatization in those countries. Figure 10.3 shows the private sector's percent share of the gross domestic product (GDP) in 26 of them.[16]

The solvency and stability of the banking sector were found to be improved by the privatization of industrial and commercial companies. Privatized companies have improved their profitability more rapidly, which has led to notable improvements in the banks' loan portfolios.[17]

And the list of government-owned businesses and activities being sold to private owners or turned over to private companies to manage and operate goes on and on. The space available here is too limited to treat the subject thoroughly; instead, we refer you to the endnotes cited in this section and to articles on privatization that frequently appear in newspapers, periodicals, and Web sites.

privatization
The transfer of public-sector assets to the private sector, the transfer of management of state activities through contracts and leases, and the contracting out of activities previously conducted by the state

Private Buyers Do Well, but an American Needs a Passport

Privatization is the sizzling political trend all over the world—that is, everywhere except in the United States. From 1985 through 2000, $500 billion worth of public assets was privatized. Since 1980, the People's Republic of China has gone from nearly 80 percent to less than 50 percent state ownership. Chile has privatized 75 percent of its state-owned enterprises, and Mexico about 33 percent. Now France, Germany, Italy, and other European countries are selling.

In most cases, the buyers are profiting. According to the equity strategist Richard Davidson of the broker Morgan Stanley, their share index rose by 19.9 percent through March 1997, while the index of privatized companies was 4.3 percent higher at 24.2

[Figure 10.3] Transition Progress

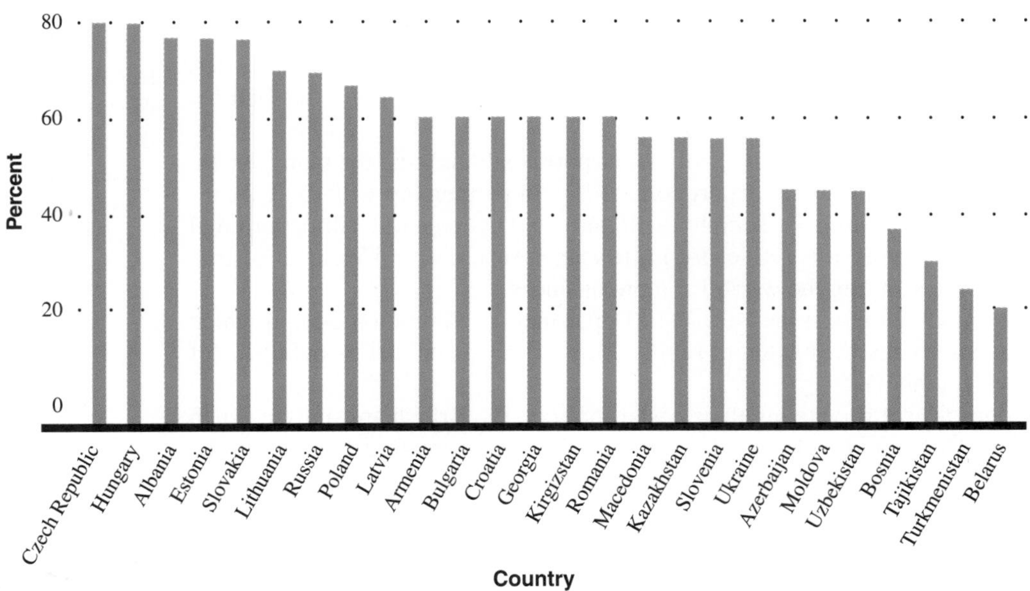

Source: From *The Economist,* December 23, 1999, p. 39. Copyright 1999 The Economist Newspaper Group, Inc. Reprinted with permission. Further reproduction prohibited. www.economist.com

percent. Davidson says that governments have become more attuned to investor needs, companies have begun to focus on shareholder value, and returns have improved.[18]

The BAA operation mentioned above has been a financial success. BAA's pretax profits have more than tripled since it was privatized, from £122 million to £418 in 1996.[19]

These are not isolated examples. A study by Alliance Capital discovered that over the past five years, stocks of privatized companies have climbed by 174 percent versus an 85 percent rise in the S&P 500. But the privatization trend has not begun in the United States by either the national or the state governments. Fortunately, American investors can partake in the trend by buying mutual funds that hold shares of the world's newly privatized companies.[20]

Privatization Anywhere and Any Way

It should be noted that privatization does not always involve ownership transfer from government to private entities. Activities previously conducted by the state may be contracted out, as Mozambique has contracted a British firm to run its customs administration, and Thailand has private companies operating some of the passenger trains of its state-owned railroad.

Governments may lease state-owned plants to private entities, as Togo has done. They may combine a joint venture with a management contract with a private group to run a previously government-operated business. Rwanda did this with its match factory.

Even unemployment services are being privatized. Australia is a leader in this field, and it has found church groups to be the most successful employment agency operators. Those groups have secured lucrative government contracts, and Tony Abbott, the employment services minister, says that community-based and charitable agencies have been about 25 percent better than the average in helping the long-term unemployed.[21]

Figure 10.4 shows privatization by geographic region. The percentages in the figure total 100 without reference to the United States; this illustrates the previously made point that neither the U.S. government nor the individual state governments are participating in the privatization trend.

[Figure 10.4] **Privatizations by Region**

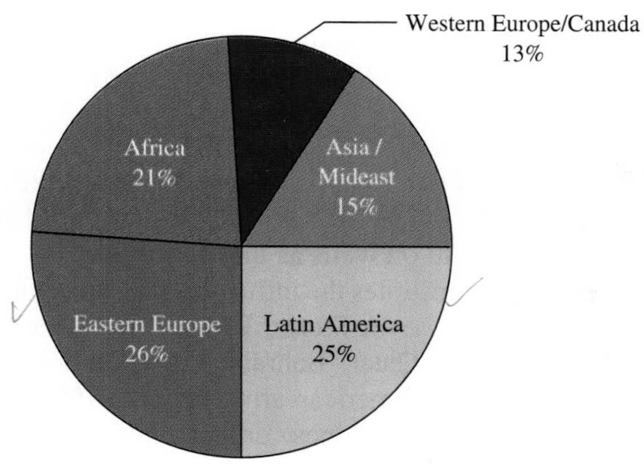

Source: "Privatization Worldwide Summary," prepared for the Transnational Corporations and Management Division of the United Nations. Used here by permission of the author, Michael S. Minor.

Nationalism

nationalism
A devotion to one's own nation, its political and economic interests or aspirations, and its social and cultural traditions

Nationalism has been called the "secular religion of our time." In most of the older countries, loyalty to one's country and pride in it were based on such shared common features as race, language, religion, and ideology. Many of the newer countries, notably in Africa, have accidental boundaries resulting from their colonial past, and within these countries, there are several tribes and languages. This has resulted in civil wars, as in Rwanda, Nigeria, and Angola, but it has not prevented these new countries from developing instant and fierce nationalism.

Nationalism is an emotion that can cloud or even prevent rational dealings with foreigners. For example, the chief of the joint staffs of the Peruvian military, when taking charge in Peru, blamed the ills of its society on foreign companies.

Some of the effects of nationalism on international companies are (1) requirements for minimum local ownership or local product assembly or manufacture, (2) reservation of certain industries for local companies, (3) preference of local suppliers for government contracts, (4) limitations on the number and types of foreign employees, (5) protectionism, using tariffs, quotas, or other devices, (6) seeking a "French solution"* instead of a foreign takeover of a local firm, and (7) in the most extreme cases, expropriation or confiscation.

Government Protection

A historical function of government, whatever its ideology, has been the protection of the economic activities—farming, mining, manufacturing, and so forth—within its geographic area of control. These activities must be protected from attacks and destruction or robbery by terrorists, bandits, revolutionaries, and foreign invaders. A war was required to free Kuwait and its oil wealth from Iraq.

Iraq Grabs for Economic-Political Power

In 1990, the Iraqi armed forces moved massively into Kuwait, quickly overwhelming the defenders of that much smaller country. Although Kuwait is small, it is oil-rich. If Iraq held Kuwait, the combined petroleum reserves of the two countries would make Iraq a major player in petroleum politics.

*The French solution is to make every effort to find a French company rather than a foreign one to take over the French firm.

An even greater prize was lying next door: Saudi Arabia, with the world's largest proved petroleum reserves. With armed forces no match for those of Iraq, Saudi Arabia might even have followed Iraqi orders without an invasion. That would have made Iraq the world's mightiest petroleum power and permitted it to influence strongly the policies and actions of Europe, Japan, North America, and most of the rest of the world.

Led by the United States and sanctioned by the United Nations (UN), an international coalition mobilized and transported armed forces to the Middle East. A short war, code-named Desert Storm, in early 1991 forced Iraqi forces out of Kuwait, although they set fire to hundreds of Kuwaiti oil wells as they retreated.

The aftermath of this war demonstrates the influence of politics on business. In gratitude for American leadership of Desert Storm, Kuwait and other Gulf Cooperation Council countries—Saudi Arabia, Qatar, Bahrain, the United Arab Emirates, and Oman—bought some $36 billion of American arms. But in a 1997 competition to sell Kuwait 72 self-propelled howitzers, a Chinese company beat out an American company's widely considered superior versions. In private conversations, Kuwaiti officials said their reasons for buying Chinese had nothing to do with range, price, or accuracy and everything to do with politics.

China suggested it would withhold its support at the United Nations for extending trade sanctions against Iraq unless Kuwait gave the estimated $300 million order to the Chinese company. "Sometimes you get to a state when you feel you're being blackmailed," a senior Kuwaiti official said. "We lean toward the U.S. equipment, but we have to find a way to please the Chinese and not upset them in the Security Council."[22]

Terrorism

terrorism
Unlawful acts of violence committed for a wide variety of reasons, including for ransom, to overthrow a government, to gain release of imprisoned colleagues, to exact revenge for real or imagined wrongs, and to punish nonbelievers of the terrorists' religion

Since the 1970s, the world has been plagued by **terrorism.** Various groups have hijacked airplanes, shot and kidnapped people, and bombed people and objects. A common denominator of these terrorist groups has been hatred of the social, economic, and political orders they find in the world.

During the 1970s and 1980s, Italy was particularly hard hit by terrorist violence directed against businesses and politicians. Between 1975 and 1982, terrorist groups almost shattered Italy's faith in its ability to govern itself without resorting to a communist or fascist police state. However, the democratic Italian government struck back successfully by creating a special 25,000-strong antiterrorist squad. Once caught, terrorists were tried, convicted, and sentenced to prison by the Italian courts.

Coinciding with those events, the attraction of terrorist groups lessened for educated, idealistic young Italians, the original source of the groups' recruits. And with their charisma fading, the groups had many penitents and defectors. As these young Italians became disenchanted, terrorist leaders turned to more conventional crime. They began cooperating with the Mafia, which is growing and becoming more feared by Italian authorities. The Bank of Italy has warned that the Mafia threatens to contaminate Italy's financial system.

Terrorism Worldwide

Italy is by no means alone as a victim of terrorism, which exists worldwide. A few of the better known gangs are the Irish Republican Army (IRA), the Hamas and other radical Islamic fundamentalist groups, the Basque separatist movement (ETA), the Japanese Red Army, and the German Red Army Faction.

All of them and others had sanctuaries in the former East Germany, other former Eastern European Soviet satellites, and the Soviet Union itself. The East German secret police, the Stasi, and the Soviet secret police, the KGB, provided financing, training, and protection to terrorist groups.

Government-Sponsored Terrorism: An Act of War

In addition to the Soviet Union and its European satellites, other countries financed, trained, and protected terrorists. They included Iran, Iraq, Libya, and Syria. In 1986, a

A woman cries on the grave of her son, a Bosnian defender who was killed in the war.
Reuters/Bettmann

British court convicted a Palestinian of trying to smuggle explosives (concealed in the baggage of his pregnant girlfriend) aboard an El Al Israel 747 aircraft. The flight from London to Tel Aviv would have been blown up over Austria. It was revealed at the trial that the material for the explosives had been brought into London in Syrian diplomatic pouches aboard the Syrian government airline; the Syrian ambassador had sanctioned or even directed the operation. In international law, government action to damage or kill in another country is an act of war.

In 2000, the U.S. State Department identified several countries that finance, sponsor, and train terrorists and/or provide sanctuaries for them. They are Afghanistan, Cuba, Iran, Iraq, Lebanon, Libya, North Korea, Sudan, and Syria.[23]

Kidnapping for Ransom

Kidnapping is another weapon used by terrorists. The victims are held for ransom, frequently very large amounts, which provides an important source of funds for the terrorists. Italian industry is not alone in being subjected to terrorism and kidnapping for ransom. For example, industry in Argentina has paid ransom of several hundred million dollars for the release of kidnapped business executives.

By 1986 Colombia and Peru had become the most dangerous places for American executives, and a long stay by a high-ranking American executive in either country is risky. Brief visits are usually fairly safe because kidnappings take a while to plan, and so top executives from the United States practice what is called commando management. They arrive in Bogota or Lima as secretly as possible, meet for a few days with local employees, and fly off before kidnappers learn of their presence.

Paying Ransom Becomes Counterproductive

The hostage business is booming. In 1999, the numbers of people taken captive increased by 6 percent over 1998, and it has gone like that for several years. Kidnapping for ransom is up by 70 percent over eight years. A remarkable deal concluded in the Philippines in 2000 explains why.

Libya's Colonel Muammar Qaddafi, trying to shake off that country's pariah status and ingratiate himself abroad, bought the release of several Western hostages held by a band of Islamist bandits in the Philippines. The price was about $1 million each. The kidnappers evidently have learned two lessons: holding a few hostages keeps the army away, and grabbing more keeps the money rolling in. Within weeks after receiving the ransom money, the Philippine kidnappers had bought new weapons and a new speedboat with which to capture more people to sell.[24]

A Successful Counterterrorist Operation

A terrorist organization not named above, the Tupac-Amaru Revolutionary Movement (MRTA), seized the residence of the Japanese ambassador to Peru in Lima. It was just before Christmas in 1996, and the ambassador was hosting a large party; 104 hostages were taken, including high-level business, church, diplomatic, and government officials.

The terrorists demanded the release of 400 MRTA members being held in Peruvian prisons, money, and safe passage out of Peru to Cuba. The Peruvian president refused their demands, and there was much argument about whether they should be more accommodating to the terrorists to secure the hostages' release without endangering lives or should use troops to storm the building. Those advocating the use of force pointed out that giving in to terrorists' demands encourages more terrorism, and not only in Peru; indeed, the Lima hostage story was being carried by the media worldwide. For example, part of the information presented in these paragraphs comes from an article in a Bangkok, Thailand, newspaper.

More evidence of the universal interest in the situation was provided by an offer by the Russian president, Boris Yeltsin, to send Russian antiterrorist troops to be part of an international force to rescue the hostages. The offer was made on Christmas day, 1996. There is no evidence one way or another whether it was intended as a Christmas gift.[25]

Regardless, Peru did not accept the Russian offer or other foreign offers. Instead, the Peruvians carried on with tough negotiations with the terrorists and tunneled under the residence, covering the digging sounds by bombarding it with loud music. The tunnel went under a ground-floor room where several of the terrorists played a game of indoor soccer each afternoon, and during a game one afternoon in April 1997, the government detonated a bomb. It caught 8 to 10 of the terrorists, and about half of them were killed.

The blast was the signal for assault troops to pour in from all sides. It was a short battle with remarkably few casualties. Although all the terrorists were killed, only two Peruvian troopers and one hostage died. Mr. Michael Radis, an expert on guerrilla groups at the Foreign Policy Research Institute in Philadelphia, says that "it will go down in the books among the great counterterrorist operations in history."[26]

Countermeasures by Industry

Insurance to cover ransom payments, antiterrorist schools, and companies to handle negotiations with kidnappers have come into being.

As kidnapping and extortion directed against businesses and governments have become common fund-raising and political techniques for terrorists, insurance against such acts has grown into a multimillion-dollar business. The world's largest kidnapping and extortion underwriting firm is located in London. The firm, Cassidy and Davis, underwriter for Lloyd's of London, says that it covers some 9,000 companies. Cassidy and Davis does not sit back and wait for claims to be filed. It runs antiterrorism training courses for executives, with subjects ranging from defensive driving techniques—escape tactics and battering through blockades—to crisis management. Country-by-country risk analyses are instantly available on international computer hookups.

Cassidy and Davis works closely with Control Risk, Ltd., a London-based security service company that advises firms and families in negotiations with kidnappers. Cassidy and Davis encourages its clients to use Control Risk services. The premiums for the insurance underwritten by Cassidy and Davis range from some $3,000 a year for $1.5 million of coverage in low-risk England to $60,000 a year for the same coverage in high-risk Peru.

Figures 10.5 and 10.6 are checklists for executives traveling to and in countries where they are at risk of being kidnapped. Figure 10.5 indicates what should be done before leaving the home country; Figure 10.6 discusses what to do once in the host country.

Inflation plunged to near zero, foreign development aid was restored, local investments started up, and an attack began on the big drug traffickers. In 1993, Gonzalo Sanchez de Lozada, the planning minister who masterminded Bolivia's anti-inflation program, was elected president. Bolivians are sensitive about privatization, particularly to foreigners, so the new government is achieving the desired results by a different route. First, the word *privatization* is not used; the program is called "Capitalization of Public Enterprises in Bolivia." Second, 50 percent equity in five previously state-owned monopolies, together with management control, was transferred to private-sector "strategic partners" that bought the equity in an international bidding process. Unlike other privatizations, the money paid for the equity went not into government coffers but into the company as fresh capital. Third, the other 50 percent was transferred to two private pension funds that will make annual pension payments called "Bonsols" to which all Bolivians are entitled.

In May 1997, thousands of elderly Bolivians flocked to collect their first Bonsols, which will be equivalent to about a third of annual per capita income. "That will make a tremendous difference, especially in the rural areas," said President Gonzalo Sanchez de Lozada.[32]

They May Thank Political Stability. Bolivia, once notorious for the frequency of its military coups, conducted in 1997 its fifth consecutive democratic general election since 1982. Over the four years leading up to 1997, far-reaching structural reforms were put in place peacefully despite strong political opposition.[33]

Traditional Hostilities

We need mention only a few of the **traditional hostilities** to illustrate their powerful impact on business and trade.

traditional hostilities
Long-standing enmities between tribes, races, religions, ideologies, or countries

Arab Countries–Israel

Israel is surrounded on three sides by Arab countries, but until the peace efforts initiated by the Egyptian Anwar Sadat, the Arab countries would not trade or have other peaceful dealings with it. Indeed, some Arab countries still boycott companies that trade with Israel, and because some of the Arab countries are extremely rich Organization of Petroleum Exporting Countries (OPEC) members, the boycott can be financially painful.*

Israel then made peace with its neighbor Jordan and made progress in negotiations with the Palestine Liberation Organization (PLO). However, those negotiations had not been successful as of the writing of the current edition of this book. Several issues remain, but the most difficult seems to be sovereignty over parts of Jerusalem.

Also endangering the negotiations is the support being given to Palestinian terrorists in Israel by the Palestinian government. Heavily armed terrorist camps operate in territory controlled by that government, and Palestinians rally frequently, calling for "death to Israel."

Hutus and Tutsis in Burundi and Rwanda

The majority Hutus and the Tutsis have been at each other's throats for many years. Burundi and Rwanda, where they constitute most of the population, were colonies of Belgium from the 19th century until after World War II. During that period, Hutu–Tutsi hostilities were kept at low levels, but they broke out in the 1990s, first in Burundi, where they were quelled, and then in 1993 and 1994 in Rwanda. The Hutus ran the government and army in Rwanda, and at least part of the army embarked on a campaign to exterminate the Tutsis. Some million people were massacred, and a Tutsi-led army coming in

*See Chapter 11 for a discussion of U.S. law dealing with this boycott.

U.S. Government Assistance to American Exporters

Small and Medium-Sized Enterprises

In 1999, the U.S. Commerce Department launched its Market Entry Program to prepare small and medium-sized firms to sell their products and services abroad by providing training, consulting, mentoring, and participation in trade missions. The Program recommends potential markets and finds buyers, distributors, agents, or partners in the market countries.

The Program will introduce firms to officials at the U.S. Export-Import Bank, which can help their customers obtain financing. At least one company set up its own business Web site by using the free Internet storefront builder at **http://www.freemerchant.com.** For more information, contact the Program at (213) 804-3966 or by E-mail at kristinhouston@mail-doc.gov. ■

Source: Annette Haddad and Scott Doggett, "Program Helps Firms Sell Abroad," *Los Angeles Times,* January 24, 2000, p. C2.

from Uganda retaliated. The Tutsi army defeated the Hutus, whose subsequent retreat led to the worst refugee situation in the world's history. Over a million Hutus swarmed and crammed into Zaire, as it was then called, where they were held in camps at the border. Cholera and dysentery took thousands of lives.

The Tutsis installed a new government in Rwanda and invited the Hutus to return. They did so slowly, but chances look slim for the cooperation between the Hutus and Tutsis that would be necessary to achieve conditions attractive to foreign investors.

Not surprisingly, this conflict spread, and in 1997 Tutsi soldiers provided the cutting edge of an army that toppled the longtime and extremely corrupt dictatorship of Mobutu Sese Seko in Zaire. The leader of that army, Laurent Kabila, proclaimed himself president and renamed the country the Democratic Republic of Congo.

Fighting among Hutus, Tutsis, and other tribal groups continued into 2001. At least some of the expense of the fighting, such as buying arms and ammunition, was met by mining and selling diamonds. Some of the part of Central Africa where the fighting is occurring is rich in diamond mines, and whichever tribe controls the mines takes out their riches.

This has led to efforts by the mining company De Beers and by several countries where diamonds are cut and prepared for market to refuse to buy "dirty diamonds" that are being used to finance the fighting. That is proving difficult to impossible because rough diamonds are nearly identical and could have come from any mine.

Tamils and Sinhalese in Sri Lanka

The Tamils form a substantial minority of the Sri Lankan population. An armed group calling itself the Tamil Tigers has been fighting a bloody series of battles with the Sri Lankan army and has committed terrorist murders and bombings of the Sinhalese population.

The Tamils want a separate state, and a large Tamil population in India has given them support. The late Indian president Rajiv Ghandi sent troops to Sri Lanka in an attempt to suppress the Tamil uprising. They failed, and the troops were withdrawn, but Ghandi gained Tamil hatred for his attempt. His murder—by a bomb hidden in a flower arrangement offered to him by a woman when he was campaigning for election in the Indian Tamil state in 1991—was blamed on the Tigers or their allies.

As with the traditional hostilities we mentioned above, the Sinhalese–Tamil battles continued into 2001. Also, as with the others, business is adversely affected; businesspeople are afraid to enter combat areas even to attempt short-term sales, and companies are even less apt to risk people on longer-term investment bases. These areas are thus deprived not only of qualified people but also of the capital and technology that would come with them.

Albanians, Bosnians, Croats, and Serbs in the Former Yugoslavia

This historical enmity was mentioned above, and they are killing each other despite UN efforts at peacemaking. There are ethnic and religious elements in these conflicts, and each group engaged in rape, torture, and murder as it overran another group. The horrible term *ethnic cleansing* has been heard often. Many of the Bosnians are Muslims as a result of Turkey's dominance in this area for several hundred years, and their conflicts with their Christian neighbors add bitterness to the situation. The Serbs are the best armed, having gotten most of the weapons of the former Yugoslav army.

NATO troops took over from ineffective UN forces, and Kosovo, a former Yugoslav province, is trying to break away and become independent. Albanians constitute the majority of the population in Kosovo, but the Serb minority controlled the province and was ethnically cleansing the Albanians until the UN and then NATO intervened. Hatred between these ethnic groups is intense, and the outcome is far from clear as Albanians seek revenge against Serbs.

South Africa

We should emphasize that the examples given above are, unfortunately, only a few of many racially based hostilities around the world. We presented another in the fifth edition of this book: the black–white strife of South African apartheid. Since that was written, South Africa has elected a new multirace government.

Most of the world imposed sanctions against investing in, lending to, or trading with South Africa as protests against apartheid. Now that it is ended, the sanctions are off, and South Africa, rich in natural resources, may again become a prosperous place for business.

International Organizations

As was discussed above, nationalism is a powerful political force that grew greatly during the middle and late 20th century and continues to grow in the 21st century. There are also international political forces with which business must contend. Here we shall cover briefly the political impact of some of the international organizations introduced in Chapter 4.

United Nations (UN)

The UN is highly politicized. The member-countries vote as blocs formed because of ideology or perceived similar objectives.

UN personnel advise member-countries on such matters as tax, monetary, and fiscal policies. The UN is active in the harmonization of laws affecting international trade. It had a hand in drafting an international commercial arbitration convention. It has drafted a code of conduct for multinational business. Any of the political ideologies we have discussed can be reflected in the content and spirit of tax, trade, and arbitration laws; conduct codes; and fiscal or monetary policies.

The Transnational Corporations Division of the UN has had a change of attitude resulting from a change in political orientation. During the early UN years, the division tended to be hostile to private international companies, saying they cheated and victimized developing countries that needed UN protection. The new, changed attitude is that developing countries should encourage investment by those companies to obtain such things as capital, technology, and management skills.

The United Nations Conference on Trade and Development (UNCTAD) is credited with having influenced the International Monetary Fund (IMF) to ease its restrictions on loans to developing countries. This is important to banks lending to and suppliers selling to developing countries.

Virtually all the specialized UN agencies are now actively advising developing countries about what to buy for their agriculture, industry, airlines, health programs, weather stations, and so forth. These are huge markets for business.

In Chapter 4, we spoke of the many peacemaking and peacekeeping operations of the UN around the world. Even if inadvertently, these military incursions have political results.

IMF, GATT/WTO, and OPEC

The IMF can have great influence on the fiscal and monetary policies of the nations that it assists, and as reported in Chapter 4, many believe its power is growing.

Although GATT (now WTO) has in general strived to lower barriers to trade, it has condoned their erection by developing countries in some cases. Import barriers are, of course, an important political force affecting multinational business operations.

The political power of OPEC was discussed in Chapter 4. We mention it here again to remind you that petroleum is now as much a political force as it is a commodity.

EU

Slowly, the member-nations of the European Union (EU) are surrendering parts of their sovereign powers to the Brussels headquarters. Mention of only a few areas will illustrate the extent of the EU's influence on business. Among other things, the EU is working to harmonize laws dealing with taxes, patents, labor conditions, competition, insurance, banking, and capital markets.

Harmonization of differing national laws is one matter, but the EU has now gone a step beyond that—to lawmaking. This is occurring in such fields as company law, antitrust, and consumer and environmental protection. Twelve of the EU member-countries have surrendered their monetary policymaking powers to the European Central Bank. The objective of some Europeans is to create a political, as well as an economic, power to rival America and Japan.

Organization for Economic Cooperation and Development (OECD)

This 29-member organization of industrialized countries has issued "Guidelines for Multinational Enterprises." Although it has been said that OECD guidelines merely create a voluntary set of principles upon which to build sound international relations, they can have a significant impact. For example, when Badger, Raytheon's subsidiary in Belgium, closed shop, it did not have enough money to meet its labor termination obligations under Belgian law. The Belgian government and labor unions used the pressure of the OECD "voluntary" guidelines to persuade Raytheon to pay Badger's obligations.

Labor

Workers and labor unions are the subject of Chapter 12, but we would be remiss if we did not mention them in connection with the political forces bearing on business. The European labor unions are ideologically oriented, usually toward the left. The American unions are said to be more pragmatic, but in practice they are extremely active politically. They supply large amounts of money and workers to support the political candidates they favor.

In Europe, the United States, and, increasingly, Japan, labor makes its political force felt not only at the polls but also in the legislatures. Unions lobby for or against laws as those laws are perceived to be for or against the interests of labor.

International Companies (ICs)

International business is not merely a passive victim of political forces. It can be a powerful force in the world political arena.

48 of World's 100 Biggest Economic Units Are Firms, Not Nations

International companies repeatedly make decisions about where to invest, where to conduct research and development, and where to manufacture products. The country or area in which an investment is made or a laboratory, research facility, or manufacturing plant is located can benefit as jobs are created, new or improved technology becomes available, or products are produced that can be exported or substituted for imports.

Of course the IC will seek the country and area where it can operate most beneficially and profitably. It will negotiate with the governments and national and local areas in which it is considering an investment or location in efforts to maximize benefits such as tax breaks, infrastructure improvements, and worker training programs.

An IC negotiating with a country may have annual sales larger than that country's GNP. You are referred to the section in Chapter 1 where annual sales of the largest companies are compared with nations' GNPs.

Large financial size carries power. However, an IC's power need not rest solely on size. It can come from the possession of scarce capital, technology, and management, plus the capability to deploy those resources around the world. An IC may have the processing, productive, distributive, and marketing abilities necessary for the successful exploitation of raw materials or for the manufacture, distribution, and marketing of certain products. Those abilities are frequently not available in developing countries. Recognition of the desirability of IC investments is growing.[34]

Country Risk Assessment (CRA)

It is arbitrary to place this subject in a chapter on political forces because **country risk assessment (CRA)** involves many risks other than political risks. It is probably important enough to warrant a separate chapter, but one of our objectives was to avoid an overlong book. We shall introduce our readers to CRA here; there is a growing literature about it, and those who are interested can find much material, to some of which we shall direct you in this section.

The political events of recent years have caused firms to concentrate much more on the CRA. Firms that had already done CRA updated and strengthened the function, and many other companies began to engage in the practice.

country risk assessment (CRA)
A bank or business having an asset in or payable from a foreign country, or considering a loan or an investment there, evaluates that country's economic situation and policies and its politics to determine how much risk exists of losing the asset or not being paid

Types of Country Risks

Country risks are increasingly political in nature. There are wars, revolutions, and coups. Less dramatic, but nevertheless important for businesses, are government changes by election of a socialist or nationalist government, which may be hostile to private business and particularly to foreign-owned business.

The risks may be economic or financial. There may be persistent balance-of-payments deficits or high inflation rates. Repayment of loans may be questionable.

Labor conditions may cause investors to pause. Labor productivity may be low, or labor unions may be militant.

Laws may be changed in regard to such subjects as taxes, currency convertibility, tariffs, quotas, and labor permits. The chances for a fair trial in local courts must be assessed.

Terrorism may be present. If it is, can the company protect its personnel and property?

Information Content for CRA

The types of information a firm will need to judge country risks vary according to the nature of its business and the length of time required for the investment, loan, or other involvement to yield a satisfactory return.

Nature of Business

Consider, for example, the needs of a hotel company compared with those of heavy-equipment manufacturers or manufacturers of personal hygiene products or mining companies. Banks have their own sets of problems and information needs. Sometimes there are variations between firms in the same industry or on a project-to-project basis. The nationality—home country—of the company may be a factor; does the host country bear a particular animus or friendly attitude toward the home country?

Length of Time Required

Export financing usually involves the shortest period of risk exposure. Typically, payments are made within 180 days—usually less—and exporters can get insurance or bank protection.

Bank loans can be short, medium, or long term. However, when the business includes host country assembly, mixing, manufacture, or extraction (oil or minerals), long-term commitments are necessary.

With long-term investment or loan commitments, there are inherent problems with risk analysis that cannot be resolved. Most such investment opportunities require 5, 10, or more years to pay off. But the utility of risk analyses of social, political, and economic factors decreases precipitously over longer time spans.

Who Does Country Risk Assessing?

General or specific analyses, macro or micro analyses, and political, social, and economic analyses have been conducted—perhaps under different names—for years. The Conference Board located bits and pieces of CRA being performed in various company departments—for example, the international division and public affairs, finance, legal, economics, planning, and product-producing departments. Sometimes the efforts were duplicative, and the people in one department were unaware that others in the company were similarly involved.

Efforts are now being made to concentrate CRA and to maximize its effectiveness for the company. These efforts include guidelines about the participation of top management.

Outside consulting and publishing firms are another source of country risk analysis. As CRA has mushroomed in perceived importance, a number of such firms have been formed or have expanded.

Some of the better-known outside consulting and publishing firms for CRA include

- Bank of America World Information Services.
- Business Environment Risk Intelligence (BERI) S.A.
- Control Risks Information Services.
- Economist Intelligence Unit (EIU).*
- Euromoney.
- Institutional Investor.
- Standard and Poor's Rating Group.
- Moody's Investor Services.[35]

In 1997, Deutsche Morgan Grenfell introduced its DB-WEB to illustrate credit risks in Eastern Europe. It identifies four risk areas in those emerging economies: fundamental, external, debt, and financial indicators.[36]

In June 1997, *The Wall Street Journal* published a section on which countries are safest to riskiest for investors. Countries were divided into five levels, from the safest in level 1 to the riskiest in level 5.[37]

*Figure 10.7 is an EIU advertisement of its *Risk Ratings Review* publication, and Figure 10.8 is a chart showing its country risk ratings for 2000.

[Figure 10.7] Assistance in Country Risk Assessment

WARNING: ONE OF THESE COUNTRIES COULD DAMAGE YOUR FINANCIAL HEALTH

You can now limit the risks to your business in 97 emerging and highly-indebted countries by subscribing to just one publication—the **Risk Ratings Review** from the Economist Intelligence Unit.

Every three months you receive ratings of the political, economic and financial risks for 97 emerging markets–providing early warnings of economies in trouble, and a spotlight on countries where conditions for trade, investment and lending are becoming more favourable.

The Risk Ratings Review–a one stop shop for reducing your risks around the world

The **Risk Ratings Review** offers you the highlights of the **Country Risk Service**, the Economist Intelligence Unit's international country credit rating service. It is an ideal introduction to the service and gives you access to all its ratings at a cost effective price.

Every three months the **Country Risk Service** publishes risk assessment reports for each of the 97 countries it covers. These project up to 180 economic and financial variables over a two year forecast horizon and include detailed ratings of political, economic and financial risk around the globe.

Identify deteriorating and improving economies–at a glance

The Risk Ratings Review summarises these findings, helping you to spot global trends and identify countries whose risk profile is changing. Each issue includes:

- **Comparative risk ratings tables**– listings of the current risk ratings scores produced by the Country Risk Service for all 97 countries;
- **Global and regional analysis**–what this quarter's rankings reveal about international and region-wide patterns of risk;
- **Up-to-date ratings focus**–an analytical summary of each country whose risk rating has changed in the previous quarter;
- **Watchlist**–early warnings of countries likely to deteriorate or improve over the next three-to-six months, and the factors that need to be monitored most carefully.

The **Risk Ratings Review**: the first place to turn for country-by-country assessments of financial solvency, political stability and economic health.

Monitor these risks for all 97 countries:

- Overall country risk
- Political risk
- Economic structure risk
- Economic policy risk
- Liquidity risk
- Currency risk
- Sovereign debt risk
- Banking risk

Countries covered in the Risk Ratings Review

Western Europe
Cyprus
Greece
Italy
Portugal
Spain
Turkey

Middle East & North Africa
Algeria
Bahrain
Egypt
Iran
Iraq
Israel
Jordan
Kuwait
Lebanon
Libya
Morocco
Oman
Qatar
Saudi Arabia
Sudan
Syria
Tunisia
UAE
Yemen

Asia
Australia
Bangladesh
China
Hong Kong
India
Indonesia
Malaysia
Myanmar
New Zealand
Pakistan
Papua New Guinea
Philippines
Singapore
South Korea
Sri Lanka
Taiwan
Thailand
Vietnam

Sub-Saharan Africa
Angola
Botswana
Cameroon
Côte d'Ivoire
Gabon
Ghana
Kenya
Malawi
Nigeria
Namibia
Senegal
South Africa
Tanzania
Zambia
Zimbabwe

Eastern Europe & the former Soviet Union
Azerbaijan
Baltic Republics: Estonia, Latvia, Lithuania
Bulgaria
Croatia
Czech Republic
Hungary
Kazakstan
Poland
Romania
Russia
Slovakia
Slovenia
Ukraine
Uzbekistan
Yugoslavia (Serbia-Montenegro),
Macedonia

Latin America & the Caribbean
Argentina
Bolivia
Brazil
Chile
Colombia
Costa Rica
Cuba
Dominican Republic
Ecuador
El Salvador
Guatemala
Honduras
Jamaica
Mexico
Nicaragua
Panama
Paraguay
Peru
Trinidad & Tobago
Uruguay
Venezuela

Keep alert to worldwide patterns of risk—subscribe to the Risk Ratings Review today

Order form

How to order your **Risk Ratings Review** subscriptions. Complete your personal details, choose your payment method and post to: The Economist Intelligence Unit, NA, Incorporated. The Economist Building, 111 West 57th Street, New York, NY 10019, USA. Alternatively, you can order by telephone on: (1.212) 554 0600, by fax on (1.212) 586 11813 or by E-mail: newyork@eiu.com

Personal details

Name (Mr/Mrs/Ms/Dr) ____________

Job title ____________

Company name ____________

Department ____________

Address ____________

____

City ____________ State ____________

Zip + 4 ____________ Country ____________

Please add zip+4 to ensure fastest possible delivery

Nature of business ____________

Tel ____________ Fax ____________

E-Mail ____________

	Quantity	Price	Sub-total
Risk Ratings Review		US $795*	
		Tax	
		Total	

Postage is included *Add applicable sales tax in Florida and Massachusetts. In Canada add 7% GST #R 132 494 238.

❒ Please send me details of the full **Country Risk Service.**

Payment details

❒ I enclose a check for US$ ________ payable to **The Economist Intelligence Unit, NA, Incorporated**

❒ Please charge US$________ to my ❒ Visa ❒ Mastercard ❒ Amex ❒ Diners Club

Account Number ____________

Signed ____________ Expiry date ____________

❒ Please proforma invoice me (Report will be sent on receipt of payment)

Billing address if different from above

____

____

❒ I do not wish to receive promotional material from other companies

E•I•U
The Economist Intelligence Unit

1ABLWA

Source: *The Economist,* December 6, 1997; p. 94. Reproduced by permission of the Economist Intelligence Unit Ltd.

[Figure 10.8] Country Risk

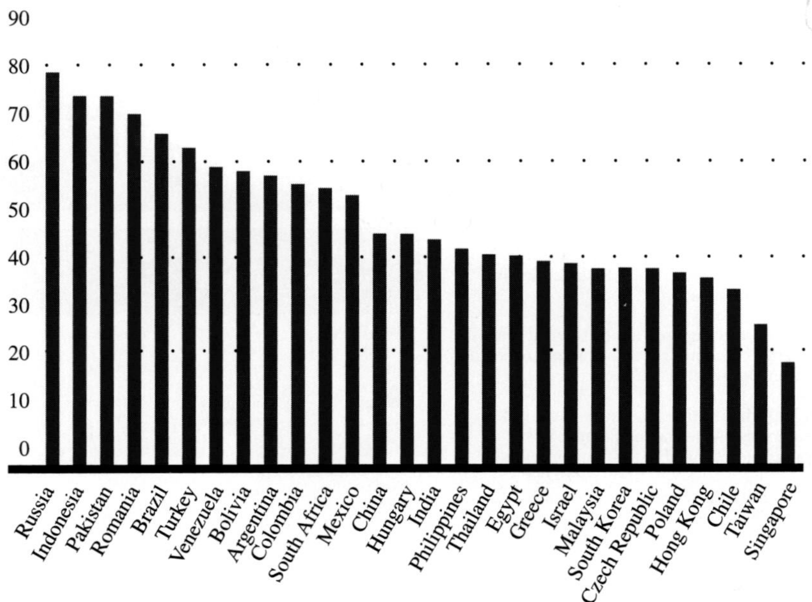

Risky economies The chart shows country-risk ratings for next year produced by the Economist Intelligence Unit, a sister company of *The Economist*. (Its new report covers a total of 93 countries.) A country's overall score takes account of 77 different indicators that reflect such factors as political stability, quality of governance, monetary and fiscal policy, regulatory policy, current-account balances, debt, financial structure and liquidity risk. Political risk has a weight of 22% in the overall score. The riskiest country in the chart is Russia, with a score of 78 out of a maximum of 100. Hot on its heels are Indonesia and Pakistan. At the other extreme, the EIU reckons that Singapore and Taiwan are the safest countries in which to invest, with scores of 16 and 24 respectively. Looking at regions as a whole, Asia, despite its recent crisis, remains the safest with an average risk rating of 48. The Middle East has an average risk score of 53, Latin America 54 and Eastern Europe 58. But Africa (60) gives the most sleepless nights. It includes two very risky countries not in the chart: Angola (93) and Nigeria (77).

Source: *The Economist,* November 13, 1999, p. 114. Copyright 1999, The Eonomist Newspaper Group, Inc. Reprinted with permission. Further reproduction prohibited. www.economist.com

Instead of or in addition to the outside consultants, a number of firms have buttressed their internal risk analysis staffs by hiring such experts as international business or political science professors or retired State Department, CIA, or military people.

Lessons of International Debt Crises

There are at least five lessons that CRA analysts should have learned. First, many developing countries are vulnerable to external shocks. One thing that has become apparent is the importance of a country's export and import structure in weathering an external economic shock. For example, the newly industrialized countries of Asia with their diversified export structures have been in a much better position to deal with the collapse of commodity prices and the erection of protectionist barriers than have been other countries with a comparable level of development but lopsided export structures (such as Indonesia and Mexico).

Second, the development of the debt crisis has shown clearly that the economic policies of debtor countries have a decisive impact on default risk. The countries that have become most deeply mired in the crisis are the ones that adopted expansionary fiscal and monetary policies. The results were inflation, current account deficits, loss of international competitiveness, and capital flight. Such has been the fate of the Philippines and the high-debt countries of Latin America.

By contrast, those countries that allowed the altered world market prices and demand conditions to take effect on their economies and adapted their economic policies to accommodate changed conditions have fared much better. Restrictive fiscal and monetary policies damped inflation, while occasional devaluations of their currencies kept trade balances under control. South Korea withstood the debt crisis through skillful economic policies.

Third, sustained economic growth is a major requirement for high-debt countries to service their debt and reduce its burden. Austerity alone cannot be a solution, economically, politically, or socially.

Fourth, the social and potential political costs of overindebtedness combined with austerity are proving high. Social and political tensions have risen sharply and threaten the survival of several democratically elected governments. That, in turn, greatly increases the danger of a debt moratorium.

The fifth lesson from debt crises for CRA analysts is the global ripple effect of seemingly independent risks or economic shocks. For example, the oil price collapse at the beginning of 1986 jacked up oil-exporting countries' default risk while lessening that risk for oil importers, thus affecting international interest and exchange rates and triggering a whole series of fiscal and monetary policy responses. The tequila effect was the phrase applied to the global ripples caused by the financial crises in the Mexican economy at the end of 1994 and into 1995.

The 1987 stock market crash caused worldwide economic reverberations. Other events that would have global effects if they were to occur include sustained changes in world interest rates, recession in major market countries, creation of debtor-country cartels, and the banking system's loss of confidence in an entire region.

[Summary]

Identify the ideological forces that affect business and understand the terminology used in discussing them.

We discussed capitalism, communism, socialism, conservative, liberal, right wing, and left wing.

Understand that although most governments own businesses, they are privatizing them in growing numbers.

Even governments that consider themselves capitalist and conservative own some businesses. But almost all governments—with the United States lagging behind—are privatizing and getting out of business.

Explain the changing sources and reasons for terrorism and the methods and growing power of terrorists.

The former Soviet Union and Eastern European satellite countries no longer finance, train, and shelter terrorists, but they have been replaced by countries such as Iran, Iraq, Libya, North Korea, and Syria. Radical Islamic fundamentalists represent a growing threat with their hatred of Christians, Jews, secularists, democrats, and the West generally. They are infuriated by the peace moves between Israel and its Arab neighbors. Nuclear terrorism is a new fear, as security has failed at nuclear sites in the former Soviet Union and enriched uranium is being stolen and smuggled around the world.

Explain steps that traveling international business executives should take to protect themselves from terrorists.

Before international business executives travel abroad and after they arrive in the host country, they should take steps to protect themselves from terrorists. See Figures 10.5 and 10.6.

Understand the importance to business of government stability and policy continuity.

Business can rarely thrive in a country with an unstable government or rapid, drastic policy changes. See the section about Bolivia.

Discuss the power sources of international organizations, labor unions, and international companies.

Large international businesses have political power, as do labor unions and international organizations such as the UN and the EU.

Understand country risk assessment by international business.

Country risk assessment is now considered a necessity by most international businesses before they commit people, money, or technology to a foreign country. CRA involves evaluating a country's economic situation and policies as well as its politics.

[Key Words]

communism (p. 348)
expropriation (p. 350)
confiscation (p. 350)
capitalism (p. 351)
socialism (p. 351)
conservative (p. 352)
right wing (p. 352)
liberal (p. 352)
left wing (p. 352)
privatization (p. 355)
nationalism (p. 357)
terrorism (p. 358)
stability (p. 363)
instability (p. 363)
traditional hostilities (p. 365)
country risk assessment (CRA) (p. 369)

[Questions]

1. a. What is ideology?
   b. Why is it important to international business?
2. a. What is the capitalist, free enterprise ideal?
   b. What is the actual situation in capitalist countries?
3. What impact can terrorism have on business?
4. Why does business fear sudden changes in government policies?
5. How can traditional hostilities affect business?
6. How can ICs use their strengths to influence government policies?
7. Is country risk assessment (CRA) an exact science? Explain.
8. a. In terms of exposure to political risk (for example, expropriation), which of the following businesses would you consider the most and least vulnerable? Explain.

   banks
   mines
   oil fields
   oil refineries
   heavy-equipment manufacturers
   hotels
   cosmetics manufacturers
   manufacturers of personal hygiene products
   automobile manufacturers

b. Are the most vulnerable businesses high-profile or low-profile? What are some ways to change the profile of a company in a foreign country?

9. Discuss the lessons CRA analysts should have learned from the world debt crises.

10. Islamic fundamentalism is a growing terrorist threat. Why?

[Internet Exercises]

Using the Internet

1. As was discussed in the text, political parties are often labeled with terms such as "right" or "left," "conservative" or "liberal," even though these terms change over time and have different meanings in different countries. It is important, however, to understand that, particularly outside the United States, countries have many different parties with many differing views. Using the Internet, find the major and minor political parties in a country of your choosing and answer the following questions:
   a. How many political parties exist?
   b. How many members of each political party are currently serving in the nation's parliament?
   c. What position has the political party taken on major issues?
2. The text discusses the importance of country risk assessments. Using the Internet, find:
   a. information on political, economic, and financial risk in countries; and
   b. corruption ranking of countries.

[Minicase 10.1]

Company Privatization

You are the chief executive officer of a company that the government has just denationalized by selling the company's stock to the company's employees. In the past, any major decision about company policy required approval by a government agency, which was time-consuming. Wages and salaries had been established by reference to civil service "equivalents," and incentive payments were unheard of. Maintenance of the plant and equipment was lax, breakdowns were frequent and expensive, and utility expenses were high.

You want the newly privatized company to be a success. Suggest some programs that you would institute to improve its chances of success.

[Chapter] 11

Legal Forces

"[N]ew areas have been opened up to international law, whilst new players have entered the arena . . . The diversification of the areas governed by international law has rendered that law more complex and more diverse. Thus human rights, environmental law, economic law, the law of the sea or space law are sometimes regarded today as specialized branches of international law."

—Judge Gilbert Guillaume, President of the International Court of Justice, addressing the General Assembly of the United Nations, October 27, 2000

Concept Previews

After reading this chapter, you should be able to:

- **appreciate** the complexity of the legal forces that confront international business
- **understand** that many taxes have purposes other than to raise revenue
- **discuss** enforcement of antitrust laws
- **appreciate** the risk of product liability legal actions, which can result in imprisonment for employees or fines for them and the company
- **recognize** the importance of being aware of peculiarities of local foreign law
- **understand** contract devices and institutions that assist in interpreting or enforcing international contracts
- **anticipate** the need and methods to protect your intellectual property
- **recognize** how industrial espionage affects international business

Courtesy of International Court

When a Local Issue Can Have International Ramifications

The world has become increasingly interrelated, and the law reflects this trend. What may appear to be a local issue may take on national and often worldwide importance. In June 1996, the Commonwealth of Massachusetts decided to take a position against what many in Massachusetts believed to be a repressive regime in Myanmar (formerly Burma). The Massachusetts legislature passed an act barring Massachusetts state entities from buying goods or services from businesses doing business with Myanmar. This included business entities having operations or franchises in Myanmar or providing any goods or services to the government of that country. Massachusetts exempted business entities providing medical supplies or international telecommunication goods or services, or reporting the news. Three months after Massachusetts passed that law, the U.S. Congress passed the Foreign Operations, Export Financing, and Related Programs Appropriations Act, which banned aid to the Myanmar government with the exception of funds for certain forms of humanitarian assistance, funds used to fight drugs, and funds used to promote human rights and democracy. Congress also directed the U.S. president to develop a strategy to bring democracy to Myanmar and improve human rights practices there. The president was further empowered to waive any sanction if it was determined that the application of that sanction would be contrary to U.S. national security interests.

The National Foreign Trade Council brought suit in the federal court in Massachusetts against Massachusetts state officials, seeking to prevent them from administering the state law. The federal district court agreed with the National Foreign Trade Council and blocked enforcement of the Massachusetts law. This decision was upheld by the federal court of appeals. The matter finally reached the U.S. Supreme Court, which agreed that enforcement of the Massachusetts law should be prevented. The Supreme Court found that the Massachusetts law was unconstitutional and noted that Congress had intended to give the president flexibility and effective authority over economic sanctions against Myanmar. The Supreme Court held that it was "simply implausible" that Congress would have gone to such lengths if it had intended to permit state statutes to "blunt the consequences of discretionary Presidential action." On the basis of the Constitution's Supremacy Clause, the Supreme Court found that the Massachusetts law conflicted with federal law and struck down the Massachusetts law. Under the Constitution, the president and Congress have the power to set foreign policy. State laws that violate those constitutional mandates will be struck down. ■

Source: U.S. Supreme Court, *Crosby v. National Foreign Trade Council,* No. 99-474, 530 U.S. 363 (2000).

Anyone studying the legal forces affecting international business soon realizes that the immensity and variety of those forces complicate the task tremendously. International business is affected by laws too numerous to count enacted by governments at all levels on virtually every subject.

Nevertheless, this text, which is an introduction to international business, would be incomplete without some discussion of the many legal forces that affect international business. We will first examine several national legal forces and then discuss some international legal forces.

An area of great concern to businesses that operate internationally is the stability of a host government and its legal system. When a business enters a country, the business needs to know whether the country's host government will be able to protect the foreign business with an adequate legal system. The legal system must be able to enforce contracts and protect basic rights of employees working for the business. In examining international legal forces, one must keep in mind that a stable government and an adequate court system are necessary to ensure a welcome environment for foreign businesses.

Although many U.S. laws affect the activities of international firms, there has not been a successful effort to coordinate them. Some are at cross-purposes, and some diminish the ability of U.S. businesses to compete with foreign companies. We will close this chapter with a brief examination of some of these laws and regulations.

We will now proceed to deal with specific legal forces. Some of them, such as taxation, concern every business and businessperson, whereas others, such as antitrust, involve fewer firms.

Some Specific National Legal Forces

Taxation

Purposes

The primary purpose of certain taxes is not necessarily to raise revenue for the government, which may surprise those who have not studied taxation. Some of the many **nonrevenue tax purposes** are to redistribute income, to discourage consumption of such products as alcohol and tobacco, to encourage consumption of domestic rather than imported goods, to discourage investment abroad, to achieve equality of the tax amounts paid by taxpayers earning comparable amounts, and to grant reciprocity to resident foreigners under a tax treaty.

nonrevenue tax purposes
Include redistributing income, discouraging consumption of products such as tobacco and alcohol, and encouraging purchase of domestic rather than imported products.

Even this short list of purposes suggests the economic and political pressures influencing government officials responsible for tax legislation and collection. Powerful groups in every country push for tax policies that favor their interests. These groups and interests differ from country to country and frequently conflict; this accounts in part for the complexity of the tax practices that affect multinationals.

National Differences of Approach

Among the many nations of the world, there are numerous differences in tax systems.

Tax Levels. For one thing, tax levels range from relatively high in some Western European countries to zero in tax havens. (A tax haven is a country in which income of defined types incurs no tax liability.) Some countries have capital gains taxes,* and some do not. Those that have them tax capital gains at different levels. Incidentally, the United States levies one of the highest long-term capital gains taxes, with some countries having no capital gains tax.

In the United States, the capital gains tax is controversial. Many argue that the tax rate should remain high because any reduction would reward the rich, the group having the most assets that have increased in price. Others argue that the capital gains tax locks in money that would be better invested elsewhere to create jobs and increase productivity. Some maintain that the United States should levy no capital gains tax,[1] following the example of several other countries.

Tax Types. There are different types of taxes. We have just introduced one: the capital gains tax. Although the United States levies a relatively high capital gains tax, it relies for most of its revenue on the income tax. As indicated by the name, this tax is levied on the income of individuals and businesses. Income taxes are common in industrialized countries. Figure 11.1 on the next page shows the tax rates on wage income in the member-countries of the Organization for Economic Cooperation and Development (OECD). Among the OECD members, the United States has a fairly low income tax rate. A generality, subject to exceptions, is that the higher the income, the higher the income tax. In the 1970s and 1980s, much discontent developed among Americans over the impact of the income tax and other taxes. Possibly as a result, there has been growing support for a value-added tax (VAT) in the U.S. Congress and Treasury.

Many suggest that the United States use a VAT similar to the VATs in effect in all European Union countries, where they are main sources of revenue. A simplified example of how a VAT works on a loaf of bread can be seen in Table 11.1 on page 381. We will assume a VAT of 10 percent. The wheat farmer sells to the miller for 30 cents the part of the wheat that eventually becomes the loaf. So far, the farmer has added 30 cents of value by planting, growing, and harvesting the wheat. The farmer sets aside 3 cents (10 percent of 30 cents) to pay the VAT. The miller makes loaves of bread out of the wheat and sells them to the wholesaler for 50 cents each. Thus, the miller has added 20 cents of value (50 cents − 30 cents) and must pay a VAT of 2 cents (10 percent of 20 cents). The wholesaler now advertises and distributes the loaves, selling them to

*A capital gain is realized when an asset is sold for an amount greater than its cost.

[Figure 11.1] Highest Tax Rates on Wage Incomes

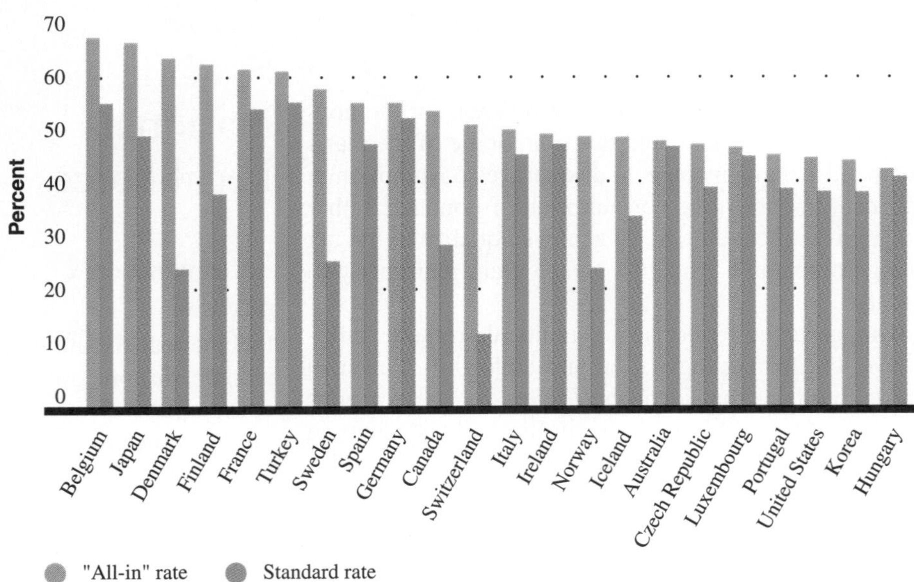

In OECD countries there is often quite a difference between the highest "all-in" rate of taxes on wage income and the highest standard rate of personal income tax imposed by central government. In Denmark the standard rate is over 20% whereas the "all-in" rate is over 60%. The standard rate in the United States is much higher than in Denmark, but the 'all-in' rate is much lower, at about 46%.

"All-in" rates include all "taxes" imposed on wage income which are above the standard rate, such as social security contributions and local taxes.

Source: From OECD, *OECD in Figures,* 1999, p. 86. Reprinted with permission of OECD Washington.

retailers for 70 cents. The wholesaler has added 20 cents of value and owes 2 cents of VAT. Finally, the retailer adds 40 cents through its display, advertising, and sales efforts and owes 4 cents of VAT. The loaf of bread is sold for $1.10 retail and has borne a cumulative VAT of 11 cents, 10 percent of $1.10.

The VAT has proponents and opponents. In general, their arguments are as follows: The proponents say the VAT is relatively simple and can be raised or lowered easily to collect the amount of income desired by the government. The opponents argue that it is a consumption-type tax that bears most heavily on the poor.

In addition, some U.S. VAT proponents argue that the present situation, in which the major European countries rely heavily on the value-added tax, is unfair to the United States because of World Trade Organization (WTO)* regulations. WTO permits a rebate of VAT when a product is exported from a country but does not permit a rebate of income taxes. The rebates enable exporting countries to offer lower-priced, more competitive goods. VAT proponents want the United States to inaugurate the VAT and lower income taxes to take advantage of those WTO rules.

Another form of tax on international companies (ICs) that has been controversial for several decades is the unitary tax imposed by several U.S. states. Most states have since repealed these tax laws under threats of retaliation by foreign governments. International tax treaties are almost universally built on the "arm's length" or "water's edge" principle: taxable profits for a subsidiary in a country will be assessed as though it were conducting its business independently. The unitary tax system, by contrast, calculates the worldwide income of the IC and then assesses the tax due in proportion to the percentage of the group's property, payroll, and sales in the state.

California was the last state to move away from the unitary principle. The 1986 and 1988 changes in California's tax laws did not eliminate the unitary approach but instead now permit ICs to choose either a water's edge or a unitary system. A company's circumstances, for instance, the sources or types of income involved, would determine which would be more advantageous.[2]

Complexity of Tax Laws and Regulations. From country to country, the complexity of tax systems differs. Many consider that of the United States to be the most complex.

*See Chapter 4 for a discussion of the World Trade Organization.

Table 11.1 Value-Added Tax on a Loaf of Bread

Stage of Production	Selling Price	Value Added	VAT at 10 Percent	Cumulative VAT
Farmer	30¢	30¢	3¢	3¢
Miller	50¢	20¢	2¢	5¢
Wholesaler	70¢	20¢	2¢	7¢
Retailer	$1.10	40¢	4¢	11¢

The Internal Revenue Code (IRC) can be found in the United States Code and includes thousands of pages. Many provisions of the IRC refer to other provisions of the IRC, making interpretation difficult. In addition, Congress frequently changes provisions of the IRC. Congress typically debates major tax legislation in every session. Once Congress approves provisions of the IRC, it leaves it up to the U.S. Department of Treasury to issue regulations to implement IRC provisions. The Department of Treasury has large numbers of staff members working to write these regulations. As with the IRC, the regulations issued by the Department of the Treasury run thousands of pages. In addition to the IRC and the regulations, there are numerous court decisions interpreting the tax laws. U.S. income tax laws are very complicated but are extremely important to anyone in business.

Who Obeys the Law? Compliance with tax laws and their enforcement vary widely. Some countries, such as Germany and the United States, are strict. Others, such as Italy and Spain, are relatively lax. The Italian practice allows a taxpayer to declare a very low taxable income to which the government counters with a very high amount. They then negotiate a compromise figure.[3] It has been said that completely honest people would go broke if they complied fully with the law. In addition to corporate income tax, businesses in Italy may find themselves paying a Chamber of Commerce tax, a license tax, a trade association tax, a stamp tax, the local tax, a rental-agreement tax, a tax for registering with the office that collects the VAT, a tax for health inspection, a tax for the accounting books, a tax for the welfare system, a tax for water, and even a tax for an awning outside. By one estimate, there are 300 separate taxes businesses are expected to pay.[4]

Other Differences. There are many other differences, too numerous to list here, but a few are tax incentives to invest in certain areas, exemptions, costs, depreciation allowances, **foreign tax credits,** timing, and double corporate taxation (taxation of the profits of a corporation and then of dividends paid to its stockholders). U.S. tax laws give U.S. taxpayers relief from possible double taxation by more than one jurisdiction. For example, if a U.S. taxpayer were living and working in Sweden, that taxpayer would be subject to tax laws both of the United States and of Sweden. Without some form of tax relief, that taxpayer could end up paying more than 100 percent of her or his income in taxes. This tax relief comes in the form of foreign tax credits and provisions of various tax treaties. U.S. tax laws allows U.S. taxpayers to take a credit against their U.S. taxes for taxes paid to another country. This is especially important because U.S. citizens and U.S. permanent residents (green card holders) are taxed on their worldwide income regardless of the source of the income and regardless of the residence of the taxpayer.

foreign tax credits
U.S. taxpayers who reside and pay income taxes in another country can credit those taxes against U.S. income tax

tax treaties
Treaties between countries that bind the governments to share information about taxpayers and cooperate in tax law enforcement; tax treaties are often called tax conventions

Tax Treaties or Conventions

Because of the innumerable differences between nations' tax practices, many of them have signed **tax treaties** or tax conventions with each other. Typically, tax treaties

[Figure 11.2] U.S. Network of Tax Treaties

The United States Has Tax Treaties with the Following Countries		
Australia	India	Pakistan
Austria	Indonesia	Philippines
Barbados	Ireland	Poland
Belgium	Israel	Portugal
Canada	Italy	Romania
China, People's Republic of [1]	Jamaica	Russia
Commonwealth of Independent States[2]	Japan	Slovak Republic
Cyprus	Kazakstan	South Africa
Czech Republic	Korea, Republic of	Spain
Denmark	Latvia	Sweden
Egypt	Lithuania	Switzerland
Estonia	Luxembourg	Thailand
Finland	Mexico	Trinidad and Tobago
France	Morocco	Tunisia
Germany	Netherlands	Turkey
Greece	New Zealand	United Kingdom
Hungary	Norway	Venezuela
Iceland		

[1]Does not include Hong Kong.
[2]The U.S.—U.S.S.R. income tax treaty applies to the countries of Armenia, Azerbaijan, Belarus, Georgia, Kyrgyzstan, Moldova, Tajikistan, Turkmenist Ukraine, and Uzbekistan.

define such things as income, source, residency, and what constitutes taxable activities in each country. They address how much each country can tax the income earned by a national of one country living or working in the other. All these treaties contain provisions for the exchange of information between the tax authorities of the two countries. The United States has tax treaties with over 50 countries. Figure 11.2 lists the countries with which the United States currently has tax treaties.

The presence or absence of a tax treaty is often a factor in international business and investment location decisions. It is now fully accepted that treaties facilitate international flows of goods, capital, services, and technology.

However, countries sign treaties for different motives. Most OECD countries regard treaties as providing a standard framework for all countries in allocating taxing jurisdiction. Tax treaties often determine which country will tax which income. Among emerging-market countries, treaties are viewed as a key tool in giving foreign investors confidence in their stability.[5]

The Disappearing Taxpayer

In the coming decades, electronic commerce—combined with the growing ease with which firms and people can shift their operations and residences from one country to another—will make it easier for people to leave countries where taxes are high or avoid taxes altogether by doing their business in cyberspace. Figure 11.3 shows you the divergence of corporate income tax rates in the world's major developed countries; bear in mind that none of them is a tax haven where taxes, corporate and individual, can be as low as zero.

Not all firms, workers, and products are equally mobile. Entrepreneurs, scientists, tennis players, and film stars may be able to uproot themselves in search of lower taxes, but the average worker is still unlikely to become a tax refugee. Thus, governments may have to cut taxes on the most mobile factors of production, notably skilled work-

[Figure 11.3] Will They Converge?

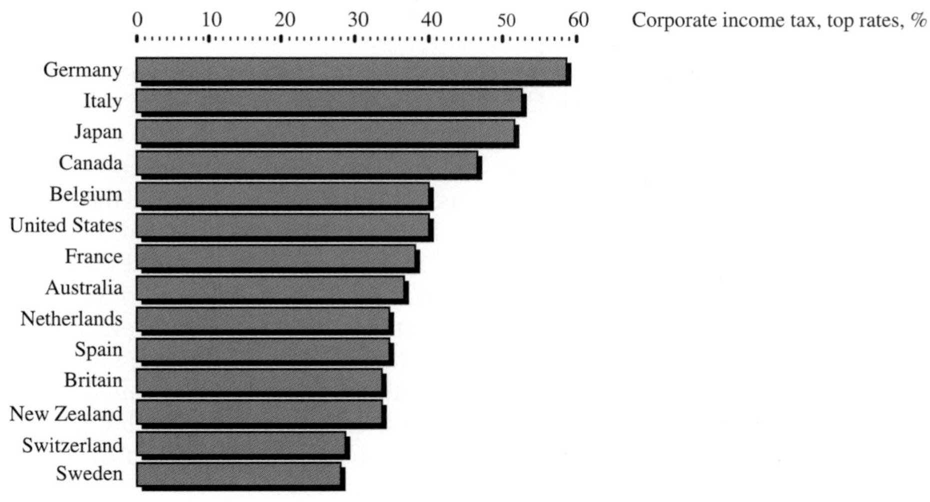

Source: *The Economist,* May 31, 1997, p. 21. © 1997 The Economist Newspaper Group, Inc. Reprinted with permission. Further reproduction is prohibited. www.economist.com

ers, while taxes on less mobile unskilled workers will have to rise. Other tax law changes being considered are to shift the tax base from income toward consumption and property.[6]

Antitrust Laws

In the tax area, it is taxpayers (here, international business) against tax collectors (governments). Antitrust actions also involve business versus government and occasionally government versus government.

U.S. Laws and Attitudes Are Different

The U.S. **antitrust laws** are stricter and more vigorously enforced than those of any other country. The U.S. Department of Justice, headed by the attorney general, is charged with the responsibility of enforcing U.S. antitrust laws. However, other countries, as well as the European Union (EU), are becoming more active in the antitrust field. In the EU, these laws sometimes are referred to as **competition policy.**

antitrust laws
Laws to prevent price-fixing, market sharing, and business monopolies

competition policy
The European Union phrase for antitrust laws

The German antitrust laws are the toughest after those of the United States, and during 1986 the German Federal Cartel Office tightened its grip—literally, in some cases. Wolfgang Kartte, president of the Cartel Office, tells the story of a raid his investigators made on the office of a heating equipment supplier. One of the supplier's managers stuffed a memo in his mouth and tried to swallow it, but a quick-thinking investigator grabbed the man by the throat and forced him to spit out the memo. Half chewed but still legible, it provided valuable evidence of illegal price-fixing.

In 1991, the European Court of Justice gave a major boost to EU efforts to inject competition into economic sectors still largely dominated by powerful state monopolies. The Court confirmed that the EU Commission can force EU member-governments to dismantle state monopolies that block progress toward an open, community-wide market.[7]

Article 81 of the Treaty of Rome outlaws any agreement or action to fix markets or distort competition. Under the authority of that article, the Commission fined the

Dutch chemicals group Akzo ECU* 7.5 million in 1991.[8] Later in 1991, empowered by Article 82, which bans abuse of dominant positions, the Commission imposed a record ECU 75 million fine on Tetra Pak, a Swiss-based liquid packaging group, for eliminating competitors in the European market.[9] That record was broken in 1994 as the EU Commission levied fines totaling $158.58 million on 19 carton-board producers. They had formed what the Commission described as Europe's "most pernicious" price-fixing cartel.[10]

Also in 1991, the Commission for the first time used its authority under a 1990 law to veto a major business transaction. Using its expanded power, it blocked the acquisition of Boeing's de Haviland subsidiary by a French-Italian consortium, Avions de Transport Regional (ATR). The Commission said the acquisition would have given ATR an unfair advantage that would have allowed it to crowd out competition.

A number of important differences in antitrust laws, regulations, and practices exist between the United States, other nations, and the EU. One difference is the effort of the United States to apply its laws extraterritorially (outside the United States). Another difference is the per se concept of the U.S. law. Under the U.S. laws, certain activities, such as price-fixing, are said to be illegal per se. This means that they are illegal even though no injury or damage results from them.

The Treaty of Rome articles dealing with restrictive trade practices do not contain the per se illegality concept of U.S. antitrust law. For example, a cartel that allows consumers a fair share of the benefits is legally acceptable in the EU. Also, the treaty is not violated by market dominance—only by misuse of that dominance to damage competitors or consumers.

Worldwide Application of U.S. Antitrust Laws

extraterritorial application of laws
When a country attempts to apply its laws to foreigners or nonresidents and to acts and activities that took place outside its borders

The U.S. government often attempts to enforce its antitrust laws outside the U.S. borders. This is referred to as **extraterritorial application of laws.** For example, in 1979, a grand jury in Washington, DC, indicted three foreign-owned ocean-shipping groups on charges of fixing prices without getting approval from the U.S. Federal Maritime Commission. The other governments, European and Japanese, protested bitterly, arguing (1) that shipping is international by definition so that the United States has no right to act unilaterally and (2) that the alleged offenses were both legal and ethical practices outside the United States.[11]

The U.S. Supreme Court on several occasions has permitted overseas application of U.S. antitrust laws.[12] Extraterritorial application has been extended in a variety of other areas, including taxation and environmental law.

EU Extraterritorial Application of Its Competition Policy

The EU Commission is charged with enforcement of EU competition policy. Like the U.S. Department of Justice, the EU Commission has increasingly sought enforcement of its competition policy abroad when there is an effect on commerce within the EU. In 1997, the U.S. Boeing Co. planned a $14 billion takeover of the U.S. McDonnell Douglas Corp. The EU Commission took the position that it had the right to approve or disapprove of the merger even though both companies were based in the United States and had no operations in Europe. People in the United States pointed out that the Europeans were applying their law extraterritorially, which was the behavior they complained about when the United States did it. The EU maintained that its authority to review the combination was based on the extensive sales both Boeing and McDonnell Douglas made in Europe.

In the end the EU approved the merger, but it exacted a price. Boeing was forced to cancel the exclusive supplier agreements it had made with American, Continental, and Delta airlines, thus, at least in theory, giving the European competitor, Airbus Industries, a chance to sell them planes.[13] Likewise, the EU Commission had to give

*The ECU (European Currency Unit) is no longer in use, having been replaced by the euro.

its approval before merger talks between America Online and Time Warner could proceed. Before its approval was given to the merger, AOL–Time Warner had to agree to sever all ties with the German media group Bertelsmann.[14]

Criminal Cases

U.S. antitrust laws contain both civil and criminal penalties.* In 1997, a decision by a U.S. federal appeals court held that *criminal* antitrust laws apply to foreign companies even if the conspiracy took place abroad. While earlier decisions had permitted U.S. antitrust laws to be used against foreign companies in *civil* cases, this decision against Nippon Paper Industries set the precedent that they could be used also to get criminal convictions.[15]

Japan's "Toothless Tiger"

Japan's Fair Trade Commission (FTC), which is supposed to enforce antitrust laws, has been nicknamed the toothless tiger. It is viewed as one of the weakest bodies in government, easily bullied by the powerful ministries of finance and international trade and industry, both of which have vested interests in ensuring that Japan's cozy ways of doing business prevail. Most of FTC's victims are small and weak; when it has investigated powerful industries such as cars, car parts, construction, glass, and paper, it has punished them at worst with raps on the knuckles and "recommendations." They are all businesses from which foreigners complain they are excluded.

A major difference between American and Japanese trust-busting is that around 90 percent of U.S. complaints are initiated by private parties, while in Japan a private antitrust action can be brought only if the FTC has investigated the case first. Because of Japan's arcane discovery laws, the only way the FTC can obtain information on a firm is to raid it. As a result, the FTC won't make a move unless it is sure the laws are being broken. Of course, it is almost impossible to be sure of that without information. Given all this, it is easy to understand why the FTC is considered to be a toothless tiger.[16]

Proposal for Global Antitrust Approval

In light of the numerous countries that impose antitrust rules worldwide, the U.S. government has proposed a world organization for clearance of antitrust issues. If approved, the organization would probably take the form of a clearinghouse for merger filings. Calls for such an entity are increasing because of the multinational nature of most large mergers.[17] In a similar vein, the World Bank has also called for a global bankruptcy agreement in light of the large number of multinational companies that have problems with creditors worldwide. It is thought that a worldwide bankruptcy agreement would make it easier for creditors and others involved in bankruptcy proceedings. Now creditors must comply with rules in various countries before receiving relief from companies in bankruptcy.[18]

Tariffs, Quotas, and Other Trade Obstacles

Although we introduced these subjects in Chapter 3, they are legal forces. For that reason, we mention them again here.

Every country has laws on one or more of these subjects. The purposes of tariffs are to raise revenue for the government and to protect domestic producers. Quotas, which limit the number or amount of imports, are for protection.

There are many other forms of protection or obstacles to trade in national laws. Some are health or packaging requirements. Others deal with language, such as the mandatory use of French on labels and in advertising, manuals, warranties, and so forth, for goods sold in France.

The U.S. Customs Service is responsible for collecting tariffs and enforcing trade laws such as quotas.
Jeff Greenberg/PhotoEdit

*Civil liability calls for payment of money damages. Criminal liability may result in fines or imprisonment.

The following list is a sampling of U.S. export products, export destinations, and the trade barriers encountered at the destinations.

Product	Destination	Barrier
Carbon steel	EU	Imports limited to 8 percent of market
Pesticides	Canada	Residue standards bar some U.S. chemicals
Machine tools	Japan	Government subsidizes domestic industry
Machine tools	Argentina	Money from sales must remain in Argentina for months
Paperboard	Japan	Specifications require smoother board than is produced in the United States

In other countries, U.S. exports may encounter weak patent or trademark protection, very high tariffs, zero quotas, quarantine periods, or a variety of other obstacles.

Of course, the United States imposes barriers against the importation of a number of products. It sometimes uses tariffs, sometimes quotas, and often a more modern form of quota called by some *"voluntary" restraint agreements* (VRAs) and by others *"voluntary" export restraints* (VERs). "Voluntary" is in quotes because these barriers are imposed by the U.S. government on the exporting countries. The inevitable result is higher costs to American consumers as exporters send only the higher-priced top of their lines and importers charge more for scarcer products.[19] The nearby Small and Medium-Sized Enterprises feature entitled, When Is a Duck Not Like a Bedspread?, demonstrates how difficult the bureaucrats at U.S. Customs and the Justice Department can make it to import a simple, harmless product even though it does not compete with anything U.S.-made.

One justification for protectionism is that it saves domestic jobs. The cost to U.S. consumers to save one job in the U.S. car industry was estimated to be $250,000.[20]

Super 301 is the popular name given to legislation aimed at preventing unreasonable or discriminatory trading practices by other countries. Super 301 gives the U.S. trade representative (USTR) power to take retaliatory action against trading partners of the United States which engage in unfair trading practices. Congress passed Super 301 in 1988 to give the president additional leverage in trade negotiations. The act requires the USTR to identify trade practices of other nations that pose unfair barriers to U.S. firms and to identify those nations that exhibit a pervasive pattern of unfair discrimination against U.S. firms. The USTR is required to negotiate with the identified countries in an attempt to remove the trade barriers. If the negotiations fail, Super 301 allows the USTR to impose punitive measures against noncooperating countries. Information on the actions of the USTR with respect to Super 301 can be found at **www.ustr.gov/reports/special/factsheets.html.**

The United States is not the only country that imposes VRAs and VERs on its trading partners—far from it. Japan, Canada, the EU countries, and many others require countries exporting to them to "voluntarily" limit the number or value of goods exported.

In 1982, the French came up with a novel protectionist device. Japanese videotape recorders were one of the French imports causing a large balance-of-payments deficit with Japan. The recorders normally entered France through the major port of Le Havre, which had a large detachment of customs officers to process imports. Then the French government issued a decree requiring all the recorders to enter France through Poitiers, which had a tiny customs post. The result was long delays that reduced the number of recorders entering France. Japan then "voluntarily" agreed to limit the number of recorders it exported to France.

Product Liability—Civil and Criminal

Manufacturers' liability for faulty or dangerous products was a boom growth area for the U.S. legal profession beginning in the 1960s. Liability insurance premiums have soared, and there are concerns that smaller, weaker manufacturing companies cannot survive.

When Is a Duck Not Like a Bedspread?

Small and Medium-Sized Enterprises

Robert Capps is president of Blue Ridge: The Item Co., which is based in Skyland, North Carolina, and employs about 20 people. In 1995, Blue Ridge tried to import from China a line of novelties called TV Ducks; these ducks are cute animals made of cloth that perch on the arms of couches. Their attached pockets can hold television remote controls and small magazines.

But the U.S. Customs officials went duck hunting and ruled that the little animals belonged in the same tariff schedule as bedspreads, which are subject to U.S. textile quotas. To bring the ducks into the United States, Capps would have had to purchase a textile quota visa which would have doubled their price and made them unprofitable.

So he hired a $250-per-hour Washington lawyer who said, "My job is to persuade the judge that TV Ducks are not like bedspreads." He succeeded, and Judge Musgrave issued a stern order directing U.S. Customs to permit Capps to bring in his novelty items. But customs officials and lawyers in Attorney General Janet Reno's Justice Department weren't about to quit or admit they had goofed. Instead, they filed an appeal with the U.S. Court of Appeals. You had to be in the courtroom to appreciate the looks of disbelief that the judges directed toward the government lawyer as she insisted that ducks are just like bedspreads.

The Court of Appeals ruled for Capps, but that did not end the negative activities of the Justice Department lawyers. They proceeded to fight to make sure the government doesn't pay the $100,000-plus legal bills they forced upon Capps.

Blue Ridge was able to stay in business by selling TV Ducks in England, New Zealand, and Australia. Capps commented, among other things, that this was "just another case of big government picking on a little guy." ■

Source: Republished with permission of *The Asian Wall Street Journal,* from *The Asian Wall Street Journal,* February 24, 1997, p. 12. Permission conveyed through Copyright Clearance Center.

Now that boom may spread to Europe, where directives of the EU Commission are pushing new **product liability** laws that would standardize and toughen existing ones. A directive (O.J. No. L 210/229) was adopted in the EU in 1985 imposing a system of **strict liability.**

There are several reasons to believe that the impact of strict liability on product designers and manufacturers in Europe and Japan will not be as heavy or severe as it is in the United States. In Europe, the directive permits the EU member-countries to allow "state-of-the-art" or "developmental risks" defenses, which allow the designer/manufacturer to prove that at the time of design or manufacture, the most modern, latest-known technology was used. The countries also are permitted to cap damages at amounts not less than 70 million ECUs.* Damages awarded by American juries have been in the hundreds of millions of dollars.

Major differences in legal procedures in the United States compared with those in Europe and Japan will limit or prevent product liability awards by European and Japanese courts. In the United States but not elsewhere, lawyers take many cases on a contingency fee basis whereby the lawyer charges the plaintiff no fee to begin representation and action in a product liability case. The lawyer is paid only when the defendant settles or loses in a trial, but then the fee is relatively large, running between one-third and one-half of the settlement or award. In addition, outside the United States, when the defendant wins a lawsuit, the plaintiff is called upon to pay all the defendant's legal fees and other costs caused by the plaintiff's action.[21]

In the United States, product liability cases are heard by juries that can award plaintiffs actual damages plus punitive damages. As the name indicates, punitive damages have the purpose of punishing the defendant, and if the plaintiff has been grievously injured or the jury's sympathy can be otherwise aroused, it may award millions of dollars to "teach the defendant a lesson." Outside the United States, product liability cases are heard by judges, not juries. Judges are less prone to emotional reactions than juries are, and even if the judge is sympathetic toward a plaintiff, punitive damages are not awarded by non–U.S. courts.[22]

product liability
Holding a company and its officers and directors liable and possibly subject to fines or imprisonment when their product causes death, injury, or damage

strict liability
Holds the designer/manufacturer liable for damages caused by a product without the need for a plaintiff to prove negligence in the product's design or manufacture

*At the exchange rate on April 11, 1995, ECU 70 million was equal to US$92 million. The ECU has since been replaced by the euro.

Punitive Damage Effects on Medicine

Multimillion-dollar punitive damage awards by U.S. courts have caused foreign firms to keep their products out of the United States. For instance, Axminster Electronics, a British firm whose devices help prevent crib death by monitoring a baby's breathing, does not sell in the United States because it cannot secure product liability insurance. Within the United States, medical research of all sorts has declined precipitously; after all, every drug company knows that if a person subsequently gets ill, there is a good chance that a jury somewhere in the United States will blame the medicine and levy huge fines.[23]

Faced with thousands of silicone breast implant lawsuits, Dow Corning, which made the implants, was forced into bankruptcy in 1994. Since then, attorneys representing women who claim illnesses caused by them have been suing Dow Chemical, which was a 50 percent owner of Dow Corning. In 1997, a New Orleans jury found that Dow Chemical knew that silicone was potentially harmful to humans.

This was the first phase of the trial. In the second phase, the jury will be asked to decide whether the implants caused the health problems suffered by the plaintiffs. The defendants cite major studies at Harvard University, the Mayo Clinic, and several other institutions which have found that women with implants are no more likely to suffer from diseases than are women without implants.[24]

As indicated at the beginning of this discussion of product liability, the EU adopted a directive in 1985, which was to be in place in 1988 in the member-countries, imposing a system of strict liability. But because the concept of strict liability is abhorrent to some cultures, the directive had not been implemented by France, Ireland, or Spain as late as 1997. In order to encourage them to pass implementing laws, the EU permits "state-of-the-art" defenses and caps on damage awards, as was mentioned above.[25]

Buyer Beware in Japan

The Japanese law on product liability is similar to that in the United States before 1963. The plaintiff must prove design or manufacturing negligence, which particularly with complex, high-tech devices is virtually impossible. The plaintiffs' difficulties are exacerbated by the failure of Japanese legal procedures to provide discovery, the process by which plaintiffs can seek defendants' documents relevant to their cases. Discovery is available to plaintiffs in U.S. courts but not in Japan or Europe.[26]

In a survey of more than 500 chief executives by the Conference Board, more than one-fifth believe strict U.S. product liability laws have caused their companies to lose business to foreign competitors.[27] But as foreign firms buy or build U.S. plants, they are being hit by the same liability and insurance problems long faced by U.S. companies.[28]

Currency Exchange Controls

Almost every country has currency exchange controls—laws dealing with the purchase and sale of foreign currencies. Most countries, including developing countries and communist countries, have too little hard foreign currency.* There is the rare country, such as Switzerland, that sometimes feels it has too much.

Exchange Control Generalities

The law of each country must be examined, but some generalizations can be made. In countries where hard foreign currency is scarce, a government agency allocates it. Typically, an importer of productive capital equipment gets priority over an importer of luxury goods.

People entering such a country must declare how much currency of any kind they are bringing in. On departure, they must declare how much they are taking out. The intent is twofold: (1) to discourage travelers from bringing in the host country's national currency bought abroad at a better exchange rate than exists inside the country and (2) to encourage them to bring in hard foreign currency. Currency exchange controls are discussed in detail in Chapter 6.

*A hard currency is readily exchangeable for any other currency in the world. Developed countries usually have hard currencies. The U.S. dollar, for example, is a hard currency. Hard currencies are discussed in Chapter 6.

Miscellaneous Laws

Individuals working abroad must be alert to avoid falling afoul of local laws and of corrupt police, army, or government officials. Some examples make the point.

A Plessey employee, a British subject, is serving a life sentence in Libya for "jeopardizing the revolution by giving information to a foreign company." Two Australians were executed in Malaysia for possession of 15 grams or more of hard drugs. Saudi Arabia and other Muslim countries strictly enforce sanctions against importing or drinking alcohol or wearing revealing clothing. Foreigners in Japan who walk out of their homes without their alien registration cards can be arrested, as happened to one man while he was carrying out the garbage. In Thailand, people can be jailed for mutilating paper money or for damaging coins that bear the picture or image of the royal prince, as was one foreigner who stopped a rolling coin with his foot. Neither *Playboy* nor *Penthouse* can be brought into Singapore.

Travelers and vacationers can also run afoul of unexpected laws in different countries. In the People's Republic of China, unmarried couples—foreigners included—face a possible 10 days in jail if they stay overnight in the same room. In Greece, travelers who exceed their credit card limits may be sentenced to prison for as long as 12 years.

A Philadelphia law firm, International Legal Defense Counsel (ILDC), has made a reputation dealing with countries where American embassies and consulates are of little legal help and where prison conditions are so squalid that survival is the first concern. One of its cases involved a Virginia photographer named Conan Owen. He was duped into transporting a package of cocaine from Colombia to Spain, where he was arrested and slapped with a stiff prison sentence. The U.S. attorney general personally interceded with no success, and Owen languished in prison for nearly two years. Then ILDC sprang him through the use of a bilateral prisoner transfer treaty that permits American inmates in foreign jails to do their time in a facility back home. Once in the United States, Owen was quickly freed.

Among ILDC publications that give travelers legal advice are *The Hassle of Your Life: A Handbook for Families of Americans Jailed Abroad* and *Know the Law: A Handbook for Hispanics Imprisoned in the United States.*[29]

public international law
Legal relations between governments

private international law
Laws governing transactions of individuals and companies that cross international borders

International Legal Forces

What Is International Law?

Before discussing international legal forces, it is important to recognize that each sovereign nation is responsible for creating and enforcing laws within its jurisdiction. Once laws cross international borders, the matter of enforcement is complicated by the necessity of agreement between nations. The same concepts that apply to domestic laws do not always apply to international law.

What is called international law can be divided into public international law and private international law. **Public international law** includes legal relations between governments, including laws concerning diplomatic relations between nations and all matters involving the rights and obligations of sovereign nations. **Private international law** includes laws governing the transactions of individuals and companies crossing international borders. For example, private international law would cover matters involved in a contract between businesses in two different countries.

treaties
Agreements between countries; may be bilateral (between two countries) or multilateral (involving more than two countries). Treaties also may be called conventions, covenants, compacts, or protocols

Sources of International Law

International law comes from several sources. The most important source is found in bilateral and multilateral **treaties** between nations. Treaties are agreements between countries and also may be called conventions, covenants, compacts, or protocols. In the United States, the Constitution gives the president the power to negotiate treaties with the advice and consent of the Senate. The Constitution also provides that treaties, once enacted, have the same status as federal laws. Both federal laws and treaties are subordinate to the Constitution, but both take precedence over state laws.

Another source of international law is customary international law. International rules derived from customs and usage over the centuries form what is called customary international law. Customary international law is especially common in areas such as maritime and admiralty law. International organizations such as the United Nations (UN) have provided an additional means for creation of international law. The UN has sponsored many conferences that have led to agreements among nations on a large range of matters, including postal delivery and use of driver licenses in other countries. The International Court of Justice, one of the organs of the United Nations, creates international law when it decides disputes brought before it by member-nations.

International Dispute Settlement

Litigation in the United States

The United States has a long tradition of using lawsuits to solve disputes between parties. Businesses in the United States have grown accustomed to resolving disputes through litigation. The United States has well-developed court systems that facilitate litigation. These court systems handle both criminal and civil matters. Criminal matters are those brought by the government against people for actions deemed criminal behavior by law. Examples include theft, burglary, and homicide. Penalties can include fines, imprisonment, and in some cases even death. Civil matters, by contrast, are disputes involving two or more parties. Examples include personal injury (called tort) actions, contract actions, and dissolution of marriage. Since civil matters entail resolution of disputes, criminal penalties are not involved. In civil matters, courts are able to award money (called damages) to the winning party. The United States uses a jury system in most criminal and most civil cases.

Litigation can be extremely complicated and expensive. In addition to the trial itself, most lawsuits involve lengthy pretrial activities, including a process called discovery. Discovery is the means of finding facts relevant to the litigation known to the other side, including obtaining documents in possession of the other side. Some discovery methods can seem quite intrusive since courts grant parties great latitude in obtaining information in the possession of the opposing side. Indeed, one reason many people outside the United States dislike litigation in the United States is the process of discovery.

Unlike most other countries, the United States has two major court systems. One is the federal court system. It includes trial courts (called district courts), at least one of which is located in every state. The federal court system also includes the federal courts of appeals, one for each of the 11 circuits and the District of Columbia. Finally, the federal court system includes the U.S. Supreme Court, which has the final word on matters before it. The United States also has a system of state courts in each state. Most litigation occurs in state courts. State courts are general courts of general jurisdiction, meaning they can hear almost any type of case. State courts usually have trial courts and a system of courts of appeal that includes intermediate and final courts of appeals. In all states except New York, the state's highest court is called the supreme court. In New York, it is called the court of appeals.

Litigation involving disputes that cross international lines can arise in both state and federal courts. Special rules exist for obtaining discovery in other countries, which vary from country to country. Some countries freely allow U.S. litigators to obtain discovery. Others have restrictions.

WISE/ALDRICH
AND FOR USING THE TERM "THE LITTLE WOMAN," YOU ARE SENTENCED TO SIX MONTHS OF BEING REFERRED TO AS "THE LITTLE MAN."
8-7

Let the punishment fit the crime.

Source: Real Life Adventures © 2000 GarLanco. Reprinted with permission of Universal Press Syndicate. All rights reserved.

One of the major problems usually involved in cross-border litigation is the question of which jurisdiction's law should apply and in which location the litigation should occur. Each country (and each state in the United States) has elaborate laws for determining which law should apply and where litigation should occur. Of course, as with any other disputed matter, the final decision on these matters rests with the court. It is for this reason that in contracts, it is prudent to include a choice of law clause and a choice of forum clause in the event of a dispute.

As was mentioned before, many people outside the United States dislike the U.S. system of discovery. For this reason, it is common for U.S. businesspeople entering into contracts with businesspeople abroad to agree that any disputes will be resolved by arbitration, not by litigation. Arbitration is a dispute resolution mechanism that is an alternative to litigation. Arbitration is usually quicker, less expensive, and more private than litigation. Arbitration is also usually binding on all parties. Arbitration is discussed further below.

Issues Surrounding Performance of Contracts

Whenever businesses enter into agreements with other businesses either in the United States or abroad, there is always the possibility that there may be problems getting the other side to perform its obligations. There is no international court with the power to enforce contracts worldwide because there is no international sovereign. Each nation in the world is a sovereign nation. For this reason, enforcing contracts that cross international lines often is quite complicated.

When contracting parties are residents of a single country, the laws of that country govern contract performance and any disputes that arise between the parties. That country's courts have jurisdiction over the parties, and the court's judgments are enforced in accordance with the country's procedures. When residents of two or more countries contract, those relatively easy solutions to disputes are not available.

United Nations Solutions

When contract disputes arise between parties from two or more countries, which country's law is applicable? Many countries, including the United States, have ratified the UN Convention on Contracts for the International Sale of Goods (CISG) to solve such problems.

The CISG established uniform legal rules to govern the formation of international sales contracts and the rights and obligations of the buyer and seller. The CISG applies automatically to all contracts for the sale of goods between traders from different countries that have ratified the CISG. This automatic application will take place unless the parties to the contract expressly exclude—opt out of—the CISG.[30]

European Union Solutions

The law applicable to contracts between EU residents is determined by an amendment to the Rome Convention, which came into effect in 1991. It established two principles. First, if the parties agree at the outset which country's law should apply, then that choice will be upheld. Second, if no such choice is made, the law of the country most closely connected with the contract will apply. A set of rules has been established to make this work in practice.[31]

Private Solutions, Arbitration

Many parties either cannot or do not wish to accept UN or EU solutions. Instead of going to court in any country, they opt for **arbitration.** At least 30 organizations now administer international arbitrations, the best known of which is the International Court of Arbitration of the International Chamber of Commerce in Paris. More than 650 disputes were filed with that body during 1996, and the number is expected to increase 15 to 20 percent annually over the next several years.[32] People and businesses may prefer arbitration for several reasons. They may be suspicious of foreign courts, but regardless of that,

arbitration
A process, agreed to by parties to a dispute in lieu of going to court, by which a neutral person or body makes a binding decision

arbitration is always faster than law courts, where cases are usually backlogged and procedures are formal. Arbitration procedures are informal. They can also be confidential, avoiding the perhaps unwelcome publicity accompanying an open court case.

Although London, New York, and Paris are traditional arbitration centers, Hong Kong is growing as one. This follows from the explosive growth of business and trade in the Pacific Rim countries and a 1991 cooperation agreement between the Hong Kong International Arbitration Center and its counterpart in the People's Republic of China.[33]

Enforcement of Foreign Arbitration Awards

Courts in countries around the world usually enforce arbitration awards, but occasionally enforcement can pose problems. One solution is the UN Convention on the Recognition and Enforcement of Foreign Arbitral Awards. The United States and most UN member-countries of industrial importance have ratified this convention. It binds ratifying countries to compel arbitration when the parties have so agreed in their contract and to enforce the resulting awards.

In instances where the contract in dispute involves investment in a country from abroad, another arbitration tribunal is available. This is the International Center for Settlement of Investment Disputes, sponsored by the World Bank. Investors were encouraged in 1986 when Indonesia proved willing to abide by a decision of the center even though an adverse opinion could have cost the country several million dollars.

Other organizations are working toward a worldwide business law. The Incoterms of the International Chamber of Commerce and its Uniform Rules and Practice on Documentary Credits now receive almost universal acceptance. The UN Commission on International Trade Law and the International Institute for the Unification of Private Law are doing much useful work. The Hague-Vishy Rules on Bills of Lading sponsored by the International Law Association have been adopted by a number of countries.[34]

Despite Legal Uncertainties, Trade Grows

Since the end of World War II, the proportion of trade as a share of global income has increased substantially. International trade continues to play an increasingly important role in the United States. For example, over 8.8 million people in the United States are employed in export-related fields, with jobs paying 15 to 17 percent more than non-export-related jobs.[35] Despite legal uncertainties of doing business in other countries, the trend indicates that international business activities will only increase in the future. It is for this reason that international businesspeople must be aware of the legal environment in which they find themselves. Legal systems vary significantly from country to country, and it is important to understand these differences. The assumptions one makes on the basis of the U.S. legal system may not apply in all countries.

Intellectual Property: Patents, Trademarks, Trade Names, Copyrights, and Trade Secrets

A patent is a government grant giving the inventor of a product or process the exclusive right to manufacture, exploit, use, and sell that invention or process. Trademarks and trade names are designs and names, often officially registered, by which merchants or manufacturers designate and differentiate their products. Copyrights are exclusive legal rights of authors, composers, creators of software, playwrights, artists, and publishers to publish and dispose of their works. Trade secrets are any information that a business wishes to hold confidential. All are referred to as **intellectual property.**

intellectual property
Patents, trademarks, trade names, copyrights, and trade secrets, all of which result from the exercise of someone's intellect

Trade secrets can be of great value, but each country deals with and protects them in its own fashion. The duration of protection differs, as do the products that may or may not be protected. Some countries permit the production process to be protected but not the product. Therefore, international companies must study and comply with the laws of each country where they may want to manufacture, create, or sell products.

Patents

In the field of patents, some degree of standardization is provided by the International Convention for the Protection of Industrial Property, sometimes referred to as the Paris Union. Some 90 countries, including the major industrial nations, adhere to this convention.

Most Latin American nations and the United States are members of the Inter-American Convention. The protection it provides is similar to that afforded by the Paris Union.

A major step toward the harmonization of patent treatment is the European Patent Organization (EPO). Members are the EU countries and Switzerland. Through EPO, an applicant for a patent need file only one application in English, French, or German to be granted patent protection in all member-countries. Before the EPO, an applicant had to file in each country in the language of that country.

The law firm of Ladas & Parry offers information about the EPO, protecting inventions in Europe, and recent EPO decisions. See **http://www.ladas.com/middle.html.**

The World Intellectual Property Organization (WIPO) is a UN agency that administers 16 international intellectual property treaties. There is also another organization called TRIPS for "trade-related aspects of intellectual property." TRIPS operates under the aegis of the World Trade Organization.

WIPO's activities are increasing, as nearly 29,000 international patent applications were filed in 1993 under the Patent Cooperation Treaty, which enables investors to apply for registration in several countries with a single application. This was five times the number in the mid-1980s, and the average number of designated countries per application jumped from 10 to 31. In addition, WIPO advises developing countries on such matters as running patent offices and drafting intellectual property legislation. Interest in developing countries about intellectual property matters has been growing.[36]

At the UN, representatives of the developing nations have been mounting attacks on the exclusivity and length of patent protection. They want to shorten the protection periods from the current 15 to 20 years down to 5 years or even 30 months. But companies in industrialized countries that are responsible for the new technology eligible for patents are resisting the changes. They point out that the only incentives they have to spend the huge amounts required to develop the technology are periods of patent protection long enough to recoup their costs and make profits.

Trademarks

Trademark protection varies from country to country, as does its duration, which may be from 10 to 20 years. Such protection is covered by the Madrid Agreement of 1891 for most of the world, though there is also the General American Convention for Trademark and Commercial Protection for the Western Hemisphere. In addition, protection may be provided on a bilateral basis in friendship, commerce, and navigation treaties.

An important step in harmonizing the rules on trademarks was taken in 1988 when regulations for a European Union trademark were drafted. A single European Trademark Office will be responsible for the recognition and protection of proprietary marks in all EU countries, including trademarks belonging to companies based in non-EU member-countries.

The Ladas & Parry law firm mentioned earlier in this chapter as a source of information about patents also offers information about trademarks.

Companies, such as Coca-Cola, have operations throughout the world, including this facility in China, and understand the importance of protecting trademarks worldwide.
Gamma Liaison

Trade Names

Trade names are protected in all countries that adhere to the Industrial Property Convention, which was mentioned above in connection with patents. Goods bearing illegal trademarks or trade names or false statements about their origin are subject to seizure at importation into these countries.

Copyrights

Copyrights get protection under the Berne Convention of 1886, which is adhered to by 55 countries, and the Universal Copyright Convention of 1954, which has been adopted by some 50 countries. The United States did not ratify the Berne Convention until 1988, by which time it was driven to do so by the need for greater protection against pirating of computer software.

Trade Secrets

Trade secrets are protected by laws in most nations. Employers everywhere use employee secrecy agreements, which in some countries are rigorously enforced.

Industrial Espionage

industrial espionage
The effort of one company to steal another company's trade secrets, for example, by attempting to bribe an employee, eavesdropping electronically on internal communications, or hacking into the target company's computer data

Industrial espionage among companies that develop and use high technology is not unusual, and it is becoming much more common, with American companies as frequent victims. In the mid-1990s, a guard standing behind the Houston home of an executive of a large U.S. defense contractor noticed two well-tailored men tossing plastic bags of garbage into their van. The guard doubted that even in that upscale neighborhood there would be custom-collected garbage.

One of the men turned out to be no less a personage than France's consul general in Houston. He claimed he was collecting fill for a hole in his backyard. The FBI suspected that he was searching trash for secrets—one well-established tactic in a vast 30-year effort by the French government to harvest U.S. scientific and military secrets.

Bell Helicopter spent years and big bucks, including some $3.5 billion of U.S. government money, researching tilt-wing aircraft technology. Japanese companies wanted that technology. Their spy technique was "tunneling," by which they set up an anonymous-looking U.S. subsidiary company and hired away Bell's disgruntled (but knowledgeable) employees. As a result, it is quite possible that a family of new aircraft that spent many years germinating in the United States may take off first in Asia.[37]

In a survey, 325 American companies reported 32 cases of theft of intellectual information per month entailing losses of some $5.1 billion. Ranked by nationality and frequency of complaints, the top perpetrators were the Chinese, Canadians, French, Indians, and Japanese.

A favorite method is to get one's spies employed by the target company; they are referred to as moles and have been identified at many U.S. companies, including IBM, Corning, and Texas Instruments. When foreign businesspeople travel and use hotels, particularly in Japan, South Korea, and China, they must be aware that the rooms may be bugged. As one traveler put it, "The whole hotel is live."[38]

Costly Intellectual Property Rip-Offs

In the heart of Istanbul's labyrinthine Covered Bazaar, two police officers sit sipping tea. A few meters away is a row of stalls piled high with brightly colored Benetton sweaters, Lacoste T-shirts, Nike and Reebok shoes, and Levi's jeans. All are counterfeit, copied from originals in hundreds of small factories in the city's back streets; the asking prices are $2 to $3. Turkey's 1995 law on intellectual property rights was supposed to have eradicated counterfeiting, but enforcement is lax.

It is estimated that financial losses caused by counterfeiting amount to 5 to 7 percent of world trade, or $250 billion to $350 billion, and it is a fast-growing business. Turkey is said to be the world's top producer of counterfeit products, followed by China, Thailand, Italy, and Colombia.

Counterfeiting causes many ills. Fake machinery parts have led to deaths; the fraud distorts competition; it reduces investment, which leads to a loss of jobs; and it reduces governments' tax revenues.

Pharmaceuticals are counterfeited and sold at prices far below those charged in legal markets. Of course, the reason for high pharmaceutical prices is the need of the companies to recoup the millions of dollars spent on research to develop drugs. If they are prevented from recouping such costs, research for new drugs and medicines will be discouraged, to say the least.[39]

International Standardizing Forces

Several international standardizing forces have already been discussed. In the tax area, there are tax conventions, or treaties, among nations. Each country tries to make each such treaty as nearly as possible like the others, and so patterns and common provisions may be found among them.

In antitrust, the EU member-nations operate under Articles 81 and 82 of the Treaty of Rome. In an unusual bilateral move, Germany and the United States signed an executive agreement on antitrust cooperation. This was the first attempt by national governments to cooperate on antitrust matters concerning firms operating in both countries. As was mentioned before, there have been proposals to create worldwide agreements on antitrust and bankruptcy.

In the field of commercial contract arbitration, we mentioned the UN Convention. If the disputed contract involves investment from one country into another, it can be submitted for arbitration by the International Center for Settlement of Investment Disputes at the World Bank, and in 1988, the UN Convention on the International Sale of Goods came into effect.

Several international patent and other agreements were pointed out. Chapter 4 covered a number of UN-related organizations and other worldwide associations. Each of them has some harmonizing or standardizing effect. The same can be said of the regional international groupings and organizations dealt with in Chapter 4.

Two standardizing organizations are the International Organization for Standardization (ISO) and the International Electrotechnical Commission (IEC). The IEC promotes standardization of measurement, materials, and equipment in almost every sphere of electrotechnology. The ISO recommends standards in other fields of technology. Most government and private procurement around the world demands products that meet IEC or ISO specifications, and therein lies a danger for U.S. companies. All IEC and ISO measurements are in the metric system, which has not been adopted in the United States, thereby imposing an additional burden on U.S. firms trying to export products without metric measurements.

U.S. Laws That Affect the International Business of U.S. Firms

Although every law relating to business arguably has some effect on international activities, some laws warrant special notice. We will look briefly at U.S. taxation laws, the Foreign Corrupt Practices Act, and the antiboycott law.

Taxation

As we have remarked, the U.S. tax system is considered by many to be the world's most complicated. That in itself makes doing business more complicated and therefore more expensive for a U.S. company than it is for companies based elsewhere.

Taxing Americans Who Work Abroad

Observing a so-called **national tax jurisdiction,** rather than a **territorial tax jurisdiction,** the United States is almost alone among countries in taxing its people according to nationality rather than on the basis of where they live and work. As was mentioned before, U.S. citizens and permanent residents (green card holders) are taxed on their worldwide income regardless of the source of the income and regardless of the residence of the taxpayer. As a result, U.S. citizens and permanent residents living or working in another country must pay taxes there and to the United States. In addition to higher tax payments, this requires the time and expense of completing two sets of complicated tax returns. In 1981, the sections of the IRC dealing with this subject were again amended. Although the burden of completing two tax returns was not lifted, the new law gave relief, starting in 1982, in the amount of American taxes to be paid by exempting the first

national tax jurisdiction
A tax system for expatriate citizens of a country whereby the country taxes them on the basis of nationality even though they live and work abroad

territorial tax jurisdiction
Expatriate citizens who neither live nor work in the country—and therefore receive none of the services for which taxes pay—are exempt from the country's taxes

$85,000 of earned income.* In 1997 this exemption again received attention from the U.S. Congress, which in 1986 had lowered it to $70,000. Starting in 1998, the new law raised the ceiling by $2,000 a year for each of the next five years, reaching $80,000 in 2002 and thereafter. After 2007, the $80,000 limit will be indexed for inflation.

When U.S. Taxes Are Anti-American. Suppose a U.S.-based multinational wants to open a new factory, store, warehouse, or office building in the United States. That would create new jobs for Americans, along with all the benefits that flow from new jobs.

But when the company's executives look at the new U.S. tax law, they hesitate because of the section dealing with allocation of interest expense. When a U.S. company with subsidiaries in many countries borrows money to finance a U.S. business, the interest is treated as if it were paid in part to finance foreign operations. That results in a partial loss of the tax deduction and thus a higher after-tax interest cost.

Foreign companies—including foreign-based multinationals—have no such requirement and can deduct 100 percent of interest on borrowings to finance a U.S. operation. Therefore, they have lower after-tax interest costs and, to that extent, can be more competitive in the United States than many U.S. companies.[40]

As was discussed previously, the U.S. tax code is extremely complicated. It is especially complicated for international tax matters. Many argue that the U.S. tax system hurts the competitiveness of U.S. businesses abroad. Certainly, the tax code complicates the lives of U.S. businesspeople operating in other countries.

Federal Employment Laws

There are numerous federal laws that attempt in some manner to prevent unwarranted discrimination in employment. Even though there is no single federal law prohibiting illegal discrimination in employment, Title VII of the federal Civil Rights Act of 1964 (Title VII) is largely recognized as the focal point of federal employment discrimination law. Title VII prohibits discrimination in employment based on race, color, religion, sex, or national origin. Other major pieces of federal employment discrimination law include the Age Discrimination in Employment Act of 1967 (ADEA) and the Americans with Disabilities Act of 1990 (ADA).

Even though Congress has the power to extend application of its laws beyond the territory of the United States, it must intend to do so and that intent must be made clear in the legislation. Congress specifically intended these federal employment laws to apply extraterritorially. Title VII, the ADEA, and the ADA generally cover U.S. citizens working for U.S. companies abroad. For example, if a woman who is a U.S. citizen is denied a promotion because of her gender while working in Germany for an American company, she may bring an action in the United States under Title VII against her employer for unlawful discrimination in employment. Congress enacted one exception to the extraterritorial application of federal employment laws, though, and that is an exception for local foreign laws. It is not a violation of U.S. law for an employer to engage in conduct that ordinarily would constitute illegal behavior if such behavior is required by local law in the country where the conduct took place. For example, certain countries prohibit women from engaging in certain activities, such as driving. If a U.S. company is complying with the laws in a nation with such laws, the U.S. company will be protected from suits in the United States for discrimination if the discrimination is necessary to comply with local laws. Exceptions to Title VII's prohibitions, however, are extremely unusual.

questionable or dubious payments
Bribes paid to government officials by companies seeking purchase contracts from those governments

Foreign Corrupt Practices Act (FCPA)

During the 1970s, revelations of **questionable or dubious payments** by American companies to foreign officials rocked governments in the Netherlands and Japan. Congress considered corporate bribery "bad business" and "unnecessary," and President Carter found it "ethically repugnant." As a result, the Foreign Corrupt Practices Act (FCPA) was passed and signed.

*Earned income includes salaries, bonuses, and commissions. Interest, dividend, and royalty income is called unearned income.

Uncertainties

There were a number of uncertainties about terms used in the FCPA. An interesting one involves *grease.* According to the FCPA's drafters, the act does not outlaw grease, or facilitating payments made solely to expedite nondiscretionary official actions. Such actions as customs clearance and telephone calls have been cited. There is no clear distinction between supposedly legal grease payments and illegal bribes. To confuse matters further, U.S. Justice Department officials have suggested that they may prosecute some grease payments anyway under earlier antibribery laws written to get at corruption in the United States.

Other doubts raised by the FCPA concerned the accounting standards it requires for compliance. That matter is connected to questions about how far management must go to learn whether any employees, subsidiaries, or agents may have violated the act; even if management were unaware of an illegal payment, it could be in violation if it "had reason to know" that some portion of a payment abroad might be used as a bribe.[41]

Other Countries' Reactions to Bribes*

No other country had a law similar to the FCPA until 1998, when the OECD adopted rules for its member-nations. Attitudes of business and government officials in Europe toward the FCPA range from amusement to incredulity, and no other government historically took a position similar to that represented by the FCPA—quite the opposite.[42] German tax collectors, for example, permit resident companies to deduct foreign bribes, which are called *sonderspesen,* or special expenses.

Leading industrial nations such as Britain, France, Germany, and Japan cited many reasons for not adopting FCPA-type laws. They claim such laws might be seen as meddling in other countries' affairs, and unlike the Americans, they weren't eager to regulate their own citizens overseas, especially in business and tax matters. The OECD Convention to combat bribery went into effect, though, on February 15, 1999. The Convention makes it a crime to bribe a foreign official in order to obtain a business deal. The Convention also seeks to eliminate deductibility for income tax purposes in individual countries for money spent for foreign bribes. Deducting money paid for foreign bribes used to be considered a legitimate business expense and was allowed in many countries. As of early 2000, 34 countries had signed the Convention, including all the world's biggest economies. Twenty countries have already changed their laws to conform to the Convention, including Germany and Japan. Laws in other countries will now be closer to the antibribery laws in the United States.

In addition to the OECD, there are others looking under corruption rocks. Transparency International (TI) was founded in 1993 with headquarters in Berlin by the former World Bank director Peter Eigen.

Moving on the principle that a little sunlight can do a lot to burn away what grows in damp corners, TI prints press reports about corruption in individual countries and maintains what it calls a Corruption Perception Index. The Index, which is based on surveys of international businesspeople, political analysts, and the general public, reflects their perceptions of corruption in countries worldwide. The TI Web site is **www.transparency.de.**

In 1997, the International Monetary Fund (IMF) issued new guidelines that direct its staff to raise corruption issues with countries seeking IMF aid. It also issued a pamphlet, *Economic Issues 6,* which stated, among other findings, that "corruption discourages investment, limits economic growth, and alters the composition of government spending, often to the detriment of future economic growth."[43]

Antiboycott Law

As a part of the hostility and wars between the Arab countries and Israel, several Arab countries boycott foreign companies that do business with Israel. They will not buy from such companies. Inasmuch as several Arab countries are extremely rich oil producers, they are very large potential markets from which sellers do not like to be excluded. In 1977, however, the United States passed an act forbidding American companies to comply with any

*Other words with similar connotations are *dash, squeeze, mordida, cumshaw,* and *baksheesh.* Bribes and questionable payments were mentioned in connection with sociocultural forces in Chapter 9.

Arab boycott law or regulation. To be more accurate, the U.S. antiboycott laws apply to all boycotts that are unsanctioned by the United States. They do not apply specifically to the Arab League boycott of Israel, but at the present time that is the principal foreign economic boycott with which American firms must be concerned. Information on the boycott can be found at the Web site of the Bureau of Export Administration of the U.S. Department of Commerce, **www.bxa.doc.gov/AntiboycottCompliance/OACRequirements.html.**

The Arab League blacklist of firms is maintained by the Damascus, Syria–based Central Boycott Office, but those firms are not the only ones with which League member-countries are not supposed to do business. The prohibition extends to any firms that do business with the blacklisted companies. The office of the U.S. trade representative states that even though the boycott is not evenly applied by all League members, it results in significant economic harm to U.S. firms in terms of lost sales, forgone opportunities, and distortion of investment decisions.[44]

Contrast American and British Attitudes

As in the case of the FCPA, few other countries have any such antiboycott law. A British House of Lords select committee studying similar legislation for Britain found 2.7 billion reasons to bury it in 1978. During 1977, British exports to Arab markets totaled £2.7 billion.[45]

Other Attitudes

In the aftermath of the Iraq–Kuwait war, some other countries seemed to come around to the U.S. view. Belgium, Canada, France, Germany, Luxembourg, and the Netherlands now forbid their companies to comply with the boycott.

Changing Attitudes

Although it has not yet occurred, problems with the antiboycott law may dissolve because of ongoing political efforts seeking a peace agreement in the Middle East. As of yet, however, the Arab League has not rescinded its declared boycott of companies that do business with Israel and the United States has not repealed its law forbidding American firms to comply with the boycott.

Some Laws and Agencies Aid U.S. Exports and Investment

The U.S. Department of Commerce actively encourages exports by U.S. companies. It is helping U.S. companies get financing support through the Export-Import Bank and political risk insurance through the Overseas Private Investment Corporation. An advocacy center tracks the 50 to 100 largest overseas projects for potential involvement by U.S. companies. Export assistance centers with better market data are active in several cities, including Baltimore, Chicago, Los Angeles, and Miami. The Commerce Department is also moving to relax more export controls, as it has done with computers.

The United States has embassies and consulates in most countries around the world. These offices can frequently be sources of valuable business information and can provide introductions to potential business partners and to host/market country government officials to whom you might want to sell or from whom you may need licenses or permits.

Common Law or Civil Law?

Historically, there has been a clear distinction between common law, which developed in England and spread to the English colonies, and civil law, which originated on the continent of Europe. Courts made common law as they decided individual cases; civil law was made by kings, princes, or legislatures issuing decrees or passing bills. The common law system tends to be more flexible than the civil law system. Judges in a common law jurisdiction have the power to *interpret* the law, while judges in a civil law jurisdiction have the power only to *apply* the law. The difference can be quite significant. Judges in common law jurisdictions have more power to expand rules to fit particular cases. The civil law, by contrast, is more rigid in its application. A judge in a civil law jurisdiction is bound by the words in the code. This strict adherence to the language of the code, though, makes the civil law system much more predictable than the common law system.

As time has passed, legislatures and government agencies in the United States have made more and more laws and regulations. The courts in turn have interpreted these laws and regulations as parties have argued about what they mean. That is the sort of procedure one finds in Europe, but vast differences in practices have developed that have less to do with the traditional common–civil law approaches than with historical government-citizen (or subject) relationships and attitudes.

European Practice

Europe has a history of thousands of years of tyranny, which recently has been covered with a veneer of democracy. People have greater reason to fear their governments in Europe than do people in the United States, and government service has more prestige. Before a new law is presented to the legislature (which, unlike legislatures in the United States, is always controlled by the same political party that controls the executive branch), consensus is achieved among most of the people, businesses, and government agencies that will be affected.

In contrast to U.S. practices, European legislation is rarely amended, and regulations are rarely revised. Courts are not as often asked to give their interpretations, and if they are, the decisions are rarely appealed. Once a consensus has been reached, it is considered very bad form to open the subject again, and those who do may find themselves left out of the consultations the next time around.

American Practice

In contrast to European custom, Americans have a weaker tradition of obeying their governments and have had very little fear of them. Americans are much more likely than Europeans to challenge laws in the courts, in the streets, or by disobedience. Legislation in the United States is a product of an ongoing adversarial proceeding, not of consensus; law is written by one independent branch of government for implementation by a second and interpretation by a third. Different political parties or people with conflicting philosophies frequently control the three different branches of government.

Laws and regulations are constantly being amended or revised by the legislatures and the agencies. Courts interpret laws in ways that are sometimes surprising; the courts may strike laws down as being unconstitutional.

In the United States, legislative power is vested in Congress. Congress has the authority to implement laws throughout the country in accordance with the power granted to it by the U.S. Constitution. The EU, by contrast, is a grouping of sovereign nations. As explained in Chapter 4, even though all EU member-nations have yielded a certain amount of sovereignty to the EU, the EU still has limited power to implement comprehensive legislation throughout the EU. That power is increasing, though. It is important to keep in mind that the EU establishes laws in a manner much different from that in the United States. The main policy-setting institution in the EU remains the Council of Ministers, which is controlled by the national governments. The EU may someday resemble the United States in terms of lawmaking, but it is not there yet.

Differences between the United States and England

As this chapter has shown, it is important to be aware of differences between laws in different parts of the world. Even countries such as the United States and the United Kingdom, which share many legal traditions, including the common law, have significant differences in the modern practice of law. Here are five differences in the legal systems between the United States and England:

1. *England has a split legal profession with barristers and solicitors.* In the United States, there is no distinction in the legal profession. Once admitted to practice,

English barrister.
A. Ramoy/Stock Boston

a lawyer in the United States can represent clients in court. In England, by contrast, clients hire solicitors to advise them on legal matters. If an appearance is necessary in most courts, though, the solicitor must hire a barrister. Thus, in England, each party in a court case must retain at least two lawyers: the solicitor and the barrister.

2. *England has no jury for civil court actions.* Pursuant to the Constitution of the United States, parties in civil actions in the United States who are seeking monetary damages generally are entitled to have their cases heard by a jury. This is not the case in England. Parties in civil cases in England can have their cases heard by a jury only in certain specific cases, which are very unusual. Criminal defendants in both countries are entitled to a jury.
3. *Payment to lawyers.* It is common in the United States for a lawyer to take a case on a contingency fee basis, which means the lawyer will recover a fee only when the client receives money through settlement or a trial. Usually, the fee is a percentage, such as one-third, of the amount recovered. England has no contingency fees. In fact, it is unethical for a solicitor or a barrister to enter into such an arrangement.
4. *Award of costs to the winner in civil litigation.* In litigation in England, the losing party must pay most (usually 60 to 70 percent) of the costs, including the attorneys' fees of the winning party. In the United States, attorneys' fees are awarded only in very limited cases, when a contract or statute provides for an award of those fees.
5. *Pretrial discovery.* There is a significant difference between the United States and England in terms of pretrial discovery. Pretrial discovery is the opportunity for the parties to learn facts known by or to obtain documents in the possession of the other party. Even though some U.S. courts are limiting discovery, compared to England, the United States allows discovery with few restrictions. In England, parties generally are entitled to receive a list of witnesses with a brief explanation of the expected testimony. In the United States, parties are able to examine witnesses before trial at what is called a deposition. Discovery in the United States is much more far-reaching than it is in England.

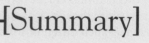

[Summary]

Appreciate the complexity of the legal forces that confront international business.

International business is affected by many thousands of laws and regulations issued by states, nations, and international organizations. Some are at cross-purposes, and some diminish the ability of firms to compete with foreign companies.

Understand that many taxes have purposes other than to raise revenue.

Certain taxes have purposes other than to raise revenues. For example, some aim to redistribute income, discourage consumption of certain products, encourage use of domestic goods, or discourage investment abroad. In addition, taxes differ from country to country. Tax treaties, or conventions, between countries can affect decisions on investment and location.

Discuss enforcement of antitrust laws.

The United States and the European Union enforce antitrust laws extraterritorially. This is a concern for companies operating in many countries.

Appreciate the risk of product liability legal actions, which can result in imprisonment for employees or fines for them and the company.

Product liability refers to the civil or criminal liability of the designer or manufacturer of a product for injury or damages it causes. In several ways, product liability is treated differently in the U.S. legal system than in other countries. For example, only in the United States does one find lawyers' contingency fees, jury trials of these cases, and punitive damages. Although the principle of strict liability has been adopted in Europe, defendants are permitted to use state-of-the-art defenses and countries can put a cap on damages. Product liability is virtually unknown in Japan.

Recognize the importance of being aware of peculiarities of local foreign law.

Miscellaneous laws in host countries can trip up foreign businesspeople or tourists. Charges can range from not carrying an alien registration card to narcotics possession.

Understand contract devices and institutions that assist in interpreting or enforcing international contracts.

International contracts should specify which country's law and courts should apply when disputes arise. The UN's CISG and the EU's Rome Convention have established rules for solving contract disputes. Arbitration is an increasingly popular solution.

Anticipate the need and methods to protect your intellectual property.

Patents, trademarks, trade names, copyrights, and trade secrets are referred to as intellectual properties. Pirating of those properties is common and is expensive for their owners. The UN's World Intellectual Property Organization (WIPO) was created to administer international property treaties, as was TRIPS, a WTO agency with a similar purpose.

Recognize how industrial espionage affects international business.

Industrial espionage is one company's attempt to steal another company's trade secrets, a crime punishable in some countries by fines or imprisonment.

[Key Words]

nonrevenue tax purposes (p. 379)
foreign tax credits (p. 381)
tax treaties (p. 381)
antitrust laws (p. 383)
competition policy (p. 383)
extraterritorial application of laws (p. 384)
product liability (p. 387)
strict liability (p. 387)
public international law (p. 389)
private international law (p. 389)
treaties (p. 389)
arbitration (p. 391)
intellectual property (p. 392)
industrial espionage (p. 394)
national tax jurisdiction (p. 395)
territorial tax jurisdiction (p. 395)
questionable or dubious payments (p. 396)

[Questions]

1. Explain some purposes of taxes other than to raise revenues.
2. Why do some people feel that a VAT should replace some or all of the U.S. income tax?
3. Why does a national tax system put citizens of that country at a disadvantage?
4. What objections do other countries have to extraterritorial application by the United States of its antitrust laws?
5. When an American traveling abroad falls afoul of the criminal laws of a foreign country, are the U.S. embassy and the U.S. consulates likely to be of much help? Where else can the traveler look for aid?
6. What are some advantages that arbitrating contract disputes may have compared to using the courts?
7. Are tariffs the only type of obstacle to international trade? If not, name some others.
8. Can product liability be criminal? If so, in what sorts of situations?
9. a. Does the Foreign Corrupt Practices Act forbid all bribes? Explain.
   b. Does the antiboycott law permit U.S. exporters to Arab countries to certify that the products are not of Israeli origin if that is true?
   c. Are attitudes and practices of Arab countries and the Arab League concerning the Israeli boycott changing? If so, to what extent?
10. a. Comparing the United States with England, what are the differences in practices in the legal systems?
    b. What are the reasons for those differences?

[Internet Exercises]

Using the Internet

1. The text discusses legal systems outside the United States, such as the European Union. Using the Internet, find information on the European Court of Justice by using the EU Web site. Discuss the following:
   a. Jurisdiction of the European Court of Justice. What issues can the European Court of Justice decide?
   b. Structure of the European Court of Justice. How are judges selected for the European Court of Justice?
2. As the text discusses, protection of patents in other countries is quite important to international business. Using the Internet, find information on rules on protection of patents in various countries.

[Minicase 11.1]

Italian Law

A California-based company is expanding very well and has just made its first export sale. All of its sales and procurement contracts up to now have contained a clause providing that if any disputes arise under the contract, they will be settled under California law and that any litigation will be in California courts.

The new foreign customer, which is Italian, objects to these all-California solutions. It says it is buying and paying for the products, so the California company should compromise and allow Italian law and courts to govern and handle any disputes.

You are the CEO of the California company, and you very much want this order. You are pleased with the service your law firm has given, but you know it has no international experience. What sorts of solutions would you suggest that your lawyers research as possible compromises between your usual all-Californian clause and the customer's wish to go all-Italian?

[Chapter]

Labor Forces

"I will build a motor car for the great multitude."

—Henry Ford

In order to get the workers he needed to make that happen, Ford shocked the industrial world in 1914 by paying an unheard of $5.00 a day at a time when the prevailing wage was $2.34 a day and by reducing the number of hours worked from nine to eight.

Source: "Our Tumultuous Century," Detroit Free Press, *www.freep.com/century/cent29_19991129.htm. November 29, 1999*

Concept Previews

After reading this chapter, you should be able to:

- **recognize** forces beyond management control that affect the availability of labor
- **understand** the reasons that cause people to leave their home countries
- **discuss** guest workers
- **understand** the principles underlying the immigration system in the United States
- **understand** how high technology is influencing workers and the workplace
- **explain** how the composition of a country's labor force affects productivity
- **name** other forces that affect productivity
- **understand** women's positions in labor forces
- **discuss** differences in labor unions from country to country
- **understand** how labor is getting a voice in management

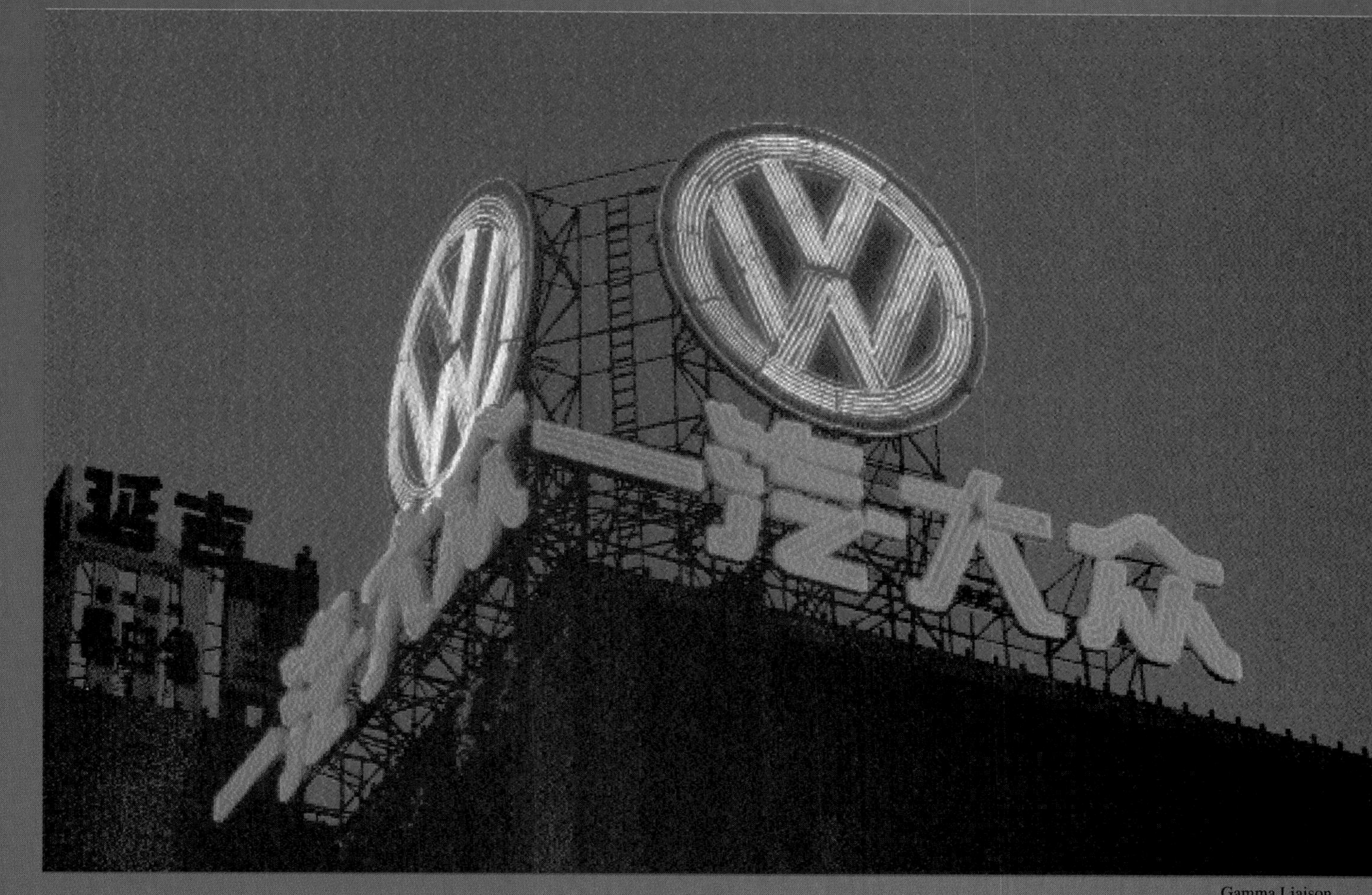

Gamma Liaison

Job Sharing, German Style

With EU-wide unemployment exceeding 10 percent, a top goal for governments across Europe and for employers is to preserve jobs. But for Germany's troubled and overstaffed Volkswagen, the only way to become competitive appeared to be slashing the domestic work force from 100,000 to 70,000.

Instead, Volkswagen and Germany's largest labor union, IG Metall, agreed on a four-day workweek as an alternative to the work-force slash. The union got its long-sought goal of a 35-hour week, and VW got a wage cost savings of 10.75 percent. VW estimates its 1994 wage cost savings at nearly $1.3 billion, and no employees needed to be laid off.[a]

If the number of working hours were an important factor in employment, then America and Japan, where the working week is longer than it is in most of Europe, would have more unemployment. In fact they have less.[b]

Sources: [a]*Crossborder Monitor,* December 22, 1993, p. 21; [b]*The Economist,* August 6, 1994, p. 56.

The quality, quantity, and composition of the available labor force are of great importance to an employer, especially if the employer must be efficient, competitive, and profitable. As we have indicated, there are government-owned plants that aim to provide employment or essential services, with profitability and competitiveness being secondary.

labor quality
The skills, education, and attitudes of available employees

labor quantity
The number of available employees with the skills required to meet an employer's business needs

Labor quality refers to the attitudes, education, and skills of available employees. **Labor quantity** refers to the number of available employees with the skills required to meet an employer's business needs. Circumstances can arise in which there are too many available workers; this can be good or bad for the business.

If there are more qualified people than a company can economically employ, its bargaining position is strengthened and it can choose the best employees at relatively low wages. On the other hand, high unemployment can cause social and political unrest, which are usually not conducive to profitable business.

Many of the labor conditions in an area are determined by the social, cultural, religious, attitudinal, and other forces we have already discussed. Other determinants of labor conditions are political and legal forces, and here we will expand on those introduced in Chapters 10 and 11.

We will look at labor availability, the reasons for its availability or scarcity, the types of labor likely to be available or scarce under different circumstances, productivity, and employer–employee relationships. These relationships are affected by employee organizations, such as labor unions. One cannot generalize about unions because they differ so greatly from country to country or even within one country.

Labor Mobility

labor mobility
The movement of people from country to country or area to area to get jobs

Classical economists assumed the immobility of labor; more complications are involved in moving people than in moving capital or most goods.

We now know, though, that **labor mobility** does exist. At least 60 million people left Europe to work and live overseas between 1850 and 1970. Between the end of World War II and the mid-1970s, some 30 million workers from southern Europe and North Africa flowed into eight northern European countries where they were needed because of the economic boom there. This movement is slowing or even reversing now. We'll further discuss these "guest workers" later in this chapter.

Another huge worker migration began during the 1970s as the sparsely populated, and newly very rich, Arab Organization of Petroleum Exporting Countries (OPEC) countries needed labor in their oil fields, for construction projects, and for required services. The countries supplying most of these workers were Egypt, Algeria, Morocco, Pakistan, and India.

Immigration into the United States continued in the 1980s and 1990s and into the 21st century. Europeans are still coming to the United States, but in much smaller numbers than they did in the 19th century. Immigrants now come from all over the world, with the largest number of legal immigrants coming each year to the United States from Mexico (91,000), Vietnam (78,000), the Philippines (59,000), and the republics of the former Soviet Union (44,000). Among these immigrants, most (nearly three-fourths) intend to reside in six states: California, New York, Texas, Florida, New Jersey, and Illinois.[1]

According to the U.S. Census Bureau, 10.4 percent of people residing in the United States are foreign-born.

Immigration

U.S. immigration policy is a good reference point for examining labor mobility not only in the United States but also throughout the world. Immigration refers to the process of leaving one's home country to reside in another country. For people who are not citizens of the United States, the United States can be a difficult country to enter. Those desiring to come to the United States must comply with strict provisions of the law in order to be admitted.

naturalization
The process of becoming a U.S. citizen

U.S. citizens have the right to live and work in any state in the United States. As discussed in Chapter 4, the European Union (EU) has four freedoms, one of which is the freedom of movement of people from one country to another within the EU. By contrast to the countries in the EU, citizens of no other country have an automatic right to enter the United States. All people who desire to enter the United States for business or pleasure have the obligation to comply with U.S. immigration laws in order to enter the United States. Even citizens of Canada and Mexico must prove their right to be in the United States. Unlike the EU, the North American Free Trade Agreement (NAFTA) among the United States, Canada, and Mexico grants no automatic right to citizens of one country to live and work in the other two countries.

New U.S. citizens at swearing-in ceremony.
Bob Daemmrich/Stock Boston

The Immigration and Naturalization Service (INS) of the U.S. Department of Justice is the federal agency responsible for all immigration matters, including naturalization. **Naturalization** deals with the process of becoming a U.S. citizen, which usually occurs after one has been admitted as an immigrant, which is also called a permanent resident, to the United States.

The INS has two sometimes conflicting missions: (1) to allow legal immigrants to enter the United States and (2) to keep out illegal immigrants. The term *illegal immigrant* or *illegal alien* refers to an individual who is in the United States without legal permission to be there. It is hard to know the number of illegal immigrants in the United States, but the INS estimates it to be about 5 million.[2] About half of all illegal immigrants in the United States entered the country legally but simply overstayed their visas. In this section, we will focus on legal immigration to the United States.

Background

The United States is a nation of immigrants. During the first century after the founding of the country, there were no significant efforts to restrict the flow of foreign nationals to the United States; the nation felt the frontier would always provide opportunities for economic growth. In the 1870s, though, the country suffered a depression, which, together with an increase in racial animosity toward Asians, led to the first restrictions on immigration, which were called the Chinese Exclusion Acts. These restrictions in the 1870s and 1880s were aimed specifically at the Chinese. Before the enactment of the Chinese Exclusion Acts, there had been a large influx of Chinese into the United States. Many of the Chinese were processed for entry at Angel Island near San Francisco, California. Angel Island often is referred to as the "Ellis Island of the West" because about one million immigrants were processed there, including about 175,000 Chinese but also many Europeans and Australians. However, unlike Ellis Island, Angel Island was not a beacon of hope for all; it was a detention center for Chinese and others awaiting return to their countries of origin. The Chinese were often engaged in hard labor, such as railroad building and mining in the Western United States. One prominent historian spoke of the contribution of the Chinese to the mining industry in Montana: "Unfortunately no study has been made of the Chinese in Montana, but there were thought to be about eight hundred of them in the territory in 1869. There was considerable hostility toward them because of their willingness to work long, hard hours for a pittance. But they were important economically because they were willing to rework the 'tailings' of the claims which white men had supposedly exhausted."[3]

Federal Law

Immigration is a federal matter in the United States, and Congress therefore has plenary power over immigration. The first comprehensive law in the United States limiting the number of immigrants permitted each year and setting criteria for their admission was passed in 1921. The criteria emphasized country of origin, favoring those countries that already were heavily represented in the U.S. population. Over the ensuing decades,

Congress amended the immigration laws many times. In the 1965 amendments, Congress abolished the national origin formula of 1921. The United States adopted a system of immigration based on family reunification and employment skills. President Lyndon Johnson, in signing the bill, said: "Those wishing to emigrate into America shall be admitted on the basis of their skills and their close relationship to those already here."

In an attempt to stop illegal immigration, Congress passed the Immigration Reform and Control Act of 1986 (IRCA), which, for the first time in U.S. history, made employment of people not authorized to work in the United States a crime for the employer. In addition to requiring employers to hire only individuals authorized to work in the United States, IRCA placed on every employer the obligation to verify the employment eligibility of potential employees before employment. This usually is done by having a potential employee complete an I-9 form. In light of fears that IRCA would result in discrimination against certain groups, Congress included antidiscrimination provisions in the act. Employers are prohibited from discriminating against those who are authorized to work in the United States. With limited exceptions (for national security purposes, for example), private employers requiring U.S. citizenship as a basis for employment are in violation of IRCA. Today, entry into the United States can be either temporary or permanent.

Nonimmigrant Visas

Nonimmigrant visas are issued to those coming to the United States for a temporary visit (usually no more than six years). Most (96 percent) visitors to the United States come for temporary visits. These visas are broken into specific categories (such as workers, students, and tourists) and are identified by letters. The major visa categories are discussed here:

B. The B visa is issued for a short-term stay, usually six months or less. The visits can be for either business (B-1) or pleasure (B-2). For example, if a businessperson were coming to attend a three-day conference in New York, a B-1 visa would be appropriate. If a noncitizen wanted to visit Yellowstone National Park on vacation, a B-2 visa would be appropriate.

E. The E visa is for noncitizens who are coming to the United States for the sole purpose of carrying on trade between the United States and a noncitizen's home country or to direct the operations of an enterprise in which a noncitizen has invested a substantial amount of money.

F. The F visa is for students.

H. The H visa is for workers. Included in the H is the H-1B visa for specialty occupations such as professionals and highly skilled workers. Many high-tech workers are admitted for temporary stays under the H-1B category. Usually, holders of the H visa are employees of a U.S.-based company that requests the visa for a noncitizen.

I. The I visa is for members of the media.

J. The J visa is for exchange scholars.

L. The L visa is for intracompany transferees. The individuals usually are sent to the United States to work in an affiliate office of the same company.

Immigrant Visas

Immigrant visas are for individuals who want to remain permanently in the United States. Individuals receiving immigrant visas are classified as permanent residents. The immigrant visa is often called a green card even though the actual card issued by the INS is not green. There are two main categories for the issuance of immigrant visas: family reunification and employment-based immigration.

refugees/asylum seekers
People who leave their home country to escape persecution

Refugees/Asylum Seekers

Throughout history, there have been flights of people from persecution. These individuals are called **refugees** or **asylum seekers.** If refugees are able to get to a safe country, they are in a position to seek asylum.

During the 1960s and 1970s, millions fled from East to West Germany, from the People's Republic of China to Hong Kong and elsewhere, and from North to South Vietnam and then as "boat people" from Vietnam to wherever they could land and hope to be accepted. In 1980, the flight of people from Cuba resumed for political reasons. Those going from Mexico to the United States and from southern Europe to northern Europe go for primarily economic reasons: better jobs and pay.

In a report released late in the year 2000, the International Organization for Migration (IOM) stated that more than 150 million people were living in another country. The IOM is an intergovernmental organization based in Geneva, Switzerland. The report noted that people are moving for several reasons, including economic globalization, population growth in developing countries, and new technology that allows immigrants to maintain contact with family members and friends in the home country. The report also indicated that immigration into industrialized countries rose rapidly during the 1990s. Immigrants make up about 10 percent of the total population in Western Europe and North America.[4]

Standard for Admission of Refugees/Asylum Seekers into the United States

In order to be admitted to the United States as a refugee or asylum seeker, one must establish a well-founded fear of persecution based on one's race, religion, nationality, membership in a particular social group, or political opinion. People who live in economically depressed countries cannot seek asylum for economic reasons.

Population Pressures

One of the most important pressures forcing people to flee is the booming population growth taking place primarily in the poor developing countries. Some 95 percent of the projected increase in the world's population from 6 billion in 1996 to over 10 billion by the year 2050 will be in those areas.[5]

Women bear most of the burdens of the baby boom, graphically illustrated by the photograph of a woman working while caring for two small children. The closely spaced pregnancies plus the constant childcare responsibilities are resulting in a growing number of female illiterates and the deterioration of female health.

These are human tragedies first and foremost. In terms of labor force efficiency and productivity, the women and children victims of these developments will be negative forces.

The burdens of women in poor countries: working while caring for two small children.
Penny Tweedie/Tony Stone Images

United Nations High Commission for Refugees (UNHCR)

The UNHCR is an organization that attempts to assist refugees. The UNHCR was created by the United Nations General Assembly in 1950 and began its work in 1951 with the mandate to lead and coordinate international action for the worldwide protection of refugees and the resolution of refugee problems. More information about the UNHCR can be found at its website, www.unhcr.ch.

Refugees Welcome?

Refugees are not welcome in many countries. The few countries willing to accept some refugees will take only limited numbers. Many refugees are poor. Even in such a relatively rich and racially diverse country as the United States, which is accepting—or getting—millions of refugees, there are difficulties. One of them is finding work for all of the new people; another is educating their children.

But Immigrants Can Help

In the 1960s and through 1990s, immigrants, both refugees and others, permitted the U.S. economy to grow faster than its long-term trend without igniting inflationary

High-tech firms often look to non-U.S. citizens to fill computer and engineering positions.
Lonnie Duks/Tony Stone Images

flames. Many of those immigrants were Latino; almost 40 percent of people hired for new jobs in 1996 were Latino even though this group makes up only about 10 percent of the U.S. population.[6] Immigrant workers in the United States work in both high- and low-skilled positions. Among the 12.7 million new jobs created in the United States between 1990 and 1998, 5.1 million (38 percent) were filled by immigrants. Without immigrants, those positions might have gone unfilled.[7]

Many high-technology firms in the United States rely on non-U.S. citizens to supply the necessary engineering and computer skills that enable those firms to excel in the new high-tech economy. As was mentioned in the immigration section, many high-tech workers come to the United States under the H-1B visa. The maximum number of H-1B visas permitted in fiscal years 1999 and 2000 was 115,000. Those visas were used up about halfway through each year because of the high demand for them, which came in large part from high-tech firms seeking new highly skilled workers. In late 2000, the United States raised the number of H-1B visas permitted each year to 195,000 for fiscal years 2001, 2002, and 2003.[8]

Guest Workers and Labor Shortages

guest workers
People who go to a foreign country legally to perform certain types of jobs

Guest Workers

Countries that receive many refugees or have high birthrates may have too many people for the available jobs, but there are also countries that have too few people. France, Germany, the Scandinavian countries, and Switzerland, all of which have low birthrates, fall into the latter category. And to those countries have legally come the so-called **guest workers** to perform certain types of jobs, usually in service, factory, or construction work.

In 1997, there were 4.6 million immigrants in France who did not qualify for French nationality, including 3.4 million from Arab countries and 206,000 people from sub-Saharan Africa. Germany had 4.6 million foreigners, of whom 1.7 million were Turks. England, Switzerland, and the Scandinavian countries also had large numbers of foreign workers and their families. Most of the guest workers are from southern Europe, North Africa, and Turkey.

Figure 12.1 shows total employment for the member-nations of the Organization for Economic Cooperation and Development. Included in Figure 12.1 is a listing of the foreign labor force. In 1998, 11.7 percent of the total labor force in the United States consisted of foreign workers.

Guest workers provide the labor host countries need, which is desirable as long as the economies are growing. But when the economies slow, as they did during the mid-1970s, 1980s, and 1990s, fewer workers are needed and problems appear. Unemployment increases among the native workers, who then want the jobs held by guest workers. It is conveniently forgotten that the guest workers took jobs the natives would not do when times were good. To appease their citizens, some countries refused to renew the guest workers' permits. In other countries, where the work was seasonal, the guest workers were deported at the end of the season instead of being permitted to stay and take other work. The French, for example, paid surplus foreign workers 10,000 francs (about $1,500) as a "go home" bonus, and Germany offered "repatriation assistance"—equivalent to about $4,000, plus a lesser amount per child—for certain unemployed foreign workers to leave.

Labor Shortages

The beginning of the 21st century saw low unemployment in many industrialized nations, including the United States. Figure 12.2 shows that the unemployment rate in the United States is less than 5 percent, which is the lowest rate in recent history. In order to meet their staffing requirements, many companies are resorting to unique avenues

[Figure 12.1] Employment

	Total labor force				Civilian employment										
	Thousands 1998	Change 1998/88 %	Female participation rate[1] (%)		Total thousands 1998	Change 1998/88 (%)	Agriculture, forestry, and fishing (%)		Industry (%)		Services (%)		Foreign labor force (% of total labor force)		
			1998	1988			1998	1988	1998	1988	1998	1988	1998	1988	
Australia	9 399	18.0	65.0	59.1	8 596	16.9	4.8	5.8	21.9	26.4	73.3	67.8	24.8[b]	25.7[b,f]	Australia
Austria	3 888	13.3	61.9	53.7	3 689	11.4	6.6	8.1	31.8	37.4	61.7	54.5	9.9	5.4	Austria
Belgium	4 350	5.4	57.8	51.2	3 720	3.0	2.4	2.8	26.0	28.3	71.5	68.9	8.8	7.2[g]	Belgium
Canada	15 692	12.3	69.4	69.1	14 326	11.8	3.7	4.4	22.4	25.8	73.9	69.8	19.2[b,c]	18.5[b,f]	Canada
Czech Republic	5 565	—	69.2	—	5 156	−1.8	5.5	12.0	41.3	47.4	53.1	40.7	—	—	Czech Republic
Denmark	2 848	−1.1	75.3	77.6	2 658	−0.1	3.6	5.8	27.0	27.2	69.4	67.1	3.2[d]	2.2	Denmark
Finland	2 532	−1.6	69.9	73.0	2 213	−8.6	6.5	9.8	27.7	30.6	65.7	59.6	—	—	Finland
France	25 869	5.4	60.2	57.1	22 382	4.0	4.4	6.6	25.2	30.3	70.4	63.3	6.1[d]	6.4	France
Germany	39 804	—	63.1	55.4[a]	35 715	—	2.8	4.0[a]	34.5	39.9[a]	62.6	56.0[a]	9.1[c]	7.0	Germany
Greece	4 446	12.2	—	43.5	3 967	8.5	17.7	26.6	23.0	27.2	59.2	46.2	—	—	Greece
Hungary	4 011	—	50.7	—	3 659	—	7.6	—	34.6	—	57.0	—	—	—	Hungary
Iceland	152	18.1	81.2	68.0	148	15.5	8.6	10.2	25.1	30.2	66.3	59.5	—	—	Iceland
Ireland	1 629	24.4	52.6	37.6	1 495	38.7	9.1	15.4	29.2	27.8	62.3	57.0	3.4[d]	2.7	Ireland
Italy	23 549	−2.9	45.0	43.2	20 157	−3.2	6.6	9.9	31.9	32.4	61.4	57.7	1.7[e]	1.3[f]	Italy
Japan	67 690	9.8	63.9	58.4	64 900	8.0	5.3	7.9	32.2	34.1	62.5	58.0	1.0	—	Japan
Korea	21 390	23.6	52.1	48.8	19 926	18.1	12.2	20.7	27.8	33.7	60.0	45.6	—	—	Korea

(Continued)

[Figure 12.1] **Employment** *(continued)*

	Total labor force				Civilian employment											
	Thousands 1998	Change 1998/88 %	Female participation rate[1] (%)		Total thousands 1998	Change 1998/88 (%)	Agriculture, forestry, and fishing (%)		Industry (%)		Services (%)		Foreign labor force (% of total labor force)		
			1998	1988			1998	1988	1998	1988	1998	1988	1998	1988	
Luxembourg	242	36.4	—	47.2	236	35.5	2.3	3.7	24.9	31.9	72.0	64.5	55.1[d]	39.9	Luxembourg
Mexico	38 244	—	42.8	—	37 137	—	19.4	—	24.7	—	55.9	—	—	—	Mexico
Netherlands	7 797	17.4	62.7	50.6	7 425	25.1	3.3	4.8	21.7	26.4	75.0	68.8	2.9	3.0	Netherlands
New Zealand	1 874	16.5	67.1	62.4	1 735	15.1	8.5	10.3	23.9	26.1	67.0	63.5	—	—	New Zealand
Norway	2 317	6.1	76.3	72.8	2 216	6.6	4.7	6.4	23.4	26.4	71.9	67.1	2.8[d]	2.3	Norway
Poland	17 285	—	59.8	—	15 354	—	19.2	—	32.1	—	48.8	—	—	—	Poland
Portugal	4 987	8.0	65.2	58.2	4 703	9.9	13.6	20.7	36.0	35.1	50.4	44.2	1.8[d]	1.0	Portugal
Spain	16 441	9.8	47.8	39.6	13 193	12.0	8.0	14.4	30.4	32.5	61.5	53.1	1.1[d]	0.4	Spain
Sweden	4 255	−4.8	72.6	80.1	3 979	−9.5	2.6	3.8	25.7	29.5	71.7	66.7	5.1	4.9	Sweden
Switzerland	3 995	10.1	70.3	58.0	3 848	6.7	4.6	5.5	26.2	33.8	69.1	57.1	17.5[d]	16.7	Switzerland
Turkey	23 013	15.7	30.9	37.0	21 084	18.7	42.3	46.5	22.8	22.3	34.9	31.2	—	—	Turkey
United Kingdom	28 944	2.4	67.2	63.7	27 009	5.5	1.7	2.3	26.5	33.0	71.8	65.1	3.9	3.4	United Kingdom
United States	138 897	12.6	71.3	67.1	131 463	14.3	2.7	2.9	23.6	26.9	73.7	70.2	11.7[b]	9.4[b,h]	United States
G7[2]	340 445	—	65.3	60.8	315 952	—	3.6	4.9	27.4	30.9	69.0	64.3	—	—	G7[2]
EU-15[2]	171 581	—	—	53.5	152 541	—	4.8	7.3	29.4	33.1	65.9	59.7	—	—	EU-15[2]
OECD Total[2]	521 104	—	—	—	482 090	—	7.8	—	27.3	—	64.9	—	—	—	OECD total[2]

Notes:

— not available
1. Defined as female labor force of all ages divided by female population age 15–64
2. Only data shown in this table are included in these totals.
a. Former West Germany only.
b. Foreign-born labor force.
c. 1996.
d. 1997.
e. 1995.
f. 1991.
g. 1989.
h. 1990.

Sources: *Labor Force Statistics: 1978–1998,* OECD, Paris, 1999; and *Trends in International Migration,* OECD, 2000.

[Figure 12.2] Unemployment Rate

	Ten-Year Averages 1982–91	Ten-Year Averages 1992–2001	1992	1993	1994	1995	1996	1997	1998	1999	2000	2001
Unemployment rate (*Percent*)												
Advanced economies	**7.0**	**6.7**	**7.1**	**7.5**	**7.4**	**7.0**	**7.0**	**6.8**	**6.7**	**6.3**	**5.9**	**5.7**
Major industrial countries	6.9	6.5	7.1	7.2	7.0	6.6	6.7	6.4	6.2	6.0	5.7	5.8
United States	7.0	5.4	7.5	6.9	6.1	5.6	5.4	4.9	4.5	4.2	4.1	4.4
Japan	2.5	3.7	2.2	2.5	2.9	3.1	3.3	3.4	4.1	4.7	5.0	5.3
Germany	7.3	8.1	6.3	7.6	8.2	7.9	8.6	9.5	9.0	8.3	7.9	7.6
France	9.5	11.2	10.3	11.6	12.3	11.7	12.4	12.5	11.7	11.3	9.8	8.8
Italy	10.5	11.1	10.7	10.1	11.1	11.6	11.6	11.7	11.8	11.4	10.7	10.1
United Kingdom	9.0	6.6	9.6	10.2	9.2	8.0	7.3	5.5	4.7	4.3	3.9	4.0
Canada	9.7	9.0	11.2	11.4	10.4	9.4	9.6	9.1	8.3	7.6	6.6	6.5
Other advanced economies	7.2	7.6	7.4	8.7	8.8	8.2	8.1	7.8	8.1	7.3	6.2	5.7
Spain	18.6	19.2	18.4	22.7	24.2	22.9	22.2	20.8	18.8	15.9	14.0	12.6
Netherlands	8.2	5.0	5.4	6.5	7.6	7.1	6.6	5.5	4.1	3.2	2.3	2.0
Belgium	9.4	8.9	7.3	8.8	10.0	9.9	9.7	9.4	9.5	9.0	8.3	7.7
Sweden	2.5	6.6	5.3	8.2	8.0	7.7	8.1	8.0	6.5	5.6	4.6	4.0
Austria	3.4	4.0	3.4	4.0	3.8	3.9	4.3	4.4	4.7	4.4	3.5	3.5
Denmark	9.2	8.4	10.9	12.0	11.9	10.1	8.6	7.8	6.4	5.6	5.4	5.5
Finland	4.9	12.6	11.7	16.4	16.6	15.4	14.6	12.6	11.4	10.3	9.0	8.2
Greece	7.6	10.2	8.7	9.7	9.6	9.1	9.8	9.7	10.8	11.7	11.5	11.3
Portugal	7.0	5.5	4.1	5.5	6.8	7.2	7.3	6.7	5.0	4.4	4.1	4.0
Ireland	15.1	9.9	15.2	15.5	14.1	12.1	11.5	9.8	7.4	5.6	4.5	4.0
Luxembourg	1.5	2.7	1.6	2.1	2.7	3.0	3.3	3.3	3.3	2.9	2.7	2.3
Switzerland	0.7	3.6	2.6	4.5	4.7	4.2	4.7	5.2	3.9	2.7	2.0	1.9
Norway	3.4	4.2	5.9	5.9	5.4	4.7	4.1	3.3	2.4	3.2	3.6	3.6
Israel	7.1	8.4	11.2	10.0	7.8	6.9	6.7	7.7	8.5	8.9	8.4	8.2
Iceland	1.1	3.3	3.0	4.4	4.8	5.0	4.3	2.8	2.9	1.9	1.8	1.8
Korea	3.3	3.5	2.4	2.8	2.4	2.0	2.0	2.6	6.8	6.3	4.2	3.5
Australia	8.1	8.6	10.8	10.9	9.8	8.5	8.6	8.6	8.0	7.2	6.7	6.6
Taiwan Province of China	2.1	2.2	1.5	1.5	1.6	1.8	2.6	2.7	2.7	2.9	2.5	2.3
Hong Kong SAR	2.5	3.2	2.0	2.0	1.9	3.2	2.8	2.2	4.7	6.1	4.0	3.1
Singapore	3.3	2.7	2.7	2.7	2.6	2.7	2.0	1.8	3.2	3.5	2.9	2.5
New Zealand	6.0	7.4	10.3	9.5	8.2	6.3	6.1	6.7	7.5	6.8	6.4	6.4
Memorandum												
Industrial countries	7.3	7.1	7.5	8.0	7.9	7.4	7.4	7.1	6.8	6.4	6.0	6.0
European Union	9.3	9.6	9.3	10.6	11.0	10.5	10.6	10.3	9.5	8.8	8.0	7.5
Euro area	9.7	10.4	9.4	10.8	11.6	11.2	11.5	11.5	10.8	9.9	9.0	8.3
Newly industrialized Asian economies	2.9	3.1	2.1	2.4	2.2	2.1	2.2	2.6	5.4	5.2	3.7	3.1

Source: From *World Economic Outlook,* IMF, September 2000, p. 278. Reprinted with permission.

to reach potential employees. Marriott sent recruiters into laundromats, bus terminals, and senior centers in southern California in an attempt to find employees for its hotels. The Walt Disney Company asked annual Disneyland pass holders if they knew anyone who wanted to work.[9]

At the same time, many are seeking ways to deal with the shortage of high-tech workers. As was mentioned above, the United States recently substantially increased the number of visas available to bring more high-skill workers into the U.S. work force. A congressional commission also investigated the problem and came to several conclusions. The commission estimated that the shortage of high-tech workers costs the United States $3 billion to $4 billion a year. One suggestion of the commission was to require that more women, minority group members, and people with disabilities be allowed to join the high-tech work force. The commission concluded that if the high-tech work force attracted the same number of women as men, there would be no shortage of high-tech workers.[10]

[Worldview] Guest Workers in Japan?

Japan does not have guest workers in the European sense, where they are legal. In Japan, they are illegal. Coming mostly from the Philippines, Bangladesh, and Pakistan, they commonly enter Japan with tourist visas, often on false passports, find jobs, and stay.

The law only prohibits migrant laborers from working in Japan; it does not prohibit employers from hiring them. So clandestine workers in Japan have no legal rights. They cannot force employers to pay fair wages or appeal to the police for help.

A Japan Labor Ministry survey showed that on average they earn less than half the wages of their Japanese coworkers. Firms save even more on labor costs because illegal workers do not receive the insurance or other benefits usually demanded by Japanese employees. These non-Japanese laborers work on average 60 to 70 hours a week in small factories, the fast-food industry, or construction.

Just as European contractors did in the 1970s, Japan's contractors and smaller manufacturers have begun to depend on cheap foreign labor to offset rising costs associated with the yen's appreciation. Even at much higher legal wages and benefits, there is a severe shortage of Japanese laborers who are willing to perform the dangerous or dirty work done by the illegals.

The situation is particularly dangerous for young women employed in the bars and massage parlors of Japan's ubiquitous "entertainment industry." As frequently happens, young women come to Japan expecting to work as waitresses or hotel clerks, but exploitative business owners take their passports away and force them to work as prostitutes.

Japan historically has relied heavily on foreign workers to fill labor shortages, but it is far from a melting pot. Thousands of Koreans and Chinese were forcibly recruited during World War II to work in factories and mines. Most of the 660,000 people of Korean and Chinese ancestry who remain in Japan are virtually indistinguishable from their Japanese neighbors. Nevertheless, they are still classified as "resident aliens" and must carry alien registration cards. ■

Source: Republished with permission of *The Asian Wall Street Journal.* From *The Asian Wall Street Journal,* December 8, 1977. p. 10. Permission conveyed through Copyright Clearance Center.

Composition of the Labor Force

When refugees flow into a country, the resulting growth of the labor force includes whatever ages, genders, and skills are able to get in. They are not coming for specific jobs; they are fleeing oppression or poverty. At the outset, the refugees may cause problems for the host country, which must try to feed, clothe, educate, and find work for them.

Some, for various reasons, remain burdens on the host country or on international refugee relief agencies. Others find more peaceful surroundings, adapt relatively quickly, and become upwardly mobile in their new society. This holds true for many of the Cuban refugees in the United States. Many believe the rehabilitation and growth of downtown Miami owe much to the Cubans' influence and work.[11]

Immigrants are said to have saved New York City, which absorbed some 113,000 of them a year during the 1990s. "This city was dying in the 1970s," says Peter D. Salins, a senior fellow at the Manhattan Institute, and demographers credit immigrants with turning around a potentially catastrophic population drain.[12]

At the end of the 20th century, New York was soaking up immigrants at nearly the same torrid pace it maintained at the beginning of the century. Instead of Italians, it's Dominicans. Instead of Irish, it's Mexicans. Instead of Russians and Poles, well, in fact, it's a new generation of Russians and Poles.[13]

labor force composition
The mix of people available to work, in terms of age, skill, gender, race, and religion

Labor Force Composition and Comparative Productivity

Another change in **labor force composition** in the United States began in the mid-1970s. The percentage of adult women in the American labor force increased by some

section [3]

10 percent during the 1970s. The increase continued, reaching 73 percent in 1989, when it ended. One reason given for the end was the disillusionment of many two-income couples with their stressful lifestyles. When interest rates dropped in the early 1990s, many seized the opportunity to refinance their mortgages and used the extra cash to work less rather than consume more.[14]

The size of the total U.S. labor force increased by 36.1 million workers between 1974 and 1997. A unique feature of U.S. labor force growth—female and male—is that many of the new workers are immigrants who speak little, if any, English in addition to being unskilled. This growth and heterogeneity of the U.S. labor force made an increase in **labor productivity** difficult but not impossible.

labor productivity
Measures how many acceptable units of a product are produced by a worker during a given time and the cost per unit

In fact, a 1995 study showed that the United States was the leader among the big economies in labor productivity in manufacturing as measured by value added per hour worked. The study compared other countries with the United States at 100. The nearest country was the Netherlands at 97, with Sweden third at 90. Australia was at the bottom of the list at 52.[15]

Unit labor costs rose for many years and then declined. This decline did not result from reduced wages or employment but from increased productivity.[16]

unit labor costs
The cost in labor to produce one unit of output

Although productivity has grown in most countries in the Organization for Economic Cooperation and Development (OECD), U.S. productivity is nonetheless still well above the European and Japanese averages, even in manufacturing. U.S. labor costs in manufacturing are currently some 30 percent below those of foreign competitors.

Human capital has been a major contributor to economic growth in the United States. Up to a quarter of income growth per worker since World War II can be attributed to better education. Although other OECD countries have also made major gains, educational attainment as a whole in the United States remains higher than it is elsewhere.

Figure 12.3 shows the percentage of working-age people who are employed in several industrialized countries. Figure 12.4 shows the annual increase in productivity in terms of output per hour in manufacturing. According to Figure 12.4, the United States

[Figure 12.3] **World of Work: Employment as Percentage of Working-Age Population, 1998**

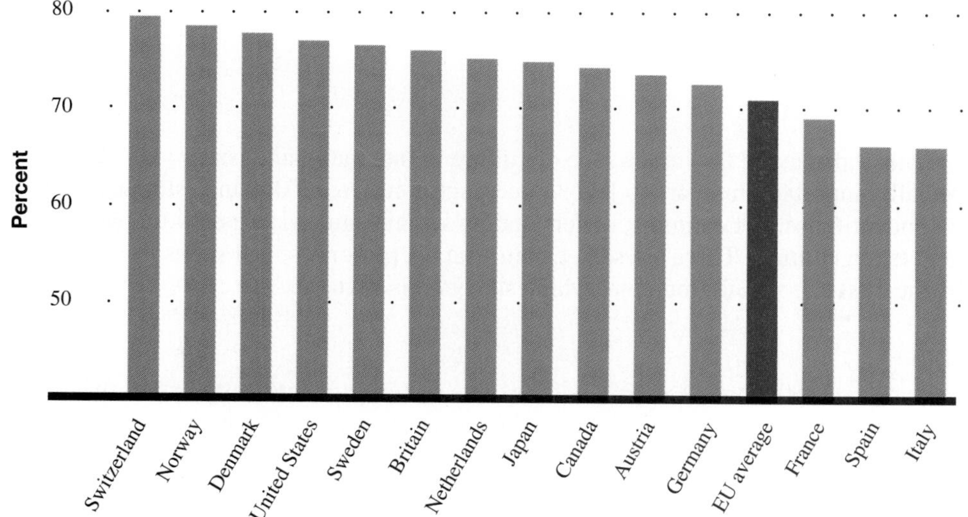

Source: From *The Economist,* March 23, 2000. © 2000 The Economist Newspaper Group, Inc. Reprinted with permission. Further reproduction prohibited. www.economist.com

[Figure 12.4] Productivity: Output Per Hour in Manufacturing

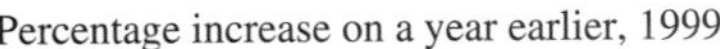

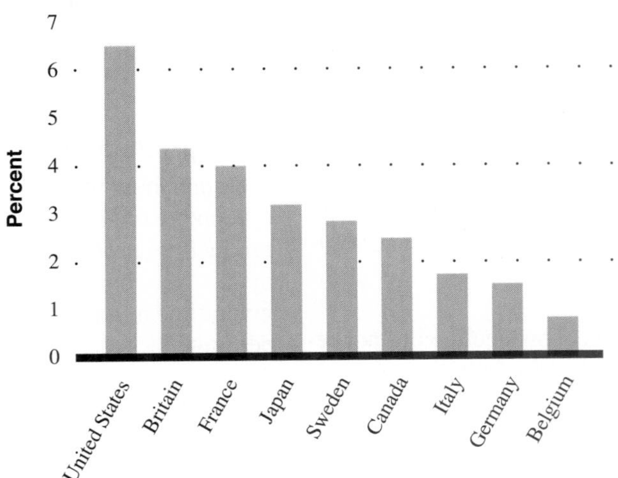

Productivity America led other rich countries in the rise in manufacturing productivity in 1999. According to preliminary data from the Bureau of Labor Statistics, American labor productivity increased by 6.2% over a year earlier. The countries with the next-biggest rises were Britain and France. Belgium came last in our table with an increase of 0.7%. In Canada, Italy, and Japan, productivity grew in 1999 after declines in 1998. Britain, France, and Sweden showed better gains in 1999 than in 1998, but productivity growth in Belgium and Germany decelerated. This seems to support the common complaint of European economists that their countries have failed to reap productivity gains from the Internet. Hours worked in manufacturing declined between 1979 and 1999 in all countries for which data were available except Canada, where hours rose at an average annual rate of 0.3%.

Source: From *The Economist,* November 18, 2000, p. 122. © 2000 The Economist Newspaper Group, Inc. Reprinted with permission. Further reproduction prohibited. www.economist.com

led other industrialized countries in the rise in productivity in 1999. *The Economist* notes that many European economists believe that Europeans have failed to reap productivity gains from the Internet.

Research and Development (R&D)

More efficient tools and machines result from more extensive and effective R&D. The R&D a company can do depends on its management policies, how many after-tax dollars are available, and whether R&D can be deducted as a pretax expense. Governments do a great deal of R&D, which can also boost productivity. A nation's tax policies can influence how much money is available to private business for R&D. They can also make immense differences in the amount available to private business to buy new plant, tools, and machines.

Social Status, Sexism, Racism, Traditional Society, or Minorities: Considerations in Employment Policies

Social Status

Chapter 9 discussed the importance of culture to international business. Culture is especially important in regard to labor forces, since culture so dominates human behavior and attitudes. For example, understanding social status is necessary to understanding certain cultures. There are societies in which a person's social status is established by the **caste** or social group into which she or he is born.

India

India presents an extreme example of the caste system, and intercaste battles that cause fatalities and home burnings still occur between upper-caste Hindus and the untouchables, whom Mahatma Gandhi called *harijans,* the children of God. Obviously, a would-be employer must tread carefully when both upper-caste Hindus and harijans are in the employee pool.

Caste remains a pervasive fact in India, which is a very populous country of growing importance in the world. Thus, we should give some more facts about caste. At the top is the Brahmin (priest, teacher), followed by the Kshatriya (variously landholder, warrior, or ruler). At the third level is the bania (businessman), which is a step above the shudra (laborer).

caste

A system under which people's place or level in a multilevel society is established at birth to be the same level or caste as that of their parents

The top three are considered upper caste, which includes 15 percent of India's population and has ruled the country for 3,000 years. Another 50 percent of the population belongs to the laboring, or shudra, caste. Roughly 20 percent are casteless or untouchables considered beyond the pale of Hindu society. The remaining 15 percent belong to other religions—11 percent are Muslim, and the others are Buddhists, Christians, Parsis, and Sikhs.

Caste rules are rigid, and those who deviate from them are shunned. Caste divides Indian society into groups whose members do not intermarry and usually will not eat with each other.

Change is occurring. The young, including the children of the brahmins and kshatriya, no longer view the civil service as the career of choice. They all want to get an MBA and go into business; money rather than power is what motivates young people.[17]

Another change is the conversion of Hindus to other religions to escape their low caste or untouchable status. The untouchables now call themselves dalits, and one champion of the dalit cause was Dr. B. R. Ambedkar, who converted thousands to Buddhism. In 1997, riots broke out in Mumbai (Bombay) and other cities in the states of Maharashtra and Gujarat in the course of which 11 dalits were killed by police. The riots were an expression of fury because a garland of shoes was hung around the neck of a statue of Dr. Ambedkar. Shoes are considered unclean in the subcontinent, and there are few insults worse than a string of dirty sandals hung around the neck.[18]

Great Britain

Some say that the class system in Great Britain is eroding, but people there are still classified by the accents they acquire at home and school. When Margaret Thatcher was elected prime minister, commentators saw fit to point out that she was "only" the daughter of a small-store owner even though her accent was "upper class," apparently acquired at Oxford University. Although class differences do not cause riots in Britain, as caste differences do in India, a foreign employer should nevertheless be conscious of the possibilities for friction arising from those differences.

Japan

In Japan, there remains an odd caste holdover from the 17th century, when the feudal Togugawa regime imposed a rigid social pecking order on the country. The warrior-administrator samurai were at the top. Below them were farmers and artisans, then merchants, and, at the very bottom, those with occupations considered dirty and distasteful, such as slaughterers, butchers, and tanners.

As in India, where discrimination against untouchables is illegal, all natives of Japan who are of the Japanese race are legally equal. However, the descendants of the lowest Japanese class remain trapped in their ghettos, working in small family firms that produce knitted garments, bamboo wares, fur and leather goods, shoes, and sandals. They call themselves *burakumin* (ghetto people) and claim they number about 3 million people living in some 6,000 ghettos. Their average income is far below that of other Japanese.

The word *burakumin* is almost never aired in the Japanese media, and foreign books that touch on the problem have all references to it deleted when they are translated into Japanese. One woman, although she was not a burakumin, lived near one of their ghettos and recorded and decried its residents' plight in speeches, articles, and a series of stories. Her name was Sue Sumii, and she died in 1997 at the age of 95. Her sad saga tells of the trials of a family of sandal makers: the poverty, the taunts, the shame of trying to buy food when shopkeepers would not touch coins that had been handled by a burakumin.

In one of her stories, when fire breaks out in their village, the neighbors stand around remarking how a burakumin fire stinks instead of helping to put out the fire. In a real-life reflection of Ms. Sumii's story, the areas worst hit by the fires that followed the Kobe earthquake of 1995 were the narrow streets and wooden shacks where the burakumin lived. Local people claimed that the firefighters doused their flames last.

[Worldview]

Sexism in Japan

In Japan, nearly 600 colleges have special courses for women. These courses teach women to be perfect "office ladies." Such women never wear jeans, drink alcohol, or smoke. They should be able to answer with a firm yes to 15 basic questions, including "When asked to do something, do you respond with a smile and 'certainly'?" and "Is your back straight?"

The colleges look ahead to the time when each student, with a smile and a straight back, will aim to be a "good wife and wise mother." She should provide comfort for her husband and school-age sons. In periods of high economic growth and labor shortages, she should be prepared to return to work, but she should gracefully accept being laid off in a recession.

Women make up only 6.7 percent of Japanese business executives. One reason is tradition, a burden for female executives in most countries. A second reason is after-hours social sessions, which are common in most countries but even more prevalent in Japan. Much of Japanese consensus decision making is accomplished during these sessions, which primarily involve drinking and talking. Female managers tend to consider them a waste of time and are somewhat uncomfortable with the behavior of their male counterparts as their inhibitions disappear. The drinking is often very heavy, and drunkenness is not considered a disgrace. Intoxicated individuals are delivered carefully home.

The discomfort goes both ways. One man in computer sales, talking about after-hours drinking sessions with his female section chief, complained, "I don't know what to talk about with her. She's not married, so I must avoid any remarks with sexual connotations. With a man, I could have a drink and talk about anything." ■

Source: From *The Economist*, June 7, 1997, p. 88. www.economist.com.

Ms. Sumii made links between the Japanese imperial family's wealth and burakumin wretchedness and between the shared religious roots of emperor worship and scorn for the burakumin. By one account, when Ms. Sumii was six, the Emperor Mejii visited the village where she lived. After he left, the villagers scrambled for souvenirs, cigarette butts adorned with the imperial seal, anything that the god-king might have touched. She spent most of her adult life exposing the fallacy of Japan's class system and inspiring sympathy for its most despised victims, the burakumin.[19]

Sexism

Acceptability of women as full participants in the work force ranges from improving acceptability in the United States and Western Europe to almost no acceptability in many countries. While sexism is far from having been eliminated, the United States has seen large strides in the status and acceptability of women in business. In other countries, however, laws, customs, attitudes, and religious beliefs continue to act as extremely hostile barriers to women in business. Sexism, the denial of equal participation in a society for women, developed as an inherent part of many cultures as they evolved as patriarchal societies. Greater awareness of the importance of providing equal opportunity for both genders and changing attitudes toward the roles of women in society in general and business in particular have made it easier for women to succeed in business in many parts of the world. Culture and tradition, though, continue to make it difficult for women in many countries.

Japan (see the Worldview) is not the only country where women are encountering major problems in making or retaining progress, as sexism is widespread throughout the world. In Pakistan, for example, one step forward has been accompanied by several steps backward. Women were banned from taking part in public sporting events in that country. A Pakistani federal court decision allowed women to serve as judges, but court procedures were changed to make the word of one male witness equal to that of two women. When women in Lahore protested this devaluation of their legal personalities, police responded with brutality, injuring thirteen.

[Figure 12.5] Women in the U.S. Labor Force

46.5%	of U.S. labor force
49.5%	of managerial and professional specialty positions
12.5%	of corporate officers
11.7%	of boards of directors
6.2%	of highest titles
4.1%	of top earners
2	of Fortune 500 CEOs (Hewlett-Packard's Carly Fiorina, Avon's Andrea Jung)

Source: From *Catalyst 2000 Census of Women Corporate Officers and Top Earners of the Fortune 500.*

It is often difficult for women to do business in Saudi Arabia and other Middle Eastern countries. For example, the law in Saudi Arabia specifically prohibits the commingling of men and women in the workplace. Women are not allowed to drive vehicles in that country.

Other backward steps in Pakistan are proposals to deny women the vote, deny them the right to drive a car (as in Saudi Arabia), and impose the death penalty for women working as prostitutes (but not for their male customers). Pakistan receives financial assistance from Saudi Arabia, and that aid is believed to strongly influence Pakistani policies. Saudi Arabian society strictly separates the sexes in education and business, and its influence is being felt in Pakistan. Segregated schools for Pakistani women are being established. An indication of what these segregated schools for women teach is provided by one college, which has banned women from physics and mathematics and has channeled them into a new course, called household accounts, instead.

In Korea, women cannot participate in rites held in memory of their own or their husbands' ancestors. They are expected, however, to prepare the food and drinks on such occasions. Many Korean shop owners are upset when a woman is the first customer of the day because they believe it is a bad omen for the day's business. Shop owners typically throw salt on the doorway after the customer leaves.

In 1997, the group known as the Taliban seized control in Afghanistan, resulting in extreme oppression of women. The Taliban forced a bank out of the country because it lent money to poor women to set up businesses. The Taliban accused the bank of "promoting shamelessness among Afghan women" and also of encouraging women to leave their husbands. In Taliban-controlled areas, women are not allowed out of the house without being accompanied by a man, and girls' schools have been closed.[20]

Even in countries where women have made some strides, their progress is not necessarily secure. When the fundamentalist Islamic government took control from the shah in Iran in 1979, it separated the sexes, ordering women to return to their strict traditional dress and roles. In recent years, women have regained some opportunities, but Iran remains a society with rigid gender roles. Even in the United States today, women have made great advancements yet continue to face discrimination, especially in advancing into the higher levels of business management. As is indicated in Figure 12.5, even though women make up 46.5 percent of the U.S. labor force, they hold a relatively small percentage of senior positions in the Fortune 500 companies.

Women's Education

Studies show a persistent correlation between the length of women's schooling and birthrates, child survival, family health, and a nation's overall prosperity. One study ranked countries by the extent of the schooling their girls received. At the top of the scale was France, where almost all girls attend secondary school and women average more than 11 years of formal education. At the bottom was Chad, a poverty-stricken African country where women have on average less than a month of schooling.[21]

Very low levels of education are almost always present in societies in which girls and young women are forced into prostitution or otherwise brutalized at a young age

[Figure 12.6] Unemployment Rates: Percent of Total Labor Force, 1998

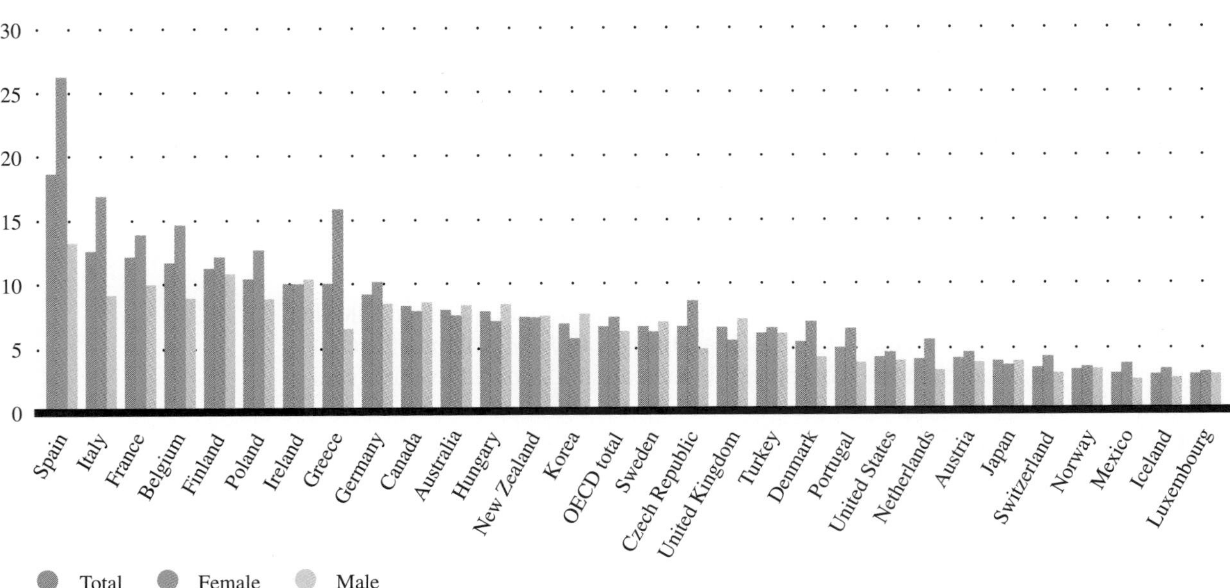

Source: From www.oecd.org/publications/figures. Reprinted with permission of OECD Washington.

by techniques such as female genital mutilation. The World Health Organization, a United Nations (UN) agency, says that people in these societies believe that they are doing the right thing for their daughters by subjecting them to genital mutilation and do not see the link between the genital mutilation of a young girl and the pain, infections, ill health, and possible death she may suffer.[22]

An increasing number of countries are realizing the importance of educating girls. The Egyptian government is integrating a successful concept of girl-friendly community schools into the formal education system. These schools use female teachers, active learning, and child-centered class management. In one region of China, villages and households that send girls to school are given priority for loans or development funds. And a promising initiative in Tanzania aims to find solutions to obstacles to the social and academic development of girls by encouraging girls to speak out about their problems.[23]

Problems Persist

As is indicated in Figure 12.6, in almost every OECD country the unemployment rate for women is higher than the rate for men. Figure 12.7 shows women still earn substantially less than men, ranging from 42 percent less in Korea to 10 percent less in Belgium.

Opportunities for Women in International Business

As in many areas, opportunities abroad are increasing for women. Progress is slow, though. According to a study conducted by Catalyst (see the Worldview), over 65 percent of human resources executives see international opportunities for white women as having increased somewhat or greatly from 1995 to 2000. Less than half, though, report similar progress for women of color.[24]

Since many now view international assignments as necessary for advancement, it is increasingly becoming important for women to accept international positions.

[Figure 12.7] **Female Wage Gap: Difference Between Female and Male Full-Time Earnings**

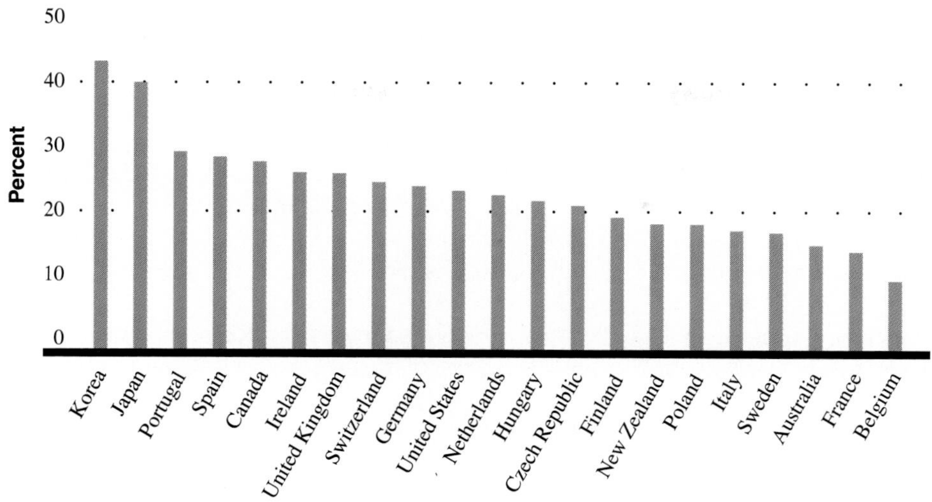

Source: From *OECD in Figures,* 1999, p. 83. Reprinted with permission of OECD Washington.

Some companies are better at providing opportunities than others are. *Working Woman* magazine cited Philip Morris as a company where 31 percent of all managers are women. With respect to international assignments, Philip Morris makes sure that women are tapped for those assignments. The chair, president, and CEO of Hewlett-Packard is Carly Fiorina. She makes Hewlett-Packard one of only two companies in the Fortune 500 with a woman as chair, president, and CEO. Hewlett-Packard, which has a strong international presence, has a long history of supporting and promoting women. For example, since Ms. Fiorina's arrival, Hewlett-Packard has gone through a restructuring. Five of the eight members of the executive committee are women.[25]

Racism

Unfortunately, examples of racial conflicts and discrimination are found worldwide. There have been black-versus-white conflicts in such places as the United States, South Africa, and Great Britain and Arab-, Indian-, or Pakistani-versus-black conflicts in Africa. Racial friction has existed because of the situation of guest workers in parts of Europe. There has been bloody conflict in Sri Lanka between Tamils and Sinhalese.

In another part of the world, Japan has come under increasing criticism for its laws denying Japanese citizenship to anyone not of the Japanese race. The largest alien group affected is the Koreans, many of whom were brought to Japan as workers when Japan occupied Korea. Now the second- and third-generation descendants of those Koreans, all of whom were born in Japan, with Japanese as their native tongue, are still considered aliens and not granted the rights and privileges of Japanese citizenship. The relatively few Vietnamese refugees permitted into Japan are beginning to feel the same racial discrimination.

Things seem to be changing for the better for Koreans in Japan as they no longer must be fingerprinted as aliens, and some local authorities, though not yet the central government, now employ Koreans. More than 80 percent of these Koreans marry Japanese, and their children are automatically Japanese. Naturalization is possible, and a growing number of Koreans are taking that route to Japanese citizenship. But a diehard, mostly pro–North Korean minority clings to Korean ways, for example, by sending their children to Korean schools dressed in traditional Korean costume.[26]

[Worldview]

U.S. Women in the Global Arena

Catalyst, a nonprofit research and advisory organization that is working to advance women in business, commissioned a study concerning U.S. women in global business.

Misconceptions about women's ability to handle international assignments and willingness to accept those assignments are key barriers to women getting selected for the global business arena. While women represent 49 percent of all managers and professionals in the United States, only 13 percent of the American managers sent abroad are women.

Survey respondents believe that women are not as "internationally mobile" as men, yet 80 percent of female expatriates have never turned down a relocation, compared to 71 percent of men. A second powerful assumption is that women encounter more work-life conflict while managing a global schedule. However, nearly half of both women and men report that they find work-life balance difficult. Finally, survey respondents believe clients outside the United States are not as comfortable doing business with women as they are with men. In fact, 76 percent of women expatriates said being a woman had a positive or neutral impact on their effectiveness overseas.

Both women and men, managers and human resources executives hold the preconceptions that emerged in this study about women's ability in the international arena. Yet paradoxically, 90 percent of female expatriates, 91 percent of women with global responsibility who haven't relocated, and 93 percent of men married to expatriates said they would accept their current assignments again. In fact, current expatriates (85 percent) and former expatriates (86 percent) believe global experience makes them more marketable to other companies.

The majority of human resources executives said they are experiencing a shortage of global managers. Almost half of all these executives said developing global talent is now a high priority at their organizations, and 80 percent agree that it will be a high priority within the next five years. Despite a need for more global managers, U.S. companies barely tap their pool of qualified women.

"The bottom line is that these stereotypes—one on top of the other—make it less likely that decision makers are going to think of women managers when they build executive global teams," said Sheila Wellington, president of Catalyst. "This is destructive because as it turns out, women want these assignments, they do well abroad, and . . . they would seize the opportunity again." ■

Source: From Catalyst, *Passport to Opportunity: U.S. Women in Global Business,* October 2000.

Discrimination against minorities has occurred in other countries as well. In Uganda, for example, the government seized the property, shops, and land of people of Indian or Pakistani heritage, drove them out, and turned the seized assets over to native Ugandan citizens.

Minorities

traditional societies
Tribal, nomadic states of people before they turn to organized agriculture or industry

minorities
Usually a relatively smaller number of people identified by race, religion, or national origin who live among a larger number of different people

Traditional societies sometimes present opportunities along with problems for employers. There are societies in which merchants, businesspeople, and bankers are looked down on and people prefer political, religious, military, professional, or agricultural careers. In such societies, outsiders may dominate commercial and banking activities. Some examples are the Indians and Pakistanis in East Africa, the Chinese in Southeast Asia, and the Greeks in Turkey.

An advantage for a foreign employer moving into these societies is that such **minorities** may be immediately available, bringing financial and managerial skills to the employer. They speak the local language and usually one or more others, and they are less nationalistic than the majority.

A disadvantage is that such people are often unpopular with the majority local population. The foreign employers can easily become too dependent on minority employees, thus becoming isolated and insulated from the real world of the majority.

[Figure 12.10] Labor Costs

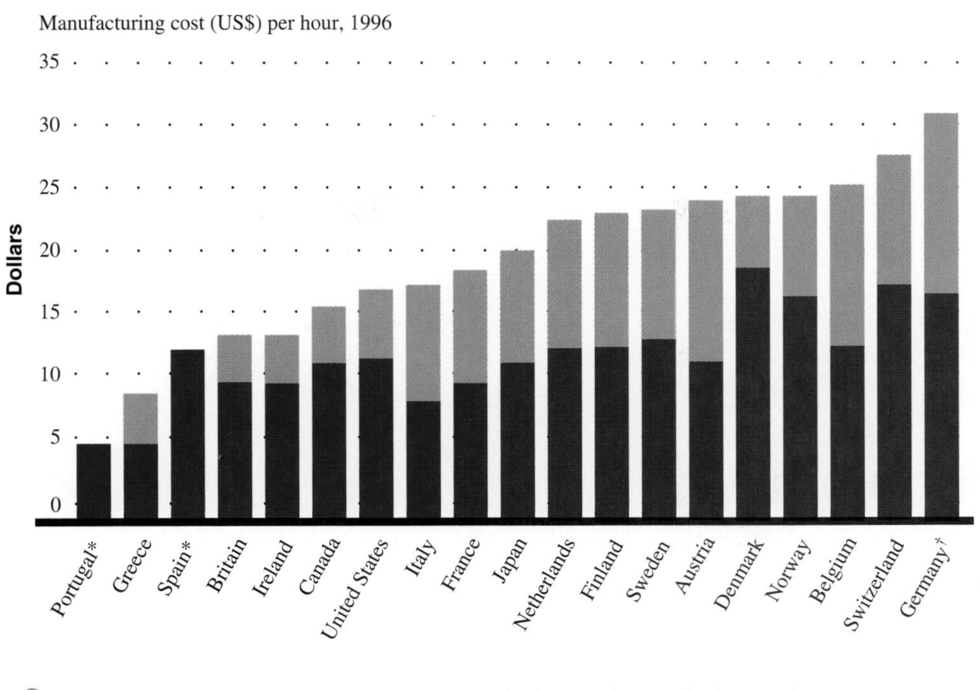

Source: From *The Economist,* May 24, 1997, p. 104. © The Economist Newspaper Group, Inc. Reprinted with permission. Further reproduction prohibited. www.economist.com

within the EU, between France, Germany, and Spain on the high end and the United Kingdom and the Netherlands much lower. Between 1970 and 1994, the EU created about 7 million jobs in the government sector while losing about 1 million in the private sector. During the same period, jobs in the North American government sectors grew by some 8 million while private-sector jobs increased by about 40 million.

The EU unemployment rate is about 9.2 percent compared to 4.2 percent in the United States and 7.6 percent in Canada. In Europe, more than 40 percent of the unemployed have been out of work for more than a year; that figure is 11 percent in the United States.

Young people fare poorly in the job markets. In Spain, almost half of those under 24 are out of work. In Italy and France, the proportion is greater than one in four.[36] One article about French unemployed youth speaks of a "generation in crisis; the young people of France are in despair, casualties of an economy that has failed them."[37]

The United Kingdom's unemployment rate is 6.1 percent, much lower than France's 11.3 percent. The wave of free-market change ushered in by Prime Minister Margaret Thatcher in the 1980s and continued by her successors, including the Labor government voted in in 1996, created a business-friendly climate in Britain, which lured many foreign companies.

It is safer to expand in Britain than on the continent because if the economy slows, companies can cut their work forces without going through the long layoff processes of France and Germany. And while employees are working, it costs the employer about $19 an hour in Britain compared with $30 in France and $37 in Germany.[38]

Companies in France and Germany complain that there is too little flexibility and too much government regulation. Berlin is undergoing a large-scale construction boom and, despite high unemployment in Germany, has 190,000 building workers from other EU countries and probably an equal number of black market workers. These workers are not only cheaper than Germans; they are also, according to building contractors, faster and more flexible, working as self-employed laborers or helping out across demarcation lines when necessary—things that German labor union practice forbids.

Relaxation of government regulation helps. A spurt of new jobs followed the limited liberalization in 1996 of shop-opening hours. Germany's bakeries, which are now allowed to open on Sunday mornings, announced in 1997 that they had employed 5,000 new workers in the past six months. Permitting the creation of private employment agencies has helped the unemployed find work.[39]

[Summary]

Recognize forces beyond management control that affect the availability of labor.

Labor quality and labor quantity are beyond a company's control. There are a finite number of employees available in any labor pool with the skills required to meet an employer's needs.

Understand the reasons that cause people to leave their home countries.

In many parts of the world, wars, revolutions, racial and ethnic battles, and political repression cause people to flee. Others go to other countries in hopes of better jobs and pay.

Discuss guest workers.

Guest workers move to a host country to perform specific types of jobs, usually in service, factory, or construction work. But when a country's economy slows, its native workers may want the jobs held by guest workers. In addition, racial friction has developed in some countries because of guest workers.

Understand the principles underlying the immigration system in the United States.

The United States admits people from throughout the world as immigrants (permanent) and nonimmigrants (temporary). Many come to the United States for employment, while others come to the United States to be reunited with family members. The United States also grants asylum to those fleeing persecution.

Understand how high technology is influencing workers and the workplace.

As high technology becomes more and more important, many companies in the United States are seeking workers from other countries to meet their staffing demands. Technology not only is creating new employment opportunities, it also is making it easier for people taking these positions to stay in touch with those back home.

Explain how the composition of a country's labor force affects productivity.

Workers may come with or without skills and abilities. The better they are, the more productive they can be.

Name other forces that affect productivity.

Productivity is affected by several forces other than workers' skills. Greater resources invested in research and development usually result in better capital equipment for workers. A country's tax policies can also influence how much money is available for R&D and other investments.

Understand women's positions in labor forces.

Since the mid-1970s, more and more women have entered the work force in most industrialized countries. Because of obstacles such as discrimination and changes in lifestyles, the growth of their numbers slowed in the 1990s. But acceptability of women in the work force is virtually nil in many other countries.

Discuss differences in labor unions from country to country.

Historically, labor unions have tended to be more political in Europe and more pragmatic in the United States, but developments during the 1990s and into the 21st century have shown much more political activism in U.S. unions. Unions have been losing membership in most of the developed countries.

Understand how labor is getting a voice in management.

Labor participation in management has grown in Europe, Japan, and, later, the United States. Industrial democracy and worker participation have recently spread in the United States. This has involved labor–management cooperation, in some instances including union officials as members of companies' boards of directors.

[Key Words]

labor quality (p. 406)
labor quantity (p. 406)
labor mobility (p. 406)
naturalization (p. 407)
refugees/asylum seekers (p. 408)
guest workers (p. 410)
labor force composition (p. 414)
labor productivity (p. 415)
unit labor costs (p. 415)
caste (p. 416)
traditional societies (p. 422)
minorities (p. 422)
labor market (p. 423)
labor unions (p. 424)
codetermination (p. 428)
works councils (p. 428)

[Questions]

1. a. How could an excess of qualified employees be beneficial for an employer?
   b. How could it be detrimental?
2. Classical economists assumed the labor factor of production to be immobile. Is this assumption correct in the modern world? Explain.
3. What are some differences between guest workers and refugees?
4. What are the reasons why people from all over the world come to the United States for temporary or permanent stays?
5. What is the effect on productivity of the influx into the work force of inexperienced, unskilled workers?

6. What effects do the levels of a country's research and development have on its relative competitiveness?
7. In several Southeast Asian and South Pacific countries, the Chinese minority is prominent in banking, finance, and business. What are the dangers for a foreign employer staffing the local company primarily with such a minority?
8. What is a major difference between unions in Europe, the United States, and Japan?
9. Unemployment rates are lower in the United Kingdom and the United States than they are in France and Germany. What are some reasons for this difference?
10. What are the prospects for effective multinational union collaboration? Discuss.
11. What are works councils?

[Internet Exercises]

Using the Internet

1. Governments around the world often get heavily involved in labor and employment issues. Using the Internet, find information on ministries of labor in a country of your choosing.
2. The text examined the importance of labor around the world. Using the Internet, find information on labor statistics throughout the world.

[Minicase 12.1]

Staffing Your Operations Abroad

Your company, an international company based in the United States, has decided to expand aggressively in Asia. It plans to source many of its raw materials, to subcontract, and to manufacture and market throughout Asia, from Japan in the north through New Zealand in the south.

You were appointed to organize and direct this major new effort and to determine where to locate the regional headquarters for the Asian division. After considerable study, you selected the island nation of Luau.

Luau's advantages are several. It is about equidistant between New Zealand and Japan. It was a British colony, so the main language is English. It has a relatively efficient telephone and telegraph system and good air service to all the major Asian destinations in which you are interested and to the United States.

Not least important, the Luau government is delighted to have your company locate and invest there. It has made very attractive tax concessions to the company and to its personnel who will move there.

The company moves in, leases one large building, and puts out invitations to bid on the construction of a larger building, which will be its permanent headquarters. Now, as you begin to work much more with the private banking and businesspeople of Luau and less with government officials, you begin to be more aware of a Luau characteristic about which you had not thought much previously. Almost all the middle- and upper-management personnel in the business and finance sector are of Chinese extraction. The native population of Luau, which constitutes the great majority, is Micronesian.

On inquiring why the Chinese are dominant in banking and business while the Micronesians stay with farming, fishing, government work, and manual labor, you are told that this is the way it developed historically. The Chinese enjoy and are good at banking and business, while the native Luauans do not like those activities and have stayed with their traditional occupations. The two groups buy and sell from and to each other, but there are almost no social relations and very little business or professional overlap between the groups. Occasionally, some of the Micronesians study abroad, and some work abroad for periods; when they return, they frequently go to work in a bank or business or take a government position.

You must staff your headquarters with middle- and lower-management people and with clerical help. You find that the only applicants for the jobs are Chinese, and you select the best available. They are quite satisfactory, and the operation gets off to a good start.

Then, as the months pass, you notice a gradual change of attitude toward you and the company among government officials and among the people in general. They have become less friendly, more evasive, and less cooperative. You ask your Chinese staff about it, but they have noticed nothing unusual.

What could be happening? Why might the Chinese staff not notice it? What might you do to improve government and public relations?

[Minicase 12.2]

Hiring Professional Workers from Abroad

Christine Lund is a Swedish citizen who lives in Stockholm, Sweden. She has been a practicing architect in Sweden for over 20 years. Ms. Lund has a bachelor's degree from an architectural school at a major U.S. university. She has been offered a position by a Los Angeles architectural firm for three years. The Los Angeles firm specializes in the design of beachfront condominiums, which is one of Ms. Lund's areas of expertise. What type of visa would be appropriate for her?

[Minicase 12.3]

Investors Desiring to Come to the United States

Amir Naguib, who is a citizen of Egypt, wants to come to the United States to set up a company selling miniature replicas of the pyramids. He believes there is a market for miniature pyramids in the United States as he thinks they would make great paperweights. He intends to invest $100,000 initially in the company and plans to direct its operations. He also plans to hire people to manufacture and distribute the pyramids. What type of visa would be appropriate for him?

[Chapter]

13

Competitive Forces

"If there is a single great fact of our era, it is the emergence of the first truly international marketplace and the struggle between the leading trading nations and blocs: the United States, Western Europe, Japan, Singapore–Taiwan–Hong Kong–Korea, Mexico–Brazil, and, potentially, China."

—*Paraphrased from H. Lewis and D. Allison*, The Real War: The Coming Battle for the New Global Economy and Why We Are in Danger of Losing

Concept Previews

After reading this chapter, you should be able to:

- **explain** why international competition has increased among the United States, Japan, the EU, and Asian nations
- **know** the areas in which the United States remains vulnerable to foreign competition
- **describe** the responsibilities of government, management, labor, and consumers in maintaining the international competitiveness of the United States
- **explain** the competitive environment in Japan, the EU, and the developing nations, including the NIEs
- **understand** the purpose of the keiretsu in Japanese industry
- **appreciate** the magnitude and danger of product counterfeiting
- **understand** the importance of industrial espionage
- **describe** the sources of competitive information

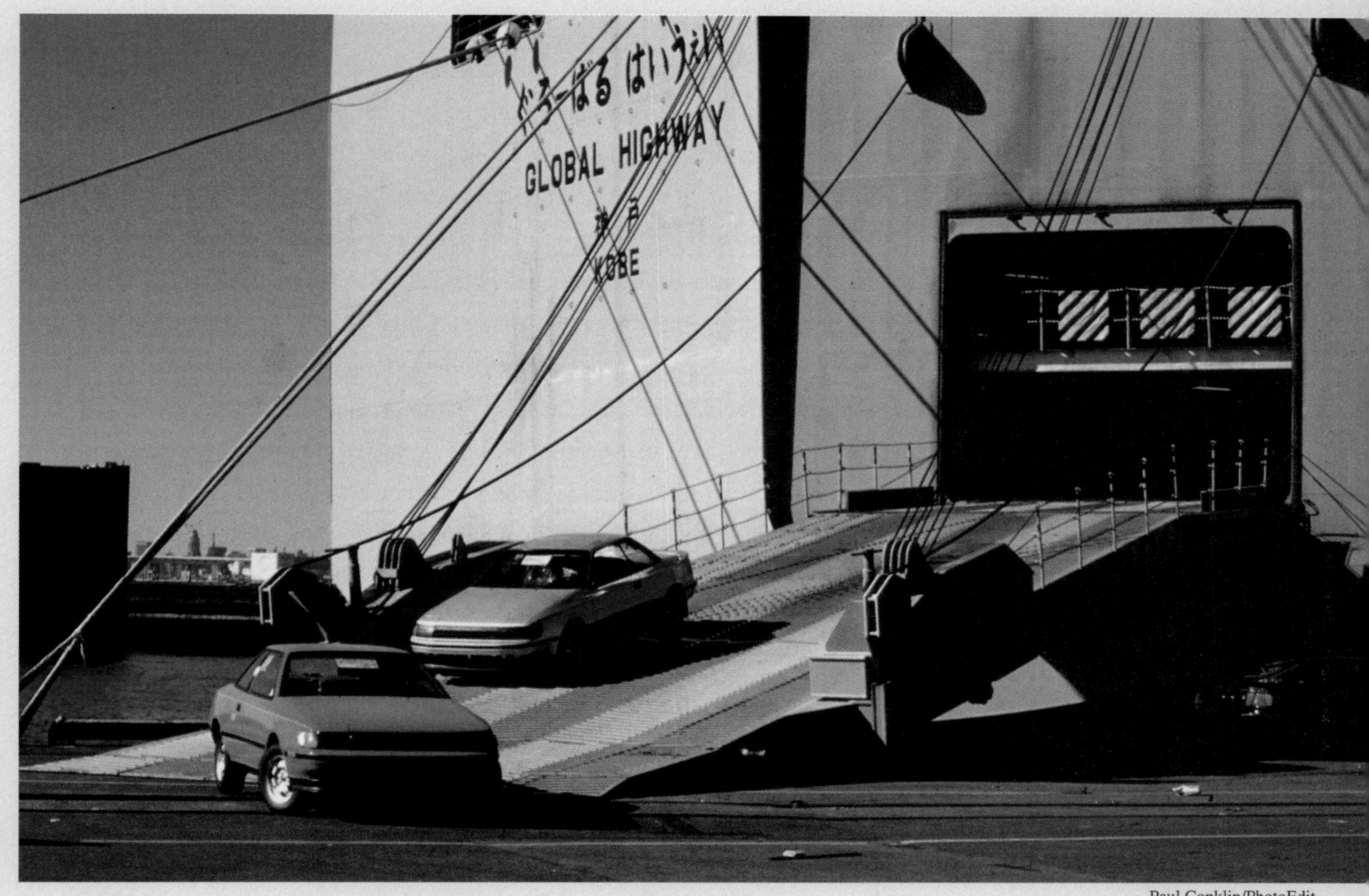

Paul Conklin/PhotoEdit

This Is War: Are Your Secrets Safe?

Executives from a top U.S. firm who were in Japan to negotiate a joint venture arrangement with a local firm were having a private meeting in one of the host's meeting rooms. Because they had so much to discuss among themselves before beginning the negotiations, the meeting went into overtime. Suddenly they heard a loud beeping sound, and according to the senior executive, "the door popped open, a guy runs in, reaches under the table, switches a tape, bows, and leaves." In another instance, a Russian spy was able to get samples of vital metal alloys by posing as a visitor and picking up metal shavings on crepe rubber soles on his walk through the plant.

Although the end of the Cold War reduced world tensions, it did not end the foreign intelligence threat to the United States. Actually, the number of countries spying on American industry has increased. For example, former Russian President Boris Yeltsin criticized Russian industry for not using effectively the technology the Russian intelligence services steal. The former head of French intelligence, Pierre Marion, admitted he set up a section to spy on American companies. "When it comes to economic and technological competition," he said, "we are competitors." He also admitted that Air France stewardesses, working as industrial spies for the state, bugged and eavesdropped on businesspeople's conversations. In addition, more than 20 French spies have been found in U.S. companies such as Corning, IBM, and Texas Instruments.

Despite the passage of the Economic Espionage Act in 1996, which made it a federal crime to provide American businesses' trade secrets to a foreign entity, the FBI says that foreign spies have increased their attacks on American industry. The major offending nations are France, Germany, Israel, China, Russia, and South Korea. Losses to American firms because of economic espionage resulting from the passage of information about product development, specifications, manufacturing processes, and marketing plans may have exceeded $300 billion in 1997. In spite of these losses, an American Society for Industrial Security study in which 325 firms with aggregate revenues of $600 billion were involved found that just 58 percent of technology firms have established security systems. The percentages for manufacturing and service firms were even lower—48 and 29 percent, respectively. Fewer than half these companies had elementary defenses, such as the controlled destruction of sensitive materials, to protect against theft from their rubbish. ■

Sources: "Industrial Espionage Is Alive and Well," *World Trade,* July 1997, pp. 24–26; "FBI Warns Companies to Beware of Espionage," *International Herald Tribune,* January 13, 1998, p. 3; "For Pills, Not Projectiles," *The Economist,* July 12, 1997, p. 22; Department of Energy, "Foreign Economic Collections and Industrial Espionage," ww.orau.unsd.gov/tmsd/trade/siginfo/se/chapt7.htm (January 17, 1998); and "China's Spies Target Corporate America," *Fortune,* March 30, 1998, pp. 118–22.

You may recall from Chapter 2 that developed nations account for nearly 70 percent of the world's international trade and over 90 percent of foreign direct investment. If you remember that section, you will understand why Kenichi Ohmae of the consulting firm McKinsey & Co. contends that for an international firm to compete in world markets, it must be present in at least two and preferably all three parts of a triad composed of the United States, Japan, and the European Union.[1] Note that the triad includes nearly all of the world's developed countries, which not only are much larger markets [about 80 percent of the world's gross national product (GNP)] than are the developing nations but also have business climates (political, financial, and legal forces) that are more favorable to business and more predictable. Figure 13.1 shows the trade patterns of the triad.

Recently, another group of countries has emerged to become a fourth important region, with a combined GNP of over $2 trillion. This group includes the newly industrialized economies (NIEs) in East Asia, consisting of the "Asian tigers" (South Korea, Taiwan, Hong Kong, and Singapore), two newly industrializing countries (NICs) (Malaysia and Thailand), and China.

Although it is true that Japan has invested heavily in the Asian Pacific nations and thus is well represented in that region, it is overly simplistic to think of Japan and the Asian NIEs as one trading bloc. In fact, our method of considering only two groups in the Pacific as being in competition is not completely adequate. Consider this: There are extremely strong trade flows (1) among the Asian NIEs themselves and (2) between those nations and the 10 members of the Association of South East Asian Nations (ASEAN).* For example, Asian NIEs export more to other Asian NIEs and ASEAN nations than they export to Japan. Firms from Asian NIEs are also important investors in ASEAN members.

In addition, a division of labor no longer exists just between Japan and the Asian countries or Japan and the ASEAN nations. Significant differences in labor costs have

*One of the Asian NIEs, Singapore, and the two emerging NICs, Malaysia and Thailand, are also members of ASEAN.

[Figure 13.1] **Intratriad Trade, 1999 (Billions of Dollars)**

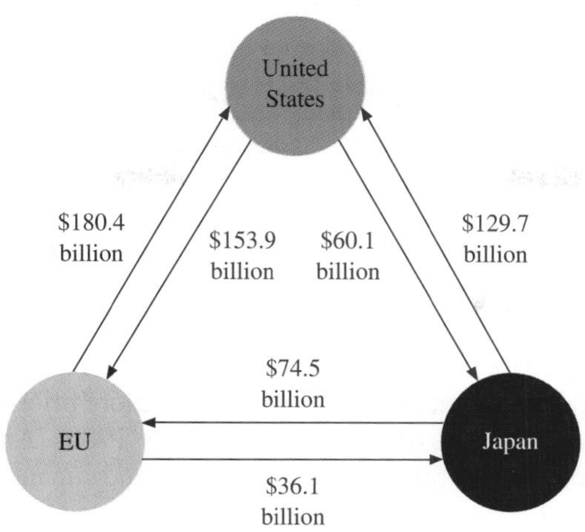

Source: United Nations, *Monthly Bulletin of Statistics,* July 2000, pp. 258–61.

also developed among the Asian NICs, NIEs, and China and between the Asian NIEs and the ASEAN nations. Rising labor costs in South Korea, for example, have forced some manufacturers to move to countries with lower labor costs, such as Indonesia and China.

> A South Korean company produces shoes under contract for Nike, L.A. Gear, and Reebok in its Indonesian plant. The owners used to make the shoes in Korea, but they moved the plant to Indonesia when Korean wages rose to $800 per month compared to the $40 per month being paid in China and Indonesia—about what the Koreans earned in the 1970s.
>
> Nike, which has no shoe production facilities of its own, has contracted with the biggest sports shoe factory in the world, the Yue Yeun complex in southern China, which also produces shoes for Reebok, Adidas, Puma, L.A. Gear, and other well-known brands around the world. Financed by the Taiwanese, the factory employs 40,000 people, 70 percent of them women. The company, which also has factories in Indonesia and Vietnam, produces a third of the world's branded shoes, such as those mentioned previously.[2]

These are some of the reasons we believe an examination of the uncontrollable competitive forces is more revealing if we study them using the four-entity format mentioned previously. Let us now examine the competition among (1) the United States, (2) the European Union, (3) Japan, and (4) the Asian NICs, NIEs, and China. While there are other nations and regions in the world economy, these four regions are responsible for the overwhelming majority of GNP and trade. They will therefore represent the primary focus of this chapter.

national (macro) competitiveness
Ability of a nation's producers to compete successfully in world markets and with imports in their own domestic markets

Competition at the Macro Level (National Competitiveness)

Nations, of course, do not compete against each other; their companies do. However, because most economic and social conditions, as well as political actions, affect the ability of all of a nation's firms to compete in world markets, it is convenient to speak of **national (macro) competitiveness.** To promote clarity in presentation within the brief space allowed in this chapter, the following sections will refer to competitiveness on a national or regional (e.g., European Union) level except where specifically noted.

United States

After World War II, the strong economic infrastructure developed by the war effort and subsequent domestic expansion and international recovery efforts resulted in sustained prosperity and competitiveness for U.S. firms in the 1950s and 1960s.

However, complacency among American managers coupled with economic development in other nations resulted in a substantial decline in the relative competitiveness of the United States in the world economy.

Declining Competitiveness in the 1970s and 1980s

In the 1970s, a lag in national competitiveness began to become apparent as imports gained a larger share of the domestic U.S. market. The extent of the decline in American competitiveness was masked, however. A growing share of the export market was achieved by American firms due to a dollar whose value was dropping relative to other major currencies at an average annual rate of 2.5 percent. When the dollar's value rose at the beginning of the 1980s, U.S. unit labor costs mounted, causing imports to increase and U.S. exports to decrease. Not until 1985, when the dollar's value again declined, did labor costs begin to fall and American exports became more price competitive.[3]

During the challenging years of the 1970s and early 1980s, American firms experienced growing competition in this country. European and Japanese firms were buying U.S. firms because the cheap dollar made them inexpensive in those countries' currencies. Moreover, the size of the American market, the availability of raw materials, the developed capital markets, and the political stability of the United States combined to attract massive foreign investment. As the value of the dollar rose and U.S. firms experienced difficulty competing in the U.S. market and overseas, protectionist sentiment grew in this country, and this provided additional impetus for foreign investors to set up U.S.-based operations.

When the dollar again fell in the late 1980s, foreign firms that were still supplying this market with exports found it difficult to compete pricewise with domestic products, and thus they too established production in the United States. Those that did not either lost sales or, if they cut prices to remain competitive, saw their profits from the United States decline. Japanese exporters of high-technology items, including automobiles, electronics, and computers, lost over 40 percent of their profits as they tried to meet U.S. prices in the face of a yen that rose from 260 per dollar to 123 in just two years.[4]

Although the overvalued dollar was one of the principal reasons for the decline in American competitiveness in the 1970s and early 1980s, it was not the only one. A number of nonprice factors, such as quality, delivery time, after-sales service, reliability of supply, and trade barriers to U.S. exports, were also responsible. In 1991, the Washington-based Council on Competitiveness (COC), a nonpartisan, nonprofit forum of 150 leaders in industry, labor, and higher education, published a study examining U.S. competitiveness. Its definition of competitiveness was "the nation's capacity to meet the test in international markets while maintaining or boosting the real incomes of its citizens."[5] After analyzing 94 critical technologies that industry experts declared were driving the U.S. economy, the COC concluded that the United States "was weak or losing badly in one-third of them." To assure the country's technological strength, a series of policy recommendations for government, industry, and academia were included in the report.

Improving Competitiveness of the United States

From the mid-1980s through the mid-1990s, efforts in the United States focused on improving the financial situation (e.g., addressing the savings and loan industry's problems, reducing the budget deficit), streamlining regulation, opening global markets, and improving industrial productivity by restructuring operations, enhancing quality, reducing costs, investing in information and computer technologies, and reducing time to market.[6]

After many of its policy recommendations were put into effect, the COC was asked to reassess the U.S. performance in critical technologies. Was the nation's competitive position improving or deteriorating? A COC study published in 1994 revealed that the United States had significantly improved its position in areas where it had been lagging and had maintained its strength in areas where it had been strong in the 1991 report.

[Figure 13.2] **Compound Annual Growth in Manufacturing Productivity, 1985–1995 Versus 1999**

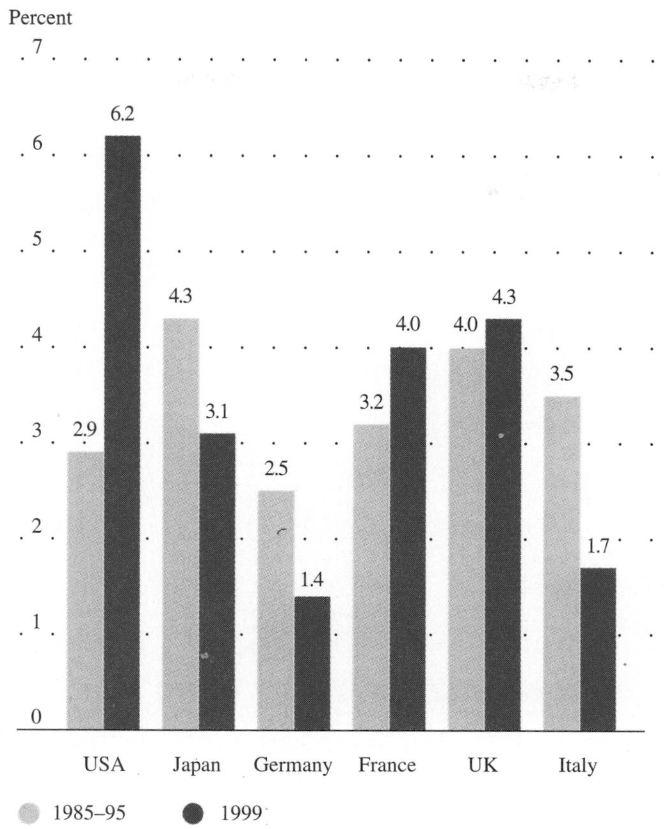

Sources: Council on Competitiveness, *Competitiveness Index 1996* (Washington, DC: Council on Competitiveness, 1996), p. 31; and Bureau of Labor Standards, "International Comparisons of Manufacturing Productivity and Unit Labor Cost Trends, 1999," http://stats.bls.gov/news.release/prod4.nr0.htm (October 31, 2000).

Flat-panel displays were the only category of electrical components in which the United States was losing badly and had made no progress by 1994.

Another study by the COC, *Competitiveness Index 1996,* provided a decadelong (1985–1995) assessment of U.S. competitiveness. This study also included a comparison of the United States with developing nations because of those nations' growing importance as both competitors and sources for growth opportunities. The Council found that the United States had increased its global market share of goods by over 23 percent, had generated a large and growing surplus in services trade (from $7 billion in 1985 to $80 billion in 1995), had led the major industrial nations in growth of industrial output during the last five years of analysis, had a lower unemployment rate than all major industrialized nations except Japan, and had strengthened its competitive position overall.

Improvements in American competitiveness in the early 1990s were followed by further improvements. For example, growth in U.S. manufacturing productivity over the 1985–95 decade was lower than the growth of other nations, including Japan, France, the United Kingdom, and Italy. By the end of the 1990s, however, the United States was the clear leader, achieving productivity growth nearly 50 percent higher than that of its nearest competitor, the United Kingdom (Figure 13.2).

Ranking American Competitiveness

In addition to the COC studies, there are other indications that the United States is regaining competitiveness on an international basis. The International Institute for Management Development (IMD), in its annual *World Competitiveness Yearbook,*

Table 13.1 The World Competitiveness Scoreboard: Ranking as of April 19, 2000

Country	Score	Ranking 2000	1999	1998	1997	1996	1995	1994
United States	100.00	1	1	1	1	1	1	1
Singapore	75.22	2	2	2	2	2	2	2
Finland	74.01	3	3	5	4	15	18	19
Netherlands	72.13	4	5	4	6	7	8	8
Switzerland	68.49	5	6	7	7	9	5	5
Luxembourg	68.09	6	4	9	12	8	—	—
Ireland	64.83	7	11	11	15	22	22	21
Germany	64.49	8	9	14	14	10	6	6
Sweden	63.86	9	14	17	16	14	12	9
Iceland	63.52	10	17	19	21	25	25	—
Canada	63.42	11	10	10	10	12	13	20
Denmark	63.38	12	8	8	8	5	7	7
Australia	63.12	13	12	15	18	21	16	16
Hong Kong	60.47	14	7	3	3	3	3	4
United Kingdom	59.36	15	15	12	11	19	15	14
Norway	57.79	16	13	6	5	6	10	126
Japan	57.36	17	16	18	9	4	4	3
Austria	57.19	18	19	22	20	16	—	—
France	54.33	19	21	21	19	20	—	—
Belgium	53.34	20	22	23	22	17	—	—
New Zealand	52.77	21	20	13	13	11	9	10
Taiwan	51.10	22	18	16	23	18	—	—
Israel	50.30	23	24	25	26	24	—	—
Spain	47.28	24	23	27	25	29	—	—
Malaysia	42.12	25	27	20	17	23	23	18
Chile	41.44	26	25	26	24	13	—	—
Hungary	40.90	27	26	28	36	39	—	—
Korea	38.36	28	38	35	30	27	—	—
Portugal	37.97	29	28	29	32	36	—	—
Italy	34.71	30	30	30	34	28	—	—
China	34.32	31	29	24	27	26	—	—

Sources: IMD, "The World Competitiveness Scoreboard," http://www.imd.ch/wcy/factors/overalldata.html (August 23, 1998); and http://www.imd.ch/wcy/ranking/ranking.cfm (April 25, 2000).

ranks the 29 Organization for Economic Cooperation and Development (OECD) members and 18 newly industrializing and emerging market economies. The ranking is based on eight factors (domestic economy, internationalization, finance, infrastructure, science and technology, management, government, and people), and there are an average of 31 criteria per factor. Table 13.1 lists the 2000 scores and the rankings from 1994 through 2000 for the 31 highest-ranked nations. The United States has consistently ranked first throughout this time period, followed by Singapore. The ratings of the other nations have varied over the years, as shown in the table.[7]

Another ranking of international competitiveness is the Global Competitiveness Report (GCR), which is published by the World Economic Forum. The GCR's rankings are based on "the ability of a country to achieve sustained high rates of growth in GDP per capita." Table 13.2 presents the 25 top-ranked nations for 2000. The United States is ranked first, replacing Singapore, which had been ranked highest in the 1996 through 1999 analyses. As you can see from an examination of Table 13.2, there has been considerable change among the 25 top-ranked nations since 1996. The United States moved up three places, while the nations that moved up the most were Ireland (+21) and the Netherlands (+13). Those declining most were New Zealand (−17) and Malaysia (−15).

Table 13.2 **Global Competitiveness Report of 25 Top-Ranked Nations**

	Growth Competitiveness Rank				
Country	2000	1999	1998	1997	1996
United States	1	2	3	3	4
Singapore	2	1	1	1	1
Luxembourg	3	7	10	11	5
Netherlands	4	9	7	12	17
Ireland	5	10	11	16	26
Finland	6	11	15	19	16
Canada	7	5	5	4	8
Hong Kong	8	3	2	2	2
United Kingdom	9	8	4	7	15
Switzerland	10	6	8	6	6
Taiwan	11	4	6	8	9
Australia	12	12	14	17	12
Sweden	13	19	23	22	21
Denmark	14	17	16	20	11
Germany	15	25	24	25	22
Norway	16	15	9	10	7
Belgium	17	24	27	31	25
Austria	18	20	20	27	19
Israel	19	28	29	24	24
New Zealand	20	13	13	5	3
Japan	21	14	12	14	13
France	22	23	22	23	23
Portugal	23	27	26	30	34
Iceland	24	18	30	38	27
Malaysia	25	16	17	9	10

Source: World Economic Forum, The Global Competitiveness Report, 2000 and 1999 editions, www.worldeconomicforum.com (November 29, 2000). Reprinted with permission of World Economic Forum.

Comparison of the 2000 rankings of the World Competitiveness Scorecard (WCS) and the GCR reveals several interesting points. The United States, Singapore, and the Netherlands are ranked consistently in the top five in each report. All of the top 20 countries in each report are in the top 25 in both reports, although there are some substantial differences in their order within the rankings. For example, Iceland is number 10 in the WCS but number 24 in the GCR. Other examples include Taiwan (WCS 22, GCR 11) and Germany (WCS 8, GCR 15). Before basing decisions on these reports, managers obviously must understand the methodologies used in each instance.

Dawn of a "New Economy"?

A disproportionate share of American economic and export growth in the last decade has been generated by a relatively small number of industries, particularly those related to information and communications technology (ICT). ICT includes a variety of sectors related to digital technology, such as computer hardware and software, wireless and wired telecommunications systems, and the Internet.

Evidence suggests that ICT accounted for up to 75 percent of the rise in U.S. productivity growth during the second half of the 1990s.[8] Some analysts have suggested that the ICT sector has provided the basis for a "new economy" characterized by a permanent increase in productivity growth, lower levels of unemployment while maintaining low inflation, and more stable growth in output. The emergence of the "new economy" has been promoted by several interrelated forces, including technological advances, liberalization of financial markets, globalization, greater flexibility in labor markets, improved management of the macroeconomy, and an environment supportive of entrepreneurship.[9]

Continued Challenges to U.S. Competitiveness

Some have characterized the emergence of the ICT-driven new economy as a development on a par with prior industrial revolutions, such as the emergence of steam power or the assembly line. Although performance of the U.S. economy has clearly been impressive, especially during the latter half of the 1990s, it may be too early to state definitively that a fundamentally new economy has emerged. The United States is experiencing steady growth associated with the longest peacetime economic expansion in its history, although there are many indications in early 2001 that this expansion may be losing steam. Despite improvements in competitiveness during the 1990s, the United States faces challenges to its efforts to maintain international competitiveness. This section identifies several key challenges to the sustained competitiveness of U.S. industry and increased American exports, as well as several important actions that can be taken by government, business, and labor to promote improved competitiveness of the United States.

innovation
The transformation of knowledge into new products, processes, and services

Innovative Capability and Investment in Research and Development. Technological **innovation** plays a central and well-recognized role in productivity improvement, long-term economic growth, and improvement of a nation's standard of living.[10] Historically, it was accepted wisdom that industrialized nations were the sources of innovation while less industrialized countries provided raw materials as well as lower-cost labor and manufacturing. However, many developing countries have begun to move from being imitators to being innovators, facilitating this progression through investment in people, research, technology, and an innovation-friendly environment.

The World Economic Forum's Economic Creativity Index 2000 ranks the United States as the leading country overall and for each of the creativity, technology, and start-up dimensions that make up this index (see Table 13.3). A study of the innovative capacity of 17 OECD economies and 8 emerging nations that was conducted in 1999 by the COC found that the United States and Switzerland had achieved sustained leadership in innovative capabilities across the three decades examined in this study.[11] However, their lead has declined over time, and further erosion is projected if current trends continue. For example, despite a sustained economic malaise in the 1990s, Japan's innovative capacity has improved dramatically since the 1970s. While certain European nations (for example, the United Kingdom, Germany, Italy, and France) have experienced declining or merely stable innovative capability, several other countries (for example, Sweden, Denmark, and Finland) have achieved world-class innovative capability. Nations such as Singapore, Taiwan, South Korea, Israel, and Ireland have invested substantially in their infrastructure to promote innovation, moving them into a position to challenge second-tier OECD economies in terms of innovative capacity. Other countries (for example, Spain, New Zealand, and an increasing number of low-wage nations) have not established themselves as strong innovators but have improved their capacity to be quick imitators of innovations that are made in other nations. In contrast, investment in the United States in fundamental bases of innovation capacity peaked in 1985. Since 1985, the United States has had a decline in the growth rate of funding for research and development (R&D) and employment, flat or declining spending on education as a percentage of the gross domestic product (GDP), and a decline in its relative international openness, and the underlying environment for technological innovation in the United States has become relatively less supportive.[12]

Much of the sustained U.S. leadership in R&D can be traced to a government-supported innovation infrastructure that emerged particularly strongly during the Cold War, including the National Aeronautics and Space Administration (NASA), the National Institutes of Health (NIH), the Department of Defense, and the U.S. university system. These efforts played a critical role in training people and promoting con-

Table 13.3 Economic Creativity Index 2000 for the 25 Top-Ranked Nations

Country	Economic Creativity Index Rank	Economic Creativity	Technology Index	Start-up Index
United States	1	2.02	2.02	2.02
Finland	2	1.73	2.02	1.43
Singapore	3	1.63	1.95	1.31
Luxembourg	4	1.44	1.37	1.51
Sweden	5	1.36	1.52	1.21
Israel	6	1.35	1.55	1.15
Ireland	7	1.31	1.74	0.87
Netherlands	8	1.26	1.20	1.32
United Kingdom	9	1.22	1.08	1.36
Iceland	10	1.16	0.80	1.51
Switzerland	11	1.11	1.62	0.60
Hong Kong	12	1.10	0.58	1.63
Denmark	13	1.07	1.25	0.88
Germany	14	1.04	1.66	0.41
Canada	15	0.99	1.21	0.77
Australia	16	0.97	0.91	1.04
Taiwan	17	0.97	0.90	1.04
Belgium	18	0.95	1.00	0.90
Norway	19	0.80	0.61	0.98
Japan	20	0.69	1.59	−0.21
Hungary	21	0.66	1.06	0.27
New Zealand	22	0.64	0.73	0.56
Malaysia	23	0.59	1.08	0.11
France	24	0.59	1.36	−0.18
Poland	25	0.56	1.14	−0.01

Source: World Economic Forum, The Global Competitiveness Report 2000, www.worldeconomicforum.com (November 29, 2000). Reprinted with permission of World Economic Forum.

sumption as well as the production of innovative new products and services. They also had important spillover effects beyond their initial areas of emphasis. For example, the Internet is the result of Department of Defense–promoted efforts to develop a decentralized communication system for government agencies and university researchers that could remain operational despite a major attack from the Soviet Union.

As a percentage of GDP, overall R&D expenditures in the United States are higher than those of other major nations and amount to over twice the amount spent by the nearest contender, Japan. Although the United States leads all nations in R&D spending, the level of expenditures on R&D as a percentage of national wealth was lower at the end of the 1990s than it had been in the early 1980s. As shown in Figure 13.3, growth in R&D spending during the economic expansion that began in 1991 has been the lowest since the early 1970s. Although there has been growth in investment in the health sciences, total expenditures on basic research have declined substantially as a percentage of GDP. Reduced funding by the federal government, particularly in the aftermath of the Cold War, has accounted for much of this decline. Indeed, the U.S. government's share declined from nearly 60 percent of total U.S. R&D expenditures in 1970 to around 30 percent in 1997.[13] Increased R&D investment by businesses has only partially made up the difference.

To address this situation, the U.S. government must reverse recent declines in support for R&D outside the health sciences area. The government should encourage initiatives that will promote private R&D spending, especially on long-term projects. Promotion of basic research in universities, independently or in cooperation with the private sector, is also essential.

[Figure 13.3] Growth in U.S. R&D Spending During Economic Expansions, 1970–1997 (Constant 1992 U.S. Dollars)

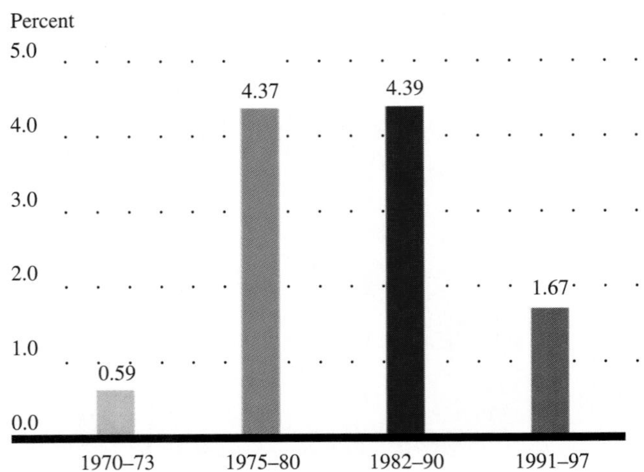

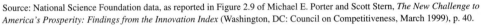

Source: National Science Foundation data, as reported in Figure 2.9 of Michael E. Porter and Scott Stern, *The New Challenge to America's Prosperity: Findings from the Innovation Index* (Washington, DC: Council on Competitiveness, March 1999), p. 40.

A Shortage of Knowledge Workers. Increased global competition has placed an increasing premium on skilled workers, particularly in scientific and technical activities. Yet the proportion of R&D workers in the total U.S. work force has been declining since the late 1980s. The increasing importance of information technology and the emergence of a service-sector-dominated economy have created an unmet demand for knowledge workers and made computer literacy a basic requirement for even many entry-level positions. The aging of the national work force has produced an urgent requirement to replace a generation of skilled workers, including the so-called baby boom generation that will reach retirement age beginning in 2005.

Within industry, managers have found that investments in education and training pay off in terms of higher productivity and noninflationary wage growth. A study done by the researchers Sandra Black and Lisa Lynch found that raising the educational level of workers in a manufacturing plant by one year raises labor productivity 8 percent. Giving employees a voice in decision making in the plant through meetings has a positive impact on labor productivity, and manufacturing plants that have a profit-sharing plan for nonmanagerial employees had labor productivity 7 percent higher than that of their competitors. Managers have found that workers like to know how they compare to their competitors. Using **benchmarking** raises labor productivity 6 percent.[14]

benchmarking
A technique for measuring a firm's performance against the performance of others that may be in the same or a completely different industry

In terms of education, the United States outspends all other industrialized nations and leads the world in the percentage of students graduating from universities. Despite this, test scores from secondary-level students have failed to improve since 1985 and compare poorly with the scores of students in other nations (see Table 13.4). Graduate school enrollments in engineering and the physical sciences have been static or declining. A growing proportion of these graduate students are from other nations, and increasingly, these graduates are returning to their native countries once they complete their studies. Industry has successfully lobbied for legislation to permit the recruitment of more than 100,000 skilled knowledge workers per year from other nations in an effort to overcome the domestic shortage of suitably skilled workers. Despite this, companies have been forced to send skilled jobs to workers in other nations. The Information Technology Association of America projected that out of 1.6 million openings, over 843,000 information technology jobs in the United States would go unfilled in 2000 due to a lack of qualified employees.[15]

Table 13.4 Who Is Head of the Global Class?

A study of 15,000 students and 1,500 schools from 21 countries, sponsored by the International Association for the Evaluation of Educational Achievement, found that factors in students' homes have more of a bearing on success than do class size, amount of homework, and other instructional factors. Listed below are the average scores at the eighth grade or its equivalent for a selection of the countries studied.

Country	Overall Average	Science Tasks	Mathematics Tasks
Singapore	71	72	70
England*	67	71	64
Australia*	65	63	66
Switzerland	65	65	66
Sweden	64	63	65
Scotland	62	64	61
Norway	62	58	65
Czech Republic	61	60	62
Canada	60	59	62
New Zealand	60	58	62
Netherlands*	60	58	62
United States*	55	55	54
Spain	54	56	52
Iran, Islamic Republic of	52	50	54
Portugal	47	47	48
Cyprus	46	49	44
International average	59	58	59

*Countries not satisfying guidelines for sample participation rates.

Source: *Performance Assessment in IEA's Third International Mathematics and Science Study (TIMSS)*, International Association for the Evaluation of Educational Achievement, September 1997, http://timss.bc.edu/TIMSS1/TIMSSPDF//Pareport.pdf.

These trends suggest a threat to the ability of the United States to sustain its role as a global leader in innovation, with potentially damaging implications for the country's economic, social, and environmental performance over time. To address these challenges, the United States must initiate significant changes and investments in primary and secondary education, as well as undertaking concerted efforts to rebuild university education in technical disciplines at the undergraduate and graduate levels.

More Conducive Regulatory Environment. The private sector, not governments or universities, is the primary engine for transforming knowledge and new ideas into wealth-creating technologies, products, and services.[16] Yet government policy and institutions such as universities can create an environment that can promote, or inhibit, firms' innovativeness.

> Strong intellectual property laws in the United States have encouraged investment in research to discover new drugs, resulting in a strong and innovative U.S. pharmaceutical industry. In contrast, unfavorable patent laws in Japan and pricing laws in France have discouraged investment in new product R&D, resulting in lower levels of innovation by those nations' pharmaceutical firms.[17]

Increasingly, the public in the United States and other OECD countries has come to realize what industry managers have been claiming for years: improving the conditions that make up the business environment is a key requirement for industrial competitiveness. A significant aspect of this environment is the creation of a more conducive macroeconomic framework by federal government. The regulatory and legal environment in the United States produces substantial and often unnecessary costs for the business sector. Indeed, regulatory costs are estimated to account for about 9 percent of U.S. GDP, and the United States ranks 18th out of 25 nations in international comparisons of national regulatory environments. The estimated costs associated with regulatory compliance increased from $561 billion in 1985 to $668 billion in 1995 and are projected to grow to $721 billion in 2000. About one-third of this amount is linked to increased paperwork requirements.[18]

Government activities per se are not harmful in regard to national competitiveness. High regulatory standards for safety, energy use, environmental protection, and other areas can promote innovation. However, critics argue that in addition to the previously mentioned encouragement of R&D and reform of education, much more remains to be done by the U.S. government. This includes tax reform (including simplifying the tax system, reducing corporate rates and taxes on personal income, broadening the tax base, and modifying tax policies affecting corporate R&D and investment spending), the opening of foreign markets, protection of intellectual property rights, reducing dependence on foreign capital, and industrial targeting, each of which will be discussed below.

Market-Opening Efforts. Another key initiative by the U.S. government would be to renew its historical leadership activities in terms of opening markets domestically and worldwide. In this regard, one measure that U.S. government officials have taken is to threaten retaliation if other governments fail to remove trade barriers to American exports. The United States had a 1999 trade deficit of $105 billion in autos and auto parts, with a major portion of that deficit associated with imports from Japanese automakers. Japan, which has had overall annual trade surpluses of $50 billion or more with the United States for the last decade ($70 billion in 1999), is constantly being pressured by American trade officials to lower nontariff barriers that hinder the efforts of U.S. firms that try to do business in that country.

> One particularly troublesome and costly barrier is the slow and cumbersome Japanese import clearance procedures. Slow processing by inspection authorities such as the Departments of Agriculture and Health, as well as nonuniform application of customs regulations throughout Japan, results in high overall clearance time. Some improvement has been made, but American trade officials continue to press for greater improvement.[19]

In addition to Japan, the United States has focused its attention on opening the markets of other nations, particularly China. While some progress has been made, these efforts must be sustained and perhaps expanded to allow effective competition by American firms and help address the record high trade deficits generated by the United States in the late 1990s and projected for the early 2000s. For example, the current account deficit was $331.5 billion in 1999 and was projected to rise to $432.8 billion, $470.5 billion, and $483.3 billion in 2000, 2001, and 2002, respectively.[20]

Protecting Intellectual Property Rights. The U.S. government has also used the threat of retaliation to promote the protection of intellectual property rights and eliminate another barrier to American exports in international markets, particularly in Asia—competition from illegal copies of U.S. products. As is discussed in the section later in this chapter "Counterfeiting and Piracy," counterfeiting has become a serious problem for companies from the United States and other nations. Various industry associations estimate that rightful patent owners from the United States lose $200 billion in sales every year.[21] According to U.S. estimates, the cost of Chinese copyright violations involving compact discs, software, and movies alone amounts to over $2 billion annually. Although China has enacted laws to protect U.S. copyrights, patents, and trademarks in response to American pressure, it has not enforced them. However, when the American government threatened to increase import duties on $2 billion of Chinese exports to the U.S., China proceeded to close illegal production facilities and confiscate millions of illegally made products.[22] The threat of retaliation against Taiwan and Korea has produced somewhat better results. Not only have both countries enacted laws to protect American patents, unlike China, these governments have exerted some effort to enforce them.

Dependence on Foreign Capital. Another area where U.S. competitiveness may be vulnerable is the nation's reliance on foreign capital. As was discussed in Chapter 2, in the late 1990s and in 2000, the United States experienced unprecedented inflows of capital from abroad. These inflows include record high levels of acquisitions of U.S. companies by firms headquartered in other nations.

This flow of capital into stocks, bonds, and other investments in the U.S. economy has been driven by a number of factors, including depreciating currencies in other regions (for example, the declining value of the euro during the first two years after its introduction) and higher projected growth and profitability opportunities in the United States. The U.S. economy could be vulnerable to changes such as renewed inflationary pressure, a rapid depreciation of the currency, slowed growth, and declines in projected corporate profits and stock prices. These changes could quickly reverse the flow of capital, possibly reducing the availability of funds for investment and choking economic growth. Some economists have suggested that the government could take actions to reverse the low national saving rate (private saving declined from over 18 percent of GDP in 1992 to nearly 13 percent in 2000),[23] thereby reducing the need for foreign capital. The government could also act to reduce the federal budget deficit, particularly during the period of strong budget surpluses being projected for the early 2000s, thereby decreasing the amount of savings consumed by the government now and over time. These actions could result in lower interest rates, which would enable U.S. firms to pay less for loans to expand production facilities and purchase more technologically advanced equipment.

Industrial Targeting. The government can also do more to support American companies that face competition from targeted industries. **Industrial targeting**, the practice of government assisting selected industries to grow by a variety of means, has been common in Europe and Japan, as well as in many developing nations. France, for example, modernized its railroad construction industry by modernizing its rail system. Equipment contracts were given only to French suppliers. Because a strong home base was built first, French suppliers were ready for the export market. Increasingly, the U.S. mass transit market is being dominated by French and Japanese businesses; both of those governments support target industries.

industrial targeting
Government practice of assisting selected industries to grow

Another industry targeted by European nations is the production of commercial aircraft. Airbus Industrie, a consortium of French, German, British, and Spanish aircraft manufacturers, produces parts that are then assembled in a giant hangar in Hamburg, Germany. Since the consortium began operations in 1970, it has received more than $13.5 billion in government aid. A Boeing official stated, "Airbus was allowed to start a program without a sufficient order base and at production rates that would force a U.S. manufacturer to shut down."[24] In 1999, for the first time in 30 years, Airbus obtained more orders for jetliners than Boeing did. After Boeing landed 625 firm orders for aircraft in 1998, versus 558 for Airbus, Airbus announced that it had firm orders for 476 planes in 1999, compared with Boeing's 391. Airbus's efforts to overcome American dominance include the 2000 launch of the 555-seat A3XX super-jumbo plane, which will be the world's biggest commercial aircraft and will end Boeing's monopoly in the jumbo-size jetliner segment. In part because of American complaints about European government subsidies to Airbus and also because Airbus needs a more flexible arrangement than the present consortium, the four partners agreed to change in 2000 to a stand-alone business capable of competing with Boeing on equal terms.[25]

European Union

When the European Economic Community was first formed in the late 1950s, one market was created out of six. Not only did the larger market attract new competitors from outside Europe, it also gave firms that had been selling in only one member-country easy access to five additional countries. Competition increased with the admission of Denmark, Ireland, and the United Kingdom in 1973 and heightened with the admission of Greece in 1981 and Spain and Portugal in 1986.

Producers of industrial, but not agricultural, products were confronted with competition from European Free Trade Area (EFTA) member-countries when the

[Worldview]

H-P TO NEC, "BONZAI!"

In 1993, Hewlett-Packard (H-P), a major American multinational producer of computers, printers, and systems, was challenged by Japan's NEC. Japan's largest computer manufacturer was going to attack H-P's leadership in computer printers in the standard Japanese manner: undercut prices with a new, better product. This is the same strategy used by Japanese manufacturers years ago to take the market from H-P after it had introduced handheld calculators.

This time the strategy failed. Months before NEC could launch its inexpensive monochrome inkjet printer, Hewlett-Packard had brought to market an improved color version and drastically cut the price by 40 percent of its best-selling black-and-white printer. NEC withdrew its printer, now overpriced and uncompetitive. The head of Canon's inkjet business explained H-P's success in this way: "H-P understood computers better; it understood American customers better. Japanese makers' culture hindered the kind of quick decision making needed in the fast-paced U.S. computer market."

When Hewlett-Packard marketers began to study the printer market, they knew the company would need a product more technologically advanced than the Oki and Seiko dot matrix printers dominating the printer market. A printer using the inkjet technology accidentally discovered by an H-P scientist the year before was the answer. The inkjet printer was cheaper and more easily adaptable for color printing, and nobody else had perfected it.

The quality of the first inkjet H-P made was bad, but because the company believed PC users wanted better-quality printouts of text and graphics, its engineers began a process of continual improvement to solve the inkjet's problems. When executives from Epson's U.S. company told their superiors in Japan that PC users would soon demand high-quality printers and that Epson should work on the inkjet technology, the response of Japanese executives was, "Who are these Americans to come over and tell us how to build our products?"

In 1988, H-P introduced the plain-paper inkjet printer, the Deskjet, that was expected to take market share from the Japanese. Instead of being positioned as competition for Japanese dot matrix printers, the Deskjet was competing with the more expensive H-P laser printers, and sales were low. In the fall of 1988, H-P managers decided to meet dot matrix printers head on. They did it with the obsessiveness of a Japanese company. Teams of H-P employees in "Beat Epson" sweatshirts studied Epson marketing practices, surveyed Epson customers, and dismantled Epson printers for engineering and design ideas. They discovered that Epson got a long life from a product by creating a broad product line made up of many variations of one basic printer.

By 1992, Japanese printer makers realized that dot matrix printers were being attacked by inkjets, whose sales were climbing while their sales fell. When they tried to enter the market with their own inkjets, they were stopped by H-P's lock on many important patents. When trying to develop print heads, engineers of the Citizen Watch Company found that H-P had filed so many patents that it was like being in a maze. "You go down this path and suddenly you're into an area that may infringe on their main patents and have to back up and start over," said a vice president of Citizen's U.S. unit.

H-P's economies of scale have allowed it to lower production costs and undercut any competitor's price. Its production experience enabled it to make continual improvements in the manufacturing process. Today's inkjet production costs are half what they were in 1988 when measured in constant dollars. These cost improvements have allowed H-P to carry out this competitive strategy: When a rival attacks, hit back fast and hard. When H-P learned that Canon was going to launch a color inkjet printer in 1993, it cut the price of its own version before the Canon version came to market.

Hewlett-Packard has 55 percent of the world market for inkjet printers. The company's success with inkjets and laser printers has made it one of the fastest-growing American multinationals. The success of the printer division's mass market approach is causing other H-P divisions to try to make the lowest-cost personal and handheld computers in the market.

H-P is just one of a number of American firms that are taking back American technologies such as cellular phones, disk drives, computer-chip-making machinery, and pagers that had been previously lost to the Japanese. ■

Sources: "How H-P Used Tactics of the Japanese to Beat Them at Their Game," *The Wall Street Journal*, September 8, 1994, p. A1; "Here's a PC for Peanuts," *Newsweek*, January 25, 1993, p. 63; and "The Invasion That Failed," *Forbes*, January 20, 1992, pp. 102–3.

[Figure 13.4] **The European Economic Area (EU and EFTA) Takes in Some 387 Million Consumers***

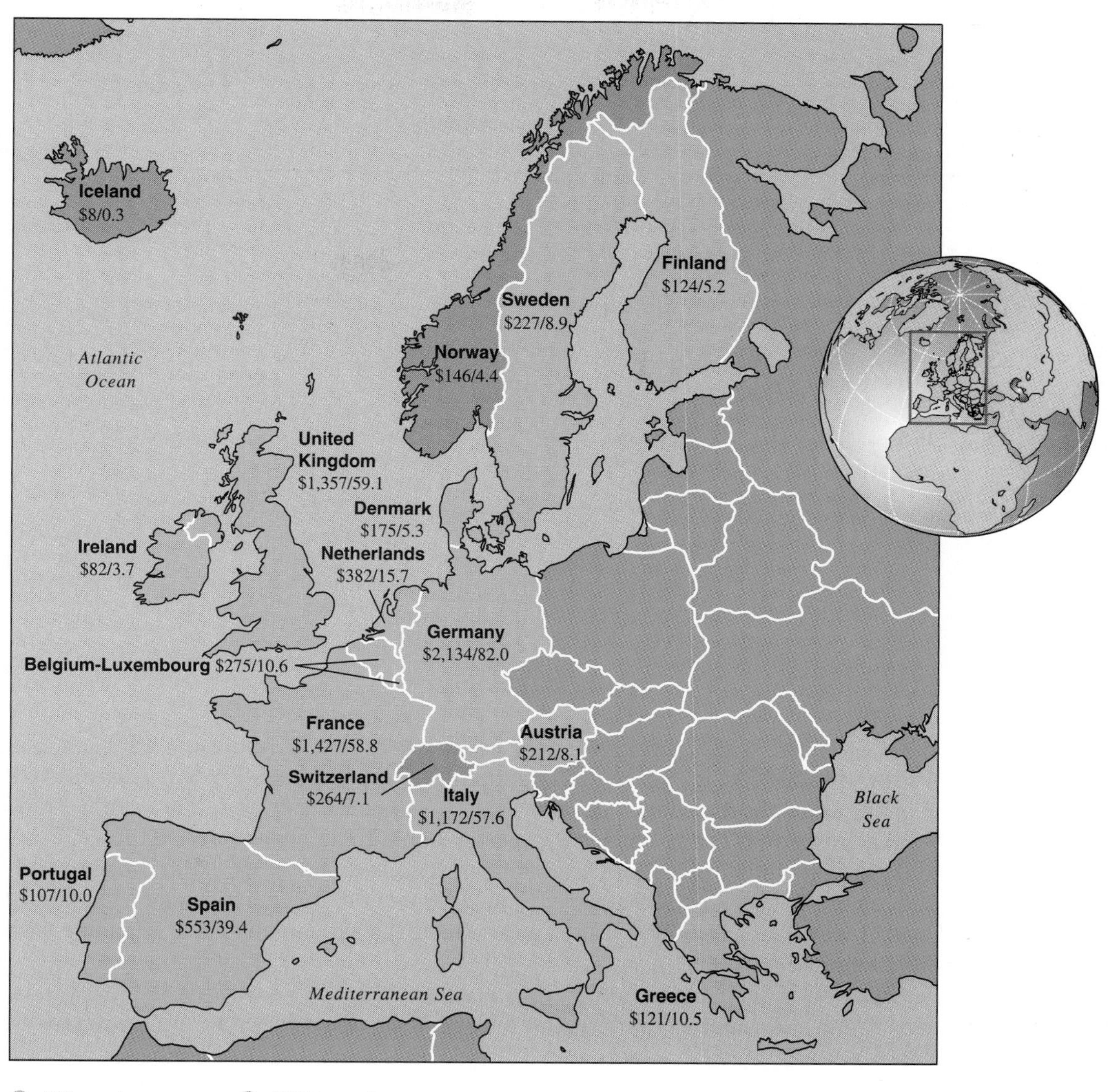

*$00 is GNP in billion dollars; 00.0 is population in millions.
Source: Data from *World Bank Atlas, 2000* (Washington, DC: World Bank, 2000), pp. 24–25, 186–89.

European Economic Zone was formed in 1984. In October 1991, a new agreement between the two groups was reached which changed the European Economic Zone to the **European Economic Area (EEA)**. With the entry of the former EFTA members Austria, Sweden, and Finland to the European Union on January 1, 1995, only three EEA members—Norway, Iceland, and Liechtenstein—are not part of the European Union (EU) (see Figure 13.4). By 2003, the EU is expected to begin adding additional members, particularly Central and Eastern European countries, ultimately incorporating 27 or more nations into a "greater Europe" trading area. Such developments can create important new opportunities for business, as well as creating new competitive challenges.

European Economic Area
A free trade area for industrial products consisting of the 15 EU nations and 3 EFTA nations

Lomé Convention
An agreement between 71 African, Caribbean, and Pacific states (ACP) and the EU by which 99.2 percent of the ACP's exports are admitted duty-free to the EU

More Competition

A preferential arrangement known as the **Lomé Convention,** begun in 1975, is a source of competition from developing nations for some European producers. This is

Table 13.5 Growth in Volume of World Merchandise Trade by Selected Regions (annual change in percentage)

Exports: Average, 1990–96	1995	1996	1997	1998	1999		Imports: Average, 1990–96	1995	1996	1997	1998	1999
5.5	**8.5**	**4.0**	**10.5**	**4.5**	**4.5**	**World**	**6.0**	**8.5**	**4.5**	—	—	—
7.0	9.5	5.5	11.0	3.5	4.5	North America*	7.0	8.0	5.5	13.0	10.5	10.5
—	—	—	19.5	11.0	13.5	Mexico	—	—	—	28.0	15.5	15.0
8.5	12.0	11.0	11.5	7.5	7.0	Latin America	11.0	3.0	10.5	22.5	8.5	−2.0
5.0	7.5	4.0	9.5	5.5	3.5	Western Europe	4.0	6.5	3.0	9.0	8.5	3.5
5.0	8.0	4.0	9.5	6.0	3.5	European Union (15)	4.0	6.0	2.5	8.5	8.5	4.0
3.5	14.5	3.5	10.5	5.0	−3.0	Transition economies	2.5	11.5	12.0	13.5	5.0	−10.0
7.0	9.5	2.5	13.0	3.5	6.0	Asia	9.5	14.0	4.5	5.5	−8.5	9.0
1.0	3.5	20.5	12.0	−1.5	2.0	Japan	6.0	12.5	2.5	1.5	−5.5	9.5
10.0	14.5	3.5	16.5	13.0	11.5	East Asian traders†	10.5	15.5	4.0	3.0	−22.5	17.5

*Canada and the United States.

†Hong Kong, the Republic of Korea, Malaysia, Singapore, Taiwan, and Thailand for 1990–1996 data. Indonesia, Republic of Korea, Malaysia, Philippines, and Thailand for 1997–1999 data.

— = data not available.

Sources: World Trade Organization, "International Trade," April 4, 1997, http://www.wto.org/intltrad/intlorg.htm (July 9, 1997); and "Developing Countries' Merchandise Exports in 1999 Expanded by 8.5%—about Twice as Fast as the Global Average," http://www.wto.org/english/news_e/pres00_e/pr175_e.htm (April 6, 2000).

a series of aid, trade, and investment treaties between 71 African, Caribbean, and Pacific nations (ACP) and the EU. Under the present agreement, virtually all ACP exports enter the EU duty-free and are not subject to quotas.[26] The World Trade Organization (WTO) has ruled that the favorable trade terms provided to ACP nations are incompatible with international trade rules. The treaty expired in 2000, although the WTO allowed the current Lomé Convention to operate under a temporary waiver while the EU and ACP attempt to reform the agreement to be compatible with WTO guidelines.[27]

One option available to Lomé Convention negotiators is to modify the treaty to be consistent with another preferential arrangement, the **Generalized System of Preferences (GSP).** Under the GSP, products from 140 developing nations not given preferential treatment under any other agreement such as the Lomé Convention are provided duty-free access to most developed nations, including EU members. Under the U.S. program, imports of these products are valued at billions of dollars annually.[28]

Generalized System of Preferences (GSP)
An agreement under the auspices of WTO under which many products of developing nations are provided duty-free access to most developed nations

European Competitiveness

It is difficult to compare the competitiveness of one country with that of 15 even when the 15 are members of a common market. However, there are some indications that the EU's competitiveness as a whole has declined relative to the United States despite the fact that several member-nations have improved their international competitive position in recent years.

During the 1990s, as shown in Table 13.5, the level of growth in the EU's export volume has lagged the level achieved by most of the world, including North America. The 1999 increase (3.5 percent) was only 37 percent of the EU's level for 1997 and 70 percent of its average for the period 1990–1996. The EU's imports have also been growing at a slower rate than have those of most of the world. The 1999 increase of 4.0 percent was the same as the average for the 1990–1996 period but less than half its performance in 1997 and 1998. Note also that the EU averages in both exports and imports have been at or below the world averages at all the times shown in Table 13.5.

The EU has had lower growth in real GDP and a higher unemployment level than the United States for each year from 1992 through 1999, and these trends are projected to continue through at least 2002. Similarly, the EU's relative fiscal surplus has been worse than that of the United States for every year from 1993 through 1999, and this situation is expected to continue through 2002 or beyond.

Another indication of the EU's competitiveness is how it compares with the United States and Japan in technology. OECD indicators for trade coverage ratios (exports/imports) for "high-tech," "medium-tech," and "low-tech" industries reveal that European firms appear to specialize in low-tech products for export, followed by medium-tech and then high-tech products. Export/import ratios for American and Japanese firms are in the reverse order.[29] European expenditures on R&D as a percentage of GDP are consistently lower than those of Japan and the United States, and government expenditures for R&D have been declining in major European nations since the early 1980s. As shown in Figure 13.5, business-funded R&D in major European countries was also lower in the late 1990s than it had been a decade before. Firms in the United States and Japan typically spend over 10 percent of their R&D budget on computers and other office equipment compared to 4.5 percent spent by Europeans.[30] The COC found that the relative innovative capacity of several European nations, including France, Italy, the Netherlands, and the United Kingdom, has been eroding over the past quarter century.[31]

Computer Intelligence, a research firm that surveys computer use at firms worldwide, finds that in a typically large business site with more than 1,000 employees, 75 percent more personal computers and five times as many local area networks are used by American compared to European firms. Moreover, because technology adoption proceeds at a slower pace in Europe than in the United States or Japan, the Europeans are falling further behind. A 2000 report by the European Commission's Economic and Financial Affairs Office found that EU expenditures per capita in 1999 on ICT were less than 60 percent of the level in the United States. The EU was found to have a permanent deficit with the United States in ICT trade, and this deficit increased in the 1990s. This report also suggested that the EU as a whole was approximately five years behind the United States in receiving economic benefits from the information and communication technologies that produced such a strong performance in the United States in the 1990s.[32] Factors limiting diffusion of ICT in the EU include an insufficient supply of skilled computer specialists, limited markets for risk financing, and administrative burdens on new companies.

Barriers to European Competitiveness

Labor Costs and Productivity. Labor costs are a key factor affecting European competitiveness. Wages, salaries, and fringe benefits are higher in 11 European countries than they are in the United States when stated in U.S. dollars. The hourly rates of nine European countries are higher than those of Japan. A common complaint in Europe is that Europe's workers are overpaid and overprotected and get too many holidays—43 days in Germany compared to 21 days in the United States and 22 days in Japan.

The high cost of labor in the EU is compounded by productivity that lags that of the United States and other competitors. As we saw in Figure 13.2, in the latter part of the 1990s (and since the mid-1980s in some cases) productivity growth in many of the largest EU nations lagged behind that in the United States and Japan. Preliminary calculations by the European Commission suggest that the EU's total growth in productivity in the 1990s was lower than it had been in the prior decade. Productivity growth from 1991 to 1995 was 2.0 percent, and it was only 1.5 percent from 1995 to 1999.[33] In the opinion of many analysts, European managers have taken too long to adapt their operations to the fierce global services competition and to match the aggressive improvements in world-class manufacturers. In a survey of executives at 594 manufacturing firms in Europe, Japan, and the United States, the respondents stated that Europe is still slow to develop new products and is poor at mixing products with services.[34]

McKinsey & Co, management consultants, released a study in which it claimed that thousands of jobs may have to be cut if industries such as the automotive, telecommunications, and banking industries are to be as efficient in France and

[Figure 13.5] **Expenditures on R&D as a Percentage of GDP, Overall and by Business Sector, 1988–1997**

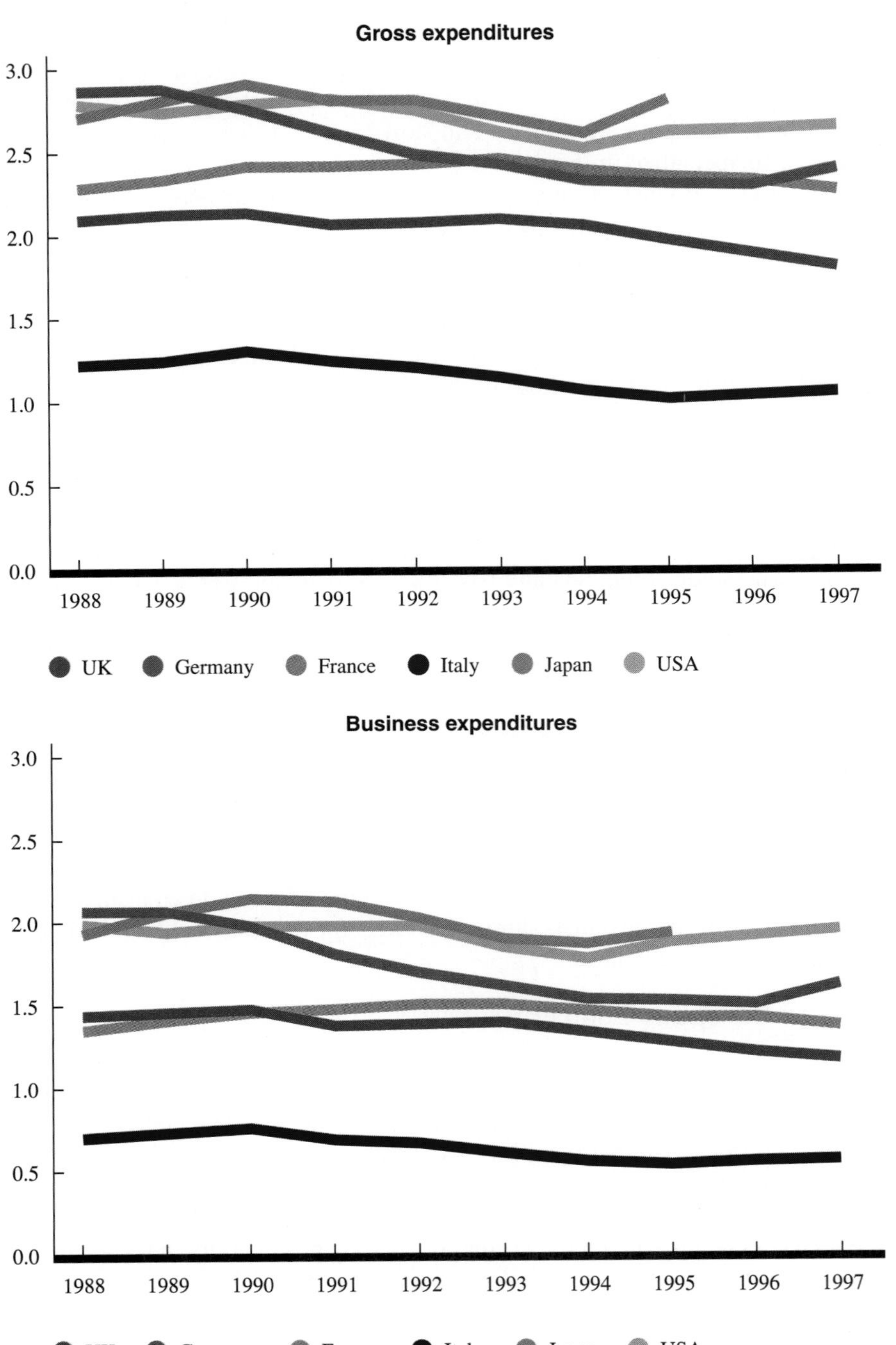

Note: Data for Italy for 1996 are provisional, and data for France and Italy for 1997 are provisional. Data for Japan are estimated and no data are available for Japan for 1996 or 1997. Data for Germany for 1997 are estimated.

Source: *SET Statistics 1999,* U.K. Office of Science and Technology, www.dti.gov.uk/ost/setstats/data/7/tab7_1.htm (November 12, 2000).

Germany as they are in Japan and the United States. The six-industry analysis implies that government regulations in both European countries hinder economic growth and increase unemployment. The automotive industry has suffered because French and German barriers to Japanese imports have protected local manufacturers from competition and thus delayed their restructuring. According to research from the Massachusetts Institute of Technology, the Japanese build a car with half as many workers as the French do and with two-thirds the number of German workers. Compared to the Japanese, the French produce 40 percent fewer goods and services per capita and the Germans produce 30 percent fewer in six major industries: autos, banking, housing, telecommunications, retailing, and software.[35]

The study puts much of the blame on another European social scheme: to obtain better levels of living for people at the lowest end of the job market, Germany and France have repeatedly increased their minimum wages over the past 25 years. In inflation-adjusted terms, minimum wages have doubled in both nations and are blamed for keeping low-skilled people out of the workplace. The report stated that if the United States raised the minimum wage to the French level from where it is now (55 percent of that level), 30 million Americans would be thrown out of work.[36] To maintain employment levels, nations such as France have passed legislation to reduce the workweek below 40 hours, and labor laws in the EU make it extremely difficult to fire employees once they have been employed for a year. U.S. companies have much greater flexibility in hiring and firing workers, allowing those companies to adjust more readily to changes in the marketplace.

Education. As we saw in Table 13.4, many European nations have achieved high standards of performance in their primary and secondary school systems, performance that often is superior to that in the United States. However, a higher percentage of the U.S. population attends university than is the case for the EU. University education in Europe also tends to be more theoretical, more rigid, and less adaptable to the changing needs of industry than is the case in the United States, and this can further harm the competitiveness of European businesses.

Conflicting Positions of Member-Nations. A constraining factor in efforts to improve overall competitiveness of the EU is continued disagreement among member-nations regarding key issues. For example, in 2000, Danish voters again voted against adopting the euro as that nation's currency, hindering efforts to extend the EU's monetary union to Denmark, the United Kingdom, and Sweden. The EU continues to have significant differences in relative economic prosperity among member-nations, complicating efforts to achieve consensus on monetary and taxation policies, economic development and industrial subsidies, expansion of the EU through adding new member-nations, and other initiatives.

Cultural Biases. One reason for Europe's technological lag is an aversion to using tools that are overly "American." Intel's European manager observed that the CEOs of several European personal computer (PC) companies don't have computers in their offices. The Computer Intelligence representative explains, "In many European companies, the goal is to rise to a high enough position where you don't have to use a PC. It's a status symbol not to use one."[37] These and other cultural biases can hinder the EU's efforts to improve competitiveness in an increasingly knowledge-driven world.

International E-Commerce in Europe. After the WTO extended the moratorium on Internet taxes, sales records were set in the year 2000. The EU's enterprise commissioner, who is responsible for small and medium-sized businesses as well as telecommunications and E-commerce, says that Europe has three to four years to overtake the United States and become completely competitive in Internet technology. EU Commission data reveal that while 30 percent of the American and Canadian populations are connected to the Internet, in most EU nations fewer than 15 percent of the people are. For the populations of France, Italy, Ireland, Spain, and Greece, the figure is 5 percent.

The development of EU E-businesses is hindered by the lack of an entrepreneurial culture and an underdeveloped risk capital market. The EU's enterprise commissioner says that it takes 11 weeks to set up a business in the EU, compared with just 11 days in the United States. The average EU legal costs for the setup (US$1,600) are three times the American costs. The commissioner is working to reduce the burden of regulation, saying, "We can't have a legal system that makes E-commerce impossible."

Nevertheless, in November 2000, a French judge ordered the U.S.-based portal Yahoo! to prevent French-based users from accessing certain parts of its Web site or face a fine of $13,000 per day.[38] This ruling could set an important precedent in terms of one nation trying to reach across borders and impose its laws on E-businesses based in other nations and could stifle efforts to fully develop E-commerce opportunities in the EU and elsewhere.

In spite of these difficulties, online shopping is growing in Europe. One research organization predicts that 9.36 million Europeans will purchase on the Internet in 2000, compared with 4.62 million in 1999. Europeans are expected to account for 43 percent of the online population by 2003, but because only 35 percent of Europe's top retailers offer online shopping, the leading American E-retailers are already operating in Europe.[39] Because of unrestricted trade between the 15 EU members, numerous American and European online retailers have started sites all over the continent that they supply from a single centralized warehouse.[40]

Signs of Improvement in European Competitiveness

Despite lagging performance relative to the United States, recently there have been signs of improving competitiveness among many of the European nations. For example, as we saw earlier in the Global Competitiveness Report (Table 13.2), 6 of the top 10 (and 15 of the top 25) nations in 2000 are from the EU or EFTA, compared to only 3 of the top 10 in 1996. Similarly, the World Competitiveness Scoreboard 2000 (Table 13.1) lists 8 European nations among the top 10 (versus 6 of 10 in 1996). At a business level, only the United States has more firms than the EU on *Fortune's* Global 500 list for 2000.[41]

Another encouraging factor regarding European competitiveness is the low level of corruption perceived to exist in many European countries. Table 13.6 shows the Corruption Perceptions Index 2000 from Transparency International. European nations account for 7 of the leading 10 nations on this list and 13 of the top 20. This can influence the competitiveness of working with (or against) European firms in the EU and elsewhere in the world.

In terms of competitiveness in innovation, the Economic Creativity Index 2000 (Table 13.3) lists 7 European nations among the world's top 10 (and 13 of the top 25). The COC found that several European nations, particularly Denmark, Finland, and Ireland, have made major gains in their innovative capacity in recent years, allowing them to gain position relative to the United States, Japan, and leading European innovation leaders such as Sweden, Switzerland, and Germany.[42] Favorable shifts in regulatory policy as well as improved investment in R&D and education are positioning the Scandinavian countries as a leading center for innovation, particularly in wireless telecommunications, where those countries are among the world's leaders.

One step that many European firms, especially the larger international companies, are taking to improve their production efficiency is to close older plants and concentrate their production at the most efficient facilities. British Telecommunications, for example, has cut 170,000 jobs and invested more than $17 billion in new technology since it was privatized in 1984. Renault, the French automaker, aroused political fury when it announced it was closing its Belgian plant, with a loss of 3,100 jobs. Renault and Peugeot Citroën chairmen, in order to cut workers from their payrolls, tried to persuade the government to provide funds to pay for the premature retirement of 40,000 French workers in their fifties. When the idea was rejected, Renault announced that it was letting nearly 3,000 workers go among its 100,000 French workers without closing any more of its plants. Peugeot Citroën made the same announcement.[43]

Although the EU experienced a subdued economic performance and continued high levels of unemployment in the 1991–1996 period, the region has had improved economic growth since that time. Strong gains have been made in employment in the late 1990s and 2000, particularly in part-time and fixed-term employment in the services sector. The creation of an additional 4 million net jobs is projected by 2002, bringing the unemployment rate EU-wide down to an estimated 7.2 percent, the best performance in over 20 years.[44] A survey of senior executives in nearly 1,500 of Europe's

Table 13.6 The Year 2000 Corruption Perceptions Index: Top 20 and Bottom 10 Countries

Rank	Country	2000 Corruption Perceptions Index Score
1	Finland	10.0
2	Denmark	9.8
3	New Zealand	9.4
3	Sweden	9.4
5	Canada	9.2
6	Iceland	9.1
6	Norway	9.1
6	Singapore	9.1
9	Netherlands	8.9
10	United Kingdom	8.7
11	Luxembourg	8.6
11	Switzerland	8.6
13	Australia	8.3
14	United States	7.8
15	Austria	7.7
15	Hong Kong	7.7
17	Germany	7.6
18	Chile	7.4
19	Ireland	7.2
20	Spain	7.0
81	Mozambique	2.2
82	Kenya	2.1
82	Russia	2.1
84	Cameroon	2.0
85	Angola	1.7
85	Indonesia	1.7
87	Azerbaijan	1.5
87	Ukraine	1.5
89	Yugoslavia	1.3
90	Nigeria	1.2

Rankings are based on multiple surveys from 1998 through 2000. The rankings are based on the degree to which corruption is perceived to exist among public officials and politicians. The index is a composite, drawing on 16 surveys from eight independent institutions. Surveys incorporate the perceptions of businesspeople, the general public, and country analysts.

Source: Transparency International, www.transparency.de/documents/cpi/2000/cpi2000.html (September 14, 2000).

largest firms revealed that they are more willing to hire more workers in the year 2000 than they had been a year earlier. Companies in Belgium, Spain, France, and the Netherlands were especially interested in hiring. When asked to compare their firms' current economic positions with the prior year's, a net 37 percent of the companies stated that the current year was better. Net figures are obtained by subtracting the replies saying it had worsened from those replying that it had improved. When asked about the year 2000, a net 51 percent of the respondents replied that their firms' economic situations were likely to improve compared with a net 31 percent a year earlier. Respondents also expect that the euro and the Internet, along with globalization, will have the biggest influence on European companies' pricing policies.[45]

Competition from Japan. Automobiles are only one facet of the Japanese onslaught in Europe. As in the United States, Japanese imports have nearly eliminated the European motorcycle industry. The EU runs a large trade deficit in electronics. Japanese cameras and watches are market leaders, and every small color TV tube used in Europe is made by Japanese electronic companies with local production facilities. Extensive investments by Japanese automobile manufacturers, including Nissan, Honda, and Toyota, have helped those firms to make rapid gains in market share during the 1990s. Additional automobile production capacity by Japanese firms is scheduled to come online in the early 2000s.

Japanese service companies have also invested in the European market and are competing with local firms in retailing, advertising, hotels, distribution, tourism, and insurance. Many have come because Japanese manufacturers frequently prefer to bring their service providers with them instead of having to use local suppliers. The president of a Japanese market research organization claims, "Toyota will bring every one of its subcontractors with it, all the way down to its construction firms and its insurance companies. Most of the service companies arriving in Europe have come to look after Japanese industry." The leading banks in Japan were among the first service companies to follow Japanese manufacturers to Europe. Advertising agencies are now following the same pattern.

European manufacturers are concerned that Japanese manufacturers are buying local distributing companies. In Japan, large electronics producers do this to control marketing and pricing. Buying distributors in Europe permits them to maintain high prices and makes it difficult for small competitors to get distribution. Barrie James, author of *The Trojan Horse,* a study of Japanese investment in Europe, says, "Over the long term, combining manufacturing with all the related services poses a greater risk for Europe than does a simple manufacturing penetration. Europe will end up facing the same oligopoly situation as Japan, under which prices rise and poorer European competitors increasingly get locked out of the market."[46]

Competition from the United States

European firms face competition from American exports as they do from Japan, but unlike Japan, U.S. companies have had European-based manufacturing facilities for a long time. European-produced General Motors (GM) and Ford cars compete in the automobile market; brands such as Heinz, Kodak, and Coca-Cola are household names (the English "hoover" their rugs instead of vacuuming them); and computer manufacturers IBM, Compaq, and Hewlett-Packard dominate the professional PC market. American firms also supply two-thirds of Europe's needs.[47] Probably because of the long-term political and cultural ties plus the fact that European multinationals have been free to invest in the United States with minimum hindrance, American companies have generally been well accepted in Europe. The occasional EC–U.S. "chicken," "pasta," "banana," and "citrus" wars have not had a serious impact on the European subsidiaries of American global and multinational firms.

Yet European governments are working to help national companies compete with American firms. They have helped Airbus in its battle against Boeing and have spent billions of dollars on research and development programs to support European industry. There are two main EU research schemes: (1) the Fourth Framework Programme for Research and Development and (2) Eureka. The Fourth Framework distributed $14.5 billion in R&D grants to fund precompetitive research over the period 1994–98 and was followed by a Fifth Framework Programme in 1999. Interestingly, European subsidiaries of foreign firms can participate with European companies, universities, or research institutions. The European Union also supports *Eureka,* an independent research program involving 20 nations, including EU members, and various firms that are involved in the research. To date, more than 2,000 organizations have participated in Eureka-related projects. Among Eureka's programs are *Eureka Audiovisual* (high-definition TV) and *Jessi* (semiconductor research). Although Jessi's purpose is to help European companies develop new microchip technology to compete against Japanese and American producers, IBM Europe is a member.[48]

Competition from Asian Nations

Companies from Asian nations that used to receive investment from Europeans taking advantage of lower labor costs are now investing in Europe. Their investments in

European electronics and automobile plants amount to billions of dollars. While firms from all the Asian tigers have production facilities in Europe, South Korea's industrial conglomerates—the **chaebol**—have been leading the Asian investment drive into Europe. Similar to the case for Japan, the chaebol have a clear preference for one country. In recent years, the United Kingdom has been receiving two-thirds of new Korean investment in Europe.[49] However, the Asian economic turmoil that began in 1997 resulted in the near collapse of the Korean economy under the weight of $150 billion in foreign debt. The four major chaebol—Daewoo, Samsung, Hyundai, and LG (formerly Lucky-Goldstar)—are responsible for over half the Korean corporate debt and have been undergoing substantial reorganization as a result, often including the sale or merger of subsidiaries.[50] As a result, many planned chaebol investments have been delayed or canceled.[51] These developments have helped to slow the onslaught into Europe of Korean and other Asian competitors, but this situation is likely to be only temporary.

chaebol
Large South Korean conglomerates, mostly family-owned and directed, that have succeeded worldwide in such fields as microchips, electronics construction, shipbuilding, and steel

Will the "New Economy" Transform Europe?

A lingering uncertainty is whether, and at what pace, the EU will experience the accelerated productivity growth that was experienced during the late 1990s in the United States. There have been several efforts aimed at structural reform and the promotion of a knowledge-based economy, including privatization, reform of labor and financial markets, and adoption of new technologies. Domestic demand has been strong, competition in the EU has intensified, prices have declined, and many nations have initiated efforts to reform the tax system.[52] To achieve its potential, the region must try to avoid sustained decline in the relative value of the euro, manage differences in policy and economic growth among member-nations, and avoid major shocks from macroeconomic events such as recession in the United States or elsewhere. If these goals are achieved, the EU may be positioned for improved productivity and sustained, noninflationary growth and the opportunity to begin closing the competitiveness gap with the United States.

Japan

Japan experienced impressive economic growth between 1960 and 1985, but in the late 1980s, the Japanese economy overexpanded and capital was misallocated. A sustained downturn resulted from the subsequent collapse of the "bubble economy," in which prices of Japanese stocks, real estate, and other property plummeted. As a result, the 1990s were difficult for Japan, with an average annual growth in real GDP of less than 1 percent from 1992 through 1999. High levels of corporate debt and stagnant domestic demand resulted in record numbers of bankruptcies (rising from 9 trillion yen in 1995 and 8 trillion in 1996 to 14 trillion yen in each of 1997, 1998, and 1999 and projected to exceed 18 trillion yen in 2000). Economists estimate that bankruptcies caused a loss of 10 percent of the nation's GDP over the five-year period 1993–1997. Unemployment increased by 135 percent between 1990 and 1999, rising from 2.0 percent of the work force to 4.7 percent. The government's fiscal budget declined from a 1.5 percent surplus in 1992 to a 7.0 percent deficit in 1999, and Japan's public debt is the highest among the OECD nations (well over 100 percent of GDP in 2000). The end of the decade saw deflation, with the largest declines occurring in the investment goods sectors. Land prices declined at double-digit rates in the late 1990s but by only 9 percent in 2000.[53]

In the past, Japanese firms were able to export the country out of its economic problems relatively easily, but the large devaluations of Southeast Asian and South Korean currencies cut into Japanese exports of automobiles, electronics, and machinery, causing Japan's trade surplus with those countries to fall sharply in 1997 and 1998. Economists had been warning that the financial crisis in Southeast Asia would depress exports, the only sector of Japan's economy that had been growing. Instead, because of large gains in its trade with the United States and the EU due to a cheap yen, the country ended 1997 with an increase in its trade surplus. As shown in Table 13.5, exports declined by 1.5 percent in 1998 due to the region's financial crisis and rebounded by only 2.0 percent in 1999 (to $403.4 billion). Despite this, as was shown in Figure 13.1, Japan had 1999 trade surpluses with the EU and the United States of $38.4 billion and $69.6 billion, respectively. With overall trade surpluses projected at $125 billion in 2000, $117 billion in 2001, and $131 billion in 2002,[54] increasing pressure is coming from abroad to open Japanese markets to competition. These trade tensions further complicate efforts by Japanese managements and government to pull the economy out of its sustained slide.

Declining Ranking on Competitiveness

The experiences of the 1990s have had a negative impact on the competitiveness ranking of Japan. As we saw earlier in the Global Competitiveness Report (Table 13.2), Japan's ranking declined from 13 to 21 between 1996 and 2000. The World Competitiveness Scorecard (Table 13.1) suggested an even greater decline in Japan's relative competitiveness, from 3 to 17 between 1994 and 2000. Below, we will address several of the factors that help explain Japan's declining competitiveness during the 1990s.

Declining Productivity. Japanese multinationals have received great praise for their operational efficiency (for example, see Chapter 20 for a discussion of Japanese production systems). As we saw in Table 13.4, Japan's educational system has produced students who perform near the top in world comparisons. Yet Japanese business encountered problems in the 1990s. As was shown in Figure 13.2, the rate of improvement in productivity declined from 4.3 percent annually between 1985 and 1995 to 3.1 percent in 1999. Part of the explanation for declining productivity is the traditional reluctance of Japanese employers to discharge loyal employees. This has resulted in overstaffing and reduced hiring of young workers, creating a mismatch of skills due to the inability to recruit younger workers with new knowledge bases.

Declining Investment in R&D. The COC ranks Japan as a leading nation in terms of international innovativeness.[55] Indeed, many Japanese companies invested heavily in R&D during the 1990s despite the overall economic problems in Japan, and they have established strong international positions as a result of their innovativeness. Historically, Japan's expenditures on R&D as a percentage of GDP have been the highest of any of the major world economies, as was suggested in Figure 13.5. Japanese investment in R&D has declined substantially since the early 1990s, however, and the proportion of GDP invested in R&D in the period 1993–1997 was lower in Japan than it was in the United States, France, and Germany.

Barriers to Innovation. As we saw in Table 13.3, Japan ranked 20th in the Economic Creativity Index 2000 and was the lowest ranked among the top 25 nations in terms of the start-up index, reflecting barriers to entrepreneurial initiative in that country. Although some progress has been made in recent years, it continues to be difficult for entrepreneurs and small businesses to gain access to capital. This problem is particularly great for businesses in emerging knowledge-based sectors, which involve higher risk and fewer assets to serve as collateral.

The costs of establishing a new manufacturing facility in Japan are also significantly higher than they are in other developed countries. As shown by the Japan External Trade Organization (Table 13.7), establishing a manufacturing facility is from 5 to 11 times more costly in Japan than it is in nations such as the United States, Germany, France, and the United Kingdom and even more costly than it is in the Asian NICs and NIEs. These higher costs can encourage businesspeople to start or expand their companies in other nations, further harming Japanese efforts to reduce unemployment and boost economic activity. This problem has been compounded by high costs for telecommunications and Internet connections in Japan, although pressure from the United States has resulted in significant reductions in charges between 2000 and 2003 and improved access for new competitors. Japanese Internet penetration continues to lag that of the United States, a situation compounded by Japan's failure to deregulate to promote competition and by barriers to the use of foreign experts in training or workplace roles.[56]

Table 13.7 International Comparisons of Initial Investment Costs in the Manufacturing Sector

		Japan	United States	United Kingdom	Germany	France
Manufacturing plant	Price of space in industrial park	100	13	12	17	2
Office	Lease guarantee	100	8	81	7	10
Setting up a company	Registration costs	100	7	139	76	2
Hiring costs	Factory manager	100	67	82	78	79
	Administrative Manager	100	11	19	44	44
	Engineers	100	20	34	81	81
	Headquarters staff, factory workers	100	18	3	5	8
Housing, school	Rent guarantee	100	12	20	25	29
	Admission fee, tuition	100	85	62	46	59
Visa	Visa fee	100	158	283	67	333
Ratio		100	14	24	20	9

Note: Japan = 100. Costs are based on a wholly owned subsidiary with 500 million yen of capital, a 5,000-square-meter factory with 3,000 square meters of factory space in an industrial park in a provincial city, 500 square meters of office space in a major city, one expatriate representative director with three dependents (spouse and two school-aged children) and 150 square meters of rental housing in a major city, and local hires of one factory manager, one administration manager, 20 engineers, clerical workers for the headquarters, and factory workers.
Source: JETRO Inward Foreign Direct Investment Survey (Tokyo: Japan External Trade Organization), www.jetro.go.jp/ip/e/access/inward_foreign_direct_investment.html (November 12, 2000).

Japan's trade in ICT, both imports and exports, has grown more slowly than that of the world as a whole. Reflecting a drop in exports within Asia due to the Asian financial crisis, as well as the movement of production to offshore sites and falling prices for semiconductors and memory chips, Japan's ICT exports grew by an average of minus 0.4 percent per year and imports grew by 0.5 percent between 1996 and 1999.[57] Between 1996 and 1999, Japan's share of the world's ICT exports declined from 15.1 percent to 12.5 percent, and its share of ICT imports declined from 7.0 percent to 5.9 percent.

Regulations and Restructuring

Despite continued pressure to promote restructuring and deregulation, limited progress was achieved by the Japanese in the 1980s and early 1990s. The keiretsu (discussed below) continued to exercise strong influence, the financial sector was insulated from international competitiveness, and inefficient, often corrupt practices characterized many public works projects. In a cultural setting that did not allow for corporate or bank failure, problems were only papered over, not resolved, which prolonged the post–bubble economy crisis and permitted a chronic lack of confidence to settle in.

Pressured by a broad recognition that the sustained economic malaise would not disappear on its own, the Japanese government recently began to promote a number of institutional changes. Efforts were undertaken to restructure the business sector. To address the more than $1 trillion in bad loans, the banking sector is being restructured.[58] Changes include a number of mergers and sales of previously bankrupt banks, although this sector continues to be plagued by nonperforming loans and weak balance sheets. The so-called "Big Bang" restructuring of the financial sector after 1997 has resulted

Selling black market CDs in Belgrade.
Art Zamur/Gamma Liaison

in a continuing surge of entry by foreign financial institutions from the United States and Europe.[59] Fidelity Investments has formed partnerships with three Japanese banks to sell mutual funds. Merrill Lynch acquired a network of 2,000 brokerage offices when their former owner, Yamaichi Securities, went bankrupt.

Another governmental restriction to competition was Japan's Large-Scale Retail Store Law. Under the original version, a small convenience store could prevent the opening of a large store in its area for up to 10 years. After three years of discussion, Toys "Я" Us, with heavy pressure from the U.S. government, persuaded the Japanese government to change the law. The revision, which limited the maximum delay to 18 months, enabled Toys "Я" Us to open its first Japanese store in 1991. Finally, at the end of 1997, the Japanese government scrapped the bill completely.[60] At that time, Toys "Я" Us had 42 stores in Japan.[61]

Japan's Keiretsu

One of Japan's best-known institutions is the **keiretsu,** a group of financially connected firms that tend to do business with themselves rather than with others. Both American businesspeople and trade officials have contended for many years that the keiretsu system contributes greatly to the huge Japanese–U.S. trade imbalance.[62]

keiretsu
A group of financially connected Japanese firms that tend to do business among themselves

The keiretsu system was an important force in the Japanese recovery after World War II and was regarded by many management experts as the source of Japanese industry's competitive strength. Historically, the keiretsu were at the center of a circular arrangement involving the government, banks, industry, and the population. The government told the banks to invest in certain companies. The companies provided lifetime employment for their employees, who put their savings in the banks, which reinvested them as ordered by the government. In return for following the orders of the government, the companies were given preferential treatment in the awarding of business licenses.

Among the important forms of keiretsu, the horizontal was the most powerful. It contained a firm from each industrial sector, all of which were grouped around a large bank that supplied up to 40 percent of the keiretsu's financing. Through cross-shareholding, keiretsu members owned up to 60 percent of each member-company's stock. This arrangement practically eliminated independent stockholders and permitted each company to pursue long-term growth without having to report regularly to stockholders as American companies must do.

The U.S. government has maintained that keiretsu groups have constructed informal barriers to the sale of foreign goods in Japan. A keiretsu such as the Toyota keiretsu has been able to assemble an automobile from parts supplied only by keiretsu members, for example. This has made it nearly impossible for potential suppliers outside the keiretsu to obtain business from Toyota. Many people in business and government feared that Japanese firms were using the keiretsu system in the United States. Ford's head of component operations complained that the Japanese still buy too many parts from Japanese suppliers that have set up operations in the United States and not enough parts from American firms. Over 250 Japanese suppliers have set up U.S. plants to serve eight Japanese auto plants.[63]

After the collapse of the "bubble economy," regulations were relaxed to permit greater access to international financial markets, and both banks and companies became less dependent on the keiretsu. As an executive of one keiretsu bank explained, in the last 10 years the percentage of cross-holdings has declined and the proportion of lending the bank gives to the companies in the keiretsu has dropped. He also said that some of the 20 firms in the keiretsu hardly borrow from his bank anymore and that three-quarters of them did not buy the bank's stock when it was trying to raise capital.

Although the keiretsu have become weaker over the last decade, they largely survived intact until 1999. Now the system is beginning to unravel. Sustained domestic economic stagnation, internationalization of capital markets, and pressure for reform of corporate governance have begun to loosen traditional relationships among affiliated members of keiretsu. In addition, many of the banks are merging and selling their cross-share holdings. Nissan, under a new chief executive officer from Renault (which purchased a controlling stake in the company), not only pulled out of its keiretsu because its bank merged with other keiretsu banks but also broke up its vertical keiretsu of suppliers. Nissan reduced the number of companies in which it owns stock from 1,394 to just 4 and the number of suppliers from 1,145 to 600. With the exception of Mitsubishi, the keiretsu now seem to accept the fact that a gradual breakup of the nation's 50-year-old industrial system is inescapable.[64]

Improving Japanese Competitiveness

During the decade of the 1990s, to improve their competitiveness when the yen declined below the critical barrier of 100 to the dollar, Japanese firms invested billions of dollars in Asian production facilities to take advantage of cheaper labor, land, and manufactured components. Their strategy was to dominate local sales with local production and keep out U.S. exports while expanding their exports to the rest of the world. Low-cost imports from their Asian subsidiaries, both finished products and components used in Japanese-made products, enabled Japanese firms to compete at home against American imports.[65] The emergence of the Asian economic crisis in 1997 hampered short-term economic returns from this strategy; however, it also provided an opportunity for further investments at reduced rates, including purchasing shares from financially strapped local partners. These actions are expected to lower overall costs and improve international competitiveness during the 2000s.

The Japanese economy began to enter a recovery phase in mid-1999, with the bottom of the cycle occurring in April 1999. Performance has remained tenuous in 2001, with continued overcapacity in many industrial sectors and sustained high personal savings rates due to individuals' uncertainty about their financial prospects. The government implemented a zero interest rate policy from February 1999 until August 2000 in an effort to stimulate economic recovery and reduce the record level of bankruptcies. The government also introduced several promotional programs, including a November 1999 public works package worth over $60 billion, in an effort to stimulate demand. Restructuring continues to put a damper on the economy, yet business profits have recovered markedly, leading to increased business investment domestically and abroad. Although much more work remains, restructuring has helped promote improved transparency and external monitoring of corporate governance, facilitating changes in traditional management practices.

Government deregulation, technological advances, diversifying consumer tastes, and increasing internationalization of Japanese society have opened up Japan to increased foreign direct investment from other nations. Major investments in the automobile industry (including Renault's acquisition of a controlling stake in Nissan) and other sectors resulted in a record high level of $12.7 billion of investment from abroad in 1999. Although less than 5 percent of the level of investment flowing into the United States ($282.5 billion in 1999), these inflows were nearly four times Japan's 1998 total of $3.3 billion.[66]

Competition from the United States and Europe

The Japanese economy has been in a repetitive cycle for the last 25 years in which the government allows the yen to fall against the dollar to boost exports while also restricting domestic growth to dampen imports. Japan's trade surplus takes off. Then the United States reacts by demanding that the Japanese government (1) allow the yen to rise against the dollar, (2) reduce restrictions on U.S. imports, (3) permit U.S. firms more freedom in doing business in Japan, and (4) stimulate its economy to increase demand. The Japanese response is to make some concessions on American imports, reduce some of the restrictions on American firms doing business in the country, and drive up the value of the yen. However, often the yen rises too much and recession results. The country was coming out of its fifth such cycle in 2001. What is the impact on American competitiveness in Japan? The following is what happened in the first part of the 1990s and is being repeated in the fifth cycle.[67]

Bargain hunting is in; high prices are out. The recession and high costs have motivated Japanese consumers and businesses to search for cheaper products and are creating new distribution channels for U.S. imports made cheaper by increased American competitiveness and the strong yen. Because of the economic slowdown, manufacturers have accumulated inventory that their conventional retailers cannot buy. Desperate to unload the merchandise, they have sought out the very discounters to whom they previously refused to sell.[68]

The continued easing of regulations and the decline in land prices have encouraged further activity by foreign firms in Japan's distribution, service, and retail sectors. At the end of 1997, the U.S. office supply superstore chains Office Max and Office Depot both established their first stores in Japan. In a challenge to the complex distribution channels that are typical in Japan (see Chapter 2), Office Max and Office Depot source their goods directly from manufacturers, bypassing wholesalers. An increasing number of foreign firms are also entering Japan's service sector, many areas of which previously were protected from competition due to regulations. Foreign firms, which are 90 percent more productive than Japanese nonmanufacturing firms and 70 percent more productive than Japanese firms as a whole, are stimulating rapid change in business practices.[69]

Many U.S. and European retailers of specialty apparel have entered Japan, opening stores in shopping centers. Other foreign firms are expanding into Japan by using retail strategies developed in the United States, such as outlet centers (shopping centers where manufacturers sell their own products at discount prices) and wholesale clubs (retail stores where members purchase goods at wholesale prices).[70] The advent of price-conscious consumers and the opening of the Japanese distribution system have attracted many U.S. companies that are enthusiastically attacking the Japanese market. Microsoft, Lotus, and Borland have taken more than half the Japanese PC software market, causing some Japanese producers to complain about unfair competition. Ironically, in a twist on common complaints about Japanese business practices, Japanese firms say that "the Americans care more about market share than profits."[71]

Competition from Asian Nations

hollowing out
Firms closing their production facilities and becoming marketing organizations for other, mostly foreign, producers

Much of the competition in Japan from Asian countries is the result of Japanese firms moving their production to those countries in the mid-1990s to avoid high labor costs at home and increase or recover their international competitiveness. Key industries, such as electronics manufacturers, are being accused of **hollowing out,** that is, closing their local production facilities and becoming marketing organizations for other, generally foreign, producers. Those companies that are continuing to do their own manufacturing are, as we discussed earlier, shifting to other countries where production costs are lower. For example, Japan produced 38.2 million videocassette recorders (VCRs) in 1989, which accounted for most of the world's market. By 1998, Japan was producing 9.6 million VCRs, a 66 percent decline.[72] Of the 3.3 million machines Sanyo produces annually, only 600,000 are Japanese-made; the remainder are produced in Indonesia, China, and Germany.[73] South Korea, which has long depended on Japan for investment and technology, is now successfully competing against it in the export of high-tech goods such as electronics, petrochemicals, machinery, and steel.[74]

> In Hong Kong, NEC is a company without a factory. The NEC subsidiary in Hong Kong supervises the production of PCs, printers, and disk drives but manufactures nothing. Some factories in China make the printer parts, and others assemble them. PC parts come from suppliers in Hong Kong and other parts of Asia, and the disk drives come from the Philippines. NEC has no investment in any of these companies producing NEC products but maintains a team of 26 roving production specialists to see that quality control and product reliability meet NEC standards.[75]

Table 13.8 Average Annual Increases in Merchandise Exports for Selected Countries, 1980–1995

	Average Annual Growth Rate, 1980–1990 (%)	Average Annual Growth Rate, 1990–1999 (%)	Growth Rate in 1997 (%)	Growth Rate in 1998 (%)	Growth Rate in 1999 (%)	Value in 1999 ($ billions)
World	4.7%	6.5%	10.5%	5.0%	5.0%	$5,473
Japan	5.0	2.5	12.0	−1.5	2.0	419
China	11.4	—	—	—	—	195
Hong Kong	15.3	9.0	6.0	−4.5	3.5	174
South Korea	—	15.0	25.0	17.0	12.0	145
Taiwan	5.9	5.5	8.0	1.0	5.0	122
Singapore	16.2	11.0	7.0	−0.5	5.5	115
Malaysia	17.8	13.5	9.5	4.0	20.0	85
Thailand	21.6	10.0	7.5	8.0	12.0	58
United States	3.6	6.5	12.0	2.5	4.5	695
Mexico	12.2	14	15	6	16	137
Germany	4.6	5.5	12.0	7.0	4.0	542

Sources: *World Development Indicators, 1997* (Washington, DC: World Bank, 1997), pp. 154–56, 158–60; and *International Trade Statistics 2000* (Geneva: World Trade Organization, 2000), pp. 17, 44, 51, 60–61, 83.

This new Japanese strategy is creating regional groups capable of competing worldwide and also ties Asian nations to the Japanese economy. Firms, such as NEC, that formerly kept their technology and high-value-added production at home are now sharing technology and supporting production networks. Instead of joint ventures, these new arrangements are bound together only with contracts that allow the partners to be flexible and autonomous. Although some of the Asian countries, especially Malaysia, welcome their ties with Japan, others remain concerned about being excessively dependent on the Japanese.[76]

Developing Nations and the NIEs

One factor that stands out in this analysis of competitive forces is that products made by Asian firms are competing strongly with the output of older, more experienced producers from Europe, the United States, and Japan. Japanese companies that have been driven by the strong yen to build plants in East Asia are increasingly exporting their output (called *reverse exports*) back to Japan, as you saw in a previous section.

U.S. investment in East Asia also has increased, rising to nearly $6 billion between 1987 and 1999. Motorola has a $400 million complex in Hong Kong, along with a dozen plants in nine other Asian nations, including Singapore and China. That company is also a leading supplier of cellular phones and high-end walkie-talkies in the region.

An Economic Crisis Hits the Region

The Asian NICs, NIEs, and China have developed rapidly over the past two decades, and as shown in Table 13.8, a major factor driving these nations' growth has been international trade. However, rapid growth in the 1980s and early 1990s was accompanied by excess capacity, high levels of debt, and rapid inflation in real estate and other asset values. Ironically, the financial system that had allowed these nations to achieve rapid growth through access to easy money, often based on political connections and other factors, was ultimately one of the main reasons for later problems. In 1997, a financial crisis in Thailand spread quickly to other Asian nations, resulting in a decline of local currencies of up to 80 percent versus the U.S. dollar. Many of these nations experienced similar declines in their stock prices, as about $400 billion in value was erased from Asian stock markets in 1997. Most of the region experienced deep economic recession as part of one of the largest economic collapses the world has ever experienced.

The International Monetary Fund came to the assistance of many of the affected nations, committing over $110 billion in short-term loans just to Thailand, Indonesia, and South Korea. To obtain these loans, the borrowing nations had to agree to a number of actions, including economic deregulation, banking reform, and tight macroeconomic policies. There was also pressure for substantial structural reforms, including reduced government spending, scaling back of government efforts at industrial targeting, reform of banking systems, removal of barriers to foreign investment, and a breakup or sell-off of indebted companies.

Recovery Is Faster Than Expected

There are signs that most of the Asian economies are emerging from the wreckage. For the first time in many cases, managements of Asian companies are concentrating on earning profits instead of trying to break production records at any price. The formerly powerful conglomerates in Korea, Indonesia, and other nations have been forced to sell off portions of their businesses to pay their debts. Banks that served as conduits for directing a country's savings to the conglomerates' favored entities must now function as normal commercial banks.[77]

In South Korea, for example, the chaebol (industrial conglomerates) have had to sell off many of their subsidiaries to reduce their huge debts. One is the Daewoo Group, which is bankrupt and is being dismantled by its creditors to liquidate over $76 billion in liabilities. Hyundai, another Korean conglomerate, has been forced to sell its majority interests in steel, oil-refining, aluminum, and chemical plants as a result of the reformist government's stopping of its formerly limitless supply of soft bank loans.[78]

Thailand is another Asian country that enacted massive legal changes affecting bankruptcy and also liberalized rules on foreign investment. Like Korea, it has established barriers separating banks and other businesses from their owners to ensure that the banks no longer function as the conglomerates' private vaults.[79]

Clearly, since 1999, a substantial economic recovery has been occurring in most Asian countries. As shown in Table 13.8, many of those nations have resorted to exporting as a means of dealing with their financial problems. These strategies have been facilitated by a booming American economy. The collapse of Asian currencies caused those countries' goods to be much less expensive than they were before the crisis, allowing Asian nations to ship vast quantities of merchandise, particularly computers and electronics goods. Indeed, in the first half of 2000, electronics goods alone accounted for 60 percent of Thailand's exports, as well as 53 percent of Hong Kong's, 34 percent of Taiwan's, 33 percent of China's, 25 percent of Malaysia's, 19 percent of Korea's, and 14 percent of Singapore's.[80] Korea, Hong Kong, and Singapore combined accounted for 22.6 percent of world exports of information technology–related goods in 1999.[81]

E-Commerce Has a Promising Future

While the Asian NIEs, NICs, and China currently lag the United States, Europe, and Japan in Internet access and E-commerce, that gap is expected to narrow in coming years. The number of Internet users in the Asia Pacific region as a whole is projected to increase from 73 million in 2000 to 233 million in 2005, which will be an average penetration rate of 8 percent.[82] China had about 17 million Internet users in 2000, compared to 15 million in Korea, and the number of users is expected to double every six months. In terms of E-commerce, Hong Kong, Korea, and Singapore have the greatest potential in the near term, especially for business-to-consumer (B2C) applications, due to the high cost of a personal computer, Internet access costs, and low income levels. Korea's B2C market is expected to rise to $10 billion by 2005, compared to $0.9 billion in 2000. Overall, by 2005, the B2C market in Asia is projected to total $57 billion, a fraction of the projected business-to-business (B2B) market of $1.2 trillion.[83] However, government actions may pose a barrier in some nations as a result of restrictive attitudes toward the Internet and E-commerce. For example, in 2000, the Chinese central government introduced regulations on foreign ownership of Internet portals, and that action could constrain that country's Web development.

Questions Remain Regarding the Future

Since mid-1997, short-term foreign debt levels have become more manageable, though still equaling 20 percent of the region's total output, and foreign exchange reserves have grown in most of the Asian nations. Korea has committed approximately $125 billion in public funds in an effort to rescue its banking sector. Some banks have been sold to foreign companies, and others have been forced to merge. While government efforts to provide stimulus packages have helped to hasten the rate of economic recovery, the result is that several nations are now running budget deficits of about 5 to 6 percent of GDP. In several nations, the pace of structural reform has been slower than anticipated and there are still too many weak banks and companies with problem loans. In many nations, output remains below precrisis levels.

It remains to be seen whether the Asian NICs and NIEs can soon regain the sustained high growth rates that existed before the crisis. Achieving that will require their governments to implement the proposed structural reforms.[84] Slowing growth in the United States, especially in high-technology sectors supplied by Asian companies, and continued economic difficulties in Japan may also limit the effectiveness of traditional national economic development strategies based on export-driven growth.

China, a Case unto Itself

China is the world's most populous nation, with over 1.3 billion people. Over the last 20 years, China has had strong sustained growth, even by comparison to the Asian NICs and NIEs. It has achieved average growth in merchandise exports of 15 percent per year during the last two decades, and as we saw in Chapter 2, it has a large trade surplus. With $87.8 billion in imports in 1999, the United States is China's largest trading partner. Indeed, exports from China to the United States grew at an average rate of 21 percent in the 1990s, and the growing trade deficit has caused concern among American politicians and businesspeople.[85] China's growth in exports of computers/peripherals and miscellaneous electronic parts, which together represented 59 percent of total exports in 1999, grew by 30 percent and 19 percent, respectively, between 1996 and 1999.[86] China's performance in international trade and as a destination for large flows of foreign direct investment helped that country to largely escape the 1997 Asian economic crisis that hit most of its neighbors.

China has been trying to join the World Trade Organization (WTO) (and its predecessor, GATT) for over 13 years. That country views WTO membership as a necessary element in its quest to establish a sustainable market economy and is preparing for anticipated entry into the WTO in 2001. However, entry will require China to eliminate many of the trade barriers and other practices that currently protect its business sector from foreign competitors. The transition will require many changes in government and business practices, and concerns remain regarding China's vulnerability to the type of currency problems that struck other Asian nations.

Counterfeiting and Piracy: A Challenge to Business Worldwide

You are in Hong Kong and see a Louis Vuitton purse or a Ralph Lauren polo shirt at half the U.S. price. Are these items genuine or fake? A special kind of competition confronting unwary consumers and international companies in both developed and developing nations is **counterfeiting.** The International Chamber of Commerce estimates that 8 percent of world trade consists of counterfeit products.[87] According to the Global

counterfeiting
Illegal use of a well-known manufacturer's brand name on copies of the firm's merchandise

Anti-Counterfeiting Group, counterfeiting and piracy cost U.S. manufacturers $200 billion per year.[88]

Besides the production of exact copies of branded items, other kinds of counterfeiting include making (1) close copies with different names, (2) reproductions that are not exact copies, and (3) imitations that are cheap copies and fool no one. As was discussed in Chapter 11, **piracy,** a kind of counterfeiting, is the copying of trade-related intellectual property protected by patents, copyrights, and trademarks. Computer software, semiconductors, videos, compact discs, and books are the kinds of products that are pirated. In Hong Kong, for example, 56 percent of all software is pirated, and in China, 91 percent of software is pirated.[89] Factories in Malaysia produce an estimated 315 million compact discs a year that are worth $300 million.[90] In 1998, 10 percent of counterfeit goods seized by U.S. Customs consisted of fashion garments and 21 percent of the total value consisted of accessories such as purses and wallets.

piracy
A kind of counterfeiting involving copying of trade-related intellectual property protected by patents, copyrights, and trademarks

> Increasingly, the sale of counterfeit goods is occurring on the Web. A spokesperson for the Anti-Counterfeiting Coalition advises, "Now that it's finally safe to buy things with your credit card over the Internet, lo and behold, what you're buying is counterfeit." There are about 25,000 Web sites selling consumer luxury products, and from 20 to 30 percent of them sell counterfeit goods or misuse a manufacturer's trademark. For example, counterfeit Gucci items have been found on nearly 300 sites. Be careful to read the fine print. Some sites call their counterfeits "replicas."[91]

Counterfeiting is extremely common in Asian nations such as South Korea, China, Hong Kong, Malaysia, Thailand, and Indonesia. Taiwan has been one of the major sources of counterfeit products, but under heavy pressure from the United States, the Taiwanese government passed strong copyright laws and banned the exportation of pirated products. Although there has been a decline in the proportion of seizures of products from Taiwan since 1999, that country remains a major source of illegal products. Malaysia passed a law in 1987 that stipulated prison terms of up to five years for copyright infringement, but courts in that nation have yet to send any offenders to jail and the levels of seized counterfeit goods from Malaysia have been increasing rapidly in the United States.[92] Organized crime, particularly Chinese crime syndicates known as Triads, has become increasingly involved in product counterfeiting. Indeed, the Federal Bureau of Investigation considers counterfeiting and other forms of theft of intellectual property to be "the crime of the 21st Century."[93]

Despite pressure from business groups and the passage of new laws in many nations which have been major sources of counterfeit goods, the problem of counterfeiting appears to be growing. The U.S. Customs Service searches only about 2 percent of all goods imported annually into the United States. Yet from the data in Table 13.9, one can see that there was a 40 percent increase in seized counterfeit goods in 1998 over the 1997 levels. From data in Table 13.9, you can see that there was a 31 percent increase from 1998 to 1999, and a further increase of nearly 100 percent is suggested by data from the first half of 2000.

Among product categories seized in 1998 and 1997, pirated software, motion pictures, and music topped the list, accounting for $22 million in contraband, 56 percent more than they did in fiscal year 1997. Table 13.9 shows that during the first half of 2000, China was the source of nearly three times the value of counterfeit items as the next largest nation, Taiwan. Malaysia was the third largest source, followed by Hong Kong and Panama.

China, the Biggest Offender

Around the world, China has earned the status of the world's biggest source of counterfeit goods. The Chinese are producing knockoffs of Microsoft software, fake cans of Coca-Cola, fake McDonald's hamburger restaurants, and even fake versions of a Jeep that Chrysler's joint venture manufactured in China.[94] Foreign companies have hired detectives, conducted raids, filed court cases, lobbied Beijing, and pressed for sanctions by their own governments against China, only to see the problem continue to escalate. Even when factories have been shut down, an industry lobbying group claims that the plants have simply been moved elsewhere in China.[95] Domestically, pirated products claim at least 90 percent of the $7 billion Chinese market for music and videos.[96] It is estimated that counter-

Table 13.9 Country of Origin of Customs Seizures in Fiscal Years 1998 and 1999 and Midyear 2000

Country of Origin	Midyear 2000 Domestic Value (% of total)	1999 Domestic Value (% of total)	1998 Domestic Value (% of total)
China	$6,804,654 (30%)	$16,030,463 (16%)	$28,951,681 (38%)
Taiwan	2,791,654 (12%)	42,237,070 (43%)	8,616,523 (11%)
Malaysia	2,320,630 (10%)	—	1,324,353 (2%)
Hong Kong	1,887,545 (8%)	2,538,155 (3%)	6,679,329 (9%)
Panama	1,881,628 (8%)	—	—
Korea	1,379,232 (6%)	3,517,935 (4%)	2,966,895 (4%)
Mexico	789,931 (3%)	—	—
France	649,956 (3%)	1,152,790 (1%)	1,132,275 (1%)
Singapore	541,817 (2%)	1,732,074 (2%)	—
Switzerland	473,075 (2%)	567,953 (1%)	582,598 (1%)
Indonesia	—	—	1,247,140 (2%)
Spain	—	—	667,027 (1%)
Poland	—	676,188 (1%)	—
India	—	1,042,150 (1%)	3,943,525 (5%)
Bangladesh	—	626,700 (1%)	—
Other countries	3,433,022 (15%)	29,407,689 (30%)	19,785,162 (26%)
Total domestic value	**$22,952,561**	**$99,539,167**	**$75,896,508**

Source: International Anti-Counterfeiting Coalition, www.iacc.org/statsnation.htm, November 29, 2000. Reprinted with permission.

feit products account for a quarter of Chinese manufacturing, and ending the production of such products could wreak havoc in some sectors of the Chinese economy.[97]

Counterfeit Products Can Be Dangerous

Is your Polo shirt or Gucci handbag real? Easy-to-copy products with high markups, such as luxury goods (Gucci, Vuitton, and Cartier), have long been counterfeited, but products now routinely copied include pesticides, fertilizers, drugs, toys, car and airplane parts, and electronic items. Besides causing legitimate manufacturers to lose sales, these fakes sometimes bring tragedy to users when, as is common, they fail to perform as well as the original. Farmers in Zaire and Kenya bought what they thought was Chevron's top-quality pesticide, which turned out to be a fake made of chalk. The two countries lost two-thirds of their cash crops for that year.

In California, a major broker of aircraft parts admitted selling counterfeit parts made in Taiwan for a General Electric jet engine used on corporate jets. He told his customers they had been manufactured by GE or other approved firms. His firm also modified parts intended for military engines that it sold to nonmilitary customers with fraudulent documentation. *Business Week* obtained a printout from a Federal Aviation Administration (FAA) (the agency responsible for airline safety) internal report stating that fake parts were involved in at least 166 U.S.-based aircraft accidents from 1973 to 1993. The FAA's solution to this overwhelming problem? Threaten to fire or demote any staff member who publicly states that fake parts are a safety threat.[98] Other cases of dangerous fake products include the following:

1. In Mexico, officials confiscated 15,000 counterfeit burn remedies because many contained sawdust or dirt and caused raging infections.
2. Nigerian pharmacists estimate that over a quarter of the 4,000 different medicines in that market are fake.
3. In Europe, hospitals and pharmacies dispensed millions of counterfeit doses of a cardiac medicine, some at only half the labeled strength.[99]

Small Is Beautiful

Small and Medium-Sized Enterprises

You probably have used products made by the Korean conglomerates Hyundai, Samsung, and LG. Perhaps you've "nuked" a TV dinner in a Samsung microwave or driven a Sonata or a Sephia, but have you ever used a computer with chips made by Mosel Vitelic or a Lite-On monitor? You probably have but don't know it because of the difference between the Korean and Taiwanese development models.

The Taiwanese government encourages small and medium-sized enterprises (SMEs) to compete in a highly competitive market, whereas the Korean government has targeted and fosters a small exclusive group of huge conglomerates. In Taiwan's case, the government has the very limited role of providing an economic environment conducive to the growth of export-oriented industries. By contrast, the Korean government has been heavily involved in keeping out foreign competition and urging the chaebol to expand. Their double-digit growth has been financed by cheap credit to businesses favored by politicians and bureaucrats, but Taiwanese firms have been financed by loans at market-determined interest rates and more by equity than by debt. While the combined sales of Korea's top 30 chaebol amounted to 48 percent of the country's output in 1996, 95 percent of Taiwan's companies are SMEs and account for 60 percent of that nation's exports.

The Asian crisis has brought to light the differences between Taiwan's model favoring SMEs and open-market competition and the Korean model promoting and protecting a few colossal conglomerates. During the last half of 1996, the South Korean won fell 73 percent against the dollar; the Taiwanese dollar dropped only 22 percent. South Korea needed an IMF bailout of $57 billion; Taiwan offered to lend $2 billion to South Korea. Small is beautiful. ■

Sources: "Kill or Cure," *The Economist,* January 19, 1998, pp. 13–14; The International Commercial Bank of China, *Economic Review,* January–February 1998, pp. 4–21; "What Asia—and the World—Must Do," *Business Week,* January 26, 1998, p. 106; and "Small Is Beautiful for Taiwan as Its Companies Skirt Asian Crisis," *International Herald Tribune,* February 2, 1998, p. 11.

Combating Imitations. Levi Strauss has probably gone further than most firms to rid the market of imitations. The company has a corporate security organization with an annual million-dollar budget to stop this unfair competition. Levi Strauss was also instrumental in forming the International Anti-Counterfeiting Coalition (IACC), which now has 60 member-firms from 11 countries. Member-firms exchange information on problems they encounter in certain markets and how they handle them. The coalition lobbies in the United States and other countries to increase the penalties for commercial counterfeiting. Because of these efforts, U.S. Customs is now empowered to seize and destroy counterfeit goods discovered at a point of entry.

In addition to the IACC, other industry groups are working to stop product counterfeiting. One is the Intellectual Property Committee comprising 13 of the largest U.S. patent holders, such as IBM, General Electric, and Pfizer (the pharmaceutical industry is one of the biggest victims of international piracy). Another group, the International Intellectual Property Alliance, represents 1,600 firms in the software, motion picture, computer, and book and music publishing industries. A third, the Business Software Alliance (BSA), estimates that annual losses caused by pirated software exceeded $12 billion worldwide in 1999 and over $59 billion from 1995 to 1999.[100] BSA claims that 39 percent of the piracy occurs in Europe, followed by 29 percent in Asia. Twenty-seven of the 70 countries listed in its latest report are said to have piracy rates over 90 percent, and of these, 8 have illegal copying rates surpassing *97 percent,* compared with the 35 percent estimated to be pirated in the United States.[101]

reverse engineering Dismantling a competitor's product to learn everything possible about it

industrial espionage Spying on a competitor to learn its trade and production secrets

Industrial Espionage

Usually, a counterfeiter can copy a patent design by **reverse engineering,** that is, taking the finished article apart, but when that is not feasible, the copier may obtain blueprints or process information by means of **industrial espionage.**

For years, companies have been acquiring information about each other by hiring competitors' employees, talking to competitors' customers, and so forth. Recently, however, intensified competition has motivated firms to become more sophisticated in this endeavor, even to the point of committing illegal acts. Mitsubishi, for example, was indicted on charges of stealing industrial secrets from Celanese, and Hitachi pleaded guilty to conspiring to transport stolen IBM technical documents to Japan. General Motors accused Jose Lopez, its former head of global purchasing, of arranging an enormous act of industrial sabotage when he and some associates left the company to join Volkswagen. German prosecutors say the documents police obtained from one of the group's apartments contained detailed information about GM's future products and data on suppliers and parts costs. After four years of dispute, GM settled with Volkswagen. Volkswagen is paying $100 million in damages, buying $1 billion in GM parts, and cutting all ties with Lopez until at least the year 2000. The U.S. Justice Department continues to investigate the case and may still charge Volkswagen.[102]

Another case was an FBI sting operation involving two representatives from a Taiwanese firm that wanted to steal information about an anticancer drug from Bristol-Myers Squibb. They thought they were dealing with a Bristol-Myers scientist who was going to provide the technical data for $200,000 cash, a $1,000 monthly retainer, and a share of future profits. When the agreement was reached, the FBI, which had been filming the operation, moved in for the arrest.[103]

Apparently, these are not isolated incidents. A 1997 survey by the American Society for Industrial Security claims that intellectual property losses from foreign and domestic espionage may total more than $300 billion. Major companies reported more than 1,100 documented and 500 suspected incidents of economic espionage. As usual, high-tech firms, especially in Silicon Valley, were the most common targets. While the FBI doesn't identify foreign governments that sponsor economic espionage, a former FBI agent named France, Germany, Russia, and South Korea as the major offenders. The FBI confirmed that economic spying by countries considered friends as well as by adversaries is increasing.[104]

There are many stories about the French government's participation in industrial espionage. European and American competitors suspect that some of the dramatic gains French companies are making in high-tech fields are due to stolen information. A secret French spy list of 49 targeted firms was published in American newspapers and authenticated by the CIA. On the list were 5 helicopter makers, 13 sensor makers, 10 producers of radar, 25 rocket and satellite manufacturers, and 2 commercial aircraft manufacturers, McDonnell-Douglas and Boeing.[105] American intelligence experts say that American businesspeople should not fly Air France because of possible bugged seats and French government spies posing as passengers and flight personnel. According to an executive of Pinkerton, a security agency, the French are very open about their industrial espionage. Government employees in France routinely enter the hotel rooms of visiting businesspeople to look through their briefcases.[106]

Analysis of the Competitive Forces

"The biggest single problem in international planning is the lack of efficient and good competitive information." This is the conclusion of *Business International*'s study of 90 worldwide companies. The study also found that many companies have no organized approach to global competitive assessment; whatever is done is diffused among the various parts of the company. The Futures Group, a consulting firm specializing in business intelligence systems (also known as competitor intelligence systems), conducted a survey in 1997 of over 100 major American firms representing a wide variety of industries. Two-thirds of the respondents had annual revenues of more than $1 billion, and 28 percent had revenues greater than $10 billion.

The company found that although only 60 percent of all respondents had organized business intelligence systems, the great majority (82 percent) of the companies with revenues of $10 billion or more had them.[107]

Is Competitor Assessment New?

Sales and marketing managers have always needed information about their competitors' products, prices, channels of distribution, and promotional strategies to plan their own marketing strategies. Sales representatives are expected to submit information on competitors' activities in their territories as part of their regular reports to headquarters. It also has been common practice to talk to competitors' customers and distributors, test competitors' products, and stop at competitors' exhibits at trade shows. Larger firms maintain company libraries whose librarians regularly scan publications and report their findings to the functional area they believe would have an interest in the information.

> One of the writers was working at Goodyear when a librarian reported reading about a patent application for vulcanizing hose that Dunlop, a competitor, had filed in South Africa. The process, although new, had already been patented elsewhere. She reasoned correctly that this new application in South Africa indicated that Dunlop was preparing to use the process, which would enable it to produce a better-quality product at a lower price in its South African plant.
>
> Inasmuch as the Goodyear—South Africa facility had nothing to equal it, the process would give Dunlop a strong competitive advantage. Headquarters immediately notified the South African affiliate, which hurriedly modernized its vulcanization process. By the time Dunlop installed its new process, the local Goodyear plant was ready. Thanks to an alert librarian, Dunlop failed to gain the competitive advantage it had expected.

competitor analysis
Principal competitors are identified, and their objectives, strengths, weaknesses, and product lines are assessed

competitor intelligence system (CIS)
Procedure for gathering, analyzing, and disseminating information about a firm's competitors

Inasmuch as gathering information about the competition has been going on for so long, what is different about present-day **competitor analysis**? Essentially, the difference lies in top management's recognition that (1) increased competition has created a need for a broader and more in-depth knowledge of competitors' activities and (2) the firm should have a **competitor intelligence system (CIS)** for gathering, analyzing, and disseminating information to everyone in the firm who needs it. Moreover, many firms hire consultants or firms specializing in competitor analysis to provide information, and others send employees to seminars to learn how to do it themselves. Some even employ former CIA agents or investigators to handle data gathering and analysis.

Sources of Information

There are five primary sources of information about the strengths, weaknesses, and threats of a firm's competitors: (1) within the firm, (2) published material, including computer databases, (3) suppliers/customers, (4) competitors' employees, and (5) direct observation or analyzing physical evidence of competitors' activities. These sources are all used in the United States and other industrialized countries, but they can be especially helpful in developing nations, which usually have a paucity of published information.

Within the Firm

As was mentioned previously, a firm's sales representatives are the best source of this kind of information. Librarians, when firms have them, can also provide input to the CIS. Another source is the technical and R&D people, who, while attending professional meetings or reading their professional journals, frequently learn of developments before they become general knowledge. Incidentally, government intelligence agencies from all countries subscribe to and analyze other nations' technical journals.

Published Material

In addition to technical journals, there are other types of published material that provide valuable information. Databases such as *Compuserve, Dialog, Dow Jones News/Retrieval, Lexis-Nexis,* and *NewsNet* enable analysts to obtain basic intelligence about sales, revenues, profits, markets, and other data needed to prepare detailed profiles of competitors. These services also enable users to create clipping folders based on search words such as the names of competitors, major customers, and suppliers or words describing a product's technology. The amount of useful information on the Internet continues to grow. Presumably, you have seen the many endnotes in this text citing Internet sources and the Internet site directory we have provided that is solely for sources of business information. England's Economist Intelligence Unit and the United States' Predicast publish useful industry reports, and under the Freedom of Information Act, American firms and their foreign competitors can get information about companies from public documents. Aerial photographs of competitors' facilities are often available from the U.S. Environmental Protection Agency (EPA) or the U.S. Geological Survey if the company is near a waterway or has done an environmental impact study. The photos may reveal an expansion or the layout of the competitor's production facilities. Be careful not to take unauthorized aerial photographs—this is trespassing and is illegal.

Suppliers/Customers

Companies frequently tell their customers in advance about new products to keep them from buying elsewhere, but often the customer passes this information on to competitors. For example, Gillette told a Canadian distributor when it planned to sell its new disposable razor in the United States. The distributor called BIC, which hurried its development and was able to begin selling its own razor shortly after Gillette did.

A company's purchasing agent can ask its suppliers how much they are producing or what they are planning to produce in the way of new products. Because buyers know how much their company buys, any added capacity or new products may be for the firm's competitors. They can also allege that they are considering giving a supplier new business if the sales representative can prove the firm has the capacity to handle it. Salespeople often are so eager for the new business that they divulge the firm's total capacity and the competitor's purchases to prove they can handle the order.

Competitors' Employees

Competitors' employees, actual or past, can provide information. Experienced human relations people pay special attention to job applicants, especially recent graduates, who reveal they have worked as interns or in summer jobs with competitors. They sometimes reveal proprietary information unknowingly. Companies also hire people away from competitors, and unscrupulous ones even advertise and hold interviews for jobs they don't have to get information from competitors' employees.

Direct Observation or Analyzing Physical Evidence

Companies sometimes have their technical people join a competitor's plant tour to get details of the production processes. A crayon company sent employees to tour a competitor's plants under assumed names. Posing as potential customers, they easily gained access and obtained valuable information about the competitor's processes; admittedly, this was unethical, although standing outside a plant to count employees and learn the number of shifts a competitor is working is not considered unethical.

We have already mentioned the common practice of reverse engineering, which is an example of analyzing physical evidence, but intelligence analysts even buy competitors' garbage. It is illegal to enter a competitor's premises to collect it, but it is permissible to obtain refuse from a trash hauler once the material has left the competitor's premises. Another interesting analysis was done by a Japanese company, which sent employees to measure the thickness of rust on train tracks leaving an American competitor's plant. They used the results to calculate the plant's output.[108]

We have pointed out when an act is legal or illegal, and we have also commented on whether, in our opinion, it was ethical. Certainly, businesspeople have a responsibility to use all ethical means to gather information about their competitors. The

Japanese owe much of their rapid progress in high technology to their ability to gather information. Mitsubishi occupies two floors of a New York office building in which dozens of people screen technical journals and contact companies for brochures and other materials. Mitsubishi and other large Japanese firms do their own microfilming and electronic scanning, which they send to their Tokyo headquarters for analysis.[109]

Benchmarking. This is an increasingly popular way for firms to measure themselves against world leaders. Whereas competitor analysis will help a firm spot differences between its performance in the market and that of its competitors, it does not provide a deep understanding of the processes that cause these differences.

Benchmarking involves several stages:

1. Management examines its firm for the aspects of the business that need improving.
2. It then looks for companies that are world leaders in performing similar processes.
3. The firm's representatives visit those companies, talk with managers and workers, and determine how they perform so well. Because the people who are going to use the newly acquired knowledge are line personnel, they, not staff people, should make these visits.

The problem, of course, is identifying which company to use as a benchmark. Some firms have been successful in choosing companies in their own industries, but often the ideal benchmark is in a related or perhaps even a completely different industry. Managers have a choice of using one or more of the four basic types of benchmarking:

1. *Internal*—comparing one operation in the firm with another. Because it is in-house, it is relatively easy to implement. It produces about a 10 percent improvement in productivity.
2. *Competitive*—comparing the firm's operation with that of a direct competitor. Obviously, this is the most difficult kind of benchmarking to do. Productivity improves about 20 percent.
3. *Functional*—comparing similar functions of firms in one's broadly defined industry: American Airlines comparing its freight handling procedure with that of Federal Express, for example. Functional benchmarking is easier to research and implement than competitive benchmarking. It generally results in about a 35 percent improvement in productivity.
4. *Generic*—comparing operations in totally unrelated industries. When Xerox decided to improve its order-filling process, it went to L.L. Bean, a mail-order house famous for filling orders quickly and correctly. Although the industries and the kinds of products were very different, Xerox saw that both firms handled a wide variety of shapes and sizes that made it necessary to pack them by hand. By learning from Bean, Xerox reduced its warehousing costs 10 percent.[110]

When Nissan's Infiniti division wanted to change the negative view many people have of service in the car industry, it went to famous service companies for its role models. McDonald's taught the Infiniti team the value of a clean, attractive facility and teamwork. Nordstrom, the department store chain, taught Infiniti the importance of rewarding employees for providing outstanding service.[111]

Although sometimes a visit to another firm will provide an idea that can be used without change, generally some adaptation will be needed. The basic purpose of benchmarking is to make managers and workers less parochial by exposing them to different ways of doing things so as to encourage creativity.

[Summary]

Explain why international competition has increased among the United States, Japan, the EU, and Asian nations.

World competition has intensified, and there are four nations and groups of nations whose firms are in worldwide competition with each other—the United States, Japan, the EU, and the NIEs and other Asian nations. Nations do not compete with each other; their firms do—but most economic and social conditions, as well as political actions, affect the ability of all a nation's firms to compete. Using the term *national competitiveness* is a convenience.

Know the areas in which the United States remains vulnerable to foreign competition.

The United States may be vulnerable due to a variety of factors, including declining investment in research and development, particularly by the government; a shortage of knowledge workers and low U.S. test scores at the secondary level; regulatory and legal requirements and the rising costs of compliance; inadequate tax reform, market-opening efforts, and protection of intellectual property rights; and a rising trade deficit and dependence on foreign capital.

Describe the responsibilities of government, management, labor, and consumers in maintaining the international competitiveness of the United States.

Government must reduce the stifling government bureaucracy that hampers business, help improve the nation's education system, reduce the double taxation of dividends, and adopt a capital gains tax to encourage investment in modern technology. Management must take a long-term view in planning and should increase its investment in R&D, employee training, and plant and equipment.

Explain the competitive environment in Japan, the EU, and the developing nations, including the NIEs.

It appears that both the Japanese and the EU countries are losing some of their competitiveness compared to the United States. Critics say Europe's competitiveness problems stem in part from the fact that European workers are overpaid and overprotected and get too many holidays, all of which raise Europe's labor costs. The expensive yen, high labor costs, and inefficient management practices are causing Japanese industry to lose its competitiveness. The developing nations and the NIEs are still recovering from the Asian economic crisis of 1997.

Understand the purpose of the keiretsu in Japanese industry.

A keiretsu is a group of financially connected Japanese firms that tend to do business among themselves. Two of the most important forms of keiretsu are the vertically integrated production group found in all Japanese automakers and the horizontal group that is a family-owned conglomerate. American businesspeople and government trade officials claim that the keiretsu system acts as a barrier to American producers trying to sell to Japanese companies. Slow domestic growth, deregulation, the opening of financial markets to international competition, and pressures for reform of corporate governance are loosening traditional keiretsu relationships.

Appreciate the magnitude and danger of product counterfeiting.

Product counterfeiting is costing industry worldwide as much as $200 billion, some experts claim. It is especially common in Asia. American producers of software, compact discs, and videos allege they are losing millions of dollars in sales annually to pirated copies produced in China.

Understand the importance of industrial espionage.

Industrial espionage is costing American firms billions annually in lost sales. General Motors accused its former global head of purchasing of sabotage when he and associates left the firm to join Volkswagen. He allegedly stole company secrets about a new small car that are said to be worth billions to Volkswagen in product development time saved. There are many reports of the French secret police spying on foreign industrialists. American and European competitors think that the gains the French are making in high-tech fields are due to information stolen by French industrial spies.

Describe the sources of competitive information.

Sources of competitive information are from within the firm, published material, customers, competitors' employees, and direct observation.

[Key Words]

national (macro) competitiveness (p. 437)
innovation (p. 442)
benchmarking (p. 444)
industrial targeting (p. 447)
European Economic Area (p. 449)
Lomé Convention (p. 449)
Generalized System of Preferences (GSP) (p. 450)
chaebol (p. 457)
keiretsu (p. 460)
hollowing out (p. 462)
counterfeiting (p. 465)
piracy (p. 466)
reverse engineering (p. 468)
industrial espionage (p. 468)
competitor analysis (p. 470)
competitor intelligence system (CIS) (p. 470)

[Questions]

1. If firms, not nations, compete worldwide, how can we speak of national competitiveness?
2. How can the U.S. government help American industry increase its competitiveness? What can industry and labor do?

3. What do you think of the commentary in the McKinsey report on the impact of the minimum wage on employment in France and Germany over the last 25 years?
4. Why is it overly simplistic to consider Japan and the other Asian countries as one trading bloc?
5. Why have some American managers claimed that the Japanese keiretsu are restraints to trade and contribute importantly to the U.S. trade deficit with Japan? Why might these concerns diminish over time?
6. What is industrial targeting? Does the United States engage in this practice?
7. Explain the relevance of counterfeiting and piracy to American business.
8. Explain the repetitive cycle through which the Japanese economy has passed five times in the last 25 years.
9. What are some information sources used in competitor analysis? What are some ethical issues involved?

[Minicase 13.1]

Wal-Mart Takes on the World

Founded by Sam Walton in 1962, Wal-Mart has developed into the largest retailer in the world, with sales of $165 billion in fiscal 2000. Embodying high levels of service, strong inventory management, and purchasing economies, Wal-Mart overpowered competitors and became the dominant firm in the U.S. retail industry. After rapid expansion during the 1980s and 1990s, however, Wal-Mart faces limits to growth in its home market and has been forced to look internationally for opportunities.

Many skeptics claimed that Wal-Mart's business practices and culture could not be transferred internationally. Yet, in its first decade of operations outside the U.S., the company's globalization efforts progressed at a rapid pace. As of January 2001, Wal-Mart had 1,068 retail units outside the United States, employing over 255,000 associates. About 14 percent of Wal-Mart's sales came from international operations, a level that is expected to increase substantially over the next decade.

Globalizing Wal-Mart: Where and How to Begin?

When Wal-Mart began to expand internationally, it had to decide which countries to target. Although the European retail market was large, to succeed there Wal-Mart would have had to take market share from established competitors. Instead, Wal-Mart deliberately selected emerging markets as their starting point for international expansion. In Latin America, they targeted nations with large populations—Mexico, Argentina, and Brazil—and in Asia they aimed at China.

Wal-Mart pursued a very deliberate entry strategy for the emerging markets. For their first international store, opened in 1991 in Mexico City, the company used a 50-50 joint venture. When they entered Brazil four years later, Wal-Mart had the majority position in a 60-40 venture. Both ventures included a partner that was a leading local retailer, to help Wal-Mart learn about retailing in Latin America. When the company subsequently entered Argentina, it was on a wholly owned basis. After gaining experience with partners, in 1997 Wal-Mart expanded further in Mexico by acquiring a controlling interest in the leading Mexican retail conglomerate, Cifra (now Wal-Mart de México). Still, learning the do's and don'ts was a difficult process. "It wasn't such a good idea to stick so closely to the domestic Wal-Mart blueprint in Argentina, or in some of the other international markets we've entered, for that matter," said the President of Wal-Mart International. "In Mexico City we sold tennis balls that wouldn't bounce right in the high altitude. We built large parking lots at some of our Mexican stores, only to realize that many of our customers there rode the bus to the store, then trudged across those large parking lots with bags full of merchandise. We responded by creating bus shuttles to drop customers off at the door. These were all mistakes that were easy to address, but we're now working smarter internationally to avoid cultural and regional problems on the front end."[i]

The Challenge of China

The lure of China, the world's most populous nation, proved too great to ignore. Wal-Mart was one of the first international retailers in China when it set up operations in

[i]"ASDA purchase leads way for Wal-Mart's international expansion," *Wal-Mart Annual Report 2000,* p. 10.

1996. Before Wal-Mart's arrival, state-owned retailers typically offered a limited range of products, often of low quality, and most stores were poorly lit, dirty, and disorganized. Concerned about their potential impact on local firms, Beijing restricted the operations of foreign retailers. These restrictions included requirements for government-backed partners and limitations on the number and location of stores. Initially, Wal-Mart's partner was Charoen Pokphand, a Thai conglomerate with massive investments in China and a strong track record with joint ventures. This venture was terminated after 18 months, due to differences regarding control. A new venture was subsequently formed with two politically connected partners, Shenzhen Economic Development Zone and Shenzhen International Trust and Investment Corporation, and Wal-Mart was able to negotiate a controlling stake in the venture. The first Chinese Wal-Mart store was in Shenzhen, a rapidly growing city bordering Hong Kong. The company chose to concentrate its initial activities in Shenzhen while it learned about Chinese retailing.

Wal-Mart had many well-publicized miscues while learning how to do business in China. For example, some household items found at American Wal-Marts are not found in the Chinese stores. "Their shopping list isn't as extensive as ours. If you ask the majority of people here what a paper towel is, they either don't know or they think it's some kind of luxury item," said the president of Wal-Mart China.[ii] The company eliminated matching kitchen towels and window curtains, since the wide variety of Chinese window sizes caused people to make their own curtains. Consumers purchased four times the number of small appliances than projected, but Wal-Mart no longer tries to sell extension ladders or a year's supply of soy sauce or shampoo to Chinese customers, who typically live in cramped apartments with limited storage space.[iii]

Operationally, the scarcity of highly modernized suppliers in China frustrated Wal-Mart's initial attempts to achieve high levels of efficiency. Bar coding was not standardized in China, and retailers had to either recode goods themselves or distribute labels to suppliers, procedures that increased costs and hindered efficiency. Pressured to appease the government's desire for local sourcing of products, while maintaining the aura of being an American shopping experience, Wal-Mart's solution was to source about 85 percent of the Chinese stores' purchases from local manufacturers but heavily weighting purchasing toward locally produced American brands (such as products from Procter & Gamble's factories in China).

Wal-Mart also learned the importance of building relationships with agencies from the central and local governments and with local communities. Bureaucratic red tape, graft, and lengthy delays in the approval process proved to be aggravating. The company learned to curry favor through actions such as inviting Chinese officials to visit Wal-Mart's headquarters in the U.S., assisting local charities, and even building a school for the local community.[iv] Wal-Mart expected its small-town folksiness to be a strong asset in China. "Price has been an issue, but there's always somebody who can undersell you. A young person who's smiling and saying, 'Can I help you?' is a big part of the equation. Most places in this country you don't get that," said the president of Wal-Mart International.[v] "Over the last two years, Wal-Mart has learned a tremendous amount about serving our Chinese customers, and our excitement about expanding in the market and in Asia has never been stronger."[vi]

Wal-Mart had 11 stores in China at the beginning of 2001, a small fraction of its worldwide retailing operations. However, the lessons Wal-Mart has learned have positioned the company to exploit future market-opening initiatives in China.

[ii]James Cox, "Great Wal-Mart of China red-letter day as East meets West in the aisles," *USA Today,* September 11, 1996, p. B1.
[iii]Peter Wonacott, "Wal-Mart finds Market Footing in China," *Wall Street Journal,* July 17, 2000, p. A31.
[iv]Ibid.
[v]James Cox, "Great Wal-Mart of China red-letter day as East meets West in the aisles," *USA Today,* September 11, 1996, p. B1.
[vi]"Wal-Mart China Expansion to Accelerate," (www.Walmartstores.com/newsstand/archive/prn_980605_chinaexpan.shtml), June 5, 1999.

Although China restricts foreign participation in its retail market and investors from abroad account for only 2.5 percent of China's total retail sales, this situation is expected to change soon.[vii] Within three years of the date China joins the World Trade Organization (WTO), these restrictions will be phased out, creating opportunity for expansion by foreign retailers. Wal-Mart's stores in Shenzhen, Dalian, and Kunming are expected ultimately to serve as regional hubs for a nationwide chain. Yet, Wal-Mart's intention is to expand slowly, trying to make friends and gain respect as they go. As Wal-Mart's head of Asian operations stated, "We are not just going to march out all over China."

A Different Approach for Entering Canada and Europe

After focusing initial international expansion efforts on large developing nations, Wal-Mart began to pursue the Canadian and European markets. Strong, entrenched competitors in these developed country markets hindered Wal-Mart's prospects for obtaining critical mass solely through internal growth. Rather than first developing their retail operations from scratch, as in Latin America and Asia, Wal-Mart entered via acquisitions. The company acquired 122 Canadian Woolco stores in 1994, and now it has a 35 percent share of the Canadian discount- and department-store retail market. In Europe, Wal-Mart entered Germany by acquiring 21 Wertkauf units in 1998 and 74 Interspar stores in 1999. The company entered the U.K. in 1999 through the acquisition of the 229-store ASDA Group. These acquisitions allowed Wal-Mart to build market share quickly within the highly advanced and competitive European retail market.[viii] From this base, additional growth is anticipated through the opening of new stores, supplemented with further acquisitions.

Although successful in rapidly building European market share, Wal-Mart still encountered difficulties. Acquiring two German companies within a year proved too much for the company to handle with its limited European infrastructure. Efforts to centralize purchasing and leverage Wal-Mart's famous competencies in information systems and inventory management were stymied by problems with suppliers that were not familiar with such practices. The introduction of Wal-Mart's "always low prices" approach met resistance from competitors and regulators. Indeed, the company was ordered by Germany's Cartel Office to raise prices, charging that Wal-Mart had helped to spark a price war by illegally selling some items below cost.[ix] Wal-Mart also challenged existing retail practices regarding hours of operation. Current laws require shops to close by 8 P.M. on weekdays and 4 P.M. on Saturdays, and to remain closed on Sundays. However, Wal-Mart stores have begun to open by 7 A.M., two hours earlier than most competitors, and the company has lobbied for additional reforms to allow later closing times. These changes have sparked vehement opposition from smaller competitors and employees' unions. As it struggled to build a strong competitive base, Wal-Mart Germany lost between $120 million and $200 million in 1999, and the losses have continued into 2001. Summing up the experience in Germany, the managing director for Wal-Mart's European business stated that, "Our progress has not been as fast or as good as we'd like it to be. But the reason we're comfortable is that we've built a platform from which we can grow the business. We want to have a serious business in Europe. Our objective is long-term market growth."[x]

[vii] "Big Chains Set for Post-WTO Scrap," *South China Morning Post,* November 3, 2000, p. 5.
[viii] "Hither and Thither: Growth vs. Maturity," *Businessworld,* December 3, 1999, p. 1.
[ix] Glenn Hall, "Wal-Mart Germany told to raise prices: Choking small retailers," *National Post,* September 9, 2000, p. D3.
[x] "Wal-Mart Plans Major Expansion in Germany," *Wall Street Journal,* July 20, 2000, p. A21.

A Successful Base for Continued Globalization Efforts

Wal-Mart's path to internationalization has been littered with challenges. The company has persevered and learned from its mistakes, however, and it seems well positioned for continued growth. As an indication of its success, in 1999, Wal-Mart ranked ninth on the *Financial Times'* "Most Respected in the World" list of companies. In 2000, the company was ranked fifth in *Fortune* magazine's "Global Most Admired All-Stars" list.[xi] There are still many potential markets for a Wal-Mart store and the company is committed to exploiting these opportunities, whether they are at home or internationally.

[xi]"Wal-Mart: A History of Growth" (www.walmartstores.com/newsstand/archive/prn_timeline.shtml), January 14, 2001.

[Chapter] 14

International Strategy, Organizational Design, and Control

"Companies don't produce strategies, just plans. No company will tell you its planning processes produce new wealth-creating strategies. The dirty little secret is that we don't have a theory of strategy creation. We just don't know how it's done."

—Gary Hamel, chairman, Strategos, international consulting firm and visiting professor of strategy and international management, London Business School

Concept Previews

After reading this chapter, you should be able to:

- **understand** international strategy, competencies, and international competitive advantage
- **describe** the steps in the global strategic planning process
- **understand** the purpose of mission statements, objectives, quantified goals, and strategies
- **describe** the new directions in strategic planning
- **discuss** the various organizational forms
- **understand** the concept of the virtual corporation
- **explain** why decisions are made where they are among parent and subsidiary units of an international company (IC)
- **understand** how an IC can maintain control of a joint venture or of a company in which the IC owns less than 50 percent of the voting stock
- **list** the types of information an IC needs to have reported to it by its units around the world

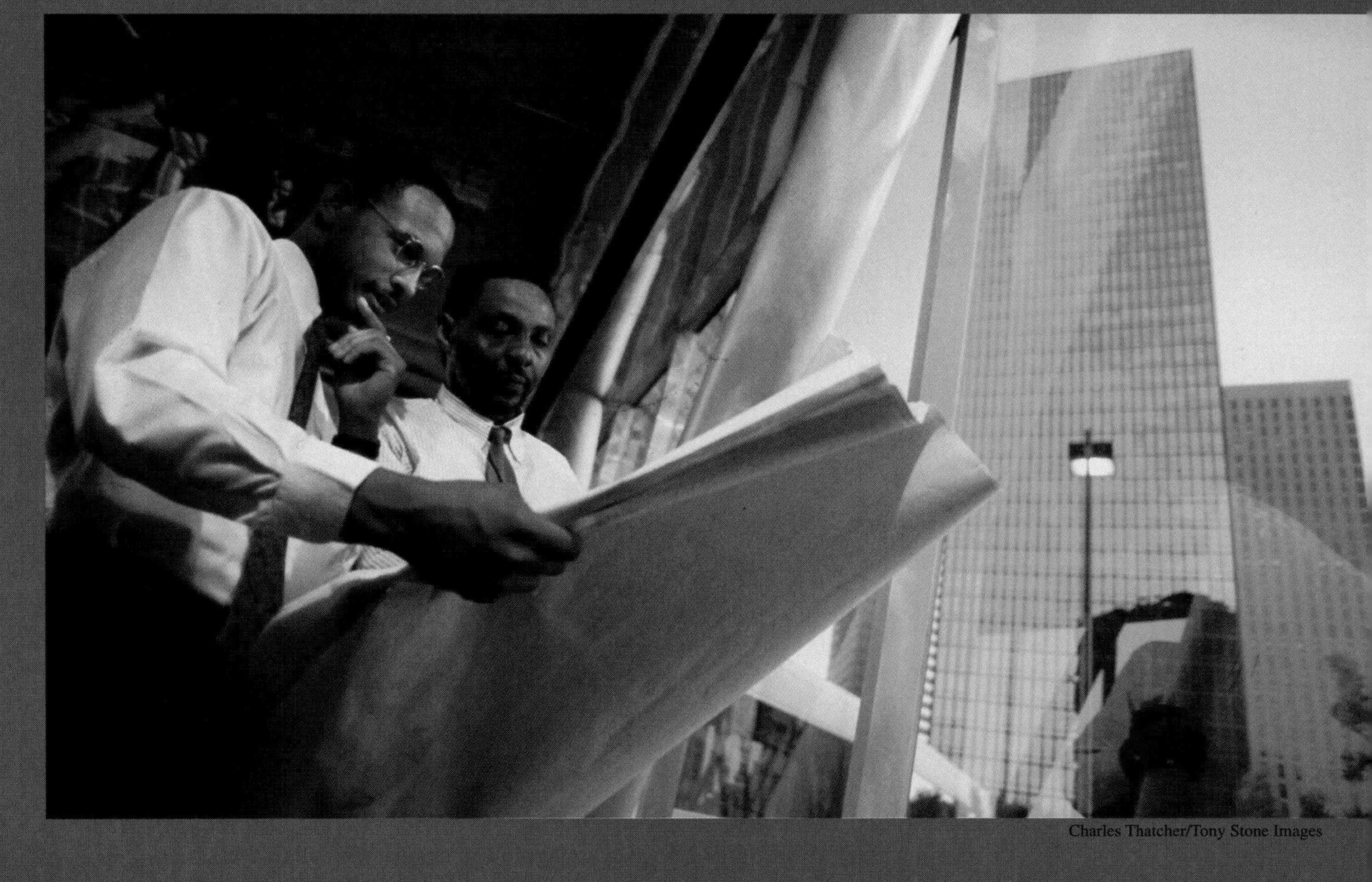
Charles Thatcher/Tony Stone Images

Is Strategic Planning Dead?

"Strategic planning is dead," say the management gurus.[a] However, a well-known business publication, *Business Week,* says, "After a decade of downsizing, Big Thinkers are back in vogue." The publication reports that "strategy is again a major focus in the quest for higher revenues and profits. Some companies are even recreating full-fledged strategic-planning groups."[b]

Who is right? How can strategic planning be dead when, according to a study of executives, consultants, and management professors, "business strategy is now the single most important management issue and will remain so for the next five years"? Vijay Govindarajan, a professor of strategy at Dartmouth College, says, "We are seeing strategy make a rebound. Strategy has become a part of the main agenda at lots of organizations today."[c]

Upon examining these statements in more detail, we find that the "strategic planning is dead" people have narrowly defined strategic planning to be the old bureaucratic variety, which Professor Gary Hamel describes as a calendar-driven ritual, not an exploration of the company's potential. He states that the old strategy-making process "works from today forward, not from the future back, implicitly assuming, whatever the evidence to the contrary, that the future will be more or less like the present."[d]

These people claim that the old process has been replaced by *strategic management,* which combines strategic thinking, strategic planning, and strategic implementation.[e] The implication, of course, is that none of the participants in the old system ever had any independent thoughts. In fact, the process has been described as "groupthink."

The new strategic planning process differs from the old one in other ways. It is no longer something that only the company's most senior executives do. Top management, at the urging of strategy consultants, is assigning strategic planning to teams of line and staff managers from different businesses and functional areas, much as it has done with process-improvement task forces and quality circles. Frequently these teams include a range of ages—from junior staff members who have shown the ability to think creatively to experienced veterans near retirement age who will "tell it like it is." Another difference between the new and the old processes: formerly, planning was a company activity done in seclusion, but now, consultants say it should include interaction with important customers and suppliers in order to gain firsthand experience with the firm's markets.

Chairman Kent C. Nelso of United Parcel Service explains why his firm is spinning out a full-fledged strategic-planning group from the company's marketing department, where it has resided: "Because we're making bigger bets in investments in technology, we can't afford to spend a whole lot of money in one direction and then find out five years later it was the wrong direction."[f] ■

Source: [a]Paul S. Forbes, "Update: Strategic Planning Is Dead," *Management Articles,* http://www.forbesgroup.com/articles/articles/plandead-695.htm (March 15, 1998). [b]"Strategic Planning," *Business Week,* August 26, 1996, p. 46. [c]Ibid. [d]Gary Hamel, "Strategy Revolution," *Harvard Business Review,* July–August 1996, p. 70. [e]Forbes, "Update: Strategic Planning Is Dead." [f]"Strategic Planning."

In the preceding three sections of this book, the primary focus has been on the broad environmental context in which international businesses compete. This discussion has included the theoretical framework for international trade and investment, the international monetary and other organizations that influence international business, and the financial, economic, physical, social, political, legal, and other institutions found in various nations. Our attention now shifts away from the external environment, and we focus instead on the business itself, including the actions managers can take to help their companies compete more effectively as international businesses.

In this chapter, we will discuss the concept of international strategy and how companies use strategic planning to improve their global competitiveness. We will also discuss the different organizational forms an international company can take and key strategic issues that managers must address in choosing among these various organizational designs. Included in the discussion will be the identification of concerns that managers have regarding their ability to control the international activities of their companies.

To succeed in today's global marketplace, a company must be able to quickly identify and exploit opportunities wherever they occur, domestically or internationally. To do this effectively, managers must fully understand why, how, and where they intend to do business, now and over time. This requires managers to have a clear understanding of the company's mission, a vision for how they intend to achieve that mission, and an understanding of how they plan to compete with other companies. To meet these challenges, managers must understand the company's strengths and weaknesses and be able to compare them accurately to those of their worldwide competitors. Strategic planning provides valuable tools that help managers address these global challenges.

The Competitive Challenge Facing Managers of International Businesses

What Is International Strategy, and Why Is It Important?

International strategy is concerned with the way firms make fundamental choices about developing and deploying scarce resources internationally.[1] International strategy involves decisions that deal with all the various functions and activities of a company, not merely a single area such as marketing or production. To be effective, a company's international strategy needs to be consistent among the various functions, products, and regional units of the company (internal consistency) as well as with the demands of the international competitive environment (external consistency).

The goal of international strategy is to achieve and maintain a unique and valuable competitive position both within a nation and globally, a position that has been termed **competitive advantage.** This suggests that the international company either must perform activities different from those of its competitors or perform the same activities in different ways. To create a competitive advantage which is sustainable over time, the international company should try to develop skills, or competencies, that (1) create value for customers and for which customers are willing to pay, (2) are rare, since competencies shared among many competitors cannot be a basis for competitive advantage, (3) are difficult to imitate or substitute for, and (4) are organized in a way that allows it to exploit fully the competitive potential of these valuable, rare, and difficult to imitate competencies.[2]

international strategy
The way firms make choices about acquiring and using scarce resources in order to achieve their international objectives.

competitive advantage
The ability of a company to have higher rates of profits than its competitors.

> WalMart has become a strong competitor in the international retailing industry because it has been able to develop more effective processes for performing critical activities, such as the logistics of tying point-of-purchase data to the company's inventory management and purchasing activities. Competitors have had continued difficulties matching WalMart's competencies, enabling WalMart to consistently earn a return on sales that is twice the average of its industry. As a result, WalMart has been able to exploit these competencies internationally by entering markets such as Canada, Mexico, Europe, and Asia.

Managers of international companies that are attempting to develop a competitive advantage face a formidable challenge: resources—time, talent, and money—are always scarce. There are many alternative ways to use these scarce resources (for example, which nations to enter, which technologies to invest in, and which products to develop), and these alternatives are not equally attractive. A company's managers are forced to make choices regarding what to do, and what *not* to do, now and over time. Different companies make different choices, and those choices have implications for each company's ability to meet the needs of customers and create a defensible competitive position internationally. Without adequate planning, managers are more likely to make decisions that do not make good sense competitively, and the company's international competitiveness may be harmed.

Why Plan Globally?

Because of the challenges mentioned, many international firms have found it necessary to institute formal global strategic planning to provide a means for top management to identify opportunities and threats from all over the world, formulate strategies to handle them, and stipulate how to finance the strategies' implementation. Global strategic plans not only provide for consistency of action among the firm's managers worldwide but also require the participants to consider the ramifications of their actions in the other geographical and functional areas of the firm. These plans provide a thorough, systematic foundation for making decisions regarding what resources and competencies to develop, when and how to develop them, and how to use those competencies to achieve competitive advantage.

Standardization and Planning

Historically, more aspects of research and development and manufacturing have been standardized and coordinated worldwide by companies than has been the case for marketing. Many top executives believe marketing strategies are best determined locally because of differences among the various foreign environments. Yet there is a growing tendency to standardize not only marketing strategies but also the total product, which leads to their inclusion in the global strategic planning process. Of course, their standardization can also be the *result* of strategic planning as the company's managers search for ways to lower costs and present a uniform company image as a global producer of quality products. Let us look at the planning process.

Global Strategic Planning Process

Global strategic planning is the primary function of managers, and the ultimate manager of strategic planning and strategy making is the firm's chief executive officer. The process of strategic planning provides a formal structure in which managers (1) analyze the company's external environments, (2) analyze the company's internal environment, (3) define the company's business and mission, (4) set corporate objectives, (5) quantify goals, (6) formulate strategies, and (7) make tactical plans. For ease of understanding, we present this as a linear process, but in actuality there is considerable flexibility in the order in which firms take up these items.

> In company planning meetings that one of the writers attended, the procedure was iterative; that is, during the analysis of the environments, committee members could skip to a later step in the planning process to discuss the impact of a new development on a present corporate objective. They then often moved backward in the process to discuss the availability of the firm's assets to take advantage of the environmental change. If they concluded that the company had such a capability, the committee would try to formulate a new strategy. If a viable strategy was developed, the members would then establish the corporate objective that the strategy was designed to attain.

Global and Domestic Planning Processes Similar

You will note that the global planning process, illustrated in Figure 14.1, has the same format as the planning process for a purely domestic firm. As you know by now, most activities of the two kinds of operations are that way. It is the variations in values of uncontrollable forces that make the activities in a worldwide corporation more complex than they are in a purely domestic firm.

Analyze Domestic, International, and Foreign Environments

Because a firm has little opportunity to control these forces, its managers must know not only what the present values of the forces are but also where the forces appear to

[Figure 14.1] The Global Strategic Planning Process

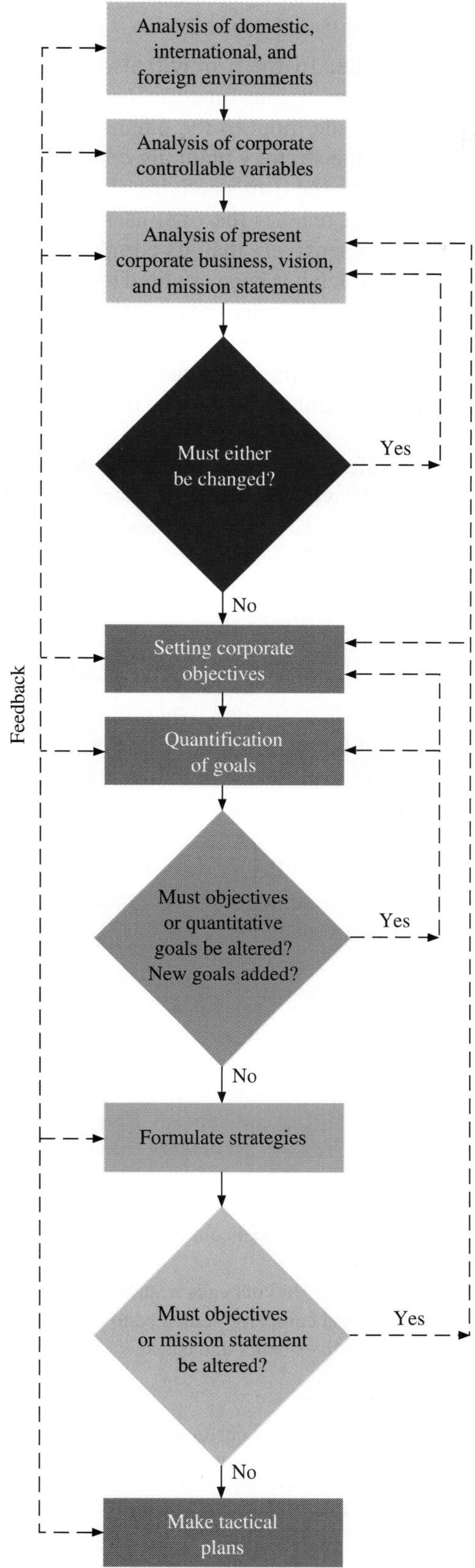

be headed. An environmental scanning process similar to the market screening process described in Chapter 15 can be used for continuous gathering of information.

Analyze Corporate Controllable Variables

An analysis of the forces controlled by the firm will also include a situational analysis and a forecast. The managers of the various functional areas will either personally submit reports on their units or provide input to the planning staff (if there is one), who will in turn prepare a report for the strategy planning committee.

Often management will analyze the firm's activities from the time raw materials enter the plant until the end product reaches the final user with the aim of finding ways to perform them better or less expensively than its competitors.

Although this analytical approach has been credited to Professor Michael Porter, the valve chain concept has been around for decades. Marketers will remember that Wroe Alderson made the same analysis in the 1960s using a unit of analysis he called *transvection.* Transvection is a series of sorts and transformations beginning with raw materials entering the factory and terminating when the finished product is in the hands of the final consumer.[3]

After the analysis of corporate controllable variables, the planning committee must answer questions such as the following: What are our strengths and weaknesses? What are our human and financial resources? Where are we with respect to our present objectives? Have we uncovered any facts that require us to delete goals, alter them, or add new ones? After completing this internal audit, the committee is ready to examine its business, vision, and **mission statements.**

mission statement
A broad statement that defines the organization's scope

Define the Corporate Business, Vision, and Mission Statements

These broad statements communicate to the corporation's stakeholders (employees, stockholders, governments, suppliers, and customers) what the company is and where it is going. Some firms combine two or all three, whereas others have separate statements. The director of planning at 3M believes that "the mission statement typically defines the scope of what you do, while the vision should be a vibrant and compelling image of the organization's purpose."[4] In any case, the planning committee must evaluate these statements against the changing realities uncovered in the external and internal analyses and then alter them when necessary.

Some Examples. Ford has a statement that says:

> Ford Motor Company enters the new millennium with a clear vision to become the world's leading consumer company for automotive products and services. This strategy puts customers first in everything the company does. By leveraging our sources of competitive advantage, we continuously drive to improve, transform and grow the business. The ultimate measure of success is delivering superior shareholder returns.[5]

Du Pont has statements defining the company and its mission:

> We're a science and technology-based global company of people who make products that make a difference in everyday life.
>
> Its mission, or "core purpose," as Du Pont calls it, states: "To be the world's most successful energy and chemistry-based company, dedicated to creating high-quality, innovative materials that make people's lives better and easier."[6]

Amazon.com states the following:

> Amazon.com seeks to be the world's most customer-centric company, where customers can find and discover anything they might want to buy online.[7]

After defining any or all of the three statements, management must then set corporate objectives.

Set Corporate Objectives

Objectives direct the firm's course of action, maintain it within the boundaries of the stated mission, and ensure its continuing existence. McDonald's states that its vision is "to be the world's best quick service restaurant experience. Being the best means providing outstanding quality, service, cleanliness and value, so that we make every customer in every restaurant smile." To achieve this vision, three objectives are presented: (1) to be the best employer for its people in each community around the world, (2) to deliver operational excellence to its customers in each of its restaurants, and (3) to achieve enduring profitable growth by expanding the brand and leveraging the strengths of the McDonald's system through innovation and technology.[8]

Intel's mission is to "do a great job for our customers, employees and stockholders by being the building block supplier to the worldwide Internet economy." Their objectives are (1) to make Intel the number one computing platform everywhere on the Internet, (2) to grow new businesses for Intel focusing on the Internet, and (3) to excel at Intel Basics.[9]

Several years ago, Goodyear Tire and Rubber Co. announced the following objectives "to strengthen its focus as a growth company capable of consistent earnings improvement":

1. Greater commitment to geographical diversity through global expansion.
2. Reduce company debt.
3. Increase operating margins.
4. Capital spending to increase productivity and production capacity.
5. Introduction of new products.[10]

How does Goodyear know whether it achieves these objectives? How much does the company expect to reduce company debt, for example?

Quantify the Objectives

When objectives can be quantified, they should be. For example, 3M's objectives include (1) growth in earnings per share of more than 10 percent a year on average, (2) growth in economic profit exceeding growth in earnings per share and return on invested capital among the highest among industrial companies, (3) at least 30 percent of sales from products introduced during the past four years, and (4) 8 percent productivity improvement per year, measured in terms of sales per employee in local currencies.[11]

Similarly, in the earlier example, the Goodyear CEO tells us that management's goal is to reduce the ratio of debt to debt plus equity to below 30 percent. He also wants to increase operating margins to 12 percent and maintain capital spending between $500 million and $700 million annually. However, he does not attempt to quantify the number of products introduced, nor does he set a goal for the amount of geographical diversity. Interestingly, the variables used to measure this last objective are the percentages of total unit sales and sales revenue made outside the United States. In 1994, they were more than 40 percent of revenue and 45 percent of unit sales.[12]

This illustrates that despite the strong preference of most top managers for verifiable objectives, they frequently do have nonquantifiable or directional goals. One of PepsiCo's objectives, for example, is to accelerate profitable growth. Although this goal is not quantified, it does set the direction for managers and requires them to formulate more specific strategies to attain it. Incidentally, objectives do tend to be more quantified as they progress down the organization to the operational level, because, for the most part, strategies at one level become the objectives for the succeeding level. Up to this point, only *what, how much,* and *when* have been stipulated. *How* these objectives are to be achieved will be determined in the formulation of strategies.

Formulate the Corporate Strategies

Generally, participants in the strategic planning process will formulate alternative **corporate strategies**, or action plans, that seem plausible considering the directions the external environmental forces are taking and the company's strengths, weaknesses, opportunities, and threats (something that endangers the business, such as a merger of

corporate strategies
Action plans to enable organizations to reach their objectives

two competitors, the bankruptcy of a major customer, or a new product that appears to make the company's product obsolete).

Suppose (1) their analysis of the external environment convinces them that the Japanese government is making it easier for foreign firms to enter the market and (2) the competitor analysis reveals that a Japanese competitor is preparing to enter the United States (or wherever the home market is). Should the firm adopt a defensive strategy of defending the home market by lowering its price there, or should it attack the competitor in its home market by establishing a subsidiary in Japan? Management may decide to pursue either strategy or both, depending on its interpretation of the situation.

When choosing among strategies, management must consider the corporate culture.[13] If it decides to put into effect a quality control system that includes quality circles and heretofore there has been little employee participation in decision making, the strategy will have to include the cost of and time for training the employees to accept this cultural change.

Strategies May Also Be General. At the corporate level, strategies, like objectives, may be rather general. Intel, for example, has stated that its strategy for growth is to "(1) drive networked PC improvements, (2) expand our branding programs, and (3) develop customer bases around the world."[14] You can be sure that the marketing and design functions, which receive these strategies as their objectives, will be required to quantify as many as possible.

scenarios
Multiple, plausible stories about the future

Scenarios. Because of the rapidity of changes in the uncontrollable variables, many managers have become dissatisfied with planning for a single set of events and have turned to **scenarios,** which are multiple, plausible stories for probable futures.[15]

Often, the "what if" questions raised reveal weaknesses in present strategies. Some of the common kinds of subjects for scenarios are large and sudden changes in sales (up or down), sudden increases in the prices of raw materials, sudden tax increases, and a change in the political party in power. Frequently, scenarios are used as a learning tool for preparing standby or contingency plans.

contingency plans
Plans for the best- or worst-case scenarios or for critical events that could have a severe impact on the firm

Contingency Plans. Many companies prepare **contingency plans** for worst- and best-case scenarios and for critical events as well. Every operator of a nuclear plant has contingency plans, as do most producers of petroleum and hazardous chemicals since such ecological disasters as the Valdez oil spill and the tragic Bhopal gas leak occurred.[16] Because of the important impact on profits of changes in the prices of jet fuel, contingency planning is a common strategic activity for domestic and international airlines.

Prepare Tactical Plans

Because strategic plans are fairly broad, tactical (also called operational) plans are a requisite for spelling out in detail how the objectives will be reached. In other words, very specific, short-term means for achieving the goals are the objective of tactical planning. For instance, if the British subsidiary of an American producer of prepared foods has as a quantitative goal a 20 percent increase in sales, its strategy might be to sell 30 percent more to institutional users. The tactical plan could include such points as hiring three new specialized sales representatives, attending four trade shows, and advertising in two industry periodicals every other month next year. This is the kind of specificity found in the tactical plan.

Management Tools

Generally, the adoption and use of management tools is discussed in planning meetings because some are useful in improving a firm's performance in critical areas. According to a survey taken of 9,000 American managers, tool usage is high and growing. The most commonly used tool (90 percent of the respondents) was the mission statement, followed by the customer satisfaction survey (90 percent). Next were total quality management (76 percent) and competitor profiling (74 percent).

[Worldview]

Rehearsing the Future

What would happen if the price of oil were to skyrocket (as it did during 2000) or suddenly crash? What are the chances of a host government nationalizing the oil industry? These are examples of scenarios—stories about possible futures—that Royal Dutch Shell employs in the planning process to force executives to question their assumptions about the environments in which the company operates.

Back in the 1970s, Shell used scenario planning as a fundamental tool for thinking strategically about the future, but when such planning went out of fashion, scenarios did, too. Now that strategic planning is back, so are scenarios, but with a difference. Formerly, the planners made the scenarios and presented them to the line managers—a kind of "show and tell." There was no involvement of the managers.[a] Now there is an emphasis in the company on getting managers to bring scenarios into their decision processes because Shell's top management is convinced that scenario building is an important management tool. Scenarios are plausible and challenging stories, but they are not forecasts; that is, they do not extrapolate from past data to make predictions.[b] In fact, they are a means to force managers to realize that their assumptions based on past experience no longer apply. Also, if managers have thought out the possible outcomes, they should be quicker to react when one of those outcomes occurs. As Shell's former planning head expresses it, "They can remember the future."[c]

Managers typically work in teams of six to eight people to build scenarios. They first agree about the decision that must be made and then gather information by reading, observing, and talking with knowledgeable people. Next, the team works to identify the driving (environmental) forces and the "critical uncertainties" (the unpredictable) and prioritizes them. Three or four scenarios are prepared, based on issues critical to the success of the decision. Each should depict a credible future and not be written to show the best-case, worst-case, and most likely situations. The team then identifies the implications of the scenarios and the leading indicators management must follow.

A member of a consulting firm that trains managers to use scenarios writes, "Using scenarios is rehearsing the future, and by recognizing the warning signs and the drama unfolding, one can avoid surprises, adapt, and act effectively. Decisions which have been pretested against a range of what fate may offer are more likely to stand the test of time, produce robust and resilient strategies, and create distinct competitive advantage. Ultimately, the end result of scenario planning is not a more accurate picture of tomorrow, but better decisions today."[d] ■

Sources: [a]"A Glimpse of Possible Futures," *Financial Times*, August 25, 1997, p. 8. [b]"20:20 Vision," *Global Scenarios*, www.shell.com/b/b2_03.html (March 15, 1998). [c]"A Glimpse of Possible Futures." [d]"Using Scenarios," *GBN Scenario Planning*, http://www.gbn.org/usingScen.html (March 20, 1998).

Managers responded that the least used tools were value chain analysis (27 percent), five forces analysis (24 percent),* mass customization (20 percent), and dynamic simulations (20 percent). According to the author, "Mass Customization and Dynamic Simulation may have low trial rates because they are relatively new, but Porter's Value Chain Analysis and Five Forces Framework have been around for at least 15 years."[17]

Strategic Plan Features and Implementation Facilitators

Sales Forecasts and Budgets

Two prominent features of the strategic plan are *sales forecasts* and *budgets.* The sales forecast not only provides management with an estimate of the revenue to be received and the units to be sold but also serves as the basis for planning in the other functional areas. Without this information, management cannot formulate the production, financial,

*Michael Porter's five forces analysis consists of using (1 and 2) bargaining power of buyers and suppliers, (3 and 4) threats of substitute products and new entrants, and (5) rivalry of firms to attempt to measure industry competitiveness. See any principles of management text.

and procurement plans. Budgets, like sales forecasts, are both a planning and a control technique. During planning, they coordinate all the functions within the firm and provide management with a detailed statement of future operating results.

Plan Implementation Facilitators

Once the plan has been prepared, it must be implemented. Two of the most important plan implementation facilitators that management employs are policies and procedures.

Policies. Policies are broad guidelines issued by upper management for the purpose of assisting lower-level managers in handling recurring problems. Because policies are broad, they permit discretionary action and interpretation. The object of a policy is to economize managerial time and promote consistency among the various operating units. If the distribution policy states that the firm's policy is to sell through wholesalers, marketing managers throughout the world know that they should normally use wholesalers and avoid selling directly to retailers. The disclosure of the widespread occurrence of bribery prompted company presidents to issue policy statements condemning this practice. Managers were put on notice by these statements that they were not to offer bribes.

Procedures. Procedures prescribe how certain activities will be carried out, thereby ensuring uniform action on the part of all corporate members. For instance, most international corporate headquarters issue procedures for their subsidiaries to follow in preparing annual reports and budgets. This assures corporate management that whether the budgets originate in Thailand, Brazil, or the United States, they will be prepared using the same format, which facilitates comparison.

Kinds of Strategic Plans

Time Horizon

Although strategic plans may be classified as short-, medium-, or long-term, there is little agreement about the length of these periods. For some, long-range planning may be for a five-year period. For others, this would be the length of a medium-term plan; their long range might cover 15 years or more. Short-range plans are usually for one to three years; however, even long-term plans are subject to review annually or more frequently if a situation requires it. Furthermore, the time horizon will vary according to the age of the firm and the stability of its market. A new venture is extremely difficult to plan for more than three years in advance, but a five- or six-year horizon is probably sufficient for a mature company in a steady market.

Level in the Organization

Each organizational level of the company will have its level of plan. For example, if there are four organizational levels, as shown in Figure 14.2, there will be four levels of plans, each of which will generally be more specific than the plan that is at the level above. In addition, the functional areas at each level will have their own plans and sometimes will be subject to the same hierarchy, depending mainly on how the company is organized.

Methods of Planning

Top-Down Planning

top-down planning Planning process that begins at the highest level in the organization and continues downward

In **top-down planning,** corporate headquarters develops and provides guidelines that include the definition of the business, the mission statement, company objectives, financial assumptions, the content of the plan, and special issues. If there is an international division, its management may be told that this division is expected to contribute $5 million in profits, for example. The division, in turn, would break this total down among the affiliates under its control. The managing director in Germany would be informed that the German operation is expected to contribute $1 million; Brazil, $300,000; and so on.

[Figure 14.2] 3M Strategic Planning Cycle

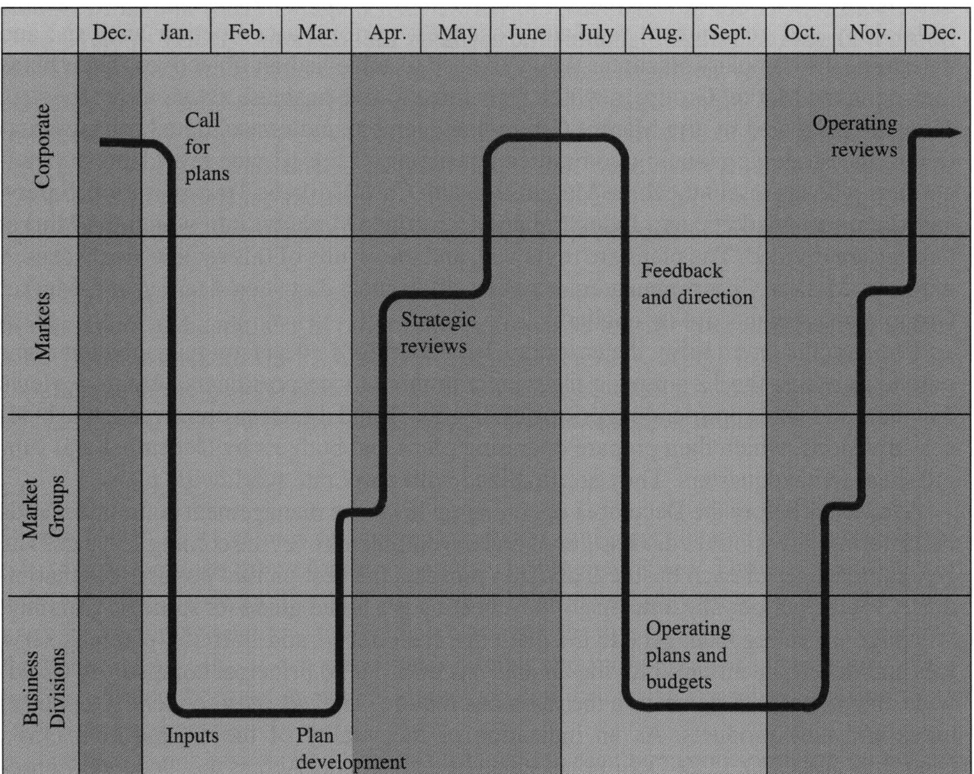

Disadvantages of top-down planning are that it restricts initiative at the lower levels and shows some insensitivity to local conditions, particularly within ethnocentric management teams. Furthermore, especially in an international company, there are so many interrelationships that consultation is necessary. Can top management, for example, decide on rationalization of manufacturing without obtaining the opinions of the local units as to its feasibility?

The advantage of top-down planning is that the home office with its global perspective should be able to formulate plans that ensure the optimal corporatewide use of the firm's scarce resources.

Bottom-Up Planning

Bottom-up planning operates in the opposite manner. The lowest operating levels inform top management about what they expect to do, and the total becomes the firm's goals. The advantage of bottom-up planning is that the people responsible for attaining the goals are formulating them. Who knows better than the subsidiaries' directors what and how much the subsidiaries can sell? Because the subsidiaries' directors set the goals with no coercion from top management, they feel obligated to make their word good. However, there is also a disadvantage. Each affiliate is free to some extent to pursue the goals it wishes to pursue, and so there is no guarantee that the sum total of all the affiliates' goals will coincide with those of headquarters. When discrepancies occur, extra time must be taken at headquarters to eliminate them. Japanese companies, particularly larger firms, almost invariably use bottom-up planning because they strive for a consensus at every level.

bottom-up planning
Planning process that begins at the lowest level in the organization and continues upward

Iterative Planning

It appears that **iterative planning** (see Figure 14.2) is becoming more popular, especially in global companies that seek to have a single global plan while operating in many diverse foreign environments. Iterative planning combines aspects of both top-down and bottom-up planning.

iterative planning
Repetition of the bottom-up or top-down planning process until all differences are reconciled

[Worldview]

From Bullets to Stories: Improving Strategic Planning at 3M

After years of working as 3M's executive director of planning, Gordon Shaw came to the conclusion that the firm's business plans were usually "to do" lists that would improve 3M's performance but did not reflect the rationale for selecting the items on the lists. For this reason, the mere listing of statements in a bullet-list format gave no indication of the thought and reasoning that went into the list's preparation.

Members of the planning committee were accustomed to using the bullet point format in their writing and presentations. This allows complex business situations to be explained by a short list of points that can be modified and clarified as they are presented. But as Shaw observes, "Bullets allow us to skip the thinking step, genially tricking ourselves into supposing we have planned them, when, in fact, we've only listed some good things to do."

Shaw also claimed that bullet lists encourage people to be intellectually lazy:

1. These documents frequently are a list of things to do that can apply to any business and fail to show how they will specifically help the company in question. For example, a 3M business unit proposed three strategies: (a) Reduce high delivered costs by continuing to reduce factory costs and product costs, (b) accelerate development costs, and (c) increase responsiveness. Undoubtedly, the managers who made this list knew what had to be done in each case. However, the people who had to support the plan and make it work did not.
2. Lists can specify only three relationships: sequence with respect to time, priority (most important to least important), and members of a set (without specifying the basis of the relationship). Moreover, the list specifies only one of those relationships at a time. Either the presenter or the audience must come up with any other relationships.
3. Lists do not include assumptions about how the items affect the business. Shaw gives an example: "Consider these major objectives from a standard five-year strategic plan:

   a. Increase market share by 25 percent.

   b. Increase profits by 30 percent.

   c. Increase new product introductions to 10 a year.

   The planners making these objectives had to have a set of assumptions about how these factors relate to each other. For example, changing the order in which these actions are taken requires a different set of assumptions. If the assumptions are not clear to all the planners, they cannot agree on the same sequence and thus on the results."

Because of the problems inherent in the list of objectives, 3M adopted "planning by narrative." First the strategic planner sets the stage as any storyteller does. This includes an analysis of the current situation, including uncontrollable environmental forces and corporate controllable variables. Then the narrator discusses the dramatic conflict. What are the obstacles to success? Once the obstacles are presented, the plan must show how the firm can conquer them and triumph. The audience is made aware of the writers' thought processes in arriving at their conclusions, and the assumptions are brought out in the open, enabling executives to evaluate the plan and then ask perceptive, incisive questions and offer valuable advice. One 3M manager stated, "If you just read bullet points, you may not get it, but if you read a narrative plan, you will. If there's a flaw in the logic, it glares out at you. With bullets, you don't know if the insight is really there or if the planner has merely given you a shopping list." 3M management believes that narrative plans can motivate and mobilize an entire organization. ■

Source: Adapted from Gordon Shaw, Robert Brown, and Philip Bromiley, "Strategic Stories: How 3M Is Rewriting Business Planning," *Harvard Business Review*, May–June 1998, pp. 41–50.

Summary of the Planning Process

Perhaps a good way to summarize the new direction in planning is to quote Frederick W. Gluck, a principal architect of the strategic management practice in the multinational management consulting firm McKinsey & Co. Gluck says that if major corporations are to develop the flexibility to compete, they must make the following major changes in the way they plan:

1. Top management must assume a more explicit strategic decision-making role, dedicating a large amount of time to deciding how things ought to be instead of listening to analyses of how they are.
2. The nature of planning must undergo a fundamental change from an exercise in forecasting to an exercise in creativity.
3. Planning processes and tools that assume a future much like the past must be replaced by a mind-set that is obsessed with being first to recognize change and turn it into a competitive advantage.
4. The role of the planner must change from being a purveyor of incrementalism to being a crusader for action and an alter ego to line management.
5. Strategic planning must be restored to the core of line management responsibilities.[26]

Organizational Design

Organizational design normally follows planning because the organization must implement the strategic plan. The planning process itself, because it encompasses an analysis of the firm's external environments as well as its strengths and weaknesses, often discloses a need to alter the organization. Changes in strategy may require changes in the organization, but the reverse is also true. For instance, a new CEO may join the firm, or the company may acquire another business. Planning and organizing are so closely related that usually the structure of the organization is treated by management as an integral part of the planning process.

Organizational Design Concerns

Two of the concerns that management faces in designing the organizational structure are (1) finding the most effective way to departmentalize to take advantage of the efficiencies gained from the specialization of labor and (2) coordinating the activities of those departments to enable the firm to meet its overall objectives. As all managers know, these two concerns run counter to each other; that is, the gain from increased specialization of labor may at times be nullified by the increased cost of coordination. It is this search for an optimum balance between them that often leads to a reorganization of the firm's structure.

Evolution of the Global Company

As was discussed in Chapter 2, companies often enter foreign markets first by exporting and then, as sales increase, by forming overseas sales companies and eventually setting up manufacturing facilities. As the firm's foreign involvement changed, its organization frequently changed. It might first have had *no one* responsible for international business; the firm's marketing department might have filled the export orders. Next, an export department might have been created, possibly in the marketing department, and when the company began to invest in various overseas locations, it could have formed an **international division** to take charge of all overseas involvement. Larger firms, such as Ford, IBM, and Goodyear, commonly organized their international divisions on a regional or geographical basis (Figure 14.3).

international division
A division in the organization that is at the same level as the domestic division and is responsible for all non-home country activities

[Figure 14.3] International Division

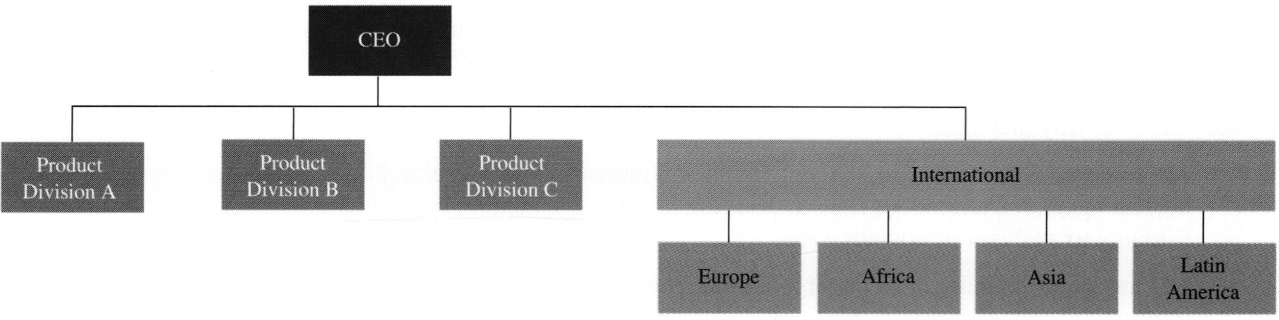

As their overseas operations increased in importance and scope, most managements, with some exceptions, felt the need to eliminate international divisions and establish worldwide organizations based on *product, region,* or *function.* Increasingly, *customer classes* are also a top-level dimension. Some service companies and financial institutions are also organized this way. At secondary, tertiary, and still lower levels, these four dimensions—plus (1) process, (2) national subsidiary, and (3) international or domestic—provide the basis for subdivisions.

Managements that changed to these types of organizations felt they would (1) be more capable of developing competitive strategies to confront the new global competition, (2) obtain lower production costs by promoting worldwide product standardization and manufacturing rationalization, and (3) enhance technology transfer and the allocation of company resources.

Global Corporate Form—Product

Frequently, this structure represents a return to preexport department times in that the domestic product division has been given responsibility for global line and staff operations. In the present-day global form, product divisions are responsible for the worldwide operations such as marketing and production of products under their control. Each division generally has regional experts, so while this organizational form avoids the duplication of product experts common in a company with an international division, it creates a duplication of area experts. Occasionally, to avoid placing regional specialists in each product division, management will have a group of managerial specialists in an international division who advise the product divisions but have no authority over them (see Figure 14.4).

Global Corporate Form—Geographical Regions

Firms in which geographical regions are the primary basis for division put the responsibility for all activities under area managers who report directly to the chief executive officer. This kind of organization simplifies the task of directing worldwide operations, because every country in the world is clearly under the control of someone who is in contact with headquarters (see Figure 14.5).

Of course, this organizational type is used for both multinational (multidomestic) and global companies. Global companies that use it consider the division in which the home country is located as just another division for purposes of resource allocation and a source of management personnel. Some U.S. global companies have created a North American division that includes Canada, Mexico, and Central American countries in addition to the United States, possibly in part to emphasize that the home country is given no preference.

The regionalized organization appears to be popular with companies that manufacture products with a rather low, or at least stable, technological content that require strong marketing ability. It is also favored by firms with diverse products, each having different product requirements, competitive environments, and political risks. Producers of con-

[Figure 14.4] Global Corporate Form—Product

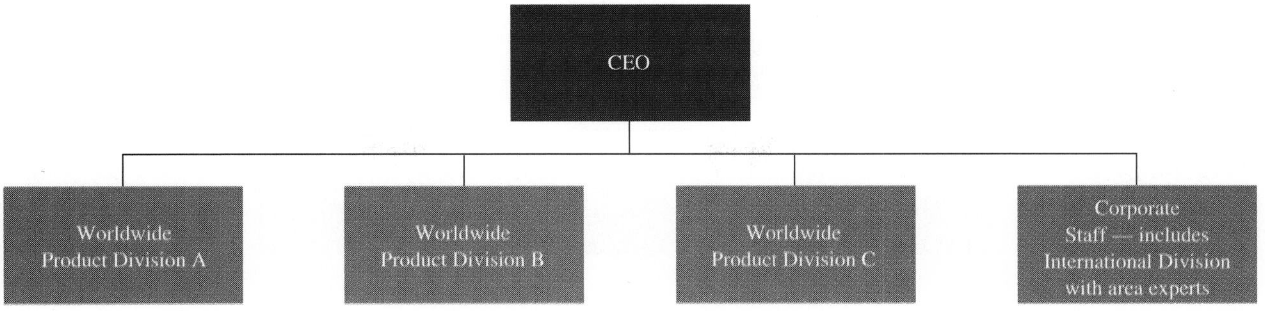

[Figure 14.5] Global Corporate Form—Geographical Regions

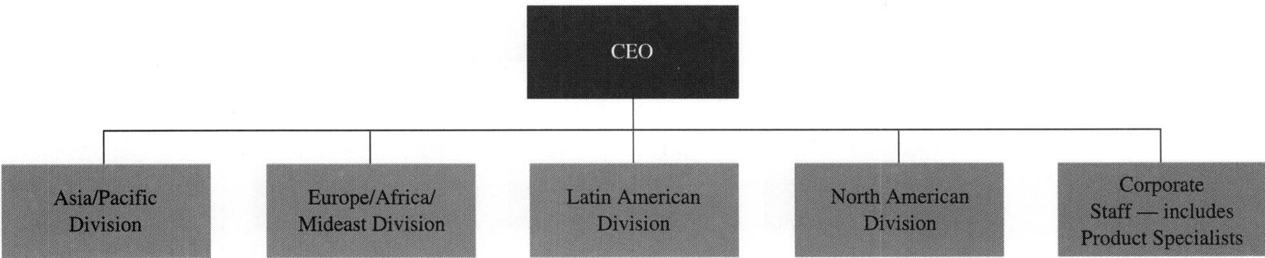

sumer products, such as prepared foods, pharmaceuticals, and household products, employ this type of organization. The disadvantage of an organization divided into geographical regions is that each region must have its own product and functional specialists so that although the duplication of area specialists found in product divisions is eliminated, duplication of product and functional specialists is necessary.

Production coordination across regions presents difficult problems, as does global product planning. To alleviate these problems, managements often place specialized product managers on the headquarters staff. Although these managers have no line authority, they do provide input to corporate decisions concerning products.

Global Corporate Form—Function

Few firms are organized by function at the top level. Those that are obviously believe worldwide functional expertise is more significant to the firm than is product or area knowledge. In this type of organization, those reporting to the CEO might be the senior executives responsible for each functional area (marketing, production, finance, and so on), as in Figure 14.6. The commonality among the users of the functional form is a narrow and highly integrated product mix, such as that of aircraft manufacturers or oil refining companies. For example, after the merger of Exxon and Mobil in November 1999, the new company restructured its operations. To improve the capital productivity of the combined organizations, ExxonMobil moved from a multifunctional, geographically based regional organization to an organization based on global functional businesses. Under the new structure, each global functional business is responsible for running its operations on a worldwide basis.[27]

Similarly, in late 1998, General Motors (GM) restructured its worldwide automobile operations. The company was trying to be "both 'global' and 'local' at the same time in order to capitalize on worldwide knowledge-sharing and to achieve economies of scale, while at the same time retaining the flexibility to tailor individual products to individual markets." To achieve these goals, GM reorganized its activities into a single global operation, GM Automotive. Functions such as

[Figure 14.6] Global Corporate Form—Function

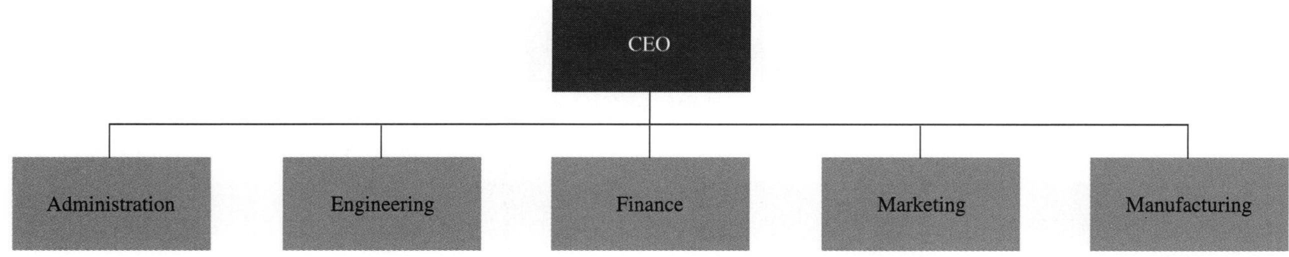

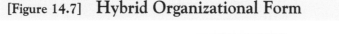

[Figure 14.7] Hybrid Organizational Form

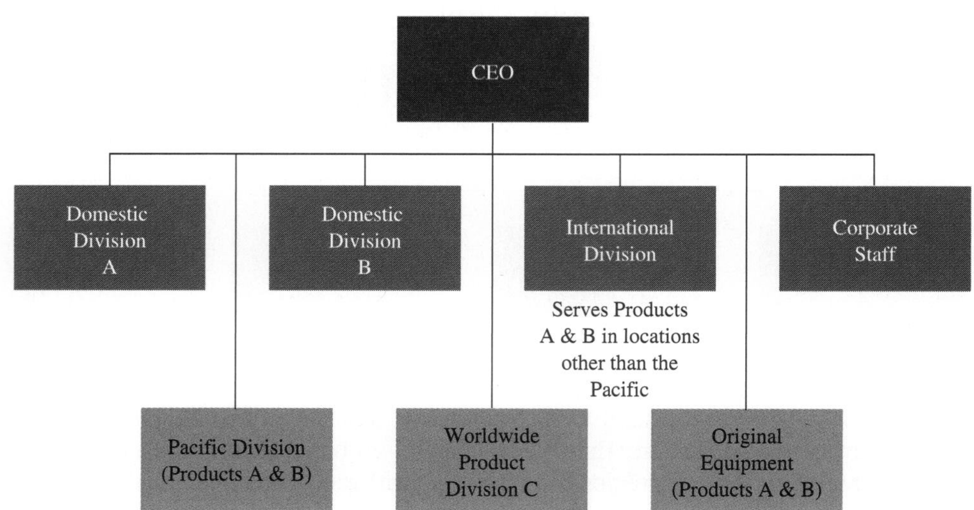

purchasing, manufacturing, engineering, research and development (R&D), human resources, and communications have been set up on a global basis, although the company has put into place mechanisms to allow "enough local control to meet the needs of local markets."[28]

Hybrid Forms

hybrid organization
Structure organized by more than one dimension at the top level

In a **hybrid organization,** a mixture of the organizational forms is used at the top level and may or may not be present at the lower levels. Figure 14.7 illustrates a simple hybrid form.

Such combinations are often the result of a regionally organized company having introduced a new and different product line that management believes can best be handled by a worldwide product division. An acquired company with distinct products and a functioning marketing network may be incorporated as a product division even though the rest of the firm is organized on a regional basis. Later, after corporate management becomes familiar with the operation, it may be regionalized.

A mixed structure may also result from the firm's selling to a sizable, homogeneous class of customers. Special divisions for handling sales to the military or to original equipment manufacturers are often established at the same level as regional or product divisions.

Recently, Ford announced a global management reorganization plan which, it says, will better serve local and regional needs. Jacques Nasser, Ford's chief executive officer, claims, "Strategic business units organized around brands and regions will help move the company forward, creating a culture that focuses on every point of contact

[Figure 14.8] Regional–Product Matrix

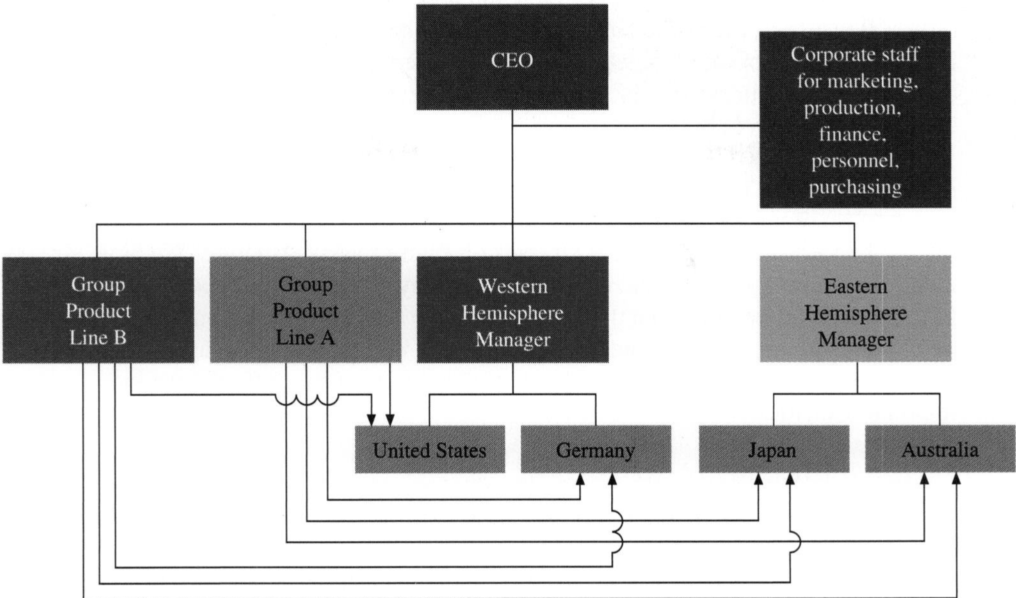

with the consumer." In recent years, Ford has been searching, like many international companies, for the optimum balance between cost-effective central management in an increasingly global industry and responsiveness to local demands. In the new organization, there are four regional business units: Ford Europe, Ford North America, Ford Asia Pacific, and Ford South America. The luxury vehicle division, which includes Aston Martin, Lincoln and Mercury, Jaguar, and Volvo, will remain a separate division, as will the service divisions: Hertz, Ford Credit, and Visteon parts.[29]

Matrix Organizations

matrix organization An organizational structure composed of one or more superimposed organizational structures in an attempt to mesh product, regional, functional, and other expertise

The **matrix organization** has evolved from management's attempt to mesh product, regional, and functional expertise while still maintaining clear lines of authority. It is called a matrix because an organization based on one or possibly two dimensions is superimposed on an organization based on another dimension. In an organization of two dimensions, such as area and product, both the area managers and the product managers will be at the same level and their responsibilities will overlap. An individual manager—say, a marketing manager in Germany—will have a multiple reporting relationship, being responsible to the area manager and in some instances to an international or worldwide marketing manager at headquarters. Figure 14.8 illustrates an extremely simple matrix organization based on two organizational dimensions. Note that the country managers are responsible to both the area managers and the product line managers.

Boeing, the largest aerospace company in the world, has an organizational structure based on a matrix of business groups/programs and functions/support services. Lines of communication flow both horizontally and vertically across these main dimensions. However, final authority rests with the top management team and the board of directors.[30] Similarly, Mitsubishi Chemical is organized as a matrix based on five business "companies" (each with various functional and product or process departments) and a number of functional departments.[31]

Problems with the Matrix. Although at one time it seemed that the matrix organizational form would enable firms to have the advantages of the product, regional, and functional forms, the disadvantages of the matrix form have kept most worldwide companies from adopting it. One problem with the matrix is that the two or three managers (if it is a three-dimensional matrix) must agree on a decision. This can lead to

matrix overlay
An organization in which top-level divisions are required to heed input from a staff composed of experts of another organizational dimension in an attempt to avoid the double-reporting difficulty of a matrix organization but still mesh two or more dimensions

less-than-optimum compromises, delayed responses, and power politics where more attention is paid to the process than to the problem. When the managers cannot agree, the problem goes higher in the organization and takes top management away from its duties. Because of these difficulties, many firms have maintained their original organizations based on product, function, region, or international division and have built into the structure accountability for the other organizational dimensions; this is called by some a **matrix overlay.**

Matrix Overlay. The matrix overlay attempts to address the problems of the matrix structure by requiring accountability of all functions in the organization while avoiding the burdensome management stresses of a pure matrix structure. We have already mentioned how a firm organized by product may have regional specialists in a staff function with the requirement that they have input to product decisions. They may even be organized in an international division, as was mentioned previously. Conversely, a regional organization would have product managers on its staff who provide input to regional decisions.[32]

strategic business unit (SBU)
Business entity with a clearly defined market, specific competitors, the ability to carry out its business mission, and a size appropriate for control by a single manager

Strategic Business Units

Strategic business units (SBUs), which originated with General Electric, are an organizational form in which product divisions have been defined as though they were distinct, independent businesses. An SBU is defined as a self-contained business entity with a clearly defined market, specific competitors, the ability to carry out its business mission, and a size appropriate for control by a single manager. Most SBUs are based on product lines, and if a product must be modified to suit different markets, a worldwide SBU may be divided into a few product/market SBUs serving various markets or groups of countries. Shell Chemical Company's SBUs, which it calls PBUs (product business units), are global.[33]

Changes in Organizational Forms

The rapidly changing business environment caused by increased global competition, customer preference for custom-made rather than mass-produced products, and faster technological change is pressuring companies to step up their search for organizational forms that will enable them to act more quickly, reduce costs, and improve the quality of product offerings. Not only are they mixing older, established forms, they are also changing to different forms, many of which are modified versions of long-established forms with new names.

What is new is the acceptance by many companies of the need for frequent reorganization. Present in these reorganizations, called *reengineering* by many, are a significant reduction in the levels of middle management, restructuring of work processes to reduce the fragmenting of the process across functional departments, empowerment of employees, and the use of computers for instant communication and swift transmittal of information. CEOs are striving to make their organizations lean, flat, fast to respond, and innovative.[34]

Royal Dutch Shell, in its biggest corporate restructuring in 30 years, dismantled its three-dimensional matrix organization of regional units, business sectors, and business functions (marketing, production, etc.) and changed to a "weakened matrix." The company stripped out the old regional lines of command and replaced them with five business organizations representing Shell's main activities: exploration and production, oil products (refining and marketing), chemicals, gas, and coal. Each of the business organizations is headed by a business committee of senior directors from the key operating companies. The national operating companies have a "dotted-line relationship" with the corporate center just described but report directly to an *international business division,* an organizational form largely discarded by experts in the organizational design of global firms.[35]

In January 2000, Coca-Cola announced a major organizational realignment that will give more responsibility and resources to local managers in the more than 200 markets where the company does business. Coke's corporate headquarters will be responsible for setting policy and strategy for the entire company, while the firm's revenue-generating units will assume all other responsibilities. For example, local managers will make decisions about products, promotion, and other functions previously controlled at headquarters.[36] Coke's CEO said, "The world in which we operate has changed dramatically, and we must change to succeed. This realignment will better enable the Company to serve the changing needs of its customers and consumers at the local level and ensure that Coca-Cola complements the local culture in every community where it is sold." As part of the realignment, 2,500 jobs in the Atlanta headquarters will be eliminated, reducing the bureaucracy and permitting greater responsiveness to political and local concerns. Coke will also sell more soft drinks that cater to local tastes. As one beverage industry analyst commented, the company has ignored local flavors for years: "The opportunities were always there. Now they've put a structure in place to go after them."[37] A company spokesperson said, "We're moving from globalization to 'multi-localization.' "[38]

Current Organizational Trends

Two organizational forms are now receiving the attention of many CEOs: the virtual corporation and the horizontal corporation.

Virtual Corporation

A **virtual corporation,** also called a network corporation, is an organization that coordinates economic activity to deliver value to customers using resources outside the traditional boundaries of the organization.[39] In other words, it relies to a great extent on third parties to conduct its business.[40] Outsourcing once was used for downsizing and cost reduction, but now companies are using it to obtain specialized expertise which they don't have but need in order to serve new markets or adopt new technology.

virtual corporation
An organization that coordinates economic activity to deliver value to customers using resources outside the traditional boundaries of the organization

The evolution of the technology infrastructure has made possible changes in the work force and working methods, such as teleworking, home offices, and flexible working practices. All these factors have contributed to the increase in virtual corporations. Global networking on the Internet has made worldwide outsourcing possible for firms of all sizes.

> Here is a real virtual corporation—it outsources practically everything. Nokia, a Finnish company that was in forest products for decades, decided to diversify into TV manufacturing in the 1980s. The business never made a profit, and so it started producing personal computers but sold the PC division. The company's CEO committed suicide, and a 38-year-old took his place. Although the company didn't know much about the technoiogy, he decided to get into digital telephones.
>
> He outsourced nearly everything—the design, marketing, chip fabrication. Amazingly, the firm became one of the world's largest telephone companies in less than two years. In spite of the fact that AT&T and the European telephone companies had spent hundreds of millions of dollars on cellular technology research, Nokia beat them in no time. It is the world's largest "manufacturer" of digital mobile phones. The firm's 1999 sales of cellular phones and other electronic products amounted to 19.77 billion euros, and sales for 2000 are projected at 21.09 billion euros.[41]

Although the name is new, the virtual corporation concept has existed for decades. It has been extremely common for a group of construction firms, each with a special area of expertise, to form a consortium to bid on a contract for constructing a road or an airfield, for example. After finishing the job, the consortium would disband. Other examples of network organizations are the various clothing and athletic shoe marketers such as DKNY, Nike, and Reebok. These latter firms are also called *modular corporations.*

The virtual corporation concept has several potential benefits. In particular, it permits greater flexibility than is associated with more typical corporate structures, and rather than building competence from the ground up and incurring high start-up costs which could limit future production decisions, virtual corporations form a network of dynamic

ACT Manufacturing: A Small Business That Grew Rapidly in Global Markets

Small and Medium-Sized Enterprises

ACT Manufacturing Inc. (ACT) provides contract electronics manufacturing (CEM) services to original equipment manufacturers. About 66 percent of ACT's business is in the global networking and telecommunications segments, with the remainder in the computer, medical equipment, and other industries. ACT's customers include large global companies such as Motorola, EMC, Alcatel, and Northern Telecom; emerging companies such as Marconi, Unisphere, and Efficient Networks; and a variety of start-up operations.

ACT began in Framingham, Massachusetts, in 1981 as a manufacturer of custom cable assembly products. In 1992, ACT was still a small manufacturing company, with net sales of $27 million. In 1991, however, this small company made an important strategic decision: it expanded into the contract assembly of printed circuit boards. This move was exceptionally timely in light of industry trends. As ACT's CEO, John Pino, said, "The direction of the electronics industry in general was away from building everything in-house."[a]

Traditionally, the manufacturing of electronics products was done in-house by large integrated companies. Rapid technological change, high levels of competition, and shorter product life cycles have caused companies to outsource manufacturing activities to specialist companies. CEMs are able to develop core competencies in specialized areas such as printed circuit board assembly, enabling them to achieve improved economies of scale, a more rapid response to technological and market changes, and other benefits.

The boom in information and communication technology sectors in the 1990s, particularly the emergence of hundreds of start-up companies in those emerging segments, created excellent growth opportunities for companies such as ACT. "The electronics manufacturing services industry has been a powerful force in providing start-up companies with the necessary manufacturing infrastructure to compete against giants such as Cisco Systems, Lucent Technologies, and others," said Jerry Labowitz, an analyst at Merrill Lynch.[b] Seeking the benefits of virtual manufacturing, start-ups often work with CEM partners such as ACT in order to quickly ramp up production in rapidly growing markets. Reflecting the trends in the industry, ACT's CEM business grew rapidly and now accounts for 95 percent of its business.

To build market share and improve operating economies in the rapidly expanding and highly competitive printed circuit board business, ACT has used strategic acquisitions to supplement internally generated growth. In 1999, ACT acquired CMC Industries (another midtier U.S. company) and selected strategic assets of GSS/Array Technologies of Thailand. In 2000, the company acquired Bull Electronics Angers. Completing these deals caused ACT's manufacturing activities to expand from three to seven countries (the United States, Mexico, Ireland, Thailand, France, Singapore, and Taiwan), for a total of 1.5 million square feet of manufacturing capacity and over 6,000 employees. After completing the GSS/Array and Bull transactions, ACT was the seventh-largest CEM provider in the world.

These acquisitions have brought more than just size, however. Through the addition of competencies from acquired companies, ACT has been able to move beyond the manufacturing of complex printed circuit boards and custom cable assemblies. The company now offers complete, customized solutions to customers, including high-end system-level assembly, systems integration, and complex logistics services. It has particular strength in managing new product introduction and emerging technologies. As Pino states, "Our goal is to continue to expand our capabilities and global footprint."[c]

ACT's stated mission (the company calls this its philosophy) is as follows:

> At ACT we are dedicated to helping our customers bring their products to

relationships which allow them to take advantage of the competencies of other organizations and respond rapidly to changing circumstances. However, this form of organization can have disadvantages, including the potential to reduce management's control over the corporation's activities (it is vulnerable to the opportunistic actions of partners, including cost increases, unintended "borrowing" of technical and other knowledge, and potential departure from the relationship at inappropriate times). From the standpoint of employees, this form of organization may replace the security of long-term employment and the promise of ever-increasing salaries with the insecurity of the market—a global market.

market faster and smarter than ever before. We redefine electronic manufacturing with value-added design, manufacturing, and logistics solutions that go far beyond the scope of traditional outsourcing.

A quick, flexible response to our customer's needs, the empowerment of our employees, and the continual development of world-class processes, form the cornerstone of our organizational philosophy. These tenets create competitive advantages for our customers and lead to the highest levels of customer and employee satisfaction.

We are committed to acting as a reliable, powerful partner—one that helps our customers around the world compete, grow, and increase market share and profits.[d]

To achieve its full potential, however, ACT has had to restructure its organization to match its broader skill base and increasingly global scope of operations. In August 2000, ACT reorganized into two geographically based divisions for manufacturing activities: (1) the Americas and (2) Europe and Asia. The company established a Global Marketing and Business Development unit to develop and integrate worldwide sales strategy and manage the company's regional direct sales forces and networks of independent representatives. To enable ACT to better manage start-up companies and their different needs, the company also established New Product Introduction (NPI) centers in three of its facilities. The NPI centers are segregated from the rest of production, enabling them to respond rapidly and effectively to changes in design or production schedules, which are common with start-ups and other companies operating in emerging technologies. Commenting on the changes, Pino said, "This new organizational structure will bring leadership and focus to the continued growth of ACT's global operations and business development efforts."[e]

For the future, Pino listed ACT's goals as follows:

It is our intention to drive revenue and profitability in excess of the marketplace. We set a minimum target for revenue expansion of about 30 percent. We believe that we will be able to expand at a higher rate than that of the rest of the industry. In fact, we have been able to do that in 1999. We exited [1999] with about a 70 percent rate of growth, and we certainly expect to be in that range or above for the year 2000. We want to continue to improve our profitability from a return of investment capital. We have a goal of 20 percent that we would like to hit. We want to utilize our assets better, so we are going to strengthen our management of the balance sheet. We are going to spend more time growing the internal customer base as well as continuing to develop through acquisition. We have a disciplined acquisition strategy in place, and we are going to continue to be acquirers. We are going to look for those companies that can complement our organization, companies that match our corporate culture, provide technologically advanced solutions to their customer set and have a "customer first" management philosophy. And certainly we are capable of meeting all financial commitments that we have. As you can see, we have set a number of goals for the company, a lot of things we are looking to achieve. We have been quite successful in doing that in the past. I do not see any reason why that will not continue.[f]

As noted by Pino, ACT's sales have been increasing at a more rapid rate than those of its main competitors in the midtier segment of CEMs. In 1999, ACT reported sales of $696 million, a 140 percent increase from 1998 sales of $291 million.[g] Building on continued strong sales growth in 2000, ACT is poised to become a $2 billion company in 2001, about 75 times larger than it was in 1992. Through intelligent strategy formulation and implementation, this small company has grown rapidly into a major international competitor. ■

Sources:[a]Hiawatha Bray, "ACT Manufacturing Inc.," *The Boston Globe,* May 20, 1997, www.boston.com/globe/business/packages/globe_100/1997/content/act.htm (December 12, 2000). [b]Claire Serant, "Outsource: Handling Start-Up's Manufacturing Needs with Care," *Electronic Buyers' News,* April 24, 2000, www.ebnonline.com/printableArticle?doc_idOEG20000424S0055 (December 13, 2000). [c]Claire Serant, "Acquisitions Boost ACT Manufacturing's 4Q Results," *Electronic Buyers' News,* February 18, 2000, www.ebnonline.com/printableArticle?doc_id=OEG20000218S0007 (December 12, 2000). [d]"Philosophy," www.actmfg.com/philosophy.htm (December 13, 2000). [e]"ACT Manufacturing, Inc. Announces New Global Organization," www.actmfg.com/articles/08_09_00.html (December 13, 2000). [f]"ACT Manufacturing to Drive Revenue and Profitability in Excess of the Marketplace," *The Wall Street Transcript,* www.twst.com/notes/articles/kak203.html (December 13, 2000). [g]Ibid.

Horizontal Corporation

Another organizational form, the **horizontal corporation,** has been adopted by some large technology-oriented global firms in highly competitive industries such as electronics and computers. Firms such as AT&T, General Electric, and Du Pont have chosen this organizational form to give them the flexibility to respond quickly to advances in technology and be product innovators.[42] In many companies *teams* are drawn from different departments to solve a problem or deliver a product.

horizontal corporation
A form of organization characterized by lateral decision processes, horizontal networks, and a strong corporatewide business philosophy

[Worldview]
How to Become More Globally Competitive

An *Industry Week* survey of senior executives in large manufacturing firms revealed that the primary strategy adopted by respondents to become more competitive globally was to concentrate on core businesses. Other structural changes adopted by about 70 percent of the companies included flattening the organization by removing layers of management, merging with other companies to form new structures, decentralizing business units, and forming new global business units.

Dow Chemical Company, which has operations in 168 countries, is an example of a firm that has made changes to become more globally competitive. In 1996, Dow changed its organizational structure from a geographic matrix to one of global business processes and 15 global business units that have individual global profit-and-loss responsibility. Management layers in the organization were reduced from 10 to 12 down to 4 to 6. Says Dow's CEO, "Dow is now making two to three times the earnings it used to make at an equivalent position in the global chemical market cycle, and we are earning the cost of capital at the trough of the cycle, something we have never done before."

Even though the division is not as popular an organizational structure as it once was, it may still offer advantages in some conditions. Herman Miller, an office furniture manufacturer ($1.8 billion in sales), put all international operations under one executive reporting directly to the CEO. The board chairman stated that under the new organization, the firm began earning a profit again after experiencing losses for five years.

Ninety percent of the executives queried stated that the strategies that have been effective in increasing their firms' global competitiveness are (1) placing profit-and-loss responsibility at lower levels in the firm, (2) reducing operating expenses, and (3) forming strategic alliances with customers, suppliers, and competitors.

Another noteworthy result was that nearly half the respondents had not adopted value chain strategies. Those who have judged the following strategies to be most effective in increasing a firm's global competitiveness:

1. Planning jointly with suppliers and customers.
2. Maintaining less inventory.
3. Managing production on a global basis.

Although 80 percent of the responding firms have limited or sole sourcing arrangements with suppliers, less than half believe that those arrangements have been effective in increasing global competitiveness. ■

Source: Adapted from "Winning the World Over," *Industry Week*, November 15, 1999, www.industryweek.com/...ntArticles.asp.articles.asp?ArticleId=656 (November 28, 1999).

This organization has been characterized as "antiorganization" because its designers are seeking to remove the constraints imposed by the conventional organizational structures. In a horizontal corporation, employees worldwide create, build, and market the company's products through a carefully cultivated system of interrelationships. Marketers in Great Britain speak directly to production people in Brazil without having to go through the home office in Germany, for example. Proponents of the horizontal organization claim lateral relationships incite innovation and new product development. They also state that the organization "puts greater decision-making responsibility in the hands of middle managers, who are not required to clear every detail and event with higher-ups. The idea is to substitute cooperation and coordination, which are in everyone's interests, for strict control and supervision."[43]

Corporate Survival into the 21st Century

Managers will make greater use of the *dynamic network structure* that breaks down the major functions of the firm into small companies coordinated by a small-sized headquarters organization. Business functions such as marketing and accounting may be provided by separate organizations connected by computers to a central office.[44] To attain the optimum level of vertical integration, a firm must focus on its core business. Anything not essential to the business can be done cheaper and faster by outside suppliers.[45]

As American companies prepare for the global battles of the 21st century, we must remember that organizations, like people, have life cycles. In their youth, they're small and fast-growing, but as they age, they often become big, complex, and out of touch with their markets. The firms of tomorrow must learn how to be large and entrepreneurial. As one CEO put it, "Small is not better; focused is better."[46]

Control

Every successful company uses controls to put its plans into effect, evaluate their effectiveness, make desirable corrections, and evaluate and reward or correct executive performance. Matters are more complicated for an international company than for a one-country operation. In earlier chapters, we brought out the complicating causes. They include different languages, cultures, and attitudes; different taxes and accounting methods; different currencies, labor costs, and market sizes; different degrees of political stability and security for personnel and property; and many more. For these reasons, international companies need controls even more than do domestic ones.

Subsidiaries, 100 Percent Owned

The words **subsidiaries** and **affiliates** sometimes are used interchangeably, and we shall examine first the control of those in which the parent has 100 percent ownership. This avoids for now the additional complications of joint ventures or subsidiaries in which the parent has less than 100 percent ownership. We shall deal with those later in the chapter.

subsidiaries
Companies controlled by other companies through ownership of enough voting stock to elect board of directors majorities

affiliates
Sometimes used interchangeably with *subsidiaries,* but more forms exist than just stock ownership

Where Are Decisions Made?

There are three possibilities. Two of them are that all decisions are made at either the international company (IC) headquarters or the subsidiary level. Theoretically, all decisions could be made at one location or the other. As common sense would indicate, they are not; instead, some decisions are made at one place, some are made at the other place, and some are made cooperatively.[47] Many variables determine which decision is made where. Some of the more significant variables are (1) product and equipment, (2) the competence of subsidiary management and reliance on that management by the IC headquarters, (3) the size of the IC and how long it has been one, (4) the detriment of a subsidiary for the benefit of the enterprise, and (5) subsidiary frustration.

Product and Equipment

As to decision location, questions of standardization of product and equipment and second markets can be important.

Standardize? As we will discuss in Chapter 16, large global manufacturers of consumer products, such as Procter & Gamble (P&G), are developing standardized products from the outset for global or at least regional markets. In these situations, the affiliates have to follow company policy. Of course, as we pointed out in the case of P&G, representatives of the affiliates have an opportunity to take part in the product design, contrary to the way new products were introduced before the globalization strategy became so popular. Then, as we explained in the discussion of the international product life cycle, new products were first introduced in the home market. After the production process was stabilized, the specifications were sent to the affiliates (second markets) for local production, where adaptations could be made if the local managements deemed them necessary for their markets.

In a firm without a global product policy, the preference of the operations management people in the home office has always been to standardize the product or at least the production process in as many overseas plants as possible, as we will explain in Chapter 20. If, however, any subsidiary can demonstrate that the profit potential is greater for a product tailored for its own market than what the company would realize from global standardization, the subsidiary ordinarily is allowed to proceed. Of course, the decision in such a case is cooperative in that the parent has the power to veto or override its subsidiary's decision.

Competence of Subsidiary Management and Headquarters' Reliance on It

Reliance on subsidiary management can depend on how well the executives know one another and how well they know company policies, on whether headquarters management feels that it understands host country conditions, on the distances between the home country and the host countries, and on how big and old the parent company is.

Moving Executives Around. Many ICs have a policy of transferring promising management personnel between parent headquarters and subsidiaries and among subsidiaries. Thus, the manager learns firsthand the policies of headquarters and the problems of putting those policies into effect at subsidiary levels.

A result of such transfers, which is difficult to measure but nevertheless important, is a network of intra-IC personal relationships. This tends to increase the confidence of executives in one another and to make communication among executives easier and less subject to error.

Another development is that some ICs have moved their regional executives into headquarters to improve communications and reduce cost.

Understanding Host Country Conditions. One element in the degree of headquarters' reliance on subsidiary management is the familiarity of headquarters with conditions in the subsidiary's host country. The less familiar or the more different conditions in the host country are perceived to be, the more likely headquarters is to rely on subsidiary management.

How Far Away Is the Host Country? Another element in the degree of headquarters' reliance on subsidiary management is the distance of the host country from home headquarters. Thus, an American parent is likely to place more reliance on the management of an Indonesian subsidiary than on the management of a Canadian subsidiary. This occurs for two reasons: American management perceives management conditions in Canada to be more easily understood than conditions in Indonesia, and Indonesia is much farther from the United States than Canada is.

Size and Age of the IC

As a rule, a large company can afford to hire more specialists, experts, and experienced executives than can a smaller one. The longer a company has been an IC, the more likely it is to have a number of experienced executives who know company policies and have worked at headquarters and in the field. Successful experience builds confidence.

In most ICs, the top positions are at headquarters, and the ablest and most persistent executives get there in time. Thus, over time, the headquarters of a successful company is run by experienced executives who are confident of their knowledge of the business in the home and host countries and in combinations thereof.

It follows that in larger, older organizations, more decisions are made at headquarters and fewer are delegated to subsidiaries. Smaller companies, in business for shorter periods of time, tend to be able to afford fewer internationally experienced executives and will not have had time to develop them internally. Smaller, newer companies have no choice but to delegate decisions to subsidiary managements. During the 1980s and early 1990s, it became something of a management fad among larger ICs also to empower subsidiary managers and decentralize. As do most fads, however, this practice faded by the mid-1990s, and ICs began to shift power to the parent in the home country.[48]

Benefiting the Enterprise to the Detriment of a Subsidiary

An IC has opportunities to source raw materials and components, locate factories, allocate orders, and govern intrafirm pricing that are not available to a non-IC. Such activities may be beneficial to the enterprise yet may result in a **subsidiary detriment.**

subsidiary detriment
A small loss for a subsidiary results in a greater gain for the total IC

Moving Production Factors. For any number of reasons, an IC may decide to move factors of production from one country to another or to expand in one country in preference to another. Tax, labor, market, currency, and political stability issues are a few possible reasons.

The subsidiary from which factors are being taken would be unenthusiastic. Its management would be slow, at best, to cut the company's capacity. Headquarters would make such decisions.

Which Subsidiary Gets the Order? Similarly, if an order—say, from an Argentine customer—could be filled from a subsidiary in France or another in South Africa or a third in Brazil, parent headquarters might decide which subsidiary gets the business. Among the considerations in the decision would be transportation costs, production costs, comparative tariff rates, customers' currency restrictions, comparative order backlogs, and taxes. Having such a decision made by IC headquarters avoids price competition among members of the same IC group.

Multicountry Production. Frequently, the size of the market in a single country is too small to permit economies of scale in manufacturing an entire industrial product for that one market. An example is Ford's production of a light vehicle for the Asian market.

In that situation, Ford negotiated with several countries to the end that one country would make one component of the vehicle for all the countries involved. Thus, one country makes the engine, a second country has the body-stamping plant, a third makes the transmission, and so forth. In this fashion, each operation achieves the efficiency and cost savings of economies of scale. Of course, this kind of multinational production demands a high degree of IC headquarters control and coordination.

Which Subsidiary Books the Profit? In certain circumstances, an IC may have some choice of two or more countries in which to declare profits. Such circumstances may arise where two or more units of the IC cooperate in supplying components or services under a contract with a customer unrelated to any part of the IC. Under these conditions, there may be opportunities to allocate higher prices to one unit or subsidiary and lower prices to another within the global price to the customer.

If the host country of one of the subsidiaries has lower taxes than the other host countries, it would be natural to try to maximize profits in the lower-tax country and minimize them in the higher-tax country. Other differences between host countries could dictate the allocation of profit to or from the subsidiaries located there. Such differences could include currency controls, labor relations, political climate, and social unrest. It is sensible to direct or allocate as much profit as reasonably possible to subsidiaries in countries with the fewest currency controls, the best labor relations and political climate, and the least social unrest.

The intrafirm transaction may also give a company choices regarding profit location. Pricing between members of the same enterprise is referred to as *transfer pricing,* and while IC headquarters could permit undirected, arm's-length negotiations between itself and its subsidiaries, that might not yield the most advantageous results for the enterprise as a whole.*

Price and profit allocation decisions like these are usually best made at parent company headquarters, which is supposed to maintain the overall view, looking out for the best interests of the enterprise. Naturally, subsidiary management does not gladly make decisions to accept lower profits, largely because its evaluation may suffer.

*Transfer pricing is discussed in Chapter 16.

The following two tables illustrate how the total IC enterprise may profit even though one subsidiary makes less. Assume a cooperative contract by which two subsidiaries are selling products and services to an outside customer for a price of $100 million. The host country of IC Alpha levies company income taxes at the rate of 50 percent, whereas IC Beta's host country taxes its income at 20 percent. The customer is in a third country, has agreed to pay $100 million, and is indifferent to how Alpha and Beta share the money. The first table below shows the enterprise's after-tax income if Alpha is paid $60 million and Beta is paid $40 million.

	Receives (in $ millions)	Tax (in $ millions)	After Tax (in $ millions)
Alpha	$60	$30	$30
Beta	40	8	32
			$62

Thus, after tax, the enterprise realizes $62 million.

The second table shows the after-tax income if Alpha is paid $40 million and Beta is paid $60 million.

	Receives (in $ millions)	Tax (in $ millions)	After Tax (in $ millions)
Alpha	$40	$20	$20
Beta	60	12	48
			$68

Thus, after taxes, the enterprise realizes $68 million.

These simple examples illustrate that the IC would be $6 million better off if it could shift $20 million of the payment from Alpha to Beta, while the customer is no worse off, as it pays $100 million in either case. Alpha, having received $20 million less payment, is $10 million worse off after taxes, but Beta is $16 million better off and the enterprise is $6 million ahead on the same contract. Given the number of countries and tax laws in the world, there are countless combinations of how such savings can be accomplished. Financial management awareness and control are the keys.

We do not mean to leave the impression that the host and home governments are unaware of or indifferent to transfer pricing and profit allocating by ICs operating within their borders. The companies must expect questioning by host and home governments and must be prepared to demonstrate that prices or allocations are reasonable. This may be done by showing that other companies charge comparable prices for the same or similar items or, if there are no similar items, by showing that costs plus profit have been used reasonably to arrive at the price. As to allocation of profits, the IC in our example would try to prove that the volume or importance of the work done by Beta or the responsibilities assumed by Beta, such as financing, after-sales service, or warranty obligations, justify the higher amount being paid to Beta. Of course, the questioning in this instance would come from the host government of Alpha if it got wind of the possibility of more taxable income for Beta and less for itself.[49]

Subsidiary Frustration

An extremely important consideration for parent company management is that the management of its subsidiaries be motivated and loyal. If all the big decisions are made, or are perceived to be made, at the IC headquarters, the managers of subsidiaries can lose incentive and prestige or face with their employees and the community. They may grow hostile and disloyal.

Therefore, even though there may be reasons for headquarters to make decisions, it should delegate as much as is reasonably possible. Management of each subsidiary should be kept thoroughly informed and be consulted seriously about decisions, negotiations, and developments in its geographical area. The mid-1990s trend for ICs to shift power away from subsidiaries toward the parent caused the forecastable frustration to subsidiary management, followed by resignations. Some companies reporting this development were IBM, European International, and CS First Boston.[50]

Joint Ventures and Subsidiaries Less Than 100 Percent Owned

A joint venture may be, as defined in Chapter 2, a corporate entity between an IC and local owners or a corporate entity between two or more companies that are foreign to the area where the joint venture is located, or it may involve one company working on a project of limited duration (constructing a dam, for example) in cooperation with one or more other companies. The other companies may be subsidiaries or affiliates, but they may also be entirely independent entities.

All the reasons for making decisions at IC headquarters, at subsidiary headquarters, or cooperatively apply equally in joint venture situations. However, headquarters will almost never have as much freedom of action and flexibility in a joint venture as it has with subsidiaries that are 100 percent owned.

Loss of Freedom and Flexibility

The reasons for that loss of freedom and flexibility are easy to see. If shareholders outside the IC own control of the affiliate, they can block efforts of IC headquarters to move production factors away, fill an export order from another affiliate or subsidiary, and so forth. Even if outside shareholders are a minority and cannot directly control the affiliate, they can bring legal or political pressures on the IC to prevent it from diminishing the affiliate's profitability for the enterprise's benefit. Likewise, the local partner in a joint venture is highly unlikely to agree with measures that penalize the joint venture for the IC's benefit.

Control Can Be Had

With less than 50 percent of the voting stock and even with no voting stock, an IC can have control. Some methods to maintain control are

- A management contract.
- Control of the finances.
- Control of the technology.
- Putting people from the IC in important executive positions.

As might be expected, ICs have encountered resistance to putting IC personnel in the important executive positions from their joint venture partners or from host governments. The natural desire of these partners and governments is that their own nationals have at least equality in the important positions and that they get training and experience in the technology and management.

Reporting

For controls to be effective, all operating units of an IC must provide headquarters with timely, accurate, and complete reports. There are many uses for the information reported. Among the types of reporting required are (1) financial, (2) technological, (3) market opportunity, and (4) political and economic.

Financial

A surplus of funds in one subsidiary should perhaps be retained there for investment or contingencies. On the other hand, such a surplus might be more useful at the parent company, in which case payment of a dividend is indicated. Or perhaps another subsidiary or affiliate needs capital, and the surplus could be lent or invested there.

Obviously, parent headquarters must know the existence and size of a surplus to determine its best use.

Technological

New technology should be reported. New technology is constantly being developed in different countries, and the subsidiary or affiliated company operating in such a country is likely to learn about it before IC headquarters hundreds or thousands of miles away does. If headquarters finds the new technology potentially valuable, it can gain competitive advantage by being the first to contact the developer for a license to use it.

Market Opportunities

The affiliates in various countries may spot new or growing markets for some product of the enterprise. This could be profitable all around, as the IC sells more of the product while the affiliate earns sales commissions. Of course, if the new market is sufficiently large, the affiliate may begin to assemble or produce the product under license from the parent company or from another affiliate.

Other market-related information that should be reported to IC headquarters includes competitors' activities, price developments, and new products of potential interest to the IC group. Also of importance is information on the subsidiary's market share and whether it is growing or shrinking, together with explanations.

Political and Economic

Not surprisingly, reports on political and economic conditions have multiplied mightily in number and importance over the past 15 or so years as revolutions—some bloody—have toppled and changed governments.[51] Democracies have replaced dictatorships, one dictator has replaced another, countries have broken apart or reunited—changes have been occurring on almost every continent.

One early example of how accurate reporting saved an American company a lot of money involved Citibank in Iran, where the bank had a representative office during the 1970s. Even though some government intelligence services were said to have been surprised when the Ayatollah Khomeini threw out the shah of Iran in 1979, the Citibank Tehran office had become aware of potential danger as early as the summer of 1978. The office first lowered the ceiling on Iranian loans and then froze any new business, even to existing customers, in the autumn of 1978.[52]

"De-Jobbing"

The conditions that created jobs 200 years ago—mass production and large organizations—are disappearing. Technology enables companies to automate production lines where many job holders used to do repetitive tasks. Instead of long production runs where the same thing has to be done again and again, firms are increasingly customizing production. Big firms, where most of the good jobs used to be, are unbundling activities and farming them out to little firms. New computer and communication technologies are **"de-jobbing"** the workplace, changing from the traditional, fixed-jobs approach to one in which teams perform tasks. And the composition of these teams changes as the tasks evolve.

de-jobbing
Replacing fixed jobs with tasks performed by evolving teams

Today's organization is rapidly being transformed from a structure built out of jobs into a field of work needing to be done. A fast-moving organization, such as Intel, will hire a person to be part of a specific project. The project will change over time, and the person's responsibilities and tasks change with it. Then the person is assigned to another project, probably before the first is finished, and then maybe to a third. As projects evolve and change, the person will work with several team leaders, keeping different schedules, being in various places, and performing a number of different tasks.

Hierarchy Implodes

Under these conditions, **hierarchy** cannot be maintained; people no longer take their cues from a job description or a supervisor's instructions. Signals come from the changing demands of the project. Workers focus their efforts and collective resources on work that needs doing, changing as that changes.

hierarchy
A body of persons organized or classified according to rank or authority

Traits of Companies with De-Jobbed Workers

They share four:

- They encourage employees to make the kinds of operating decisions that used to be reserved for managers.
- They give employees the information they need to make such decisions.
- They give employees lots of training to create the kind of understanding of business and financial issues that used to concern only an owner or executive.
- They give employees a stake in the fruits of their labor—a share of the profits.[53]

Managing in a World out of Control

The Internet may be the closest thing to a working anarchy the world has ever seen. Nobody owns it, nobody runs it, and most of its half-billion or so citizens get along by dint of online etiquette, not rules and regulations. Etiquette, however, has not prevented some users from copping names generally associated with others. The coppers may be pretenders, competitors, speculators hoping that the name might one day be worth something, or just pranksters. Some legal battles for names involve Kaplan Educational Center, which found its name had been taken by its chief competitor, Princeton Review; MCI, whose name was registered by its rival, Sprint; and MTV, which was beaten to that name registration by a former employee.[54]

Internet has been built up without any central control because the U.S. Defense Department wanted to ensure it could survive a nuclear attack. The Net has proved to be a paragon of hothouse expansion and constant evolution. Though it may be messier and less efficient than a similar system designed and run by an agency or company, this organically grown network is also more adaptable and less susceptible to a systemwide crash.

The consequences for management in a world out of control, such as Internet, are discussed in a book by Kevin Kelly titled *Out of Control: The Rise of Neo-Biological Civilization.* Among the points made in a review of the book is a recipe developed at MIT for devising a system of distributed control: (1) do simple things first, (2) learn to do them flawlessly, (3) add new layers of activity over the results of the simple task, (4) don't change the simple things, (5) make the new layer work as flawlessly as the simple one, and (6) repeat ad infinitum. Many organizations would benefit by adopting organizing principles as deceptively simple as these.

Increasingly, the most successful companies, like the machines and programs so many of them now make, and the networks on which they all will rely will advance only by evolving and adapting in this organic, bottom-up way. Successful leaders will have to relinquish control. They will have to honor error because a breakthrough may at first be indistinguishable from a mistake. They must constantly seek disequilibrium.[55]

Control: Yes and No

We have spoken of control within the IC family of parent, subsidiaries, affiliates, and joint ventures. This deals with where decisions are made on a variety of subjects under different circumstances. Timely and accurate reporting to the parent is necessary for success of the IC family. The trend in this area of control is toward centralized decision making, with more being done by the parent.

The other control of which we have spoken involves the design, production, and order-filling functions of companies. Here the explosion of software, computer networks, and information technology, including the Internet, has tended to decentralize and de-job organizations. More and more, workers do evolving tasks with changing teams of other workers. Hierarchies dissolve and successful leaders relinquish control as workers are trained and encouraged to cope with evolving tasks and rewarded for coping well.

[Summary]

Understand international strategy, competencies, and international competitive advantage.

International strategy is concerned with the way in which firms make fundamental choices about developing and deploying scarce resources internationally. The goal of international strategy is to create a competitive advantage that is sustainable over time. To do this, the international company should try to develop skills, or competencies, that are valuable, rare, and difficult to imitate and which the organization is able to exploit fully.

Describe the steps in the global strategic planning process.

Global strategic planning provides a formal structure in which managers (1) analyze the company's external environment, (2) analyze the company's internal environment, (3) define the company's business and mission, (4) set corporate objectives, (5) quantify goals, (6) formulate strategies, and (7) make tactical plans.

Understand the purpose of mission statements, objectives, quantified goals, and strategies.

Statements of the corporate business, vision, and mission communicate to the firm's stakeholders what the company is and where it is going. A firm's objectives direct its course of action, and its strategies enable management to reach its objectives.

Describe the new directions in strategic planning.

Operating managers, not planners, now do the planning. Firms use less structured formats and much shorter documents. Managers are more concerned with issues, strategies, and implementation.

Discuss the various organizational forms.

Companies may (1) have an international division, (2) be organized by product, function, or region, or (3) have a mixture of them (hybrid form). To attain a balance between product and regional expertise, some managements have tried a matrix form of organization. Its disadvantages, however, have caused many managements to put a matrix overlay over traditional product, regional, or functional form instead of using the matrix.

Understanding the concept of the virtual corporation.

A virtual corporation enables companies to come together quickly to take advantage of a specific marketing opportunity. Because each member concentrates on what it does best, a virtual corporation can have capabilities superior to those of any member. Once the opportunity ends, the virtual corporation normally will disband.

Explain why decisions are made where they are among parent and subsidiary units of an international company (IC).

Several considerations govern where decisions are made in an IC family of organizations. They include desirability of standardizing products as opposed to differentiating them for different markets, the competence of organization managements, the size and age of the IC, the benefit of one part of the family to the detriment of another, and building confidence or avoiding frustration of management.

Understand how an IC can maintain control of a joint venture or of a company in which the IC owns less than 50 percent of the voting stock.

Control can be maintained over a joint venture or a company in which the IC owns less than 50 percent of the voting stock by several devices, including a management contract, control of the finances, control of the technology, and putting people from the IC in key executive positions.

List the types of information an IC needs to have reported to it by its units around the world.

Subsidiaries should report to the IC information about financial conditions, technological developments, market opportunities and developments, and economic and political conditions.

[Key Words]

international strategy (p. 483)
competitive advantage (p. 483)
mission statement (p. 486)
corporate strategies (p. 487)
scenarios (p. 488)
contingency plans (p. 488)
top-down planning (p. 490)
bottom-up planning (p. 491)
iterative planning (p. 491)
international division (p. 495)
hybrid organization (p. 498)
matrix organization (p. 499)
matrix overlay (p. 500)
strategic business unit (SBU) (p. 500)
virtual corporation (p. 501)
horizontal corporation (p. 503)
subsidiaries (p. 505)
affiliates (p. 505)
subsidiary detriment (p. 507)
de-jobbing (p. 510)
hierarchy (p. 511)

[Questions]

1. Suppose the competitor analysis reveals that the American subsidiary of your firm's German competitor is about to broaden its product mix in the American market by introducing a new line against which your company has not previously had to compete in the home market. The environmental analysis shows that the dollar–mark exchange rate is going to continue to make American exports expensive in Germany. Do you recommend a defensive strategy, or do you attack your competitor in its home market? How will you implement your strategy?
2. You are the CEO of the Jones Petrochemical Company and have just finished studying next year's plans of your foreign subsidiaries. You are pleased that the Israeli plan is so optimistic because that subsidiary contributes heavily to your company's income. But OPEC is meeting next month. Should you ask your planning committee, which meets tomorrow, to construct some scenarios? If so, about what?
3. Your firm has used bottom-up planning for years, but the subsidiaries' plans differ with respect to approaches to goals and assumptions—even the time frames are different. How can you, the CEO, get them to agree on these points and still get their individual input?
4. Your matrix organization isn't working; decisions are taking too long, and it seems to you that instead of best solutions, you're getting compromises. What can you, the CEO, do?
5. You are the CEO of Mancon Incorporated, and you have just acquired Pozoli, the Italian small-appliance maker (electric shavers, small household and personal care appliances). It has been in business 30 years and has manufacturing plants in Italy, Mexico, Ireland, and Spain. Its output is sold in more than 100 markets worldwide, including the United States. Your company is now organized into two product groups—shaving, personal care, and an international division at the top level. How are you going to include Pozoli in your organization?
6. It is obvious that in formulating new strategies, management may uncover a need to change its organization. Can you describe some situations where the reverse may be true?
7. In determining whether decisions will be made by the parent company or by its subsidiaries, what are the considerations when equipment and products are standardized worldwide rather than tailored to individual national circumstances and markets?
8. a. In an IC, what are some decisions that could result in detriment for a subsidiary but greater benefit for the enterprise?
   b. In such circumstances, where will the decision be made—at IC headquarters or at the affected subsidiary?
9. What measures can be utilized to control subsidiaries that are less than 100 percent owned by the firm or joint venture partners in which the firm has no ownership?
10. Explain the argument that the world is de-jobbing.

[Internet Exercises]

Using the Internet

1. Du Pont's mission, or "core purpose," as Du Pont calls it, appears in this chapter.
   a. What is the company's quantified objective (goal)?
   b. Is there more than one quantified objective?
   c. What are the strategies it plans to employ to attain the goal?
2. The Economist Intelligence Unit and Andersen Consulting studied management of customer relationships in more than 200 companies worldwide (see endnote 42).
   a. Why do many executives say that functional and organizational structures stand in the way of their efforts to build relationships with their customers?
   b. How are firms dealing with fragmentation of the activities that are part of serving the customer?
   c. According to the report, effective customer relationship management must be based on a process for establishing the targeting of the "best customers."
      (1) Who are the best customers?
      (2) What will these companies do with those who are not their best customers?

[Minicase 14.1]

Electrex, Incorporated—Must It Reorganize?

Electrex, Inc., manufactures electronic and electrical connectors used on such diverse products as computers, home appliances, telecommunications, and the air bag and antiskid systems of American cars. The company has been in business since 1965. The table provides the important financial information for the last five years.

For some time, Electrex had been exporting to the Far East, where its major markets are Japan, Singapore, and Taiwan. When its foreign sales were confined to exports, the company functioned well with an export department whose manager reported to the company's marketing manager. In 1996, however, other American firms tried to enter the market, and there were rumors that a Japanese firm was searching for a licensor in the United States to supply it with manufacturing technology. Electrex decided to set up its first foreign plant in Japan. When it did, it hired financial and marketing people with Japanese experience and established an international division at headquarters to oversee the Japanese operation. The president felt that the situation would be repeated in Taiwan, Singapore, and Thailand. These were all good export markets at the time, but it was reasonable to suppose that some competitor would soon set up manufacturing facilities in one or more of them. Having a small international division with some

Far East expertise that is responsible for monitoring these markets would help the firm avoid being surprised by a competitor's move.

After the Japanese Electrex plant was in production, more Japanese firms were willing to do business with the company than had been when it had served the market through exports. In fact, the major portion of the 2000 sales increase was due to improved sales to the Japanese. However, the new customers also brought the company into a new, higher level of competition than it had known before. The Japanese competitors were bringing out new products at a considerably faster rate than Electrex was. The president wondered if horizontal linkages across functions, such as the automakers have used to reduce their design time, might help his firm. Also, on his trips to Japan, the marketing people told him things about the market and the competitors that were not being sent to the Electrex home office.

It was obvious to the president that overseas production and growth in overseas sales demanded a reorganization of the firm. Even though the company had only one plant in Japan, the president was confident that other plants would soon be needed. How should the company be organized to handle the new foreign production facilities? How can Electrex reduce the time needed to bring new designs to market?

Five-Year Financial Highlight Summary (in $ millions)

	2000	1999	1998	1997	1996
Net sales	$353.0	$298.2	$271.9	$257.4	$231.1
Gross profit	134.1	116.3	110.3	106.7	94.9
Selling, general, and administrative expense	70.5	61.2	55.8	51.8	45.1
Income from operations	63.6	55.1	54.5	54.9	49.8
Income taxes	23.9	20.9	20.9	21.8	20.9
Effective tax rate (%)	37.6	37.9	38.3	39.7	42.0
Net income	39.7	34.2	33.6	33.1	28.9

[Minicase 14.2]

Competition within the IC

Worldwide (W) is an IC with subsidiary manufacturing plants in several countries around the world. W has just won a very large contract to supply locomotives to Paraguay, which is modernizing its entire railway system with financing from the World Bank.

W's home country is the United States, and it could manufacture parts of or the complete locomotives in its U.S. plants. W subsidiary companies in Spain, Argentina, and Australia could also manufacture parts or the locomotives. The managers of all those subsidiaries know about the big new contract, and each is eager to get the work involved in performing it.

A meeting of the subsidiary chief executive officers (CEOs) is called at W's headquarters in New York to discuss which plant or plants will get the work. The manager of the American locomotive division is also at the meeting, and she makes a strong case that her plant needs the work. It has laid off 3,000 workers, and this big job would permit it to recall them. In addition, the American factory has all the latest technology, some of which has not been shared with the subsidiaries.

Each CEO argues that there is unemployment in his or her host country, and as responsible citizens, they must hire more local people. That, moreover, would reduce hostility in the host country and give them defenses against left-wing attacks on foreign-owned companies. One subsidiary CEO suggests that each subsidiary and the American division enter competitive bids and let Paraguayan Railways make the decision.

You are the CEO of W and have the responsibility for allocating parts of or all the work to one or more of the plants. List and explain the considerations that will govern your decisions.

[Chapter]

15

Assessing and Analyzing Markets

"We believe that all roads will eventually lead to the Internet."

—*Ann Lewnes, manager of Intel's worldwide advertising group,* World Opinion News *quotes,* http://www.worldopinion.com/news?cmd=item&id=2737.

Concept Previews

After reading this chapter, you should be able to:

- **discuss** environmental analysis and two types of market screening
- **explain** market indicators and market factors
- **describe** some statistical techniques for estimating market demand and grouping similar markets
- **appreciate** the value to businesspeople of trade missions and trade fairs
- **discuss** some of the problems market researchers encounter in foreign markets
- **understand** the difference between country screening and segment screening
- **identify** the sources of information for the screening process
- **appreciate** the utility of the Internet as a source of market research data

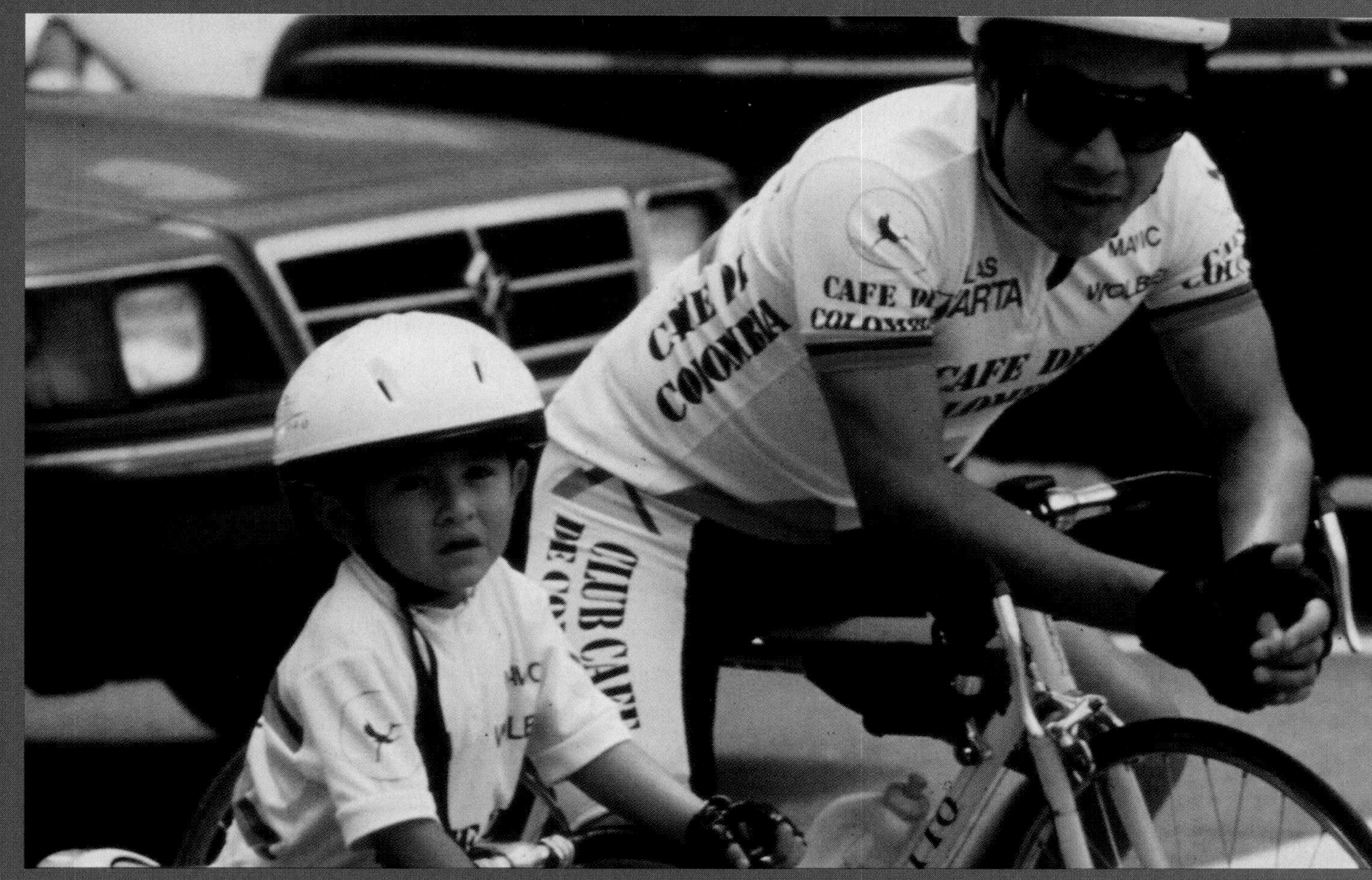

Bob Daemmrich/Stock Boston

Grassroots Marketing Research

Entrepreneur Peter Johns, a 30-year veteran in international marketing, had the idea of distributing mail-order catalogs for upscale U.S. firms in Mexico. He felt that because of the improvement in the Mexican economy, the rich would want to buy foreign-made luxury goods. He also knew that well-to-do Mexicans regularly make trips to the United States to load up on things they cannot get in their country. In fact, there is an axiom: The richer they are, the farther inland they go in the United States. However, when Johns went to confirm his beliefs with hard data, the market veteran found none to his liking. Government data were of no help.

The other alternative was personal observation, and so Johns visited the affluent neighborhoods and shopping areas to see for himself. The satellite dishes and imported sports cars, along with other information he gathered, led him to the conclusion that his target market was about 300,000 families.

Johns formed a company to distribute the catalogs of 20 American firms, Choices Unlimited, in which Mexican investors owned 60 percent. But now he had a second problem. He needed mailing lists, but he couldn't find what he needed in Mexico. This time Johns went to the Mexican investors in his own company. They gave him memberships in the city's exclusive golf clubs. He also obtained directories of the parents of the students at some of the exclusive private schools. The information he gathered enabled him to make a flashy debut at a fancy members-only nightclub. After a fashion show followed by heavy food and drink, 800 people each put down $28 in pesos to become charter members. They'll get catalogs, promotional discounts, and more fashion-show invitations. Choices Unlimited has pledged to make deliveries from the United States in 15 days and has hired Federal Express to do it. Mexican Customs has also promised to give its packages fast service.

The entrepreneur rightly predicted that the North American Free Trade Agreement would give his business a big boost because it would eliminate or greatly reduce Mexico's 15 percent import duty on clothing and 20 percent duty on luxury goods. What he didn't count on, however, was Mexico's 40 percent devaluation of the peso, which raised the peso prices of imported products paid for in dollars over 60 percent. An item costing 100 pesos before the devaluation would now cost 160 pesos.

Johns and Mexicans involved in importing were hoping that (1) the $50 billion rescue package from the IMF, the Bank for International Settlements, and the United States would stabilize the peso and (2) a cheaper peso in terms of the dollar would enable Mexico to export its way out of the financial crisis. By 1998, Mexico had recovered substantially from the 1994 crisis and was displaying strong economic growth despite the Asian crisis. The inflation rate had dropped, the unemployment rate was down to 3 percent, and retail sales were up 10 percent in 1997. It seems that Johns was right after all, although the peso has continued to slide (it is now hovering at 10 to the dollar), the devaluation has been gradual, and devaluation has helped make Mexican products cheaper abroad. ■

Source: "Macroeconomic Forecasts for 1998," *Review of the Economic Situation in Mexico,* Mexico City: Banco Nacional de Mexico, January 1998, pp. 18–32; Ed Yardeni, "Mexican Business Indicators," *Dr. Ed Yardeni's Online Chart Room,* February 2, 1998, www.yardeni.com/country.htm#Mexico (February 12, 1998); "The Egg on Zedillo's Face," *The Economist,* January 7, 1995, p. 31; "Putting Mexico Together Again," *The Economist,* pp. 65–67; and "Grass-Roots Marketing Yields Clients in Mexico City," *The Wall Street Journal,* October 24, 1991, p. B2.

market screening
A version of environmental scanning in which the firm identifies desirable markets by using the environmental forces to eliminate the less desirable markets

environmental scanning
A procedure in which a firm scans the world for changes in the environmental forces that might affect it

This anecdote illustrates the difficulties experienced marketers from industrialized nations have when they do market assessment and analysis in developing nations, even one as advanced as Mexico. It also shows that experienced international marketers like Johns will not be stopped by lack of data but will use whatever methods are available to get what they need. Often these methods are quite ingenious. Note how Johns compiled his mailing list at no cost when he could not find what he needed. Later in this chapter, we shall look at other problems marketers have in doing research across cultures.

The market research Johns did is the first step in the market screening process: determining the basic need potential. We shall describe this process fully in the next section. **Market screening** is a modified version of environmental scanning in which the firm identifies markets by using the environmental forces to eliminate the less desirable markets. **Environmental scanning,** from which market screening is derived, is a procedure in which a firm scans the world for changes in the environmental forces that might affect it.[1]

[Figure 15.1] Selection of Foreign Markets

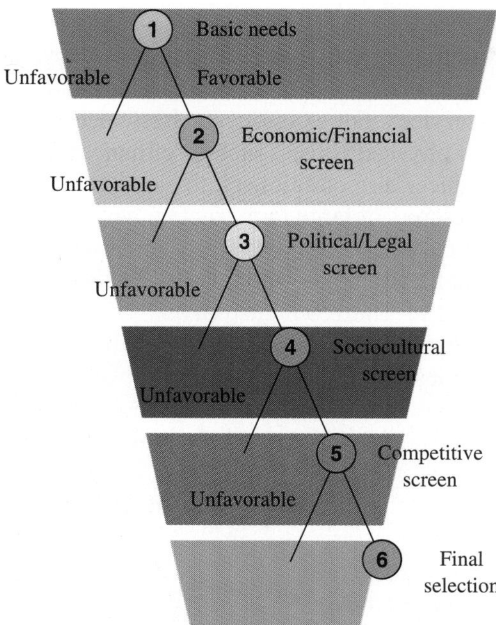

For some time, environmental scanning has been used by management during the planning process to provide information about world threats and opportunities. Those who do environmental scanning professionally may belong to such organizations as the Society of Competitive Intelligence Professionals (SCIP). In addition, private environmental scanning services are available from a number of private firms. Examples of such service providers include Summit Analytical Associates (www.s2a.com) and Stratfor, Inc. (www.stratfor.com).

Market screening assists two different kinds of firms. One is selling exclusively in the domestic market but believes it might increase sales by expanding into overseas markets. The other is already a multinational but wants to be certain changing conditions are not creating markets about which its management is unaware. In both situations, managers require an ordered, relatively fast method of analyzing and assessing the nearly 200 countries to pinpoint the most suitable prospects.

Market Screening

Market screening is a method of market analysis and assessment that permits management to identify a small number of desirable markets by eliminating those judged to be less attractive. This is accomplished by subjecting the markets to a series of screenings based on the environmental forces examined in Section Three. Although these forces may be placed in any order, the arrangement suggested in Figure 15.1 is designed to progress from the least to the most difficult analysis based on the accessibility and subjectivity of the data. In this way, the smallest number of candidates is left for the final, most difficult screening.

country screening
Using countries as the basis for market selection.

segment screening
Using market segments as the basis for market selection.

Two Types of Screening

In this chapter we will look at two types of market screening procedures. The first, which could be called **country screening,** takes countries as the relevant unit of analysis. The second, which we might call **segment screening,** is based on a subnational analysis of groups of consumers.

Initial Screening

Basic Need Potential

An initial screening based on the basic need potential is a logical first step, because if the need is lacking, no reasonable expenditure of effort and money will enable the firm to market its goods or services. For example, the basic need potential of certain goods is dependent on various physical forces, such as climate, topography, and natural resources. If the firm produces air conditioners, the analyst will look for countries with warm climates. Manufacturers of large farm tractors would not consider Switzerland a likely prospect because of its mountainous terrain, and only countries known to possess gold deposits would be potential customers for gold-dredging equipment.

Generally, producers of specialized industrial materials or equipment experience little difficulty in assessing their basic need potential. A builder of cement kilns, for example, can obtain the names and addresses of cement plants worldwide merely by contacting the Portland Cement Association in Chicago. A list of firms in an industry, often on a worldwide basis, is available either from the industry association or from specialized trade journals.

This is certainly straightforward, but what about less specialized products that are widely consumed?

Foreign Trade and Investment

If the nature of the good or service is such that a definite basic need potential cannot be readily established, analysts can learn from the United Nations' *International Trade Statistics Yearbook,* Volume II, which countries export and which import their firms' products and the dollar quantities. Furthermore, annual dollar values are given for the past five years, enabling analysts to establish trends for projecting future values. The *Yearbook* uses the United Nations Standard International Trade Classification system based on 1,312 subgroups identified by five-digit codes. These are combined progressively into 177 groups with three-digit codes, 56 divisions with two-digit codes, and 10 sections (one digit). Table 15.1 reproduces a page from the *Yearbook* showing the chocolates group, code 073.

Analysts who want to know where American competitors are exporting their firms' products can go to the International Trade Administration's (ITA) site on the Internet, www.ita.doc.gov. Endnote 11 in Chapter 2 gives the exact addresses within the ITA for four useful documents. The U.S. Department of Commerce also has the report *U.S. Exports of Merchandise* on the National Trade Data Bank (NTDB), which is available online for a subscription fee.

This information is especially useful, as it gives both units and dollar value, permitting the analyst to calculate the average price of the unit exported. It also lists more countries importing from and exporting to the United States than the old hard-copy report did and in addition states what part of the amount exported to each destination passes through each U.S. Customs district. Because it is required by law to publish foreign trade statistics, Commerce compiles and releases foreign trade statistics on a monthly and cumulative basis in its report *U.S. International Trade in Goods and Services,* commonly referred to as the *FT900.* Although not available in hard copy, it is published on the Bureau of the Census's Internet site as a press release.[2]

For help in their search for markets, analysts can obtain from the nearest Department of Commerce office numerous studies prepared by U.S. embassies. *Annual Worldwide Industry Reviews* and *International Market Research Reports* indicate major markets for many products. The *Country Market Surveys* indicate products for which there is a good market in a given country. We shall discuss these publications in greater detail in Chapter 17.

Other countries publish similar data. For example, the data office of the European Community, Eurostat, publishes an annual, *External Trade,* and JETRO, the Japanese External Trade Organization, publishes a wide assortment of trade and industry data, many of which are put on its Internet site. You can find many other sources in the

Table 15.1 Page from *UN International Trade Statistics Yearbook*

073 Chocolate and Products

Trade by Commodity in Million U.S. Dollars—Commerce Par Produit en Millions De Dollars E.U.

Countries—Pays	Imports—Importations					Countries—Pays	Exports–Exportations				
	1994	1995	1996	1997	1998		1994	1995	1996	1997	1998
World	5832.7	6925.9	7317.6	7077.9	6942.7	Monde	6723.9	7987.7	8572.6	7778.3	7244.0
Africa	41.1	47.9	48.1	47.6	52.4	Afrique	37.0	30.5	37.3	48.1	41.1
Americas	801.9	975.8	1034.7	1115.0	1176.5	Amériques	649.9	690.8	797.8	918.3	916.1
North America	547.5	628.1	710.4	818.8	869.8	Amérique du Nord	539.3	544.0	619.1	697.9	670.9
LAIA	206.5	280.2	276.9	247.3	256.7	ALAI	103.4	138.7	166.2	208.0	229.9
CACM	9.1	10.9	13.0	14.5	17.4	MCAC	4.4	4.7	6.0	6.3	8.8
Caribbean	28.0	29.4	19.3	21.6	19.6	Caraibes	2.7	3.4	6.3	6.1	6.4
Rest of America	10.8	27.2	15.2	12.9	13.0	Autre Amérique			0.1		0.1
Asia excl fmr USSR	721.1	856.7	967.1	941.8	783.2	Asie anc, URSS exclus	290.0	341.5	353.0	342.6	282.8
Middle East	137.5	190.1	213.6	216.9	214.5	Moyen-Orient	80.7	120.7	118.6	122.4	100.4
Asia former USSR	31.5	80.7	90.7	52.4	48.4	Asie ancienne URSS	1.8	2.7	1.6	1.6	1.5
Europe excl fmr USSR	3928.8	4467.8	4571.5	4388.4	4487.4	Europe anc. URSS exclus	5534.8	6687.6	7103.9	6206.8	5790.8
European Union	3537.7	4001.4	4083.3	3917.5	4022.8	Union Européenne	5026.0	6070.2	6425.7	5520.7	5140.9
Eastern Europe	163.5	200.7	222.5	200.3	194.4	Europe de l'Est	148.2	210.2	276.7	338.2	257.4
Rest of Europe	227.6	265.7	265.7	270.7	270.2	Autre de l'Europe	360.6	407.2	401.4	347.9	392.6
Europe former USSR	218.4	393.1	486.0	394.8	261.2	Europe ancienne URSS	84.6	112.3	128.6	126.4	105.6
Oceania	90.0	103.9	119.6	137.9	133.5	Océanie	125.7	122.3	150.3	134.5	106.2
France, Monaco	770.8	980.3	961.5	903.5	926.2	Germany/Allemagne	1142.0	1251.7	1583.3	1305.9	1149.9
Germany/Allemagne	838.2	815.3	842.3	908.1	903.4	Belgium–Luxembourg	827.8	1035.6	1080.9	958.0	959.5
United Kingdom	514.7	544.8	567.2	545.1	541.8	France, Monaco	734.1	1123.4	1028.1	824.8	782.1
USA/Etats-Unis d'Amer	332.5	403.0	460.3	548.2	593.2	Netherlands/Pays-Bas	648.2	741.7	655.1	571.7	510.8
Japan/Japon	257.3	319.3	357.9	317.7	286.7	United Kingdom	564.6	596.6	612.3	599.7	579.2
Netherlands/Pays-Bas	269.5	303.6	302.3	262.8	257.1	Italy/Italie	337.0	520.1	544.2	418.6	351.1
Belgium–Luxembourg	169.1	232.3	268.4	259.8	261.1	USA/Etats-Unis d'Amer	353.3	320.0	354.8	377.3	325.3
Canada	212.9	223.9	248.2	269.6	274.6	Switzerland, Liechtenst.	273.1	322.4	322.1	274.3	315.6
Italy/Italie	181.9	191.3	187.2	160.7	184.7	Canada	186.0	223.9	264.3	320.6	345.6
Ukraine	×34.3	×141.3	×217.0	×180.2	×100.8	Ireland/Irlande	218.6	206.7	214.2	188.5	196.0
Russian Federation	×154.5	×186.3	190.4	152.6	109.6	Austria/Autriche	107.3	95.1	186.5	218.8	210.4
Austria/Autriche	126.1	151.6	195.5	153.3	186.9	Sweden/Suède	136.9	152.2	160.7	125.3	122.4
Spain/Espagne	155.1	170.0	166.2	149.7	163.2	Poland/Pologne	36.2	82.9	140.0	213.5	146.3
Denmark/Danemark	139.7	172.3	147.4	132.9	142.5	Spain/Espagne	97.1	126.4	149.1	138.0	129.7
Ireland/Irlande	114.8	119.6	120.7	128.7	141.2	Australia/Australie	96.2	96.6	110.2	102.7	76.7
Brazil/Brésil	23.5	134.9	120.0	87.9	82.8	Finland/Finlande	102.1	104.5	106.1	93.0	68.6
Sweden/Suède	110.7	111.5	114.4	104.9	111.6	Turkey/Turquie	48.5	80.0	87.5	93.1	71.3
China, Hong Kong SAR	96.8	100.9	112.0	101.3	73.5	Denmark/Danemark	82.5	85.1	74.8	61.1	66.4
Portugal	65.9	88.0	85.4	90.4	94.4	Argentina/Argentine	19.1	41.0	54.8	82.5	108.2
Norway, Svalbard and JM	74.7	78.9	87.0	77.2	76.2	Singapore/Singapour	48.6	53.9	60.1	54.5	53.9
Australia/Australie	57.4	64.3	80.3	96.3	91.8	China, Hong Kong SAR	47.3	54.4	52.4	51.4	37.0
Korea, Republic of	56.6	60.9	78.1	81.2	46.0	Czech Republic	45.2	53.7	54.9	44.0	41.9
Greece/Grèce	44.7	70.2	74.5	67.0	62.7	Brazil/Brésil	43.9	47.4	45.3	58.6	53.5
Switzerland, Liechtenst.	57.9	65.3	66.7	63.9	66.8	Russian Federation	×40.6	×48.7	53.5	47.7	35.7
Poland/Pologne	35.6	51.2	70.1	55.2	44.7	Hungary/Hongrie	38.8	38.4	46.2	40.3	34.8
Mexico/Mexique	90.4	54.7	59.6	58.2	75.1	Lithuania/Lituanie	21.0	35.2	46.7	41.0	19.9
Czech Republic	40.1	54.1	62.5	54.4	57.7	Norway, Svalbard and JM	40.0	40.2	39.1	32.0	35.0
Singapore/Singapour	48.3	47.4	55.5	58.3	39.2	Korea, Republic of	26.2	29.1	36.9	33.4	23.5
Finland/Finlande	36.4	50.8	50.4	50.6	45.9	New Zealand	29.5	25.7	40.1	31.8	29.2
Kuwait/Koweit	33.4	40.6	50.1	45.6	×33.9	Slovakia/Slovaquie	27.7	34.9	28.6	28.1	22.7
United Arab Emirates	×32.8	×43.8	×45.6	×44.3	×48.2	So. African Customs Un	27.7	22.8	26.6	31.1	×26.4
Saudi Arabia	13.1	38.3	41.4	×42.9	×43.5	Malaysia/Malaisie	25.4	23.4	26.3	24.0	13.3
Philippines	29.0	31.3	26.2	50.0	26.4	Greece/Grèce	24.1	29.2	28.5	15.5	13.2
Slovakia/Slovaquie	28.4	36.2	35.1	34.0	34.1	Mexico/Mexique	12.4	18.0	25.8	25.5	23.6
Israel/Israël	24.8	30.3	35.5	38.0	39.7	Chile/Chili	19.7	20.9	24.0	23.8	25.9
Yugoslavia/Yougoslavie	×28.2	×29.1	29.9	44.5	×42.9	Israel/Israël	32.9	28.7	24.9	14.9	10.5
Slovenia/Slovénie	31.3	37.2	34.4	31.9	35.2	Croatia/Croatie	18.6	20.4	21.0	21.5	20.9
Argentina/Argentine	54.9	38.0	35.0	30.0	26.3	Ukraine	×7.6	×9.9	×10.5	×16.4	×27.4
Hungary/Hongrie	30.1	27.0	34.9	39.8	38.8	Yugoslavia/Yougoslavie	×13.1	×12.1	11.1	11.5	×12.7
New Zealand	23.4	29.3	31.1	35.2	33.1	United Arab Emirates	×11.8	×13.5	×6.6	×10.8	×13.7

x = Estimate.

Source: *International Trade Statistics Yearbook*, 1998 (New York: United Nations, 1999).

book's Internet directory under the sections (1) "Country Data," (2) countries listed under the appropriate continent, and (3) "Economic Data."

Imports Don't Completely Measure Market Potential. Even when a basic need is clearly indicated, most experienced researchers will still investigate the trade flows to have an idea of the magnitude of present sales.

Management is aware, of course, that imports alone are rarely a measure of the full market potential. Myriad reasons are responsible, among which are lack of foreign exchange, high prices (duties and markups), and political pressure.

Moreover, import data indicate only that a country has been buying certain products from abroad and are no guarantee that it will continue to do so. Managements know that a competitor may decide to produce locally, which in many markets will cause imports to cease. Change in a country's political structure also may stop imports, as we saw in the case of Iran, where orders worth billions of dollars were suddenly canceled. Nevertheless, when there is no local production, import data do enable the firm to know how much is currently being purchased and provide management with an estimate, though a conservative one, of the immediate market potential at the going price. If local production is being considered and calculations show that goods produced in the country could be sold at a lower price, the firm can reasonably expect to sell more than the quantity being imported.

Second Screening—Financial and Economic Forces

After the initial screening, the analyst will have a much smaller list of prospects. This list may be further reduced by a second screening based on the financial and economic forces. Trends in inflation, exchange, and interest rates are among the major financial points of concern. The analyst should consider other financial factors, such as credit availability, paying habits of customers, and rates of return on similar investments. It should be noted that this screening is not a complete financial analysis. That will come later if the market analysis and assessment disclose that a country has sufficient potential for capital investment.

Economic data may be employed in a number of ways, but two measures of market demand based on them are especially useful. These are *market indicators* and *market factors*. Other methods for estimating demand depending on economic data are *trend analysis* and *cluster analysis*.

Market Indicators

market indicators
Economic data used to measure relative market strengths of countries or geographic areas

Market indicators are economic data that serve as yardsticks for measuring the relative market strengths of various geographic areas. A well-known American example is the Buying Power Index published in the annual "Survey of Buying Power" by Sales & Marketing Management. The purpose of this index is to enable marketers to compare the relative buying power of counties and cities in the United States.

Somewhat similarly, we attempted to develop an index of e-commerce potential for Latin America so that the countries in the region could be compared. The results appear in Table 15.2. In this methodology, we assembled data on twenty Latin American countries and then ranked the countries against each other. We wanted to include indicators of the strength and growth rate of the overall economy, as well as factors related more specifically to e-commerce or to communications that would aid the growth of e-commerce. We developed three indexes. Each indicator is given equal weight in each index.

Market size = size of the urban population + electricity consumption

Market growth rate = average growth rate in commercial energy use + real growth rate in GDP

E-commerce readiness = mobile phones per 1,000 + number of PCs per 1,000 + Internet hosts per million people

Table 15.2 E-Commerce Potential: Rankings for Latin America

Countries	Market Size	Market Growth Rate	E-Commerce Readiness	Overall E-Commerce Potential
South America				
Argentina	4	10	1	2
Bolivia	16	9	19	16
Brazil	1	12	6	3
Chile	5	1	2	1
Colombia	8	17	7	12
Ecuador	13	16	14	15
Paraguay	12	15	11	14
Peru	11	7	11	11
Uruguay	7	13	4	6
Venezuela	3	19	4	9
Caribbean				
Dominican Republic	14	3	8	6
Haiti	20	14	15	18
Jamaica	6	8	13	9
Central America				
Costa Rica	9	6	9	6
El Salvador	15	4	16	12
Guatemala	16	11	17	16
Honduras	18	18	20	19
Mexico	2	14	3	3
Nicaragua	19	20	18	19
Panama	10	2	10	5

Source: Michael S. Minor and Alexandra Brandt, "A Possible Index of E-Commerce Potential for Latin America," Working Paper, January 29, 2001. Reprinted with permission of Michigan State University-CIBER.

The rankings on these three indexes were then utilized to form a composite ranking. We called this composite ranking E-commerce potential. As you can see in Table 15.2, utilizing our methodology the countries with the most e-commerce potential appear to be Chile, Brazil, Argentina, and Mexico, while Honduras and Nicaragua appear to have the least potential.

Market Factors

Market factors are similar to market indicators except that they tend to correlate highly with the market demand for a given product. If the analyst of a foreign market has no factor for that market, he or she usually can use one from the domestic market to get a reasonable approximation. Moreover, an analyst who works for a multinational firm may be able to obtain market factors developed by comparable subsidiaries. To be able to transfer these relationships to the country under study, the analyst must assume that the underlying conditions affecting demand are similar in the market.

We can illustrate this process, which is called **estimation by analogy,** by using the following example. If a supplier of personal computers knows that one-fifth of all home computers are replaced every year in the United States, he or she might use the same relationship to estimate demand for replacement computers in a new overseas market. If there are 3 million existing home computers in the new market, the analyst might forecast that 3 million $\times$ 0.20, or 600,000, replacement home computers will be sold annually. The constant in the country under study may be somewhat different (it usually is), but with this approach, the estimates will be in the right ballpark. Many such factors exist, and generally research personnel, either in the domestic operation or in foreign subsidiaries, are familiar with them.

Trend Analysis

When the historical growth rates of either the pertinent economic variables or imports of a product are known, future growth can be forecast by means of **trend analysis.** A

market factors
Economic data that correlate highly with market demand for a product

estimation by analogy
Using a market factor that is successful in one market to estimate demand in a similar market

trend analysis
Statistical technique by which successive observations of a variable at regular time intervals are analyzed to establish regular patterns that are used for establishing future values

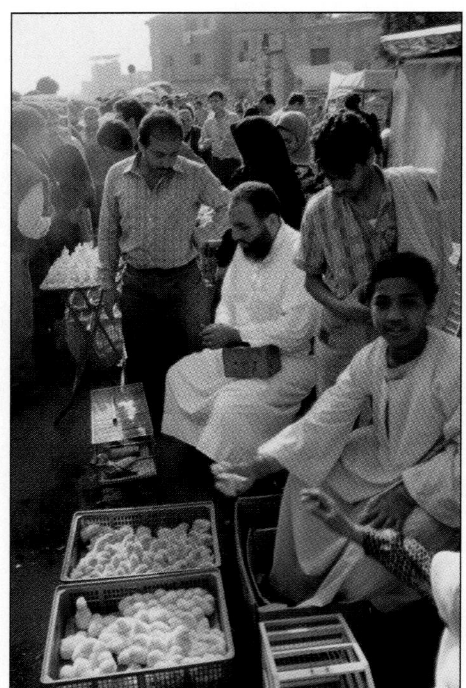
Muslim men sell baby chicks at open market in Cairo, Egypt.
Bachmann/PhotoEdit

time series may be constructed similarly to the way a regression model is made, or the arithmetic mean of past growth rates may be applied to historical data. Caution is advised when using this second method because if the average annual growth rate is applied mechanically, in just a few years the dependent variable may reach an incredible size. For example, a 5 percent growth rate compounded annually will result in a doubling of the original value in only 15 years.

Inasmuch as trend analysis is based on the assumption that past conditions affecting the dependent variable will remain constant, the analyst will generally modify the outcome to take into account any changes that can be foreseen. Often there are obvious constraints that will limit upward growth, one of which is the near certainty that competitors will enter the market if large increases in demand continue for very long.

Cluster Analysis and Other Multivariate Techniques

As multinationals extend their presence to more markets, managers in all functional areas are searching for ways to group countries and geographic regions by common characteristics to simplify their control. **Cluster analysis,** for which various computer programs are available, divides objects (market areas, individuals, customers, and other variables) into groups so that the variables within each group are similar. Marketers, for example, use cluster analysis to identify a group of markets where a single promotional approach can be employed, attorneys can use it to group nations according to similarities in certain types of laws, and so forth. Multidimensional scaling, factor analysis, and conjoint analysis are other techniques for examining differences and similarities among markets.

cluster analysis
Statistical technique that divides objects into groups so that the objects within each group are similar

Periodic Updating

If the estimates are altered appreciably in the periodic updatings that all long-term forecasts undergo, management may change the extent of the firm's involvement to be in line with the new estimates. Fortunately, the alternative forms of participation in a market permit the firm to become progressively more involved, with corresponding increases in investment. Most companies can enter a market in stages, perhaps in this sequence: exporting, establishment of a foreign sales company, local assembly, and, finally, manufacturing. Even when the decision is whether to produce overseas, management may plan to assemble a combination of imported and domestically produced parts initially and then progressively to manufacture more components locally as demand rises. Automobile manufacturers have begun a number of foreign operations employing this strategy.

Third Screening—Political and Legal Forces

The elements of the political and legal forces that can eliminate a nation from further consideration are numerous.

Entry Barriers

Import restrictions can be positive or negative, depending on whether management is considering exporting (can the firm's products enter the country?) or setting up a foreign plant (will competitive imports be kept out?). If one of management's objectives is 100 percent ownership, will the nation's laws permit it, or is some local participation required? Will the government accept a minority local ownership, or must a minimum of 51 percent of the subsidiary be in the hands of nationals? Are there laws that reserve certain industries for either the government or its citizens?[3] Is the host government demanding that the foreign owner turn over technology to its proposed affiliate that it wishes to keep at the home plant? Perhaps the host government has local content restrictions that the prospective investor considers excessive. There may be a government-owned company that would compete with the proposed plant. Depending on the circumstances and how strongly management wishes to enter the market, any one of these conditions may be sufficient cause for eliminating a nation from further consideration.

Vicente Fox, the first non-PRI President of Mexico in 71 years. Corbis/Sygma

Profit Remittance Barriers

When there are no objectionable requisites for entry, a nation may still be excluded if there are what management believes to be undue restrictions on the repatriation of earnings. Limits linked to the amount of foreign investment or other criteria may be set, or the nation may have a history of inability to provide foreign exchange for profit remittances.

Policy Stability

Another factor of importance to management in studying the possibilities of investing in a country is the stability of government policy. Is there continuity in policy when a new president takes office, for example? What is the political climate? Is the government stable, or is there infighting among government leaders? How about the public? Is there visible unrest? Do the armed forces have a history of intervention when there are public disturbances? Business can adapt to the form of government and thrive as long as the conditions are stable. But instability creates uncertainty, and this complicates planning. An often-heard complaint of businesspeople is, "They've changed the rules again."

It is important to make a distinction here between political stability and policy stability. Rulers may come and go, but if the policies that affect multinationals don't change very much, these political changes really may not be important. Indeed, if one measures political stability in terms of changes in leadership at the top, the United States is politically unstable compared to many countries!

Sources of analysis on political and policy stability are numerous. Some, such as Stratfor, have already been mentioned. In addition, Business Environment Risk Intelligence S.A. (www.beri.com) and Political Risk Services (www.polrisk.com) publish rankings comparing countries on the issue of political risk.

Fourth Screening—Sociocultural Forces

A screening of the remaining candidates on the basis of sociocultural factors is arduous. First, sociocultural factors are fairly subjective. Second, "data" are difficult to assemble, particularly from a distance. The analyst, unless he or she is a specialist in the country, must rely on the opinions of others. It is possible to hire consultants, who typically are "old hands" with experience in the country or region. Also, U.S. Department of Commerce specialists can provide some limited assistance, and professional organizations and universities frequently hold seminars to explain the sociocultural aspects of doing business in a particular area or country. Reading *Overseas Business Reports* (U.S. Department of Commerce), international business publications (*Business International* and *The Economist*), and specialized books will augment the analyst's sociocultural knowledge. In addition, there are numerous sites in your Internet directory under "Culture" and "Country Data." The use of a checklist of the principal sociocultural components as explained in Chapter 9 will serve as a reminder of the many factors the analyst must consider in this screening.

Although there are many difficulties, it is possible that recent immigrants or students from foreign countries may be used to shed light on potential sociocultural issues.

> One of the authors took a visiting speaker who was originally from Japan to visit a local firm. This business, which manufactured dessert items such as individual cherry pies,

wanted to break into the Japanese market but had not been successful. The Japanese speaker tasted the product and told them firmly that their cherry pie was too sweet for Japanese palates. We found that the company had never actually asked a Japanese person for a reaction to its products! Although the company needed to confirm this single opinion by using other methods, the taster nonetheless offered insight into an issue about which the firm was unaware.

The biggest danger, of course, is that immigrants and students have been affected by their residence abroad. Therefore, they are not necessarily reliable indicators of the reaction your product might receive from an audience "back home."

After the fourth screening, the analyst should have a list of countries for which an industry demand appears to exist. However, what management really wants to know is which of these countries seem to be the best prospects for the *firm's* products. A fifth screening based on the competitive forces will help provide this information.

Fifth Screening—Competitive Forces

In this screening, the analyst examines markets on the basis of such elements of the competitive forces as

1. The number, size, and financial strength of the competitors.
2. Their market shares.
3. Their marketing strategies.
4. The apparent effectiveness of their promotional programs.
5. The quality levels of their product lines.
6. The source of their products—imported or locally produced.
7. Their pricing policies.
8. The levels of their after-sales service.
9. Their distribution channels.
10. Their coverage of the market. (Could market segmentation produce niches that are currently poorly served?)

Concerning item 10, it may be important to ask whether there are regional or ethnic subcultures in a particular foreign country. These regional or ethnic subcultures may be natural or at least identifiable segments for which specific marketing programs may be successful. This is analogous to the fact that there are sufficient Hispanic, Chinese, and other subcultures in the United States to merit the importation of Chinese and Latin American products into the United States. Perhaps other countries have significant immigrant or subcultural populations whose needs you already understand and can serve. As an example, Japan has a small but growing population of immigrants from Latin America whose parents emigrated from Japan to Latin America in earlier times. These returnees tend to preserve their Latin heritage in Japan and might provide a market niche for firms whose strength is marketing to Latin Americans rather than to the Japanese.

Countries in which management believes strong competitors make a profitable operation difficult to attain are eliminated unless management (1) is following a strategy of being present wherever its global competitors are or (2) believes entering a competitor's home market will distract the competitor's attention from its home market, a reason for foreign investment we discussed in Chapter 3 (cross investment).

Final Selection of New Markets

While much can be accomplished through analysis, there is no substitute for personal visits to markets that appear to have the best potential. An executive of the firm should visit those countries that still appear to be good prospects. Before leaving, this person will review the data from the various screenings along with any new information that the researcher can supply. On the bases of this review and experience in making similar domestic decisions, the executive will prepare a list of points on which information must be obtained on arrival. Management will want the facts uncovered by the desk study (the five screenings) to be corroborated and will expect a firsthand report on the market, which will include information on competitive activity and an appraisal of the suitability of the firm's present marketing mix and the availability of ancillary facilities (warehousing, service agencies, media, credit, and so forth).

Field Trip

The field trip should not be hurried; as much time should be allotted to this part of the study as would be spent on a similar domestic field trip. The point is to try to develop a "feel" for what is going on, and this can't be accomplished quickly. For example, while Japanese youths model themselves after American basketball stars by wearing Nike sneakers, it appears that they change into off-brand sneakers when they actually play basketball. This type of insight is not likely to develop as a result of armchair analysis.

Government-Sponsored Trade Missions and Trade Fairs

An important mission of foreign diplomatic ministries, such as the U.S. Department of State and the government department representing industry (the Department of Commerce in the United States), is to promote a nation's foreign trade. This is why commercial officers stationed in U.S. embassies report to both State and Commerce. One of the many means of assisting American firms is to sponsor a **trade mission.**

trade mission
A group of businesspeople and/or government officials (state or federal) that visits a market in search of business opportunities

When U.S. Department of Commerce trade specialists perceive an overseas market opportunity for an industry, they will organize a trade mission. The purpose is to send a group of executives from firms in the industry to a country or group of countries to learn firsthand about the market, meet important customers face to face, and make contacts with people interested in representing their products. Because of discounted air fares, hotels, and so forth, the cost to the firm is less than what it would pay if it went on its own. Moreover, the impact of a group visit is greater than that of an individual visit. Before the mission's arrival, consulate or embassy officials will have publicized the visit and made contact with local companies they believe are interested. State governments, trade associations, chambers of commerce, and other export-oriented organizations also organize trade missions.

Probably every nation in the world holds a **trade fair** periodically. Usually each nation has a specifically marked area (Chinese pavilion, Argentine pavilion, etc.) at the fairgrounds where its exhibitors have their own booths staffed by company sales representatives. Usually, trade fairs are open to the public, but during certain hours (generally mornings), entrance is limited to businesspeople interested in doing business with the exhibitors.

trade fair
A large exhibition, generally held at the same place and same time periodically, at which companies maintain booths to promote the sale of their products

While most fairs in developing countries are general, with displays of many kinds of products, those in Europe are specialized. A famous example is the annual CeBIT computer and telecommunications trade fair—the largest computer-related trade fair in the world—held annually in Hannover, Germany. Over 830,000 people made the trip to this show in 2001 alone to see exhibits from 8,106 exhibitors drawn from about 60 countries.[4]

Besides making contact with prospective buyers and agents (direct sales are often concluded), most exhibitors use these fairs to learn more about the market and gather competitive intelligence. They not only receive feedback from visitors to their exhibits but have the opportunity to observe their competitors in action.[5]

Sometimes Local Research is Required

For many situations, the executive's report will be the final input to the information on which the decision is based. Occasionally, however, the proposed human and financial resource commitments are so great that management will insist on gathering

Some Tips on Market Research

Small and Medium-Sized Enterprises

Wonder how to begin to get that elusive "feel" for a country from survey data? As we mentioned, one way is to do it yourself via surveys and personal visits. Two other methods involve the use of an outside firm. Under one scenario, you can hire an outside firm to do customized survey research for your firm's needs. The second involves using surveys that are administered only partially, or not all, with your specific firm in mind.

Customized Surveys

Many firms which can do multi-country surveys on behalf of clients belong to ESOMAR (www.esomar.nl/), the acronym for the European Society of Opinion and Marketing Research. Originally member-firms were European, but there are now 4,000 members in over 100 countries.

General Surveys

General surveys are not done with a specific firm in mind, and they are of three types. The first type is the *omnibus survey.* Omnibus surveys are regularly scheduled surveys conducted by research agencies with questions from different clients (that is, they are wholly or partially "syndicated"). Since several firms contribute questions, the cost is spread across several users and the surveys are relatively fast. However, these surveys can ask only a limited number of questions that are directly relevant to a particular client, and the sample may not be representative of a particular firm's potential target market. As an indication, the ESOMAR directory lists 9 firms in Argentina and 23 firms in Japan that do onmibus surveys.

One example of a firm involved in administering omnibus surveys is A. C. Neilsen (www.acneilsen.com). Although we may know Neilsen best from the "Neilsen ratings," its TV-watching media measurement service, the firm is the largest marketing research firm in the world according to the Honimichl 25 list. The Honomichl Global Top 25 list of marketing/opinion research organizations is published annually in an August edition of the American Marketing Association's *Marketing News.* It offers services in over 100 countries. Neilsen does an omnibus survey in China, among other countries. Another familiar firm—the Gallup Organization (www.gallup.com)—is involved in this type of research in a variety of countries.

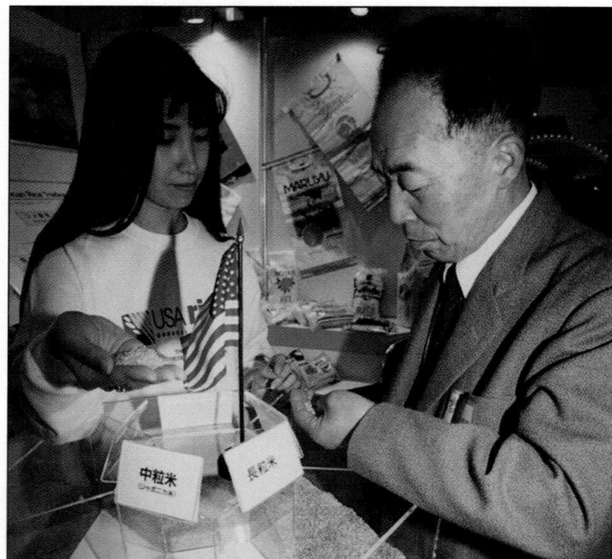

A Japanese farming specialist takes a close look at grains of American rice displayed in an exhibit booth at a U.S. food fair in Tokyo.
Reuters/Bettmann

data in the potential market rather than depending solely on the desk and field reports.[6] This would undoubtedly be the position of a consumer products manufacturer that envisions entering a large competitive market of an industrialized country. It might also be the recommendation of the executive making the field trip if he or she discovered that market conditions were substantially different from those to which the firm was accustomed. Often, in face-to-face interviews, information is revealed that would never be written. In these situations, research in the local market not only will supply information on market definition and projection but also will assist in the formulation of an effective marketing mix.

Research in the Local Market

When a firm's research personnel have had no experience in the country, management should hire a local research group to do the work unless there is a subsidiary in a neighboring country from which a research team may be borrowed. Generally, home country research techniques may be used, though they may need to be adapted to local conditions. It is imperative, therefore, that the person in charge of the project have experience either in that country or in one that is culturally similar and preferably in the same geographic area.

If secondary data are unavailable, the researchers must collect primary data, and here they face other complications caused by *cultural problems* and *technical difficulties.*

In a second type of noncustomized general survey, market research firms do surveys of their own devising which they then market to a variety of firms. An example of Neilsen's work in this type of survey is the recent Asian Target Markets Survey of well-to-do customers in seven Asian capital cities, from Jakarta and Manila to Taipei. Among other items, this survey established that the 3.5 million well-to do persons in large Asian cities now have over 84 percent ownership of home computers. In fact, Neilsen can even track TV-watching habits in China and India. Another firm which does industry-level surveys spanning a number of countries is Frost & Sullivan (www.frost.com). For example, Frost & Sullivan recently published a report on the world wireless local area network (LAN) market.

Nonprofit Surveys

A third type of survey is administered by a government or a nongovernmental agency and generally is not administered for profit. The Eurobarmometer surveys (**europa.eu.int/comm/dg10.epo**) are administered several times a year to literally thousands of respondents in European countries, under the auspices of the European Commission. Recent reports of Eurobarometer results with implications for consumer behavior include reports on attitudes toward vacations, food product safety, the elderly, and the family. In addition, a separate Eurobarmometer is administered for virtually all Central and Eastern European countries. Although these surveys are not specifically directed toward consumption issues, they are free. In 1996 the first Latino barómetro for Latin America (http://www.mori.co.uk/) was conducted.

The Internet

The number of firms which do surveys on or about the Internet is increasing. For example, Nielsen has a subsidiary devoted to research in Internet marketing called Neilsen NetRatings (**www.neilsen-netratings.com**). One of its recent studies found that New Zealand and Ireland lead the world in click rates for Internet ad banners. At some point in the future, the technology of Internet surveys may offer any firm the opportunity to do its own surveys anywhere in the world. However, at present the penetration of the Internet is generally limited to well-to-do persons in most countries. It is not currently possible to rely on the Internet to provide access to all target markets in all countries. ■

Cultural Problems. If the researchers are from one culture and are working in another, they may encounter some cultural problems. When they are not proficient in the local language or dialect, the research instrument or the respondents' answers must be translated. As we learned in the chapter on sociocultural forces, a number of languages may be spoken in a country, and even in countries where only one language is used, a word's meaning may change from one region to another.

Other cultural problems plague researchers as they try to collect data. The low level of literacy in many developing nations makes the use of mail questionnaires virtually impossible. If a husband is interviewed in a country where the wife makes the buying decisions, the data obtained from him are worthless. Nor is it always clear who should be interviewed. In certain Muslim countries where multiple wives are permitted, finding the right person to interview can be problematic. Respondents sometimes refuse to answer questions because of their general distrust of strangers. In other instances, the custom of politeness toward everyone will cause respondents to give answers calculated to please the interviewer: This is known as *social desirability bias.*

Often, people have practical reasons for not wanting to be interviewed. In some countries, income taxes are based on the apparent worth of individuals as measured by their tangible assets. In such countries, when asked if there is a stereo or TV in the household, the respondent may suspect the interviewer of being a tax assessor and refuse to answer. To overcome such a problem, experienced researchers often hire college students as interviewers because their manner of speech and their dress correctly identify them as what they are.

Technical Difficulties. As if the cultural problems were not enough, researchers may also encounter technical difficulties. First, up-to-date maps are often unavailable. The streets chosen to be sampled may have three or four different names along their length, and the houses may not be numbered. In Japan, it is said, only cab drivers can find street addresses.

[Worldview]
A Role for "Infomediaries"?

It is somewhat possible that Internet infomediaries could, in the future, provide a new avenue for global market research. Infomediaries are the "factories" of new digital information production. A rudimentary version of an infomediary is an online bookseller that uses the information consumers provide to make suggestions on further book purchases or priceline.com, which organizes markets for those willing to sell, say, airline tickets and consumers wanting to travel. Other rudimentary examples are the Personallogic.com division of America Online and AskJeeves™.

True infomediaries don't exist today but might develop along the following lines. Say you're a consumer in any country and you buy things on the Web regularly. You sign up for a membership with an infomediary. The infomediary provides software for your computer which tracks everything you do on the Web—which sites you visit, which pages you view, what products you look at, and what you buy. The infomediary collects this information and adds it to thousands or millions of other consumer profiles. The program processes all these data in ways that are meaningful to consumer product vendors, who use it to do a better job of offering you products and services that you actually want.

This would provide a new avenue for market research and a way for firms to get their hands on data about consumers in any country. Infomediaries may work best in markets that are the most fragmented—that is, where buyers and sellers know each other the least—and a firm marketing in a foreign market certainly represents a situation in which neither party knows the other very well. ■

Source: The ideas expressed here were influenced by "B2BCommerce: The Next Frontier," *Business 2.0,* www.business2.com/content/magazine/indepth/1999/09/01/16838 (September 1, 1999); and Bill Whelan, "Infomediaries Help Consumers Rule Online," www.sunworld.com/sunworldonline/swol-07-1999/swol-07-bookshelf_p.html (July, 1999).

Telephone surveys can be a formidable undertaking, because in many countries only the wealthy have telephones and the telephone directories are frequently out of date. It is not only in developing nations that telephones are hard to get. In Belgium, a woman broke the national record when she applied for a telephone and received it in just two weeks. As the four millionth telephone subscriber, she was showered with gifts. While she celebrated, 31,154 applicants were waiting to be connected. Delays of two years are common.[7] In such countries as Brazil and Mexico, researchers often have problems using their own phones because overloaded circuits make it next to impossible to get a line.

> While living in São Paulo, one of the authors wanted to call a number in Santos, an hour's drive away. The assistant to his secretary, whose main job was to dial for an outside line, had tried to place the call all morning. Finally, at noon, he drove to Santos, completed his business, and returned to the office to find his assistant still dialing.

Mail surveys can be troublesome too, as mail deliveries within a city may take weeks or are sometimes not even made.

> The postal service in Italy has been so slow (two weeks for a letter to go from Rome to Milan) that Italian firms have used private couriers to go to Switzerland to dispatch their foreign mail.

Mail questionnaires are not well received in Chile, where the recipient is required to pay the postman for each letter delivered. The response to a mail survey is often low by American standards in countries where the respondent must go to the post office to mail a letter, for example, Brazil. To increase returns, firms often offer such premiums as lottery tickets or product samples to persons who complete a mail questionnaire.

In some developing nations, researchers may have to obtain governmental permission to conduct interviews and, in some cases, submit questionnaires for prior approval. Some countries prohibit certain kinds of questions. For example, you cannot ask Egyptians about the ownership of consumer durables, and in Saudi Arabia you are not permitted to ask questions about nationality.[8]

Research as Practiced

The existence of hindrances to marketing research does not mean it is not carried out in foreign markets. As you might surmise from the discussion of the availability of secondary data, marketing research is highly developed in industrialized nations, where markets are large and incorrect decisions are costly. Problems like those we have mentioned are prevalent in the developing nations, but they are well known to those who live there. It does not take long for the newcomer to become aware of them either, because longtime residents are quick to point them out.

Analysts tend to do less research and use simpler techniques in these nations because often the firm is in a seller's market, which means everything produced can be sold with a minimum of effort. Moreover, competition is frequently less intense in developing nations because (1) there are fewer competitors and (2) managements are struggling with problems other than marketing, which keep them from devoting more time to the marketing function. Even now in Mexico, an important market for American firms, marketing research is unpopular. When it is done, the preferred method is house-to-house surveying.[9]

Although the situation is changing, the most common technique continues to be a combination of trend analysis and the querying of knowledgeable persons such as salespeople, channel members, and customers. Researchers then adjust the findings on the basis of subjective considerations.

Segment Screening

As was mentioned earlier, when a company intends to do business in several countries, managers can choose two broad market screening approaches: country segments or market segments. In the first approach, "Brazil" may be viewed as a target market segment.

Using the second approach, while Brazil is the physical location of a large group of consumers, the important variables for segmentation are commonalities in needs and wants among consumers *across nationalities.* These consumers may reside in different countries and speak different languages, but they have similar needs for a product or service. From this perspective, age, income, and psychographics (lifestyles) are the essential means of identifying market segments. The relevant marketing question is not where they reside but whether they share similar wants and needs. The targeted consumers may be global teens, middle-class executives, or young families with small children: Each of these segments may share wants and needs across borders. An example comes from "phone surfers"—young Japanese who actively use their mobile phones to surf the Internet. The small phone screen and tiny keys will be a big turnoff for older computer users in the West who are used to a laptop or a larger screen. But youngsters in the West are growing up with television games, Game Boys, and Tamagotchis, and so they will readily adapt to the small screens and tiny buttons that are a part of using cell phones and an Internet device.[10]

Because we tend to organize the world mentally in terms of countries, we naturally tend to want to analyze markets as country segments. It is much more difficult to think of ourselves as market segments which extend across borders. Also, as was mentioned in the discussion of sociocultural differences, these data can be difficult to secure. Nonetheless, it is important to do this because this approach is the logical outgrowth of the marketing concept. And the fact that certain types of data are difficult to gather doesn't mean that the data can be ignored. There is an old saying about research: "If you can count it, that ain't it." In our context, the easy-to-generate data are not necessarily the important data.

Among the criteria for these segments are that they should be

1. *Definable.* We should be able to identify and measure segments. The more we rely not on socioeconomic indicators but on lifestyle (psychographic) differences, the more difficult this becomes but the more accurate the resulting analysis is likely to be.

2. *Large.* Segments should be large enough to be worth the effort needed to serve a segment. Of course, as we get closer to flexible manufacturing, the need to find large segments is beginning to recede. Further, the segments should have the potential for growth in the future.

3. *Accessible.* If we literally cannot reach our target segment for either promotional or distribution purposes, we will be unsuccessful.

4. *Actionable.* If we cannot bring components of marketing programs (the 4 Ps of product, promotion, place, and price) to bear, we may not be successful. For example, in Mexico, the price of tortillas is controlled by the government. Therefore, competition on the price variable is impossible. We cannot penetrate the Mexican market for the standard tortilla by offering a lower price.

5. *Capturable.* Although we would love to discover market segments whose needs are completely unmet, in many cases these market segments are already being served. Nonetheless, we may still be able to compete. Where segments are completely "captured" by the competition, however, our task is much more difficult.[11]

Two Screening Methods, Reconsidered

In the final analysis, our view of the rest of the world is organized along national lines. However, it may be useful to attempt to leave that viewpoint behind when examining international markets. With the increasing recognition of the existence of subcultures *within* nations and similarities between subcultures *across* nations, the international businessperson may wish to expand his or her horizon beyond the conventional view of the nation as the relevant "unit of analysis."

The next chapter takes up a series of related questions. Are our needs and desires becoming more and more alike, or are the differences in consumption preferences between us more relevant than the similarities? We turn next to that discussion.

[Summary]

Discuss environmental analysis and two types of market screening.

A complete market analysis and assessment as described in this chapter would be made by a firm that either is contemplating entering the foreign market for the first time or is already a multinational but wants to monitor world markets systematically to avoid overlooking marketing opportunities and threats. Many of the data requirements for a foreign decision are the same as those for a similar domestic decision, though it is likely that additional information about some of the international and foreign environmental forces will be needed.

Essentially, the screening process consists of examining the various forces in succession and eliminating countries at each step. The sequence of screening based on (1) basic need potential, (2) financial and economic forces, (3) political and legal forces, (4) sociocultural forces, (5) competitive forces, and (6) personal visits is ordered so as to have a successively smaller number of prospects to consider at each of the succeedingly more difficult and expensive stages.

Explain market indicators and market factors.

Market indicators are economic data used to measure relative market strengths of countries or geographic areas. Market factors are economic data that correlate highly with the market demand for a product.

Describe some statistical techniques for estimating market demand and grouping similar markets.

Some statistical techniques for estimating market demand and grouping similar markets are trend analysis and cluster analysis.

Appreciate the value to businesspeople of trade missions and trade fairs.

Trade missions and trade fairs enable businesspeople to visit a market inexpensively, make sales, obtain overseas representation, and observe competitors' activities.

Discuss some of the problems market researchers encounter in foreign markets.

Cultural problems, such as a low level of literacy and distrust of strangers, complicate the data-gathering process, as do technical difficulties, such as a lack of maps, telephone directories, and adequate mail service. These hindrances to marketing research do not prevent the work from being done. There is a tendency in many markets, however, to do less research and use simpler techniques.

Understand the difference between country screening and segment screening.

If we utilize country screening, we assume that countries are homogeneous units (that is, "everyone living in Mexico or Chad is essentially the same"). In segment screening, we focus our attention not on the nation as a homogeneous unit but on groups of people with similar wants and desires (market segments) across as well as within countries.

Identify the sources of information for the screening process.

The sources of information for the screening process are the environmental forces.

Appreciate the utility of the Internet as a source of market research data.

Both the Small and Medium-Sized Enterprises and the Worldview articles in this chapter offer insights into how the Internet is used—or may be used—to generate information. However, in many countries the Internet is used only by relatively well-to-do and well-educated persons. What are the implications for our ability to do market research directly with potential consumers on the Internet?

[Key Words]

market screening (p. 520)
environmental scanning (p. 520)
country screening (p. 521)
segment screening (p. 521)
market indicators (p. 524)
market factors (p. 525)
estimation by analogy (p. 525)
trend analysis (p. 525)
cluster analysis (p. 526)
trade mission (p. 529)
trade fair (p. 529)

[Questions]

1. Select a country and a product that you believe your firm can market there. Make a list of the sources of information you will use for each screening.
2. What is the basis for the order of screenings presented in the text?
3. A firm's export manager finds, by examining the UN's *International Trade Statistics Yearbook,* that the company's competitors are exporting. Is there a way the manager can learn to which countries the U.S. competitors are exporting?
4. Do a country's imports completely measure the market potential for a product? Why or why not?
5. What are some barriers related to the political and legal forces that may eliminate a country from further consideration?
6. What is the reason for making personal visits to markets that survive the first five screenings?
7. Why should a firm's management consider going on a trade mission or exhibiting in a trade fair?
8. What are the two principal kinds of complications that researchers face when they collect primary data in a foreign market? Give examples.
9. What do the market size index and the market intensity index tell you?

[Internet Exercises]

Using the Internet

1. The U.S. Department of Commerce is emphasizing 10 Big Emerging Markets.
   a. What is the reason for the emphasis?
   b. What are the countries involved?
   c. Which important industrial sectors offer promising sales opportunities?
2. According to the revised FT900 for January, 2001:
   a. Were total U.S. exports greater or less than total imports for (1) cars, (2) trucks, and (3) car parts?
   b. Which nation was the largest customer of U.S. vehicles? Which nation was second?
   c. Which nation had the largest sales of vehicles to the United States? Which nation was second?
   d. Which nation purchased the most auto parts from U.S. manufacturers? Which nation was second?

[Minicase 15.1]

The Sugar Daddy Chocolate Company

Jack Carlson started Sugar Daddy Chocolate Company five years ago and is now selling about $1 million annually. Carlson would like to expand sales, but the U.S. market is very competitive. He has a friend with a small business who is now making 20 percent of his sales overseas. He wonders if any chocolates are exported.

To find out, he calls a friend of his who is a professor of international business at the university and tells him that he wants to find out if chocolate is being exported. He asks the professor to research the following questions:

1. Is chocolate being exported?
2. Which are the six largest importing nations?
3. Which of these are growing markets?
4. Carlson's export competition would probably come from which countries?

His friend tells him to meet him in the reference section of the university library. When Carlson arrives, the professor has open the UN's *International Trade Statistics Yearbook* to the page showing the international trade in chocolate (Table 15.1 in this chapter).

[Appendix]

Sources of Information Used in Screenings

I–II. First and second screenings (basic need potential, economic and financial forces).

A. WTO, www.wto.org.

B. IMF, www.imf.org.

1. *Direction of Trade Statistics.*
2. *International Financial Statistics.*
3. *World Economic Outlook.*

C. OECD.

1. *Frequently Requested Statistics,* http://www.oecd.org/std/fas.htm.
2. *Economic Surveys* (summary of each member plus links to extensive economic data sources), www.oecd.org/eco/surv/esu.htm.

D. UN.

1. *International Trade Statistics Yearbook.*
2. *Statistical Yearbook, Demographic Yearbook.*

3. *World Investment Report.*

4. *UNCTAD Trade and Development Report.*

5. *Social Indicators,* www.un.org/Depts/unsd/global.htm

E. EU.

1. *Eurostat,* www.europa.eu.int.

F. World Bank (annual publications), www.worldbank.org.

1. *World Development Indicators* (also on CD).

2. *Atlas.*

3. *World Development Tables.*

G. Development banks.

1. African Development Bank, www.afdb.org.

2. Asian Development Bank, www.adb.org.

(a) Other information on Asia is available at APEC member statistics, www.apecsec.org, and Pacific Basin Economic Council, www.pbec.org.

3. Inter-American Development Bank, www.iadb.org/int/sta/ENGLISH/staweb/index.htm.

H. CIA Country Factbook, www.odci.gov/cia/publications/factbook/index.html.

I. Heritage Foundation Index of Economic Freedom, http://index.heritage.org.

J. Small Business Administration, Office of International Trade, www.sba.gov/oit/.

K. Trade Compass, www.tradecompass.com.

L. U.S. Department of Commerce.

1. *International Trade Administration,* www.ita.doc.gov.

2. *Export Today,* www.exporttoday.com.

3. *National Trade Data Bank* (*NTDB*), CD-ROM or www.stat-usa.gov.

M. Monitor, London, England.

1. *Europe Marketing Data & Statistics* (annual).

2. *International Marketing Data & Statistics* (annual).

N. Commercial officers of foreign embassies in Washington, DC.

O. Trade associations.

P. Banks with international departments.

Q. Chambers of commerce, such as the German-American Chamber of Commerce in New York City and the Mexican-American Chamber of Commerce in Mexico City.

R. The Economist Intelligence Unit, www.eiu.com.

S. Many state governments have trade offices with market specialists and good libraries.

T. American embassies produce *Country Commercial Guides.*

U. Your company's suppliers and customers have data they might share.

V. Big 5 accounting firms sell studies that they conduct, and some publish newsletters.

III. Political and legal forces.

A. Business Environment Risk Index, www.beri.com.

B. Political Risk Group: *Political Risk Country Reports,* www.prsgroup.com.

C. European Union: *Europa,* http://europa.eu.int/index-en.htm.

D. International Chamber of Commerce, various publications.

E. Association newsletters.

F. Major city newspapers.

   1. *The Financial Times,* www.ft.com.

G. Business magazines.

   1. *Business Week,* www.businessweek.com.

   2. *The Economist,* www.economist.com.

   3. *Far Eastern Economic Review,* www.feer.com.

   4. *Forbes,* www.forbes.com.

H. Oceana Publishers, international legal publications, www.oceanalaw.com.

I. International economic law Web sources, www.fletcher.tufts.edu/inter_econ_law/iellinks.htm.

J. Laws on international trade and individual countries, treaties, guide.lp.findlaw.com/12international.

K. Corruption perception and bribery indexes, www.transparency.de/documents/cpi/2000/cpi2000/html.

IV. Cultural forces.

A. Brigham Young University: *Culturegrams,* www.culturegrams.com.

B. Business magazines.

C. Major city newspapers.

D. *Web of Culture* (body language, gestures, languages), www.webofculture.com/worldsmart/index.html.

E. Consider direct market research via the Internet provided that your products are directed toward the more affluent/younger customers who currently use the Internet.

V. Competitive forces.

A. Most of the sources listed in I are useful here as well.

B. Talk with knowledgeable people, but be careful. You may be given misinformation on purpose.

[Chapter]

16

Marketing Internationally

"But when it comes to questions of taste and, especially, aesthetic preference, consumers do not like averages . . . The lure of a universal product is a false allure."

—Kenichi Ohmae

Concept Previews

After reading this chapter, you should be able to:

- **understand** why there are differences between domestic and international marketing
- **explain** why international marketing managers may wish to standardize the marketing mix
- **comprehend** why it is often impossible to standardize the marketing mix worldwide
- **appreciate** the importance of distinguishing among the total product, the physical product, and the brand name
- **explain** why consumer products generally require greater modification for international sales than industrial products or services
- **discuss** the product strategies that can be formed from three product alternatives and three kinds of promotional messages
- **explain** "glocal" advertising strategies
- **understand** some of the effects the Internet may have on international marketing
- **discuss** the distribution strategies of international marketers

Alex Vincent/Sygma

Procter & Gamble's Path to Globalization

There have been some false starts and even some failures, but now Procter & Gamble's global marketing efforts are bringing results. The company, ranked 65 in *Fortune*'s "World's Largest Corporations" and 18 in its "Largest U.S. Industrial Corporations," obtained 51 percent of its $35.3 billion in total sales from non-U.S. operations. This is all the more notable inasmuch as P&G faces more pressures in many foreign markets than it does in the United States. There are more competitors in Europe because of the ease of shipping products across borders. For example, in France, P&G competes against Swedish, Danish, and Italian firms in many of its product categories. For years, although the situation has now changed, in countries such as Belgium, Germany, Italy, and Japan, the use of premiums and gifts for promotion was either banned or severely restricted.

In the 1940s, P&G's market strategy was to export its core products to build demand and then establish local sales companies or production facilities. None of those products was launched with global distribution in mind. Whether the products were imported or produced locally, P&G had a philosophy of employing overseas the same policies and procedures that had been successful in the United States. As a result, it took the company 15 years to get Pampers into 70 countries. However, in the early 1990s, Edwin Artzt, then P&G's CEO, changed the firm's marketing strategy. Instead of waiting to introduce a new product worldwide until after it had accumulated marketing experience in a country, the company tried to introduce products on a worldwide scale early in their development. The aim of this strategy was to avoid giving competitors time to react in all other markets. As Artzt put it, "If P&G were introducing Pampers today, it would plan to get the product into world markets in five years or less."

At times the company used a regional rather than a global approach, changing many of its products to suit the regional markets. Camay's smell, Crest's flavor, and Head & Shoulders' formula are some examples of products that varied from one region to another, as did the company's marketing strategy. Occasionally, contrary to its product launch policy, P&G has recycled ad campaigns previously used in the United States. When the firm introduced Orange Crush in Peru, it used a TV spot showing a small boy who promises to save his soccer-playing brother's Orange Crush but then succumbs to temptation and drinks it himself. It was credited with playing an important role in a 60 percent sales increase.

Does P&G's strategy work? According to its Web site, "P&G markets approximately 300 brands to nearly five billion consumers in over 140 countries." In addition, P&G is working hard on mass customization. In 1999 it launched reflect.com, a personalized beauty care products line, on the Internet. It has also launched Millstone Blends, which allows consumers to develop a "tasteprint" for coffee, after which a personal blend is developed (personalblends.com). ■

Sources: www.pg.com/main.jhtml and www.pg.com/investors/fast_facts (December 1, 2000); "Preparing to Win in the 21st Century," Procter & Gamble Annual Report, www.pg.com/info/financial_Center/annual_report/ourshareholders/preparing.html (February 19, 1998); "P&G to Get Ahead by Marketing," *Financial Times,* June 5, 1997, p. 21; and "Make it Simple," *Business Week,* September 9, 1996, pp. 96–104.

The opening section illustrates how P&G has changed its marketing strategy from (1) using the same procedures and policies overseas that have proved successful in the United States to (2) making global plans, adjusting them for regions, and then adapting them to satisfy local demands.

Whether a policy or technique is first designed for global use and then adapted for local market differences or, as in the case of the Orange Crush advertisement, the idea comes from the home country and then is used overseas, marketers must know where to look for possible differences between marketing domestically and marketing internationally. Sometimes the differences are great; at other times there are no differences.

Certainly there are some strong commonalities. Isn't it true that marketers everywhere must (1) know their markets, (2) develop products or services to satisfy customers' needs, (3) price the products or services so that they are readily acceptable in the market, (4) make them available to the buyers, and (5) inform potential customers and persuade them to buy?

Added Complexities of International Marketing

Although the basic functions of domestic and international marketing are the same, the international markets served often differ widely because of the great variations in the uncontrollable environmental forces that we examined in Section Three. Moreover, even the forces we think of as controllable vary within wide limits: distribution channels to which the marketer is accustomed are unavailable, certain aspects of the product may be different, the promotional mixes are often dissimilar, and distinct cost structures may require that different prices be set.

The international marketing manager's task is complex. He or she frequently must plan and control a variety of marketing strategies rather than one and then coordinate and integrate those strategies into a single marketing program. Even the marketing managers of global firms such as P&G who utilize a single worldwide strategy must know enough about the uncontrollable variables to be able to make changes in its implementation when necessary.

Both global and multinational marketing managers, like their domestic counterparts, must develop marketing strategies by assessing the firm's potential foreign markets and analyzing the many alternative marketing mixes. Their aim is to select target markets that the firm can serve at a profit and formulate combinations of tactics for product, price, promotion, and distribution channels that will best serve those markets. In Chapter 15, we examined the market assessment and selection process; in this chapter, we shall study the formulation of the marketing mix.

The Marketing Mix (What and How to Sell)

As we indicated above, the marketing mix consists of a set of strategy decisions made in the areas of product, promotion, pricing, and distribution for the purpose of satisfying the customers in a target market. The number of variables included in these four areas is extremely large, making possible hundreds of combinations. Often the domestic operation has already established a successful marketing mix, and the temptation to follow the same procedures overseas is strong. Yet as we have seen, important differences between the domestic and foreign environments may make a wholesale transfer of the mix impossible. The question that the international marketing manager must resolve is, "Can we standardize worldwide, must we make some changes, or must we formulate a completely different marketing mix?"

Standardization, Adaptation, or Completely Different?

Management would prefer global standardization of the marketing mix; that is, it would prefer to employ the same marketing mix in all of the firm's operations because standardization can produce significant cost savings. If the product sold in the domestic market can be exported, there can be longer production runs, which lower manufacturing costs. Even when the standard product is manufactured overseas, production costs will be lower because the extra research and design expense of either adapting domestic products or designing new ones for foreign sales will be avoided.

> Generally, R&D is still highly concentrated in the home country, although some internationals have had overseas research facilities for years. When a firm's R&D is concentrated in the home country, the important product changes have to be made there. Also, a product specification is rarely frozen (look at the changes in automobiles in a single model year). Notifying all the production facilities worldwide about these modifications is difficult, and it is much more complex when the product is not standardized.

If advertising campaigns, promotional materials (catalogs, point-of-purchase displays), and sales training programs can be standardized, the expensive creative work

[Figure 16.1] **Components of the Total Product**

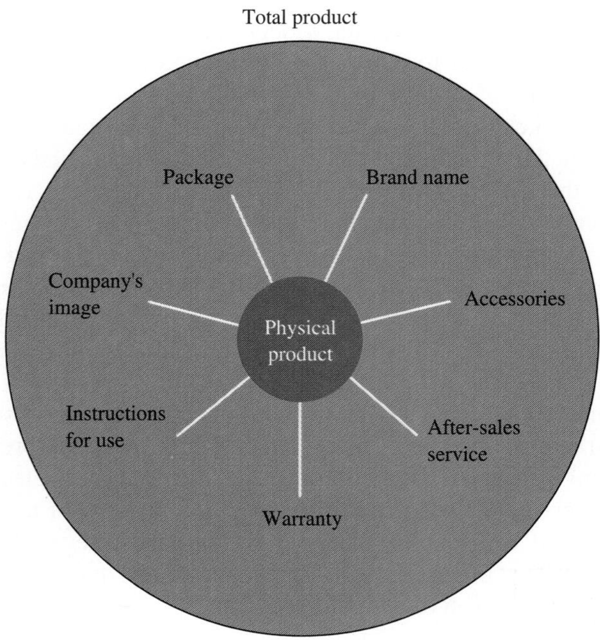

and artwork need be done only once. A standardized corporate visual identity (CVI) (firm name, slogan, and graphics) can help project a consistent image for a multinational with publics dispersed across geographic locales.[1] Standardized pricing strategies for firms that serve markets from several different foreign subsidiaries prevent the embarrassment of having an important customer receive two distinct quotations for the same product. In summary, the benefits from standardization of the marketing mix are (1) lower costs, (2) easier control and coordination from headquarters, and (3) reduction of the time spent preparing the marketing plan.

In spite of the advantages of standardization, many firms find that the opening quote by Kenichi Ohmae is accurate: Standardization is seldom as easy as it seems. Many firms find it necessary to modify the present marketing mix or develop a new one. The extent of the changes needed depends in part on the type of product, the environmental forces, and the degree of market penetration desired by management. Further, given the fact that standardization is in a state of tension with the marketing principle, we probably should not be particularly disappointed that complete standardization is nearly never possible.

Even the firm often touted as the exemplar of the standardized product, Coca-Cola, found that its increasingly standardized strategy had run its course. According to Coca-Cola's chair, Douglas Daft: "[A]s the century was drawing to a close, the world had changed course, and we had not. The world was demanding greater flexibility, responsiveness and local sensitivity, while we were further consolidating decisionmaking and standardizing our practices . . . The next big evolutionary step of 'going global' now has to be 'going local.' "[2]

Product Strategies

The product is the central focus of the marketing mix. If it fails to satisfy the needs of consumers, no amount of promotion, price cutting, or distribution will persuade them to buy. Consumers will not repurchase a detergent if the clothes do not come out as clean as TV commercials say they will. They will not be deceived by advertisements announcing friendly service when experience demonstrates otherwise.

control, and reduced 36 warehouses in Europe to 8, both European sales and operating margins improved. However, in the United States, the firm makes $10 on every $100 of sales; in Europe, it earns about $2.30 on that amount of revenue.[10]

While some international firms, such as Kodak and Campbell, have been extremely successful in employing the same brand name, label, and colors worldwide, other firms learn they must change names, labels, or colors because of cultural differences. Gold appears frequently on packages in Latin America because Latin Americans view it as a symbol of quality and prestige. In the Netherlands blue is considered warm and feminine, but the Swedes consider it masculine and cold.

> Procter & Gamble found that a gold package has value in Europe too after it launched its Crest Tartar Control Formula in the United Kingdom in a silver box, which was followed two months later by Colgate's equivalent in a gold box. Sheepish P&G officials, agreeing that Colgate's choice of gold was better than their silver, explained that silver was required because that was how the product was packaged in the United States.[11]

Even if the colors can remain the same, instructions on labels, of course, must be translated into the language of the market. Firms selling in areas where two or more languages are spoken, such as Canada and Switzerland, may need to use multilingual labels. Where instructions are not required, as in the case of some consumer or industrial products whose use is well known, there is an advantage to printing the label in the language of the country best known for the product. French labels on perfumes and English labels on industrial goods help strengthen the product's image.

> A Mexican firm in which one of the writers had an interest copied an American brand of penetrating oil that was the best-selling import, even to the blue color. It put a label in English on the can. Then, to comply with the law, a gummed sticker saying *Envasado en Mexico* (can filled in Mexico) was placed over part of the label. The Mexican product, unlike most locally made industrial products, had excellent acceptance from the start.

A perfectly good brand name may have to be scrapped because of its unfavorable connotations in another language. An American product failed to make it in Sweden because its name translated to "enema." In Latin America, a product had to be taken off the market when the manufacturer found that the name meant "jackass oil." Of course, this problem occurs in both directions, as a Belgian brewery found when it tried to introduce its Delerium Tremens lager to the U.S. market. American authorities told the company the name was an incitement to drinking. They also said that calling another beer Guillotine was like an American brewery calling its beer "electric chair."[12]

Sometimes a firm will not use a perfectly good name because someone has invented a story about its impropriety in foreign markets. This is what happened with the Nova. As the story goes, Chevrolet couldn't sell Novas in (the storyteller picks a Spanish-speaking country) because Nova means *no va* ("doesn't go") in Spanish. What the person doesn't realize is that the two are pronounced very differently—*Nova* has the accent on the first syllable, whereas the accent for *no va* falls on the *va.* Therefore, to someone speaking Spanish, the words have very different meanings. Most native Spanish-speaking people connect *nova* with "star," which is probably what General Motors had in mind. You may be surprised to learn that Pemex, the government-owned oil monopoly that is the exclusive refiner and retailer of gasoline in Mexico once called its regular gasoline *Nova.*

Pemex gasoline doesn't go.
Victoria Ball

An important difference in the social forces to which American marketers are not accustomed is people's preference in other nations for making daily visits to small neighborhood specialty shops and large, open markets where they can socialize while shopping. More frequent buying permits smaller packages, which is important to a shopper who has no automobile in which to carry purchases. However, this custom is changing in Europe, where changing consumption patterns are

[Worldview]

USING OUR WASHING MACHINE FOR WHAT?

International washing machine manufacturers such as Whirlpool, Maytag, and Electrolux acknowledge that there are differences as well as similarities in preferences among American, European, and Latin American buyers of their products. Spin speeds differ, and Europeans want machines that load from the front, whereas Americans have used top-loaders in their homes and Latin Americans have used simple, easy-to-operate machines.

However, all consumers want to get cleaner clothing with machines that don't damage clothes. Maytag, in a press release, announced that it was introducing a "laundry product for the 21st century." Its new front-loader "has more capacity, is easier to load and unload, is gentle on clothing, and it gets clothes cleaner." Yes, but can the consumer churn more buttermilk in it?

Say what? Well, Maytag is going to market the washer in India, isn't it? One unsuspecting washer manufacturer in India was obtaining respectable sales nationwide but noticed that in one region the reported results were much higher than the marketing department's forecast. Believing that the numbers were wrong, the marketers investigated the region and found that the numbers were correct, but for reasons they never would have expected. People didn't have more dirty clothes to wash than in other areas, but they did like buttermilk. What they knew that the manufacturer didn't was that the company's washing machines were extremely efficient buttermilk churns. ■

Source: Maytag, "Maytag Introduces Laundry Product for 21st Century," *Company News*, www.prnewswire.com/cgi-bin/stories.pl?ACCT=105&STORY=www.story/79339&EDATE (February 22, 1998); and "License-Raj," *Global Competitor*, May 1995, pp. 33–38.

demanding the kinds of assortments that only a large store can offer. Shopping frequency is also slowing as European women are finding that they have less free time than previously. As we mentioned in Chapter 13, the solution has been the huge combination supermarket–discount house (e.g., *hypermarché* in France) with ample parking and generally located in the suburbs.

A similar situation had been occurring in Mexico, especially after the signing of the North American Free Trade Agreement (NAFTA) and the lifting of many of the country's import restrictions. Enormous crowds, anxious to buy at lower prices, showed up at the Wal-Mart and Kmart stores when they first opened in 1993. So many people tried to enter the Monterrey Wal-Mart on opening day that store employees had to bar the doors to control the crowd.[13] However, Mexicans living in Monterrey or farther north still come to shop in Texas border-city Wal-Marts where prices are lower.[14]

One can easily draw a parallel to the situation which began in the 1940s in the United States. The same conditions of rising incomes, a growing middle class, and an increasing number of working wives have combined to put a premium on the shopper's time, and just as occurred in the United States, mass merchandising, and catalog and internet shopping have moved in to fill this need.

Legal Forces. Legal forces can be a formidable constraint in the design of product strategies because if the firm fails to adhere to a country's laws governing the product, it will be unable to do business in that country. Laws concerning pollution, consumer protection, and operator safety are being enacted rapidly in many parts of the world and limit the marketer's freedom to standardize the product mix internationally. For example, American machinery manufacturers exporting to Sweden have found their operator safety requirements to be even stricter than those required by the Occupational Safety and Health Act (OSHA), so that if they wish to market in Sweden, they must produce a special model. We have previously mentioned that product standards set ostensibly to protect a nation's citizens can be very effective in protecting indigenous industry from foreign competitors.

Laws prohibiting certain classes of imports are common in developing nations, as potential exporters learn when they research the world for markets. Products considered luxuries, as well as products already being manufactured, are among the first to be excluded from importation, but such laws also affect local production.

Foods and pharmaceuticals are especially influenced by laws concerning purity and labeling. Food products sold in Canada, whether imported or produced locally, are subject to strict rules that require both English and French on the labels as well as metric and inch-pound units. The law even dictates the space permitted between the number and the unit—16 oz. is correct, but 16oz. is not. The Venezuelan government has decreed that the manufacturer or the importer must affix to the package the maximum retail price at which the product can be sold. Because of Saudi Arabians' preoccupation with avoiding food containing pork, the label of any product containing animal fat or meat that is sold in Saudi Arabia must state the kind of animal used or state that no swine products were used.

Legal forces also may prevent a worldwide firm from employing its brand name in all its overseas markets. Managements accustomed to the American law, which establishes the right to a brand name by priority in use, are surprised to learn that in code law countries, a brand belongs to the person registering it first. Thus, the marketer may go into foreign markets expecting to use the company's long-established brand name only to find that someone else owns it. The name may have been registered by someone who is employing it legitimately for his or her own products, or it may have been pirated, that is, registered by someone who hopes to profit by selling the name back to the originating firm.

To avoid this predicament, the firm must register its brand names in every country where it wants to use them or where it might use them in the future. And this must be done rapidly. The Paris Convention grants a firm that has registered a name in one country only six months' priority in registering it elsewhere. To be certain that it has enough names for new products, Unilever, the English-Dutch manufacturer of personal care products, has over 100,000 trademarks registered throughout the world, most of which are not in use but are kept in reserve.

The use of domain names on the Internet shows that these problems have not decreased. A recent study found that American Express, for example, had registered the domain name "americanexpress" in 19 countries, while in 11 others the name is registered to someone other than American Express. In a more extreme example, CBS has 4 registrations, but others have 46. Even more disconcerting is that both of these companies are at risk in over 200 other countries where the names had not been registered at all as of early 2000. When kanji characters became an option for registering Japanese domain names, tiny Web Japan Co. got a head start by registering some 100 domain names, including those of major corporations.[15]

Economic Forces. The great disparity in income throughout the world is an important obstacle to worldwide product standardization. Many products from the industrialized countries are simply too expensive for consumers in developing countries, and so if the firm wishes to achieve market penetration, it must either simplify the product or produce a different, less costly one.

When Gillette discovered that only 8 percent of Mexican men used shaving cream (the rest use soapy water), it introduced a plastic tube of shaving cream at half the price of its aerosol can. Now more than twice that percentage use the less expensive package, and Gillette is selling the tube in other parts of Latin America. Because many Latin American customers can't afford to buy American-sized packages, the company sells packages of single razor blades and half-ounce packages of Silkience shampoo. Use of the plastic squeeze bottle, "the poor man's aerosol," is common where incomes are low.[16]

Market size influences the product mix, and in the poorer countries, the populations not only are frequently smaller but also contain a large number of people who can only purchase the bare necessities of life, thereby making the market even smaller. This means that normally the foreign subsidiary cannot afford to produce as complete a product mix as does the parent. Most automobile manufacturers assemble only the least expensive line and broaden the local product mix by importing, when permitted, the luxury cars. All international firms practice this marketing technique whenever possible because a captive foreign sales organization is available to promote the sales of the home organization's exports and because the revenue derived helps pay the subsidiary's overhead.

Boeing's 737 became the best-selling commercial jet in history partly because its engineers redesigned it for Third World aviation after its sales to developed nations dropped off. The runways in developing countries were too short for the original design and, being made of asphalt rather than concrete, were also too soft. By redesigning the wings to allow shorter takeoffs and landings and by selling 1 or 2 at a time instead of the batches of 20 or 30 which airlines in the developed nations order, Boeing built a reputation with developing countries' airlines, which later began to buy Boeing's larger planes.

Physical Forces. Physical forces, such as climate and terrain, also militate against international product standardization. Where the heat is intense, gasoline-driven machinery and automobiles must be fitted with larger radiators for extra cooling capacity.

The heat and high humidity in many parts of the tropics require that electrical equipment be built with extra-heavy insulation. Consumer goods that are affected by moisture must be specially packaged to resist its penetration. Thus, one finds pills wrapped individually in foil and baked goods packaged in tin boxes to prevent their degradation by moisture.

High altitudes frequently require product alteration. Food manufacturers have found that they must change their cooking instructions for people who live at high altitudes because at such altitudes it takes much longer to cook and bake. The thinner atmosphere requires producers of cake mixes to include less yeast. Gasoline and diesel motors generate less power at high altitudes, and so the manufacturer must often supply a larger engine.

Mountainous terrain implies high-cost highways, and so in the poorer countries, roads of the quality we know are nonexistent. Trucks traveling poorer-quality roads need tires with thicker treads and heavy-duty suspensions. Because of the rough ride, packaging must be stronger than that used in the United States. From these examples, we can appreciate that even though an unchanged product may be culturally and economically acceptable in a market, the effect of the physical forces alone may be strong enough to require some product modification.

Because of space limitations, it is impossible to examine the influence of every environmental force on foreign product strategies. We believe sufficient practical examples have been offered to give the reader an idea of their pervasiveness in the design of the entire marketing mix. In fact, as we will show at the end of this chapter, a useful guide in the marketing mix preparation is a matrix in which the marketing mix variables are tabulated against the environmental forces.

Promotional Strategies

promotion
All forms of communication between a firm and its publics

Promotion, one of the basic elements of the marketing mix, is communication that secures understanding between a firm and its publics to bring about a favorable buying action and achieve long-lasting confidence in the firm and the product or service it provides. Note that this definition employs the plural, *publics,* because the seller's promotional efforts must be directed to more than just the ultimate consumers and the channel of distribution members. Managements have awakened to the fact that the old advice of always maintaining a low profile in a foreign country is not necessarily the best course of action. Many companies have changed this strategy and are now making the general public, special interest groups, and governments aware of their public service activities.

Because promotion both influences and is influenced by the other marketing mix variables, it is possible to formulate nine distinct strategies by combining the three alternatives of (1) marketing the same physical product everywhere, (2) adapting the physical product for foreign markets, and (3) designing a different physical product with (*a*) the same, (*b*) adapted, or (*c*) different messages.[17] Let us examine the six strategies most commonly used.

1. *Same product—same message.* When marketers find that target markets vary little with respect to product use and consumer attitudes, they can offer the same product and use the same promotional appeals in all markets. Avon, Maidenform, and A.T. Cross follow this strategy.
2. *Same product—different message.* The same product may satisfy a different need or be used differently elsewhere. This means the product may be left unchanged but a different message is required. Honda's campaign "You meet the nicest people on a Honda" appealed to Americans who used their motorcycles as pleasure vehicles, but in Brazil, Honda stresses economy as it tries to make its product a means of basic transportation.
3. *Product adaptation—same message.* In cases where the product serves the same function but must be adapted to different conditions, the same message is employed with a changed product. In Japan, Lever Brothers puts Lux soap in fancy boxes because much of it is sold for gifts.
4. *Product adaptation—message adaptation.* In some cases, both the product and the promotional message must be modified for foreign markets. In Latin America, Tang is especially sweetened, premixed, and ready to drink in pouches. Unlike Americans, Latin Americans do not drink it for breakfast. There it is promoted as a drink for mealtimes and for throughout the day but not for breakfast.
5. *Different product—same message.* As we pointed out in our discussion of the economic forces' influence on product strategies, the potential customers in many markets cannot afford the product as manufactured in the firm's home country. The product may also be too technologically advanced to gain widespread acceptance. To overcome these obstacles, companies have frequently produced a very distinct product for these markets. The previously mentioned low-cost plastic squeeze bottle and inexpensive manually operated washing machines are two examples. The promotional message, however, can be very similar to what is used in the developed countries if the product performs the same functions.
6. *Different product for the same use—different message.* Frequently, the different product requires a different message as well. Welding torches rather than automatic welding machines would be sold on the basis of low acquisition cost rather than high output per labor-hour. The governments of developing countries faced with high unemployment would be persuaded by a message emphasizing the job-creating possibilities of labor-intensive processes rather than the labor saving of highly automated machinery.

The tools for communicating these messages—the promotional mix—are advertising, personal selling, sales promotion, public relations, and publicity. No one of these tools is inherently superior to the others, though circumstances in a given situation may dictate that one of them be emphasized more than the others. Just as in the case of the product strategies, the composition of the promotional mix will depend on the type of product, the environmental forces, and the amount of market penetration desired.

Advertising

Among all the promotional mix elements, **advertising** is the one with the greatest similarities worldwide. This is the case because most advertising everywhere is based on American practices. U.S. ad agencies have greatly aided the global propagation of American techniques as they have followed their domestic customers overseas. Today, the major American agencies are all global, with wholly owned subsidiaries, joint ventures, and working agreements with local agencies.[18]

advertising
Paid, nonpersonal presentation of ideas, goods, or services by an identified sponsor

Table 16.1 **World's Top 15 Creative Interactive Ad Agencies (Ranked by Awards Won)**

Rank 1999	Agency	Headquarters	Awards Won
1	Ogilvy Interactive Worldwide	New York	58
2	Hyperinteractive	London	35
3	Nicholson NY	New York	32
4	U.S. Interactive	New York	31
5	Elephant Seven Multimedia	Hamburg	26
6	USWeb/CKS	San Francisco	25
7	Agency.com	New York	24
8	Euro RSCG DSW Partners	Salt Lake City	23
9	Red Sky Interactive	San Francisco	22
10	Disney Interactive	Los Angeles	22
11	Bates Interactive	London	21
12	Microsoft Corp.	Redmond, WA	21
13	USWeb/CKS	Portland, OR	19
14	Studio Archetype	San Francisco	18
15	Lowe and Partners/SMS	New York	17

Source: Reprinted with permission from the July 26, 1999 issue of *Advertising Age.* © Crain Communications Inc., 1999.

A different analysis provides a similar story. According to *AdAge,* among the 100 leading interactive (Internet) advertising agencies in the world, 61 are U.S.-based, 12 are based in the United Kingdom, and Germany and Brazil have 8 and 3, respectively. Table 16.1 shows the top 15 such agencies.

Global and Regional Brands. Manufacturers are increasingly using global or regional brands for a number of reasons:

1. Cost is most often cited. By producing one TV commercial for use across a region, a firm can save up to 50 percent of the production cost.
2. There is a better chance of obtaining one regional source to do high-quality work than of finding sources in various countries that will work to the same high standard.
3. Some marketing managers believe their companies must have a single image throughout a region.
4. Companies are establishing regionalized organizations where many functions, such as marketing, are centralized.
5. Global and regional satellite and cable television are becoming available.[19]

Economies of scale are one reason some firms emphasize the regional or global standardization of advertising. Coca-Cola, for example, estimates that it saves over $8 million annually in the cost of thinking up new imagery by repeating the same theme everywhere.

The head of a consulting firm specializing in brands and corporate identity has a different idea. He says, "There are too many businesses out there doing the same thing. Global branding is a way of saying your company makes a difference, which moves you up the pecking order."[20] Look at the value *The Financial Times* places on what it calls the world's most valuable brands (Table 16.2).

Global or National. Even though there is a trend toward using more global brands, a debate continues among international marketers about using global, regional, or national brands. Companies that acquired successful national brands on purchasing the

Table 16.2 Comparing Global Brand Values, 1997–2000

Rank 2000 (1997)	Brand	Value (billions)	Rank 2000 (1997)	Brand	Value (billions)
1 (1)	Coca-Cola	72.5	11 (2)	Marlboro	22.1
2 (*)	Microsoft	70.2	12 (*)	Mercedes	21.1
3 (3)	IBM	53.2	13 (16)	Hewlett-Packard	20.6
4 (8)	Intel	39.0	14 (*)	Cisco Systems	20.0
5 (*)	Nokia	38.5	15 (*)	Toyota	18.9
6 (15)	General Electric	38.1	16 (*)	Citibank	18.9
7 (*)	Ford	36.4	17 (9)	Gillette	17.4
8 (5)	Disney	33.6	18 (6)	Sony	16.4
9 (4)	McDonald's	27.9	19 (*)	American Express	16.1
10 (13)	AT&T	25.5	20 (*)	Honda	15.2

*Did not appear in the top 20 in 1997.

Source: "Shimmering Symbols of the Modern Age," *The Financial Times,* October 17, 1997, p. 12: and "Coca-Cola Loses Its Fizz," *The Financial Times,* July 18, 2000, p. 14.

original owner have been extremely cautious about converting them to their global brands. Depending on the circumstances, management may stay with national brands, convert to global brands, or use a combination of both.[21] Nestlé is an example of a large global firm that uses both.

> In an interview with *The Financial Times,* Nestlé's CEO, Peter Brabeck, stated that he recognizes that the company can achieve considerable economies of scale in purchasing, production, and distribution with a strong corporate brand. However, he also understands that Nestlé's brands must appeal to consumers' emotions "by projecting a familiar closeness and they cannot do so if they are not in tune with the ethnic, social, and religious background of the people who purchase them."
>
> Nestlé tries to achieve both consumer familiarity and marketing efficiency by using two brands on a single product: (1) a *local brand* that may be familiar and appeal only to a small group of consumers and (2) a *corporate strategic brand* such as Nestlé or Nescafé. Brabeck explains, "At headquarters, we establish a hierarchy in the ranking of brands and the more strategic their character, the deeper our involvement in their positioning, design, and technological development. But giving life to our brands, making them relevant to our customers is the responsibility of the local management, which enjoys a high degree of autonomy."[22]

Private Brands. Private brands have become such serious competitors for manufacturers' brands that they are responsible for a shift in power from manufacturers to retailers. In Japan large supermarket chains, such as the Daiei group with more than 6,000 outlets, are stocking private-branded food, household goods, and clothing. They are also making alliances with international retailers who have their own branded products. Wal-Mart, for example, has an agreement with Ito-Yokado, a large Japanese retailer, to supply Wal-Mart branded goods.[23]

Private labels have captured a third of the British and Swiss food markets and a fifth of the French and German markets. The trend toward private labels is also catching on in Spain and the Netherlands. In 1996 SPAR, the world's largest food retailer (sales of $27.8 billion), with headquarters in the Netherlands, launched its own private label in 27 nations. No other retail organization has had an international private brand distributed in as many national markets.[24]

Availability of Media. Satellite TV broadcasters are making it possible for numerous programming networks to provide service to millions of households in dozens of countries. Star TV, TVB, and ABN broadcast programs in Chinese and English and also carry cable networks, such as Turner, ESPN, and HBO, with which they reach 3 billion people in Asia. A British satellite TV firm, Sky Broadcasting, transmits programs to

European cable companies and directly to homes with satellite dishes. One of the major programming networks using satellite TV broadcasting is CNN, which reaches 78 million households in over 100 countries. MTV calculates its audience to be 210 million people in 78 countries. Its Asian subsidiary broadcasts in Mandarin and English; MTV Latino's programs are in Spanish. Fox, Discovery, ESPN, and HBO are other programmers that broadcast internationally and sell time to advertisers.[25] The Middle East Broadcast Center, started in 1992, is the only satellite TV network that broadcasts Western-style news, entertainment, and advertising to Muslim countries in Arabic. Although the owners are Saudis, the Arabic female newscasters are not required to wear head coverings.[26]

There are also more international print media available. *The European,* a daily newspaper; the international edition of *The Herald Tribune;* the Asian and European editions of *The Wall Street Journal;* and the international editions of the *Manchester Guardian* and *The Financial Times* are some of the newspapers with wide circulation. The *Reader's Digest* has 48 foreign editions, and *Elle* has 32. Because all editions of each magazine are written for readers with similar demographics, all editions attract similar advertisers.

Pepsi advertising on billboards in Saudi Arabia.
Frank Spooner/Liaison Agency

Advertisers can also go to other media to reach their markets. Cinema advertising is heavily used in many parts of the world, as are billboards. In the Middle East, where media options are limited, videotape ads are rapidly becoming an integral part of the media mix. Advertisers penetrate this lucrative market by buying spots on popular videotapes. Three or four breaks with six or seven spots each are created at the beginning, middle, and end of the film. Three-quarters of the households in the United Arab Emirates, Saudi Arabia, and Kuwait have videocassette recorders, and in the first three months after release, a well-received videotape can draw an audience of 1 million viewers in Saudi Arabia alone. In a number of developing countries, automobiles equipped with loudspeakers circulate through the cities announcing products and street signs are furnished by advertisers that hang their messages on them. Homeowners can get a free coat of paint by permitting advertisers to put ads on their walls. Where mail delivery is reliable, direct mail is a powerful medium, as are trade fairs. Probably one of the most ingenious campaigns ever was that of a tea company that gave away thousands of printed prayers with a tea commercial on the other side to pilgrims bound for Mecca.

The point is that media of some kind are available in every country, and the local managers and ad agencies are familiar with the advantages of each kind. Media selection is extremely difficult for international advertising managers who try to standardize their media mix from the home office. We have mentioned only some of the problems, but from these you can appreciate that the variation in media availability is a strong reason for leaving this part of the advertising program to the local organization.

Internet Advertising. We mentioned the potential of the Internet as a market research tool in Chapter 13, and it has potential as an advertising medium as well. With well over 100 million Internet hosts worldwide and with most of the world's Internet users outside the United States, this medium is increasingly useful. Among the appealing factors of online advertising in the international sphere are the following:

1. An affluent, reachable audience. A high number of readers in a wide variety of countries read English or other common languages well (although it's becoming clear that native-language sites are strongly preferred).
2. Web contacts feature interactivity, which shrinks distance. Unlike TV or newspaper ads, Internet communications are two-way. And they are cheap.
3. The possibility exists of involving customers in determining which messages and information they receive. For this reason, there is some possibility that

company Web offerings will, in effect, be tailor-made by the user and therefore are customized, increasing the application of the marketing concept.

4. Although the Internet doesn't reach all possible groups, for some groups it may be among the best media choices. For teenagers in particular, Internet advertising can be important because teenagers spend less time watching TV than any other demographic group, preferring to spend time on the Internet or playing computer games.[27]

At the same time, there are other problems. For example, one way a bank generates a sense of trust is by building an imposing edifice of bricks and mortar. This will be trickier to do on the Internet. In fact, because Internet communications eliminate nonverbal signals, they may do little or nothing to generate trust.

Type of Product. Buyers of industrial goods and luxury products usually act on the same motives the world over; thus, these products lend themselves to the standardized approach. This enables manufacturers of capital goods, such as General Electric and Caterpillar, to prepare international campaigns that require very little modification in the various markets. Certain consumer goods markets are similar too, as we saw in the previous section. However, another set of characteristics also permits firms to use the same appeals and sales arguments worldwide: when the product is low-priced, is consumed in the same way, and is bought for the same reasons. Examples of such products are gasoline, soft drinks, detergents, cosmetics, and airline services. Firms such as Exxon (Esso overseas), Coca-Cola, Avon, and Levi Strauss have for years used the international approach successfully. Generally, the only changes they have made are a translation into the local language and the use of indigenous models.

Foreign Environmental Forces. Like variations in media availability, foreign environmental forces act as deterrents to the international standardization of advertising, and as you would expect, among the most influential of these forces are the *sociocultural* forces, which we examined in Chapter 9.

A basic cultural decision for the marketer is whether to position the product as foreign or local, and which way to go seems to depend on the country, the product type, and the target market. In Germany, for example, consumers are not at all impressed by the carmaker that announces it has American know-how. "After all," reason the Germans, "if so many Americans prefer BMW and Mercedes over U.S. cars, why shouldn't we?" At the same time, such purely American products as bourbon, fast-food restaurants, and blue jeans have made tremendous inroads in Germany and the rest of Europe.

Similarly, in Japan and elsewhere in the Far East, the American identity of consumer products enhances their image. The young and the status-conscious prefer the casual American look in clothing and seek the American label that identifies the wearer as belonging to the "in group." The influence of American-style fast-food restaurants on Japanese youth was emphasized in a survey taken by the Japanese Ministry of Agriculture, which found that more than 50 percent of the country's teenagers would rather eat Western foods than the traditional dishes. U.S.-based fast-food restaurants such as McDonald's (Japan's largest restaurant business), Dairy Queen, Mister Donut, and Kentucky Fried Chicken account for half this business. McDonald's alone is grossing over $3 billion annually, more than 10 percent of the company's global sales.[28]

The experience of the suppliers to the youth market already indicates that this too is essentially an international market segment, much like the market for luxury goods. The director of MTV Europe says that "18-year-olds in Paris have more in common with 18-year-olds in New York than with their own parents. They buy the same products, go to the same movies, listen to the same music, sip the same colas. Global advertising merely works on that premise." Almost all MTV Europe's 200 advertisers run unified English-language campaigns across its 28-nation broadcast area.[29] This means marketers can formulate global advertising campaigns for these consumers that will require little more than a translation into the local language. Before making the decision

Are these teens in Japan or the United States? Japan. But, like teens in the United States, they wear Levi's and carry American skateboards.
Catherine Karnow/Woodfin Camp

concerning local versus foreign identity, however, management should check with local personnel on a country-by-country basis.

Inasmuch as communication, the reason for advertising, is impossible if the language is not understood, translations must be made into the language of the consumers. Unfortunately for the advertiser, almost every language varies from one country to another. The same word may be perfectly apt in one country while signifying something completely different or even vulgar in another, as illustrated in Chapter 9. To avoid translation errors, the experienced advertising manager will use (1) a back translation and (2) plenty of illustrations with short copy.

Because a nation's laws generally reflect public opinion, closely allied to the cultural forces are the legal forces, which exert an extremely pervasive influence on advertising. We have seen how laws affect media availability, but they also restrict the kinds of products that can be advertised and even the copy employed in the advertisements.

American firms accustomed to using comparative advertising at home are surprised to find that legal restrictions on this technique exist in some markets. Since the early 1990s Pepsi-Cola has used comparative advertising to knock Coca-Cola, and wherever possible, Coke has used the courts to stop the ads.

PepsiCo launched a series of TV commercials in 1995 aimed at testing the comparative advertising laws of 30 countries. The ads presented the competitor's product in a way that is specifically prohibited in some countries as unfair advertising. The marketing head of Pepsi-Cola said that the company "intended to push the envelope on comparison advertising in markets around the world."[30] Because of the grueling legal battle between Pepsi-Cola and Coca-Cola over the Pepsi Challenge campaign as well as other conflicts over comparative advertising, existing laws in various Latin American countries were found to be inadequate. To avoid the passage of more laws, members of the advertising industry have established self-regulatory bodies in a number of these nations to settle disputes out of court.[31] In Europe, the European Commission authorized comparative advertising subject to restrictions because some members permitted it while others did not. Germany's comparative advertising law is so strict that Goodyear couldn't even use its multinational tire campaign stating that nylon tire cord is stronger than steel. Incredibly, the steel wire manufacturers complained of "unfair competition."

Advertisers in the Islamic nations have had to be resourceful to avoid censorship. The use of women's photos in advertisements is not forbidden, but the models are usually Western—preferably blondes or redheads. "Erotic" sound effects are not permitted: a TV soft-drink commercial with a girl licking her lips to show she liked the taste was declared "obscene." In Pakistan, women models may advertise only women's products on TV. They cannot advertise cars or men's cologne, for example. Imagine Ford trying to sell its Mercury with a slinky male posed seductively behind the wheel, or how about an all-male Old Spice commercial?[32]

Globalization versus Localization. With so many obstacles to international standardization, what should be the approach of the international advertising manager? The opinion of some experts seems to be that good ideas and good promotions can cross international borders. Robert Trebus, an ad agency executive, believes that far too often businesspeople are convinced that to be successful in different markets, they must approach each market differently.[33] However, the director of multinational accounts at McCann-Erickson claims that social classes across different countries have shared sensibilities: "A male middle executive in Italy has more in common with a male middle executive in the U.K. than with a farmer in Italy. It is those shared sensibilities that make global branding possible."[34]

This school of thought looks for similarities across segments and countries to capitalize on them by providing promotional themes with worldwide appeal, the strategy now followed by global corporations. A second school of thought believes that even though human nature is the same everywhere, it is also true that a Spaniard will remain a Spaniard and a Belgian a Belgian. Thus, it is preferable to develop separate appeals to take advantage of the differences among customers in different cultures and countries.

Neither Purely Global Nor Purely Local. You probably have already gathered from this discussion that for most firms neither a purely global nor a purely local campaign is the best way to handle international advertising. In fact, the president of a large international ad agency stated long ago, "About 15 percent of the multinational companies have global approaches, meaning campaigns will be roughly the same everywhere. Another 15 percent have strictly local approaches. But these two groups are rapidly disappearing into a group we call 'glocal,' meaning advertisers that have developed a common strategy for large regions."[35] Coca-Cola says simply, "Think globally, but act locally."

Gillette's Panregional Approach. Gillette has its advertising organized in the following regional and cultural clusters: pan-Latin America, pan-Middle East, pan-Africa, and pan-Atlantic. The international advertising manager says the arrangement is based on the belief that the company can identify the same needs and buying motives among consumers in regions or countries linked by culture, consumers' habits, and level of market development for their products. Gillette might use the same European-style advertising for Australia and South Africa, but in Asia it would link developing economies such as the Philippines, Indonesia, Thailand, and Malaysia. It will market the Asian tigers—Singapore, Hong Kong, and Taiwan—together but handle Japan, China, and India separately.

Gillette, which sells 800 products in 200 countries, is trying to approximate a global marketing strategy with its panregional strategy while allowing for regional and national differences. A vice president of Gillette's ad agency, who is also the firm's associate media director, explains Gillette's approach this way: "Our strategy is to develop the best media plans for each country, but then look for pangeographic opportunities to enhance the coverage."[36]

Programmed-Management Approach. Another middle-ground advertising strategy is what some call the **programmed-management approach,** in which the home office and the foreign subsidiaries agree on marketing objectives, after which each puts together a tentative advertising campaign. This is submitted to the home office for review and suggestions. The campaign is then market tested locally, and the results are submitted to the home office, which reviews them and offers comments. The subsidiary then submits a complete campaign to the home office for review. When the home of-

programmed-management approach
A middle-ground advertising strategy between globally standardized and entirely local programs.

fice is satisfied, the budget is approved and the subsidiary begins implementing the campaign. The result may be a highly standardized campaign for all markets or one that has been individualized to the extent necessary to cope with local market conditions. The programmed-management approach gives the home office a chance to standardize those parts of the campaign that can be standardized but still permits flexibility in responding to different marketing conditions.

Personal Selling

Along with advertising, personal selling constitutes a principal component of the promotional mix. The importance of this promotional tool compared to advertising depends to a great extent on the relative costs, the funds available, media availability, and the type of product sold.

Just as in the United States, manufacturers of industrial products rely more on personal selling than on advertising to communicate with their overseas markets. However, producers of consumer products may also emphasize personal selling overseas, especially in the developing countries, because salespeople in those countries will often work for less compensation than would be demanded in the home country. A newcomer to marketing must be careful nonetheless to consider all the expenses in maintaining a salesperson, as expense items such as automobiles and their maintenance (rough treatment on bad roads) frequently may be three or four times the U.S. cost. Fringe benefits are commonly stipulated by law, and these too often constitute a higher percentage of the base wage in other countries.

Personal Selling and the Internet. The Internet would seem to eliminate the need for personal selling, but some evidence suggests that that may not be the case. Consider the fact that successful personal selling depends on establishing trust. Although the Internet makes communication easier, it may make building trust harder. Computer-mediated communication transmits much less nonverbal information than does face-to-face communication, and this nonverbal communication transmits much information about emotions, cooperation, and trustworthiness. Eye contact, nods, hesitation—measured in milliseconds—are lost. Also, the feedback which allows a person to change a message while it is being delivered is lost. Even high-quality video—which is not likely to arrive soon in any case—reduces but doesn't eliminate weak social cues and the feeling of psychological distance resulting from computer-mediated communication. These considerations led one group of authors to conclude that computer-mediated communication will actually require more frequent face-to-face encounters so that deep relationships are built which allow both parties to trust the other in the bleaker, less informative Internet setting.[37]

International Standardization. By and large, the organization of an overseas sales force, sales presentation, and training methods are very similar to those employed in the home country.

> Avon follows the same plan of person-to-person selling in Venezuela or in Russia that it does in the United States and is extremely successful with it. When Avon entered Mexico, many of the local experts predicted that its plan would fail. The Mexican middle-class housewife would be out of the home shopping and playing bridge. The wall around the house would keep the Avon lady from reaching the front door, and when she rang the bell, the maid would not let her in. Other American firms had used this approach and had failed for these reasons. However, Avon made small but important changes. It mounted a massive advertising campaign to educate Mexicans as to what they could expect from the visits before sending its salespeople out. Although the advertisements were the same as those in the United States, the advertising campaign was more extensive because the Mexican housewife had to be taught a new concept. This was not the common door-to-door salesperson whom she knew but a professional trained to help her look beautiful. Avon recruited educated middle-class women as representatives and trained them well. They were encouraged to visit their friends, much as Tupperware representatives do. What was essentially an American plan with slight changes for cultural differences made Avon's entry into the Mexican market an unqualified success.[38]

Other firms also follow their home country approach. Missionary salespeople from pharmaceutical manufacturers such as Pfizer and Upjohn introduce their products to physicians, just as they do in the United States. Salespeople calling on channel members perform the same tasks of informing middlemen, setting up point-of-purchase displays, and fighting for shelf space as do their American counterparts.

China was identified as the number one growth opportunity for Avon ladies in the 1990s.
Dan Groshong/Corbis Sygma

Dell Computer is selling computers in Japan and Europe by mail and telemarketing, although the company's vice president for international operations remembers, "In every country, they told us mail orders would not work." There was also a question about Dell's low price in Europe. Dell executives found that European buyers have a long-established prejudice: high price equals good quality, low price means shoddy quality. Yet Dell has surprised its competitors with its success in both markets. Starting in the last half of 1992, the firm's European sales, according to the latest report, amounted to 26 percent of its total revenue, and sales in the Asian Pacific region (Japan is the major component) accounted for 6 percent.[39]

Recruitment. Recruiting salespeople in foreign countries is at times more difficult than recruiting them at home because sales managers frequently have to cope with the stigma attached to selling that exists in some areas.

Another instance of the influence of cultural forces on recruiting is the need to hire salespeople who are culturally acceptable to customers and channel members. This can be difficult and costly in an already small market that is further subdivided into several distinct cultures with different customs and even languages, as we saw in the chapter on physical forces. If a cultural pocket will support a salesperson at all, the experienced sales manager will make every effort to recruit a person indigenous to the region.

American firms are aided in recruitment by their reputation for having excellent training programs. These programs generally come from the home office and are adapted to local conditions. When the product is highly technical, the new employees are often sent to the home office for training. Of course, the opportunity to take such a trip is also an effective recruiting tool.

Sales Promotion

sales promotion
Selling aids, including displays, premiums, contests, and gifts

Sales promotion provides the selling aids for the marketing function and includes such activities as the preparation of point-of-purchase displays, contests, premiums, trade show exhibits, cents-off offers, and coupons.

The international standardization of the sales promotion function is not difficult, because experience has shown that what is successful in the United States generally proves effective overseas. Couponing is a good example. Several European markets and Canada are experiencing rapid growth. Annual redemption of 18.5 coupons per household in Belgium and 15.9 per household in the United Kingdom is far below the 80.9 in the United States. In Italy and Spain, redemption is only 4.3 and 1.5, respectively. One major difference is the method of distribution. In the United States the free-standing insert is the most frequently employed, whereas in Europe coupons are distributed in stores, usually on the package itself. Newcomers to Europe should check each country's laws concerning coupons inasmuch as they are illegal or their use is severely restricted in a number of markets.[40]

When marketers are considering transferring sales promotion techniques to other markets, they must consider some cultural constraints.

Sociocultural and Economic Constraints. Cultural and economic constraints make some sales promotions difficult to use. If a premium is to fulfill the objective of being a sales aid for the product, it must be meaningful to the purchaser. A gadget to be used in the kitchen might be valued by an American but will not be particularly attractive to a

Latin American with two maids to do the housework. Putting the prize inside the package is no guarantee that it will be there when the purchaser takes the package home.

> While living in Mexico, one of the writers bought a product for the plastic toy it contained. When he opened the package at home, there was no toy. Examining the package closely, he found that a small slit had been made in the top. Where labor costs and store revenues are low, the income from the sale of these premiums is an extra profit for the retailer.

Contests, raffles, and games, however, have been extremely successful in countries where people love to play the odds. If Latin Americans or the Irish will buy a lottery ticket week after week, hoping to win the grand prize playing against odds of 500,000 to 1, why shouldn't they participate in a contest that costs them nothing to enter? Point-of-purchase displays are well accepted by retailers, though many establishments are so small that there is simply no place to put all the displays that are offered to them. Sales promotion may not be as sophisticated overseas as it is in the United States, and our experience indicates that even American subsidiaries do not make sufficient use of the ideas coming from headquarters. The marketing manager who prepares a well-planned program after studying the constraints of the local markets can expect excellent results from the time and money invested.

Two Unsuccessful Sales Promotions. In the 1990s there have been two famous, expensive examples of sales promotions that went wrong: Hoover in the United Kingdom and Pepsi-Cola in the Philippines.

Hoover in the UK. Hoover's promotional campaign is probably the most disastrous sales promotion in history. In the fall of 1992, the company offered two free air tickets to continental Europe or the United States to anyone spending at least £100 ($150) on Hoover products. Customers spending £300 would also receive free car rentals and hotel rooms. Inasmuch as the cheapest pair of tickets cost £500, 200,000 customers rushed to buy inexpensive vacuum cleaners for £120. Hoover's mistake was to assume that most people would not collect their tickets after reading the offer's fine print laying down the conditions about when the flight could be taken and which hotels could be used.

So many customers were infuriated about delays in obtaining tickets that Maytag, Hoover's owner, sent a team from the U.S. headquarters that fired the managing director and set up a task force of 250 people to issue the tickets. Maytag first announced it would take a $30 million charge against profits to pay for the ill-fated promotion but later said it would cost $72.6 million.[41]

Pepsi-Cola in the Philippines. In February 1992, the Pepsi bottler in the Philippines began a promotion called "Number Fever," which would award cash prizes for winning numbers under bottle caps. When the company launched the promotion, it had only 16 percent of the market. But by April the promotion had been so successful (Pepsi's market share rose to 23 percent), the firm extended it to a second stage of an additional five weeks. On May 25, 1992, the winning number, 349, was drawn by computer and announced. Unfortunately, 349 had been printed on 900,000 caps, half of which carried a 1 million peso ($37,700) prize. A Pepsi employee discovered the error and tried to withdraw the number, but a news show had already announced it.

Because of the error, the company faced paying the winners $18 billion. It quickly suggested an offer of $19 to each person with a 349 cap. Since June 1992 the company has paid out $10 million, but still many people are not satisfied. PepsiCo, anxious to distance itself from the affair, says the promotion is a local problem. Pepsi's market share, which had gone to 25 percent, plunged to 16 percent.[42]

public relations
Various methods of communicating with the firm's publics to secure a favorable impression

Public Relations

Public relations is the firm's communications and relationships with its various publics, including the governments where it operates, or as one writer has put it, "Public relations is the marketing of the firm." Although American internationals have had organized public relations programs for many years in the United States, they have paid much less attention to this important function elsewhere.

Ironically, it is on the whole not true that they have neglected public service activities through their foreign subsidiaries—only that they have failed to inform their publics of what they are doing. Exxon has for years sponsored the study of foreign art students in the United States, and the ITT International Fellowship Program, started in 1973, has enabled more than 750 students from 54 countries to pursue advanced degrees in the United States and abroad.

Overseas subsidiaries of American firms support public service activities locally. In Japan, Coca-Cola spends $5 million annually on good works such as programs for children and those with disabilities. IBM Japan puts 1 percent of its profits into good works. Procter & Gamble contributes millions of dollars annually to community projects in over 60 countries.[43]

Nationalism and antimultinational feeling in many countries have made it imperative for companies with international operations to improve their communications to their nonbusiness publics with more effective public relations programs.

International pharmaceutical manufacturers are often viewed suspiciously by the public in developing nations. They are viewed as alleviating suffering, but they are making a profit at the poor people's expense. To improve its image, Warner-Lambert began a program in Africa called Tropicare that trained local health care providers in preventive medicine with audiovisual materials. In each country, the company organized a commission of experts from national and international health organizations to ensure the quality of the educational material used in the program. The African program was so successful that Warner-Lambert later introduced it in Latin America.

One of the most vexing problems for firms is how to deal with critics of their operations and motives. Some try to defuse criticism by holding regularly scheduled meetings at which topics of interest are debated. Others prefer to meet with critics privately, though they may find themselves caught in a never-ending relationship in which the critics continually escalate their demands. This is especially true of single-issue groups, whose existence depends on the continuance of the issue.

A successful strategy employed by some firms has been to address the issue without dealing directly with the critics. Instead, they work with international or governmental agencies. For example, in China recently a number of foreign firms which have achieved success—among them Toshiba, Philips, and Canon—have found themselves under fire by the Chinese media. Scott Kronick of Ogilvy Public Relations Worldwide recommends that if the coverage is too unbalanced, firms should complain to the Propaganda Department. Although the Department is not actually part of the government, it is an arm of the Communist Party apparatus and its head is an alternate member of the Politburo.[44] Another alternative is to do nothing. If the criticism receives no publicity, it may die from lack of interest. However, sometimes it is necessary for a libeled company to defend its reputation in court. McDonald's was the victim when, in the 1980s, Helen Steel and Dave Morris in London started distributing leaflets accusing the company of starving the Third World, exploiting children in its advertising, and destroying the Central American rain forests. It was also cruel to animals, they alleged, because at times chickens were still conscious when their throats were cut.

McDonald's sued Steel and Morris, a gardener and a postman, in 1994. It became the longest trial in history, ending two and a half years later. McDonald's was awarded $98,000 in damages in a case it had spent $16 billion to pursue. Despite the award (which McDonald's has never collected), there is now a major anti-Mcdonald's Web site (www.McSpotlight.org) dedicated to protests against McDonald's, and in fact Steel and Morris maintain that October 16 has become Worldwide Anti-McDonald's Day.[45]

Pricing Strategies

Pricing, the third element of the marketing mix, is an important and complex consideration in formulating the marketing strategy. Pricing decisions affect other corporate functions, directly determine the firm's gross revenue, and are a major determinant of profits.

Pricing, a Controllable Variable

Effective price setting consists of more than mechanically adding a standard markup to a cost. To obtain the maximum benefits from pricing, management must regard it in the same manner as it does other controllable variables; that is, pricing is one of the marketing mix elements that can be varied to achieve the marketing objectives of the firm.

For instance, if the marketer wishes to position a product as a high-quality item, setting a relatively high price will reinforce promotion that emphasizes quality. However, combining a recognizably low price with a promotional emphasis on quality could result in an incongruous pairing that would adversely affect its credibility with the consumer. Pricing can also be a determinant in the choice of middlemen, because if the firm requires a wholesaler to take title to, stock, promote, and deliver the merchandise, it must give the wholesaler a much larger trade discount than would be demanded by a broker, whose services are much more limited.

These examples illustrate one of the reasons for the complexity of price setting: the interaction of pricing with the other elements of the marketing mix. In addition, two other sets of forces influence this variable: (1) interaction between marketing and the other functional areas of the firm and (2) environmental forces.

Interaction between Marketing and the Other Functional Areas. To illustrate this point, look at the following:

1. The finance people want prices that are both profitable and conducive to a steady cash flow.
2. Production supervisors want prices that create large sales volumes, which permit long production runs.
3. The legal department worries about possible antitrust violations when different prices are set according to type of customer.
4. The tax people are concerned with the effects of prices on tax loads.
5. The domestic sales manager wants export prices to be high enough to avoid having to compete with company products that are purchased for export and then diverted to the domestic market (one aspect of parallel importing).

The marketer must address all these concerns and also consider the impact of the legal and other environmental forces that we examined in Section Three. Table 16.3 at the end of this chapter examines this aspect of pricing in greater detail.

International Standardization

Companies that pursue a policy of unifying corporate pricing procedures worldwide know that pricing is acted on by the same forces that militate against the international standardization of the other marketing mix components. Pricing for the overseas markets is more complex because managements must be concerned with two kinds of pricing: (1) **foreign national pricing,** which is domestic pricing in another country, and (2) **international pricing** for exports.

foreign national pricing
Local pricing in another country

international pricing
setting prices of goods for export for both unrelated and related firms.

Foreign National Pricing. Some foreign governments fix prices on just about everything, while others are concerned only with essential goods. In nations with laws on unfair competition, the minimum sales price may be controlled rather than the maximum. The German law is so comprehensive that under certain conditions even premiums and cents-off coupons may be prohibited because they violate the minimum price requirements. The international marketer must be watchful of a recent tendency of many nations, especially European Union (EU) members, to open their markets to price competition by weakening and even abolishing retail price maintenance laws.

Prices can vary because of cost differentials on opposite sides of a border. One government may levy higher import duties on imported raw materials or may subsidize public utilities, while another may not. Differences in labor legislation cause labor costs to vary. Competition among local suppliers may be intense in one market, permitting the affiliate to buy inputs at better prices than those paid by an affiliate in another market.

Competition on the selling side is also diverse. Frequently, an affiliate in one market will face heavy local competition and be limited in the price it can charge, while in a neighboring market a lack of competitors will allow another affiliate to charge a much higher price. As regional economic groupings reduce trade barriers among members, such opportunities are becoming fewer because firms must meet regional as well as local competition.

One thing European firms cannot do is agree to fix prices in an effort to limit competition. The EU Commission has imposed fines as high as $116.7 million for price fixing and collaboration. The record fine on a single company is $93 million on Tetra Pak, a Swedish packaging firm, in 1991.[46]

Because a firm usually does not introduce a new product simultaneously in all markets, the same product will not be in the same stage of the product life cycle everywhere. In markets where it is in the introductory stage, there is an opportunity to charge a high "skimming" price or a low "penetration" price, depending on such factors as market objectives, patent protection, price elasticity of demand, and competition. As the product reaches the maturity or decline stage, the price may be lowered if doing so permits a satisfactory return. Because life cycles vary among markets, prices too will be different.

International Pricing

International pricing involves the setting of prices for goods produced in one country and sold in another. The pricing of exports to unrelated customers falls in this category and will be treated separately in the chapter on exporting. A special kind of exporting, *intracorporate sales,* is exceedingly common among worldwide companies as they attempt to require subsidiaries to specialize in the manufacture of some products while importing others. Their imports may consist of components that are assembled into the end product, such as engines made in one country that are mounted in car bodies built in another, or they may be finished products imported to complement the product mix of an affiliate. No matter what the end use is, problems exist in setting a **transfer price.**

transfer price
Intracorporate price, or the price of a good or service sold by one affiliate to another, the home office to an affiliate, or vice versa

Because it is possible for the firm as a whole to gain while both the buying and the selling subsidiaries "lose" (receive prices that are lower than would be obtained through an outside transaction), the tendency is for transfer prices to be set at headquarters. The reason for this apparent anomaly is that the company obtains a profit from *both* the seller and the buyer.

The selling affiliate would like to charge other subsidiaries the same price it charges all customers, but when combined with transportation costs and import duties, such a price may make it impossible for the importing subsidiary to compete in its market. If headquarters dictates that a lower-than-market transfer price be charged, the seller will be unhappy because its profit-and-loss statement suffers. This can be a very real headache to personnel whose promotion bonuses depend on the bottom line.

Both foreign governments and the U.S. government are also interested in profits and the part transfer prices play in their realization because profits affect the amount of taxes paid. American and foreign tax agents have become aware that because of differences in tax structures, a firm can obtain meaningful profits by ordering a subsidiary in a country with high corporate taxes to sell at cost to a subsidiary in a country where corporate taxes are lower. The profit is earned where less income tax is paid, and the company clearly gains.

A study by two Florida International University professors found that high invoice prices on American imports and low prices on U.S. exports to avoid U.S. income taxes may have cost this country $40 billion in tax revenues. For example, razor blades from Israel were invoiced at 3 cents, while identical blades from Panama were priced at $29.35 each. Spark plugs going to Taiwan were billed at *1 cent* each. Would you believe that importers of Japanese instant-print cameras paid $2,538 *each* or that American importers paid $720 for a bottle of salad dressing? Not only is there no profit

[Figure 16.3] **Hiding Profits with Transfer Pricing**

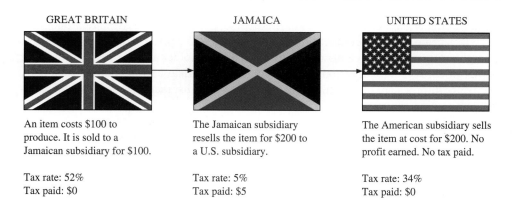

GREAT BRITAIN	JAMAICA	UNITED STATES
An item costs $100 to produce. It is sold to a Jamaican subsidiary for $100.	The Jamaican subsidiary resells the item for $200 to a U.S. subsidiary.	The American subsidiary sells the item at cost for $200. No profit earned. No tax paid.
Tax rate: 52% Tax paid: $0	Tax rate: 5% Tax paid: $5	Tax rate: 34% Tax paid: $0

to be taxed in these transactions, high import prices enable money launderers to send large sums of money out of the country.[47] Figure 16.3 shows how firms can hide profits with transfer pricing.

Increasingly, of course, the Internet is redefining the options. It is a tremendous tool for comparing prices—already sites can scan up to 300 outlets for prices on certain goods—and so national boundaries may mean less and less. In a sense, world prices for consumers may be on the way to being achieved. The effect extends to business-to-business pricing as well.

Distribution Strategies

The development of distribution strategies is difficult in the home country, but it is even more so internationally, where marketing managers must concern themselves with two functions rather than one: (1) getting the products *to* foreign markets (exporting) and (2) distributing the products *within* each market.

Interdependence of Distribution Decisions

In making decisions on distribution, care must be taken to analyze their interdependence with the other marketing mix variables. For example, if the product requires considerable after-sales servicing, the firm will want to sell through dealers that have the facilities, personnel, and capital to purchase equipment and spare parts and train servicepeople. Channel decisions are critical because they are long-term decisions; once established, they are far less easy to change than those made for price, product, and promotion.

International Standardization

Although management would prefer to standardize distribution patterns internationally, there are two fundamental constraints on doing so: (1) the variation in the availability of channel members among the firm's markets and (2) the inconsistency of the influence of the environmental forces. Because of these constraints, international managers have found it best to establish a basic but flexible overall policy. The subsidiaries then implement this policy and design channel strategies to meet local conditions.

Availability of Channel Members. As a starting point in their channel design, local managers have the successful distribution system used in the domestic operation. Headquarters' support for a policy of employing the same channels worldwide will be especially strong when the entire marketing mix has been built around a particular channel type, such as direct sales force or franchised operators. Encyclopaedia Britannica and McDonald's are examples of firms that consider their distribution systems inviolate, so locally there is little latitude in planning channel strategies.

Foreign Environmental Forces. Environmental differences among markets add to the difficulty in standardizing distribution channels. Changes caused by the cultural forces generally occur over time, but those caused by the legal forces can be radical and quick and can dramatically slow trends responding to cultural demands.

To illustrate, hypermarkets, which are changing distribution patterns in Europe and particularly in France numbered only 11 in that country in 1972. The combination of lower prices and one-stop shopping caught on with the French consumer, and 51 hypermarkets were opened in 1973. Manufacturers that saw a quick end to small shopkeepers failed to appreciate their political power. The Royer Law, passed in 1973, gave local urban commissions, often dominated by small merchants, the power to refuse construction permits for supermarkets and hypermarkets. After the law took effect, only 40 percent of large-store applications were approved.

Although the trend toward more giant stores did not stop, the growth certainly slowed. There were only about 1,000 hypermarkets in 1993 when France's prime minister announced a freeze on new construction. Both major hypermarket chains immediately complained about the order, even though France's retail sector is saturated and has little room for growth. A new law banning the opening of new stores above 300 square meters was passed in 1996 to keep small shopkeepers from being driven out of business.[48]

Japan's Large Scale Retailers Law, very similar to the French law, had also slowed the opening of large retailers. However, because of pressure from the U.S. trade representative, and the trade talks called the Structural Impediments Initiative (SII), the Japanese Ministry of International Trade and Industry suddenly found it could reduce the period during which small retailers could block the opening of new stores in their neighborhoods from an incredible 10 years to a maximum of 18 months. The Japanese government scrapped the law completely in 1997.

On the other hand, Japan—which has been behind the United States in terms of Internet use—is catching up, and one result is that retail stores are now being regarded as superfluous. When Sony launched its $2,000 electronic pet *Aibo* (Partner) in 1999, it sold out of stock in 20 minutes on the Internet. None ever were sent to stores. Sony has decided to set up an online store—SonyStyle.com—which will cannibalize sales by Sony's own chain of 2,000 retail stores. In fact, Sony is regarded as being in better position than Matsushita, which has 20,500 stores, all of which are seen as a future liability.[49]

Another restriction of distribution has been tried in the EU. Manufacturers have attempted to prevent distributors from selling across national borders, but the Commission has prohibited them from doing so by invoking EU antitrust laws. Exclusive distributorships have been permitted, but every time the manufacturer has included a clause prohibiting the distributor from exporting to another EU country, the clause has been stricken from the contract. In effect, a firm that has two factories in the EU with different costs, and thus distinct prices, is practically powerless to prevent products from the lower-cost affiliate from competing with higher-cost products from the other affiliate.

Economic differences also make international standardization difficult, although marketers can adapt to economic changes. In Japan, high prices have forced women to find jobs, and they no longer have time to shop and prepare the traditional Japanese foods. They fill their needs by purchasing more convenience foods advertised on TV with home delivery or by going to the more than 50 chains of convenience stores. The largest, 7-Eleven, has over 8,500 stores, many of which are run by former small shopkeepers. These convenience stores are also learning to take advantage of the Internet. Many Japanese are reluctant to use credit cards for online transactions, and so convenience stores (*combini*) serve as pickup centers where online orders can be picked up and paid for in cash. Worldwide, marketers are seeing cultural barriers fall as economic conditions force housewives to obtain employment to supplement household income. The premium that outside employment places on their time is leading them to prefer one-stop shopping, labor-saving devices, and convenience foods. The result is an upheaval in the way goods are distributed, but American marketers that have U.S. experience as a guide are in a position to make inroads on their foreign competitors, for which this is a new phenomenon.

Can retailing be globalized? Retailers such as France's Carrefour, with stores in France, Spain, Brazil, Argentina, and the United States, think it can. So do Safeway, Gucci, Cartier, Benetton, and Toys "Я" Us, which have made aggressive penetration in Canada, Europe, Hong Kong, and Singapore. Kaufhof, the German retailing giant, has 100 shoe stores located in Austria, France, Switzerland, and Germany and is also the leading mail-order shoe retailer in Europe.

Disintermediation

This long and difficult word refers to the unraveling of traditional distribution structures and is most often the result of being able to combine the Internet with fast delivery services such as FedEx and UPS. Increasingly, these tools are shaking up traditional distribution channels and making it possible to offer rapid service with, or without, a full-blown dedicated distribution structure. As has been pointed out, a deadly disease can spread worldwide in a matter of days since for all intents and purposes, no one in the world is ever one day from an airport which will allow that person to travel fairly quickly to any other city in the world. In the same way, the increasing ability to ship products quickly may mean that the lack of dedicated channels makes less and less difference over time.

At the same time, there are difficulties from the end users' perspective which still have to be ironed out. Sam Milford paid $110 for a CD-ROM from a reputable U.S. vendor but found that the cost of getting the CD-ROM from Heathrow Airport to his home in Brighton was $159. Forrester Research estimates that 85 percent of online companies are not capable of shipping across borders yet.[50]

Channel Selection

Direct or Indirect Marketing

The first decision that management must make is whether to use middlemen, because it frequently has the option of marketing directly to the final user. Sales to original equipment manufacturers (OEMs)* and governments are, for the most part, made directly, as are the sales of high-priced industrial products such as turbines and locomotives, because the firm is dealing with relatively few customers and transactions but with large dollar value. Even in these cases, export sales may be consummated by local agents if (1) management believes this is politically expedient or (2) the country's laws demand it.

Other types of industrial products and consumer goods are marketed indirectly. The channel members are selected on the basis of their market coverage, cost, and susceptibility to company control. They must also, of course, perform the functions required by management.

Factors Influencing Channel Selection

The factors that influence the selection of market channels may be classified as the characteristics of the market, the product, the company, and the middlemen.

Market Characteristics. The obvious place to start in channel selection is at the target markets. Which of the available alternatives offer the best coverage? Because of the variance in the target markets, the firm will most likely require multiple channels. Large retailers, governments, and OEMs may be handled by the company sales force or manufacturers' agents, while smaller retailers are supplied through wholesalers.

Product Characteristics. A low-cost product sold in small quantities per transaction generally requires long channels, but if the goods are perishable, short channels are preferable. If the product is highly technical, it may be impossible to obtain knowledgeable middlemen, and the manufacturer will be forced either to sell directly through company-owned distributors or to train independent middlemen. Caterpillar has enjoyed tremendous success by choosing the second alternative.

*Original equipment manufacturers buy components that are incorporated into the products they produce (for example, spark plugs to an automobile manufacturer).

Company Characteristics. A firm that has adequate financial and managerial resources is in a good position to employ its own sales force or agents. A financially weak company must use middlemen that take title to and pay for the goods. If management is inexperienced in selling to certain markets, it must employ middlemen who have that experience.

Middlemen's Characteristics. Most industrial equipment, large household appliances, and automobiles require considerable after-sales servicing, and much of the firm's success in marketing depends on it. If the firm is not prepared to provide this service, it cannot use agents. The same is true for warehousing and promotion to the final user. If the firm is unable to perform these functions or perceives a cost advantage in not performing them, it must select middlemen that will service, warehouse, and promote its products.

It may be that no channel members are available to reach the firm's target markets and perform the desired functions. If there are none, management must decide to (1) desist from entering the market, (2) select other target markets, or (3) create a new channel. For example, if a frozen-food processor finds that cold-storage facilities are nonexistent, it can either abandon the market or persuade middlemen to acquire the facilities. In a number of overseas markets, firms have purchased the equipment and rented, leased, or sold it on easy terms to distributors and retailers.

> An Italian cheese producer in Brazil not only supplied cold-storage equipment but also established gathering facilities for the dairy farmers. The company provides veterinarians and dairy experts to teach the dairy farmers how to maintain their herds and increase output. Nestlé has similar programs in its developing country markets.

Foreign Environmental Forces and Marketing Mix Matrix

The matrix[51] shown in Table 16.3 summarizes many of the constraints on the internationalization of the marketing mix that have been discussed in this chapter and in Section Three. Table 16.3 will serve as a reminder of the many factors marketing managers should consider when they are contemplating the standardization of marketing mix elements.

Table 16.3 Environmental Constraints to International Standardization of Marketing Mix

Factors Limiting Standardization	Product	Price	Distribution	Personal Selling	Promotion
1. Physical forces	1. Climatic conditions—special packaging, extra insulation, mildew protection, extra cooling capacity, special lubricants, dust protection, special instructions 2. Difficult terrain—stronger parts, larger engines, stronger packing	1. Special product requirements add to costs 2. Difficult terrain—extra transportation costs, higher sales expense (car maintenance, longer travel time, more per diem expense)	1. Difficult terrain—less customer mobility, requiring more outlets, each with more stock 2. Varying climatic conditions—more stock needed when distinct products required for different climates	1. Buyers widely dispersed or concentrated—affects territory and sales force size 2. Difficult terrain—high travel expense, longer travel time, fewer daily sales calls 3. Separate cultures created by physical barriers—salespeople from each culture may be needed	1. Cultural pockets created by barriers—separate ads for languages, dialects, words, customs 2. Different climates—distinct advertising themes

[16] chapter

Table 16.3 *(Continued)*

Factors Limiting Standardization	Product	Price	Distribution	Personal Selling	Promotion
2. Sociocultural forces	1. Consumer attitudes toward product 2. Colors of product and package—varying significance 3. Languages—labels, instructions 4. Religion—consumption patterns 5. Attitudes toward time—differences in acceptance of timesaving products 6. Attitudes toward change—acceptance of new products 7. Educational levels—ability to comprehend instructions, ability to use product 8. Tastes and customs—product use and consumption 9. Different buying habits—package size 10. Who is decision maker? 11. Rural–urban population mix	1. Cultural objections to product—lower prices to penetrate market 2. Lower educational level, lower income—lower prices for mass market 3. Attitudes toward bargaining—affects list prices 4. Customers' attitude toward price	1. More and perhaps specialized outlets to market to various subcultures 2. Buyers accustomed to bargaining—requires small retailers 3. Attitudes toward change—varying acceptance of new kinds of outlets 4. Different buying habits—different types of outlets	1. Separate cultures—separate salespeople 2. Varying attitudes toward work, time, achievement, and wealth among cultures—difficult to motivate and control sales force 3. Different buying behavior—different kinds of sales forces 4. Cultural stigma attached to selling?	1. Language, different or same but with words having different connotations—advertisements, labels, instructions 2. Literacy, low—simple labels, instructions, ads with plenty of graphics 3. Symbolism—responses differ 4. Colors—significances differ 5. Attitudes toward advertising 6. Buying influence—gender, committee, family 7. Cultural pockets—different promotions 8. Religion—taboos and restrictions vary 9. Attitudes toward foreign products and firms
3. Legal political forces	1. Some products prohibited 2. Certain features required or prohibited 3. Label and packaging requirements 4. Varying product standards 5. Varying patent, copyright, and trademark laws 6. Varying import duties 7. Varying import restrictions 8. Local production required of all or part of product	1. Varying retail price maintenance laws 2. Government-controlled prices or markups 3. Antitrust laws 4. Import duties 5. Tax laws 6. Transfer pricing controls	1. Some kinds of channel members outlawed 2. Markups government-controlled 3. Retail price maintenance 4. Turnover taxes 5. Only government-owned channels permitted for some products 6. Restrictions on channel members—number, lines handled, licenses for each line	1. Laws governing discharge of salespeople 2. Laws requiring compensation on discharging salespeople 3. Laws requiring profit sharing, overtime, working conditions 4. Restrictions on channel members	1. Use of languages 2. Legal limits to expenditures 3. Taxes on advertising 4. Prohibition of promotion for some products 5. Special legal requirements for some products (cigarettes, pharmaceuticals) 6. Media availability 7. Trademark laws

Factors Limiting Standardization	Product	Price	Distribution	Personal Selling	Promotion
	9. Requirements to use local inputs that are different from home country inputs 10. Cultural stigma attached to brand name or artwork?		7. Laws on canceling contracts of channel members		8. Taxes that discriminate against some kinds of promotion 9. Controls on language or claims used in ads for some products
4. Economic forces	1. Purchasing power—package size, product sophistication, quality level 2. Wages—varying requirements for labor-saving products 3. Condition of infrastructure—heavier products, hand- instead of power-operated 4. Market size—varying width of product mix	1. Different prices 2. Price elasticity of demand	1. Availability of outlets 2. Size of inventory 3. Size of outlets 4. Dispersion of outlets 5. Extent of self-service 6. Types of outlets 7. Length of channels	1. Sales force expense 2. Availability of employees in labor market	1. Media availability 2. Funds available 3. Emphasis on saving time 4. Experience with products 5. TV, radio ownership 6. Print media readership 7. Quality of media 8. Excessive costs to reach certain market segments
5. Competitive forces	1. Rate of new product introduction 2. Rate of product improvement 3. Quality levels 4. Package size 5. Strength in market	1. Competitors' prices 2. Number of competitors 3. Importance of price in competitor's marketing mix	1. Competitors' control of channel members 2. Competitors' margins to channel members 3. Competitors' choice of channel members	1. Competitors' sales force—number and ability 2. Competitors' emphasis on personal selling in promotional mix 3. Competitors' rates and methods of compensation	1. Competitors' promotional expenditures 2. Competitors' promotional mix 3. Competitors' choice of media
6. Distributive forces	1. Product servicing requirements 2. Package size 3. Branding—dealers' brands	1. Margins required by channel members 2. Special payments required—stocking, promotional	1. Availability of channel members 2. Number of company distribution centers 3. Market coverage by channel members 4. Demands of channel members	1. Size of sales force 2. Kind and quality of sales force	1. Kinds of promotion 2. Amounts of promotion

[Summary]

Understand why there are differences between domestic and international marketing.

Whether a policy or a technique is designed for global use or is first used in the home market and then used overseas, marketers must know where to look for possible differences between marketing domestically and marketing internationally. Sometimes there are great differences; sometimes there are none. Although the basic functions of marketing are the same for all markets, international markets can differ greatly because of the variations in the uncontrollable environmental forces. The marketing manager must decide if the marketing program can be standardized worldwide, if some changes must be made, or if a completely different marketing mix must be prepared.

Explain why international marketing managers may wish to standardize the marketing mix.

International marketing managers prefer to standardize the marketing mix regionally or worldwide because there can be considerable cost savings from marketing the same product, using the same promotional material and the same advertising. A standardized marketing mix is easier to control, and less time is spent preparing the marketing plan.

Comprehend why it is often impossible to standardize the marketing mix worldwide.

A manager may not be able to standardize the marketing mix worldwide because of differences in the environmental forces. The amount of change depends considerably on the product type and the degree of market penetration desired by the manager.

Appreciate the importance of distinguishing among the total product, the physical product, and the brand name.

Much of the confusion about whether a global firm can have global products arises because the discussants do not differentiate between the physical and total products. A total product is easier than a physical product to standardize. A brand name or a product concept may be standardized even though the physical product varies among markets. Also, a firm may have to use a different brand name in a market because its present one has a bad connotation or because it may already be copyrighted by someone else.

Explain why consumer products generally require greater modification for international sales than industrial products or services.

Industrial products and services generally can be marketed globally with less change than can consumer products because they are less sensitive to the foreign environment, as Figure 16.2 indicates.

Discuss the product strategies that can be formed from three product alternatives and three kinds of promotional messages.

Six commonly used promotional strategies can be formulated by combining the three alternatives of marketing the same product everywhere, adapting it, or designing a new product with the same, adapted, or different message.

Explain "glocal" advertising strategies.

International advertising agencies will design an international program for an advertiser and then make local adjustments that local managers deem necessary. The programmed-management approach is an advertising strategy for combining inputs from global advertising advocates of the home office with the opinions of local managers.

Understand some of the effects the Internet may have on international marketing.

Among those mentioned are (1) making more pricing data available worldwide, (2) potentially making traditional channel structures less important, and (3) making the offering much more personalized and therefore more in line with the marketing concept.

Discuss the distribution strategies of international marketers.

Although an international firm would prefer to standardize its distribution patterns internationally, the facts that the same kinds of channel members are not available everywhere and that environmental forces vary among markets make standardization difficult or impossible at times.

[Key Words]

total product (p. 545)
promotion (p. 552)
advertising (p. 553)
programmed-management approach (p. 559)
sales promotion (p. 561)
public relations (p. 562)
foreign national pricing (p. 564)
international pricing (p. 564)
transfer price (p. 565)

[Questions]

1. "Consumers are not standardized globally; therefore, with global brands, you either get lowest common denominator advertising or you get advertising that's right somewhere but wrong elsewhere." This is an actual statement by a CEO of an international advertising agency. What's your opinion?
2. What future do you see for global advertising?
3. Are there any advantages to standardizing the marketing mix worldwide?
4. Why are manufacturers increasing their use of global and regional brands?
5. What is the basis for Gillette's taking its panregional approach?
6. What is a generality about similarities of social and cultural values in a country?
7. Why is food retailing changing in Europe and Japan?
8. Why must a marketer consider the economic forces when formulating a product strategy? Give some examples.
9. Based on the discussion in the personal selling section about problems with Internet communication, which of the following two firms is more likely to be successful? Firm A expects to use the Internet as a tool to continue the relationships with its foreign customers that were first set up in person. Firm B expects to use the Internet to make a first sale to overseas buyers. Firm salesmen will then make personal selling trips to those firms which have already proved they are worth a visit because they have made a first purchase over the Internet.
10. Compare the amount of tax paid in the transactions shown in Figure 16.3 with a straight sale by the British subsidiary for $100 to the U.S. subsidiary, which then sells the item for $200.

[Internet Exercises]

Using the Internet

1. In *Advertising Age*'s "Dataplace," the table "Top Global Marketers in Latin America" shows that Unilever, the British–Dutch consumer products firm, spent more in 1998 advertising in Argentina and Chile than did any other advertiser.
   a. Are there any of the eight countries where Unilever doesn't lead in spending on advertising?

b. Does P&G lead in advertising expenditures in any Latin American nation?
c. According to the *Advertising Age* table "Top 100 Global Marketers," which are the five largest spenders on advertising in the world?
d. Are all five firms consumer products manufacturers?
e. Compare the total spending in 1998 by P&G and Unilever. In what area, U.S. or non-U.S., is there a greater difference between the two companies' spending?

2. According to the section "Preparing to Win in the 21st Century" in the P&G annual report,
   a. Does P&G have any global brands that are market leaders in a national market, or are national brands the national market leaders?
   b. What does management say about constant improvement of products with respect to market leadership?
   c. Unlike pharmaceutical companies, P&G is in a low-tech industry—consumer products. How many patents did the company file for in 1995?
   d. As a careful marketer, does P&G management say the firm tests a product innovation in a national market overseas before going worldwide with it?

[Minicase 16.1]

U.S. Pharmaceutical of Korea*

U.S. Pharmaceutical of Korea (USPK) was formed in 1969. Its one manufacturing plant is located just outside Seoul, the capital. Although the company distributes its products throughout South Korea, 40 percent of its total sales of $5 million were made in the capital last year.

There are no governmental restrictions on whom the company can sell to. The only requirement is that the wholesaler, retailer, or end user have a business license and a taxation number. Of the 400 wholesalers in the country, 130 are customers of USPK, accounting for 46 percent of the company's total sales. The company also sells directly to 2,100 of the country's 10,000 retailers; these account for 45 percent of total sales. The remaining sales are made directly to high-volume end users, such as hospitals and clinics.

Tom Sloane, marketing manager of USPK, would prefer to make about 90 percent of the company's sales directly to retailers and the remaining 10 percent directly to high-volume users. He believes, however, that this strategy is not possible because there are so many small retailers. Not only is the sales volume per retailer small, there is also a risk involved in extending them credit. USPK tends to deal directly with large urban retailers and leaves most of the nonurban retailers to the wholesalers.

However, the use of wholesalers bothers Sloane for two reasons: (1) He has to give them larger discounts than he gives retailers that buy directly from the firm,

*Based on an actual situation in Korea.

and (2) because of the intense competition (300 pharmaceutical manufacturers in Korea), his wholesalers frequently demand larger discounts as the price for remaining loyal to USPK.

This intense competition affects another aspect of USPK's operations—collecting receivables. USPK has found that many wholesalers collect quickly from retailers but delay paying USPK. Instead, they invest in ventures that offer high short-term returns. For example, lending to individuals can bring them interest rates of up to 3 percent a month. The company's receivables, meanwhile, range from 75 to 130 days. Wholesalers are also the cause of another problem. Many are understaffed and have to rely on "drug peddlers" for sales. The drug peddlers (there are perhaps 4,000 just in Seoul) make most of their money either by cutting the wholesalers' margins (selling at lower than recommended prices) or by bartering USPK's products for other pharmaceuticals. They do this by finding retail outlets where products are sold for less than the printed price. They exchange USPK's products at a discount for other drugs, which they sell to other retail outlets at a profit. As a result, USPK's products end up on retailers' shelves at prices lower than those that the company and its reputable wholesalers are selling them for.

The pharmaceutical industry has made some progress in persuading wholesalers and retailers to adhere to company price lists, but nonadherence is still a serious problem. One issue that manufacturers have not been able to resolve yet is the manner in which demands from hospitals and physicians for gifts should be handled.

Sloane believes the industry can do much to solve these problems, although intense competition has thus far kept the pharmaceutical manufacturers from joining together to map out a solution.

1. What should Tom Sloane and U.S. Pharmaceutical of Korea do to improve collections from wholesalers?
2. How would you handle the distribution problem?
3. Can anything be done through firms in the industry to improve the situation?
4. How would you handle the demands for gifts?

[Minicase 16.2]

An Ethical Situation**

The Swiss pharmaceutical global corporation Hoffman-La Roche has made a major breakthrough in the relief of a serious disabling disease that affects 3 percent of the world's population. Its new product, Tigason, is the first product that effectively controls severe cases of psoriasis and dyskeratoses, skin disorders that cause severe flaking of the skin. Sufferers from this disease frequently retreat from society because of fear of rejection, thus losing their families and jobs. Tigason does not cure the disease, but it causes the symptoms to disappear.

**This is an actual situation.

There is one potential problem. Because of the risk of damage to unborn babies, women should not take the drug for one year before conception or during pregnancy. Hoffman-La Roche is well aware of the potential for harm to the company if the product is misused. It has seen the problems of another Swiss firm, Nestlé. After much discussion, the company has decided the product is too important to keep off the market. It is, after all, the product that gives the greatest relief to sufferers.

The marketing department is asked to formulate a strategy for disseminating product information and controlling Tigason's use.

As the marketing manager, what do you recommend?

[Chapter]

17

Export and Import Practices

Speaking on why so many American firms don't do business outside the United States: "The biggest nontariff barrier for Americans in the world is the attitude of the CEO."

—Kenneth Butterworth, CEO of Loctite (80 percent of profits and 60 percent of sales from overseas)

Concept Previews

After reading this chapter, you should be able to:

- **explain** why firms export and the three problem areas of exporting
- **identify** the sources of export counseling
- **describe** the main elements of the export sales assistance program of the U.S. Department of Commerce
- **discuss** the meaning of the various terms of sale
- **identify** some sources of export financing
- **describe** the activities of a foreign freight forwarder
- **understand** the kinds of export documents required
- **discuss** some innovations in materials handling in sea and air transport
- **identify** import sources
- **explain** the Harmonized Tariff Schedule of the United States (HTSUSA)

States. When domestic business starts to boom again, they neglect their export trade or relegate it to a secondary place. Such neglect can seriously harm the business and motivation of their overseas representatives, strangle a U.S. company's own export trade, and leave a firm without recourse when domestic business falls off once more. Even if domestic business remains strong, the company may eventually realize that it has succeeded only in shutting off a valuable source of additional profits.

6. **Failure to treat international distributors on an equal basis with domestic counterparts.** Often, companies carry out institutional advertising campaigns, special discount offers, sales incentive programs, special credit term programs, warranty offers, and so forth in the U.S. market but fail to make similar assistances available to their international distributors. This is a mistake that can destroy the vitality of overseas marketing efforts.
7. **Assuming that a given market technique and product will automatically be successful in all countries.** What works in one market may not work in others. Each market has to be treated separately to ensure maximum success.
8. **Unwillingness to modify products to meet the regulations or cultural preferences of other countries.** Local safety and security codes, as well as import restrictions, cannot be ignored by foreign distributors. If necessary modifications are not made at the factory, the distributor must do them—usually at greater cost and perhaps not as well. It should also be noted that the resulting smaller profit margin makes the account less attractive.
9. **Failure to print service, sale, and warranty messages in locally understood languages.** Although a distributor's top management may speak English, it is unlikely that all sales personnel (let alone service personnel) have this capability. Without a clear understanding of sales messages or service instructions, these persons may be less effective in performing their functions.
10. **Failure to consider the use of an export management company.** If a firm decides it cannot afford its own export department (or has tried one unsuccessfully), it should consider the possibility of appointing an appropriate export management company (EMC).
11. **Failure to consider licensing or joint venture agreements.** Import restrictions in some countries, insufficient personnel/financial resources, or an overly limited product line can cause many companies to dismiss international marketing as unfeasible. Yet many products that compete on a national basis in the United States can be marketed successfully in most markets of the world. A licensing or joint venture arrangement may be the simple, profitable answer to any reservations. In general, all that is needed for success is flexibility in using the proper combination of marketing techniques.
12. **Failure to provide readily available servicing for the product.** A product without the necessary service support can acquire a bad reputation in a short period, potentially preventing further sales. ■

Source: Adapted from *A Basic Guide to Exporting*, NTC Books.

- To meet actual or prospective customers' requests for the firm to export—This type of *accidental exporting* is fairly common. A foreign buyer often will search for something it cannot find locally by consulting the *Thomas Register,* a publication listing American producers for hundreds of products. Every American consulate and local American chamber of commerce (French-American, Mexican-American, and so forth) has a copy.
- To offset cyclical sales of the domestic market.
- To achieve additional sales, which allow the firm to use its excess production capacity to lower unit fixed costs.
- To extend a product's life cycle by exporting to countries where technology is less advanced.
- To distract foreign competitors that are in the firm's home market by entering their home markets.

- To partake in the kind of success the firm's management has seen others achieve by exporting.
- To improve equipment utilization rates.

Why Don't They Export?

The two major reasons U.S. firms give for not exporting are (1) preoccupation with the vast American market and (2) a reluctance to become involved in a new and unknown operation. When nonexporting firms are asked why they are not active in international markets, they generally mention the following as problem areas: (1) locating foreign markets, (2) payment and financing procedures, and (3) export procedures. A group of small businesses gave somewhat different but related reasons. Ninety percent of the respondents to a survey of the National Small Business United, a 65,000-member advocacy group, stated they do not export; the majority said the reasons are that they do not know where to start (locating foreign markets), fear the complexity (payment, financing, and export procedures), or do not know that information and federal support are readily available.[3]

Although considerable assistance is available from the federal and state departments of commerce, banks, the Small Business Administration, Small Business Development Centers (does your school have one?), private consultants (your international business professor may consult), and numerous other sources, some of which we mentioned in Chapter 15, too few managers are taking advantage of this assistance. Let us examine the three problem areas.

Locating Foreign Markets

The first step in locating foreign markets, whether for export or for foreign manufacturing, is to determine whether a market exists for the firm's products. The initial screening step described in Chapter 15 indicated a procedure to follow that will pose no problem for an experienced market analyst who is well acquainted with the available sources of information and assistance. However, newcomers to exporting, especially smaller firms, may still be at a loss as to how to begin; for them, there are a number of export assistance programs available.

Sources of Export Counseling

Trade Information Center

Individuals and firms new to exporting can begin their search for export counseling by calling the U.S. Department of Commerce's Trade Information Center (TIC). The federal government has set this up as the first stop for information about all federal export assistance programs as well as country and regional market information. Before calling the TIC at 1-800-TRADE to talk with a trade specialist, an individual is advised to visit the Trade Information Center website at www.ita.doc.gov/td/tic/.

Trade Information Center Web Site. Among the items you will find at the TIC index page are links to government export programs, trade promotion events, and trade lead information. For example, there are links to 150 sites for trade leads. Go to www.ita.doc.gov/TICFrameset.html. Click on "Export Resources" and then on "Internet Guide to Trade Leads." The aim of the TIC website is to inform the inexperienced about the available resources before they contact the TIC directly for assistance.

Firms that are already exporting and desire to expand their overseas business may bypass the Trade Information Center and go directly to the nearest district office of the Commerce Department's International Trade Administration (ITA). The ITA is the primary U.S. government agency responsible for assisting firms that already are exporting.

International Trade Administration

The ITA offers a wide range of export promotion activities that include export counseling, analysis of foreign markets, assessment of industry competitiveness, and development of market opportunities and sales representation through export promotion events. Three units of ITA work together to provide these services:

1. *International Economic Policy*—Country desk officers in this unit are specialists in specific countries. They keep current on the economic and commercial conditions of their assigned countries so that they can offer information on trade and investment potential to firms that wish to sell to them.
2. *Trade Development*—This unit promotes the trade interests of American industries and offers information on markets and trade practices worldwide. It is divided into seven sectors: aerospace, automotive affairs and consumer goods, basic industries, capital goods and international construction, science and electronics, services, and textiles and apparel. Industry desk officers work with manufacturing and service industry representatives and associations to identify trade opportunities by product or service, industry sector, and market. They also develop export marketing plans and programs. Besides counseling American businesses in exporting, the unit's industry experts conduct executive trade missions, trade fairs, and marketing seminars.
3. *U.S. and Foreign Commercial Service (US&FCS)*—There are 105 district and branch offices throughout the United States and Puerto Rico that have trade specialists to help firms assess their export potential, select markets, locate overseas representatives, and obtain information on the various steps in exporting. Through a district office, a firm has access to all the assistance available in the Commerce Department. For example, the ITA's U.S. and Foreign Commercial Service has commercial officers working in 92 countries who can provide background information on foreign companies and assist in finding foreign representatives, conducting market research, and identifying trade and investment opportunities for American firms. The district offices also conduct export workshops and keep businesspeople informed about domestic and overseas trade events that offer potential for promoting American products.

Small Business Administration

The Office of International Trade of the Small Business Administration (SBA) offers assistance through SBA district offices. The Office of International Trade also works through

1. SCORE programs—Experienced executives offer free one-on-one counseling to small firms.
2. SBDC/SBI programs—Small Business Development Centers (SBDCs) in many universities and colleges give export counseling, especially to inexperienced newcomers. Business students in Small Business Institutes (SBIs) provide in-depth, long-term counseling under faculty supervision.

Department of Agriculture

Like the Department of Commerce, the Department of Agriculture has a single contact point, Ag Exporter Assistance, within its Foreign Agriculture Service (FAS) for agricultural exporters seeking export assistance. Commerce and Agriculture programs are similar in many ways.

Department of Commerce Export Assistance Program

Foreign Market Research

After learning about the company and its products, the international trade specialist might advise the potential exporter to consult the National Trade Data Bank (NTDB), a service that selects the most recent trade promotions, "how to" publications, and international trade and economic data from 15 federal agencies and puts them on one CD-ROM that is updated monthly. The NTDB provides (1) a comprehensive guide for new exporters and (2) a source of specific product and regional information for experienced exporters searching for new markets. It also contains the Foreign Traders Index—a list of foreign importers with descriptions of each one and the products it wishes to import. From this list, the exporter can prepare a mailing list of those interested in its products and then make a bulk mailing. The NTDB is usually available in university SBDCs offering export assistance and in the government documents sections of university libraries. An individual can subscribe to the NTDB as part of the trade and economic information available at the Commerce website, www.stat-usa.gov, for $175 annually or receive CD-ROM discs monthly for an annual subscription fee of $575.[4]

The trade specialist might also suggest using the Trade Opportunities Program (TOP), which provides current sales leads from overseas firms that want to buy or represent American firms. These leads are published in the industry newspaper, *The Journal of Commerce,* and also appear on the Department of Commerce's Stat-USA, available by subscription on the Internet and in the National Trade Data Bank CD-ROM. Another possibility is advertising in *Commercial News,* a catalog-magazine published 10 times annually to promote American products and services in overseas markets. For information, go to www.cnewsusa.com.[5] See also the assistance available from the Commercial Service of the Department of Commerce at www.usatrade.gov/uscs.

Smaller Number of Potential Markets. When the research has identified a small number of potential markets, the firm may then research them by using *Country Commercial Guides* stored on the NTDB, or they can be accessed at the State Department's site at www.state.gov/www/services.html. Click on "Business." The NTDB also has over 10,000 *Market Research Reports* on a wide range of industries in many countries. If there is no *Country Commercial Guide* for the country of interest, a document on the NTDB titled *Country Marketing Plans* is accessible under the *Market Research Reports* series. Another useful publication is *Business America,* a Commerce biweekly magazine whose "International Commerce" section contains announcements about (1) U.S. promotions abroad in which the firm can participate, (2) foreign concerns looking for licensors, joint venture partners, or distributorships, and (3) opportunities to make direct sales.

Direct or Indirect Exporting

When it has been established that there is an existing or potential market for its goods, the firm must choose between exporting indirectly through U.S.-based exporters and exporting directly using its own staff. If it opts for indirect exporting as a way to test the market, the trade specialist can provide assistance in locating one of the types of exporters listed in Chapter 13. However, should the firm prefer to set up its own export operation, it must then obtain overseas distribution.

The exporter may, as we mentioned previously, try a broad-based mailing to solicit representatives or use the Department of Commerce Agent/Distributor Search service for a fee of $250 per market. The exporters may then obtain information covering their commercial activities and competence by asking the Department of Commerce to supply an International Company Profile.[6] Credit reporting agencies, such as Dun & Bradstreet, FCIB (Finance, Credit, and International Business Association), and the exporter's bank, will also supply credit information.

If a firm wants to make a foreign trip, Commerce offers the *Gold Key Service* through many U.S. embassies. This is custom-tailored for managers of American companies who are coming to visit the country and includes orientation briefings, market research, introductions to potential partners, and assistance in developing a marketing strategy for the particular country. The local Commerce District Office can make the arrangements.

The Foreign Agricultural Service of the U.S. Department of Agriculture offers similar services to potential exporters of agricultural products.

Show and Sell

The Department of Commerce also organizes trade events that are helpful in both locating foreign representatives and making sales. There are four kinds:

1. *U.S. pavilions.* Commerce selects about 100 global trade fairs every year to recruit American companies for a U.S. pavilion. Preference is given to fairs in viable markets suitable for firms that are ready to export. Exhibitors receive extensive support from Commerce in management and overseas promotional campaigns to attract business audiences.
2. *Trade missions.* These focus on an industry sector. Participants are given detailed marketing information, advanced publicity, logistical support, and prearranged appointments with potential buyers and government officials. Generally, a mission will consist of 5 to 12 business executives.
3. *Product literature center.* Commerce trade development specialists represent U.S. companies at various international trade shows, distributing literature. They then tell the companies who the interested visitors were for their follow-up.
4. *Reverse trade missions.* The U.S. Trade Development Agency may fund visits to the United States by representatives of foreign governments to meet with American industry and government representatives. The foreign officials represent purchasing authorities interested in buying U.S. equipment for specific projects.

Other Sources of Assistance

Other sources of assistance available to the exporter include the following.

World Trade Centers Association

The World Trade Centers Association, another aid to marketing for the new exporter, was founded by the New York–New Jersey Port Authority, which has licensed over 300 centers worldwide. Through membership, exporters and importers have access to an online trading system. Exporters need only a computer and a modem to put offers to sell in an electronic database, and importers anywhere can send messages to the exporters' mailboxes accepting advertised prices or initiating electronic negotiations. Access can be gained with a local telephone in 800 cities in 100 countries.

District Export Councils

The Department of Commerce has 55 district export councils composed of volunteer business and trade experts who assist in workshops and also arrange for consultation between experienced and prospective exporters.[7]

State Governments

All states have export development programs that offer assistance to exporters by providing sales leads, locating overseas representatives, and counseling. Twenty-eight states also have export-financing programs, and more are setting them up.[8]

Export Marketing Plan

As soon as possible, an export marketing plan must be drawn up. An experienced firm will already have a plan in operation, but newcomers will usually need to wait until they have accumulated at least some information from foreign market research.

Same as Domestic Marketing Plan

Essentially, the export marketing plan is the same as the domestic marketing plan. It should be specific about (1) the markets to be developed, (2) the marketing strategy for serving them, and (3) the tactics required to make the strategy operational. Sales forecasts and budgets, pricing policies, product characteristics, promotional plans, and de-

Various Types of Experts Help Small Firms Export

Small and Medium-Sized Enterprises

David Kratka, president of MMO Music Group, a small producer of sing-along tapes for karaoke machines in Elmsford, New York, didn't have to search for foreign business; foreign customers came to him. Although this seems like an enviable situation, in reality, Kratka figures the company probably lost foreign sales in the 1980s because he was too busy attending to the domestic market. He didn't have time to answer faxes and telephone calls from Asia and Europe.

A year after Kratka finally decided he could no longer handle the foreign inquiries alone, he hired an international sales director. Now foreign sales constitute about 15 percent of the firm's total $8 million sales. This is up from 5 percent before he was hired.

Other companies find it easier and more economical to get exporting help from an outsider. A consulting firm, Export Resource Associates, is teaching exporting techniques to CoBatCo, a waffle griddle maker in Illinois with 21 employees. Exports amounted to 13 percent of total sales in 1993 compared to no foreign sales in 1990. "I think to some extent there were some opportunities in the late 80s that could have been pursued if we had the background to pursue them," said the president. "We didn't have knowledge of what a letter of credit even was."

Other small-firm managers without the time or international expertise to handle foreign sales turn to export management companies (EMCs) that typically handle everything from sales and distribution to credit and shipping. They usually charge a fee of between 10 and 15 percent of the shipment's value. The advantage of this approach is that experts handle the export function. The disadvantage, however, is that the control of the company's export business lies in the hands of outsiders. ■

Source: From *The Wall Street Journal,* July 7, 1994, B2. Republished with permission of *The Wall Street Journal.* Permission conveyed throughout the Copyright Clearance Center.

tails on arrangements with foreign representatives are required. In other words, the export marketing plan will spell out what must be done and when, who should do it, and how much money will be spent. An outline for an export marketing plan appears in the Appendix at the end of this chapter.

Marketing Mix

Because the comments in Chapter 16 concerning the marketing mix are valid for exporters, there is no need for a detailed discussion here. Two aspects that do require some explanation, however, are *export pricing* and *sales agreements for foreign representatives.*

Pricing Policies. Pricing is a problem even for experienced exporters. Noncompetitive prices cause sales to be lost to foreign competitors, but incorrect pricing can also cause the exporter to lose money on a sale.

terms of sale
Conditions of a sale that stipulate the point where all costs and risks are borne by buyer

One new area of concern for many firms beginning to export is the need to quote **terms of sale** that differ from those normally used. For foreign transactions, the exporter needs to be familiar with INCOTERMS, 13 trade terms that describe the responsibilities of the buyer and seller in international trade. They were created by the International Chamber of Commerce and are revised every 10 years: the latest revision is INCOTERMS 2000.

Terms of Sale. As an example, for domestic sales, the company may be quoting FOB factory, which means all costs and risks from that point on are borne by the buyer. The INCOTERM equivalent is EX-Works. Foreign customers, however, may insist on one of the following terms of sale:[9]

1. *FAS* (*free alongside ship, port of call*). The seller pays all the transportation and delivery expense up to the ship's side and clears the goods for export (new in INCOTERMS 2000).
2. *CIF* (*cost, insurance, freight, foreign port*). The seller quotes a price that includes the cost of the goods, insurance, and all transportation and miscellaneous charges to the named foreign port in the country of final destination.

3. *CFR* (*cost and freight, foreign port*). This is similar to CIF except that the buyer purchases the insurance either because it can obtain it at a lower cost or because its government, to save foreign exchange, insists that it use a local insurance company.
4. *DAF* (*delivered at frontier*). This is a common term used by exporters to Canada and Mexico. The seller quotes a price that covers all costs up to the border where the shipment is delivered to the buyer's representative. The buyer's responsibility is to arrange with its representative for receiving the goods after they are cleared for export, carry them across the border, and clear them for importation and make delivery to the buyer.

CIF and CFR terms of sale are more convenient for foreign buyers because to establish their cost, they merely have to add the import duties, landing charges, and freight from the port of arrival to their warehouse.

However, these terms can present a problem for new exporters if they forget the miscellaneous costs—wharf storage and handling charges, freight forwarder's charges, and consular fees—incurred in making a CIF shipment and simply add freight, insurance, and export packing costs to the domestic selling price. The resulting price may be too low, but more often it will be too high, because the domestic marketing and general administrative costs included in the domestic selling price are frequently greater than the actual cost of making the export sale.

The preferred pricing method is the use of the *factory door cost* (production cost without domestic marketing and general administrative costs), to which are added the direct cost of making the export sale, a percentage of the general administrative overhead, and profit. This percentage can be derived from managers' estimates of the part of their total time spent on export matters. The minimum FOB price will be the sum of these costs plus the required profit. If research in a market has shown either that there is little competition or that competitive prices are higher, then of course the exporter is free to charge a high price in that market (price skim) or set a low price to gain a larger percentage of the market (penetration pricing). The course of action taken will depend on the firm's sales objectives, just as it does in the domestic market.

Sales Agreement. The sales agreement should specify as simply as possible the duties of the representative and the firm. Most of what is contained in the contract for a domestic representative can be used in export also, but special attention must be paid to two points: (1) designation of the responsibilities for patent and trademark registration and (2) designation of the country and state, if applicable, whose laws will govern a contractual dispute. To be absolutely safe, the firm should register all patents and trademarks. Policing them may be left to the local representative if management so chooses. However, the firm should have the help of an experienced international attorney when drawing up an agreement.

U.S. exporters would prefer to stipulate the laws of the United States and their home state, but many nations, especially those of Latin America, will not permit this (Calvo Doctrine). The Calvo Doctrine, promulgated by Calvo, an Argentine jurist, holds that trying cases locally under foreign laws should not be permitted because it gives the foreign company an advantage over local firms, which must be tried under local laws. If an American state can be designated, its laws may be followed even though the dispute is adjudicated in a foreign country. The presiding judge will have the pertinent parts of the law translated or will call on witnesses who are known experts in the area of law involved.

Payment and Financing Procedures

The second major problem area concerns payment and financing procedures.

Export Payment Terms

Payment terms, as every marketer knows, are often a decisive factor in obtaining an order. As a sales official of an international grain exporter put it, "If you give credit to a guy who is broke, he'll pay any price for your product." This is somewhat exaggerated, but customers will often pay higher prices when terms are more lenient. This is especially significant in countries where capital is scarce and interest rates are high. The kinds of payment terms offered by exporters to foreign buyers are (1) cash in advance, (2) open account, (3) consignment, (4) letters of credit, and (5) documentary drafts.

Cash in Advance

When the credit standing of the buyer is not known or is uncertain, cash in advance is desirable. However, very few buyers will accept these terms, because part of their working capital is tied up until the merchandise has been received and sold. Furthermore, they have no guarantee that they will receive what they ordered. As a result, few customers will pay cash in advance unless the order is small or is for a product of special manufacture.

Open Account

When a sale is made on open account, the seller assumes all of the risk, and therefore these terms should be offered only to reliable customers in economically stable countries. The exporter's capital, of course, is tied up until payment has been received.

However, exporters that insist on less risky payment terms, such as a letter of credit, may find that they are losing business to competitors who do sell on open account, which is becoming the preferred export payment term. Well-known global firms such as Mercedes Benz do not accept the extra cost of obtaining letters of credit and give their business to suppliers that offer open account terms.

Exporters can get credit reports and credit information on foreign firms from agencies in the United States and other countries. Among the American agencies that prepare reports are Dun & Bradstreet, FCIB-NACM, Global Scan, and Experian. Eurogate and Asia Company Profiles furnish reports for European and Asian firms, respectively.[10]

Consignment

This follows the procedure, well known in the United States, by which goods are shipped to the buyer and payment is not made until they have been sold. All of the risk is assumed by the seller, and such terms should not be offered without making the same extensive investigation of the buyer and country that is recommended for open account terms. Multinationals frequently sell goods to their subsidiaries on this basis.

Letters of Credit

Only cash in advance offers more protection to the seller than does an export **letter of credit (L/C)**. This document is issued by the buyer's bank, which promises to pay the seller a specified amount when the bank has received certain documents stipulated in the letter of credit by a specified time.

Confirmed and Irrevocable. Generally, the seller will request that the letter of credit be **confirmed** and **irrevocable.** Irrevocable means that once the seller has accepted the credit, the customer cannot alter or cancel it without the seller's consent. Figure 17.1 is an example of a bank's confirmation of an irrevocable letter of credit. If the letter of credit is *not* confirmed, the correspondent bank (Merchants National Bank of Mobile) has no obligation to pay the seller (Smith & Co.) when it receives the documents listed in the letter of credit. Only the issuing bank (Banco Americano in Bogota) is responsible. If the seller (Smith & Co.) wishes to be able to collect from an American bank, it will insist that the credit be confirmed by such a bank. This is generally done by the correspondent bank, as it was in Figure 17.1. In this case, when the Merchants National Bank of Mobile confirmed the credit, it undertook an obligation to pay Smith & Co. if all the documents listed in the letter were presented on or before the stipulated date.

Note that nothing is mentioned about the goods themselves; the buyer has stipulated only that an **air waybill** issued by the carrier be presented as proof that shipment has been made. Even if bank officials knew that the plane had crashed after the takeoff,

letter of credit (L/C)
Document issued by the buyer's bank in which the bank promises to pay the seller a specified amount under specified conditions

confirmed
Act of a correspondent bank in the seller's country by which it agrees to honor the issuing bank's letter of credit

irrevocable
A stipulation that a letter of credit cannot be canceled

air waybill
A bill of lading issued by an air carrier

[Figure 17.1] Letter of Credit

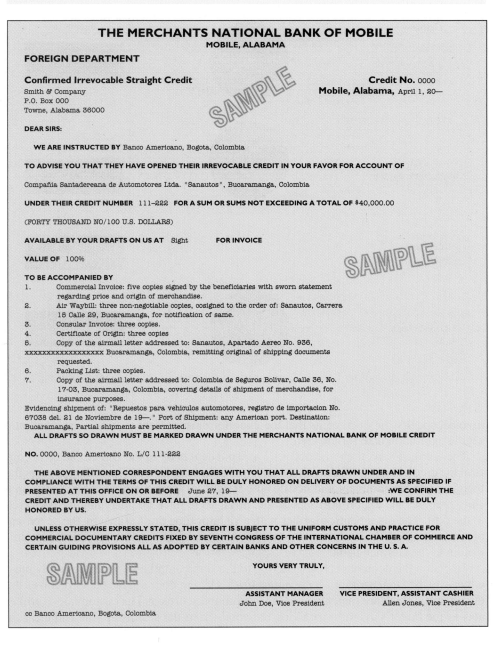

THE MERCHANTS NATIONAL BANK OF MOBILE
MOBILE, ALABAMA

FOREIGN DEPARTMENT

Confirmed Irrevocable Straight Credit
Smith & Company
P.O. Box 000
Towne, Alabama 36000

Credit No. 0000
Mobile, Alabama, April 1, 20—

SAMPLE

DEAR SIRS:

WE ARE INSTRUCTED BY Banco Americano, Bogota, Colombia

TO ADVISE YOU THAT THEY HAVE OPENED THEIR IRREVOCABLE CREDIT IN YOUR FAVOR FOR ACCOUNT OF

Compañia Santadereana de Automotores Ltda. "Sanautos", Bucaramanga, Colombia

UNDER THEIR CREDIT NUMBER 111-222 **FOR A SUM OR SUMS NOT EXCEEDING A TOTAL OF** $40,000.00

(FORTY THOUSAND NO/100 U.S. DOLLARS)

AVAILABLE BY YOUR DRAFTS ON US AT Sight **FOR INVOICE**

VALUE OF 100%

SAMPLE

TO BE ACCOMPANIED BY

1. Commercial Invoice: five copies signed by the beneficiaries with sworn statement regarding price and origin of merchandise.
2. Air Waybill: three non-negotiable copies, cosigned to the order of: Sanautos, Carrera 15 Calle 29, Bucaramanga, for notification of same.
3. Consular Invoice: three copies.
4. Certificate of Origin: three copies
5. Copy of the airmail letter addressed to: Sanautos, Apartado Aereo No. 936, xxxxxxxxxxxxxxxxxx Bucaramanga, Colombia, remitting original of shipping documents requested.
6. Packing List: three copies.
7. Copy of the airmail letter addressed to: Colombia de Seguros Bolivar, Calle 36, No. 17-03, Bucaramanga, Colombia, covering details of shipment of merchandise, for insurance purposes.

Evidencing shipment of: "Repuestos para vehiculos automotores, registro de importacion No. 67038 del. 21 de Noviembre de 19—." Port of Shipment: any American port. Destination: Bucaramanga, Partial shipments are permitted.

ALL DRAFTS SO DRAWN MUST BE MARKED DRAWN UNDER THE MERCHANTS NATIONAL BANK OF MOBILE CREDIT

NO. 0000, Banco Americano No. L/C 111-222

THE ABOVE MENTIONED CORRESPONDENT ENGAGES WITH YOU THAT ALL DRAFTS DRAWN UNDER AND IN COMPLIANCE WITH THE TERMS OF THIS CREDIT WILL BE DULY HONORED ON DELIVERY OF DOCUMENTS AS SPECIFIED IF PRESENTED AT THIS OFFICE ON OR BEFORE June 27, 19— **:WE CONFIRM THE CREDIT AND THEREBY UNDERTAKE THAT ALL DRAFTS DRAWN AND PRESENTED AS ABOVE SPECIFIED WILL BE DULY HONORED BY US.**

UNLESS OTHERWISE EXPRESSLY STATED, THIS CREDIT IS SUBJECT TO THE UNIFORM CUSTOMS AND PRACTICE FOR COMMERCIAL DOCUMENTARY CREDITS FIXED BY SEVENTH CONGRESS OF THE INTERNATIONAL CHAMBER OF COMMERCE AND CERTAIN GUIDING PROVISIONS ALL AS ADOPTED BY CERTAIN BANKS AND OTHER CONCERNS IN THE U. S. A.

SAMPLE

YOURS VERY TRULY,

ASSISTANT MANAGER
John Doe, Vice President

VICE PRESIDENT, ASSISTANT CASHIER
Allen Jones, Vice President

cc Banco Americano, Bogota, Colombia

they would still have to pay Smith & Co. *Banks are concerned with documents, not merchandise.*

Before opening a letter of credit, a buyer frequently requests a **pro forma invoice.** This is the exporter's formal quotation containing a description of the merchandise, price, delivery time, proposed method of shipment, ports of exit and entry, and terms of sale. It is more than a quotation, however. Generally, the bank will use it when opening a letter of credit, and in countries requiring import licenses or permits to purchase foreign exchange, government officials will insist on receiving copies.

pro forma invoice
Exporter's formal quotation containing a description of the merchandise, price, delivery time, method of shipping, terms of sale, and points of exit and entry

Letter of Credit Transactions. Figure 17.2 illustrates the routes taken by the merchandise, letter of credit, and documents in a letter of credit transaction.

When a German buyer accepts the terms of sale that provide for a confirmed and irrevocable letter of credit, it goes to its bank to arrange for opening the required letter. The buyer will furnish the bank with the information contained in the pro forma

[Figure 17.2] Letter of Credit Transaction

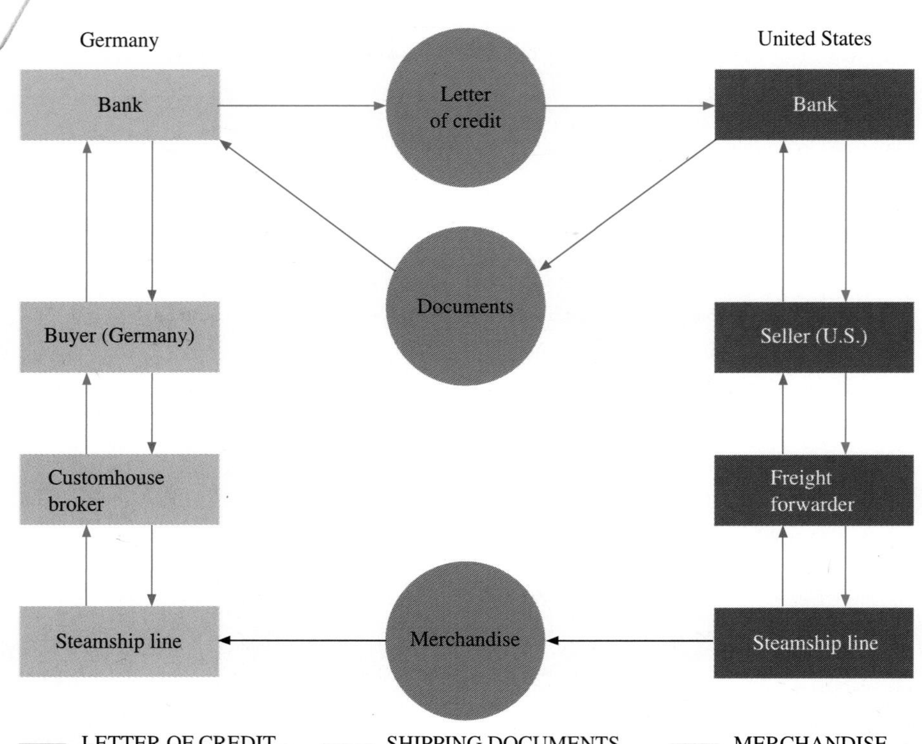

invoice, specify the documents that the exporter must present to obtain payment, and set the expiration date for the credit.

The German bank then instructs its correspondent bank in the United States to confirm the credit and inform the seller that it has been established. The seller prepares the merchandise for shipment and notifies the freight forwarder, which books space on a ship, prepares the export documents, and arranges to have the merchandise delivered to the port. The documents, together with a sight or time draft drawn by the seller, are presented to the U.S. bank, which pays the seller and forwards the documents for collection to the German bank.

To obtain the documents that give title to the shipment, the buyer in Germany must either pay the *sight draft* or accept a *time draft.* Having done so, the buyer receives the documents, which are then given to the customhouse broker. The customhouse broker acts as the buyer's agent in receiving the goods from the steamship line and clearing them through German customs.

Documentary Drafts

When the exporter believes the political and commercial risks are not sufficient to require a letter of credit, the exporter may agree to payment on a documentary draft basis, which is less costly to the buyer.

export draft
An unconditional order that is drawn by the seller on the buyer to pay the draft's amount on presentation (**sight draft**) or at an agreed future date (**time draft**) and that must be paid before the buyer receives shipping documents

An **export draft,** shown in Figure 17.3, is an unconditional order drawn by the seller on the buyer instructing the buyer to pay the amount of the order on presentation (**sight draft**) or at an agreed future date (**time draft**). Generally, the seller will ask its bank to send the draft and documents to a bank in the buyer's country, which will proceed with the collection as described in the letter of credit transaction.

Although documentary draft and letter of credit terms are similar, there is one important difference. A confirmed letter of credit guarantees payment to the seller if the seller conforms to its requirements, but there is no such guarantee with documentary drafts. An unscrupulous buyer can refuse to pay the drafts when presented and then attempt to bargain with the seller for a lower price. The seller must then acquiesce, try to

Dump the L/Cs; Pay with Plastic!

Small and Medium-Sized Enterprises

For many years, the safe but costly and laborious way to guarantee both payment and shipment of an export or import order has been with letter of credit (L/C) payment terms. Even though L/C processing has been modernized with the development of electronic documentation, it is still too much of a burden for many small and medium-size enterprises. For them, credit cards eliminate the need for the time-consuming and more expensive L/C process.

For example, the president of small manufacturing company said that if his company hadn't accepted payment by credit card, it couldn't have done business in 95 countries. He's also pleased that with the immediate completion of the sale paid by plastic, the firm avoids foreign exchange conversion costs that could occur if there were a change in the exchange rate between the time of the sale and the time of conversion of the currency. Credit card companies guarantee that payment is made directly to the seller's bank account within 72 hours at the daily U.S. dollar rate, avoiding conversion losses and increasing cash flow. ■

Source: "GBF Visa Card," GBF Merchant Program, 222.gbfvisa.com/home.html (October 8, 2000); and "Credit Card," *Setting Payment Terms,* Tradesport, www.tradesport.org/ts/trade_expert/details/payment/other.html (October 8, 2000).

[Figure 17.3] **Sight Draft**

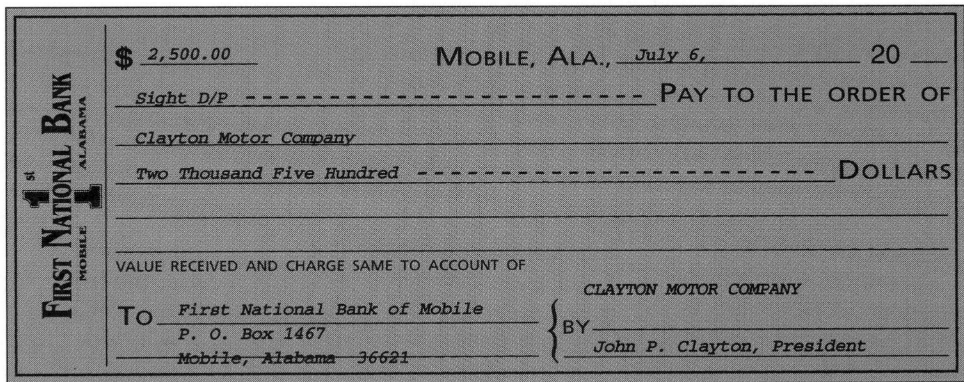

FIRST NATIONAL BANK
MOBILE ALABAMA

$ 2,500.00 MOBILE, ALA., July 6, 20

Sight D/P PAY TO THE ORDER OF

Clayton Motor Company

Two Thousand Five Hundred DOLLARS

VALUE RECEIVED AND CHARGE SAME TO ACCOUNT OF

CLAYTON MOTOR COMPANY

TO First National Bank of Mobile
P. O. Box 1467
Mobile, Alabama 36621

BY John P. Clayton, President

find another buyer, pay a large freight bill to bring back the goods, or abandon them. If the seller chooses the last alternative, customs will auction off the goods, and chances are that the original buyer will be able to acquire them at a bargain price. The seller, of course, receives nothing.

Risk/Cost Trade-Off of Export Payment Terms

You have seen that the risks and costs vary inversely among the various export payment terms. Figure 17.4 illustrates this risk/cost trade-off.

Export Financing

Although exporters would prefer to sell on the almost riskless letter of credit terms, increased foreign competition and the universally tight money situation are forcing them to offer credit. To do so, they must be familiar with the available sources and kinds of export financing, both private and public.

Private Source

Commercial banks have always been a source of export financing through loans for working capital and the discounting of time drafts. A bank may discount an export time draft, pay the seller and keep it until maturity, or, if it is the bank on which the draft is drawn, "accept" it. By accepting a time draft, a bank assumes the responsibility for

[Figure 17.4] **Export Payment Terms Risk/Cost Tradeoff**

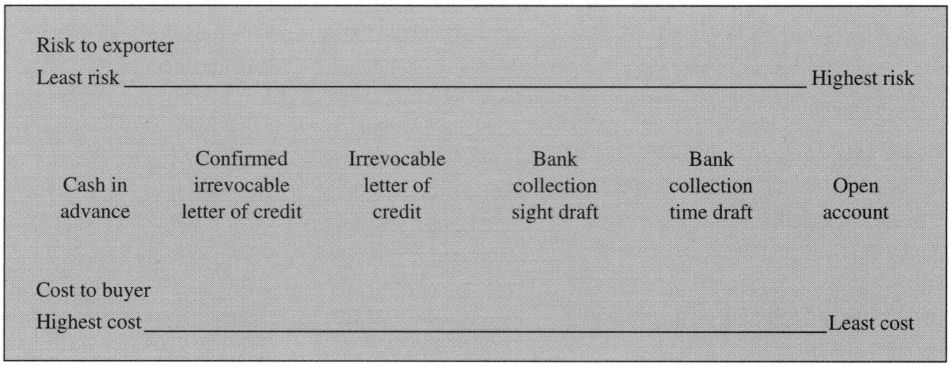

Risk to exporter Least risk					Highest risk
Cash in advance	Confirmed irrevocable letter of credit	Irrevocable letter of credit	Bank collection sight draft	Bank collection time draft	Open account
Cost to buyer Highest cost					Least cost

Source: *Business America* (U.S. Dept. of Commerce Publication), February 1995.

banker's acceptance
A time draft with maturity of less than 270 days that has been accepted by the bank on which the draft was drawn, thus becoming the accepting bank's obligation; may be bought and sold at a discount in the financial markets like other commercial paper

factoring
Discounting without recourse an account receivable

forfaiting
Purchasing without recourse an account receivable whose credit terms are longer than the 90 to 180 days usual in factoring; unlike factoring, political and transfer risks are borne by the forfaiter

Eximbank
Principal federal government agency that aids American exporters by means of loans, guarantees, and insurance programs

making payment at maturity of the draft. The accepting bank may or may not purchase (at a discount) the draft. If it does not, the exporter can sell a **banker's acceptance** readily in the open market. In recent years, new types of financing have been developed: factoring and forfaiting.

Factoring. This financing technique permits the exporter to be more competitive by selling on open account rather than by means of the more costly letter of credit method. **Factoring,** which has long been used in the United States to provide working capital to manufacturers short of cash, is now being employed in international trade. Factoring is essentially discounting *without* recourse because it is the sale of export accounts receivable to a third party, which assumes the credit risk. A factor may be a factoring house or a special department in a commercial bank.

Under the export factoring arrangement, the seller passes its order to the factor for approval of the credit risk. Once the order has been approved, the exporter has complete protection against bad debts and political risk. The customer pays the factor, which in effect acts as the exporter's credit and collection department. The period of settlement generally does not exceed 180 days.

Forfaiting. **Forfaiting** denotes the purchase of obligations that arise from the sale of goods and services and fall due at some date beyond the 90 to 180 days that is customary for factoring. These receivables are usually in the form of trade drafts or promissory notes with maturities ranging from six months to five years.

Because it is sold without recourse, forfaited debt is nearly always accompanied by bank security in the form of a guarantee or aval. Whereas the guarantee is a separate document, the aval is a promise to pay that is written directly in the document ("per aval" and the signature).

The forfaiter purchases the bill and discounts it for the entire credit period. Thus, the exporter, through forfaiting, has converted its credit-based sale into a cash transaction.

Although banks have traditionally concentrated on short-term financing, they have become involved in medium- and even long-term financing because numerous government and government-assisted organizations are offering export credit guarantees and insurance against commercial (customer goes bankrupt and can't pay) and political (government overthrown and foreign exchange unavailable to customer) risks.

Export-Import Bank

The U.S. Export-Import Bank (**Eximbank**) is the principal government agency responsible for aiding the export of American goods and services through a variety of loan, guarantee, and insurance programs. Generally, its programs are available to any American export firm regardless of size.

Direct and Intermediary Loans. The Eximbank provides two types of loans: (1) direct loans to foreign buyers of American exports and (2) intermediary loans to responsible parties, such as a foreign government lending agency that relends to foreign buyers of capital goods and related services (for example, a maintenance contract for a jet passenger plane). Both programs cover up to 85 percent of the value of the exported goods and services, with repayment terms of one year or more.

Working Capital Guarantee. This program helps small businesses obtain working capital to cover their export sales. It guarantees working capital loans extended by banks to eligible exporters with exportable inventory or export receivables as collateral.

Guarantees. Eximbank's guarantee provides repayment protection for private-sector loans to buyers of U.S. capital equipment and related services. The guarantee is available alone or may be combined with an Eximbank direct or intermediary loan.

Export Credit Insurance. An exporter may reduce its financing risks by purchasing one of several policies to protect itself against the political and commercial risks of a foreign buyer defaulting on payment. The coverage may be comprehensive or limited to political risk only.

Since its inception in 1934, the Eximbank has supported more than $300 billion in American exports.[11] Every industrialized nation and many that are industrializing have similar banks. Another government agency, the Small Business Administration, operates loan guarantee and direct loan programs to assist small-business exporters.

Other Government Incentives

Other government incentives for trade, although not strictly a part of export financing, are certainly closely related to it. These are the Overseas Private Investment Corporation (OPIC), the Foreign Sales Corporation (FSC), and the foreign trade zone (FTZ).

Overseas Private Investment Corporation (OPIC)

The **Overseas Private Investment Corporation (OPIC)** is a government corporation formed to stimulate private investment in developing countries. It offers investors insurance against expropriation, currency inconvertibility, and damages from wars or revolutions. OPIC also offers specialized insurance for American service contractors and exporters operating in foreign countries. Exports of capital equipment and semiprocessed raw materials generally follow these investments.

Overseas Private Investment Corporation (OPIC)
Government corporation that offers American investors in developing countries insurance against expropriation, currency inconvertibility, and damages from wars and revolutions

Foreign Sales Corporation (FSC)

The **Foreign Sales Corporation (FSC)** was authorized by the Tax Reform Act of 1984. It replaced the Domestic International Sales Corporation (DISC), which U.S. trading partners complained violated the General Agreement on Tariffs and Trade.

Unlike its DISC predecessor, an FSC must be located either in a U.S. possession other than Puerto Rico or in a foreign country that has an information exchange agreement with the United States. The FSC's shareholders' and directors' meetings must be held outside the United States, and its principal bank account must be maintained outside the United States.

The portion of the FSC's income that is exempt from U.S. corporate taxation is 30 percent if the FSC buys from independent suppliers or uses the Section 482* arm's-length pricing rule with related suppliers.

In 1976, the predecessor to the FSC, the Domestic International Sales Corporation, was declared an illegal export subsidy and was replaced by the United States in 1984. The European Union contested the legality of the FSC for years and finally asked a World

Foreign Sales Corporation (FSC)
Special corporate form authorized by the federal government that provides tax advantages for exporting firms

*See Chapter 16 for details on Section 482.

Trade Organization (WTO) panel to look at the issue in October 1998. In 1999, the panel reported that the FSC constituted a prohibited export subsidy. The United States appealed the decision, and on February 24 the WTO Appellate Body confirmed the previous ruling that tax breaks for exporters by means of the FSC violate WTO rules on subsidies. This was the biggest case the United States had ever lost before the WTO.

On September 30, 2000, the United States and the European Union reached an agreement regarding procedures for reviewing whether the repeal and replacement legislation forwarded to Congress is consistent with WTO requirements. The United States also requested an extension of the compliance period until November to allow Congress to complete passage of the legislation.[12]

Foreign Trade Zones

For centuries, various forms of duty-free areas have existed in many parts of the world to facilitate trade by lessening the effect of customs restrictions. These customs-privileged areas may be free ports, transit zones, free perimeters, export processing zones, or free trade zones. In each instance, a specific and limited area is involved, into which imported goods may be brought without the payment of import duties. There are hundreds of these areas in 72 countries. Of the five types, the free trade zone is the most common.

free trade zone
An area designated by the government of a country for duty-free entry of any nonprohibited good

foreign trade zone (FTZ)
American version of a free trade zone

The **free trade zone** is an enclosed area considered to be outside the customs territory of the country in which it is located. Goods of foreign origin may be brought into the zone pending eventual transshipment, reexportation, or importation into the country. While the goods are in the zone, no import duties need be paid.

The American version, called the **foreign trade zone (FTZ),** has been growing in popularity, and there are now over 600 of these zones in operation.* Many are situated at seaports, but some are located at inland distribution points.

Goods brought into the FTZ may be stored, inspected, repackaged, or combined with American components. Because of differences in the import tariff schedule, the finished product often pays less duty than what would be charged for the disassembled parts. Bicycles have been assembled in the Kansas City FTZ for that reason. Importers of machinery and automobiles improve their cash flow by storing spare parts in an FTZ, because duty is not paid until they are withdrawn.

Although the advantages of the FTZ to importers are well known, its benefits to exporters appear to have been overlooked. Foreign trade zones can provide accelerated export status for purposes of excise tax rebates and customs drawbacks. Manufacturers of such items as tires, trucks, and tobacco products are required to pay federal excise taxes when these items are produced, but the taxes are rebated if the items are exported. Firms that include imported parts in their finished products must pay duty on the imports, but this duty is returned when the product is exported (customs drawback). The recovery of this money takes time, however, and meanwhile the exporter can have considerable capital tied up in excise taxes and import duties. Because a product is considered exported as soon as it enters an FTZ, the exporter can immediately apply for a rebate or a drawback while waiting to make an export sale. Although U.S. Customs has had the duty-drawback program in place for 200 years, many firms do not claim the money they're owed. As a result, each year a billion dollars in customs-duty refunds goes unclaimed.[13]

If assembly or manufacturing is done in the FTZ using imported components, no duties need ever be paid when the finished product is exported. This is also the purpose of the previously mentioned export processing zones in which firms use cheap local labor for assembly. There are various such zones in China, for example.

Export Procedures

When nonexporters complain about the complexity of export procedures, they are generally referring to documentation. Instead of the two documents (the freight bill and the bill of lading) to which they are accustomed when shipping domestically, they are sud-

*Including subzones for individual plants.

denly confronted by five to six times as many documents for a foreign shipment. According to an Organization for Economic Cooperation and Development (OECD) study, the average overseas transaction requires 35 documents with a total of 360 copies. The study states that the "paper costs" of international trade come to between 1.4 percent and 5.7 percent of the value of the trade. "Exports move on a sea of documents" is a popular saying in the industry. Although the extra burden may be handled by the traffic department, many firms give all or at least part of the work to a foreign freight forwarder.

Foreign Freight Forwarders

Foreign freight forwarders act as agents for exporters. They prepare documents, book space with a carrier, and in general act as the firm's export traffic department. If asked, they will offer advice about markets, import and export regulations, the best mode of transport, and export packing, and they will supply cargo insurance. After shipment, they forward all documents to the importer or to the paying bank, according to the exporter's requirements.

foreign freight forwarders
Independent businesses that handle export shipments for compensation

Export Documents

Correct documentation is vital to the success of any export shipment. For discussion purposes, we shall divide export documents into two categories: (1) shipping documents and (2) collection documents.

Shipping Documents

Shipping documents are prepared by exporters or their freight forwarders so that the shipment may pass through U.S. Customs, be loaded on the carrier, and be sent to its destination. They include the domestic bill of lading, export packing list, export licenses, export bill of lading, and insurance certificate. Inasmuch as the first two documents are nearly the same as those used in domestic traffic, we shall limit our discussion to the export licenses, the insurance certificate, and the export bill of lading. Note, however, that a domestic bill of lading for goods to be exported must contain a statement by the seller that those goods will not be diverted to another destination. Export package marks and the latest allowable arrival date in the port of export should be noted. The export packing list differs from the domestic list in that it is much more detailed with respect to the weights and measurements of each package. The material in each package must be itemized.

Shipper's Export Declaration (SED). This document is required by the Department of Commerce to control exports and supply export statistics. An SED contains the following:

1. Names and addresses of the shipper and consignee
2. U.S. port of exit and foreign port of unloading
3. Description and value of the goods
4. Export license number and bill of lading number
5. Carrier transporting the merchandise

Shippers or their agents (foreign freight forwarders) must deliver the SED to the carrier, which turns it in to U.S. Customs with the carrier's manifest (list of the vessel's cargo) before the carrier leaves the United States.

Export Licenses. All exported goods with the exception of those going to U.S. possessions or Canada (with a few exceptions) require export licenses—either a *general export license* or a *validated export license.*

Most products can be exported under a **general export license,** for which no special authorization is necessary. The correct general license symbol, which is obtainable

general export license
Any export license covering export commodities for which a validated license is not required; no formal application is required

from the Department of Commerce district office, is merely written in the *shipper's export declaration.* This document, which must be filed with U.S. Customs, indicates that there is an authorization to export and also provides the statistical information for the Bureau of Census. For strategic materials and all shipments to unfriendly countries, a **validated export license** is mandatory. This is a special authorization for a specific shipment and is issued only on formal application to the Department of Commerce's Office of Export Administration for scarce materials, strategic goods, and technology or to the Department of State for war materials.

validated export license
A required document issued by the U.S. government authorizing the export of specified commodities

Export bill of Lading. The **export bill of lading (B/L)** serves three purposes: it is (1) a contract for carriage between the shipper and the carrier, (2) a receipt from the carrier for the goods shipped, and (3) a certificate of ownership. Bills of lading for foreign shipments called *air waybills* (air shipments) or *ocean bills of lading* (steamships) are issued when the shipments are made.

export bill of lading (B/L)
Contract of carriage between shipper and carrier: straight bill of lading is nonnegotiable; endorsed "to order" bill gives holder claim on merchandise

Ocean bills of lading may be either "straight" or "to order," but air waybills are always straight. A straight bill of lading is nonnegotiable, and only the person stipulated in it may obtain the merchandise on arrival. An order bill of lading, however, is negotiable. It can be endorsed like a check or left blank. In this case, the holder of the original bill of lading is the owner of the merchandise. Sight draft or letter of credit shipments require "to order" bills marked "Clean on Board" by the steamship company, which means there is no apparent damage to the shipment and it has actually been loaded onto the vessel.

Insurance Certificate. The insurance certificate is evidence that the shipment is insured against loss or damage while in transit. Unlike domestic carriers, oceangoing steamship companies assume no responsibility for the merchandise they carry unless the loss is caused by their negligence.

Marine insurance on an international transaction may be arranged by either the exporter or the importer, depending on the terms of sale. The laws of a country often require the importer to buy such insurance, thus protecting the local insurance industry and saving foreign exchange. If the exporter has sold on sight draft terms, it is at risk while the goods are in transit. In this case, the firm should buy contingent interest insurance to protect it in the event that the shipment is lost or damaged and it is unable to collect from the buyer. We believe that the exporter selling on CFR terms (the buyer purchases the insurance) should also buy contingent interest insurance to protect itself in case the buyer's insurance does not cover all risks. The premiums are low because damages are paid only on what is not covered by the buyer's policy.

Broadly speaking, there are three kinds of marine insurance policies: basic named perils, broad named perils, and all risks.

1. *Basic named perils* includes perils of the sea, fires, jettisons, explosions, and hurricanes.
2. *Broad named perils* includes theft, pilferage, nondelivery, breakage, and leakage in addition to the basic perils. Both policies contain a clause that determines the extent to which losses caused by an insured peril will be paid. The purchaser of the insurance may request either (*a*) free of particular average (excluding partial loss) or (*b*) with particular average (covering partial loss). Obviously, the rates differ.
3. *All risks* covers all physical loss or damage from any external cause and is more expensive than the policies previously mentioned. War risks are covered under a separate contract.

For the sake of convenience, the occasional exporter will ask the forwarder to arrange for insurance, but when shipments begin on a regular basis, the shipper can economize by going directly to a marine insurance broker. The broker, acting as the shipper's agent, will draw up a contract to fit the shipper's needs by choosing appropriate clauses from among the hundreds that are available.

The premiums charged depend on a number of factors, among which are the goods insured, the destination, the age of the ship, whether the goods are stowed on deck or under deck, the volume of business (there are volume discounts), how the goods are packed, and the number of claims the shipper has filed. Brokers will sometimes admit that in the long run it is preferable not to file numerous small claims, even if justified, because the higher premiums charged for future shipments will be greater than the money recovered.

Because neither the policies nor the premiums are standard, it is highly recommended that the exporter obtain various quotations.

Automated Export System (AES). The total cost of the paperwork for a single shipment has been estimated at between $150 and $300. Just preparing the SED is said to cost $18. Since the Census Bureau collects over $6.5 million SEDs annually, exporters are spending $120 million on just this form. In addition, studies indicate that one in two export documents contains errors that must be corrected by government employees.

To eliminate errors and reduce preparation costs, U.S. Customs designed the Automated Export System (AES), which uses Electronic Data Interchange (EDI) to facilitate the movement of U.S. exports. This is a one-stop export filing system—a single information collection and processing center for the electronic filing of the export shipment documentation required by the U.S. government. The use of AES is currently voluntary, but it has the goal of paperless reporting of export information by the year 2002.[14]

Collection Documents

The seller is required to provide the buyer with these documents to receive payment. For a letter of credit transaction, the collection documents must be submitted to a bank, but to collect against documentary drafts, anyone may be designated to act on the seller's behalf. A few exporters send their drafts overseas to a representative or bank for collection, but it is preferable to have a bank in the exporter's country forward them to its correspondent bank in the city of destination.

First of all, the collection costs are usually lower because the correspondent bank charges the exporter's bank less than it would charge the exporter. Second, because of the correspondent relationship between the banks, the foreign bank will generally exert a greater effort to collect the money on time. Should the exporter wish to change instructions to the foreign bank, the private cable codes and tests of banks permit new instructions to be authenticated and acted on quickly, whereas a cable from the exporter to a foreign bank would probably be ignored until it had been confirmed by a letter with a signature that could be checked for authenticity.

The documents required for collection vary among countries and among customers, but some of the most common are (1) commercial invoices, (2) consular invoices, (3) certificates of origin, and (4) inspection certificates.

Commercial Invoices. Commercial invoices for export orders are similar to domestic invoices but include additional information, such as the origin of the goods, export packing marks, and a clause stating that the goods will not be diverted to another country. Invoices for letter of credit sales will name the bank and the credit numbers. Some importing countries require the commercial invoice to be in their language and to be visaed by their local consul.

Consular Invoices. A few countries require both the commercial invoice and a special form called the *consular invoice.* These forms are purchased from the consul, prepared in the language of the country, and then visaed by the consul.

Certificates of Origin. Although the commercial invoice carries a statement regarding the origin of the merchandise, a number of foreign governments require a separate certificate of origin. This document is commonly issued by the local chamber of commerce and visaed by the consul.

Inspection Certificates. Inspection certificates are frequently required by buyers of grain, foodstuffs, and live animals. They are issued by the Department of Agriculture in the United States. Purchasers of machinery or products containing a specified combination of ingredients may insist that an American engineering firm or laboratory inspect the merchandise and certify that it is exactly as ordered.

Export Shipments

Most newcomers are so preoccupied with making a sale and handling the extra paperwork needed when exporting that they fail to be concerned about the physical movement of their goods. Yet if they knew about the advances in material-handling techniques, they might not only save money but also reach markets they previously could not serve.

For example, do you want to reduce handling costs? Do you want to reduce pilferage, always a problem in both the port of exit and the port of entry?

> One of the writers, a crew member of a merchant ship docked in an American port to discharge cargo, was leaving the ship when he heard a tremendous thump. The stevedores who were unloading the ship were picking up a large crate with the ship's winch and dropping it on the ground to break it open. Obviously, they suspected that it contained valuable merchandise. Within a few hours of a ship's arrival to unload, you can see peddlers in the street offering merchandise that arrived on the ship. You can purchase bananas, for example, outside the dock area soon after their arrival.

One means of drastically reducing both theft and handling costs is to use containers.

Containers

Containers are large boxes—8 by 8 feet in cross-section by 10, 20, or 40 feet in length—that the seller fills with the shipment in its own warehouse. Airlines also provide smaller containers with rounded cross-sections for a better fit in the fuselage. The containers are then sealed and opened only when the goods arrive at their final destination. Containers will be picked up by a tractor-trailer or a railroad for delivery to shipside, where they will be loaded aboard ship. From the port of entry, railroads or trucks will deliver them, often unopened even for customs inspection, to the buyer's warehouse. In most countries, customs officials will go to the warehouse to examine the shipment. This not only reduces handling time, it also minimizes the risks of damage and theft because the buyer's own employees unload the containers. If the importer or exporter has a warehouse on a river too shallow for ocean vessels, it can save time and expense by loading containers on barges, which are towed to the harbor, where a LASH vessel is anchored.

LASH

LASH (lighter aboard ship) vessels give exporters and importers direct access to ocean freight service even though they are located on shallow inland waterways. Sixty-foot-

Should you export using ocean freight or air freight? Many people are surprised to learn that in addition to being quicker, air freight is often cheaper than ocean freight.
Courtesy European Commission Delegation, Washington, D.C.

[Worldview]

SHOES FOR PEOPLE WITH TWO LEFT FEET

For days, cargo thieves were watching construction crews enlarging one of Los Angeles's large container terminals. Toward the end of the work, the crews began moving the fences out to the expanded perimeter. When they ran out of heavy-security fence, they used lightweight fencing temporarily. This was the chance the thieves had been waiting for. That night, they cut the fence and drove a tractor-trailer truck up to a line of containers. After breaking into a number of them, they found one full of sports shoes that retailed for $150 a pair. They connected it to their tractor-trailer and escaped in the darkness.

But it was the importer who had the last laugh. A week later, the police found the abandoned container with its cargo intact. The thieves didn't know that the importer routinely shipped all its left shoes in one container and its right shoes in another. They had stolen a container with left shoes. Buy expensive high-tech global positioning devices to know where your container is? No, use cheap low-tech methods. Ship all left shoes. ■

Source: "Sneaking Up on Security," www.internationalbusiness.com/feb/log297.htm (February 20, 1998).

long barges are towed to inland locations, loaded, and towed back to deep water, where they are loaded aboard anchored LASH ships. Exporters that are not located in deep-water ports should check to see if this service is available. Not only will they decrease their risks, they may gain from their competitors those customers facing the same problems because they too are located far from seaports. This is especially true in less developed countries, where oceangoing vessels may wait in anchor a month or more for docking space. Not only do customers have to wait for the merchandise, freight charges will be higher because the ship has a long, unproductive wait. All the expenses of operating the vessel, which can amount to thousands of dollars daily, are included in a demurrage charge added to the exporter's or importer's normal freight charge.

RO-RO

Another innovation in cargo handling is the RO-RO (roll on–roll off) ship, which permits loaded trailers and any equipment on wheels to be driven onto this specially designed vessel. RO-RO service has brought the benefits of containerization that we discussed to ports that have been unable to invest in the expensive lifting equipment required for containers. Innovative exporters might be able to combine their container shipments with other exporters' shipments of rolling stock. Of course, they must first know that RO-RO vessels exist.

Air Freight

Air freight has had a profound effect on international business because it permits shipments that once required 30 days to arrive in 1 day. Huge freight planes carry payloads of 200,000 pounds, most of which goes either in containers or on pallets. Airlines guarantee overnight delivery from New York to many European airports and claim that their planes can be completely loaded or unloaded within 45 minutes.

Many newcomers to exporting use ocean freight rather than air freight because ocean freight is so much cheaper. But if they compare the total costs of each mode, they frequently find that air freight is less costly. Total cost components that may be lower for air freight include the following:

1. *Insurance rates*—less chance of damage.
2. *Packing*—can go in domestic packaging instead of the heavier, more costly export packing, which the exporter may have to pay to have done by an outside firm.

Table 17.2 Sea-Air Total Cost Comparison (Shipment of Spare Parts)

	Ocean Freight (with warehousing)	Air Freight (no warehousing)
Warehouse administrative costs	$ 850	—
Warehouse rent	1,400	—
Inventory costs		
Taxes and insurance	630	$ 330
Inventory financing	240	160
Inventory obsolescence	1,500	0*
Seller's warehouse and handling costs	1,550	950
Transportation	350	2,000
Packaging and handling	250	100
Cargo insurance	60	30
Customs duties	110	107
Total	$6,940	$3,677

*Minimal.

3. *Customs duties*—when calculated on gross weights.
4. *Replacement costs for damaged goods*—less chance of damaging the shipment. Mercedes ships many of its automobiles to the United States by air freight.
5. *Inventory costs*—rapid delivery by air freight often obviates the need for expensive warehouses.

In addition, customers will be more satisfied when they receive shipments sooner. There is less chance of dissatisfaction caused by damage in transit or a delay while a damaged shipment is repaired or replaced. Machinery shipped by air does not require a heavy coat of grease to protect it from the elements, as does machinery sent by ship. The protective coating is extremely difficult to remove. Table 17.2 illustrates how the total cost of air freight may be lower than that of ocean freight.

Even when the total costs based on these items are higher for air freight, it may still be advantageous to ship by air when factors other than the conventional expense, inventory, and capital are considered:

1. *Production and opportunity costs,* although somewhat more difficult to calculate, are properly a part of the total cost. Getting the product to the buyer more quickly results in faster payment, which speeds up the return on investment and improves cash flow. The firm's capital is released more quickly and can be invested in other profit-making ventures or used to repay borrowed capital, thus reducing interest payments. Production equipment may be assembled and sent by air so that it goes into production sooner without the transit and setup delays associated with ocean shipments, a strong sales argument.
2. *The firm may be air-dependent;* that is, the exporter is in business only because of air freight. Suppliers of perishable food products to Europe, Japan, and the Middle East are in this category, as are suppliers of live animals (newly hatched poultry and prize bulls) and fresh flowers, a big, legal Colombian export. *Without air freight, these firms would be out of business.*
3. *The products may be air-dependent* because the market itself is perishable. Consumer products with extremely short life cycles (high-fashion and fad items) are examples, but many industrial products also fit into this category. A computer, for example, is perishable to the extent that the time it loses between the final assembly and the installation at the customer's location is time during which it is not earning income (the leasing fee).

4. The sales argument that *spare parts and factory technical personnel are available within a few hours* is a strong one for an exporting firm that has to compete with overseas manufacturers.

Importing

In one sense, importers are the reverse of exporters; they sell domestically and buy in foreign markets. However, many of their concerns are similar. As in the case of exporters, there are small firms whose only business is to import, and there are global corporations for which the importing of millions of dollars of components and raw materials every year is just one of their functions.

How does the prospective importer identify import sources? In a number of ways:

1. If similar imported products are already in the market, go to a retailer that sells them and examine the product label to see where it is made. U.S. law requires that the country of origin be clearly marked on each product or on its container if product marking is not feasible (individual cigarettes, for example).

   Once you know where the product is produced, call the nearest consul or embassy of that country and request the names of manufacturers. One of the principal duties of all foreign government representatives is to promote exports. Some countries publish newsletters in which products are offered for export. Ask to be on their mailing lists. You can also call foreign chambers of commerce in your country (the German-American Chamber of Commerce in New York City is an example). The Japan External Trade Organization (JETRO), which provides information on Japanese exporters, has a number of offices in the United States and other countries. Foreign governments sponsor trade shows in many countries, as we mentioned in our discussion of how the U.S. Department of Commerce assists exporters. Visit these as well as industry shows in your home country. Once you have the names and addresses of foreign manufacturers, you can write to them for quotations.

2. If the product is not being imported, you should contact all the sources listed in item 1. The only difference is that you will have to contact more countries. Banks, especially those with strong international departments, may publish newsletters with offers to buy and sell from overseas firms.

3. You can use the electronic bulletin boards of the World Trade Centers. For a fee, you can put your name and what you wish to buy in their computerized data banks, and that information will be seen around the world. The Internet has scores of sites where exporters from other countries offer their products for importation.

4. Accidental importing also takes place. When you visit a foreign country, look for products that may have a market at home. Finding one could put you into a new business, one that makes foreign traveling tax-deductible.

Let's look at some of the technical aspects of importing for which customhouse brokers can provide assistance.

Customhouse Brokers

In every nation, there are **customhouse brokers** just as there are foreign freight forwarders, but instead of helping exporters to export (the function of foreign freight forwarders), they help importers to import. The functions of the two are very similar; in fact, a number of firms provide both services. In the United States, both are licensed: customhouse brokers are licensed by U.S. Customs after passing an extensive examination, and foreign freight forwarders are licensed by the U.S. Maritime Administration after passing an examination.

customhouse brokers
Independent businesses that handle import shipments for compensation

Principal Activity

Acting as the agent for the importer, customhouse brokers bring the imported goods through customs, which requires them to know well the many import regulations and the extensive Tariff Schedule mentioned in Chapter 2. If a customs official places the import in a category requiring higher import duties than the importer had planned on paying, the importing firm may not be able to compete pricewise and still make a profit. Generally, customs evaluators everywhere use units for products that carry specific duties and the invoice price as the basis for ad valorem duties. As we explained in Chapter 2, there are some exceptions.

The practice of U.S. Customs is to use the transaction price, which appears on the commercial invoice accompanying the shipment, plus any other charges not included in the transaction price. These may be royalty or license fees, packing, or any assists. *Assist* is the U.S. Customs term applied to any item that the buyer provides free or at reduced cost for use in the production or sale of merchandise for export to this country. Examples are molds and dies sent overseas to produce a specific product, a common practice of importers that want the goods produced using their design, and components and parts that the buyer provides for incorporation in the finished article.

American-made goods can be returned to this country duty-free; if they have been improved in any way, however, the importers must pay import duties. Mexico's twin-plant concept would not exist if Congress had not passed a law exempting American firms from paying import duties on the American components in finished products that are assembled in Mexico and exported to the United States.

Other Activities

Customhouse brokers can also provide other services, such as arranging transportation for the goods after they have left Customs or even transportation for the goods from a foreign country if the exporter has not done so. Another important function is to know when imports are subject to import quotas and how much of the quota has been filled at the time of the import. No matter at which port the goods arrive, U.S. Customs, aided by a computer network to all American ports, knows immediately the quantity that has been imported. Merchandise subject to import quotas can be on the dock of an American port awaiting clearance through Customs; if the quota fills anywhere meanwhile, those goods cannot be imported for the rest of the fiscal year. The would-be importer must (1) put them in a **bonded warehouse** or a foreign trade zone, where merchandise can be stored without paying duty, and wait for the rest of the year, (2) abandon them, or (3) send them to another country. Importers of high-fashion clothing have lost millions of dollars because the quotas were filled and they could not sell the clothing until the following year—by then, it was out of fashion.

bonded warehouse
Authorized by customs authorities for storage of goods on which payment of import duties is deferred until the goods are removed

The Automated Commercial System (ACS). Customs has another system—ACS—that it uses to track, control, and process all commercial goods imported into the United States. ACS reduces the paperwork, cuts costs, and facilitates merchandise processing. Importers that use the system to file import documents can also pay the custom fees and import duties electronically all in one transaction. Like AES, ACS interfaces with other government agencies to transfer data electronically on import transactions for faster cargo release. An Automated Manifest System speeds the flow of cargo and entry processing, with the result that cargo remains on the dock for less time before its release to the importers.[15]

Import Duties

Every importer should know (1) how U.S. Customs calculates import duties and (2) the importance of the product classification. This requires knowing the Harmonized Tariff Schedule of the United States (HTSUSA), the American version of the global tariff code, the Harmonized System.

Harmonized System

The Harmonized System consists of 5,019 six-digit headings and subheadings that all developed nations must use. The United States further subdivides the six-digit headings into 8,800 eight-digit classification lines and 12,000 ten-digit statistical reporting numbers. There are interpretative notes that must be followed in determining how goods are to be classified in the system. An importing firm that feels it is paying excessive import duties because its product has been incorrectly classified by customs officials can take the matter to court if it cannot reach an agreement with the officials. Similarly, an exporter can also have its agent in the importing country take the case before that country's courts. Any controversy can be brought before the Customs Cooperation Committee, where contracting countries to the Harmonized System can present written views, make oral arguments, and then vote on the goods' classification.[16]

HTSUSA

Each product has its own unique HTSUSA number. Figure 17.5 shows a page from the HTSUSA. All member-countries use the same system, and so it is possible to describe the product in any language by using the first six digits. The other four digits are for use just in this country. The HTSUSA also shows the *reporting units,* which U.S. Customs uses in its paperwork. The last three columns have to do with the rate of duty.

The percentages in the "General" column are the rates the United States charges for products coming from GATT members, the most favored nations. The "Special" column is for nations that receive preferential treatment; the rates are even lower than those for the most favored nation. The abbreviations indicate which nations they are:

1. A: a General System of Preferences beneficiary country (developing nation).
2. E: Caribbean Basin Economic Recovery Act (concessions providing for no or low duty for participating Caribbean Basin nations).
3. CA: Canada (NAFTA).
4. IL: Israel (Free Trade Area).
5. J: Andean Trade Preference Act (Colombia, Ecuador, Bolivia, Peru, and Venezuela).
6. MX: Mexico (NAFTA).

Finally, column 2 lists rates for nations that are not friends of the United States: Cuba, Vietnam, Afghanistan, Laos, North Korea, Kampuchea, and Azerbaijan. Note that these duty rates are considerably higher. Small wonder that China is fighting to remain a most favored nation.

A prospective importer should follow these rules:

1. Disclose fully to the U.S. Customs Service all foreign and financial arrangements before passing the goods through U.S. Customs. The penalties for fraud are high.
2. Ask the advice of a customhouse broker *before* making the transaction. Frequently, a simple change in the product can result in much lower import duties. For example, if you are an importer of jeans, you will pay higher duties if the label is outside the back pocket instead of under the belt. If the words on the label are stylized, duties are more than they are when the words are in simple block letters. Any clothing that is ornamented pays more duty. This is why one importer brings in plain sports shirts and sews on an animal figure after they are in the United States.
3. Calculate carefully the landed price in advance. If there is a doubt about the import category, the importer can ask U.S. Customs to determine the category in advance and to put it in writing—just as you can obtain advanced rulings from the Internal Revenue Service (IRS). At the time of importation, customs inspectors must respect this determination. Many customs procedures are like those of the IRS. Both have similar procedures for appealing their decisions, for example. This is no coincidence—both are under the secretary of the treasury.[17]

[Figure 17.5] Page from the HTSUSA

XVI
84–62

HARMONIZED TARIFF SCHEDULE of the UNITED STATES (1995)
Annotated for Statistical Reporting Purposes

Heading/ Subheading	Stat. Suf-fix	Article Description	Units of Quantity	Rates of Duty 1 General	Rates of Duty 1 Special	2
8461		Machine tools for planing, shaping, slotting, broaching, gear cutting, gear grinding or gear finishing, sawing, cutting-off and other machine tools working by removing metal, sintered metal carbides or cerments, not elsewhere specified or included:				
8461.10		Planing machines:				
8461.10.40		Numerically controlled		4.4%	Free (A,CA,E,IL,J, MX)	30%
	20	Used or rebuilt	No.			
	60	Other	No.			
8461.10.80		Other		4.4%	Free (A,CA,E,IL,J, MX)	30%
	20	Used or rebuilt	No.			
	40	Other, valued under $3,025 each	No.			
	80	Other	No.			
8461.20		Shaping or slotting machines:				
8461.20.40	00	Numerically controlled	No.	4.4%	Free (A,CA,E,IL,J, MX)	30%
8461.20.80		Other		4.4%	Free (A,CA,E,IL,J, MX)	30%
	30	Used or rebuilt	No.			
	70	Other, valued under $3,025 each	No.			
	90	Other	No.			
8461.30		Broaching machines:				
8461.30.40		Numerically controlled		4.4%	Free (A,CA,E,IL,J, MX)	30%
	20	Used or rebuilt	No.			
	60	Other	No.			
8461.30.80		Other		4.4%	Free (A,CA,E,IL,J, MX)	30%
	20	Used or rebuilt	No.			
	40	Other, valued under $3,025 each	No.			
	80	Other	No.			
8461.40		Gear cutting, gear grinding or gear finishing machines:				
8461.40.10		Gear cutting machines		5.8%	Free (A,CA,E,IL,J, MX)	40%
	10	Used or rebuilt	No.			
		Other:				
	20	For bevel gears	No.			
		Other:				
	30	Gear hobbers	No.			
	40	Gear shapers	No.			
	60	Other	No.			
8461.40.50		Gear grinding or finishing machines		4.4%	Free (A,CA,E,IL,J, MX)	30%
	20	Used or rebuilt	No.			
	40	Other, valued under $3,025 each	No.			
		Other:				
	50	For bevel gears	No.			
	70	Other	No.			
8461.50		Sawing or cutting-off machines:				
8461.50.40		Numerically controlled		4.4%	Free (A,CA,E,IL,J, MX)	30%
	10	Used or rebuilt	No.			
	50	Other	No.			
8461.50.80		Other		4.4%	Free (A,CA,E,IL,J, MX)	30%
	10	Used or rebuilt	No.			
	20	Other, valued under $3,025 each	No.			
	90	Other	No.			
8461.90		Other:				
8461.90.40		Numerically controlled		4.4%	Free (A,CA,E,IL,J, MX)	30%
	10	Used or rebuilt	No.			
	40	Other	No.			
8461.90.80		Other		4.4%	Free (A,CA,E,IL,J, MX)	30%
	10	Used or rebuilt	No.			
	20	Other, valued under $3,025 each	No.			
	80	Other	No.			

Source: Harmonized Tariff Schedule of the United States (Washington, DC: U.S. Government Printing Office, 1995), p. 84–62.

[Summary]

Explain why firms export and the three problems of exporting.

Smaller firms, like larger ones, export to increase sales. Some begin to export accidentally, while others seek out foreign customers. Large multinationals export to serve markets where they have no manufacturing plants or the local plant does not produce all of the product mix. Some host governments require an affiliate to export, and many firms export to remain competitive in the home market. Exporting is also an inexpensive way to test foreign markets. A product's life can be extended by exporting the product to markets with less advanced technology. The three problem areas of exporting are (1) locating foreign markets, (2) payment and financing procedures, and (3) export procedures.

Identify the sources of export counseling.

The Trade Information Center, Small Business Administration, Small Business Development Centers in universities, Department of Agriculture, state offices for export assistance, World Trade Centers Association, and Trade Point Global Network are some sources of export counseling.

Describe the main elements of the export sales assistance program of the U.S. Department of Commerce.

The Department of Commerce, the federal department in charge of export assistance, offers many programs covering all aspects of exporting. These include services that aid in conducting market research, such as the National Trade Data Bank, the Comparison Shopping Service, and various Commerce publications. Commerce can also assist in locating foreign representatives and making sales through trade fairs, matchmaker programs, and catalog and video shows.

Discuss the meaning of the various terms of sale.

Various terms of sale are possible in exporting. FAS (free alongside ship) means the seller pays all transportation expenses to ship's side and requires all the sellers to clear the goods for export. CIF (cost, insurance, and freight) means the seller quotes a price that includes cost of goods, insurance, and transportation to a specified destination. CFR (cost and freight) is like CIF except that the buyer pays insurance costs. DAF (delivered at frontier) means that the seller's obligations are met when the goods have arrived at the border and have been cleared for export. The buyer's responsibility is to arrange for its forwarder to pick up the goods after they are cleared for export, clear them for importation, and make delivery.

Identify some sources of export financing.

Some sources of export financing are commercial banks, factors, forfaiting, the Export-Import Bank (Eximbank), and the Small Business Administration.

Describe the activities of a foreign freight forwarder.

Foreign freight forwarders act as agents for exporters. They prepare documents, book space on carriers, and function as a firm's export traffic department.

Understand the kinds of export documents required.

Correct documentation is vital to the success of any export shipment. Shipping documents include export packing list, export licenses, export bills of lading, shipper's export declaration, and insurance certificates. Collection documents include commercial invoices, consular invoices, certificates of origin, and inspection certificates.

Discuss some innovations in materials handling in sea and air transport.

Innovations in transportation and materials handling enable exporters to reach new markets and reduce theft and cost. These include the use of containers and LASH and RO-RO vessels.

Identify import sources.

Prospective importers can identify sources in a number of ways. They can examine the product label to see where the product is made and then contact the nearest embassy of that country to request the name of the manufacturer. Foreign chambers of commerce and trade organizations provide information on their countries' exporters. Electronic bulletin boards and data banks are also useful.

Explain the Harmonized Tariff Schedule of the United States (HTSUSA).

The HTSUSA is the American version of the Harmonized System used by nations worldwide for classifying imported products. There is a sample page from the HTSUSA in the text.

[Key Words]

terms of sale (p. 588)
letter of credit (L/C) (p. 590)
confirmed (p. 590)
irrevocable (p. 590)
air waybill (p. 590)
pro forma invoice (p. 591)
export, sight, and time drafts (p. 592)
banker's acceptance (p. 594)
factoring (p. 594)
forfaiting (p. 594)
Eximbank (p. 594)
Overseas Private Investment Corporation (OPIC) (p. 595)
Foreign Sales Corporation (FSC) (p. 595)
free trade zone (p. 596)
foreign trade zone (FTZ) (p. 596)
foreign freight forwarders (p. 597)
general export license (p. 597)
validated export license (p. 598)
export bill of lading (B/L) (p. 598)
customhouse brokers (p. 603)
bonded warehouse (p. 604)

[Questions]

1. What are the common terms of sale quoted by exporters? For each, explain to what point the seller must pay all transportation and delivery costs. Where does the responsibility for loss or damage pass to the buyer?
2. a. Explain the various export payment terms that are available.
   b. Which two offer the most protection to the seller?
3. What is the procedure for a letter of credit transaction?
4. The manager of the international department of the McAllen Bank learns on the way to work that the ship on which a local exporter shipped some goods has sunk. The manager has received all the documents required in the letter of credit and is ready to pay the exporter for the shipment. In view of the news about the ship, the manager now knows that the foreign customer will never receive the goods. Should the manager pay the exporter, or should he withhold payment and notify the overseas customer?
5. What is a foreign trade zone? Check with a customhouse broker or a U.S. Customs official or do some research in the library to find out the advantages of a foreign trade zone over a bonded warehouse.
6. What are the purposes of an export bill of lading?
7. An importer brings plain sports shirts to this country because the import duty is lower than it is for shirts with adornments. It then sews on a figure of a fox in this country. Should the importer do this operation in a foreign trade zone?
8. How would you find sources for a product that you want to import?
9. What does a customhouse broker do?
10. An importer in Vancouver, Washington, has the following dollar quotations from three manufacturers of gear-cutting machines. All prices are FOB border of each exporter's country. Disregarding transportation costs, which is the least expensive after paying import duty? See Figure 17.5 for appropriate import duties.
    a. $5,000 from Germany.
    b. $5,500 from Canada.
    c. $4,000 from Azerbaijan.

[Internet Exercises]

Using the Internet

1. a. What does U.S. Customs do for the *exporter?*
   b. What does the Automated Export System do for the exporter?
   c. Does the AES replace the paper SED?

d. Will the AES hold up an exporter's cargo until shipment is approved?
e. For certain shipments, other government agencies require the filing of data at the time of shipment. Must the exporter continue to file data with the other agencies as usual?

2. a. A new customer requests you, the exporter, to quote the firm a price DAF. What does this mean?
b. When do sellers fulfill their obligation to deliver the goods with payment terms of "Delivered Duty Unpaid"?
c. What does the INCOTERM "DELIVERED EX QUAY (DUTY PAID)" require of the seller?
d. How does the term in part *c* differ from FAS, Port of Exit?
e. What distinguishes Groups C, D, E, and F from each other?

[Minicase 17.1]

State Manufacturing Export Sales Price

State Manufacturing Company, a producer of farm equipment, had just received an inquiry from a large distributor in Italy. The quantity on which the distributor wanted a price was sufficiently large that Jim Mason, the sales manager, felt he had to respond. He knew the inquiry was genuine, because he had called two of the companies that the distributor said he represented, and both had assured him that the Italian firm was a serious one. It paid its bills regularly with no problems. Both companies were selling to the firm on open account terms.

Mason's problem was that he had never quoted on a sale for export before. His first impulse was to take the regular FOB factory price and add the cost of the extra-heavy export packing plus the inland freight cost to the nearest U.S. port. This price should enable the company to make money if he quoted the price FAS port of exit.

However, the terms of sale were bothering him. The traffic manager had called a foreign freight forwarder to learn about the frequency of sailings to Italy, and during the conversation she had suggested to the traffic manager that she might be able to help Mason. When Mason called her, he learned that because of competition, many firms like State Manufacturing were quoting CIF foreign port as a convenience to the importer. She asked him what payment terms he would quote, and he replied that his credit manager had suggested an irrevocable, confirmed letter of credit to be sure of receiving payment for the sale. He admitted that the distributor, however, had asked for payment against a 90-day time draft.

The foreign freight forwarder urged Mason to consider quoting CIF port of entry in Italy with payment as requested by the distributor to be more competitive. She informed him that he could get insurance to protect the company against commercial risk. To help him calculate a CIF price, she offered to give him the various charges if he would tell her the weight and value of his shipment FOB factory. He replied that the total price was $21,500 and that the gross weight, including the container, was 3,629 kilos.

Two hours later, she called to give him the following charges:

1	Containerization	$ 200.00
2	Inland freight less handling	798.00
3	Forwarding and documentation	90.00
4	Ocean freight	2,633.00
5	Commercial risk insurance	105.00
6	Marine insurance—total of items	167.15
	1−5 × 1.1 = $27,858.60 at 60¢/$100*	

During that time, Mason had been thinking about the competition. Could he lower the FOB price for an export sale? He looked at the cost figures. Sales expense amounted to 20 percent of the sales price. Couldn't this be deducted on a foreign order? Research and development amounted to 10 percent. Should this be charged? Advertising and promotional expense amounted to another 10 percent. What about that? Because this was an unsolicited inquiry, there was no selling expense for this sale except for his and the secretary's time. Mason felt that it wasn't worth calculating this time.

If you were Jim Mason, how would you calculate the CIF port of entry price?

*Total coverage of marine insurance is commonly calculated on the basis of the total price plus 10 percent.

4. Market share.
5. Profit and loss forecasts.

B. Characteristics of ideal target markets.
1. GNP/capita.
2. GNP/capita growth rate.
3. Size of target market.

C. Identify, assess, and select target markets.
1. Market contact programs.
(a) U.S. Department of Commerce.
(b) World Trade Centers.
(c) Chamber of Commerce.
(d) Company's bank.
(e) State's export assistance program.
(f) Small Business Administration.
(g) Small Business Development Center in local university.
(h) Export hotline directory.
2. Market screening.
(a) First screening—basic need potential.
(b) Second screening—financial and economic forces.
(1) GNP/capita growth rate.
(2) Size of target market.
(3) Growth rate of target market.
(4) Exchange rate trends.
(5) Trends in inflation and interest rates.
(c) Third screening—political and legal forces.
(1) Import restrictions.
(2) Product standards.
(3) Price controls.
(4) Government and public attitude toward buying American products.
(d) Fourth screening—sociocultural forces.
(1) Attitudes and beliefs.
(2) Education.
(3) Material culture.
(4) Languages.
(e) Fifth screening—competitive forces.
(1) Size, number, and financial strength of competitors.
(2) Competitors' market shares.
(3) Effectiveness of competitors' marketing mixes.
(4) Levels of after-sales service.
(5) Competitors' market coverage—Can market segmentation produce niches that are now poorly attended?
(f) Field trips to best prospects.
(1) Department of Commerce trade mission.
(2) Trade missions organized by state or trade association.

D. Export marketing strategies.
1. Product lines to export.
2. Export pricing methods.

3. Channels of distribution.
   (a) Direct exporting.
   (b) Indirect exporting.
4. Promotion methods.
5. After-sales and warranty policies.
6. Buyer financing methods.
7. Methods for ongoing competitor analysis.
8. Sales forecast.

VII. Export financial plan.

- **A.** Pro forma profit and loss statement.
- **B.** Pro forma cash flow analysis.
- **C.** Break-even analysis.

VIII. Export performance evaluation.

- **A.** Frequency.
  - **1.** Markets.
  - **2.** Product lines.
  - **3.** Export personnel.
- **B.** Variables to be measured.
  - **1.** Sales by units and dollar volume in each market.
  - **2.** Sales growth rates in each market.
  - **3.** Product line profitability.
  - **4.** Market share.
  - **5.** Competitors' efforts in each market.
  - **6.** Actual results compared to budgeted results.

[Chapter]

18

Human Resource Management

"The West can push to end child labor in a Nike factory, but where do the youngsters go then? Poverty is more dangerous for those kids than working in a Nike factory."

—*Rana Jawad Asghar, "It's Harsh, but Some Children Must Work,"* Los Angeles Times, *January 20, 2000, p. B9*

Concept Previews

After reading this chapter, you should be able to:

- **remember** some of the regional or cultural differences in labor conditions we shall present
- **understand** why some economies are better at job creation than others, which causes differing unemployment rates
- **understand** the difficulties of finding qualified executives for international companies (ICs) and the importance of foreign language knowledge
- **compare** home country, host country, and third country nationals as IC executives
- **realize** the growing role of women in international business
- **realize** the increasing importance of accommodating the trailing spouse of an expatriate executive
- **remember** some of the complications of compensation packages for expatriate executives

Dennis Halliman/FPG International

Executives with the Right Stuff in Big Demand

This is the case everywhere, but it is particularly true in developing economies. One can look at China and Latin America as examples.

Kodak's Chinese operation brought in Western managers who were excellent with the technical aspects of their jobs. Nevertheless, they failed miserably because they did not understand the culture of the country.

In an attempt to solve the problem, Kodak and other foreign companies recruit Chinese-speaking staff from Asian and other countries. But there are still cultural considerations, says Kay Kutt, managing director of Cendant Intercultural Assignment Services, Asia-Pacific division. "It's almost worse than sending a Westerner, to send someone who has the Chinese language but not Chinese values," as she puts it.

Hundreds of non–Latin American businesses trying to operate in that region have openings for bilingual executives. These companies are looking for people who can operate in a dual mode, combining U.S. efficiency and business culture with the Latin

Reality Differs from Politicians' Proclamations

At the World Trade Organization (WTO) meeting in Seattle in 1999, President Clinton declared that the WTO's policies have removed 7,000 Pakistani children from softball-making factories. He claimed that those children have gone back to school, but at least one expert says that is not where they went. This expert estimates that less than 10 percent of those children have gone back to school. His statement of reality is that "children's rights activists are successful in removing these kids from factories—where they may have higher wages, better working environments, and chances to learn higher skills—and pushing them into a bleak future."[9]

Both the World Bank and UNICEF have moved closer to this point of view. The World Bank says that children's work can be in their own interests and that a family's survival may depend on it. UNICEF advocates banning only work that can harm children's development. It goes on to observe that forcing children out of factories and into schools may actually hurt them; unless their families are compensated for the lost income, such a policy can worsen their destitution.[10]

Children and Chickens

Labor trainers for international companies (ICs) in developing nations have found that the people learn industrial skills rapidly. More difficult is teaching new workers who come from farms and villages how to adjust socially and psychologically to factory life. Some of these workers must be taught not only job skills but also the concept of time. They are not accustomed to reporting to work at the same time and place each workday or to meeting production schedules. They must be introduced to factory teamwork and to an industrial hierarchy. Frequently, the company must compromise and not attempt to change customary farm and village practices too quickly and completely.

A Spanish company opened a factory in Guatemala, hired local people, and tried to operate as if it were in Europe. The Spanish management installed work hours and production routines and schedules that had worked efficiently in Spain. But in Guatemala, in its early stage of economic development, the procedures were nearly disastrous.

The people refused to work and became hostile. Guatemalan troops were needed to protect the factory. Management at last considered local needs and compromised, and mutually satisfactory solutions were found.

American executives if they get to heaven.
Source: *Financial Times*, June 2, 1997, p. 14. © Banx. Reprinted with permission.

The solutions included four-hour breaks between two daily work periods. During the breaks, the male employees took care of their farms and gardens and the female employees attended to household needs and cared for their children. As another part of the solution, the employees were willing to work on Saturdays to make up production lost during the breaks.

Through compromise and patience, European management, operating in a preindustrial setting, was able to achieve satisfactory production. It studied, negotiated, and adapted to local needs. The alternatives were low production and perhaps even a destroyed factory.

Staffing: The Good News and the Difficulties

For those of you wanting jobs in international business, particularly those who want to live and work abroad, there is good news in a study by William M. Mercer. The study reports that 90 percent of American-based ICs plan to boost expatriate assignments by the year 2000.[11] William M. Mercer is the U.K. arm of the Mercer Consulting Group, the world's largest benefits consultancy, which is based in Chicago. The group is owned by Marsh and McLennan, the world's biggest insurance broker.

Finding the right people to manage an organization can be difficult under any circumstances, but it is especially difficult to find good managers of overseas operations. Such positions require more and different skills than do purely domestic executive jobs. The right persons need to be bicultural, with knowledge of the business practices in the home country plus an understanding of business practices and customs in the host country. And to truly understand a culture, any culture, it is necessary to speak the language of its people. Only with a good grasp of the language can one understand the subtleties and humor and know what is really going on in the host country.

Figure 18.1 shows an advertisement by the city of Berlin for international companies to set up headquarters there. A major attraction is the available expertise in 20 languages spoken in Central and Eastern Europe.

The successful manager of a foreign affiliate must be able to operate efficiently in one culture and explain operations in that culture to executives in another culture. Such managers exist, and they may be found in (1) the home country, (2) the host country, or (3) a third country.

Figure 18.2 shows a page from an international business/finance publication that contains advertisements for openings—job opportunities—at a number of institutions. The geographical locations include Azerbaijan, Greece, Japan, "job hunting internationally," and the United Kingdom. In this and numerous other sources, hundreds of employment opportunities are advertised every day.

Sources of Managers

Home Country

Most ICs utilize citizens of their own countries, called **home country nationals,** in many foreign management and technical positions even though at first such personnel are usually not knowledgeable about the host country culture and language. Many such expatriates have adapted, learned the language, and become thoroughly accepted in the host country. Of course, it would not be necessary for a host country citizen to adapt, but for a variety of reasons IC headquarters frequently needs or wants its own nationals in executive or technical positions abroad.

home country nationals
The country in which an IC has its worldwide headquarters is called the home country. Employees who are citizens of the home country are called home country nationals

Host Country Nationals Unavailable. A foreign subsidiary often cannot find suitable host country personnel for management jobs, and in such instances the parent headquarters will send out its people to manage until local personnel can be found and trained. Those are full-time jobs, but other circumstances call for temporary help from headquarters. Labor negotiators and other specialists may be sent to troubleshoot such problems as product warranty, international contracts, taxes, accounting, and reporting.

[Figure 18.1] City of Berlin's Advertisement to Attract International Business

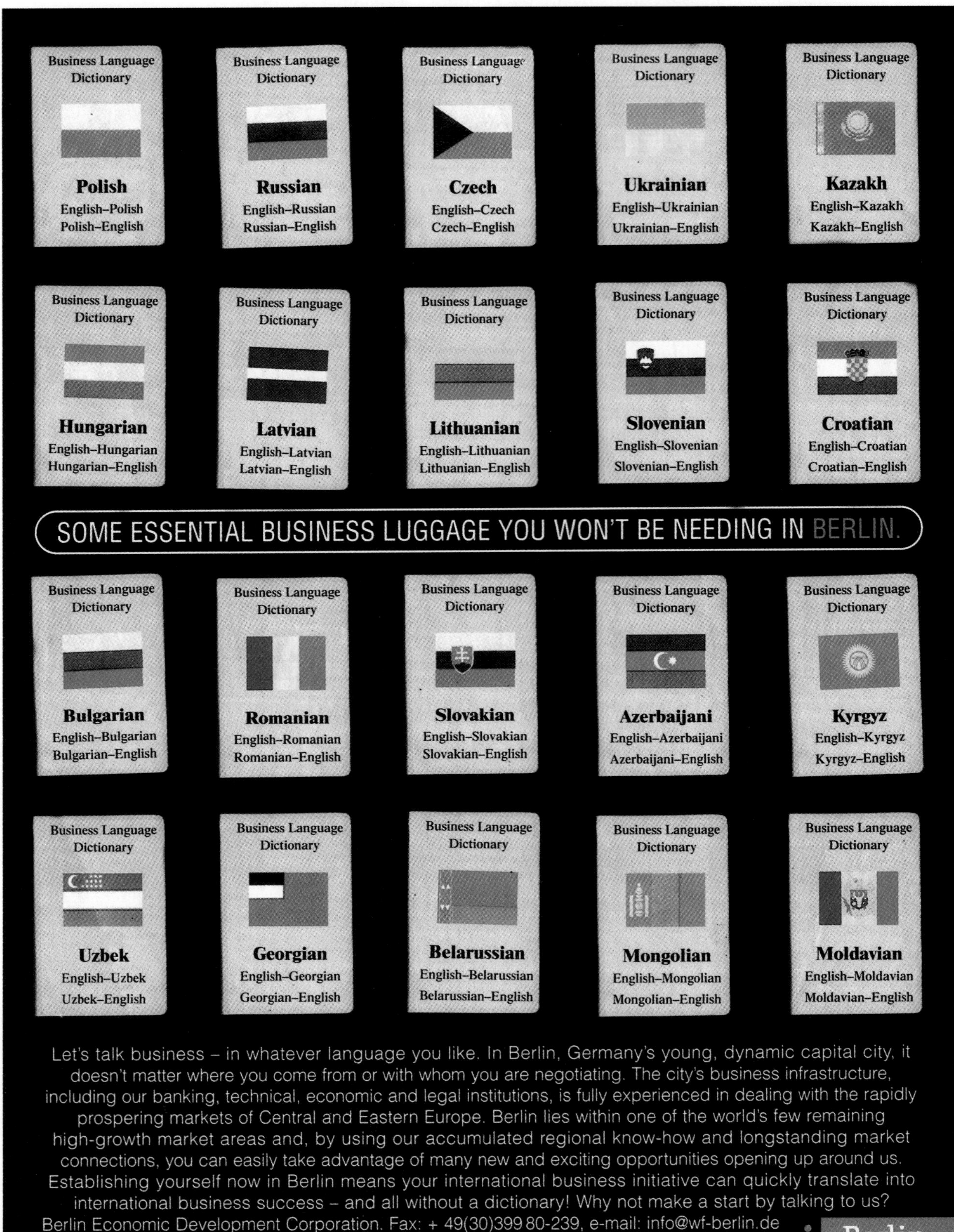

Courtesy of Berlin Economic Development Corporation.

[Figure 18.2] Job Opportunities

OPPORTUNITIES FOR

ECONOMISTS, PLANNERS AND ENGINEERS

We are a Tokyo-based consulting firm with full-time and project-based positions available in developing countries for economists, planners and engineers. We work in various sectors (e.g. transport, environment, education, tourism, energy) and offer excellent remuneration.

If interested, please send a detailed CV to:

PADECO Co., Ltd., Izumikan Sanbancho Bldg.
3-8 Sanbancho, Chiyoda-ku, Tokyo 102-0075
Fax: 81-3-3238-9422 Email: admin@padeco.co.jp
Homepage: http://www.padeco.co.jp

CENTRE OF PLANNING AND ECONOMIC RESEARCH
ATHENS, GREECE

Research Officers in Economics

The Centre of Planning and Economic Research is seeking to appoint up to 13 Research Officers in the following areas of economics:

Macroeconomics, Public Economics, Industrial Economics, Monetary Economics, Applied Econometrics, Economics with emphasis to Social Policy, Applied Microeconomics, Labour Economics.

Applicants should hold a Ph.D. degree and be Greek or EU nationals.

The closing date for applications is the 10th of July, 2000.

For further details please contact: tel. 0030 1 3643771; fax 0030 1 3630122; e-mail: kepe@kepe.gr

Founded in 1823, Birkbeck is based in Bloomsbury and has the highest proportion of research active staff of any college or university in the greater London area.

Lecturer/Senior Lecturer/ Reader in Management

The department of Management is seeking to make an appointment in any area of management or business. You will teach challenging, experienced students at undergraduate, postgraduate and PhD level and contribute to the research reputation of the department and the School of Management and Organizational Psychology as a whole.

Applicants should have a PhD, or equivalent, in a relevant social science area and have developed, or for appointment at lecturer level show evidence of developing, an international research programme and publications.

Salary ranges: £19,372 to £24,713 pa or £25,655 to £32,199 pa or £33,697 to £37,804 pa inc, depending on qualifications and experience.

For details and application forms please send a large (A4) sae to the Personnel Department, Ref: CMB143/G, Birkbeck, Malet Street, Bloomsbury, London WC1E 7HX.
Closing date: 27 June 2000
Birkbeck web site: http://www.bbk.ac.uk

JOB HUNTING INTERNATIONALLY?

Executive $75K-500K+. Career searching into, within or out of Asia / Europe / M.East / U.S.? Contact for **Free** Info & Critique

www.careerpath.co.uk

	Fax:	Email:
USA/Canada	+1 202 4781698	cpamerica@careerpath.co.uk
Europe	+44 20 75048280	cpeurope@careerpath.co.uk
Asia / M. East / Aus	+66 2 2674688	cpasia@bkk.loxinfo.co.th

Commercial Research analyst

A leading international commodity trade house with a global presence in the sugar market as principal traders, brokers and refiners is seeking a highly numerate graduate with demonstrable analytical and presentation skills. Working in the research department, initially the role requires you to develop detailed knowledge of the European Community legislative environment though it is vitally important to identify commercial opportunities and develop direct links with our clients. The successful candidate will have a good degree in Economics or closely related discipline, excellent communication and computer skills and a keen interest in agriculture policy. We will provide full in-house training, travel opportunities and a competitive salary and benefits package.

Send a cv to Box 4106, 25 St James St, London SW1A 1HG, England

Executive Director, AZERBAIJAN

Open Society Institute seeks an Executive Director for its national foundation in Baku, Azerbaijan. The executive director, in conjunction with and under direction of OSI Azerbaijan's board of directors, develops strategy, plans and implementation for operating and grantmaking programs. The director supervises staff; interacts with foundation board of directors; oversees the foundation's annual budget.

REQUIRES: Fluent English and Azeri, Turkish and/or Russian; 4+ years ngo management; 2+ years field exp. in Central and Eastern Europe or preferably, in the former Soviet Union; exp. working with a board; strong financial management, organizational, interpersonal and writing skills; BA with Masters or other advanced degree preferred. Extensive travel.

Send cover letter/CV to: **Open Society Institute**
Human Resources - Code AZERB, 400 W. 59th Street, NY, NY 10019, or fax to: (212) 548-4607.

PEMBROKE COLLEGE AND THE JUDGE INSTITUTE OF MANAGEMENT STUDIES
CAMBRIDGE

The Bristol Myers Squibb Research Fellowship In Pharmaco-Economics

Bristol Myers Squibb are supporting a Research Fellowship in Pharmaco-Economics to be held jointly at Pembroke College and The Judge Institute of Management Studies. The appointment will run from 1 October 2000 or as soon as possible thereafter.

The Judge Institute of Management Studies is the University of Cambridge's business school. It aims to be an internationally-recognised centre for research and education of the highest quality to provide a forum for the debate of key management issues by leaders from around the world.

Pembroke College is one of the constituent colleges of the University of Cambridge, and has strong accademic connections with the corporate world.

Applications are sought from candidates with a strong research record in the field of health/pharmaco-economics. The appointment is for an initial 3-year term, with the possibility of renewal thereafter. Salary is negotiable depending on experience.

Completed applications should reach the College by 24 July 2000. Further particulars and application forms are available from the Senior Tutor's Secretary, Pembroke College, Cambridge CB2 1RF (pat.whitby@pem.cam.ac.uk).

Pembroke College is an equal opportunities employer.

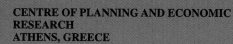

Source: *The Economist,* June 10, 2000, p. 103.

Teams may be sent from the home country to assist with new plant start-up, and they would probably stay until subsidiary personnel were trained to run and maintain the new facilities.

Training for Headquarters. Another reason for using home country citizens abroad is to broaden their experience in preparation for becoming high-level managers at headquarters. Firms that get large parts of their earnings from international sources require top executives who have a worldwide perspective, business and political. It is difficult to impossible to acquire that sort of perspective without living and working abroad for a substantial period of time.

Headquarters' Representatives. Some firms, although their policy is to employ host country nationals in most positions, want at least one home country manager (commonly the general manager or the finance officer) in their foreign subsidiaries. If new technology for the subsidiary is involved, the parent company will probably station at least one of its technologically qualified experts at the subsidiary until its local personnel learn the technology. In this way, the home office can be confident that someone is immediately available to explain headquarters' policies and procedures, see that they are observed, and interpret what is happening locally for the IC's management. Positions that an IC must take or demands that it must make are sometimes not popular with a host government. It can seem unpatriotic for a host country national to do such things, whereas the host government can understand, and sometimes accept, such positions or demands from a foreigner.

> One of the authors remembers the relief expressed by the Argentinean executives of an Argentine subsidiary of an American IC because an American manager was present to press the Argentine government for what seemed to be unusually extensive payment guarantees. The contract was for a product partly manufactured and assembled in Argentina but mostly manufactured in the United States and imported into Argentina from the United States. The Argentinean executives feared that the very specific and high-level payment guarantees would antagonize government officials. The subsidiary was an Argentine company, subject to that country's laws and dependent in part on business from government departments and government-owned companies. Its managers were residents and would stay in Argentina, while the American was there only until the signing of this contract and the guarantees. After he flew away, the local people could blame him and the American parent IC, thus deflecting anger and resentment from themselves.

Host Country

host country nationals
Subsidiaries within the IC family of companies often are located in countries other than the home country. They are called host countries, and employee citizens of the host countries are called host country nationals

When **host country nationals** are employed, there is no problem of their being unfamiliar with local customs, culture, and language. Furthermore, the first costs of employing them are generally lower (compared to the costs of employing home country nationals), although considerable training costs are sometimes necessary. If there is a strong feeling of nationalism in the host country, having nationals as managers can make the subsidiary seem less foreign.

The government development plans and laws of some countries demand that employment in all sectors and at all levels reflect the racial composition of the society. In other words, more skilled and managerial slots must be given to the local people. If foreign-owned firms in Indonesia fail to hire enough *pribumi* (indigenous Indonesians), those firms are likely to encounter difficulties with reentry permits for foreign employees as well as with other government licenses and permits that they need. Bribery requests have been known to increase until more pribumi were hired and promoted. Malaysia threatens to revoke the operating licenses of foreign-owned firms that fail to have a satisfactory number of *bumiputra* (indigenous Malays) in sufficiently elevated jobs.

A disadvantage of hiring local managers is that they are often unfamiliar with the home country of the IC and with its policies and practices. Differences in attitudes and values, as discussed in Chapter 9, can cause them to act in ways that surprise or displease headquarters. Also, local managers may create their own upward immobility if, because of strong cultural or family ties, they are reluctant to accept promotions that would require them to leave the country to work at parent headquarters or at another subsidiary.

A new problem has developed for foreign-owned companies that hire and train local, host country people. The best of these people may be pirated away by local firms or other IC subsidiaries, as local executive recruiters are constantly on the lookout to make raids.

Finally, there can be a conflict of loyalty between the host country and the employer. For example, the host country national may give preference to a local supplier even though imported products may be less expensive or of better quality. Local managers may oppose headquarters' requests to set low transfer prices in order to lower taxes payable to the host government.

Third Country

The disadvantages often encountered when using employees from the home or host country can sometimes be avoided by sending **third country nationals** to fill management posts. A Chilean going to Argentina would have little cultural or language difficulty, but IC headquarters should be careful not to rely too heavily on similarities in language as a guide to similarities in other aspects of cultures. Mexicans, for example, would have to make considerable adjustments if they were transferred to Argentina, and they would find a move to Spain even more difficult. This is because the Mexican culture is far less European than that of either Argentina or Chile. Although the latter two cultures are certainly not identical, they do have many similarities. A fair generalization is that after an executive has adapted once to a new culture and language, a second or succeeding adaptation is easier.

third country nationals
An employee who is a citizen of neither the home nor the host country

An employer should not count on cost savings in using third country nationals. Although they may come from countries where salary scales are lower, in such countries as Brazil and most of the nations of northwestern Europe, salaries may be higher than American companies are paying at comparable position levels. Furthermore, many multinationals give international status* to both home country nationals and third country nationals, who then receive the same perquisites and compensation packages for the same job.

Selection and Training

The selection and training of managers vary somewhat, depending on whether the candidate is from the home country, the host country, or a third country.

Home Country

Relatively few recent college graduates are hired for the express purpose of being sent overseas. Usually they spend a number of years in the domestic (parent) company, and they may get into the company's international operations by design and persistence, by luck, or by a combination of those elements. They may first be assigned to the international division at the firm's headquarters, where they handle problems submitted by foreign affiliates and meet visiting overseas personnel.

If the company feels that it probably will send home country employees abroad, it will frequently encourage them to study the language and culture of the country to which they are going. Such employees will probably be sent on short trips abroad to handle special assignments and to be exposed to foreign surroundings. Newly hired home country nationals with prior overseas experience may undergo similar but shorter training periods.[12]

It is increasingly possible for American ICs to supplement their in-house training for overseas work with courses in American business schools. In recognition of the growing importance of international business, those schools are expanding the number and scope of international business courses they offer. In addition, a number of university-level business schools are now operating in other countries.

*International status is discussed later in this chapter.

A large problem that has plagued employers is caused by the families of executives transferred overseas. Even though the employee may adapt to and enjoy the foreign experience, the family may not, and an unhappy family may sour the employee on the job or split up the marriage. In either event, the company may have to ship the family back home at great expense—seldom less than $25,000. Consequently, many companies try to assess whether the executive's family can adapt to the foreign ambience before assigning the executive abroad. This is part of the subject of expatriates that is dealt with later in this chapter.

Host Country

The same general criteria for selecting home country employees apply to host country nationals. Usually, however, the training of host country nationals will differ from that of home country nationals in that host country nationals are more likely to lack knowledge of advanced business techniques and of the company.

Host Country Nationals Hired in the Home Country. Many multinationals try to solve the business technique problem by hiring host country students on their graduation from home country business schools. After being hired, these new employees are usually sent to IC headquarters to receive indoctrination in the firm's policies and procedures as well as on-the-job training in a specific function, such as finance, marketing, or production.

Host Country Nationals Hired in the Host Country. Because the number of host country citizens graduating from home country universities is limited, multinationals must also recruit locally for their management positions. To impart knowledge of business techniques, the company may do one or more things. It may set up in-house training programs in the host country subsidiary, or it may utilize business courses in the host country's universities. The IC may also send new employees to home country business schools or to parent company training programs. In addition, employees who show promise will be sent repeatedly to the parent company headquarters, divisions, and other subsidiaries to observe the various enterprise operations and meet the other executives with whom they will be communicating during their careers. Such visits are also learning experiences for the home office and the other subsidiaries.

Third Country

Hiring personnel who are citizens of neither the home country nor the host country is often advantageous. Third country nationals may accept lower wages and benefits than will employees from the home country, and they may come from a culture similar to that of the host country. In addition, they may have worked for another unit of the IC and thus be familiar with its policies, procedures, and people.

The use of third country nationals has become particularly prevalent in the developing countries because of shortages of literate, not to mention skilled, locals. It can be an advantage to get someone already residing in the country who has the necessary work permits and knowledge of the local languages and customs.

Host Country Attitudes. If the host government emphasizes employment of its own citizens, third country nationals will be no more welcome than will home country people. Actually, third country nationals could face an additional obstacle in obtaining necessary work permits. For example, the host government can understand that the German parent company of a subsidiary would want some German executives to look after its interest in the host country. It may be harder to convince the government that a third country native is any better for the parent than a local executive would be.

Generalizations Difficult. We must be careful with generalizations about third country personnel, partly because people achieve that status in different ways. They may be foreigners hired in the home country and sent to a host country subsidiary either because they have had previous experience there or because that country's culture is similar to their own. Third country nationals may have originally been home country personnel who were sent abroad and became dissatisfied with the job but not with the host country. After leaving the firm that sent them abroad, they take positions with subsidiaries of multinationals from different home countries. Another way in which third country nationals can be created is by promotion within an IC. For instance, if a Spanish executive of the Spanish subsidiary of an Italian multinational is promoted to be general manager of the Italian firm's Colombian subsidiary, the Spanish executive is then a third country national.

As multinationals increasingly take the **geocentric** view toward promoting (according to ability and not nationality), we are certain to see greater use of third country nationals. This development will be accelerated as more and more executives of all nationalities gain experience outside their native lands. Another, and growing, source for third country nationals is the heterogeneous body of international agencies. As indicated in Chapter 4, these agencies deal with virtually every field of human endeavor, and all member-countries send their nationals as representatives to the headquarters and branch office cities all over the world. Many of those people become available to, or can be hired away by, international companies.

geocentric
As used here, related to hiring and promoting employees on the basis of ability and experience without considering race or citizenship

Expatriates

expatriate
A person living outside of his or her country of citizenship

Becoming an Expatriate, or Expat, as They Are Sometimes Called

You are happy and proud; you can hardly wait to get back to your office to phone your family with the news. Your boss has called you in and said, "We have a problem in Asia we need you to solve."

You are doing well with the company in the home, domestic market, but now the company has discovered markets away from home, and you haven't seen anything away from home since you and your college friend backpacked in the Argentine mountains to Bariloche. You've read about dining at Singapore's Raffles Hotel with the ghost of Somerset Maugham, exploring Bangkok's temples, and enjoying Hong Kong's Peninsula Hotel's Rolls Royce service and harbor views.

Your family will love it, and the foreign experience will be your passport to your company's top executive positions. Your career will be made. Right?

Only maybe. You must be very careful. For too many employees who take foreign assignments, it's out of sight, out of mind. But these assignments can be passports to the top if you take the right steps before you make the move.

If at all possible, arrange with someone fairly high in the company hierarchy to be your mentor. That person should keep you advised of changes and developments in the company at home and should keep your name in consideration and not forgotten there.

Before you take the job, you should insist that your bosses tell you exactly what the company expects you to accomplish. Are you to get a plant up and running, arrange customer financing, negotiate investment, or perhaps groom a host country replacement?

Of course, there is the chance that despite all your efforts and precautions, your company will forget or not value you. Realizing this possibility, you should have been profiting from your foreign assignment by doing your job well; learning new markets; gaining proficiency in the language, which will permit you to better understand the culture; and networking. The networking can be done by being active in chambers of commerce, social clubs, and sports clubs.

All this will make you valuable to other companies and make them aware of you. You have received a million dollars' worth of training paid for by your company, and you and other companies can utilize it. After all, this is an important source of third country national executives.[13]

The Expatriate's Family

Nine out of ten expatriates' failures are family-related. The stress an overseas move places on spouses and children will ultimately affect the employees no matter how dedicated they may be to the company. Unhappy spouses are the biggest reason for employees asking to go home early, and moving expenses for high-level executives can run into the hundreds of thousands of dollars. Even worse, the company is losing a "million-dollar corporate-training investment" in the executive.

In recognition of all this, some companies have begun to prepare and assist these families. Assistance may take the form of training in the culture and language of the host country. House hunting help may be given, and the new transplants should be taken on grocery and hardware shopping trips with locals and expats who have been in the host country for a while. Locals can teach you the social norms and where to shop and not to shop. Expats can teach you where to get things only expats want.[14]

The kinds of detailed assistance needed by expatriate families moving to Hong Kong are available from HK Homefront Ltd. That company's clientele is mainly from international institutions that are moving employees from Europe, the United States, and other Asian locations.

Their services begin with home finding, orientation, and leasehold management; they help expats get utilities hooked up and hire a maid. They inform clients about schools, social organizations, and cultural societies and direct them to supposedly hard-to-find items such as toilet paper and cornflakes.[15]

Expatriate Children May Suffer the Most

An overseas stint that may be seen as critical for career advancement can wreak havoc with children's lives, and so companies are increasing their focus on easing the disruptions faced by kids. An approach used by Bennett Group, a Cendant Corp. unit in Chicago, is to get the children of a family about to be transferred to a foreign city in touch with expatriate children who have already settled successfully into that city. Motorola will reimburse expatriate families for home personal computers which their children can use to stay in touch with friends by E-mail.[16]

Trailing Spouses in Two-Career Families

The number of two-career families is growing, and that can complicate matters when one spouse is offered a juicy job abroad. In efforts to ease the problem, some companies are starting programs that give trailing spouses more help in adjusting. Such help may take the form of job-hunting assistance in the host country, writing CVs, identifying career opportunities, or giving tips on local interview techniques. If all else fails, some companies even hire a trailing spouse themselves. An added complication is that in many countries, the employee's spouse does not have the legal right to work, as work permits for foreigners may be difficult to impossible to acquire.[17]

You Can't Go Home Again. Or at Least It Frequently Hurts

There is reverse culture shock when an expatriate returns to the home company and country. The expatriate will have gained new skills and knowledge, and the company's attitudes and people will have changed.

That's why planning for an expat's return should start before the overseas assignment begins. The person and the employer should discuss up front how the assignment will fit the employee's long-range career goals and how the company will handle the return. When expats come back, companies have to understand that they are going to be different and harness their new knowledge.[18]

Above, we spoke of the pain suffered by an expat family's children; returning home can prove even more traumatic. That is especially true for those who have spent their formative years abroad. Repatriation counseling is available which includes distinct children's programs and begins months before the family heads home.[19]

language trap
A situation in which a person doing international business can speak only his or her home language

Language Training

American companies are taking more seriously the language abilities of their employees. But neither they nor most Australian, British, Canadian, and New Zealand firms are sufficiently serious. The English speakers are stuck in a **language trap.**

The English language has become the *lingua franca* of the world; it is everybody's second language. The high ground in the modern world is held by people who speak an international language well and have an impenetrable language of their own. Hungary went its own way within the Soviet empire since few Russians had a clue about what the Hungarian dissidents were saying. Israel knows what the Arabs are planning in Arabic; most Arabs are flummoxed by Hebrew. The Japanese are wonderfully protected by their language as they move abroad selling and investing with particular gusto in the English-speaking world.

The French have at long last got the message. Suddenly, waiters in obscure bistros insist on speaking English. They are taking the battle to the enemy. Success is not persuading others to speak your language; it is persuading them that it is unnecessary to try.

None of this means that English has taken over European life. According to the EU, only 47 percent of Western Europeans (including the British and Irish) speak English well enough to carry on a conversation. If you want to sell shampoo or cell phones, you have to do it in Danish, French, German, Greek, Italian, Portuguese, Spanish, or Swedish. Even the British and U.S. media companies that stand to benefit most from the spread of English have been hedging their bets; CNN broadcasts in Spanish, and *The Financial Times* has launched a daily German-language edition.

As a cautionary tale for English speakers, you should recall that in the 1980s, ambitious university students the world over were studying Japanese in order to be able to do business with what was soon to be the world's foremost technological, financial, and economic power. Oops! Or, for those who made the effort to learn Japanese, *Otto*![20]

When trying to sell to potential customers, it is much better to speak their language. As English speakers try to sell abroad, it is far more likely that their customers will speak English than that the English speakers will be able to speak the customers' language. Customers can then hide behind their language during negotiations.

Women

The subject of staffing the executive offices of modern companies is not completely covered without a look at the growing role of women. About half the students in American business schools are now women; they have moved into the managements of banks, businesses, and government agencies and have been at least as successful as their male counterparts. Old-girl networks are now in place alongside the old-boy networks, providing role models and helping younger female managers.

Some assistance is available for women in international business. Membership in organizations such as the Partnership of Women Entrepreneurs and the National Foundation for Women Business Owners has been rising steeply in recent years. Another organization is Women in International Trade (WIT), based in Washington, DC.

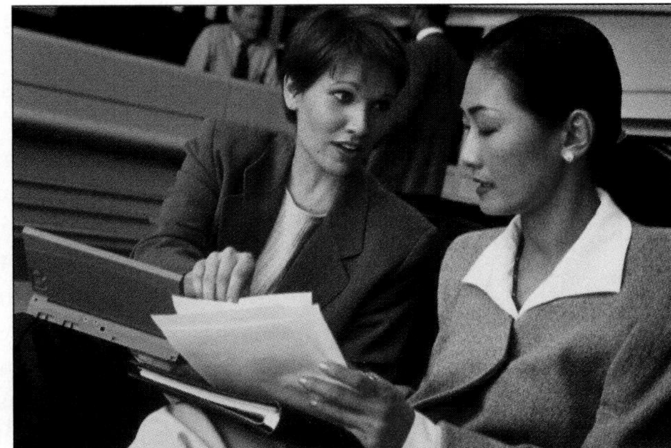
Female executives are accepting foreign positions more frequently.
Thatcher Fisher/Tony Stone Images.

Adrienne Braumiller, a customs lawyer in Dallas and a member of WIT, says it is still difficult for Latin American businessmen to deal with women in positions of authority or responsibility. She says they "are very uncomfortable with us."[21]

That sort of attitude may be part of the reason that the percentage of women in their prime childbearing years who are in the labor force topped out in 1989, ending—for now anyway—a rapid quarter-century rise. Another part of the reason, according to Williams College economist Diane Macunovich, is that men now in their twenties are part of a small generation and enjoy a scarcity premium in the job market. Hence, their wages have been rising so that a wife's income is no longer needed to achieve their desired standard of living.[22]

glass ceiling
An unwritten and therefore invisible, but nevertheless real, ceiling in an organization's executive hierarchy above which females are rarely promoted

Still another reason for women to opt out of the executive rat race is referred to as the **glass ceiling.** Organizations could incur serious legal and public relations difficulties if they wrote or otherwise expressed levels in their executive hierarchy above which women would not be promoted. Nevertheless, very small percentages of women rise to CEO levels or even close to them. The reason for that, it is alleged, is that many organizations put a real but invisible—therefore "glass"—ceiling on how high females can be promoted.

A feeling of not belonging is driving women out of organizations. The difficulty women face in tapping into informal information networks at a corporation is subtle. They are not officially shut out, but a lot of conversations about what's going on in a company happen in places women are not likely to frequent, such as the bar near the office and the golf course over the weekend.

One woman who solved that sort of problem was Cathy Minehan, who was bored to tears when she began her career at the Federal Reserve Bank of Boston. All the small talk centered on the previous night's baseball, basketball, or football scores.

By 1997, in her third year as the bank's chief executive, things had changed. She says, "Under me, we've hired a lot more women, and we're more likely to talk about the latest sale at Bloomingdale's [the retail chain] than sports." Her attitude about whether that might bore her male employees is not recorded.

Female Executives Are on Their Way through the Ceiling. Will They Want What They Find There?

Women are being propelled into positions of corporate power by two forces: rapid technological change and globalization.

The biggest pool of workers in the United States with the skills required by those forces is women. For the first time, the group of women between the ages of 25 and 35 have more education than do their male counterparts. The numbers of women earning doctorates and entering law and medical schools are growing, and by 1998, women held 46 percent of executive, administrative, and managerial positions, up from 34 percent in 1983.[23]

But Lucy Kellaway, a syndicated columnist for *The Financial Times* and other publications, has her doubts about women wanting what they get after rising above the ceiling. She says, "Ten years ago we talked passionately about the glass ceiling, believing that there were fixed barriers to advancement, that a male conspiracy was at work. But now I'm not so sure. The real reason there are so few women at the top is that they have seen what it's like, and don't fancy it particularly."[24]

Evidence is mounting that growing numbers of women are abandoning corporate life, and one now hears about a "brain drain" of talented female managers from corporations. While some are taking temporary breaks until their children reach school age, more and more are starting their own businesses.

Ironically, the tough climb up the first rungs of the corporate ladder often prepares women to succeed as entrepreneurs better than it prepares men. One woman who worked for two large companies before starting her own consulting company believes this is the case. She says that to succeed as a female manager, she was forced to take more risks than her male colleagues: "The need for risk taking that was instilled early on made me better suited to start my own business."[25]

The women remaining in management are being transferred by their employers more often, and their husbands are more frequently the trailing spouses who move with their wives. In 1997, the percentage of male trailing spouses was 16.2 percent, up from 10.9 percent in 1993. More women also are being transferred abroad. Twelve percent of foreign assignments were taken by women in 1997, up from 5 percent the year before, and the proportion of women is expected to be 22 percent by the year 2005.

As was indicated in Chapter 12, attitudes toward and treatment of women differ vastly from one culture or religion to another. A review of that material in Chapter 12 could be helpful at this point.

The rise of India's knowledge-based economy has transformed job prospects for women. With the accent on intellect, educated women have been filling top jobs not only in technology-based companies and dot-coms but also in financial services, where information technology (IT) has helped the industry modernize rapidly. The liberaliza-

[Figure 18.3] Women in Parliament*

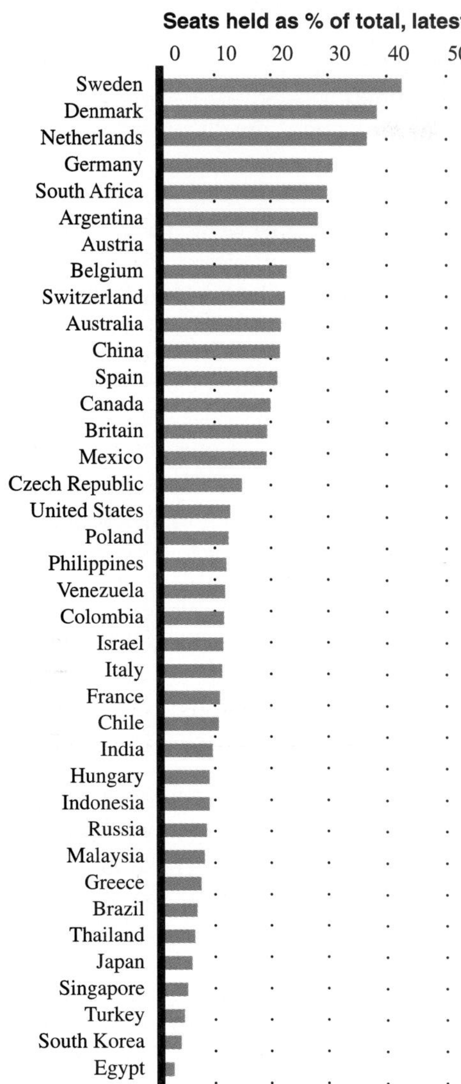

WOMEN IN POLITICS

Northern European countries have the highest proportion of female politicians, according to the Inter-Parliamentary Union, a Swiss-based organization. Sweden tops the list: more than 40% of its parliamentarians are women. More than half of the Swedish cabinet are women. In Denmark, the Netherlands and Germany more than 30% of parliamentarians are women. In contrast, the female share is only 13% in the United States, 11% in France and 5% in Japan. Among poorer countries, South Africa has the highest proportion of women in politics. One in three of South Africa's lawmakers are female. Argentina (28%) and China (22%) are not far behind. However, less than 6% of Brazilian lawmakers are women, and only 4% of South Koreans.

*Lower or single house

Source: From *The Economist,* March 11, 2000, p. 116. www.economist.com

tion of the Indian economy has opened the way for ICs whose attitude toward women has rubbed off on Indian companies.[26]

Another measure of the prevalence of women in positions of authority is the proportion of their membership in national parliaments. Figure 18.3 shows the percentages of seats held, with Sweden having the highest and Egypt the lowest.

Résumés: How to Avoid Getting Hired

The résumés of most job applicants are probably reasonably accurate, although people are taught how to put their best foot forward and present themselves in the best light. Of course, light can be too bright or not at all bright.

Robert Half International, a worldwide executive search firm based in Menlo Park, California, collects and publishes bloopers from real résumés it has seen. There follows a sampling of the types of statements you do not want to send out:

"I demand a salary commiserate with my extensive experience."

"I have lurnt Word Perfect 6.0, computor and spreadsheat progroms."

"Received a plague for Salesperson of the Year."

"Reason for leaving last job: Maturity leave."

"Wholly responsible for two (2) failed financial institutions."

"Failed bar exam with relatively high grades."

"It's best for employers that I not work with people."

"Let's meet, so you can 'ooh' and 'aah' over my experience."

"You will want me to be Head Honcho in no time."

"Am a perfectionist and rarely if if ever foreget details."

"I was working for my mom until she decided to move."

"Marital status: single. Unmarried. Unengaged. Uninvolved. No commitments."

"I have an excellent track record, although I am not a horse."

"I am loyal to my employer at all costs. . . Please feel free to respond to my résumé on my office voice mail."

"I have become completely paranoid, trusting completely no one and absolutely nothing."

"My goal is to be a meteorologist. But since I possess no training in meteorology, I suppose I should try stock brokerage."

"I procrastinate, especially when the task is unpleasant."

"As indicted, I have over five years of analyzing investments."

"Personal interests: donating blood. Fourteen gallons so far."

"Instrumental in ruining entire operation for a Midwest chain store."

"Note: Please don't misconstrue my 14 jobs as 'job-hopping.' I have never quit a job."

"Marital status: often. Children: various."

"Reason for leaving last job: They insisted that all employees get to work by 8:45 every morning. Could not work under those conditions."

"The company made me a scapegoat, just like my three previous employers."

"Finished eighth in my class of ten."

"References: None. I've left a path of destruction behind me."[27]

Selection Dos and Don'ts

Executives who should know better sometimes assume that all nationalities work within a framework of common cultures and business practices. Instant communication of information, supersonic travel, and the emergence of international financial institutions have created a global economy.

Yet this economic interdependence does not translate into a common "business culture." Business standards and practices reflect the cultures in which they are rooted. Their nuances vary widely by continent, by country, and even by region.

An executive with no cross-cultural experience can, regardless of other professional credentials, unwittingly wreak havoc with corporate plans abroad. The ability of a company to succeed in another country rests heavily on the managers' abilities to function in that country's culture. An executive search firm has drawn up a checklist of dos and don'ts in selecting executives for foreign operations.

- Do promote from within. All things being equal, selecting a known employee reduces risk. The employee knows the company, and the company knows the employee's strengths and weaknesses. The weaknesses of a new person may not be evident at first.
- Don't promote an insider if the outsider is clearly better qualified. "John's been doing a good job in New York, and he's always liked London" is not good enough. It can be a costly approach.

- Don't be blinded by language fluency. Just because a candidate is fluent in the host country's language does not mean he or she is the best person for the job. Unless your business is the local Berlitz franchise, the candidate must have the requisite technical and managerial skills.
- Do assess the total person. Functional skills, language proficiency, and knowledge of the international business environment are all important. With regard to international business savvy, third country nationals are sometimes better qualified than people born in the host country who have not lived and worked abroad. It has been noted that Scandinavians, Dutch, and Swiss are disproportionately represented in international business management positions. They come from small countries with limited markets, and so their education and business experience have been geared to the outside world. As a group, these executives have an outlook that is more cosmopolitan than nationalistic.[28]

The decade of the 2000s began with high demand by international business for scarce executive talent. Nevertheless, one successful recruiter advises companies not to go begging, not to oversell. Peter Lefkowitz teaches senior executives how to lasso the talent in sessions at his Tall Pony Ranch outside Kansas City, MO. The cost of a course there runs up to $50,000.

Mr. Lefkowitz's tips include the following:

- *Don't sell the job.* Let candidates sell themselves.
- *Don't do an interview.* Let candidates give you an "inner view" by listening to descriptions of their experiences and responsibilities.
- *Don't sell perks.* Bring-your-pet-to-work benefits won't win candidates. Sell the opportunity to do meaningful work with other smart, talented people.[29]

Although there is no denying fundamental differences in cultures, some say good managers share the same skills worldwide. "The skills are the same," says Jane Wilson of Clark Wilson Publishing, which publishes materials that help companies rate managers' skills in clarifying and communicating goals, planning, problem solving, giving feedback, and tending to details. Support for her point of view can be found in the background of the top executives of several large companies. The CEO of Goodyear Tire and Rubber worked in Belgium, Canada, France, and Morocco for 27 of his 30 years with the company. Gillette's CEO spent 20 of his 35 years with the company in Australia, Canada, Colombia, Hong Kong, and the United Kingdom. The Outboard Marine CEO spent 24 years in Europe on his way up the corporate ladder. One more example is the Mobil CEO, who for 17 of his 34 years with Mobil worked in Italy, Japan, and Saudi Arabia.[30]

Compensation

Establishing a compensation plan that is equitable and consistent and yet does not overcompensate the overseas executive is a challenging, complex task. The method favored by the majority of American ICs has been to pay a base salary equal to that paid to a domestic counterpart and then, in the belief that no one should be worse off for accepting foreign employment, to add a variety of allowances and bonuses.

Salaries

The practice of paying home country nationals the same salaries as their domestic counterparts permits worldwide consistency for this part of the compensation package. Because of the increasing use of third country nationals, those personnel are generally treated in the same way.

Some firms take the equal-pay-for-equal-work concept one step further and pay the same base salaries to host country nationals. In countries that legislate yearly bonuses

[Figure 18.4] Cost of Living

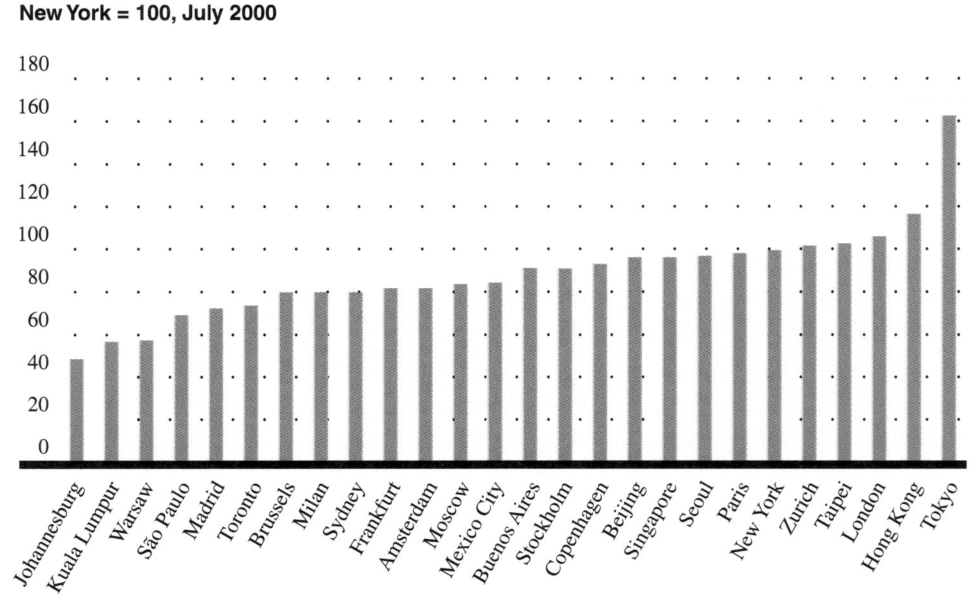

LIVING EXPENSES
Tokyo retains its crown as the world's most expensive city, according to a twice-yearly survey by the Economist Intelligence Unit (a sister company of *The Economist*). The survey expresses the cost of living for expatriate executives as a percentage of the cost in New York. Only a selection of the 127 surveyed cities are shown in the chart. On the back of an economic recovery in East Asia, Seoul's position in the complete table rose from 36th last year to 14th, with an index of 98 against New York's 100. Appreciation of the dollar against the euro resulted in New York leap-frogging Paris, whose overall rank fell from seventh to 12th. London is once again the most expensive city in the European Union though Oslo eclipses it in Europe as a whole.

Source: From *The Economist,* July 22, 2000, p. 98. © 2000 The Economist Newspaper Group, Inc. Reprinted with permission. Further reproduction prohibited. www.economist.com.

and family allowances for their citizens, a local national may receive what appears to be a higher salary than is paid the *expatriate,* although companies usually make extra payments to prevent expatriates from falling behind in this regard. In Great Britain, it is the practice to pay executives relatively lower salaries and to provide them with expensive perquisites, such as chauffeured automobiles, housing, and club memberships. A number of American companies follow British practices in compensating their executives working in Britain.

Allowances

allowances
Employee compensation payments added to base salaries because of higher expenses encountered when living abroad

Allowances are payments made to compensate expatriates for the extra costs they must incur to live as well abroad as they did in the home country. The most common allowances are for housing, cost of living, tax differentials, education, and moving.

Housing Allowances

Housing allowances are designed to permit executives to live in houses as good as those they had at home. Typically, the firm will pay all of the rent that is in excess of 15 percent of the executive's salary.

Cost-of-Living Allowances

Cost-of-living allowances are based on differences in the prices paid for food, utilities, transportation, entertainment, clothing, personal services, and medical expenses overseas compared to the prices paid for these items in the headquarters' city. Many ICs use the U.S. Department of State index, which is based on the cost of these items in Washington, DC, but have found it is not altogether satisfactory. For one thing, critics claim this index is not adjusted often enough to account for either the rapid inflation in some countries or the changes in relative currency values. Another objection is that the index does not include many cities in which the firm operates. As a result, many companies take their own surveys or use data from the United Nations, the World Bank, the International Monetary Fund, or private consulting firms. Figures and comparisons on costs of living, prices, and wages can also be found in private publications (see Figure 18.4).

Allowances for Tax Differentials

ICs pay tax differentials when the host country taxes are higher than the taxes that the expatriates would pay on the same compensation and consumption at home. The objective is to ensure that expatriates will not have less after-tax take-home pay in the host country than they would at home. This can create a considerable extra financial burden on an American parent company because, among other things, the U.S. Internal Revenue Code treats tax allowances as additional taxable income. There are other tax disincentives for Americans to work abroad.*

Education Allowances

Expatriates are naturally concerned that their children receive educations at least equal to those they would get in their home countries, and many want their children taught in their native language. Primary and secondary schools with teachers from most industrialized home countries are available in many cities around the world, but these are private schools and therefore charge tuition. ICs either pay the tuition or, if there are enough expatriate children, operate their own schools. For decades, petroleum companies in the Mideast and Venezuela have maintained schools for their employees' children.

Moving and Orientation Allowances

Companies generally pay the total costs of transferring their employees overseas. These costs include transporting the family, moving household effects, and maintaining the family in a hotel on a full expense account until the household effects arrive. Some firms find it less expensive to send the household effects by air rather than by ship because the reduction in hotel expenses more than compensates for the higher cost of air freight. It has also been found that moving into a house sooner raises the employee's morale.

Companies may also pay for some orientation of the employees and their families. Companies frequently pay for language instruction, and some will provide the family with guidance on the intricacies of everyday living, such as shopping, hiring domestic help, and sending children to school.

Bonuses

Bonuses (or premiums), unlike allowances, are paid by firms in recognition that expatriates and their families undergo some hardships and inconveniences and make sacrifices while living abroad. Bonuses include overseas premiums, contract termination payments, and home leave reimbursement.

bonuses
Expatriate employee compensation payments in addition to base salaries and allowances because of hardship, inconvenience, or danger

Overseas Premiums

Overseas premiums are additional payments to expatriates and are generally established as a percentage of the base salary. They range from 10 to 25 percent. If the living conditions are extremely disagreeable, the company may pay larger premiums for hardship posts.

Contract Termination Payments

These payments are made as inducements for employees to stay on their jobs and work out the periods of their overseas contracts. The payments are made at the end of the contract periods only if the employees have worked out their contracts. Such bonuses are used in the construction and petroleum industries and by other firms that have contracts requiring work abroad for a specific period of time or for a specific project. They may also be used if the foreign post is a hardship or not a particularly desirable one.

Home Leave[31]

ICs that post home country—and sometimes third country—nationals in foreign countries make it a practice to pay for periodic trips back to the home country by such em-

*For more on this subject and other effects of U.S. laws on American ICs, see the taxation section in Chapter 11.

ployees and their families. The reasons for this are twofold. One, companies do not want employees and their families to lose touch with the home country and its culture. Two, companies want to have employees spend at least a few days at company headquarters to renew relationships with headquarters' personnel and catch up with new company policies and practices.

Some firms grant three-month home leaves after an employee has been abroad about three years, but it is a more common practice to give two to four weeks' leave each year. All transportation costs are paid to and from the executive's hometown, and all expenses are paid during the executive's stay at company headquarters.

Compensation Packages Can Be Complicated

compensation packages
For expatriate employees: can incorporate many types of payments or reimbursements and must take into consideration exchange rates and inflation

One might think from the discussion to this point that **compensation packages,** while costly—the extras may total 50 percent or more of the base salary—are fairly straightforward in their calculation. Nothing could be further from the truth.

What Percentage?

All allowances and a percentage of the base salary are usually paid in the host country currency. What should this percentage be? In practice, it varies from 65 to 75 percent, with the remainder being banked wherever the employee wishes. One reason for these practices is to decrease the local portion of the salary, thereby lowering host country income taxes and giving the appearance to government authorities and local employees that there is less difference between the salaries of local and foreign employees than is actually the case. Another reason is that expatriate employees have various expenses that must be paid in home country currency. Such expenses include professional society memberships, purchases during home leave, and tuition and other costs for children in home country universities.

What Exchange Rate?

Inasmuch as most of the expatriate's compensation is usually denominated in the host country currency but established in terms of the home country currency to achieve comparable compensation throughout the enterprise, a currency exchange rate must be chosen. In countries whose currencies are freely convertible into other currencies, this presents no serious problem, although the experienced expatriate will argue that an exchange rate covers only international transactions and may not represent a true purchasing power parity between the local and home country currencies. For instance, such items as bread and milk are rarely traded internationally, and living costs and inflation rates may be much higher in the host country than in the home country. International companies attempt to compensate for such differences in the cost-of-living allowances.

More difficult problems must be solved in countries that have exchange controls and nonconvertible currencies. Without exception, those currencies are overvalued at the official rate, and if the firm uses that rate, its expatriate employees are certain to be shortchanged. Reference may be made to the free market rate for the host country currency in free currency markets in, for example, the United States or Switzerland or to the black market rate in the host country, but these do not give the final answers. In the end, all companies must pay their expatriate employees enough to enable them to live as well as others who have similar positions in other firms, regardless of how the amount is calculated.

A common compensation component at many American companies is a stock plan that gives employees opportunities to acquire the company's stock on favorable terms. Such programs are designed to increase loyalty and productivity, but they sometimes run into problems outside the United States.

Share ownership is unknown or restricted in numerous countries. PepsiCo's vice president of compensation and benefits says, "We had to develop a customized approach in every country we operate in." Du Pont discovered it could not give stock options in 25 of 53 nations, primarily because those countries' laws ban or limit ownership of foreign shares. Reader's Digest Association and Colgate-Palmolive are designing global stock programs country by country.

Japanese companies are now offering American-style stock option plans to their most prized employees. That development was caused by a ruling by Japanese tax authorities that the employees' options will not be taxed unless they are converted into shares that subsequently rise in price and are then sold.[32]

France traditionally has relied on the base salary to compensate its managers, but that practice is giving way to proportionately larger annual bonuses. Long-term incentives in France are usually in the form of stock options, but French tax laws are limiting their value, as, for example, they are taxed on unrealized gains.[33]

Compensation of Third Country Nationals

Although some companies have different compensation plans for third country nationals, there is a trend toward treating them the same as home country expatriates. In either event, there are areas in which problems can arise. One of these areas is the calculation of income tax differentials when an American expatriate is compared with an expatriate from another country. This results from the unique American government practices of taxing U.S. citizens even though they live and work abroad and treating tax differential payments made to those citizens as additional taxable income. No other major country taxes its nationals in those ways.

Another possible problem area is the home leave bonus. The two purposes of home leave are to prevent expatriates from losing touch with their native cultures and to have them visit IC headquarters. A third country national must visit two countries instead of only one to achieve both purposes, and the additional costs can be substantial. Compare the cost of sending an Australian employee home from Mexico with that required to send an American from Mexico to Dallas.

Regardless of problems, the use of third country nationals is growing in popularity. As businesses race to enlarge their ranks of qualified international managers, third country nationals are in greater demand. They often win jobs because they speak several languages and know an industry or country well.

The numbers of third country nationals employed as executives by ICs continue to grow, and the possible combinations of nationalities and host countries are virtually limitless. For examples, see the end of the "Selection Dos and Don'ts" section above.

International Status

In all of this discussion, we have been describing compensation for expatriates who have been granted **international status.** Merely being from another country does not automatically qualify an employee for all the benefits we have mentioned. A subsidiary may hire home country nationals or third country nationals and pay them the same as it pays host country employees. However, managements have found that although an American, for example, may agree initially to take a job and be paid on the local scale, sooner or later bad feeling and friction will develop as that person sees fellow Americans enjoying international status perquisites to which he or she is not entitled.

international status
Entitles the expatriate employee to all the allowances and bonuses applicable to the place of residence and employment

Sometimes firms promote host country employees to international status even without transferring them abroad. This is a means of rewarding valuable people and preventing them from leaving the company for better jobs elsewhere.

Thus, international status means being paid some or all the allowances and bonuses we have discussed, and there can be other sorts of payments as individual circumstances and people's imaginations combine to create them. The executives' compensation package is sufficiently important and complicated to have become a specialization in the personnel management field; at one firm, the title is "International Employee Benefits Consultant."

Help is available from outside the IC. From time to time, the large consulting firms publish pamphlets advising about the transfer of executives to specific countries.

[Figure 18.5] **Assistance for Executives Abroad**

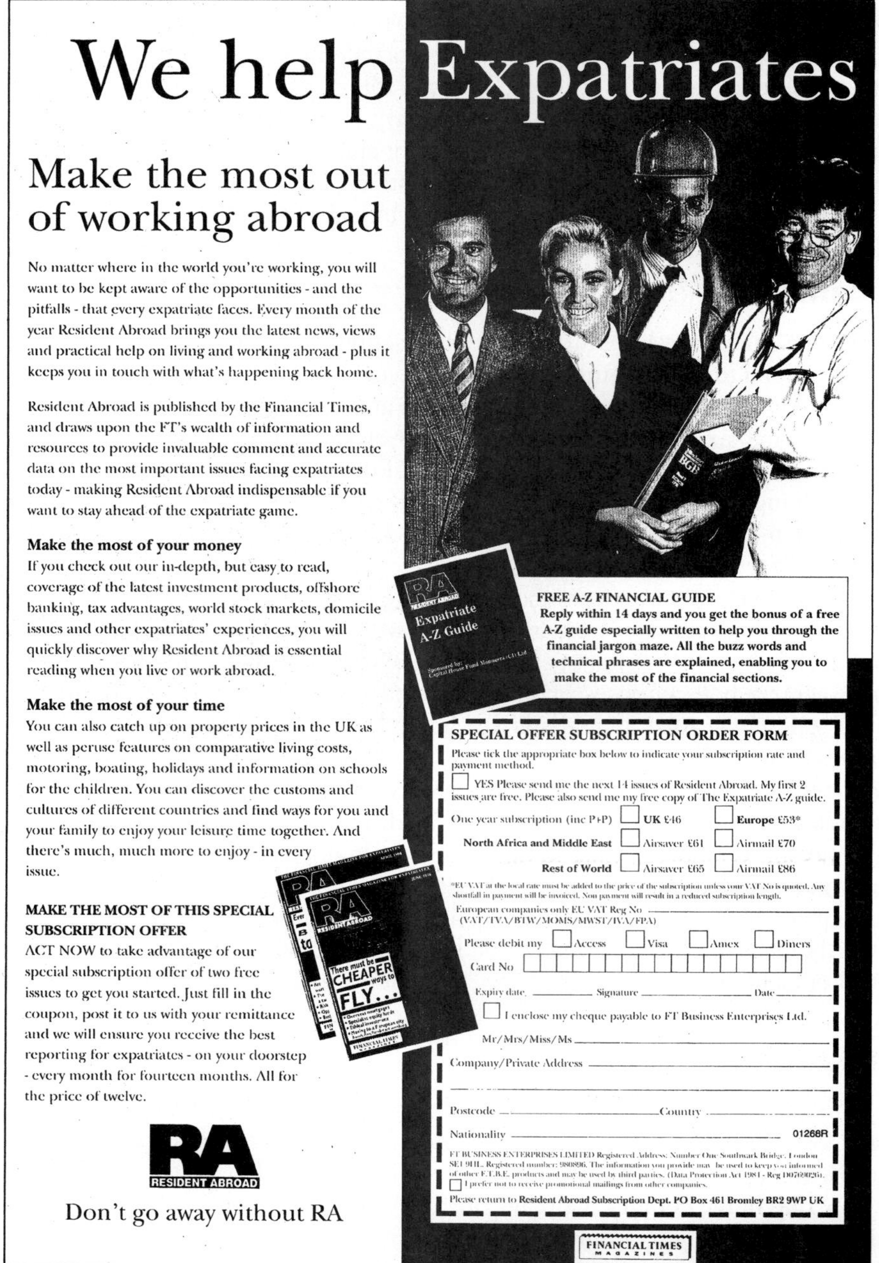

Source: From *Financial Times,* August 20, 2000. Reprinted with permission of *Financial Times.*

Another sort of help is illustrated by the advertisement "We Help Expatriates" shown in Figure 18.5.

Figure 18.6 compares the remuneration of chief executive officers (CEOs) in 24 countries. Note that the CEOs of U.S.-based companies do far better than do those of companies based in other industrial countries. But surprisingly, America's lead was limited to CEO pay. The pay of other American company managers was comparable to that of most others.

Perks

These originated in the perquisites of the medieval lords of the manor, whose workers paid parts of their profits or produce to the lords to be allowed to continue working.

[Figure 18.6] Chief Executives' Pay

EXECUTIVE PAY

Chief executives receive far more pay relative to workers on the factory floor in America than in other countries. A survey of Standard & Poor's 500 leading companies finds that, on average, top American bosses take home 475 times more than workers. A study conducted by Towers Perrin, an international consultancy, shows that European bosses take only 11 to 24 times as much as their underlings. Several South-East Asian and Latin American countries fall between the extremes. Both reports take into account incentive packages composed of shares and share options. One example is Charles Wang, boss of Computer Associates; he took a mere $4.6m in salary and bonus in 1999, but added over $650m in long-term, performance-based compensation.

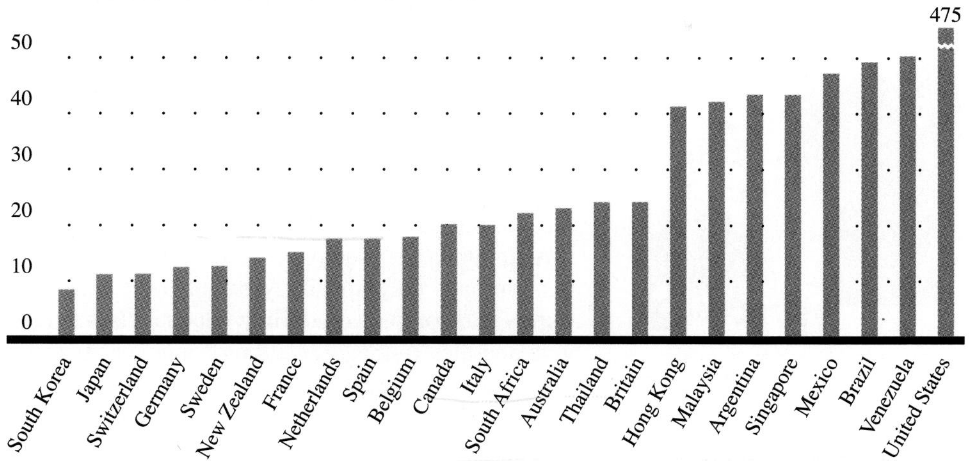

Source: From *The Economist,* September 30, 2000, p. 110. © 2000 The Economist Newspaper Group, Inc. Reprinted with permission. Further reproduction prohibited. www.economist.com.

Today, perks are symbols of rank in the corporate hierarchy and are used to compensate executives while minimizing taxes. Among the most common perks are

Cars, which higher up the organization ladder come with chauffeurs.

Private pension plan.

Retirement payment.

Life insurance.

Health insurance.

Company house or apartment.

Directorship of a foreign subsidiary.

Seminar holiday travel.

Club memberships.

Hidden slush fund (such funds may be illegal, but some corporations are said to have them).

What's Important to You?

While working abroad as an executive of an American multinational, one of the authors had a colleague who was an American expatriate married to a French woman. They had raised a family in several countries where they had been assigned by the company. Together with some other cosmopolites, they devised a table of items deemed important to at least one of them in choosing a city for the location of a company facility that employs foreigners.

The list included the usual items, such as cost of living, safety of personnel, medical facilities, housing, and schools. It also included such other items as availability of good wine at reasonable prices, quality of theater and whether it was live or cinema, number

Source: *Financial Times,* May 2, 1997; p. 29. © Roger Beale. Reprinted with permission.

and type of one-star or better (*Michelin Guide*)* restaurants, type and accessibility of sports facilities for both participants and viewers, and shopping facilities for fashionable clothes.

The table of items was circulated informally throughout the firm's many locations, and many cities in its network were graded as to each item on a 1-to-10 scale. When the New York headquarters saw the table, there was much mirth and merriment; suggestions—perhaps not all of them serious—were made as to additional items about which they would like information when they visited the cities.

However, the mirth and merriment subsided as more and more executives being assigned or reassigned abroad used the table to demand better compensation packages. Some even refused transfers because of the ratings given a city.

Also important to employees may be the number of vacation days they are likely to get from country to country and comparisons of how much it costs to celebrate and then to treat a resulting hangover. As to vacation days, Europeans are well ahead of Americans and Japanese. The average Japanese is entitled to 15 days a year and usually takes fewer, while the average American takes about 20 days. In the European vacation league, the Germans are tops with 40 days; the Irish are at the bottom with 27 days but are still well ahead of the Americans and Japanese.

As to the comparative costs of celebrating and treating hangovers, Table 18.1 shows Helsinki to be the most expensive and Milan the cheapest. The study gave a choice of

Table 18.1 The Price of Overindulgence around the World (in pounds sterling)

	75 cl. Scotch	75 cl. Gin	Average Indulgence Cost	12 Alka-Seltzers	100 Aspirins	16 oz. Coffee	Average Treatment Cost	Average Full Cost
Helsinki	30.83£	25.12£	27.98£	1.00£	3.66£	2.12£	2.26£	30.24£
Stockholm	30.09	22.47	26.28	0.77	2.99	2.07	1.94	28.22
Copenhagen	27.53	15.58	21.56	0.72	5.37	2.72	2.94	24.50
Singapore	22.87	18.89	20.88	1.20	4.62	2.60	2.81	24.69
Tokyo	18.51	11.65	15.08	—	9.71	6.04	7.88	22.96
Moscow	23.42	7.88	15.65	1.35	6.15	4.95	4.15	19.80
Sydney	17.11	10.14	13.63	1.22	3.21	3.37	2.60	16.23
Vienna	15.25	8.25	11.75	1.61	4.60	2.96	3.06	14.81
London	14.78	9.97	12.38	1.41	2.92	2.43	2.25	14.63
Cairo	14.25	10.90	12.58	0.23	1.96	3.56	1.92	14.50
Hong Kong	12.60	10.12	11.36	1.10	3.80	3.28	2.73	14.09
Amsterdam	11.97	9.02	10.50	1.36	7.42	1.69	3.49	13.99
Frankfurt	11.03	7.53	9.28	1.85	6.83	2.54	3.74	13.02
New York	11.22	9.83	10.53	1.03	3.42	2.32	2.26	12.79
Toronto	12.11	9.77	10.94	1.03	2.12	2.17	1.77	12.71
Brussels	12.54	8.79	10.67	1.07	3.04	1.91	2.01	12.68
Madrid	11.92	6.63	9.28	1.82	5.17	2.04	3.01	12.29
Paris	12.02	8.58	10.30	1.02	3.39	1.21	1.87	12.17
Milan	8.53	5.21	6.87	1.63	8.09	3.04	4.25	11.12

Source: From *Financial Times,* July 21, 1997, p. 22. Reprinted with permission of *Financial Times.*

*The *Michelin Guide* rates restaurants and hotels in France and neighboring countries.

[Figure 18.7] Comparative Business Environment in 25 Cities

DOING BUSINESS

In the past five years, Hong Kong has had the best business environment in the world, according to the Economist Intelligence Unit, a sister company of *The Economist.* But between now and 2004, thinks the EIU, Hong Kong will lose top spot to—perhaps surprisingly—the Netherlands. The EIU says that the Dutch business environment has no obvious weaknesses: its political system is stable, its labour market flexible and its financial sector efficient. Hong Kong will slip to sixth as the adverse effects on business of the territory's return to China start to be felt. The United States and Canada are ranked third and fourth, so that North America will remain the best region of the world in which to do business in 2000-04. Africa and the Middle East will be worst.

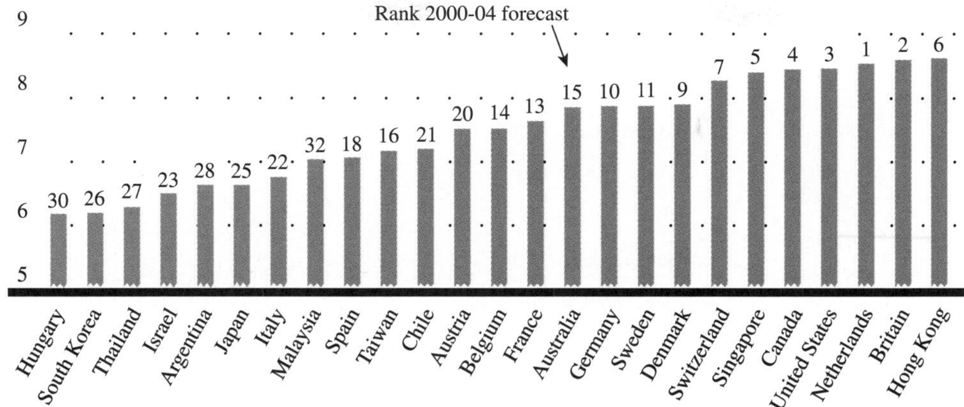

Source: From *The Economist,* January 29, 2000, p. 124. www.economist.com.

celebratory beverages—scotch or gin—and three possible treatments—Alka-Seltzer, aspirin, and coffee.

Also of importance in decisions on where to locate a business operation are considerations such as cost of living, business environment, and office rents. Figure 18.4 shows cost-of-living comparisons for a number of the world's cities. The survey compares the prices of goods and services typically consumed by the families of executives being sent abroad. You will note that although Tokyo and Hong Kong are the most expensive, living in emerging countries is not always cheap.

In rating business environments, the Economist Intelligence Unit (EIU) uses indicators such as market potential, tax and labor market policies, infrastructures, skills, and political stability. For eight years up to 2000, the EIU rated Hong Kong as the best place in the world to conduct business, but in 1997 Hong Kong reverted to the People's Republic of China (PRC), becoming Hong Kong, China. Because of the uncertainties attendant on that change, the EIU forecasts that Hong Kong will drop to sixth on the table by 2004. It predicts that the Netherlands will be the most business-friendly, followed by the United Kingdom, the United States, Canada, and Singapore.

Despite labor market problems and less attractive market opportunities, the quality of the business environment in West European and North American countries remains higher than that in emerging markets because those countries possess sophisticated institutions, such as advanced financial sectors, reliable legal systems, and political stability, that companies value. Figure 18.7 gives the EIU's rankings for 2000 and forecasts for 2004.

Office rents could be included as a part of the business environment, but they are measured separately and may be of great interest. You can see commercial property rents compared in Figure 18.8.

There are numerous sources of information available about living, managing, and working abroad. One is Meridian Resources Associates, which offers videos and resource books. Titles available from Meridian include "Managing in China," "Working with China," "Working with Japan," "Globally Speaking," "Working with Americans," "Living in Asia," "Assignment USA," and "Information on Consulting and Training Services." They can be contacted by phone at (800) 626-2047, by fax at (415) 749-0124, or at **www.mera.com**.

[Figure 18.8] Paying the Price for Office Space

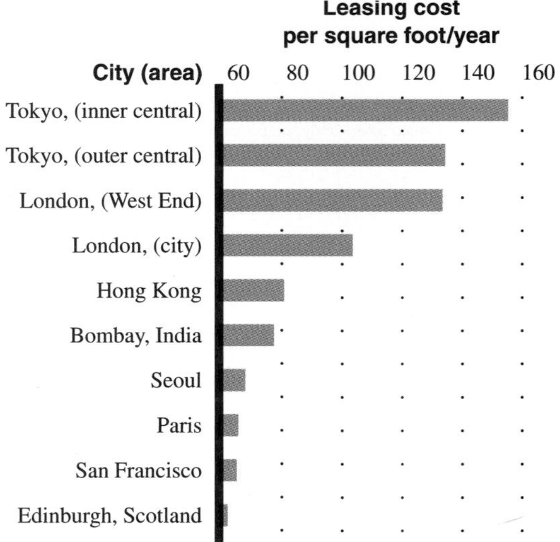

Source: Bloomberg News, *Los Angeles Times,* August 10, 2000, p. C3.

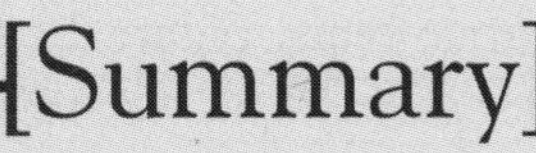

[Summary]

Remember some of the regional or cultural differences in labor conditions we shall present.

a. The Japanese jobs-for-life culture is changing.
b. There is still a huge wage gap between the neighboring countries Germany and Poland.
c. The International Federation of Free Trade Unions estimates there are 250 million child (between 4 and 15 years old) laborers, mostly in the developing countries.
d. Labor conditions in the PRC are reportedly very bad.
e. ICs from developed countries must adjust their labor practices to succeed in developing countries.

Understand why some economies are better at job creation than others, which causes differing unemployment rates.

The United States has created many more new jobs than has Western Europe and some more than has Japan since 1980. Europe's sluggish job creation is blamed by the OECD and McKinsey Management Consultancy on high minimum wages, generous unemployment benefits, restrictive employment protection laws, and product market barriers.

Understand the difficulties of finding qualified executives for international companies (ICs) and the importance of foreign language knowledge.

Knowledge of a people's language is essential to understand its culture and to know what's going on, as every effective manager must.

Compare home country, host country, and third country nationals as IC executives.

Sources of IC executives may be the home country, host countries, or third countries, and their differing culture, language, ability, and experience can strengthen IC management.

Realize the growing role of women in international business.

Women are increasingly important as IC executives and are being transferred, with trailing spouses, by their employers both domestically and internationally.

Realize the increasing importance of accommodating the trailing spouse of an expatriate executive.

The growing prevalence of two-career families is complicating problems of accommodating the spouse of an executive who is being transferred to another country.

Remember some of the complications of compensation packages for expatriate executives.

Expatriate manager compensation packages can be extremely complicated. Among other sources of complication are fluctuating currency exchange rates and differing inflation rates. Basic elements of those packages are salaries, allowances, and bonuses.

[Key Words]

Japan's jobs-for-life culture (p. 619)
child labor (p. 619)
home country nationals (p. 621)
host country nationals (p. 624)
third country nationals (p. 625)
geocentric (p. 627)
expatriate (p. 627)
language trap (p. 628)
glass ceiling (p. 629)
allowances (p. 634)
bonuses (p. 635)
compensation packages (p. 636)
international status (p. 637)

[Questions]

1. Analyze arguments made by representatives of Nepal and other poor countries in justifying the child labor they utilize.
2. What adjustments in personnel practices did the discussed Spanish company's Guatemalan subsidiary make? Why?
3. Why have problems involving the trailing spouses of expatriate executives become more numerous? What are some companies doing to solve those problems?

4. In staffing a multinational organization for service outside the IC home country, what are some advantages and disadvantages of hiring home country personnel?
5. What is the English language trap?
6. Why has there been an increasing use of third country nationals in the foreign operations of ICs?
7. Why are expatriate employees frequently paid more than their colleagues at equivalent job levels in the home office?
8. Why are compensation packages for expatriates more complicated than those for domestic employees?
9. Women executives face obstacles to assignment and promotion both in the home country and in host countries. What additional obstacle applies to the latter?
10. What are some of the quality-of-life issues executives should consider before taking their families into an expatriate experience?

[Internet Exercises]

Using the Internet

1. As the text explains, cost of living worldwide is of great importance to international business. Using the Internet, find information on the varying costs of living around the world. For example, the Web site at http://homefair.com/home provides comparisons of living costs between two cities. According to this Web site, a person making $30,000 a year in Long Beach, California, would need to make how much in Oslo, Norway, to maintain the same standard of living?
2. a. The text discusses issues confronting women working overseas. Using the Internet, find information involving women working abroad and organizations for women in international business.

   b. The role and status of women vary from one country to another. Using the Internet, find information on the participation of women in various activities in other countries.

[Minicase 18.1]

Female Executives in International Business

Suppose you are the chief executive officer (CEO) of an American multinational. On your staff and in the U.S. operating divisions of your company are several bright, able, dedicated female executives. They are also ambitious, and in your company, international experience is a must before an executive can hope to get into top management.

An opening comes up for the position of executive vice president in the company's Mexican subsidiary. One of the women on your staff applies for the position, and she is well qualified for the job, better than anyone else in the company. Would you give her the position? What are the arguments pro and con?

Another position becomes available, this one as treasurer of the Japanese subsidiary. The chief financial officer of the company's California division applies for this job. She has performed to everyone's satisfaction, and she seems thoroughly qualified to become the treasurer in Japan. In addition, she speaks and writes Japanese. She is the daughter of a Japanese mother and an American father, and they encouraged her to become fluent in both English and Japanese.

Would you give her the job? Why or why not?

[Chapter]

19

Financial Management

"Ten minutes is a long-term outlook."

—Foreign currency dealers, Manufacturers Hanover Trust Company

Concept Previews

After reading this chapter, you should be able to:

- **realize** that the currencies of countries change in value in terms of each other
- **understand** how currency value changes affect international business transactions
- **recognize** the tremendous importance of financial management to an international company (IC)
- **know** about financial management tools
- **understand** the growing use of derivatives as hedging devices
- **explain** how financial executives meet, network, and cooperate with their counterparts in other organizations to protect and/or benefit their organizations in derivatives operations.
- **understand** why exporters sometimes accept payment in forms other than money
- **differentiate** between hard, convertible currencies and soft, nonconvertible ones
- **explain** the growing importance of international finance centers to ICs

© Photodisc

The "Achète" Incident

David Edwards was born in Wichita Falls, Texas, but was intrigued by international business and finance. He worked his way up the ladder of Citibank's international operation, where he moved into a senior slot in Paris as head of *les cambistes,* as the fast-and-furious currency exchange traders are called. His boldness and quick mind equipped him well for this high-pressure operation, and he did very well for his employer and for himself. Occasionally, however, his Wichita Falls French got him in trouble. He tells of one occasion when Citibank's currency trader at the Bourse,* who was a Frenchman, phoned him and reported that the U.S. dollar bids were going down fast. Edwards shouted into the telephone, "Aw, shit!" and slammed down the receiver. A few seconds later, the trader called Edwards on another phone and reported proudly that he had bought a large block of U.S. dollars. "You did what?" Edwards yelled, to which the startled trader protested, "But you said, '*achète.*' "† That evening, Edwards

**Bourse* is the French word for stock and currency markets.
†*Achète* means "buy" in French.

Intra-IC Hedge. A rapidly growing practice is for international companies to seek an internal hedge within their own network of parent, subsidiary, and affiliated companies. Suppose that in our NK–US$ case the financial manager found that one of the IC's companies owed about NK9 million, payable about the time when the NK9 million was receivable under the export contract. The NK payable by one unit of the IC could then be hedged (netted) against the NK receivable carried by the other IC unit. Thus, two hedges are achieved at no outside cost, and the bank, option, or IMM fees are avoided.

A Covered Position. Even though the exporter in the above forward hedge example does not have any NKs at the time it enters the hedge contract, it does have the Norwegian importer's obligation to pay the NK9 million, which can be delivered to the other party to the hedge contract. If you have the funds (NK9 million) when you enter the hedge contract or they are due from another business transaction on or before the due date under your hedge contract (as here), you are in a "covered" position.[3]

An Uncovered Position. A financial manager can also use the foreign exchange market to take advantage of an expected rise or fall in the relative value of a currency. There will then be created an "uncovered" long or short position. For example, if the financial manager of an American company believes the NK will appreciate in value in the next few months, the procedure would be to go long on the NK at the spot rate, NK9 = US$1. This is a contract whereby the company buys, say, NK9 million for US$1 million, with both currencies to be delivered at a future date. If the NK appreciates to NK8 = US$1, the financial manager was correct, and the NK9 million received by the company is worth $1,250,000. The company pays, as agreed, $1 million. If the financial manager believes the NK will depreciate in the next few months, the procedure would be to short NKs at the spot rate. An uncovered short position results when you sell money or any other commodity without having it either on hand or due you under another business transaction.

Using the same rate (NK9 = US$1) and the same amount (NK9 million), the company agrees to deliver NK9 million at a future date in return for US$1 million. If, in fact, the NK depreciates to NK10 = US$1, the financial manager was again correct. The company can buy the NK9 million for approximately $830,000. The company will be paid, as agreed, $1 million.

Both of the above stories had happy endings for the company, but it exposed itself to risk. Short-term currency value movements are extremely uncertain in both direction and amount, and those company stories (and perhaps the financial manager) could have had sad endings if the currencies had moved in the other direction. People who study currency markets and deal in them daily tend to be modest in their forecasts of short-term movements.

We have interviewed and talked at length with foreign exchange market officers, bank traders, and bank economists in America, Asia, and Europe. Almost all of them expressed definite views, opinions, and forecasts about long-term currency value changes. Not one of them would hazard more than a guess about tomorrow's prices.

Credit or Money Market Hedge

As indicated by its name, the credit or money market hedge involves credit—borrowing money. The company desiring a hedge is the borrower. The credit or money market hedge may be illustrated by the same transaction used above to discuss the forward exchange market hedge.

The Norwegian importer will pay NK9 million to the American exporter for the goods in 180 days. With the money market hedge, the exporter will borrow NK9 million from an Oslo bank on the day of the sale to the Norwegian importer.* The exporter will immediately convert to US$s at the current NK9 = US$1 rate, giving it the $1 mil-

*Actually, the amount borrowed will usually be less than NK9 million. It will be an amount that, plus interest for 180 days, will total NK9 million at the end of that period. Thus, the NK9 million payment from the importer will exactly repay the loan, with no odd amounts plus or minus.

lion selling price, but it owes NK9 million to the Norwegian bank, due in 180 days. That will be repaid with the Norwegian importer's NK9 million payment.

The exporter has a variety of opportunities for the use of the $1 million. It can lend it, put it in certificates of deposit, use it in a swap (see below), or use it as internal operating capital. The financial manager will study all the opportunities to find which will be most beneficial.

Before a money market hedge is used, the exporter must compare the interest rates in its and the importer's countries. If the interest on the exporter's borrowing in the importer's country is significantly higher than the amount the exporter can earn on the money in its country, the cost of this type of hedge may be too great.

Other comparisons and checks should be made before borrowing the NK from an Oslo bank. Even though the NK is not one of the most widely traded currencies, the financial manager should inquire of banks in major Eurocurrency centers (such as London, Paris, Zurich, and Frankfurt) to ascertain whether NKs could be borrowed at a lower interest cost. And in the case of NKs, other Scandinavian financial centers—Copenhagen, Helsinki, and Stockholm—should be checked for competitive bids.

Just as in the foreign exchange market hedge situation, an IC should check its company units to learn whether any of them has an NK balance that could be lent internally, that is, from the unit with the balance to the unit with the NK foreign exchange exposure. Thus, interest payments to banks outside the IC could be avoided.

Acceleration or Delay of Payment

If an importer expects the currency in its country to depreciate in terms of the currency of its foreign supplier, it probably will be motivated to buy the necessary foreign currency as soon as it can. This assumes the importer must pay in the currency of the exporter, the opposite of our assumption in the hedging discussions.

Which Way Will the Exchange Rates Go? If the importer agreed to pay $1 million when the exchange rate was NK9 = US$1, its cost at that time would be NK9 million. If, before payment is due, the rate drops to NK10 = US$1, the cost will be NK10 million. The importer, then, would be tempted to pay early or, if possible, to make the currency exchange at once and use the foreign currency until the payment due date.

Of course, the opposite would be the case if the importer expects the NK to strengthen from the NK9 = US$1 rate at the time of the purchase contract. It would be motivated to delay payment and to delay conversion from NKs to US$s. For example, if the rate goes to NK8 = US$1, the necessary $1 million will cost only NK8 million. Payment accelerations or delays are frequently called **leads** or **lags.**

leads
Immediate purchases of a foreign currency to satisfy a future need because the buyer believes it will strengthen vis-à-vis the home currency

lags
Delayed purchases of a foreign currency to satisfy a future need because the buyer believes it will weaken vis-à-vis the home currency

Unrelated Companies. Although independent, unrelated companies use acceleration or delay on each other, one may be doing so at the expense of the other. Usually, however, the exporter is indifferent as to the method used by the importer to protect itself against currency risk as long as payment is received on time in the agreed currency. The IC, by contrast, may be able to realize enterprisewide benefit using payment leads and lags.

Within an IC. For purposes of examining potential payment accelerations or delays between different country operations of one IC, we should differentiate two types of ICs. At one extreme is the IC that operates a coordinated, integrated worldwide business with the objective of the greatest profit for the total enterprise. At the other extreme is the independent operation of each part of the IC as its own separate profit center.

As was pointed out above, international payment leads and lags between independent companies are usually of no concern to the exporter as long as it receives payment as agreed. The same would be true of IC units that operate autonomously. But an integrated, coordinated IC can benefit the enterprise as a whole by cooperating in payment leads or lags. The overall IC objective is to get its money out of weak currencies and into strong currencies as quickly as reasonably possible.

Thus, instead of incurring the hedging costs incurred by independent companies while awaiting the future day of payment, IC units can make payment immediately if trading out of a weak currency or delay payment until the payment date if trading out of a strong currency. If the profit of the unit paying immediately suffers from loss of interest on the money or shortage of operating capital (manager compensation and promotion frequently depend on profit), adjustment can be made to recognize that the IC gained as a result of the cooperation of that management's IC unit.

Effects of Leads and Lags on Foreign Exchange Markets. When an importer in a weak currency country buys from an exporter in a strong currency country with payment in the future, the usual practice is to convert or hedge immediately. And by selling the currency expected to go down in value and buying the one expected to go up, the importer helps realize those expectations; the prophecies are self-fulfilling.

The opposite is done when the importer in a country with a strong currency buys from a country with a weak currency. Now the importer will hold on to its perceived strong currency until the last moment and not buy the weak currency till then. Again, this strengthens the perceived strong currency and weakens the other currency.

Objectives of Intra-IC Payments. Within the strictures of applicable laws and the minimum working capital requirements of the parent and affiliates,[4] ICs can maximize their currency strengths and minimize their currency weaknesses.[5] Their objectives are to

1. Keep as much money as is reasonably possible in countries with high interest rates. This is done to avoid borrowing at high rates or perhaps to have capital to lend at those rates.
2. Keep as much money as is reasonably possible in countries where credit is difficult to obtain. If the IC unit in such a country needs capital, it may be able to generate it internally.
3. Maximize holdings of hard, strong currencies, which may appreciate in value in terms of soft, weak currencies. Minimize, as much as reasonably possible, holdings of the latter. This objective may conflict with the first objective because strong currencies are usually available at lower interest rates than are weak ones. Financial management must consider all the conditions, needs, and expectations and make a balanced judgment.
4. Minimize holdings of currencies that either are subject to currency exchange controls or can be expected to be subject to them during the period in which the company will hold those currencies.

Exposure Netting

exposure netting
Taking open positions in two currencies that are expected to balance each other

Exposure netting is the acceptance of open positions* in two or more currencies that are considered to balance one another and therefore require no further internal or external hedging. Basically, there are two ways to accomplish this: (1) currency groups and (2) a combination of a strong currency and a weak currency.

Currency Groups. Some groups of currencies tend to move in close conjunction with one another even during floating rate periods.[6] For example, some developing country currencies are pegged to the currency of their most important developed country trading partner.

Before 1999, most Western European countries tried to coordinate the movements of their currencies in terms of each other in the European Monetary System. Beginning in 1999, 11 of the 15 European Union (EU) member-countries agreed to begin a transition from their national currencies to the new common currency, the euro, in what is called the euro zone. The four countries that remained outside the euro zone as they decided whether, when, and how to join continued to attempt currency value coordina-

*An *open* position exists when the company has greater assets than liabilities (or greater liabilities than assets) in one currency. A *closed,* or *covered,* position exists when assets and liabilities in a currency are equal.

tion between their currencies and the euro. Thus, a financial manager could attempt currency netting with a simultaneous long of the British pound and a short of the euro.

A Strong Currency and a Weak Currency. A second exposure netting possibility involves two payables (or two receivables), one in a currently strong currency and the other in a weaker one. The hope is that weakness in one will offset the strength of the other.

How does financial management decide which currency will be strong and which will be weak? Forecasting relative currency values is fraught with peril; just ask the "experts" and look at the euro. The euro was launched amid much fanfare in January 1999 at US$1.16 = 1 euro. There was much speculation that it would become at least the coleading world currency with the US$, and some forecast that it would replace the US$ as the strong, world reserve currency. Contrary to expectations, the euro depreciated steadily to lows in late 2000 of around US82¢ = 1 euro.

This is not the place to discuss why that happened, and certainly the authors disclaim the expertise to be better forecasters, but this situation well illustrates the danger of relative currency value forecasting over even short periods of time. Nevertheless, financial managers may want to try, and there have been and will be successes.

To put this into perspective, over the past 100 years, currencies other than the US$ have been strong. They include the British pound, the French franc, the German mark, gold, the Japanese yen, and the Swiss franc. And of course, they and the euro may rise in the future.

An advantage of exposure netting is that it avoids the costs of hedging. It is also more risky; the currencies may not behave as expected during the periods of the open receivables or payables.

Price Adjustments

Sales management often desires to make sales in a country whose currency is expected to be devalued. In such a situation, financial management finds that neither hedging nor exposure netting is possible or economical. Within the limitations of competition and the customer's budget, it may be possible to make price adjustments—to raise the selling price in the customer's currency. The hope is that the additional amount will compensate for the expected drop in value of the customer's currency.

Price Adjustments within an IC Group. If an IC is of the coordinated, integrated type, there is much opportunity to adjust selling prices in intraenterprise transactions between the parent and its affiliated companies or between affiliates. The selling prices are raised or lowered in anticipation of changes in currency exchange rates, thereby maximizing gains and minimizing losses.

Government Reactions to Intraenterprise Price Adjustments. Such intraenterprise pricing practices are often used for purposes of (1) realizing higher profits in countries with lower tax rates and harder currencies and (2) decreasing import duties. Tax and customs officials have become more knowledgeable about such practices and now have the power to disregard prices that they consider unreasonably low or high. They then levy taxes or tariffs on what they determine to be reasonable profits or prices. Therefore, companies must use such practices carefully and with discretion; financial management should be able to substantiate its prices with convincing cost data. Some writers do not recommend aggressive use of transfer pricing* for foreign exchange management.

The alternatives the financial manager for an American exporter should consider to reduce the risk of exchange losses are shown in Figure 19.2. We use the transaction discussed above, in which an American exporter sold $1 million of goods to a Norwegian importer. At the time of sale, the exchange rate was $1 = 9 Norwegian krone. The sales contract called for the Norwegian importer to pay the American exporter NK9 million in six months, which placed the currency exchange risk on the exporter.

*Transfer pricing is a term for the pricing involved when one unit of an IC buys from another. See the discussion of transfer pricing in Chapter 16.

[Figure 19.2] **Hedging Currency Risks**

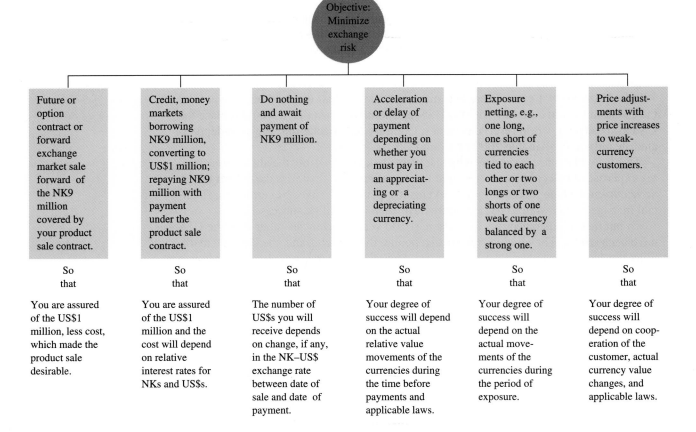

Objective: Minimize exchange risk					
Future or option contract or forward exchange market sale forward of the NK9 million covered by your product sale contract.	Credit, money markets borrowing NK9 million, converting to US$1 million; repaying NK9 million with payment under the product sale contract.	Do nothing and await payment of NK9 million.	Acceleration or delay of payment depending on whether you must pay in an appreciating or a depreciating currency.	Exposure netting, e.g., one long, one short of currencies tied to each other or two longs or two shorts of one weak currency balanced by a strong one.	Price adjustments with price increases to weak-currency customers.
So that	So that	So that	So that	So that	So that
You are assured of the US$1 million, less cost, which made the product sale desirable.	You are assured of the US$1 million and the cost will depend on relative interest rates for NKs and US$s.	The number of US$s you will receive depends on change, if any, in the NK–US$ exchange rate between date of sale and date of payment.	Your degree of success will depend on the actual relative value movements of the currencies during the time before payments and applicable laws.	Your degree of success will depend on the actual movements of the currencies during the period of exposure.	Your degree of success will depend on cooperation of the customer, actual currency value changes, and applicable laws.

Only for Big Business?

Generally, only larger companies can afford the expertise and deal in big enough amounts to make currency risk hedging practical. However, during the 1990s, a new development brought some hedging possibilities within the reach of medium-sized and small businesses.

In January 1990, the U.S. Federal Reserve allowed American banks to hold foreign currency deposits in the United States. It is difficult or even impossible for a smaller firm to open a modest account at a foreign bank, but it is much less intimidating to deal with the firm's regular, local bank.

Now, to protect against a drop in the US$'s value, an importer from France can buy the number of French francs that will be needed to pay the French exporter. They can be held in its local account, earning interest until needed.

Translation Risks

We have just examined the risks that an international business incurs when it buys and sells between two or more countries and agrees to either make or receive a future payment in a foreign currency. The purchase or sale is a transaction, and the currency value change risk is called a transaction risk.

Financial statements of ICs must be stated in one currency, just as are the statements of any domestic business. The IC may have businesses and assets in several currencies, such as German marks, French francs, and Japanese yen, but its financial statements would be meaningless for most people if all those currencies were used. One must be chosen, and the values of the others must be translated into the chosen currency.

Sooner or later, companies with international operations will have assets, liabilities, revenues, and expenses in more than one currency. The financial statements of an American IC must translate assets and so forth from the currencies of their locations into US$s.

The **translation risks** can be illustrated by assuming that an American opens a Canadian dollar (C$) bank account of C$1 million at a time when the exchange rate is C$1 = US$1. If, one year later, the exchange rate has changed to C$1.10 = US$1 and the bank balance is still C$1 million, the American IC still has its C$1 million. However, the company must report financially in US$s, and the Canadian bank account is now worth only about US$909,090.

translation risks
The losses or gains that can result from restating the values of the assets and liabilities/payables and receivables arising from investments abroad from one currency to another

It does not follow from the drop in the relative value of the Canadian dollar in this example that the investment in Canada was unwise. It may be profitable, growing, and gaining market share. The American may be very pleased with the Canadian investment and have no intention of liquidating it or may even be considering adding to it. After all, Canadian assets are now less expensive in US$ terms than they were at the time of the original investment.

Realistic Information

Ongoing translating and reporting bring up to date the values in US$s of previously reported assets and so forth. Management must base important decisions, such as dividends, pricing, new investment, and asset location, on the updating of all such asset and earnings values. It is unrealistic for management to base key decisions on the assumption that exchange rates have not changed and will not change.

Management Fears

Managers fear that shareholders and analysts will regard translated and reported foreign exchange losses as speculation or, worse, bad management. It is difficult to explain that reported losses are irrelevant or should be ignored. Even though reserves are not permitted under present U.S. accounting practices, many managers are attempting to insulate financial statements from foreign exchange market fluctuations by other means.

Some of these means are the same as those discussed above in connection with transaction risks. Management can hedge currencies, accelerate or delay payments, net exposures, or adjust prices. There are other means that can be used against transaction risks, but these methods are more often used in translation situations. Management can neutralize the company's balance sheet through the use of swaps.

Neutralizing the Balance Sheet

Neutralizing the balance sheet means endeavoring to have monetary assets in a given currency approximate monetary liabilities in that currency. In that condition, a fall in the currency value of assets will be matched by the fall in payment obligations; thus, the translation risk is avoided.

neutralizing the balance sheet
Having monetary assets in amounts approximately equal to monetary liabilities

However, before financial management neutralizes its balance sheet to avoid translation risk, it must look to the business needs of the parent and subsidiary companies. The ongoing business flow of and need for capital, the cost of capital from country to country, payrolls, payables and receivables, optimum location for new investment, and dozens of other business considerations must be factored in before an attempt is made to neutralize the balance sheets of all subsidiaries. In other words, maximizing the profit of the enterprise should be more important than avoiding translation risk when they conflict.

Swaps

Swaps may be used to protect against transaction risks, are more likely to be used against translation risks, but are most likely to be used to raise or transfer capital. Therefore, we shall treat swaps separately and examine several types: (1) spot and forward market swaps, (2) parallel loans, and (3) bank swaps. Interest rate swaps are dealt with on page 660 in the "Capital Raising and Investing" section.

swaps
Trades of assets and liabilities in different currencies or interest rate structures to lessen risks or lower costs

[Figure 19.3] **Parallel Loans by Two Parent Companies (Each to the Subsidiary of the Other)**

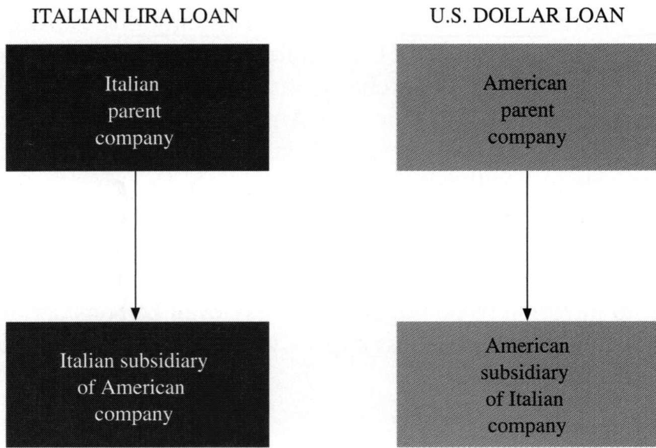

Spot and Forward Market Swaps

Suppose an American parent wants to lend Italian lira (IL) to its Italian subsidiary and avoid currency exchange risk. The parent will buy IL in the spot market and lend them to the subsidiary. At the same time, the parent will short the same amount of IL (buying US$s for forward delivery) for the period of the loan. The short lira position is covered with the lira repaid by the subsidiary, and the parent receives the dollars. The cost will depend on the discount rate in the forward market compared to the spot market rate.

Parallel Loans

Keeping the American parent and its Italian subsidiary of the previous example, let's add an Italian parent company and its American subsidiary. Assume that each parent wants to lend to its subsidiary in the subsidiary's currency. This can be accomplished without using the foreign exchange market. The Italian parent lends the agreed amount in lira to the Italian subsidiary of the American parent. At the same time and with the same loan maturity, the American parent lends the same amount (at the spot IL–US$ rate) in US$s to the American subsidiary of the Italian parent. Figure 19.3 illustrates this.

As you see, each loan is made and repaid in one currency, thus avoiding foreign exchange risk. Each loan should have the right of offset, which means that if either subsidiary defaults on its repayment, the other subsidiary can withhold its repayment. This avoids the need for parent company guarantees.

This sort of parallel loan swap can be adapted to many circumstances and can involve more than two countries or companies. If a subsidiary in a blocked-currency country has a surplus of that currency in its local operation, perhaps the local subsidiary of another IC needs capital.[7] The other IC would like to provide that capital but would not like to convert more of its hard currency into a soft currency. The subsidiary of the first IC lends its surplus currency to the subsidiary of the second IC. The parent company of the second IC lends the parent company of the first IC an equivalent amount in some other currency that it can use. Figure 19.4 illustrates this.[8]

Interest may or may not be charged on swaps. That usually depends on whether interest rates in the two countries are similar or are widely different. In the latter situation, the borrower getting the higher-cost currency might pay an equivalently higher rate of interest on repayment.

You may have observed that we have not mentioned banks in our discussion of swaps. These company-to-company loans are competition for commercial banks, but some banks will facilitate negotiations or act as a broker between clients in arranging

Table 19.2 Traded Contracts

Exchange	Jan.–Mar. 1999	Jan.–Mar. 2000	% Change
Eurex (Germany and Switzerland)	83,362,786	121,534,446	45.79
CBOE (US)	55,036,896	92,396,487	67.88
CBOT (US)	69,349,073	68,708,615	−0.92
Paris Bourse SA* (France)	49,342,833	63,043,304	27.77
CME (US)	50,881,235	59,312,855	16.57
Amex (US)	28,145,093	51,243,572	82.07
Liffe (UK)	35,473,560	32,902,760	−7.25
KSE (S Korea)	20,854,158	29,432,191	41.13
PSX (US)	16,891,255	29,312,983	73.54
Nymex (US)	25,720,933	27,291,232	6.11

Source: Futures Industry Association.
*Includes Matif and Monep.

Derivatives against Fickle Weather?

The U.S. Treasury Department estimates that 70 percent of American companies are affected by the weather. Bombardier, the snowmobile manufacturer, buys a snow derivative by which it can offer cash back to customers if snowfall is less than half the norm. The bank Societé Générale sells weather derivatives to European and Japanese customers to hedge power companies against warm weather, retail companies against adverse temperatures, ski resorts against lack of snow, food and beverage companies against fluctuating temperatures, and flower exhibitions against wind. As these examples illustrate, the potential size of weather derivatives markets is enormous.[15]

There are derivative exchanges around the world. Table 19.2 shows the location of the 10 top exchanges ranked by size in 1995 and 1996.

Financial Executives' Datebooks: Networking

It takes two to tango. It also takes two to efficiently and successfully execute parallel loans, bank swaps, interest rate swaps, and currency swaps. Where do financial executives turn to find partners when they want to protect their organizations with hedges, swaps, or other derivatives? In many cases, their international banks are the answer. In an increasing number of instances, they are finding partners at meetings such as the Risk Management Conference, an advertisement for which you can see in Figure 19.5.

Conferences such as this are held in cities around the world frequently every year. They are sponsored by publications such as the *Financial Times, Euromoney,* the *Asian Wall Street Journal,* and *Business International* and by international financial houses.

At such meetings, the financial executives meet their counterparts from other ICs as well as people representing banks, other financial organizations, and international agencies such as the World Bank and regional development banks. Even though the executives cannot meet and come to know all the participants at large conferences, they are provided a directory of all the people who registered together with the information about how to contact them. More and more, such contacts and information are providing the partners they need to protect their organizations and/or profit from derivatives operations.

Sales without Money

A number of countries desire goods and products for which they do not have the convertible currency to pay. That has not prevented efforts by many suppliers to sell to them anyway. Such countries are usually less developed and poor. There are two main nonmonetary trade themes: countertrade and industrial cooperation.

[Figure 19.5] Protecting Against International Financial Risk

The 16th Annual
Risk Management
Conference
An End-User's Forum

RMC

January 26 - 29, 2000
South Seas Plantation
Captiva Island, Florida
Register Today!
If you are interested in learning more about the effectiveness of exchange-traded derivatives and financial risk management, this is the conference to attend.
For complete conference program details, call 800-OPTIONS or visit either of the following web sites.
www.cbot.com/rmc
www.cboe.com/rmc

Source: From *Financial Times,* January 8–9, 2000, p. 5. Reprinted with permission of *Financial Times.*

Countertrade

countertrade
International trade in which at least part of the payment is in some form other than hard, convertible currency

Countertrade usually involves two or more contracts, one for the purchase of developed country products or services and one or more for the purchase of developing country products or services. We have identified six varieties of countertrade. They are called (1) counterpurchase, (2) compensation, (3) barter, (4) switch, (5) offset, and (6) clearing account arrangements. All involve to a greater or lesser degree the substitution of developing country goods, products, or services for scarce developed country money. They may be relatively simple, involving only two countries or companies, or quite complex, calling for a number of countries, companies, currencies, and contracts.

Counterpurchase agreements helped PepsiCo enter the Eastern European market. As a result, the company continues to grow and expand its operations in that region. For example, this Pepsi-Cola truck is one of a fleet of 70 vehicles based in Warsaw, Poland.
Courtesy Ryder System, Inc.

Counterpurchase

In counterpurchase situations, the goods supplied by the developing country are not produced by or out of the goods or products imported from the developed country. An example of counterpurchase is PepsiCo's arrangement with Russia, to which PepsiCo sells the concentrate for the drink, which is then bottled and sold in that country. In exchange, PepsiCo has exclusive rights to export Russian vodka for sale in the West. In 1990, the two parties renewed and expanded the agreement, increasing the amounts of Pepsi-Cola and vodka to be sold and adding a new element. PepsiCo committed itself to buying at least 10 Russian-built freighters and tankers. PepsiCo intends to lease them on the world market through a Norwegian partner.

In 1992, PepsiCo made a similar deal with Ukraine to sell $1 billion of Ukraine-built ships and to use part of the proceeds to buy soft-drink equipment and build five Pepsi bottling plants in Ukraine. A difference between the Ukrainian and the Russian deals is that another part of the Ukrainian ship sale proceeds will finance the opening of 100 Pepsi-owned Pizza Hut restaurants in that republic.[16]

Uganda wanted 18 helicopters to help stamp out elephant and rhino poaching but didn't have the $25 million to pay for them. The problem was solved by Gary Pacific, head of countertrade for McDonnell Douglas Helicopter. Pacific helped set up several local projects that generate hard currency, including a plant that will process Nile perch, and a factory to turn pineapple and passion fruit into concentrate. He then found buyers of those products in Europe, and delivery of the helicopters began in 1994.[17]

Compensation

Such transactions call for payment by the developing country in products produced by developed country equipment. The products made in the developing country by the developed country equipment are shipped to the developed country in payment for the equipment. Dresser Industries has a compensation agreement with Poland for tractors. Poland is paying with tractors and other machines that Dresser then markets.

Barter

Barter is an ancient form of commerce and the simplest sort of countertrade. The developing country sends products to the developed country that are equal in value to the products delivered by the developed country to the developing country.

Switch

Frequently, the goods delivered by the developing country are not easily usable or salable. Then a third party is brought in to dispose of them. This process is called *switch trading.*

Offset

The offset form occurs when the importing nation requires a portion of the materials, components, or subassemblies of a product to be procured in the local (importer's) market. The exporter may set up or cooperate in setting up a parts manufacturing and assembly facility in the importing country.

Clearing Account Arrangements

These are used to facilitate the exchange of products over a specified time period. When the period ends, any balance outstanding must be cleared by the purchase of additional goods or settled by a cash payment. The bank or broker acts as an intermediary to facilitate settlement of the clearing accounts by finding markets for counterpurchased goods or by converting goods or cash payments into products desired by the country with a surplus.

How Important Is Countertrade?

Frequently, countertrade agreements and their executions are not reported publicly. Indeed, the parties often prefer privacy and confidentiality for competitive reasons and to avoid setting precedents for future deals. Therefore, estimates of the extent of countertrade vary widely. The U.S. Commerce Department estimates that between 20 and 30 percent of world trade is now subject to some form of countertrade and that the proportion could reach 50 percent in 15 years.

Major U.S. firms report transactions involving some form of countertrade. *Business Week* and General Electric each independently estimate the volume at 30 percent of world trade. By far the lowest estimate, 8 percent, was made by the World Trade Organization.

Regardless of which estimate is nearest the truth, the value of countertrade is very large. Apply any of the estimates to the over $4.10 trillion volume of world trade and the result is big.[18]

An indication of the growing importance of countertrade is the growth of the American Countertrade Association (ACA), most of whose members are Fortune 500 heavyweights, including the top U.S. exporters. But more and more smaller companies are joining, including many that had not previously thought much about countertrade or even exporting. Figure 19.6 shows ACA membership percentages by industry.

U.S. Government's Positions on Countertrade. We say "positions" because different agencies contradict each other and Congress contradicts itself. The Treasury Department is flatly opposed to countertrade, the Commerce Department helps companies engage in it, and the Export-Import Bank has no policy for dealing with it. In Congress, legislation has been introduced both to curtail countertrade and to encourage countertrade of U.S. surplus agricultural commodities.

Other Governments' Positions on Countertrade. The governments of most developing countries either encourage or require countertrade, but so also do such industrialized countries as Australia and New Zealand. No country forbids countertrade.

Twin Problems. The age-old twin problems with goods coming from the developing country side of countertrade transactions are product quality and delivery reliability. In general, there are two ways the developed country side is coping with those problems.

One solution is inspection of the goods before they leave the developing country plant by a reliable third-party organization. Two such organizations are the Paris-based Bureau Veritas and the Societé Generale de Surveillance, whose main office is in Geneva.

Roger Gyarmaty of Veritas says, "We go back to the production process to see if the goods are being made to specifications. We see to it that delivery times and terms are being met. And we check the packaging and loading to be sure the goods are not dam-

[Figure 19.6] American Countertrade Association Membership by Industry

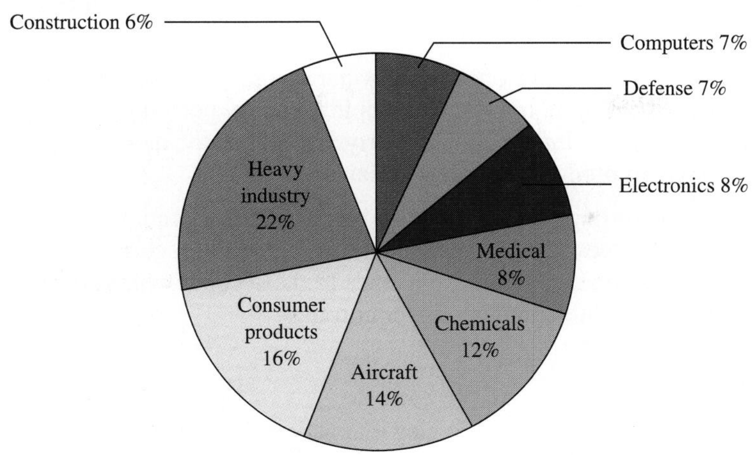

Source: From "Why Countertrade Is Getting Hot," by Shelley Neumeier, *Fortune*, June 29, 1992, p. 25. Reprinted with permission of *Fortune*.

aged at those points. Companies can save up to two or three times the cost of our services just through fewer headaches when they receive the goods."

A second solution is growing in popularity. The Eastern European banking structure is developing, and the developed country countertrade party is increasingly getting a guarantee of quality and delivery from a bank in the developing country. When such a guarantee has been given, the bank takes a stern interest in the product's production line to avoid having to come up with precious foreign exchange in the event of quality or delivery that is not in accordance with the contract.

New Directions

Not all countertrade is between developed countries and developing countries. There is trade of Angolan coffee for Russian equipment, and developing countries frequently have agreements encouraging trade with each other, such as those between Argentina and Brazil and among the Association of Southeast Asian Nations (ASEAN) member-countries.

Alan Linger, a Lloyds Bank countertrade manager, believes such business could become triangular by including developed countries. For example, developed country goods would be exported to an Eastern European country, products of which would go to a developing country, which would then complete the triangle by shipping its commodities to the developed country.

Industrial Cooperation

Industrial cooperation, which developing countries favor, requires long-term relationships, with part or all of the production being done in the developing country involved. Part of the resulting products are sold in the developing countries or the Third World.

industrial cooperation
Long-term relationships between developed country companies and developing country plants in which some or all production is done in the developing country plant

We have identified five different industrial cooperation methods.

1. *Joint venture.* Two or more companies or state agencies combine assets to form a new and distinct economic entity, and they share management, profits, and losses.
2. *Coproduction and specialization.* The factory in the developing country produces certain agreed-on components of a product, while a company in the developed country produces the other components. The product is then assembled at both locations for their respective markets.
3. *Subcontracting.* The developing country factory manufactures a product according to specifications of the developed country company and delivers the product to the developed country company, which then markets it.

4. *Licensing.* The developing country and developed country parties enter into a license agreement whereby the developing country enterprise uses developed country technology to manufacture a product. The developed country company is paid a license royalty fee in money or in product. The latter method is preferred by the developing country.
5. *Turnkey plants.* The developed country party is responsible for building the entire plant, starting it, training developing country personnel, and turning over the keys to the developing country party. Of course, the developing country wants to pay in products of the new plant.

Two threads run through countertrade and industrial cooperation. The first is that the developing country does not have enough hard, convertible currency to buy what it wants from the developed country. That leads to the second, which is the effort of the developing country to substitute goods for currency.

International Finance Center

international finance centers
Handle most or all international financial transactions for all units of an IC

A number of new developments are forcing international companies to pay more attention to financial management. International financial management has become more and more different from domestic financial management, and in several such companies, the finance operation has become a profit center and is no longer merely a service. Some of the new developments are (1) floating exchange rates, whose fluctuations are sometimes volatile, (2) growth in the number of capital and foreign exchange markets where an IC can shop for lower interest costs and better currency rates, (3) different and changing inflation rates from country to country, (4) advances in electronic cash management systems, (5) realization by financial managers that through innovative management of temporarily idle cash balances of the IC units, they can increase yields and the enterprise's profit, and (6) the explosive growth of the use of derivatives to protect against commodity, currency, interest rate, and other risks. As a result, many ICs have established **international finance centers.**

Volatile, Floating Currency Exchange Rates

An international finance center can take advantage of volatile, floating currency exchange rates to make money for the IC in several ways. It would be aware of which currencies are most susceptible to sudden weakness, avoid borrowing in undervalued currencies, and maximize short-term assets in strong currencies. This is currency exposure management.

Capital and Exchange Markets

Like any company, an IC needs to raise capital from time to time. Unlike most domestic companies, it needs to exchange currencies. Given the proliferation of capital and exchange markets, the international finance center should advise and direct the parent and affiliates where to raise and exchange money at the lowest costs.

Inflation Rates

Inflation goes up and inflation goes down, and while it's going up in one country, it's going down in another. The international finance center should be aware of all those trends and advise and direct the IC system how to protect assets and profits from monetary erosion and other economic and political risks.

Electronic Cash Management

Currency exposure management is being simplified. New technology is permitting the creation of worldwide networks that enable firms to transfer funds electronically. The international finance center should evaluate and use the best of those developing systems. Some of them are Electronic Funds Transfer Network, Society for Worldwide Interbank Financial Telecommunications, Clearing House Automated Payment System, and Clearing House Interbank Payments Transfer.

Using Derivatives Correctly

As was indicated earlier in this chapter, the use of derivatives is multiplying rapidly. They can be used to protect against, among other things, commodity price changes, currency exchange rate fluctuations, and interest rate changes. But they can be complex and can cause losses rather than provide protection. ICs or other organizations that want derivative protection should hire experts.

Other Uses of the International Finance Center

Mentioned above are only a few of the possible functions of an international finance center. Here are some others:

1. *Handle internal and external invoicing.* The center can make complex decisions about financing international trade among the IC units and between them and outside suppliers and customers. All data on imports and exports can be channeled through the center, which can determine which currencies will be used and how the trades will be financed.
2. *Help weak currency affiliate.* An affiliate with a weak currency could have difficulty obtaining needed imports. By placing itself in the trade chain, the center can arrange the financing needed by such an affiliate.
3. *Strengthen affiliate evaluation and reporting systems.* The center is in a unique position to understand and interpret the performance of affiliates in countries around the world. Inherent differences are exacerbated by volatile exchange rates, different inflation rates, varying tax laws and accounting rules, transfer price policies, and a host of environmental factors. IC decisions about transfer pricing, choosing one subsidiary over another to compete for a contract, or adding capital to one subsidiary rather than another also complicate performance evaluations, with which the international finance center can assist.

[Summary]

Realize that the currencies of countries change in value in terms of each other.

Currency exchange rates, the cost of one currency in terms of others, fluctuate constantly.

Understand how currency value changes affect international business transactions.

Anyone who has the obligation to pay or the right to receive a foreign currency in the future has a currency exchange risk. The risk may arise out of transactions (e.g., export or import contracts, in which case it is called a transaction risk). Or it may arise out of longer-term investments that are the subjects of financial statements, in which case it is called a translation risk.

Recognize the tremendous importance of financial management to an international company (IC).

Financial management is vital to the success of ICs and has moved from being merely a service to being a profit center.

Know about financial management tools.

Financial management tools include derivatives, hedges, payment timing, exposure netting, price adjustments, balance sheet neutralizing, and swaps.

Understand the growing use of derivatives as hedging devices.

Derivative hedges include such devices as forward, future, and credit hedges.

Explain how financial executives meet, network, and cooperate with their counterparts in other organizations to protect and/or benefit their organizations in derivatives operations.

Financial management conferences are held frequently in cities around the world. At them, the financial executives can meet or become aware of their counterparts from other organizations with whom to cooperate.

Understand why exporters sometimes accept payment in forms other than money.

Buyers frequently don't have or don't want to use hard, convertible currency and wish to pay in goods or services instead of money. The generic term for this is countertrade.

Differentiate between hard, convertible currencies and soft, nonconvertible ones.

Hard, convertible currencies are accepted all around the world at uniform exchange rates. Soft, nonconvertible currencies are rarely of any use outside the country of issue.

Explain the growing importance of international finance centers to ICs.

An IC's international finance center accumulates the expertise and information to transact all international financial dealings of all the IC's units most profitably and at lowest cost.

[Key Words]

fluctuating exchange rates (p. 649)
transaction risks (p. 649)
hedging (p. 649)
leads (p. 653)
lags (p. 653
exposure netting (p. 654)
translation risks (p. 657)
neutralizing the balance sheet (p. 657)
swaps (p. 657)
equity capital (p. 659)
debt capital (p. 659)
derivatives (p. 662)
countertrade (p. 664)
industrial cooperation (p. 667)
international finance centers (p. 668)

[Questions]

1. Why is an exporter that is to be paid in six months in a foreign currency worried about fluctuating foreign exchange rates?
2. Are there ways in which this exporter can protect itself? If so, what are they?
3. How does the credit or money market hedge work?

4. Why is acceleration or delay of payments more useful to an IC than to smaller, separate companies?
5. How would you accomplish exposure netting with currencies of two countries that tend to go up and down together in value?
6. Why is the price adjustment device more useful to an IC than to smaller, separate companies?
7. Some argue that translation gains or losses are not important so long as they have not been realized and are only accounting entries. What is the other side of that argument?
8. Is the parallel loan a sort of swap? How does it work?
9. How and why would a seller make a sale to a buyer that has no money the seller can use?
10. Developed country partners in countertrade contracts have had problems with quality and timely delivery of goods from the developing country partners. How are they trying to deal with those problems?

[Internet Exercises]

Using the Internet

1. The text discusses the importance of managing currency fluctuations as they may change rapidly even within one trading day. Using the Internet, find information on currency trading and how quickly trading occurs. For example, CNNfn's Web site lists the value of currency trading and the time of the last trade.
2. As the text points out, fluctuating currency exchange rates may be a result of many factors. Using the Internet, examine the economy of a country in order to determine how changes in exchange rates could be predicted by an international manager.

[Minicase 19.1]

Dealing with the Transaction Risk Caused by Fluctuations of Relative Currency Values

You are the finance manager of an American multinational. Your company has sold US$1 million of its product to a French importer. The rate of exchange on the day of sale is US$1 = FF5, so on that day the 1 million U.S. dollars equals 5 million French francs.

The contract calls for the French importer to pay your company FF5 million six months from the date of sale. Therefore, your company bears the transaction risk of a change in the currency exchange rates between the US$ and the FF.

Assume your company has no need for French francs and will want U.S. dollars no later than the payment date. Assume further that you do not wish to carry the transaction risk. Give two methods by which you might protect your company from that risk.

[Chapter]

20

Global Operations Management: The Third Industrial Revolution

"Inspection with the aim of finding the bad ones and throwing them out is too late, ineffective, costly. Quality comes not from inspection, but from improvement of the process."
—Dr. W. Edwards Deming.

Concept Previews

After reading this chapter, you should be able to:

- **describe** the five global sourcing arrangements
- **appreciate** the importance of the added costs of global sourcing
- **understand** the increasing role of electronic purchasing for global sourcing
- **understand** the Japanese efforts to improve quality and lower costs
- **know** the just-in-time (JIT) production system
- **comprehend** the problems with JIT
- **understand** synchronous manufacturing
- **identify** the impediments to global standardization of production processes and procedures
- **understand** the importance of intermediate and appropriate technology
- **know** the two general classes of activities, productive and supportive, that must be performed in all manufacturing systems

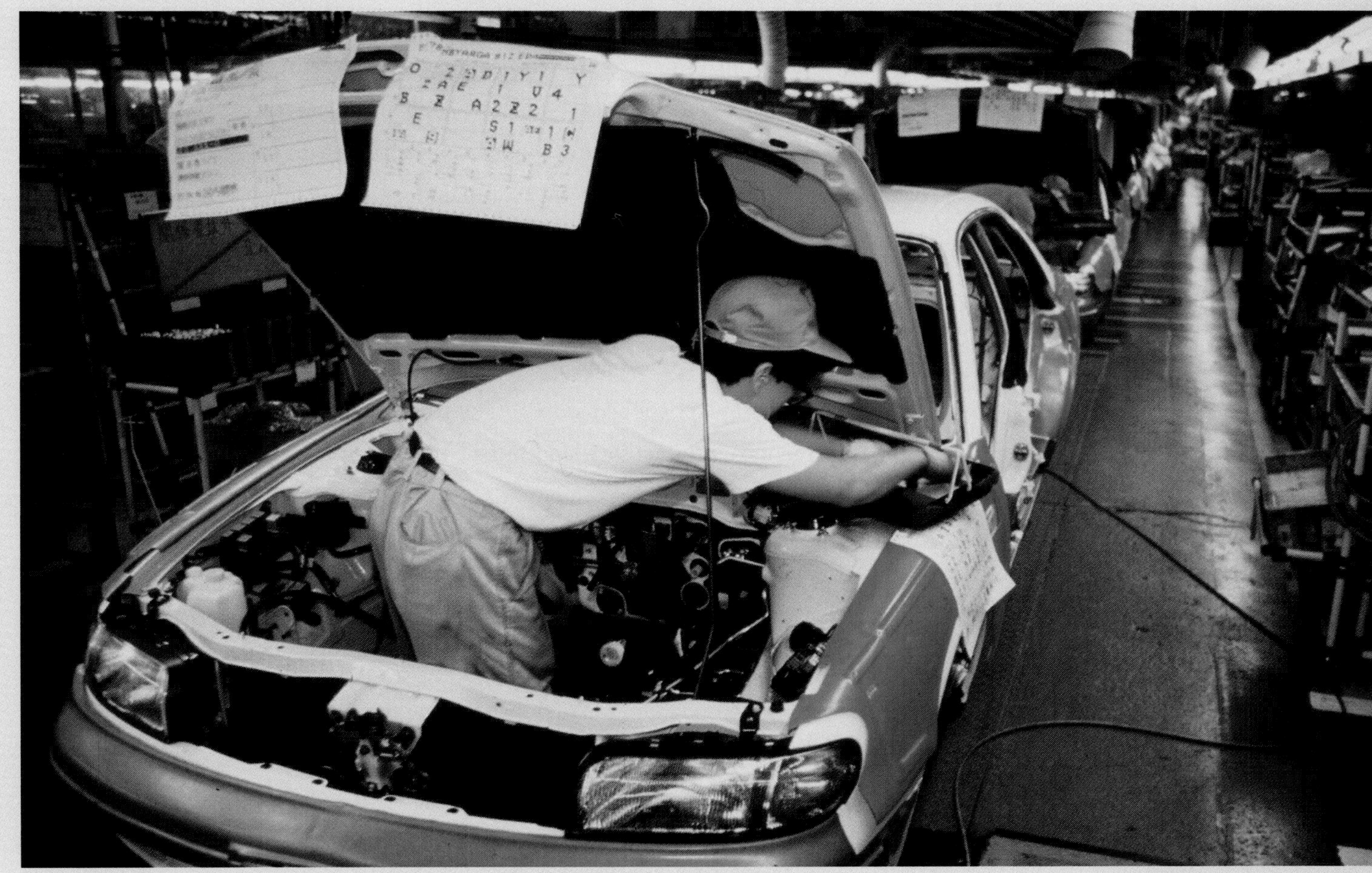

Andy Sachs/Tony Stone Images

Outsourcing: Growth by Building on Existing Businesses

In the early 1980s, Johnson Controls was known for heating controls and plastic containers, not for automotive products. Until 1985 automobile manufacturers made car seats in their own factories, and it was then that Johnson and another company, Lear, conceived the idea of supplying those essential parts of a car's interior for them.

Now the company estimates that 80 percent of the seating in American-made cars is outsourced, while in Europe the comparable proportion is 70 percent. According to the company, demand from automakers for a single supplier of seating systems is expected to grow "due to opportunities system integration creates for cost reduction, parts consolidation, weight reduction, quality and safety improvements, enhanced functionality, and vehicle differentiation." As Johnson's customers move overseas, they expect Johnson to supply them from local facilities. In response, the company has established over 130 seat-making plants, most of which are in the United States and Europe. Many are satellite plants located close to big car factories, to which the seats are delivered straight to the assembly line as needed. To manage the complexity of a global production system, the company is creating a standardized business operating system and a single, global infrastructure, thus helping to eliminate variation and inefficiencies across factories.

Johnson is striving to increase the input of its engineers to the design work so that it can use the results in the seats of other car manufacturers. "Three years ago, 80 percent of our development work was done on behalf of individual customers and only 20 percent was our own proprietary designs," says Johnson's president. "Today the proportion is about 60:40 and our goal is to turn this to 20:80." In 1999, the company launched an Internet-based database that employees worldwide can use to post and retrieve factory-tested best practices and ideas for improving performance in such areas as quality, cost, timelines, productivity, and morale of employees. Another private Web site allows the company's suppliers to provide real-time status updates, generates progress reports, and helps program managers quickly identify problems.

Another strategy has been to expand its role from supplying seating to include non-seating areas of car interiors (roof interiors and trim). This is part of a move to supply a "total interior" service to automakers. A further step in this direction is the introduction of a satellite-based communications system built into a car's interior.

Johnson Controls, building on the knowledge that its existing customers are its largest source of growth, has expanded its outsourcing to include the operation and maintenance of commercial buildings full-time for customers for which it once was the source for just heating and ventilation controls. It is now the world's leading supplier of integrated facility management, with a portfolio of over 1.2 billion square feet of building space in 35 nations. ■

Source: Johnson Controls, "Letter to Shareholders," *Annual Report 1997,* www.johnsoncontrols.com/annualreports/ (March 4, 1998); and "Automotive" and "Controls," *Annual Report 1999,* www.johnsoncontrols.com/annualreports/ (November 24, 2000); "Manufacturing: Going International Can Spread Risks," *Financial Times,* January 13, 1998, www.ft.com/search97cgi/ (March 4, 1998); and "Case Study: Johnson Controls," *Financial Times,* February 23, 1998, www.ft.com/search97cgi/ (March 4, 1998).

As firms continue to enter global markets, global competition increases. This forces management of both international and domestic companies to search for ways to lower costs while improving their products to remain competitive. Often the solution is *outsourcing,* that is, hiring others to do noncore activities instead of doing them in-house. Commonly, outsourcing firms provide key components of data processing, logistics, human relations, and accounting, although any activity in the value chain can be outsourced. Actually, the difference between outsourcing and sourcing is minimal. As you saw in the opening section, Johnson Controls outsources automobile interiors for car manufacturers and the maintenance and administration of commercial buildings for the buildings' owners.

> An interesting outsourcing firm is Wackenhut, a supplier of numerous security services in over 50 countries. Some of its activities include selecting, training, and supervising security guards; operating airport inspection systems; and providing theft protection in retail stores. In addition to serving embassies from a variety of other nations, Wackenhut has a contract with the U.S. State Department to provide security personnel and security-related services to over 20 overseas U.S. embassies that were formerly protected by the Marines. In 1993, Wackenhut began operating in Russia, and it extended its operations to China in the following year. The company now has operations in the United States and 56 other countries on six continents.[1]

Sourcing Globally

Reasons for Sourcing Globally

Although the primary reason for sourcing globally is to obtain lower prices, there are others. Perhaps certain products the company requires may not be available locally and must be imported. Another possibility is that the firm's foreign competitors are using components of better quality or design than those available in the home country.[2] To be competitive, the company may also have to source these components or production machinery in foreign countries. Table 20.1 presents the five most important reasons given and the percentages of respondents for each reason in a survey of 149 American companies that do foreign sourcing.

Note that although the primary reason for global sourcing given by American manufacturers is to obtain lower prices, half the respondents believed that foreign suppliers had products not available locally and about one-fourth felt that they could buy higher-tech and better-quality products overseas.

Outsourcing decisions, including the decision to use global sources of supply, are extensions of the make-or-buy decisions of earlier eras. The pros and cons of these make-or-buy decisions usually included comparisons of costs as well as managerial control of confidential product design specifications, delivered quantity, quality, design, and delivery time and method. Other considerations include the manufacturing expertise required to make the raw material or components and the added cost of not being able to take advantage of the scale or larger volumes a vendor may have. In global purchasing, these issues are exacerbated by such factors as distance, different languages between buyer and seller, and different national laws and regulations. Over time, many organizations have developed the ability to manage these obstacles fully or in part, thus enabling global outsourcing to become a viable option for an increasing number of firms.

The lure of global sourcing is the existence of suppliers with improved competitiveness in terms of cost, quality, timeliness, and other relevant dimensions. For example, certain nations may provide access to lower-cost or better-quality minerals or other important raw materials or components compared to what might be available domestically (such as bauxite in Jamaica or dynamic random-access memory chips in South Korea). In addition, the existence of industrially less developed countries with inexpensive and abundant unskilled labor may provide an attractive source of supply for labor-intensive products with low skill requirements. This helps explain why many labor-intensive operations (such as the assembly of athletic shoes or men's dress shirts) have moved away from the more industrialized countries, where labor is more expensive. As these countries develop industrially, and some have developed rather rapidly, they have typically moved forward on the product and process continuum from high-labor-content products made with light unsophisticated process equipment, such as sewing machines, to more sophisticated processes and more complex, lower-labor-content machinery.

Table 20.1 Five Most Important Reasons for Sourcing Globally

Reason	Percentage of Respondents
1. Lower price available from foreign sources	74%
2. Availability of foreign products not available locally	49
3. Firm's worldwide operation and attitude	28
4. Advanced technology available from foreign sources	28
5. Higher-quality products available from foreign sources	25

Source: Reprinted with permission from the publisher National Association of Purchasing Management. "International Purchasing: Benefits, Requirements, and Challenges," by Laura M. Biron and Stanley E. Fawcett, Spring 1993, Volume 29, #2, p. 34.

Topsy Tail—A Real Virtual Company

Small and Medium-Sized Enterprises

No firm is too small or too large to use outsourcing. Today nearly any organization can get access to resources. In the global economy of the 1990s and 2000s, knowledge and expertise differentiate companies—not the size and scope of the resources they own. Small companies are using outsourcing to obtain all the capabilities of large ones without the expense and delay of acquiring and managing each new resource.

There must be few companies that utilize outsourcing to the extent that a small Texas company, Topsy Tail, does. With only three employees, it has sold more than $100 million worth of its hairstyling products since 1991. The "company" is a carefully structured network of 20 outside vendors who handle everything from production to the servicing of retail accounts. Practically everything the firm does—design, production, packaging, sales, and distribution—is handled by subcontractors. Tomima Edmark, head of Topsy Tail, says her company could not have grown so swiftly in any other way. ■

Source: Outsourcing Institute, "The Networked Organization," *Outsourcing: How Industry Leaders Are Reshaping the American Corporation*, www.outsourcing.com/getstart/95seintr.html (March 3, 1998); and "The Outing of Outsourcing," *The Economist*, November 25, 1995, pp. 57–58.

The rate at which developing nations shift to more sophisticated processes is often more rapid than the initial emergence of these processes in a developed country. In part, this may be due to an emerging nation's ability to transfer technology and processes previously invented and commercialized in the more developed nations, thus avoiding the cost and time of inventing these technologies on its own. As was discussed in Chapter 10, there can be important implications for nations that may be losing jobs as a result of the migration of developing nations into more sophisticated, higher-value sectors. Many times, a worker put out of a high-labor-content job in a more industrially developed nation may lack the ability or training to move up the ladder to a more sophisticated job. Governments, concerned with the potential loss of jobs, may attempt to take actions to prevent or delay movement of the work to the developing country.

Global Sourcing Arrangements

As was suggested in Chapter 2, any of the following arrangements can provide a firm with foreign products:

1. *Wholly owned subsidiary*—May be established in a country with low-cost labor to supply components to the home country plant, or the subsidiary may produce a product not made in the home country.
2. *Overseas joint venture*—Established where labor costs are lower than those in the home country to supply components to the home country.
3. *In-bond plant contractor*—Home country plant sends components to be machined and assembled or only assembled by an independent contractor in an in-bond plant.
4. *Overseas independent contractor*—Common in the clothing industry, in which firms with no production facilities, such as DKNY, Nike, and Liz Claiborne, contract with foreign manufacturers to make clothing to their specifications with their labels.
5. *Independent overseas manufacturer.*

Importance of Global Sourcing

As was discussed in Chapter 13, there is a strong relationship between global sourcing and ownership of the foreign sources. Here are some additional data about American industry. In 1998, U.S. multinational corporations (MNCs) imported $158.1 billion (44 percent of all imports by U.S. MNCs) from their overseas subsidiaries. In the same

[Worldview]

Chasing the Sun

"Big Ben strikes 5, and a team of engineers in London saves the latest files on a major design project and heads home to their flats. At about that time, a second team is pouring its first cups of coffee in rainy Seattle, eight time zones behind, and setting to work where the Brits left off. At the end of their eight-hour day, the Americans flip the proverbial baton over the Great Wall to a Beijing team, who will later complete the 24-hour cycle by giving way to the London team arriving for breakfast."[a]

Sound far-fetched or futuristic? Think again, because this type of activity is occurring in a growing number of multinational corporations. Driven by increasing global competition and pressure to reduce concept-to-market cycle time, many international competitors—particularly in high-technology sectors such as information technology—have been forced to fundamentally rethink the way they structure their operations. The result is an approach termed global, concurrent engineering, or "chasing the sun" in more common terms.

Companies such as Hewlett-Packard (H-P) are trying to gain an advantage over their competitors by developing systems that permit around-the-clock development of new products. As stated by Mark Canepa, who is responsible for workstation systems strategy at H-P, "There's enormous pressure to make better and better products, faster than the competition, and time to market is the biggest differentiator."[b] In rolling out its latest major initiative, the Open Enterprise Computing program, H-P is using a "virtual" team of specialists from around the world who are linked with each other—and with an array of international customers and partners—regardless of location and time.

Leveraging 24-hour global computer networks, project-focused Web sites, and teams of engineers and other technical personnel located at various offices around the globe, companies such as H-P are attempting to enable around-the-clock communication among clients and coworkers and thereby facilitate continuous real-time engineering enhancements, updating of blueprints, and related project management activities. In essence, they are attempting to revolutionize the way business is conducted.

Implemented properly, these new approaches can yield valuable cross-fertilization of ideas to stimulate productivity and innovation among international teams, produce staggering reductions in lead time for new projects, and deliver a flood of new and enhanced products and services into the market ahead of competitors. The result: a powerful advantage in the demanding global competitive marketplace. ■

Source: [a]Ray Bert, "Around the World in 24 Hours," *ASEE Prism*, American Society of Engineering Education, March 2000, www.asee.org/prism/march/html/feature2.html (May 10, 2000).

[b]David Evans, "Chasing the Sun," *Computer Weekly*, April 27, 1995, p. 33

year, imports by U.S. MNCs from their foreign affiliates totaled \$185.4 billion (42 percent of all imports by U.S. MNCs).[3]

In U.S. industry, the proportion of purchased materials in the overall cost of goods sold has been rising for several decades, from an average of 40 percent in 1945 to 50 percent in 1960 and 55 to 79 percent today.[4] There are several reasons for this phenomenon, including greater complexity of products and increasing pressure for firms to focus on their core business and outsource other activities in which they lack strong competitive ability. In addition, competitive pressures and an emphasis on reduced concept-to-market cycle times in many product and service sectors have resulted in a rapid increase in the number of new products that are made available to the market. It has been estimated that at least 50 percent of products currently on the market were not available five years ago. This development has created additional pressure to locate suppliers worldwide that can provide inputs at competitive prices and quality and with quick responsiveness to market changes.

Finding Global Sources

The import sources discussed in Chapter 17 are the ones a professional purchasing agent would contact to learn about independent foreign sources. Foreign consulates and embassies are especially useful in furnishing the names of national firms searching for foreign customers. Many countries have programs to promote their industries similar to those of the U.S. Department of Commerce. As part of their sales promotional programs, local branches of foreign banks will generally assist in locating sources in their home countries when requested. Some even have newsletters with offers from firms in the home country to sell as well as buy.

The Increasing Use of Electronic Purchasing for Global Sourcing

Simply entering "exporter" and the name of the product in a search engine will bring up the Web sites of dozens of exporters around the world that have online catalogs and information on how to order their products. There are also buyers, some of them from large companies, looking for products. In recent years, many firms have set up electronic procurement (E-procurement) exchanges, individually or in conjunction with other firms, to identify potential suppliers or customers and facilitate efficient and dynamic interactions among these prospective buyers and suppliers. For example, aerospace and defense industry giants BAE Systems, The Boeing Company, Lockheed Martin Corporation, and Raytheon have a combined annual procurement budget of $71 billion and more than 37,000 suppliers and hundreds of airline and government customers. In 2000, those four companies formed Exostar, a business-to-business (B2B) electronic marketplace, to reduce procurement costs, streamline supply chains, and reach new markets. Other ambitious B2B E-procurement projects have been announced in automobile manufacturing (e.g., Covisint, an integrated auto parts supplier exchange developed by Ford, DaimlerChrysler, and General Motors), chemicals (e.g., ChemConnect and CheMatch.com), computers (e.g., ehitex, a mix of suppliers, buyers, and other companies, including Compaq, Gateway, Hewlett-Packard, AMD, Hitachi, Samsung, Quantum, Western Digital, NEC, SCI Systems, and Solectron), steel, insurance, petroleum, hospital supplies, electric utilities, and a wide range of other industries. Forrester Research predicts that B2B exchanges will ultimately account for 53 percent of all online B2B transactions.[5]

In many companies, the purchasing function has been neglected for many years, often being viewed as a prime candidate for outsourcing to other firms. However, purchasing is increasingly being viewed as a strategic function, a trend encouraged by rapid developments in E-procurement. While directly production-oriented goods have been the focus of management attention for many years, the purchasing of goods and services that are not part of finished goods—termed indirect procurement—is also critical. Including such items as maintenance, repair, operating supplies, office equipment, and other services and supplies, indirect procurement can account for as much as 70 percent of the total purchasing expenditures in a company. Although total global expenditure on nonproduction items has been estimated at $1.4 trillion, many organizations have continued to rely on traditional paper-based processes for indirect procurement despite their cost and inefficiency.[6]

Options for Global Electronic Procurement

Among the most basic transactions that can occur over electronic purchasing exchanges are catalog purchases. Suppliers will provide a catalog of the products available, and buyers can access, review, and place orders for desired items at a listed price. The supplier can keep the catalog updated in real time, adjusting prices according to inventory levels and the need to move particular products. Electronic exchanges can also permit buyers and suppliers to interact through a standard bid/quote system in which buyers can post their purchasing needs online for all prospective suppliers to view and the suppliers can then submit private quotes to the buyer. The buyer can then select among the submitted quotations on the basis of price, delivery times, or other factors. Industry-sponsored exchanges could also facilitate obtaining letters of credit, contracting for logistics and distribution, and monitoring daily prices and order flows, among other services.

Benefits of Global Electronic Procurement Systems

The benefits of electronic purchasing initiatives can be quite substantial. For example, Oracle Corporation announced that it would save $2 billion in the year 2000 due to companywide E-business initiatives that have allowed the company to streamline operations, cut costs, and improve productivity in supply chain management and customer response.[7] Hewlett-Packard estimates that high-technology industries can reduce purchasing costs by at least 40 percent by using B2B exchanges.[8] A study by American Express and Ernst & Young reported that firms that switched from manual purchase orders to automated and streamlined electronic procurement systems could reduce transaction processing costs by up to 95 percent.[9] Participants in a chemical B2B exchange reported average cost savings of 15 percent of the total value of their long-term and spot transactions, as well as reducing the trading cycle time from 6 weeks to 2 weeks.[10] British Telecom, one of the largest corporate buyers in Europe with annual purchases of $8.8 billion, is using B2B procurement to reduce its supply base, improve internal purchasing processes, and reduce the average cost of a purchasing transaction from $113 to an estimated $8.[11] During the first year of deployment, many organizations have reported more than a 300 percent return on investment for automated Internet procurement systems.[12]

> When you look at a large company like General Motors, for example, they are managing hundreds or perhaps thousands of buying agents and hundreds of different buying scenarios. Every agent has a different authority for buying different products and a different relationship with different suppliers. It's hard to enforce a buying discipline and make sure agents are operating underneath the operations. . . Electronic buying removes that one step from the personal relationship and makes the discipline easier to follow. Automation makes it more supervisable.[13]

Smaller companies are also using the Internet to purchase raw materials as well as to sell their products to customers, often on a worldwide basis. Indeed, the emergence of broadly accessible industry B2B exchanges may be particularly beneficial to smaller, resource-constrained suppliers that might be unable to establish and maintain competitively viable electronic sourcing or purchasing exchanges of their own or to otherwise exploit the potential benefits of global supplier or buyer markets. Developments such as E-procurement exchanges have opened the door for many smaller suppliers, which now have to spend very little to get into the market, lowering barriers to entry to domestic and international market opportunities. As asserted by Amanda Mesler, managing director of KPMG Consulting in Houston, Texas, "The promise of an exchange is that it allows them (smaller companies) to leverage their size further and get into more markets, especially globally and internationally, than they ever have before."[14]

Business-to-business electronic commerce has been growing rapidly since the late 1990s and is projected to grow in the United States alone from $43 billion in 1998 to $1.3 trillion in revenues by 2003 (an increase from 0.2 percent to 9.4 percent of total business sales during that five-year time period).[15] The pace of B2B development in Europe has been slower than that in the United States, but Europe is expected to close that gap quickly, reaching a projected $1.2 billion in revenues by 2004.[16]

Overall, emerging industry-based B2B exchanges can help optimize the supply chain across an entire network of organizations, not merely within a single company. These exchanges can create value by aggregating the purchasing power of buyers, improving process efficiency, integrating supply chains, enhancing content dissemination, and improving overall market efficiency within and across nations. For example, the potential cost savings from a fully integrated make-to-order system for automobiles, from raw materials to ultimate consumer, are estimated at $1,000 to $3,000 per vehicle.[17]

Problems with Global Sourcing

Although global sourcing is a standard procedure for half the U.S. firms with sales over $10 million, it does have some disadvantages.[18] Inasmuch as lower price is the primary reason companies make foreign purchases, they may be surprised that what initially appeared to be a lower price is not really lower once all the costs connected to the purchase are considered. For purchases of capital goods, such as manufacturing equipment, many U.S. buying organizations now use "life cycle costing" to analyze purchasing decisions through the life of the purchased item, including trade-in or future estimated salvage value. Even on components, firms increasingly are including full costing, including the use of activity-based costing systems, to ensure that all the costs associated with foreign sourcing (e.g., transportation, insurance, increased inventory levels to insulate against delays in delivery) are fully recognized when they make purchasing decisions.

Added Costs

The buyer must understand the terms of sale discussed in Chapter 17 because international freight, insurance, and packing can add as much as 10 to 12 percent to the quoted price, depending on the sales term used. The following is a list of the costs of importing, with an estimate of the percentage of the quoted price that each cost adds:

1. International freight, insurance, and packing (10–12%).
2. Import duties (0–50%).
3. Customhouse broker's fees (3–5%).
4. Transit or pipeline inventory (5–15%).
5. Cost of letter of credit (1%).
6. International travel and communication costs (2–8%).
7. Company import specialists (5%).
8. Reworking of products out of specification (0–15%).

Explanation of Added Costs. To be certain of the cost of freight, insurance, and packing, the prospective importer should request a quotation with sales terms of CIF port of entry and stipulate that the merchandise be packed for export unless all shipments will be sent by air freight. As discussed in Chapter 17, import duties can be extremely high if the exporting country is in column 2 of the Harmonized Tariff Schedule for the United States (HTSUSA) (see Figure 17.5). Unless the goods enter duty-free, the duty must be added as part of the landed cost. To estimate the import duty, the importer should ask the customhouse broker for assistance. Brokers have experience in customs classification and usually can get nonbinding opinions from the customs inspectors with whom they work. If the product will be imported regularly, the importer should ask Customs to provide a binding tariff classification. This will be made in writing and must be honored by Customs officials.

Costs for inventory in the pipeline will vary according to the exporter's delivery promise. If it can ship from stock and air freight is a viable means, the importer may be able to work with only two weeks' inventory. If, however, the exporter must produce to fill the order and ship by ocean freight, it may need two months' inventory. Carrying costs include the opportunity cost of capital, the cost of storage facilities, insurance, pilferage, depreciation, taxes, and handling.

If there is considerable import activity, the importer may want to set up an import group of employees to be in charge of the operation. One other item that requires explanation is the rework expense and scrap charges. Sometimes a foreign exporter will submit a sample of the article it is quoting that is perfect in every respect, yet the actual shipment may include various pieces out of specification. If the importer has not made arrangements in the purchasing contract for rebates or replacement, the costs can escalate severely.

> Boeing had such a problem with a Japanese firm. After purchasing a particular subassembly domestically for years with no problems, Boeing decided to buy the part from a Japanese manufacturer. It soon found that the Japanese firm's quality and delivery performance were poor. Boeing's engineers wished they had stayed with the American supplier.[19]

Other Disadvantages

One disadvantage an importer should not have to face is an increase in price because the home currency has lost value as a result of exchange rate fluctuation. For example, if an American importer requires the exporter to quote dollar prices, the importer has no exchange rate risk. However, if the firm has a large volume of imports and the dollar is unstable, management may want a quotation in foreign currency. In that case, the chief financial officer of the importing company probably will protect the company from exchange rate risk by using one of the hedging techniques discussed in the last chapter. Hedging has been used for many years by companies that operate internationally, particularly if their raw materials include one or more of the commodities traded on established commodities markets. In most cases, this hedging has not been done for speculative reasons but to protect the company from the risk of rapid price fluctuations.

The emergence of E-procurement has also been accompanied by problems. E-procurement and electronic commerce as a whole cannot be isolated from the company's overall business system. Many early efforts at developing E-procurement systems have been done in isolation and have subsequently failed to deliver on their potential. Successful electronic commerce initiatives include connections to traditional systems for fulfilling procurement and other value chain activities, as well as considerations on how to manage the transition to new, electronic approaches. The traditional functions of purchasing—supplier determination, analysis, and selection—still have to be accomplished before the actual purchasing via E-procurement. In most instances, a company may be able to use the Internet for quicker data acquisition about possible suppliers and generally from a much broader information base than was previously available in a timely manner. Ensuring that a supplier is selected which can meet all the company's conditions for its raw material in terms of quality, delivery, price, and so forth, remains a challenge, particularly in a broad-scale E-procurement network involving suppliers with which the company is not familiar.

Security also is often a significant concern for E-procurement. For B2B electronic commerce to achieve its full potential, access to the company's internal systems from outside is critical. Companies are wary of opening up the details of their business—including pricing, inventory, or design specifications—to competitors, as well as risking the loss of brand equity and margins. As one supplier commented,

> Let's see, you want me to put all my products and prices online so my customers can beat me about the head and shoulders. Then I can commoditize myself even more to take my razor-thin margins down to microscopic levels. Finally, I get to pay transactions fees for this privilege. . . What am I missing?[20]

In addition, exposing internal business systems to access via the Internet can expose the firm to a wide range of potential security issues, such as unauthorized entry ("hacking") and fraudulent orders. Although extensive research and development efforts have been undertaken in encryption technology and other technology and processes to ensure integrity, much progress still remains to be achieved before these systems can be considered fully secure.

Different country standards are also of concern in attempting to implement international E-procurement systems. For example, a study by Price WaterhouseCoopers, conducted for the European Commission, revealed that only 3 of 15 nations in the European Union accepted E-mail invoices as documentation for authorizing return of the 15 percent to 25 percent value-added tax collected in various member-nations. In most nations, a paper document was required to receive the tax refunds, and the rules are not harmonized between countries.[21] Governmental concerns with potential anti-competitive effects of collaboration among competitors may also cause problems for industrywide B2B exchanges.

U.S. Firms That Have Returned

Many U.S. firms have brought their overseas manufacturing facilities back to the United States. GE Fanuc, a producer of robots, took over the production of a programmable logic

simplified product lines and designed the products to use as many of the same parts as possible. This also contributed to the company suppliers' acceptance of the JIT concept because they received fewer but larger orders, which permitted longer, less costly (fewer production changeovers) production runs.

6. For just-in-time to be successful, manufacturers had to have the cooperation of their suppliers. They could not follow the common American practice of having numerous vendors, which buyers often play against one another to get the best price. Japanese firms used fewer vendors and sought to establish close relationships with them, including calling them in during the design of the product.

7. To lower costs, improve quality, and lower production times, Japanese managements required product designers, production managers, purchasing people, and marketers to work as a team. They realized that something better than the American and European "bucket brigade" was needed. That term stems from an analogy between the ancient method of putting out fires and the process by which an idea becomes a product in many firms.

   The research laboratory gets an idea. It passes the idea to the engineering department, which converts it to a design with all parts specified. Manufacturing gets the specifications from engineering and figures out how to make the product. Responsibility for selling it is "dumped" on marketing, with little interaction or communication between functions.

8. Getting these people together enabled suppliers to suggest using the lower-cost standard parts they regularly produce, manufacturing to indicate when a design change could simplify the production process, and marketing to contribute the customer's viewpoint, *all before the first product was produced.*[30]

Improve Quality

To improve quality, Japanese managers had to use a human relations approach different from the one common in the United States and Europe. Everyone—from top management to workers—had to be committed to quality. Getting worker involvement was not especially difficult thanks to the Japanese practice of lifetime employment and the social benefits that large Japanese companies offer their employees.

The concept they adopted originated, like so many others, in the United States. **Total quality management (TQM),** a companywide management approach to ensure quality throughout the organization, was invented in the Bell Laboratories in the 1920s.

total quality management (TQM)
Managing the entire organization so that it excels on all dimensions of product and services that are important to the customer

Teams are necessary in the implementation of TQM, and one useful kind of team is the **quality circle,** an idea of Ishikawa, a Japanese quality expert.[31] Look at how the president of Komatsu, Caterpillar's Japanese competitor, describes the use of quality circles in his company.

quality circle (quality control circle)
Small work groups that meet periodically to discuss ways to improve their functional areas and the quality of the product

> The objective of the quality circle is to take part of the responsibility for the quality goal of each section: "Quality circle members are aware of the extent to which their achievement of their objectives will contribute to the results of their department, and also to the business of the company as a whole."
>
> A small group of employees, led by a foreman who has previously received quality control education, independently undertakes quality control activities. The circle's activities are divided among subdivisions of the circle led by a person junior to the foreman. Here is an example that illustrates that quality circles are used in all functional areas, not just in manufacturing.
>
> One day, telephone operators received complaints from outside callers regarding delays in answering telephones, so they surveyed company employees, who confirmed that the complaints were valid. They then studied the average time they were taking to answer a call and found that it was 7.4 seconds. They called the telephone company, which informed them that its standard was three seconds. The quality circle then discussed how to reach the three-second standard.[32]

Problems with Implementing the Japanese JIT System

Many American manufacturers rushed to Japan to study the just-in-time "miracle" and mistakenly copied only one part of it: the narrow focus on scheduling goods inventories, called by some "little JIT." They failed to realize that what is important is "big JIT," a *total system* covering the management of people, materials, and relations with suppliers (also called *lean* production).[33] Moreover, many did not understand that JIT includes TQM, of which continuous improvement is an integral part.

Another difficulty was the difference in attitudes (a cultural force) between Japanese and Western managers. American managers and unions still valued highly the specialization of worker functions based on **Taylor's scientific management system.** This system contradicts the principles of quality circles: (1) participative decision making and (2) problem-solving capabilities of workers. Americans, pressured for quick results, were disappointed when quality circles didn't offer immediate solutions for improvement. The practice of not guaranteeing long-term employment also made it more difficult to attain company loyalty for JIT.[34]

Taylor's scientific management system
A system based on scientific measurements that prescribes a division of work whereby planning is done by managers and plan execution is left to supervisors and workers

A further problem in implementing JIT systems was failure to train and integrate suppliers into the system. For example, one automobile company in Michigan had parts shipped from its vendors by truck from Canada. The Michigan factory was geared up for JIT, but no one told the supplier's shipping department in Canada to ship according to the new JIT production schedule. Since performance of the shipping coordinator in the Canadian company was assessed on the basis of the amount of trucking costs, the shipments were not sent until the trucks were full. The company had to reevaluate the trucking operation from Canada so that shipments would be made just in time, thus increasing the costs of transportation as a result of implementing JIT.

Advanced Production Technology—United States

Problems with JIT

American production experts also realized that there were problems with JIT itself:

1. JIT is restricted to operations that produce the same parts repeatedly because it is a *balanced* system; that is, all operations are designed to produce the same quantity of parts. Yet as Westinghouse saw when visiting Mitsubishi, repetitive operations may appear only in parts of the manufacturing process. It is far less useful for job shops (firms or departments within larger firms that specialize in producing small numbers of custom-designed products)* in which there is no dominant flow of production through the processes.
2. Because JIT is a balanced system, if one operation stops, the entire production line stops—there is no inventory to keep succeeding operations working.
3. Achieving a balanced system is difficult because production capacities differ among the various classes of machines. It may require five lathes to keep one punch press busy, for example, and it takes dozens of tire-building machines to use the output of just one calender, a huge machine (similar in size to a newspaper printing press) that rubberizes the fabric used in making tires. This problem is less severe for large production units, of course.
4. JIT makes no allowances for contingencies, and so every piece must be defect-free when it is received and delivery promises must be kept. **Preventive (planned) maintenance** is crucial. A sudden machine breakdown will stop the entire production process.

   Toyota found out how vulnerable its just-in-time system is to the failure of just one supplier to deliver a part at the planned time. A fire at one of its keiretsu members, the exclusive producer of its brake parts, shut down all of the company's auto plants in Japan, causing it to lose

preventive (planned) maintenance
Maintenance done according to plan, not when machines break down

*Job shop also refers to a production system in which departments are organized around specific operations (grinding, drilling, and so forth).

a week's production. Not only did the fire paralyze Toyota's manufacturing activities, it caused hundreds of other Toyota suppliers to stop the production of its parts.

The company's suppliers are given an approximate monthly production schedule and then receive the final order on a daily or even hourly basis, according to the flow of production on a given day. Toyota holds merely a half day's supplies at any one time. The company had a similar problem the year before, when an earthquake stopped delivery of many of its supplies.

After the fire, Toyota's chairman acknowledged that the just-in-time inventory system needed improvement. His company had to give orders to more than one supplier to prevent further crippling stoppages caused by a lack of parts. The single supplier concept, of course, has been a key component of its kereitsu network.[35]

5. Much trial and error are required to put the system into effect.[36]

Synchronous Manufacturing

synchronous manufacturing
An entire manufacturing system with unbalanced operations that emphasizes total system performance

bottleneck
Operation in a manufacturing system whose output sets the limit for the entire system's output

The problems with JIT, especially the long time required for its installation in a manufacturing system, caused some American firms to realize that something else was needed to assist them in gaining market share lost to the Japanese. Many turned to **synchronous manufacturing,** also called the theory of constraints (TOC), a scheduling and manufacturing control system that seeks to locate and then eliminate or minimize any constraints to greater production output, such as machines, people, tools, and facilities. The system's output is determined by and limited to the output of the slowest operation (**bottleneck**) that is working at full capacity; this is similar to how the speed of a convoy of vehicles is limited to that of the slowest vehicle. For the convoy to go any faster, the speed of the slowest or bottleneck operation needs to be improved first.

A computer program developed by Dr. Goldtratt, the originator of TOC, schedules work, taking into consideration bottleneck and nonbottleneck operations. This makes scheduling much faster because production schedules and simulation can be done on a computer instead of having to arrive at schedules by trial and error, as is necessary with JIT. Also, once a bottleneck is discovered, the operations manager can concentrate on increasing the production rate of that process. After resolving that, the manager can repeat the process on the next-slowest operation.[37]

Instead of attempting to achieve a balanced system like JIT, in which the capacities of all operations are equal, synchronous manufacturing aims to balance the *product flow* through the system, which leaves output levels of the various operations *unbalanced.* For example, with the bottleneck operation producing at full capacity, perhaps only 60 percent capacity is needed at another operation. Because there is no reason for this operation to produce over 60 percent of its capacity, it is stopped at that point; anything more would be unwanted inventory. Inasmuch as work is assigned to each operation rather than to the entire system, as in JIT, there is no need for more work in process than that which is actually being worked on. Inventory may also be placed near the bottleneck to avoid any shutdown in this crucial operation, and sometimes, unlike JIT, there may even be a quality control inspector to check the bottleneck operation's input.

As we mentioned previously, management's attention is focused on the bottleneck rather than on the other operations, because a production increase at the bottleneck means an increase for the entire production system; an increase in a nonbottleneck operation only adds to that machine's idle time.

Note another important difference between JIT and synchronous manufacturing: A defective part or component at any point in the production process can shut down a JIT system. But because a synchronous manufacturing system has excess capacity in all operations except at the bottleneck, any defective part produced before the bottleneck can be remade, and thus the entire system is not stopped.

Incidentally, as firms adopt new manufacturing techniques such as synchronous manufacturing, they find that traditional accounting methods are inadequate to measure the costs of overhead. Managements are turning to *activity-based costing* to allocate the overhead burden according to its components, which vary among products.

Soft Manufacturing

In the new American factory, software and labor have become more important than production machines. Robots, if present, play only a supporting role. An IBM manufacturing executive explains: "We're not as enamored with automation as we were in the early 1980s." The firm found after research that it is more cost-efficient to use hand labor with software networks than to use robots.

Soft manufacturing has made plants extremely agile. A firm can customize products one at a time while producing them at mass-production speeds. For example, the Motorola factory for pagers in Florida receives orders from dealers and Motorola sales representatives by E-mail or a toll-free phone line. The data are digitalized and flow to the assembly line, where robots select the components for humans to assemble. Orders are often completed in 80 minutes, permitting customers to receive them the same day they order them.

Soft manufacturing has enabled the United States to regain the lead in manufactured exports from Japan and Germany for the first time in a decade. In industries as diverse as computers, pagers, and construction equipment, Japanese and European manufacturers are rushing to copy American techniques.[38]

European Production Technology

According to knowledgeable sources, European manufacturers are about two years behind their American counterparts.[39] However, increasingly they are recognizing that they must make substantial rather than incremental changes in processes and organizations to reach the high-performance levels of American and Japanese companies. In Germany, for example, the economic crisis caused by high wages, short working hours, and a strong mark forced managements into **reengineering, delayering,** and outsourcing to regain global competitiveness.[40] Note that reengineering calls for discontinuous thinking and is imposed from the top down, totally the opposite of the continuous improvement associated with TQM.

reengineering
A radical redesign of business processes to achieve dramatic improvements in critical measures of performance, such as cost, quality, service, and speed

delayering
Removing levels of middle management

The Single Market Program that lowered internal trade barriers among European Union (EU) members has enabled European manufacturers to consolidate their operations to reduce costs. Because of the improvements in European distribution services, firms can supply all Europe from a single European manufacturing facility. As they close national plants, manufacturers are eliminating national distribution centers and factories. What were formerly national functions, such as purchasing, inventory management, and logistics management, are becoming pan-European functions.[41] IBM Europe, for example, has located all its personal computer (PC) production in Scotland. Its factory in France produces all the mainframes for the European market and is one of only three IBM plants in the world making them (the U.S. and the Japanese plants are the other two).

Comparisons of Productivity and Competitiveness

Inasmuch as European managements have access to the same advanced production technology and management techniques that U.S. managements do, there should not be an appreciable difference in performance between U.S. and European companies. Although European company results improved in the late 1990s, important gaps in performance remained as the 20th century ended, and there are still some key areas where Europe is lagging.

Governments Need to Make Structural Changes

One is the necessity for European governments to combat high unemployment and create an environment for business expansion by making structural changes such as more deregulation, lower taxes, and less rigid work laws. In general, companies in Europe still have not downsized as their American counterparts have done for the past 10 years. Another difference is the composition of their gross domestic products (GDPs). As was discussed in Chapter 13, in the United States, high technology, which creates high-paid jobs, accounts for nearly a third of GDP. In contrast, high tech's share of output in Europe is less than 15 percent.

Europe Has Fallen Farther Behind

Two recent studies claim that European industry has fallen farther behind in world competitiveness. As you read in Chapter 13, McKinsey and Co. claims that there is a large and growing gap between the performance of six industries in France and Germany and that of the world's leaders. The study states that Germany produces 30 percent fewer goods and services per capita than the leaders do and has 20 percent lower labor productivity. France is in a worse position. It lags the leaders by 40 percent in production per capita and 20 percent in productivity. As shown in Chapter 13, productivity growth rates in the United States during the late 1990s were 50 percent to more than 300 percent above those of the leading European nations.

A study in 1998 by the European employers' federation blamed the European nations for failing to restructure their economies to face increasing global competition. The report criticized France's strategy of trying to reduce unemployment by imposing shorter working hours, pointing out that Germans work fewer hours than do other Europeans and have an extremely high unemployment rate. Longer hours have not created high unemployment in the American and Japanese economies, however.[42]

International Effort to Improve Quality and Lower Costs

Companies all over the world have successfully put into place JIT systems or have highly synchronized their manufacturing systems. Moreover, they have installed computer-integrated manufacturing (CIM), utilizing computers and robots to further improve productivity and quality. The Worldview example describes Ford's breakthrough that will reduce its development costs for new models by $200 million annually.[43]

Western Firms That Are Succeeding

General Motors, General Electric, Ford, IBM, Motorola—the list is long of American firms that have synchronous manufacturing and a TQM system. Many have also reengineered and downsized to improve their global competitiveness.

In 1988, Corning, the glass manufacturer, copied Japan's extensive automation because, as the firm's executive president says, "The Japanese were better than us in manufacturing." However, management soon found that heavy automation undermined motivation of employees in the United States. To involve workers, Corning let any worker sign a purchase order up to $500 without authorization, eliminated time clocks, created just one job classification with one manager for 60 employees, and trained each employee to handle as many as 15 different jobs. Management also sought employee involvement in selecting manufacturing technology. "There were places where we could have robotized, but we decided against it. Even in boring and repetitive jobs, we have moved away from automation because humans adapt and robots don't," says the plant manager.

The plant has increased its productivity at a rate of 25 percent annually, and its integration of employees and technology has attracted so many American, Japanese, and European companies that every month it conducts a tour—for a fee. Representatives from production, design, marketing, and suppliers work jointly on new products, a technique called *concurrent engineering.* As a result, new-product introduction, which used to take three years, now is done in one.[44]

Examples of multinational firms from Europe that are using synchronous manufacturing systems include Electrolux (Swedish), Volkswagen (German), and Rover (English). Fiat recently opened a $3 billion plant in southern Italy in an effort to instill different work practices. The company spent $64 million training workers and engineers to work in independent, multiskilled teams. Fiat's personnel chief says, "Top-down decision making is dead. Problems are solved by teams actually working on production."[45]

Cognizant Technology Solutions: Sourcing Low-Cost Talent Internationally to Achieve Global Competitive Advantage

Small and Medium-Sized Enterprises

India has become a global center for high-technology businesses in recent years. Exports of computer software and services increased from $150 million in 1992 to $3.9 billion in 1999, with over 60 percent of that amount going to the United States. Companies such as Microsoft, Oracle, and Sun have established research and development (R&D) facilities in Bangalore, Calcutta, and other Indian cities in an effort to utilize inexpensive and well-trained Indian engineers instead of expensive talent in the United States.

One company seeking to exploit this opportunity is Cognizant Technology Solutions of Teaneck, New Jersey. With an electrical engineering degree from Cambridge and an MBA from Harvard Business School, the company's chairman and CEO, Kumar Mahadeva, was well prepared to build a technology-based business. Observing the thriving software industry that was emerging in India in the early 1990s, Mahadeva recognized an opportunity. He realized that he could achieve a strong cost advantage over other U.S. companies by employing talented entry-level programmers in India for $6,000 per year, compared to an average salary in the United States of about $50,000.

Providing software development and maintenance services, Cognizant competes on the basis of price, speed, and agility. The centerpiece of the company's operations is an innovative "offshore-onshore" business model. Under this model, a modest proportion of the company's more than 2,000 computer science and engineering professionals work at customer sites in the United States or other Western nations, and the remainder work at one of its eight development centers in India.

Once a contract has been signed, a global "virtual project team" is set up. About 20 percent of the team is located at the client's site, mainly Indian nationals who come for a couple of years to handle project management activities and manage client relationships on a daily basis. The remainder of the team is located in India, where software development, coding, maintenance, and other activities are completed on an around-the-clock, seven-days-a-week basis. This approach allows Cognizant's project managers to interact intensely with its clients during working hours in the West, intimately understanding the clients' strategies and needs, while prototype development, coding, and system upgrading activities are conducted overnight.

To facilitate effective management of the offshore and on-site components of the multinational team, the company has set up a satellite and fiber-optic cable–based voice/data communications infrastructure, including E-mail and videoconferencing capabilities. To minimize misunderstandings and other problems as thoughts are translated from one culture to another, Cognizant's recruitment efforts target English-speaking students from computer science, engineering, and information technology programs at leading Indian universities. The company also provides extensive project management training programs. In addition, the company has a proprietary Project Management Tool that allows project managers to monitor the workflow of individual team members and track the status of components and various development activities.

Despite a fiercely competitive marketplace, Cognizant has achieved sustained success with its innovative business model. In early 2000, the six-year-old company had 57 clients, primarily in health care, insurance, and information services, including a number of prominent domestic and international companies such as Nielsen Media Research, the Body Shop, and Northwest Airlines. Revenues were approximately $90 million and growing more rapidly than those of the industry as a whole, and profits were strong. In 1999, Cognizant was named the best small company in the United States in the *Forbes* magazine listing of the "200 Best Small Companies." ■

Sources: Interviews with executives at Cognizant Technology Solutions; and Alex Salkever, "Recognizing Cognizant as a High-Tech Bargain," *Business Week,* March 28, 2000. www.businessweek.com/bwdaily/dnflash/mar2000/sw00328.htm (May 15, 2000).

Reasons for Global Standardization of Manufacturing Systems

Standards are documented agreements containing technical specifications or other precise criteria that will be used consistently as guidelines, rules, or definitions of the characteristics of a product, process, or service. Standards help ensure that materials, products,

SKF, a major bearing manufacturer with headquarters in Sweden, was able to reduce the number of types of ball bearings produced in five major overseas subsidiaries years ago from 50,000 to 20,000. Of the 20,000 remaining types, 7,000 have been rationalized among the five plants, and the other 13,000 are produced solely by one or another subsidiary for its local customers.[47]

These examples illustrate that for manufacturing rationalization to be possible, the product mix must first be rationalized; that is, the firm must elect to produce products that are identical worldwide or regionwide. Once this has been done, each subsidiary can be assigned to produce certain components for other foreign plants, thus attaining a higher volume with a lower production cost than would be possible if it manufactured the complete product for its national market only. Obviously, this strategy is not viable when consumers' tastes and preferences differ markedly among markets. For less differentiated products, however, manufacturing rationalization permits economies of scale in production and engineering that would otherwise be impossible. Nissan Motors has been able to employ the most modern methods, including CAM,* in its Mexican motor plant because of the high input it obtains through exports (80 percent of the total) to Tennessee, Japan, and Latin America. And Ford supplies engines for all Ford–Europe from one plant in England.[48]

Purchasing. When foreign subsidiaries are unable to purchase raw materials and machinery locally, they generally look for assistance from the purchasing department at headquarters. Because unified processes require the same materials everywhere, buyers can handle foreign requirements by simply increasing their regular orders to their usual suppliers and passing on the volume discounts to the subsidiaries. However, when special materials are required, purchasing agents must search out new vendors and place smaller orders, often at higher prices.

Control

All the advantages of global standardization cited thus far also pertain to the other functions of management. Three aspects of control—quality, production, and maintenance—merit additional discussion.

Quality Control. When production equipment is similar, home office control of quality in foreign affiliates is less difficult because management can expect all plants to adhere to the same standard. The home office can compare the periodic reports that all affiliates submit and quickly spot deviations from the norm that require remedial action, such as a large number of product rejects. Separate standards for each plant because of equipment differences are unnecessary.

Production and Maintenance Control. A single standard also lessens the task of maintenance and production control. The same machinery should produce at the same rate of output and have the same frequency of maintenance no matter where it is located. In practice, there will be deviations because of the human and physical factors (dust, humidity, temperature), but at least similar machinery permits the home office to establish standards by which to determine the effectiveness of local managements. Furthermore, the maintenance experience of other production units in regard to the frequency of overhauls and the stock of spare parts needed will help plants avoid costly, unforeseen stoppages from sudden breakdowns.

Planning

When a new plant can be built that is a duplicate of others already functioning, the planning and design will be both simpler and quicker because it is essentially a repetition of work already done:

1. Design engineers need only copy the drawings and lists of materials that they have in their files.

*CAM—computer-assisted manufacturing—generally includes automated materials handling and programmable robots.

2. Vendors will be requested to furnish equipment that they have supplied previously.
3. The technical department can send the current manufacturing specifications without alteration.
4. Labor trainers experienced in the operation of the machinery can be sent to the new location without undergoing special training on new equipment.
5. Reasonably accurate forecasts of plant erection time and output can be based on experience with existing facilities.

In other words, the duplication of existing plants greatly reduces the engineering time required in planning and designing the new facilities and eliminates many of the start-up difficulties inherent in any new operation. To be sure, a newly designed plant causes problems when it is erected domestically, but those problems tend to be greater when the plant is located in a different environment at a great distance from headquarters. Just how important the savings from plant duplication are was emphasized in a study of the chemical and refining industries that indicated that the cost of technology transfer was lowered by 34 and 19 percent for the second and third start-ups, respectively.[49]

Since the case for global standardization of production is so strong, why do differences among plants in the same company persist?

Impediments to Globalization of Manufacturing Facilities

Generally, it is easier for international corporations to standardize the concepts of total quality management and synchronous manufacturing in their overseas affiliates than it is to standardize the actual manufacturing facilities. Units of an international multiplant operation differ in size, machinery, and procedures because of the intervention of the foreign environmental forces, especially the economic, cultural, and political forces.

Environmental Forces

Let us examine the impact of the three kinds of forces just mentioned.

Economic Forces. The most important element of the economic forces that impedes production standardization is the wide range of market sizes, discussed in Chapter 16.

> A number of studies confirmed by personal experience have shown that the foremost criterion for plant design is the output desired. Once this is known, the engineering department of a multiplant operation will check to see whether a factory already has been built with a capacity similar to the output specified. If so, this facility will serve as a design standard for the new plant, though modifications may be made to eliminate any problems encountered in the original design. Many large multiplant firms actually have standard designs for large, medium, and small production outputs.

To cope with the great variety of production requirements, the designer generally has the option of selecting either a *capital-intensive process* incorporating automated, high-semimanual output machinery or a *labor-intensive process* employing more people and general-purpose equipment with lower productive capacity. The automated machinery is severely limited in flexibility (variety of products and range of sizes), but once set up, it will turn out in a few days what may be a year's supply for some markets.[50] For many processes, this problem may be resolved by installing one machine of the type used by the hundreds in the larger home plant. However, sometimes this option is not available; some processes use only one or two large machines, even in manufacturing facilities with large output, as we mentioned in the discussion of standardized manufacturing. Until recently, when the option was not available, plant designers had to choose between the high-output specialized machinery and the lower-output general-purpose machines mentioned earlier. The major differences are that general-purpose machines require skills that are built into a special-purpose machine. The general-purpose machine usually produces a product of lower quality and higher per-unit costs than does the special-purpose machine.

A third alternative is available: computer-integrated manufacturing, which many international firms are using. However, its cost and high technological content generally limit its application to the industrialized nations and the more advanced developing nations. CIM systems enable a machine to make one part as easily as another in random order on an instruction from a bar code reader of the kind used in supermarkets. This reduces to one the economic batch quantity—the minimum number of a part that can be made economically by a factory. There is a limit, nevertheless, to the variety of shapes, sizes, and materials that can be accommodated.

Another economic factor that influences the designer's selection of processes is the *cost of production.* Automation tends to increase the productivity per worker because it requires less labor and results in higher output per machine. But if the desired output requires that the machines be operated only a fraction of the time, the high capital costs of automated equipment may result in excessive production costs even though labor costs are low. In situations where production costs favor semimanual equipment, the designer may be compelled to install high-capacity machines instead because of a lack of floor space. Generally, the space occupied by a few high-capacity machines is less than that required for the greater number of semimanual machines needed to produce the same output. However, because the correct type and quality of process materials are indispensable for specialized machinery, the engineers cannot recommend this equipment if such materials are unobtainable either locally or through importation. Occasionally, management will bypass this obstacle by means of **backward vertical integration;** that is, manufacturing capacity to produce essential inputs will be included in the plant design even though it would be preferable from an economic standpoint to purchase those materials from outside vendors. For example, a textile factory might include a facility for producing nylon fibers.

backward vertical integration
Establishing facilities to manufacture inputs used in the production of a firm's final products

The economic forces we have described are fundamental considerations in plant design, yet elements of the cultural and political forces may be sufficiently significant to override decisions based on purely economic reasoning.

Cultural Forces. When a factory is to be built in an industrialized nation where there is a sizable market and high labor costs, capital-intensive processes will undoubtedly be employed. However, such processes may also be employed in developing countries, which commonly lack skilled workers despite their abundant supply of labor. This situation favors the use of specialized machines because although a few highly skilled persons are needed for maintenance and setup, the job of *attending* these machines (starting, feeding stock) can be performed by unskilled workers after a short training period. In contrast, general-purpose machinery requires many more skilled operators.

These operators could be trained in technical schools, but the low prestige of such employment, a cultural characteristic, affects both the demand for and the supply of vocational education. Students do not demand it, and the traditional elitist attitude of the educational administrators in many developing nations causes resources to be directed to professional education instead of to the trades where they are needed.

Firms that attempt to reduce their requirements for skilled workers by installing automatic machinery are of course left vulnerable to another cultural characteristic of the developing countries: absenteeism. If the setup and maintenance crews fail to report to work, the entire production line may be shut down. Some managers resolve this problem by training a few extra people as backups. Having extra personnel is viewed as production insurance necessary to keep the plant in operation. This extra expense may be far less than the expense of handling the greater number of labor–management problems resulting from a larger work force in a nonautomated factory with a similar capacity.

These economic and cultural variables, important as they are, are not the only considerations of management; the requirements of the host government must be met if the proposed plant is to become a reality.

[Worldview]

GM's New Global Plant Design Strategy—Make 'em Alike

Unlike its age-old plant design strategy, General Motors has a new one for the 21st century—make them alike. For years, GM plants were designed by autonomous groups of executives and engineers who rarely talked to each other. The result was a group of plants, each with its own characteristics.

This method of designing plants has changed. The company is building so many plants in various parts of the world that management decided to save money by globalizing plant design, that is, building essentially the same plants simultaneously in China, Argentina, Poland, and Thailand. The assembly lines are so much alike that if the Polish plant has a problem with a robot, for example, its engineers can probably get help by calling one of the other three plants because they are working with the same equipment. It is true that numerous multiplant internationals, such as Gillette and General Tire, have used similar designs in more than one location for years, but GM's cookie cutter design and construction methods for four plants simultaneously are groundbreaking.

Another indication of how international companies' policies are changing with the globalization of the market is the fact that the factories are state-of-the-art. Formerly, foreign manufacturing subsidiaries located in poorer countries would use older technology to build older models. The products were simpler, were frequently of an obsolete design, and were often produced with hand-me-down, overhauled machinery from plants in the home country or other industrialized nations. GM's plants in Latin America produced the Chevy Chevette for years after it had been discontinued in the United States.

The four new plants, however, were designed by Brazilian and German engineers who were trying to imitate the German plant where GM implemented the lean manufacturing techniques it learned from its joint venture with Toyota in the early 1990s. The German plant, now the company's most efficient, assembles cars twice as fast as most of its North American assembly facilities.

Another advantage of the new strategy—the total cost of the Argentine plant is only $350 million compared to GM's rule-of-thumb $1 billion price for a new assembly plant of any size. And this price includes a new high-tech press that stamps metal parts more quickly than any other GM press plus an engine plant that delivers to the assembly line with air-conditioning, transmission, and fan belts already installed.

Although the four new plants were designed to be as similar as possible, there are some differences because local conditions in the four countries are different. These differences range from special efforts to protect machinery in Thailand from rust due to that country's extreme humidity to special arrangements set up to compensate for China's poor transportation system. GM's director of lean operations explains, "We are going to have things delivered to our Shanghai plant by bicycle." ■

Source: Republished with permission of *The Wall Street Journal*. From *The Wall Street Journal*, August 4, 1997, p. A1. Permission conveyed through the Copyright Clearance Center.

Political Forces. When planning a new manufacturing facility in a developing country, management is frequently confronted by an intriguing paradox. Although the country desperately needs new job creation, which favors labor-intensive processes, government officials often insist on the most modern equipment. Local pride may be the cause, or it may be that these officials, wishing to see the new firm export, believe that only a factory with advanced technology can compete in world markets. They not only may be reluctant to take chances on "inferior" or untried alternatives, they also may feel that low-productivity technology will keep the country dependent on the industrialized countries. In some developing countries, this fear has been formalized by laws prohibiting the importation of used machinery. Vietnam passed such laws recently.[51]

Some Design Solutions

More often than not, after consideration of the environmental variables, the resultant plant design will be a hybrid or one using intermediate technology.

Hybrid Design. Commonly, in designing plants for developing countries, engineers will use a hybrid of capital-intensive processes when they are considered essential to ensure product quality and labor-intensive processes to take advantage of the abundance of unskilled labor. For example, they may stipulate machine welding rather than hand welding but then use semimanual equipment for the painting, packaging, and materials handling.

Intermediate Technology. In recent years, the press of a growing population and the rise in capital costs have forced the governments of developing nations to search for something less than highly automated processes. They are becoming convinced that there should be something midway between the capital- and labor-intensive processes that will create more jobs, require less capital, but still produce the desired product quality. Governments are urging investors to consider an **intermediate technology,** which, unfortunately, is not readily available in the industrialized nations. This means that the international companies (ICs) cannot transfer the technology with which they are familiar but must develop new and different manufacturing methods. It is also possible that the savings in reduced capital costs of the intermediate technology may be nullified by higher start-up costs and the greater expense of its transfer.

intermediate technology
Production methods between capital- and labor-intensive methods

Appropriate Technology

One global corporation, Philips in the Netherlands, has worked systematically to match a country's markets with its resources and ability to produce certain components to obtain an optimal technological mix. A pilot plant devises commercially viable production patterns based on the factors that enable foreign subsidiaries to manufacture small volumes with processes less automated than those of the home plant.

Rather than search for an intermediate technology, the emphasis of Philips and others is on employing the **appropriate technology,** which can range from the most advanced to the most primitive, depending on the economic, sociocultural, and political variables. For some products, the superiority in productivity and product quality of the modern process is so marked that it makes the labor-intensive method totally inappropriate. Compare resource mapping by satellites with geologists on horseback, for example. Yet in the case of sugar refining, it was found in India that for the same amount of capital, either a large plant capable of producing 12,000 tons of sugar annually with 900 employees or 47 small plants with an output of 30,000 tons employing 10,000 workers could be built.[52]

appropriate technology
Production methods—intermediate, capital-, or labor-intensive (or a mixture)—considered most suitable for an area according to its cultural, political, and economic situation

Table 20.2 compares appropriate technology and capital-intensive technology with respect to cost, number of workers, and cost per job for various industries. Note that the differences are significant.

Does this mean that the government of a developing nation should urge a company to adopt a less capital-intensive process? It depends. It is possible that the cost per unit produced will be higher with this process. In this case, government administration must choose between (1) the use of the less capital-intensive technology to save scarce capital and create more jobs and (2) the more capital-intensive processes that will provide a less expensive product for its citizens. The choice obviously depends on government priorities.

These examples help substantiate a growing belief that there is no universally appropriate technology. In fact, proponents of this concept state that what may be suitable for the cultural, political, and economic situation in one region is not necessarily applicable even in another area of the same country. The concept's effect on attempts to standardize production facilities worldwide is obvious.

Local Manufacturing System

Basis for Organization

Except for plants in large industrialized nations, the local manufacturing organization is commonly a scaled-down version of that found in the parent company. If the firm is organized by product companies or divisions (tires, industrial products, chemicals) in

Table 20.2 **Comparison of Appropriate Technology (AT) and Capital-Intensive Technology (CIT)**

Industry	Annual Output of Plant	Ratios: Cost, AT Plant/Cost, CIT Plant	Ratios: No. Workers, AT Plant/No. Workers, CIT Plant	Ratios: Cost per Job, AT Plant/Cost per Job, CIT Plant
Brick making	16 million bricks	0.2	3.2	0.1
Cotton spinning	2,000 tons	0.3	2.5	0.1
Sugar processing	50,000 tons	0.6	4.8	0.1
Cotton weaving	40 million square yards	0.5	2.1	0.2
Corn milling	36,000 tons	0.4	1.5	0.3
Shoes	300,000 pairs	0.5	1.4	0.4
Leather processing	600,000 hides	0.7	1.7	0.6
Beer brewing	200,000 hectoliters	0.6	0.9	0.7
Fertilizer	528,000 tons of urea	0.9	1.0	0.9

Source: Calculated from Tables 2 and 3, Howard Pack, *Macroeconomic Implications of Factor Substitution in Industrial Processes,* World Bank Staff Working Paper No. 377 (March 1980).

its home nation, the subsidiary will be divided into product departments. Manufacturing firms that use process organizations (departmentalized according to production processes) in the domestic operation will set up a similar structure in their foreign affiliates. In a paper-box factory, separate departments will cut the logs, produce the paper, and assemble the boxes. The only noticeable difference between the foreign and domestic operations is that in the foreign plant all these processes are more likely to be at one location because of the smaller size of each department.

Horizontal and Vertical Integration

The local manufacturing organization is rarely integrated either vertically or horizontally to the extent the parent is. Some vertical integration is traditional, as in the case of the paper-box factory, and some will occur if it is necessary to assure a supply of raw materials. In this situation, the subsidiary might be more vertically integrated than the parent, which depends on outside sources for many of its inputs. However, the additional investment is a deterrent to vertical integration, as are the extra profits gained by supplying inputs to these captive customers from the home plants. Some countries prohibit vertical integration for certain industries. Mexico for years prohibited automobile manufacturers from owning producers of car parts. However, as a result of the North American Free Trade Agreement (NAFTA), the government has rescinded many of its restrictions on investment by foreigners. Nevertheless, the severe restrictions on private investment (Mexican or foreign) in the petroleum and petrochemical industry still exist and keep producers of products that use petrochemicals from achieving backward vertical integration. While foreign-owned firms can produce products from petrochemicals, they cannot own more than 40 percent of the companies that produce the petrochemicals, such as synthetic resins and synthetic rubber.[53]

There are countries that require a percentage of local content in finished products. When the subsidiary cannot meet the requirement by local sourcing, it may be forced to produce components that its parent does not.

Horizontal integration is much less prevalent in the foreign subsidiaries, although restaurant chains, banks, food-processing plants, and other industries characterized by small production units will, of course, integrate horizontally in the manner of the domestic company. Overseas affiliates themselves become conglomerates when the parent acquires a multinational.

The design of a manufacturing system influences the flow and efficiency of activities in a plant.
Verdios/Verdios & Associates/Tony Stone Images

Design of the Manufacturing System

A *manufacturing system* is essentially a functionally related group of activities for creating value. Although the manufacturing system as described below is basically one for producing tangible goods, nearly everything that is said applies equally to the production of services. Factors involved in the efficient operation of a manufacturing system include

1. Plant location.
2. Plant layout.
3. Materials handling.
4. Human element.

Plant Location. Plant location is significant because of its effect on both production and distribution costs, which are frequently in conflict. The gain in government incentives and in the lower land and labor costs obtained by locating away from major cities may be offset by the increased expense of warehousing and transportation to serve those markets. Management will, after ascertaining that adequate labor, raw materials, water, and power are available, seek the least-cost location, or the one for which the sum of production and transfer costs is minimized. Management's first choice may then be modified by market requirements, the influence of competitors' locations, employee preference (climate, recreational facilities), and conditions imposed by the local authorities.

Governments that are anxious to limit the congestion of large urban areas may either prohibit firms from locating in the major cities or offer them important financial inducement to locate elsewhere.

> Businesses that establish plants in the Mezzogiorno (southern Italy) can obtain soft loans, tax exemptions, and outright grants of up to 40 percent of the fixed investment. Nearly all the European nations and some nations in Latin America offer similar advantages. Mexico offers a special one-time deduction for the depreciation of fixed assets to all firms located *outside* the Federal District, Guadalajara, and Monterrey during the first two years of operation. This is an incentive for companies to locate outside those three cities.[54]

export processing zones
Specific and limited areas into which imported components may be brought for further processing; the finished product must be reexported to avoid payment of import duties

Firms that have come to a country to take advantage of low labor costs and export their production have a limited selection of plant locations. They must locate in **export processing zones,** such as Mexico's in-bond manufacturing zones, most of which are on the Mexican-American border. Similar zones exist in South Korea, Taiwan, Singapore, and some 50 other nations.

Plant Layout. Modern practice dictates that the arrangement of machinery, personnel, and service facilities should be made before the erection of the building. In this way, the building is accommodated to the layout that is judged most capable of obtaining a smoothly functioning production system.

The designer must attempt to obtain the maximum utility from costly building space while providing room for the future expansion of each department. Space can become critical very quickly if forecasts, especially for new products, prove to have been unduly pessimistic. Managements of plants located in developing countries may attempt to stint on space for employees' facilities, reasoning that the workers' standard of living in these countries is lower and that they will accept less just to have employment. Often, however, foreign labor laws are more demanding than those of the home country.

Materials Handling. Considerable savings in production costs can be achieved by a careful planning of materials handling, which, as you have seen, is a major consideration in synchronous manufacturing. Operations managers often failed to appreciate that inefficient handling of materials may cause excessive inventories of partly finished parts to accumulate at some workstations, while at others expensive machinery was idle for lack of work (bottleneck). This concerned marketers too, because poor materials handling can result in late deliveries and damaged goods, which in turn lead to order cancellation and a loss of customers. Therefore, marketers must also be included in the total quality control approach that we discussed earlier in this chapter.

Human Element. The effectiveness of the manufacturing system depends on people, who are in turn affected by the system. Productivity suffers when there is extreme heat or cold, excessive noise, or faulty illumination. Colors also influence human behavior—pale colors are restful and unobtrusive, whereas bright colors attract attention. Plant designers take advantage of this fact by painting the walls of the working areas pale blue and green but marking exits with bright yellow and painting safety equipment red. This practice is accepted nearly everywhere, although, as we indicated in the sociocultural chapter, color connotations vary among cultures.

For safety and ease of operation, controls of imported machinery must frequently be altered to accommodate smaller workers. Extra lifting devices, unnecessary in the home country, may be required. Where illiteracy is a problem, safety signs must include pictures. For example, a picture of a burning cigarette with a red line through it may substitute for a "no smoking" sign. Plants in multilingual nations and plants that employ large numbers of foreign workers will require warnings in more than one language.

Because of the prohibitive cost of automobiles in many developing nations, employees ride bicycles to work, and so bicycle stands must be provided in parking lots. Special dietary kitchens are necessary when workers from more than one culture work together. These and other special conditions caused by environmental differences must be reckoned with in the design of the manufacturing system.

Operation of the Manufacturing System

Once the manufacturing system has been put into operation, two general classes of activities, *productive* and *supportive,* must be performed.

Manufacturing Activities. After the initial trial period, during which workers become familiar with the manufacturing processes, management will expect the system to produce at a rate sufficient to satisfy market demand. It is the function of the line organization—from operations manager to first-level supervisor—to work with labor, raw materials, and machinery to produce on time the required amount of product with the desired quality at the budgeted cost.

Obstacles to Meeting Manufacturing Standards. Management must be prepared to deal with any obstacle to meeting the manufacturing standards. Among these obstacles are (1) low output, (2) inferior quality, and (3) excessive manufacturing costs.

Low Output. Any number of factors may be responsible for the system's failure to meet the design standards for output, and these factors can be the source of managerial uncertainty.

1. Raw materials suppliers may fail to meet delivery dates or may furnish material out of specification. This is a common occurrence in the sellers' markets of developing countries, but it is also occasionally a problem in the industrialized countries. The purchasing department must attempt to educate the vendor about the importance of delivery dates and specifications, although the effectiveness of this strategy is limited when, as is often the case in developing nations, there is only one supplier. Increasing the price paid and sending technicians to assist the vendor generally improve this situation.

When the automobile plants in Mexico were required to incorporate locally made parts into the product, they not only provided their own technical assistance to vendors but also arranged for licensing agreements from U.S. suppliers and even guaranteed bank loans enabling the vendors to buy production machinery. This tremendous assistance program was a leading factor in creating the Mexican parts industry.

2. Poor coordination of production scheduling slows the delivery of finished products when, for example, completely assembled automobiles wait for bumpers. Scheduling personnel may require additional training or closer supervision. Often, scheduling personnel—or any production workers, for that matter—are unaware of the importance of their jobs because they have not been shown "the big picture." Firms find that teaching employees why they do what they do, as well as how, pays off in creating a better attitude, which results in higher productivity. This has become crucial as firms strive for participative management, which is essential to synchronous manufacturing.

   Cultural forces of attitude toward authority and the great difference between the educational levels, common in many countries, establish a gulf between managers and workers. In fact, this is one of the reasons Japanese affiliates have had trouble introducing their production methods in the United States, where distances between managers and workers are much smaller than they are in most developing nations. Getting the participative management necessary for JIT and synchronous manufacturing will necessitate workers making sizable cultural changes, which in our opinion will require many years to attain.

   Another cultural problem is the desire to please everyone and the aversion to long-range planning. You have seen the importance of planning for the success of JIT, and you also learned that firm production schedules at least a month long are requisite. The desire to please everyone prevalent in some cultures tends to cause neglect of the schedule while production stops to attend the latest request from a customer. Moreover, because the markets are smaller in developing countries than they are in industrialized nations, product variations will have to be pared even more, and production systems will have to be even more flexible, if possible.

3. *Absenteeism,* always a problem for production managers everywhere in meeting production standards, has become even more significant in a bottleneck operation of a synchronous manufacturing system. Imagine the problems that occur when an entire department is idled because workers are at home helping the extended family with the harvest. When poor transportation systems make getting to work difficult, companies frequently provide transportation. To counteract absences due to illness and injury, they subsidize workers' lunches—prepared by trained nutritionists—and provide special shoes and protective clothing. Of course, management has the problem of educating workers not to remove the restraining apparel that they have never used before.

   Low morale conducive to high absenteeism will result if foreign managers trying to introduce the participative management necessary for synchronous manufacturing fail to assume the role of *patron* that most workers in developing countries expect. When employees have personal problems, they assume that the boss, not the personnel office, will find a solution. Personal debts, marital problems, and difficulties with the police are all part of manager–employee relations.

   All too often, expatriate managers accept high absenteeism and low productivity as the norm instead of attempting to correct them. Yet those who apply all the corrective means used at home, making adjustments for the foreign environment when necessary, do achieve notable success. One corrective measure, the discharge of unsatisfactory workers, is frequently impossible to apply because of legal constraints, but a consistent, energetic program of employee training, good union and labor relations, and the use of such morale builders as employee recognition, company reunions, sponsorship of team sports, and even suggestion boxes with rewards can be as successful in a foreign location as in the domestic operation.

Inferior Product Quality. Good quality is relative. What passes for good quality in the industrialized nations may actually be poor quality where a lack of maintenance and operating skills requires looser bearing fits and strong but more unwieldy parts. If the product or service satisfies the purpose for which it is purchased, the buyer considers it to be of good quality.

> In World War II, the American military found that the Japanese submachine gun, poorly finished except at the working surfaces, was as effective a weapon as the American Thompson, which was finely finished all over. A gun collector would consider the American weapon to be of higher quality, but was it of higher quality from the Japanese standpoint?

Product quality standards are not set arbitrarily. It is the responsibility of the marketers, after studying their target market, to choose the price–quality combination they believe is most apt to satisfy that market. On the basis of this information, the quality standards for incoming materials, in-process items, and finished products should be established.

When the headquarters of global corporations insist that all foreign subsidiaries maintain the high-quality standards of the domestic plants, a number of problems can occur. Production may have to accept inputs of poorer quality when there is no alternative source of supply and then rework them. As we have pointed out, quality tolerances are especially tight for automated machinery. Finished-product standards set by a home office concerned about maintaining its global reputation can cause a product to be too costly for the local market. Many globals resolve this problem by permitting the subsidiary to manufacture products of lower quality under different brand names. If they wish the local plant to be a part of a worldwide logistic system, they may require a special quality to be produced for export. In some areas, "export quality" still denotes a superior product. Quality control, by the way, is not left exclusively in the hands of the subsidiary. Nearly all worldwide corporations require their foreign plants to submit samples of the finished product for testing on a regular basis.

Excessive Manufacturing Costs. Any manufacturing cost that exceeds the budgeted cost is excessive and naturally is of concern to the marketing and financial manager as well as to production personnel. Low output for any of the reasons we have discussed may be the cause, but the fault may also lie with the assumptions underlying the budget. Overoptimistic sales forecasts, the failure of suppliers to meet delivery dates, the failure of the government to issue import permits for essential raw materials in time, and unforeseen water or power failure are a few of the reasons output may be lower than expected.

Managements have always tried to limit inventories of raw materials, spare parts for plant machinery, and finished products, and those managements with synchronous manufacturing systems have a goal of almost complete elimination. But when there is uncertainty of supply, as in most developing nations, stocks of these items can quickly get out of control. Production tends to overstock inputs to avoid the expense of changing production schedules when a given raw material has been exhausted. Maintenance personnel lay in an excessive stock of spare parts because they worry about not having something when they need it. Marketers, fearful of the frequent delays in manufacturing, overreact by building up finished goods inventories to avoid lost sales. When sales decrease, manufacturing may continue to produce finished products rather than lay off workers because the labor laws in many countries, unlike American labor laws, make employee layoffs both difficult and costly. In countries where skilled workers are in short supply, management does not dare to lay them off even if the law permits because these people will obtain employment elsewhere. The only alternative in the short run is to keep the factory running.

Finance, the one headquarters department that would ordinarily act to limit inventory building, will not move aggressively to stop this practice in countries afflicted with hyperinflation. It knows that under this condition, sizable profits can be made by being short in cash and long in inventory.

Supportive Activities. Every manufacturing system requires staff units to provide the *supportive activities* essential to its operation. Two of these, quality control and inventory control, were examined in the previous section. Let us look now at the purchasing, maintenance, and technical functions.

Purchasing. Manufacturing depends on the purchasing department to procure the raw materials, component parts, supplies, and machinery it requires to produce the finished product. The inability to obtain these materials when needed can result in costly shutdowns and lost sales. If the buyers agree to prices higher than what competitors are paying, the firm must either sell the finished product at higher prices or price competitively and earn less profit. The quality of the finished product may suffer if the quality of the purchased materials is inadequate.

For many years, some have referred to purchasing as the "management of outside manufacturing," and this was never more true than it is today with the globalization of industry. If the purchasing function is to fit in with the rest of the global operations of a firm, it must increasingly behave in the manner of a manager of manufacturing. In the past, the purchasing function often was responsible only for buying the cheapest possible inputs. However, as discussed in this chapter, there are many other considerations besides cost that need to be managed by the purchasing function.

Even in the industrialized countries before JIT was introduced, purchasing agents rarely could satisfy all of their companies' needs by waiting for the suppliers' representatives to come to them. They had to seek out and develop suppliers by visiting their plants and arranging for their companies' production and technical personnel to discuss matériel problems with the vendors' counterparts. In the developing countries, where many suppliers do not retain a sales force because they can sell everything they produce, supplier development assumes greater importance. The ability to locate vendors can easily compensate for a lack of other skills that management would require of a buyer at home.

When the firm depends heavily on imported materials, the prime criterion for hiring will be the purchasing agents' knowledge of import procedures and their connections with key government officials. The purchasing agents must constantly monitor government actions that can affect the availability of foreign exchange. They will often buy as much as possible of regularly consumed materials because they know they can always sell the excess to others, possibly at a profit.

Whether to fill the critical position of purchasing agent with a local citizen or with someone from the home office is often the subject of considerable debate at headquarters. A native has the advantage of being better acquainted with the local supply sources and government officials, but he or she might suffer from such cultural disadvantages as a tendency to favor members of the extended family or to accept as a normal business practice the giving (scarce supply) or receiving (plentiful supply) of bribes. An employee from the home office, in contrast, will be experienced in company purchasing procedures and should be free of these cultural disadvantages. Managers are not so naive as to believe that belonging to a certain culture guarantees that an individual will or will not engage in unethical activities. However, the tendency to commit these acts may be greater when there are no cultural constraints.

Maintenance. A second function supporting manufacturing is the maintenance of buildings and equipment. The goal of maintenance management is to ensure an acceptable level of production. Several possibilities are available for accomplishing this task. As was noted several times in this chapter, JIT has caused other parts of the manufacturing function to assume greater importance, and maintenance of plant production capacity is one of these parts. Before JIT, inventory was the solution to many managerial problems by hiding the causes and effects of these problems. The removal by JIT systems of inventory as a buffer has forced industry to give greater consideration to these problem areas, one of which is the maintenance of anticipated processing capacity. This may entail the prevention of unscheduled work stoppages caused by equipment failure.

There are two primary alternatives for dealing with maintenance problems. The first option is planned maintenance or preventive maintenance. The objective here is to prevent failure before it occurs, because failure is more expensive to repair and is disruptive to production schedules. The second alternative is breakdown maintenance. That is, when a machine or another element in the production process fails, it will be repaired. Although we have all heard the saying "If it works, don't fix it," this is seldom the best maintenance alternative. There are situations when companies let a process go until failure, such as light bulbs—we do not usually replace them until they fail. However, in production activities it is often appropriate to have a redundant or backup system.

In general, companies are concerned with maintenance because unanticipated system failure and downtime are a drain on scarce productive capacity. In a global context, there may be difficulty in obtaining imported spare parts and machinery, threatening the continued productive ability of a firm. As a result, the machine shops of many maintenance departments may actually manufacture some of these items in order to keep machines operating.

> General Tire–Spain began building tire molds for its own use but became so proficient that it was soon selling them to other affiliates. General Motors subsidiaries are regularly supplied with tools and dies made by GM in Mexico.

It is common practice in industrialized countries to establish preventive maintenance programs in which machinery is shut down according to plan and worn parts are replaced. Such programs are especially important for a synchronous manufacturing system, as you know. With advance notice of a shutdown, the manufacturing department can schedule around the machine, or by working the machine overtime, the department can temporarily build up inventories, permitting the manufacturing process to continue during its overhaul. In other words, the company is able to maintain an acceptable level of output to service the anticipated demands of customers.

This concept is not widely accepted in developing countries, where firms seem to take a fatalistic attitude toward equipment: "If it breaks down, we'll repair it." This may be attributable to the concept that preventive maintenance in most instances requires a greater degree of skill and knowledge than does breakdown maintenance.

Furthermore, in a seller's market, maintenance personnel are pressured by production and marketing managers to keep machinery running. This short-term view allows no time for scheduled shutdowns. Subsidiaries that do practice preventive maintenance with overhaul periods based on headquarters' standards frequently find these standards inadequate because of local operating conditions (humidity, dust, and temperature) and the manner in which the operators handle the machinery. When the amount of spare parts ordered with the machinery is based on domestic experience, it is often insufficient because of differing local conditions in other nations, including the skill and training of the local machine operators and maintenance workers.

In one sense, proper maintenance is more critical than 100 percent attendance of workers. The absence of one worker from a group of six interchangeable workers usually will not halt manufacturing, but if a key machine for which there is no substitute suddenly breaks down, the entire plant can be idled.

Technical Function. The function of the technical department is to provide operations management with manufacturing specifications. Usually, technical personnel are also responsible for checking the quality of inputs and the finished product. The task of the technical department in a foreign subsidiary is not simply one of maintaining a file of specifications sent by the home office, because difficulty in obtaining the same kinds and quality of raw materials as those used by the home plants may require substitutions that necessitate the complete rewriting of specifications.

> When a synthetic rubber plant was established in Mexico to produce some kinds of synthetic rubber, the government banned imports of all synthetic rubbers. Technical departments worked day and night to produce specifications that enabled the tire companies to substitute the few types available locally for the many kinds formerly imported.

The affiliate's technical manager is a key figure in the maintenance of product quality and thus is extremely influential in selecting sources of supply. Global and multidomestic companies go to great lengths in persuading host governments and joint venture partners of the need to place one of their people in this position. In this way, they are certain to keep the affiliate as a captive customer purchasing all the inputs that the more highly integrated parent manufactures.

[Summary]

Describe the five global sourcing arrangements.

A firm may establish a wholly owned subsidiary in a low-labor-cost country to supply components to the home country plant or to supply a product not produced in the home country. An overseas joint venture may be established in a country where labor costs are lower to supply components to the home country. The firm may send components to be machined and assembled by an independent contractor in an in-bond plant. The firm may contract with an independent contractor overseas to manufacture products to its specifications. The firm may buy from an independent overseas manufacturer.

Appreciate the importance of the added costs of global sourcing.

International freight, insurance, and packing may add 10 to 12 percent to the quoted price, depending on the sales term used. Import duties, customhouse broker's fees, cost of letter of credit, cost of inventory in the pipeline, and international travel are some of the other added costs.

Understand the increasing role of electronic purchasing for global sourcing.

The establishment of electronic purchasing systems on a company or industry basis can influence the number and type of suppliers available internationally to firms. Although there are a number of challenges to their use, electronic purchasing systems can produce significant reductions in the costs of inputs, both direct and indirect products and services. These systems can also permit the optimization of supply chains across networks of organizations, not merely within a single company.

Understand the Japanese efforts to improve quality and lower costs.

Japanese manufacturers realized that because of the limited size of Japan's economy and its lack of natural resources, they would have to export to grow. To do so, they would have to be competitive with other nations, which meant improving their product quality and lowering their costs. To achieve these goals, they created a production system, just-in-time, based primarily on American production concepts.

Know the just-in-time (JIT) production system.

JIT requires coordinated management of materials, people, and suppliers. JIT's goal is to eliminate inventories, reduce process and setup times, and use participative management to ensure worker input and loyalty to the firm. JIT includes total quality management (TQM), of which continuous improvement is an integral part.

Comprehend the problems with JIT.

JIT is restricted to repetitive operations. It is a balanced system, and so if one operation stops, the whole production line stops. But it is difficult to achieve a balanced system. In addition, JIT makes no allowances for contingencies. A sudden breakdown will stop the entire production system. Finally, it is a slow process to put JIT into effect.

Understand synchronous manufacturing.

The goal of synchronous manufacturing is unbalanced manufacturing scheduling rather than the balanced scheduling of JIT; attention is focused on the bottleneck of the manufacturing system, and scheduling for the entire operation is controlled by the output of the bottleneck operation.

Identify the impediments to global standardization of production processes and procedures.

Differences in the foreign environmental forces, especially the economic, cultural, and political forces, cause units of an international multiplant operation to differ in size, machinery, and procedures.

Understand the importance of intermediate and appropriate technology.

Governments of developing nations, preoccupied with high unemployment and rising capital costs, are urging investors to consider an intermediate technology rather than the highly automated processes of the industrialized nations. The multinationals' response in some instances has been to search for an appropriate technology, which matches a country's market with its resources. Under this concept, the production processes used may vary from the most advanced to the most primitive, depending on the influence of the economic, sociocultural, and political variables.

Know the two general classes of activities, productive and supportive, that must be performed in all manufacturing systems.

A manufacturing system is essentially a functionally related group of activities for creating value. After the system is operable, two general classes of activities, productive and supportive, must be performed. Productive activities are all those functions that are part of the manufacturing process. Among the important supportive activities are purchasing, maintenance, and the technical function.

[Key Words]

just-in-time (JIT) (p. 683)
total quality management (TQM) (p. 684)
quality circle (p. 684)
Taylor's scientific management system (p. 685)
preventive (planned) maintenance (p. 685)
synchronous manufacturing (p. 686)
bottleneck (p. 686)
reengineering (p. 687)
delayering (p. 687)
manufacturing rationalization (p. 691)
backward vertical integration (p. 694)
intermediate technology (p. 696)
appropriate technology (p. 696)
export processing zones (p. 698)

[Questions]

1. What are the trade-offs for a firm that uses a just-in-time production system?
2. Why does the cost of raw materials represent about 55 percent to 79 percent of the cost of goods sold in U.S. industry, and why has this proportion been increasing over time?
3. Who is responsible for inventory? Where does the cost of carrying inventory show up, on the balance sheet or the income statement?

4. What are the costs of carrying inventory? Is the Japanese version of the cost of carrying inventory in agreement with your calculation? (*Hint:* Start your carrying cost calculation with the opportunity cost of invested capital.)
5. What advantages does synchronous manufacturing have over JIT?
6. What does quality in a pickup truck mean to you? To a farmer in Africa?
7. What difficulties do you see for global firms when they implement synchronous manufacturing in their plants located in developing countries? Are there any advantages that are more valuable to them than to plants in industrialized nations?
8. What is the benefit to a buyer company and to a vendor company of standards such as ISO 9000?
9. What is the connection between manufacturers' insistence on receiving components with zero defects from outside suppliers and JIT?
10. What are the advantages to a worldwide firm of global standardization of its production facilities?
11. Discuss the influence of the uncontrollable environmental forces in global standardization of a firm's production facilities.
12. Why might manufacturing costs be excessive?
13. Who should be in charge of the purchasing function of an overseas affiliate, a local person or someone from the home office? Why?
14. What is the importance of preventive maintenance? Why might it be difficult to establish a preventive program in an overseas plant?
15. Do you know of any situations for which breakdown maintenance is a viable alternative?

[Internet Exercises]

Using the Internet

1. a. What is the maximum percentage of a Mexican firm's stock that a foreigner can own?
   b. What is the maximum amount a Mexican subsidiary may remit of its profits and dividends to its foreign parent in a fiscal year?
   c. What are the maximum hours in a standard workweek that are permitted by law in Mexico?
   d. What percentage of their normal daily wages are workers paid during their vacation period in Mexico?
   e. What are the incentives offered by the Mexican government to investors in an in-bond plant?

[Minicase 20.1]

Penwick–El Pais

Maquinas para el Hogar Penwick is a manufacturing subsidiary of Penwick Home Appliances in Boston. It is located in El Pais, a nation with 25 million inhabitants whose GNP per capita is $1,480. The country's annual inflation rate is about 30 percent, but the local company makes a good profit, in part because it keeps large stocks of components and raw materials purchased as much as 12 months before they are needed for production. The finished products are sold at prices set as if the raw materials and components had been purchased recently; hence the high profits. Penwick's competitors use the same strategy.

Penwick–El Pais has three competitors, none of which produces as complete a product mix or as many variations in each of the product lines of refrigerators, kitchen stoves, and washing machines as does the local Penwick plant. José Garcia, the local marketing manager, is proud that Penwick–El Pais makes as many kinds of products and variations of products as the much larger home plant, and he has told the managing director of the local company that it is the wide product mix that maintains Penwick–El Pais's number-one position in sales. It is true that Manuel Cardenas, the local operations manager, and Garcia frequently have heated discussions because Cardenas wants to make fewer product variations. Garcia accuses him of wanting to make black stoves like Henry Ford made black cars, but Cardenas claims he could double his output if he could make fewer kinds of products with fewer variations. Cardenas knows the value of long manufacturing runs and tries to get them. Garcia retorts that if Cardenas would pay attention to what he wants instead of making what Cardenas wants to make, he could sell more.

This is a sore spot with Cardenas because he tries hard to produce a new product according to Garcia's written request. If Garcia's memo says he wants a new size refrigerator in three colors to be available with or without beverage coolers or ice cube makers, these are the models Cardenas asks the product design department to design and make production specifications for. True, Garcia at one time or other has asked to attend meetings with Cardenas and his staff, but Cardenas considers this a waste of time. After all, he doesn't waste the design department's time by asking to attend their meetings; why should a salesperson attend his meetings? He has enough problems with the high prices for parts that the purchasing department gives him. When he complains, they tell him that everything he orders is special manufacture for the vendors. Cardenas says that's their problem; this is what the design department specifies, and this is what he has to use to build the product.

Cardenas has more pressing problems. Headquarters has adopted a new manufacturing system, synchronous manufacturing, and now wants him to do the same. In fact, he had to send his assistant manager to Boston for a month's training. Now she and the design manager, who also went, are back, and they have brought one of the home office experts with them. They're all going to have a long meeting with him this afternoon. Cardenas has read about synchronous manufacturing in technical journals and feels it does seem to have some advantages. But all of them have been in highly industrialized nations, and there are a lot of cultural and economic differences between El Pais and those countries.

You might role-play this case. Imagine you are one of the group of three that has come from Boston. Even though you know the local plant has orders to convert to synchronous manufacturing, you still have to win over the local personnel.

1. What will you say?
2. Can you think of any advantages that might be even more important for the local plant than they are for the larger home plant?
3. What problems do you foresee in putting synchronous manufacturing in place?

Your Future

The preparation of the 8th edition of this international business book coincides with a powerful attack on the results of the growth of international business. We believe that such a book at such a time should acquaint its readers with arguments on both sides, because their resolution will have a great effect on the international business managed or dealt with by those readers and on their lives. What is being attacked and defended with counterattacks is called globalization.

The attackers argue that globalization means the rape of the planet and the exploitation of the poor. They say it has caused a rise in inequality. The counterattackers argue that those statements not merely are wrong but are examples of the big lie—a proposition that is the opposite of the truth.

The former Mexican president, Ernesto Zedillo, put it as follows: "A peculiar alliance has recently come to life. Forces from the extreme left, extreme right, environmentalists and labor, and groups of developed countries are gathering around a common endeavor: to save the people of developing countries from development." He said that they are tied together by "globaphobia" and that their revealing common denominator is protection.

President Zedillo identifies the true targets of the globaphobic groups as trade with and investment in developing countries. He says that their success would be tragic for the poor countries and their poor people, because "what is clear from historical evidence is that in every case where a poor nation has significantly overcome its poverty, it has been achieved by engaging in production for export markets and opening itself to the influx of foreign goods, investment, and technology—that is, by participating in globalization."

Globalization as the Cause of Rich–Poor Inequality

Jay Mazur, president of the Union of Needletrades, Industrial and Textile Employees of the United States, says globalization does cause inequality. He argues that it has dramatically increased inequality between and within nations.

That the gap between world's rich and poor is huge is unquestionable. The antiglobalizers claim that globalization has caused that gap to increase. They propose that the way to halt this malign trend is to stop integration altogether or to load a host of labor and social standards on it. But their proposals fly in the face of evidence.

As Martin Wolf of *The Financial Times* points out, the 1980s and 1990s were the first decades in the last two centuries in which global inequality declined rather than rose. Major reasons for this were the rise in living standards in China and India. World Bank figures show that the number of people living on less than $1 a day in East Asia fell from 418 million in 1987 to 278 million in 1998 even after the 1997–98 Asian financial crises.

As Globalization Creates Jobs in Poor Countries, Is Unemployment Growing in Rich Countries?

Unemployment numbers demonstrate that is not the case. Despite its long recession, Japan's historically low unemployment rate has remained comparatively low. Relatively high unemployment in the European Union has fallen in the late 1990s and into the 2000s. Unemployment in the United States has remained low at around 4 percent for several years.

Has Globalization Caused Destruction of the Environment?

A difficulty caused by the North American Free Trade Agreement (NAFTA) and the maquiladora program which began before NAFTA has been pollution along the Mexico–United States border. Damage to the environment has been caused by the many new production facilities and the movement of thousands of Mexicans to that area to work in them.

Although both the Mexican and U.S. governments are responding by cleaning up the pollution and protecting the environment, the damage is mostly on the Mexican side of the border. Therefore, the Mexican government's attitude toward the problem is extremely relevant. It has been stated by former President Zedillo, who says, "Economic integration tends to favor, not worsen the environment. Since trade favors economic growth, it brings about at least part of the necessary means to preserve the environment. The better off people are, the more they demand a clean environment. Furthermore, it is not uncommon that employment opportunities in export activities encourage people to give up highly polluting marginal occupations."

Can Globalization Be Forced on a Country?

No. Countries can and do reject globalization. Some that have done this are Myanmar, the Democratic Republic of Congo, Sierra Leone, Rwanda, Madagascar, Guinea-Bissau, Algeria, the Republic of Congo, Burundi, Albania, Syria, and Ukraine. They are among the most impoverished countries in the world. As an article in *The Financial Times* puts it, "they are victims of their refusal to globalize."

Globalization Has Powerful Enemies

Because of ideology, perceived self-interest, or misinformation, protesters have taken to the streets and have been effective. They wrecked the Seattle World Trade Organization trade talks in 1999 and made their presence felt at International Monetary Fund/World Bank meetings in Washington, DC, and Prague in 2000.

Those organizations are not merely listening to the activists but increasingly are pandering to them, adjusting both their policies and the way those policies are presented to the public.

The protesters' outpourings of anticapitalist sentiments are meeting next to no intellectual resistance from official quarters. Governments are apologizing for globalization and promising to civilize it. The civilizing actions by rich-country governments probably will take the form of adding rules ostensibly to protect labor and the environment to the international trading regime.

If this comes about, it will be over the objections of developing country governments, because most of those governments have come around to the idea that trade (real globalization) is good. The rich countries—Europe, Japan, the United States, and others—are saying, in effect, that now that the poor countries have decided they would like to reduce poverty as quickly as possible, they won't be allowed to because that would inconvenience the rich.

Globalization and You

Your future as participants in international business or teachers of it will be strongly affected by the battles about globalization and their outcome. There will be opportunities and jobs, but the things you will be doing and/or teaching will depend on the outcomes. The second half of the twentieth century saw a tremendous expansion of international investment and trade. Those developments were accompanied and assisted by reductions in investment and trade barriers. That creates one sort of world in which to work and teach.

If the protesters have their way, the barrier reductions will be reversed. More and more of your time will be spent dealing with government regulations, restrictions, and taxes. That would be a very different world.

[Endnotes]

[Chapter 1]

1. 3—Unilever (British–Dutch), 7—Grupo Carso (Mexican), 8—Laidlaw (Canadian), 10—Campbell (US), 16—Diego (British).

2. Gordon R. Walker and Mark A. Fox, *Globalization: An Analytical Framework,* www.law.indiana.edu/glsj/vol3/no2/walker.html. (July 3, 2000)

3. A. Coskin Samli, Richard Still, and John S. Hill, *International Marketing* (New York: Macmillan, 1993), p. 210; and Thomas Hout, Michael E. Porter, and Eileen Rudden, "How Global Companies Win Out," *Harvard Business Review,* September–October 1982, pp. 98–110.

4. "Developed Countries Boost Foreign Direct Investment by 46 Per Cent to New Record," *UNCTAD Press Release,* TAD/INF/2826, September 23, 1999, p. 5, www.unctad.org/en/press/pr2826.htm (August 2, 2000).

5. Anne-Wil Harzing, "An Empirical Analysis and Extension of the Bartlett and Goshal Typology of Multinational Corporations," *Journal of International Business Studies,* First Quarter 2000, pp. 101–19; and C. A. Bartlett and S. Goshal, *Managing across Borders: The Transnational Solution* (Boston: Harvard Business School Press, 1989).

6. "Organization and Corporate Governance," *Unilever Annual Accounts 1996,* http://www.unilever.com (August 15, 1997).

7. "A Bit of Background," Shell home page, http://www.shell.com (August 15, 1997).

8. "Argentina/Brazil Binational Companies," *MERCOSUR-Binational Companies,* http://www.americasnet.com/mauritz/mercosur/english/page14.html (August 14, 1997); and "History Conformation," *Seguros de Pichincha S.A.,* http://www3.satnet.net/segurospichincha/usseguro.htm.

9. "The Growth of Global Industry," *The Wheel Extended,* no. 4, 1989, p. 11.

10. "Multinationals Come into Their Own," *Financial Times,* December 6, 2000, p. 16.

11. Mira Wilkins, *The Maturing of the Multinational Enterprise, 1940–1970* (Cambridge, MA: Harvard University Press, 1974), pp. 1–83.

12. "American Business Abroad," *Financial World,* June 25, 1991, p. 45.

13. Christopher Tungendhat, *The Multinationals* (New York: Random House, 1972), p. 12.

14. Bayer home page, http://www.bayer.com (August 16, 1997).

15. Fred W. Riggs, "Globalization Is a Fuzzy Term but It May Convey Special Meanings," *The Theme of the IPSA World Congress 2000,* July 1999, www2.hawaii.edu/~fredr/ipsaglo.htm (July 29, 2000).

16. R. F. M. Lubbers, "General Introduction," *The Globalization of Economy and Society,* December 30, 1996, www.globalize.org/globview.htm (August 8, 1997).

17. Matthew J. Slaughter and Phillip Swagel, *Does Globalization Lower Wages and Export Jobs?* (Washington, DC: IMF, 1997), p. 1.

18. Daniel Yergin, "The Word of the Week," *Daily Davos Home Views,* February 3, 1999, www.dailydavos.com/nw-srv/printed/special/davos/vw; and Daniel Yergin, "The Word of the Week," Newsweek.com, www.dailydavos.com/nw-srv/printed/special/davos/vw/vw0199tu_1.htm.

19. Terence Brake, Danielle Walker, and Thomas Walker, *Doing Business Internationally* (Burr Ridge, IL: Richard D. Irwin, 1995), p. 8.

20. *Cisco Annual Report,* 1999, www.cisco.com (July 31, 2000).

21. "Herding Cats," *Forbes,* July 24, 2000, pp. 108–10; "Ford's Model E," *Forbes,* July 17, 2000, pp. 30–34; "At Ford, E-Commerce Is Job 1," *Business Week,* February 28, 2000, pp. 74–78; and "Seller Beware," *The Economist,* March 4, 2000, pp. 61–62.

22. "Shell and BP in Plan for Global Exchange," *Financial Times,* April 12, 2000, p. 17; and "Seller Beware," p. 110.

23. "World FDI Grows 25 Per Cent in 1999, Surpassing US800 Billion," *UNCTAD Press Release,* TAD/INF/2837, February 8, 2000, www.unctad.org/en/press/pr_2837.htm (August 3, 2000).

24. "Press Briefing by George Kell on 1999 World Investment Report," *Press Briefing,* September 27, 1999, http://srch0.un.org:80/plweb-cgi/fastweb.

25. UNCTAD, *World Investment Report 1997* (New York: United Nations, 1997), p. XV.

26. "International Production Drives Globalization," *UNCTAD Press Release,* TAD/INF2820, September 23, 1999, www.unctad.org/en/press/pr2820en.htm (August 2, 2000).

27. Michael Minor, *Changes in Developing Country Regimes for Foreign Investment* (Greenville: University of South Carolina, 1990), p. 15.

28. "The Largest Industrial Companies in the World," *Fortune,* August 10, 1981, pp. 205–18; and "The Global 500 List," *Fortune 500 2000,* www.fortune.com/fortune/global500 (August 4, 2000).

29. "The Global Hundred," *Business Week,* July 12, 1999, p. 51; and "The Top 100 Companies," *Business Week Archives,* July 7, 1997,

www.businessweek.com/1997/b35341 3.htm (August 6, 2000).

—Internet Appendix

1. "The Total Librarian," *The Economist,* September 14, 1996, p. 12.
2. Fritz Erickson and John A. Vonk, *Effective Internet* (Chicago: Richard D. Irwin, 1996), p. 35.

[Chapter 2]

1. *World Investment Report 1997* (New York: United Nations, 1997), pp. 6–7.
2. The Programme on Transnational Corporations uses the stock of foreign direct investment as a measure of the productive capacity of international corporations in foreign countries. Washington, DC: International Monetary Fund, p. 13.
3. *Annual Report 2000* (Geneva, Switzerland: World Trade Organization), p. 13, www.wto.org/english/res_e/anrep_e/anre00_e.pdf.
4. *29th Survey of Overseas Business Activities* (Tokyo: Ministry of International Trade and Industry, fiscal 1999).
5. Yukio Ohnuma, "Trading Their Way to the Top," *Japan Update,* October 1992, pp. 20–21; and "Sogo-Shosha Begin Global Metamorphosis," *Japan Update,* December 1992, pp. 22–23.
6. "Trade between Japan and ASEAN4 in main products," *JETRO White Paper on Foreign Direct Investment 2000* (Tokyo: Japan External Trade Organization, 2000), p. 39.
7. *Monthly Bulletin of Statistics* (New York: United Nations, July 2000), pp. 260–61.
8. *Monthly Bulletin of Statistics* (New York: United Nations, July 2000), pp. 260–61.
9. *Monthly Bulletin of Statistics* (New York: United Nations, July 2000), pp. 260–61.
10. *JETRO White Paper on Foreign Direct Investment 2000* (Tokyo: Japan External Trade Organization, 2000), p. 12.
11. Internet URLs are as follows:
a. Office of Trade & Economic Analysis, www.ita.doc.gov/td/industry/otea.
b. U.S. Foreign Trade Highlights, www.ita.doc.gov/industry/otea/usfth.
c. U.S. Commodity Trade with Top 80 Trading Partners, www.ita.doc.gov/td/industry/otea/usfth/top80cty/top80cty.html.
d. U.S. Industry and Trade Outlook 2000, www.ita.doc.gov/td/industry/otea/outlook/index.html.
12. Telephone conversation with the International Trade Administration office, October 14, 1997.
13. Russell B. Scholl, "The International Investment Position of the United States at Yearend 1999," *Survey of Current Business,* July 2000, pp. 46–56, www.bea.doc.gov/bea/pubs.htm.
14. *World Investment Report 1996,* pp. xx–xxiv.
15. *Outward Direct Investment by Country & Region* (Tokyo: Ministry of Finance, June 1, 2000), www.mof.go.jp/english/fdi/e1c008h2.htm (November 13, 2000).
16. "Technical Notes," *World Development Report 1994* (Washington, DC: World Bank, 1994), p. 231.
17. Ibid., p. 232.
18. "Bangalore Bytes," *The Economist,* March 23, 1996, p. 67; and "The Growth of the Global Office," *World Investment Report 1996,* p. 107.
19. Warner-Lambert, *Annual Report 1990,* p. 25.
20. "The Goose That Laid the Golden Pill," *Forbes,* May 9, 1994, pp. 50–52.
21. "International Performance Outshines Domestic Results," *Business International,* September 29, 1986, p. 305.
22. "The 100 Largest U.S. Multinationals," *Forbes,* July 18, 1994, pp. 276–79.
23. "The 100 Largest U.S. Multinationals," *Forbes,* July 28, 1997, pp. 218–20; and July 15, 1996, pp. 288–90.
24. "The 100 Largest Foreign Investors in the U.S.," *Forbes,* July 28, 1997, p. 222.
25. "A Muffin on Wheels," *Financial Times,* January 10, 1992, p. 12.
26. "Toyota's Camry: Made in the USA—Sort Of," *Business Week,* November 22, 1993, p. 6.
27. "The Revenge of Big Yellow," *The Economist,* November 10, 1990, pp. 77–78.
28. "Zenith to Shift TV Assembly Work out of U.S. Plant," *The Wall Street Journal,* October 31, 1991, p. A13.
29. "The Border," *Business Week,* May 12, 1997, pp. 64–74; and "About the Maquiladora Industry," www.maquila.com/insider.html (November 11, 2000).
30. "Maquilas Face Uncertainty under NAFTA," *McAllen Monitor,* August 17, 1994, p. 1C.
31. "Maquilas and NAFTA," *Twin Plant News,* 1996 annual, pp. 19–21.
32. "New Trends in the Maquilas," *Twin Plant News,* August 1944, p. 28.
33. "Second Report to Congress on the Operation of the Caribbean Basin Economic Recovery Act," www.ustr.gov/reports/cbera/index.html (February 28, 1997).
34. *Guidebook to the Andean Trade Preference Act* (Washington, DC: Department of Commerce, July 1992), pp. 1–6.
35. "Growth Triangle Cooperation Makes Progress," *Indonesian News Quarterly,* Autumn 1993/Winter 1994, p. 13; and Asian Development Bank, *ADB Quarterly Review,* January 1994, p. 13.
36. "U.S. Companies See 1992 as an Opportunity," *San Jose Mercury News,* March 26, 1989, p. 1.
37. "Bruised in Brazil: Ford Slips as Market Booms," *The Wall Street Journal,* December 13, 1996, p. A10; and "Ford and VW Split Up Venture in Latin America, *The Wall Street Journal,* December 2, 1994, p. A8.
38. "Cafe au Lait, a Croissant—and Trix," *Business Week,* August 24, 1992, p. 50.
39. "Merck Has an Ache in Japan," *Business Week,* March 18, 1985, pp. 42–48.
40. "Van Heusen-Polgat JV First to Take Advantage of U.S.–Israel FTA," *Business International,* August 18, 1986, p. 262.
41. One of the writers, who was employed by the Mexican affiliate of an American company, which held 33 percent equity in the affiliate, was asked by the Mexican secretary of commerce why the Mexican plant was not exporting to Guatemala. The reason, which he could not disclose, was that the company served the Guatemalan market from wholly owned plants in the United States and thus kept all the profits. A

hurried call to Akron gave him permission to do some exporting to Guatemala to appease the Mexican government, but he was asked "not to try too hard."

42. "The Great Patent Plague," *Forbes ASAP,* September 1993, pp. 59–66.

43. "Cross-License Agreement Expected to Bring More Than $1 Billion to TI over Next 10 Years," May 23, 1999 press release, www.ti.com/corp/docs/press/company/1999/c99024.shtml (November 20, 2000).

44. U.S. Census Bureau, *FT900—U.S. International Trade in Goods and Services* final report for 1999, Exhibit 2, www.census.gov/foreign-trade/Press-Release/99_press_releases/Final_Revisions_1999/exh2.txt.

45. To learn more about Pierre Cardin's businesses, visit "Designer with a Midas Touch" at www.vivelavie.com/vivestories/pcardin.html.

46. McDonald's Reports Global Results," October 19, 2000, www.mcdonalds.com/corporate/press/financial/2000/10192000/index.html.

47. "Chip Makers Unite in Project to Raise Computer Power to New Levels," *International Herald Tribune,* September 12, 1997, p. 15.

48. Dan Gillmor, "Formidable force aims at Microsoft," *The Arizona Republic,* July 6, 1998, page E1; "Symbian Cellphone Alliance faces growing threat from Microsoft," *Wall Street Journal,* November 6, 2000, pp. B1, B4.

49. "Stake in TV-Tube Venture Sold to Japan's Toshiba," *The Wall Street Journal,* November 1, 1988, p. A27.

50. For discussion of challenges in managing international joint ventures and alliances, see Colette A. Frayne & J. Michael Geringer, 1995, "Challenges Facing General Managers of International Joint Ventures," In M. Mendenhall & G. Oddou (Eds.), *Readings and Cases in International Human Resource Management,* Cincinnati, OH: South-Western, 2nd edition, pp. 85–97; J. Michael Geringer & C. Patrick Woodcock, 1995, "Agency Costs and the Structure and Performance of International Joint Ventures," *Group Decision and Negotiation,* 4 (5), pp. 453–467; Colette A. Frayne & J. Michael Geringer, 1993, "Joint Venture General Managers: Key Issues in Research and Training," in K.M. Rowland, B. Shaw & P. Kirkbride (Eds.), *Research in Personnel and Human Resources Management,* Supplement 3, Greenwich, CN: JAI Press, pp. 301–321; and J. Michael Geringer & Louis Hebert, 1989, "Control and Performance of International Joint Ventures," *Journal of International Business Studies,* 20 (2) (Summer), pp. 235–254.

51. "Making Global Alliances Work," *Fortune,* December 17, 1990, pp. 121–26.

52. "Is U.S. Business Giving Away Its Technology—Again?" *Fortune,* September 11, 1989, p. 10.

53. "Revolution in Japanese Retailing," *Fortune,* February 7, 1994, pp. 143–46.

54. "What Is Sogo Shosha?" www.fjt.co.jp/~jftc_sogo.htm (February 9, 1998).

55. Mitsui & Co., Ltd. *Investors Guide,* www.mitsui.co.jp/tkabz/english/investor/97finan/97arsf.htm (February 8, 1998); and Mitsubishi Corporation, *Annual Report,* www.mitsubishi.co.jp/ar/anurep96/5_1.html (February 9, 1998).

56. "Exports That Aren't Going Anywhere," *Business Week,* December 2, 1885, pp. 121–24.

57. Ibid., p. 121.

[Chapter 3]

1. Government administrators involved in project evaluation are increasingly applying socioeconomic rather than purely financial criteria. For example, social rates of discount and opportunity costs are considered rather than the pure costs of borrowing money. Although marketing managers do not have to be development economists any more than they need to be specialists in marketing research, they should have a knowledge of the basic concepts.

2. "Fortress of Mercantilism," *Insight,* July 18, 1988, pp. 15–17.

3. David Ricardo, "The Principles of Political Economy and Taxation," in *International Trade Theory: Hume to Ohlin,* ed. William R. Allen (New York: Random House, 1965), pp. 62–67.

4. The idea that only hours of labor determine production costs is known as the *labor theory of value.* In fairness to Ricardo, we must admit that he included the cost of capital as "embodied labor" in his labor costs. Actually, as shown in the section "Introducing Money," the theory of comparative advantage can be explained by the cost of all factors of production.

5. Eli F. Heckscher, "The Effect of Foreign Trade on the Distribution of Income," *Economisk Tidskrift,* XXI, 1919, pp. 497–512; and Bertil Ohlin, *Interregional and International Trade* (Cambridge, MA: Harvard University Press, 1933).

6. The economist Bela Belassa, in his *Stages Approach to Comparative Advantage,* published by the World Bank in 1977, found in a study of 26 developed and developing nations that "the intercountry differences in the structure of exports are in a large part explained by differences in physical and human capital endowments."

7. J. Sachs and H. Shatz, "Trade and Jobs in U.S. Manufacturing," cited in *The Economist,* October 1, 1994, p. 19.

8. "While Toyota Loses Its Hold," *Business Week,* April 26, 1993, p. 28.

9. Louis Wells, "A Product Life Cycle for International Trade," *Journal of Marketing,* July 1968, pp. 1–6.

10. Many new products come not from the manufacturer's laboratories but from its suppliers of machinery and raw materials.

11. Belassa, *Stages Approach to Comparative Advantage,* pp. 26–27.

12. Richard B. Chase and Nicholas J. Aquilano, *Production and Operations Management,* 7th ed. (Burr Ridge, IL: Irwin, 1995), pp. 321–22.

13. Gerard Tellis and Peter Golder, "First to Market, First to Fail? Real Causes of Enduring Marketing Leadership," *Sloan Management Review,* 37, no. 2, cited in "Why First May Not Last," *The Economist,* March 16, 1996, p. 65.

14. Dennis R. Appleyard and Alfred J. Field, *International Economics* (Homewood, IL: Irwin, 1992), pp. 226–29.

15. John H. Dunning, "The Competitive Advantage of Countries and the Activities of Transnational Corporations," *Transnational*

Corporations, February 1992, pp. 135–68.

16. John H. Dunning, *The Globalization of Business* (London: Routledge, 1993), p. 106.

17. "Footwear Industry Tells Congress 'Shoe Gap' Threatens U.S. Defense," *The Wall Street Journal,* August 24, 1984, p. 21.

18. "Mexican Labor's Hidden Costs," *Fortune,* October 17, 1994, p. 32.

19. "Brie and Hormones," *The Economist,* January 7, 1989, pp. 21–22.

20. *National Trade Estimate Report on Foreign Trade Barriers* (Washington, DC: United States Trade Representative, 2000), pp. 95–96, www.ustr.gov/reports/nte/2000/eu.pdf (August 25, 2000).

21. "Europe's Burden," *The Economist,* May 22, 1999, p. 84.

22. "EU Leads Surge in Anti-Dumping Claims," *Financial Times,* April 17, 2000, p. 3; and "Dumping Duties on China," *Financial Times,* February 6, 1997, p. 19.

23. "The New Rules of Trade," *National Review,* April 18, 1994, pp. 40–44.

24. "The Jumbo War," *The Economist,* June 15, 1991, pp. 65–66.

25. "Airbus to Build 555-Passenger Jetliner," *The Columbian,* June 23, 2000, p. A1; "EADS Makes Debut Selling Superjumbos," *International Herald Tribune,* June 24–25, 2000, p. 11; and "Birth of a Giant," *Business Week,* July 10, 2000, pp. 170–76.

26. "Summary of the Final Act of the Uruguay Round," www.fas.usda.gov/itp/policy/gatt/sum_fact.html#cAgreement (October 23, 1997); and "World Trading Environment and Developing Asia," www.asiandevbank.org/ado97/ado-06.htm (October 23, 1997).

27. "Draped in Import Quotas," *Seattle Times,* February 27, 1994, p. D1.

28. "Textile Group Loses New Fight against The Limited," *Journal of Commerce,* May 29, 1998, www.joc.com/issues/980529/, (December 18, 2000).

29. Center for Responsive Politics, "The Politics of Sugar," www.crp.org/pubs/sugar/sugar06.html (October 24, 1997).

30. "The Agreement on Textiles and Clothing," May 22, 1997, www.wto.org/wto/goods/textiles.htm (October 23, 1997); and "A Summary of the Final Act of the Uruguay Round," www.fas.usda.gov/itp/policy/gatt/sum_fact.html#cAgreement (December 18, 2000).

31. Office of the U.S. Trade Representative, "The 1997 Estimate Report on Foreign Trade Barriers", pp. 108–09, www.ustr.gov/reports/nte/1997/contents.html (October 26, 1997).

32. European Union, "Market Access Sectoral and Trade Barriers Database," http://mkaccdb.eu.int/general/mac.pl (September 21, 1997).

33. "A Bitter Taste," *The Economist,* February 19, 1994, p. 27; and "The Fanjuls of Palm Beach: The Family with a Sweet Tooth," *Forbes,* May 14, 1990, p. 14.

34. The OECD published *Costs and Benefits of Protection,* which evaluates a wide range of studies on import restrictions of manufactured goods in OECD countries.

35. "Classification of Economies," *The World Bank Group—Development Data,* www.worldbank.org/data/databytopic/class.htm (August 30, 2000).

36. "Light on the Shadows," *The Economist,* May 3, 1997, pp. 63–64.

37. "Everybody's Doing It," *International Management,* July–August 1987, p. 27.

38. "Light on the Shadows," p. 63.

39. "Tapping the Resources of Mexico's Underground Economy," *The Wall Street Journal,* December 30, 1988, p. A7.

40. World Bank, "Structure of Consumption in PPP Terms," *2000 World Development Indicators* (Washington, DC: World Bank, 2000), p. 224.

41. Charles Kindleberger and Bruce Herrick, *Economic Development* (New York: McGraw-Hill, 1977), p. 1.

42. United Nations Development Program, "Human Development Index 1999 Rankings," www.undp.org/undp/hdro/HDI.html.

43. Charles Kindleberger, *American Business Abroad* (New York: Yale University Press, 1969), pp. 43–44.

44. Stephen Hymer, *The International Operations of International Firms: A Study in Direct Investment* (Cambridge, MA: MIT Press, 1976).

45. Ricard Caves, "International Corporations: The Industrial Economics of Foreign Investment," *Economica,* February 1971, pp. 5–6.

46. F. T. Knickerbocker, *Oligopolistic Reaction and Multinational Enterprise* (Boston: Harvard Business School, 1973).

47. E. M. Graham, "Transatlantic Investments by Multinational Firms: A Rivalistic Phenomenon," *Journal of Post-Keynesian Economics,* Fall 1978, pp. 82–99.

48. P. Buckley and M. Casson, *The Future of Multinational Enterprise* (New York: Macmillan, 1976).

49. R. Z. Aliber, "A Theory of Direct Investment," *The International Corporation* (Cambridge, MA: MIT Press, 1970), pp. 17–34.

50. A. Rugman, *International Diversification and the Multinational Enterprise* (Lexington, MA: Lexington Books, 1979).

51. John H. Dunning, *International Production and the Multinational Enterprise* (London: George Allen & Unwin, 1981), pp. 109–10.

[Chapter 4]

1. United Nations, www.un.org.

2. The World Bank Group Multilateral Development Banks, www.worldbank.org/html/extdr/institutions/mdb.htm.

3. The World Bank Group, www.worldbank.org.

4. Article I of the Articles of Agreement of the International Finance Corporation (Washington, DC, June 20, 1956), p. 3.

5. IFC General Policies (Washington, DC: IFC, 1970).

6. The World Bank/PRDMG, *Transition 7,* no. 11–12 (November–December 1996), pp. 20–22.

7. The World Bank Group, www.worldbank.org/html/extdr/about/wbgis.htm.

8. The World Bank Group, www.worldbank.org/icsid/about/about.htm.

9. Melanie Tammen, "Privatize the World Bank," *The Wall Street Journal,* May 17, 1991, p. A14.

10. "Time to Roll Out a New Model," *The Economist,* March 15, 1997, pp. 71–72.

11. Leslie Crawford, "Chaotic Bank Threatens Africa Soft

Loans," *Financial Times,* May 26, 1997, pp. 1, 14.

12. "The Asian Development Bank: Help Yourselves," *The Economist,* May 4, 1996, p. 78.

13. Kevin Done, "EBRD Wins Approval for Doubling of Capital Base," *Financial Times,* April 16, 1996, p. 2; and "Role for EBRD," *Financial Times,* April 11, 1997, p. 15.

14. Inter-American Development Bank, www.iadb.org/exr/english/ABOUTIDB/about_idb.htm.

15. *United Nations Monetary and Finance Conference, Bretton Woods, New Hampshire, July 1 to 22, 1944,* Department of State Publication 287, Conference Series 55 (Washington, DC: Department of State, 1944).

16. A. Acheson et al., *Bretton Woods Revisited* (Toronto: University of Toronto Press, 1972).

17. Oscar L. Altman, "Quotas in the International Monetary Fund," *International Monetary Fund Staff Papers 5,* no. 2 (1956).

18. Leland M. Goodrich and Edward Hambro, *Charter of the United Nations: Commentary and Documents,* rev. ed. (Boston: World Peace Foundation, 1949), p. 349.

19. For a discussion of how surveillance is working, see "Surveillance Strengthened to Meet New Challenges," *IMF Survey,* September 1996, pp. 7–10.

20. Mansoor Ijaz, "The IMF's Recipe for Disaster," *The Wall Street Journal,* June 10, 1996, p. A18; and "IMF Conditionality Can Signal Policy Credibility to Markets," *IMF Survey,* March 24, 1997, pp. 81–83.

21. Richard Lapper, "BIS Sees Acceptance of More Bond Market Risk," *Financial Times,* February 28, 1997, p. 6.

22. "The Bank for International Settlements: A Profile of an International Institution," CH 4002 Basel, June 1990, pp. 1–8.

23. Peter Marsh, "New East Meets Old West at Central Bankers' Bank," *Financial Times,* July 9, 1991, p. 2.

24. Keith Bradsher, "U.S. Role Grows in Discreet Bank," *International Herald Tribune,* August 7, 1995, p. 4; and www.bis.org/press/p960909b.htm (April 13, 1997).

25. Richard N. Gardner, *Sterling-Dollar Diplomacy* (New York: Oxford University Press, 1956).

26. Gerard Curzon, *Multilateral Commercial Diplomacy* (New York: Praeger, 1965).

27. Bernard Norwood, "The Kennedy Round: A Try at Linear Trade Negotiations," *Journal of Law and Economics,* October 12, 1966, pp. 297–319; Ernest M. Preeg, "*Traders and Diplomats* (Washington, DC: Brookings Institution, 1970); John W. Evans, *The Kennedy Round in American Trade Policy: The Twilight of GATT?* (Cambridge, MA: Harvard University Press, 1971); Sidney Golt, *The GATT Negotiations, 1973–1974: A Guide to the Issues* (London, Washington, and Ottawa: British–North America Committee, 1974); and B. Balassa and M. E. Dreinin, "Trade Liberalization under the Kennedy Round: The Static Effects," *Review of Economics and Statistics,* May 1967, pp. 125–37.

28. "GATT Comes Right," *The Economist,* December 18, 1993, pp. 13–14.

29. Guy de Jonquières, "WTO Urged to Act on Regional Pacts," *Financial Times,* February 6, 1997, p. 10.

30. "WTO in the Wake of Seattle," *The Asian Wall Street Journal, Weekly Edition,* December 13–19, 1999, p. 5.

31. "EU Slips Up over Banana Imports." *Financial Times,* July 18, 2000, p. 7.

32. Perez Alfonze, "The Organization of Petroleum Exporting Countries," (Caracas) *Monthly Bulletin,* no. 2 (1966).

33. *International Petroleum Encyclopedia,* 1979, pp. 194–95, Table 6.

34. Luis Vallenilla, *Oil: The Making of a New Economic Order* (New York: McGraw-Hill, 1975).

35. James Cook, "Comeuppance," *Forbes,* May 9, 1983, pp. 55–56.

36. "The Impact of Lower Oil Prices," *IMF World Economic Outlook,* May 1994, pp. 20–21.

37. "Crude Oil Production, OPEC and Non-OPEC," *World Economic Outlook,* October 1996, pp. 141–42; International Monetary Fund, Washington, DC.

38. Derek Urwin, *The Community of Europe: A History of European Integration since 1945* (New York: Longman, 1991), p. 8.

39. Martin Walker, "George Marshall: His Plan Helped Rebuild Europe," *Europe,* April 1997, pp. 22–23; Martin Walker, "From Acheson to Albright," ibid., pp. 24–25; Alex Krause, "Interview Maurice Schumann," ibid. pp. 26–27; and "Interview Albert Beveridge, Head of the George Marshall Foundation," ibid, p. 29.

40. Wendell H. McCulloch, Jr., "United States of Europe?" *Backgrounder,* no. 706, the Heritage Foundation, May 5, 1989.

41. Tony Snape, "Customers Fraud Unit to Plug EU Gaps," *The European,* February 27–March 5, 1997, p. 31.

42. Wendell H. McCulloch, Jr., and Donald A. Ball, "Canada–United States Free Trade Agreement: Add Mexico?" *Proceedings of the International Trade and Finance Association Annual Meeting,* May 30–June 2, 1991, Volume 1, pp. 1–14.

43. Jonathan Friedland, "Chile Is Relaxed on NAFTA as Chief Begins U.S. Visit," *The Wall Street Journal,* February 24, 1997, p. A18.

44. Nancy Dunne, "Canada Takes Free Trade Trial Alone," *Financial Times,* April 11, 1997, p. 6.

45. John P. Sweeney, "U.S. Needs Fast Track Authority Now," *Backgrounder 1027 Update,* the Heritage Foundation, February 24, 1997, p. 3.

46. Organization of American States, www.oas.org.

47. Stephen Fidler, "Trade Pact Sets the Pace for Integration," *Financial Times,* February 4, 1997, p. 12; and "Mercosur Survey," *Financial Times,* February 4, 1997, pp. 12–14.

[Chapter 5]

1. Charles N. Henning, William Pigott, and Robert Haney Scott, *International Financial Management* (New York: McGraw-Hill, 1978), p. 149.

2. Gillian O'Connor, "Increasing Gold Demand Is Easier Said Than Done," *Financial Times Survey,* June 28, 2000, p. I.

3. Albert C. Whitaker, *Foreign Exchange,* 2nd ed. (New York: Appleton-Century-Crofts, 1933), p. 157.

4. Jacques Rueff, *The Wall Street Journal,* June 5, 1969, pp. 6, 9.

5. John Mueller, "The Reserve Currency Curse," *The Wall Street Journal,* September 4, 1986, p. 26.

6. "Sell Some Gold," *The Wall Street Journal,* September 4, 1986, p. 26.

7. "Taking in the Biscuits," *The Economist,* May 11, 1991, p. 79.

8. K. K. Sharma and R. C. Murthy, "India Sends 25 Tonnes of Gold to London," *Financial Times,* July 9, 1991, p. 3.

9. David Aviel, "Naysayers Can't Tarnish the Value of Gold," *The Asian Wall Street Journal,* August 19, 1996, p. 15.

10. *Articles of Agreement, International Monetary Fund* (Washington, DC: IMF, 1944), Article I.

11. Robert Z. Aliber, *The Future of the Dollar as an International Currency* (New York: Praeger, 1966).

12. For a discussion of how the pars were set, see Henning et al., *International Financial Management,* pp. 108, 218.

13. Theodore Sorenson, *Kennedy* (New York: Harper & Row, 1965), p. 408. See also *Maintaining the Strength of the United States Dollar in a Strong Free World Economy* (Washington, DC: U.S. Treasury Department, January 1968), p. xi; and *Economic Report of the President,* January 1964, p. 139.

14. *Federal Reserve Bulletin,* September 1969 and January 1974.

15. Ibid., December 1971 and January 1974.

16. Ibid., January 1974, p. A75.

17. This was perceived by the French economist Jacques Rueff, who also forecast the results; see endnote 4.

18. William Safire, *Before the Fall* (New York: Belmont City Books, 1975), p. 514. The size of the British request has been questioned; see Charles Coombs, *The Arena of International Finance* (New York: Wiley, 1976), p. 218, where Coombs says that the Bank of England request was for cover of only US$750 million.

19. Wilson E. Schmidt, "The Night We Floated," International Institute for Economic Research, Original Paper 9, October 1977.

20. Ibid., p. 7.

21. For detailed accounts of the international monetary system during the 1971–73 period, see Coombs, *Arena of International Finance,* chap. 12; and Robert Solomon, *The International Monetary System* (New York: Harper & Row, 1977), chaps. 12–15.

22. For discussions of the varieties and methods of clean or dirty floats plus comparisons of float versus peg, see, for example, Weir M. Brown, *World Afloat; National Policies Ruling the Waves,* Essays in International Finance, no. 116 (Princeton, NJ: International Finance Section, Department of Economics, Princeton University, May 1976); Harry G. Johnson, *Further Essays in Monetary Economics* (Winchester, MA: Allen & Unwin, 1972); Anthony M. Lanyi, *The Case for Floating Exchange Reconsidered,* Essays in International Finance, no. 72 (February 1976); Raymond F. Mikesell and Henry M. Goldstein, *Rules for a Floating Regime,* Essays in International Finance, no. 109 (March 1975); and "Economics Brief: To Fix to Float," *The Economist,* January 9, 1988, pp. 66–67.

23. Wendell H. McCulloch Jr., "American Exports: Why Have They Lagged?" A Study for the Subcommittee on Trade, Productivity, and Economic Growth of the Joint Economic Committee, Congress of the United States, May 14, 1985.

24. Peter Norman, "Adjusting to a New Climate," *Financial Times,* April 29, 1991, section IV, p. 1.

25. David Fairlamb, "Tame the Currency Markets? Think Again," *Business Week,* April 24, 2000, p. 86.

26. Stanley W. Black, *Floating Exchange Rates and National Economic Policy* (New Haven: Yale University Press, 1977), pp. 23–26, 49–50, 129–30, 149–50, 154–56, and 173–74.

27. Ibid.

28. Michael R. Sesit, "The Robust Dollar and the World: What's in It for You," *The Wall Street Journal,* March 4, 1997, p. C1.

29. *The Wall Street Journal,* August 29, 2000, p. C11.

30. Ibid.

31. "Asian Economies: Happy Neighbors," *The Economist,* August 26, 2000, p. 63.

32. James Kynge, "Foreign Exchange Growth in Asia," *Financial Times,* September 1, 2000, p. 5.

33. *IMF Survey,* October 1993, pp. 9–11.

34. "Some Facts about the SDR," *IMF Survey,* April 1, 1996.

35. "Some Facts about the SDR," *IMF Survey,* April 1, 1996.

36. Giscard d'Estaing, "The ECU and the European Monetary System," *Bulletin, Swiss Banking Magazine,* November 1989, pp. 11–13.

37. "When Ecu Plus EMU Equals Euro," *The European,* August 1–7, 1996, p. 17.

38. Gillian Tett, "Isle of Man to Issue First Euro," *Financial Times,* February 29, 1996, p. 7.

39. Gillian Tett, "Euro Will Not Be Easy Money," *Financial Times,* September 9, 1996, p. 3.

40. Wilhelm Nolling, "The Test Tube Currency," *Financial Times,* May 19, 1997, p. 14.

41. William Pfaff, "A Common European Currency Doesn't Make Political Sense," *International Herald Tribune,* December 2, 1996, p. 10.

42. Klaus Engelen, "Ignore Impact of the Euro at Your Peril," *The European,* March 27–April 2, 1997, p. 21. For a comprehensive discussion of the euro, see "The Euro: A Stable Currency for Europe," Special Report by *Deutsche Bank Research,* February 12, 1997.

[Chapter 6]

1. "Dollar's Embrace Leaves Ecuadoreans Tender for Passing of Their Sucre," *Financial Times,* September 21, 2000, p. 9.

2. "Colombia Raids Counterfeiters," Associated Press, November 18, 2000.

3. Discussed by Robert Z. Aliber, *The International Money Game,* 2nd ed. (New York: Basic Books, 1976), pp. 189–90.

4. Samuel I. Katz, " 'Managed Floating' as an Interim International Exchange Rate Regime, 1973–1975," *New York University Bulletin,* 1975–3 (New York: Center for the Study of Financial Institutions, New York University, 1975), pp. 13–14.

5. Vermont Royster, "Thinking Things Over, 'A Thrice-Told Tale,' " *The Wall Street Journal,* May 10, 1978, p. 18.

6. "Recent Developments in Latin America," Bank for International Settlements, *67th Annual Report,*

April 1, 1996–March 31, 1997, June 9, 1997, pp. 35–36.

7. Georg Junge and Max Schieler, "The Real Choices Facing the Debtor Countries," *Economic and Financial Prospects,* April–May 1990, pp. 1–5.

8. "Brady Bonds," Bank for International Settlements, *66th Annual Report, April 1, 1995–March 31, 1996,* June 10, 1996, p. 123.

9. Brian Bollen, "Debt Traders Look to Eastern Europe," *Euromoney,* November 1993, pp. 50–52.

10. Ben Edwards, "The Age of the Exotic Sovereign Borrower," *Euromoney,* March 1994, pp. 127–30.

11. Michael R. Pakko, "Debt Relief," *International Economic Trends,* Federal Reserve Bank of St. Louis, November 1996, p. 1.

12. Alan Abelson, "Do the Wrong Thing, Young Bankers," *Barron's,* September 25, 1989, pp. 1 and 53.

13. "Emerging Market Indicators: Foreign Debt," *The Economist,* April 26, 1997, p. 110.

14. "U.S. Foreign Debt Rose 26.6% in 1996: Strong Dollar Blamed," *The Wall Street Journal,* July 1, 1997, p. A2.

[Chapter 7]

1. Many of these factors also affect domestic firms, but multinational firms are generally more vulnerable and usually must act more quickly.

2. If management is interested in a country as a possible site for investment, it will require the same detailed information it does for an area where the firm is already doing business.

3. *International Bibliography, Information, Documentation (IBID),* an excellent bibliography, is published quarterly by UNIPUB. It includes abstracts of publications and studies containing economic and demographic data.

4. "Table 1.9—Relation of Gross Domestic Product, National Income, and Personal Income," www.bea.doc.gov/bea/dn/nipatbls/nip1-9.htm (November 16, 1996).

5. The World Bank staff has worked to make the data comparable. Wherever possible, the staff has used consumption rather than income. *World Development Indicators 1997* (Washington, DC: World Bank, 1997), p. 57.

6. Azizur Rahman Khan, Keith Griffin, and Carl Riskin, "Income Distribution in Urban China during the Period of Economic Reform and Globalization," *AEA Papers and Proceedings* 89(2), 1999, pp. 296–300.

7. *World Development Indicators 1997,* p. 109.

8. "The Swoosh Index for Emerging Markets," *Business Week,* May 5, 1997, p. 8; "Pangs of Conscience," *Business Week,* July 29, 1996, pp. 46–47; "Nike, Inc.," *The Wall Street Journal,* September 23, 1997, p. B12; and "Where Asia Goes from Here," *Fortune,* November 24, 1997, p. 104.

9. You can make your own table for countries not listed in Table 7.6 by first getting the average hourly earnings in national currency from the U.S. Department of Labor, Bureau of Statistics, *Handbook of Labor Statistics.* However, the data in this publication lag considerably, so you then go to the latest issue of *International Financial Statistics,* published monthly by the IMF. Here, for each country listed in the *Handbook,* you can find a very recent index of average hourly costs. Multiplying a ratio of the IMF's index values by the latest value in national currency in the *Handbook,* you can derive more recent values in local currency. Then you go back to the IMF publication and select the average exchange rates for the years you are comparing and convert national currencies to dollars. You will find differences between *Business Europe*'s figures and the results you obtain by this method. We're not sure why, but obviously *Business Europe* either used different exchange rates or obtained different values expressed in national currency (probably the exchange rates). This illustrates the problem in expressing any national statistic in dollars.

10. "Debt Sustainability," *World Development Indicators 1997,* p. 225.

11. "Korea's Past Policies Are Unable to Remedy Today's Economic Ills," *The Wall Street Journal,* November 24, 1997, p. A1.

12. "Viva las Pampas," *Forbes,* October 28, 1991, p. 106.

13. "Latin America's New Currency," *The Economist,* October 29, 1988, p. 87.

14. "Hidden Horrors," *The Economist,* October 22, 1994, p. 95.

15. Developed nations are not immune. France, the Netherlands, and Belgium have faced this problem.

16. "Table 2.2: Population Dynamics," *World Development Indicators 1997,* pp. 38–40.

17. "No. 1325: Population by Country," www.census.gov/statab/freq/96s1325.txt (December 7, 1997).

18. "Whirlpool Jumps into the Global Market," *The European,* November 1–3, 1991, p. 25; "Planning for Global Expansion at Whirlpool," *Business International,* April 15, 1991; and "Whirlpool Is Gathering a Global Momentum," *The New York Times,* April 23, 1989, p. 10.

19. "Population Policy: Country Experience," *Finance & Development,* September 1984, p. 19.

20. "Table 2.2: Population Dynamics," *World Development Indicators 1997,* pp. 36–38.

21. "The Graying of Japan: Pension Lab for a Cost-Conscious World," *The International Herald Tribune,* September 3, 1997, p. 1.

22. *World Development Indicators 1997,* pp. 6–9.

23. Ibid., pp. 114–16.

24. "Strictly Speaking, Wal-Mart May Need Lessons in French," *The Wall Street Journal,* April 13, 1994, p. B7; and "Wal-Mart Again Runs into Language-Law Trouble," *The Wall Street Journal,* June 24, 1994, p. A4.

[Chapter 8]

1. Robert Bartels, ed., *Comparative Marketing: Wholesaling in 15 Countries* (Homewood, IL: Richard D. Irwin, 1963), p. 4.

2. "Austria as a Business Location," *Report* (Vienna: Bank Austria, June 1994), pp. 12–13.

3. "The Challenge of Enlargement: Commission Opinion on Finland's Application for Membership," *Bulletin of the European Communities,* June 1992, p. 47.

4. "The Challenge of Enlargement: Commission Opinion on Austria's Application for Membership," *Bulletin of the European Communities,* April 1992, pp. 10–11.

5. OECD, *Monthly Bulletin of Statistics,* June 1994, pp. 44–52.

6. When a sales engineer from Madrid and one of the writers went to Barcelona, the Detroit of Spain, on a business trip, we were accompanied on our visits to customers by our salesman from Barcelona. Our meetings with customers always followed the same pattern. The Barcelona salesman would begin the meeting by telling the customer we were from Madrid and did not speak Catalan, the local language. The meeting would proceed in Spanish until either the customer or our local salesman, in searching for a word in Spanish, would use the more familiar (to him) word in Catalan. This would trigger the other to begin speaking in Catalan (completely unintelligible to anyone speaking only Spanish), and the sales engineer and the writer would be completely in the dark as to what was being discussed. After a moment, the local salesman and the customer would realize what they were doing and apologize. The discussions in Spanish would be resumed, and then the switch to Catalan would be repeated. If our local salesman had not been present to smooth over these lapses and provide the necessary empathy with the customer, these meetings would have been disastrous.

7. "Spain's Regions," *The Economist,* November 16, 1996, pp. 55–56.

8. "Spain Firm on Terrorism after Basque Killing," *Financial Times,* July 3, 2000, p. 2; "Basque Separatists Renew Violent Campaign in Spain," *The Columbian,* July 19, 2000, p. A8; and "Spain's Aznar Says ETA Seeks 'Ethnic Cleansing,' " *Lycos News,* September 1, 2000, http://news.lycos.com/ (September 3, 2000).

9. Belgium (97 percent), Israel (91 percent), Uruguay (91 percent), Netherlands (89 percent), United Kingdom (89 percent), Argentina (89 percent), Germany (87 percent), and Venezuela (86 percent). *World Development Indicators,* pp. 26–28.

10. Australia has no north–south railway mainly because there is little population and economic activity in the center of the country to support one. There is an east–west coastal system in the more populous southern region that was completed partly because the federal government feared the western states might secede from the Australian union. The system, however, has the same problems as those of other large developing nations, such as India and Brazil. There are three different gauges along its length, with a few disconnected feeder lines going inland from the ports to mining and farm districts. Goods in transit between Sydney and Perth take 14 days when, because of the distance, they should take 5. Some unification has been done, but it is not complete. Goods and passengers still must be transferred at some state borders.

11. *World Development Indicators 2000,* pp. 10–11.

12. "River to Nowhere," *The Columbian,* July 20, 2000, p. A8.

13. Intergovernmental Hidrovia Committee, "Hidrovia Information," www.ssdnet.com.ar/hidrovia/index2.htm (September 14, 2000).

14. "Chinese Press Raps Huge Dam Project," *The Oregonian,* March 18, 1999, p. A13; and "Another Controversy Strikes Huge Dam Project in China," *The Columbian,* May 8, 2000, p. A5.

15. "Bolivia Doesn't See New Ties with Chile," *International Herald Tribune,* April 26, 1999, p. 6.

16. Rhoads Murphey, *The Scope of Geography,* 2nd ed. (Skokie, IL: Rand McNally, 1973), pp. 188–89.

17. Andrew M. Karmack, *The Tropics and Economic Development* (Washington, DC: World Bank, 1976), p. 5.

18. Joseph Butler, *Economic Geography* (New York: John Wiley & Sons, 1980), p. 108.

19. "Volume of World Petroleum Reserves," http://hypertextbook.com/facts/2000/EvanAbel.shtml (September 16, 2000).

20. "Third 'Major' Oil Discovery Is Made at El Nar in Sudan," *The Wall Street Journal,* January 21, 1997, p. B5b; "Treasure under the Sea," *Financial Times,* May 1, 1997, p. 11; and "Pulling Oil from Davy Jones' Locker," *Business Week,* October 30, 1995, pp. 74–76.

21. "Technology Set to Bring Oil Sands to Full Potential," *Financial Times,* April 11, 2000, p. 32; "Canada-Open-Pit Mining Equipment—Marketing Assessment," http://strategis.ic.gc.ca/cgi-bin/allsite/b, pp. 4–5 (September 16, 2000); and "*Canada,*" Energy Information Administration, www.eia.doe.gov/emeu/cabs/canada.html (September 16, 2000).

22. "Australian Oil Shale," Suncor Energy Company, www.suncor.com/about/about_australia.html (September 16, 2000); "Australian Oil Fields," Action for Public Transport, "www.cs.su.oz.au/~jimd/apt/energy.html (September 17, 2000); and "Oil Shale Resources of Nova Scotia," www.gov.ns.ca\natr/meb/90eg3a.htm.

23. "Oil-from-Coal," Sasol, www.gas2liquids.com/oil.htm (September 16, 2000); and "Sasol Oil-from-Coal Process," Sasol, www.sasol.com.co.za/process/oil/oil.html (September 18, 2000).

24. "Chevron in JV with Sasol on GTL," *Alexander's Gas & Oil Connections,* July 19, 1999, www.gasandoil.com/goc/company/cna93014.htm (September 16, 2000); and "Chevron, Sasol Set Natural-Gas Accord," *The Wall Street Journal,* June 10, 1999, p. A2.

25. "Coal," *International Energy Outlook 2000* (Washington, DC: Energy Information Administration), www.eia.doe.gov/oiaf/ieo/coal.html (September 19, 2000); and "Nuclear Power," *International Energy Outlook 2000* (Washington, DC: Energy Information Administration), www.eia.doe.gov/oiaf/ieo/nuclear.html (September 19, 2000).

26. "Natural Gas," *International Energy Outlook 2000,* www.eia.doe.gov/oiaf/ieo/nat_gas.html (September 19, 2000).

27. "1999 Best Year Ever for Wind Energy," *Global Wind Energy Market Report,* American Wind Energy Association, www.awea.org/faq/global99.html (September 20, 2000); "Annual Solar Thermal and Photovoltaic Manufacturing Activities Tables, 1999," Energy Information Administration, www.eia.doe.gov/cneaf/...renewables/page/solar/solarphoto_tab.html (September 20, 2000); and "Table 10.7 Photovoltaic Cell and Module Shipments by Type, Price, and Trade, 1982–1998," *Annual Energy Review 1999,* Energy Information Administration, www.eia.doe.gov/fuelrenewables.html (September 20, 2000).

28. "Underwater Gold," www.questacon.edu.au/innovaus/c4s4_004.html (September 21, 2000); "Stacks of Treasures," *Sydney Morning Herald,* June 4, 1999, www.smh.com.au/news/9906/04/features/features1.html (September 21/2000); "Namibian Minerals Corporation," *MBendi Profile,* www.mbendi.co.za/orgs/cbi7.htm (September 21, 2000); and "NAMCO—Exploiting Profitable Diamond Niche," *Bull and Bear Financial Reporter,* www.thebullandbear.com/bb-reporter/bbfr-archive/nameco-1.html (September 21, 2000).

29. "World's First Gasoline-to-Fuel Cell Power Demonstration," *Technical Accomplishments—Fuel Cells,* USCAR, www.uscar.org/pngv/technical/gasoline.htm (September 23, 2000); "PNGV," *USCAR,* www.uscar.org/pngn/index.htm (September 23, 2000); and "Who Is USCAR?" *USCAR,* www.uscar.org/uscar/whois.htm (September 23, 2000).

30. "Brazil Balks at International Pressure," *The Wall Street Journal,* February 13, 1989, p. A7B.

31. "Luxury, Calm, and Speed: It's the Chunnel Train," *Business Week,* November 14, 1994, p. 143; and "On the Right Track," *International Management,* July–August 1994, p. 19.

32. "Majestic Bridge Links More Than Nation," *The Wall Street Journal Europe,* May 26–27, 2000, p. 5; "Sweden's Ice Age Comes to an End," *Financial Times,* June 24–25, 2000, p. 9; and "Scandinavia Linked to Rest of Europe," *Dawn-International,* www.dawn.com/2000/07/04/int10.htm (September 24, 2000).

33. "Union Carbide, India Reach $470 Million Settlement," *The Wall Street Journal,* February 15, 1989, p. B12.

34. "Union Carbide Sued in U.S. for 1984 Bophal Gas Release," *Corporate Watch,* www.corpwatch.org/trac/bhopal/lawsuit.html (September 24, 2000).

35. "World's Worst Nuclear Disaster," www.tiac.net/users/chernobl/WWND.html (December 31, 1997).

36. "Cold Comfort for Ukraine in Shutdown of Chernobyl," *The Oregonian,* December 15, 2000, p. A3.

37. "Alaska Oil Spill," *Management Review,* April 1990, pp. 13–14.

38. "Exxon Is Told to Pay $5 Billion for Valdez Spill," *The Wall Street Journal,* September 19, 1994, p. A2.

39. "Lakes of Spilled Oil Plunge Kuwait into Ever-Deeper Mess," *The Wall Street Journal,* August 12, 1991, p. A8.

40. "Persian Gulf War Leaves Behind Ecologically Ravaged Landscape," *San Antonio Express-News,* November 12, 1994, p. 9A.

41. "Deadly Cyanide Spill in Tisa River," *Halifax Chronical Herald,* February 14, 2000, www.canoe.ca/AllAboutCanoesNewsFeb00/14_spill.html (September 24, 2000); and "Romanian Cyanide Spill Poisons Danube Region," February 13, 2000, www.forests.org/archives/europe/romcyspi.htm (September 24, 2000).

42. "Anderson Reflects on Managing Bhopal," *Industry Week,* October 13, 1986, p. 21.

[Chapter 9]

1. "How to Win Friends and Influence Clients," *The European,* January 21–27, 1994, p. 11.

2. I. Brady and B. Isaac, *A Reader in Cultural Change,* vol. 1 (Cambridge, MA: Schenkman Publishing, 1975), p. x.

3. V. Barnouw, *An Introduction to Anthropology* (Homewood, IL: Dorsey Press, 1975), p. 5.

4. "Cultural Traits," *Future Culture,* www.wepworld.com/future/tcoc.htm (January 2, 1998).

5. Vern Terpstra and K. David, *The Cultural Environment of International Business* (Cincinnati: South-Western Publishing, 1985), p. 7.

6. E. T. Hall, *Beyond Culture* (Garden City, NY: Doubleday, 1977), p. 54.

7. "Make It Simple," *Business Week,* September 9, 1996, pp. 96–104; "P&G Viewed China as a National Market and Is Conquering It," *The Wall Street Journal,* September 12, 1995, p. A1; "P&G Rewrites the Marketing Rules," *Fortune,* November 6, 1989, pp. 34–46; and "After Early Stumbles, P&G Is Making Inroads Overseas," *The Wall Street Journal,* February 6, 1989, p. B1.

8. "P&G's Joy Makes an Unlikely Splash in Japan," *The Wall Street Journal,* December 12, 1997, p. B1.

9. "Monsieur Mickey," *Time,* March 25, 1991, pp. 48–49.

10. "Crème de la Crème, Sans MBA," *Financial Times,* December 29, 1997, p. 9.

11. "National versus Corporate Implications for Human Resource Management," *Human Resource Management,* Summer 1988, pp. 232–45.

12. One of the writers installed in a Spanish factory new production equipment that was to replace old but still serviceable machinery. Before leaving for a week's work in Madrid, he tested the equipment, trained some workers to use it, and advised the supervisor that it was ready. On his return, he was surprised to find that the new equipment was not being used. The supervisor explained that the old machinery was working well and he didn't want to "disrupt production." Actually, the new equipment was easier to use and would greatly increase output. Realizing that drastic action was called for, the writer grabbed a sledgehammer and made a token effort to destroy the old equipment. Only then did the supervisor get the message. Admittedly, the action was unorthodox, but it did bring immediate results. Not wanting to replace a still serviceable object with a new object, even when the new object is superior, is a common attitude in many countries.

13. "Mouse Trap," *The Wall Street Journal,* March 10, 1994, p. A12.

14. This classification depends in part on M. J. Herskovits, *Man and His Works* (New York: Alfred A. Knopf, 1952), p. 634. It was embellished by anthropologists at the University of South Alabama.

15. "Nike Recalls Shoes Bearing Logo That Muslims Found Offensive," *The Oregonian,* June 25, 1997, p. A18.

16. Anita Snow, "Ad Featuring 'Che' Guevara Sparks Furor," *The Monitor,* August 10, 2000, p. 8a.

17. Herskovits, *Man and His Works,* p. 414.

18. "Cultural Factors," *Business Travel Abroad,* http://sys1.tpusa.com/dir01/basicgui/guide08.html (January 6, 1998).

19. "The Middle East Mirage," *International Management,* April 1989, p. 21.

20. Sanjyot P. Dunung, *Doing Business in Asia: The Complete Guide* (New York: Lexington Books, 1995).

21. "Middle East Mirage," p. 23.

22. "Revolution in Mexico City: The One-Hour Lunch," *International Herald Tribune,* October 20, 1999, p. 14.

23. "Boom Times Erode Spain's Siesta Time," *The Oregonian,* December 26, 1999, p. A24.

24. Thomas E. Maher and Yim Yu Wong, "The Impact of Cultural Differences on the Growing Tensions between Japan and the United States," *SAM Advanced Management Journal,* Winter 1994, p. 45.

25. "German View: You Americans Work Too Hard—and for What?" *The Wall Street Journal,* July 14, 1994, p. B1.

26. "Average Annual Hours in Manufacturing, 12 Countries, 1950–1996," *Foreign Labor Statistics,* http://stats.bls.gov/news.release/prod4.t06.htm (January 7, 1998); "Working Hours per Full Working Week," *Japan 1997* (Tokyo: Keizai Koho Center, 1997), p. 97; and "Hours of Actual Work per Month," Japan Ministry of Labor, jin.jcic.or.jp/stats/09LAB41.html.

27. It is difficult to translate adequately the connotations of the two words. No one proudly says he is an *obrero* even if he earns more than an *empleado* who is a file clerk.

28. "How the Japanese Are Changing," *Fortune,* Pacific Rim, 1990, pp. 15–22.

29. Samia Nakhoul, "Born to Be Untouchable," *The Financial Times,* July 22–23, 2000, pp. I, III.

30. Pravin K. Shah, "Religions of India," *Jain BBS Email Bulletin,* August 1994, http://SunSITE.sut.ac.jp.pub/academic/rel...dia/jain/world_religions/ (June 6, 1997); and "History and Practices," *Sikhism in Brief,* www.sikhs.org/summary.htm (March 16, 2001).

31. "Taoism," *Chinese Religions,* www.gio.gov.tw/info/yearbook/f_html/ch25_2.html#ch25_0 (February 9, 1997).

32. Minda Zetlin, "Feng Shui: Smart Business or Superstition?" *Management Review,* August 1995, pp. 26–27.

33. "Children of the Islamic Revolution: A Survey of Iran," *The Economist,* January 18, 1997, pp. 1–15.

34. "World Wire," *The Wall Street Journal,* January 10, 1995, p. A17.

35. "Iran, Iraq Engage in Power Struggle to Select Spiritual Leader of Shiites," *The Wall Street Journal,* February 11, 1994, p. A12.

36. "Malaysian Malady: When the Spirit Hits, a Scapegoat Suffers," *The Wall Street Journal,* March 3, 1980, p. 1.

37. "Cummins Joins Fiat in $300m Engine Venture," *Financial Times,* May 2, 1996, p. 1; and "Compaq to Shift Some Computer Output to Its Houston Facility from Singapore," *The Wall Street Journal,* February 25, 1994, p. B4.

38. Ronald F. Smith, "Appropriate Technology Transfer," http://members.tripod.com/~Appropriatetech/Appropriate_Technology_Transfer (January 8, 1998); and "Where Technology Is the Appropriate Word," *The Economist,* April 18, 1987, p. 83.

39. Smith, "Appropriate Technology," p. 2; and "How to Sell Soap in India," *The Economist,* September 10, 1988, p. 82.

40. Jennifer W. Spencer, "Knowledge Flows in the Global Innovation System: Do U.S. Firms Share More Scientific Knowledge Than Their Japanese Rivals?" *Journal of International Business Studies,* Third Quarter 2000, pp. 521–30.

41. "Programme on Transnational Corporations," *World Investment Report 1993* (New York: United Nations, 1993), p. 85.

42. "The Internet Economy Indicators," www.internetindicators.com/key_findings_june_00.html.

43. Joseph Coleman, "Liquor Stores Phasing Out Beer Vending Machines," *The McAllen Monitor,* June 2, 2000, p. 6A.

44. "Indicators on Literacy," United Nations, 1997, www.un.org/Depts/unsd/social/literacy.htm (December 15, 1997).

45. "Let Open Doors Swing Both Ways," *The Wall Street Journal,* June 15, 1988, p. 12.

46. "Costly Brain Drain," *Development Forum* (Geneva: United Nations, March 1982), p. 12.

47. *Science and Engineering Indicators—2000,* Appendix Table 3-23, www.nsf.gov/sbe/srs/seind00/start.htm.

48. "Migration of Foreign Scientists and Engineers to the United States," http://econ.bu/ied/saesum.htm (January 10, 1998); "Immigrant Scientists, Engineers, and Technicians, 1993," www.nsf.gov/sbe/srs/nsf96322/nsf96322.htm#cht3 (January 11, 1998); and "The Arab Brain Drain," *Arab View,* www.arab.net/arabview/articles/tash9.html (January 3, 1998).

49. "India Seeks to Reverse Its Brain Drain," *Financial Times,* June 27, 1996, p. 4; and "Return of the Natives," *The Wall Street Journal,* May 24, 1993, p. R14.

50. "Reverse Brain Drain," www.gyaid.org/english/braind.htm (January 3, 1998); and "Reverse Brain Drain Association," www.nectec.or.th/users/pong/RBD/purpose.html (January 3, 1998).

51. "What's Worrying the Swiss?" *Bulletin* (Zurich: Crédit Suisse, April 1988), pp. 4–5.

52. "Do the Swiss Want to Join the EU After All?" *Bulletin* (Zurich: Crédit Suisse, January 1955), pp. 10–12.

53. Clare Nullis, "Swiss Divided on Language Issues for Their Children," *The Monitor,* November 4, 2000, p. 5A.

54. "Euro-Tongues Wag in English," *The Economist,* October 25, 1997, p. 60; and "Business Favors English and German," *International Herald Tribune,* March 19, 1997, p. 11.

55. "Pulling Down the Language Barrier," *International Management,* July–August 1994, p. 42.

56. "Why Speaking English Is No Longer Enough," *International Management,* November 1986, p. 42.

57. This mistake was caught before it was published locally, but an incident happened to one of the writers, newly arrived in Brazil, that did go all over the country. The ad manager, a Brazilian, brought him a campaign emphasizing that car owners should maintain 24 pounds per square inch in their tires to get maximum wear. To really get the point across, life-size figures of a tire company salesman were made up, with the name of the company and a large "24" printed across his chest. Care was taken to get these figures out to the dealers, who were to set them up on a "D day." The writer, sitting in his São Paulo office, proud of the unusually good coordina-

tion of the campaign, began receiving calls from competitors asking what type of people worked in his company. Over the laughter came the message—24 in Brazilian Portuguese means homosexual.

58. "French Watchdogs Seek to Limit English Web Sites," *The Mexico City News,* January 8, 1997, p. 32; and "French Lobby Loses Case," *Financial Times,* June 10, 1997, p. 2.

59. "The Coming Global Tongue," *The Economist,* December 21, 1996, pp. 75–78.

60. "Wal-Mart Again Runs into Language-Law Trouble," *The Wall Street Journal,* June 24, 1994, p. A4.

61. "Well, Excuse Moi! English Suffers Kick in Derriere," *The Wall Street Journal,* February 24, 1994, p. A12; and "Firm Cultural Ownership Rules Wanted by Minister but Not Cabinet," *Vancouver (Canada) Sun,* April 30, 1994, p. B12.

62. "A Little Bad English Goes a Long Way in Japan's Boutiques," *The Wall Street Journal,* May 5, 1993, p. A1.

63. "Gestures Around the World," www.webofculture.com/refs/gestures.html (March 19, 2001).

64. Gillian Tett, "Mori Gaffe May Hit Ruling Party's Poll Hopes," *The Financial Times,* June 9, 2000, p. 16.

65. E. T. Hall, *The Hidden Dimension* (Garden City, NY: Doubleday, 1969), pp. 134–35.

66. One of the writers, who lived in Latin America for 15 years, was surprised to read this statement in *The Silent Language in Overseas Business* by E. T. Hall. His Mexican wife, who had lived on both sides of the border, absolutely refuted it, so when he went to Ecuador as a consultant, he was careful to observe conversational distances. In no instance did he note any appreciable difference.

67. "A Global Guide to Gift Giving," *Los Angeles Times,* December 1, 1993, p. D4; and Roger Axtel, ed., *Do's and Taboos Around the World,* 2nd ed. (New York: John Wiley & Sons, 1990), pp. 113–47.

68. Neil H. Jacoby, Peter Nehemkis, and Richard Eells, *Bribery and Extortion in World Business* (New York: Macmillan, 1977), pp. 174–75.

69. The 1988 amendment to the Foreign Corrupt Practices Act specifies permissible payments. www.usdoj.gov/criminal/fraud/fcpa (March 19, 2001).

70. "Transparency International," www.transparency.de/ (January 3, 1998).

71. "Transparency International Publishes 1997 Corruption Perception Index," www.transparency.de/press/1997.31.7.cpi.html (August 4, 1997).

72. Herskovits, *Man and His Works,* p. 303.

73. Geert Hofstede, "Cultural Dimensions in Management and Planning," *Asia Pacific Journal of Management,* January 1984, p. 83.

74. Ibid., p. 83.

75. Lisa Hoecklin, *Managing Cultural Differences* (Wokingham, England: Addison-Wesley Publishing, 1995), pp. 28–30.

76. Ibid., p. 31.

77. Rose Knotts and Sheryann Tomlin, "A Comparison of TQM Practices in U.S. and Mexican Companies," *Production and Inventory Management Journal,* First Quarter, 1994, p. 54.

78. Hofstede, p. 85.

79. Hoecklin, pp. 31–32.

80. Ibid., pp. 31 and 36.

81. Hofstede, pp. 81 and 84.

[Chapter 10]

1. Ian Brownlie, *Principles of Public International Law* (Oxford, England: Oxford University Press, 1966), pp. 435–36.

2. "Why Planned Economies Fail," *The Economist,* June 25, 1988, p. 67. See also "Wounded Pride: Why Communism Fell," *The Economist,* May 25, 1991, pp. 98–99.

3. Jack Lowenstein, "Ready to Join the Big League?" *Euromoney,* October 1990, pp. 66–73.

4. Roman Rollnick and Dierdre Mooney, "Le Pen on Long March to Paris," *The European,* February 13–19, 1997, p. 3.

5. "Europe Wheels to the Right," *The Economist,* May 10, 1997, p. 45.

6. "France's Fading Reds," *The Economist,* May 10, 1997, p. 47.

7. *The Right Guide,* 4th ed. (Ann Arbor, MI: Economics America, 2000); and *The Left Guide,* 3rd ed. (Ann Arbor, MI: Economics America, 2001).

8. Richard L. Holman, "EC Widens Business Control," *The Wall Street Journal,* July 25, 1991, p. A10.

9. "Thatcher's Sales," *Business Week,* December 10, 1990, p. 26.

10. Jill Leovy, "Lockheed Looks to Expand Its Airport Business," *Los Angeles Times,* May 31, 1994, pp. D1, 6.

11. Hilary Clarke, "Europe Flies Its Airport Revolution to the World," *The European,* May 22–28, 1997, p. 15.

12. Martin Dickson, "America's Sale of the Century," *Financial Times,* June 1, 1992, p. 12.

13. Frederick Studemann, "German Postal Sell-Off Nearer as Parties Agree," *The European,* February 11–17, 1994, p. 16.

14. Roger Matthews, "Mozambique Brings in the British," *Financial Times,* June 17, 1997, p. 9.

15. Kathy Chen, "Cracking Open the Door," *The Asian Wall Street Journal,* April 14, 1997, p. 5.

16. "Going Private," *The Economist,* December 23, 1999, p. 38.

17. Gerhard Pohl, Robert Anderson, Stijn Claessens, and Simeon Djankov, "Privatisation and Restructuring in Central and Eastern Europe," *World Bank Technical Paper No. 386* (Washington, DC: World Bank, June 1997); and Kevin Done, "Europe's Privatisation Fast Track," *Financial Times,* July 4, 1997, p. 10.

18. Chris Butler, "Privatisation Shares Begin to Perform," *The European,* May 1–7, 1997, p. 25.

19. Clarke, "Europe Flies."

20. Gekko, "Random Walk: Wall Street," *National Review,* June 27, 1994, p. 26.

21. Virginia Marsh and Shawn Dorman, "Church Groups Catch the Privatization Spirit," *Financial Times,* January 8–9, 2000, p. 3.

22. John Lancaster, "U.S. Arms Sales in Gulf Risk Being Eroded by China and Others," *International Herald Tribune,* July 17, 1997, p. 6.

23. James Phillips and James H. Anderson, "International Terrorism: Containing and Defeating Terrorist Threats," *Issues 2000,* the Heritage Foundation, Washington, DC, August 2000.

24. "The Price of Paying Ransoms," *The Economist,* September 2, 2000, p. 17.

25. "Peru: Release Leads to Diplomatic Row," *Bangkok Post,* December 27, 1996, p. 9.

26. Jose de Cordoba, Thomas T. Vogel Jr., and Matt Moffett, "Peru's

Hostage Rescue: A Study in Counter-Terrorism," *The Wall Street Journal,* April 24, 1997, p. A14.

27. Sue Zesiger, "Freeze," *Fortune,* April 28, 1997, pp. 417–20.

28. Michael Bond, "Europe Alert over Threat of Nuclear Terrorism," *The European,* March 10–24, 1994, pp. 1 and 2.

29. Phillips and Anderson, "International Terrorism."

30. Jonathan Friedland, "High Growth Gains New Meaning in Bolivia," *The Wall Street Journal,* December 6, 1996, p. A12.

31. Sally Bowen, "Dream of Port Kickstarts Bolivian Soybean Boom," *Financial Times,* November 20, 1996, p. 5.

32. Sally Bowen, "Bolivia's Pensioners See Benefit of Sell-Offs," *Financial Times,* May 6, 1997, p. 8.

33. Sally Bowen, "Haggling Ahead in Bolivia Poll," *Financial Times,* May 31–June 1, 1997, p. 3.

34. David Wessel, "Flow of Capital to Developing Nations Surges Even as Aid to Poorest Shrinks," *The Wall Street Journal,* March 24, 1997, p. A5.

35. http://www.duke/edu/~charvey/Country_risk/pol/pol.htm; and http://www.polrisk.com/products.htm.

36. "Eastern Europe: New DB-WEB Illustrates Credit Risk," *Deutsche Morgan Grenfell: Economics,* April 28, 1997, pp. 15–18.

37. "Global Investing: The Game of Risk," *The Wall Street Journal,* June 26, 1997, pp. R1–18.

[Chapter 11]

1. Jack Kemp, "Greenspan Is Right: Abolish Capital Gains Taxes," *The Wall Street Journal,* February 24, 1997, p. A22.

2. George Graham, "UK Still Unhappy with California Tax Proposals" and "Unitary v. Water's Edge: Seeking a Company Tax Deal, *Financial Times,* August 21–22, 1993, p. 2.

3. Chris Endean, "Italians Urged to Stop Tax-Dodging Friends," *The European,* June 2, 1991, p. 4.

4. Madelaine Drohan, "The Fine Art of Avoiding Bewildering Italian Taxes," *The Globe and Mail,* September 28, 1996, p. D4.

5. Jonathan Schwarz, "Stimuli for Freer Trade," *Financial Times,* May 20, 1994, p. II.

6. "The Disappearing Taxpayer," *The Economist,* May 31, 1997, p. 15; and "Disappearing Taxes," *The Economist,* May 31, 1997, pp. 21–23.

7. Richard L. Holman, "EC Antitrust Efforts Boosted," *The Wall Street Journal,* March 20, 1991, p. A17; and "EC Court Reinforces Commission's Antitrust Clout," *Eurecom,* April 1991, p. 1.

8. Andrew Hill, "Predatory Pricing Judgment Confirmed," *Financial Times,* July 5, 1991, p. 2.

9. Andrew Hill, "Tetra Pak: Swiss Precision in Seeing Off Its Competitors," *Financial Times,* July 21, 1991, p. 2; and Martin Du Bois and Brian Coleman, "EC Blocks Sale of a Boeing Unit to French-Italian Joint Venture," *The Wall Street Journal,* October 3, 1991, p. A14.

10. Emma Tucker, "Price-Fixing Cartel Given Record Fine by Brussels," *Financial Times,* July 14, 1994, pp. 1, 18.

11. *The Economist,* June 9, 1979, pp. 91–92.

12. For example, see *Continental Ore Co. v. Union Carbide & Carbon Corp.,* 370 U.S. 690 (1962); *Timberline Lumber Co. v. Bank of America,* 549 F.2d 597 (9th Cir. 1976); and *United States v. Aluminum Co. of America,* 148 F.2d 416 (2d Cir. 1945).

13. Jeff Cole and Helene Cooper, "U.S., EU Open Aircraft-Subsidy Talks as Europe Weighs Status of Boeing Deal," *The Wall Street Journal,* April 28, 1997, p. A20.

14. "Brussels Clears AOL–Time Warner Merger," *Financial Times,* October 12, 2000, p. 24.

15. John R. Wilke, "U.S. Court Rules Antitrust Laws Apply to Foreigners," *The Wall Street Journal,* March 19, 1997, p. B6.

16. "Japan's Fair Trade Commission, Pussycat," *The Economist,* October 23, 1993, pp. 85–86.

17. "U.S. Endorses a Global Approach to Antitrust," *The Wall Street Journal,* September 15, 2000, p. A15; and "Call to Align Global Policy on Competition," *Financial Times,* September 15, 2000, p. 6.

18. "Plan for Global Insolvency Accord," *Financial Times,* October 26, 2000, p. 4.

19. Thomas G. Donlan, "Not So Free Trade: U.S. Preaches What It Doesn't Always Practice," *Barron's,* June 27, 1988, pp. 70–71.

20. "The American Car Industry's Own Goal," *The Economist,* February 6, 1988, p. 69. For a good discussion of protectionism, see Robert Z. Lawrence and Robert E. Litan, "Why Protectionism Doesn't Pay," *Harvard Business Review,* May–June 1987, pp. 60–67.

21. Sandra N. Hurd and Frances E. Zollers, "Desperately Seeking Harmony: The European Community's Search for Uniformity in Product Liability Law," *American Business Law Journal 30* (1992) pp. 35–68.

22. Ibid.

23. "Product Liability," *The Economist,* May 25, 1996, p. 67; and Katherine Dowling, "Wide-Ranging Suits against Manufacturers May Keep Lifesaving Medical Devices on the Shelf and Out of Reach," *The Wall Street Journal,* August 19, 1997, p. A4.

24. David R. Olmos, "Dow Chemical Dealt Defeat in Important Trial," *Los Angeles Times,* August 19, 1997, pp. A1, 19.

25. Barbara Crutchfield George, "The Legislative Process of the European Union: Its Social and Cultural Dimension," *Rocky Mountain Regional Academy of Legal Studies in Business Conference,* September 16, 1994.

26. Barbara Crutchfield George and Linda McCallister, "The Effect of Cultural Attitudes on Product Liability Laws," *Southwestern Association of Administrative Disciplines,* March 4, 1993.

27. Carolyn Lochhead, "Strict Liability Causing Firms to Give up on Promising Ideas," *The Washington Times,* August 22, 1988, p. B5.

28. Steven P. Galante, "American Insurance Crisis Begins to Hurt European Firms with Operations Here," *The Wall Street Journal,* December 29, 1985, p. 12; and Patrick Cockburn, "The Tricky Waters of U.S. Liability Insurance," *Financial Times,* March 29, 1990, p. 21.

29. Tom Dunkel, "Saving Hapless Americans Abroad," *Insight,* March 26, 1990, pp. 47–49.

30. Mark A. Goldstein, "The UN Sales Convention," *Business America,* November 21, 1988, pp. 12–13.

31. Lucy Kellaway, "EC Legal Convention on Contracts Approved," *Financial Times,* January 30, 1991, p. 7.

32. "Firms Specify Arbitration for International Fights," *The Wall Street Journal,* August 4, 1997, p. A8.

33. Michael Moser, "A Good Place to Make Peace," *Euromoney,* July 1991, special supplement, pp. 50–54.

34. A. H. Herman, "Growth in International Trade Law," *Financial Times,* March 30, 1989, p. 10.

35. Trade Promotion Coordinating Committee, "The National Export Strategy: Staying the Course," *Sixth Annual Report to the United States Congress,* October 1998.

36. Frances Williams, "GATT Joins Battle for Right to Protect," *Financial Times,* July 7, 1994, p. 7.

37. Alan Farnham, "Spy vs. Spy: Are Your Company's Secrets Safe?" *Fortune,* February 17, 1997, p. 136.

38. Erich Eichman, "Business and Intelligence," *The Wall Street Journal,* April 3, 1997, p. A16.

39. Sandra Smith, "Brand-Name Pirates Plunder Open Borders," *The European,* June 19–25, 1997, p. 4.

40. "When We Wear the Black Hats," *The Wall Street Journal,* March 22, 1990, p. A16.

41. Barbara Crutchfield George, "The U.S. Foreign Corrupt Practices Act: The Price Business Is Paying for the Unilateral Criminalization of Bribery," *International Journal of Management,* September 1987, pp. 391–402; and "Some Guidelines on Dealing with Graft," *Business International,* February 25, 1983, p. 62.

42. Wendell H. McCulloch Jr., interviews conducted in Europe during July and August 1995.

43. "Over the Border," *The Economist,* August 16, 1997, p. 36; land Paolo Mauro, "Why Worry about Corruption?" *Economic Issues 6,* International Monetary Fund, February 1997.

44. "The Arab League Boycott of Israel," www.ustr.gov/reports/nte/1996/arab.html.

45. *The Economist,* September 2, 1978, p. 101.

[Chapter 12]

1. American Immigration Lawyers Association, www.aila.org/about immigration.html.

2. INS, www.ins.usdoj.gov/graphics/aboutins/statistics/illegalalien/index.htm.

3. K. Ross Toole, *Montana: Uncommon Land* (Tulsa-University of Oklahoma Press, 1984), pp. 72–73.

4. Frances Williams, "150m Living in Foreign Countries," *Financial Times,* November 2, 2000, p. 6.

5. Bromwen Maddox, "UN Warns of World's Creaking Cradle," *Financial Times,* August 12, 1997, p. 6.

6. "Immigrant Assistance," *The Economist,* March 29, 1997, p. 28.

7. www.ailf.org/global/newecon.

8. 8 U.S.C. § 1184(g) (2000).

9. Leslie Earnest, "Tourism Firms Battle for Low-Skill Workers," *Arizona Republic,* November 18, 2000, p. D2.

10. Sharon Gaudin, "Solving the IT Labor Shortage," CNN.com, July 17, 2000.

11. Anthony Ramirez, "Making It," *The Wall Street Journal,* May 20, 1980, pp. 1, 27.

12. Blaine Harden and Jay Mathews, "New Mix Enlivens N.Y. Melting Pot," *The Washington Post,* May 26, 1997, pp. A1, 14.

13. Ibid.

14. Joseph Spiers, "Women Chill Out," *Fortune,* June 27, 1994, p. 20.

15. "Who's Producing Now?" *The Economist,* February 22, 1997, p. 87.

16. Michael C. Jensen, "A Revolution Only Markets Could Love," *The Wall Street Journal,* January 3, 1994, p. 6.

17. Gurcharan Das, "Indians Get Ahead," *The Wall Street Journal,* August 14, 1997, p. A12.

18. "India: Casteing Stones," *The Economist,* July 19, 1997, p. 38.

19. "Obituary: Sue Sumii," *The Economist,* July 5, 1997, p. 84.

20. Kasra Naji, "Taliban Ousts Bank That Lends to Women," *Financial Times,* September 16, 1997, p. 6.

21. John Thor Dahlburg, "Closing the Education Gap for Women," *Los Angeles Times,* April 12, 1994, pp. H1 and 5.

22. Ethan Bronner, "Summit Seeks End to Female Mutilation," *Press Telegram,* September 11, 1994, pp. A1 and 4.

23. "Women and Girls: Education, Not Discrimination," *OECD Observer* (electronic edition), November 3, 2000.

24. Catalyst, *Passport to Opportunity: U.S. Women in Global Business,* October 2000.

25. Joanne Cleaver, "The Top Twenty-Five Companies for Executive Women," *Working Woman,* December 2000–January 2001, pp. 58–60, 64–67.

26. "Friends, Koreans, Countrymen," *The Economist,* November 9, 1996, p. 41.

27. "China Bars Efforts to Unionize, Study Says," *The Wall Street Journal,* April 10, 1997, p. A10.

28. Everett M. Kassalow, *Trade Unions and Industrial Relations: An International Comparison* (New York: Random House, 1969).

29. David Shribman, "Politics: Big Labor Gets Its Act Together," *Fortune,* September 29, 1997, pp. 60, 64.

30. Aaron Bernstein, "Labor's Labors Aren't Lost," *Business Week,* November 27, 2000, p. 86.

31. Linda Grant, "Unhappy in Japan," *Fortune,* January 13, 1997, p. 142.

32. "Beer, Sandwiches and Statistics," *The Economist,* July 12, 1997, p. 70; and see "Labor Unions Still Struggle Worldwide," *Los Angeles Times,* November 4, 1997, p. D15.

33. "Trade-Unions: US-UK Alliance Signed," *Financial Times,* July 1, 1997, p. 10.

34. Stephen S. Golub, "International Labor Standards and International Trade," IMF Web site, www.imf.org; and see "Can Harmonized Labor Standards Boost Trade and Income?" *IMF Survey,* June 9, 1997, pp. 169, 179, 180.

35. Jesus Sanchez and Donald Wontat, "Chrysler to Drop Union President's Spot on Its Board," *Los Angeles Times,* March 14, 1991, p. D1.

36. "Europe Labour Isn't Working," *The Economist,* April 5, 1997, pp. 21–23.

37. Mark Porter, Stephanie Theobold, and Julie Read, "Abandoned," *The European,* August 7–13, 1997, pp. 8–12.

38. Douglas Lavin, "Tale of Two Job Markets: Why England Works, France Doesn't," *The Wall Street Journal,* August 7, 1997, p. A10; and see "The Great Job Massacre," *The European,* October 16–22, 1997, p. 5.

39. "German Jobs: Odd Men In," *The Economist,* June 14, 1997, pp. 71–72.

[Chapter 13]

1. Kenichi Ohmae, *Triad Power: The Coming Shape of Global Competition* (New York: Free Press, 1985).

2. Personal telephone interview with Saucony representative, January 20, 1997; "Nike's Lead: Just Follow It?" *Fortune,* September 8, 1997, p. 188; "Follow Nike's Footsteps to Find Asian Growth," *International Herald Tribune,* March 17, 1997, p. 13; "Chinese Symbol of 'Success,' " *International Herald Tribune,* February 28, 1997, p. 17; "The World Less Traveled," *The Oregonian,* December 1, 1996, p. D1; and "The Sole of a Company," *U.S. News & World Report,* April 22, 1996, p. 64.

3. "Competitiveness: Getting It Back," *Fortune,* April 27, 1987, pp. 217–23.

4. "Waiting for the Yen to Stop Pummeling the Profits," *Business Week,* June 1, 1987, pp. 58–59.

5. Council on Competitiveness, *Competitiveness Index 1996* (Washington, DC: Council on Competitiveness, 1996), p. vii.

6. OECD, "Policies for Industrial Development and Competitiveness," www.oecd.org/dsti/sti/industry/indcomp/prod/overview.htm (January 23, 1998).

7. *The World Competitiveness Yearbook* (Lausanne, Switzerland: International Institute for Management Development, 2000), www.imd.ch/wcy.ranking/ranking.cfm (April 25, 2000).

8. *The EU Economy: 2000 Review,* European Commission Economic and Financial Affairs Office, Luxembourg, europa.eu.int/comm./economy_finance/document/review/2000review.htm (December 3, 2000).

9. Ibid.

10. Michael E. Porter and Scott Stern, *The New Challenge to America's Prosperity: Findings from the Innovation Index* (Washington, DC: Council on Competitiveness, March 1999).

11. Ibid.

12. Ibid.

13. SET Statistics 1999, U.K. Office of Science and Technology, www.dti.gov.uk/ost/setstats/data/7/tab7_1.htm; and Michael E. Porter and Scott Stern, op. cit., p. 43.

14. Department of Labor, "Capital Spending Is Back Up," *Generating Productivity Growth,* September 10, 1996, www.dol.gov/dol/_sec/public/media/reports/grow.htm (January 24, 1998).

15. Marc Ballon, "U.S. High-Tech Jobs Going Abroad," *Los Angeles Times,* April 24, 2000, pp. C1, C4.

16. Porter and Stern, op. cit.

17. Ibid., p. 13.

18. Ibid., pp. 67–69.

19. U.S. Trade Representative, "Japan," *1997 National Trade Estimate on Foreign Trade Barriers,* www.ustr.gov/reports/nte/1997/japan/pdf (January 20, 1998).

20. *OECD Economic Outlook 68,* November 2000, Table I.2.

21. David K. Freedman, "Fakers' Paradise," *Forbes.com,* April 5, 1999, www.forbes.com/asap/1999/0405/048.html (December 2, 2000).

22. "This Is One Showdown the White House Can't Duck," *Business Week,* April 8, 1996, p. 52; U.S. Trade Representative, "People's Republic of China," *1997 National Trade Estimate on Foreign Trade Barriers,* www.ustr.gov/reports/nte/1997/china.pdf (January 20, 1998); and "Microsoft Says Raid in China Uncovered a Factory Counterfeiting Its Software," *International Herald Tribune,* May 1, 1996, p. 1.

23. Martin Wolf, "Risking a Hard Landing," *Financial Times,* December 6, 2000, p. 14.

24. "Airbus Subsidies Are Invisible to Radar," *The Wall Street Journal,* March 4, 1994, p. A7.

25. "A Boom Ends?" *The Economist,* January 17, 1998, p. 58; "Rivalry between Boeing, Airbus Takes New Direction," *The Wall Street Journal,* April 30, 1997, p. B4; and "Airbus Boasts Year of Record Orders," *Financial Times,* January 7, 1998, p. 6.

26. "EU Issues Green Paper on Lomé Convention," *AfricaNews,* November 22, 1997, www.africanews.org/atlarge/stories/19971122_feat.html (January 26, 1998); and "Special Issue on the Revised Lomé Convention," *The Courier,* January–February 1996, pp. 1–24.

27. "EU, ACP Meet for Lomé Talks," International Centre for Trade and Sustainable Development, www.ictsd.org/html/story1.15-02-99.htm (December 4, 2000); and "Trade-EU: WTO rules used to kill Lomé Convention, NGOs Say," www.oneworld.org/ips2/Oct99/13_20_055.html (December 8, 2000).

28. Office of the United States Trade Representative, "Generalized System of Preference Enhancements Benefits Sub-Saharan Africa," June 5, 1997, www.ustr.gov/releases/1997/06/97-52.pdf (January 20, 1998); and USTR, "Generalized System of Preferences—Frequently Asked Questions," April 5, 1996, www.ustr.gov/reports/gsp/faq.html (April 2, 1997).

29. OECD, "OECD in Figures," *The OECD Observer,* 1997 edition, pp. 60–61, www.oecd.org/publications/observer/figures/tm_e.htm.

30. "Business in Europe Survey," *The Economist,* November 23, 1996, pp. 1–16.

31. Porter and Stern, op. cit., pp. 33–37.

32. *The EU Economy: 2000 Review,* European Commission Economic and Financial Affairs Office, Luxembourg, europa.eu.int/comm./economy_finance/document/review/2000review.htm (December 3, 2000).

33. Ibid., pp. 20–21.

34. "1994 Manufacturing Futures Survey," *The Economist,* October 29, 1994, p. 74.

35. "France, Germany Must Cut More Jobs to Improve Efficiency, Report Suggests," *The Wall Street Journal,* March 14, 1997, p. 9A.

36. "What Ails Europe? A Surfeit of Rules, Study Says," *International Herald Tribune,* March 14, 1997, p. 13.

37. "Europe's Technology Gap Is Getting Scary," *Fortune,* March 17, 1997, pp. 26–27.

38. Pierre-Antoine Souchard, "Yahoo! Ordered to Limit French Use," *The Washington Post,* November 20, 2000, www.washingtonpost.com/wp-dyn/articles/A45727-2000Nov20.html (November 29, 2000).

39. "Is 2000 the Year of International E-Commerce?" *E-Commerce Times,* www.ecommercetimes.com/news/articles/991213-2.shtml (January 8, 2000).

40. "E-Commerce Discovers Europe," *International Tribune,* December 24–27, 1999, p. 15.

41. "Global 500," www.fortune.com/global500.

42. Porter and Stern, op. cit., pp. 33–37.

43. "Europe's Great Car War," *The Economist,* March 8, 1997, pp. 69–70.

44. *The EU Economy: 2000 Review,* European Commission Economic and

Financial Affairs Office, Luxembourg, europa.eu.int/comm./economy_finance/document/review/2000review.htm (December 3, 2000), p. 7; and *OECD Economic Outlook 68,* November 2000, Table I.4.

45. "European Business Bullish on Growth," *Financial Times,* November 11, 1999, p. 2.

46. "The Latest from Japan," *International Management,* March 1991, pp. 29–32.

47. "PC Makers Target Businesses in Europe," *The Wall Street Journal,* March 17, 1997, p. B9; and "Europe's Software Debacle," *The Economist,* November 12, 1994, pp. 37–38.

48. "Focus on Competitiveness," *Financial Times,* June 27, 1996, p. 11.

49. "South Korean Investment in Europe," *Financial Times,* October 6, 1997, p. 1.

50. "Korea Inc. Balks," *Business Week,* January 19, 1998, pp. 44–45.

51. "Asian Fallout Sets Region's New Challenge," *Financial Times,* January 22, 1998, p. 9.

52. *The EU Economy,* op. cit.

53. "Japan," *OECD Economic Outlook 68,* November 2000.

54. Ibid.

55. Porter and Stern, op. cit.

56. *JETRO White Paper on Foreign Direct Investment,* Tokyo: Japan External Trade Organization, 2000, p. 42.

57. Ibid., pp. 22–26.

58. David E. Sanger, "Japan's Bad Debt Is Now Estimated Near $1 Trillion," *New York Times,* July 30, 1998, pp. A1, 8.

59. *JETRO White Paper on Foreign Direct Investment* (Tokyo: Japan External Trade Organization, 1999).

60. JETRO, "The Large-Scale Retail Law," www.jetro.go.jp/Changing/2.html (June 16, 1997).

61. "Govt Must Press Ahead with Reforms," *The Yomiuri Report,* December 30, 1997, www.gwjapan.com/yomiuri/rptdy.html; and Toys " Я " Us, "Store Directory," www.toysrus.com/about_us/intl-stores.html (February 3, 1998).

62. "An Appropriate Corporate and Financial Strategy for Successfully Investing in the Japanese Market," *Business Economics,* July 1994, pp. 50–55; and "Learning from Japan," *Business Week,* January 27, 1992, pp. 52–60.

63. "Japanese Auto Makers Buy More U.S. Parts," *The Wall Street Journal,* August 24, 1993, p. A2.

64. "Great Asset Now Being Derided as Liability," *Financial Times,* December 17, 1999, p. 11; "Disintegration of the Keiretsu System," *Financial Times,* December 14, 1999, p. XXXIX; and "The Circle Is Broken," *Financial Times,* November 9, 1999, p. 14.

65. "The Cheap Buck Gives Japan a Yen for Asia," *Business Week,* May 23, 1994, p. 52.

66. "Inward Foreign Direct Investment," Japanese External Trade Organization, www.jetro.go.jp/ip/e/access/inward_foreign_direct_investment.html (November 12, 2000).

67. "Japanese Repeat," *Financial Times,* August 23, 1997, p. 6; and "Bailout of Asia Is Likely to Fail, as Perhaps It Should," *International Herald Tribune,* January 13, 1998, p. 8.

68. "What? Everyday Bargains? This Can't be Japan," *Business Week,* September 6, 1993, p. 41.

69. *JETRO White Paper on Foreign Direct Investment,* op. cit., Figure III–13.

70. Ibid.

71. "Making Inroads," *The Wall Street Journal,* April 15, 1994, p. A1.

72. "Dwindling Trade Surplus," *Trends in Japan,* www2.nttca.com:8010/infomofa/trends96/honbun/tj960901.html (February 6, 1998).

73. "Sanyo Shifting Production," *Japan Newsbriefs,* www.nb.pacifica.com/jnews/japannewsbriefs010396_460.shtml (February 6, 1998).

74. "Korea's Export Boom Is Hurting—and Helping—Japan," *Business Week,* August 8, 1994, p. 16.

75. "The Sun Rises in the East," *Global Competitor,* Spring 1994, pp. 27–31.

76. "Not so Fast," *The Economist,* January 18, 1997, p. 37; and "The Sun Rises in the East," p. 30.

77. "Special Report—Rebuilding Asia," *Business Week On-Line,* November 29, 1999, www.businessweek.com (November 22, 1999).

78. "The Death of Daewoo," *The Economist,* August 21, 1999, pp. 55–59.

79. "Special Report—Rebuilding Asia," *Business Week On-Line,* November 29, 1999, www.businessweek.com (November 22, 1999).

80. "Asia's Rollercoaster Rides," *The Economist,* October 21, 2000, www.economist.com/displayStory.cfm?Story_ID=398067, (November 5, 2000).

81. *JETRO White Paper on Foreign Direct Investment,* op. cit., p. 24.

82. Andrew Fisher, "Gap Widens between 'Haves' and 'Have-Nots,' " *Financial Times,* December 6, 2000, p. XXIX.

83. Ibid.

84. "From Crisis to Recovery in the Emerging Market Economies," *World Economic Outlook 1999* (Washington, DC: International Monetary Fund, 1999), pp. 54–57.

85. *International Trade Statistics 2000* (Geneva: World Trade Organization, 2000), p. 86.

86. *JETRO White Paper on Foreign Direct Investment,* op. cit., p. 22.

87. David H. Freedman, "Faker's Paradise," *Forbes.com,* April 5, 1999, www.forbes.com/asap/1999/0405/048.html (December 2, 2000).

88. Sathnam Sanghera, "Counterfeit Goods Cost EU $400bn," *Financial Times,* April 20, 2000, p. 3; and Freedman, "Faker's Paradise."

89. "Hong Kong Hit by Piracy," *Financial Times,* May 30, 2000, p. 8.

90. Eric Ellis, "Digital Underground," *Time,* May 29, 2000, www.cnn.com/ASIANOW/time/magazine/2000/0529/malaysia.piracy.html (June 6, 2000).

91. Freedman, "Faker's Paradise."

92. Ellis, "Digital Underground."

93. "Organized Crime and Product Counterfeiting," www.iacc.org/organized_crime.html (December 2, 2000).

94. "Copy to Come," *The Economist,* January 7, 1995, p. 51.

95. "A Case for Copying," *The Economist,* November 23, 1996, p. 73.

96. Anthony Kuhn and Tyler Marshall, "China's New Tune Encourages U.S. Entertainment Industry," *Los Angeles Times,* November 25, 2000, pp. C1, C3.

97. Richard McGregor, "China's Movie Pirates Turn to Home for New Cinema Plunder," *Financial Times,* November 20, 2000, p. 16.

98. "WARNING!" *Business Week,* June 10, 1996, pp. 84–87.

99. "A $5 Billion Dose That Doesn't Help," *The Economist,* May 2, 1992, pp. 85–86; and "A Really Nasty Business," *Business Week,* November 5, 1990, pp. 36–43.

100. Eric Ellis, "Digital underground," *Time,* May 29, 2000, www.cnn.com/ASIANOW/time/magazine/2000/0529/malaysia.piracy.html (June 6, 2000).

101. BSA, "BSA 1994 Software Piracy Estimates," www.livelinks.com/livelinks/bsa/94spe.html (February 8, 1998).

102. "GM Agreed to VW Pact to Avoid Further Costs, Risks," *The Wall Street Journal,* January 13, 1997, p. B4; and "VW 'Lucky' to Escape with $100m Pay-Out to GM," *Financial Times,* January 12, 1997, p. 2.

103. "Corporate Spies Feel a Sting," *Business Week,* July 14, 1997, pp. 75–77; and "For Pills, Not Projectiles," *The Economist,* July 12, 1997, p. 22.

104. "FBI Warns Companies to Beware of Espionage," *International Herald Tribune,* January 13, 1998, p. 3.

105. "French Suspected of Spying," *McAllen Monitor,* April 18, 1994, p. C1.

106. "The Lure of the Steal," *U.S. News & World Report,* March 4, 1996, pp. 45–48; and "Industrial Spies Come in for the Gold," *Business Mexico,* August 1994, p. 6.

107. Futures Group, "Ostriches and Eagles 1997," www.tfg.com/pubs/docs/O_EIII-97.html (January 30, 1998).

108. "George Smiley Joins the Firm," *Newsweek,* May 2, 1988, pp. 46–47.

109. "Still a Distant Second," *Across the Board,* November 1991, pp. 42–47.

110. "10 Steps to Best-Practices Benchmarking," *Quality Digest,* February 1996, pp. 23–28.

111. "What Ronald McDonald, Mickey Mouse Taught Nissan," *Business International,* February 22, 1993, pp. 57–58.

[Chapter 14]

1. For a discussion of strategy, see Michael E. Porter, "What Is Strategy?" *Harvard Business Review,* November–December, 1996, pp. 61–78.

2. Jay B. Barney, "Looking Inside for Competitive Advantage," *Academy of Management Executive,* 9(4): 49–61, 1995.

3. Wroe Alderson, *Dynamic Marketing Behavior* (Homewood, IL: Richard D. Irwin, 1965), pp. 75–97. In the late 1970s, McCarthy and other writers of "principles of marketing" texts discussed the use of transvection as a unit of analysis.

4. "Rethinking Vision and Mission," *Planning Review,* September–October 1994, pp. 9–11.

5. "Customer-Focuses Strategy," www.ford.com/finaninvest/stockholder/stock99/special_pg3.htm (December 12, 2000).

6. Du Pont, *Annual Report,* 1997; and *Du Pont Direction Statement,* http://www.dupont.com/corp/glb-company/statement.html (March 20, 1998).

7. "Company Information: About Amazon.com," www.iredge.com/IREdge/IREdge.asp?c=002239 (December 12, 2000).

8. "About McDonald's," www.mcdonalds.com/corporate/corp.html (December 12, 2000).

9. "Top Company Questions," www.Intel.com/intel/company/corp1.htm (December 12, 2000).

10. Goodyear Tire & Rubber, *Annual Report,* 1994, pp. 2–4.

11. "About 3M: Frequently Asked Questions," www.corporate-ir.net/ireye/ir_site.zhtml?ticker=MMM&script=1800 (December 12, 2000).

12. Goodyear Tire and Rubber.

13. "Using Quality Circles to Develop an Action Plan Required for Leading Organizations," *IM,* September–October 1992, pp. 8–10.

14. Intel, *Annual Report,* 1996, p. 1.

15. "Style and Strategy: New Metaphors, New Insights," *European Management Journal,* August 1996, p. 351.

16. "Many Multinationals Are Failing to Plan for All Contingencies," *Business Insurance,* November 6, 1995, p. 4.

17. "Managing the Management Tools," *Planning Review,* September–October 1994, pp. 20–24.

18. 3M, "Chairman's Letter," *3M Annual Report 1999,* p. 12.

19. "The New Breed of Strategic Planner," *Business Week,* September 19, 1984, p. 62.

20. "Strategic Planning," *Business Week,* August 26, 1996, pp. 46–52.

21. "The New Breed of Strategic Planner," p. 64.

22. Ibid., p. 66.

23. Alfred Chan, "As in Chess, Strategic Planning Is a Good Move," *Enterprise 50,* http://biztimes.asial.com/bizcentre/Enterprise50/plan9701.html. (March 19, 1998).

24. Andrew Campbell and Marcus Alexander, "What's Wrong with Strategy?" *Harvard Business Review,* November–December 1997, p. 46.

25. "20-20 Vision," *Global Scenarios,* www.shell.com/b/b2_03.html (March 15, 1998); and P. W. Beck, "Corporate Planning for an Uncertain Certain Future," *Long-Range Planning,* August 1982, p. 14.

26. Frederick W. Gluck, "A Fresh Look at Strategic Management," *Journal of Business Strategy,* Fall 1985, p. 6.

27. "To Our Shareholders," *ExxonMobil 1999 Annual Report,* www.exxonmobil.com/shareholder_publications/c_annual_99/c_shareholder.html (December 12, 2000).

28. "Global," *General Motors Annual Report 1999,* www.gm.com/company/investor_information/annual_reports/ar1999/global/index.htm (December 12, 2000).

29. "Ford to Focus on Regional Markets in Global Revamp," *Financial Times,* October 16–17, 1999, p. 1.

30. *Boeing Company 1999 Annual Report,* www.boeing.com/companyoffices/financial/finreports/annual/99annualreport/board.html (December 12, 2000).

31. "Organization," www.m-kagaku.co.jp/english/aboutmcc/corp/orgnz.htm (December 12, 2000).

32. "The Myth of the Horizontal Organization," *Canadian Business Review,* Winter 1994, pp. 28–31; and "Seven Organizational Alternatives for MNCs in the 1990s," *Business International,* February 13, 1989, p. 46.

33. "Shell Moves to Think Globally, Act Locally," *Company Overview,* www.shellchemicals.com/CMM/WEB/GLOBCHEM.NSF/global/article1.htm (March 15, 1998); and Christopher Barlett and Sumantra Goshal, *Transnational Management,* 2nd ed. (Burr Ridge, IL: Richard D. Irwin, 1995), p. 352.

34. Arthur A. Thompson and A. J. Strickland, *Crafting and Implementing Strategy,* 6th ed. (Burr Ridge, IL: Richard D. Irwin, 1995), p. 276.

35. "Prised out of its Shell," *Financial Times,* February 16, 1996, p. 11; and "Barons Swept out of Fiefdoms," *Financial Times,* March 30, 1995, p. 15.

36. "Daft Shakes Up Coke, Pushing Local Decisions," *International Herald Tribune,* February 7, 2000, p. 13.

37. "The Coca Cola Company Announces Major Organizational Realignment," Press Release, www.thecoca-colacompany.com/news/NewsDetail3.asp?Newskey=165 (February 8, 2000).

38. "Global Firms Are Too Big to Act Like Businesses," *The Oregonian,* January 30, 2000, p. D1.

39. "The Question Is Not If, but When," *Financial Times,* June 14, 1997, p. XII.

40. "Executives Unprepared for Managing Virtual Corporations," *Andersen Consulting Web Site,* May 27, 1997, www.ac.com/topstories/currnews/ts_97-0527.html (February 20, 1998).

41. "Press Releases," *Nokia Web Site,* www.nokia.com/news/news_htmls (March 25, 1998); "Turn Your Company into a Cybercorp," *Computerworld,* October 9, 1995, p. 32; *Nokia Corporation Annual Report 1999,* p. 3; and "Nokia Corporation Revenue History," E-Trade Quotes and Research, www.etrade.com (December 12, 2000).

42. "Closer to the Customer, Closer to the Goal," *Andersen Consulting Outlook,* www.ac.com/outlook/o_clos_1.html (February 20, 1998); and "The Horizontal Corporation," *Business Week,* December 20, 1993, pp. 76–81.

43. "Mapping Is the Key to Going Horizontal," *HCI Consulting,* www.hci.com.au/hcisite/mappingisthe.htm (March 25, 1998); and "Jack Welch Reinvents General Electric Again," *The Economist,* March 30, 1991, p. 59.

44. Daniel Robey and Carol A. Sales, *Designing Organizations,* 4th ed. (Burr Ridge, IL: Richard D. Irwin, 1994), Chapter 16.

45. "Is Big Still Good?" *Fortune,* April 20, 1992, p. 52.

46. Ibid., p. 60.

47. Louis Kehoe, "Radical Change of IBM Format," *Financial Times,* November 21, 1991, p. 27.

48. Richard L. Hudson and Joann S. Lublin, "Power at Multinationals Shifts to Home Office," *The Wall Street Journal,* September 9, 1994, pp. B1, B3.

49. Teresa Watanabe, "IRS Seeks More Power to Probe Foreign Firms," *Los Angeles Times,* February 22, 1991, pp. D1, D12.

50. Richard L. Hudson, ". . . Power . . . ," *The Wall Street Journal,* September 9, 1994, p. B1.

51. Richard Thomas Cupitt, "Foreign Political Risk Assessment," *The International Trade Journal,* Summer 1990, pp. 341–56.

52. Richard F. Janssen, "U.S. Lenders Taking New Looks at Risks from Political, Social Upheavals Abroad," *The Wall Street Journal,* March 13, 1979, p. 7.

53. William Bridges, "The End of the Job," *Fortune,* September 19, 1994, pp. 62–74.

54. "Mess.com," *The Economist,* October 15, 1994, p. 82.

55. Rick Tetzeli, "Managing in a World out of Control," *Fortune,* September 5, 1994, p. 111.

[Chapter 15]

1. A good introduction to scanning is Chun Wei Choo, "The Art of Scanning the Environment," *ASIS Bulletin,* www.asis.org/Bulletin/Feb-99/choo.html (November 20, 2000).

2. U.S. Census Bureau, "FT900—U.S. International Trade in Goods and Services," www.census.gov/foreign-trade.press.html (November 17, 2000).

3. Virtually all governments have barriers to foreign direct investment and at the same time offer a variety of incentives to potential foreign investors. For example, Mexico currently restricts foreign investment in the petroleum industry. For a recent review, see Steven Globerman and Daniel M. Shapiro, "The Impact of Government Policies on Foreign Direct Investment: The Canadian Experience," *Journal of International Business Studies,* Third Quarter 1999, pp. 513–32.

4. "CeBIT 2001," www.cebit.de/ (April 2, 2001); and "CeBit 2000 Focuses on the Internet," *Financial Times,* Feb. 2, 200, p. XX.

5. "REC—More about Exhibitions," www.reedexpo.com/exhibitions.html (February 14, 1998).

6. Secondary data and sometimes primary data will be gathered on a field trip, but the visitor rarely has the time or ability to conduct a complete field study.

7. "New Record," *The European,* August 2–4, 1991, p. 11.

8. "Third World Research is Difficult, but It's Possible," *Marketing News,* August 26, 1997, p. 51.

9. "Data Collection Methods Hold Key to Research in Mexico," *Marketing Today,* April 1994, p. 28.

10. Emiko Terazano, "A Wave of Phone Surfing," *Financial Times,* February 11, 2000, p. 8.

11. This approach was inspired by Masaaki Kotabe and Kristiaan Helsen, *Global Marketing Management* (New York: Wiley, 2001), p. 219.

[Chapter 16]

1. T. C. Melewar and John Saunders, "International Corporate Visual Identity: Standardization or Localization?" *Journal of International Business Studies,* Third Quarter 1999, pp. 583–98.

2. Douglas Daft, "Back to Classic Coke," *Financial Times,* March 27, 2000, p. 16.

3. "Multinational, Not Global," *The Economist,* December 24, 1988, p. 99; and "Nestle Shows How to Gobble Markets," *Fortune,* January 16, 1989, p. 75.

4. One of the authors went to pick up his car in a repair shop and asked the mechanic whether he had test-driven it after finishing the repair. Much to his surprise, the mechanic answered that he had not—he didn't know how to drive!

5. When General Tire was an American company, it used to do a good business in the United States selling tires for antique cars. The company imported the tires from its foreign subsidiaries, where they were in regular production to supply the old cars still on the road in those countries.

6. "New Andersen Consulting Executive Team Reflects Strong Growth Worldwide," newsroom.ac.com/news/Dynamicpressrelease.cfm?ID=6 (December 1, 2000).

7. Ernst & Young, "Our Worldwide Leadership (as of Sept. 30, 1997)," *Ernst & Young LLP Introductions,* www.ey.com/intro/world.htmb (February 21, 1998).

8. See their annual reports at www.visa.com, www.mastercard.com, and americanexpress.com.

9. "Call it Worldpool," *Business Week,* November 29, 1994, pp. 98–99.

10. Whirlpool press releases, www.Whirlpoolcorplcom/ics/news/shownews.cgi?ID=886516277 (February 23, 1998) and www.cob.ohio.edu/~ mgt300/cases/Whirlpool.htm (December 5, 2000).

11. "A Global Comeback," *Advertising Age,* August 20, 1987, p. 146.

12. "Belgium's Strong Drinks," *International Management,* June 1992, p. 65.

13. "Tough Sale," *The Wall Street Journal,* July 29, 1994, p. A1.

14. "Some Companies Look North to Benefit from Devaluation," *McAllen Monitor,* January 29, 1995, p. 1F.

15. http://currents.net/newstoday/00/03/07/news4.html (December 1, 2000); and http://globalarchive.ft.com/globalarchive/article.html?id=001205001403 (December 5, 2000).

16. Gillete, *Annual Report 1994,* p. 38.

17. Warren J. Keegan, "Multinational Product Planning Strategic Alternatives," *Journal of Marketing,* January 1969, pp. 56–62, combines these strategies to formulate five product and promotional strategies.

18. "World's Top 50 Advertising Organizations," *Advertising Age,* www.adage.com/dataplace/archives/dp097.html (February 22, 1998).

19. "Think Globally, Act Locally," *Financial Times,* June 30, 1997, p. 12; and "Remixing the Message," *Business Asia,* February 15, 1993, p. 4.

20. "Shimmering Symbols of the Modern Age," *Financial Times,* October 17, 1997, p. 12.

21. "PR's Place on the Map," *Marketing (Choosing and Using PR Supplement),* February 17, 1994.

22. "Striking a Balance between Familiarity and Efficiency," *Financial Times,* October 17, 1997, p. 12.

23. "Japan's Brands Feel the Pinch, Too," *Financial Times,* April 23, 1994, p. 8.

24. "SPAR Eurobrands Sold throughout Europe," *Internationale SPAR Centrale,* www.spar-int.com/isc/uk/consumer/index.asp (February 24, 1998).

25. "Big Guns Target a Sky Wars Victory," *Financial Times,* December 19, 1997, p. 5; "Satellite Television in Asia," *The Economist,* February 3, 1996, pp. 53–55; and "Pay TV Goes South," *Business Week,* December 6, 1994, pp. 174–75.

26. "Western-Style News, Entertainment Is Dished Out to Arab Viewers Via MBC," *The Wall Street Journal,* March 5, 1992, p. A12.

27. The best theoretical discussion of the Internet's potential remains Donna L. Hoffman and Thomas P. Novak, "Marketing in Hypermedia Computer-Mediated Environments," *Journal of Marketing* 60: 3 (July 1996), pp. 50–68.

28. 1996 annual report.

29. "Moving from Global Brands to Global Bands," *Marketing News,* July 3, 1995, p. 30; and "Selling to the World," *The Wall Street Journal,* August 27, 1992, p. A1.

30. "PepsiCo's New Campaign to Knock Rival Coca-Cola," *Financial Times,* January 19, 1995, p. 12.

31. "Mexico Unleashes Watchdog to Avoid Legal Ad Disputes," *Advertising Age,* September 18, 1995, p. 16.

32. "No Women, No Alcohol: Learning Saudi Taboos before Placing Ads," *International Advertiser,* February 1986, pp. 11–12. These stipulations were confirmed in conversations with Saudi Arabians and South Asians in December 2000.

33. Robert S. Trebus, "Can a Good Ad Campaign Cross Borders?" *Advertising World,* Spring 1978, pp. 6–8.

34. "Ad Agencies Take on the World," *International Management,* April 1994, pp. 50–52.

35. "World Brands, *Advertising Age,* February 2, 1992, p. 33.

36. "Gillette Tries to Smooth Analyst Fears on Profit Growth," *The Wall Street Journal,* September 24, 1997, p. B4; and "Gillette Knows Shaving—and How to Turn Out Hot New Products," *Fortune,* October 14, 1996, pp. 207–10.

37. Robert D. Putnam, *Bowling Alone: The Collapse and Revival of American Community* (New York: Simon & Schuster, 2000), especially chap. 9.

38. "Operation Highlights," *Avon Annual Report,* www.avon.com (February 25, 1998).

39. "Annual Report," *Dell Computer,* www.dell.com (February 25, 1998); and "Dell Finds U.S. Strategy Works in Europe," *The Wall Street Journal,* February 3, 1997. p. A8.

40. "Opening Up the World of Coupon Redemption," *Marketing,* June 1994, pp. 30–31.

41. "After the Dust Has Settled," *Financial Times,* April 28, 1994, p. 9; and "Hoover Free Flight Offer Cost Company $48.2 m," *Financial Times,* April 21, 1994, p. 6.

42. "Number Fever Leaves Pepsi Drinkers Cold," *Financial Times,* June 2, 1994, p. 8; and "Pepsi in the Philippines," *Business Asia,* March 1994, pp. 6–7.

43. Procter & Gamble, "Leading in Our Communities," *Annual Report,* www.pg.com/info/financial_ center/annual_report/newsbriefs/leading.html (February 19, 1998).

44. Richard McGregor, "China's Paper Tigers Swift to Bite," *Financial Times,* August 23, 2000, p. 9.

45. "McDonald's Wins Case against U.K. Activists," *International Herald Tribune,* June 20, 1997, p. 1; "McDonald's Wins Its Libel Case against Two Activists in the UK," *The Wall Street Journal,* June 20, 1997, p. B2; and www.McSpotlight.org (November 20, 2000).

46. "EU Penalizes 16 Steel Firms over Pricing," *The Wall Street Journal,* February 17, 1994, p. A12.

47. "Salad Oil, $720," *Forbes,* August 14, 1995, p. 56.

48. "Not at Any Price," *The Economist,* April 6, 1995, p. 70.

49. Alexandra Nusbaum and Naoko Nakamae, "Store Wars in Cyberspace," *Financial Times,* February 8, 2000, p. 18.

50. Avi Machlis, "Cross-Border Regulations Create Hurdle for Cybershoppers," *Financial Times,* February 16, 2000, p. 7.

51. The idea for this matrix came to one of the writers when he was working on the first edition of this book. It is a checklist to help those working on the standardization of an element of the marketing mix to remember the impact of the uncontrollable forces. He wishes he had such a tool when he was an international marketing manager.

[Chapter 17]

1. "1999 Annual Report," IBM, www.ibm.com (October 3, 2000); and "A

Profile of U.S. Exporting Companies," *United States Department of Commerce News,* April 28, 1999, www.census.gov/foreign-trade/misc/edbrel-9697.pdf (October 3, 2000).

2. Telephone conversation with Ford International representative.

3. National Small Business United, "About NSBU," www.nsbu.org (February 27, 1998); and "Selling Abroad," *U.S. News & World Report,* March 2, 1992, p. 64.

4. "National Trade Data Bank," *Stat-USA Electronic Information Products,* www.stat-usw.gov (October 3, 2000).

5. *Commercial News USA,* U.S. Commercial Service, www.cnewsusa.com (October 3, 2000).

6. "International Company Profiles," *Commerce Services Give U.S. Exporters a Leading Edge in World Markets,* www.usatrade.gov/uscs/uscsicp.html (October 4, 2000).

7. "District Export Councils," *General Export Counseling and Assistance,* Trade Information Center, www.ita.doc.gov/TIC Frameset.html (October 4, 2000).

8. "National Export Directory," Trade Information Center, http://tradeinfo.doc.gov/ticwsbsite/NED.NSF/. Click on "By State." (October 4, 2000).

9. "INCOTERMS," www.united-shipping.com/glossary/incoterms.htm (October 5, 2000); "INCOTERMS 2000," www.malaysiaexports.com/inex9.6.incoterms.htm (October 5, 2000); and "The 13 Incoterms," World Cargo Alliance, www.worldcargoalliance.com/library/incoterms/incoterms.htm (October 5, 2000).

10. Ruth A. Pagell, "Finding International Credit Information," March 1998, www.nacm.org/bcmag/bcarchives/1998/articles1998/mar/mar98art9.html (October 5, 2000).

11. Eximbank, "General Fact Sheet," www.exim.gov/general.html (October 6, 2000).

12. "WTO Appellate Body Confirms That US Import Subsidies Breach International Trade Rules," *News Releases,* February 24, 2000, www.eurounion.org/news/press/2000/2000008.htm (October 7, 2000); "US Loses WTO Appeal on Foreign Sales Corporation," *Eurocom,* March 2000, the European Delegation of the European Commission to the United States, www.eurunion.org/news/eurocom/2000/eurocom0300.htm (October 7, 2000); and "U.S.-E.U. Reach Agreement on FSC Procedures," *USTR Press Release,* September 30, 2000, Office of the USTR, www.ustr.gov/releases/2000/09/00-65.pdf (October 7, 2000).

13. "Duty Drawback," *Foreign Trade,* September 1994, p. 53; and "How to Take Advantage of Duty Drawbacks," *Traffic Management,* September 1990, p. 59.

14. "An Introduction to AES," *Importing and Exporting,* U.S. Customs Service, www.customs.gov/impoexpo/impoexpo.htm (October 7, 2000).

15. "Automated Commercial System," U.S. Customs, www.customs.treas.gov/impoe-expo/acs/acs_intro.htm (October 7, 2000).

16. "New Tariff Code Streamlines Global Trading System," *Business America,* November 23, 1987, pp. 2–5.

17. Discussion with U.S. Customs officials Gilbert Medina and Carlos Baraja at Hidalgo, Texas, on March 10, 1995.

[Chapter 18]

1. David Holley, "Lifetime Employment Fading Fast in Japan," *Los Angeles Times,* January 24, 1994, p. D3; Andrew Fisher, "The End of a Tradition," *Financial Times,* July 20, 1994, p. 10; and Sara Olkon, "More Jobs Eliminated in Japan," *The Wall Street Journal,* December 29, 1994, p. A6.

2. David Holley, "Pink Slip in Japan: A Trip into Psychological Abyss," *The Los Angeles Times,* January 2, 1994, pp. A1, A10.

3. "The Amazing Portable Sarariman," *The Economist,* November 20, 1990, pp. 71–72.

4. Alex Harvey, Michiyo Nakamoto, and Gillian Teft, "Fall in Japan Births May Hit Labour Force," *Financial Times,* March 23, 2000, p. 8.

5. David Marsh, "A Crossroad of Frustrations," *Financial Times,* February 28, 1994, p. 13.

6. Frances Williams, "Rise in Child Labour to 250m," *Financial Times,* November 12, 1996, p. 7.

7. John-Thor Dahlburg, "Trading with Tiny Hands," *Los Angeles Times,* July 12, 1994, pp. H1, H4.

8. *The State of the World's Children 1997* (Oxford, UK: Oxford University Press, 1997); and see Mark Suzman, "Unicef Urges Multinationals to Adopt Child Labour Code," *Financial Times,* December 12, 1996, p. 5.

9. Rana Jawad Asghar, "Perspectives on the Third World," *Los Angeles Times,* January 20, 2000, p. B9.

10. "Kids Need Liquidity, Too," *The Economist,* September 16, 2000, p. 86.

11. Frederick Rose, "The Checkoff," *The Wall Street Journal,* June 10, 1997, p. A1.

12. Lisa Wood, "Search for Worldly-Wise Company Executives," *Financial Times,* April 9, 1991, p. 15.

13. Linda Grant, "That Overseas Job Could Derail Your Career," *Fortune,* April 14, 1997, p. 166.

14. Hal Lipper, "Helping Expats Survive China," *The Asian Wall Street Journal,* September 22, 1997, pp. 1, 11; and Richard Donkin, "Expatriate Blues," *Financial Times,* May 5, 1997, p. 1.

15. "Making Executives Feel They Have Arrived," *Hong Kong Trader,* July 2000, p. 8.

16. Joann S. Lublin, "To Smooth a Transfer Abroad, a New Focus on Kids," *The Wall Street Journal,* January 26, 1999, pp. B1, 14.

17. Victoria Griffith, "Move Me, Move My Spouse," *Financial Times,* April 28, 1997, p. 10.

18. Annette Haddad and Scott Doggett, "Road Home Hard after Working Overseas," *Los Angeles Times,* March 13, 2000, p. C2.

19. Lublin, "To Smooth a Transfer," op cit.

20. Justin Fox, "The Triumph of English," *Fortune,* September 18, 2000, pp. 209–12.

21. Lesli Hicks, "Women Confront Gender Barriers South of the Border," *McAllen Monitor,* November 2, 1994, p. 1C.

22. "Women Chill Out," *Fortune,* June 27, 1994, p. 20; and Richard Donkin, "Women 'Opting Out' of Careers in Management," *Financial Times,* May 3, 1994, p. 8.

23. Christopher Farrell, "Women in the Workplace: Is Parity Finally in Sight?" *Business Week,* August 9, 1999, p. 35; and Gene Koretz, "Women in the Boardroom," *Business Week,* September 25, 2000, p. 30.

24. Lucy Kellaway, "Ownership Disowned," *Financial Times,* July 12, 1999, p. 8.

25. Victoria Griffith, "A Sense of Belonging," *Financial Times,* September 15, 1997, p. 12; and see Marla Tratzer, "Men Are from Marrakech," *Los Angeles Times,* November 3, 1997, Business Part II, p. 8.

26. Khozem Merchant, "Women in India: A Handle on Power," *Financial Times,* September 6, 2000, p. 10.

27. Anne Fisher, "Stupid Résumé Tricks: How to Avoid Getting Hired," *Fortune,* July 21, 1997, p. 117.

28. Fortunat F. Mueller-Maerkl, "Dos and Don'ts in Selecting Managers for Foreign Operations," in *U.S.-German Economic Survey* (New York: German/American Chamber of Commerce, 1984), pp. 123–25.

29. "Headhunting Rope Tricks," *Los Angeles Times,* September 10, 2000, p. G1.

30. Joann S. Lublin, "An Overseas Stint Can Be a Ticket to the Top," *The Wall Street Journal,* January 29, 1996, p. B1.

31. Some writers regard paid home leave as an allowance, but our experience convinces us that it is a bonus, because ICs consistently give more frequent or longer home leaves to employees working in less desirable assignments.

32. "Share Buybacks in Japan Exercised," *The Economist,* August 2, 1997, pp. 59–60.

33. "Top Executive Compensation: Canada, France, the United Kingdom and the United States," the Conference Board Research Report #1250-99-RR, http://www.conference-board.org/search/dpress.cfm?pressid-4509 (February 2, 2000).

[Chapter 19]

1. There is almost always some cost for protection, and an important management function is to compare the magnitude of the risk with the cost of protection against it.

2. If you were dealing in a currency more actively traded than the krone, such as the British, Canadian, French, Japanese, Swiss, or German currency, you would use the 180-day futures quotation for that currency.

3. Covered positions are also referred to as "square" or "perfect" positions.

4. In every IC, there is one central company at the top of the organization. That company is called the parent company. The other companies are referred to as affiliated or subsidiary companies.

5. The power of ICs to control the timing and currencies of payment and asset accumulation has not been ignored by governments. In furtherance of their tax and exchange control policies, most countries have legal limits on acceleration, delays, and intra-IC netting.

6. Currencies may be fixed in value in terms of each other by international agreement; if there are no such agreements, they are said to float.

7. A blocked-currency situation arises either because there is no satisfactory market for the currency or because of a country's laws.

8. In such circumstances, the equivalent amount is subject to some negotiation because a blocked, noncovertible currency does not have a free-market spot or other exchange rate, which would be used when dealing with two convertible currencies.

9. When equity securities (stock) are issued, part of the ownership is being sold. No money is being borrowed that must be repaid, as is the case when debt securities (bonds) are issued.

10. The international, or Euro-type, capital market has been created by national currencies being traded, borrowed, and lent outside their countries of origin. Thus, U.S. dollars outside the United States are Eurodollars, and German deutsche marks outside Germany are Euromarks.

11. Richard Lapper, "TVA, EIB Find Winning Formula," *Financial Times,* September 12, 1996, p. 22.

12. "Derivatives," *Financial Times Survey,* June 27, 1997, pp. I–VIII.

13. Philip Coggan, "In Defense of Derivatives," *Financial Times,* October 30, 1997, p. 20; see also Phil Rivett and Jonathon Davies, "Credit Derivatives," http://www.coopers.co.uk/coopers/financia...vices/bankersdigest/credit_w96/index.html (February 23, 1997).

14. Christopher Swann, "Derivatives in Demand to Beat Fickle Currencies," *Financial Times,* September 22, 2000. p. XXVII.

15. Claire, Smith, "Weather Derivatives: An Enormous Potential," *Financial Times,* June 28, 2000, p. VI.

16. Michael McCarthy Jr., "Pepsi Seeking to Boost Sales to Ukrainians," *The Wall Street Journal,* October 23, 1992, p. A10.

17. Shelley Neumeier, "Why Countertrade Is Getting Hot," *Fortune,* June 29, 1992, p. 25.

18. Renato Ruggiero, "The High Stakes of World Trade," *The Wall Street Journal,* April 28, 1997, p. A18.

[Chapter 20]

1. www.wackenhut.com (November 24, 2000).

2. "Buy Global, Skip Local," *CIO Magazine,* April 1, 1996, www.cio.com/cio/ciomag/archive/archive_apr_1_96_global.html (March 3, 1998).

3. Raymond J. Mataloni, Jr., "U.S. Multinational Companies Operations in 1998," *Survey of Current Business* (Washington, DC: Bureau of Economic Analysis, U.S. Department of Commerce, July 2000), p. 29.

4. L. J. Krajewski and L. P. Ritzman, *Operations Management,* 5th ed. (Addison-Wesley, 1999), p. 456; and J. Heizer and B. Render, *Principles of Operations Management,* 4th ed. (Prentice-Hall, 2001), p. 436, Table 11.2.

5. Peter D. Henig, "Revenge of the Bricks," *Red Herring,* August 2000, www.redherring.com/mag/issue81/mag-revenge-81.html (November 25, 2000).

6. "E-procurement: The Transformation of Corporate Purchasing," *Fortune,* www.fortune.com/fortune/sections/eprocurement/index.html (November 24, 2000).

7. Sam Jaffe, "Oracle: A B2B Rebirth That Few Foretold," *Business Week,* April 6, 2000, www.businessweek.com (November 24, 2000).

8. Henig, "Revenge of the Bricks."

9. "Companies Can Pare Process Costs by 95 Percent When Purchasing Supplies, American Express Study Reveals," May 25, 1999, home3.americanexpress.com/corp/latestnews/purch-process.asp (November 24, 2000).

10. "Ciba Specialty Chemicals Uses ChemConnect for Annual Long Term

Contracts," September 27, 2000, www.chemconnect.com/about/press-releases/sept27-00.html.

11. Ibid.; and "E-Procurement."

12. Ibid.

13. Philip Verges, CEO of VergeTech, quoted in Hailey Lynne McKeefry, "The Integration of Net Markets and Exchanges—E-Markets Not Only Create Economies of Volume—They Can Help You Go Global, Too," *VAR Business,* September 18, 2000, www.techweb.com/se/directlink.cgi/VAR20000918S0018 (November 25, 2000).

14. Ibid.

15. Ibid. Estimate in 1999 market study by Forrester Research, quoted in Jaffe, "Oracle."

16. William Echikson, "FreeMarkets Help to Foment Europe's B2B Revolution," *Business Week,* March 7, 2000, www.businesssweek.com:/ebiz/0003/ec0307.htm (November 24, 2000).

17. Estimate from PriceWaterhouse Coopers study on trends in the motor vehicle business, cited in "How the Internet Will Change the Motor Industry and Lop Thousands off New Car Prices," *CarToday.com,* May 17, 2000, www.cartoday.com/livenews/news/00/05/17.2.asp (November 24, 2000).

18. Richard B. Chase and Nicholas J. Aquilano, *Production and Operations Management,* 7th ed. (Burr Ridge, IL: Richard D. Irwin, 1995), p. 716.

19. "Global Sourcing at Second Glance," *Global Competitor,* Summer 1994, pp. 70–74.

20. Henig, "Revenge of the Bricks."

21. Ibid.; and "E-Procurement."

22. "U.S. Companies Come Home," *Fortune,* December 30, 1991, pp. 106–12.

23. "Du Pont Sets Up S.A. Site," *San Antonio Express-News,* October 27, 1994, p. 1F.

24. "Shingo's Message," *TQM: An Integrated Internet System,* www.dmu.ac.uk/dept/schools/business/corporate/tqmex/shingo.htm (January 26, 1998).

25. "Deming's Message," *TQM: An Integrated Internet System,* www.dmu.ac.uk/dept/schools/business/corporate/tqmex/deming.htm (January 26, 1998); and Lloyd Dobyns and Clare Crawford-Mason, *Quality or Else* (Boston: Houghton Mifflin, 1991), pp. 10–17.

26. Chase and Aquilano, *Production and Operations Management,* 6th ed., p. 229.

27. J. M. Juran, "A History of Managing for Quality in the United States," *Quality Digest,* December 1995, pp. 34–45; and *Quality or Else,* p. 18.

28. Shigeo Shingo, *Non-Stock Production: The Shingo System for Continuous Improvement* (Cambridge, MA: Productivity Press, 1988), p. 36.

29. Chase and Aquilano, *Production and Operations Management,* 7th ed., p. 240.

30. "Innovation," *Business Week,* Special Issue, June 1989, p. 107.

31. "Ishikawa's Message," *TQM: An Internet Integrated System,* www.dmu.ac.uk/dept/schools/business/corporate/tqmex/ish.htm (January 26, 1998).

32. "Motivation Systems for Small-Group Quality Control Activities," *Japan Economic Journal,* June 28, 1988, pp. 33–35.

33. Chase and Aquilano, *Production and Operations Management,* 7th ed., p. 240.

34. Franklin Strier, "Quality Circles in the United States: Fad or Fixture?" *Business Forum,* Summer 1984, pp. 19–23.

35. "Toyota to Recalibrate 'Just-in-Time,' " *International Herald Tribune,* February 8–9, 1997, p. 9; and "Brakes on a Toyota," *Financial Times,* February 7, 1997, p. 8.

36. Chase and Aquilano, *Production and Operations Management,* 5th ed., pp. 736–68.

37. "Bottlenecks," http://members.aol.com/williamfla/bottle.htm (March 3, 1998); and Chase and Aquilano, *Production and Operations Management,* 7th ed., pp. 755–65.

38. "Digital Factory," *Fortune,* November 14, 1994, pp. 93–108.

39. "Ringing the Changes," *International Management,* September 1994, p. 59.

40. "Herr Lazarus," *The Economist,* March 18, 1995, pp. 63–64.

41. "Lean, Mean, and Mobile," *The Journal of European Business,* July–August 1993, pp. 53–56.

42. "Workers Pay for Europe's Rigidities," *Financial Times,* February 13, 1998, p. 2; "What Ails Europe? A Surfeit of Rules, Study Says," *The International Herald Tribune,* March 14, 1997, p. 13; and "France, Germany Must Cut More Jobs to Improve Efficiency, Report Says," *The Wall Street Journal,* March 14, 1997, p. 9A.

43. "Ford's Assembly Lines Will Now Be Virtually Foolproof," *Financial Times,* April 14, 1997, p. 1.

44. "A Select Few Poised to Lead Business in the 90s," *The Wall Street Journal,* Centennial Edition, June 23, 1989, p. A3.

45. "The Winds of Change Below Everywhere," *Business Week,* October 17, 1994, pp. 92–93.

46. Jay Heizer and Barry Render, *Principles of Operations Management,* (4th ed., Upper Saddle River, NJ: Prentice Hall, 2001. p. 173.

47. Conversation with SKF executive.

48. Conversation with Ford International representatives.

49. D. J. Teece, "Technology Transfer by Multinational Firms," reprinted in M. Casson (ed.), *The International Library of Critical Writings in Economics 1* (England: Edward Elgar Publishing, 1990), pp. 185–204.

50. A highly automated machine may make only one or two sizes or types of a product, whereas a general-purpose machine may be capable of producing not only all sizes of a product but other products as well. Its output, however, may be as little as 1 percent of that of a specialized machine.

51. "Vietnam Bans Used Imports," *Financial Times,* January 21, 1996, p. 4.

52. This does not mean that unit production costs are lower in the small plants, and certainly the coordination of their activities will be formidable. The example does illustrate the extreme range of possibilities when capital costs are a primary consideration. From Colin Norman, *Soft Technology, Hard Choice* (Washington, DC: Worldwatch Institute, June 1978), p. 14.

53. "Petrochemicals in Mexico," *Investing in Mexico,* http://bancomext-mtl.com/bancomext/invest.htm (March 9, 1998).

54. "Mexico: A Basic Guide for Foreign Investors," *Investing in Mexico,* http://bancomext-mtl.com/bancomext/invest.htm (March 9, 1998).

[Glossary]

Absolute advantage The advantage enjoyed by a country because it can produce a product at a lower cost than can other countries.

accidental exposure Export business obtained through no effort of the exporter.

accounting exposure The total net of accounting statement items on which loss could occur because of changes in currency exchange rates.

adjustment assistance Financial and technical assistance to workers, firms, and communities to help them adjust to import competition.

ad valorem tariff or duty Literally "according to the value." A method in which customs duties or tariffs are established and charged as a percentage of the value of imported goods.

advertising Paid, nonpersonal presentation of ideas, goods, or services by an identified sponsor.

advising bank The bank that notifies the beneficiary of the opening of a letter of credit. The advising bank makes no payment commitment.

aesthetics A culture's sense of beauty and good taste.

affiliated company May be a subsidiary or a company in which an IC has less than 100 percent ownership.

A.G. Aktien-Gesellschaft. A joint stock company in Germany.

agency office An office of a foreign bank in the United States that cannot accept domestic deposits. It seeks business for the bank when U.S. companies operate internationally.

air waybill For goods shipped by air, performs the functions of a bill of lading in land surface transport or of a marine bill of lading in water transport.

allowances Extra payments to expatriate employees to meet the higher costs they incur abroad.

American depository receipt (ADR) Stock of a foreign corporation is deposited at an American bank. The bank issues an ADR, not the corporation's stock certificate, to an American investor who buys shares of that corporation. The stock certificate is kept at the bank.

antiboycott law An American law against complying with the Arab countries' boycott of Israel.

antitrust laws Laws to prevent business from engaging in such practices as price-fixing and market sharing.

appreciation An increase in the value of one asset in terms of another.

apprenticeship program Enables a person to learn a job skill by working with a skilled worker.

appropriate technology The technology—advanced, intermediate, or primitive—that most fits the society using it.

arbitrage The simultaneous purchase and sale of something in two (or more) markets at a time when it is selling (being bought) at different prices in the markets. Profit is the price differential minus the cost.

arbitration The settlement of a dispute between parties by a third, presumably unbiased, party, not a court of law.

arm's-length transaction A transaction between two or more unrelated parties. (A transaction between two subsidiaries of an IC would not be an arm's-length transaction.)

Asian religions The primary Asian religions are Hinduism, Buddhism, Jainism, and Sikhism (India); Confucianism and Taoism (China); and Shintoism (Japan).

associations Social units based on age, sex, or common interest, not on kinship.

Back-to-back letter of credit (L/C) A paying bank that will pay the exporter opens a back-to-back L/C based on the underlying L/C the exporter's supplier (a manufacturer, for example) may be paid.

back-to-back loans A unit of one IC lends to a unit of a second IC, and at the same time and in equivalent amounts, another unit of the second IC lends to another unit of the first.

backward vertical integration Es-tablishing facilities to manufacture inputs used in the production of a firm's final products.

balance of payments (BOP) A financial statement that compares all reported payments by residents of one country to residents of other countries with payments to domestic residents by foreign residents. If more money has been paid out than received, the BOP is in deficit. If the opposite condition exists, the BOP is in surplus.

banker's acceptance A draft drawn, for example, by an exporter on an importer's bank. If the bank accepts the draft, the bank has agreed to pay in accordance with its terms.

bank swaps To avoid currency exchange problems, a bank in a soft-currency country will lend to an IC subsidiary there. The IC or its bank will make hard currency available to the lending bank outside the soft-currency country.

barter The exchange of goods or services for goods or services. No money is used.

bill of exchange (draft) An unconditional written order calling on the party to whom it is addressed to pay on demand or at a future date a sum of money to the order of a named party or to the bearer. Examples are acceptances or the commercial bank check.

bill of lading (B/L) A receipt given by a carrier of goods received and contract for their delivery. Usually a B/L is made to the order of someone and is negotiable. The B/L is also a document of title with which the holder may claim the goods from the carrier.

blocked account Financial assets that cannot be transferred into another currency or out of the country without the government's permission.

bonded warehouse Warehouse authorized by customs authorities for storage of goods on which payment of import duties is deferred until the goods are removed.

bonds: (1) Eurobond A long-term bond marketed internationally in countries other than the country of the currency in which it is denominated. The issue is not subject to national restrictions. **(2) zero-coupon bonds** Pay no periodic interest (hence their name), so the total yield is obtained entirely as capital gain on the final maturity date. **(3) dual-currency bonds** Denominated in one currency but pay interest in another currency at a fixed rate of exchange. Dual-currency bonds can also pay redemption proceeds in a different currency than the currency of denomination. **(4) floating-rate bonds** The most commonly issued instrument, the interest coupons on which are adjusted regularly according to the level of some base interest rate plus a fixed spread.

bonuses Extra payments to expatriates because of hardships and inconveniences encountered in some foreign postings.

boomerang effect Refers to the fact that technology sold to companies in another nation may be used to produce goods that will then compete with those of the seller of the technology.

bottleneck Operation in production system whose output sets limit for entire system's output.

bottom-up planning Planning process that begins at the lowest level in the organization and continues upward.

brain drain The loss by a country of its most intelligent and best educated people.

branch office An office or department of a company at a location away from headquarters. It is a part of the company and not a separate legal entity, as is a subsidiary, an affiliate, or a joint venture.

Bretton Woods A resort in New Hampshire at which bank and treasury officials of the major Allied powers met near the end of World War II. There they established the International Monetary Fund, the World Bank, and an international monetary system.

bribes Gifts or payments to induce the receiver to do something illegal for the giver.

buffer stock A supply of a commodity that the executive of a commodity agreement tries to accumulate and hold so that when the price of the commodity begins to rise above desirable levels, sales can be made from that stock to dampen the price rise.

Canadian Shield A massive land area of bedrock covering one-half of Canada's landmass.

CAP Common agricultural policy.

capital-intensive Describes pro-cesses that require a high concentration of capital relative to labor per unit of output and products produced by such processes. The opposite is labor-intensive.

capitalism All possible activities are performed by private business or persons rather than by a government.

cartel An organization of suppliers that controls the supply and price of a commodity. To be successful, a cartel should have relatively few members who control most of the export supply of the commodity, the members must observe the cartel rules, and the commodity must be a necessity with a price-inelastic demand.

caste system An aspect of Hinduism by which the entire society is divided into four groups plus the outcasts, and each is assigned a certain class of work.

central banks Government institutions with authority over the size and growth of the national monetary stock. Central banks frequently regulate commercial banks and usually act as the government's fiscal agent.

centrally planned economy Governments plan and direct almost all economic activity and usually own the factors of production.

centrally planned markets Markets in which there is almost no free-market activity and the government owns all major factors of production, controls labor, and tries to plan all activity.

central reserve assets Gold, SDRs, ECUs, or hard foreign currencies held in a nation's treasury.

certificate of review Legal document issued by U.S. Department of Commerce that grants immunity from state and federal antitrust prosecution to export trading companies.

chaebol Large South Korean conglomerates, frequently family-owned and directed, that have succeeded worldwide in such fields as microchips, electronics, construction, and shipbuilding. Korean law prohibits banks from being part of chaebol.

clearing The process of transmitting, reconciling, and, in some cases, confirming payment orders prior to settlement, possibly including netting of instructions and the establishment of final positions for settlement. Sometimes the term is used (imprecisely) to include settlement.

clearinghouse A central location or central processing mechanism through which financial institutions agree to exchange payment instructions. The institutions settle for items exchanged at a designated time based on the rules and procedures of the clearinghouse. In some cases, the clearinghouse may assume significant counterparty, financial, or risk management responsibilities for the clearing system.

clearing system A set of procedures whereby financial institutions present and exchange data and/or documents relating to funds or securities transfers to other financial institutions. The procedures often also include a mechanism for the calculation of participants' bilateral and/or multilateral net positions with a view to facilitating the settlement of their obligations on a net basis.

CIF (cost, insurance, and freight) A term used in the delivery of goods from one party to another. The price includes the costs of the goods, the maritime or other appropriate transportation, the insurance premium, and the freight charges to the destination.

CIS Commonwealth of Independent States.

climate The meteorological conditions, including temperature, precipitation, and wind, that prevail in a region.

cluster analysis Statistical technique dividing objects into groups so that the objects within each group are similar.

COCOM Voluntary group of most NATO nations that administers a common set of export controls to prevent transfer of sensitive goods to hostile nations. In 1994, after the end of the Cold

War, COCOM went out of existence. A number of developments are causing some NATO members to consider reviving it. Such developments include modernization of the PRC armed forces, fears of a Russian military revival, and the discovery that at least one of the so-called rogue countries, Iraq, developed arms of mass destruction, including nuclear, biological, and chemical weapons.

codetermination A system in which representatives of labor participate in the management of a company.

collection documents All documents submitted to a buyer for the purpose of receiving payment for a shipment.

collective bargaining Bargaining between an employer and a labor union about employee wages and working conditions.

commodity agreement An agreement between the producers and consumers of a commodity (for example, tin, cocoa, or rubber) to regulate the production, price, and trade of the commodity.

common external tariff Under an agreement reached by a group of nations, such as the EU, the same level of tariffs is imposed by these nations on all goods imported from other nations.

communism A theory of a classless society conceived by Marx. Lenin, Stalin, and others developed it differently.

comparative advantage Unless a country has the same absolute advantage in producing all goods and services, there would be some goods and services in which it had less relative advantage. It would gain by importing those and exporting the ones in which it had an absolute advantage or the greatest relative advantage.

compensation A form of countertrade involving payment in goods and cash.

compensatory financing A program to assist countries in financial difficulties due to drops in export earnings because of natural causes, such as drought, or because of international market price decreases. The IMF and the EU have compensatory financing programs.

compensatory trade Any transaction that involves asset transfer as a condition of purchase.

competition policy The European versions of American antitrust laws.

competitive alliance Cooperation between competitors for specific purposes.

competitor analysis Process in which principal competitors are identified and their objectives, strengths, weaknesses, and product lines are assessed.

competitor intelligence system (CIS) Procedure for gathering, analyzing, and disseminating information about a firm's competitors.

compound duty A form of import duty consisting of an ad valorem duty and a specific duty.

confirmed Act of a correspondent bank in the seller's country by which it agrees to honor the issuing bank's letter of credit.

confirmed letter of credit (L/C) An L/C confirmed by a bank other than the opening bank. Thus, it is an obligation of more than one bank.

confiscation Seizure by a government of foreign-owned assets that is not followed by prompt, effective, and adequate compensation.

Confucian work ethic Same as the Protestant work ethic. The term is used in Asian nations where Confucianism is a major religion.

conservative In American political usage, a conservative advocates minimum government activity.

contingency plan Plan for the best- or worst-case scenarios or for critical events that could have a severe impact on the firm.

contract manufacturing Manufacturing of a product or component by one company for another company. The two companies may or may not be related by stock ownership, common parent, or otherwise.

controllable forces The forces internal to the firm that management administers to adapt to changes in the uncontrollable environmental forces.

convertible currencies Currencies that may be changed for or converted into other currencies, at least for current account payments, without government permission.

cooperative exporters Established international manufacturers who export other manufacturers' goods as well as their own.

coproduction A form of industrial cooperation in which two or more factories produce components for a final product.

corporate strategy Action plan to enable an organization to reach its objectives.

cottage industry Production away from a central factory, typically in the worker's own home or cottage. Workers are paid on a piece-rate basis, or so much for each unit produced.

counterfeiting Illegal use of a well-known manufacturer's brand name on copies of a firm's merchandise.

countertrade A transaction in which goods are exchanged for goods. Payment by a purchaser is entirely or partially in goods instead of hard currencies for products or technology from other countries.

countervailing duty An additional amount of tariff levied on an import that is found to have benefited from an export subsidy.

country risk assessment (CRA) Evaluating the risks before lending or investing in a country.

country screening Takes countries as the relevant unit of analysis for market screening.

covered investment or interest arbitrage Investment in a second currency that is "covered" by a forward sale of that currency to protect against exchange rate fluctuations. Profit depends on interest rate differentials minus the discount or plus the premium on a forward sale.

covering Buying or selling foreign currencies in amounts equivalent to future payments to be made or received. A means of protection against loss due to fluctuations in currency exchange rates.

credit or money market hedge Hedging by borrowing the currency of risk, converting it immediately to the ultimately desired currency, and repaying the loan when payment is received.

cross investment Foreign direct investment made by oligopolistic firms in each other's home country as a defense measure.

cross rate The direct exchange rate between two non–U.S. dollar currencies. It is determined by observing the U.S. dollar exchange rate for each of the other two currencies and, from those rates, computing their direct exchange rate.

culture The rules, techniques, institutions, and artifacts that characterize human populations.

currency area The group of countries whose currencies are pegged to any one developed country currency. Many developing countries peg the value of their currency to that of their major developing countries' trading partner.

currency exchange controls A government's controls over how much foreign currency its residents or visitors can have and how much they must pay for it.

currency swap The exchange of one currency into another at an agreed rate and a reversal of that exchange at the same rate at the end of the swap contract period.

customhouse broker Independent business that handles import shipments for compensation.

customs union An arrangement between two or more countries whereby they eliminate tariffs and other import restrictions on one another's goods and establish a common tariff on the goods from all other countries.

Debt capital Money raised by selling bonds, the principal and interest on which must be repaid.

debt default When a debtor fails or refuses to pay a debt.

debt rescheduling Defaulted debt is renegotiated, giving the debtor a longer time to pay, a lower interest rate, or both.

delayering Removing levels of middle management.

demonstration effect The result of having seen others with desirable goods.

demurrage Charge assessed by a carrier on an exporter or an importer for excess time taken to unload or load a vessel.

depreciation of a currency A decline in the value of a currency in terms of another currency or in terms of gold. *Depreciation* and *devaluation* are used interchangeably.

derivatives A contract, the value of which changes in concert with the price movements in a related or underlying commodity or financial instrument. The term covers standardized exchange-traded futures and options as well as over-the-counter swaps, options, and other customized instruments.

devaluation Depreciation of a currency by official government action.

developed A classification for all industrialized nations, that is, those that are more developed technically.

developed countries (DCs) Industrialized countries.

developing A classification for the world's lower-income nations that are less technically developed.

development banks Banks that aid developing countries in economic development. They may lend or invest money and encourage local ownership. They may be worldwide, regional, or national.

direct exporting The exporting of goods and services by the firm that produces them.

direct investment Sufficient investment to obtain at least some voice in management. The U.S. government considers 10 percent or more equity in a foreign company to be direct investment.

dirty float A currency that floats in value in terms of other currencies but is not free of government intervention. Governments intervene to "smooth" or "manage" fluctuations or to maintain desired exchange rates.

discretionary income The amount of income remaining after paying taxes and making essential purchases.

disposable income The amount of income remaining after taxes.

distributors Independent importers who buy for their own account for resale.

district export councils Groups of volunteer businesspeople in every state that are appointed by the U.S. Department of Commerce to assist exporters.

documentary drafts Drafts accompanied by such documents as invoices, bills of lading, inspection certificates, and insurance papers.

domestication Term used to indicate process in which a host government brings pressure to force a foreign owner to turn over partial ownership to the host country government or host country citizens.

domestic environment All the uncontrollable forces originating in the home country that surround and influence the firm's life and development.

domestic international sales corporation (DISC) A subsidiary corporation of a U.S. company that is incorporated in a state of the United States for the purpose of exporting from the United States. DISCs are given certain tax advantages. Generally, they have been superseded by foreign sales corporations.

drafts (bills of exchange) Orders drawn by a drawer that order a second party, the drawee, to pay a sum of money to a payee. The payee may be the same party as the drawer.

drawback The reimbursement of the tariff paid on an imported component that is later exported. When a component is imported into the United States, a tariff is levied on it and paid by the importer. If that component is later exported, the exporter is entitled to get 99 percent of the tariff amount from U.S. Customs.

drawee See drafts.

drawer See drafts.

dumping Selling abroad at prices lower than those charged in the home or other markets.

duties (tariffs) Amounts charged when goods are imported into a country. If such duties are based on the values of the goods, they are called ad valorem. If they are based on the number of items imported, they are called specified.

Earned income Income derived from efforts, labor, sales, or active participation in business. Salaries, wages, bonuses, and commissions are examples. Unearned income is a return on investment of money or time. Examples are interest, dividends, and royalties. The distinction is important for purposes of U.S. taxation of American residents abroad.

East-West trade Trade between the centrally planned economies of the communist bloc (East) and the more market-oriented economies of the OECD nations (West). Recent developments, such as the breakup of the Soviet Union and the end of the COMECON trade bloc that it dominated, have reduced the number of avowedly communist countries. Many of those countries are trying to achieve market economies and democracy, but progress is slow and difficult at best.

Economic and monetary union (EMU) A number of European countries are replacing their national currencies with the euro and subjecting their national banks to the European Central Bank (ECB).

Edge Act corporation A subsidiary of a U.S. commercial bank that operates in a foreign country. The Edge subsidiary, operating abroad, is free of restraints of U.S. law and may perform whatever services and functions are legal in the countries where it operates.

employee facilities Schools, cafeterias, housing, recreation, or other employer-provided facilities.

environment All the forces surrounding and influencing the life and development of the firm.

environmental scanning Procedure in which a firm scans the world for changes in the environmental forces that might affect it.

equity capital Money raised by selling corporate stock that represents ownership of the corporation.

equity-related bonds Bonds that are convertible at the option of the holder into other securities of the issuer, usually common stock-type equity. Called *convertibles* in the United States.

Erasmus European Union action scheme for the mobility of university students.

escape clause A legal provision concerning products whose tariffs have been reduced. If, thereafter, imports increase and threaten the domestic producers of those products, the escape clause permits the tariffs to be put back up.

estimation by analogy Using a market factor that is successful in one market to estimate demand in a similar market.

ethnocentricity A belief in the superiority of one's own ethnic group.

euro The name of the single currency that will replace national currencies of European countries which become part of the economic and monetary union (EMU).

Eurobonds Bonds that are issued outside the restriction applying to domestic offerings and are syndicated and traded mostly from London. Most of these bonds are denominated in U.S. dollars.

Eurocurrency A currency being used or traded outside the country that issued it.

Eurodollar The U.S. dollar is the most widely used Eurocurrency.

European Central Bank (ECB) The bank which will replace or oversee the national banks of countries which become part of the EMU.

European Currency Unit (ECU) A currency unit established by the European Monetary System. Its value is determined by reference to the value of a "basket" of currencies. The currencies in the basket are those of the system's member-countries.

European Economic Area The European Free Trade Area consisting of the EU and EFTA.

European Monetary Cooperation Fund (EMCF) Lends assistance to EMS member-countries that have difficulties in keeping their currencies within the agreed value relationships.

European Monetary System (EMS) A system, established in 1979, under which West European countries agreed to keep their currency values within an established range in relation to one another.

European Union (EU) Supranational entity of 15 (as of the beginning of 2001) European countries working toward European economic and political integration.

EU Commission EU executive institution that runs the day-to-day operations of the EU.

EU Council of Ministers EU policy-setting institution.

EU Court of Justice EU court that decides issues arising from the Treaty of Rome (which established the predecessor of the EU) as amended.

EU Parliament EU institution containing representatives popularly elected from the member-nations.

exchange rate The price of one currency stated in another currency.

exchange rate risk In activities involving two or more currencies, the risk that losses can occur as a result of changes in their relative value.

Eximbank (Export-Import Bank) Principal federal government agency that aids American exporters by means of loans, guarantees, and insurance programs.

export bill of lading (B/L) Contract of carriage between shipper and carrier. Straight bill of lading is nonnegotiable; an endorsed "to-order" bill gives the holder claim on merchandise.

export draft An unconditional order drawn by the seller on the buyer to pay the draft's amount on presentation (sight draft) or at an agreed future date (time draft) that must be paid before the buyer receives shipping documents.

export incentives Subsidies or tax rebates paid by governments to companies to encourage them to export.

export licenses A government document that permits the exporter to export designated goods to certain destinations. In the United States, the export license will be either a general export license or a validated export license.

export management company A company that acts as the export department for other companies. It performs all export-related services for its customers except supplying the product.

export processing zones Specific and limited areas into which imported components may be brought for further processing. The finished product must be reexported to avoid payment of import duties.

export trading company A firm established principally to export domestic goods and services and help unrelated companies export their products.

exposure netting An open position in two or more currencies whose strengths and weaknesses are thought to balance one another.

expropriation Seizure by a government of foreign-owned assets. Such seizure is not contrary to international law if it is followed by prompt, adequate, and effective compensation. If not, it is called confiscation.

extended family Includes relatives beyond the parents and children.

extortion The demand for payments to keep the demander from causing harm to the payer.

extraterritorial application of laws Attempts by a government to apply its laws outside its territorial borders.

Factor A buyer, at a discount, of a company's receivables with short-term maturities of no longer than a year.

factor endowment A country is or is not endowed with one or more of the factors of production, capital, labor, and natural resources.

factoring Discounting without recourse an account receivable.

factory door cost The production cost of a good or service to which marketing and general administrative costs have not been added.

firm surveillance The IMF has the power to monitor the exchange rate policies of member-nations.

fiscal policies Government policies about the collection and spending of money.

fixed currency exchange rates A system under which the values of currencies in terms of other currencies are fixed by intergovernmental agreement and by governmental intervention in the currency exchange markets.

fixed interest rate An interest rate that is set when a loan is made and remains the same for the life of the loan regardless of whether other interest rates rise or fall.

floating currency exchange rates A system in which the values of currencies in terms of other currencies are determined by the supply of and demand for the currencies in currency markets. If governments do not intervene in the markets, the float is said to be *clean.* If they do intervene, the float is said to be *dirty.*

floating interest rates A loan situation in which the interest rate set when a loan is made may rise or fall as the interest rates of some reference, such as LIBOR or the prime rate, vary. Sometimes called *variable rates.*

floating-rate notes or bonds Debt instruments with floating or variable interest rates. The interest rates are pegged to a fluctuating interest rate, such as the six-month LIBOR rate.

fluctuating exchange rates See *floating exchange rates.*

Foreign Corrupt Practices Act of 1977 An American law against making questionable payments when American companies do business abroad.

foreign exchange The exchanges of the currency of one country for that of another country.

foreign exchange rates Prices of one currency in terms of other currencies.

foreign exchange reserves Gold, SDRs, U.S. dollars, and other convertible currencies held in a nation's treasury.

foreign financing Occurs when a foreign company or other borrower comes to a nation's capital market and borrows in the local currency, for example, when an Italian company borrows U.S. dollars in New York or French francs in Paris.

foreign freight forwarder Indepen-dent business that handles export shipments for compensation.

foreign national pricing Local pricing in another country.

Foreign Sales Corporation (FSC) A corporation provided for in the Tax Reform Act of 1984. The FSC replaces the domestic international sales corporation (DISC) as a tax incentive for exporters.

foreign tax credits The credit an American taxpayer may take against American income tax for tax levied on the same income by a foreign government.

foreign trade zone (FTZ) American version of a free trade zone. In an FTZ, goods may be imported and manufactured or handled and changed in any way. No tariff need be paid unless and until the goods are removed from the FTZ into the country where the FTZ is located.

forfaiting Has the same purposes and procedures as factoring, which is the sale by an exporter of its accounts receivable for immediate cash. However, there are two important differences: (1) factoring involves credit terms of no more than 180 days, while forfaiting may involve years; (2) factoring does not usually cover political and transfer risks, while forfaiting does.

forward contract A contract to exchange one currency for another currency at an agreed exchange rate at a future date, usually 30, 90, or 180 days. May be used to hedge. See *forward rate.*

forward rate The cost today for a commitment by one party to deliver to or take from another party an agreed amount of a currency at a fixed future date. This rate is established by the forward contract.

franchising A franchisee pays a franchisor for the right to use the franchisor's logo, procedures, materials, and advertising.

free trade zone An area designated by the government of a country for duty-free entry of any nonprohibited goods.

friendship, commerce, and navigation (FCN) treaties The basic agreements between nations about such matters as treatment of each others' citizens or companies.

fringe benefits Payments or other benefits given to employees over and above base wages.

futures contract An agreement between a buyer and a seller to exchange a particular good for a particular price at a specified future date.

General export license Any export license covering export commodities for which a validated license is not required. No formal application is required.

generalized system of preferences (GSP) An agreement under the auspices of WTO under which many products of developing nations are provided duty-free access to developed nations.

general trading companies Exist in many countries, including the United States, though the Japanese versions of these companies, called *sogo shosha* in Japanese, are the best known. For many years, the sogo shosha have imported and distributed commodities and products for use by Japanese industries and consumers, sought foreign customers for Japanese companies, and exported to other companies.

geocentric As used in this book, hiring and promoting employees because of their abilities without reference to their nationality or race.

gilts Technically, British and Irish government securities, though the term also includes issues of local British authorities.

global company A company that markets a standardized product worldwide and allows only minimum adaptations to local conditions and tastes from country to country. Its financial, marketing, and advertising strategies are global with little differentiation among countries or areas as to product. Other authors, particularly when writing about the automobile industry, mean the company's ability to source parts and components from subsidiaries in several countries for assembly in the market country or area.

globalization The decision to become and the process of becoming a global company.

globality The circumstance of having become a global company.

GmbH Gesellschaft mit beschrankter Haftung (organization with limited ability). A German form of business organization.

GNP/capita The gross national product of a nation divided by its population (an arithmetic mean).

gold exchange standard The system established at Bretton Woods whereby the value of one currency (the U.S. dollar) was set in terms of gold. The United States held gold and agreed that when another country accumulated U.S. dollars, it could exchange them for gold at the set value.

gold standard A system under which currency values are set in terms of gold and each country agrees that if a second country accumulates more of a first country's currency than it wants for other purposes, the second country can exchange the first country's currency for that amount of the first country's gold.

gold tranche The amount of gold paid by a country as its contributed capital in the International Monetary Fund.

gray market Where goods are sold that either are legal but unauthorized imports bearing domestic manufacturers' trade names or are exports diverted to the domestic market.

gross domestic product (GDP) The market value of a country's output attributable to factors of production located in the country's territory. It differs from GNP by the exclusion of net factor income payments, such as interest and dividends received from, or paid to, the rest of the world. See *gross national product (GNP).*

gross national product (GNP) The market value of all the final goods and services produced by a national economy over a period of time, usually a year.

Group of 5 The term used for meetings of the finance ministers and central bank governors of France, the Federal Republic of Germany, Japan, the United Kingdom, and the United States.

Group of 7 (G7) The Group of 5 plus Canada and Italy.

Group of 10 The Group of 7 plus Belgium, the Netherlands, and Sweden.

Group of 77 Had its origins in the caucus of 75 developing countries that met in 1964 to prepare for UNCTAD. After the first UNCTAD meeting, the caucus grew to 77.

groups (*grupos* in Spanish-speaking countries) Conglomerates or a number of firms that together form a vertically integrated marketing and production system. Groups are common in Europe and Latin America. Frequently owned by immediate family members or a small investment combine. See *chaebol.*

guest workers Foreign workers who are brought into a country by legal means to perform needed labor.

Hard currency A currency that is freely convertible into other currencies.

hard loans Loans that must be repaid in a hard currency at market interest rates.

hedging Selling forward currency exchange, borrowing, or using other means to protect against losses from possible currency exchange rate changes that affect the values of assets and liabilities.

hierarchy A system in which there are several layers of authority between the lowest rank (say, the peasants or untouchables) and the highest rank (say, king, commissar, or brahmin).

hit list or Super 301 Refers to Section 301 of the U.S. 1988 Trade Act, which requires the U.S. trade representative to prepare a list of countries that systematically restrict access of American products to their markets.

hollowing out Refers to the practice of firms that close their production facilities and become marketing organizations for other producers, mostly foreign.

home country The country where the parent company's headquarters are located.

horizontal corporations A form of organization characterized by lateral decision processes, horizontal networks, and a strong corporatewide business philosophy.

host country The country in which foreign investment is made.

human-needs approach A way to economic development that includes the elimination of poverty and unemployment as well as an increase in income.

hybrid organization A structure organized by more than one dimension at the top level.

hypermarkets Huge combination supermarkets and discount stores where soft and hard goods are sold.

Import substitution An industrialization policy followed by some developing nations by which the government encourages the local production of substitutes for imported goods. High import duties protect local producers from import competition.

incentive pay plans Plans that pay employees more for achieving certain goals.

income distribution A measure of how a nation's income is apportioned among its people. It is commonly reported as the percentage of income received by population quintiles.

INCOTERMS A publication of the International Chamber of Commerce setting forth recommended standard definitions for the major trade terms used in international trade.

indexing Taking into account the effect of inflation on assets and liabilities and adjusting the amounts of these items to preserve their original relationships.

indicative plans Planning done by governments in collaboration with industry. It is essentially a forecast of the direction the economy is expected to take. An indicative plan does not control economic activity as in centrally planned economies, and firms are free to make their own decisions.

indirect exporting The exporting of goods and services through various types of home-based exporters.

industrial cooperation A long-term relationship with a company in a developed country in which a developing country produces products for its own market, exports to the West, or both.

industrial espionage Stealing trade, process, customer, pricing, or technology secrets from a business.

industrial targeting Government practice of assisting selected industries to grow.

information glut There is too much information to absorb or it is not properly classified or organized.

infrastructure The fundamental underpinnings of an economy—roads, railroads, communications, water supplies, energy supplies, and so forth.

in-house training programs Programs provided by an employer on its own property.

instability As used in this book, occurs when a government is likely to be ovethrown by a revolution or coup.

insurance certificate Evidence that marine insurance has been obtained to cover stipulated risks during transit.

interest arbitrage Lending in another country to take advantage of higher interest rates. Such arbitrage tends to equalize interest rates.

interest rate swap A transaction in which two parties exchange interest payment streams of differing character based on an underlying principal amount. The three main types are coupon swaps (fixed rate to floating rate in the same currency), basis swaps (one floating rate index to another floating rate index in the same currency), and cross-currency interest rate swaps (fixed or floating rate in one currency or fixed or floating rate in another currency).

intermediate technology Production method between capital- and labor-intensive methods.

internalization theory An extension of the market imperfection theory, which claims that to obtain a higher return on its investment, a firm will transfer its superior knowledge to a foreign subsidiary rather than sell it on the open market.

international division A division in the organization that is at the same level as the domestic division in the firm and is responsible for all non-home-country activities.

international environment The interaction between the domestic and foreign environmental forces.

international finance center A multinational's or global's office that handles most of the international money transactions for all the firm's units.

international financing Occurs when a borrower raises capital in the Eurocurrency or Eurobond markets, outside the restrictions that are applied to domestic or foreign offerings. See *foreign financing.*

international law A body of principles and practices that have been generally accepted by countries in their relations with other countries and with citizens of other countries.

international management information system Organized process of gathering, storing, processing, and disseminating information about international operations to managers to assist them in making business decisions.

international monetary system The agreements, practices, laws, customs, and institutions that deal with money (debts, payments, investments) internationally.

international product life cycle (IPLC) A theory that helps explain both trade flows and foreign direct investment on the basis of a product's position in the four stages of (1) exports of an industrialized nation, (2) beginning of foreign production, (3) foreign competition in export markets, and (4) import competition in the country where the product was introduced originally.

international status Confers extra perquisites and privileges on an IC's top employees.

Internet A global web of computer networks with some 10 million host computers. It has created a new form of communication but is neither organized by any organization nor regulated by any government or agency.

intervention currency A currency bought or sold by a country (not necessarily the one issued by it) to influence the value of its own currency.

intraenterprise transaction A transaction between two or more units of the same IC.

irrevocable A letter of credit that cannot be canceled.

Islam A religion whose practitioners are called Muhammadans or Muslims. They are found worldwide but are predominant across North Africa, throughout the Middle East, and in Pakistan and Indonesia. Muslims believe the future is ordained by Allah (God). The Koran, a collection of Allah's revelations to Muhammad, the founder of Islam, is accepted as God's eternal word.

iterative planning Repetition of the bottom-up or top-down planning process until all differences are reconciled.

J curve A curve illustrating the theory that immediately after a country devalues its currency, its imports become more expensive and its exports cheaper, thus worsening a BOP deficit. As the country's exports increase, it earns more money and the deficit bottoms out and becomes a surplus up the right side of the J.

joint venture May be (1) a corporate entity between an IC and local owners, (2) a corporate entity between two or more ICs that are foreign to the area where the joint venture is located, or (3) a cooperative undertaking between two or more firms for a limited-duration project.

just-in-time (JIT) A balanced system in which there is little or no delay time or inventory.

Key currencies Those held extensively as foreign exchange reserves.

Labor force composition The different sorts of available laborers, differentiated in terms of skill, age, race, or gender.

labor-intensive Describes products whose production requires a relatively large amount of labor and a relatively small amount of capital. Also describes the manufacturing process.

labor market The labor available in an area.

labor mobility The movement of labor from one location to another.

labor productivity How much a labor force produces in a given time period.

labor quality The skill and industriousness of labor.

labor quantity The number of available laborers.

labor unions Organizations of laborers that represent and negotiate for workers.

lags As used in this book, delaying conversion when payment is to be made in another currency in the belief the other currency will cost less when needed.

landlocked Refers to a nation bordered on all of its frontiers by land.

LASH Specially designed oceangoing vessel for carrying barges.

leads As used in this book, converting immediately when payment is to be made in another currency in the belief the other currency will cost more when needed.

left wing Extremely liberal, in the American sense of the word.

less developed countries (LDCs) Countries with low per capita income, low levels of industrialization, high illiteracy, and usually political instability.

letter of credit (L/C) A letter issued by a bank indicating that the bank will accept drafts (make payments) under specified circumstances.

liberal In American political usage, a liberal advocates extensive government intervention in business and society.

licensing A contractual arrangement in which one firm, the licensor, grants access to its patents, trademarks, or technology to another firm, the licensee, for a fee, usually called a royalty.

lingua franca A foreign language used to communicate among diverse cultures that speak different languages.

linkage In international marketing, the creation of demand in a second national market by movement of the product or the customer into that market.

Lombard rate The interest rate that a central bank charges other banks on loans secured by government and other selected securities.

Lomé convention An agreement between 70 African, Caribbean, and Pacific states and the EU by means of which 99.2 percent of the former group's exports are admitted duty-free to the EU.

London Interbank Offered Rate (LIBOR) The interest rate the most creditworthy banks charge one another for loans of Eurodollars over-night in the London market. LIBOR is a cornerstone in the pricing on money market issues and other short-term debt issues by both government and business borrowers. Interest is often stated to be LIBOR plus a fraction.

long position The position taken when a party buys something for future delivery. This may be done in the expectation that the item bought will increase in value. It may also be done to hedge a currency risk.

Managed float See *floating exchange rates. Managed* is a more decorous word than *dirty.*

managed trade Trade managed in some way by governments.

management contract An agreement by which one firm provides management in all or specific areas to another company for a fee.

management information system (MIS) The computerized system through which multinational or global executives get timely, relevant information about all the company's units.

manufacturers' agents Independent sales representatives of various noncompeting suppliers.

manufacturing rationalization Division of production among a number of production units, enabling each to produce components for all of a firm's assembly plants.

maquiladora (in-bond plant) Introduced by the Mexican government to create jobs for its people. Plants along the Mexican-American border cooperate, with the plant on the American side doing the capital-intensive work and the Mexican plant doing the labor-intensive production.

market economies Economies characterized by a relatively large, free (nongovernmental) market sector. There is no such thing as a totally free market; all governments regulate, tax, and intervene in various ways.

market factors Economic data that correlate highly with market demand for a product.

market indicators Economic data used to measure relative market strengths of countries or geographical areas.

market method to correct BOP deficit Deflate the economy and devalue the currency.

market screening A version of environmental scanning in which the firm identifies desirable markets by using the environmental forces to eliminate the less desirable markets.

Marshall Plan The U.S. aid program that helped European countries reconstruct after World War II. Cooperation among the European countries was a forerunner of the EC.

material culture Refers to all human-made objects and is concerned with how people make things (technology) and who makes what and why (economics).

matrix organization An organizational structure composed of one or more organizational structures superimposed over one another in an attempt to mesh product, regional, functional, and other expertise.

matrix overlay An organization whose top-level divisions are required to heed input from a staff composed of experts of another organizational dimension. It attempts to avoid the double-reporting difficulty of a matrix organization but still mesh two or more dimensions.

mercantilism The economic philosophy that equates the possession of gold or other international monetary assets with wealth. It also holds that trade activities should be directed or controlled by the government.

merchant banks Combine long- and short-term financing with the underwriting and distributing of securities.

minorities As used in this book, a group of people of one race or religion living in an area populated by a larger number of people of a different race or religion.

mission statement A broad statement defining an organization's scope.

mitbestimmung German for *codetermination.*The Germans pioneered codetermination, and their word for it is frequently used.

monetary aggregate A composite monetary variable used as a measure of the monetary supply (and as such, sometimes adopted as an intermediate monetary policy objective as an indicator of monetary conditions) that includes a varying range of liquid assets, depending on its definition. Monetary aggregates range from narrow to broad. The narrowly defined aggregate M1 typically includes currency and demand deposits.

monetary policies Government policies regulating whether the country's money supply grows and, if so, how fast.

money laundering The attempt to conceal or disguise the ownership or source of the proceeds of criminal activity and integrate them into legitimate financial systems in such a way that they cannot be distinguished from assets acquired by legitimate means. Typically, this involves the conversion of cash-based proceeds into account-based forms of money.

money markets Places where currencies are traded or capital is raised.

monopolistic advantage theory The idea that foreign direct investment is made by firms in oligopolistic industries that possess technical and other advantages over indigenous firms.

most favored nation (MFN) The policy of nondiscrimination in international commercial policy, extending to all nations the same customs and tariff treatments that are extended to the most favored nation.

multinational economic union A group of nations that have reduced barriers to intergroup trade and are cooperating in economic matters.

multinational, company or enterprise (MNC or MNE) Terms used by some authors to mean an organization consisting of a parent company in a home country that owns relatively autonomous subsidiaries in various host countries.

National (macro) competitiveness Ability of a nation's producers to compete successfully in the world markets and with imports in their own domestic markets.

national economic plans Plans prepared by governments that state their economic goals and means for reaching them for periods of usually up to five years.

nationalism A strong attachment to and support of one's country.

nationalization Government take-over of private property.

national tax jurisdiction Taxation on the basis of nationality regardless of where in the world a taxpayer's income is earned or where the activities of the taxpayer take place.

natural resources Anything supplied by nature on which people depend.

net negative international investment position Residents of a country have less investment abroad than nonresidents have in the country.

neutralizing the balance sheet Having the assets in a given currency approximate the liabilities in that currency.

newly industrializing countries (NICs) A group of middle-income nations with high growth in manufacturing. Much of their production goes to high-income, industrialized nations.

newly industrialized economies (NIEs) The four Asian tigers—Hong Kong, South Korea, Taiwan, and Singapore.

nonmarket economy The World Bank designation for a communist nation.

nonmarket measures Use of currency controls, tariffs, or quotas to correct a BOP deficit.

nonrecourse financing Financing in which the factor assumes the full responsibility and all the risk of collecting from a third party. See *forfaiting.*

nonrevenue tax purposes Use of a tax to encourage some perceived socially desirable end, such as home ownership, or to discourage something undesirable, such as tobacco.

nontariff barriers (NTBs) Con-straints on imports other than import duties, such as quotas, product standards, orderly marketing arrangements, customs and administrative procedures, and government participation in trade.

North American Free Trade Agreement (NAFTA) The agreement creating a free trade area that includes Canada, Mexico, and the United States.

note issuance facility (NIF) Medium-term arrangements that enable borrowers to issue paper, typically of three or six months' maturity, in their own names. A group of underwriting banks guarantees the availability of funds to the borrower by purchasing any unsold notes or by providing standby credit.

Off-premises training The employer sends workers away from its property to a school or other site to be trained.

offshore banking The use of banks located in other countries, particularly tax havens such as the Caymans and the Bahamas.

offshore funds Investment funds whose shares are usually denominated in U.S. dollars but located and sold outside the United States. There are tax and securities-registration reasons for such funds.

on-the-job training Employees learn a job by performing it under supervision.

opening bank The bank that opens a letter of credit (L/C). This bank will honor (pay) drafts drawn under the L/C if specified conditions are met.

orderly marketing agreements (OMAs) Compacts negotiated between two or more nations under whose terms the exporting nation or nations agree to limit exports of specified goods to the importing nation. They are sometimes called *voluntary export agreements (VEAs).*

Organization for Economic Cooperation and Development (OECD) Organization of primarily developed countries dedicated to promoting economic expansion of its member-countries.

Overseas Private Insurance Cor-poration (OPIC) A U.S. government corporation that offers American investors in developing countries insurance against expropriation, currency inconvertibility, and damages from wars and revolutions.

overvalued currency A currency whose value is kept higher by government action than it would be in a free market.

Paper gold See *special drawing rights (SDRs).*

parallel importing The importing of a product by an independent operator that is not part of the manufacturer's channel of distribution. The parallel importer may compete with the authorized importer or with a subsidiary of the foreign manufacturer that produces the product in the local market.

parent company A company that owns subsidiary companies.

par value The value that a government, by agreement or regulation, sets on its currency in terms of other currencies. At Bretton Woods, other currencies were assigned par values in terms of the U.S. dollar.

paternalism A system in which a chief, sheik, or other authority figure cares for all the people as if he were their father.

pegged exchange rate An exchange rate in which a country's currency is fixed in terms of another country's currency. Frequently, the other country is a major trading partner or a country with which there was a colonial relationship.

peril point In U.S. law, a point below which a tariff cannot be lowered without causing or threatening serious injury to U.S. producers of competitive products.

physical product The basic physical product produced by a firm's production system. It does not include attributes added after production, such as packaging, brand name, service, and financing.

political risks The risks to a business and its employees that stem from political unrest in an area. As a result of such unrest, the markets or supplies of the business may be disrupted or the business may be nationalized and its employees may lose their jobs or be kidnapped, injured, or even killed.

population density A measure of the number of inhabitants per area unit (inhabitants per kilometer or mile).

population distribution A measure of how the inhabitants are distributed over a nation's area.

polymetallic deposits Deposits that contain a number of metals.

portfolio investment The purchase of stocks and bonds to obtain a return in the money invested. The investors are not interested in assuming control of the firm.

preindustrial societies A designation that can signify anything from traditional societies through societies in the early stages of agricultural and industrial organization.

preventive (planned) maintenance Maintenance done according to plan, not when a machine breaks down.

price and wage controls Govern-ment limits on prices that may be charged and wages that may be paid.

private international law Laws governing transactions of individuals and companies crossing international borders.

privatization When a government transfers ownership, operation, or both of a government-owned enterprise to private owners/operators.

product liability Liability of a product's manufacturer for damage caused by the product.

pro forma invoice Exporter's formal quotation containing a description of the merchandise, price, delivery time, method of shipping, terms of sale, and points of entry.

programmed-management approach A middle-ground advertising strategy between globally standardized and entirely local programs.

promotion All forms of communication between a firm and its publics.

promotional mix A blend of the promotional methods a firm uses to sell its products.

Protestant work ethic The duty of Christians to glorify God by hard work and the practice of thrift.

Public international law Legal relations between nations.

public relations Various methods of communicating with the firm's publics to secure a favorable impression.

purchasing power parity The relative ability of one unit of two countries' currencies to purchase similar goods. From this relative ability is derived an indication of what the market exchange rate between the two currencies should be.

Quality circles (quality control circles) Small work groups that meet periodically to discuss ways to improve their functional areas in the firm and the quality of the products.

questionable or dubious payments Bribes.

quota (1) A imitation on imports by number or by weight; for example, only so many of a given item or only so many pounds or kilos may be imported. (2) At the IMF, each member-nation has a quota that determines the amount of its subscription and how much it can borrow.

Reengineering A radical redesign of business processes to achieve dramatic improvements in critical measures of performance, such as cost, quality, service, or speed.

regional dualism A situation in which some regions of a nation have high productivity and high incomes while other regions of the same country have little economic development and lower incomes.

reinvoicing Centralizing all international invoicing by an IC. The reinvoicing center decides which currencies should be used and where, how, and when.

repatriation The transfer home of assets held abroad.

representative office An office of an out-of-state or foreign bank that is not permitted to conduct direct banking functions. The purpose of such an office is to solicit business for its parent bank, where it can conduct such functions.

revaluation of a currency An increase in a currency's value in terms of other currencies. See *devaluation.*

reverse engineering Dismantling a competitor's product to learn everything possible about it.

reverse imports Products made by a multinational's overseas subsidiaries that are exported to the home country.

revocable letters of credit (L/Cs) L/Cs that the opening bank may revoke at any time without notice to the beneficiary.

Rhine waterway A system of rivers and canals that is the main transportation artery of Europe.

right wing Extremely conservative politically.

robotics Machines, usually computer controlled, doing work previously done by human workers.

RO-RO Specially designed oceangoing vessel that permits any equipment on wheels to be rolled on board.

rural-to-urban shift Describes the movement of a nation's population from rural areas to cities.

S.A. Société Anonyme, Sociedad Anomina, or Societa Anomina. Joint-stock companies (in French, Spanish, and Italian, respectively).

safe haven The currency of a country that is politically secure is called a *safe haven currency.*

sales company A corporate entity established in a foreign country by the parent company to sell goods or services imported from the parent company and other foreign affiliates.

sales promotion Selling aids, including displays, premiums, contests, and gifts.

S.A.R.L. Société à Responsibilité Limitée.

scenario Description of a possible future. Managers often use most likely, worst, and best cases for the purpose of planning.

securitization The term is most often used to mean the process by which traditional bank assets, mainly loans or mortgages, are converted into negotiable securities. More broadly, refers to the development of markets for a variety of new negotiable instruments.

segment screening (new) Takes sub-national or cross-national groups of consumers with similar consumption preferences as the relevant unit of analysis.

self-reference criterion Uncon-scious reference to one's own cultural values when judging behavioral actions of others in a new and different environment.

shale A fissile (capable of being split) rock composed of laminated layers of claylike, fine-grained sediment.

short position The position of a party when it has sold something it does not own. This is for future delivery in the expectation that the item sold will decrease in price. It is also done to hedge a currency risk.

sight draft A bill of exchange that is payable immediately on presentation or demand. A bank check is a sight draft.

skilled labor Employees trained in needed skills.

Smithsonian agreement New agreements on currency par values, the value of gold, and tariffs reached by the major trading countries at the Smithsonian Institution in Washington, DC, in December 1971. When the United States closed the "gold window" in August 1971, the world currency exchanges were thrown into turmoil, and such agreements became necessary.

snake During the 1970s, several West European countries agreed to keep the values of their currencies within established ranges in terms of one another. The currencies would all float in value in terms of other currencies, for example, the U.S. dollar and the Japanese yen.

socialism A theory of society in which the government owns or directs most of the factors of production.

soft currency A currency that is not freely convertible into other currencies. Such a currency is usually subject to national currency controls.

soft loans Loans like those granted by the IDA. These loans may have grace periods during which no payments need be made; they may bear low or no interest; and they may be repayable in a soft currency.

sogo shosha The Japanese term for general trading companies.

sovereign debt The debt of a national government.

sovereign immunity The immunity of a government from lawsuits in the courts of its own country or other countries unless it submits voluntarily. Such immunity is particularly likely to exist if the government limits itself to governmental functions as opposed to economic ones.

sovereignty The power of each national government over the land within its borders and over the people and organizations within those borders.

special drawing rights (SDRs) Accounting entries at the IMF. SDRs are treated as reserve assets and are credited or debited to member-countries' accounts. Sometimes cal-led *paper gold,* they permit liquidity to be created by agreement at the IMF rather than having it depend on the U.S. BOP deficit.

specific tariff or duty A method of measuring customs duties or tariffs by number or weight instead of by value. Thus, the amount of the tariff or duty is based on how many units or how many pounds or kilos are imported, regardless of their value. See *ad valorem tariff or duty.*

spot rate or spot quotation The rate of exchange between two currencies for delivery, one for the other, within two business days.

stability As used in this book, occurs when a government is not likely to be overturned by a revolution or a coup.

standardization of the marketing mix The utilization of the same pricing, product, distribution, and promotional strategies in all markets where the firm does business.

sterilization The use by a central bank of operations (such as open market sales) to reduce bank reserves (liquidity) it has created through another financial transaction, such as the purchase of foreign currency.

straight bonds or notes Issues with a fixed, not floating, coupon or interest rate.

strategic business unit (SBU) Business entity with a clearly defined market, specific competitors, the ability to carry out its business mission, and a size appropriate for control by a single manager.

subcontracting Prime manufacturers' purchase of components from other suppliers. Used in industrial cooperation.

subsidiaries Companies owned by another company, which is referred to as the parent company.

subsidiary detriment A subsidiary is deprived of a potential advantage so that the IC as a whole may enjoy a greater advantage.

subsidies, export Financial encouragement to export. Such subsidies can take the form of lower taxes, tax rebates, or direct payments.

superstores Name given to hypermarkets in Japan and in some parts of Europe and the United States.

swaps Are of two basic kinds: interest rate swaps and currency swaps. Interest rate swaps typically exchange fixed-rate for floating-rate payments. Currency swaps are accords to deliver one currency against another currency at certain intervals.

swing In a bilateral trade agreement, the leeway provided for mutual extension of credit.

switch trade A type of countertrade utilized when a country lacks sufficient hard currency to pay for its imports. When it can acquire from a third country products desired by its creditor country, it switches shipment of those products to the creditor country. Its debt to the creditor country is thereby paid.

synchronous manufacturing An entire manufacturing process with unbalanced operations. Total system performance is emphasized.

Takeoff A phase in the development of a developing country when its infrastructure has been sufficiently developed, enough interacting industries have been established, and domestic capital formation exceeds consumption so that the country's own momentum carries the development process onward.

tariff quota A tariff that has a lower rate until the end of a specified period or until a specified amount of the commodity has been imported. At that point, the rate increases.

tariffs See *duties.*

tax haven A country that has low or no taxes on income from foreign sources or capital gains.

tax incentives The tax holidays that developing countries sometimes give companies and their managements if they will invest in the country or that developed countries sometimes give them to induce investment in an area of high unemployment or to encourage exports.

tax treaty A treaty between two countries in which each country usually lowers certain taxes on residents who are nationals of the other and the countries agree to cooperate in tax matters such as enforcement.

Taylor's scientific management system A system based on scientific measurements that prescribes a division of work whereby planning is done by managers and plan execution is left to supervisors and workers.

technological dualism The presence in a country of industries using modern technology while others employ more primitive methods.

terms of sale Conditions of a sale that stipulate the point where all costs and risks are borne by the buyer.

terms of trade The real quantities of exports that are required to pay for a given amount of imports.

territorial tax jurisdiction The levying of tax on taxpayers while living and working in the territory of the taxing government. Income earned while living and working elsewhere is not taxed or is taxed at a lower rate.

terrorism The use by nongovernment forces of murder, kidnapping, and destruction to publicize or gain political goals or money.

third country nationals Citizens of neither the home country nor the host country.

tied loans or grants Loans or grants that the borrower or recipient must spend in the country that made them.

time draft An unconditional order drawn by the seller on the buyer to pay the draft's amount at an agreed future date.

top-down planning Planning process that begins at the highest level in the organization and continues downward.

topography The surface features of a region, such as mountains, deserts, plains, and bodies of water.

total product What the customer buys; it includes the physical product, brand name, after-sale service, warranty, instructions for use, the company image, and the package.

total quality management (TQM) A system that integrates the development, maintenance, and improvement of quality among all functional areas of the firm.

trade acceptance A draft similar to a banker's acceptance, the difference being that no bank is involved. The exporter presents the draft to the importer for its acceptance to pay the amount stated at a fixed future date.

trade bloc A group of countries with special trading rules among them, such as the EU.

trade deficit/surplus A trade deficit is an excess of merchandise imports over exports. A trade surplus is the opposite.

trade fair A large exhibition generally held periodically at the same place and time at which companies maintain booths to promote the sale of their products.

trade mission Group of businesspeople, government officials (state and federal), or both that visits a foreign market in search of business opportunities.

trading at a discount When a currency costs less in the forward market than the spot cost.

trading at a premium When a currency costs more in the forward market than the spot cost.

trading companies Firms that develop international trade and serve as intermediaries between foreign buyers and domestic sellers, and vice versa.

traditional economy An area in a most rudimentary state. In such an economy, the people are typically nomadic, agriculture is at a bare subsistence level, and industry is virtually nonexistent.

traditional hostilities When nations, races, or religions have been in conflict for long periods.

transaction risk The risk run in international trade that changes in relative currency values will cause losses.

transfer price The price charged by one unit of an IC for goods or services that it sells to another unit of the same IC.

translation risk The apparent losses or gains that can result from the restatement of values from one currency into another, even if there are no transactions, when the currencies change in value relative to each other. Translation risks are common with long-term foreign investments as foreign currency values are translated to the investor's financial statements in its home currency.

transnationals Used by the UN and some others to connote organizations variously called global, multinational, worldwide companies, or ICs.

Treaty of Rome Established the EU.

trend analysis Statistical technique by which successive observations of a variable at regular time intervals are analyzed for the purpose of establishing regular patterns used for establishing future values.

twin plants Along the Mexican–American border, the plant on the U.S. side does the high-tech, capital-intensive part of production, while the Mexican plant, also called a *maquiladora,* does the labor-intensive part.

Unbalanced growth theory The idea that economic growth can be attained by deliberately creating an imbalance in the economy through investment in an industry that will require further investment in supporting industries to reduce the imbalance.

uncontrollable forces The external forces in the domestic and foreign environments over which management has no direct control.

underground economy The part of a nation's income that, underreported or unreported, is not measured by official statistics.

undervalued currency A currency that has been oversold because of emotional selling or a currency whose value a government tries to keep below market to make its country's exports less expensive and more competitive.

unit labor cost The labor cost to produce one unit of output.

unskilled labor Employees without needed skills.

unspoken language Nonverbal communication, such as gestures and body language.

untouchables Lowest-caste Indians. Mahatma Gandhi called them *harijans,* the children of God.

Uruguay Round The round of GATT negotiations that held its first meeting in Uruguay in 1986.

Validated export license A required document issued by the U.S. government authorizing the export of specified commodities.

value-added tax (VAT) A tax levied at each stage in the production of a product. The tax is on the value added to the product by that stage.

variable levy Import duties set at the differences between world market prices and local government-supported prices. Used by the European Union on grain imports to ensure that they have no price advantage over locally grown grains.

vehicle currency A currency used in international transactions to make quotes and payments. The U.S. dollar is the currency most often used.

venture capital Money invested, usually in equity, in a new, relatively high-risk undertaking.

vertically integrated Describes a firm that produces its own inputs (such as subassemblies) for its subsequent manufacturing processes.

vertical mobility An individual's opportunities to move upward in a society to a higher caste or a higher social status.

virtual corporation A temporary group of independent companies including manufacturers, marketers, suppliers, customers, and competitors, connected by a computer network, for the purpose of designing, manufacturing and marketing a product.

voluntary export agreements (VEAs) See *orderly marketing agreements.*

Watch list List containing items of interest concerning uncontrollable variables of special interest to the firm.

Webb-Pomerene Act Exempts from U.S. antitrust laws those associations among business competitors engaged in export trade. They must not restrain trade within the United States or the trade of any other U.S. competitors.

works council A directive issued by the EU in 1995 required all firms with more than 1,000 employees to set up a consultative mechanism if at least 150 of a firm's employees are in two or more member-states. The aim, says the directive, is to "improve the right to information and to consultation."

World Trade Organization (WTO) The organization that succeeded the General Agreement on Tariffs and Trade (GATT) as a result of the successful completion of the Uruguay Round of GATT negotiations.

worldwide companies Used by some authors to connote the organizations referred to by others as globals, multinationals, transnationals, or ICs.

Zaibatsu Centralized, family-dominated, monopolistic economic groups that dominated the Japanese economy until the end of World War II, at which time they were broken up. As time passed, however, the units of the old zaibatsu drifted back together, and they now cooperate within the group much as they did before their dissolution.

zero-coupon bonds Bonds that are issued at a heavy discount and pay no interest but are redeemable at par at a future date.

[Name Index]

[Company Index]

Q

R

S

T

U

V

W

X

Y-Z

[Subject Index]

C

D

E

F

G

H

I

J

K

L

M

Q

R

S

T